The Concise
Evangelical Dictionary of Theology

The Concise Evangelical Dictionary of Theology

Edited by
Walter A. Elwell

Abridged by
Peter Toon

BAKER BOOK HOUSE
Grand Rapids, Michigan 49516

Printed in the United States of America

Library of Congress Cataloging in Publication Data

Evangelical Dictionary of Theology
The Concise Evangelical dictionary of theology / edited by Walter A. Elwell ; abridged by Peter Toon.
p. cm.
Abridgment of: Evangelical dictionary of theology / edited by Walter A. Elwell, c 1984
ISBN 0-8010-3210-5
1. Theology—Dictionaries. 2. Evangelicalism—Dictionaries. I. Elwell, Walter A. II. Toon, Peter, 1939– . III. Title.
BR95.E87 1991
230'.046—dc20 91-26424
CIP

Preface

The *Concise Evangelical Dictionary of Theology* fills a small but important niche on the reference shelf. It is designed to provide tightly-written, down-to-basics definitions of theological terms, descriptions of organizations and movements, summaries of ideas, and biographies of leaders. It is a condensation of the *Evangelical Dictionary of Theology*—reedited, reorganized, and updated.

The *Concise EDT* is a direct descendant of *Baker's Dictionary of Theology*, which pioneered a new idea in theological works when it rolled off the presses in 1964. Its authors were theologians who explained and applied theological terms for those who had not studied in a seminary classroom. The *Dictionary of Theology* was born in an era when the young evangelical movement was testing its wings and finding its voice. Many contributors to Baker's dictionary were at that moment contributing to a quiet revolution within Christendom.

By 1984, when Baker Book House introduced the *Evangelical Dictionary of Theology*, the new era was well underway. Christians who felt isolated and unfulfilled in old ecclesiastical pigeonholes found a solidarity under the banner of "evangelicalism."

That is why the *EDT* and the *Concise EDT* identifiy themselves as "evangelical." Evangelicalism has matured as a world ecumenical movement. Its people stand together in the essentials of faith and witness, even as they stand apart in individual theological and cultural contexts. The evangelical spirit transcends denominations; its diversity nearly defies theological description; its vision pervades all of life.

No wonder the preface to the *EDT* observed: "After several decades of trying to find answers for our deepest questions in everything from biochemistry to computer science, it has dawned upon us once more that these questions are theological and that only theological answers will do."

The generous reception afforded the *EDT* stimulated the idea that its essence could be distilled in a shorter format for quick reference. This idea was debated for some time. After all, wasn't the *EDT* itself a "short format," a one-volume compendium of the essential details of theology? But requests persisted, resulting in the publication of this volume.

The format of the *Concise EDT* generally follows that of the *EDT*. Fewer than 200 articles, deemed to be of relatively minor importance for a general audience, were removed. Sufficient material from each contribution has been retained so that it remains factual and as informative as possible. Dr. Peter Toon, a skilled and competent theologian in his own right, undertook the sensitive task of paring the original articles down to size.

Preface

The *Concise EDT* is not a substitute for the *EDT*, but a handbook that provides summary statements for those who want the most basic information. For a more complete treatment of the subjects, or bibliographies of key English-language works, readers should continue to consult the *EDT*.

Needless to say, in a work written by more than 160 people, differences of opinion appear. Such differences are part of that evangelical diversity, and no attempt has been made to enforce uniformity. Nothing in *EDT*, though, casts doubt on any fundamental truth of the Christian faith or on the absolute trustworthiness of the Bible.

Contributors

Adie, Douglas K. Ph. D., University of Chicago. Professor of economics, Ohio University, Athens.

Akers, John N. Ph.D., University of Edinburgh. Special assistant, The Billy Graham Evangelistic Association, Montreat, N.C., office.

Allis, Oswald T. Ph.D., University of Berlin. Late professor of Old Testament, Westminster Theological Seminary, Philadelphia, Pennsylvania.

Allison, C. FitzSimons. D.Phil., Oxford University. Former bishop, Episcopal Diocese of South Carolina, Charleston.

Archer, Gleason Leonard, Jr. Ph.D., University of Aberdeen. Professor emeritus of Old Testament and Semitic languages, Trinity Evangelical Divinity School, Deerfield, Illinois.

Atkinson, David J. Ph.D., University of London. Fellow and chaplain, Corpus Christi College, Oxford, England.

Babbage, Stuart Barton. Ph.D., University of London; Th.D., Australian College of Theology. Registrar, Australian College of Theology, Sydney.

Baird, John S. S.T.D., Temple University, Denise Professor of Homiletics and Ministry, University of Dubuque (Iowa) Theological Seminary.

Baker, William H. Th.D., Dallas Theological Seminary. Professor of Bible and theology, Moody Bible Institute, Chicago, Illinois.

Barabas, Steven. Th.D., Princeton Theological Seminary. Late professor of theology, Wheaton (Ill.) College.

Beegle, Dewey M. Ph.D., Johns Hopkins University. Professor emeritus of Old Testament, Wesley Theological Seminary, Washington, D.C.

Benner, David G. Ph.D., York University. Professor of psychology, Redeemer College, Ancaster, Ontario.

Benton, W. Wilson, Jr. Ph.D., University of Edinburgh. Senior pastor, Kirk of the Hills Presbyterian Church, St. Louis, Missouri, and adjunct professor, Covenant Theological Seminary, St. Louis.

Bishop, Russell K. Ph.D., McGill University. Professor of history, Gordon College, Wenham, Massachusetts.

Blaising, Craig A. Th.D., Dallas Theological Seminary. Assistant professor of systematic theology, Dallas (Tex.) Theological Seminary.

Bloesch, Donald G. Ph.D., University of Chicago. Professor of theology, University of Dubuque (Iowa) Theological Seminary.

Boettner, Loraine. Th.M., Princeton Theological Seminary. Late theological writer.

Borchert, Gerald L. Ph.D., Princeton Theological Seminary. Professor of New Testament interpretation, Southern Baptist Theological Seminary, Louisville, Kentucky.

Brandon, Owen Rupert. M.Litt., University of Durham. Late librarian and lecturer, London College of Divinity.

Contributors

Bromiley, Geoffrey W. Ph.D., Litt.D., University of Edinburgh. Senior professor of church history and historical theology, Fuller Theological Seminary, Pasadena, California.

Broomall, Wick. Th.M., Princeton Theological Seminary. Late minister, Westminster Presbyterian Church, Augusta, Georgia.

Brown, Colin. Ph.D., University of Bristol. Professor of systematic theology, Fuller Theological Seminary, Pasadena, California.

Bruce, F. F. M.A., University of Aberdeen; M.A., Cambridge University; M.A., University of Manchester. Late Rylands Professor of Biblical Criticism and Exegesis, University of Manchester, England.

Burge, Gary M. Ph.D., University of Aberdeen. Karl A. Olsson Professor of Religious Studies and associate professor of New Testament, North Park (Ill.) College.

Burke, Gary T. Ph.D., University of Iowa. Former associate professor of religion, Eastern New Mexico University, Portales.

Butman, Richard Eugene. Ph.D., Fuller Theological Seminary. Associate Professor of Psychology, Wheaton (Ill.) College.

Cameron, William John. M.A., University of Edinburgh. Professor emeritus of New Testament language, literature and theology, Free Church of Scotland College, Edinburgh.

Carson, D. A. Ph.D., Cambridge University. Professor of New Testament, Trinity Evangelical Divinity School, Deerfield, Illinois.

Caulley, Thomas Scott. Dr.Theol., University of Tübingen. Associate professor of New Testament, Manhattan (Kan.) Christian College.

Chappell, Paul G. Ph.D., Drew University. Dean and professor of church history, School of Theology, Oral Roberts University, Tulsa, Oklahoma.

Clark, Gordon H. Ph.D., University of Pennsylvania. Late professor of philosophy, Butler University, Indianapolis, Indiana, and chairman of philosophy, Covenant College, Lookout Mountain, Tennessee.

Cleveland, Howard Z. Th.D., Dallas Theological Seminary. Late chairman, Language Department, Oak Hills Christian Training School, Bemidji, Minnesota.

Clouse, Robert G. Ph.D., University of Iowa. Professor of history, Indiana State University, Terre Haute.

Coates, Richard John. M.A., University of Bristol. Late vicar of Christ Church, Weston-Super-Mare, Somerset, England; lecturer, Tyndale Hall, Bristol, England.

Collins, George Norman MacLeod. B.D., Knox College. Professor emeritus of church history, Free Church of Scotland College, Edinburgh.

Colquhoun, Frank. M.A., Durham University. Canon emeritus, Norwich Cathedral, Norwich, England.

Corduan, Winfried. Ph.D., Rice University. Associate professor of philosophy and religion, Taylor University, Upland, Indiana.

Craigie, Peter C. Ph.D., McMaster University. Late dean, Faculty of Humanities, University of Calgary, Alberta.

Crum, Terrelle B. M.A., Harvard University. Late dean, Providence-Barrington Bible College, Providence, Rhode Island.

Cruz, Virgil. Ph.D., Free University. Professor of New Testament, Louisville (Ky.) Presbyterian Seminary.

Culbertson, Robert G. Ph.D., University of Cincinnati. Former professor of criminal justice sciences, Illinois State University, Normal.

Davids, Peter H. Ph.D., University of Manchester. Langley (British Columbia) Vineyard Christian Fellowship.

Davis, Creath. M.Div., Southwestern Baptist Theological Seminary. Late executive director, Christian Concern Foundation, Dallas, Texas.

De Koster, Lester. Ph.D., University of Michigan. Editor emeritus, *The Banner*.

Demarest, Bruce A. Ph.D., University of Manchester. Professor of systematic theology, Denver (Colo.) Seminary.

DeVries, Paul Henry. Ph.D., University of Virginia. Former associate professor of philosophy, Wheaton (Ill.) College.

Diehl, David W. Ph.D., Harvard Seminary Foundation. Former professor of religion, King's College, Briarcliff Manor, New York.

Dieter, Melvin E. Ph.D., Temple University. Professor emeritus of Church History and Historical Theology, Asbury Theological Seminary, Wilmore, Kentucky.

Donnelly, John Patrick, S.J. Ph.D., University of Wisconsin. Professor of history, Marquette University, Milwaukee, Wisconsin.

Douglas, J. D. Ph.D., Hartford Seminary Foundation. Lecturer, Singapore Bible College.

Drickamer, John M. Th.D., Concordia Seminary, St. Louis. Pastor, Good Shepherd Lutheran Church, Erie, Kansas.

Dunbar, David G. Ph.D., Drew University. President, Biblical Seminary, Hatfield, Pa.

Dyrness, William A. D.Theol., Strasbourg University. Dean, School of Theology, Fuller Theological Seminary, Pasadena, California.

Earle, Ralph. Th.D., Gordon Divinity School. Distinguished professor emeritus of New Testament, Nazarene Theological Seminary, Kansas City, Missouri.

Edman, V. Raymond. Ph.D., Clark University. Late president, Wheaton (Ill.) College.

Eller, David B. Ph.D., Miami University. Senior editor, Macmillan/McGraw-Hill Publishing Co.

Elwell, Walter A. Ph.D., University of Edinburgh. Professor of biblical and theological studies, Wheaton (Ill.) College.

Enroth, Ronald M. Ph.D., University of Kentucky. Professor of sociology, Westmont College, Santa Barbara, California.

Erickson, Millard J. Ph.D., Northwestern University. Dean and professor of theology, Bethel Theological Seminary, St. Paul, Minnesota.

Estep, William R., Jr. Th.D., Southwestern Baptist Theological Seminary. Professor of church history, Southwestern Baptist Theological Seminary, Fort Worth, Texas.

Farrer, Michael Robert Wedlake. M.A., Oxford University. Vicar, St. Paul's Vicarage, Cambridge, England.

Feinberg, Charles L. Th.D., Dallas Theological Seminary; Ph.D., Johns Hopkins University. Dean emeritus and professor emeritus of Semitics and Old Testament, Talbot Theological Seminary, La Mirada, California.

Feinberg, John S. Ph.D., University of Chicago. Chairman, Department of Systematic Theology, and associate professor of biblical and systematic theology, Trinity Evangelical Divinity School, Deerfield, Illinois.

Feinberg, Paul D. Th.D., Dallas Theological Seminary. Professor of biblical and systematic theology, Trinity Evangelical Divinity School, Deerfield, Illinois.

Ferguson, Duncan S. Ph.D., University of Edinburgh. Chairman, Committee on Higher Education, Presbyterian Church (USA), Louisville, Kentucky.

Ferguson, Everett. Ph.D., Harvard University. Professor emeritus, Abilene (Tex.) Christian University.

Field, David H. B.A., Cambridge University. Vice-principal, Oak Hill College, London, England.

Finger, Thomas N. Ph.D., Claremont School of theology. Visiting professor of theology, Eastern Mennonite Seminary, Harrisburg, Virginia.

Fisher, Fred Lewis. Th.D., Southwestern Baptist Theological Seminary. Late director, Southern California Center, Golden Gate Baptist Theological, Seminary, Mill Valley, California.

Fletcher, David B. Ph.D., University of Illinois. Associate professor of philosophy, Wheaton (Ill.) College.

Frame, John M. M.Phil., Yale University. Professor of apologetics and systematic theology, Westminster Theological Seminary-West, Escondido, California.

Franklin, Stephen T. Ph.D., University of Chicago. Minister and former professor of systematic theology, Wheaton (Ill.) College.

Freundt, Albert H., Jr. M.Div., Columbia Theological Seminary. Professor of church history, Reformed Theological Seminary, Jackson, Mississippi.

Fry, C. George. Ph.D., Ohio State University; D.Min., Winebrenner Theological Seminary. Protestant chaplain, St. Francis College, Fort Wayne, Indiana.

Gallatin, Harlie Kay. Ph.D., University of Illinois. Senior professor of history and chairman, Department of History and Political Science, Southwest Baptist University, Bolivar, Missouri.

Gasque, W. Ward. Ph.D., University of Manchester. Provost, Eastern College, St. David's, Pennsylvania.

Geisler, Norman L. Ph.D., Loyola University of Chicago. Former dean, Liberty Center for Christian Scholarship, Liberty University, Lynchburg, Virginia.

German, Terence J. Ph.D., Oxford University. Former professor of systematic theology, Marquette University, Milwaukee, Wisconsin.

Gerstner, John F. Ph.D., Harvard University. Professor-at-large, Ligonier Valley Study Center, Ligonier, Pennsylvania, and adjunct professor, Reformed Theological Seminary, Orlando, Florida.

Gill, David W. Ph.D., University of Southern California. Writer and former dean, New College, Berkeley, California.

Glasser, Arthur F. D.D., Covenant Theological Seminary. Dean emeritus, School of World Mission, Fuller Theological Seminary, Pasadena, California.

Goddard, Burton L. Th.D., Harvard University. Dean emeritus and professor of biblical languages and exegesis, Gordon-Conwell Theological Seminary, South Hamilton, Massachusetts.

Goldberg, Louis. Th.D., Grace Theological Seminary. Professor of theology and Jewish studies, Moody Bible Institute, Chicago, Illinois.

Gouvea, Fernando Q. M.A., University of São Paulo, Former assistant professor of mathematics, University of São Paulo, Brazil.

Granberg, Lars I. Ph.D., University of Chicago. Professor emeritus of psychology, Hope College, Holland, Michigan.

Grider, J. Kenneth. Ph.D., Glasgow University. Professor of theology, Nazarene Theological Seminary, Kansas City, Missouri.

Griffith, Howard. M. Div., Gordon-Conwell Theological Seminary. Pastor, All Saints Reformed Church, Richmond, Virginia.

Grudem, Wayne A. Ph.D., Cambridge University. Associate professor of biblical and systematic theology, Trinity Evangelical Divinity School, Deerfield, Illinois.

Gruenler, Royce G. Ph.D., University of Aberdeen. Professor of New Testament, Gordon-Conwell Theological Seminary, South Hamilton, Massachusetts.

Gundry, Stanley N. S.T.D., Lutheran School of Theology at Chicago. General manager, Book Division, and publisher, Academic and Professional Books, Zondervan Publishing House, Grand Rapids, Michigan.

Guthrie, Donald. Ph.D., University of London. Former vice-principal, London (England) Bible College.

Habermas, Gary R. Ph.D., Michigan State University. Chairman and professor, Department of Philosophy and Apologetics, Liberty University, Lynchburg, Virginia.

Hall, Joseph H. Th.D., Concordia Seminary, St. Louis. Associate professor of church history and librarian, Knox Theological Seminary, Fort Lauderdale, Florida.

Harm, Frederick R. Ph.D., De Paul University; D.Min, Faith Lutheran Seminary. Visiting professor of systematic theology, Concordia Seminary, St. Louis, Missouri; pastor, St. John Lutheran Church, Drake, Missouri.

Harris, R. Laird. Ph.D., Dropsie College. Late professor of Old Testament, Covenant Theological Seminary, St. Louis, Missouri.

Harrison, Everett F. Th.D., Dallas Theological Seminary; Ph.D., University of Pennsylvania. Late professor of New Testament, Fuller Theological Seminary, Pasadena, California.

Harrison, Roland Kenneth. Ph.D., University of London. Professor emeritus, Old Testament, Wycliffe College, Toronto, Ontario.

Hasel, Gerhard F. Ph.D., Vanderbilt University. Professor of Old Testament, and biblical theology, Theological Seminary, Andrews University, Barrien Springs, Michigan.

Hawthorne, Gerald F. Ph.D., University of Chicago. Professor of Greek, Wheaton (Ill.) College.

Hein, Rolland N. Ph.D., Purdue University. Professor of English, Wheaton (Ill.) College.

Heinze, Rudolph W. Ph.D., University of Iowa. College dean and senior tutor, Oak Hill College, Southgate, London, England.

Henry, Carl F. H. Th.D., Northern Baptist Theological Seminary; Ph.D., Boston University. Visiting professor of biblical and systematic theology, Trinity Evangelical Divinity School, Deerfield, Illinois.

Hesselgrave, David J. Ph.D., University of Minnesota. Professor of mission, Trinity Evangelical Divinity School, Deerfield, Illinois.

Hexham, Irving. Ph.D., University of Bristol. Professor of religious studies, University of Calgary, Alberta.

Higginson, Richard Edwin. B.D., University of London. Former lecturer, Tyndale Hall, Bristol, England.

Hoehner, Harold W. Th.D., Dallas Theological Seminary; Ph.D., Cambridge University. Professor of New Testament Studies, Dallas (Tex.) Theological Seminary.

Hoffecker, W. Andrew. Ph.D., Brown University. Professor of religion, Grove City (Pa.) College.

Hoover, Arlie J. Ph.D., University of Texas. Professor of history, Abilene (Tex.) Christian University.

Hope, Norman V. Ph.D., University of Edinburgh. Late professor of church history, Princeton (N.J.) Theological Seminary.

Horn, Carl, III. J.D., University of South Carolina. Attorney, Civil Rights Division, United States Department of Justice, Washington, D.C.

Houston, James M. D.Phil., Oxford University. Professor of spiritual theology, Regent College, Vancouver, British Columbia.

Howe, E. Margaret. Ph.D., University of Manchester. Professor, Department of Philosophy and Religion, Western Kentucky University, Bowling Green.

Hubbard, David A. Ph.D., St. Andrews University. President, Fuller Theological Seminary, Pasadena, California.

Hughes, Philip Edgcumbe. D.Litt., University of Cape Town; Th.D., Australian College of theology. Late professor, Trinity Episcopal School for Ministry, Ambridge, Pennsylvania.

Hummel, Horace D. Ph.D., Johns Hopkins University. Professor of Old Testament exegesis, Concordia Seminary, St. Louis, Missouri.

Imbach, Stuart R. Diploma in Bible, Prairie Bible Institute. Communications Department director, Overseas Missionary Fellowship, Singapore.

Inch, Morris A. Ph.D., Boston University. Former professor of theology, Wheaton (Ill.) College.

Jewett, Paul K. Ph.D., Harvard University. Professor of systematic theology, Fuller Theological Seminary, Pasadena, California.

Johnson, James E. Ph.D., Syracuse University. Professor of history, Bethel College, St. Paul, Minnesota.

Johnson, John F. Th.D., Concordia Seminary, St. Louis; Ph.D., St. Louis University. President, Concordia Seminary, St. Louis, Missouri.

Johnson, S. Lewis. Th.D., Dallas Theological Seminary. Professor emeritus of New Testament studies, Dallas Theological Seminary.

Johnston, Robert K. Ph.D., Duke University. Dean, North Park Theological Seminary, Chicago, Illinois.

Justice, William G., Jr. D. Min., Luther Rice Seminary. Ph.D., D. Litt., Oxford Graduate School. Director, Tri-County Counseling Center, Knoxville, Tennessee, and adjunct professor, Oxford Graduate School, Dayton, Tennessee.

Kantzer, Kenneth S. Ph.D., Harvard University. Dean emeritus, Trinity Evangelical Divinity School, Deerfield, Illinois.

Kelly, Douglas F. Ph.D., University of Edinburgh. Professor of systematic theology, Reformed Theological Seminary, Jackson, Mississippi.

Kent, Homer A., Jr. Th.D., Grace Theological Seminary. Professor emeritus, New Testament and Greek, Grace Theological Seminary, Winona Lake, Indiana.

Kerr, David W. Th.D., Harvard University. Late professor of Old Testament, Gordon Divinity School, Beverly Farms, Massachusetts.

Kerr, William Nigel. Th.D., Northern Baptist Theological Seminary; Ph.D.,

University of Edinburgh. Professor emeritus of church history and missions, Gordon-Conwell Theological Seminary, South Hamilton, Massachusetts.

Kevan, Ernest F. Ph.D., University of London. Late principal, London (England) Bible College.

Klooster, Fred H. Th.D., Free University. Professor emeritus, systematic theology, Calvin Theological Seminary, Grand Rapids, Michigan.

Klotz, John W. Ph.D., University of Pittsburgh. Professor emeritus, School for Graduate Studies, Concordia Seminary, St. Louis, Missouri.

Knight, George W., III. Th.D., Free University. Professor of New Testament, Knox Theological Seminary, Fort Lauderdale, Florida.

Knox, D. Broughton. D.Phil., Oxford University. Principal emeritus, Moore College, Sydney, Australia.

Kroeger, Catherine Clark. Ph.D., University of Minnesota. Adjunct professor, Gordon-Conwell Theological Seminary, South Hamilton, Massachusetts.

Kroeger, Richard C. S.T.M., University of Iowa. Retired assistant professor of religion, Eastern New Mexico University, Portales.

Kromminga, Carl Gerhard. Th.D., Free University. Professor emeritus, practical theology, Calvin Theological Seminary, Grand Rapids, Michigan.

Kubricht, Paul. Ph.D., Ohio State University. Professor of history, LeTourneau College, Longview, Texas.

Kuhn, Harold Barnes. Ph.D., Harvard University. Professor emeritus of philosophy of religion, Asbury Theological Seminary, Wilmore, Kentucky.

Kyle, Richard. Ph.D., University of New Mexico. Professor of history and religion, Tabor College, Hillsboro, Kansas.

La Bar, Martin. Ph.D., University of Wisconsin, Madison. Professor of science, Central (S.C.) Wesleyan College.

Ladd, George Eldon. Ph.D., Harvard University. Late professor of New Testament theology and exegesis, Fuller Theological Seminary, Pasadena, California.

Lamorte, André. Th.D., Montpelier University. Late professor of theology, Aix-en-Provence, France.

Laurin, Robert B. Ph.D., St. Andrews University. Late dean, American Baptist Seminary of the West, Berkeley, California.

Lewis, Gordon R. Ph.D., Syracuse University. Professor of systematic theology and Christian philosophy, Denver (Colo.) Seminary.

Liefeld, Walter L. Ph.D., Columbia University. Professor of New Testament, Trinity Evangelical Divinity School, Deerfield, Illinois.

Lightner, Robert P. Th.D., Dallas Theological Seminary. Professor of systematic theology, Dallas (Tex.) Theological Seminary.

Linder, Robert D. Ph.D., University of Iowa. Professor of history, Kansas State University, Manhattan.

Lowery, David K. Th.M., Dallas Theological Seminary. Professor of New Testament studies, Dallas (Tex.) Theological Seminary.

Lundin, Roger W. Ph.D., University of Connecticut. Professor of English, Wheaton (Ill.) College.

Lyon, Robert W. Ph.D., St. Andrews University. Professor of New Testament interpretation, Asbury Theological Seminary, Wilmore, Kentucky.

McClelland, Scott E. Ph.D., University of Edinburgh. Associate professor of biblical studies, King's College, Briarcliff Manor, New York.

McComiskey, Thomas Edward. Ph.D., Brandeis University. Professor of Semitic languages and Old Testament, Trinity Evangelical Divinity School, Deerfield, Illinois.

McDonald, H. D. Ph.D., D.D., University of London. Formerly vice-principal, London (England) Bible College.

Macdonald, Michael H. Ph.D., University of Washington. Professor of philosophy and European studies, Seattle (Wash.) Pacific University.

McGavran, Donald A. Ph.D., Columbia University. Late dean, Fuller Theological Seminary, Pasadena, California.

McIntire, C. T. Ph.D., University of Pennsylvania. Professor of history, Trinity College, University of Toronto, Ontario.

McKim, Donald K. Ph.D., University of Pittsburgh. Theologian, Presbyterian Church (USA).

McRay, John R. Ph.D., University of Chicago. Professor of New Testament and archaeology, Wheaton (Ill.) College Graduate School.

Magnuson, Norris A. Ph.D., University of Minnesota. Professor of church history, Bethel Theological Seminary, St. Paul, Minnesota.

Marchant, George John Charles. B.D., University of Durham. Archdeacon emeritus, Durham (England) Cathedral.

Mare, W. Harold. Ph.D., University of Pennsylvania. Professor emeritus of New Testament, Covenant Theological Seminary, St. Louis, Missouri.

Marshall, Caroline T. Ph.D., University of Virginia. Professor of history, James Madison University, Harrisonburg, Virginia.

Martin, Dennis D. Ph.D., University of Waterloo. Assistant professor of theology, Loyola University, Chicago.

Masselink, William. Th.D., Free University; Ph.D., Southern Baptist Theological Seminary. Late teacher of reformed doctrine, Reformed Bible College, Grand Rapids, Michigan.

Mathew, C. V. Th.M., Serampore University. Lecturer in religion and society, Union Biblical Seminary, Pune, India.

Mennell, James E. Ph.D., University of Iowa. Professor of history, Slippery Rock (Pa.) University.

Mickey, Paul A. Ph.D., Princeton Theological Seminary. Associate professor of pastoral theology, Duke University Divinity School, Durham, North Carolina.

Miller, Douglas J. Ph.D., Claremont School of Theology. Former professor of Christian social ethics, Eastern Baptist Theological Seminary, Philadelphia, Pennsylvania.

Moberg, David O. Ph.D., University of Minnesota. Professor of sociology, Marquette University, Milwaukee, Wisconsin.

Morris, Leon. Ph.D., Cambridge University. Retired principal, Ridley College, Melbourne, Australia.

Motyer, J. A. B.D., Trinity College, Dublin. Minister, Christ Church, Wesbourne, Dorset, England.

Motyer, Stephen. M.Litt., University of Bristol. Lecturer in New Testament, Oak Hill College, London, England.

Mounce, Robert H. Ph.D., University of Aberdeen. President emeritus, Whitworth College, Spane, Washington.

Mounce, William D. Ph.D., University of Aberdeen. Professor of religion and philosophy, Azusa Pacific University, Azusa, California.

Moyer, James C. Ph.D., Brandeis University. Professor of religious studies, Southwestern Missouri State University, Springfield.

Mueller, J. Theodore. Th.D., Xenia Theological Seminary. Ph.D., Webster University. Late professor of doctrinal and exegetical theology, Concordia Seminary, St. Louis, Missouri.

Nicole, Roger R. Th.D., Ph.D., Harvard University. Visiting professor of theology, Reformed Theological Seminary, Orlando, Florida.

Noll, Mark A. Ph.D., Vanderbilt University. Professor of history and church history, Wheaton (Ill.) College.

Noll, Stephen F. Ph.D., University of Manchester. Associate professor of biblical studies, Trinity Episcopal School for Ministry, Ambridge, Pennsylvania.

Obitts, Stanley R. Ph.D., University of Edinburgh. Professor of philosophy, Westmont College, Santa Barbara, California.

Oliver, O. Guy, Jr. B.D., Louisville Presbyterian Theological Seminary. Pastor and former professor of Christian mission, Erskine Theological Seminary, Due West, South Carolina.

Omanson, Roger L. Ph. D., Southern Baptist Theological Seminary. Translation consultant, United Bible Societies.

Osborne, Grant R. Ph.D., University of Aberdeen. Professor of New Testament, Trinity Evangelical Divinity School, Deerfield, Illinois.

Osterhaven, M. Eugene. Th.D., Princeton Theological Seminary. Professor emeritus, systematic theology, Western Theological Seminary, Holland, Michigan.

Packer, James I. D.Phil., Oxford University. Professor of historical and systematic theology. Regent College. Vancouver, British Columbia.

Parker, Thomas Henry Louis. D.D., Cambridge University. Late vicar of Oakington, rector of Great and Little Panton, and vicar of Brothertoft, Cambridge, England.

Payne, J. Barton. Ph.D., Princeton Theological Seminary. Late professor of Old Testament, Covenant Theological Seminary, St. Louis, Missouri.

Pfeiffer, Charles F. Ph.D., Dropsie College. Late professor of Hebrew and Oriental languages, Harvard University, Cambridge, Massachusetts.

Pierard, Richard V. Ph.D., University of Iowa. Professor of history, Indiana State University, Terre Haute.

Piggin, F. Stuart. Ph.D., University of London. Master, Robert Menzies College, Macquarie University, Australia.

Preus, Robert D. Ph.D., University of Edinburgh; D. Theol., Strasbourg University. Former president, Concordia Theological Seminary, St. Louis, Missouri.

Proctor, William Cecil Gibbon. B.D., Trinity College, Dublin. Formerly lecturer in the Divinity School, Trinity College, Dublin, Ireland.

Pun, Pattle P. T. Ph.D., State University of New York, Buffalo. Professor of biology, Wheaton (Ill.) College.

Rausch, David A. Ph.D., Kent State University. Professor of church history and Jewish studies, Ashland (Ohio) University.

Rayburn, Robert G. Th.D., Dallas Theological Seminary. Late president and professor of practical theology, Covenant Theological Seminary, St. Louis Missouri.

Rayburn, Robert S. Ph.D., University of Aberdeen. Pastor, Faith Presbyterian Church (PCA), Tacoma, Washington.

Rehwinkel, Alfred Martin. B.D., St. Stephen's Theological College. Late professor of theology, Concordia Seminary, St. Louis, Missouri.

Reid, William Stanford. Ph.D., University of Pennsylvania. Professor emeritus of history, University of Guelph, Ontario.

Rennie, Ian S. Ph.D., University of Toronto. Vice-president and academic dean, Ontario Theological Seminary, Willowdale.

Renwick, Alexander MacDonald. D.D., University of Edinburgh. Late professor of church history, Free Church of Scotland College, Edinburgh.

Reymond, Robert L. Ph.D., Bob Jones University. Professor of systematic theology, Knox Theological Seminary, Fort Lauderdale, Florida.

Ringenberg, William C. Ph.D., Michigan State University. Chair, Department of History, director, honors program, Taylor University, Upland, Indiana.

Ro, Bong Rin. Th.D., Concordia Seminary, St. Louis. Executive secretary, Asia Theological Association, Seoul, Korea.

Roberts, Robert C. Ph.D., Yale University. Professor of Philosophy and Psychology, Wheaton (Ill.) College.

Robinson, William Childs. Th.D., Harvard University. Late professor of church history and polity, Columbia (S.C.) Theological Seminary.

Ross, Alexander. M.A., University of Edinburgh. Late professor, New Testament exegesis, Free Church of Scotland College, Edinburgh.

Rule, Andrew Kerr. Ph.D., University of Edinburgh. Late professor of church history and apologetics, Louisville (Ky.) Presbyterian Theological Seminary.

Ryrie, Charles C. Th.D., Dallas Theological Seminary; Ph.D., University of Edinburgh. Professor emeritus of systematic theology, Dallas Theological Seminary.

Saucy, Robert L. Th.D., Dallas Theological Seminary. Professor of systematic theology, Talbot Theological Seminary, La Mirada, California.

Schnucker, Robert V. Ph.D., University of Iowa. Professor of history and religion, director, Thomas Jefferson University Press, Northeast Missouri State University, Kirksville.

Scholer, David M. Th.D., Harvard Divinity School. Distinguished professor of New Testament and early church history, North Park College and Theological Seminary, Chicago, Illinois.

Scott, J. Julius, Jr. Ph.D., University of Manchester. Professor of biblical and historical studies, Wheaton (Ill.) College Graduate School.

Seerveld, Calvin G. Ph.D., Free University. Senior member in philosophical aesthetics, Institute for Christian Studies, Toronto, Ontario.

Shelley, Bruce L. Ph.D., University of Iowa. Professor of church history, Denver (Colo.) Seminary.

Shelton, R. Larry. Th.D., Fuller Theological Seminary. Dean, School of Religion, Seattle Pacific University, Seattle, Washington.

Singer, C. Gregg. Ph.D., University of Pennsylvania. Professor of church history and historical theology, Greenville (S.C.) Presbyterian Theological Seminary.

Skillen, James W. Ph.D., Duke University. Executive director, Association for Public Justice, Washington, D.C.

Skoglund, Elizabeth R. M.A., MFCC, Pasadena College. Contributing editor,

Christian Herald and marriage, family and child counselor and writer, Burbank, California.

Smith, Stephen M. Ph.D., Claremont School of Theology. Associate professor of systematic theology and ethics, Trinity Episcopal School for Ministry, Ambridge, Pennsylvania.

Smith, Wilbur M. D.D., Dallas Theological Seminary. Late professor of English Bible, Fuller Theological Seminary, Pasadena, California.

Spiceland, James D. Ph.D., Oxford University. Associate professor of philosophy, Western Kentucky University, Bowling Green.

Sprunger, Keith L. Ph.D., University of Illinois. Oswald H. Wedel Professor of History, Bethel College, North Newton, Kansas.

Stanton, Gerry B. Th.D., Dallas Theological Seminary. Professor of missions, Oral Roberts University, Tulsa, Oklahoma.

Steeves, Paul D. Ph.D., University of Kansas. Professor of history, Stetson University, DeLand, Florida.

Stein, Robert H. Ph.D., Princeton Theological Seminary. Professor of New Testament, Bethel Theological Seminary, St. Paul, Minnesota.

Synan, Vinson. Ph.D., University of Georgia. Professor of Pentecostal and charismatic studies, Oral Roberts University, Tulsa, Oklahoma.

Taylor, Stephen. M.A., Wheaton College.

Tenney, Merrill C. Ph.D., Harvard University. Late professor of Bible and theology, Wheaton (Ill.) College.

Thomas, Robert L. Th.D., Dallas Theological Seminary. Professor of New Testament, The Master's Seminary, Panorama City, California.

Thomson, J. G. S. S. Ph.D., University of Edinburgh. Former professor of Hebrew and Old Testament. Columbia (S.C.) Theological Seminary.

Tinder, Donald G. Ph.D., Yale University. Professor, Evangelical Theological Faculty, Louvain, Belgium, and Tyndale Theological Seminary, Amsterdam, the Netherlands.

Tongue, Denis Harold. M.A., Cambridge University. Former lecturer in New Testament, Tyndale Hall, Bristol, England.

Toon, Peter. D.Phil., Oxford University. Director, Department of Systematic Theology, Nashotah House, Madison, Wisconsin.

Troutman, Richard L. Ph.D., University of Kentucky. Professor and head of History Department, Western Kentucky University, Bowling Green.

Tuttle, Robert G., Jr. Ph.D., University of Bristol. E. Stanley Jones Professor of Evangelism, Garrett Evangelical Theological Seminary, Evanston, Illinois.

Unger, Merrill F. Ph.D., Johns Hopkins University; Th.D., Dallas Theological Seminary. Late chairman, Old Testament Department, Dallas (Tex.) Theological Seminary.

Van Engen, John. Ph.D., University of California, Los Angeles. Director, Medieval Institute, University of Notre Dame, Indiana.

VanGemeren, Willem A. Ph.D., University of Wisconsin, Madison. Professor of Old Testament, Reformed Theological Seminary, Jackson, Mississippi.

VanderMolen, Ronald J. Ph.D., Michigan State University. Professor of history, California State University, Stanislaus, California.

Vos, Howard F. Th.D., Dallas Theological Seminary; Ph.D., Northwestern University. Professor of history and archaeology, King's College, Briarcliff Manor, New York.

Waetjen, Herman Charles. Th.D., University of Tübingen. Robert S. Dollar Professor of New Testament, San Francisco (Calif.) Theological Seminary and Graduate Theological Union.

Wallace, David H. Ph.D., University of Edinburgh. Former associate professor of Biblical theology, California Baptist Theological Seminary, Covina.

Wallace, Ronald Stewart. Ph.D., University of Edinburgh. Professor emeritus of biblical theology, Columbia (S.C.) Theological Seminary.

Walls, Andrew Finlay. B. Litt., Cambridge University. Professor of religious studies, University of Aberdeen Scotland.

Walter, Victor L. Th.M., Princeton Theological Seminary. Senior pastor, Cheyenne (Wyo.) Evangelical Free Church.

Walvoord, John F. Th.D., Dallas Theological Seminary; D.D., Wheaton College. Chancellor and professor emeritus, systematic theology, Dallas (Tex.) Theological Seminary.

Ward, Wayne E. Th.D., Southern Baptist Theological Seminary. Senior professor of Christian theology, Southern Baptist Theological Seminary, Louisville, Kentucky.

Weaver, J. Denny. Ph.D., Duke University. Professor of religion, Bluffton (Ohio) College.

Weber, Timothy P. Ph.D., University of Chicago. Professor of church history, Denver (Colo.) Seminary.

Webster, Douglas D. Ph.D., University of Toronto. Adjunct lecturer in theology and ethics, Ontario Theological Seminary, Willowdale; pastor, Evangelical Community Church, Bloomington, Ind.

Weinrich, William C. Th.D., University of Basel. Associate professor of historical theology and early Church history and patristic studies, Concordia Theological Seminary, Fort Wayne, Indiana.

Wenger, J. C. Th.D., University of Zurich. Late professor of historical theology, Goshen Biblical Seminary, Elkhart, Indiana.

Wheaton, David H. M.A., University of London. Principal, Oak Hill College, London, England.

White, R. E. O. B.D., University of London. Former principal, Baptist Theological College of Scotland.

White, Ronald C. Jr. Ph.D., Princeton University. Former director of continuing education, Princeton (N. J.) Theological Seminary.

Whitlock, Luder G., Jr. D.Min, Vanderbilt University. President, Reformed Theological Seminary, Jackson, Mississippi.

Williams, J. Rodman. Ph.D., Columbia University. Professor of theology, Regent University, Virginia Beach, Virginia.

Wilson, Marvin R. Ph.D., Brandeis University. Ockenga Professor of Biblical Studies, Gordon College, Wenham, Massachusetts.

Wolf, Herbert M. Ph.D., Brandeis University. Professor of theological studies, Wheaton (Ill.) College.

Wood, James E., Jr. Ph.D., Southern Baptist Theological Seminary. Simon and Ethel Bunn Professor of Church-State Studies and director, Institute of Church-State Studies, Baylor University, Waco, Texas.

Woolley, Paul. Th.M., Princeton Theological Seminary. Late professor of church history, Westminster Theological Seminary, Philadelphia, Pennsylvania.

Woudstra, Marten H. Th.D., Westminster Theological Seminary. Professor emeritus, Old Testament studies, Calvin Theological Seminary, Grand Rapids, Michigan.

Wright, David F. M.A., Cambridge University. Senior lecturer in ecclesiastical history and dean, faculty of divinity, New College, University of Edinburgh, Scotland.

Wright, John Stafford. M.A., Cambridge University. Late principal, Tyndale Hall, Bristol, England.

Wyngaarden, Martin J. Ph.D., University of Pennsylvania. Late professor of Old Testament interpretation, Calvin Theological Seminary, Grand Rapids, Michigan.

Youngblood, Ronald F. Ph.D., Dropsie College. Professor of Old Testament and Hebrew, Bethel Seminary West, San Diego, California.

Zerner, Ruth. Ph.D., University of California, Berkeley. Professor of history, Lehman College, City University of New York.

Aa

Abaddon. (Heb.; lit. "the destroyer"; Gk. *Apollyon*) A satanic angel who appears as king of a horde of hellish locust-monsters sent to plague rebellious humanity (Rev. 9:11). In the OT abaddon occurs as an epithet for the grave, Sheol, or Hades. It signifies "death," "ruin" or "destruction" (Job 26:6; 28:22; 31:12; Ps. 88:11; Prov. 15:11; 27:20).

G. L. ARCHER, JR.

See also BAAL-ZEBUB; SATAN.

Abba. (Aram. "my father"; Gk. *patēr*) Occurs in Jesus' Gethsemane prayer (Mark 14:36), and for the cry of the Spirit in the heart of a Christian (Rom. 8:15; Gal. 4:6). In each case it is used in conjunction with the Greek equivalent.

R. EARLE

See also FATHER, GOD AS; GOD, NAMES OF.

Abelard, Peter (1079–1142). Philosopher, theologian, and teacher. Peter Abelard lived in constant personal turmoil and confrontation with authority. Born in Brittany, he studied with some of the most respected theologians of his day and became the brightest intellectual star of the Cathedral School of Paris. But for a tragic love affair and marriage, he undoubtedly would have been the dominant thinker of the century.

Abelard mediated between nominalist and realist philosophies, distinguishing between a mental concept and the objective reality it represents. He also developed what is usually called the moral influence theory of the atonement. Abelard's conception was that in Christ God showed his love in voluntarily assuming the burden of suffering brought on by human sin. This free act of God's grace demands no human response or compensation for sin—instead it awakens in people gratitude and love for God.

Abelard's *Sic et Non* (*Yes and No*), written around 1120, paved the way for Thomas Aquinas and medieval scholasticism in its strong defense of the role of reason as well as faith in theology. Abelard argued that simply quoting traditional church fathers did not in itself determine truth; intellectual skills must also be applied to the problem.

R. D. LINDER

See also ATONEMENT, THEORIES OF THE; REALISM; SCHOLASTICISM.

Abomination of Desolation. (Gk. *bdelygma tēs erēmoseōs)* This precise form is found in the KJV in Matt. 24:15 and Mark 13:14, but the idea is expressed in Luke 21:20. The phrase is undoubtedly taken from Dan. 11:31 and 12:11, where the KJV reads "the abomination that maketh desolate"; it is possible also that Dan. 8:13 and 9:27 contribute to the conception. Most expositors regard the passages in Daniel as allusions to the desecration of the temple by Antiochus Epiphanes. On Dec. 15, 168 B.C., a pagan altar to Zeus Olympios was built on the site of the great altar of burnt sacrifices; 10 days later heathen sacrifice was offered on it.

The passages in the NT are predictive, so are not exhausted by the historical fulfillment of the intertestamental period. The Greek phrase may be rendered "a detestable thing that brings desolation."

On the principle of interpreting the texts of Matthew and Mark by Luke 21:20, therefore, the "abomination of desolation" must mean the destruction of Jerusalem by Roman troops. Fulfillment began under Cestius (Gallus) in A.D. 66, continued under Vespasian (A.D. 68), and the city was utterly devastated by Titus (A.D. 70). It was the encirclement (*kykloumenēn*) of Jerusalem by besieging forces of the Roman army that constituted the sign. The participle is in the present tense and shows that the Christians were to flee when they saw the city "being compassed" with armies.

E. F. KEVAN

See also ANTICHRIST.

Abortion. An abortion is an induced termination of pregnancy in a manner designed to kill the embryo or fetus. Although miscarriage is sometimes referred to as "involuntary" abortion, Christian ethical concerns involve "voluntary abortion."

Harold O. J. Brown summarizes the historic Christian view of abortion by observing: "The overwhelming consensus of the spiritual leaders of Protestantism, from the Reformation to the present, is clearly antiabortion. There is very little doubt among biblically oriented Protestants that abortion is an attack on the image of God in the developing child and is a great evil" (*Human Life Review,* Fall 1976, 131).

Karl Barth's view is normative: "The unborn child is from the first a child. It is still developing and has no independent life. But it is a man and not a thing, nor a mere part of the mother's body. . . . He who destroys germinating life kills a man" (*Church Dogmatics*, 3.4.415ff.).

Advocates of a liberal abortion policy make three key arguments in support of their position. (1) The abortion decision is within the woman's "freedom of choice" (or "right of privacy" or her "right of control over her own body"). The antiabortion response is that one's freedom to act is limited by another's right not to be acted upon. Abortion thus involves the rights of both the mother and child. Any conception of the unborn child as a mere appendage of the mother's body is rejected; the unborn child is considered a valuable human being. (2) We may not impose a particular view of morality or value system upon law in a pluralistic society. The antiabortion response is that there is no position in which "values neutrality" is possible. It is not a question of *whether* but *whose* morality or values will be reflected in law and public policy. (3) It is necessary to protect the "quality of life" of the mother and those children who are allowed to be born. This "quality-of-life" ethic stands in contrast to the traditional Judeo-Christian "sanctity-of-life" ethic. The quality of life argument is normally raised in connection with so-called hard cases (pregnancy resulting from rape, incest, or teenage sex, where birth defects seem likely, or where the mother has a history of child abuse) and has been effective as an emotional appeal to many who are sensitive to human suffering. Proponents argue that it is compassionate for professionals to be given the legal right to determine which "products of conception" should be "terminated." The antiabortion response is to reject as morally and theologically repugnant the contention that fetuses' right to life depends upon their being "wanted," upon their genetic or physical endowment, or upon how much it will cost their parents or society to rear them.

C. HORN, III

Abraham's Bosom. In Luke 16:22–23, Jesus speaks of Lazarus being carried by the angels into *Abraham's bosom* to the heavenly banquet. Reclining at table at Abraham's side (cf. John 13:23), Lazarus is thus enjoying the privileges of a guest of honor (cf. Matt. 8:11). Jesus draws a clear distinction between Hades as a place of torment and Abraham's bosom as one of rest and intimate fellowship. He makes clear that the two are not simply separate divisions or compartments of the same place.

M. H. WOUDSTRA

See also INTERMEDIATE STATE.

Absolution. (Lat. *absolvo*, "to loosen or set free") The forgiveness of sins. One who is absolved is truly free in that no accusation of sin can be made. The term is used in the Roman Catholic doctrine of the remission from sin available through the church and its sacraments.

In the Bible. All sin is sin against God ("Against thee, thee only, have I sinned" [Ps. 51:4, KJV]), and therefore sin can only be forgiven in the last analysis by God.

But one's sin affects others as well as offending God. In particular the sins of a Christian affect the church and the person's relationship with the church. The Lord's teaching concerning forgiveness links the disciples' forgiveness of one another with God's forgiveness (Matt. 6:12). In saying, "Whatever you bind on earth will be bound in heaven, and whatever you loose on earth will be loosed in heaven" (Matt. 16:19; 18:18), Jesus commissions ministry which is connected in John 20:21–23 with the inspiration of the Holy Spirit.

In the Church. In early church practice the penitent made public confession of sin before the congregation and was received back by the congregation with prayer and the laying on of hands by the bishop. In time a natural alternative to public confession was for the penitent to confess privately before the bishop or a presbyter. From the 8th century priests took on a more judicial role, inquiring into every aspect of the penitent's life. Absolution took on a declaratory form as distinct from the earlier precatory form. Thomas Aquinas was the first formally to defend this type of absolution, which is still used in the priest's declaration: *Ego te absolvo a peccatis tuis in nomine Patris et Filii et Spiritus Sancti.*

In declaring that no human priest stands between the individual and God, the Reformers sought to restore forgiveness to its scriptural and early church usage. The confessional and its declaratory form of absolution were abolished in Protestant churches. This stirring of the conscience to repentance is mainly affected by preaching and prayer. Any declaration of forgiveness takes the form of a proclamation of the Bible's promises.

W. C. G. PROCTOR

See also ATONEMENT; FORGIVENESS; PENITENCE; REPENTANCE.

Abyss. See BOTTOMLESS PIT.

Accommodation. The characteristic of biblical literature in which a writer, for purposes of simplification, adjusts language to the limitations of readers without compromising truth. Thus, in theology God may be described through anthropomorphic reference to physical properties (hands, eyes, etc.). In cosmology facts of nature may be described in language of appearance instead of science (the sun "sets"). In ethics a stronger Christian may accommodate to the scruples of a weaker (1 Cor. 8; Gal. 2:3–5). In teaching, the language of parable may be used to convey deeper spiritual mysteries to the unenlightened (Matt. 13:10–17).

W. BROOMALL

See also ANTHROPOMORPHISM.

Accountability. See RESPONSIBILITY.

Accountability, Age of. See AGE OF ACCOUNTABILITY.

Acolyte. See MINOR ORDERS.

Active Obedience of Christ. See OBEDIENCE OF CHRIST.

Acts of Uniformity. See UNIFORMITY, ACTS OF.

Adam. (Heb.; lit. "man") The Hebrew word transliterated "Adam" is found about 560 times in the OT. In the overwhelming majority it means "man" or "humankind." It is a proper name in some instances—Gen. 4:1; 1 Chron. 1:1; Luke 3:37; Jude 14.

Adam in OT Teaching. The creation narratives tell us that *Adam* as head of the human race is made of dust from the ground and so is related to the rest of creation (Gen. 2:7, 19), as well as to God (Gen. 1:27; cf. 2:7). Adam has "dominion" over the lower forms of creation (Gen. 1:26, 28), an authority symbolized in the naming of the other creatures. The fall passage (Gen. 3) speaks of the seriousness of Adam's sin and of its permanent effects. This is not a topic to which there is frequent reference in the OT, but there is a fundamental presupposition that every individual is a sinner which marks off the literature of the Hebrews from other literatures of antiquity. The solidarity of Adam with his descendants is in the background throughout the OT, as is the connection between sin and death.

Adam in Intertestamental and NT Thought. During the intertestamental period there are striking expressions of solidarity with Adam, such as Ezra's impassioned exclamation: "O Adam, what have you done? For though it was you who sinned, the fall was not yours alone, but ours also who are your descendants" (2 Esd. 7:48 [118]; cf. 3:21; 4:30; Wis. 2:23–24; the blame is assigned to Eve in Sir. 25:24). Adam was seen not as a lone sinner, but as one who influenced all humanity.

In 1 Tim. 2:13–14 the subordinate place of woman is argued from two facts: (1) Adam was created first, and (2) Eve was deceived though Adam was not. This passage presumes that the Genesis stories tell us something of permanent significance about all men and women. Rom. 5 stresses the connection of humanity at large with Adam. It was through that one man that sin came into the world, and the consequence of his sin was death. This happened long before the law was given, so death cannot merely be law-breaking. Of the resurrection Paul writes: "As in Adam all die, even so in Christ shall all be made alive" (1 Cor. 15:22, KJV). Rom. 5 states that Adam was the head of the race and brought death to everyone in it; Christ is the head of the new humanity and brought life to all within it.

Scriptural use of "Adam," then, stresses the solidarity in sin of the human race. It reminds us that the human race had a beginning and that all its history from the very first is marked by sin. But "the last Adam" has replaced sin with righteousness and death with life.

L. MORRIS

See also ADAM, THE LAST; FALL OF MAN; MAN, ORIGIN OF; SIN.

Adam, The Last. In 1 Cor. 15:45 Paul refers to Jesus Christ as "the last Adam" (*ho eschatos Adam*) in contrast to "the first man Adam" (*ho prōtos anthrōpos Adam*). In this antithetic parallelism lies a continuity of humanity, but the second person who represents the new humanity so far excels the first that he is described as the one who became an active "life-giving spirit" (*pneuma zōopoioun*), where the original Adam (Gen. 2:7) became only "a natural living being" (*psychēn zōsan*). The contrast is heightened in 1 Cor. 15:46–49 (see also 1 Cor. 15:21–22; Rom. 5:14–19).

R. G. GRUENLER

See also ADAM; INCARNATION.

Administration, Gift of. See SPIRITUAL GIFTS.

Adonai. See GOD, NAMES OF.

Adoption. A relatively infrequent term in the Scriptures, "adoption" is of theological importance in relating how God made Israel and makes Christians his "sons" and "heirs."

In the OT. "Adoption" does not appear in the OT, nor was adoption provided for in Israelite law. Examples which do occur come from outside the Israelite culture (Eliezer in Gen. 15:1–4; Moses in Exod. 2:10; Genubath in 1 Kings 11:20; Esther in Esther 2:7, 15).

For Israel as a whole there was a consciousness of having been chosen by God as his "son" (Isa. 1:2; Jer. 3:19; Hos. 11:1). Likewise the kings succeeding David were ascribed sonship before God (2 Sam. 7:14; 1 Chron. 28:6; Ps. 89:27). Ps. 2:7 uses "You are my son," which is probably the adoption formula used in the enthronement ceremony of each successive Davidic ruler. Together these ideas laid the basis for later NT usage of adoption imagery.

In the NT. In the NT the term "adoption" (*huiothesia*) is strictly a Pauline idea, occurring in Rom. 8:15, 23; 9:4; Gal. 4:5; and Eph. 1:5. In Greek and Roman society adoption was relatively common, at least among the upper classes. Adoption conferred rights and came with a list of duties as well.

Paul proclaims adoption as deliverance from the past, a status and way of life in the present, and a hope for the future. It describes the process of becoming a son of God (cf. John 1:12; 1 John 3:1–2) and receiving an inheritance from God (cf. Col. 3:24).

P. H. Davids

Adoptionist, Adoptionism. The theory that Jesus was a normal man who was selected to become the Son of God. The earliest extant expression of this position is *The Shepherd of Hermas* (A.D. 150). It taught that the Redeemer was a virtuous man chosen by God, to be united with God's Spirit. He was by divine decree adopted as Son and exalted to lordship.

This view was perpetuated in the 2d and 3d centuries by dynamic monarchians, who taught that Christ was a mere man on whom the power of God came and who was then adopted or constituted "the Son of God." A leader in that general movement was Theodotus, who came to Rome from Byzantium in about 190, teaching the virgin birth but asserting that Jesus became the Son of God only after he was tested as a human. Theodotus was excommunicated and his theology failed to win many followers.

The heresy technically called as Adoptionism originated in Spain in the 8th century, where it troubled the Spanish and Frankish churches. Elipandus, bishop of Toledo from ca. 780, expressed the view that Christ was an adopted Son; Felix, bishop of Urgel in the Pyrenees, held a similar position. Their teachings were condemned by three synods under Charlemagne. Both recanted as ordered by Pope Adrian I. Extensive efforts were required to bring their numerous following back into the fold. The effects of the controversy lasted for decades in Toledo.

H. F. Vos

Adultery. In Scripture voluntary cohabitation of a married person with any other than his or her lawful spouse. The Bible sometimes designates adultery as *porneia*, "fornication" (1 Cor. 5:1), though this properly designates any sexual intercourse between persons not married to one another. Scripture distinguishes between *pornoi* ("fornicators"), and *moichoi* ("adulterers"), as in 1 Cor. 6:9.

Adultery is forbidden in Scripture, especially in the interest of the sanctity of the home and family (Exod. 20:14; Deut. 5:18). Lev. 18:20 condemns self-defilement by lying with a neighbor's spouse. The penalty for the offense was death (Lev. 20:10; John 8:5). The moral law condemns adulterous practices committed with the eye and the heart (Job 31:1, 7) as well as in action. Christ emphasized such chastity in the Sermon on the Mount (Matt. 5:28), where he pronounced guilty anyone who looked upon a woman lustfully.

When our Lord testified against the lax divorce practices of the Jews who followed the loose interpretation of Deut. 24:1–3 advocated by Hillel, in Matt. 5:32; 19:9 he supported the stricter school of Shammai in justifying divorce only in cases of adultery. The NT warns against all sexual immorality in 1 Cor. 6:9; Heb. 13:4, and James 4:4.

J. T. MUELLER

See also FORNICATION; DIVORCE; MARRIAGE, THEOLOGY OF.

Advent. (Lat., *adventus*, "coming, arrival") The season of the ecclesiastical year for preparation to celebrate the birth of Jesus Christ (Christmas), a time when the church engages in self-examination in expectation of Christ's second coming. It begins in the West on the Sunday nearest to St. Andrew's Day (Nov. 30) and always includes four Sundays. In the East the period is longer, beginning earlier in November.

P. TOON

See also CHRISTIAN YEAR.

Adventism. The belief that Christ's personal second coming is imminent and will inaugurate a millennial kingdom and the end of the age. Chiliasm, apocalypticism, and millennialism are cognate theological terms. Similar beliefs have been espoused by diverse groups throughout Christian history (e.g., Montanists, Anabaptists, Fifth Monarchy Men, Plymouth Brethren and other premillennialists, and Jehovah's Witnesses).

Adventism is most commonly used to denote the movement which sprang up in the 1830s from the teachings of William Miller, a Baptist minister in New York. Miller and his successor leaders prophesied exact years and even dates for the return of Christ. In the wake of several disappointments many, including Miller, abandoned the church. Under Hiram Edson and the prophecies of Ellen Gould (Harmon) White, the movement achieved new fervor.

Two major bodies represent the movement today—the Advent Christian Church and the numerically predominant Seventh-day Adventists. Adventists have been especially known for their health-care ministries. Such dietary concerns as proscription of coffee and tea and advocacy of vegetarianism predated other health movements. Modern Adventist theologians have tended to regard individual prophecies as subject to the judgment of Scripture, and Seventh-day Adventists are considered by some evangelicals to be within the pale of orthodoxy.

M. E. DIETER

See also SABBATARIANISM; SOUL SLEEP; WHITE, ELLEN GOULD; MILLENNIUM, VIEWS OF THE; ANNIHILATIONISM.

Advent of Christ. See BIRTH OF JESUS CHRIST; SECOND COMING OF CHRIST.

Advocate. See HOLY SPIRIT.

Aeon. See AGE, AGES.

Aesthetics, Christian View of. Aesthetics is the philosophical study of the beautiful and of fine arts. Christian and secular aesthetic theories differ in that Christian aesthetics relates beauty to the lordship of Jesus Christ.

Development of a Theology of Beauty. Platonic thought first reflected on beauty but set up what became perhaps the major stumbling block to a fruitful theory of art.

Plato lost the possibility of a down-to-earth sense of beauty and a trustworthy hermeneutic for imagination when he posited that absolute beauty lies outside the visible, temporal world. A good

Greek mind would pursue this transcendent perfection until it came to contemplate the unspeakably well-proportioned, noetic form of beauty itself. Then one's immortal soul would be saved from the curse of bodily, earthly transience (*Symposium*, 209e–212a). Platonic conceptions of beauty were brought into the church by the Hellenist Plotinus and Augustine. Thomas Aquinas's doctrine of beauty retained Plato's highly mathematical dogma. Proportion, perfection, and brilliance were attributes of God the Son by which beauty could be judged in the mundane forms.

John Calvin understood the visible beauty of creation to mirror God's glory; art then became a gift of God's general revelation. The 1898 Princeton lectures of Abraham Kuyper followed Calvin and formulated an idealism which has become the tradition among evangelical Protestant thinkers; art's mystical task is to remind those homesick for heaven of the beauty that was lost and the perfect luster that is coming. Christian thinkers who adopt a theology of beauty are beset by the problems which attend natural theology and all theodicies: How radical and disfiguring is the reality of sin? Can beautiful nature and art be evil? If human art is beautiful, is it not naturally good?

Struggle for a Foolproof Hermeneutics. Modern debate in aesthetic theory has largely converted beauty into a problem of individual taste. There is doubt that the mind can be sure its critical analysis of beauty is correct. Immanuel Kant saw taste as autonomous. A person's view of beauty was a source of personal satisfaction but not objective knowledge.

Romantic idealists (e.g., Johann Herder and Friedrich Schelling) supported the existence of artistic genius and intellectually intuitive creativity that transcends examination. Positivists discounted any truth which could not be reduced to neutral technical description. Marxist thinkers saw more clearly than most Christians that the perspective of the artist permeates any work, and its merit can be judged on that basis. Christians working in literary theory and the aesthetics of art and literary criticism, as well as ordinary expositors of the Bible, have usually followed secular trends at a distance. Idealists express concern for the spiritual content of art without regard for technical details translated into Bultmannian attempts to get to the *kerygma* core of Scripture.

Other seekers of truth, whether in the arts or exposition, follow these and other aesthetic philosophies, contributing to the modern theological confusion.

Problems of Systematic Aesthetic Theory. Christian aesthetic theory assumes that the world is created and revealed in God. There must be objective standards for aesthetic reality, for the style of ordinary life, and for the construction of artworks. Biblical Christian aesthetic analysis also recognizes that performers and critics, leaders in style and composers, have breathed a holy or evil spirit into what they produce which needs to be examined to determine whether the work has served the public with insight or a curse.

One attempt to systemize art views the incarnation of Jesus Christ as the paradigm for artistic acts. Artists give form and sensation to spiritual content. Such a theology of transcendental beauty likens God to artist and treats all art as essentially sacramental. Perhaps the most radically Christian aesthetic philosophy yet developed asserts that artists are called to imaginatively mime and interpret with nuance the things and events in creation. Artists are understood not as imitators of Christ taking on flesh but as diaconal workers skilled in forming symbols pregnant with meaning for whoever has eyes to see and ears to hear. Artworks are metaphors and parables that can be critiqued as expressions of committed human subjects under Christ's rule. If the artwork is vain, it needs to be charitably humbled; if weak, it should be aided by informed wisdom; if fruitful, it should be praised with thanks.

Such an aesthetic theory encompasses any genre of arts and literature. Portraiture can serve, as can monuments, advertising, and liturgy. Theater, concerts, paintings, and novels make their own special contributions. The ultimate arbiter of aesthetic quality becomes God's judgment of a work's redemptive fruit on the final Lord's day.

C. G. SEERVELD

Affliction. See PAIN.

Affusion. See BAPTISM, MODES OF.

Agape. See LOVE FEAST; LOVE.

Age, Ages. (Heb. *'ôlām*; Gk. *aiōn*) A long, indefinite period of time, past or future, whose limits are determined only by the context or nature of the thing spoken of.

OT Usage. *Undefined Past.* Amos 9:11 foresees the restoration of the tabernacle of David as in "days of antiquity." The expression "from antiquity" can refer to events in the indefinite past (Josh. 24:2; Jer. 2:20; Jer. 28:8). It can also include the whole sweep of human history (Isa. 64:4; Joel 2:2). The word is used of God's acts and relationship with Israel in the undefined past (Ps. 25:6; Isa. 63:16) or to refer to the totality of God's dealings with humanity (Isa. 63:19); it can simply designate indefinite time (Isa. 42:14).

Indefinite Future. An indeterminate future is seen in 1 Sam. 13:13; Isa. 32:14. Enduring without end are God's salvation (Isa. 51:6–8), his dwelling in Jerusalem (1 Chron. 23:25), his covenants (Gen. 17:7; Isa. 55:3), the Mosaic institution (Exod. 27:21; 30:21; Lev. 3:17; 10:9; Num. 10:8), the passover observance (Exod. 12:24), Solomon's temple (1 Kings 9:3; 2 Kings 21:7), the Holy City (Ps. 125:1), and Messiah's rule (Ps. 45:6; Isa. 9:7). That some of these institutions passed away illustrates that precise meaning is to be derived from its context.

When applied to the existence of God, the full idea of eternity emerges (Deut. 32:40; Isa. 40:28; Dan. 12:7). The plural *ages* intensifies the idea of an unending future: Ps. 145:13; Isa. 26:4; 45:17; Dan. 9:24.

Past and Future. The indefinite past and future, "from antiquity and unto futurity," are brought together, referring to the existence of God (Pss. 90:2; 106:48); God's love (Ps. 103:17); praise to God (Neh. 9:5); the promise of the land of Israel (Jer. 7:7; 25:5).

NT Usage. Aiōn *as Indefinite Time.* The age of the prophets is "from the age," that is, from long ago (Luke 1:70; Acts 3:21). God's revelation to Israel was "from the age" (Acts 15:18).

The expression "unto the age" occurs 27 times. In Matt. 21:19; Mark 3:29; John 13:8; 1 Cor. 8:13 it means "never." In other contexts the idea of a future eternity is apparent (John 6:51, 58; 10:22; 2 Cor. 9:9; Heb. 5:6; 6:20).

The plural, "ages," strengthens the idea of endlessness. (1) In the past: "before the ages" (1 Cor. 2:7); "from the ages" (Col. 1:26; Eph. 3:9). (2) In the future: "unto the ages" (Luke 1:33; Rom. 1:25; 9:5; 11:36; 2 Cor. 11:31; Heb. 13:8). Jude 25 reads "unto all the ages." The parallelism of ages and generations in Col. 1:26 suggests that the plural form conceives of time as consisting of a succession of many ages or generations.

The eternity of the future is further strengthened by doubling the form: (1) in the singular: "unto the age of the age" (Heb. 1:8); (2) in the plural: "unto the ages of the ages." This expression occurs 21 times.

The lordship of God over all time is seen in the expression "king of the ages" (1 Tim. 1:17; Rev. 15:3).

Aiōn *as a Segment of Time.* Theologically the most important usage of *aiōn* in the NT is when it designates two periods: this age and the age to come within the eschatological character of the work of redemption. This idiom views redemptive history as two distinct and contrasting periods of time.

This age will come to its end with the parousia of Christ (Matt. 24:3). At the consummation of this age the Son of Man will send his angels to separate the wicked from the righteous (Matt. 13:39–42).

The age to come will be the age of eternal life (Luke 20:34–35; see Mark 10:30). In that age the righteous will "shine like the sun in the kingdom of their Father" (Matt. 13:43, NIV). Mark 10:30 equates the age to come with both eternal life and the kingdom of God; and in Matt. 25:46 the righteous inherit the kingdom of God and enter into eternal life when the Son of man comes in his glory (Matt. 25:31) at the end of this age (Matt. 25:41). This dualistic structure is shared with contemporary Judaism (see 4 Esd. 6:7–9; 7:20–31), but it is implicit in the OT, which sees the world in need of a miraculous transformation by the direct act of God before God's people can enjoy the fullness of the redemptive blessings (Isa. 65:17–25).

At one important point the NT stands apart from its Jewish environment: In Christ the blessings of the age to come have entered into this evil age. Jesus, who will come in glory as the Son of man to inaugurate the age to come, has already appeared on earth in humility to bring the life of the age to come. We already taste the powers of the coming age (Heb. 6:5). Through the death of Christ we are now delivered from this present evil age (Gal. 1:4). We are no longer to be conformed to this age but are to be transformed by an inner power (Rom. 12:2). Therefore, eternal life, which belongs to the age to come (Matt. 25:46; Mark 10:30; John 12:25; Rom. 2:7), is a present possession (John 3:36; 6:47). Justification has already been accomplished (Rom. 3:24; 5:1), freeing us from fear of the judgment at the end of this age (Matt. 12:36–37; Rom. 8:33–34). Salvation belongs to the future (Rom. 13:11; 1 Pet. 1:5, 9), but it also is present (2 Cor. 6:2; Eph. 2:8). The kingdom of God, which belongs to the age to come (Matt. 25:34; 1 Cor. 15:50), has invaded this age, bringing its blessings in advance (Matt. 12:28; Luke 17:20; Col. 1:13; Rom. 14:17). Christians live in two ages; they enjoy the powers of the age to come while living in the end of this age.

G. E. LADD

See also TIME; ETERNITY; KINGDOM OF CHRIST, GOD, HEAVEN; SECOND COMING OF CHRIST; THIS AGE, THE AGE TO COME; TIME.

Age, This. See THIS AGE, THE AGE TO COME.

Age of Accountability, The. The stage of life at which moral consciousness emerges and with it responsibility for conduct before God. This is not a fixed age, but relates to the mental and social ability in the individual, to go beyond mere imitation of the behavior of others to evaluate choices on moral and spiritual bases. See Rom. 1:20; 2:20; 2 Cor. 5:10.

G. M. BURGE

Age of Man. See MAN, ORIGIN OF.

Aging, Christian View of. The aging of the world's population is paralleled by rapid graying of church membership. Challenging opportunities for Christian ministries with and for the aged emerge from applying biblical values to current realities.

Demographic Data. United Nations studies reveal an accelerating increase in the world's aging population. In 1975, 343.151 million or 8.5 percent of the population were past age 60; by the year 2000 the figure is expected to be 579.995

million or 9.4 percent. The increases will be much greater in Africa, Latin America, and South Asia than in Europe and North America, where already significant increases will bring the proportion past age 60 years to about one-fifth of the population.

In the U.S. the percentage of people past age 65 increased by 27.9 percent from 1970 to 1980, while the percentage of those under age 65 increased only 9.7 percent. In 1980, 25.544 million people (11.3 percent or one in every nine) were past age 65. The proportions ranged widely from a low of 2.3 percent in Alaska to a high of 17.3 percent in Florida, but there is a much wider spread in local communities; in some, more than one-fourth of the population are past age 65.

The proportion of church membership past 65 is generally higher for several reasons. (1) Many churches do not include young children in their membership. (2) Older people tend to retain their membership more tenaciously than young adults. (3) On the basis of several criteria, they are the most religious segment of the population. Graying hair and wrinkled skin characterize a majority of the active members in many congregations.

In 1900 average life expectancy at birth was 47.3 years in the U.S. By 1978 it had risen to 73.3, but for women it was 77.2, compared to 69.5 for men. There were 1.333 million widowers past 65 in 1980, compared with 7.121 million widows. Women also greatly exceed men among the elderly divorced and single populations. These differences have profound implications for churches.

Social Circumstances. Much poverty among the elderly is invisible. They tend to retain middle-class attitudes and try to remain self-sufficient, keeping up the appearance of an earlier lifestyle so well that their economic plight is overlooked by others. Inflation eats away the buying power of savings; except for Social Security benefits, income seldom increases with rising costs. Poverty among young adults can be viewed as temporary; among the elderly it is permanent and hopeless.

Economic problems influence self-concepts. Retirement not only brings reduced income but also contributes to a loss of personal identity (who am I without a job title?), feelings of inferiority, and a spirit of self-pity.

The necessity to live on a reduced income affects other activities. Retired people usually have extra discretionary time to spend, yet cost may prevent participation in social activities. Some save money on food at the expense of a balanced diet, which in turn increases susceptibility to illness. Telephone subscriptions may have to be cancelled or services reduced, restricting communication with others. They may also avoid making advisable medical appointments if costs exceed insurance coverage.

Biblical Values. The Ten Commandments mandate respect for parents (Exod. 20:12; Deut. 5:16), and the Mosaic law commanded respect for the elderly (Lev. 19:32). Some Christians interpret these and related passages (e.g., Eph. 6:1–3; 1 Tim. 5:3–16) to mean that all responsibility for the aging resides in their own children. Many, however, have no children or none who can care for their needs. About 6 percent of the elderly have never married, and one-tenth of those who did marry did not have children. Children also may have died, have become incapacitated, or be living under financial and physical disabilities of their own old age.

The law to love our neighbor as we love ourselves pertains to all ages as a two-way relationship. The elderly can share in the joy that comes from giving to others if they are helped to discover opportunities for service. Biblical ethics imply that Christians should work *with* the aging, not merely provide services *to* them. Doing for others what we would want them to do for us (Matt. 7:12) requires respect for their individual uniqueness, autonomy, interdependencies, and abilities. No single approach to ministry fits everyone; alternatives enable each older person to choose what best fits personal desires and needs.

Ministries with and for the Aging. The range of potential and actual services to the aging by churches is extremely broad. Besides ministries that serve all ages, church-sponsored housing, nursing care facilities, and home care services help to meet needs at various levels of care. Most gerontologists recommend that people be helped to remain in their own homes as long as possible, both to promote their sense of well-being and to reduce economic costs. Volunteer services and exchanges of labor can help meet this need. A daily telephone reassurance call and regular assistance with housework, laundry, bathing, home maintenance, and transportation can extend the years during which many are capable of residing at home.

Senior citizen programs help to meet many physical, material, educational, social, psychic, and spiritual needs when they are wisely planned and directed. They also give older persons the opportunity to serve others. Day care services can provide for the daytime needs of dependent older persons while household members are at work or school. Churches can supplement public social service programs and in the process provide older persons with the opportunity to help others, thus helping themselves.

The elderly should be remembered in all church ministries, including evangelism. They are an important asset. Their presence is a living witness to God's faithfulness. Their prayers provide important support to the pastor and other leaders. The active service of the "young old" can significantly enlarge the scope of church ministries. As their spiritual needs are met, they in turn minister to the needs of others.

D. O. MOBERG

Agnosticism. Although etymologically applicable to any kind of skepticism, the term was coined in 1869 by T. H. Huxley to signify religious skepticism. Huxley taught that no person can know whether God exists.

Agnosticism can refer to: (1) the suspension of judgment on all ultimate issues, including God, free will, or immortality; (2) a secularistic attitude, such as the belief that God is irrelevant to the life of modern man; (3) a strongly anti-Christian and anticlerical attitude; (4) roughly synonymous with atheism.

P. D. FEINBERG

See also GOD, ARGUMENTS FOR THE EXISTENCE OF; PASCAL'S WAGER.

Agricola, Johann (ca. 1494–1566). German reformer, theologian, pastor, and teacher. Johann Agricola (family name Schneider or Schnitter) was born in Eisleben, Germany, more than a decade after Martin Luther. Agricola went to Wittenberg in 1515 to study with Luther and remained there for 10 years. In 1536 Luther invited him back to Wittenberg to teach theology.

It was during his second Wittenberg period that Agricola became the center of what was to become the first major theological dispute in the Lutheran movement—the so-called antinomian controversy.

The antinomian controversy lasted intermittently from 1537 to 1540 when, just ahead of a trial for heresy, Agricola hastily left Wittenberg for Berlin to become court preacher for the elector Joachim II of Brandenburg. Agricola argued that people were sufficiently motivated by hearing of Christ's sacrifice for their sins and that the preaching of the law was unnecessary and perhaps even harmful. Agricola backed down from some of his more radical statements, but he and Luther remained estranged.

R. D. LINDER

See also ANTINOMIANISM; LUTHER, MARTIN.

Aids, Gift of. See SPIRITUAL GIFTS.

À Kempis, Thomas. See THOMAS À KEMPIS.

Albertus Magnus (1193–1280). Dominican scholar, theologian, and churchman. Albert was the dominant intellectual of his age and an early champion of the right of scholars to use reason in the search for truth. A Swabian of noble birth, he became a monk (1223), attended the University of Paris and taught there from 1245 to 1248. His most famous student was Thomas Aquinas. In 1248 he returned to Cologne to establish a new course of studies for the Dominicans and later served as head of the order for the German province.

The scientific works of Aristotle and commentaries on them by Islamic scholars were then becoming known in the universities of Europe. He was the first to master this material, sharing his understanding in many of the 21 massive volumes that he wrote. The most significant of his works were his explanation of Aristotle's scientific writings and his attempt to harmonize theology and philosophy in the *Summa theologiae*.

R. G. CLOUSE

See also SCHOLASTICISM.

Alcohol, Drinking of. Consumption of ethyl alcohol (ethanol) as a beverage ingredient. It is both an energy source and a drug that affects the central nervous system and depresses sensory functions. The desired effects of alcoholic drinks are a sense of euphoria; an easing of tension, stress, and worry; a general elevation of spirits; and the relaxation of barriers among people, promoting fellowship within a group. Excessive use impairs speech and motor control and produces outbursts of aggressive behavior and finally unconsciousness. Alcoholism is a condition in which an individual's dependence upon alcohol interferes significantly with his or her physical and mental health, interpersonal relations, and social and economic functioning. Addiction leads to serious medical complications, including insanity or death. Specialists are divided as to whether the underlying causes of alcoholism are primarily physical (a disease or genetic factors) or moral and psychological (sin or personality disorders).

Strong Drink in the Bible. The only alcoholic beverage identified by name in the Bible is wine (*yayin* and *tîrôš*, OT; *oinos*, LXX and NT). Another word, *šēkār*, is translated "strong drink" in the KJV and "beer" in the NIV. No evidence whatsoever supports the notion that the wine mentioned in the Bible was unfermented grape juice.

It was used symbolically in the OT as a token of God's blessing (Gen. 27:28) and was acceptable as an offering (Exod. 29:40). Metaphorically, it represents something good prepared for those who receive it (Prov. 9:5; Isa. 55:1). Jesus performed his first miracle at Cana by changing water to wine (John 2:1–11), referred to the current practice of putting new wine in new wineskins (Matt. 9:17; Mark 2:22), was caricatured by his enemies as a tippler (Matt. 11:19; Luke 7:34), and at the Last Supper offered a cup of wine in remembrance of his shed blood (Matt. 26:27–29; Mark 14:23–25; Luke 22:20; 1 Cor. 11:25–26). Scripture observes that wine gladdens the heart (Ps. 104:15), refreshes those in anguish (Prov. 31:6), and possesses medicinal value (1 Tim. 5:23).

Scripture also points to the peril of drinking alcohol. It befuddles the mind (Isa. 28:7), prevents rulers from acting wisely (Prov. 31:4–5), causes poverty

(Prov. 23:21), and leads to sexual immorality (Eph. 5:18) and humiliation (Gen. 9:21; 19:30–38). It was called a mocker that led one astray and destroyed his understanding (Prov. 20:1; Hos. 4:11). Metaphorically it symbolizes the adulteries of "the whore of Babylon" (Rev. 17:2).

Drunkenness and Temperance. Scripture unequivocally condemns immoderate use of strong drink. Followers of Christ are commanded not to get drunk on wine but to be filled with the Holy Spirit (Eph. 5:18), and they should not even associate with those who call themselves "brothers" but are drunkards (1 Cor. 5:11). Drunkenness is associated with the participation in darkness and not in the kingdom of God (Rom. 13:12–13; 1 Cor. 6:10; Gal. 5:21). Church leaders must not drink excessively (1 Tim. 3:3, 8; Titus 1:7; 2:3). The destructive impact of alcoholism is vividly described in Prov. 23:29–35.

The biblical norm is temperance, which means self-control and moderation in all behavior, not total abstinence from beverage alcohol (Gal. 5:23; Titus 2:2; 2 Pet. 1:6).

R. V. PIERARD

Alcuin (ca. 735–804). Christian scholar and educator during the reign of Charlemagne. Alcuin became a trusted adviser to Charlemagne, and directed the establishment of many schools. In 796 he became abbot of the Monastery of St. Martin of Tours, which became a center of medieval scholarship. Of special significance was his leadership of a group of scholars who revised the text of the Latin Vulgate Bible, making use of the most reliable manuscripts available. He also was responsible for the development of the Caroline minuscule script, the forerunner of Roman typefaces. Some of his liturgical innovations made a lasting impact on Roman Catholic worship.

J. N. AKERS

Alexander, Archibald (1772–1851). The first professor at Princeton Theological Seminary and progenitor of the "Princeton Theology," which guided American Presbyterian theology for over a century. Alexander came to the seminary in 1812 after service as an itinerant evangelist in Virginia, as president of Hampden-Sidney College (1796–1807), and as pastor of Pine Street Presbyterian Church in Philadelphia (1807–12). His successors in Princeton's chair of theology—Charles Hodge, Archibald Alexander Hodge, and B. B. Warfield—expanded, clarified, and deepened the major themes of his thought but did not go measurably beyond them.

M. A. NOLL

See also PRINCETON THEOLOGY, OLD.

Alexandrian Theology. Bible interpretation and metaphysical system dependent on Greek philosophical thought. The indications are that Christianity was well established in middle Egypt by A.D. 150 and that Alexandria was its port of entry and supporting base.

Clement of Alexandria became head of the catechetical school about 190. A philosopher throughout his life, Clement saw Greek philosophy as a preparation for Christ, and a witness to divine truth. Plato was a cherished guide.

Around 202 Clement was succeeded in the catechetical school by Origen. A biblical student and exegete of great ability, Origen produced the *Hexapla* text of the OT. He wrote on all the biblical books, finding three senses or levels on which Scripture might be interpreted—literal, moral, and allegorical. The Bible was inspired, useful, and true in every letter, but the literal interpretation was not necessarily the correct one. Indebted, like Clement, to the Greeks, Origen was not as admiringly dependent upon them. His conception was of a great spiritual universe, presided over by a beneficent, wise, and personal being. Alexandrian Christology finds its beginnings with Origen.

By the incarnation the Logos is the mediator of redemption. He took to himself a human soul in a union that was a "natural union." It was, therefore, proper to say that the Son of God was born an infant, that he died (*De princ.* 2.6.2–3). By teaching, example, offering himself a propitiatory victim to God, and paying the devil a ransom, Christ saves men. Men gradually free themselves from the earthly by purging meditation, abstinence, and the vision of God. Although this world is neither the first nor the last of a series, all things will ultimately be restored.

After Origen's departure from Alexandria his disciples diverged. One group tended to deny the eternal generation of the Logos. Dionysius, bishop of Alexandria (247–65), sympathized with this party and declared the Logos to be a creation of the Father. When the presbyter Arius began, perhaps about 317, to proclaim that the Logos was a creation in time, differing from the Father in being, he attracted interest and disciples, but Bishop Alexander opposed Arius. Following the Council of Nicea in 325, Athanasius (bishop from 328) became the champion of the Nicene conclusion that the Son was *homoousios* (of the same Being) with the Father.

From this time on, Alexandria emphasized vigorously the identity in being of the Father and the Son. Athanasius presented, in his *On the Incarnation of the Logos*, the indispensability of the union of true God with true man for the Christian doctrine of salvation through the life and death of Christ. The Savior must be wholly God and wholly man.

Later, the unity of the personality of Christ became increasingly an Alexandrian emphasis and was strongly stressed by Cyril, who became bishop in 412. The Logos took a full human nature upon himself, but the result was a natural union and Cyril loved the formula *mia physis* (one nature), one even though originally *ek duo* (out of two). The incarnation was to the end of salvation. His most famous writing is his series of 12 anathemas against Nestorius, attacking what appeared to him denials of the unity and full deity of Christ and of the crucifixion and resurrection of the Word. In 433 Cyril accepted, with the Antioch leaders, a profession of faith which declared that a unity of the two natures of Christ had come into existence and used the term for which Cyril had so vigorously contended against Nestorius, *Theotokos* (God-bearer), as a description of the Virgin Mary.

The Alexandrian school with its Platonic emphasis was the popular school of its time. In its more moderate form it set the christological pattern for many centuries. The love of allegorical interpretation was characteristic. The intervention of the divine in the temporal was stressed, and the union of the natures of Christ with overriding emphasis on the divine component was dangerously accented.

P. WOOLLEY

See also ATHANASIUS; CLEMENT OF ALEXANDRIA; CYRIL OF ALEXANDRIA; LOGOS; MONARCHIANISM; MONOPHYSITISM; MONOTHELITISM; ORIGEN.

All. Inclusive or total extent or number. Hebrew and Greek words represented by "all" in English translations are among the most frequently used in Scripture. No conviction was held more firmly by the Hebrews than that the God of Israel created, sustains, and directs all things in heaven and on earth, visible and invisible. Even his special selection of Israel is not to be seen as an act of exclusivity but that "in thee shall all the families of the earth be blessed" through Israel's hearing of the Word of God (Gen. 12:3).

The theme is particularly expressed in reference to redemption. The total healing of the consequences of the fall is the fundamental vision of the prophets: In the restoration the wolf will lie down with the lamb (Isa. 11:6–7), nations shall no longer learn war (Isa. 2:4), and all will know the Lord (Jer. 31:34).

The same themes are expressed Christocentrically in the NT. All creation has come into being through Christ as mediator (John 1:3; 1 Cor. 8:6; Col. 1:16; Heb. 1:2). The created order is sustained through him (Heb. 1:3; Col. 1:17). The totality of creation is to experience reconciliation through his blood (Col. 1:20; cf. Rom. 8:21–22; Eph. 1:10). The call to repentance and faith goes out to all nations (Matt. 28:19–20; Luke 24:47; Acts 17:30). Finally, there is the vision of the day when every knee shall bow and every tongue confess the lordship of Jesus Christ. Such material is not to sustain a universalism but to declare the totality of the lordship of Christ and the inclusiveness of the call to faith.

R. W. LYON

See also MANY.

Allegory. An oral or literary device which attempts to express immaterial truths in pictorial forms. Allegory usually occurs as an extended metaphor in narrative form; examples can be found in both the OT and NT (for example, in Ps. 80 Israel is a *vine* from Egypt; in John 10:1–16 Jesus is the *Good Shepherd*). The device allows point-for-point comparison between intangibles and tangible representations which are recognizable to the intended audience.

The literary use of allegory should be distinguished from the method of interpretation known as "allegorizing." This method is characterized by the search for a deeper meaning than is apparent in the literal statements of a text.

Allegorizing originated in Greece (6th century B.C.), influenced Judaism through Philo at Alexandria (2d century B.C.), and entered Christian use through such notables as Origen, Jerome, and Augustine.

S. E. MCCLELLAND

Alleluia, Alleluiah. See HALLELUJAH.

All Saints Day. From early times the church commemorated its great leaders and heroes, especially those who had suffered martyrdom, by observing the dates of their death. This gave rise to the sanctoral section of the liturgical calendar.

Because there were other Christians whose faith and service (and even martyrdom) went unrecorded, and because some centers of the church gained more martyrs than could be commemorated in the days of the year, the practice of a general commemoration on All Saints Day developed. Originally celebrated on May 13, this festival was transferred in 835 to Nov. 1 in the Western Church, and medieval ideas of purgatory led to the following day being observed as All Souls Day, when the souls in purgatory were remembered. In the Eastern Church All Saints Day is the first Sunday following Pentecost.

At the Reformation All Souls Day was dropped. Reformed churches use All Saints Day to thank God for the faithful departed.

D. H. WHEATON

See also CHRISTIAN YEAR; HALLOWEEN.

Almighty. See GOD, NAMES OF.

Alms, Almsgiving. Benevolent acts of mercy which compassionately meet the needs of the poor. Almsgiving has played a major role among the people of God in response to the mercy God has already exhibited. Thus the term for alms, *eleēmosynē* (appearing 13 times in the NT), is related to the word for *mercy* (*eleos*).

In the OT generosity to the poor was strongly commended (Deut. 15:7–11; Ps. 112:9). But to ensure a comprehensive system of welfare, the Mosaic Law established institutions to provide for the needy: (1) the law stipulated that arable lands, vineyards, and orchards were to be left fallow every seventh year "for the poor" (Exod. 23:10–11); (2) every third year a tithe of the land's produce was to go to the poor (Deut. 14:22–29); (3) the poor could eat their fill as they passed through a neighbor's vineyard or field (Deut. 23:24–25); (4) at harvest the gleanings, the borders, and the corners of the fields were to be left for the poor (Lev. 19:9–10).

In Jesus' day an impressive system of welfare tended the poor. In addition to the OT legislation, synagogues filled "poor chests" each sabbath, a daily "poor bowl" circulated with food, and weekly a "poor basket" brought food and clothing to the needy. Jesus affirmed this activity completely (Matt. 6:1–4; John 13:29) and commended liberality in almsgiving (Matt. 5:42; Luke 6:38). Jesus' encounters with Zacchaeus (Luke 19:1–10) and the rich young ruler (Matt. 19:16–22) no doubt illustrate his attitude to those who had severely abused the Jewish system. Jesus cautioned against almsgiving for the sake of recognition (Matt. 6:2–3) and taught that alms can never be substituted for authentic spiritual piety (Luke 11:41–42; Matt. 5:23–24).

It seems clear that the generous almsgiving of Judaism provided the impetus for the communal lifestyle of the early Christian church. Possessions were sold and the proceeds distributed (Acts 2:45; 4:32). Ananias and Sapphira were no doubt examples of false participation (Acts 5:1–11), and Acts 6 describes an administrative adjustment to the distribution of aid.

For Paul, an important theological connection existed between the mercy shown by God (Eph. 2:4–9; Titus 3:5) and the mercy surrounding almsgiving: the believer should pass on the mercy he has received (Rom. 12:1; 2 Cor. 8:1–4). James similarly exhorts the believer to be "full of mercy and good fruit" (3:17 NIV; cf. Heb. 13:16) because to reject mercy is to invite the merciless judgment of God on oneself (2:13).

G. M. BURGE

Alpha and Omega. (Gk. *to Alpha kai to Ō*, found in Rev. 1:8; 21:6, and 22:13) In this phrase is probably a reference to the Jewish employment of the first and last letters of the Hebrew alphabet to indicate the totality of a thing. The essential meaning is, "I am the first, and I am the last; apart from me there is no God" (Isa. 44:6 NIV). Thus it is a claim that the one to whom it refers is the Eternal One—God himself.

S. L. JOHNSON

See also GOD, DOCTRINE OF; GOD, NAMES OF.

Altar. (Heb. *mizbēah*, "a place of slaughter or sacrifice;" Gk. *bōmos*, only used in Acts 17:23 and in LXX; *thysiastērion*, "a place of sacrifice")

In the OT. *Materials and Forms*. There were two basic types of altars in the OT. The first was an altar of no prescribed shape or material, constructed of earth and stones. This type of altar generally had a nonpriestly or lay use (Gen. 8:20; Exod. 20:24–26). The second type had a prescribed form and was made of wood and bronze or wood and gold. In particular, the two altars associated with the tabernacle and its priestly service (and that of its temple successors) followed definite patterns and were constructed by skilled craftsmen.

At Mount Sinai God revealed to Moses the specifications for two altars associated with the tabernacle and the priestly ministry. Directions even specified who was to do the construction and how the work would proceed (Exod. 31:2–5, 9). The bronze altar or altar of burnt offerings was 7.5 feet square, 4.5 feet tall, made of acacia wood covered with bronze, and had horns on the four top corners. It was constructed so that it could be carried and stood between the entrance to the courtyard and the door of the tabernacle. The animal and cereal offerings were made here (Exod. 27:1–8; 38:1–7; 40:6, 29). Sacrifices offered here (Lev. 1–7) signified that atonement for sin was necessary before one could enter the presence of God.

The second altar was the gold altar or altar of incense. It was 18 inches square, 3 feet high, made of acacia wood covered with gold, and had four horns on the top corners. It too could be carried. It was placed by the curtain separating the Holy Place from the Holy of Holies (Exod. 40:5, 26; Heb. 9:4). On the gold altar the high priest offered incense morning and evening and once a year applied atoning blood to its horns (Exod. 30:1–10; 40:5, 26–27). The smoke of incense filling the tabernacle signified offered prayer (cf. Rev. 8:3).

It is not known what happened to either the bronze or gold altars of the tabernacle, but Solomon's temple was provided with altars serving the same functions. The new bronze altar was larger (30 feet square and 15 feet high, 2 Chron. 4:1), but little is known of the new gold altar except that it was made of cedar overlaid with gold (1 Kings 6:20–22). The returned exiles presumably restored both altars in the second temple (Ezra 3:3; cf. 1 Macc. 1:21, 54; 4:44–49).

In the NT. Most NT references to altars are to those in Herod's temple. Luke 1:11 speaks of the altar of incense and Jesus refers to burnt offerings in Matt. 5:23–24 and 23:18–20. But there are also references to the altar of incense in the heavenly temple (Rev. 6:9; 8:3–5; 9:13; 14:18; 16:7). There is no altar of burnt offering, for atonement is complete, but the prayers of the saints like the incense of the gold altar rise to God.

The perception of the communion table as an altar came to prevail in both Eastern Orthodoxy and Roman Catholicism. Protestant traditions that stress the "real presence" of Christ in the elements are likely to speak of the communion table as an altar. As such it is the focal point of worship in the Lord's Supper and in congregational prayers, praise, thanksgiving, and the offering of gifts. Traditions that understand the elements in more symbolic and/or spiritual terms are more likely to speak simply of "the Lord's table."

Churches within the revivalist Protestant tradition use the term "altar" to refer to the place where the individual offers himself to God—thus "the altar call."

S. N. GUNDRY

See also LORD'S SUPPER; LORD'S SUPPER, VIEWS OF; OFFERINGS AND SACRIFICES IN BIBLE TIMES.

Althaus, Paul (1888–1966). German Lutheran theologian. Born in Obershagen, near Hannover, he was the son of Paul Althaus, Sr., also a well-known theologian. Chief influences on his thought were his father, Carl Strange, and Adolf Schlatter. He taught at the universities of Göttingen (1914–20), Rostock (1920–25), and Erlangen (1925–66). In 1926 he succeeded Karl Holl as president of the *Luthergesellschaft*, where he remained as a major figure for the rest of his active life. He was cofounder of the *Zeitschrift für systematische Theologie*, wrote extensively on systematic theology and eschatology, and published sermons and devotional works.

W. W. GASQUE

Ambrose (ca. 340–397). A leading foe of Arianism. Born of a Roman noble family he became governor of Aemilia-Liguria, with headquarters at Milan. He was consecrated bishop of Milan on Dec. 7, 374, over his own objections. He chose to receive his office from the hands of a Catholic bishop and worked against the Arian party until his death. Backed by two able Roman popes, Damasus (366–84) and Siricius (384–99), Ambrose lived to see Arianism largely defeated in the Western Church. In 390 he set a critical precedent by forcing the Catholic emperor Theodosius to do public penance for his slaughter of 7000 persons at the Thessalonican circus, insisting that the emperor was within the church and not over it. Augustine was instructed and baptized by Ambrose.

Because of his classical education Ambrose was fluent in Greek and Latin. He introduced the thinking of Greek Christianity into the Latin Church and thus played a crucial role in the unity of the church, even as the empire foundered. Thirty-five treatises, 91 of his episcopal letters, and a few of his hymns survive.

V. L. WALTER

See also ARIANISM.

Amen. (Heb. *āmēn,* "reliable, sure, true"; Gk., *amēn,* "truly") By itself the term was used as a formula ("Surely!" "In very truth!") at the end of (1) a doxology, such as "Blessed be Jehovah forever," where it signifies: "Yes indeed!" or, "May it be so in very truth!"); cf. Pss. 41:13; 72:19; 89:52; 106:48; 1 Chron. 16:36 and Neh. 8:6; (2) a decree or expression of royal purpose, where the obedient listener indicates his hearty assent and cooperation (1 Kings 1:36; Jer. 11:5). The usage is the same in the NT.

Isa. 65:16 speaks of the God of amen, meaning that God speaks the truth and carries out his word; cf. Rev. 3:14. Jesus introduces matters of importance with *amēn, legō hymin* ("Truly, I say unto you"), affirming the truthfulness of what he is about to say (e.g., John 1:51; 5:19, 24, 25).

G. L. ARCHER, JR.

Ames, William (1576–1633). English Puritan preacher and theologian. In 1610 Ames was expelled from Cambridge because of his Puritanism, and took refuge in the Netherlands, joining the large English-Scottish refugee community. He served first as a military chaplain and then as professor of theology at the University of Franeker (1622–33), where he earned a doctor of theology degree.

Known as "the Learned Doctor Ames" because of his great intellectual stature among Puritans, he combined Calvinist doctrine, Ramist philosophy (from Peter Ramus), and Puritan practical divinity. His best known books are *The Marrow of Sacred Divinity* (1627), and *Conscience, or Cases of Conscience* (1630). Ames stressed that theology must combine orthodox doctrine and moral practice.

K. L. SPRUNGER

Amillennialism. See MILLENNIUM, VIEWS OF THE.

Amish. SEE MENNONITES.

Amsdorf, Nicholas von (1483–1565). German Lutheran Reformer. When Luther arrived at Wittenberg, he and Amsdorf became close friends. Amsdorf accompanied Luther to the Leipzig debate in 1519, was at Worms with him in 1521, and assisted him with his translation of the OT.

The Elector John Frederick appointed Amsdorf first bishop to the Lutheran diocese of Naumburg-Zeitz. After Luther's death he was expelled from his diocese (1547), returned to Magdeburg where much of his previous reforming activity had been carried on, and led the opposition to the compromising tendencies of Melanchthon and the Philippist party.

From 1552 until his death Amsdorf lived in Eisenach, without formal office but acknowledged as "secret bishop of the Lutheran Church."

J. F. JOHNSON

See also MAJORISTIC CONTROVERSY.

Amyraldianism. A system of Reformed theology based on the premise that God wills all to be saved if they believe, propounded by the French theologian Moise Amyraut and associates at the Saumur Academy in the 17th century.

Amyraut took issue with contemporary Calvinists who shaped their system of theology around the decree of predestination. He insisted that the chief doctrine of Christian theology is not predestination but the faith which justifies. For Amyraut predestination is only an inscrutable mystery which helps explain why some accept Christ while others reject him.

The Saumur school postulated a covenant with three successive steps in God's saving program in history: (1) The covenant of nature established between God and Adam involved obedience to the divine law as disclosed in the natural order. (2) The covenant of law between God and Israel focused on adherence to the written law of Moses. (3) The covenant of grace established between God and all people requires faith in the finished work of Christ. In Amyraldianism the threefold covenant of grace was further divided into two parts: a conditional covenant of universal grace and an unconditional covenant of particular grace. The former required fulfillment of law as a condition of faith. The latter, grounded in God's good pleasure, does not call for the condition of faith; rather it creates faith in the elect. Amyraut's covenant theology—particularly his division of the covenant of grace into a universal conditional covenant and a particular unconditional covenant—provided the basis for the unique feature of Amyraldianism, namely, the doctrine of hypothetical universal predestination.

Some later Reformed theologians, such as Charles Hodge, W. G. T. Shedd, and B. B. Warfield, insisted that Amyraldianism was an inconsistent synthesis of Arminianism and Calvinism. Others, however, such as H. Heppe, R. Baxter, S. Hopkins, A. H. Strong, and L. S. Chafer, maintained that it represents a return to the true spirit of Holy Scripture.

B. A. Demarest

See also Amyraut, Moise; Atonement, Extent of the.

Amyraut, Moise (1596–1664). French Protestant theologian. Born in Bourgueil in 1633, Amyraut was installed as professor of theology at Saumur. Under the leadership of Amyraut and his colleagues L. Cappel and J. de la Place the Saumur Academy became the leading theological school of French Protestantism. A prolific writer, Amyraut published some 30 books in addition to a number of sermons and essays. Chief among his works are *A Treatise Concerning Religions* (1631), *A Short Treatise on Predestination* (1634), and the six-volume *Christian Ethics* (1652–60).

Staunch opposition arose to Amyraut's teaching on universal grace in Switzerland, the Netherlands, and in France itself. Amyraut was tried for heresy at three national synods in 1637, 1644, and 1659, but was acquitted in each case. The *Formula Helvetic Consensus* (1675) was prepared by the Swiss Reformed Church largely to counter the Saumurian theology of Amyraut and his colleagues.

B. A. Demarest

See also Amyraldianism.

Anabaptists. See Radical Reformation.

Analogia Fidei. See Analogy of Faith.

Analogy. Similarity. Analogous language expresses a meaning that is similar, but neither identical, which would be called *univocal language,* or completely different, which would be called *equivocal language*. With respect to religious language there are two kinds of analogies, metaphysical and metaphorical. The former apply to God literally and the latter do not. For instance, in the sentence "God is good" the term "good" applies to God literally. But in the sentence "God is a rock" the term "rock" applies to God only metaphorically. Likewise, when the Scriptures refer to God's arms, ears, and eyes, these are only metaphorical analogies usually called anthropomorphisms.

N. L. Geisler

Analogy of Faith. (1) The extent of an individual's faith. Paul in Rom. 12:6 teaches that he who has the gift of prophecy should prophesy "in proportion to his faith." The apostle enjoins the believer to exercise his gift of prophecy to the extent that individual faith will allow. The "proportion" or "analogy of faith" (*analogia tēs pisteōs*) thus is similar to the "measure of faith" (*metron pisteōs*) mentioned in Rom. 12:3.

(2) The general hermeneutical principle that an obscure biblical text may be illumined by other, clearer Scripture texts. Since God is the author of Holy Scripture, what is taught in one Scripture cannot contradict what is taught in another Scripture. The meaning of a given text often is established only after a careful consideration of other passages which speak to the issue. As an extension of this principle Augustine insisted that the interpretation of Scripture never violates the rule of faith summarized in the Apostles' Creed. If Scripture is alleged to mean something contrary to the universally accepted body of Christian truth, the validity of one's exegesis is suspect. Luther argued that the primary interpreter of Scripture must be Scripture, rather than any sources outside of Scripture. Reformers used the analogy of faith principle to condemn Roman Catholicism for its insistence that the Bible must be interpreted in accordance with the corpus of tradition. The analogy of faith exegetical principle is violated by imposition of any meanings not intended by the biblical writer.

B. A. DEMAREST

Anathema. See CURSE.

Ancient of Days. See GOD, NAMES OF.

Anderson, Robert (1841–1918). Presbyterian layman who made an impact for the gospel through criminology, preaching, and writing.

Born in Dublin, he became a barrister and adviser to the British Home Office on Irish political terrorism. He later headed Scotland Yard's Criminal Investigation Department (1888–1901). Anderson wrote extensively but centered his efforts on the fields of apologetics and Bible prophecy. He had a deep respect for the fundamental truths of the Bible and boldly attacked higher criticism. He was a leading popularizer of dispensational Bible interpretation.

Among his works are *The Coming Prince*, *Daniel in the Critic's Den*, *The Bible and Modern Criticism*, *The Silence of God*, and *The Gospel and Its Ministries*.

H. F. VOS

Andover Controversy. A theological dispute over liberal theology and the doctrine that those who have not heard the gospel will get a second chance after death. The controversy lasted from 1886 to 1892, involving faculty of Andover Theological Seminary, led by E. C. Smyth, and exemplified the transition from New England Calvinism to liberal theology. In 1884 the *Andover Review*, a theological journal published by the faculty for the purpose of rethinking and restating Christian theology in contemporary terms, published a series of editorials by members of the faculty exploring central Christian doctrines under the title "Progressive Orthodoxy." The controversy centered on promotion of a view of "future probation" but ultimately it involved an evolution-based rethinking of the nature of God, humanity, Christian mission, and the world which redefined salvation and attempted to point theology toward a more hopeful view of the progress of humanity. The dismissal of Smyth in the investigation culminated in a Massachusetts Supreme Court decision in 1891 which ordered that Smyth be reinstated.

L. G. WHITLOCK, JR.

Andreae, James (1528–1590). German Lutheran scholar. Andreae served as professor of theology at the University of

Tübingen, led the Lutheran movement in Württemberg, and was a major contributor to the Formula of Concord (1577).

In 1557 Andreae published his first book, *A Short and Simple Statement Concerning the Lord's Supper,* in which he attempted to formulate a doctrine of the Lord's Supper consistent with Lutheran theology without offending the Calvinists. His main contribution to Lutheran unity was made through his *Six Christian Sermons* of 1573. These sermons treated the subjects over which the disputes had developed among the Lutherans. In the winter of 1573–74 the sermons were recast into a more academic format entitled the Swabian Concord. This was revised by several Lutheran theologians in 1575–76, culminating in the Torgau Book and the Belgic Book, which together became the Formula of Concord.

J. F. JOHNSON

See also CONCORD, FORMULA OF.

Angel. (Heb. *mal'ak*; Gk. *angelos*) A human or a heavenly messenger. In the NT, except in Luke 7:24; 9:52; and perhaps in the letters to the angels of the seven churches in Revelation (e.g., Rev. 1:20), it denotes heavenly beings.

The words chosen to denote angels indicates their primary function; they are God's messengers or ambassadors. They belong to his heavenly court and service. Their mission in heaven is to praise him (Rev. 5:11–14). They devote themselves to doing his will (Ps. 103:20), and in this activity they behold his face (Matt. 18:10). They also have a mission on earth. They accompany God in his work of creation (Job 38:7), though they themselves are creatures (Ps. 148:2, 5). They also assist in God's providential ordering of affairs (Dan. 12:1). Above all they are active in the divine work of reconciliation (from Gen. 19:1–2 onward). In fulfillment of their mission they declare God's words (e.g., Luke 1:26–27) and do his work (e.g., Matt. 28:2). Heb. 1:14 describes them as "ministering spirits."

The function of angels may be seen clearly in their role in the incarnation. They are present at the nativity and at the resurrection and ascension. They also assist the church in its early ministry (e.g., Acts 5:19; 10:3). Throughout Revelation they are shown to play an important part in events of the end time. Finally they will come with Christ when he returns in glory (Matt. 24:31) and separate the righteous from the wicked (Matt. 13:41, 49). They accompany and declare Christ in his work of reconciliation, praising God and summoning men and women to participate in their worship (Luke 1:46).

Belonging to the heavenly sphere, they cannot be properly conceived of in earthly terms. They belong fully to God. The two angelic names, Michael and Gabriel, end with *el*, emphasizing that they are *God's* angels. As God's they are called "elect" in 1 Tim. 5:21. Yet Scripture warns against worship of these fellow servants (Col. 2:18; Rev. 19:10).

Some distinctions among rank and ministry are made among the heavenly beings. Some are referred to as archangels; others are referred to simply as angels (1 Thess. 4:16; Jude 9). Seraphim are mentioned in Isa. 6:2. Cherubim guarded Eden after the expulsion of Adam and Eve (Gen. 3:24). They form God's chariot at his descent (Ps. 18:10). Figures of cherubim adorned the ark (Exod. 25:17–22) and Solomon's temple (1 Kings 6:23–28), so that Yahweh is said to be enthroned between the cherubim (1 Sam. 4:4; Ps. 80:1).

Of angels named, Michael is called "the great prince" (Dan. 12:1) and the other angels seem to be led by him (Rev. 12:7). Gabriel, the other angel named in canonical Scripture, is the angel of the annunciation (Luke 1:26). The apocryphal writings provide three more angelic names, Raphael, Uriel, and Jeremiel. Tob. 12:15 calls Raphael one of the holy angels who present the prayers of the saints (cf. the seven who stand before God in Rev. 8:2 and the possible link between these seven and the "chief princes" of Dan. 10:13).

Has there been a fall of angels? Jude 6 suggests this, and Irenaeus (*Against Heresies* 4.37.1) and many fathers took this view. Certainly the Bible speaks of the dragon and his angels (Rev. 12:7–9) and also of powers of evil (Eph. 6:12). While there is much about angels we do not know, we can assume that there is a real kingdom of evil in grotesque caricature of the angelic kingdom. These angels and their leader were defeated at the cross (Col. 2:15) and will finally be condemned (Matt. 25:41).

G. W. Bromiley

See also Angel of the Lord.

Angel of the Lord. (Heb. *mal'ak YHWH*) In the OT and NT the angel of the Lord is represented as acting on behalf of the nation of Israel as well as of individuals. The lack of precise data in the OT with regard to the identification of this figure and his relationship to Yahweh has given rise to a number of conclusions.

Many understand the angel of the Lord as a true theophany. From the time of Justin Martyr on, the figure has been regarded as the preincarnate Logos. It is beyond question that the angel of the Lord must be identified in some way with God (Gen. 16:13; Judg. 6:14–24; 13:21–22), yet he is distinguished from God in that God refers to the angel (Exod. 23:23; 32:34), speaks to him (2 Sam. 24:16; 1 Chron. 21:15, 27), and the angel speaks to Yahweh (Zech. 1:12). The evidence for the view that the angel of the Lord is a preincarnate appearance of Christ is basically analogical and falls short of being conclusive. The NT does not clearly make that identification. It is best to see the angel as a self-manifestation of Yahweh in a form that would communicate his immanence and direct concern to those to whom he ministered.

T. E. McComiskey

See also Angel; Theophany.

Anger. A human emotion rich in Hebrew terminology, being represented by seven words, but by only two in Greek. Because the nose was prominent in the hard breathing accompanying an increase in blood adrenalin, anger was most commonly rendered by "nose," "nostril" (Heb. *'ap*). The intensity of anger was expressed by such words as "fury," "heat," "rage," "burn with anger" (Heb. *hēmâ, hārâ, 'ebrâ, zā'ap, qāsap)* or "be irritated," "be grieved" (*pa 'ām*). The NT employs *thymos* to describe emotionally intense wrath and *orgē* as anger which is the consequence of a moral judgment, but in the LXX the two terms were interchangeable.

The anger of God is a deliberate reaction to all that violates his holy nature. His covenant people were commanded to imitate God's holiness (Lev. 11:44), and when they failed to do so, they felt his anger, whether through natural circumstances (Num. 21:6) or other nations (Isa. 10:5). Even God's chosen servants experienced God's punishing wrath, as with Moses (Exod. 4:14), Miriam (Num. 12:9–10), Jonah (Jonah 1:4), and others. All violations of the covenant agreement exposed the Israelites to God's anger, which could only be averted by true repentance.

Jesus became angry with his disciples when they forbade children to be brought to him (Mark 10:14) and with the hardhearted members of the Capernaum synagogue (Mark 3:5). Similar expressions of anger were directed at the Sadducees (Mark 12:24–27), the scribes and Pharisees (Matt. 23:13–36), and Peter (Matt. 16:23), and on each occasion represented his rejection of unrighteousness. Human anger could be selfish (Gen. 4:5; Num. 24:10), righteous (Exod. 16:20; 2 Sam. 12:5), or a combination of both (Gen. 34:7; 2 Sam. 13:21). In the NT anger is usually condemned (Col. 3:8; James 1:19–20).

R. K. HARRISON

Anglican Communion. A worldwide fellowship of churches in communion with the archbishop of Canterbury (England). Bishops of churches within the communion have normally gathered each decade since 1867 for the Lambeth Conference.

Bishops are the chief officers of Anglican churches. Archbishops or presiding bishops function as "first among equals" with national or provincial responsibilities and administrative authority. Only bishops may ordain clergy and consecrate other bishops. Some dioceses have assistant bishops called coadjutor or suffragan bishops. A suffragan bishop does not automatically succeed the diocesan bishop, whereas the coadjutor does.

The basic unit in the church is the parish congregation and rector. The diocese is that group of parishes under a bishop whose representatives meet each year for a diocesan convention (or synod). Bishops are elected at these synods in most Anglican churches, but some bishops are still appointed, as in the Church of England.

The *Book of Common Prayer,* in one of its many derived forms, is used by all Anglican churches. It is regarded as the distinctive embodiment of Anglican doctrine, following the principle of "the rule of prayer is the rule of belief" (*lex orandi, lex credendi*). The Holy Scripture is declared to be the Word of God and to contain all that is necessary to salvation. The Nicene and Apostles' Creeds are accepted as confessing the faith of Scripture and classical Christianity. The Thirty-Nine Articles are not required for explicit assent in most of the communion, but they are regarded as an important historical and theological signpost.

Worship in Anglican churches varies widely but is characterized by an attempt to follow the liturgical year; that is, from Advent and the nativity (Christmas) through the manifestation of Christ to the Gentiles (Epiphany), Lent, Easter, and Pentecost. Readings from both Testaments are required at all normal services. The Lord's Supper, or Holy Eucharist, is generally regarded as the central service and over the last century has come to be held with increasing frequency. The norm for public worship is to stand to sing, sit to listen, and kneel to pray.

The wide diversity within Anglicanism is reflected by the astonishing growth and evangelical character of the church in East Africa, the highly sacramental and Anglo-Catholic tradition of the Province of South Africa, the liberal spirit and discomfort with classical expressions of orthodoxy on the part of some North American and British theologians and bishops, and the conservative evangelicals who retain an unyielding loyalty to Scripture and the Thirty-Nine Articles.

C. F. ALLISON

See also ANGLO-CATHOLICISM; BOOK OF COMMON PRAYER; HIGH CHURCH MOVEMENT; LATITUDINARIANISM; LOW CHURCH; THIRTY-NINE ARTICLES, THE.

Anglo-Catholicism. The modern name for a "high-church" tradition within Anglicanism that regarded the episcopacy as the essence of the church. It was first termed the Tractarian or Oxford Movement. Edward Pusey, John Keble, and John Henry Newman were the leaders of this transition from the older high churchmanship, with its emphasis on the established Erastian church-state relationship, to an emphasis upon the distinctive claims of the church's authority in apostolic succession of bishops. Ordination by bishops was seen to be of the *esse* of the church, without which a church is not a church. Less appreciation was given to the principles of the Anglican Reformation.

Two major works indicate the best in scholarship and theological emphasis of this tradition: *Lux Mundi* (1889) and *Essays Catholic and Critical* (1926).

Four modern strands of Anglo-Catholicism have been discerned: (1) The Cambridge Camden Society and its successors, who lay great and somewhat romantic emphasis upon English history and pre-Reformation English rites and vestments; (2) liberal Anglo-Catholicism, which is less authoritarian and more friendly to liberal theology; (3) evangelical Catholics, who attempt to blend the biblical teachings on grace and gospel with the classical dogmas and distinctive ritual; (4) pro-Roman Anglo-Catholicism, whose main aim is the reunion of Anglicanism with Roman Catholicism.

Anglo-Catholicism has emphasized the doctrine of the incarnation, sacramental theology, and ecclesiastical polity.

C. F. ALLISON

See also ANGLICAN COMMUNION; HIGH CHURCH MOVEMENT; KEBLE, JOHN; OXFORD MOVEMENT; NEWMAN, JOHN HENRY; PUSEY, EDWARD BOUVERIE.

Anguish. See PAIN.

Annihilationism. (From Lat. *nihil*, "nothing") The position that some, if not all, human souls will cease to exist after death. This takes three main forms: (1) All human beings inevitably cease to exist altogether at death (materialist); (2) while human beings are naturally mortal, God imparts to the redeemed the gift of immortality and allows the rest of humanity to sink into nothingness (conditional immortality); (3) humanity, being created immortal, fulfil their destiny in salvation, while the reprobates fall into nonexistence through a direct act of God or through the corrosive effect of evil (annihilationism proper). The distinction between tenets of conditionalism and annihilationism become muddled, and these two terms are commonly used as practical synonyms. A fourth view is that God will finally extinguish all evil and redeem all rational beings (universalism). Historic orthodoxy has always maintained both that human souls will eternally endure and that their destiny is irrevocably sealed at death.

R. NICOLE

See also ADVENTISM; CONDITIONAL IMMORTALITY; INTERMEDIATE STATE.

Anoint, Anointing. (Heb. *māšaḥ, dāšan, sûḵ, mišḥâ*; Gk. *aleiphō, enchriō, chrisma*) The ancient Near East custom of rubbing persons or objects with plain or perfumed oil in dedication or for medicinal, preservative, or cosmetic purposes.

In the OT. Anointing with oil set apart persons and objects to divine service. Elaborately prepared oils were used to dedicate the tabernacle, its furniture, and vessels (Exod. 30:22–33; 40:10–11), together with those from the high-priestly class of Levi who were to serve in it (Exod. 28:40–42; 29:1–46; 30:30–33). There are also scattered references to the anointing of prophets (1 Chron. 19:16; Isa. 61:1). More frequent are references to the anointing of kings, from the beginning of the monarchy (1 Sam. 10:1; 16:13; 1 Kings. 1:39). As "anointed of the Lord" such kings were assured of succession and elevated to an inviolable status (1 Sam. 24:6; 26:9, 11, 16).

The ancient Hebrews also looked forward to the coming of a king from the line of David who would be specially anointed of God to bring in his kingdom, and to this figure was given a name borrowed from the Hebrew word for anointing, *Messiah*. OT prophetic descriptions of the Messiah vary widely in emphasis and content. Often depicted as a great and just king (Pss. 2; 7; 72; 110; Zech. 3), he invariably enjoys a unique relationship with God the Father and is fully endowed with extraordinary spiritual and charismatic gifts (Isa. 9:1–7; 11:1–5; Mic. 5:1–5).

In the NT. The entire NT testifies to the fact that Jesus of Nazareth was that Messiah. The equivalent Greek term for the "anointed one" (*Christos*) was applied to Jesus in every book except 3 John. Among the Greco-Roman communities, where its original meaning was probably not understood, it quickly lost the article and became a part of Jesus' name.

In Church History. Such numerous references to anointing in Scripture could not fail to have an impact upon Christians. Beginning in the 8th and 9th centuries kings and bishops were anointed with chrism (holy oil) upon their elevation into office. They were considered the vicars or place-holders of Christ, set apart, like the kings and high priests of the OT, for divine service.

From at least the year 200 on, the church practiced a postbaptismal anointing (see 2 Cor. 1:21; 1 John 2:20–27) and laying on of hands (see Acts 8:14–17; 19:1–6) in order to confer the gift of the Holy Spirit. In the early church and still in Eastern churches, this was not clearly distinguished from the baptism itself, and the rite took its name from the anointing or, more accurately, from the chrism it employed. In the Middle Ages the Western or Catholic Church separated this rite from baptism and elevated it to the sacrament of confirmation, through which, its theologians taught, an increased or fortifying grace of the Spirit was conferred upon children or young adults.

The command to anoint the sick found in James 5:14 together with a suggestive reference in Mark 6:13 led to a practice which in the Catholic Church eventually came to be known as "extreme unction" and since Vatican Council II is once again called the "anointing of the sick."

J. Van Engen

Anselm of Canterbury (1033–1109). Medieval theologian. Anselm served in turn as prior (1063–78) and abbot (1078–93) at Bec in Normandy before reluctantly agreeing to succeed Lanfranc as archbishop of Canterbury (1093–1109). His 12 theological treatises, 19 prayers, and three meditations, together with many of his 375 letters, rank as literary masterpieces. His prayers and meditations transformed the formal liturgical prayer of the early Middle Ages into a more intimate and intense expression of personal devotion to Christ, Mary, and the saints. His letters likewise became models for the sophisticated expression of warm personal and religious friendships. His theological works, on the other hand, were marked not so much by personal warmth as intuitive intellectual insight, clarity of exposition, and rigorous argument.

He always proceeded as one who already possessed faith and sought understanding; this tag ("faith seeking understanding") was borrowed from an old Latin rendering of Isa. 7:9.

His theological works include *Monologion* (Soliloquy), *Proslogion* (Colloquy), and *Cur Deus Homo* (Why God Became Man). Setting aside all knowledge of Jesus Christ, Anselm attempted to produce necessary reasons for the coming of a God-man and his atoning sacrifice. The injury dealt to God's honor by the human fall into sin required humanity itself to render satisfaction to an upright God; yet only God himself could adequately make amends. Hence the God-man whose innocent sacrifice potentially made satisfaction for all people. His "satisfaction" theory of the atonement effectively refuted early medieval notions of the devil's "rights" over fallen humankind and also displaced earlier Eastern emphases upon Christ as victor. Indeed this satisfaction theory shaped nearly all Catholic and Protestant thought on redemptive theology down to modern times.

J. VAN ENGEN

Anthropology. See MAN, DOCTRINE OF.

Anthropomorphism. (from Gk. *anthrōpos*, man, and *morphē*, form) Metaphoric conceptions of God as having human form (Exod. 15:3; Num. 12:8) with feet (Gen. 3:8; Exod. 24:10), hands (Exod. 24:11; Josh. 4:24), mouth (Num. 12:8; Jer. 7:13), and heart (Hos. 11:8), but in a wider sense the term also includes human attributes and emotions (Gen. 2:2; 6:6; Exod. 20:5; Hos. 11:8).

Anthropomorphic concepts were "absolutely necessary if the God of Israel was to remain a God of the individual Israelite as well as of the people as a whole. . . . For the average worshipper . . . it is very essential that his god be a divinity who can sympathize with his human feelings and emotions, a being whom he can love and fear alternately, and to whom he can transfer the holiest emotions connected with memories of father and mother and friend" (W. F. Albright, *From the Stone Age to Christianity*; 2d ed., p. 202). It is precisely in the area of the personal that theism, as expressed in Christianity, must ever think in anthropomorphic terms. To regard God solely as Absolute Being or the Great Unknown is to refer to *him* or *it*, but to think of God as literally personal, one with whom we can fellowship, is to say *Thou*.

"To say that God is completely different from us is as absurd as to say that he is completely like us" (D. E. Trueblood, *Philosophy of Religion*, p. 270). Jesus said those who saw him saw the Father (John 14:9). Finite people will ever cling to the anthropomorphism of the incarnation and the concept of God as Father (Matt. 7:11), but at the same time they will realize the impossibility of absolute, complete comprehension of God, "for my thoughts are not your thoughts, neither are your ways my ways, says the Lord" (Isa. 55:8 NIV).

D. M. BEEGLE

Anthroposophy. A religious and philosophical mysticism based on the theosophical ideas of Rudolf Steiner (1861–1925).

Like theosophy from which it came, anthroposophy includes elements from Hinduism, Neo-Platonism, Gnosticism, and Sufism. It affirms the existence of spiritual as well as material worlds and teaches that salvation consists of escaping the confines of the material world by obtaining esoteric spiritual knowledge about the true nature of things.

Whereas theosophy views Christ as only one of many *avatars*, anthroposophy teaches that Christ is the only avatar, an exalted solar being (*Sonnenwesen*) who entered human history as the full revelation of the spiritual world. Contact with Christ brings deeper penetration into his own knowledge of reality. Thus for anthroposophists celebration of the Eucharist has ultimate significance.

Anthroposophy was condemned by the Roman Catholic Church in 1919. Followers are most numerous in Germany, Britain, and the U.S.

T. P. WEBER

Antichrist. (Gk. *Antichristos*) Although the term *Antichrist* occurs only in the Johannine letters, the conception of an archopponent of God and his Messiah is found in both Testaments and in intertestamental writings. Opposition is reflected in *anti*, which probably means "against," not "instead of," although both ideas may be present: Posing as Christ, Antichrist opposes Christ.

OT Background. Because Christ is not fully revealed, the OT offers no complete portrait of Antichrist but furnishes materials for the picture in descriptions of personal or national opposition to God.

Belial. Certain individuals, infamous for wickedness, are called "sons of [or men of] Belial" (Heb. *bĕlîya'al,* "without worth," "useless"). See Deut. 13:13; Judg. 19:22; 20:13; 1 Sam. 1:16.

Foreign Enemies. Opposition to God's kingdom is opposition to him. The nations' vain plot against the Lord's anointed king in Ps. 2 may be a foreshadowing of the Antichrist idea.

The Little Horn. (Dan. 7:8-21). This appears to denote God's final enemy. Further, the portrait of this "king of the north" (Dan. 11), the personification of evil, has helped significantly to shape the NT figure of Antichrist.

Intertestamental Elaboration. Two emphases appear in the Apocrypha and Pseudepigrapha: (1) Rome replaces Syria as the national enemy, and Pompey supplants Antiochus IV as the epitome of opposition to God; (2) Belial (Beliar) is personified as a satanic spirit.

The "lawless one" (2 Thess. 2:8) has been connected with Beliar, which rabbinic tradition interpreted as "without yoke," that is, refusing the law's yoke. This connection seems strengthened by the LXX translation of *belial* by *paranomos,* "lawbreaker" (e.g., Deut. 13:13). However, Paul distinguishes Beliar from the lawless one: Beliar is a synonym of Satan (2 Cor. 6:15), while Satan and the lawless one are differentiated (2 Thess. 2:9).

NT Development. *The Gospels.* References to Christ's opponent are neither numerous nor specific. The disciples are warned that false Christs will attempt to deceive even the elect (Matt. 24:24; Mark 13:22). Similarly, Christ speaks of one who comes in his own name, whom the Jews receive (John 5:43).

2 Thessalonians. The outstanding characteristic given by Paul of Christ's archenemy, is contempt of law. Two names—"man of lawlessness" (preferable to "man of sin") and "the lawless one" (2 Thess. 2:3, 8–9)—stress this anarchistic attitude, recalling Dan. 7:25, where the little horn tries to change the times and law. Furthermore, Antichrist makes exclusive claim to deity (2 Thess. 2:4) in terms reminiscent of Dan. 7:25; 11:36. Paul does not picture a pseudo-Messiah posing as God's messenger, but a pseudo-God viciously opposing all other religion.

He deceives many by wonders (2 Thess. 2:9–10). Antichrist will work miracles by satanic power, and many will worship him as God.

One of Antichrist's names—"son of perdition" (2 Thess. 2:3; cf. John 17:12)—reveals his destiny: Christ will slay him by his breath and the brightness of his appearing (2 Thess. 2:8; Rev. 19:15, 20; cf. Isa. 11:4).

Antichrist is the personal culmination of a principle of rebellion already working secretly—"the mystery of lawlessness" (2 Thess. 2:7). When God's restraining hand which preserves law and order is withdrawn, this spirit of satanic lawlessness will become incarnate in "the lawless one."

The Johannine Letters. Though John recognized the expectation of a single Antichrist, he turns his attention to the many Antichrists who have come denying that Jesus is the Christ and thus denying the true nature of both Father and Son (1 John 2:18, 22; 4:3).

Revelation. The apocalyptist's beast (Rev. 13), dependent in spirit and detail on Daniel, combines the characteristics of all four OT beasts. He is more than a person: his seven heads are seven kings (Rev. 17:10–12). The beast himself is an eighth king, springing from one of the seven. This complicated picture suggests that the beast symbolizes worldly power, the anti-God spirit of a nationalistic ambition which will become incarnate in one great demagogue—Antichrist. John adds at least one important element—the false prophet, a second beast who works under the authority of Antichrist, as Antichrist gains his authority from the dragon, Satan (Rev. 13:2, 11–12). After directing Antichrist's political and religious enterprises, the false prophet shares his fate at Christ's advent (Rev. 19:20).

Christian Interpretation. The fathers generally believed in a personal Antichrist. His identity hinged on whether the "mystery of lawlessness" was interpreted politically or religiously. The Reformers equated Antichrist with the papacy, as had some medieval theologians.

In the ideal or symbolic view, Antichrist is an ageless personification of evil, not identifiable with one nation, institution, or individual.

Futurists hold that idealists fail to stress sufficiently the culmination of this hostility in a personal adversary. They believe that Antichrist will usher in a period of great tribulation at history's close.

D. A. HUBBARD

See also ABOMINATION OF DESOLATION.

Antinomianism. (from Gk. *anti*, "against," and *nomos*, "law") The doctrine that it is not necessary for Christians to preach and/or obey the moral law of the OT. There have been several justifications for this view: (1) Once persons are justified by faith in Christ, they no longer have any obligation toward the moral law. A variant is that since Christ has raised believers above the positive precepts of the law, they need to be obedient only to the immediate guidance of the Holy Spirit, who will keep them from sin (cf. 1 Cor. 6; Gal. 3). (2) The law actually came from the demiurge (as in Gnosticism) and not from the true, loving Father, so it is a Christian's duty to disobey it. (3) Since sin is inevitable anyway, there is no need to resist it. Some contend that God, in his eternal decree, willed sin, so it would be presumptuous to resist it. (4) The law is unnecessary and, indeed, is contrary to the gospel of Jesus Christ.

The two most famous antinomian controversies in Christian history occurred in the 16th and 17th centuries, and involved Martin Luther and Anne Hutchinson, respectively. Luther coined the term *antinomianism* in his theological struggle with his former student, Johann Agricola. In the early days of the Reformation Luther had taught that, after NT times, the moral law had only the negative value of preparing sinners for grace by making them aware of their sin. Agricola denied even this function, believing that repentance should be induced only through the preaching of the gospel of salvation by grace through faith in Christ. Partly in response, Luther began to stress the role of the law and discipline in the life of a Christian, refuting antinomian views most clearly in *Against the Antinomians* (1539). The Lutheran Formula of Concord in 1577 recognized a threefold use of the law: (1) to reveal sin, (2) to establish general decency in society at large, and (3) to provide a rule of life for those regenerated through faith.

Anne Marbury Hutchinson emigrated to Massachusetts Bay Colony in 1634. At the time, the New England Puritans were attempting to clarify the place of "preparation for conversion" in covenant theology. They had come to the conclusion that salvation lay in fulfilling the conditions of God's covenant with humankind, including preparation for justification and a conscious effort toward sanctification. To some, including Hutchinson, this seemed like an overemphasis on the observance of the law, and she condemned it as a "covenant of works." Instead, she stressed the "covenant of grace," which she said was apart from the works of the law. At a synod of Congregational churches in 1637 Hutchinson was condemned as an antinomian, enthusiast, and heretic, and banished from the colony. In 1638 she moved to Rhode Island.

In the 20th century some have viewed existentialist ethics, situation ethics, and moral relativism as forms of antinomianism because these either reject or diminish the normative force of moral law. Most orthodox Christians today agree that the law serves at least the twin purposes of establishing the fact of human sin and of providing moral guidelines for Christian living.

R. D. LINDER

See also AGRICOLA, JOHANN; JUSTIFICATION; SANCTIFICATION.

Antiochene Theology. A rationalistic, literal-historical school of biblical interpretation, arising as a counterpoint to Alexandrian allegorical, mystical hermeneutics. A stress in affirming the full humanity of Christ made Antioch the birthplace of grammaticohistorical exegesis and expository preaching.

Ignatius was bishop of Antioch in the early 2d century. In his seven epistles he is eager to defend the full deity and full humanity of Christ. He particularly warns against docetism. Later in the century, Theophilus developed the Logos doctrine, referring to the logos *prophorikos* and used *trias* to apply to the Godhead.

Three quarters of a century later Paul of Samosata as bishop theorized that the Logos was a divine force—part of the mind of the Father—dwelling in Jesus from his birth, but apart from the Virgin. Jesus manifested himself as *energeia* and was not to be worshiped, though he was endowed greatly with the Logos. His unity with God is one of purpose, of will, of love. While it is possible for Paul to speak of one *prosōpon* (person) of God and the Logos, and to use the term *homoousios* (of the same Being) of Christ and the Father, yet the Logos and the Son were not identical. Paul of Samosata was excommunicated and came to lose most of his influence. Paul's opponents did not approve the term *homoousios*, later to become a touchstone of orthodoxy.

A schoolmaster, Lucian, next came to prominence in Antioch. Lucian conceived of Christ on a higher plane than did Paul. Whether he considered him as equal with the Father in deity is questionable. His work on the text of the Greek Bible was extensive, and he favored the historical and critical interpretation of the Scriptures.

Following the Council of Nicea, Antioch exhibited wide differences of opinion on the Arian question, but in this atmosphere John Chrysostom grew to maturity with extraordinary ability as a preacher. Emphasizing the moral values of Christianity, he continued the stress on historical exegesis. One of Chrysostom's teachers, the presbyter Diodorus, became bishop of Tarsus and was recognized as a "normal" theologian by the Council of Constantinople in 381. But he did not find an adequate expression for the relationship between the divine and human natures of Christ. There seemed almost to be a dual personality in his conception. Theodore, later bishop of Mopsuestia, developed historical criticism much further. He failed to find the doctrine of the Trinity in the OT, and minimized the messianic intimations in the Psalms. But he put heavy stress upon the importance of textual and historical study as a basis for exegesis. Theodore emphasized the difference between God and man. The Logos humbled himself and became man. The *prosōpon* of the man is complete and so is that of the Godhead. His disciple Theodoret's exegesis is in the best historical tradition, his apologetic writing clear and well organized. He stressed the infinite difference between God and man. His christological views were unquestionably influenced by his friend Nestorius, the most prominent representative of the Antiochene school. Impetuous, self-confident, full of energy, Nestorius was not a scholar. He emphasized the humanity of Jesus, but it is reasonably clear that what he intended to express was not heretical. The union of Godhead and manhood in Christ is voluntary, but it can be said that there is one *prosōpon* of Jesus Christ. Nestorius campaigned against the term *Theotokos* (God-bearer) as applied to the Virgin Mary, yet he agreed that, if properly understood, the term was unobjectionable. It was the violence of his emphases, with their stress on the separateness of the human and the divine in Christ, which was dangerous.

Justinian's *Edict of the Three Chapters* in 543 was unfair to the School of Antioch in its condemnations of the writings of Theodore and Theodoret. The Council of Constantinople of 553 (Fifth Ecumenical) condemned writings of the Antioch school on the basis of falsified and mutilated quotations.

The separation from the imperial church of the bishops who led the Nestorian schism and the capture of Antioch in 637 by the rising power of Islam checked the further distinctive development of the School of Antioch. Its Aristotelian emphasis on rationality, on ethical quality, and on man's free agency was not popular. Yet it is to be valued for its stress on the genuine continuance in the Second Person of the properties of each nature and for its insistence upon the importance of grammaticohistorical exegesis.

P. WOOLLEY

See also LOGOS; MONARCHIANISM; NESTORIUS, NESTORIANISM.

Antipaedobaptism. See BAPTISM, BELIEVERS'.

Anti-Semitism. The term was introduced in 1879 by Wilhelm Marr, a German political agitator, to designate anti-Jewish campaigns in Europe. It came to be applied to hostility and hatred directed toward Jews since before the Christian era.

The first major example of anti-Semitism occurred when the Seleucid Antiochus IV Epiphanes (175–163 B.C.) attempted to hellenize Jews, who found Greek idolatry as abhorrent as they later found Roman emperor worship. Jews were viewed as the great dissenters of the Mediterranean world. To pagans they became objects of discrimination and contempt.

The Jewish revolt of A.D. 66–70 resulted in the death, exile, or slavery of thousands of Jews. Such hardship was thought by the rapidly expanding Gentile church to be chastisement, proof of divine rejection. Gradually the church came to see itself as superseding a "dead" and "legalistic" Judaism. Triumphantly, the church stood over the synagogue as the new Israel, heir to the covenant promises. This cut off Christians from Jews, who failed to understand messianic redemption in terms of a suffering Servant and refused to believe that God had forever cast away his chosen.

In the Middle Ages, Jews were largely excluded from society. They sought to avoid social, economic, and ecclesiastical pressures by living behind ghetto walls. They were, however, permitted to practice usury. This led Christians to accuse them of being a pariah people. Jews were required to wear a distinctive hat or patch sewn on their clothing. They were accused of having a peculiar smell, in contrast to the "odor of sanctity." Jews were also maligned as "Christ-killers," desecraters of the host, murderers of Christian infants, spreaders of the black plague, poisoners of wells, and sucklers of sows. Since then the Jewish people have been persecuted in most European countries at one time or another.

The Holocaust of the 20th century is an event unparalleled in anti-Semitist history. Nazi propaganda stated that the human race must be "purified" by ridding it of Jews. The final solution to the

Jewish problem was camps, gas chambers, and crematoria. Between 1933, when Hitler came to power, and the end of World War II, 6 million Jewish lives were destroyed. Today in Jerusalem the Yad Vashem (the name is taken from Isa. 56:5) remembers victims and conducts Holocaust research and documentation.

Despite reaction to the Holocaust and reforms in Eastern Europe during the 1980s, anti-Semitism persists as a worldwide phenomenon, particularly in Europe and the U.S. It also further complicates Jewish-Arab tensions in the Middle East. The Anti-Defamation League and other agencies are organized to confront prejudice and to promote understanding between Jews and Gentiles.

M. R. WILSON

Antitrinitarianism. See UNITARIANISM.

Antitype. See TYPE, TYPOLOGY.

Apocalyptic. (from Gk. *apokalypsis*, "unveiling") Literature containing real or alleged revelations of heavenly secrets or events attending the end of the world and the inauguration of the kingdom of God. The term is derived from Rev. 1:1 which refers specifically to the Revelation of John, but the word is applied by modern scholars to a group of Jewish books which contain similar literary and eschatological characteristics. Not all of the literature popularly called apocalyptic belongs in that classification.

Historical Background. Many apocalypses were produced by unknown Jewish authors between 200 B.C. and A.D. 100 in imitation of the Book of Daniel. The apocalypses arose out of a three-part historical-theological problem: (1) monastic Judaism desired to see restoration of Israel through a righteous remnant; (2) unprecedented suffering and political bondage were continuing in an apparently righteous Israel; (3) God no longer seemed to be sending prophets nor speaking to explain the nation's plight.

Literary Characteristics. Apocalyptic as a genre of literature succeeded the prophetic. At some points apocalyptic is a development of elements in prophecy; at other points it departs from the prophetic character. No sharp line can be drawn between the two types, and characterizations of apocalyptic differ considerably but include these elements: (1) *Revelations.* The seer must learn the solution to the problems of evil and the coming of the kingdom through dreams, visions, or heavenly journeys with angelic guides. (2) *Imitative Literary Character.* The visions are literary fictions which imitate prophetic visions. Generally, prophecy was first spoken, while apocalypses were written. (3) *Pseudonymity.* The apocalyptists attributed their revelations to OT saints to validate the message to their own generation. (4) *Symbolism.* Symbolism becomes the main stock in trade, particularly for outlining the course of history disguising names of rulers then in power. (5) *Rewritten History.* The apocalyptists sometimes rewrote history from the perspective of the distant past as though it were future prophecy anticipating the coming of the kingdom in their own day.

Religious Characteristics. Apocalyptic eschatology's contrast of the present time of suffering with the future time of salvation is so radical that it is dualistically described as two ages: "this age" and "the age to come." The transition from this age of evil to the coming age of the kingdom of God will be accomplished only by God's supernatural intervention. The apocalyptists do not view the present against the background of the future. Their viewpoint encompasses the entire sweep of history, for they interpret history theologically. The apocalypses are theological treatises rather than historical documents.

It is not correct to call the apocalyptists pessimists, for they never lost their confidence that God would finally triumph and bring his kingdom. They concluded that God had withdrawn from his people in the present age and that salvation could be expected only in the age to come (Enoch 89:56–75). This evil age, however, has been predetermined and must run its course. God is waiting the passing of the times which he has decreed before breaking in to aid the righteous (4 Ezra 4:36–37).

The NT Apocalypse. The Revelation of John shares numerous traits with Jewish apocalypses but at important points stands apart from them.

The author designates his book as a prophecy (1:3; 22:7, 10, 18–19). John is not pseudonymous. The author merely signs his name: "John to the seven churches in the province of Asia" (1:4). John also differs from the apocalyptic treatment of the future. A true apocalyptic retraces history under the guise of prophecy. John takes his stand in his own environment, addresses his contemporaries, and looks prophetically into the future.

He embodies the prophetic tension between history and eschatology. The beast is Rome and at the same time an eschatological Antichrist which cannot be fully equated with historical Rome. John shares the optimism of the gospel rather than the pessimism of apocalyptic thought. While John prophesies that the satanic evil of the age will descend in fury upon God's people, he does not see an age abandoned to evil. On the contrary, history has become the scene of the divine redemption.

Finally, the Apocalypse possesses prophetic moral urgency. It does indeed promise a future salvation but not one which can be taken for granted. The seven letters strike a note of warning and a demand for repentance (2:5, 16, 21–22; 3:3, 19).

There are, it seems, a prophetic and a nonprophetic apocalyptic literature, and the Apocalypse of the NT stands in the first type.

G. E. LADD

See also ESCHATOLOGY.

Apocrypha, New Testament. (Gk. *ta apokrypha*, "the hidden things") A substantial collection of works published under the names of apostolic writers from the 2d century on. Most were deliberate fabrications without serious claim to canonicity. Hence, in this connection the word "apocrypha" is used in its meaning of untrue or spurious.

NT Apocrypha likely arose primarily for two reasons. Some sought to answer questions regarding Christ and his life on which the canonical Gospels were silent or to supply details concerning the apostles omitted from the Acts. Also, those with heretical tendencies sought to embed their views in works attributed to Christ and the apostles. Gnostics particularly advanced their cause in this way.

More than 50 apocryphal gospels are known. A few have been preserved in their entirety, others in fragments, and the rest only by name. Numerous acts of the Apostles were composed. Among the better known is the collection of five called the Leucian Acts because they were collected by Leucius. These fragmentary works include the Acts of Paul, John, Andrew, Peter, and Thomas.

Apocryphal epistles are not so numerous because it was harder to fabricate them with any appearance of authenticity. Apocalypses were modeled somewhat on the Revelation of John.

One of the most significant finds of NT apocryphal works occurred in 1946 at Nag Hammadi, about 30 miles north of Luxor in Egypt. This included 37 complete and five fragmentary works, generally with a Gnostic bias. All in Coptic, they were translations from Greek originals.

H. F. Vos

See also Apocrypha, Old Testament; Gnosticism; Bible, Canon of.

Apocrypha, Old Testament. Some 13 books comprise the Apocrypha: 1 and 2 Esdras, Tobit, Judith, the rest of Esther, the Wisdom of Solomon, Ecclesiasticus (which is also entitled The Wisdom of Jesus the Son of Sirach), Baruch, the Letter of Jeremiah, the Additions to Daniel, the Prayer of Manasses, and 1 and 2 Maccabees.

The Jews uniformly denied canonical status to these books, so they never were found in the Hebrew Bible. Manuscripts of the LXX included them, however, as an addendum to the canonical OT. In the 2d century A.D. the first Latin Bibles were translated from the LXX and so included the Apocrypha. Jerome's Vulgate distinguished between the *libri ecclesiastici* and the *libri canonici* with the result that the Apocrypha was accorded a secondary status.

In 1548 the Council of Trent recognized the Apocrypha, excepting 1 and 2 Esdras and the Prayer of Manasses, as having unqualified canonical status. The Reformers repudiated the Apocrypha as unworthy and contradictory to the doctrines of truly canonical Scripture; however, Luther did admit that they were "profitable and good to read." The Coverdale and Geneva Bibles included the Apocrypha but set them apart from the canonical books of the OT. After much debate the British and Foreign Bible Society decided in 1827 to exclude the Apocrypha; soon afterward the American branch concurred, and this action generally set the pattern for modern English Bible editions. Among Protestant communions only the Anglican Church makes some use of the Apocrypha today.

Many literary genres appear in the Apocrypha: popular narrative, religious history and philosophy, morality stories, poetic and didactic lyrics, wisdom literature, and apocalyptic. Most of these books were written in Palestine between 300 B.C. and A.D. 100.

D. H. Wallace

See also Apocrypha, New Testament; Bible, Canon of.

Apokatastasis. (Gk. *apokatastasis*, "restoration") Found in the NT only in Acts 3:21: "Jesus . . . must remain in heaven until the time comes for God to restore everything, as he promised long ago through his holy prophets" (NIV).

Peter asserted that at Christ's parousia would come the restoration of all that was proclaimed by the OT prophets—conversion of the Jews, gathering of the elect, righteous reign of the Messiah on earth, and creation of a new heaven and a new earth.

B. A. Demarest

See also Universalism.

Apollinarianism. A christological heresy of the 4th century which effectively allowed Christ only a divine nature and no human initiative. It was originated by Apollinaris (or Apollinarius) the Younger (ca. 310–ca. 390).

The central deviation of Apollinarianism began in a Platonic trichotomy. Man was seen to be body, sensitive soul, and rational soul. Apollinaris felt that if one failed to diminish the human nature of Jesus in some way, a dualism had to result. Furthermore, if one taught that Christ was a complete man, then Jesus had a human rational soul in which free will resided; and wherever there was free will, there was sin. Therefore, it followed that the Logos assumed only a body and its closely connected sensitive soul. The Logos or Word himself took the place of the rational soul (or spirit or *nous*) in the manhood of Jesus. Thus one can speak of "the one sole nature incarnate of the

Word of God." This doctrine was developed by Apollinaris in his *Demonstration of the Divine Incarnation* (376).

Apollinaris was a prolific writer, but following his anathematization in 381 his works were assiduously sought out and burned. Thus Apollinarianism leaves little literature except as cited in the works of its critics. The general principle on which Apollinarianism was condemned was the Eastern perception that "that which is not assumed is not healed." If the Logos did not assume the rational soul of the man Jesus, then the death of Christ could not heal or redeem the rational souls of men.

V. L. WALTER

See also CHALCEDON, COUNCIL OF.

Apollyon. See ABADDON.

Apologetics. A systematic defense or justification of the divine origin and the authority of the Christian faith. Peter commanded Christians to be ready to give a reason for the hope they have (1 Pet. 3:15). Broadly defined, apologetics is a part of evangelism.

Christianity is a worldview that asserts some very precise things—that the cosmos is not eternal and self-explanatory, that a Creator exists, that he chose a people and revealed himself and worked miracles among them, and that he incarnated himself at a precise time in history. The substantiation of such claims involves two classes of apologetics, the *subjective* and the *objective*.

The Subjective School. Luther, Pascal, Lessing, Kierkegaard, Brunner, and Barth doubted that the unbeliever can be "argued into belief." They stressed the operation of the Holy Spirit or the unique personal experience of grace, the inward, subjective encounter with God. They minimized human wisdom and rejected most traditional philosophy and classical logic, stressing the supernatural over natural theology and theistic proofs, since sin has blinded the eyes of man so that his reason cannot function properly.

The Objective School. Objective fact and external realities are theistic proofs to those in the objectivist camp, but there are two differing schools here.

The Natural Theology School. Such thinkers as Thomas Aquinas, Joseph Butler, F. R. Tennant, and William Paley followed an empirical tradition in philosophy from Aristotle, believing that reason was, perhaps, weakened by the fall but not severely crippled.

The Revelation School. Augustine, Calvin, Abraham Kuyper, and E. J. Carnell borrow insights from both the subjective school and the natural theology school. They distrust unregenerate reason, yet appreciate the role of concrete facts. As Luther said, "Prior to faith and a knowledge of God, reason is darkness, but in believers it is an excellent instrument. Just as all gifts and instruments of nature are evil in godless men, so they are good in believers."

Objectivists tend to use the same body of evidence when they do apologetics; they differ on how and when proofs persuade the unbeliever.

A. J. HOOVER

See also EVIL, PROBLEM OF; GOD, ARGUMENTS FOR THE EXISTENCE OF; THEODICY.

Apostasy. A deliberate repudiation and abandonment of professed faith (Heb. 3:12). Isa. 1:2–4 and Jer. 2:1–9 are among numerous defections of Israel. Perhaps the most notorious NT example is Judas Iscariot. Others include Demas (2 Tim. 4:10) and Hymenaeus and Alexander (1 Tim. 1:20). The apostles warned about the rise of apostasy in the church, culminating in the appearance of the man of sin (1 Tim. 4:1–3; 2 Thess. 2:3). There are also references to the consequences of falling away (Heb. 6:5–8; 10:26).

L. G. WHITLOCK, JR.

Apostle, Apostleship. (Gk. *apostolos*, from *apostellein*, "to send") Whereas several NT words express such ideas as dispatch, release, or dismiss, *apostellein* emphasizes *commission*—authority of and responsibility to the sender. So an apostle is properly one sent on a definite mission, in which he acts with full authority on behalf of the sender and is accountable to him. Biblical use of *apostle* is almost entirely confined to the NT, where it occurs 79 times: 10 in the Gospels, 28 in Acts, 38 in the epistles, and three in the Revelation of John.

Christ as Apostle. In Heb. 3:1 Jesus is called "the apostle . . . of our confession." Repeatedly he made the claim of being sent by the Father.

The Twelve as Apostles. Called "disciples" in the Gospels, for their primary function during Christ's ministry was to be with him and learn of him, the Twelve are also apostles because Jesus imparted to them his authority to preach and to cast out demons (Mark 3:14–15; 6:30).

The number 12 recalls the 12 tribes of Israel, but the basis of leadership is no longer tribal, but personal and spiritual. Evidently the college of apostles was regarded as fixed in number, for Jesus spoke of 12 thrones in the coming age (Matt. 19:28; cf. Rev. 21:14). Judas was replaced by Matthias (Acts 1:15–26).

Apostles receive first mention in the lists of spiritual gifts (1 Cor. 12:28; Eph. 4:11). Their duties were preaching, teaching, and administration. Their preaching rested on their association with Christ and the instruction received from him, and included their witness to his resurrection (Acts 1:22). Their converts passed immediately under their instruction (Acts 2:42). Broadly speaking, in the area of administration, they were responsible for the life, discipline, and welfare of the Christian community (Acts 5:1–11).

Paul as Apostle. Paul's apostleship was by direct appointment of Christ (Gal. 1:1) and the Gentile world was specifically his sphere of labor (Rom. 1:5; Gal. 1:16; 2:8). His apostleship was recognized by the Jerusalem authorities, but he never asserted membership among the Twelve (1 Cor. 15:11). He bore witness to the resurrection because his call came from the risen Christ (1 Cor. 9:1; Acts 26:16–18).

Other Apostles. It is reasonably clear that in addition to the Twelve, Paul and James had the leading recognition as apostles. Others might be included under special circumstances—e.g., Barnabas, Silvanus, and Timothy—but warrant is lacking for making "apostle" the equivalent of "missionary."

E. F. Harrison

See also Apostolic Succession; Church, Authority in.

Apostles' Creed. Summary of Christian belief. The modern form is from about A.D. 700. However, segments of it date as early as the 2d century. The most important predecessor of the Apostles' Creed was the Old Roman Creed, from the latter half of the 2d century. The Apostles' Creed was associated with entrance into the fellowship as a confession of faith for those to be baptized. Catechetical instruction was often based on its tenets. In time the creed became a "rule of faith" to give continuity to Christian teachings and to clearly separate true faith from heretical deviations. By the 6th or 7th century the creed had come to be accepted as a part of the official liturgy of the Western Church. Likewise, it was used by devout individuals, along with the Lord's Prayer, in morning and evening devotions. The churches of the Reformation included it in doctrinal collections and used it in worship.

O. G. Oliver, Jr.

See also Creed, Creeds.

Apostleship, Gift of. See Spiritual Gifts.

Apostolic Succession. A claim that an ecclesiastical leader's authority derives from episcopal consecration of bishop to bishop in an unbroken chain from the apostles. This theory of ministry arose ca. A.D. 170–200. Gnostics claimed to possess a secret tradition handed down to them from the apostles. As a counterclaim the Catholic Church pointed to each bishop as a true successor to the apostle who had founded the see and therefore to the truth the apostles taught. The bishop, as an authoritative teacher, preserved the apostolic tradition. He was also a guardian of the apostolic Scriptures and the creed. As the last links with the apostles were dying out this emphasis on apostolic teaching and practice was natural. In the 3d century the emphasis changed from the open succession of teachers to the bishops as the personal successors of the apostles. This development owed much to the advocacy of Cyprian, bishop of Carthage (248–58).

R. E. HIGGINSON

See also CHURCH, AUTHORITY IN.

Aquinas, Thomas. See THOMAS AQUINAS.

Archangel. See ANGEL.

Archbishop. See BISHOP; CHURCH OFFICERS.

Archdeacon. See CHURCH OFFICERS; DEACON, DEACONESS.

Archpriest. See CHURCH OFFICERS.

Arianism. A christological heresy teaching that the Logos was a being created in time and sharing no substance with the Father. This subordinationist theory originated in the teaching of Arius (d. 336), a presbyter in Alexandria (312–25). Arius was a thoroughgoing Greek rationalist who studied in Alexandria, the center for Origen's teachings on the subordination of the Son to the Father. Origen had balanced his theology by insisting on the eternal generation of the Son. Arius lost that balance. Similar views are continued by unitarians and the Jehovah's Witnesses.

Between 318 and 323 Arius first came into conflict with Bishop Alexander over the nature of Christ. A truce was attempted between the leaders, but in Mar. 324 Alexander convened a provincial synod which anathematized Arius and in Feb. 325 Arius was condemned at a synod in Antioch. The Emperor Constantine intervened by calling the first ecumenical council, the Council of Nicea, on May 20, 325, which condemned Arius and his teaching. Athanasius, a member of Alexander's staff at Nicea, took little part in the council, but as bishop of Alexandria from 328, he was the unremitting foe of Arianism.

Arius was banished to Illyricum where he continued to write, teach, and appeal to an broadening circle of political and ecclesiastical adherents. Around 332 or 333 Constantine opened direct contact with Arius, and in 335 the two met at Nicomedia. Arius presented a confession which Constantine considered sufficiently orthodox to allow reconsideration. The Synod of Jerusalem readmitted Arius to communion as he lay dying in Constantinople. Since Arian views were being advanced by many bishops and members of the court, the furor did not diminish.

The Council of Nicea's confession "in one Lord Jesus Christ the Son of God, begotten of the Father, only-begotten, that is from the substance of the Father" denied Arius's central assertion that an immutable God could not communicate or share attributes with any other being. The council's "true God from true God, begotten not made" set aside Arius's contention that, since God was immutable and unknowable, Christ had to be a created being, made out of nothing by God, first in the created order, but created. This allowed only a limited preexistence of the Logos. The Logos was incarnate in the Christ, but, asserted Arius, "there was once when he was not."

Nicea's "of one substance with the Father" made the Greek term *homoousios* the catchword of the orthodox. Arianism developed two parties, one of which taught that Christ was of a substance *like* the Father (*homoiousios*). A more extreme wing insisted that, as a created being, Christ was unlike the Father in substance (*anomoios*). Arius himself would have belonged to the more moderate party.

The council anathematized anyone who taught that Christ was created, that he matured in his understanding of the divine plan according to the Scriptures and therefore could not be part of the unchanging God, or that Jesus was given the honorary title "Son of God."

Arianism could have triumphed. Beginning with Constantius, the court was often Arian. Five times Arians drove Athanasius into exile. Synods at Antioch in 341 and Arles in 353 repudiated Nicea. In 360 in Constantinople all earlier creeds were disavowed and the term "substance" (*ousia*) was outlawed. The Son was simply declared to be "like the Father who begot him."

The orthodox counterattack pointed out that Arian theology reduced Christ to a demigod and in effect introduced polytheism, since Christ was worshiped among Arians as among the orthodox. The most telling argument was Athanasius's battle cry that only God, very God, truly God Incarnate could reconcile and redeem fallen man to holy God. The Cappadocian fathers—Basil the Great, Gregory of Nyssa, Gregory of Nazianzus—brought a final resolution. They distinguished the concept of substance (*ousia*) from the concept of person (*hypostasis*) and thus allowed the orthodox defenders of the original Nicene formula to unite with moderate Arians in understanding God as one substance and three persons. Christ therefore was of one substance with the Father (*homoousion*) but a distinct person. With this understanding the Council of Constantinople in 381 was able to reaffirm the Nicene Creed. Emperor Theodosius I joined the orthodox and Arianism began to wane.

The long struggle was continued by Ulfilas, a missionary to the Germanic tribes. Ulfilas taught the similarity of the Son to the Father and the total subordination of the Holy Spirit to the Visigoths north of the Danube, and they carried this semi-Arianism back into Italy. The Vandals were taught by Visigoth priests and in 409 carried the same semi-Arianism across the Pyrenees into Spain. It was not until the end of the 7th century that orthodoxy was to finally absorb Arianism, and it never fully disappeared.

V. L. Walter

See also Athanasius; Nicea, Council of.

Aristotle, Aristotelianism. The Greek philosopher Aristotle (384–322 B.C.) was the son of the court physician to the king of Macedon. At age 17 he went to Plato's Academy in Athens, where he remained for 20 years (367–347) as a student and then a teacher. After the death of Plato he spent 12 years away from Athens, serving three years as tutor to the son of Philip II of Macedon, Alexander the Great. In 335 he returned to Athens to open a new school called the Lyceum, where he taught for the next 12 years.

Classification of the Writings. Aristotle's writings may be divided into four major groups: (1) logical treatises, commonly called the Organon (including *Categories*, *De interpretatione*, *Prior Analytics*, *Posterior Analytics*, and *Topics*); (2) natural philosophy and science (including *On Coming into Being and Passing Away*, *De caelo*, *Physics*, *De historia animalium*, *De partibus animalium*, *De generatione animalium*, and *De anima on human nature*); (3) a collection of works known as the *Metaphysics*, and (4) works on ethics and politics (the most important of these are *Eudemian Ethics*, *Nicomachean Ethics*, *Politics*, *Rhetoric*, and the fragmentary *Politics*).

Logic. Aristotle sees logic, not as a definite part of philosophy, but rather, as a methodological tool for all science and philosophy. His logic may be divided into (1) basic modes of being that are apprehended by single concepts and definitions (*Categories*), (2) the union and separation of these modes of being as expressed by judgments (*De interpretatione*), and (3) the way the mind passes from reasoning about known truth to about unknown (*Prior and Posterior Analytics*).

Natural Philosophy. Nature, for Aristotle, is characterized by change so natural philosophy is fundamentally an analysis of the process of change. Change may be explained in terms of the material cause or matter from which the thing has evolved, the formal cause which gives shape or structure, the efficient cause which imposes form on the matter, and the final cause which is the ultimate end to which that substance emerges. The final cause is what requires the efficient cause to act in a certain way.

Change turns the potential into the actual. Since there is movement from potentiality to actuality, there must be an external efficient cause that accounts for an object's origin and continued existence. Aristotle held that an efficient cause was needed for the physical universe as a whole. Therefore, there must be a first, unmoved mover, who is not subject to change. Because there is regularity throughout nature, it may be concluded that this first cause is intelligent.

The highest earthly being is the human. Aristotle gives a whole treatise, *De anima*, to the study of human nature. The human soul unites three parts. (1) The vegetative part allows the human to take nourishment, grow, and reproduce. (2) The animal part gives the ability to sense and desire and to move from place to place. (3) Through the rational part distinctively human functions are possible.

Metaphysics. The most fundamental reality is being itself. All categories are restricted kinds of being. Everything, whether it changes or is unchanging, whether it is quantitative or nonquantitative, falls within metaphysics. From this perspective the most basic structure of the world is understood. The foundation of reality is not an abstract essence but an individual substance. Individual substances are a combination of matter and form.

God, or the first mover, is the first cause of all finite existence. He is total actuality and lacks all potentiality; otherwise there would be the need for something prior to himself to actualize him. The actualization of potential involves change. Since God is only actuality he must be changeless, eternal, and immaterial because matter is a form of potency. Being immaterial, he is a mind, not dependent on external objects for reflection but contemplating his own perfect being.

Practical Philosophy. The proper guide to action is individual ethics. Aristotle's mature reflection is recorded in the *Nicomachean Ethics*.

The goal toward which all strive is happiness or well-being. Happiness is the operation of all parts of human nature under reason for an entire life. This requires the learning of basic moral virtues, which are the rational habits to act in a certain way. At first the habit comes from without. Parents punish and reward behavior, but moral virtue has not really been learned until the habit is internalized and the act done for its own sake.

Every virtue is the mean between two extremes. Courage is the mean between cowardice and foolhardiness. With passions guided and controlled by reason and good fortune, a happy life may be lived. However, the intellectual virtues, since they are most distinctly human, are the crowning pleasures of a happy life. Contemplation and prayer are the fundamental intellectual virtues because they underlie the rest.

Aristotelianism. During the early Middle Ages, Aristotle's logical works received great attention. Contrasts between substance and accident, matter and form, became important theological distinctions. In the 13th century the influence of Aristotle increased with translation of his works into Latin from Arabic and the availability of commentaries by major Islamic philosophers. For example, the work of Averroes (1126–98) was more honored in the West than in his homeland. Albertus Magnus came in contact with Averroes' commentaries on Aristotle at the University of Paris, but, it was Albertus's pupil, Thomas Aquinas, who produced a synthesis of Christian and Aristotelian thought. Aristotelianism also got a bad name through Averroes, who advocated the eternality of the universe, leading the church to condemn the work of Aristotle and Averroes in 1277.

With the canonization of Aquinas and the study of his works Aristotelianism regained favor. The influence of Aristotle can be seen in the scholastic theologians Duns Scotus and William of Ockham. During the Renaissance the emphasis on humanism and classical languages led to the scholarly revival of interest in Plato and Aristotle. Much Protestant theology owed its general methodology and structure to Aristotelianism in the late 16th and 17th centuries.

The 16th through the 18th centuries saw another reaction in the West against Aristotelianism. The response was at least partly the result of the astronomical views of such thinkers as Copernicus (1473–1543), whose views were in conflict with many of those of Aristotle. The Catholic Church, however, put its seal of approval on Aquinas's work with Pope Leo XIII's encyclical *Aeterni patris* in 1879.

P. D. FEINBERG

See also ALBERTUS MAGNUS; AVERROES; DUNS SCOTUS, JOHN; NEO-PLATONISM; SCHOLASTICISM; THOMAS AQUINAS; WILLIAM OF OCKHAM.

Arius. See ARIANISM.

Armageddon. (Gk. *harmagedōn*) Prophetic battlefield mentioned only in Rev. 16:16, where the prophet describes a confrontation of "the kings of the whole world" who are inspired to do battle by demonic spirits.

The name does not appear in any extant Hebrew writing. It is popularly thought to refer to the mountain (*har*) of Megiddo (*magedōn*). This has merit in that Megiddo was a military stronghold (Josh. 12:21; 17:11; Judg. 1:27; 1 Kings 9:15) and many famous battles were fought in the area: between Israel and Sisera (Judg. 5:19) as well as Josiah and the Pharaoh Neco (2 Kings 23:29). On the other hand, R. H. Charles wonders if a corruption in the language (*ar himdah*, "city of desire"; or *har migdo*, "his fruitful mountain") should not point to Jerusalem, "the mountain of Israel." Prophetic expectation seems to point to a climactic battle in the neighborhood of Zion (Joel 3:2; Zech. 14:2; 1 Enoch 56:7). If the apocalyptic imagery of Rev. 16–20 derives from Ezek. 38-39, we have a picture of the final battle in the "mountains of Israel" (Ezek. 38:7–23; 39:2). Still others (e.g., G. R. Beasley-Murray) suggest that no geographic locality is meant; rather, this name stands for an event. Here the culmination of history is found in the final clash between the forces of God and Satan/evil. In contemporary popular theology the term often adopts this symbolic meaning.

G. M. BURGE

Arminianism. The teaching of the Dutch theologian Jacobus (also Jakob or James) Arminius (1560–1609) and the movement which stemmed from it .

Arminianism is a distinct Protestant theology which teaches conditional predestination, in which the predetermination of the destiny of individuals is based on God's foreknowledge of whether they will freely accept or reject Christ. Arminius stressed the human freedom to choose salvation, proclaiming that Christ's atonement is unlimited in its benefits but that believers may lose their salvation and be eternally lost.

A spillover from Calvinism into Arminianism has occurred in America in recent decades. Many Arminians whose theology is not very precise say that Christ paid the penalty for our sins, though strict Arminianism teaches that Christ "suffered for us." Until relatively recently the Arminian tradition emphasized infant baptism, considered as the sacrament which helps implement prevenient grace and restrains the child until evangelical conversion occurs. The adoption of full biblical inerrancy and dispensationalism are also late developments.

About 8 million Arminians constitute the Christian Holiness Association. This movement strongly defends Christ's virgin birth, miracles, bodily resurrection, and substitutionary atonement (his suffering for the punishment believers would have received); the dynamic inspiration and infallibility of Scripture; justification by grace alone through faith alone; and the final destinies of heaven and hell.

J. K. GRIDER

See also ARMINIUS, JACOBUS; METHODISM; WESLEYAN TRADITION, THE.

Arminius, Jacobus (Jakob or James) (1560–1609). Dutch theologian. Born in Oudewater, the Netherlands, Arminius was educated at the universities of Marburg (1575) and Leiden (1576–81), at the academy at Geneva (1582, 1584–86), and at Basel (1582–83). He was pastor of an Amsterdam congregation (1588–1603), and a professor at the University of Leiden from 1603 until his death. His *Declaration of Sentiments* of 1608 gave his arguments against supralapsarianism (the view that each person's destiny was determined by God prior to Adam's fall). It also sought to secure favorable status in the United Netherlands for his own kind of conditional predestination teaching.

Arminius was the ablest exponent of the teaching that God's predestination of the destiny of individuals is based on his foreknowledge of the way in which they will freely (in the context of prevenient grace) accept or reject Christ. This view was popularized by John Wesley and the Methodists and guides denominations which constitute the Christian Holiness Association.

J. K. GRIDER

See also ARMINIANISM.

Armstrongism. Officially the Worldwide Church of God, founded by Herbert W. Armstrong and best known for its magazine, *The Plain Truth*, and radio broadcast, "The World Tomorrow." With headquarters at Ambassador College in Pasadena, California, Armstrongism is a blend of Adventist and Jehovah's Witnesses doctrines and a form of British Israelitism.

I. HEXHAM

See also ADVENTISM; JEHOVAH'S WITNESSES.

Articles, The Thirty-Nine. See THIRTY-NINE ARTICLES, THE.

Articles of Religion. The standards of doctrine of the United Methodist Church. The Articles began as John Wesley's abridgment of the Thirty-Nine Articles of the Church of England for use in the American Methodist Episcopal

Church organized in 1784; Wesley reduced the Thirty-Nine Articles to 24. The organizing conference added Article 23, outlining the church's relationships with the newly formed American government.

The only change in the original doctrinal statement has been the Confession of Faith of the United Brethren Church in the *Book of Discipline* at the formation of the United Methodist Church in 1968. This addition introduced into the official doctrinal statement of the church, for the first time, an article on Christian perfection—a doctrine central to Wesleyan theology but never before part of the doctrines of the *Discipline*.

M. E. DIETER

See also WESLEY, JOHN; WESLEYAN TRADITION, THE.

Asbury, Francis (1745-1816). The father of Methodism in the U.S. Asbury arrived in the American colonies in 1771 and rapidly assumed leadership among the four Methodist missionaries. He was convinced that preachers should go where the gospel most needed to be heard—in taverns, jails, fields, and by the wayside. His authoritarian leadership and the strength of his example set the style for the itinerant Methodist minister in early America.

In 1784 Wesley appointed Asbury and Thomas Coke as "general superintendents" of the Methodists in the U.S. In December of that year at the historic Christmas Conference in Baltimore, the Methodist Episcopal Church in America was officially organized under Asbury. From that time the church grew rapidly, particularly west of the mountains. Asbury preached God's free grace, humankind's liberty to accept or reject that grace, and the Christian's need to strive for the abolition of willful sin after conversion. Asbury organized the Methodist "circuit riders" and early supported camp meetings and revivals as means of evangelism. At Asbury's arrival in America four Methodist ministers cared for about 300 laypeople; when he died there were 2000 ministers and more than 200,000 Methodists.

M. A. NOLL

See also METHODISM.

Ascension Day. Jesus ascended into heaven on the 40th day after his resurrection (Acts 1:3, 9), and 10 days before the descent of the Holy Spirit at Pentecost (Acts 2:1). During the 3d and early 4th centuries the festival of Pentecost apparently commemorated both the ascension and the descent of the Holy Spirit, ideas juxtaposed in Eph. 4:8–11. Toward the end of the 4th century the two events were celebrated separately, with Ascension Day on the 40th day after Easter.

D. H. WHEATON

See also CHRISTIAN YEAR.

Ascension of Christ. The end of Christ's postresurrection appearances and departure of his physical presence. Luke describes this event in a word or two in Luke 24:51 and more fully in Acts 1:9.

John 3:13; 6:62, and 20:17 speak of the approaching ascension. Paul describes the result of the ascension; the Lord permeates the universe with his presence and power (Eph. 4:10). Such phrases (ASV) as "received up in glory" (1 Tim. 3:16), "gone into heaven" (1 Pet. 3:22), and "passed through the heavens" (Heb. 4:14) refer to the same event. Paul exhorts the Colossian believers to "seek the things that are above, where Christ is, seated on the right hand of God" (Col. 3:1, ERV).

The Heidelberg Catechism suggests three benefits we receive from the ascension. (1) Christ is our Advocate in the presence of his Father (Rom. 8:34; 1 John 2:1; Heb. 7:25). As our High Priest he offered on the cross the one perfect and final sacrifice for sins (Heb. 10:12), and now continues his priestly ministry in heaven. As King-Priest he communicates, through the Holy Spirit, to all believers the gifts and blessings which he died to win for them. (2) Christ represents our fleshly bodies in heaven, a pledge of the time when "he, as our Head, will also take us, His members, up to Himself." (3) He sends his Spirit, as the earnest of the promised inheritance.

A. ROSS

See also RESURRECTION OF CHRIST.

Ascetical Theology. In Roman Catholic thought the study of the ordinary means of Christian perfection. Its purpose is to probe the disciplined renunciation of personal desires, the imitation of Christ, and the pursuit of charity. It is distinguished since the 17th century from *moral theology*, which deals with the avoidance of mortal and venial sins and duties essential for salvation, and *mystical theology*, which studies the extraordinary grace of God leading to infused contemplation.

The borderline between moral and ascetical theology is hazy at best, while its distinction from mystical theology is often denied altogether. Ascetical theology is usually divided into the *purgative*, *illuminative*, and *unitive* ways. The purgative way, which stresses the cleansing of the soul from serious sin, overlaps moral theology; the unitive way, which focuses on union with God, easily includes mystical theology. Only the illuminative way, the practice of positive Christian virtue, is distinctively ascetical.

P. H. DAVIDS

See also DEVOTIO MODERNA; ILLUMINATIVE WAY, THE; MYSTICISM; PURGATIVE WAY, THE; SPIRITUALITY; UNIO MYSTICA; UNITIVE WAY, THE.

Aseity of God. See GOD, ATTRIBUTES OF.

Ash Wednesday. A day of penitence signified by the dabbing of ashes on the forehead and traditionally marking the beginning of Lent. The day was originally part of the discipline of public penitence and came to be used generally from the 10th century. The ash recalls Gen. 3:19's reminder that humans are of dust .

D. H. WHEATON

See also CHRISTIAN YEAR.

Asian Theology. Indigenization of the Christian message through a number of distinctive, Asian-culture-based theologies. The International Missionary Council in Jerusalem in 1930 stressed that the Christian message must be expressed in national and cultural patterns. This emphasis on using indigenous art forms and structures was carried into the area of theology. In the early 1970s the Theological Education Fund promoted "contextualization" of God's revelation to the various world cultural contexts during its Third Mandate Period (1972–77). Contextualization indigenized theology within missions, hermeneutics, and educational method and structure.

Proponents argue that the Scriptures came through a specific cultural form, Judaism and Hellenism. Therefore the gospel must be translated or contextualized for the Asian cultures. Theologies claiming to represent Asian cultural forms include the *pain of God theology* (Japan), *water buffalo theology* (Thailand), *third-eye theology* (for the Chinese), *minjung theology* (Korea), and *theology of change* (Taiwan). There are also national theologies, developed for India, Burma, Sri Lanka, and other areas. Asian theologies have proliferated since the 1960s. Increasingly, evangelical theologians have reacted against the concept of Asian theology, although some within evangelicalism insist careful theological indigenization is needed.

Syncretistic Theology. Some Christian theologians and other religious thinkers have tried to syncretize Christianity with Hinduism, Buddhism, or Islam to contextualize theology. The Programme Unit on Faith and Witness of the World Council of Churches (WCC) has sponsored a number of dialogues with the leaders of other religions. Some meetings have resulted in a mutual acceptance of beliefs. The scope of Hinduism and Buddhism is large enough to accommodate all other religions including Christianity.

Accommodation Theology. Accommodation attempts to contextualize theology in the same ways a hotel accommodates a guest. Theological accommodation considers prevailing customs and religious practices of another culture and adopts as many of them as possible. Christian attempts to accommodate are observable particularly in Buddhist countries. The accommodation of Asian religious terminologies and concepts such as *dharma, Tien Chu, anicca, dukkha,* and *anatta* into Christian theology can be acceptable to many Christians as long as biblical meaning is incorporated. Yet the question of where to draw the line between syncretism and accommodation depends on whether the person is willing to accept the unique revelation of God in Jesus Christ and in the Scriptures in his accommodation.

Situational Theology. The main thrust of ecumenical theology in Asia is toward liberation from social injustice, economic exploitation, political oppression, and racial discrimination. Minjung theology is a Korean version of liberation theology which presents Jesus Christ as liberator of the oppressed.

Conclusion. The key issue surrounding development of an Asian theology is whether contextualization can preserve biblical and historical doctrines without compromise. In OT times the ark was carried by ox cart. Today in several countries the ark would be carried by rickshaw, horse, motorcycle, or car. Yet the meaning of the ark must not be changed. Many liberal theologians are trying to change the ark itself. Asian Christians must listen to, evaluate, and be open-minded to different Asian theological views on contextualization and yet, without compromise, be faithful to the gospel and proclaim it in love.

B. R. Ro

See also Pain of God Theology.

Assumption of Mary. See Mary, Assumption of.

Assurance. Assurance of faith or salvation is the humble confidence of the believer in Christ that, notwithstanding his mortal sinful condition, he is irrevocably a child of God and an heir of heaven. The doctrine of spiritual assurance is particularly taught by Paul, John, and the writer of Hebrews. Paul relates the Spirit of adoption to the assurance of sonship (Rom. 8:15–17; Gal. 4:6).

Assurance of salvation has both an objective and a subjective basis. First, on the objective authority of the Word of God the believer can know that God chose him from the foundation of the world, and that Christ made full atonement for his sins, rose from the dead for his justification, lives to make intercession, and will come again to receive him to glory. Assurance also involves the deep personal conviction created by the Holy Spirit of forgiveness, adoption, and eternal salvation. However, one may be genuinely saved but lack full assurance of salvation (1 John 5:13). The doctrine of assurance was given full treatment by Luther, Calvin, and most Reformation theologians. The Council of Trent rejected the teaching that a Christian may be certain of salvation. John Wesley stressed assurance through the internal witness of the Holy Spirit and a life lived without voluntary sin.

B. A. Demarest

See also Backsliding; Perseverance.

Astrology. The ancient art of divination through studying the influence of stars and planets and their relative positions in the heavens on persons or events. Some astrologists conclude that the planets exert an actual influence, while others believe that celestial movements and positions only indicate how a person or event will fare. Astronomy seeks information about the heavenly bodies and laws governing their movements, while astrology seeks meaning in the relationship of heavenly bodies to people and events on earth.

The OT condemns the worship of heavenly bodies (see, e.g., Deut. 4:19; 17:2–5; 2 Kings 17:16), a practice that Manasseh introduced in the southern kingdom (2 Kings 21:5) and Josiah removed (2 Kings 23:5). Jeremiah refers to Hebrew worship of the "queen of heaven" (Ishtar, the planet Venus; 7:18; 44:17–19) and to worship of heavenly bodies (8:2; 19:13). But such worship is not astrology. Isaiah referred specifically to stargazers "who divide the heavens" and who distinguished the signs of the zodiac (47:13). He declared that they could not even save themselves. Hebrews were to seek their God directly. Astrologers indirectly were condemned in Daniel's day when they could not meet the demands of Nebuchadnezzar. Daniel through divine enablement stepped into the gap (2:27; 4:7; 5:7, 11).

Magi, perhaps Median priests, saw Jesus' star in the east (Matt. 2:1–2). Whether it was a nova, a comet, a conjunction of planets (e.g., Jupiter, Mars, and Saturn), or just some supernatural light, it signified to them the birth of a great ruler among the Jews. This isolated sign is no endorsement of astrology.

H. F. Vos

See also Occult, The.

Athanasian Creed. One of the three ecumenical creeds widely used in Western Christendom as a profession of the orthodox faith. It is also referred to as the *Symbolum Quicunque* because the first words of the Latin text read, *Quicunque vult salvus esse* . . . ["Whoever wishes to be saved . . ."].

According to (false) tradition Athanasius, bishop of Alexandria in the 4th century, was the author of the creed. The oldest known instance of the use of this name is in the first canon of the Synod of Autun, ca. 670, where it is called the "faith" of St. Athanasius. The creed was probably formulated ca. 500 in south Gaul. It was likely influenced by theologians of Lerins and deals with Arianism and Nestorianism. The creed was counted as one of the three classic creeds by the time of the Reformation. Lutheran and Reformed confessional statements recognize its authority. However, the contemporary liturgical use of the creed is largely confined to the Roman and Anglican communions.

The creed is composed of 40 carefully modeled clauses or verses, each a distinct proposition. The first section centers on the doctrine of God as Trinity, excluding unorthodox viewpoints and expressing Augustinian insights. The second section expresses faith in the incarnation by affirming the doctrinal conclusions reached in controversies regarding the divinity and the humanity of Jesus. The creed affirms that the incarnation was a union of two distinctly different natures, the divine and the human, each complete in itself, without either losing its identity.

J. F. Johnson

See also Athanasius; Creed, Creeds; Filioque; Homoousion.

Athanasius (ca. 296–373). Bishop of Alexandria from 328 to 373. An uncompromising foe of Arianism, regarded as the greatest theologian of his time.

As a young man Athanasius plunged into writing and produced theological works of lasting importance. One was the *Contra Gentiles*, a defense of Christianity against paganism; another was the *De incarnatione*, an attempt to explain the doctrine of redemption. During this period Athanasius was the secretary and confidant of his bishop, Alexander. In this capacity he attended the first general council at Nicea in 325. At the council the anti-Arian party led by Bishop Alexander won a resounding victory over Arian subordinationism. The council affirmed that the Son of God was "of one substance with the Father," both sharing alike the fundamental nature of deity. In 328 Alexander died and Athanasius succeeded him in the see.

The tenure of Athanasius as bishop of Alexandria was marked by five periods of exile. His vigorous defense of the Nicene formula caused him to be a target for the supporters of Arius, who rallied after the council. However, during his 46 years as bishop there were enough years of relative peace for Athanasius to accomplish much as a theologian. He was a churchman and a pastor rather than a systematic or speculative theologian. His works are pastoral, exegetical, polemical, and even biographical; there is no single treatise that attempts to present the totality of his theology. Nevertheless, for Athanasius the truth or falsity of a doctrine is to be judged on the basis of the degree to which it expresses Christian monotheism and the doctrine of salvation.

J. F. JOHNSON

See also ARIANISM; ATHANASIAN CREED; HOMOOUSION; NICEA, COUNCIL OF.

Atheism. (Gk. *atheos*, "without God") Used in Eph. 2:12 in the plural form to designate the condition of being without the true God.

Four modern senses of "atheism" may be identified: (1) *Classical atheism* is not a general denial of God's existence but rejects the god of a particular nation. Early Christians were repeatedly called atheists because they refused to acknowledge Roman gods. In this sense Cicero called Socrates and Diagoras of Athens atheists. (2) *Philosophical atheism* denies existence of a personal, self-conscious deity (not a principle, first cause, or force). (3) *Dogmatic atheism* is the absolute denial of God's existence. This position is rare. People have more often declared themselves agnostics or secularists. Those who have claimed this view include the 18th-century French atheists. (4) *Practical atheism* lives life, whatever the belief system, as though there is no God. There is complete indifference, often outspoken and defiant, to God's claims on life (Ps. 14:1).

P. D. FEINBERG

Atheism, Christian. See DEATH OF GOD THEOLOGY.

Atonement. (Heb. *kippūr*; related to Gk. *katallagē, hilasmos, hilastērion*) The expression "to make atonement" is frequent only in Exodus, Leviticus, and Numbers, but the basic idea is widespread. In the OT sin is dealt with by the offering of sacrifice. Thus the burnt offering will be accepted "to make atonement" (Lev. 1:4), as also the sin offering and the guilt offering (Lev. 4:20; 7:7) and especially the sacrifices on the day of atonement (Lev. 16).

In the NT the principle on which atonement is effected is that the sacrifice of animals cannot avail for sin (Heb. 10:4), but has been replaced by the perfect sacrifice of Christ (Heb. 9:26; 10:5–10). Christ paid sin's penalty (Rom. 3:25–26; 6:23; Gal. 3:13). He redeemed us (Eph. 1:7), paying the price that sets us free (1 Cor. 6:20; Gal. 5:1). He made a new covenant (Heb. 9:15). He won the victory (1 Cor. 15:55–57), turning away God's wrath (Rom. 3:25), and reconciling believers to God (Eph. 2:16). His love and endurance of suffering further set the theme for the Christian's response to atonement (Luke 9:23; 1 Pet. 2:21).

L. MORRIS

See also ATONEMENT, EXTENT OF THE; ATONEMENT, THEORIES OF THE; BLOOD, SACRIFICIAL ASPECTS OF.

Atonement, Day of. (Heb. *yom kippūr*, lit. "day of coverings, propitiations") The only fast day prescribed by Mosaic law (Lev. 16; 23:26–32; Num. 29:7–11), celebrated on the 10th day of Tishri with abstinence and worship and referred to in the NT as "the fast" (Acts 27:9). This day speaks of the Lord's gracious concern both to deal fully with his people's sins and to make them fully aware that they stand before him, accepted and covered in respect of all iniquity, transgression, and sin (Lev. 16:21). The day of atonement (Lev. 16) centered on the high priest's sprinkling of blood on the mercy seat and the ritual of the two goats (vv. 7–10, 15–17, 20–22). One goat is sacrificed as a "sin offering" (vv. 9, 15) and the other is sent off as the "scapegoat" into the wilderness (vv. 10, 24).

J. A. MOTYER

See also BLOOD, CHRIST'S; OFFERINGS AND SACRIFICES IN BIBLE TIMES.

Atonement, Extent of the. Two views surround the extent of Christ's redemption. Either the death of Jesus was intended to secure salvation for a limited number (Augustinian, Calvinist) or for everyone (Arminian). The first view is sometimes called "limited" or "particular" atonement because, while redemption is available to all, a particular group (the elect) effectively benefits. The second view is sometimes referred to as "unlimited" or "general" atonement since redemption is determined to be for humanity in general.

Particular. The doctrine that Jesus' death was sufficient for the elect in particular arose as an implication of the doctrine of election and the satisfaction theory of the atonement. The Synod of Dort (1618–19) gave the succinct definition of the view, stating that Christ's death was "sufficient for all but efficient for the elect."

General. The doctrine of general redemption argues that the death of Christ was designed to include all humankind, whether or not all believe. To those who savingly believe it is redemptively applied, and to those who do not believe it provides the benefits of common grace and the removal of any excuse for being lost. God loved them and Christ died for them; they are lost because they refused to accept the salvation that is sincerely offered to them in Christ.

Summary. Both views try to preserve something of theological importance. Defenders of limited atonement stress human inability to come to God since the fall, God's initiative in election, and the certainty of salvation. If salvation depended on our work, all would be lost. The defenders of general redemption guard the fairness of God. Salvation is no less certain if Christ died for all. It is the decision to reject it that brings about condemnation, and faith that puts one in a saving relationship with Christ who died that we might live. E. A. Litton attempts to mediate the two views in this fashion: "The most extreme Calvinist may grant that there is room for all if they will come in; the most extreme Arminian must grant that redemption, in its full Scriptural meaning, is not the privilege of all men" (*Introduction to Dogmatic Theology*, p. 236).

W. A. ELWELL

See also AMYRALDIANISM; ARMINIANISM; ATONEMENT; ATONEMENT, THEORIES OF THE; PROPITIATION.

Atonement, Limited. See ATONEMENT, EXTENT OF THE.

Atonement, Theories of the. Central to the Bible is the question, "How can sinful people ever be accepted by a holy God?" The Bible takes sin seriously as a barrier (Isa. 59:2) humanity was able to erect but is quite unable to demolish. Scripture insists that God has made the way whereby sinners may find pardon. Salvation is never seen as a human achievement. In the OT sacrifice had no merit in itself (see. Heb. 10:4), but was given as a reminder of sin's seriousness and God's forgiveness through blood (Lev. 17:11). In the NT the cross is central. Each writer shows from his own perspective that it is the death of Christ and not human achievement that brings salvation.

Theories of the atonement attempt to understand redemption under one of three heads: (1) The essence of the atonement is the effect of the cross on the believer. (2) Atonement is a victory of some sort. (3) Christ satisfied God's holiness and justice. Some prefer a twofold classification, differentiating subjective theories which emphasize the effect on the believer, from objective theories which stress what the atonement achieves outside the individual.

The Subjective View or Moral Influence Theory. While there are many variations, this theory emphasizes the effect of Christ's cross on the sinner. The view is generally attributed to Abelard, who emphasized the love of God, and is sometimes called the moral influence theory, or exemplarism. When we look at the cross we see the greatness of the divine love. This delivers us from fear and kindles in us an answering love. We respond to love with love and no longer live in selfishness and sin. Taken by itself this theory is inadequate, but not untrue. It is important to respond to the love of Christ seen on the cross and to feel the compelling force of his example.

The Victory Theory. People belong to Satan, but God offered his Son as a ransom, a bargain the evil one eagerly accepted. When, however, Satan got Christ down into hell he found that he could not hold him. On the third day Christ rose triumphant and left Satan without either his original prisoners or the ransom he had accepted in their stead. This view has been variously called the devil ransom theory, the classical theory, or the fishhook theory of the atonement. This metaphor delighted some of the fathers, but after Anselm (see below) it faded from view. It was not until quite recent times that Gustaf Aulén with his *Christus Victor* showed that behind the grotesque metaphors there is an important truth. In the end Christ's atoning work means victory, conquering the hosts of evil and sin.

The Satisfaction Theory. In the 11th century Anselm, archbishop of Canterbury, wrote *Cur Deus Homo?* ("Why did God Become Man?"). In it he subjected the patristic view of the victory theory to severe criticism. He saw sin as dishonoring the majesty of God. A sovereign may be ready in his private capacity to forgive an insult or an injury, but because he is a sovereign he cannot. The state has been dishonored in its head. Appropriate satisfaction must be offered. God is the sovereign Ruler of all, and it is not proper for God to remit any irregularity in his kingdom. Anselm argued that the insult sin has given to God is so great that only one who is God can provide satisfaction; but, it was committed by man and so a man should do so. Thus he concluded that one who is both God and man is needed.

Penal Substitution. The Protestant Reformers agreed with Anselm that sin is a very serious matter, but they saw it as a breaking of God's law rather than as an insult to God's honor. The moral law, they held, is not to be taken lightly (Rom. 6:23), and this is the problem. Sinners lay under a curse, and it seemed clear that the essence of Christ's saving work consisted in his taking the sinner's place (Gal. 3:13). The Reformers did not hesitate to speak of Christ as having borne the sinner's punishment or as having appeased the wrath of God.

Sacrifice. There is much about sacrifice in the OT and not a little in the NT. Some insist that this gives the key to understanding the atonement. It is certainly true that the Bible regards Christ's saving act as a sacrifice, and this must enter into any satisfying theory. But unless it is supplemented, it is an explanation that does not explain. How does sacrifice save? The answer is not obvious.

Governmental Theory. Hugo Grotius (d. 1645) argued that Christ did not bear human punishment but suffered as a penal example whereby the law was honored while sinners were pardoned. His view is called "governmental" because Grotius envisions God as a ruler or a head of government who passed a law that sin demands death. Because God did not want sinners to die, he relaxed that rule and accepted the death of Christ instead.

Summary. Each view, in its own way, recognizes that the atonement is vast and deep, but none could explain it fully. Even together they only represent a beginning comprehension of the vastness of salvation.

L. MORRIS

See also BLOOD, CHRIST'S; CROSS, CRUCIFIXION.

Attributes, Communication of. See COMMUNICATION OF ATTRIBUTES, COMMUNICATIO IDIOMATUM.

Attributes of God. See GOD, ATTRIBUTES OF.

Auburn Affirmation (1924)**.** A document issued by liberal Presbyterian ministers in opposition to what they believed was a fundamentalist assault on the church's unity and liberty. Meeting in Auburn, New York, 150 clergy published *An Affirmation* in Jan. 1924, which distinguished between the *facts* of religion and the *theories* (i.e., the theological formulations) devised to explain them. While holding earnestly to the five "great facts and doctrines," the signers argued that the General Assembly had erred in 1923 in forcing particular conservative theories on the whole church.

T. P. WEBER

See also FUNDAMENTALISM; LIBERALISM, THEOLOGICAL.

Auburn Declaration (1837)**.** A statement by New School Presbyterians seeking to prove their loyalty to the Calvinist standards of the church. In the early 19th century Presbyterians in the U.S. divided into Old and New School parties over revivalism, interdenominational cooperation, and conformity to the Westminster Confession. In the mid-1830s the PCUSA split into Old School and New School churches, amid much rancor. Forced from their denomination, in Aug. 1837, about 200 New School ministers and laypeople met in Auburn, New York, to protest the action of the Old School in the General Assembly and proclaim their faithfulness to Presbyterian standards.

T. P. WEBER

See also NEW HAVEN THEOLOGY; NEW SCHOOL THEOLOGY; OLD SCHOOL THEOLOGY; TAYLOR, NATHANIEL WILLIAM.

Augsburg Confession (1530)**.** The basic Lutheran confession of faith or statement of what is believed in loyalty to Christ and his Word. It was presented at the Diet of Augsburg in 1530. Philip Melanchthon was its author, but its teachings are clearly those of Martin Luther.

The Augsburg Confession was read publicly at the diet in German on the afternoon of June 25, 1530, and it was signed by seven princes and representatives of two independent cities. The confession was not intended to present the teachings of any governmental authority. It stated what was being taught in the churches in those parts of Germany. The first article begins: "The churches among us teach with great consensus . . . " (Lat. text). In addition to a preface and a brief conclusion the Augsburg Confession has

28 articles. The first 21 present the Lutheran teaching and reject contrary doctrines. The last seven reject abuses in Christian life. In 1531, responding to a Roman Catholic answer, *The Confutation*, Melanchthon published the *Apology of the Augsburg Confession*, which deals with the controverted issues at greater length.

J. M. DRICKAMER

See also CONFESSIONS OF FAITH; LUTHER, MARTIN; MELANCHTHON, PHILIP.

Augustine of Canterbury (d. 604–9 [?]). First archbishop of Canterbury. Augustine began as prior of Pope Gregory the Great's Monastery of St. Andrew in Rome. He lacked Gregory's intense desire for world missions but obediently accepted papal appointment to head a mission to England. After turning back once in fear of the "savage" English, Augustine landed in Thanet early in 597, where he was received by King Aethelbert of Kent, whose queen, Bertha, was a Christian. She and her chaplain, the Frankish bishop Liudhard, gave the missionary monks a living place and authority to preach in Canterbury. Aethelbert was soon converted, and his subjects were baptized by the thousands. Christ Church and the Monastery of Saints Peter and Paul (which now bears Augustine's name) was built, and in 604 bishops for London and Rochester were consecrated. Augustine failed to unite all of England's British and Celtic Christians under Rome. In 597 Gregory consecrated Augustine as bishop and in 601 gave him authority over all English bishops. The archbishop developed the first English rite and laid down financial procedures which became standard in the Roman Church.

Augustine of Hippo (354–430). North African theologian. Augustine was born in Tagaste, North Africa (Algeria), to Patricius, a pagan, and Monica, a Christian. He taught grammar and rhetoric in North Africa (373–82) and then in Rome (383), where he abandoned the Manichaeans and became a skeptic. He moved to Milan to teach (384), where he was later influenced by reading Neo-Platonic philosophy and by Ambrose's sermons. He was converted through Rom. 13:13–14, baptized by Ambrose (387), and reunited with his mother, who died shortly thereafter.

Augustine was ordained a priest in Hippo, North Africa (391), where he established a monastery and later became bishop (395). The rest of his life can best be seen by the controversies he engaged in and the writings he produced. Augustine died Aug. 28, 430, as the Vandals laid siege to Rome.

Major Writings. Augustine's works fall roughly into three periods.

First Period (386–96). He wrote philosophical dialogues, anti-Manichaean works, and such theological and exegetical works as *On Faith and Symbol* (393).

Second Period (396–411). His later anti-Manichaean writings and such ecclesiastical writings as *On Baptism* (400) and *On the Unity of the Church* (405) were written, plus *Confessions* (398–99) and *On the Trinity* (400–416).

Third Period (411–30). The works in the final period of Augustine's writings were largely anti-Pelagian. They include *On Grace and Free Will* (426), *On Rebuke and Grace* (426), *On Predestination of the Saints* (428–29), and *On the Gift of Perseverance* (428–29). The last writings in this period are theological and exegetical, including perhaps his greatest work, *The City of God* (413–26).

Translations of Augustine's works can be found in numerous sources, including *Ancient Christian Writers; Catholic University of America Patristic Studies; The Works of Aurelius Augustinus; The Fathers of the Church; Library of Christian Classics;* and *A Select Library of Nicene and Post-Nicene Fathers.*

Augustine is the father of all succeeding expressions of orthodox Western theology, both Catholic and Protestant.

N. L. GEISLER

See also JANSENISM; PELAGIUS, PELAGIANISM.

Aulén, Gustaf Emanuel Hildebrand (1879–1978). Swedish theologian and scholar. Professor of theology at the University of Lund (1913–33) and bishop in Strängnas (1933–52), he returned to teaching at Lund and also continued his leading role in the ecumenical movement, playing an important part in the first assembly of the World Council of Churches (1948). Aulén's *Faith of the Christian Church* was first published in 1923. The English translation of the 5th Swedish ed. is still a model of ecumenical Lutheran theology. He is best remembered for his classic analysis of theories of the atonement in *Christus Victor*, written while still a professor at the University of Lund (1930).

S. M. SMITH

Authority in the Bible. See BIBLE, AUTHORITY OF.

Authority in the Church. See CHURCH, AUTHORITY IN.

Authority of the Bible. See BIBLE, AUTHORITY OF.

Auxiliary Bishop. See BISHOP; CHURCH OFFICERS.

Awakenings, The Great. See GREAT AWAKENINGS, THE.

Awe. (usually Heb. *yir'â*; Gk. *phobos*) A profound reverence and respect for God. This acute reverence is characterized by solemn wonder mingled with dread in view of the great and terrible presence of the Supreme Being. Awe is the most characteristic meaning of the term "fear" in the Bible and is based upon one's recognition and awareness of the holiness and supreme majesty of God (Gen. 20:11; Ps. 34:11; Acts 9:31; Rom. 3:18). Foundational to this sense of holy fear is a person's perception of God's unmerited and gratuitous love toward him (2 Cor. 7:1).

P. G. CHAPPELL

See also FEAR; NUMINOUS, THE.

Azusa Street Revival. The event beginning modern Pentecostalism at an abandoned Methodist church at 312 Azusa Street in the industrial section of Los Angeles in 1906. William J. Seymour, black Holiness preacher, founded the Apostolic Faith Gospel Mission on Azusa Street, where a new emphasis on the work of the Holy Spirit rapidly became a local sensation and eventually a worldwide phenomenon. The revival which began on Azusa Street in 1906 rapidly attracted attention from secular media. More important, it soon attracted thousands of visitors from around the world, who often went back to their homelands proclaiming the need for a special post-conversion baptism of the Holy Spirit. Meetings at Azusa Street, which went on daily for three years, were marked by spontaneous prayer and preaching, a nearly unprecedented cooperation between blacks and whites, and the active participation of women.

M. A. NOLL

See also PENTECOSTALISM.

Bb

Baal-zebub. (Sem. *bă'al zĕbûb*, "Lord of flies") *Bă'al* (lord) was the Canaanite god of fertility and fire, one of the chief deities of the area (2 Kings 1:6). *Zĕbûb* means fly or poisonous insect. In Mark 3:22 (Matt. 12:24; cf. 9:34; Luke 11:15) the Pharisees denigrate Jesus and attempt to explain his power over demons as itself of demonic origin by attributing it to Beelzebub. Here Beelzebub (and its archaic form Be-Elzebub) clearly means Satan.

J. J. Scott, Jr.

See also Satan.

Babylon. Ancient capital of Mesopotamia in what is now Iraq. Scripture uses the city in historic, prophetic, and symbolic (or typical) senses. Historically, the term referred to the great city on the Euphrates River, to the kingdom, or to its surrounding plain of Babylonia. The empire was used by God to judge Judah. The rise of Nebuchadnezzar in Babylon began the time of the Gentiles (Jer. 27:1–11; Dan. 2:37–38). The destruction of Babylon is foretold in Isa. 13:17–22; Jer. 25:12–14. The city fell to the Medes in 539 B.C. Three primary passages (Isa. 13; 14; 47; Jer. 50; 51; Rev. 16:17–19:5) predict Babylon's ultimate destiny. The exact meaning of "Babylon" in Revelation has long been disputed. Suggestions include the Roman Empire, Roman Catholic Church, and apostate Christendom.

W. M. Smith

See also Eschatology; Second Coming of Christ.

Backsliding. A temporary lapse in belief. Such passages as Jer. 5:6; 8:5; Hos. 11:7; 14:4 use four Hebrew words which can be translated "backsliding," "apostasy," "turning away," or "faithlessness." In the OT it primarily concerns Israel's forsaking of its covenant relation with Yahweh, analogous to breaking a marriage vow (Jer. 3:6–22). Examples of backsliding or apostasy in the OT include Saul (1 Sam. 15:11–28), Solomon (1 Kings 11:4–40), Rehoboam (2 Chron. 12:1–2), and Asa (2 Chron. 16:7–9). There are numerous NT examples of believers who draw away from fellowship with the Lord—e.g., the disciples (Matt. 26:56), Peter (Matt. 26:69–75), Demas (2 Tim. 4:10), Corinthian Christians (2 Cor. 12:20–21), and churches in Asia (Rev. 2:4, 14–15, 20).

Causes of spiritual backsliding include forgetfulness (Ezek. 23:35), unbelief (Heb. 3:12), bitterness (Heb. 12:15), preoccupation with the world (2 Tim. 4:10), love of money (1 Tim. 6:10), and seductive philosophies (Col. 2:8). Backsliding displeases the Lord (Heb. 10:38), grieves the Holy Spirit (Eph. 4:30), and incurs divine punishment (Lev. 26:18–39). It can be prevented by abiding in Christ (John 15:4–7), spiritual alertness (Eph. 6:18), constant prayer (1 Thess. 5:17), and maintaining a good conscience (1 Tim. 1:19).

B. A. Demarest

See also Assurance; Perseverance.

Baillie, John (1886–1960)**.** Scottish theologian and divinity professor (1934) and principal (1950) at New College, Edinburgh. One of the Church of Scotland's greatest scholars of this century, Baillie was said in theological outlook to have combined the old liberalism and Barthianism with a strong mystical tendency. He warmly supported the ecumenical movement and became president of the World Council of Churches. He is best remembered for *A Diary of Private Prayer* (1936) and *Invitation to Pilgrimage* (1942).

J. D. DOUGLAS

Banquet, Messianic. See MARRIAGE FEAST OF THE LAMB.

Baptism. (from Gk. *baptisma*) The sacrament of washing in water from the earliest days (Acts 2:41) has been the rite of Christian initiation. Its origins variously have been traced to OT purifications, Jewish sects, and pagan washings, but baptism as practiced by Christians definitely begins with John the Baptist. Christ, by precedent (Matt. 3:13) and precept (Matt. 28:19), authorizes its observance.

In essence baptism consists in washing or going in or under the baptismal water in the name of Christ (Acts 19:5) or the Trinity (Matt. 28:19). The disagreement is among those who practice "covenant baptism" of children of believers, those who baptize children as a saving ordinance, and those who insist upon a personal confession as a prerequisite.

NT discussions of baptism refer to three OT types: the flood (1 Pet. 3:19–20), the Red Sea (1 Cor. 10:1–2), and circumcision (Col. 2:11–12). These all refer in different ways to the divine covenant, to its provisional fulfillment in a divine act of judgment and grace, and to the coming and definitive fulfillment in the baptism of the cross.

Scripture also offers different but interrelated associations: (1) *Washing* (Titus 3:5). The cleansing water is linked with the blood of Christ and to the purifying action of the Spirit (see 1 John 5:6, 8). (2) *Initiation, adoption,* or *regeneration* (John 3:5). (3) *Death and emergence to new life* (Rom. 6:3–4). In all three themes the witness of the act is to the work of God in the substitutionary death and resurrection of Christ. This identification with sinners in judgment and renewal is what Jesus accepts when he comes to the baptism of John and fulfils when he takes his place between two thieves on the cross (Luke 12:50). Here we have the real baptism of the NT, which makes possible the baptism of our identification with Christ and underlies and is attested by the outward sign.

G. W. BROMILEY

See also BAPTISM, BELIEVERS'; BAPTISM, INFANT; BAPTISM, MODES OF; BAPTISMAL REGENERATION; BAPTISM FOR THE DEAD.

Baptism, Believers'. Where the gospel is first preached or Christian profession has lapsed, baptism is always administered on confession of penitence and faith. In this sense, baptism of adults on profession of faith has been the norm in all the church. Yet many see believers' baptism as the only true form.

Those who practice believers-only baptism differ primarily with the view that the sacrament has actual saving power and with the Calvinist doctrine that Christians stand in covenantal relation to God, with their children. Several arguments are used to support this position:

(1) Jesus' commission to baptize (Matt. 28:19) set baptism in the context of making disciples and said nothing about infants.

(2) The meaning of baptism in Rom. 6:1–11 is that in repentance and faith the believer is identified with Jesus Christ in his death, burial, and resurrection. To infants, who cannot hear the Word and properly respond, to speak of baptism into the death and resurrection of Christ seems misleading.

(3) Christ's blessing of the children shows us that the gospel is for little ones, but it says nothing whatever about

administering baptism (Mark 10:13–16). Luke 1:41 suggests that God may work in infants, but it gives no warrant to suppose that baptism may be given before this work finds expression in individual repentance and faith. The children of Christians are reckoned in some sense "holy" by God (1 Cor. 7:14), but there is no baptismal identification with Jesus Christ in death and resurrection.

(4) Reference to household baptisms (e.g., Acts 10:47–48; 16:30–34) does not say that the infants were present when the Word was preached or that any infants were baptized.

(5) Theologically, the insistence upon believers' baptism in all cases seems better calculated to avoid error. Only when there is personal confession before baptism can it be seen that repentance and faith are necessary to salvation and that these do not come magically but through hearing the Word of God.

The stress of believers' baptism is that it marks a step from darkness and death to light and life. The recipient's decision is thus confirmed and identification made with the regenerate, true church. The believer is encouraged to walk in new life.

G. W. Bromiley

See also Baptism; Baptism, Infant; Baptismal Regeneration.

Baptism, Infant. In Protestant theology, the baptism practiced by Calvinists which signifies that the children of believers are holy under the covenantal relation between God and his people.

In a missionary situation the first subjects of baptism are always converts, but as early as Irenaeus and Origen with a reference back to the apostles, the children of professing believers have been baptized. While some theologies have practiced theories of baptismal regeneration, orthodox Christians also find warrant for infant baptism.

(1) In the OT God deals with families rather than individuals. Noah's family is received with him into the ark (cf. 1 Pet. 3:20–21). Abraham's children are expressly brought under the covenant and marked with the covenantal sign and seal of circumcision (Gen. 17; cf. Col. 2:11–12). All Israel passes through the Red Sea, a foreshadowing of baptism, according to 1 Cor. 10:1–2.

(2) Jesus himself becomes an infant, and receives and blesses small children (Matt. 19:13–15). He says the things of God are revealed to babes rather than the wise and prudent (Luke 10:21).

(3) Peter directly identifies the Christian relationship with the Abrahamic covenant (Acts 2:38–39). If children had been excluded from that covenant it would have been noted. Yet in fact the household baptisms seem to include children as a matter of course.

(4) Baptism is not primarily a sign of repentance and faith but a covenant sign (like circumcision, only expanded beyond the males), and therefore a sign of the work of God which precedes conversion. It also is a witness of the parents' and the church's faith in the substitutionary work of Christ and the regenerative work of the Holy Spirit, which is done for the elect before they believe.

Infant or paedobaptism does not remove the necessity that the child will, when mature, make a personal confession of faith. It also sets strict responsibilities on home, church, and Christian school toward those sealed.

G. W. Bromiley

See also Baptism; Baptism, Believers'.

Baptism, Modes of. There are, generally speaking, two opinions regarding the proper manner of administering baptism: that only immersion is lawful and that the mode is a matter of indifference.

The immersionist position is founded on three arguments. (1) The word *bap-*

tizein means "to immerse" and therefore the command to baptize is itself a command to immerse. (2) Baptism signifies union with Christ in his burial and resurrection (Rom. 6:4; Col. 2:12); only sinking under and coming up out of the water adequately express the symbolism of the sacrament. (3) In the early church immersion was the primary mode.

The second position essentially negates these arguments. It denies the immersionist insistence that baptism is rightly administered only by immersion, contending that in the NT baptism, in its external form, is simply a washing, a cleansing, which can as well be effected by pouring (affusion) or sprinkling (aspersion) as by immersion.

R. S. RAYBURN

See also BAPTISM.

Baptismal Regeneration. Twice in the NT a connection is made between water, or washing in water, and regeneration (John 3:5; Titus 3:5). The phrase is open to misunderstanding but may be appropriate with the understanding that the new life of the Christian is in Christ born, crucified, and risen for us. Incorporation into Christ is the work of the Holy Spirit. The true baptism behind the sacramental rite is this saving action of Christ and the Holy Spirit. The rite itself, in conjunction with the word, attests this work and is a means used by the Holy Spirit to its outworking in the believer. Baptism is not regeneration, however, nor is regeneration baptism, except in this deeper sense and context.

G. W. BROMILEY

See also BAPTISM.

Baptism for the Dead. Most identified now with the rite among members of the Church of Jesus Christ of Latter-Day Saints, a vicarious baptism which assumes both the necessity of baptism for salvation and the opportunity for salvation after death. It arises out of Paul's question in 1 Cor. 15:29: "If there is no resurrection, what will those do who are baptized for the dead?" Various interpretations have been suggested. Some take it that the apostle refers to a practice of vicarious baptism as later reported among the Marcionites and Novatianists. On this view, he is not approving it, but sarcastically using it for the sake of argument. Others construe it as reference to baptism of the dying or the administration of the sacrament over graves of the saints. Most commentators try to avoid any connection with actual practice. Baptism is to fill up the ranks left vacant by the dead, or under the inspiration of their witness, or with a view to death and resurrection in Christ, or more specifically in token that we are dead but may seek our new and true life in the resurrected Christ. Whatever the exact signification, the wider meaning is undoubtedly that baptism is a witness to the resurrection. Baptism loses its meaning if death is not followed by resurrection.

G. W. BROMILEY

Baptism of [in/with] the Spirit. Among the greatest blessings conferred by the Christian gospel is the personal indwelling and enduement of the divine Spirit. Scripture identifies the Holy Spirit as active in creation and in history, and occasionally coming upon people with supernatural enabling power. The Spirit was promised to be a particular endowment of the Messiah (Isa. 11:2; 61:1–3), and other prophets extended a similar promise to all God's people (Joel 2:28–29; cf. Ezek. 36:26–27).

The Spirit descended in a graphic way at Jesus' baptism (Matt. 3:16; Mark 1:10; Luke 3:22; John 1:32; cf. Acts 10:38), linking water baptism and the reception of the Spirit in Christian experience. John contrasted water and the more significant Spirit baptism (Matt. 3:11). His thought was repeated by Jesus (Acts 1:5), Peter (Acts 11:16), John (1:26, 33) and

Paul (Acts 19:4–6; cf. 1 Cor. 12:13). Here reception of the Holy Spirit is no longer the alternative to a water baptism of repentance, but its fulfillment. Baptism by water was known as a rite of initiation into the people of God, so the initial experience of the Spirit's indwelling and enduement came to be called a "baptism in" or "with" the Holy Spirit.

In Greek, the preposition is here ambiguous: *en* may be local, meaning "within" water or Spirit; or instrumental, meaning "by means of" water or Spirit.

In Modern Experience. A slightly different phrase, "the baptism of the Spirit," has replaced the scriptural phrases in Pentecostal and charismatic circles. This new expression places less emphasis upon the indwelling of the Spirit, with the illumination of mind (John 14:26; 16:8–15), the refinement of character (the fruit of the Spirit, Gal. 5:22–23; love, 1 Cor. 12:27–13:13), and the gifts of peace, power, and joy that the Spirit bestows. While not denying these, Pentecostal believers specifically associate Spirit baptism with enabling supernatural powers. These include gifts, abilities, and emotional resources, manifest in spiritual healing, speaking in unknown tongues, prophesying, leadership, exuberant emotion, and other forms of equipment for service.

Opinion is divided also on how and when the initial reception of the Spirit may be expected. Historically it has been taught that indwelling comes with conversion. Some insist that, in the NT pattern of initiation, reception of the Spirit accompanies baptism in water.

Others insist that the baptism of the Spirit is an experience subsequent to conversion and entirely independent of water baptism, possibly replacing it. It is a second blessing, an "infilling" of the Spirit, supplementing conversion as the young Christian advances to maturity.

R. E. O. White

See also Charismatic Movement; Holy Spirit; Pentecostalism; Spiritual Gifts.

Baptist Tradition, The. The convictions of Baptists are based primarily on the spiritual nature of the church, and the practice of believers' baptism arises only as a corollary. The themes of Baptist theology include:

Membership of the Church. The church is composed of those who have been born again by the Holy Spirit and who have been brought to personal and saving faith in the Lord Jesus Christ. A living and direct acquaintance with Christ is, therefore, basic to church membership.

Nature of the Church. Members of the church are joined by God into a fellowship of life and service under the lordship of Christ. The church is perceived most clearly in its local manifestation.

Government of the Church. Christ is the only head of the church. The local church is autonomous, a principle of government sometimes described as the "congregational order of the churches." Government of the church through the mind of the local congregation is not to be equated with the humanistic concept of democracy, but through the voice of the Holy Spirit in the hearts of the members in each local assembly. Whereas in a strictly democratic order of church government there would be a government of the church *by* the church, the Baptist position makes recognition of Christ's rule in the church *through* the church.

Ordinances of the Church. Believers' baptism and the Lord's Supper are normally regarded as the only two, though it would be more proper to include the ordinance of preaching.

Ministry of the Church. The ministry is as broad as the fellowship of the church, yet for the purposes of leadership the term "ministry" has been reserved for those who have the responsibility of oversight and instruction. Pastors and deacons are chosen and appointed by the local church, though their appointment is frequently made in the wider context of the fellowship of Baptist churches. A Baptist minister becomes so by virtue of an inward call of God which, in turn, receives confirmation in the outward call of a church. Public acknowledgment of this call of God is given in a service of ordination.

Ecumenicity of the Church. Baptist organizations are largely voluntary, cooperative ventures with no legal binding force over their members. This allows for freedom and concerted action to exist at the same time. Hence Baptist denominations are simply collections of individual Baptist churches. Cooperation with other groups is based on the merits of each case.

E. F. KEVAN

See also BAPTISM, BELIEVERS'; LANDMARKISM.

Barclay, William (1907–1978). Scottish biblical scholar. From 1947 he lectured in NT at Glasgow University, where he was promoted to professor in 1964. His *Daily Study Bible* (NT) won acclaim worldwide and was published in many languages. Barclay always urged his students to have some nonreligious interests and to keep abreast of current topics. Doctrinally, he was a universalist who rejected the substitutionary view of the atonement. Reticent about the authority of Scripture, he rejected also the virgin birth and regarded miracles as merely symbolic of what Jesus can still do in the world.

J. D. DOUGLAS

Barmen, Declaration of (1934). A declaration of the Confessing Church in Germany against National Socialism, formulated at the Synod of Barmen in 1934. At the Braune Synod in Saxony (1933), the *Deutsche Christen* (German Christians) had attempted to provide Hitler's National Socialist movement with a theological justification. The Barmen Confession, which contains six main paragraphs, resisted the subordination of the Christian gospel and church to any political or social movement, stressing the absolute necessity for submission to, and dependence upon, Jesus Christ as the living Word of God. It also emphasizes the Scriptures, each paragraph developing a scriptural theme. The church, it proclaims, cannot recognize any source of final divine revelation other than Jesus Christ. He alone must be its Lord. It was in large part written by the theologian Karl Barth.

J. D. SPICELAND

See also BARTH, KARL; NEO-ORTHODOXY.

Barnhouse, Donald Grey (1895–1960). American Bible teacher. In 1927 Barnhouse went to Tenth Presbyterian Church in downtown Philadelphia and from this church, where he continued the rest of his life, built his national and international empire. Through most of his career he spoke over radio networks of up to 455 stations, using the Bible expository method of teaching. The popularity of these broadcasts and later telecasts led to many invitations to conduct Bible conferences, and the increasing demand of these conferences led him, after 1940, to be absent from his pulpit six months a year. He founded and edited two magazines, *Revelation* and *Eternity*. Barnhouse's theology was an eclectic yet independent mix of dispensationalism, Calvinism, and fundamentalism.

W. C. RINGENBERG

Barth, Karl (1886–1968). German theologian. In 1919 he published the first edition of *Der Romerbrief* which is recognized as the beginning of neo-orthodoxy, or dialectical theology. By 1930 Barth was teaching in Bonn, where he allied with the Confessing Church against

Hitler's National Socialism. In 1934 the opposition produced the Barmen Declaration, basically written by Barth. The next year he was expelled from Germany and went to Basel. He wrote more than 500 books, articles, and papers, the most famous being the 13-volume *Church Dogmatics*.

There are at least three key ideas in his early thought critical for his later writings. (1) God is absolute, transcendent, and sovereign, while humanity is sin-dominated. (2) A dialectical theological method poses truth as a series of paradoxes. For example, the infinite became the finite; eternity entered time; God became human. Such paradoxes create tension, in which one finds both a crisis and truth. (3) The individual discovers in the tension of the dialectic a crisis of existence, judgment, separation, belief/unbelief, and acceptance/rejection of the ultimate truth of God concerning humanity as revealed in the Word.

Barth's view of the absolute sovereignty of God coupled with his view of the fall meant the will, emotions, and reason were ruined and incapable of allowing one to discover God. Humans respond to God's self-disclosure but have no role in the self-disclosure. The Christocentric Word is the only source of the knowledge of God. Christ is God's Word incarnate; the Word is in Scripture but Scripture is not necessarily the Word; and the Word is that of proclamation. The Word is God's communication to humans, his self-disclosure in Jesus Christ, the one and only revelation. Humans are totally dependent upon it. The content of the Word is judgment and grace. The Word descends; it does not ascend from creation. As the Word, Jesus Christ is the *God*-man, and as the God-*man* takes humanity into partnership with God. This was part of the original covenant broken by the fall but restored in the Word made flesh. The Bible, seen as inspired, unique, to be taken with great seriousness, is not to be confused with the Word. It is a human document and becomes the Word only as the Holy Spirit testifies to it; thus use of higher and lower criticism is permissible and necessary.

R. V. SCHNUCKER

See also BARMEN, DECLARATION OF; BRUNNER, HEINRICH EMIL; NEO-ORTHODOXY.

Basel, First Confession of (1534)**.** A 12-article statement of the Protestant faith composed by Oswald Myconius in 1532 and approved and published by the city council of Basel, Switzerland, in 1534 as the official creed of the city. It remained so until 1872. The nearby German city of Mühlhausen approved it in 1536 so it is also known as the Confession of Mühlhausen. The confession is a simple, warm expression of the Protestant faith expressed in contrast to both Roman Catholicism and Anabaptism. The articles deal with God, man, providence, Christ, the church, the Lord's Supper, church discipline, the state, faith and works, the final judgment, God's commands, and infant baptism.

F. H. KLOOSTER

See also CONFESSIONS OF FAITH.

Basil the Great (ca. 330–379)**.** Theologian, Cappadocian monk, and bishop of Caesarea from 370. He was born into a wealthy Christian family in Pontus. Basil is known for contributions in three fields. (1) He introduced the idea of a communal monasticism based on love, holiness, and obedience, which replaced individual asceticism. The Rule of St. Basil remains the basic structure of Eastern monasticism. (2) He established the principle of social concern for both monastic communities and for bishops. (3) He defended orthodox doctrine, particularly the doctrine of the Trinity. In *De Spiritu Sancto* he defended the deity of the Holy Spirit. In this defense of the faith he gave exact meanings to the terms for the Trinity, fixing the formula of one substance (*ousia*) and three persons (*hypostaseis*) and thus preparing the way for the Council of Constantinople (381). His books, homilies (especially on the Psalms), commentary on Isa. 1–6, and letters revealed the heart of a learned man, but also a loving Christian.

P. H. DAVIDS

See also CAPPADOCIAN FATHERS.

Bavinck, Herman (1854–1921). Theologian of the neo-Calvinist revival initiated a century ago in the Dutch Reformed Church and still represented in North America by the Christian Reformed Church. Trained at the University of Leiden and the Theological Seminary at Kampen, Bavinck served a church at Franeker (1881–82) before becoming professor of systematic theology at Kampen (1882–1902) and then at the Free University of Amsterdam (1902–20). His major work was *Gereformeerde Dogmatiek (Reformed Dogmatics)* first published between 1895 and 1901, of which only the second of the four volumes has been translated into English as *The Doctrine of God.*

J. VAN ENGEN

Baxter, Richard (1615–1691). English Puritan pastor. His ministry at Kidderminster (1641–60) was marked by a dramatic transformation of the whole life of the community. He supported Parliament in its battle against the king, serving briefly as a military chaplain. He sided with the Nonconformist party and was eventually ejected from the Church of England along with 2000 other clergy in 1662. Throughout his ministry Baxter sought to increase cooperation and tolerance among Episcopalians, Presbyterians, and Independents. Three of his writings have been reprinted frequently. *The Saint's Everlasting Rest* (1650) expounds "the blessed state of the Saints in their enjoyment of God in glory." It continues to be one of the classics of Christian devotional literature. *The Reformed Pastor* (1656) describes the oversight pastors are to exercise over themselves and their flock. *A Call to the Unconverted* (1657) shows Baxter's evangelistic concern. It consists of an earnest and reasoned appeal to the unconverted to turn to God and accept his mercy.

O. G. OLIVER, JR.

Beatification. A legal process in the Roman Catholic Church whereby a departed "servant of God" is adjudged worth of public veneration. Beatified ("blessed") persons are recognized only in particular churches, dioceses, or regions, and are distinguished iconographically by a simple circular diadem. In the ancient and medieval church such cults sprang up locally and often spontaneously. Since the 17th century the Roman See, specifically the Congregation of Rites, has controlled the process, which is the first and most significant step toward full canonization.

J. VAN ENGEN

See also CANONIZATION.

Beatific Vision. (Lat. *visio Dei*) In traditional Roman Catholic theology the direct, face-to-face knowledge of the triune God. This occurs for all the redeemed in heaven and is the final fruition of the Christian life revealing God as he is in himself. Catholics traditionally have believed in temporary beatific visions by some saints on earth. In recent years Roman Catholic and Protestant scholars alike have interpreted the biblical language (e.g., Deut. 34:10; 1 Cor. 13:12) much more broadly, as living joyfully and everlastingly in the immediate presence of God.

J. VAN ENGEN

Beelzebub, Beelzebul. See BAAL-ZEBUB.

Being. The quality of existing, the most general property common to everything that is. In early Greek philosophy being was usually contrasted with becoming or change. Being was associated with perfection, and perfection could not change, since any change would be for the worse.

The nature of being was a central issue in the development of natural theology in the late Middle Ages. God is pure actuality, and as such is immutable. He is a *necessary being* in that he needs nothing outside of his own being for his existence. All other beings are *contingent beings*; they depend on something or someone outside themselves for their existence. This distinction becomes fundamental to the cosmological argument. This argument was developed in two directions. As a causal argument, it has been argued that a contingent being needs a first, necessary cause or an infinite regress results. As a contingency argument, it is maintained that a contingent being can only be explained with reference to a necessary being who needs no explanation.

In modern theology the concept of being has taken a quite different course. For example, P. Tillich insisted that God is "being itself" or "the ground of being." As such, Tillich's God is "the God beyond the God of theism." Process theology attempts to synthesize God's being with his becoming. God is thought to be di- or bipolar. The static pole gives the subjective aim and potentiality to objects in reality. The dynamic pole is in constant becoming. Through it, said A. N. Whitehead, God "prehends" or adds to himself something from all actual entities and so is in the "process" of growing in beingness by taking into himself value left by the perishing of objects. Whitehead sees in God the supreme actual entity.

P. D. FEINBERG

Belgic Confession (1561). Also known as the Walloon Confession, an apology by Guido de Bres for the faith of persecuted Reformed Christians in the Lowlands who formed the "churches under the cross." Translated from French into Dutch in 1562, it gained synodical approval at Antwerp in 1566, at Wesel in 1568, at Emden in 1571, and definitively at Dordrecht in 1618. Together with the Heidelberg Catechism and the Canons of Dort, it provides the confessional foundation for Dutch Reformed churches, and remains binding for members of the Christian Reformed Church in North America. Like Calvin's *Institutes*, the text breaks down roughly into three parts: the triune God and knowledge of him from Scripture (arts. 1–9), Christ's work of creation and redemption (arts. 10–23), and the Spirit's work of sanctification in and through the Christian church (arts. 24–37).

J. VAN ENGEN

See also CONFESSIONS OF FAITH.

Belief, Believe. See FAITH.

Believer. See CHRISTIANS, NAMES OF.

Benediction. A pronouncement of divine blessing by God or his representative. The Aaronic benediction was given to Aaron and his sons as part of their ministry, through which they put God's name upon the people (Num. 6:22–27). The NT parallel is the apostolic benediction (2 Cor. 13:14), which emphasizes the Trinity. In modern times the Roman Catholic Church has introduced the Benediction of the Blessed Sacrament. The priest, having taken the host and placed it in the monstrance, incenses the sacrament. After appropriate singing and prayer, the priest makes the sign of the cross with the monstrance (still containing the host) over the people. This benediction is given in silence.

E. F. HARRISON

Berdyaev, Nikolai Aleksandrovich (1874–1948). Russian personalist philosopher-theologian. Born in Kiev, he was exiled by the czarist government as a Marxist in 1898. After the Bolshevik Revolution he was professor of philosophy at Moscow University until deported to Europe by the Soviets in 1922 because of the Christian premises of his socialism. Berdyaev lived as an unwilling exile in France until his death, where he propagated his thought as director of the Religious-Philosophical Academy and editor of the journal *The Way* and the YMCA Press. A freethinker in early years, Berdyaev embraced the Russian Orthodox Church on the eve of World War I.

In more than 20 books and dozens of articles Berdyaev presented no orderly system; this is in line with his confession that his vocation was "to proclaim not a doctrine but a view." His radical stress is on freedom and creativity. He spoke of freedom as uncreated, independent of God, and eternal. It is the nothingness (*Ungrund*) out of which God produced his good creation; it also is the occasion for evil and thus pain and suffering. Creativity constitutes the likeness between God and humanity. Christ destroyed the radical disjunction between man and God and joined the two in the task of transforming "this evil and stricken world."

P. D. STEEVES

See also ORTHODOX TRADITION, THE.

Berkeley, George (1685–1753). Irish philosopher who presented classic arguments in favor of idealist metaphysics. He produced most of his philosophical works early in life: *An Essay Towards a New Theory of Vision* (1709) and *A Treatise Concerning the Principles of Human Knowledge* (1710). He also attempted to establish a college in Bermuda and served as an Anglican bishop in Cloyne, Ireland, beginning in 1734. Berkeley's basic doctrine is that for something to exist, it must be perceived. If something is an odor it must be smelled; if it is a color it must be seen. Moreover, sense information is the only basis for knowledge. We have no way of claiming that there is some material object that we sense because we cannot get beyond our senses to find out.

Berkeley said things things do not cease to exist when no human is present to perceive them because God continues to perceive them. God also coordinates our ordinary perceptions to give them a lawlike regularity. This regularity simplifies the world for God, who does not have to maintain both a material world and our ability to perceive the world. He merely maintains our perceptions.

P. H. DEVRIES

Berkhof, Louis (1873–1957). Theologian of the Christian Reformed Church. In 1906 Berkhof began a 38-year teaching career at Calvin Theological Seminary, Grand Rapids, Mich., serving also as the first president of the seminary from 1931 until his retirement in 1944. He taught both OT and NT. In 1926 Berkhof became professor of dogmatics or systematic theology and is best known as a systematic theologian. In 1932 his class lectures were published in two volumes as *Reformed Dogmatics*. A revised and expanded edition appeared in 1938 as a single volume entitled *Systematic Theology*. Berkhof followed in the line of John Calvin and embraced the development of Reformed theology by the Dutch theologians Abraham Kuyper and Herman Bavinck.

F. H. KLOOSTER

See also BAVINCK, HERMAN; KUYPER, ABRAHAM; REFORMED TRADITION, THE.

Bernard of Clairvaux (1090–1153). Medieval mystic and monastic reformer. He was so well loved that he was canonized in 1174 and made Doctor of the Church in 1830, but Bernard was preeminently a monk. He founded the monastery at Clairvaux but was active in a broad spectrum of endeavor. He helped to heal the papal schism of 1130; was the "hammer of heretics" including Henry of Lausanne, Arnold of Brescia, and Peter Abelard; wrote voluminous mystical, theological, and devotional works, and carried on an extensive personal correspondence with emperors, popes, wayward monks, and theologians. As a man of action, contemplation, mystical experience, doctrinal orthodoxy, and administrative skill, Bernard was the theological personification of the "medieval synthesis" for Dante. Among hymns attributed to him are "Jesus, the Very Thought of Thee," "O Sacred Head Sore Wounded," and "Jesus Thou Joy of Loving Hearts."

C. F. ALLISON

See also MYSTICISM; SPIRITUALITY.

Beza, Theodore (1519–1605). The undisputed leader in Geneva as John Calvin's successor. Beza served as professor of Greek at the Academy of Lausanne from 1549 to 1558, when he was called to the post of both rector and professor at the newly formed Academy of Geneva. His chief contributions to the Swiss Reformation were securing Calvin's gains in Geneva and solidifying the Presbyterian system.

Beza's doctrine of the church may be found in his three-volume collection *Tractationes Theologicae*, especially in his *Ad Tractationem de Ministrorum Evangelii . . . Responsio*, where he takes Anglican prelacy to task. Other key scholarly works are his 1582 edition of the Greek NT and his three-volume *Histoire ecclésiastique des églises réformées . . . de France*. Concern for the welfare of the church prompted volumes of sermons, commentary, a French translation of many psalms for the Huguenot Psalter, a joint translation with Calvin of the French NT, and an influential confession of faith.

J. H. HALL

Bible. (from Gk. *biblios*, *biblion*, "roll" or "book") The terms originally referred to a roll of papyrus or byblis, a reed-like plant whose inner bark was dried and fashioned into a writing material. The word as referring to the record of divine revelation is ecclesiastical in origin, but its roots go back into the OT. In Dan. 9:2 *ta biblia* (Gk. text) refers to the prophetic writings. In the prologue to Sirach it refers generally to the OT Scriptures. This usage passed into the Christian church (2 Clem. 14:2) and about the turn of the 5th century was extended to include the entire body of canonical writings of the Old and New Testaments. The expression *ta biblia* passed into the vocabulary of the Western Church, and its neuter plural came to be regarded as a feminine singular. In this form the term passed into the languages of modern Europe. This change reflected the growing conception of the Bible as one utterance of God rather than a multitude of voices speaking for him.

R. H. MOUNCE

See also BIBLE, AUTHORITY OF; BIBLE, CANON OF; BIBLE, INERRANCY AND INFALLIBILITY OF; BIBLE, INSPIRATION OF; WORD, WORD OF GOD, WORD OF THE LORD.

Bible, Authority of. Authority may be bestowed or inherent. When Jesus was asked by what authority he taught and acted (Matt. 21:23–24) the implication was that his authority was external. In the declaration that Jesus taught with authority (Matt. 7:29) and "with authority and power" expelled unclean spirits (Luke 4:36) the authority was regarded as an ontological authority, inherent in his being.

In the Bible both aspects of authority are combined, because the Bible points beyond itself to God and so has a conferred authority, yet also has authority in itself as the embodiment of God's self-disclosure (2 Tim. 3:16–17). In God all authority is finally located. But what God is, is made known only in his self-disclosure. Revelation is, therefore, the key to God's authority, and revelation and authority may be regarded as two sides of the same reality. In revelation God declares his authority.

OT prophets found certainty in God's revelation; in their message they knew they declared God's authoritative will, proclaiming what God required of his people. For Christian faith that authority is expressed in Christ. This progressive unveiling of God, which culminated in Christ, has been given perpetual form in the biblical writings (Heb. 1:1–2). Scripture consequently participates in God's authority and is decisively vindicated as authoritative by its relation to Christ.

By his attitude to and use of the OT Christ truly validated its divinity. NT writers accepted it and quoted it (2 Pet. 1:20–21), and they, as the inspired interpreters of Christ's person and work, put their own writings on an equal footing with the OT Scriptures as divinely authoritative (2 Cor. 12:19; 1 Thess. 2:13; 2 Thess. 2:15; 3:14).

H. D. McDonald

See also Bible, Inerrancy and Infallibility of; Bible, Inspiration of.

Bible, Canon of. Biblical books acknowledged by the early church as the rule of faith and practice. Both Jews and Christians have canons of sacred writings. The Jewish canon consists of 39 books; the Christian consists of 66 for Protestants and 80 for Roman Catholics (whose canon includes the Apocrypha).

OT Canon. The faith of Israel existed independently of a book for hundreds of years between the time of Moses, who was the first known Hebrew to commit sacred history to writing (Exod. 24:4, 7).

The modern English Protestant Bible follows the order of the Latin Vulgate and the content of the Hebrew Bible. It is important to remember that the OT was more than 1000 years in writing, the oldest parts being written by Moses and the latest after the Babylonian exile. Therefore, the Jews lived their faith without a closed canon of Scriptures, such a canon not being considered essential to the practice of religion. The books finally were collected, evidently, as an act of providence historically prompted by the emergence of apocryphal and pseudepigraphical literature in the intertestamental period. By the time of Jesus the OT, called Tanaach by modern Judaism, consisted of the law, prophets, and writings (cf. Luke 24:44).

NT Canon. The earliest list of NT books containing only 27 appeared in A.D. 367 in a letter of Athanasius, bishop of Alexandria. The order was: Gospels, Acts, General Epistles, Pauline Epistles, Revelation. The NT canon was not formed by conciliar decision. The earliest ecumenical council, Nicea in 325, did not discuss the canon. The first undisputed decision of a council on the canon seems to be Carthage in 397, which decreed that nothing should be read in the church as Scripture except the canonical writings. Then the 27 books of the NT are listed as canonical. The council could list only those books that were generally regarded by the consensus of use as canon. The formation of the NT canon must, therefore, be regarded as a process rather than an event, and a historical rather than a biblical matter.

J. R. McRay

See also Apocrypha.

Bible, Inerrancy and Infallibility of. The two words most often used to express the nature of scriptural authority, "inerrant" and "infallible," are approximately synonymous, but they are used differently. In Roman Catholic theology "inerrant" is applied to the Bible, "infallible" to the church, particularly in the teaching function of pope and *magisterium*. Since Protestants reject the infallibility of pope and church, the word is used of the Scriptures. "Infallible" has been championed by those who hold to what B. B. Warfield called limited inspiration but what today is called limited inerrancy. They limit the Bible's inerrancy to matters of faith and practice, particularly soteriological issues.

Definition of Inerrancy. Inerrancy is the view that the Bible, in its original autographs and correctly interpreted, is entirely true in all it affirms, whether in doctrine or ethics or to the social, physical, or life sciences. Probably the most important aspect of this definition is its definition of inerrancy in terms of truth and falsity rather than in terms of error.

Arguments for Inerrancy. Arguments for inerrancy are biblical and historical.

The Biblical Argument. (1) The Bible teaches its own inspiration by God (2 Tim. 3:16). (2) The Bible teaches its own authority (Matt. 5:17–20; John 10:34–35). While both passages emphasize the Bible's authority, this authority can only be justified by or grounded in inerrancy. Something that contains errors cannot be absolutely authoritative. (3) Inerrancy follows from what the Bible says about God's character. The Scriptures teach that God cannot lie (Num. 23:19; 1 Sam. 15:29; Titus 1:2; Heb. 6:18). If, then, the Bible is from God, it must be inerrant and infallible.

The Historical Argument. Biblical inerrancy has been the view of the church throughout its history. As part of the corpus of orthodox doctrine, the position has until relatively recently seldom been questioned and so was assumed and seldom defended through church history. Nevertheless, in each period of the church's history clear affirmations of the doctrine can be found.

P. D. Feinberg

See also Bible, Authority of; Bible, Inspiration of.

Bible, Inspiration of. The theological idea of inspiration, like its correlative revelation, presupposes a personal mind and will acting to communicate. Thus inspiration is a supernatural influence of the Holy Spirit upon writers, so that what they write under that influence is trustworthy and authoritative.

Biblical Teaching. The conception of "inspiration" is firmly embedded in the Bible. The word *theopneustos* (lit. "God-breathed-out," 2 Tim. 3:16) affirms God as author of Scripture. The biblical sense is far stronger than the modern definition, which lends to the term "inspiration" merely a dynamic or functional significance. The apostle Paul does not hesitate to speak of the sacred Hebrew writings as the words of God (Rom. 3:2). Biblical prophecy is declared to be more sure than even the testimony of eyewitnesses of Christ's glory (2 Pet. 1:17–21).

Jesus' View of Scripture. In John 10:34–35, Jesus singles out an obscure passage in Ps. 82:6 to reinforce the point that "the Scripture cannot be broken." The reference is doubly significant because it discredits the modern bias against identifying Scripture as the word of God, on the ground that this assertedly dishonors the supreme revelation of God in the incarnate Christ. Jesus of Nazareth, while speaking of himself as indeed the one "the Father consecrated and sent into the world" (John 10:36, RSV), nonetheless asserts that the whole of Scripture is of irrefragable authority. Objective students of Jesus' view of Scripture must conclude with Reinhold Seeberg: "Jesus himself describes and employs the Old Testament as an infallible authority" (*Text-book of the History of Doctrines*, 1.82).

OT View. The OT prophets are marked off by their unswerving assurance that they were spokesmen for the living God. The constantly repeated formula "thus says the Lord" leaves no doubt that they considered themselves chosen agents of divine self-communication. The classic example of this assurance is Moses, who is the founder of prophetic religion. He mediates the law and mandates the priestly and sacrificial elements of revealed religion in the firm belief that he promulgates the will of God. In speaking for God he is "like God" to Israel and to Pharaoh, with Aaron as his prophet (Exod. 4:14–16; 7:1–2).

The Old and the New. NT observations about Scripture speak primarily of the OT canon. But the apostles extended the claim to divine inspiration. Jesus spoke of a further ministry of teaching by the Spirit (John 14:26; 16:13). The apostles assert confidently that they speak by the Spirit (1 Pet. 1:12). They ascribe both the form and matter of their teaching to the Spirit (1 Cor. 2:13). They assume a divine authority (1 Thess. 4:2, 14; 2 Thess. 3:6, 12); acceptance of their written commands is a test of spiritual obedience (1 Cor. 14:37). They even refer to each other's writings with the same regard as for the OT (1 Tim. 5:18, for example, quotes from Luke 10:7 as Scripture, and 2 Pet. 3:16 places the Pauline epistles with "the other scriptures").

Historical View. The view that the Bible as a whole and in every part is the word of God written was assumed until the rise of modern critical theories a century ago. The historic evangelical view affirms that, alongside the special divine revelation in saving acts, God's disclosure has taken the form of truths and words. This revelation is communicated in a restricted canon of trustworthy writings, deeding fallen man an authentic exposition of God and his relations with man. Scripture itself is viewed as an integral part of God's redemptive activity, a special form of revelation, a unique mode of divine disclosure. In fact, it becomes a decisive factor in God's redemptive activity, interpreting and unifying the whole series of redemptive deeds, and exhibiting their divine meaning and significance.

Critical Theories. Higher criticism has shown itself far more efficient in creating a naive faith in the existence of manuscripts for which there is no overt evidence (e.g., J, E, P, D, Q, 1st-century nonsupernaturalistic "gospels" and 2d-century supernaturalistic redactions) than in sustaining the Christian community's confidence in the only manuscripts the church has received as a sacred trust. Perhaps the most significant gain in our generation is the new disposition to approach Scripture in terms of primitive witness instead of remote reconstruction. While it can shed no additional light on the mode of the Spirit's operation on the chosen writers, biblical criticism may provide a commentary on the nature and extent of that inspiration, and on the range of the trustworthiness of Scripture.

C. F. H. Henry

See also Bible, Inerrancy and Infallibility of; Plenary Inspiration; Verbal Inspiration.

Biblical Theology Movement. A movement from the 1940s to the early 1960s of scholars in North America and Europe who shared liberal, critical assumptions but who attempted to relate theology to biblical studies. This way of doing theology was fundamentally concerned with doing justice to the theological dimension of the Bible, which previous generations of liberal scholars had neglected. The movement reflected an interest of European neo-orthodox theologians from the 1920s. Neo-orthodoxy and the biblical theology movement shared the concern to understand the Bible as a fully human book to be investigated with the fully immanent historical-critical method and yet to see the Bible as a vehicle or witness of the divine Word. The modern naturalistic-evolutionary worldview as developed by natural science, modern philosophy, and critical history were meshed with the view of a God who gives meaning and coherence to this world in his personal acts in history.

Characteristics. Typical features common to the movement included:

Reaction to Liberalism. It was a reaction against the study of the Bible in previous liberal theology where the source criticism of the historical-critical method atomized the biblical text into separate sources, frequently consisting of small isolated entities or fragments of documents.

Alliance with Neo-orthodoxy. The neo-orthodox reaction against Protestant liberalism's reduction of the Christian faith to universal human and religious truths and moral values became a powerful impetus for the movement. It was fostered by Karl Barth and Emil Brunner in Europe and H. Richard Niebuhr and Reinhold Niebuhr in America.

Greek versus Hebrew Thought. It constantly opposed the influence of modern philosophy and its constructs as modes to understand biblical thought. It also tended strongly to reject an understanding of the Bible on the basis of Greek thought and its categories. Although the NT was written in Greek, the Hebrew mentality was common to both Testaments. The idea of the Hebrew mentality led to significant studies of words in both Testaments.

The Bible within Its Culture. It emphasized the distinctiveness of the Bible in its environment. The consensus emerged that when there is borrowing or even syncretism, or when there are similarities, the differences between the literature of Israel and that of the surrounding nations are far more remarkable than its points of contacts. The movement claimed that the most significant things in Israel were not the things it held in common with its neighbors but the things where it differed from them.

Biblical Unity. It took seriously the unity of both Testaments. This was unity in diversity, a unity of divine revelation given in the context of history and through the medium of human personality.

Revelation in History. Its concept of divine revelation in history stressed divine self-disclosure without propositional revelation, using the neo-orthodox concept of encounter without propositional content. God's revelational encounter in history bridged the gap between past and present in that Israel's history became the church's history and subsequently our modern history. In the church's liturgy the believer and the community of faith participate in the same redemptive event by means of recital.

Decline and Evaluation. There is no easy way to evaluate the biblical theology movement because it is part of a trend in modern liberal theology and in part the neo-orthodox movement. It was a major attempt for a full generation to correct liberal theology from within. It did not succeed because it ultimately remained a captive of the basic thought patterns, presuppositions, and methods of liberal theology itself. It did add impetus to more recent attempts to show the basic method of the historical-critical method is bankrupt (W. Wink) or announce its end (G. Maier) and seek for new methods of study of the Bible and its theology, whether a theological-historical method (G. F. Hasel) or structuralism (D. Patte).

G. F. HASEL

See also NEO-ORTHODOXY.

Binding and Loosing. Terms used by Christ for the exercise of disciplinary authority bestowed with the keys of the kingdom, first to Peter in Matt. 16:19, then to all the disciples in 18:18. What is implied is the authority to exclude from, as well as to reinstate in, the community of believers. Related to the Matthean sense of binding and loosing is John 20:23. Exclusion from the community is always due to some offense and, therefore, presupposes the retaining of sins, while readmission includes forgiveness. This understanding of binding and loosing is found among the church fathers—Tertullian, Cyprian, and Origen. In the Reformation, Luther likewise interpreted this power as (1) that of retaining and remitting sins, and (2) granted to all Christians to be exercised in preaching and private absolution. The Council of Trent recognized the former but declared that Matt. 18:18 applied only to bishops and priests.

H. C. WAETJEN

See also KEYS OF THE KINGDOM.

Bioethics. An interdisciplinary collaborative field that uses medicine, philosophy, law, and theology to resolve difficult ethical and moral questions raised in the context of modern health care. In one sense bioethics is very new. The questions debated, however, are timeless: What is the nature and value of human life? How are we to understand and respond to human suffering and imperfection? Where there are differences of opinion—for example, on whether to extend routine medical care to handicapped newborns—who decides? Technology and the general secularization of society have made bioethics a strategic area for thoughtful Christian involvement.

A surprisingly high number of bioethical issues draw intense public interest: abortion, euthanasia, genetic engineering, "test-tube babies," treatment of handicapped newborns, and population control. Other issues include the use of "surrogate mothers" who are artificially inseminated and give birth for another individual or couple, sperm banks (including one which carries only the sperm of "geniuses"), fetal experimentation, legal claims of "wrongful birth" (alleging failed contraception—the defense being, in part, that the mother could have aborted), amniocentesis, and cryogenics (the practice of freezing bodies in the hope that a future "cure" for death will enable them to be brought back to life and health).

The Christian begins by assuming that God the Creator loves his creation. This is what we mean when we contend for the "sanctity of life." The most fundamental conflicts in bioethics are a result of the modern replacement of the "sanctity-of-life" assumption of the Judeo-Christian ethic with a "quality-of-life ethic." Jews, Christians, and anyone wishing to preserve the accumulated moral consensus of Western civilization must reject this ethical position. Bioethical issues may not be all black and white, but neither are they all gray. The quality-of-life ethic, which is little more than warmed-over relativism or situation ethics, must be unequivocally rejected by Christians seeking to make a faithful and responsible contribution to bioethics.

C. HORN, III

See also ABORTION; ETHICAL SYSTEMS, CHRISTIAN; EUTHANASIA; SITUATION ETHICS; SOCIAL ETHICS.

Birth, New. See REGENERATION.

Bishop. An overseer (pastor, shepherd) of the church. In the NT period it appears that the title "bishop" described the function of the presbyter (elder). In Acts 20:17–28 and Titus 1:5–7 these two terms may be interchangeable. Qualifications and duties for the work are supplied in 1 Tim. 3:2 and Titus 1:7 and primarily rate to character and ability to teach.

A clear distinction between the offices of bishop and presbyter is seen in the letters of Ignatius, who was the sole bishop of Antioch. Written ca. 117 they testify to the emergence (at least in Antioch) of what is called the monarchical episcopate. Each church had a bishop, who was assisted by presbyters and deacons. Thus there was a threefold order of ordained ministry. The bishop was the chief celebrant in worship, the chief pastor of the flock, and the chief administrator of the people of God and their possessions. The episcopate as distinct from the presbyterate also developed a theology of apostolic succession. By ca. 150 it was widely held that bishops were the direct successors of the apostles and the chief guardians of church teaching. This particular theology was expanded in later centuries.

However we account for the origin of bishops as chief pastors, they were universal in the church from early times until the 16th century. As the church expanded and adopted the geographical divisions of the Roman Empire, bishops became chief pastors of all the churches within an area. Those bishops in important cities or with large dioceses were called by such titles as pope, patriarch, metropolitan, and archbishop. Suffragan, auxiliary, assistant, and coadjutor bishops developed as assisting offices under the bishop.

During the Protestant Reformation some new churches abandoned the office of bishop, arguing that in the NT there is no distinction between a bishop and a presbyter. This approach has been dominant within Protestantism. However, the title "bishop" is used in certain Protestant denominations where there is no claim that the bishops are in the apostolic succession. Here the word means either pastor or chief pastor.

P. Toon

See also Church Officers; Elder.

Black Theology. A theology of liberation committed to the amelioration of the condition of black people and consciously locked in battle with white racism, which is considered to be a religion called "white religion," "whitianity," or "Christianity" (in contrast to true Christianity). From the earliest period of blacks in America, deliberate distortions of Christianity were perpetrated to preserve the master-slave relationship.

Rationale. Beginning with the generally accepted principle that the God of Israel and the church acts in history to effect salvation, black theologians contend that to view salvation as having an exclusively "spiritual" connotation truncates its meaning. They proclaim salvation's economic, political, and social dimensions particularly seeing these dimensions evident in the exodus. The conclusion is drawn that God's election of his people and his liberation of them from bondage are inextricably related; God is not neutral!

A NT case is made for Jesus' intentional identification with those in social bondage, based both upon the accusations of his enemies (Matt. 11:19) and upon his own teaching. Luke 4:18–19 functions as the primary text for black theology (and for most theologies of liberation), for here it is perceived that Jesus' work is essentially one of liberation.

Both Testaments are viewed as recognizing God's liberating activity as integral to understanding his dealing with his people. Thus, it may be assumed that Christ's radical identification would be with blackness in the 20th century. Just as identification with Israel clearly spoke of God's siding with the weak and the oppressed in the ancient world, so his identification with blackness would be the most effective and easily discerned symbol of that choice in contemporary American society. Obedience to God requires of Christians a similar identification with the poor and oppressed, that is, with blackness.

Origin. Black theology's origin and founder are debated. James Cone is most influential in the late 20th century due to the number of his publications and their importance as formulations. However, not everyone would grant him the status of originator. William Jones, for example, who observes that one's identification of a founder has unmistakable implications for one's definition of black theology, sees the 1964 publication of *Black Religion* as the beginning, with author Joseph Washington as founder.

Appraisal. Black theology is regarded as one of a very few authentically indigenous North American theological movements. In the future it will undergo revision through its internal dialogue and continuing research into its African roots. Confrontation with adversaries will also have an impact on it, as will dialogue with feminist theology, Latin American theology of liberation, African theology, and similar groups. These movements received inspiration and strategy from black theology and now influence it from their respective positions.

The primary focus of black theology remains, however, a biblically mandated message of liberation. While acknowledging that blacks as well as whites are sinners, in the contemporary social setting, it is particularly the white who must be called to a repentance that will relinquish racial intolerance and identify with blackness.

V. Cruz

See also Liberation Theology.

Blasphemy. Slander or insult, particularly that which detracts from the glory and honor of God; the opposite of praising or blessing God. A Hebrew could blaspheme God directly by insulting "the Name" or indirectly by flaunting God's law (Num. 15:30), but in either case blasphemy, as idolatry (the ultimate blasphemy, Isa. 65:7; 66:3; Ezek. 20:27), was punishable by death by stoning (Lev. 24:10–23; 1 Kings 21:9–10). In the NT blasphemy occurs in its wider meaning as well as its specifically religious sense, for people are also slandered (Rom. 3:8; 1 Cor. 10:30; Eph. 4:31; Titus 3:2). The most common form of blasphemy in the NT, however, is blasphemy of God. God may be directly insulted (Rev. 13:6; 16:9), his Word mocked (Titus 2:5), or his revelation and its bearer derided (Moses in Acts 6:11; Paul in 1 Cor. 4:12–13). When Jesus forgave sins (Mark 2:7) he was accused of blasphemy on the grounds that he, being a man, made himself God (John 10:33–36). The same charge was the basis of his condemnation at his trial (Mark 14:61–64), for the Sanhedrin judged his claim to be Christ a mockery of God. The real blasphemy to the NT writers was the mockery of Jesus (Matt. 27:39; Mark 15:29; Luke 23:39), which continues in the persecutors of the church who mock the baptismal vow "Jesus is Lord" (James 2:7) or try to force Christians to curse it (cf. Acts 26:11).

P. H. Davids

Blasphemy Against the Holy Spirit. The willful and conscious rejection of God's activity and its attribution to the devil. The sin is mentioned in Matt. 12:31; Mark 3:28–29; Luke 12:10. The Pharisees saw a notable miracle and heard Jesus' own teaching, but they chose darkness (John 3:19) and called good evil (Isa. 5:20) by attributing the miracle to the devil. It is the enlightened, willful, high-handed nature of such sin that makes it unforgivable (not forgiven at death, as the Jews thought, but punished through eternity).

P. H. Davids

See also Sin unto Death; Eternal Sin.

Blood, Christ's. A modern theological question has arisen over whether "the blood of Christ" refers to the death of Christ or the life of Christ released from the body. Some hold that the second is the view of the OT, which is taken over into the NT.

Lev. 17:11 is cited: "For the life of the flesh is in the blood; and I have given it for you upon the altar to make atonement for your souls; for it is the blood that makes atonement, by reason of the life." (RSV) It is claimed that this and similar passages show that Hebrews thought life resided in the blood so that the life of a sacrificed animal was being released from the body so that it might be presented to God. Further, it is contended that when we read in the NT of the blood of Christ, we should understand that Christ's life was set free for a higher purpose, that of bringing salvation.

Against this view, the OT employs the word *dām,* "blood," 362 times, of which 203 refer to death and violence, 103 to the blood of sacrifices, seven connect life and blood, with which we should link 17 which refer to eating meat with blood (as Lev. 17:14). The remaining 32 examples do not bear on our problem. When a Hebrew heard the word "blood," the most likely association would be with death. The passages that link blood with life are exceptional. The universal OT view is that sin is so serious that it is punished by death: "The soul that sins shall die" (Ezek. 18:20). The shedding of blood in the sacrifices most naturally attaches to this penalty. Indeed, most accounts of sacrifices mention the death of the victim, saying nothing about its life (e.g., Lev. 1:5).

The largest group of the 98 occurrences of the word in the NT is that for death by violence (25 times). The blood of animal sacrifices (12 times) will also point to death if our conclusions from the OT are valid. Some of the references to the blood of Christ must signify his death. Thus Col. 1:20 refers to "the blood of his cross." Little blood was shed in crucifixion, so that must mean his death. Paul speaks of being "justified by his blood" and "saved by him from the wrath of God," statements parallel to "reconciled to God by the death of his Son" and "saved by his life" (Rom. 5:9–10). There are references to death in the immediate context and this is surely the force of "blood" also. Other passages where "blood" plainly means the death of Christ include John 6:53–56; Acts 5:28; Eph. 2:13; 1 John 5:6; Rev. 1:5; 19:13. References to Christ's blood as a sacrifice (e.g., Rom. 3:25) also point to death, as Heb. 9:14–22 shows.

There is no reasonable doubt that blood points, not to life set free, but to life given up in death. References to blood are a vivid way of saying that we owe our salvation to the death of Christ.

L. MORRIS

See also ATONEMENT; BLOOD, SACRIFICIAL ASPECTS OF.

Blood, Avenger of. See AVENGER OF BLOOD.

Blood, Sacrificial Aspects of. Lev. 17:11 is the OT's central statement about the significance of blood in the sacrificial system, and what it asserts remains true throughout the regulations for individual sacrifices. (1) The blood of sacrifice is a divine provision: "I have given it to you." This counters any theory of sacrifice which sees in it a human gift designed to attract or excite divine favor. (2) The use of blood in sacrifice is a price-paying act, to make atonement. The verb (*kippūr*) takes its meaning from the related noun (*kōper*), "redemption price" (cf. Exod. 21:30; 30:12; Job 33:24). It means to pay whatever price cancels the offense. If the blood pays the price, then its significance is life forfeited or laid down in payment for sin. (3) The shedding of the blood of sacrifice is a substitutionary act. The last clause of Lev. 17:11 should be translated either the blood "makes atonement at the cost of the life" (i.e., the animal's life), or "makes atonement in the place of the life" (i.e., the sinner's life). For the use of the Hebrew preposition *bĕ* of price paying, see 1 Kings 2:23; Prov. 7:23; of exact equivalence or substitution, see Deut. 19:21; 2 Sam. 14:7. Heb. 9:11–18 confirms in the NT the symbolism of blood as death and applies Lev. 17:11 to the sacrifice of the Lord Jesus Christ.

J. A. MOTYER

See also ATONEMENT; BLOOD, CHRIST'S.

Bodily Presence. See LORD'S SUPPER, VIEWS OF.

Bodily Resurrection. See RESURRECTION OF THE DEAD.

Bodily Resurrection of Christ. See RESURRECTION OF CHRIST.

Body, Biblical View of the. In the OT there is no single term corresponding to the NT *sōma*, the physical body, which is distinct from the soul and/or spirit. The Hebrew terms *bāsār* ("flesh") in Lev. 14:9; 15:2; *nibĕlâ* ("corpse, carcass") in 1 Kings 13:22, 24; and *gĕwīyâ* ("body, corpse") in 1 Sam. 31:10, 12 are among those most frequently translated *sōma* in the LXX and "body" in some of the English translations.

Man is more than just a body; he is physical and immaterial, body and soul and/or spirit. The scriptural dualism is not the same as Greek dualism, where the soul is the prisoner of the body, but rather the body is the instrument through which the immaterial expresses itself. The material and immaterial parts of a person are on a par. Both need redemption and both live eternally. Man is not just body or just soul/spirit but the combination of them.

The distinction between "body" and "flesh" (*sarx*) is important. (1) The body, which can be transformed, is the dwelling place of the Holy Spirit (Rom. 8:11; 1 Cor. 6:19), whereas in the flesh nothing good dwells (Rom. 7:18). (2) The body is for the Lord and is to glorify him (1 Cor. 6:13, 20), whereas the flesh cannot please God (Rom. 8:8). (3) The body is to be an instrument of righteousness (Rom. 6:12–13), whereas the flesh only serves as a beachhead for sin (Gal. 5:13) and is at enmity with God (Rom. 8:7; Gal. 5:16–17). (4) The body awaits redemption and resurrection (Rom. 8:23; 1 Cor. 15:35–49), whereas the flesh cannot be resurrected (1 Cor. 15:50) but is destined for death. (5) The body will face the judgment seat of Christ (2 Cor. 5:10). J. A. T. Robinson stated it succinctly: "While *sarx* stands for man, in the solidarity of the creation, in his distance from God, *sōma* stands for man, in the solidarity of creation, as made for God" (*The Body*, p. 31).

In 1 Cor. 15:35–49 the resurrected body is contrasted with the preresurrected body, which is described as a "soulish body" or a material body governed by the soul. The resurrected body is described as a "spiritual body" (1 Cor. 15:44). It is immortal and designed for a heavenly existence (1 Cor. 15:50–53).

Body of Christ. Jesus' body could be seen, touched, and heard (1 John 1:1–3; John 1:14). In his resurrected body Christ breathed (John 20:22), ate (Luke 24:42–43), and was recognizable (John 20:27–29), but it also was different because he was not always immediately recognizable (Luke 24:16–31; John 20:14; 21:4); he could walk through doors or walls (John 20:19, 26; Luke 24:36) and rapidly traverse great distances (Matt. 28:7–10). The NT specifically speaks of Christ's physical body in connection with his death (Matt. 27:58–59; Mark 15:43–46; Luke 23:52; 24:3, 23; John 19:38, 40; 20:12; Col. 1:22; Heb. 10:10). At the Last Supper, after he broke the bread, Jesus said, "This is my body" (Matt. 26:26; Mark 14:22; Luke 22:19; 1 Cor. 11:24). With the Passover meal being the setting of that Last Supper, the breaking of the bread symbolized the sacrifice of Jesus' body as a substitutionary death for all mankind.

Sōma also refers to the church as the body of Christ (Rom. 12:5; 1 Cor. 10:16–17; 12:12–27; Eph. 1:23; 2:16; 4:4, 12, 16; 5:23, 30; Col. 1:18, 24; 2:19; 3:15). As described in this metaphor, believers are united by the Holy Spirit to Christ in one body.

H. W. HOEHNER

See also MAN, DOCTRINE OF; FLESH.

Body, Soul, and Spirit. See MAN, DOCTRINE OF; TRICHOTOMY.

Body and Soul. See MAN, DOCTRINE OF; DICHOTOMY.

Body of Christ. See CHURCH, THE.

Boehme, Jakob (1575–1624). German Lutheran mystic and theosophist. His mystical insights led him to write numerous books, including *Aurora, On the Three Principles of Divine Being, Six Theosophical Points, Six Mystical Points,* and *The Way to Christ*.

His thought centers on myth and symbol, rather than concepts, which makes his contemplations difficult to understand. He stresses the unity of good and evil, theorizing an elaborate sevenfold system to explain the divine activity as reflected in nature. These seven qualities divide into two triads, a higher and a lower, between which there is creative energy called the flash. The lower group consists of individualization, diffusion, and the struggle between the two. The higher triad consists of love, expression, and the kingdom of God. People must choose between the lower world of sensation, or die to self and live on the higher plane. The true Christian life is an imitation of the sacrifice and triumph of Christ. Boehme's influence has been very great in Germany, where the pietist, romantic, and idealist movements each owed something to his teaching. In England the Cambridge Platonists, John Milton, Isaac Newton, William Blake, William Law, and the Behmenists followed his ideas.

R. G. CLOUSE

See also MYSTICISM.

Bonaventure (1221–1274). Franciscan theologian and head of the Order; Doctor of the Church (Seraphicus); canonized in 1482. Bonaventure's main written works were a commentary on the *Book of Sentences* of Peter Lombard, *Journey of the Mind to God*, and *Life of St. Francis of Assisi*. One central theme of his theology is the ascent of the human soul toward God. In this pilgrimage there are three stages. (1) Reason can deduce God's existence from creation. (2) Since man is made in God's image, the soul turns inward toward memory, intellect, and will. (3) The individual finally goes beyond reason to mystical contemplation of the divine presence. Mysticism is the pure gift of the Holy Spirit. Although Bonaventure allowed Aristotle a limited place, his viewpoint is fundamentally Augustinian in its basic religious orientation and philosophical principles.

N. V. HOPE

Bonhoeffer, Dietrich (1906–1945). German Lutheran pastor and theologian. Born in Breslau, Germany, Bonhoeffer was executed in a Nazi concentration camp and did not attain international recognition until the posthumous publication and translation of *Letters and Papers from Prison* (1951). This volume of his collected correspondence, smuggled out of his prison cell in Berlin-Tegel, was never intended for publication, yet became the most popular of his many books. His two years as a Nazi prisoner (1943–45), although initially a time of intense spiritual testing, led Bonhoeffer to develop a routine of disciplined contemplation and creativity, resulting in writings on contemporary and future challenges facing the church. Assessing Christianity's role in "a world come of age," Bonhoeffer's prison letters described a Christian as "a man for others" and the church as existing "for others." "Who is Christ for us today?" was his piercing query. One of Bonhoeffer's most divergently understood concepts concerns a nonreligious interpretation of Christianity, "Religionless Christianity." His primary point was that Christ did not call his people to a "religion" but to life. The cost of this discipleship in the world, as opposed to "cheap grace," was explored in *The Cost of Discipleship* (published 1948). Bonhoeffer has contributed to conservative and liberal Christian thought, secularist writings, and Marxism. He also has been a source of inspiration for Christians under oppressive political regimes and for Christians in the Third World, especially in Latin America. Liberation theology owes much to his life and thought.

R. ZERNER

See also LIBERATION THEOLOGY

Book of Common Order. Liturgical handbooks used by the Church of Scotland and other Presbyterian churches. The first book to bear this title was published by authority of the General Assembly of the Church of Scotland in 1562 and contained texts for the administration of the sacraments. Two years later it was expanded to include metrical psalms and versions of other portions of Scripture. The *Book of Common Order* was never an absolute formulary like the *Book of Common Prayer* in England, but rather a standard and model of worship; the minister was given freedom for extempore prayer as well as flexibility of usage. This led to free types of services during the 18th and 19th centuries, but the 20th century saw the resurrection of the *Book of Common Order* as a guide.

D. H. WHEATON

Book of Common Prayer. A title given specifically to three guides in the Church of England and generally applied to books in other provinces of the Anglican Communion. In 1549 the English Parliament passed an Act of Uniformity requiring the clergy to use from the Feast of Pentecost that year "the Booke of the Common Prayer and Administracion of the Sacramentes and other Rites and Ceremonies of the Church after the Use of the Church of England." This revised and reformed handbook of worship was largely the work of the archbishop of Canterbury, Thomas Cranmer. In his preface, Cranmer explained that the book was to provide prayer in the common tongue. Previously worship of the Church of England had been almost entirely in Latin, and also it was to bring a common form of worship to every diocese, which also had been lacking.

In conducting worship the clergy had previously needed the missal (for the Mass), breviary (for daily offices), manual (for the occasional offices), and pontifical (for episcopal services). The new book contained all of these except the ordinal, which was published separately in 1550 and revised in 1552 and 1662. It included a calendar and lectionary and the litany, together with Coverdale's translation of the Psalter. Protestants felt the 1549 edition did not go far enough in its reforms so Cranmer produced a second prayer book in 1552 in which the Protestant position was more clearly adopted. These books are known as the First and Second Prayer Books of King Edward VI.

When Mary Tudor ascended the English throne in 1553, this second prayer book was proscribed as she reestablished the Roman Catholic teaching and practices; leading Protestants were martyred. In 1559 Elizabeth I restored the second book with minor alterations. During the next century with the accession of James I in 1603 and the restoration of Charles 2 in 1660 the ongoing struggle between extreme Puritans and Episcopalians smoldered continuously, and the Hampton Court (1604) and Savoy (1661) conferences were held in an attempt to resolve the matters at issue. In the end relatively few changes were made, and the 1662 Act of Uniformity introduced a third *Book of Common Prayer* which was basically that of 1552 in its theological emphasis. This continues to be the *first* Prayer Book of the Church of England.

D. H. WHEATON

Book of Concord. See CONCORD, BOOK OF.

Book of Life. Record kept in ancient cities of living citizens; after death their names were marked out of the book of the living. This idea appears in Exod. 32:32–33; Ps. 69:28; Isa. 4:3. From the idea of being recorded in God's book of the living (or the righteous) comes the sense of belonging to God's eternal kingdom or possessing eternal life (Dan. 12:1; Luke 10:20; Phil. 4:3; Heb. 12:23; Rev. 13:8; 17:8; 20:15; 21:27). For Christ to say that he will never blot out the overcomer's name from the book of life (Rev. 3:5) is the strongest affirmation that death can never separate us from Christ and his life (cf. Rom. 8:38–39).

A. F. JOHNSON

Booth, Catherine (1829–1890). "Mother of the Salvation Army." Born Catherine Mumford in Derbyshire, she married William Booth in 1855 and played a prominent part in founding what became the Salvation Army in 1878. She defended the right of women to preach and fought the exploitation of women and children (she was the mother of eight). Within the Army she consolidated the principle that women have absolute equality with men in privilege, position, and dignity, and she won the sympathy of the upper classes for the new movement.

J. D. DOUGLAS

See also BOOTH, WILLIAM.

Booth, William (1829–1912). Founder of the Salvation Army. Born in Nottingham, he grew up amid poverty, became a pawnbroker's assistant, was converted at 15, and became a Methodist pastor. Aided by Catherine, he began the Christian Mission as a rescue operation in London's East End. Renamed the Salvation Army 13 years later (1878), it waged war against poverty and sin. In 1890 he published *In Darkest England—and the Way Out*, which set the tone for the Army's increasing emphasis on its social program. His Army spread throughout the world, but Booth remained very much in control. He spent most of his last years traveling the world, preaching and promoting Army work.

J. D. DOUGLAS

See also BOOTH, CATHERINE.

Born Again. See REGENERATION.

Bottomless Pit. (Heb. *tĕhôm*; Gk. *abyssos*, "the deep") (1) A prison for Satan and certain demons (Luke 8:31; Rev. 10:1, 3; cf. 2 Pet. 2:4; Jude 6); (2) the realm of the dead which the living cannot enter (Rom. 10:7), the place from which the beast or Antichrist arises (Rev. 11:7; 17:8). That God imprisons and releases the demonic spirits signifies his ultimate power over the satanic realm. The concept provides an additional image to hell as the place of terror filled with demons. Hell (Gehenna) is the eschatological fiery destination of all the wicked (human and demon), while the abyss is the present abode of demonic spirits.

A. F. JOHNSON

See also DEEP, THE; HELL.

Bousset, Wilhelm (1865–1920). German NT scholar and leader (with W. Wrede, H. Gunkel, J. Weiss, and W. Heitmüller) of the history-of-religions approach to biblical study. He taught at Göttingen (1896–1916) and Geissen (1916–20). He attempted to show that primitive Christianity can only be understood against the background of late Judaism and hellenistic religious syncretism. A significant change took place in the early church as Gentile hero worshipers transferred their allegiance from other "lords" to Jesus the Lord (*Kyrios*). The disappointment of the early Palestinian church when the parousia of the Son of man failed to materialize hastened this decisive development in early Christianity.

W. W. GASQUE

Branch. (esp. Heb. *nēṣer, ṣemaḥ*, Gk. *klēma, klados*) The translation of more than 20 Hebrew and Greek words, usually referring to various trees, vines, or shrubs. *Nēṣer* is used figuratively, of a royal scion in Isa. 11:1. *Ṣemaḥ* is used of Messiah in Isa. 4:2; Jer. 23:5; 33:15; and Zech. 3:8; 6:12. Christ calls his followers to an intimate vital union with himself, typified as the union of the tender *klēma* branch with the vine. Some use a literal exegesis of John 15:2 to deny eternal security, but the point of the simile is to emphasize the necessity of abiding in him. In Rom. 11 Israel is likened to a *klados* olive branch cast off during this age while the Gentile church is grafted in, but to be grafted in again when the Redeemer will come out of Zion (Rom. 11:26).

R. L. HARRIS

See also MESSIAH.

Breaking of Bread. See LORD'S SUPPER.

Brethren of the Common Life. A religious society in the Netherlands between the 14th and early 17th centuries. Gerhard Groote, an unordained preacher, was the first leader of the new community, which consisted of clergy and laity. Members took no vows, joined no religious order, but sought to live in God's presence a life of total dedication and to prepare themselves for eternal life. This mystic strain was complemented by active philanthropy toward the poor and by the setting up of hostels for students. Brethren schools were among the best of the 15th century. The humanist scholar Erasmus was among the students there. Thomas à Kempis, another student and subsequently a member, wrote *Imitation of Christ*, which reflects the movement's spirit and ideals. Known sometimes as the *Devotio Moderna*, the movement was overtaken by the Reformation, and died out in the 17th century.

J. D. DOUGLAS

See also DEVOTIO MODERNA; THOMAS À KEMPIS; GROOTE, GERARD.

Bride of Christ. See CHURCH, THE.

Brother. See CHRISTIANS, NAMES OF.

Brown, William Adams (1865–1943). American Presbyterian theologian and social and ecumenical activist. He was perhaps the most influential and thoroughly representative liberal theologian of his time. Brown emphasized the life, personality, and certain teachings of the historical Jesus rather than traditional orthodox doctrines about Christ. He was confident that God works uniquely through Jesus to promote transformation in the lives of his followers, and through them to introduce gradually a better social order, the kingdom of God. Brown worked among slum dwellers and supported such causes as the labor movement. He saw denominations as impediments to the practical task of the church, so he promoted the emerging ecumenical movement. His *Christian Theology in Outline* (1906) was one of the most widely used texts of liberal theology.

D. G. TINDER

See also LIBERALISM, THEOLOGICAL.

Brunner, Heinrich Emil (1889–1966). Swiss Reformed theologian. With Karl Barth and Rudolf Bultmann, he was a developer of the theology of crisis, dialectical theology, neo-orthodoxy, and Barthian theology. Barth and Brunner each developed his thought independently. From 1924–55 he was professor of systematic and practical theology at the University of Zurich, frequently lectured in Europe, Britain, and America, and in 1953–55 served as visiting professor at the newly established International Christian University in Tokyo.

Brunner published at least 396 books and scholarly journal articles, of which 23 books were translated into English. *The Mediator* (1927), which was the first attempt to treat the doctrine of Christ in terms of the new dialectical theology, established his reputation. Brunner's thought was characterized by a high Christology, an emphasis on personal encounter in Jesus Christ as the centerpiece of faith, an ethical system that balanced individualism and community, and a view of the church as a fellowship of persons in Christ which had been constituted (wrongly) by men as an external organization. His doctrine of man stressed the paradoxical nature of man as both in the image of God and a sinner, an individual and a member of a community.

His greatest impact has been in the field of Christology and in his insistence that God can be known only through personal encounter. In Christology, Brunner attacked theological liberalism's humanistic and essentially unitarian picture of Jesus. He attempted a fresh restatement of what he regarded as the indispensable Christian belief that the appearance of Jesus Christ was unique and unrepeatable—that Jesus was not just a great teacher or a humanitarian martyr but the one and only incarnation of the Word of God. Brunner stressed the incarnation and the resurrection as cornerstones of Christian faith and accepted the definition of Chalcedon that Jesus Christ is at once true God and true man. His theology is presented in *Dogmatics* (3 vols.).

Orthodox Christians are indebted to Brunner for his criticism of theological liberalism's sentimental and degrading portrayal of Jesus, its optimistic view of humanity, and its idea of history as inevitably progress into the kingdom of God. Brunner restated for the 20th century many historic Christian doctrines: sin, the incarnation and resurrection of Christ, the centrality of Jesus in salvation, the need for a personal faith, and the church as a fellowship rather than an institution. He also reestablished the Scriptures as the norm for faith and practice in Christian churches. However, Brunner has been sharply criticized by more orthodox theologians on several counts, for example, his rejection of such doctrines as the virgin birth and hell.

R. D. LINDER

See also BARTH, KARL; NEO-ORTHODOXY.

Buber, Martin (1878–1965). Jewish religious thinker. Raised in central Europe during the early years of Zionism, Buber became involved with that movement. In 1938 he left Germany to become professor of sociology at the Hebrew University of Jerusalem. There he enjoyed a distinguished career as a proponent of what he took to be the true Hebrew humanism, expressed in the Hasidic teaching that "God is to be seen in everything, and reached by every pure deed." Particularly through his *I and Thou*, Buber's ideas on true life as relation became known. He claims that in one's life with nature, with other persons, and with spiritual existences, a person can become an "I" only when the object with which one has to do is seen as a "Thou" rather than as an "it." In and through such relational events there is a meeting with the absolute Other, the eternal Thou, God. This is not so much a mystical union, or the transcendent becoming immanent, as it is an existential encounter in faith. Buber's concept of the "I-Thou" relationship has been adopted by several Christian theologians, notably Friedrich Gogarten, Karl Heim, Karl Barth, Dietrich Bonhoeffer, and Rudolf Bultmann.

S. R. OBITTS

Bucer, Martin (1491–1551). Continental and English Reformer. Influenced by Luther initially and then by Zwingli, Bucer became a mediating Protestant theologian. His mediating position thrust

Bucer into several conciliatory efforts on the Continent and in England. With Wolfgang Capito he coauthored the Tetrapolitan Confession (1530), drawn up at the Diet of Augsburg to effect reconciliation between the Reformed and evangelical wings. Again in the Concord of Wittenberg (1536) he collaborated with Melanchthon to assist Saxon Lutheran theologians in achieving unity over the doctrine of the bodily/spiritual presence of Christ in the sacrament. In England he developed a doctrine of the church as a living extension of the incarnation, committed to transforming the entire political and social order with its stress on discipline, visibility, and transformation of personal and corporate entities. These views were published posthumously as *De regno Christi* (1557).

P. A. MICKEY

See also TETRAPOLITAN CONFESSION; WITTENBERG, CONCORD OF.

Buchman, Frank. See MORAL RE-ARMAMENT.

Bulgakov, Sergei Nikolaevich (1870–1944). Russian economist and theologian. Though a son of a Russian Orthodox priest, he abandoned the views of the church during his early life. Bulgakov's intellectual pilgrimage took him from Marxism to idealism to Christian mysticism. He came to believe that the world was animated by a world soul and that God had created the world out of nothing. During his later years his goal was to interpret the main teachings of the Christian church in the light of the doctrine of Holy Wisdom, whom he identified as a third being who mediated between the beings of God and the cosmos.

H. F. VOS

Bullinger, Johann Heinrich (1504–1575). Swiss Reformer. Bullinger succeeded Zwingli at Zurich and played a major role in the Protestant Reformation. His *Decades*, 50 long sermons dealing with the major tenets of Christian doctrine, were published during 1549–51 and soon translated into English, Dutch, and French. In England the *Decades* served as the officially appointed theological guide for clergy who had not obtained a master's degree. Bullinger and Calvin sought to avert potential schisms in the Protestant movement through their proposal of the Zurich Agreement (1549). They agreed that believers receive Christ spiritually and are united to him through the Lord's Supper. Later Bullinger authored the Second Helvetic Confession (1566), which united Calvinistic churches throughout Europe.

O. G. OLIVER, JR.

See also HELVETIC CONFESSIONS; ZURICH AGREEMENT.

Bultmann, Rudolf (1884–1976). German theologian. Professor in the University of Marburg, he was known for his historical and interpretive writings on the NT, but he was at heart a churchman, seeking by his scholarship to make the Christian message live for his contemporaries. In Bultmann's view the most pressing task facing theologians in the 20th century was to discover a conception of the NT which could be understood by laypeople, and then to work out the details of this interpretation. Bultmann believed that he had found such a conceptuality in the existentialist philosophy of Martin Heidegger, and spent most of his career interpreting the NT using historical-critical methods to cleanse the text of elements which resisted existentialism. NT ideas such as the resurrection of the body, blood atonement for sins, everlasting life, an ethical ideal of human nature, and a salvation history only mislead people about what salvation really is. These are primitive, "mythological" ideas which need to be reinterpreted in existentialist terms. In the 1940s he began to call this interpretive activity "demythologizing," and it is this process for which Bultmann is best known.

R. C. Roberts

See also Demythologization; Existentialism; New Hermeneutic, The.

Bunyan, John (1628–1688). English Puritan. Although he had a bare minimum of education, Bunyan probed the depths of the gospel of grace in the Bible. Active as a lay preacher in the Parliamentary army and during the Commonwealth, he continued to preach during the Restoration and was imprisoned 12 years for doing so. Offered freedom if he would no longer preach, he replied, "If I am freed today I will preach tomorrow." During his imprisonment he wrote *Pilgrim's Progress; Grace Abounding to the Chief of Sinners*, a spiritual autobiography; and *Defense of Justification by Faith*. Later he wrote *The Holy War*. He is appreciated for his literary genius by scholars who seldom appreciate his doctrine. The unforgettable imagery and blended thought and passion were grounded in Reformation teachings.

C. F. Allison

Burnt Offering. See Offerings and Sacrifices in Bible Times.

Bushnell, Horace (1802–1876). Known as "the father of American theological liberalism." Bushnell was a complex figure who incorporated into his thought many traditional Puritan elements that later theological conservatives would also preserve. His theology combined the Puritan sense of covenant, influences from Europe and England, a great confidence in the future of America, and an organic view of God's work in history. He was pastor of North Church, Hartford. Bushnell's major works spell out the main currents of his thought. *Christian Nurture* (1847) focused new attention on the religious training of young people. His most important theological work followed soon thereafter, a "Dissertation of Language" prefaced to *God in Christ* (1849). This essay contended that human language is inadequate to the realities of spiritual existence. *Nature and the Supernatural* (1858) suggested that all things, natural and supernatural, shared a common spiritual character. His *Vicarious Sacrifice* (1866) arose out of a deep sense of tragedy at the unfolding of the Civil War combined with a lifetime's reflection on the nature of Christ's work. His conclusion was that the death of Christ was intended primarily as an example for the human race to follow in self-giving sacrifice.

M. A. Noll

See also Liberalism, Theological.

Butler, Joseph (1692–1752). English churchman, rationalist philosopher, and opponent of deism. Butler lived during the "golden age of English deism," and he sought to cut the ground from under his deistic opponents. His great literary effort was *The Analogy of Religion Natural and Revealed to the Constitution and Course of Nature* (1736). He took the position that the order in nature is paralleled by the order in revelation, intimating that God was author of both. He argued that the order and beauty of nature reveal a creating intelligence with some conscious design in view. Butler was also intensely practical, as his *Fifteen Sermons Preached at the Rolls Chapel* (1726) demonstrates. In this he sought to justify to practical men the common virtues (such as benevolence and compassion).

H. F. Vos

See also Deism.

Cc

Call, Calling. (Heb. *qārā*; Gk., primary, *kaleō*, "call"; *klēsis*, "calling") The developed biblical idea is that God summons by his word and compels by his power, those who must take part in or enjoy the benefits of his gracious redemptive purposes.

In the OT. Israel is identified as a family, called first from heathendom in Abraham (Isa. 51:2), and then from Egyptian bondage (Hos. 11:1), to be God's (Isa. 43:1), serving him and enjoying his favor. This conviction is most fully stated in Isa. 40–55. The calling of individuals is mentioned only in connection with Israel's corporate destiny, either as the prototype of it (Abraham, Isa. 51:2), or as a summons to further it and bring the Gentiles to share it (Cyrus, Isa. 46:11; 48:15; the servant, 42:6; 49:1).

In the NT. Calling in the NT has to do with God's approach to the individual. In the Synoptics and Acts God's verbal summons, spoken by Christ or in his name, is to repentance, faith, salvation, and service (Mark 1:20; 2:17; Luke 5:32; Acts 2:39). The "called" (*klētoi*) in Matt. 22:14 receive this summons; the "chosen" (*eklektoi*) respond. In the epistles and Revelation, however, the concept is broadened. The verb "call" and the noun "calling" (*klēsis*) now refer to the effective call of faith through the gospel by the Holy Spirit, who unites men to Christ according to God's gracious purpose in election (Rom. 8:30; 1 Cor. 1:9; Gal. 1:15; 2 Thess. 2:13–14; 2 Tim. 1:9; Heb. 9:15; 1 Pet. 2:9; 2 Pet. 1:3). The called are the elect believers (Rom. 1:6–7; 8:28; Jude 1; Rev. 17:14). This upward calling to freedom and felicity (1 Cor. 7:22; Gal. 5:13; Phil. 3:14; Thess. 2:12; Heb. 3:1; 1 Pet. 5:10) has ethical implications. It demands a worthy walk (Eph. 4:1) in holiness, patience, peace (Col. 3:15; 1 Thess. 4:7; 1 Pet. 1:15; 2:21) and sustained moral exertion (Phil. 3:14; 1 Tim. 6:12).

The terminology of calling has two subordinate NT applications: (1) God calls and designates individuals to particular functions and offices in his redemptive plan (apostleship, Rom. 1:1; missionary preaching, Acts 13:2; 16:10; high priesthood, Heb. 5:4; cf. the calling of Cyrus and of Bezaleel in Exod. 31:2); (2) God's call takes into account the individual's external circumstances and state of life (1 Cor. 1:26; 7:20).

J. I. PACKER

See also ELECT, ELECTION; VOCATION.

Calovius, Abraham (1612–1686). German Lutheran theologian. A leading representative of 17th-century Lutheran orthodoxy, Calovius joined the faculty of the University of Wittenberg as professor of theology in 1650. He became primarius and superintendent. Calovius was rigidly orthodox, but known for his personal, practical piety. He was sympathetic with the pietism of Johann Arndt and Philipp Jakob Spener. His concern for orthodoxy extended to the most precise details of theological formulation. He regarded each Bible-based teaching as a fundamental of the faith.

S. N. GUNDRY

See also SCHOLASTICISM, PROTESTANT.

Calvin, John (1509–1564). Protestant reformer and father of Reformed theology. Born in Noyon, Picardy, he was trained as a humanist scholar and lawyer. The point of his conversion is uncertain, but he identified with the Protestants in the early 1530s and wrote the first edition of *Institutes of the Christian Religion* in 1536, prefaced by a letter to Francis I defending the French Protestants. Against his wishes he was convinced to settle in Geneva to aid the Reformer Guillaume Farel, and in a dispute over the city's immorality the two were banished. Geneva's government begged him to return in 1541 as pastor of the Église St. Pierre. Thereafter he spent much of his time preaching; yet his greatest influence came from his writings. He wrote commentaries on 23 OT books and on all of the NT except the Apocalypse. He produced a large number of pamphlets—devotional, doctrinal, and polemical. But most important, his *Institutes* went through five editions, expanding from a small book of six chapters to 79 chapters in 1559. Calvin translated the original Latin versions into French. All these works were widely distributed and read throughout Europe.

Through his writings, Calvin's impact on the church remains vast. He is most influential for his doctrine of the Holy Spirit, a system of Augustinian theology so identified with Calvin that it came to be called "Calvinism," and his lucid political and social views, which call for Christian influence in every aspect of life and society.

W. S. Reid

See also Calvinism.

Calvinism. John Calvin, often regarded as "the systematizer of the Reformation," brought together biblical doctrine as no other Reformer. He was not an ivory-tower scholar but a pastor who thought and wrote his theological works with an eye to the edification of the Christian church. His views have not always been popular and have at times been grossly misrepresented, but all Reformed and Presbyterian churches look back to him as the founder of their biblical-theological doctrinal position.

Scripture. The formal principle and source of Calvin's theological system is embodied in the Latin phrase *sola Scriptura* (Scripture only). In a strict sense Calvin was primarily a biblical theologian. He rejected the medieval interpretation system of allegorizing, spiritualizing, and moralizing, insisting that the literal meaning of the words be taken in their historical context. He sought a theology that would set forth in a systematic form the teaching of Scripture. The stress upon the Scriptures was the result of his belief that they were the Word of God and therefore were the final authority for belief and action. Further, the individual comes to recognize the Bible as the Word of God not primarily because of logical, historical, or other arguments but by the enlightenment of the Holy Spirit's "internal testimony."

God. The triunity of God in Father, Son, and Holy Spirit, the same in substance and equal in power and glory is the keystone of Calvinism. God is sovereign, perfect in all respects, and possessor of all power, righteousness, and holiness. He is eternal and completely self-sufficient. Therefore, he is subject neither to time nor to any other beings, nor is he reducible to spatiotemporal categories for human understanding and analysis. To his creatures God must always be mysterious, except insofar as he reveals himself to them. As God sovereignly sustains all his creation, so in his providence he rules and guides it to accomplish his ultimate purposes that all things might be to his glory alone (*soli Deo gloria*). This rule included even the free actions of human beings, so that history might achieve the end determined from all eternity.

Humanity. Human beings were created in the image of God, with true knowledge, righteousness, and holiness, and as the stewards of God's handiwork. God entered into a covenant relationship with Adam, promising blessing, in return for which he was to rule over and subdue nature under the sovereign authority of God. Yet Adam chose to declare his independence and asserted himself as an independent being and thus fell under the judgment of God. The outcome was condemnation and a total corruption over the entire human race, which Adam represented in the covenant. This, however, did not frustrate God's plans and purposes. Already in eternity he had chosen a great number of these fallen creatures for himself, to be reconciled to him. To God's chosen ones the Holy Spirit is sent, not only to enlighten them to understand the gospel set forth in the Scriptures, but to enable them to accept God's promise of forgiveness. By this "effectual calling" they come to faith in Christ as the one who has redeemed them, trusting in him alone as the one who has met all God's requirements on their behalf. Thus it is by faith alone (*sola fidei*) that they are saved, through the regenerating power of the Holy Spirit. Thereafter, they are to glorify him in thought, word, and deed.

The Church. God's people now live as citizens of his kingdom, called to serve him in the world through the church. This obligation is laid upon both adult believers and their children, as it was with OT Israel under the Abrahamic covenant. The covenantal sign and seal is baptism, which signifies entry into the membership of the visible body of Christ's people for both children and adults. For adults baptism is upon confession; for children it anticipates their confession as adult believers. The Lord's Supper is the continuing sacrament in which Christ's people partake in witness to him and remember his redemptive work for them. Calvinists have tended toward government by teaching elders, and elders who rule or supervise, both elected by the church.

Calvinism in History. Calvin most clearly defined his thoughts in his *Institutes of the Christian Religion.* Subsequently Calvinists added various confessions, such as the *Heidelberg Catechism* (1563), the *Canons of the Synod of Dort* (1618), and the *Westminster Confession* and *Catechisms* (1647–48). Theologians also have elaborated various points. The 19th century in particular saw a considerable expansion of Calvinistic thought under the influence of Abraham Kuyper and Herman Bavinck in the Netherlands, Auguste Lecerf in France, and A. A. Hodge, Charles Hodge, and B. B. Warfield in the United States. Calvin's influence has implications for all of life and thought.

W. S. REID

See also CALVIN, JOHN; REFORMED TRADITION, THE.

Calvinistic Methodism. A Welsh movement begun by Griffith Jones (1684–1761), Howell Harris (1714–73), and Daniel Rowlands (1713–90), who had significant contacts with English Methodists. It predated English Methodism by about 20 years. In 1795 the group separated from the state church and in 1823 adopted a confession of faith patterned after the *Westminster Confession.* The Calvinistic Methodist or Presbyterian Church of Wales remains active in educational, missionary, social, and political work, with a predominantly Welsh constituency of 1350 congregations.

P. A. MICKEY

See also CALVINISM; METHODISM; REFORMED TRADITION, THE; WHITEFIELD, GEORGE.

Cambridge Platonists. A philosophical and theological movement in 17th-century England. The leaders were graduates of Cambridge University inspired by Thomas Hobbes, and each was an Anglican clergyman. Major leaders were Ralph Cudworth and Henry More. Others included Benjamin Whichcote, John Smith, Nathaniel Culverwel, and Peter Sterry. They were committed not so much to particular doctrines as to a general Platonistic perspective: a love of truth, a contempt for worldliness, and a concern for justice. They believed goodness to be eternal and emphasized the moral life as the essence of Christianity. They trusted heavily in human reason and rejected the English empiricists' belief that the mind has no innate capacities for knowledge because that suggested a materialistic picture of human nature. They sought to give full weight to human rationality. They attacked Calvinism for setting faith above reason.

P. H. deVries

Campbell, Alexander (1788–1866). A founder of the Christian Church (Disciples of Christ). Joining the Christian Association of Washington (Pennsylvania), which his father Thomas Campbell started, Campbell was ordained to its ministry in 1812, speedily sharing his father's leadership and doing itinerant preaching in Kentucky, Ohio, Indiana, West Virginia, and Tennessee. His converts called themselves "Disciples of Christ" (others called them Campbellites). He expounded his ideas in two monthly magazines, *The Christian Baptist* (1823–30) and its successor, *The Millennial Harbinger* (1830–64). In 1840 he founded Bethany College in West Virginia, serving as its president for over 20 years. Church membership was based on personal confession of Jesus Christ as divine Savior and baptism by immersion. He declared baptism to be both an act of obedience to Christ's command, and "a means of receiving a formal, distinct, and specific absolution, or release from guilt." The local congregation was seen as the basic unit of Christianity, completely autonomous but expected to cooperate with other Christians. Two classes of office-bearers were recognized: bishops or elders to give congregational leadership in matters spiritual and deacons to handle temporal concerns. The Lord's Supper was to be observed weekly.

From 1832 the "Disciples of Christ" united with "the Christians" to form the Christian Church (Disciples of Christ), the largest indigenous body having its inception in America.

N. V. Hope

Campbell, John McLeod (1800–1872). Scottish theologian. After five years as minister of Row (modern Rhu), he was arraigned before Dumbarton presbytery and found guilty of preaching "the doctrine of universal atonement and pardon through the death of Christ, and also the doctrine that assurance is of the essence of faith and necessary to salvation." The next general assembly (1831) deposed Campbell from the ministry. His zeal and saintliness, acknowledged even by opponents, were reflected in his ministry in an independent congregation in Glasgow (1833–59). He wrote *The Nature of the Atonement* in 1856. In it he argued that Christ had effected the requisite repentance on behalf of humanity and had fulfilled the condition of forgiveness. This move away from a legal interpretation of the doctrine reportedly created "a brighter, clearer, theological atmosphere purged of Calvinistic gloom." Hailed by James Denney and others as one of Scotland's greatest theologians, Campbell was partially rehabilitated by 1869, when Glasgow University made him an honorary D.D. His book on the atonement has gone through many editions.

J. D. Douglas

Campbellites. See CAMPBELL, ALEXANDER.

Camp Meetings. See REVIVALISM.

Canon. See CHURCH OFFICERS.

Canonization. A legal process in the Roman Catholic Church whereby a departed "servant of God" is declared a "saint." Such persons are entered into the "canon" or catalog of saints invoked at the celebration of Mass. In beatification the individual is declared to have had heroic virtue and miraculous power; saints must have performed at least two additional miracles. Beatification is usually a preliminary step toward canonization. Since Vatican Council I canonization is considered an infallible papal act, guaranteeing that saints are indeed worthy of veneration and able to intercede for the faithful. The beatified receive only local recognition, while saints are venerated throughout the Catholic Church. The cult of the beatified is permitted, while that of the saints is mandated. Saints alone become patrons of churches.

J. VAN ENGEN

See also BEATIFICATION.

Canon of the Bible. See BIBLE, CANON OF.

Capital Punishment. The penalty of death for the commission of a crime. In the OT persons were put to death for sacrificing to false gods (Exod. 22:20), blasphemy (Lev. 24:14), witchcraft (Exod. 22:18), sabbath-breaking (Num. 15:32), and similar offenses. On the other hand, Cain was not put to death for slaying his brother Abel. The death penalty was not appropriate for a homicide without malice (Deut. 19:1–7). Those opposing capital punishment contend Jesus opposed to the death penalty, saying in the case of the adulteress that only the perfect might put her to death (John 8:2–11).

The most frequent secular arguments supporting the death penalty are that the threat of death deters people from committing offenses, saves lives because even sentenced to life imprisonment murderers may kill other prisoners and guards, and that execution is cheaper than incarceration. Those opposed to capital punishment see the first two arguments as unsubstantiated by any study. Though the cost of incarcerating a person on death row is great, an inmate can contribute to dependents and make restitution payments under a properly administered system. Specifically Judeo-Christian arguments are that God has established humans as his image bearers and life as holy and inviolable (Gen. 9:5–6). Those who oppose capital punishment contend that the death penalty devalues the worth of life.

R. G. CULBERTSON

Cappadocian Fathers. Three theologians of the 4th century. Basil the Great and Gregory of Nyssa were brothers; Gregory of Nazianzus was their friend from youth. Basil and Gregory of Nazianzus are now classed (along with John Chrysostom and Athanasius) as Doctors of the Greek Church. The Cappadocian fathers mediated Origen's best thought with orthodoxy. By insisting on the formula "three persons but one essence" they preserved that Nicene Trinitarian orthodoxy from Arian and semi-Arian corruption.

V. L. WALTER

See also BASIL THE GREAT; GREGORY OF NAZIANZUS; GREGORY OF NYSSA; ORIGEN.

Cardinal. A senior official of the Roman Catholic Church, who is now always a bishop. Each member is nominated by the pope and since 1962 has been raised to the office of bishop if he did not hold it already. In the 16th century there was a fixed rule of 70 cardinals, but now there are more than 100. As a body they advise the pope, help in the Vatican, and when a vacancy arises they elect the new pope (who is usually one of their number). They wear a special cassock and red skull cap and have the title of "Eminence."

P. TOON

See also CHURCH OFFICERS.

Carlstadt, Andreas Bodenstein von (1477–1541). German Protestant Reformer. A teacher at the new University of Wittenberg, he conferred on Luther the doctor of theology degree in 1512. Like Luther, he underwent a spiritual transformation in which he repudiated his Thomist beliefs and became a supporter of the mobilizing Protestant movement. A natural leader, Carlstadt led the Wittenberg community in reform. On Christmas 1521 he celebrated communion in the Castle Church without priestly dress and without sacrifice or elevation of the host. He even offered the cup to the laity. In Jan. 1522 he married and instructed that all ministers should marry. He also opposed church music, religious images, begging, and religious fraternities. While Luther could endorse many of these changes in the next few years, he believed Carlstadt's reforms to be dangerous to the movement at that juncture. In Sept. 1524 the Saxon authorities banished Carlstadt, forcing him to leave behind his child and a pregnant wife. Allowed to return in 1525 on the condition that he would not lecture, he was again forced to leave and finally settled in Switzerland. Here his symbolic understanding of communion was welcomed, and he held a professorship at Basel from 1534 to his death.

D. A. RAUSCH

See also LUTHER, MARTIN; REFORMATION, PROTESTANT.

Carnell, Edward John (1919–1967). American evangelical theologian. He aimed to correct certain fundamentalist emphases and to restate orthodox theology in an intelligent and persuasive manner. Carnell began teaching in 1945 at Gordon College and Divinity School. In 1948 he moved to Fuller Theological Seminary, where he remained until his death, serving as president (1954–59). Carnell first came to prominence in 1948 with *An Introduction to Christian Apologetics*, which became a standard textbook for apologetics. He next wrote *A Philosophy of the Christian Religion* (1952). *Christian Commitment* (1957), and *The Kingdom of Love and the Pride of Life* (1960) preserved Carnell's respect for propositional revelation but broadened his apologetic to include "knowledge by acquaintance" and a more existential defense of Christianity's answer to the human moral predicament.

B. L. SHELLEY

Caroline Divines. Seventeenth-century theologians named for the period under Charles I and Charles II. In practice the term more widely refers to high church Anglicans writing generally in the 17th century. The term became current during the Tractarian movement in the 19th century. The massive scholarship and extensive learning of these men was demonstrated by publication in the 19th century of the multivolume *Library of Anglo-Catholic Theology*. They were seen to exemplify an Anglicanism which had appropriated the value of the Reformation, avoided the excesses of Puritanism, and provided Christendom with a "middle way" between Geneva and Rome. Among the leading figures were Lancelot Andrewes (1555–1626) and William Laud (1573–1645).

C. F. ALLISON

See also LAUD, WILLIAM.

Casuistry. The application of general ethical laws to specific life situations. Aristotle called attention to what he termed the need for equity, and the search for methods to decide what is a right or wrong act has been an important part of the study of ethics. It has been called the goal of ethics. Christianity, as any other system with moral values, must engage in casuistry. One of the earliest examples is Paul's rulings about the eating of meat sacrificed to idols and the remarriage of divorced persons. In the Roman Catholic Church casuistry has been a particular concern because of the need for both priests and penitents to know the church's position on guilt and obligations.

S. R. OBITTS

Catechisms. (Gk. *katēcheō*, "to instruct") A catechism is a popular manual of instruction in Christian beliefs, normally in question-and-answer form. Such manuals developed in the early 16th century, but catechetical teaching or catechesis originated early as converts were prepared for baptism.

The formal catechumenate period of instruction (cf. Hippolytus, *Apostolic Tradition*) by the 4th and 5th centuries incorporated quasiliturgical ceremonies in which oral transmission (*traditio*) of the Creed and Lord's Prayer by the catechist was recited (*redditio*) by the catechumen. The system was designed to safeguard the integrity of the church and the secret discipline (*disciplina arcani*) of its inner life. Concentrated preparation prior to baptism at Easter (the origin of Lent) survives in a series of catechetical addresses by Cyril of Jerusalem, Ambrose, Chrysostom, and Theodore of Mopsuestia. Augustine wrote *How to Catechize the Uninstructed* and Gregory of Nyssa his *Great Catechetical Oration.*

As infant baptism became the norm, the catechumenate declined. During the medieval era no regular ecclesiastical catechesis was provided for children, though there were popular teaching materials. An explosion of catechism production took place in the Reformation; many Lutheran pastors compiled their own. The most influential was Luther's Small Catechism of 1529, published a month after his Great Catechism, which was based on a series of sermons of 1528. Both were intended as aids to pastors. The Small Catechism dealt with the Decalogue, Apostles' Creed, Lord's Prayer, and sacraments, standard ingredients of subsequent Protestant catechisms.

Catechisms were anti-Roman from the outset. From around 1530 a catechism for the young was regarded as a salient mark of the reform movement's break with the past, and was regularly one of the first innovations of reformed states and cities. In the Genevan Reformation Calvin produced a French catechism in 1537 (Lat. 1538) and a simpler 1541 form (Lat. 1545). He reordered the four sections so that Decalogue followed Creed, stressing the law as a guide for Christian life.

The Shorter and Larger Catechisms of the Westminster Assembly (1647) largely displaced all others in Reformed and Presbyterian churches. They abandon the Creed but incorporate other traditional ingredients, while exactingly defining God's decrees and Calvinistic doctrines. The Shorter Catechism has exercised unparalleled influence in Scottish-based churches.

The Catholic Counter-Reformation produced catechisms, although the Catechism of the Council of Trent (1566) is a polemical confession and manual for clerical use. The most enduring document proved to be *The Sum of Christian Doctrine* (1555) of the Jesuit Peter Canisius. Most Roman catechisms are local, with none attaining general use. In the wake of Vatican Council II the General Catechetical Directory issued by Paul VI in 1971 laid down guidelines for local hierarchies to follow.

In about 1640 Peter Mogilas, the metropolitan of Kiev, produced a catechetical *Orthodox Confession of the Catholic and Apostolic Eastern Church*, which became standard throughout the

Greek and Russian churches from the Synod of Jerusalem (1672). Its three heads are faith (Nicene Creed), hope (Lord's Prayer and Beatitudes), and love (including the Decalogue). It was eventually superseded in the 19th century by the *Christian Catechism of the Orthodox Catholic Eastern Greco-Russian Church,* compiled in 1823 by Philaret, the scholarly and saintly metropolitan of Kiev. A revised version was finally approved in 1839. It follows the pattern of Mogilas's work. Philaret produced a shorter catechism in 1840.

With diversification of teaching methods, catechisms declined in the 20th century or became more aids for teachers than precise patterns for learning.

D. F. WRIGHT

See also CONFESSIONS OF FAITH; LUTHER'S SMALL CATECHISM; WESTMINSTER CATECHISMS.

Catholic. (from Gk. *katholikos,* "throughout the whole," "general")

1. Universal, in distinction from the local congregation. This is its meaning in the first occurrence in a Christian setting: "Wherever Jesus Christ is, there is the catholic church" (Ignatius *Smyr.* 8:2). The Nicene Creed defines the church as "one holy catholic and apostolic" affirming a sense of universality and unity in spite of wide diffusion. This idea was continued in the 7th-century Apostles' Creed. The catholic epistles of the NT were so designated by Origen, Eusebius, and others to indicate that they were intended for the whole church, rather than a local congregation.

2. Orthodox or true. The designation "Roman Catholic" emerged in connection with the controversy between Rome and the Anglican Church, which insisted on its right to use the term catholic as linking it with the ancient apostolic church.

3. In modern usage a member of the Roman Catholic Church.

4. An ecumenical or open spirit or outlook, in contrast to that which is regarded as rigidly narrow.

5. "Old Catholics" are a group of small national churches who have separated from Rome and retained episcopal succession.

E. F. HARRISON

Catholic Church, Roman. See ROMAN CATHOLICISM.

Catholicism, Liberal. Response by some Catholic intellectuals to the French Revolution and 19th-century European liberalism. Also, a reform Catholicism which has long contended with Roman Catholic traditions and theology deemed conservative and authoritarian.

The pioneer of the movement was the passionate French priest H. F. R. de Lamennais (1782–1854), who developed a new apologetic for Catholicism. The Catholic religion, he maintained, is not evidenced chiefly by miracles and fulfilled prophecies but by its capacity to perpetuate those beliefs which humankind has found essential to an ordered social life: monotheism, the difference between good and evil, immortality of the soul, and reward or punishment in a future life.

C. R. F. de Montalembert (1810–70), historian and publicist, entered the French Parliament in 1837 seeking to catholicize liberals and to liberalize Catholics. His greatest political victory was passage in 1850 of the Falloux law, which allowed a Catholic secondary education system independent of the state. Liberal Catholics were committed to education and emphasized preaching, then unusual in the Roman Catholic Church. The greatest liberal Catholic preacher was the Dominican J. B. H. Lacordaire (1801–61), who attracted vast crowds, especially to his Lenten conferences at Notre Dame Cathedral. The majority of liberal Catholics remained orthodox, seeking to modernize the church through the political emancipation of the laity and the separation of church and state. A later generation of liberal Catholics, including Lord Acton (1834–1902) in England and J. J. I. von Döllinger (1799–1890) in Germany, advocated autonomy for the laity in doctrinal matters.

The currents of liberal Catholicism led at the beginning of the 20th century to stormier waters of Catholic modernism, which tended to be antidogmatic and anthropocentric. The leading Catholic modernists—Alfred Loisy, George Tyrrell, Baron Friedrich von Hügel, Edouard Le Roy, Maurice Blondel, and Ernesto Buonaiuti—sought to reconcile traditional doctrine with the results of critical exegesis.

The papacy has consistently criticized and frequently condemned liberal Catholicism for its rationalism and naturalism.

F. S. PIGGIN

See also ROMAN CATHOLICISM; TYRRELL, GEORGE; VON HÜGEL, FRIEDRICH; ULTRAMONTANISM.

Celibacy. The state of being unmarried for purposes of religious devotion and ethical purity. Since the 4th century celibacy has been required of Roman Catholic clergy. The Eastern Church has not imposed celibacy upon clergy ordained after marriage. The Protestant Reformers denied the biblical validity of imposed celibacy. The NT teaches both the normalcy of marriage and the value of celibacy. John the Baptizer, Paul, and Jesus might be cited as examples of celibates. Further, in Matt. 19 and 1 Cor. 7 the Scriptures speak of the value of celibacy. Both Paul (1 Cor. 7:7) and Jesus (Matt. 19:12) indicate such celibacy is a gift from God not given to all persons. Those receiving the gift are to forgo the married state for the sake of greater freedom from worldly entanglements to serve God.

O. G. OLIVER, JR.

Cereal Offering. See OFFERINGS AND SACRIFICES IN BIBLE TIMES.

Ceremonial Law. See LAW, BIBLICAL CONCEPT OF.

Chafer, Lewis Sperry (1871–1952). American Presbyterian preacher and educator. As a gospel singer and evangelist, he came under the influence of C. I. Scofield. In 1922 Chafer moved to Dallas, Texas, to establish the Dallas Theological Seminary, which came into existence in 1924. He served as president and professor of systematic theology until his death. Chafer's theology may be characterized as biblical, Calvinistic, premillennial, and dispensational; but chiefly he was a strong exponent of the grace of God. He wrote an eight-volume *Systematic Theology* (1947) which still is widely used as an explanation of dispensational, premillennial theology.

C. C. RYRIE

See also DISPENSATION, DISPENSATIONALISM.

Chalcedon, Council of (451). The 4th ecumenical council, summoned by the Eastern emperor Marcion to establish ecclesiastical unity in the East. Its formulation, the Chalcedonian Definition, remains the highest orthodox statement explaining the two natures in the one Person of Christ.

More than 500 bishops and several papal legates attended the Oct. meeting. There was general consensus simply to ratify the Nicene tradition interpreted by Constantinople, along with the letters of Cyril of Alexandria to Nestorius and John of Antioch and Pope Leo's letter to Flavian (the so-called Tome, or *Epistola Dogmatica*). However, the imperial commissioners deemed it necessary to unity that the faith be defined as it related to the Person of Christ.

The council proceeded in three steps. (1) It reaffirmed the Nicene tradition; (2) it accepted as orthodox the letters of Cyril and Leo; (3) it provided a Definition of the doctrine of the Person of Christ as one Person with two natures.

J. H. HALL

See also COUNCILS, CHURCH.

Channing, William Ellery (1780–1842). The most important spokesman for Unitarianism in America in the first half of the 19th century. In 1803 he became the minister of Boston's Federal Street Congregational Church, where he remained for the rest of his life. His presence along with a liberal Harvard College made Boston the Unitarian stronghold. He denied the traditional doctrine of the Trinity and he qualified severely the sense in which Christ should be considered divine. He affirmed the perfectibility of humanity, the fatherhood of God, and the moral perfection of Christ. Yet he continued to affirm the reality of the resurrection and genuineness of other NT miracles, which for him constituted solid rational proof for the supernatural character of Christianity. Channing's moderate and temperate personality did much to spread his views.

M. A. NOLL

See also UNITARIANISM.

Charismata. See SPIRITUAL GIFTS.

Charismatic Movement. (from Gk. *charisma*, "gift of grace") A renewal movement within historic churches that began in the 1950s. The movement was at first often termed "neo-Pentecostal"; it came to be referred to as the "charismatic renewal" or the "charismatic renewal movement" with participants described as "charismatics."

In the U.S. significant charismatic renewals began in 1960, when national publicity was given to the ministry of Dennis Bennett, then Episcopal rector in Van Nuys, California. The movement grew within many churches: Episcopal, Lutheran, and Presbyterian (early 1960s); Roman Catholic (beginning in 1967); and Greek Orthodox (about 1971). The movement affected almost every historic church and spread to many churches and countries beyond the U.S. This continuing growth resulted in a multiplicity of national, regional, and local conferences, the production of a wide range of literature, and increasing attention to doctrinal and theological questions both within and outside the movement. Since 1960 well over 100 official denominational documents on the charismatic movement have been produced.

The background of the charismatic movement is "classical Pentecostal" emphases on baptism with (or in) the Holy Spirit as an endowment of power subsequent to conversion, speaking in tongues as initial evidence of this baptism, and the continuing validity of the spiritual gifts (charismata) of 1 Cor. 12:8–10. Because of such distinctive emphases these early "Pentecostals" found no place in the mainline churches. They either freely left or were forced out and founded their own—such denominations as the Assemblies of God, the Pentecostal Holiness Church, the Church of God (Cleveland, Tennessee), the Church of God in Christ, and the International Church of the Foursquare Gospel. The charismatic movement, while related historically and doctrinally to classical Pentecostalism, has largely stayed within the historic church bodies or has spilled over into interdenominational church fellowships. In neither case has there been any significant movement toward the classical Pentecostal churches. Hence the charismatic movement exists almost totally outside official Pentecostal denominations.

Special Emphases. *Baptism with the Holy Spirit.* This is understood to result from "the gift of the Holy Spirit," wherein the Spirit is freely "poured out," "falls upon," "comes on," "anoints," "endues" the believer with "power from on high." This event/experience is the moment of initiation into the Spirit-filled life. Spirit baptism is said to occur either at conversion or subsequently.

Speaking in Tongues (Glossolalia). Glossolalia are generally understood to be communication with God in language other than one known to the speaker. A person does the speaking, but it is claimed that the Holy Spirit gives the utterance. It is the language of transcendent prayer and praise. In tongues there is speech to God which goes beyond the mental to the spiritual. Speaking in tongues is understood, not as irrational, but as suprarational utterance. It is not the forsaking of the rational for the nonsensical—hence gibberish—but the fulfillment and transcendence of the rational in the spiritual. Most persons in the charismatic movement view speaking in tongues as directly connected with the event of Spirit baptism. The Scriptures in Acts which specifically record speaking in tongues (2:4; 10:46; 19:6) state that it occurred with persons who had just received the gift of the Holy Spirit.

Spiritual Gifts. All in the charismatic movement claim that each spiritual gift mentioned in Scripture is or should be operational in the Christian community. Biblical charismata include a wide range of gifts described in Rom. 12:6–8; 1 Cor. 12–14, and 1 Pet. 4:10–11. (*Charisma* is also used in Rom. 1:11; 5:15–16; 6:23; 1 Cor. 1:7; 7:7; 2 Cor. 1:11; 1 Tim. 4:14; 2 Tim. 1:6; *charismata* [pl.] in Rom. 11:29.) All these gifts, charismatics hold, should function in the body of Christ. Charismatics generally recognize that spiritual gifts cannot substitute for spiritual fruit of Christian maturity described in Gal. 5:22–23.

J. R. Williams

See also Baptism of [in/with] the Spirit; Pentecostalism; Spiritual Gifts; Tongues, Speaking in.

Chasten, Chastisement. See Discipline.

Chemnitz, Martin (1522–1586). Lutheran theologian and educator, superintendent pastor at Brunswick, and a leading influence in consolidating Lutheran doctrine and practice in the generation after Luther's death. There is some truth to a saying among Lutherans that "if Martin Chemnitz had not come along, Martin Luther would hardly have survived." Chemnitz was an important churchman and preacher, but his abiding significance rests on his study of Roman Catholic theology and decrees rising from the Council of Trent, *Examen Concilii Tridentini,* and his large part in the writing and acceptance of the Formula of Concord in 1577.

J. F. Johnson

See also Concord, Formula of.

Cherub, Cherubim. See Angel.

Chesterton, Gilbert Keith (1874–1936). Christian writer and apologist. Against theological liberalism he argued that belief in sin as well as in goodness was more favorable to social reform than was the woolly optimism that refused to recognize evil. He held that the acid test of all religions lay in the question: What do they *deny*? Chesterton's writings used whimsy and paradox to cast statements bizarre enough to pass the readers' defenses and explode devastatingly within their minds. He became a Roman Catholic in 1922. Most of his theological works came afterward, including *The Everlasting Man* (1925) and *Avowals and Denials* (1934). C. S. Lewis and Ronald Knox acknowledged their intellectual and spiritual debt to him.

J. D. Douglas

Chief Priest. See Priests and Levites.

Chiliasm. See Millennium, Views of the.

Choose, Chosen. See Elect, Election.

Christ, Jesus. See Jesus Christ.

Christ, Offices of. See Offices of Christ.

Christening. (from Gk. *chriō*, "anoint") (1) The anointing with oil (the chrism) by a bishop when baptism, anointing, and sometimes the laying on of hands were all administered as one rite in the ancient church. (2) Middle English used the word loosely as an equivalent to baptism (i.e., making a Christian). The word came to be applied to the giving of the name in baptism, and from the 16th century has been used as a synonym for "naming."

D. H. WHEATON

Christian. See CHRISTIANS, NAMES OF.

Christian Calendar. See CHRISTIAN YEAR.

Christian Ethics. See ETHICAL SYSTEMS, CHRISTIAN.

Christianity and Culture. Culture is usually understood in relation to Christianity as the total pattern of a people's behavior. Culture includes all behavior learned and transmitted through symbols (rites, artifacts, language, etc.) within a particular group. It focuses on ideas or assumptions that comprise a worldview.

Biblical and Theological Framework. *OT.* The Bible has no word for culture as such, but the early chapters of Genesis present the created order as an interrelated community in which relations with God, the earth, and other people played a part. The disobedience of Adam and Eve resulted in a disordered community and a culture that reflected human pride (Gen. 11:4). From the choosing of Abraham to the deliverance from Egypt, God's purpose was to restore and renew the created order through a people reflecting his character. God is not concerned to give his people a special culture, but to intervene and reveal his will so existing institutions and practices can be reformed to be suitable vehicles of his glory. This meant that much from neighboring cultures had to be forbidden; even institutions Israel had in common with its neighbors—such as the priesthood or kingship—were transformed under God's instructions (e.g., Deut. 17:14–20).

NT. God's desire to redeem and restore human cultural patterns is implied in the ministry of Christ, who came to realize the redemptive purpose of the OT. His earth-shattering recreative work focused on the resurrection, ascension, and Pentecost, which fulfilled the OT promises for covenant life and community. The oft-repeated remark that the NT is indifferent to culture holds only for a very narrow view of culture. The Christian experience with Christ was seen to have great implications for culture (cf. Paul's advice to Philemon). If the OT vision of earthly and human renewal is borne in mind, it can be seen that Christ's earthly work started a process of transformation that will be gloriously completed when he returns to judge the world, a consummation which by our response of faith and obedience we are already made to taste.

Types of Response. The history of encounter between Christianity and culture shows certain typical responses based in theology and historical contingencies. Three typical views have influenced evangelical thinking.

Anabaptist. Throughout Christian history a radical and rigorist stream has emphasized the fallen character of the world order and the need for alternative structures that more closely follow the model of the church's crucified Lord. Most clearly expressed in the Radical Reformation, that view has continued through churches in the anabaptist or pietist traditions. Watchman Nee expressed the extreme view in teaching that salvation means the total severance of a person from the world's system. The Christian in the world is in an alien environment—like a diver in water—and so should develop an attitude of detachment. The earthly work of the Christian is always under death sentence; the only hope is in God's final deliverance. A more moderate proponent, Jacques Ellul, visualizes civilization as a fallen city awaiting renewal in the New Jerusalem. Christians work, realizing "we are participating in a work of death which is under a curse." For J. H. Yoder, Jesus came to effect a social revolution, not by encountering powers but by forming a new voluntary community. Christ founded a new order with alternative patterns of leadership and lifestyle that will eventually condemn and displace the old, dying order. The way of the cross is an "alternative to both insurrection and quietism." This view has given clear expression to the apocalyptic and transcendent elements of Christianity, and many representatives have exerted a strong prophetic influence, though they have hesitated to engage in active public efforts to improve existing conditions.

Anglo-Catholic. Other Christians have distinguished between the spheres of grace and nature, believing human culture is indifferent to religious values. John Henry Newman (1801–90) gave a classic expression to this view, claiming that culture has value on its own (natural) level but cannot be the locus of virtue: "Intellectual cultivation is not the cause or proper antecedent of anything supernatural." C. S. Lewis (1898–1963) took a similar view. He said culture must be dispensed with the minute it conflicts with the service of God. The good of culture may be analogous to Christian good but it is not the same, and he was uncertain how the two could be reconciled. In such a view spiritual values have priority, but there is no critical perspectives shaped by Christian truth. The result supports the cultural status quo.

Reformed. Justin Martyr (100–65) expressed the conviction that culture could be taken captive to the lordship of Christ. Emphasizing the power of God and the victorious work of Christ, this view is more optimistic about human structures, feeling that the most depraved institutions lie within Christ's kingship. John Calvin (1509–64) in *Institutes of the Christian Religion* gave classic expression to this position, and Abraham Kuyper (1837–1920) developed its 20th-century implications. This is the view of all Reformed theological traditions. The self-glorification of God is the center of Reformed thinking about culture. Human labor collectively exhibits the image of God and by common grace is given to honor Christ as mediator of creation. Culture can be the means to control the influence of sin. Because of Christ's work to restore creation, the triumph of Christ's restored kingship at the second coming has a beginning now. Kuyper said genuine development in society will carry over into eternity (Rev. 21:24), even in the midst of spiritual apostasy. This view has made Reformed churches influential on societies where they are present and exhibits an attractive emphasis on the lordship of Christ and the actuality of his kingdom. Its weakness is a tendency to triumphalism that underestimates the power and extent of evil.

Christians through the ages have sought a faith large enough to encompass a view of God as Creator and Sustainer, Christ as both Logos and Lord, and redemption of the sinner and the created order. Such a view leads to a realistic optimism and balanced perspective. Scripture is the norm for all peoples and times, but its supracultural element must always be expressed in cultural form, even if those forms are transformed as the Holy Spirit applies the reality of the kingdom.

W. A. DYRNESS

Christian Liberty. See LIBERTY, CHRISTIAN.

Christians, Names of. *Christian.* (Gk. *Christianos*) The name by which followers of Jesus Christ are now generally known achieved preeminence gradually. According to Acts 11:26 the name originated in Antioch. The narrative of Agrippa uses it in Acts 26:28. First Pet. 4:16 is the only other occurrence in the NT, again with the suggestion of use by unbelievers. From Roman writers (Tacitus, *Annals* 15.44; Suetonius, *Nero* 16; Pliny, *Epistles* 10.96) comes evidence that "Christian" was in common use among Roman citizens by the reign of Nero and elsewhere in the empire by the end of the 1st century.

Disciple. (Gk. *mathētēs*) The characteristic name for those who gathered around Jesus during his ministry was "disciple." He was the teacher or master; they were his disciples, a term involving too much personal attachment and commitment to be rendered adequately by "pupil." The name carried over into Acts, where it frequently has the general sense of Christian (cf. Acts 14:21). The use of the term in Acts for those who had no acquaintance with Jesus during the days of his flesh reminds that the relationship of Christians to the exalted Christ is not essentially different from that enjoyed by those who walked with him on the earth.

Brother. (Gk. *adelphos*) This word occurs as frequently as "disciple" in Acts. The parallel use of these titles, as in Acts 18:27, indicates that as technical terms they were virtually synonymous. Unlike "disciple," however, "brother" survived as a common self-designation in the rest of the NT and in early Christian literature. As a title it expresses the spiritual bond among believers and the obligation to love one another (Rom. 12:10; 1 Pet. 3:8). Christians did not always live up to this name (1 Cor. 6:8).

Saint. (Gk. *hagios*) This title appears almost exclusively in the plural as a collective. It is an OT name for God's people and derives from the doctrines of God's intrinsic holiness and the holiness of his people by reason of their relationship to him (Deut. 7:6; Lev. 19:2; 20:26). In the NT also the fundamental idea of sainthood is separation to God or belonging to God. The holiness of Christians is objective (1 Cor. 7:14). They are saints or holy by virtue of their being people of God (Eph. 2:19–22), chosen and loved by God (Col. 3:12), called (Rom. 1:7), in Christ (1 Cor. 1:30; Phil. 1:1), and the objects of the work of the Holy Spirit (2 Thess. 2:13). The ethical dimension, subjective holiness, is secondary, though no less important (Eph. 5:3; Heb. 12:14). The name survived as a general title for Christians only through the 2d century. Perhaps as a result of the juxtaposition of sainthood and martyrdom in Revelation (16:6; 17:6), it gradually became an honorific title for confessors, martyrs, and ascetics.

Believer. (Gk. *pistos*) This name is rooted in the OT (Gen. 15:6; Isa. 7:9; Hab. 2:4). In the verbal form (e.g., Acts 5:14, *pisteuontes*) it draws a connection with faith as trust and confidence in God's mercy, apprehended in Christ (cf. John 20:31; Rom. 3:22). The absolute form (e.g., Acts 16:1; Eph. 1:1 *pistos*) is ambiguous. It can mean "believer" or "faithful, trustworthy." In certain occurrences it definitely is used in a technical sense as a title for Christians (2 Cor. 6:15; 1 Tim. 4:10, 12).

Follower of the Way. Six times in Acts, all in connection with Paul, the Christian faith and community are designated "the Way" (*he hodos,* 9:2; 19:9, 23; 22:4; 24:14, 22). By implication Christians might be called "followers of the Way."

Friend. (Gk. *hoi philoi*) In Acts 27:3 and 3 John 15 this may mean acquaintances, rather than Christians, but in John 15:13–15; James 2:23 faith and obedience bring the title of friend of God.

Nazarene. Clearly a slur in Acts 24:5, in this the church found itself bearing its master's reproach (cf. John 1:46).

Designations. A large number of designations for Christians never achieved the status of names by which Christians addressed one another or were addressed by unbelievers. Some of the more theologically important of these are "children of God" (Rom. 8:16; 1 John 3:1), "servant" (Acts 4:29; Rom. 1:1), "soldier" (2 Tim. 2:3), "heir" (Rom. 8:17; Gal. 3:29), and "elect" (1 Pet. 1:1). Other designations identify Christians with OT Israel, among which may be mentioned "people of God" (Rom. 9:25), "sons of God" (Rom. 8:19; Gal. 3:26), "children of promise" (Gal. 4:28), "sons of Abraham" (Gal. 3:7), "seed of Abraham" (Gal. 3:29), "Israel" (Gal. 6:16; Heb. 8:8), and "circumcision" (Phil. 3:3). Finally, there are descriptive phrases such as "those who call upon the name of our Lord Jesus Christ" (1 Cor. 1:2) and "those who obey God's commandments and hold to the testimony of Jesus" (Rev. 12:17).

R. S. RAYBURN

Christian Science. See CHURCH OF CHRIST, SCIENTIST.

Christian Socialism. See SOCIALISM, CHRISTIAN.

Christian Year. The liturgical calendar of various seasons and holy days, especially as designated by high church communions. It begins on the first Sunday of Advent, and its central feast is Easter. The various feast days memorialize aspects of the life of Jesus Christ and various saints. Seasons and feasts all have a liturgical aspect since each ultimately revolves around worship of God. Pius XII in *Mediator Dei* insists that the year of the church is not a boring record of a previous time period, but rather a vibrant reliving of events. These would especially include the death, resurrection, and ascension of Christ and the coming of the Holy Spirit at Pentecost.

In the Roman Catholic calendar there are two levels in the year. One deals with the feasts of Jesus Christ, the other with feasts of Mary and the saints. Feasts of the saints grew out of local celebrations. As these communities corresponded, they began to copy feasts and to devise a kind of sequence. Pius V schematized the year in the 16th century. By the 20th century there were more than 250 feasts and Pius X stressed the fact that all feasts had to be centered ultimately upon Jesus Christ. In 1960 some feasts of the saints were dropped for various reasons, and Vatican Council II attempted to further simplify the calendar.

Many feast days are movable in the sense that they can happen on various dates within the year, but some feasts are fixed to a particular day in the year. Easter is the most notable movable feast, whereas Christmas is the most notable fixed feast day. Some fixed feast days cannot be celebrated if they occur on a Sunday because Sundays always celebrate God as Father, Son, and Holy Spirit. The feasts always must draw one to reflect upon God as Father, Son, and Holy Spirit in one way or another. Further, the most important parts of the Christian year celebrate the historical aspects of the redeeming power of Jesus Christ in union with events in his own life. Every Sunday celebrates the paschal event of Jesus Christ.

The Easter Season. The Sunday called *Septuagesima* begins the season of preparation for Easter, and the Easter celebration extends to Pentecost. Easter celebrates Christ's passion and death within the context of his resurrection. Holy Week begins with Palm Sunday, remembering the advance of Jesus toward his death. Holy Thursday celebrates the Last Supper and involves the washing of feet in remembrance of Christ, who washed the feet of his apostles to demonstrate his humility and servanthood. Good Friday celebrates the passion and death of Christ. For Roman Catholics the veneration of the cross is the most moving experience of Good Friday. Holy Saturday consists in quiet and reflective preparation for Easter itself. Easter is celebrated as an octave lasting eight days. Each day deals with various aspects of the resurrected Christ. The entire Easter season is to be a period of joy culminating in the happiness surrounding the placing of Jesus at the right hand of God. The season closes with Pentecost, which celebrates the coming of the Holy Spirit to the early Christians.

The Christmas Season. The Christmas period is second in importance to Easter, although it has more secular importance. The Christmas season celebrates the birth of Christ and his childhood. The Christmas season developed later than did the Easter season, although the feast was originally a pagan Roman holy day celebrated yearly on December 25. The Advent period deals with the coming of Christ and the preparation of the faithful to receive him in their hearts. His incarnation celebrates not only his human birth but also his existence through all eternity. Advent recognizes sin but combines confession with joy that the Savior came. The feast of the Epiphany ends the Christmas season.

Feasts of the Saints. Many of the less important feast days recall the early martyrs and various aspects of the life of the Virgin Mary. One of the first feasts somewhat related to Mary was the Feast of the Purification, which has Jesus as its central aspect. The Feast of the Assumption was celebrated as early as the 8th century.

T. J. GERMAN

See also ADVENT; ALL SAINTS DAY; ASCENSION DAY; CHRISTMAS; EASTER; GOOD FRIDAY; HALLOWEEN; HOLY SATURDAY; HOLY WEEK; LENT; MAUNDY THURSDAY; PALM SUNDAY; PENTECOST.

Christmas. The day observed to commemorate the birth of Jesus Christ. The Scriptures do not reveal the exact date of Christ's birth, and the early Christians had no fixed time for observing it. By the late 4th century Christmas was generally observed, although on differing dates in different locales. Dec. 25 eventually became the officially recognized date because it coincided with the pagan festivals celebrating Saturnalia and the winter solstice. The church thereby offered the people a Christian alternative to pagan festivities and reinterpreted many of their symbols and actions. For example, Malachi's picture of Jesus Christ as the "Sun of Righteousness" (4:2) replaced the sun god, Sol Invictus. In every period of Christian history the observance of Christmas has been opposed by some, usually because of its pagan associations and lack of scriptural warrant.

O. G. OLIVER, JR.

See also CHRISTIAN YEAR.

Christology. ***NT Christology.*** NT writers indicate who Jesus is by describing the significance of the work he came to do and the office he came to fulfill. Amidst the varied descriptions of his work and office, usually in OT terms, there is a unified blending of one aspect with another, and a progressively enriched development.

Jesus in the Gospels. His humanity is taken for granted in the Synoptic Gospels, as if it could not occur to question it. He lies in a cradle, grows, learns, hungers, and feels emotion (Luke 2:40; 7:9; Mark 2:15; 14:33; 15:34). He dies and is buried. But elsewhere his true humanity is specifically witnessed to as against unbelief (John 1:14; Gal. 4:4), or neglect of its significance (Heb. 2:9, 17; 4:15; 5:7–8; 12:2). Nevertheless there is an emphasis that he is sinless and utterly different from others. His coming is absolutely decisive for every individual he encounters and for the destiny of the world (John 3:16–18; 10:27–28; 12:31; 16:11; 1 John 3:8). In his coming the kingdom of God has come (Matt. 16:28;

Mark 1:15; Luke 22:30), signified by miracles (Luke 11:20). In speaking his thoughts he utters the eternal word of God (Matt. 5:22, 28; 24:35). He has authority even to forgive sins (Mark 2:1–12).

Christ. In the events set in motion in his earthly career God's purpose and covenant with Israel is fulfilled. Jesus of Nazareth is the One anointed with the Spirit and power (Acts 10:38) to be the true Messiah or Christ (John 1:41; Rom. 9:5) of his people. He is the true prophet (Mark 9:7; Luke 13:33; John 6:14), priest (John 17; Hebrews), and king (Matt. 2:2; 21:5; 27:11). Certain messianic titles are used by him and of him in preference to others. He particularly receives from his contemporaries the titles "Christ" (Mark 8:29), "Son of David" (Matt. 9:27; 12:23; 15:22; cf. Luke 1:32; Rom. 1:3; Rev. 5:5).

Son of Man. Jesus used the title "Son of man" of himself more than any other. In some OT passages the phrase simply means "man" (e.g., Ps. 8:4), as do some of Jesus' uses of it (e.g., Matt. 8:20). Most contexts indicate that in using this title Jesus is thinking of Dan. 7:13, where the "Son of man" is a heavenly figure, both an individual and the ideal representative of the people of God. In Jewish apocalyptic tradition this Son of man is regarded as a preexistent one who will come at the end of the age (cf. Mark 14:62). Jesus sometimes uses this title to emphasize his authority (Mark 2:10; 2:28). At other times he is emphasizing his humility (Mark 10:45; Luke 19:10; 9:58). In John the title is used of his preexistence, his descent into humiliation (John 3:13–14; 6:62), his role of uniting heaven and earth (John 1:51), and his coming again (John 5:27; 6:27).

Servant. Jesus' self-identification often recalls the suffering servant of Isaiah (Matt. 12:18; Mark 10:45; Luke 24:26). He is a representative of the people both as priest and sacrifice for the sins of the world (John 1:29; Isa. 53). Jesus is explicitly called the "servant" in the early preaching of the church (Acts 3:13, 26; 4:27, 30), and the thought of him as such was also in Paul's mind (cf. Rom. 4:25; 5:19; 2 Cor. 5:21).

Son of God. This is the title given by the heavenly voice at his baptism and transfiguration (Mark 1:11; 9:7), by Peter (Matt. 16:16), by the demons (Mark 5:7), and by the centurion (Mark 15:39). This title is messianic. In the OT, both Israel (Exod. 4:22; Hos. 11:1) and the king (Ps. 2:7; 2 Sam. 7:14) are "sons." But the title also reflects the unique filial consciousness of Jesus (cf. Matt. 11:27; Mark 13:32; 14:36; Ps. 2:7). He is not simply a son but *the* Son (John 20:17). This consciousness, which is revealed at high points in the Synoptic Gospels, is the continuous conscious background of Jesus' life in John. The Son and the Father are one (John 5:19, 30; 16:32) in will (4:34; 6:38; 7:28; 8:42; 13:3), in activity (14:10), and in giving eternal life (10:28–30).

Lord. Paul most frequently refers to Jesus as "Lord." His lordship extends over history and the powers of evil (Col. 2:15; 1 Cor. 2:6–8; 8:5–6; 15:24). He must be Lord in the life of the church (Eph. 6:7; 1 Cor. 7:10, 25). As Lord he will judge (2 Thess. 1:7). After the resurrection and ascension Jesus was almost spontaneously described as "Lord" (Acts 2:32–36.; Phil. 2:9–11). The early church prayed to him as to God (Acts 7:59–60; 1 Cor. 1:2).

Word. The statement, "The Word became flesh" (John 1:14), relates Jesus to the wisdom of God in the OT (Prov. 8) and to the law of God (Deut. 30:11–14; Isa. 2:3). In these the Word is declared by which God creates, reveals himself, and fulfills his will (Ps. 33:6; Isa. 55:10–11). There is a close relationship between word and event. In the NT it becomes clearer that the Word is not merely a message but is Christ himself (cf. Eph. 3:17 and Col. 3:16; 1 Pet. 1:3

and 23). Col. 1 and Heb. 1 echo John 1; Christ was the agent of God's creative activity from the beginning.

Patristic Christology. The developed doctrine of Christ came slowly and through controversy over concepts and the words which defined them.

Origen had a decisive influence in the development of Christology in the East. He taught the eternal generation of the Son from the Father and used the term *homoousios*. His complicated doctrine viewed Christ as an intermediate being, who spanned the distance between the utterly transcendent being of God and the created world. Both sides in the later Arian controversy, which began ca. 318, were influenced by Origen.

Arius denied the possibility of any divine emanation, or contact with the world, or of any distinction within the Godhead. Therefore the Word is made out of nothing before time. Though called God, he is not very God. Arius denied to Christ a human soul. The Council of Nicea (325) condemned Arius by insisting that the Son was not simply the "first born of all creation" but was indeed "of one essence with the Father." In his long struggle against Arianism, Athanasius sought to uphold the unity of essence of the Father and Son by basing his argument, not on a philosophical doctrine of the nature of the Logos, but on the nature of the redemption accomplished by the Word in the flesh. Only God himself, taking on human flesh and dying and rising in our flesh, can effect a redemption that consists in being saved from sin and corruption and death, and in being raised to share the nature of God himself.

The relation of the deity and humanity of Jesus was resolved at the Council of Chalcedon (451), which taught one Christ in two natures united in one person or hypostasis, yet remaining "without confusion, without conversion, without division, without separation." This was later clarified to mean that the human nature is enhypostatic—subsisting in and through the divine nature. Further, Chalcedon declared, there are two wills—a human and a divine—in the one Christ.

Further Development. Luther's Christology was based on Christ as true God and true man in inseparable unity. Yet there was a "communication of attributes" (*communicatio idiomatum*) between the Father and Son, so that God the Father's qualities or attributes were shared in the divine and human natures in Christ, a mutual interpenetration of divineness and humanity. This verged on the commingling of natures which Chalcedon had avoided. Calvin also approved of the orthodox statements of the church councils. He stressed that in the incarnation God did not suspend nor alter his normal function of upholding the universe. He insisted that the two natures in Christ are distinct, though never separate. Yet in the unity of person in Christ, one nature is so closely involved in the other that the human nature can be spoken of as partaking of divine all attributes.

Here is a divergence in teaching. The Lutherans focused on a union of two natures in which the human nature is assumed into the divine. The Reformed began with the divine person, which assumed humanity. Reformed saw a direct union between the natures, adding to the patristic conception of the *communicatio idiomatum* the concept of the *communicatio operationum* in which the properties of the two natures coincide in one person. Reformed could speak of an active communion between the natures without teaching a doctrine of mutual interpenetration. The *communicatio operationum* (which came to be adopted by Lutherans) corrects patristic theology's rather static way of speaking of the hypostatic union, seeing the person and work of Christ in inseparable unity. The divine and human natures interact in the work of atoning and reconciling. The natures cooperate in such a way that Christ is fully sufficient in himself to mediate between God and fallen humanity by the distinctive effectiveness of both natures. Incarnation and atonement are essentially complementary.

Liberal theologies from the early 19th century tried to depart from the Chalcedonian doctrine of the two natures to protect the humanity of Jesus portrayed in the Gospels. They found in Chalcedon's formula terminology alien both to Scripture and to current modes of expression. Karl Barth and others resisted this tendency, insisting that Chalcedon's apparently paradoxical formula is meant to point toward the mystery of the unique relationship of grace set up between the divine and human in the person and work of the God-man. This mystery must not be thought of apart from atonement, for it is perfected and worked out in history through the whole work of Christ crucified, risen, and ascended. Neo-orthodoxy sees in this mystery the same sort of unity as that given to the church through the Spirit, making Christology a model for the doctrine of the church and of the sacraments. This recognizes the truth that any view of Jesus Christ sets the pattern for all else in a theological system, giving it coherence and unity.

Much recent NT study has been undertaken in the belief that the Gospels provide sufficient historical detail to give us a reliable picture of the kind of man Jesus actually was, allowing a genuine understanding of his humanity as a basis for Christology. Wolfhart Pannenberg has criticized Barth and others for beginning their Christology by first assuming the Trinity and the incarnation and then arguing downward, viewing the humanity of Jesus against this transcendent background. Pannenberg himself believes a presupposition of the divinity of Jesus will inevitably mar Christology with disjunction and paradox, posing insoluble problems in the unity of his person and obscuring his true humanity. Pannenberg seeks a "Christology from below," moving from Jesus' life and death toward his transformation in his resurrection and exaltation through the grace of God. Pannenberg assumes there are legendary elements in the Gospel history (e.g., the virgin birth). He stresses the need to interpret Jesus and his death from the standpoint of our own experience of history, as well as from the standpoint of the OT. Karl Rahner, on the Roman Catholic side, also begins with the humanity of Jesus based on anthropology.

Do the NT accounts allow such a one-sided approach? That the "Word became flesh" implies that the flesh cannot be apart from the Word nor the Word apart from the flesh. The biblical witness must determine both approach and the method of investigation. Hans Frei produced a study in Christology in which he attempts to face the problems of our approach to the Gospel narratives. He insists that Jesus Christ is known to the Christian believer in a manner that allows personal knowledge but also surpasses knowledge. Moreover, "we can no longer think of God except as we think of Jesus at the same time nor of Jesus except in reference to God." Frei insists that, while we can think of other people rightly without them being present, we cannot properly think of Jesus as not being present. We cannot know his identify without being in his presence.

R. S. WALLACE

See also JESUS CHRIST; LOGOS; MESSIAH; WORD, WORD OF GOD, WORD OF THE LORD.

Chrysostom, John (ca. 347–407). Preacher, patriarch of Constantinople, and a father of the Greek Church. At Antioch, after 386, he began preaching, and his rhetorical skills, amplified by his scholarship and piety, earned him a reputation as a biblical expositor. Sixth-century churchmen began to refer to him as "Chrysostomos" ("golden-mouthed"). Reformers used his thought and exegetical approach to the study of Scripture. In 398 John became patriarch of Constantinople. He labored to reform the laxness of the clergy and the corrupt life of the city. Soon powerful enemies conspired against him and in 404, after defying an imperial order, Chrysostom was exiled to the eastern frontier, where he died from exposure and exhaustion.

H. K. GALLATIN

See also ANTIOCHENE THEOLOGY.

Church, Authority in. ***Locus of Authority.*** The strongest authorities in the earliest churches seem to have been the apostles (i.e., the Twelve, Matthias replacing Judas, plus Paul). Their authority extended beyond the local congregations and congregations they had been instrumental in founding; but it was not without limit. The objective truth of the gospel, Paul insists, enjoys antecedent authority; if even an apostle tampers with that, he is to be reckoned anathema (Gal. 1:8–9).

NT prophets likewise enjoyed wide authority. Some may have been itinerant. "Prophecy" in the NT ranges from Spirit-empowered preaching to direct propositional messages from God; but the degree or kind of inspiration and authority accorded the prophet were limited. It is impossible to conceive of 1 Cor. 14:29 being applied to OT prophets or to NT apostles.

Those who consistently seem to have enjoyed the greatest authority in the local congregation were the ruling elders (also labeled bishops or overseers) and teaching elders or pastors (Acts 20:17–28; cf. Eph. 4:11; 1 Tim. 3:1–7; Titus 1:5, 7; 1 Pet. 5:1–2). In a typical list of qualifications for this office (e.g., 1 Tim. 3:1–7) almost every entry is mandated elsewhere of *all* believers. What is distinctive is that (1) elders must not be novices, and (2) elders must be able to teach, which presupposes a grasp of the gospel and of the Scriptures and an ability to communicate them. The sphere of responsibility and authority for these bishops-elders-pastors is the local church; there is little compelling evidence that a bishop, for instance, unlike elders, exerted authority over several congregations. A plurality of elders, if not mandated, appears to have been common, and perhaps the norm. However, the word "elder" is also used of specific leaders—Peter in 1 Pet. 5:1 and James in Acts 15.

Deacons may trace the origin of their office and function to the appointment of the seven (Acts 6), but this is uncertain. When lists of qualifications are presented (e.g., 1 Tim. 3:8–13), stress is laid (as with elders) on features which signify spiritual maturity, except that teaching is not required. Deacons were responsible to serve in a variety of subsidiary roles, but enjoyed no church-recognized teaching authority akin to that of elders.

Patterns of Authority. Historically one of three avenues has been followed, with variations, to relate these two offices/functions—elder-pastor-overseer and deacon—to the authority of the local church or to other churches.

Congregationalism places most day-to-day authority ultimately in the hands of the congregation. In part this is a reaction against the interposition of a priestly class between God and believers; the priesthood of all believers (1 Pet. 2:9) is central. Churches decide, alongside apostles and elders (Acts 15:22); churches are responsible to guard against false teachers (Galatians; 2 Cor. 10–13; 2 John); churches become the final court of appeal (Matt. 18:17); even when the apostle Paul wants discipline to be exercised, he appeals to the entire local church in solemn assembly (1 Cor. 5:4).

Episcopacy labels its chief ministers bishops and lesser ones presbyters (or priests) and deacons. Some within this camp see the function of the bishops as heir to that of the apostles; others point to the intermediate roles of Timothy and Titus in the Pastoral Epistles—elders with power to appoint elders (Titus 1:5). The bishop-priest-deacon hierarchical ministry was defended as early as Ignatius (ca. A.D. 110).

Presbyterianism points out that presbyters in the NT occupy the most important place after the apostles; and in any location the plurality of presbyters (or elders) seems to argue for a group of presbyters who exercised general oversight over the congregation in the area (1 Thess. 5:12–13; Heb. 13:17).

Each of these prevailing patterns raises questions. Presbyterianism has raised an inference from Scripture to the status of principle. Episcopacy makes disjunctions between bishop and elder that cannot be defended from the NT. Congregationalism tends to read principles of majority vote into NT churches.

Spheres of Authority. Whatever the type, ecclesiastical authority operates primarily in three spheres. (1) Early churches exercised discipline, which ranged from private admonition (e.g., Gal. 6:1) to excommunication and the handing over of a person to Satan (e.g., 1 Cor. 5:5; cf. Matt. 16:19; 18:18). (2) They held responsibility for and authority over matters of internal order—arranging collection of monies for poor relief (2 Cor. 8–9) or administering the Lord's Supper (1 Cor. 11:20–26). (3) Churches had some responsibility and authority in the selection of deacons and elders and delegates (e.g., Acts 6:3–6; 15:22; 1 Cor. 16:3).

There is great fluidity possible in the authority structure of the church, but at least two boundaries are fixed: (1) The church is not at liberty to ignore, countermand, or contravene the authority of the gospel without calling into question its own status as church. (2) The church of the NT self-sufficiently administers itself under the foundational authority of Christ, but it does not expect to have compulsory power over the surrounding world. It is to express authority toward the world, but that authority is to be felt through the transformed and redemptive lives of its members.

D. A. CARSON

See also CHURCH DISCIPLINE; CHURCH GOVERNMENT.

Church, The. (from Gk. *kyriakos*, "belonging to the Lord"; in OT, Heb. *qāhāl*, "assembly of God's people;" LXX, Gk. *ekklēsia*, "a public assembly" or *synagōgē*, "congregation"; in NT, Gk. *ekklēsia*) In the Hebrew OT *qāhāl* designates the assembly of God's people (e.g., Deut. 10:4; 23:2–3; 31:30; Ps. 22:22), and the LXX Greek OT, translates this word with both *ekklēsia* and *synagōgē*. In the NT *ekklēsia* may signify a public assembly (Acts 19:32, 39, 41) or the assembly of the Israelites (Acts 7:38; Heb. 2:12). Usually it designates the Christian church, both local (e.g., Matt. 18:17; Acts 15:41; Rom. 16:16; 1 Cor. 4:17; 7:17; 14:33; Col. 4:15) and universal (e.g., Matt. 16:18; Acts 20:28; 1 Cor. 12:28; 15:9; Eph. 1:22).

Origin. According to Matthew, the only Gospel to use the word *ekklēsia*, the origin of the church goes back to Jesus himself (Matt. 16:18). Did Jesus intend to found the church? It may be claimed that critical study of the Gospels reveals that Jesus probably did not give teachings for the purpose of establishing and ordering the church. Rather his whole life and teaching provide the foundations upon which the church was created and called into being through its faith in the risen Lord.

Nature. A multiplicity of NT images and concepts contribute to an understanding of the nature of the church. In the appendix of *Images of the Church in the New Testament,* Paul Minear lists 96 images which he classifies as (1) minor images, (2) the people of God, (3) the new creation, (4) the fellowship in faith, and (5) the body of Christ. For example, the church is pictured as the salt of the earth, a letter from Christ, branches of the vine, the elect lady, the bride of Christ, exiles, ambassadors, a chosen race, the holy temple, a priesthood, the new creation, fighters against Satan, the sanctified slaves, friends, sons of God, the household of God, members of Christ, a spiritual body. A few major concepts hold these many images together, however. According to the Council of Constantinople (381) and reaffirmed at Ephesus (431) and Chalcedon (451), the church is "one, holy, catholic, and apostolic."

The Church Is One. According to *World Christian Encyclopedia* (1982), there were an estimated 1900 church denominations at the beginning of the 20th century. Today there are an estimated 22,000. Despite all this seeming disunion, the NT witness is clear regarding the unity of the church. The Gospel of John speaks of one shepherd and one flock (10:16), and Jesus prays that his followers may be one even as Father and Son are one (17:20–26, c.f. Acts 4:32; Gal. 3:27–28). Perhaps the most stirring passage on this point is Eph. 4:4–6: "There is one body and one Spirit—just as you were called to one hope when you were called—one Lord, one faith, one baptism; one God and Father of all, who is over all and through all and in all" (NIV). Unity, however, does not demand uniformity. From the beginning the church manifested itself in local churches (e.g., Jerusalem, Antioch, Corinth); the one church had no uniformity of worship, structures, or theology.

The Church Is Holy. To be holy is to be separated from what is profane and to be dedicated to the service of God. It does not mean sinlessness (Phil. 3:12). Despite their serious problems, Paul called the Corinthian Christians "sanctified" and "saints." Christians are holy in that they are separated for God's service and set apart by God (2 Thess. 2:13; Col. 3:12).

The Church Is Catholic. (from Lat. *catholicus* and Gk. *katholikos,* "universal") Although the word is not used in the NT to describe the church, the concept is biblical. Ignatius of Antioch wrote in the early 2d century, "Wherever the bishop is, there his people should be, just as where Jesus Christ is, there is the Catholic Church" (*Smyr.* 8.2). Only from the 3d century on was "catholic" used in a polemical sense to refer to those who were "orthodox" as opposed to schismatics and heretics. To speak of the catholicity of the church is thus to refer to the entire church, which is universal and has a common identity of origin, lordship, and purpose.

The Church Is Apostolic. Eph. 2:20 states that the church is "built on the foundation of the apostles and prophets, with Christ Jesus himself as the chief cornerstone." To claim that the church is apostolic is not to assert a direct line of succession but to recognize that the message and the mission of the apostles as mediated through Scripture must be that of the whole church.

The adjectives "one, holy, catholic, apostolic" are terms specific enough to describe the essential nature of the church and yet allow for differences within denominations and churches in the ways in which each fulfills the mission and ministry of the church in the world.

The Body of Christ. Only Paul uses this term. It is significant that he speaks of the church as the "body of Christ" but never as a "body of Christians." Christians are one body in Christ with many members (Rom. 12:4–5; 1 Cor. 12:27).

Indeed, the church is the body of Christ (Eph. 1:22–23; 4:12), who is the head of the body (Eph. 5:23; Col. 1:18); and the body is dependent on its head for its life and growth (Col. 2:19). The church is never directly called the bride of Christ, but is so understood by Paul's analogy in which the husband-wife relationship is said to be like the Christ-church relationship (Eph. 5:22–33). Husband and wife are to be one flesh, and this is the same regarding Christ and the church (Eph. 5:31–32). Christians form a unity both with Christ and with one another, and Christ is acknowledged as both the authority who stands over the church and the one who gives life and growth. This image is a strong assertion of the need for the diverse gifts God gives to the church.

Purpose. The church has a dual purpose; it is to be a holy priesthood (1 Pet. 2:5) and it is to be a missionary people, declaring "the praises of him who called you out of darkness into his marvelous light" (1 Pet. 2:9, NIV).

R. L. Omanson

See also Denominationalism.

Church and State. Differentiation between secular and religious institutions is ancient. The state has been concerned primarily with temporal life as an end in itself; the church has been concerned with temporal life as a means to spiritual ends. A certain tension exists implicitly in any society that contains these two institutions, even when there is no attempt to separate them.

The issue of the most desirable relationship between church and state is older than the Christian faith, and has been a persistent theme in its history. Jesus' dictum to "render therefore to Caesar the things that are Caesar's, and to God the things that are God's" (Matt. 22:21) marked the beginning of a new epoch in the history of relations between religion and the state. For the first time, a formal distinction was made between the obligations owed to both. Jesus did not indicate where the line of demarcation lay; and theologians and scholars have argued the issue since the 4th century. The resulting discussions lie as an almost impenetrable historical-theological swamp. The debate is especially intense in highly pluralistic societies.

Historical Background. Christian thinkers made no attempt to formulate a theory of church-state relations until Christianity became a state religion in the 4th century. The removal of the capital from Rome to Constantinople (Byzantium) in 330, and other factors, led to a different conception of church-state relations in the East than in the West. In the Eastern Roman Empire (later the Byzantine Empire) and consequently in Eastern Orthodoxy the prevailing theory was caesaropapism—supreme authority over the church, even in doctrinal matters, lay with the secular ruler. In the West, the church had more freedom from direct civil control. Here Bishop Gelasius I initially stated the doctrine of the two swords in 494: "There are two powers by which this world is chiefly ruled; the sacred authority of the popes and the royal power. Of these the priestly power is much more important because it has to render account for the kings of men themselves at the divine tribunal. . . . You know that it behooves you, in matters concerning the reception and reverent administration of the sacraments, to be obedient to the ecclesiastical authority rather than to control it."

During the Middle Ages (ca. 500–1500) the theory of the two spheres, the spiritual and the temporal, was generally accepted, but the question of supremacy remained undefined. The state was universally considered a Christian institution, obligated to nourish, protect, and further the faith. Church law held that the state was obligated to punish heretics, and this obligation was accepted by the state. But there was endless debate among theologians and canon lawyers over the real meaning of Gelasius's two swords.

The Reformation and Its Aftermath. The Protestant Reformers challenged the authority of the church in general and the papacy in particular in both spiritual and political realms. This further diminished the ability of the church to control in political affairs. In place of late medieval theory of ultimate pontifical authority in church-state matters, Reformers posited different approaches. Martin Luther sharply distinguished the temporal from the spiritual but considered many ecclesiastical functions, such as administration, to be nonessentials. Therefore, in most Lutheran states the princes supervised church affairs. John Calvin made a clearer break with the state, believing it the duty of magistrates to maintain peace, protect the church, and follow biblical guidelines in civil affairs. In general, Geneva and the Reformed churches of Europe avoided civil domination. The Church of England substituted the king for the pope as head of the church and designated king and parliament to regulate ecclesiastical government, worship, and discipline.

Anabaptists and other radical Reformers insisted that the correct biblical emphasis was to separate the spheres completely. Their position seemed so anarchical that they were severely persecuted by all other parties, Protestant and Catholic alike. In turn, the Anabaptists passed on their views on church and state to related movements in 17th-century England—Baptists, Quakers, and Independents. More than any other religious group in the 17th and 18th centuries, those of Baptist views—John Smyth, Thomas Helwys, Leonard Busher, John Murton, John Bunyan, John Clarke, Roger Williams, Isaac Backus, and John Leland, among others—championed the concept that the logical corollary to the doctrine of religious liberty was the principle of the separation of church and state.

The 18th-century Enlightenment natural rights theorists such as John Locke popularized the view that civil government was rooted in a social contract rather than in God's appointment. Armed with this concept, states tended to make the church subservient to the common good of society and came to expect institutional religion to steer clear of political issues. However, the development of this view around the world was uneven, and attempts at state control of the church recurred. Only in the U.S. did the government clearly agree to a system that sought to guarantee religious freedom through separation of church and state.

The American Experiment. Conditions in the American colonies prior to 1776 were not favorable to the establishment of a single church. Individual colonies had an established church—Congregationalism in New England and the Church of England in most other places. However, there was no state church in Rhode Island, Pennsylvania, New Jersey, or Delaware, and elsewhere large numbers of Baptists and Quakers opposed those that existed. By the time of the revolution, when the new states wrote their constitutions, most had disestablished their churches. Gradually all did.

The Constitution forbade religious tests for public office and its First Amendment provided that "Congress shall make no law respecting an establishment of religion, or prohibiting the free exercise thereof." A new experiment in church-state relations had been inaugurated with backing from Baptists, Mennonites, Quakers, Methodists and Presbyterians, and the support of the founding fathers—some of whom were rationalists who wanted to protect the state from clerical domination.

The original intentions of the founding fathers and their supporters are now debated. Thomas Jefferson and his party and most Christians evidently assumed some sort of "wall of separation" should be maintained for the good of the republic and the health of true religion. They considered that government best which governed least and sought to minimize conflict between politics and religion. They did not try to segregate religion from national life, and the nation was mostly religiously homogeneous. Many now argue that there was actually no unanimity among the founders and it is impossible to determine the original intent of the Constitution.

As America became religiously and culturally heterogeneous in the 20th century, the view of a rather rigorous separation of church and state was increasingly challenged. Secularists seek radical separation to exclude anything religious from national life; others arguing for a more porous wall to allow for a virile civil religion in national affairs. This new period of church-state relations might be traced to the 1920s, with roots dating much earlier. Legally and politically, it stems from 1940, when a landmark decision by the Supreme Court (*Cantwell et al. vs. State of Conn.*) shifted church-state cases from state to federal jurisdiction. Since then the court has dealt with a number of critical religious issues: laws governing business on Sundays, taxation of church property, religion and prayers in the public schools, public support for parochial education, church lobbying, conscientious objection, abortion, pornography and censorship, and resistance to war taxes.

Contrasts. Islam, Hinduism, and most other major religions have not produced a doctrine of separation of church and state. In many Muslim countries there is no separation whatever. In others there is formal separation of institutions but a close link in terms of favored treatment and anticonversion laws.

R. D. LINDER

See also CHURCH, THE; CIVIL RELIGION; GOVERNMENT.

Church Councils. See COUNCILS, CHURCH.

Church Discipline. An ecclesiastical function mandated by the Great Commission to make disciples (Matt. 28:19–20). A disciple is voluntarily subservient to the master, and the supervision of conduct by the church endeavors to school disciples in the Lord's revealed will. The universal form of discipline is the preaching of the Word. All discipline seeks to nurture the evidence of saving faith in the fruit of good works (James 2:17). It further guards the church (Acts 20:28) through its leaders. The believer is required to pay heed to their admonition (Heb. 13:17).

The process of formal ecclesiastical discipline extends from loving admonition (Gal. 6:1) to excommunication (1 Cor. 5:13). Patterned on Matt. 18:15–17, steps move from private counsel by representatives of the congregation's ruling body, through meeting with that body, announcement of the offense to the congregation (usually at first anonymously) with request for prayer, to public naming of the disciplinee, culminating in eventual excommunication—assuming there is a continuing refusal to acknowledge and deal with the sin.

L. DE KOSTER

Church Government. There are three types of church government—episcopal, presbyterian, and congregational—each of which takes on features from the others. Episcopalianism, for example, rules partly through delegated presbyters in its synods and elsewhere, and its congregations have many functions of their own. Congregations also play a large role in Presbyterian churches, and moderators convene Presbyterian elders, a type of episcopal supervision. Congregational and Baptist churches join in associations or unions, which employ a hierarchical management style. Yet general categories do apply.

Episcopacy. In this system the chief ministers are bishops. Other ministers are presbyters (priests) and deacons. These offices are derived from the NT, although in Scripture bishops and presbyters seem to be bearers of the same office. Those who see an episcopal system in the NT point to the function of the apostles, which some think was passed on to bishops. Timothy and Titus may have held somewhat transitional authority between the apostles and the later bishops. The apostles are said to have ordained by the laying on of hands (Acts 6:6; 14:23; 1 Tim. 4:14). On this view the apostles were the supreme ministers in the early church, and took care that suitable men were ordained to the ministry. To some they entrusted the power to ordain and so provided for the continuance of the ministry.

Episcopacy undoubtedly developed early and was practically universal. When divisions appeared, notably the great schism in 1054 when the Orthodox Church in the East separated from the Roman Catholic Church in the West, both continue to be episcopal and hold to the doctrine of apostolic succession. But there are differences. The Orthodox Church is a federation of self-governing churches, each with its own patriarch. The Roman Catholic Church is centralized, its bishops appointed by the pope.

At the Reformation the Church of England rejected Roman supremacy but retained the historic episcopate. Some Lutherans opted for an episcopal system without the historic succession. Other churches have bishops—for example some Methodist churches—also rejecting the historic succession.

Presbyterianism. This representative system of government emphasizes elders, or presbyters. In the NT presbyters or bishops form the principal local ministry. In each place there appears to have been a group of ruling presbyters which was in charge of local church affairs (Heb. 13:17; 1 Thess. 5:12–13). From the account of the Council of Jerusalem in Acts 15 arose the synod of presbyters delegated by associated churches.

In the Swiss Reformation John Calvin organized the four churches in Geneva with a fourfold ministry: the pastor, the doctor (or teacher), the deacon, and the presbyter (ruling elder). This was not a full presbyterian system but laid its foundation. Presbyterianism developed in Switzerland, Germany, France, the Netherlands, and Scotland. Churches with Reformed theology are usually Presbyterian and associate voluntarily with one another on the basis of shared doctrinal standards, such as the *Belgic Confession*, *Heidelberg Catechism*, or *Westminster Confession*. The congregation elects ruling elders, who as a body form a session, council, or consistory which governs. Its moderator is usually the minister, the "teaching elder," who is chosen and called by the congregation. He is, however, ordained by the presbytery or classis, which consists of all teaching and delegated ruling elders from the congregations within its jurisdiction. The Presbytery sends delegates to the denominational-level body, the synod or general assembly. Parity between teaching and ruling elders is characteristic of Presbyterian government.

Congregationalism. Congregational rule as a system appeared after the Reformation. Its chief scriptural buttresses are the headship of Christ over the church (e.g., Col. 1:18) and the priesthood of all believers (1 Pet. 2:9). Congregational government thus seeks a theocratic ideal in which the people rule, conscious that they are acting under and for Jesus Christ.

In the Reformation many decisively rejected the idea of a state church and saw believers as forming a "gathered church." An Englishman and a founder of Puritan separatism, Robert Browne, published the foundational *Treatise of Reformation without Tarrying for Anie* (1582), which affirmed the principle of the gathered church, its independence of bishops and magistrates, and its right to ordain its ministers. Denied freedom to put this into practice in England, many of these "pilgrims" crossed into Holland. From Leiden they launched the historic emigration to America in 1620. Thousands of persecuted Puritans followed, establishing congregationalism in the new world. Congregationalism is much wider than the church that bears the name. Baptists and many other denominations have congregational polity. There is a great variety in congregational government. Many groups empower the diaconate with some administrative authority and congregational groups form district and denominational associations, with staff and agencies.

Conclusion. In the NT church there were elements of the episcopal, presbyterian, and congregational systems and each developed. Modern Christians may hold fast to their particular church polity and rejoice in its values, taking care not to unchurch others whose reading of the evidence is different.

L. Morris

See also Church, Authority in; Church Officers.

Church Growth Movement. An international educational effort to teach Christians to apply principles from Scripture, management, and other disciplines to evangelism and discipleship in their local church situation.

Origin. The Church Growth Movement was conceived when Donald McGavran, a missionary to India, noticed that though missionaries were doing a tremendous amount of good work to feed, teach, heal, and help people, little church growth resulted. After 26 years of study and work, in Jan. 1961 McGavran established the Institute of Church Growth at Northwest Christian College, Eugene, Oregon. The modern Church Growth Movement was born at Winona Lake, Indiana, in September 1961 when McGavran shared his vision with executives of the Evangelical Foreign Missions Association. An annual Church Growth Seminar at Winona Lake was established. During the next 10 years more than 1000 career missionaries attended this educational program.

In the spring of 1965 Fuller Theological Seminary called McGavran to be the founding dean of a Graduate School of World Mission. He gathered Alan Tippett, Ralph Winter, Charles Kraft, J. Edwin Orr, Arthur Glasser, and C. Peter Wagner to organize a multidimensional study center for effective evangelism. *Understanding Church Growth,* the definitive book on church growth, appeared in 1970. The graduate program drew working churchmen from around the world to Fuller. Each had to produce an original thesis or dissertation on ministry in their own culture or missions context as a degree requirement. The best of these were published, adding enormously to Christian understanding of specific situations around the globe. Through books, education, and seminars the movement equipped a new generation of pastors, missionaries, national leaders, mission executives, and professors of mission.

Church Growth in America. In 1971 C. Peter Wagner organized a similar effort specifically for North America. Wagner and McGavran formed seminary classes for clergy and lay leaders. Win Arn established the Institute of American Church Growth and was soon holding church growth seminars across America. The Fuller Evangelistic Association was founded to promote American church growth as a most needed aspect of effective evangelism.

Methods. The world is a vast mosaic made up of tens of thousands of different pieces. The church grows differently in every piece. Each piece requires a different method. Some of the more universal might include: (1) It is essential to measure and see what is happening in society and the church. (2) The culture to be reached must be understood. (3) The gospel message must be contextualized—presented so that culture can understand it. (4) The congregation will grow fastest if its people are culturally homogenous. (5) Friendship evangelism is vital to win the lost. (6) It is helpful to set denominational and local church goals. (7) At least some laity must be involved in purposeful evangelism, empowered to their spiritual gifts.

D. A. McGavran

See also Missiology.

Church of Christ, Scientist. A religion centered in the teachings of Mary Baker Eddy (1821–1910) and her book *Science and Health, with a Key to the Scriptures* (1875). Eddy claimed that direct revelation had given her understanding of an element of healing lost from primitive Christianity. In 1876 Eddy formed the Christian Scientists Association and three years later chartered the Church of Christ, Scientist. The church was reorganized into its present form in 1892. The First Church of Christ, Scientist, of Boston is known as the "mother church," and each local "branch" is independently governed. The tenets and bylaws of the church were incorporated by Eddy into the church manual of 1895.

Theologically, the Church of Christ, Scientist, agrees with few tenets of orthodox Christianity. It assigns novel metaphysical meanings to traditional terms. The sources of authority are Eddy's writings, which are considered divine revelation, and the Bible as allegorically interpreted through her works. God is a monistic spirit, and there was no physical incarnation. All matter or flesh is an illusion, as is all sickness, sin, and death. Nothing can exist which is not good. Each person is on a plane of equality with God in his origin, character, and eternity. Heaven and hell are states of present thought, not future dwelling places. Salvation is the understanding that life is wholly derived from God the Spirit and is not mortal and material.

There is no clergy or priesthood, nor preaching. Readers recite selections from the Bible and Science and Health. Baptism means spiritual purification of daily life and the Eucharist is silent spiritual communion with God.

P. G. Chappell

See also Eddy, Mary Baker.

Church Officers. *Archbishop.* One who presides over a "province" in the Anglican or Roman churches, a geographical area in which several dioceses are joined administratively. The bishop of the chief see or archdiocese is the archbishop or metropolitan.

Archdeacon. A cleric who exercises delegated administrative authority under a bishop. Duties are of a general disciplinary character, including responsibility for diocesan property.

Archpriest. The senior pastor of a city or a similar position of preeminence.

Auxiliary Bishop. A bishop who assists the diocesan bishop.

Bishop. In NT times the leader of a congregation; also called an elder; in episcopal polity the chief pastor over several churches in a geographical area. Bishops of important areas may be called a pope, patriarch, metropolitan, or archbishop.

Canon. A member of the chapter of a cathedral. Appointment is by nomination or election. "Residentiary canons" form part of the salaried staff of a cathedral and have general responsibility for maintenance of services.

Cardinal. In the Roman Catholic Church the official rank immediately below the pope and, assembled in consistory, his immediate counselors. When a vacancy occurs they meet in secret session to elect a pope. There are three ranks: cardinal-priests, cardinal-deacons, and cardinal-bishops.

Coadjutor Bishop. An administrative bishop who assists the diocesan bishop. In the Roman Catholic Church since Vatican Council II the coadjutor bishop has the right of succession whereas an auxiliary bishop does not.

Curate. Originally a clergyman who had the "cure" of souls; today a deacon or priest who assists a parochial clergyman.

Deacon, Deaconess. A designation for offices emphasizing service in nearly every Roman Catholic and Protestant communion, modeled on a similar office in the Jewish synagogue and NT church (Acts 6:1–6; 1 Tim. 3:8–13).

Dean. The head of a cathedral church immediately under the bishop who presides over the chapter and is responsible for the order of the cathedral.

Elder. A position of spiritual care, protection and administrative leadership, in the NT church, synonymous with bishop or presbyter (Titus 1:5–9).

Metropolitan. A bishop exercising provincial (not merely diocesan) powers; an archbishop or primate.

Moderator. In Presbyterian polity the elder who presides over a session, presbytery, synod, or General Assembly. The primary responsibility is the order of meetings.

Patriarch. (1) Bishops of the five chief sees: Rome, Alexandria, Antioch, Constantinople, and Jerusalem. (2) The head of an Eastern orthodox communion.

Prebendary. The occupant of a cathedral benefice.

Presbyter. Elder.

Rector. (1) Anglican parish minister. (2) Head of a Jesuit house.

Rural Dean. The clergyman appointed by a bishop as a link between the bishop and the clergy of a small area.

Suffragan Bishop. The bishop who officially assists a diocesan bishop and who has a specific title.

Superintendent. The senior pastor in a given area in the Lutheran and Methodist systems.

Vicar. The priest of a parish with the same status and duties as a rector.

S. B. BABBAGE

See also BISHOP; CARDINAL; CHURCH GOVERNMENT; CLERGY; DEACON, DEACONESS; ELDER; MAJOR ORDERS; MINISTER; MINOR ORDERS; ORDERS, HOLY; ORDAIN, ORDINATION; PAPACY; PATRIARCH.

Church of Jesus Christ of Latter-day Saints. See MORMONISM.

Circumcision. (1) Removal of the male's foreskin as a seal of the Abrahamic covenant (Gen. 17:10–14; Exod. 4:24–26; Josh. 5:2–5). (2) Internal renewal in righteousness (Deut. 10:16; 30:6). In the NT literal circumcision is explained as a sign of faith (Rom. 4:10–11) which lost its relevance when Christ came (Gal. 5:6). No NT believer can be compelled to submit to it (Acts 15:3–21; cf. Gal. 2:3), and its fulfillment applies equally to Jewish and Gentile Christians (Phil. 3:3) in baptism (Col. 2:11–12).

M. H. WOUDSTRA

See also ISRAEL, THE NEW.

Civil Disobedience. Intentional acts prohibited by the civil authority or refusal to perform an act required by the civil authority because of conscience. Civil disobedience may be carried out by an individual or a group, and it may involve a specific issue or the general right of the authorities to govern.

For Christian ethics two commands are involved: (1) Christians are called to unqualified obedience to God (Deut. 13:4; Jer. 7:23; John 14:15). (2) Christians are called to submit to governing authorities as God's agents, even where the civil authority is not Christian (cf. Rom. 13:1–7; 1 Pet. 2:13–17). Civil disobedience becomes an issue when God commands something which the civil authority prohibits or the civil authority commands what God prohibits. Daniel's illegal prayer (Dan. 6), Peter's illegal preaching (Acts 5:27–32), and Paul's refusal to leave his prison cell as ordered (Acts 16:35–40) are biblical examples of civil disobedience.

While the basic principle is clear—"We must obey God rather than men" (Acts 5:29)—discernment is necessary to distinguish biblically warranted civil disobedience from a mere rationalization of illegal protest growing out of other motives and interests. If it becomes apparent that there is a real conflict between the demands of biblical justice and love and the demands of the state, and if all available legal avenues of reform are exhausted, then civil disobedience may be warranted.

D. W. GILL

See also SOCIAL ETHICS.

Civil Religion. Also called civic, public, or political religion; the widespread acceptance by a people of a body of religio-political traits connected with the national history and destiny. Civil religion relates the society to some ultimate meaning; it interprets the society, integrates the symbols, rituals, values, norms, and allegiances that function which unify community life, and transcends all internal conflicts and differences. A civil religion is distinctive in that: (1) It has reference to the state's power yet focuses on more transcendent meaning behind the power. Theoretically it justifies power and is a basis for criticizing those who exercise power. (2) "Civil" faith must in some sense be independent of the church as such or it will merely be an ecclesiastical legitimization of the state. (3) It must be genuinely a "religion" or it is mere secular nationalism. Its "civil theology" must provide the society with meaning and a destiny, interpreting the historical experience, and affording a dynamic uniqueness and identity. Reduced to its bare essentials, civil religion means a consensus of religious sentiments, concepts, and symbols are directly or indirectly, consciously or unconsciously, used for political purposes. Civil religion claims a "general" religious faith, while the "particular" faith of sectarian or denominational groups claim the allegiance of only a segment of population.

Supporters of civil religion insist that the ideas of transcendence and covenant hold the nation accountable, cement an otherwise heterogeneous society, challenge the country to fulfill its most noble ideals, and serve as instruments in the hands of wise political leaders to inspire people to higher levels of achievement. Critics condemn it for idolizing the nation, distorting patriotic enthusiasm and falsifying national history to make it fit civil religion preconceptions, reducing God to the level of a tribal deity, providing a tool for public leaders to drum up support for questionable policies and ventures, and ignoring the needs of suppressed minorities within the national community. Many regard a biblical, evangelical faith and civil religion as incompatible.

R. V. PIERARD

Civil Rights. An entitlement citizens possess over against the state or other citizens. Civil rights are consigned by a constitution or statutory law. More general rights, such as the classic ones to freedom of speech, press, religion, and assembly, are commonly called "civil liberties." More often civil rights designate specific rights that have emerged from the moral claims of powerless social groups, especially those that have been historically subjected to unfair treatment. Some argue that civil rights should be limited to the more procedural questions such as due process under the law. Others assert that they must include the requirements for equal material resources, or at least equal access to conditions by which one's social well-being is guaranteed. The debate about what constitutes one's civil rights underlies much of the civil strife in the modern world.

In Western Political Thought. Civil rights laws in the West rest upon fundamental moral principles nurtured in the natural law tradition. By the 18th century natural law theory reached its political height. John Locke believed that all humans are the workmanship of the one all-powerful and wise Maker and, consequently, the state of nature has a law of which nothing is more evident than that all people are equal. All rights and duties humans owe each other in the sociopolitical realm are derived from this claim. Both the U.S. and French declarations of independence affirm as "self-evident" truths or "simple and incontestable principles" that "all men are created equal" or are "born and remain free and equal in rights." Undergirding these truths was the declared assumption that all people possess an "equal station to which the laws of nature and nature's God entitle them."

In the Bible. The emphasis upon human rights is also rooted in the Judeo-Christian faith. The Mosaic law not only established procedural guarantees before the law, but granted the powerless certain economic claims against the wealthy. Thus, the hungry had the right to glean food (Lev. 19:9–10; Deut. 23:24; 24:19–22; Matt. 12:1). Debtors could expect their loans canceled after seven years (Deut. 15:7–11). Sojourners, widows, and orphans were given special rights to the food brought to the temple as a tithe (Deut. 14:28–29).

Unfortunately, the rights of the poor were often neglected or even despised. The prophets, however, became an eloquent moral force in reaffirming the civil rights tradition. Their visions of the holy God radicalized their understanding of sin and sensitized them to the extent of economic exploitation occurring in the land (Isa. 5:16; 6:3–5; Jer. 22:13–16; Ezek. 18:5–18; Mic. 3:1–4). Proverbs and religious hymns also highlight that concern (Prov. 14:31; 29:7; Ps. 15; 113:7–9).

The NT reflects the same position. The teachings of Jesus are well within the prophetic focus and are highly critical of unjust treatment for disenfranchised groups. He reminded his adversaries that a human being is of great value (Matt. 12:12; Luke 14:5). Jesus saw himself as the champion of the underclasses, the messianic liberator of the oppressed (Luke 4:18). Jesus' teachings and activities continually reinforced the moral standing of the penniless (Mark 12:41–44), the diseased (Matt. 14:13–14), the aged (Matt. 15:4–6), women (John 4:7–9), children (Mark 10:13–14), and other socially weak groups such as prisoners (Matt. 25:36) and the blind (Matt. 11:4–6). The writings of Paul and the communal practices of the early church (Acts 2:44–45; 4:34–35) mediated the same moral and theological grounding for civil rights as was found in the OT and the teachings of Jesus. Paul's theological affirmations of human equality were unequivocal (Gal. 3:28; 1 Cor. 7:3–4; 2 Cor. 8:13–15).

D. J. Miller

Clement of Alexandria (Titus Flavius Clemens, ca. 150–ca. 215). Greek theologian and writer. Clement was the first significant representative of the Alexandrian theological tradition. Born of pagan parents in Athens, Clement went to Alexandria, where he succeeded his teacher Pantaenus as head of the Catechetical School. In 202 persecution forced him to leave Alexandria, apparently never to return. Clement is important for his positive approach to philosophy which laid the foundations for Christian humanism and for the idea of philosophy as "handmaid" to theology. The idea of the Logos dominates his thinking. The divine Logos, creator of all things, guides all good men and causes all right thought.

W. C. WEINRICH

See also ALEXANDRIAN THEOLOGY.

Clergy. (from Gk. *klēros*, "a lot," an ambiguous word referring to choice by lot or simply choice; thus, the concept of "the Lord's chosen") In the NT the word is not used of a restricted group, and in 1 Pet. 5:3 the plural is used of God's people as a whole. But by the time of Tertullian (ca. 155–220) it was used of ordained office-bearers in the church.

L. MORRIS

Clergy, Secular. See SECULAR CLERGY.

Coadjutor Bishop. See BISHOP; CHURCH OFFICERS.

Cocceius, Johannes (1603–1669). Linguist and biblical theologian. Johann Koch (latinized to Cocceius) was born in Bremen and was professor of Oriental languages at Bremen, Franeker, and Leiden. Cocceius's views are set forth in his *Doctrine of the Covenant and Testaments of God* (1648) and in his *Commentary on the Epistle to the Romans* (1655). Using a strict exegetical method, he developed a biblical theology in which he distinguished three different periods in the history of God's dealings with his people. In his relationship to humankind God established a covenant of works with Adam. This was supplanted by a covenant of grace made with Moses in which there were three periods—before, during, and after Moses' time. The new covenant is given in Jesus Christ.

M. E. OSTERHAVEN

See also COVENANT THEOLOGY.

Cohabitation. Persons living together in a sexual relationship who are not married. While cohabitation represents only a small percentage of American households, it nearly tripled (from 500,000 to 1.5 million residences) from 1972–82. In 1982, 25 percent of students on college campuses reported that they had lived with someone of the opposite sex. Cohabitation covers a wide variety of relationships from temporary casual arrangements of convenience to more committed lifelong substitutes for marriage.

The rising incidence of cohabitation is variously explained as the result of a general breakdown in personal morality or of broader social forces. The changing sexual values and patterns, the emphasis upon individual human growth, the liberalization of living arrangements on college campuses, the phenomenon of extended adolescence and later marriage, more effective contraception, and the high cost of housing are all factors. Tax and social security laws often tend to discourage some couples from marrying.

The moral problem of unwed people living together is grounded in the historical Christian belief that sexual activity outside marriage is an offense against God's law and a disservice to one's partner. Nevertheless, many people who cohabit justify their action by asserting that love is the key ingredient of their relationship and a marriage license contributes scarcely anything to that love. While Christians have usually insisted that sexual activity must be nurtured by love, they have also maintained that its most sublime meaning is achieved when it is linked to marriage.

Throughout the Scriptures, God's relation to humans is described in covenantal terms with concrete stipulations. Marriage is one of the more significant legal covenants which God has provided. Thus, the claim is only partially true that human ties are made in heaven apart from the concrete legal arrangements. Rather they are also made on earth, as affirmed by God as Creator of both heaven and earth. God's original command in creation was that male and female unite in covenantal partnership, or marriage. This bond bestowed meaning upon their sexual activity as expressed by the phrase "one flesh" (Gen. 2:24).

Cohabitation is a form of social interaction which may communicate that the individuals are important to each other, but they are not so important that they wish to leap into a relationship of ultimacy and permanence. In cohabitation sexual expression is a structurally false symbol of a totally committed relationship. Many Christians believe that the church should respond to cohabitation by neither condoning nor condemning the people who practice it. Rather it should oppose those questionable social forces which tend to encourage and even subsidize it. In this view parents, relatives, friends, and the church are urged to continue a gospel ministry of care to those who live together outside of marriage, helping the couple to deal with their own individual circumstances, while addressing the broader social trends which tend to perpetuate this lifestyle.

D. J. MILLER

See also MARRIAGE, THEOLOGY OF.

Coke, Thomas (1747–1814). Methodist preacher and missionary. Coke was probably the most important figure in the spread of worldwide Methodism in the generation following the death of John Wesley. Born in Brecon, Wales, he graduated from Jesus College, Oxford, in 1768, was ordained an Anglican priest in 1772, and formally joined the Methodists in 1777 and moved to London to become Wesley's assistant during the latter's declining years. Coke was less an innovator than a zealous promoter and organizer. He helped establish Methodist missions from England and America to Ireland, Africa, the West Indies, and elsewhere during the formative period of Methodist missionary expansion.

W. C. RINGENBERG

See also METHODISM.

Comforter. See HOLY SPIRIT.

Command, Commandment. See LAW, BIBLICAL CONCEPT OF.

Commission, The Great. See GREAT COMMISSION, THE.

Common Grace. See GRACE.

Common Order, Book of. See BOOK OF COMMON ORDER.

Common Prayer, Book of. See BOOK OF COMMON PRAYER.

Communication of Attributes (*Communicatio Idiomatum*). The principle that whatever can be attributed to (said about) either the divine or the human nature in Christ is to be attributed to the entire person. Whatever is true of either nature is true of the person. This doctrine is more characteristic of Lutheran than Reformed theology. Categories common among Lutherans are:

Genus Idiomaticum (Category of Attributes). The properties of each nature are ascribed to the person, using any of his names or titles. Christians may thus confess that the Lord of glory was crucified (1 Cor. 2:8).

Genus Maiestaticion (Category of Majesty). The divine attributes are communicated (given) to Christ's human nature. Christ received according to his human nature the omnipotence, omniscience, and omnipresence which he possessed as true God (Matt. 11:27; 28:18–20; John 3:34–35; Col. 1:19). The divine nature does not receive human limitations because God cannot change. Reformed theologians claim that Christ's human nature received only finite gifts, not divine attributes.

Genus Apotelesmaticum (Category of Works). What Christ did for our salvation he did as the God-man. All his works for us are his works as God and man (Gal. 4:4; Heb. 2:14–15; 1 John 3:8). Reformed theologians have tended to designate Christ's acts as the acts of one nature or the other.

J. M. DRICKAMER

Communion, Holy. See LORD'S SUPPER.

Communion of Saints, The. The phrase is probably the latest addition to the Apostles' Creed, not being attested before the 5th century. It is absent from all the Eastern creeds. The traditional, and probably the best, interpretation refers the phrase to the union of all believers, living or dead, in Christ, stressing their common life in Christ and their sharing of all the blessings of God. Some medieval interpreters, including Thomas Aquinas, read the phrase as "the communion in holy things" (a reading which the Latin text allows), referring it to the sacraments, especially the Eucharist.

F. Q. GOUVEA

See also APOSTLES' CREED; FELLOWSHIP; PRAYERS FOR THE DEAD.

Communitarianism, Community of Goods. In the NT church Christian life centered on worship. In the wake of Pentecost a desire to worship God appears to have led to a spontaneous sharing of goods in the church of Jerusalem (Acts 2:42–47; 4:32–37). This sharing was interpreted as a manifestation of the work of the Holy Spirit (Acts 5:3). Throughout the NT writings the welfare of other Christians is of constant concern. Hospitality and aid are continually advocated (1 Cor. 16). In American religious history communal groups have played an important role. These include the Shakers, who followed the teachings of Mother Ann Lee (1736–84), and the perfectionist Oneida Community of John Humphrey Noyes (1811–86). Although heretical in terms of traditional Christian theology, both groups had considerable social impact. The Shakers are credited with inventing the washing machine, while the Oneida Community developed silver plating and became an important industrial enterprise.

I. HEXHAM

See also SOCIALISM, CHRISTIAN; MONASTICISM.

Comparative Religion. The origin of comparative religion may trace to the 6th-century Greek thinker Xenophanes, who noted that different peoples tend to depict God in their own image, but not until the 19th century did the study of comparative religion begin in earnest. Under the influence of evolutionary theory a number of scholars found what they believed to be evolutionary links between various religious traditions. Chief among these theorists were F. Max Müller, E. B. Tylor, and J. G. Fraser. The discipline gained rapid academic recognition, and chairs were established in various institutions, particularly new universities of North America. In Britain the subject tended to serve the needs of the empire and was closely linked to the study of Asian languages. In Germany it took the form of the history of religions, as an adjunct to Christian theology. In the U.S., influenced by such institutions as the University of Chicago, it became an important element in the liberal consensus. As an undergraduate subject, comparative religion became popular in the late 1960s and early 1970s, with new religious studies departments opening in many universities in Britain and North America.

I. HEXHAM

Concomitance. A technical term used in the eucharistic theology of Roman Catholicism to describe the presence of both the body and blood of Christ in each of the species of bread and wine, and thus to afford a theological justification for the denial of the cup to the laity. More widely, it denotes the presence of the whole Christ, that is, his human soul and Godhead, together with the body and blood in virtue of the hypostatic union.

G. W. BROMILEY

See also LORD'S SUPPER, VIEWS OF; REAL PRESENCE; TRANSUBSTANTIATION; HYPOSTASIS.

Concord, Book of (1580). Also called *The Confessions of the Evangelical Lutheran Church* (German) or *Concordia* (Latin); all the generally accepted symbols of the Lutheran Church. The *Book of Concord* comprises : (1) the Apostles' Creed (7th century); (2) the Niceno-Constantinopolitan Creed (381); (3) the Athanasian Creed (ca. 350–600); (4) Luther's Large and Small Catechisms (1529); (5) the Augsburg Confession (1530); (6) the Apology of the Augsburg Confession (1531); (7) the Smalcald Articles (1537); (8) the "Treatise on the Power and Primacy of the Pope" (1537); (9) the Formula of Concord (1577).

R. D. PREUS

See also CONCORD, FORMULA OF.

Concord, Formula of (1577). Unifying confession which settled the doctrinal position of the Evangelical Lutheran Church. It was completed in 1577 and was published in the *Book of Concord*, culminating 30 years of theological labor by hundreds of theologians on doctrinal controversies which beset Lutheranism after Luther's death. Its 12 articles of faith teach: (1) original sin (affirming total depravity); (2) bondage of the will (affirming salvation by grace alone); (3) justification (stressing the forensic nature of justification); (4) the relation of good works to salvation; (5) the distinction between law and gospel; (6) the third use of the law (i.e., the necessity of preaching law in the Christian community); (7) the Lord's Supper (confessing the Lutheran doctrine of the sacramental union and the real presence); (8) the person of Christ (emphasizing the communication of attributes of the two natures); (9) the descent into hell (Christ's actual descent and victory over the forces of evil); (10) adiaphora; (11) predestination (to salvation by grace for Christ's sake, but not to hell); (12) various heresies.

R. D. PREUS

See also CONCORD, BOOK OF.

Concursus. (Concurrence; Lat. *concursus divinus*) Relationship between the divine activity and that of finite creatures within God's providential control of the world. Scripture frequently speaks about the absolute sovereignty of God; it also emphasizes the reality of human decision and responsibility. It is predominantly a Lutheran philosophical doctrine.

M. E. OSTERHAVEN

Condemnation. See JUDGMENT.

Conditional Immortality. The doctrine that immortality was not a natural human endowment at creation but is God's gift to the redeemed who believe in Christ. Those who do not receive Christ ultimately lose all consciousness or existence. This teaching enjoyed some popularity in the 19th century through the writings of E. White, J. B. Heard, and the prebendaries Constable and Row in England, Richard Rothe in Germany, A. Sabatier in France, E. Petavel and C. Secretan in Switzerland, and in the U.S. through C. F. Hudson, W. R. Huntington, C. C. Baker, L. W. Bacon, and Horace Bushnell. Conditionalists appeal to the Scriptures: (1) Only God is said to be immortal (1 Tim. 6:16); (2) eternal life is described as a gift from God imparted only to the believing person (John 10:27–28; 17:3; Rom. 2:7; 6:22–23; Gal. 6:8); and (3) the wicked are said to "perish" or to be "destroyed," which is taken to mean the nonredeemed will be reduced to nonexistence. The doctrine of the resurrection of the wicked to condemnation argues against conditional immortality (John 5:28–29; cf. Rev. 20:6). It is this doctrine of resurrection which strikes a blow at both the Greek concept of the immortality of the soul and the conditional immortality viewpoint.

A. F. JOHNSON

See also ANNIHILATIONISM.

Confessions of Faith. Variations on the term "confession" are found in the NT (e.g., 1 Tim. 3:16; 6:13). In the early church the word was used to describe the testimony of martyrs as they were about to meet their deaths. Its most common usage, however, designates the formal statements of Christian faith written by Protestants since the earliest days of the Reformation. As such, "confessions" are closely related to creeds, which most frequently refer to statements Christians have recognized—the Apostles' Creed, the Nicene Creed, and (less frequently) the Athanasian Creed. The technical term "symbol" is a general designation for any formal statement—whether creed, confession, or catechism—which sets apart the community which professes it from those who do not.

The Reformation and Confessions. Conditions in the 16th century were ripe for the composition of confessions. The publications of Reformation leaders brought momentous theological questions to the fore. When entire communities, or just the leaders, turned to their teachings, an immediate demand arose for uncomplicated yet authoritative statements of the new faith. In addition, the very nature of the Reformation and the very character of the 16th century stimulated the urge to write confessions. The Reformers posed Scripture as the ultimate authority for all of life, even if this undercut received tradition. Several generations of academicians had also raised troubling issues in philosophy. New statements of Christian belief were needed, not just to reorient Christian life, but to reposition Christianity within the forces of early modern Europe. Thus the great outpouring of confessions in the first century and a half of Protestantism performed a variety of functions. Authoritative statements of Christian belief enshrined the new ideas of the theologians in forms that could provide regular instruction for the common faithful.

The Confessions of Protestants. In Switzerland, Ulrich Zwingli superintended the publication of four confessional documents—the Sixty-Seven Articles of Zurich in 1523 (to bring his own canton to break with Rome), the Ten Theses of Berne in 1528 (to solidify reform in that city), the Confession of Faith to Charles V in 1530 (to inform the emperor of Protestant convictions), and the Exposition of the Faith to King Francis I in 1531 (to move the French sovereign to a more even-handed attitude toward Protestants). Martin Luther published his Small Catechism in 1529 after a disappointing tour of Saxony revealed gross ignorance of elemental biblical material, let alone the main Reformation principles. And in 1530 the Protestant princes of Germany confessed their faith before the emperor at Augsburg in a confession written by Philip Melanchthon which has stood as the touchstone of Lutheran theology ever since. The same pattern appeared in other Protestant regions.

The very nature of Protestantism as a politically diverse movement prevented the formulation of a single inclusive confession. Yet in the Reformation's "second generation" considerable consolidation did occur around such documents as the Lutheran *Book of Concord* and the Reformed Second Helvetic Confession and Heidelberg Catechism.

The writing of confessions never stopped, especially in the U.S. The profusion of new denominations or the branching off of old bodies into new configurations has caused frequent new compositions. American Congregationalists, Baptists, Methodists, and Presbyterians, among others, have rewritten Old World creeds to fit the New World situation (e.g., the Congregationalist Saybrook Platform of 1708 or the American Presbyterian revisions of the Westminster Confession in 1788). Others composed new documents (e.g., the New Hampshire Confession of Faith for Baptists in 1833). Confessionlike statements also served as the charters for new denominations (e.g., Thomas Campbell's "Declaration and Address" of 1809 which helped found the Disciples of Christ). They have written confessions in response to shifting theological perceptions (e.g., the Presbyterian Confession of 1967). However, the writing of confessions is not by any means an exclusively American enterprise. Two of the most significant Protestant confessions of the 20th century were the Barmen Declaration in 1934, in which German "confessing Christians" announced their determination to live by the Word of God, and the Lausanne Covenant of 1974, which expressed the faith of evangelicals from around the world on theological and social matters.

The Place of Confessions in the Churches. Given the diversity of Protestants, it is not surprising that the heirs of the Reformation also put confessions to use in diverse ways. Some of the differences can be explained by the circumstances of their composition. Others arise from differing Protestant attitudes toward confessions themselves as well as to authority in the church. In the past the denominations of greater centralization (episcopal or presbyterian) tended to place more weight on confessions than those of greater decentralization (congregational). But now some of the historically confessional bodies sit much looser to statements of faith than do independent churches and organizations.

The Propriety of Confessions. Confessions have served Protestants as bridges between scriptural revelation and particular cultures. They arise in response to a need for understanding Christian teaching concerning a particular problem or in a particular place. As such, many confessions have had their hour in the sun and passed quietly away. Others, because of affective power or balanced judiciousness, have endured. Some of these have become so important to their communions that in practice it is nearly unthinkable to challenge the confession openly while remaining a member in good standing. Yet even in these cases Protestants insist, as the great student of the creeds Philip Schaff once put it, that "the authority of symbols, as of all human compositions, is relative and limited. It is not coordinate with, but always subordinate to, the Bible, as the only infallible rule of the Christian faith and practice." The realization that confessions err, combined with Protestant allegiance to Scripture, has led some groups to disparage confessions entirely. All Protestant bodies have operated under the authority of either formal, written confessions or informal, unwritten standards that function as confessions. In summary, although Protestants do not regard confessions as absolute authorities in matters of faith and practice, many of them have found confessions to be valuable introductions to Christian belief, helpful summaries of Scripture, and dependable guides to the Christian life.

M. A. Noll

See also Augsburg Confession; Concord, Book of; Confession of 1967, The;

Heidelberg Catechism; Helvetic Confessions; Irish Articles; Luther's Small Catechism; New Hampshire Confession; Scots Confession; Smalcald Articles, The; Thirty-nine Articles, The; Westminster Confession of Faith.

Confirmation. One of the seven sacraments of both the Roman Catholic and Eastern Orthodox church. The Roman Church teaches that it was instituted by Christ, through his disciples, for the church. Its early history is somewhat uncertain, and only gradually did it receive recognition as a sacrament. It was given a sacramental status by Peter Lombard in the 12th century and by Thomas Aquinas in the 13th century, and finally by the Council of Trent in the 16th century. One of the two sacraments administered by a bishop in the Roman Catholic Church, its purpose is to make those who have been baptized in the faith strong soldiers of Jesus Christ. It is administered to children before they receive their first communion, generally at about age 12. Concerning it Aquinas wrote: "Confirmation is to baptism what growth is to generation." It is administered according to this form: "I sign thee with the sign of the Cross and confirm thee with the chrism of salvation." It is only administered once. According to Roman Catholic theology, sanctifying grace is increased in the soul, and a special sacramental grace consisting of the seven gifts of the Holy Spirit is conferred upon the recipient. This has recently been reaffirmed by Pope Paul VI in the Apostolic Constitution on the Sacrament of Confirmation (1971), where he says, "Through the sacrament of confirmation, those who have been born anew in baptism receive the inexpressible Gift, the Holy Spirit himself, by which they are endowed . . . with special strength."

In the Lutheran Church confirmation is administered at about age 13 or 14 and admits the recipient to communion. In the Episcopal Church it is a sacramental rite completing baptism.

C. G. Singer

See also Sacrament; Baptism.

Congregationalism. See Church Government.

Conscience. Moral awareness. According to Rom. 2:14–15 conscience is innate and universal, not the product of environment, training, habit, or education, though it is influenced by these factors. It has three functions: (1) Obligatory. It urges man to do that which he regards as right and restrains him from doing that which he regards as wrong. (2) Judicial. Conscience passes judgment upon man's decisions and acts. (3) Executive. Conscience executes its judgment in the heart of man. It condemns his action when in conflict with his conviction by causing an inward disquietude, distress, shame, or remorse. It commends when man has acted in conformity with his convictions. Conscience is a gift of God. It is a guardian of morality, justice, and decency and testifies to the existence of God.

A. M. Rehwinkel

Conscientious Objection. See Pacifism.

Consensus Tigurinus. See Zurich Agreement.

Conservation. That continual activity of God whereby he maintains in existence the things which he has created, together with the forms, properties, and powers with which he has endowed them. While conservation presupposes creation, it is distinguished from it. In creation God acted to bring the universe into existence; in conservation God acts to sustain what he has created. In creation God is the sole cause of the universe, but in conservation there is a cooperation and concurrence of the first with second causes. In Scripture the two concepts, although inseparably related, are never confused: "all things were created by him . . . and by him all things consist" (Col. 1:16–17, KJV).

W. W. BENTON, JR.

See also CREATION, DOCTRINE OF; GOD, DOCTRINE OF.

Constantinople, Council of (381). The gathering in Constantinople of 150 Eastern bishops at the request of the Emperor Theodosius I was later regarded by the Council of Chalcedon (451) as the second great ecumenical council of the church. It marked the end of over 50 years of Arian political and theological dominance in the East, the restoration of Nicene orthodoxy, and the acceptance of a doctrine of the Holy Spirit. The path of history from Nicea to Constantinople is twisted with various political and theological figures and several theological and synodal skirmishes between Arianism and orthodoxy.

The theology of the Council of Constantinople is set forth first by the condemnation of various heresies then troubling the church. More positively, it was expressed in a published statement of doctrine, a *tomos,* and the creed of the council. Unfortunately, the *tomos* is no longer extant except for what is reflected of it in the letter of the synod of 382. The creed is to be found not in the records of Constantinople, but in those of the Council of Chalcedon (451), where a creed attributed to Constantinople was read along with the Nicene Creed. What is read in churches today as the Nicene Creed is more appropriately named the Niceno-Constantinopolitan Creed. The pneumatological emendation of the Nicene faith followed the example of Basil by limiting itself to biblical words and phrases. The Spirit is confessed to be the "Lord" and "Life-giver," the one "who with the Father and the Son is together worshiped and together glorified." Besides the reaffirmation of Nicene orthodoxy, this statement made possible a full Trinitarian doctrine for the East.

C. A. BLAISING

See also APOLLINARIANISM; ARIANISM; HOMOOUSION; NICEA, COUNCIL OF; MONARCHIANISM.

Consubstantiation. See LORD'S SUPPER, VIEWS OF.

Consummation of the Age. See ESCHATOLOGY.

Contextualization of Theology. An Oct. 1970, circular letter from Nikos A. Nissiotis (then director of the Ecumenical Institute of the World Council of Churches) regarding the imminent 1971 consultation on "Dogmatic or Contextual Theology" in Switzerland emphasized the need for a new point of departure in theologizing. His concern, reinforced by the consultation, was to give preference to a "contextual or experiential" theology that grows out of the contemporary historical scene and thought, in contrast to systematic or dogmatic theologies aimed at discovering the biblical tradition and confessional statements based on the biblical text.

Roots of contextualized theology are found in the Christian-Marxist dialogue, the impetus given to the secularization of the theology by Vatican II, social encyclicals dealing with the *aggiornamento* (modernization) of the church in the world, the economic and sociopolitical analyses of Latin America at the Medellín meeting of CELAM (1968), and the Uppsala General Assembly of the WCC (1968). Precursors of the kind of contextualization advocated in the conciliar movement include the theology of hope, the theology of liberation, and black theology. The aegis of theologizing has been located in praxis within the world rather than in the exegesis of Scripture. And mission has become a matter of discerning what God is doing in the contemporary world and participating in that task rather than participating in a missionary task delineated in the NT.

More conservative scholars saw potential gains in contextualized theology but also new digressions from the biblical mandate. The International Congress on World Evangelization in Lausanne (1972) gave some attention to contextualization. Brought together by the Lausanne Continuation Committee, a group of mostly conservative theologians and missiologists meeting at Willowbank, Bermuda (1974), studied the issues growing out of the developing contextualization theory and practice. It is understood, for example, that theologies developed in the Third World will give special attention to such issues as demonism, sorcery, and ancestor veneration. Yet theological reflection without epistemological control and revelatory givens can lay no valid claim to being Christian. Western and Third World theologians who base their teachings on Scripture may indeed develop different theologies, but these theologies will be complementary, not contradictory. Moreover, these Western and Third World theologians will be in a position to encourage one another to a richer understanding of the person, purpose, and provision of God and to challenge one another to faithfulness to his Word.

While adaptation to cultural contexts and existential situations is incumbent upon theology and missiology, adherence to the Scriptures must be viewed as basic to all authentic theologizing and missionizing.

D. J. HESSELGRAVE

Contingency Argument for God. See GOD, ARGUMENTS FOR THE EXISTENCE OF.

Contingent Being. See BEING.

Continuous Creation. See CREATION, DOCTRINE OF.

Contribution, Gift of. See SPIRITUAL GIFTS.

Contrition. Sorrow for sin because it is displeasing to God. A person may repent of sin out of fear of punishment or because he has offended a just and holy God. The term "attrition" is used in Roman Catholic theology (from the Middle Ages) to denote the first, and "contrition" the second. Attrition does not necessarily understand sin as evil but seeks to avoid unpleasant consequences to oneself. Such an attitude does not constitute penitence in the true sense (cf. 2 Cor. 7:9–10). Contrition is the proper attitude, and indicates real love of God and desire to please him.

W. C. G. PROCTOR

See also PENITENCE; REPENTANCE.

Conversion. (Heb. *šûb*, "to turn back," "return"; *niham*, "to regret"; Gk. *epistrephō*, "to turn towards"; *metanoeō*, "to renew mind and heart") An integral concept in the Bible. A key passage in the Synoptic Gospels is Matt. 18:3, in the KJV translated: "Except ye be converted, and become as little children, ye shall not enter into the kingdom of heaven." The NEB begins, "Unless you turn round. . . ."

In Reformation theology conversion was understood as the human response to regeneration, the infusion of new life into the soul. Conversion was held to be dependent on grace, an act empowered and directed. Calvinism was inclined to portray this grace as irresistible, with the result that conversion became a virtually spontaneous turning of the one who was elected to receive grace. Martin Luther believed conversion could be aborted and that one could fall away. Both John Calvin and Luther envisaged the whole Christian life as a life of conversion. Later evangelicals associated conversion with a crisis experience that inaugurates the new life in Christ. In some circles it was regarded as an event involving total transformation. In the Holiness Movement conversion was seen as the initiation of Christian life and entire sanctification as the fulfillment of Christian life.

Conversion is both an event and a process. It signifies the action of the Holy Spirit upon us, by which we are moved to respond to Jesus Christ in faith. It includes the continuing work of the Holy Spirit within us, purifying us and remolding us in the image of Christ. This work of purification is accomplished as we repent and cling to Christ anew. Conversion is personal and social. It basically connotes a change in our relationship with God as well as in our attitudes toward others. It entails accepting Christ as Savior from sin and also as Lord of all of life. Conversion is also the beginning of a Christian's ascent to perfection. Such perfection is the goal of continuing and maintaining a conversion that is never completed in this life. Evangelical theology contends that Christians progress toward perfection, but we never attain it as a realized goal. Even the converted need to repent, turn again to Christ, and be cleansed anew (cf. Ps. 51:10–12; Luke 17:3–4; 22:32; Rom. 13:14; Eph. 4:22–24; Rev. 2:4–5, 16; 3:19).

D. G. Bloesch

See also Faith; Grace; Justification; Regeneration; Salvation; Sanctification.

Cooperation, Ecclesiastical. See Ecumenism.

Correction. See Discipline.

Cosmological Argument for God. See God, Arguments for the Existence of.

Councils, Church. Conferences called by church leaders to guide the church. The first council took place in Jerusalem (ca. A.D. 50) to oppose Judaizing efforts (Acts 15). Its findings were normative for the entire early church. However, it must be distinguished from succeeding councils in that it had apostolic leadership.

A council may be either ecumenical and thus represent the entire church, or it may be local, having regional or local representation. For example, 12 regional councils met to discuss the Arian heresy between the ecumenical councils of Nicea in 325 and Constantinople in 381. Historically, councils have been called by emperors, popes, and bishops. The first seven councils were convoked in the East by emperors and were thus typical of Eastern caesaropapism (state over church). In the Western Church the pope typically convened councils, except for a time during the Great Schism (1378–1417) when the plurality of bishops both convened councils and deposed popes (conciliarism). Indeed, the Council of Constance in 1415 proclaimed the superiority of general councils over the pope. But their supremacy was short-lived. By 1500 the pontiff had overcome the conciliar movement and was again convening councils.

The most significant of the early councils were Nicea (325) and Chalcedon (451). The former settled the issue of the nature of Christ as God, whereas the latter dealt with the twofold natures of Christ and their unity. Subsequent councils found it necessary to consolidate the gains of Chalcedon and to oppose further christological errors. These councils terminated with the Third Council of Constantinople in 680–81. In the West the Second Synod of Orange (529) was significant in combating semi-Pelagianism and setting forth the gracious character of salvation apart from works. Although it was not officially ecumenical, its declarations prevailed *de jure* but not *de facto* in the Roman Catholic Church down to the Reformation era.

The Council of Trent, 1545–63, should be viewed as both a counter to the Protestant Reformation and an establishing of key tenets of Roman Catholicism. Vatican Council I (1869–70) made official what had long been practiced—

papal infallibility. Vatican Council II (1962–65) was attended by both traditional and radical Roman Catholics. Its more open stance toward the Bible is hailed by most Protestants as salutary. Thus the term used at Vatican II, *aggiornamento* (modernization), has to some extent been realized in post-Vatican II Roman Catholicism.

J. H. HALL

See also ECUMENICAL COUNCILS; CONSTANTINOPLE, COUNCIL OF; CHALCEDON, COUNCIL OF; EPHESUS, COUNCIL OF; NICEA, COUNCIL OF; TRENT, COUNCIL OF; VATICAN COUNCIL I; VATICAN COUNCIL II.

Counter-Reformation. The Roman Catholic revival of the 16th century in reaction to the Protestant challenge. The movement is also labeled the Catholic Reformation and the Catholic renaissance, since elements of Catholic reform and revival predated the Protestant Reformation and were, like Protestantism, a response to the widespread aspiration for religious regeneration pervading late 15th-century Europe. It is now understood that the Protestant and Catholic reformations had many similarities and drew on a common past: the revival of preaching exemplified in such pre-Reformation preachers as Jan Hus, Bernardino of Siena, and Savonarola; Christ-centered, practical mysticism of the *Devotio Moderna*, and the movement for ecclesiastical reform headed by Cardinal Ximénez de Cisneros in Spain and reforming bishops in France and Germany.

Two of the three great instruments of the Counter-Reformation stemmed from Spain, the Society of Jesus and the Inquisition. The third was the Council of Trent (1545) after constant pressure from the Emperor Charles V. The corrupt hierarchy of the Roman Catholic Church was dramatically reformed in the wake of the Council of Trent. Dioceses mushroomed in areas where there was felt to be a particular Protestant threat. Bishops carried out frequent visitations of their dioceses and established seminaries for the training of clergy. The number of church buildings and clergy increased markedly. Some Protestant gains were reversed under the direction of such theologians as Robert Bellarmine (1542–1621) and Peter Canisius (1521–97). The Counter-Reformation in general, and the Council of Trent in particular, strengthened the position of the pope and the forces of clericalism and authoritarianism, but it also genuinely supplemented the church's spiritual foundations.

F. S. PIGGIN

See also REFORMATION, PROTESTANT; SOCIETY OF JESUS, THE; TRENT, COUNCIL OF.

Covenant. (Heb. *bĕrît*; Gk. *diathēkē*) A compact or agreement binding two parties. In relations between God and humanity it denotes a gracious undertaking entered into by God with himself for the benefit and blessing of human beings, and involves those who by faith receive the promises and commit themselves to obligations the covenant involves.

In the OT. The OT covenant is unalterable and permanently binding. It constituted a divine announcement of God's will to extend the benefits of his grace to individuals or nations. The human part was to personally commit to God as an absolute obligation. The characteristic statement of this relationship occurs in the formula "I will be their God and they shall be my people" (cf. Jer. 11:4; 24:7; 30:22; 32:38; Ezek. 11:20; 14:11; 36:28; 37:23; Zech. 8:8). This signifies that God unreservedly gives himself to his people and that they in turn give themselves to him and belong to him. Thus they are his "peculiar treasure" (*sĕgullâ*—Exod. 19:5; Deut. 7:6; 14:2; 26:18; Ps. 135:4; Mal. 3:17). His motive in adopting them as his covenant children is lovingkindness or "covenant-love" (*ḥesed*), a term with which *bĕrît* is often associated (cf. Deut. 7:9; 1 Kings 8:23; Dan. 9:4).

This triumphantly enduring quality of the covenant of grace is especially set forth by the prophets in the form of the "new covenant." In the classic passage on this theme (Jer. 31:31–37) the earliest phase of the covenant effected at Sinai is shown to have been temporary and provisional because of the flagrant violation of it by the Israelite nation as a whole, and because of their failure to know or acknowledge God as their personal Lord and Savior. But there is a time coming when God will put his holy law into human hearts so that their cordial inclination and desire will be to live according to his holy standard. Moreover he shall beget within them a sense of adoption, so that they shall have a personal knowledge and love of him that will not require artificial human teaching. The carrying out of this redeeming purpose is as sure as the continued existence of sun, moon, and stars, or even of the foundations of heaven itself.

In the NT. Since the ordinary Greek word for "contract" or "compact" (*synthēkē*) implied equality on the part of the contracting parties, the Greek-speaking Jews preferred *diathēkē* (coming from *diatithemai*, "to make a disposition of one's own property") in the sense of a unilateral enactment. In secular Greek this word usually meant "will" or "testament," but even classical authors like Aristophanes (*Birds* 439) occasionally used it of a covenant wherein one of the two parties had an overwhelming superiority over the other and could dictate his own terms. Hence NT terminology signifies more specifically than the OT an arrangement made by one party with plenary power, which the other party may accept or reject but cannot alter.

G. L. ARCHER, JR.

See also COVENANT, THE NEW; COVENANT THEOLOGY.

Covenant, The New. Jeremiah first speaks of a new covenant in his prophecy of a great future work of God's salvation (Jer. 31:31–34). Jeremiah's new covenant prophecy has strong affinities with other prophetic texts that depict the triumph and consummation of the kingdom of God in the world (cf. Isa. 11:6–9; 54:11–15; 59:20–21; Jer. 32:36–41; 33:14–26; Ezek. 16:59–63). The term is found six times in the NT (1 Cor. 11:25; 2 Cor. 3:6; Heb. 8:8; 9:15; 12:24; and the disputed reading in Luke 22:20) though the idea of a new covenant is present elsewhere (cf. Rom. 11:27; Gal. 4:21–31). In 2 Cor. 3:4–18 the new covenant is contrasted with the old covenant in the context of Paul's contrasting his ministry with that of Moses. By the time of Tertullian, "Old Covenant" (*Vetus Testamentum*) and "New Covenant" (*Novum Testamentum*) designate the pre-Christian and Christian Scriptures, respectively. In Christian theology generally the new covenant has been identified with the Christian dispensation, the religio-historical economy introduced by Christ and the apostles. Accordingly, it is the fulfillment of the promises of the old covenant and is better by degrees than that former covenant by virtue of its clearer view of Christ and redemption, its richer experience of the Holy Spirit, and by the greater liberty which it grants to believers.

R. S. RAYBURN

See also COVENANT.

Covenant of Grace. See COVENANT THEOLOGY.

Covenant of Redemption. See COVENANT THEOLOGY.

Covenant of Works. See COVENANT THEOLOGY.

Covenant Theology. The doctrine of the covenant was one of the theological contributions that came to the church through the Reformation of the 16th century. Undeveloped earlier, it made its appearance in the writings of Ulrich Zwingli (1484–1531) and Johann Bullinger (1504–75), who were driven to the subject by Anabaptists. It passed to Calvin and other Reformers, was further developed by their successors, and played a dominant role in much Reformed theology of the 17th century. It came to be known as "covenant," or "federal," theology. Covenant theology sees the relation of God to humankind as a compact which God established as a reflection of the relationship among the three persons of the Trinity. This emphasis on God's covenantal dealings with the human race tended to soften what seemed a harshness in earlier Reformed theology, with its emphasis on sovereignty and predestination. From Switzerland covenant theology proceeded to Germany, the Netherlands, and the British Isles. Among its early and most influential advocates were, besides Zwingli and Bullinger, Kaspar Olevianus (1536–87) (*Concerning the Nature of the Covenant of Grace Between God and the Elect,* 1585), Johannes Cocceius (1603–69) (*Doctrine of the Covenant and Testaments of God,* 1648), and Witsius (*The Oeconomy of the Covenants,* 1685). It was taken up into the Westminster Confession and came to have an important place in the theologies of Scotland and New England.

The Covenant of Works. Having created man in his own image as a free creature with knowledge, righteousness, and holiness, God entered into covenant with Adam that he might bestow upon him further blessing. Called variously the Edenic covenant, the covenant of nature, the covenant of life, or preferably the covenant of works, this pact consisted of (1) a promise of eternal life upon the condition of perfect obedience through a probationary period; (2) the threat of death upon disobedience; and (3) the sacrament of the tree of life, or, in addition, the sacraments of paradise and the tree of the knowledge of good and evil.

The Covenant of Redemption. In an eternal pact between God the Father and God the Son human salvation was secured. The Father appointed the Son to be the mediator, the Second Adam, whose life would be given for the salvation of the world, and the Son accepted the commission, promising that he would do the work which the Father had given him to do and fulfill all righteousness by obeying the law of God.

The Covenant of Grace. This covenant has been made by God with humankind, offering life and salvation through Christ to all who believe. Inasmuch as none can believe without the special grace of God, it is more exact to say that the covenant of grace is made by God with elect believers. Jesus said that all the Father had given him would come to him and that those who come would be accepted (John 6:37). Herein is seen the close relation between the covenant of grace and the covenant of redemption, with the former resting on the latter.

Although the covenant of grace includes various dispensations of history, it is essentially one. From the promise in the garden (Gen. 3:15), through the covenant made with Noah (Gen. 6–9), to the covenant established with Abraham, there is abundant evidence of God's grace. With Abraham a new beginning is made, which the Sinaitic covenant implements and strengthens. At Sinai the covenant assumes a national form stressing the law of God. This is not intended to alter the gracious character of the covenant, however (Gal. 3:17–18), but it is to train Israel until the time when God himself would appear in its midst. In Jesus the new form of the covenant that had been promised by the prophets is manifest, and the temporary nature of the old form of the covenant disappears (Jer. 31:31–34; Heb. 8). While there is unity and continuity in the covenant of grace throughout history, the coming of Christ and the subsequent gift of the Holy Spirit have brought rich gifts unknown in an earlier age. These are a foretaste of future blessedness (Rev. 21:1).

M. E. OSTERHAVEN

See also COVENANT.

Creation, Doctrine of. The opening verse of the Bible and the opening sentence of the Apostles' Creed confess God as Creator. In Scripture the theme of God as Creator of the "heavens and the earth" (Gen. 1:1) is prominent in both OT (Isa. 40:28; 42:5; 45:18) and NT (Mark 13:19; Rev. 10:6). God is the Creator of humans (Gen. 1:27; 5:2; Isa. 45:12; Mal. 2:10; Mark 10:6), of Israel (Isa. 43:15), of "all things" (Eph. 3:9; Col. 1:16; Rev. 4:11). Creation occurs by God's word (Gen. 1:3); when he speaks, all comes into being (Pss. 33:9; 148:5). Creation is the work of the triune God (John 1; Heb. 11:3).

Theologically, this doctrine of creation as an act of the triune God is of great importance. The church's three creedal statements joined creation and redemption in one living God. The Apostles' Creed added the phrase "maker of heaven and earth" to the old Roman Creed and recognized the Creator as the Father of Jesus Christ. The Nicene Trinitarian statement (A.D. 325) spoke of the "maker of all things visible and invisible" who is "of the same substance" (*homoousios*) as the Son. The Council of Chalcedon (A.D. 451), after affirming earlier creeds that identified God as ruler and maker of heaven and earth, confessed Jesus Christ as "very God and very man," thus uniting Creator and Redeemer.

Theology of Creation. Since God as Creator explains the existence of the world and humanity, the activity of creation establishes our deepest, most essential relation to God as Creator and thus Lord. The doctrine of God as Creator is perhaps the most basic conception of God. From the affirmation of God as Creator *ex nihilo* a number of points follow. Langdon Gilkey has cited three major dimensions of what this means theologically.

God Is the Source of All That There Is. No other principle or power can be coequal or coeternal with God. No other thing may be worshiped.

Creatures Are Dependent Yet Real and Good. Human freedom and intelligence is a gift which may be used either to affirm or deny the fundamental relationship of existence, dependence on God.

God Creates in Freedom and with Purpose. Creation was a free act of the free God. The act expressed the character of God, which is variously described but which finds its primary focus in love (1 John 4:16), specifically love for the world in Jesus Christ (John 3:16). In creation and sustaining creation, God is working out his ultimate purposes.

Contemporary Thought on Creation. Contemporary conversations between theologians and philosophers and between theologians and scientists have often addressed matters of creation in relation to such diverse issues as time, evolution, origins of the cosmos, the nature of human knowledge, and language about God. T. F. Torrance, in studies of the relation of theology and science, cites three "masterful ideas" developed in the early church from the doctrines of the incarnation and creation *ex nihilo* which have had a powerful and determinative influence on both natural science and theology: (1) *The Rational Unity of the Universe.* God is the ultimate source of order and rationality. (2) *The Contingent Rationality or Intelligibility of the Universe.* There is an intrinsic order in the universe which can be probed and discovered through science. (3) *The Contingent Freedom of the Universe.* God does not need the universe to be, but the universe is completely dependent on God for its origin and continuity. The freedom to explore the universe is given to creatures, and that contingent freedom embraces inexhaustible possibilities of discovery that can lead to the praise and glory of the Creator.

D. K. McKim

See also God, Doctrine of.

Creation, New; Creature, New. See New Creation, New Creature.

Creationism. See Soul.

Creed, Creeds. (from Lat. *credo*, "I believe") The form is active, denoting not just a body of beliefs but confession of faith. It is also individual; creeds may take the plural form of "we believe," but the term comes from the 1st-person singular.

Biblical Basis. Scripture offers rudimentary creedal forms that provide models for later statements. The *Shema* (Deut. 6:4–9) is a creed, and many scholars regard Deut. 26:5–9 as a little credo. In the NT references to "traditions" (2 Thess. 2:15), the "word of the Lord" (Gal. 6:6), and the "preaching" (Rom. 16:25) suggest a common message already formed a focus for faith. Confession of Jesus as Christ (John 1:41), Son of God (Acts 8:37), Lord (Rom. 10:9), and God (John 20:28; Rom. 9:5; Titus 2:13) constitutes an obvious starting point for creedal development.

Creedal Functions. *Baptismal.* A creed offered candidates the opportunity to confess as demanded in Rom. 10:9–10. At first the form of words would vary, but familiar patterns soon began to develop.

Instructional. With a view to the baptismal confession, creeds came to serve as a syllabus for catechetical instruction in Christian doctrine. The level of teaching might vary from simple exposition to the advanced theological presentation of the *Catecheses* of Cyril of Jerusalem.

Doctrinal. The rise of heresies helped to expand the first rudimentary statements into the more developed formulas of later centuries. These modifications gave the creeds a new function as a key to the proper understanding of Scripture (Tertullian) and as tests of orthodoxy for the clergy.

Liturgical. Being used in baptism, creeds had from the very first a liturgical function. It was seen, however, that confession of faith is a constituent of all true worship. This led to the incorporation of the Nicene Creed into the Eucharist.

The Three Creeds. Three creeds from the early church have achieved particular prominence.

Apostles'. In its present form it is known only from about 700 and seems to have come from Gaul or Spain. It came into regular use in the West, and the Reformers gave it their sanction in catechisms, confessions, and liturgies.

Nicene. Despite its name, the Nicene Creed must be distinguished from the creed of Nicea (325). Yet it embodies in altered form, without the anathemas, the christological teaching which Nicea adopted in answer to Arianism. The West on its own added the *filioque* clause ("and from the Son") to the statement on the Holy Spirit, but the East never conceded its orthodoxy or the validity of its mode of insertion. In both East and West this creed became the primary eucharistic confession.

Athanasian. Also known as Quicunque Vult. The creed inaccurately attributed to Athanasius is commonly thought to be a 4th- or 5th-century canticle. As a more direct statement on the Trinity it became a test of the orthodoxy and competence of the clergy in the West at least from the 7th century. The Reformers valued it highly, but the East did not recognize it, and in general its catechetical and liturgical usefulness has been limited.

Conclusion. The dangers of creed-making are obvious. Creeds can become formal, complex, and abstract. They can be almost illimitably expanded. They can be superimposed on Scripture. Properly handled, however, they facilitate public confession, form a succinct basis of teaching, safeguard pure doctrine, and constitute an appropriate focus for the church's fellowship in faith.

G. W. BROMILEY

See also APOSTLES' CREED; ATHANASIAN CREED; CONFESSIONS OF FAITH; FILIOQUE; NICEA, COUNCIL OF.

Crisis Theology. See NEO-ORTHODOXY.

Cross, Crucifixion. Execution upon a pole, frame, scaffolding, or a natural tree, exposing the condemned to public derision. In many cases the individual was put to death through some other means and all or a part of the body (usually the head) was displayed. In other circumstances it became the actual means of execution. Because of both the effect of crucifixion upon the body and the lengthy period which usually elapsed before death, it represented the most painful, cruel, and barbaric form of execution. In one form or another it is known to have been practiced by such groups as the Indians, Scythians, Celts, Germani, Britanni, and Taurians, but is most closely associated with the Persians, Carthaginians, Phoenicians, Greeks, and especially the Romans. Some evidence suggests that it may have been associated with religious human sacrifice as well as punishment.

The disgrace associated with crucifixion in the ancient world can hardly be overstated. It was usually reserved for slaves, criminals of the worst sort from the lowest levels of society, military deserters, and traitors. Rarely were Roman citizens, no matter what their crime, crucified. Among the Jews it carried the additional stigma of an understood divine curse (Deut. 21:23). Thus, the idea of a crucified Messiah posed a special problem for Jews (cf. Gal. 3:13; 1 Cor. 1:23).

Significance of the Cross. NT writers assume the historicity of the crucifixion of Jesus and focus their attention upon its significance. In it they understand that Christ endured the ultimate of humiliation and degradation (Phil. 2:6–8). Yet, they affirm, the crucifixion of Jesus, the Messiah (Christ), was the will and act of God, with eternal and cosmic significance. At the simplest level, the crucifixion of Jesus was the means by which God provided salvation, the forgiveness of sins (cf. 1 Cor. 15:3). Christ crucified becomes the summary of the Christian message (1 Cor. 2:2). The cross of Jesus, the beloved Son of God, is the supreme demonstration of the love God has for sinful humanity (cf. John 3:16). In Jesus' death God deals concretely with the sin and guilt which offends his holiness and separates creature from Creator. Because of the cross God becomes both the righteous and just Judge and, at the same time, the one who makes forgiveness available and justifies believers (cf. Rom. 3:26). The condemning legal demands set against man have been "canceled," nailed to the cross (Col. 2:14). The word of the cross is God's word of reconciliation (2 Cor. 5:19). The cross is also the symbol of discipleship: "If anyone would come after me, he must deny himself and take up his cross and follow me" (Mark 8:34; cf. Matt. 10:38; Luke 14:27).

J. J. SCOTT, JR.

Crucifixion. See CROSS, CRUCIFIXION.

Cults. (1) The term "cult" was originally used by Ernst Troeltsch in *The Social Teaching of the Christian Churches* (1912), to classify religious groups as "church," "sect," and "cult." For Troeltsch the cult represents a mystical or spiritual religion that appeals to intellectuals and the educated classes. At the heart of a cult is a spirituality which seeks to enliven a dead orthodoxy. Thus for Troeltsch the early Martin Luther, many Puritans, and pietism are examples of cultic religion. In a similar sense students of comparative religion study the "cultic" practice of ancient Israel, the early church, any other group.

(2) The term is more generally used by evangelicals of groups whose teachings are so heretical as to remain outside of historic Christianity. In Jan van Baalen's *The Chaos of Cults* (1938), van Baalen expounds the beliefs and critiques theosophy, Christian Science, Mormonism, and Jehovah's Witnesses as "cults." Many similar works have since appeared.

(3) In a similar, even more derogatory sense, the word has been picked up by secularists in various societies as a label for Christians and especially Christians who evangelize. In anticonversion laws conversion to cults involves any form of change in lifestyle brought about by a religious conversion.

While a relatively new term, "cult" is such a vague, overused, and negative idea as to virtually be worthless in communication. In outreach to members of heretical groups the expression "new religious movements" has become preferred. To express Christian opposition to their teachings on theological grounds the ancient idea of "heretic" or a new expression, "spiritual counterfeits," may be more helpful. Such a procedure would move the debate from psychological theories that can be used by secularists against Christianity to the arena of theological discussion and religious argument.

I. HEXHAM

See also HERESY; SECT, SECTARIANISM.

Culture and Christianity. See CHRISTIANITY AND CULTURE.

Curate. See CHURCH OFFICERS.

Curse. (Heb. n. *qĕlālâ, ḥāram*; v. *'ārar*; Gk. n. *katara, anathema*; v. *kataraomai*) (1) An imprecation or express wish for evil. If directed against God, it is blasphemy (Job 1:5, 11; 2:5, 9). Curses in OT times were considered to have an innate power. One regular use of the word is in contrast to blessing. Before the people of Israel entered Canaan they were given the choice of obedience and God's blessing or disobedience and the curse. The curse was placed symbolically on Mount Ebal, while the blessings were attached to Mount Gerizim (Deut. 27:13–26). The rarity of the curse in the NT is in keeping with the spirit of the new age (Matt. 21:19–22.; Mark 11:12–21). The curse has a definite christological reference. Paul states that Christ became a curse for us (Gal. 3:13) by bearing the penalty of the law (Deut. 21:23).

(2) An act of dedicating or devoting to God. Things or persons thus devoted could not be used for private purposes (Lev. 27:28). In time of war a city was devoted to the Lord. All men were killed (Deut. 20:12–14); the site of the city itself might be cursed (Josh. 6:26); children and virgins might be spared (Deut. 21:11–12); all objects of pagan religion destroyed (Deut. 7:25); other metals might be devoted to worship (Josh. 6:24); and whatever was devoted to destruction was under God's ban (Josh. 6:18; 7; 1 Kings 16:34). The Canaanites as a nation were set under such a curse (Josh. 2:10; 6:17). The curse indicates a thing devoted to an exclusively sacred use. It amounts to a vow. Compare the consecration of John the Baptist (Luke 1:15), and the misuse of the vow among the people of Israel by an evasion instituted by their religious leaders (Mark 7:10–12).

(3) In NT usage the most extreme excommunication involved anathema, a curse of eternal condemnation (John 9:22; 12:42; 16:2; Matt. 18:17; Gal. 1:8–9).

C. L. FEINBERG

Cyprian (ca. 200–258). North African church leader, martyr. Caecilius Cyprianus was born to a wealthy and highly cultured pagan family. After distinguishing himself as a master of rhetoric, he was converted to Christianity and renounced his wealth and pagan culture. He was quickly raised through the presbyterate to become bishop of Carthage in about 248. He had an influential pastoral ministry and produced various writings before his martyrdom in 258. In his handling of certain pastoral and schismatic problems his views decisively shaped ecclesiology through the Middle Ages.

In dealing with the Novatian schism over lapsed Christians Cyprian advocated degrees of penance. He also contended that the unity of the church was episcopal, not theological. Oneness was in the unity of the college of bishops, and leaving the bishops meant leaving the church. There are two versions of Cyprian's argument in *On the Unity of the Church*, both apparently genuinely Cyprian. The papal version is that he argues for the primacy of Peter, the other that he contends for coequality among all apostles and therefore all bishops. Cyprian added: "He is not a Christian who is not in Christ's church"; "He cannot have God for his father who has not the church for his mother," and "There is no salvation outside the church."

C. A. Blaising

See also Donatism; Novatian Schism.

Cyril of Alexandria (d. 444). Patriarch of Alexandria (412–44). Cyril's patriarchate was racked by controversy with Nestorius regarding the person of Christ. It reached a climax with the Council of Ephesus in 431, an eruption of deep-seated theological differences between Antioch and Alexandria. In 428 Cyril accused Nestorius, patriarch of Constantinople, of heresy because he insisted that Mary could be called *Christotokos* but not *Theotokos*. Cyril was determined to recognize the unity of Christ which he feared Nestorius compromised in distinguishing between the divine and human natures.

The Roman Synod of 430 appointed Cyril as representative to ask Nestorius to recant. Ensuing correspondence between the two became increasingly intense, including reciprocal anathemas. The controversy stirred up such troubles that a general council was called by imperial order to settle the matter. When the council met Cyril quickly convened the body and condemned and deposed Nestorius before Syrian delegates sympathetic to Nestorius could arrive. The action was reversed, but Nestorius was ultimately exiled. A Formula of Union was eventually agreed upon which affirmed a "hypostatic union" in which the humanity and divinity of Christ were seen as two distinct, inseparable natures. Cyril abided by the compromise but retained views which opened the way for the monophysite position to predominate in Alexandrian theology after his death.

L. G. Whitlock, Jr.

See also Adoptionism; Alexandrian Theology; Antiochene Theology; Ephesus, Council of; Hypostatic Union; Nestorius, Nestorianism.

Dd

Damnation. See JUDGMENT; HELL.

Darby, John Nelson (1800–1882). English dispensationalist leader of the separatist Plymouth Brethren (Darbyite) movement. His ideas pervaded late 19th-century millenarianism in England and America and contributed to American fundamentalism.

Leaving the Anglican Church in Ireland, he joined the Brethren movement. Under his forceful leadership Brethren groups grew rapidly. After 1840 sharp divisions between Darby and other Brethren teachers erupted over increasingly narrow theological and ecclesiastical questions. As a result Darby became the leader of the Exclusive group after a bitter controversy with B. W. Newton.

Darby popularized dispensationalism and proselytized converts to Brethrenism in travels to Europe, New Zealand, Canada, and the U.S. between 1862 and 1877. His views gained gradual acceptance, as his basic assumptions of verbal inspiration of Scripture, human depravity, and the sovereignty of God's grace were seemingly compatible with traditional Calvinism. His eschatological views were propagated through a series of prophecy conferences, such as the Niagara Bible Conference, an evangelical fellowship which met annually from 1883 to 1897.

W. A. HOFFECKER

See also DISPENSATION, DISPENSATIONALISM; FUNDAMENTALISM; NIAGARA CONFERENCES; TRIBULATION.

"Dark Night of the Soul." A period of apparent spiritual aridity, named from the title of a book by John of the Cross. The contemplative life is often at first a life of great spiritual experiences. Conversion is exciting as the works of evil are stripped away and the person experiences God's power in physical provision and spiritual experience (from visions to the simple perception of God's love and fellowship). Growth in spiritual knowledge and insight is perceptible. Then comes a period when God seems distant or even absent. One who had been experiencing great spiritual fervor now experiences nothing. The person feels utterly sinful, unworthy, and unfit for God's presence. This period was described in the older literature as aridity, or dryness in the soul. John of the Cross calls it "the dark night of the soul." The experience can bring maturity, self-abandonment, and purification.

P. H. DAVIDS

See also JOHN OF THE CROSS; MYSTICISM.

Day of Atonement. See ATONEMENT, DAY OF.

Day of Christ, God, the Lord. A future, anticipated divine visitation of judgment or restoration. Semitic thought often designates events of importance with the term "day." These could be decisive events in Israel's history (the day of Jerusalem's destruction, Ps. 137:7) or random events which took on symbolic value (the day of trouble, Ps. 27:5). Among Israel's prophets the term often took on an eschatological tenor, describing a future climactic day of judgment (Isa. 2:12). This day of the Lord was anticipated by Israel as a future day of

Yahweh's visitation. But as the earliest reference in Amos (5:18–20) makes clear, this visitation would not reaffirm Israel's hopes. Jerusalem would be destroyed (Amos 2:5) and foreign powers would raze Israel (3:9–11). Other prophets confirmed this same picture (Isa. 2:12; Zech. 14:1). Joel writes that "the day of the Lord is near; it will come like destruction from the Almighty" (1:15, NIV). Zephaniah in particular gives this theme increased attention when he describes the coming catastrophe (1:7, 14) and employs images descriptive of an impending battle (1:10, 16; 2:5–15).

Alongside this desperate outlook, however, another prophetic word is evident. The prophets not only view historical events as ushering in the day of the Lord's visitation, but they look to an ultimate eschatological event. Even for Amos this will be a day of universal judgment (8:8–9; 9:5) when at last salvation and genuine hope will come to Israel: "In that day I will restore David's fallen tent. I will repair its broken places, restore its ruins, and build it as it used to be" (Amos 9:11 NIV; see Zeph. 3:9–20). Therefore this "day" is both near and far, both historical and eschatological for Israel. It may be a divine visitation within history as well as a final visitation that climaxes history.

The NT maintains this expectation but adds that the second coming of Jesus Christ (or the parousia) will hallmark the day of the Lord. It will be a day of revealing (1 Cor. 1:8; 5:5; cf. 2 Thess. 2:2) and thus "the day of the Lord Jesus" (2 Cor. 1:14) or simply "the day of Christ" (Phil. 1:10; 2:16). It will be a day of surprise (1 Thess. 5:2; 2 Pet. 3:10), ushering in a climactic battle (Rev. 16:14) and universal judgment (2 Pet. 3:12). This surprising climactic denouement to history parallels the eschatological Son of man sayings in the Gospels ("For the Son of Man in his day will be like the lightning, which flashes and lights up the sky from one end to the other" Luke 17:24 NIV).

The most important development in NT eschatology is the early Christian view that the eschatological era had been inaugurated with the coming of Christ and the Spirit. Thus in Acts 2, Peter can cite Joel 2 and interpret the experiences of Pentecost in light of eschatological fulfillment. This parallels the OT notion of a special divine visitation within history. But still, while the promise may be partially realized, NT writers are clear that its fulfillment is future. Thus while the church has already acquired some benefits of the day of the Lord, it still awaits a thoroughgoing future bestowal at the second coming of Christ.

G. M. Burge

See also Eschatology; Last Day, Days; Realized Eschatology; Second Coming of Christ.

Days, Last. See Last Day, Days.

Deacon, Deaconess. (Gk. *diakoneō,* "to serve"; *diakonia,* "service"; *diakonos,* "server") While the office of elder was adopted from the Jewish synagogue, the early church instituted something new with an order of deacons. The word group surrounding *diakoneō* initially referred to a waiter at a meal (John 2:5, 9). Christians are to be known as servants (*diakonoi*) of Christ (John 12:26), who himself was a *diakonos* (Rom. 15:8; Gal. 2:17) but directed each of us to serve in a similar fashion (Mark 9:35; 10:43; cf. 2 Cor. 3:6; 11:23; Col. 1:7).

The beginnings of a formal diaconate, or formal office of deacons, may be traced to Acts 6. A problem in distribution of aid led to the appointment of seven leaders who would free the apostles from "waiting on tables." The body elected seven, who were ordained by the apostles. From Jerusalem the diaconate spread to the Gentile churches. Phil. 1:1 lists the deacons alongside the bishops in Paul's greeting and suggests two adjacent offices. In 1 Tim. 3:8–13 there is a substantial paragraph devoted to the role of the deacon. In the patristic era the office was soon formalized (1 Clem. 42:4; Hermas, *Visions* 3, 5:1; *Similitudes* 9, 26:2; and Ignatius, *Eph.* 2:1; *Mag.* 6:1; 13:1; *Trall.* 2:3; 3:1; 7:2; *Pol.* 6:1).

It is certain that women served actively as deacons. This is clear not only in Rom. 16:1, where the deaconess Phoebe is commended, but in 1 Tim. 3:11, where an order of women deacons (*gynaikas hosautos*) may be in view. A parallel development is found in 1 Tim. 5:3–16, where widows were recognized for their service. The patristic church organized an independent order of deaconesses (Syriac Didascalia) from the 4th century.

G. M. BURGE

See also CHURCH, AUTHORITY IN; CHURCH OFFICERS; MAJOR ORDERS.

Dead, Abode of the. See SHEOL.

Dead, Prayers for the. See PRAYERS FOR THE DEAD.

Dean. See CHURCH OFFICERS.

Death. Death has preoccupied Christian thought for centuries, either in its physical aspects as the cessation of bodily life and how one ought to prepare for it or in its spiritual aspects as separation from God and how it may be overcome. These perspectives developed out of a variety of strands in the biblical literature.

OT and Intertestamental Periods. In the OT death is usually seen as a natural part of human existence: Adam was not seen as created immortal. The goal was to live a long, full life and to die in peace. An early death was a great evil (2 Kings 20:1–11) and indicated God's judgment for sin (Gen. 2–3; Deut. 30:15; Jer. 21:8; Ezek. 18:21–32).

In the intertestamental period the idea that death itself is an evil, first seen in Eccles. 3:19–29, grows under Greek influence and further reflection. Not just premature death, but all death is the result of sin (2 Apoc. Bar. 54:19; 2 Esd. 3:7). There is also the growth of the idea that the whole person does not die, but only his body. The soul lives on either to await resurrection (1 Enoch 102) or to enjoy its natural immortality free from the body (Wis. 3:4; 4:1; 4 Macc. 16:13; 17:12).

The NT. In the NT, which focuses on a crucified and resurrected Lord, death is a power dominating the present life of the individual, not just something that happens at the end of life. People live in separation from God, a spiritual death; estrangement from God is the common factor in all natural human life (life according to the flesh, Rom. 8:6; 1 John 3:14). Sin and its resulting death lives within the person despite God's law (Rom. 7:9; 1 Cor. 15:56; James 1:15). The archrebel Satan is the lord of death (Heb. 2:14); indeed death itself may be seen as a demonic power (1 Cor. 15:26–27; Rev. 6:8; 20:13–14).

The good news in the NT is that Christ who did not need to die (since he was sinless) entered into death (1 Cor. 5:7; Phil. 2:8; 1 Pet. 3:18), dying "for us" (Mark 10:45; Rom. 5:6; 1 Thess. 5:10; Heb. 2:9), and conquered the devil and death, ascending with power over them (Heb. 2:14–15; Rev. 1:17–18, the keys of death). Christians are still mortal, so they die physically, but they die "in Christ" (1 Thess. 4:16) or "fall asleep" (John 11:11–14; Acts 7:60; 1 Cor. 7:39; 15:6, 18, 20, 51; 1 Thess. 4:13–15). Physical death is an enemy potentially conquered by Christ, but still undefeated in individual physical experience (Rom. 8:9–11; 1 Cor. 15:26). It cannot separate the Christian from Christ, but rather puts him even closer to Christ (Rom. 8:38–39; 2 Cor. 5:1–10; Phil. 1:20–21), who as the resurrected one will call all believers back to transformed physical life as well as the spiritual life they already enjoy (1 Cor. 15:20; Col. 1:12).

The Church. Thus the death of martyrs could be celebrated and the death of the faithful, while sorrowful, could be spoken of with confidence and joy. Death was not denied nor sorrow suppressed, but death was seen as hopeful, an event in Christ for which one could prepare. This idea produced a literature on holy dying and elaborate descriptions of the deathbeds of holy persons. For the Christian death was an enemy whose sting had been pulled; death could be faced with confidence and hope.

P. H. DAVIDS

See also ABRAHAM'S BOSOM; DEAD, ABODE OF THE; DEATH, THE SECOND; HADES; HELL; INTERMEDIATE STATE; PARADISE; SHEOL.

Death, The Second. (Rev. 2:11; 20:6, 14; 21:8). The "lake of fire" into which are placed at the end of God's judgment all those not found in God's book of life and, finally, death and Hades themselves. The second death has no claim on God's people. The expression presupposes that the first death is physical death at the end of one's life.

D. M. SCHOLER

See also FINAL STATE; HELL; LAKE OF FIRE; LAST JUDGMENT, THE.

Death of Christ. See ATONEMENT; ATONEMENT, THEORIES OF THE; CROSS, CRUCIFIXION.

Death of God Theology. A radical theology movement that flourished in the mid-1960s. It never attracted a large following, did not find a unified expression, and passed from the scene as quickly and dramatically as it had arisen. There is even disagreement as to its major representatives. However, its idea had been incipient in Western philosophy and theology for some time—the suggestion that the reality of a transcendent God at best could not be known and at worst did not exist at all.

The definition of the death of God theology is as varied as those who proclaimed God's demise. Since Friedrich Nietzsche, theologians had occasionally said "God is dead" to express his seeming unreality for an increasing number of people. But the idea of God's death began to have special prominence in 1957 when Gabriel Vahanian published a book entitled *God Is Dead.*

Thomas J. J. Altizer (*The Gospel of Christian Atheism*) said God is dead in that he has ceased to exist as a transcendent, supernatural being. Rather, he has become fully immanent in the world. The result is an essential identity between the human and the divine. For William Hamilton (*God Is Dead*) the death of God describes a common, subjective feeling in humanity that the reality of God and language describing God are meaningless. Nontheistic explanations have been substituted for theistic ones. This trend is irreversible, and everyone must come to terms with the historical-cultural death of God. Paul van Buren (*The Secular Meaning of the Gospel*) is usually associated with death of God theology, although he himself disavowed this connection. In his article "Christian Education *Post Mortem Dei*" he proposes an approach to Christian education that assumes "the death of God" and that "God is gone." The real significance of these writers was that their modern theologies, by giving up the essential elements of Christian belief in God, had logically become antitheologies. When the death of God theologies passed off the scene, the commitment to secularism remained and manifested itself in other forms of secular theology in the late 1960s and 1970s.

S. N. GUNDRY

See also BONHOEFFER, DIETRICH; BULTMANN, RUDOLF; EXISTENTIALISM; SECULARISM, SECULAR HUMANISM; TILLICH, PAUL.

Death Penalty. See CAPITAL PUNISHMENT.

Decalogue, The. See TEN COMMANDMENTS, THE.

Decrees of God. God's comprehensive plan for the world and its history, sovereignly established in eternity. Paul refers to "the plan of him who works out everything in conformity with the purpose of his will" (Eph. 1:11 NIV). The Westminster Shorter Catechism provides this classic definition: "The decrees of God are his eternal purpose, according to the counsel of his will, whereby, for his own glory, he hath foreordained whatsoever comes to pass" (Q.7).

The relation of eternity and time, of divine sovereignty and human responsibility, makes understanding of God's eternal decree difficult. The decree is not eternal in exactly the same sense that God is eternal. The decree results from the free, sovereign will of God; it must be distinguished therefore from the necessary acts of God within the divine Trinity. The decree of God must also be distinguished from its execution in history. For example, the decree to create is not the actual creation. Another important distinction arises when human agents are used in carrying out God's decree. Some decreed events occur by God's direct agency (for example, creation, regeneration, and the comings of Jesus Christ); other decreed events are carried out in history through obedient human agents who live according to God's law, or through sinful, disobedient human action, as in the crucifixion of Jesus Christ.

Scriptural references to God's decree generally relate to historical situations for the purpose of promoting comfort, security, assurance, and trust. According to the psalmist, "The Lord foils the plans of the nations; he thwarts the purposes of the peoples. But the plans of the Lord stand firm forever, the purposes of his heart through all generations" (Ps. 33:10–11, NIV). "Many are the plans in a man's heart, but it is the Lord's purpose that prevails" (Prov. 19:21, NIV). The eternal decrees of God also justify predictive prophecy.

Augustinian, Reformed theology sets the doctrine of God's eternal decrees alongside the doctrines of God's sovereignty and predestination. Pelagian and liberal theology deny this doctrine as inconsistent with human freedom and meaningful history. Semi-Pelagian and Arminian theologies restrict God's decree to foreknowledge of future events and compromise it by way of human initiative and cooperation.

F. H. KLOOSTER

See also ELECT, ELECTION; PREDESTINATION; REPROBATION; SOVEREIGNTY OF GOD; SUPRALAPSARIANISM.

Deep, The. (Heb. *ṣûlă, mĕṣûlâ, tĕhôm*; Gk. *abyssos*) In the OT, most frequently a reference to the sea. The suggestion that *tĕhôm* connotes a mythological water chaos is linguistically difficult. The root *thm* occurs in Ugaritic meaning only "sea." In the NT *abyssos* is translated "the deep" in Luke 8:31, connoting a place of incarceration of demonic spirits (cf. Rev. 9:1–6), and Rom. 10:7 refers to the realm of the dead. The words *bathos* and *bythos* also refer to the sea.

T. E. MCCOMISKEY

See also BOTTOMLESS PIT.

Deism. As distinguished from theism, polytheism, and pantheism, a natural religion or the acceptance of religious knowledge acquired solely by the use of reason. The authority of revelation through God, Scripture, or church teaching is rejected. The basic doctrines of deism are: (1) the belief in a supreme being; (2) the obligation to worship; (3) the obligation of ethical conduct; (4) the need for repentance from sins, and (5) divine rewards and punishments in this life and the next. These five points were stated by Lord Herbert of Cherbury, often called the father of deism.

In England at the beginning of the 18th century this general religious attitude turned more militant, particularly in the works of John Toland, Lord Shaftesbury, Matthew Tindal, Thomas Woolston, and Anthony Collins. The ideal of these deists was a sober natural religion without many of the basic tenets of Christianity. Deism was transmitted to Germany primarily through translations of Shaftesbury's works. Important German deists were Gottfreid Leibnitz, Hermann Reimarus, and Gotthold Lessing. François-Marie Voltaire is generally considered to be the greatest of the French deists. Even though he consistently called himself a theist, Voltaire was in the tradition of the British deists, never attacking the existence of God but always the corruptions of the church. By the end of the 18th century deism had become a dominant religious attitude among intellectual and upper-class Americans.

The rationalism of deism continued into the 20th century as a stress on mechanism—the tendency to explain almost everything by analogy to a machine. So-called higher criticism may also be traced to deism. Although deism is not widely held, its significance has been great.

M. H. MACDONALD

See also ENLIGHTENMENT, THE; KANT, IMMANUEL; LEIBNITZ, GOTTFRIED WILHELM; LESSING, GOTTHOLD EPHRAIM.

Deity of Christ. See CHRISTOLOGY.

Deliverance, Deliverer. (Heb. *yĕšûʿâ*, *tĕšûʿâ*, "safety;" *pĕlêtâ*, "escape;" *môšîaʿ*; *mĕpallēṭ*; *maṣṣîl*; Gk. *rhyomenos*; *bytrōtēs*, "deliverer") The liberation of Israel from Egypt established the type for deliverance. In Israel's history God does not free an individual or group from bondage merely to provide relief from an embarrassing or potentially disastrous situation. He liberates people so that they might be free from their former life to serve him alone. This concept was fundamental to the Sinai covenant, and has been an abiding principle of spirituality ever since. The most prominent deliverer in the OT is God, who enters into a covenant with his people and promises to them a Messiah to bring about the ultimate redemption. The deliverer thus makes for the sinner a way of escape (Ps. 40:17; cf. 1 Cor. 10:13) and intervenes to save his people from their perils (Judg. 2:16; 3:9; Isa. 43:1–2). Those who serve as human agents of deliverance receive their authority and power from God (Isa. 49:3–6).

God delivers his people from a wide variety of troubles and afflictions (see Pss. 33:19; 34:6; 107:6, 13, 19), and promises to liberate even creation from its bondage to decay (Rom. 8:21), reversing the law of entropy. In Matt. 6:13 the heavenly Father delivers the believer "from the evil [one]." Deliverance from sin and the works of the devil is emphasized by Paul more fully in such passages as Acts 16:31; Eph. 2:8; and 1 Thess. 1:10.

R. K. HARRISON

Deluge, The. See FLOOD, THE.

Demiurge. (from Gk. *dēmiourgos*, "craftsman" or "creator" in Heb. 11:10) God's creative activity. Plato and Epictetus employ the term to refer to the craftsmanship of the phenomenal or visible world by the divine. The gnostics, however, used the term in a derogatory sense to refer to the lower deity responsible for the creation of the world after the fall or straying of Sophia in the upper realm of deity. For the gnostics the world is a negative place formed by a negative creator from which escape is necessary.

G. L. BORCHERT

See also GNOSTICISM.

Demon, Demon Possession. The existence and work of supernatural beings subservient to Satan. There are two major theories for the origin of such beings. (1) A multitude of angels fell into sin, prompted by Lucifer's rebellion against God (Matt. 25:41; 2 Pet. 2:4; Rev. 12:7–9). (2) Demons are the unnatural offspring of angels and antediluvian women (Gen. 6:2; Jude 6). These beings sent forth evil spirits from their bodies once they were destroyed in battle or in the flood. The Jewish Apocalyptic work 1 Enoch is a major source for this view (10:11–14; cf. "the watchers," 16:1; 86:1–4). This concept was accepted by the Christian apologist Justin Martyr and even influenced the views of Thomas Aquinas.

Origen developed the concept of a pre-cosmic rebellion, understanding all intelligent creatures (human and angelic) as being created with a free will. The diversity of these creatures' relationship to God is directly related to Lucifer's fall (*De princips* 2.9.6). Thus, demons are those angelic beings who were fully carried away with Satan's apostasy. This became the prevailing Christian view, adopted by, among others, Augustine (*De genesi ad literem* 3.10) and Peter Lombard (*Sentences* 2.6).

The NT consistently speaks of a conflict between two realms, the kingdom of Satan, the prince of this world, and the kingdom of God, which through the incarnation of Jesus Christ has broken into Satan's realm. The NT rests solely within the Hebrew understanding that these beings are of a completely evil nature and are destined to share in the destruction which God has prepared for Satan (Matt. 25:41).

Possession. The majority of references to demonic activity in the NT occur in the Synoptic Gospels and deal with confrontations between Jesus and the demon-possessed. The Synoptic record of Jesus' encounters with demons includes: (1) physical or mental affliction—nakedness, mental anguish, and masochism (Matt. 8:28–33; Mark 5:1–10; Luke 8:26–39), inability to speak (Matt. 9:32; 12:22; Mark 9:17), blindness (Matt. 12:22), and lunacy (Matt. 4:24; 17:15). (2) The demon recognizing and fearing Jesus (Mark 1:24; 5:7; Luke 4:34; 8:28). (3) Jesus' power over the demons is demonstrated, usually by their exorcism through the power of his word (Matt. 4:24; 8:16; Mark 7:30) or by Jesus' permission for them to depart (Matt. 8:32; Mark 5:13; Luke 8:32).

The ability of Jesus and his followers to exercise authority over demons is established as an eschatological sign of the kingdom's presence (Matt. 12:22; Luke 10:17) and is a cause for some of the popularity of Jesus' mission (Luke 4:36). Exorcism, however, is usually associated with Jesus' healing ministry and that of the apostles. A distinction between demon possession and insanity (or other diseases) is implied.

Modern Views. Belief or disbelief in the existence of demons and in Satan himself distinguishes the modern liberal from the fundamental and evangelical traditions. On the liberal side much of what was termed demonic in Scripture is now identified with psychological illnesses that were unknown to the 1st-century mind. Jesus' actions, it is argued, actually amounted only to his accommodation to the contemporary beliefs of the Palestinian peasant and in no way reflected his own opinion as to the cause of individual afflictions.

However, with the increase of interest in, and practice of, occultism, the conservative acceptance of the existence of both Satan and demons appears to be confirmed. Deliverance from demonic subjection involves the confession of an individual's faith in Christ as Savior, the confession and repentance of the occult involvement, and reception of the liberation that can be found in Christ.

S. E. McClelland

See also Occult, The; Satan; Satanism and Witchcraft.

Demythologization. A technical term, usually associated with the interpretive principles of Rudolf Bultmann, and which dates from his lecture published in English as "New Testament and Mythology" (see *Kerygma and Myth*, pp. 1–44). Bultmann's thesis is that contemporary humanity, which depends upon a scientific worldview, cannot accept the mythological worldview of the Bible. Myth for Bultmann means the use of language symbols or images of this world and this life to conceptualize the divine or the otherworldly. Thus, ideas such as God's transcendence or heaven and hell are described in spatial terms that pertain to an ancient three-story *Weltanschauung* (concept of the universe or reality).

Bultmann's concern was not the elimination of myth, as the English word "demythologize" might suggest. Rather, he sought a reinterpretation of the mythological language of the Bible. The cosmological categories of the Bible, for Bultmann, must be reinterpreted in anthropological (human-oriented) or existential (personal) categories. Thus, the fall of Adam is basically a statement of human sinfulness and finitude. The purpose of demythologization, accordingly, is the reinterpretation of the biblical images to provide self-understanding for the scientific mind of the 20th century. Bultmann's goal of reinterpreting the biblical myths was to highlight the nature of faith.

Important to Bultmann's demythologizing thesis is his understanding of history. Unlike English, the German language provided Bultmann with two words for "history." The first, *Historie*, is used to refer to the facts of history. The second, *Geschichte*, implies the meaning or significance of an event. By using these two words it is possible to differentiate between the meaning of an event and an actual fact. Thus, Easter may be a faith event (*Geschichte*) without the resurrection being a fact (*Historie*). A *geschichtliche* event is not unimportant. In fact, for Bultmann it is the basis of existential meaning. Statements which sound like *Historie* in the Bible, however, may have no reference to facticity. Bultmann holds some, such as the empty tomb and the virgin birth, to be mere "legends" which arose in the Christian community to support the "myths" of the resurrection and the incarnation. Both myths are part of the church's larger mythological formula known as "Jesus Christ."

G. L. Borchert

See also Bultmann, Rudolf; Myth; New Hermeneutic, The.

Denney, James (1856–1917). Scottish theologian. In 1897 he became professor of systematic and pastoral theology at Glasgow Divinity College, moving to NT three years later. He served as principal from 1915 to 1917. Chief among his writings are a commentary on Romans, *The Expositor's Greek Testament* (1900), *The Death of Christ* (1902), *The Atonement and the Modern Mind* (1903), *Jesus and the Gospel* (1908), and *The Christian Doctrine of Reconciliation* (1917). His contribution lies in his exposition of the significance of the work of Christ and his defense of the doctrine of the substitutionary atonement. Christ's death on the cross is a revelation, not merely of the love of God, but also of his righteousness. Denney accepted the basic approach of modern biblical criticism (minus its attendant skepticism). In Denney's ideal the evangelists are the theologians and the theologians, evangelists. He had no use for a theology which could not be preached and did not lead men and women to commit themselves unreservedly to the God who has revealed himself in the cross of Calvary.

W. W. Gasque

Denominationalism. Associations of congregations with a common heritage. A true denomination does not claim to be the only legitimate expression of the church. A denominational heritage normally includes doctrinal, experiential or organizational emphases and frequently includes common ethnicity, language, social class, and geographical origin. However, normally these common features come to gain great diversity in time. This often results in wide differences within a denomination, despite organizational unity.

Denominationalism is a comparatively recent phenomenon. The theological distinction between the church visible and invisible, made by John Wycliffe (1329–84) and Jan Hus (1373–1415) and elaborated by the Protestant Reformers, underlies the practice and defense of denominationalism that emerged in the 17th century. The 18th-century revivals associated with John Wesley (1703–91) and George Whitefield (1714–70) greatly encouraged the practice, especially in America, where it became dominant.

In theory denominationalism is sharply contrasted with two much older approaches, catholicism and sectarianism. Catholic or national churches at the period of their greatest growth are almost always supported, or "established," by the civil government, whether imperial or tribal or national. Those in national state churches see themselves as embracing from infancy all Christians within their territories, in contrast with voluntary nature of individual affiliation in a denomination. The Roman Catholic Church in Italy, Spain, and Poland is a prime example; in the U.S. Roman Catholicism is a denomination.

In theory denominationalism is also sharply distinguishable from sectarianism. Each sect sees itself as the only legitimate institutional expression of the followers of Christ. Unlike catholic churches, sects have never embraced more than a small percentage of any population. Besides attracting to its ranks the once clearly distinct catholic churches and some sects, denominationalism has brought forth other institutional responses. These are related to the obvious discrepancy between denominational distinctiveness (or rivalry) and the biblical portrayal of a unity among Christians, a unity observable by the world (John 17:20–23).

One response has been to oppose denominations and urge all Christians to meet simply as churches of Christ, Christian churches, churches of God, disciples, brethren, Bible churches, evangelical churches, and similar inclusive names. Another response has been for local congregations to remain organizationally independent but to engage in cooperative endeavors with other Christian organizations near and far that have a variety of denominational links. The practicality of congregational independency has been enhanced in this century by the growing numbers and kinds of nondenominational specialized ministries. Another response has been to promote more visible unity through ecumenicity. The ecumenical movement has seen many denominations merge, sometimes across family lines, and allowed denominational cooperation at the higher official levels. Generally speaking, the nondenominational specialized ministries are unambiguously evangelical, while the promoters of conciliar ecumenism are not.

Denominational identity is not nearly so accurate a predicter of theological stance, worship style, organizational preference, or social class as it once was. There is no indication that denominations will soon disappear, but neither does it appear that anyone is eager to justify them theologically.

D. G. Tinder

See also Ecumenism.

Deontological Ethics. See Duty.

Depravity, Total. Helplessness before God because of sin. The concept of total depravity does not mean depraved people cannot or do not perform actions that are good in either humankind's or God's sight. But no such action can gain favor with God for salvation. It does not mean fallen humanity has no conscience which judges between good and evil. But that conscience has been affected by the fall so that it is not a reliable guide. Neither does it mean people indulge in every form or sin or in any sin to the greatest extent possible. Positively *total* depravity means that the corruption has extended to all aspects of human nature, corrupting the entire being; and total *depravity* means that because of that corruption there is nothing any person can do to merit saving favor with God. The Bible teaches this concept of total depravity in many places. The Lord recognized good people (Matt. 22:10), yet he labeled his own disciples as evil men (Matt. 7:11). The mind is affected (Rom. 1:28; Eph. 4:18), the conscience is unclean (Heb. 9:14), the heart is deceitful (Jer. 17:9), and by nature humankind is subject to wrath (Eph. 2:3).

C. C. Ryrie

See also Sin.

Descartes, René (1596–1650). French philosopher. Modern philosophy is generally said to have begun with René Descartes, for he was occupied with problems which, in his opinion, would be solved by reason alone. He considered himself a philosopher and mathematician, not a theologian. His fundamental aim was to attain philosophical truth through reason.

Descartes' way of doing philosophy began with a methodological skepticism. Having subjected to doubt all that can be doubted, he arrived at the "simple" and indubitable proposition: *Cogito, ergo sum* (I think, therefore I am). However much I doubt, I must exist. Otherwise I could not doubt. Thus my existence is proven in the act of doubting. The *cogito, ergo sum* is therefore the indubitable truth on which Descartes proposed to found his philosophy. Next Descartes attempted to prove the existence of God. This illustrates an essential feature of his thought and is very significant to later developments in philosophy. So far Descartes had established only that he existed as a thinking being; now he proceeded entirely from the contents of his own consciousness to prove the existence of something else. Descartes proceeded in this "transcendental" way, proving first the existence of God and then working deductively from God's existence to other contingent beings and the "external" world. His method of working from the data of consciousness has remained important to subsequent thinkers, becoming the basis for many later subjectivist and idealist developments.

M. H. MacDonald

Descent into Hell (Hades). In the NT Hades indicates the abode of the dead and is roughly equivalent to Sheol in the OT. Christ's descent into Hades after his crucifixion and death has a solid foundation in both Scripture and the early church. In the NT it is attested in Acts 2:31; Eph. 4:9–10, and 1 Pet. 3:19–20. The passages in Ephesians and 1 Peter seem to indicate the extension of the saving work of reconciliation and redemption to the souls in the nether world of Hades.

In the Gospels reference is made to saints in the tombs (the nether world) who were raised with Jesus (Matt. 27:51–53; John 5:25–29). Jesus also spoke of forgiveness in this world and in the world to come (Matt. 12:31–32). He confidently expected that the gates of Hades could not prevail or hold out against his church (Matt. 16:18). In the Book of Revelation it is said that Christ possesses the keys to the underworld and can open its gates (Rev. 1:18). Similarly, an angel is given the key to the bottomless pit in order to open it (Rev. 9:11; 20:1).

The descent into Hades was not universally accepted as part of the Apostles' Creed until the 8th century, though it is mentioned in local forms of that creed in patristic times. It was almost universally affirmed by the church fathers, including Polycarp, Justin Martyr, Origen, Hermas, Irenaeus, Cyprian, Tertullian, Hippolytus, Clement of Alexandria, Athanasius, Ambrose, and Augustine. The earliest patristic references to the descent occur in the epistles of Ignatius about the beginning of the 2d century. There was disagreement about who benefited from Christ's descent. Many restricted Christ's redemptive activity to the OT patriarchs and prophets (Ignatius of Antioch, Irenaeus, Tertullian). Others held that those who had died before the great flood were redeemed (the Alexandrian theologians and Origen). Some thought that Jesus Christ redeemed all the dead except the very wicked (Melito, Gregory of Nazianzus, Marcion, Ephraem). Cyril of Alexandria spoke of Christ "spoiling all Hades," "emptying the insatiable recesses of Death," and "leaving the devil desolate and alone."

In medieval thought the idea of an intermediate state of Hades was supplanted by heaven, hell, purgatory, the limbo of the patriarchs, and the limbo of unbaptized children. At one point Martin Luther taught with Philip Melanchthon that Christ's preaching in Hades, as referred to in 1 Peter, might have saved the nobler heathen. In a sermon at Torgau in April 1533 Luther spoke of the descent of the whole Christ into hell, where he demolished hell and bound the devil. Luther and Lutheran orthodoxy saw the descent as the first stage in Christ's exaltation. Flacius, Calovius, and many other Lutheran theologians regarded the descent as a damnatory manifestation of judgment against the rejected.

In Reformed theology the descent into Hades has generally been interpreted as a figurative expression of the unutterable sufferings of Christ in his humanity. Following Calvin, it saw the descent as part of the humiliation of Christ, not as the first stage of his exalted state as in Lutheranism.

To believe in the literal descent of Christ into Hades for the purpose of offering redemption does not imply universalism. Most of those who have held to this belief admit the possibility of rejecting the offer of salvation given by Christ. Again, this is not to be confounded with the doctrine of a second chance. What the descent doctrine affirms is the universality of a first chance, an opportunity for salvation for those who have never heard the gospel in its fullness.

D. G. BLOESCH

See also DEAD, ABODE OF THE; HELL; LIMBO; PARADISE; PURGATORY; SPIRITS IN PRISON.

Descent of Man. See MAN, ORIGIN OF.

Desire. The self in its longing to possess and enjoy some object or to fulfil some need or prized goal. God has created the human brain with specialized neural systems that govern desires, including the common drives of hunger, thirst, rest, and sex. Desire is so essential to human experience that some have described the self as being simply the aggregate of its desires.

The NT writers continue the Hebrew tradition that human desires are normal dimensions of the created self (Matt. 13:17; Luke 16:21; Phil. 1:22–23). Jesus not only spoke favorably of human longings, but he felt them himself (Luke 17:22; 22:15). However, both Jesus and Paul affirmed that desires are the primary medium of sin in the fallen world

(Mark 4:19; John 8:44; Eph. 2:3; Titus 2:12). They are good, but they become evil when directed away from others to pure self-interest. These desires "of the flesh" are referred to as "deceitful" (Eph. 4:22), "evil" (Col. 3:5), "hurtful" (1 Tim. 6:9), "worldly" (Titus 2:12), "youthful" (2 Tim. 2:22), and "sinful" (Rom. 13:14).

In redemption Christ's spirit confronts the demonic powers in the arena of the desiring self (Rom. 7:7–8; Eph. 4:22–24; James 1:14–15; 2 Pet. 2:18; 1 John 2:15). The desires of the spirit (love, joy, peace . . .) battle those of the flesh (fornication, idolatry, envy . . .) and the battle itself was won by his death and resurrection (Gal. 5:16–25). Thus, through the grace of God in Christ, the Christian is freed from surrendering to the fallen selfish desires. God takes possession of the person by seizing the desiring self and reshaping those desires into love for the neighbor (Gal. 5:13–15).

D. J. MILLER

See also FLESH.

Despair. Utter hopelessness caused by tragic events or guilt. In Scriptures despair is described in such rich but bitter terms and images as "languish," "wailing," "anguish," "terror," "desolation," "gloom," "dwelling in darkness," "cowering in ashes," "torn to pieces," "wormwood and gall," "teeth grinding on gravel," "depths of the pit," "soul in tumult," "gnashing of teeth," "heavy chains" (see Lamentations). The "woe" cry, one of the more intense expressions of despair in the Bible, was often uttered by the prophets to intensify the hopelessness of those who despise God's justice (Amos 5:18). The future woes will bring such an avalanche of despair that the earth's inhabitants will scream for the mountains to bury them (Rev. 6:15–17; 8:13).

While hopelessness usually characterizes those alienated from God and experience God's wrath, there are moments when the person of faith reaches the boundaries of despair. In the presence of the holy God, Isaiah envisions his own uncleanness and is driven to declare, "Woe is me" (Isa. 6:5). Events can strike with such devastating force that both Job and Jeremiah curse the day of their birth and wish they had died in delivery (Job 3; Jer. 20:14–18). That the Christian often lives near the edge of despair was noted by Augustine and theologically developed by Martin Luther. Luther maintained that despair (*Anfechtung*) is a redeeming force in the sinner. One of the most profound and influential theological discussions of despair is encountered in Søren Kierkegaard's *The Sickness unto Death*. He analyzes in great detail the forms or stages of despair, and argues that underlying all despair is not the felt deprivation of earthly misfortune, but rather a desperation at the loss of the true self and of the eternal God who constitutes the self. Nevertheless, despair is the "passageway to faith" which intensifies to bring one nearer to salvation. Kierkegaard's analysis of despair greatly influenced later writers.

When driven to darkness by unforeseen events the Rom. 8 response for a Christian is, "What is God going to do through me now?" Thus, the believer humbly accepts God's sovereignty with the expectation that circumstances are instruments of God's redemptive change in a fragmented and misery-congested world.

D. J. MILLER

Determinism. See FREEDOM, FREE WILL, AND DETERMINISM.

Devil. See SATAN.

Devil Ransom Theory. See ATONEMENT, THEORIES OF THE.

Devotio Moderna. A devotional movement of the 15th and 16th centuries, chiefly associated with the Brethren of the Common Life; their founder, Gerard

Groote, and their best-known writer, Thomas à Kempis. The *Devotio Moderna* was strongly Augustinian in tone, but without his stress on predestination. The chief marks of the movement included: (1) a focus on devotion to Christ, including meditation on his passion; (2) an emphasis on obeying Christ's commands and therefore on holiness, simplicity, and community; (3) a strong involvement in individual piety and spiritual life; (4) a call to repentance and reform, and (5) elements of nominalism, Christian humanism, and Franciscan asceticism. The lasting value of this movement has been the literature it produced and its influence over Anabaptists and other Reformers.

P. H. DAVIDS

See also BRETHREN OF THE COMMON LIFE; GROOTE, GERARD; THOMAS À KEMPIS.

Dialectical Theology. See NEO-ORTHODOXY.

Dichotomy. (Gk. *dicha*, in two; *temnein*, cut) Division into two parts. In theology it is that view of human nature which holds that people have two fundamental parts to their beings: body and soul. Thus, the actual relationship between body and soul becomes a crucial question.

W. E. WARD

See also MAN, DOCTRINE OF; TRICHOTOMY.

Diocese. (Gk. *diokēsis*, administrative unit) A territorial unit of an episcopal church, which is administered by a bishop. The word was adopted from the territorial divisions of the Roman Empire, but only gradually achieved common usage in the church. It is the basic unit of Roman, Orthodox, Anglican, Old Catholic, and some Lutheran churches.

P. TOON

See also BISHOP; CHURCH OFFICERS.

Dionysius the Pseudo-Areopagite. An influential source from which the Christian Platonism of the early church was transmitted to the Middle Ages. The "pseudo-Dionysius" was mistakenly identified as Dionysius the Areopagite who was converted by Paul (Acts 17:34). Instead, he lived ca. 500, probably in Syria. His writings paved the way for Christian mysticism and became standard theological authorities in the Eastern Church. Their Latin translation by John Scotus Erigena made them widely known in the West. Theologians such as Hugh of St. Victor, Bonaventure, Meister Eckhart, Albertus Magnus, and Thomas Aquinas knew the writings and used them. Major themes of the pseudo-Dionysian writings include the hierarchical pattern of the universe, the soul's intimate union with God, and humanity's eventual deification. These are found in the treatises *Celestial Hierarchy*, *Ecclesiastical Hierarchy*, *Divine Names*, and *Mystical Theology*.

D. K. MCKIM

See also MYSTICISM; NEOPLATONISM.

Discerning of Spirits. See SPIRITUAL GIFTS.

Disciple. See CHRISTIANS, NAMES OF.

Discipline. (Heb. *yāsar, mûsār*; Gk. *paideuō, paideia*) Instruction and correction that improves, molds, strengthens, and perfects character. It is the moral education obtained by the enforcement of obedience through supervision and control. Usually the concept is translated chastening, chastisement, and instruction. The discipline of the believer on the part of the heavenly Father is frequently illustrated by the correction made by the human father (Deut. 8:5; Pss. 6:1; 38:1). The disciple is taught not to despise the chastening of the Almighty (Job 5:17; Prov. 3:11). The value of discipline by a parent is stressed in Prov. 19:18. The OT teaching is amplified in the NT, especially in Heb. 12:3–12, by considering carefully the suffering endured by the Savior. Discipline may be severe but not disastrous (Ps. 118:18; 2 Cor. 6:9), and such chastisement delivers from condemnation with the world (1 Cor. 11:32). The purpose of discipline is the correction, the improvement, the obedience, the faith, and the faithfulness of God's child. The outcome is blessing (Job 5:17; Ps. 94:12) and assurance (Rev. 3:19).

V. R. EDMAN

See also CHURCH DISCIPLINE.

Discipline, Church. See CHURCH DISCIPLINE.

Dispensation, Dispensationalism. The idea that God's administration of the history is accomplished in the unfolding of various dispensations or stewardship arrangements. The world is seen as a household administered by God in connection with several stages of revelation that mark off the different economies in the outworking of his total program. These economies are the dispensations. From God's viewpoint a dispensation is an economy; from the human viewpoint it is a responsibility to the revelation given at the time. Thus a dispensation may be defined as "a distinguishable economy in the outworking of God's program."

Number of Dispensations. There is disagreement among dispensationalists, but at least three dispensations (as commonly understood in dispensationalism) are seen in Paul's writing: one preceding the present time (Col. 1:25–26), the present arrangement (Eph. 3:2), and a future administration (Eph. 1:10). These three require a fourth—one before the law, and a prelaw dispensation would seem to need to be divided into pre- and postfall economies. Thus five administrations are distinguished (at least within a premillennial understanding of Scripture). Seven are counted to include the times after the Noahic flood and after the call of Abraham.

Essential Characteristics. Dispensational theology grows out of a literal hermeneutical principle which does not exclude the use of figures of speech, but insists that behind every figure is a literal meaning. Dispensationalists distinguish God's program for Israel from his program for the church. Thus the church did not begin in the OT but on the day of Pentecost, and the church does not fulfill promises made to Israel in the OT. Most dispensationalists teach that the basis of salvation in every dispensation is the death of Christ and the requirement for salvation is always faith. It is the content of faith that changes.

Origins. Unsystematic dispensational statements can be found from the writings of the church fathers on, but as a system dispensationalism developed in the early part of the 18th century in the writings of Pierre Poiret, John Edwards, and Isaac Watts. John Nelson Darby in the 19th century systematized the concept. His work was the foundation for such later dispensationalists such as James H. Brookes, James M. Gray, C. I. Scofield, and L. S. Chafer.

C. C. RYRIE

See also DARBY, JOHN NELSON; ULTRADISPENSATIONALISM.

Divine Presence. See PRESENCE, DIVINE.

Divinity of Christ. See CHRISTOLOGY.

Divorce. In the early centuries of the Christian era, the evidence points to a rejection of divorce with right of remarriage. By the 6th century the Eastern Church had developed a tradition of allowing divorce with right of remarriage for a variety of causes, and the Eastern Orthodox tradition today has introduced the concept of the "moral death" of a marriage.

The Western Church, however, held that marriage was indissoluble. Augustine, who developed the view of marriage as a sacrament, regarded marriage as a permanent moral obligation which *should not* be dissolved. The medieval church developed a sacramental view that marriage was absolutely indissoluble and *could not* be dissolved. This view still is held by Christians of Catholic traditions. In the Middle Ages a complex set of procedures for dispensation and annulment grew up to evade or overcome the law of indissolubility. Continental Reformers sought a more biblical understanding of the nature of marriage. They rejected the elevation of marriage to the status of sacrament and disagreed with the absolute indissolubility of marriage. They objected to the annulment procedures that brought the divine ideal of permanence into disrepute, believing that the NT allowed divorce with right of remarriage in certain circumstances.

OT Background. Pentateuchal laws governing sexual relationships appear to be framed to preserve the view that a man and a woman are united in a permanent, lifelong, exclusive union. Deut. 24:1–4, the background to some of the material in the Gospels, must be understood in this context. Its legislation is mainly concerned with remarriage. A woman who has been divorced by her husband because of some "indecency" (probably some serious sexual misconduct short of adultery) and who subsequently marries another, who also divorces her, may not return to her first husband. The paragraph recognizes that divorces happen, though it does not command or encourage them. It regulates divorce (the bill of divorcement) to protect the wife. The curious prohibition about subsequent remarriage to the first husband may curb some custom of "lending out" wives for a time.

NT Teaching. In the NT context the OT law was held dear (although it was variously interpreted) and Greco-Roman customs also exercised influence. Mark 10:12 coincides with the Roman permission for women as well as men to initiate divorce, but Matt. 19:9, written for a Jewish readership, does not say this.

In Jesus' day there was a dispute between Pharisaic schools about the interpretation of Deut. 24:1–4 and its permissible grounds for divorce. This lies behind the way Matthew frames the question in 19:3: "Is it lawful for a man to divorce his wife for any and every reason?" (par. Mark 10:2). The Shammaite Pharisees interpreted the Deuteronomic legislation strictly: divorce was permitted only for serious sexual sin. The more liberal Hillelite Pharisees' interpretation permitted divorce for the most trivial of reasons.

Jesus responds to the Pharisees' question about the grounds for divorce by referring back to God's intention in creation (Matt. 19:4; Mark 10:6). In contrast to the usual concentration on the externals of legalities, disciplines, and ceremonies, the biblical emphasis is on covenant relationship. Marriage language is used to describe God's covenant relationship with his people; God's relationship with his people, Christ's with his church, is given as the pattern for marriage. A covenant is a personal relationship within a publicly known structure, based on promises given and accepted. It is to this personal relationship that Gen. 2:24 (see Matt. 19:5) points when it summarizes marriage as "leaving father and mother" (public declaration, the social dimension); "cleaving" (committed covenant love-faithfulness); "becoming one flesh" (a unitary partnership, symbolized by and deepened through sexual union). Jesus sets this verse in the theological context of creation (Gen. 1:27). Marriage answers to God's creation pattern for personal sexual relationship. God's ideal is for a lifelong, exclusive union.

Jesus also brings divorce and remarriage under the heading of adultery

(Matt. 19:9; see 5:27–32). The Pharisees had trivialized divorce by reducing their concerns to the level of grounds for divorce and to the need for a certificate. Jesus says that in the light of God's creation intention every breaking of the commitment of "one flesh," every "putting away" (*apolyō*) of one's partner, is sin. The commandment "You shall not commit adultery" means "You shall not break the one-flesh." Divorce, therefore, is covenant unfaithfulness, a serious and sinful act. It is argued that in circumstances in which sin traps us so that no way open is "good," divorce may be a "lesser-evil" choice. However, taking the divine covenant as guide, divorce is never obligatory; even the sin of sexual unfaithfulness (Hosea's wife) can be an occasion for forgiveness and reconciliation.

Grounds for Divorce. There are exceptive clauses in Matt. 5:32 and 19:9 (except on the ground of *porneia*). There is disagreement about the meaning of this phrase, although it seems most likely to refer to serious sexual sin, including adultery. But why do not Mark, Luke, and Paul refer to it? The best explanation seems to be that Matthew, with his particular concern for his Jewish readership, refers to the civil requirement on a Jewish husband to divorce his wife if she was unfaithful to him. Mark and Luke may have assumed the exception. The exceptive clause points to the sort of concession to which Deut. 24:1–4 also referred. It recognizes that, despite being a sinful departure from God's intention for marriage, divorce may sometimes be permitted in a sinful world. Is divorce permitted only for *porneia*? The Deuteronomic law was framed largely to prevent *cruelty*; Matthew points us to *unlawful sexual misbehavior*; Paul seems to allow divorce as a consequence of *desertion* (1 Cor. 7:15). These may serve as paradigms to clarify the extreme seriousness with which the question of divorce should be approached. They suggest the sort of circumstances which might allow the moral permissibility of divorce as a last resort. Recognition of the persistent "hardness of heart" in a sin-affected society requires recognition of the human impossibility of healing some broken relationships.

D. J. ATKINSON

See also MARRIAGE, THEOLOGY OF; REMARRIAGE; SEPARATION, MARITAL.

Docetism. A theological belief among some in the early church that the sufferings and human aspects of Christ were imaginary or apparent instead of being part of a real incarnation. The basic thesis of such docetics was that if Christ suffered he was not divine and if he was God he could not suffer. Docetism was an integral part of gnosticism. It was a major reason for the Definition of Chalcedon (A.D. 451) explicit teaching that Jesus Christ was "truly God and truly man."

G. L. BORCHERT

See also CHALCEDON, COUNCIL OF; GNOSTICISM.

Dogma. (Gk. *dogma*, "decree, ordinance, decision, or command" in Luke 2:1; Acts 16:4; 17:7; Eph. 2:15; Col. 2:14; Heb. 11:23) In late Greek philosophy *dogma* was also identified as the doctrinal propositions that expressed the official viewpoint of a particular teacher or school. Christian theology came to adopt Greek usage. Basil the Great (ca. 329–79) distinguished between the Christian kerygma and dogma propositions of faith. The church's first sanctioning of "dogmatic" statements was in 325 at the Council of Nicea, where the consubstantiality of the Son with the Father was stated as a confession of faith.

In the Middle Ages the Western Church developed the view of the *depositum fidei* ("deposit of faith"), in which the church was seen as having been entrusted with a certain treasury of truths whose ramifications could be rightfully developed by the church. Eventually, through the Council of Trent (1545–63) and the Vatican Council I (1870), dogmatic pronouncements came to be considered infallible. Protestantism rejected the association of dogma with infallible ecclesiastical pronouncements. In Reformation thought all dogmas must be tested against the revelation of God in Scripture. As Karl Barth observed, "The Word of God is above dogma as the heavens are above the earth" (*Church Dogmatics*, 1.1, p. 306). Dogma has come to mean an expression of doctrinal truth, yet without claims to infallibility.

D. K. McKim

See also Dogmatics; Systematic Theology.

Dogmatics. That branch of theology which attempts to express the beliefs and doctrines (dogmas) of the Christian faith as "the whole counsel of God" (Acts 20:27) in an organized or systematic way. This discipline is now more commonly called "systematic theology" or simply "theology." Dogmatics or systematic theology generally deals with the doctrines of revelation (prolegomena), God (theology proper), humankind (anthropology), the person and work of Jesus Christ (Christology), the Holy Spirit and the application of salvation (soteriology), the church and the means of grace (ecclesiology), and the intermediate state and the second coming of Christ (eschatology). Even when using different terms and organizational arrangements, all systematic theologians deal with these subjects. They are generally concerned with the biblical sources and support of the doctrines of faith, with the history of the development of such doctrines, with contrasting dogmas from other faith communities, and with the views of other theologians. Because this discipline is concerned with the whole as well as with specific doctrines, systematic theology always reflects a particular faith community—Roman Catholic, Eastern Orthodox, Lutheran, Reformed, liberal, neo-orthodox, or existentialist, for example.

F. H. Klooster

See also Dogma; Systematic Theology.

Donatism. A schism in the North African Church originating in the early 4th century and named after Donatus, the second bishop of the movement. Donatists were rigorists who sought to maintain a pure church, free from all infection by those leaders who had compromised in times of persecution. They even rebaptized those who had already received baptism. They were judged to be too intolerant by church leaders, and such theologians as Augustine wrote against them. However, the movement was widespread in North Africa until the invasion by the Arabs in the 7th–8th centuries when it was eliminated along with the Catholic Church.

P. Toon

See also Augustine of Hippo; Cyprian; Tertullian.

Doorkeeper. See Minor Orders.

Dooyeweerd, Herman (1894–1977). Dutch Reformed philosopher. In 1926 he was appointed to the chair of legal philosophy at the Free University, a position which he occupied until his retirement in 1965. Dooyeweerd is best known for his four-volume *A New Critique of Theoretical Thought* (1953–58). Although his attempt to establish a Christian philosophy has been neglected by the philosophical establishment and many Christian groups, Dooyeweerd generated a small but dedicated following. His most widely known pupils were Hans Rookmaaker and Cornelius Van Til, and Francis Schaeffer popularized his ideas. Dooyeweerd was an innovative thinker who boldly faced the intellectuals of his day. His writing demands concentration and a familiarity with Western intellectual history, which he boldly challenges from a Christian perspective. The best-known part of his work is his transcendental critique of Western thought. Although many criticisms can be made of Dooyeweerd's work, he appears to be one of the few conservative Christians who have attempted to challenge the intellectual ideas of his day while remaining loyal to the faith. The value of his work lies not in his solutions but in the foundation he lays for creative interaction with modern thought.

I. HEXHAM

See also KUYPER, ABRAHAM.

Dorner, Isaac August (1809–1884). German Lutheran theologian. In 1839 he accepted a full professorship at Kiel, moving in 1843 to Königsberg, in 1847 to Bonn, and in 1853 to Göttingen. In 1862 he was appointed to a chair at Berlin, where he taught until his retirement in 1883. Dorner was a cofounder of the journal *Jahrbucher für deutscher Theologie* in 1856 and was active in this publication until it was discontinued in 1878. He wrote treatises on various aspects of theological history, particularly *History of the Development of the Doctrine of the Person of Christ* (5 vols., 1846–50), and *The History of Protestant Theology* (2 vols., 1867). He expounded his constructive theology in *A System of Christian Doctrine* (4 vols., 1879–81).

N. V. HOPE

Dort, Synod of (1618–1619). An international church assembly called by the States General of The Netherlands to settle ecclesiastical and doctrinal matters troubling the Reformed Church of the Netherlands. It consisted of 35 pastors and a number of elders from the Dutch churches, five theological professors from the Netherlands, 18 deputies from the States General, and 27 foreign delegates. Problems that faced the synod were complex. (1) It had to deal with Erastianism, the control of the church by the state. (2) It had to wrestle with an anticonfessional humanism. (3) It had to wrestle with fundamental Christian doctrine. Predestination was the doctrine most attacked, especially that part of it known as reprobation. Its critics were known as Remonstrants or Arminians. The Remonstrants expected to be recognized as equals and that the synod would be a conference to discuss disputed questions. Instead, the synod summoned the Remonstrants to appear as defendants, and in due time their doctrines were condemned. The Canons of Dort set forth: (1) Unconditional election and faith are a gift of God. (2) While the death of Christ is abundantly sufficient to expiate the sins of the whole world, its saving efficacy is limited to the elect. (3, 4) All are so corrupted by sin that they cannot effect their salvation; in sovereign grace God calls and regenerates them to newness of life. (5) Those thus saved are preserved until the end; there is assurance of salvation even while believers are troubled by many infirmities. Dort thus preserved the Augustinian doctrines of sin and grace.

M. E. OSTERHAVEN

See also ARMINIANISM; CALVINISM; REMONSTRANTS.

Double Predestination. See ELECT, ELECTION.

Doubt, Religious. Just as belief may be propositional or personal, so one may doubt with respect to propositions or persons and objects.

(1) Doubt of a person may be *propositional* doubt. To doubt God may mean nothing more than doubting the truth of the proposition "God exists." But doubt of a person often involves distrust more than disbelief. The doubter expresses a lack of dependence and a lack of trust in God's reliability. There are various forms of propositional doubt. Philosophical doubt includes what may be called

definitive or skeptical doubt. Provisional doubt (exemplified in the method of Descartes) calls items into question for the sake of reaching a more dependable conclusion. With provisional doubt there is skepticism in order to learn. The skeptic does not *have an answer* and thinks there *is no answer* and could be none. Examples of skeptical doubt are rare in Scripture, but the Bible is replete with cases of provisional doubt. The doubt of Thomas seems to fit this category, and it is important to note that there is not one word of rebuke to Thomas from the Lord or one word of repentance by Thomas. Evidently such doubt is not sinful.

(2) There also is a doubt equivalent to *denial*. The individual does not pose a question in order to learn, nor in skepticism. Instead, doubts are meant as veiled assertions of denial. Such doubt simply refuses to accept the presence of evidence (the skeptic's point is that there is no evidence). The Pharisees' continuing requests for signs from Jesus despite all the previous miracles performed provides an example. In the face of evidence they refused to accept the evidence. Jesus responded by rebuking them and refusing to give another sign (Matt. 12:38–42).

(3) There is what may be labeled *ignorant* doubt. It is doubt which seeks evidence in the face of evidence. The individual has enough evidence to believe but still thinks there is some alternate explanation that will resolve all doubt. The doubter does not know what a final explanation would be, and does not realize that the answer is already in hand. Such doubt is without rational ground. It is ignorant in that the person doubting is looking for something further but cannot explain what the something would be.

Several elements are involved in doubting. The most obvious is the rational or intellectual. On the other hand, one may still doubt in the face of evidence, even evidence which he fully understands. In such a case it seems proper to argue that there are emotional or volitional problems as well. That is, one may know the truth but not be comfortable with the way such a truth makes him feel, so belief is withheld. Or it may be that one understands admitting the truth implies a painful change of lifestyle. Doubt is chosen to avoid such commitment, a volitional problem.

J. S. FEINBERG

See also FAITH; GOD, ARGUMENTS FOR THE EXISTENCE OF.

Doxology. (from Gk. *doxa*, "glory") An ascription of praise to the three persons of the Trinity. In its commonest form it dates to the 4th century and is known as the *Gloria Patri* or "Lesser Doxology": "Glory be to the Father, and to the Son, and to the Holy Ghost: As it was in the beginning, is now, and ever shall be, world without end. Amen." The so-called Greater Doxology is the *Gloria in Excelsis*: "Glory be to God on high."

F. COLQUHOUN

See also WORSHIP IN THE CHURCH.

Drechsel, Thomas. See ZWICKAU PROPHETS.

Drink Offering. See OFFERINGS AND SACRIFICES IN BIBLE TIMES.

Drunkenness. See ALCOHOL, DRINKING OF.

Dualism. An interpretation or system of belief based on two opposing factors or principles. There are usually no intermediate degrees between the two extremes. Three major types of dualism exist: metaphysical, epistemological or epistemic, and ethical or ethicoreligious.

Metaphysical dualism asserts that the universe is best explained as the relation of two irreducible elements, usually considered to be mind and matter. Matter occupies space and moves; mind is conscious experience—two qualitatively different orders of reality. Epistemological dualism holds that the idea of an object is radically different from the real object itself. The "object" of knowledge is known only through the mediation of "ideas." Ethical or ethicoreligious dualism asserts that there are two mutually hostile forces or beings in the world—the one being the source of all good, the other the source of all evil. The most clear-cut type of ethicoreligious dualism is that of the ancient Iranian religion, Zoroastrianism.

Christian theology generally accepts a modified moral dualism, recognizing God as supremely good and Satan as a deteriorated creature bent everywhere upon the intrusion of evil. This, however, is not dualism as usually defined since Christian theology does not consider Satan to be ultimate or original, and sees him ultimately excluded from the universe.

H. B. KUHN

See also MANICHAEISM; NESTORIANISM; ZOROASTRIANISM.

Dulia. Reverence paid to saints directly in prayer or through their images or icons. This is less than the special reverence (*hyperdulia*) paid to the Virgin Mary and of a lower nature than the *latria* (true worship) given to God.

P. TOON

See also HYPERDULIA; LATRIA.

Duns Scotus, John (1266–1308). Franciscan scholastic theologian. His teaching is preserved in a commentary on the *Sentences* of Peter Lombard, glosses on Aristotelian texts, and disputations about various subjects. Scotus's ideas were formed in an atmosphere of opposition to the earlier philosophical position of Thomas Aquinas. Scotus felt that faith was a matter of the will rather than a process based on logical proofs. Even though he relied on some arguments for the existence of God, he taught that the most basic Christian truths, such as the resurrection and immortality, must be accepted by faith. Emphasizing the love of God, he used this characteristic to explain creation, grace, the incarnation, and heaven. He developed the doctrine of the immaculate conception. Given the title *Doctor Subtilis* by admirers, Scotus was ridiculed by the humanists and Protestant Reformers who used his name as an epithet, calling someone whose ideas are obscure a "duns" or dunce.

R. G. CLOUSE

See also SCHOLASTICISM.

Duty. Moral necessity or requirement. Duties are reasons for action but do not in themselves cause action. One could have a duty to act in a certain way without acting in that way or even being inclined to so act. Generally when people speak of duties they think in terms of deontological ethics. According to deontological ethics one ought to give primary focus to rules and principles in making moral decisions.

The most outstanding representative of the deontological approach was Immanuel Kant. According to Kant, we should not seek to acquire happiness but to be worthy of it through developing a will that acts only on the basis of duty. One's duties are defined by the basic moral law, which he called the "categorical imperative." This basic principle is categorical in that it applies to every person at every time and is unresponsive to desired goals or what is deemed prudent.

An alternative to the deontological approach is teleological ethics—focusing primarily on the results or consequences of our actions. Moral principles become for teleologists important practical rules of thumb for acquiring valued results. The critical thing is to discover what results are most valuable. Some seek personal happiness; others seek the greatest total happiness for a group of people; still others seek the advancement of the kingdom of God, reconciliation, the glorification of God, or the growth of love relationships. Teleologists argue that fulfilling one of these goals is our highest duty and that our commitment to any rule should depend on how effectively the rule helps achieve the highest goal. Critics argue that teleologists merely seek to justify their means by the ends they desire.

A third approach to ethics might be called ontological ethics, which argues that humans have both duties to obey rules and duties to achieve goals. Moral duties must then be derived from laws of nature—laws humans can discover within themselves or in relation to God or the world.

To talk about duties or laws implies a duty or law *to* someone. Ethics seems pointless without responsibility to another being. Certainly people have duties to themselves and to other humans, but the seriousness of ethical responsibility suggests an ongoing duty to a greater being. Kant argued that in order to understand the role of ethical duty, it is necessary to believe in the existence of a Supreme Judge who observes our actions in every circumstance. In addition, Kant believed that ethics necessarily include a belief in immortality so that beyond this life we are able to receive the rewards for our actions.

P. H. DEVRIES

See also CHRISTIAN; ETHICAL SYSTEMS, ETHICS; ETHICS, BIBLICAL; SITUATION ETHICS.

Ee

Earth, Age of. In the 17th century James Ussher suggested that the earth was created in 4004 B.C. Such estimates require assumptions: the data are complete and accurate; the days of Gen. 1 were brief and consecutive; the events described in Gen. 1 began soon after the formation of the earth, and so on. Bible genealogies cannot legitimately be used to construct chronologies. Comparison shows names omitted (compare Matt. 1:8 and 1 Chron. 3:10–12). It would appear that the earth's age, then, cannot be deduced unequivocally from biblical evidence. Most scientists, including some who hold to the verbal inspiration of the Bible, believe that the dates proposed by various kinds of geological evidence are approximately correct and that the earth is 5 billion years old or older. Others, questioning the conclusions of radioactive dating and historical geology, argue for various more recent dates.

M. La Bar

See also Gap Theory.

Earth, New. See New Heavens and New Earth.

Easter. The day and season commemorating the resurrection of Christ. As the oldest and most important movable feast, it determines the arrangement of the Christian liturgical year. Originally Easter was a one-night celebration (like passover), recalling both the death and resurrection of Christ. The ceremony included the lighting of the paschal candle, prayer, readings from Scripture, and the joyful celebrating of Eucharist. This became the ideal occasion for baptisms (with resurrection life symbolized by white robes) and led to the lengthening of the brief preparatory period into the 40 days of Lent. Accordingly, after the 4th century the unitary feast was broken into several parts and the resurrection came to be celebrated separately on Sunday morning, with Eastertide extending another 40 or 50 days. Over the centuries popular customs reflecting pagan spring folklore (Easter egg and rabbit) as well as Jewish and Christian sources were added.

R. K. Bishop

See also Christian Year.

Ebionites. (possibly from Heb. *'ebyônîm*, "poor men") A sect of Jewish Christian ascetics who chose poverty as a way of life. Ebionites drew their theology from Deut. 18:15 and their lifestyle from Matt. 5:3; Luke 4:18; 7:22. They accepted Jesus of Nazareth as the "prophet like me from among you." Further, they seem to have been a continuation of the Judaizers. They came into relative prominence after A.D. 70 and waned after the 4th century. In addition to accepting Jesus as the prophetic successor to Moses (whether virgin born or born of Joseph) and practicing asceticism, particularly poverty, Ebionites tended to deny the preexistence of the Logos. They venerated Jerusalem, saw Christianity as obedience to a moral code that was higher than or fulfilled the law, saw Jesus as adopted to be the Anointed One at baptism, taught that Jesus was selected because he kept the law perfectly, and stressed the Epistle of James, rejecting Paul's soteriology.

V. L. Walter

See also Adoptionism; Judaizers.

Eck, Johann (1486–1543). Roman Catholic apologist. Born Johann Maier at Eck (or Egg) in Swabia, Eck is remembered as an opponent of Martin Luther. At first friendly with Luther, he replied to the Ninety-Five Theses with the tract *Obelisks* (1518). Speaking for the papacy at the Leipzig Disputation (1519), Eck displayed a fine memory, sound learning, and a tactical mastery of debate. He forced Luther to admit some solidarity with Jan Hus (1373–1415) and to set Scripture above popes, councils, and fathers. Eck helped secure Luther's condemnation in the bull *Exsurge Domine* (1520) and defended papal authority in the treatise *On the Primacy of Peter* (1521). He then composed a frequently republished work (1525), *A Manual of Commonplaces against Luther and the Other Enemies of the Church* (Philip Melanchthon and Ulrich Zwingli). At the Diet of Augsburg (1530) he presented 404 propositions against Luther and wrote a *Confutation* of the Confession.

G. W. Bromiley

See also Leipzig Disputation; Luther, Martin.

Eckhart, Meister. See Meister Eckhart.

Ecumenical Councils. Originally summoned by emperors to promote unity, the early councils were intended to represent the whole church. Later the Roman Catholic canon law came to stipulate that an ecumenical council must be convened by the pope. Because of this switch in policy and representation, Christians have disagreed on which councils were "ecumenical." While the Roman Catholic Church accepts 21, the Coptic, Syrian, and Armenian churches accept only the first three in the Roman Catholic list. Most Protestants and Eastern Orthodox accept the first seven.

The first eight councils, called by emperors and representing Eastern and Western bishops, were Nicea I (325); Constantinople I (381); Ephesus (431); Chalcedon (451); Constantinople II (553); Constantinople III (680–81); Nicea II (787); and Constantinople IV (869–70). With Lateran Council I (1123) the papacy assumed control, continuing this policy with Lateran II (1139); Lateran III (1179); Lateran IV (1215); Lyon I (1245); Lyon II (1274); and Vienne (1311–12). During the conciliar movement, when the papacy had reached a low ebb, the councils of Constance (1414–18) and Basel (called 1431, transferred to Ferrara in 1438 and Florence in 1439) were convened. During the 16th century Lateran Council V (1512–17) and the Council of Trent (1545–63) were called to meet challenges to the Roman Church. The papacy has since convened two councils, nearly a century apart—Vatican I (1869–70) and Vatican II (1962–65).

D. A. Rausch

See also Councils, Church.

Ecumenism. (from Gk. *oikoumenē*, "the entire inhabited earth," Matt. 24:14; Acts 17:6; Heb. 2:5) The organized attempt to bring about the cooperation and unity among Christians.

The Modern Ecumenical Movement. Under the leadership of American Methodist John R. Mott, delegates to the International Missionary Conference in Edinburgh (1910) caught a vision for Christian unity. Three organizations were established to continue the work. The International Missionary Council (Lake Mohonk, New York, 1921) attempted to bring about cooperation between Protestant mission agencies; the Conference on Life and Work (Stockholm, 1925) sought to unify efforts to solve social, economic, and political problems, and the Conference on Faith and Order (Lausanne, 1927) addressed the theological bases of church unity. By 1937 the conferences on Life and Work and Faith and Order agreed that a more inclusive organization was needed and proposed establishment of a World Council of Churches (WCC). The coming of World War II interrupted implementation, but in 1948, 351 delegates representing 147 denominations from 44 countries gathered in Amsterdam and formed the World Council, under the leadership of W. A. Visser't Hooft. General Assemblies of the WCC were held at Evanston, Illinois (1954), New Delhi, India (1961), Uppsala, Sweden (1968), Nairobi, Kenya (1975), and Vancouver, British Columbia (1983). At the New Delhi assembly the Russian Orthodox Church joined the WCC, the International Missionary Council was brought under WCC control, and the confessional "Basis" was adopted: "The World Council of Churches is a fellowship of Churches which confess the Lord Jesus Christ as God and Savior according to the Scriptures and therefore seek to fulfill together their common calling to the glory of one God, Father, Son, and Holy Spirit."

Conspicuously absent from most of these ecumenical endeavors has been the Roman Catholic Church. Disagreements over the primacy of the Roman pontiff, the meaning and practice of the Eucharist, and the like have kept Roman Catholic and Protestant ecumenists apart. At Vatican Council II, Pope John XXIII opened the door to greater ecumenical dialogue. In the Council's Decree on Ecumenism (1964), Rome maintained its traditional insistence that "only through the Catholic Church of Christ, the universal aid to salvation, can the means of salvation be reached in all their fulness." But for the first time it was willing to recognize that there were authentic Christians ("separated brethren") outside the Roman fold.

Evangelicals and Ecumenism. Conservative evangelicals also remain outside the WCC. This reticence does not mean evangelicals are against collective action. Since the evangelical awakenings of the 18th century evangelicals have cooperated in evangelism and foreign missions. In the 1940s American evangelicals founded two cooperative organizations, the National Association of Evangelicals (NAE) and the American Council of Christian Churches (ACCC). In 1951 the World Evangelical Fellowship (WEF) was organized. Membership in the WEF is open to national evangelical fellowships that subscribe to an orthodox statement of faith. The WEF assists in theological education around the world, undertakes humanitarian relief, and promotes Bible and evangelistic ministries.

On the whole, however, evangelicals seem more interested in promoting evangelism. Growing out of the ministry of Billy Graham, the World Congress on Evangelism was held in Berlin in 1966, drawing delegates from more than 100 countries. In 1974 more than 2700 participated in the International Congress on World Evangelization in Lausanne, Switzerland. The Lausanne congress marked a new maturity in evangelical unity efforts.

T. P. WEBER

See also MOTT, JOHN RALEIGH.

Eddy, Mary Baker (1821–1910). Founder of the Church of Christ, Scientist. Born Mary Morse Baker, she was reared in a devout Congregationalist home, but later rejected her parents' strict Calvinism. Suffering poor health throughout most of her life, Mary was preoccupied with questions of health. In search of healing she submitted herself to the metaphysical teachings of Phineas P. Quimby and was healed. Suffering a serious fall in 1866, she was healed by reading the Bible and practicing metaphysical principles. She regarded that incident as the discovery of Christian Science. Her metaphysical system gradually evolved and was published as *Sci-*

ence and Health with Key to the Scriptures* in 1875. Although her followers consider this work as divinely inspired, critics contend that it is deeply indebted to the works of Francis Lieber and Quimby. The following year she founded the Christian Scientist Association, which three years later became the Church of Christ, Scientist.

P. G. CHAPPELL

See also CHURCH OF CHRIST, SCIENTIST.

Edwards, Jonathan (1703–1758). American theologian and revivalist. Edwards produced one of the most thorough and compelling bodies of theological writing in the history of America. A Congregationalist pastor, his first charge was Northampton, Massachusetts, where he served until dismissed in 1750 in a controversy over standards for church admission. He then labored in frontier Stockbridge, Massachusetts, as minister to congregations of Indians and whites. His death from inoculation for smallpox came on Mr. 22, 1758, only a few weeks after he began his work as president of the College of New Jersey.

Edwards' claim to be regarded as America's greatest evangelical theologian, and perhaps the greatest of any variety, rests on both the depth and breadth of his writing and his importance for both practical and theoretical religion. He was the theologian of the First Great Awakening and the 18th century's most powerful exponent of experimental Calvinism. The ongoing publication of a definitive edition of Edwards' works by Yale University Press makes clear how large his contributions were, not only in several divisions of theology defined more narrowly, but also in metaphysics, ethics, and psychology.

Theology. Edwards is most often studied for his Augustinian description of human sinfulness and divine all-sufficiency. He held that the root of human sinfulness was antagonism toward God; God was justified in condemning sinners who scorned the work of Christ on their behalf; conversion meant a radical change of the heart; true Christianity involved not just an understanding of God and the facts of Scripture but a new "sense" of divine beauty, holiness, and truth. Edwards summarized many of these insights in *A Careful and Strict Inquiry into the Modern Prevailing Notions of that Freedom of Will* (1754).

In a posthumously published volume, *Original Sin* (1758), Edwards defended the view of human nature which underlay the argument in *Freedom of Will.* This volume contended that all humanity was present in Adam at the fall and that all people, as a consequence, shared the bent toward sinning which Adam had brought upon himself.

Psychology. Edwards' examination of religious psychology arose directly out of his experiences in the Northampton revivals and in the colonial Great Awakening as a whole. In 1746 he published *A Treatise on the Religious Affections,* which has been likened in its acuity to William James' *Varieties of Religious Experience.* This volume argued that true religion resides in the heart, or the seat of affections, emotions, and inclinations and scrutinized the kinds of religious emotions that are largely irrelevant to true spirituality. The book closed with a description of 12 "marks" of true religion.

Metaphysics. Edwards' metaphysical speculations have been largely ignored in the subsequent history of American evangelical theology, but they represent a compelling effort to view reality in strictly theistic terms. Edwards recorded most of his metaphysical work in notebooks which have begun to be published only in recent years. But these more substantial reflections are consonant with modes of thought present in *Freedom of Will* and other works published during his life. Edwards' most important metaphysical commitment was to idealism. Physical reality and physical laws are not self-explanatory but are the result of God's constant and voluntary choices. With this conviction Edwards was still able to accept most of Newtonian science.

Ethics. Most of the major themes of Edwards' theology came together in the ethical interests which dominated the last period of his life. In particular he was concerned to argue against "the new moral philosophy" of the Enlightenment. This argued that human beings possessed some natural faculty or sense which, when cultivated properly, could point the way to a truly virtuous life. In response to this tendency, which was the ethical counterpart to the generally ameliorative views of human nature prominent in his century, Edwards strongly contended that true virtue could not be understood apart from God and his revelation. It was Edwards' argument, especially in the posthumously published *Nature of True Virtue* (1765), that genuine morality arises only from God's regenerating mercy.

The theology of Jonathan Edwards remains of great interest, both for historians and for some modern theologians, especially those who sense a need for a renewed presentation of philosophically sophisticated Calvinistic and Augustinian theology in the modern world.

M. A. NOLL

See also GREAT AWAKENINGS, THE; NEW ENGLAND THEOLOGY.

Effectual Calling. See CALL, CALLING.

Efficacious Grace. See GRACE.

Egotism. See SELF-ESTEEM, SELF-LOVE.

El. See GOD, NAMES OF.

Elder. (Heb. *zāqēn*, lit. "beard"; Gk. *presbyteros*) ***In the OT.*** The "elders of the people" or "elders of Israel" are frequently associated with Moses' leadership (Exod. 3:16; 4:29; 17:5; 18:12; 19:7; 24:1, 11; Num. 11:16). They later administer local government (Judg. 8:14; Josh. 20:4; Ruth 4:2) and have a hand in national affairs (1 Sam. 4:3) even after the institution of the monarchy (1 Sam. 8:4; 30:26; 2 Sam. 3:17; 5:3; 1 Kings 21:8). They are prominent during the exile (Jer. 29:1; Ezek. 8:1; 14:1; 20:1) and after the return are associated with the governor (Ezra 5:9–11; 6:7) and with local administration (Ezra 10:14). They have certain juridical functions (Deut. 22:15; 25:7–10) and are associated with the judges, who are probably appointed from their number, in the administration and execution of justice (Deut. 16:18; 21:2–9; Ezra 7:25; 10:14). They are also associated with Moses and Aaron in conveying the word of God to the people (Exod. 3:16–18; 4:29; 19:7) and in representing the people before God (Exod. 17:5; 24:1; Num. 11:16) on great occasions. They see to passover arrangements (Exod. 12:21). In the Maccabean period the title "elders of Israel" is used of the members of the Jewish Sanhedrin, which was regarded as having been set up by Moses in his appointment of the 70 elders (Num. 11:16–30).

In the NT. Elders or "presbyters" appear early in the life of the church, taking their place along with the apostles, prophets, and teachers. At Jerusalem they are associated with James in the government of the local church after the manner of the synagogue (Acts 11:30; 21:18), but in association with the apostles they share in the wider government of the church (Acts 15:2, 6, 23; 16:4). An apostle can be a presbyter (1 Pet. 5:1). The presbyters whom Paul addressed at Ephesus (Acts 20:17–35) and those addressed in 1 Peter and Titus have a decisive place in church life. They share in the ministry of Christ toward the flock (1 Pet. 5:1–4; Acts 20:28; Eph. 4:11).

It is often asserted that in Gentile churches the name *episkopos* is used as a substitute for *presbyteros* with identical meaning. The words seem to be interchangeable in Acts 20:17, 28; and Titus 1:5–9. But though all *episkopoi* are undoubtedly *presbyteroi*, it is not clear whether the reverse is always true. The word *presbyteros* denotes rather the status of eldership while *episkopos* denotes the function of at least some elders. There may have been elders who were not *episkopoi*.

In 1 Tim. 5:17 teaching as well as oversight is regarded as a function of the presbyter. It is likely that when apostles, teachers, and prophets ceased to be able to minister to the whole church, the function of teaching and preaching fell on the presbyters, and thus the office and qualifications of those holding it would develop. This, again, may have led to distinction within the presbyterate. The presidency of the body of presbyters, in both the ordering of the congregation and the celebration of the Lord's Supper, would tend to become a permanent office held by one man.

The "elder" in 2 John and 3 John may refer to someone highly esteemed within the church. The 24 elders of the Book of Revelation are examples of how all authority should humbly adore God and the Lamb (Rev. 4:10; 5:8–10; 19:4).

R. S. Wallace

See also Church Government.

Elect, Election. Scripture employs a rich vocabulary to express several aspects of God's sovereign election, choice, and predestination. Five types of election are distinguished: (1) "elect angels" (1 Tim. 5:21); (2) election to service or office, as in God's choice of David as Israel's king (1 Sam. 16:7–12) and Jesus' choice of disciples and apostles (Luke 6:13; John 6:70; 15:16; Acts 9:15; 15:7); (3) election of Abraham's descendants to form the theocratic nation of Israel (Deut. 4:37; 7:6–7; 10:15; 1 Kings 3:8; Isa. 44:1–2; 45:4; 65:9, 15, 22; Amos 3:2; Acts 13:17; Rom. 9:1–5); (4) election of the Messiah (Isa. 42:1; Matt. 12:18; Luke 9:35; 23:35 1 Pet. 1:20; 2:4, 6); (5) election to salvation. The most common NT reference to election is God's eternal election of certain persons to salvation in Jesus Christ. The most comprehensive texts are Eph. 1:3–11 and Rom. 8:28–11:36.

Principles of Election. There are six main features of election: (1) Election is a sovereign, eternal decree of God. The elect have been predestined according to God's plan (Eph. 1:11). (2) The human race is utterly fallen; election involves God's gracious rescue plan. It is not based on human works or God's foreknowledge of works (Rom. 9:11). The elect are chosen to be holy, adopted as children (Eph. 1:4–5). (3) Election is "election in Christ"; it involves rescue from sin and guilt and receiving salvation. (4) Election involves both the elect's salvation and the means to that end; the elect are those whom God "foreknew . . . predestined . . . called . . . justified . . . glorified" (Rom. 8:29–30). The preaching of the gospel is indispensable in effecting God's election (Rom. 10:14–17; Acts 18:9–11). (5) Election is individual, personal, specific, and particular. Ephesians refers repeatedly to "us" and "we" in connection with election (1:4–5, 12). Particular, personal election leads to the believer's comfort and does not promote carelessness or false confidence. (6) The ultimate goal of election is the glory and praise of God. Election to salvation involves personal security, but Scripture makes clear that it is "to the praise of his glorious grace" that everything leads (Eph. 1:6).

F. H. Klooster

See also Decrees of God; Predestination; Reprobation; Supralapsarianism; Sovereignty of God.

El-Eloe-Israel. See GOD, NAMES OF.

El Elyon. See GOD, NAMES OF.

Elements, Elemental Spirits. (Gk. *ta stoicheia*, lit. "belonging to a series," Gal. 4:3, 9; Col. 2:8, 20) Greeks used the term to describe, among other things, the order of letters in the alphabet, and the elementary principles ("ABCs") of any science or system. The meaning Paul attaches to *stoicheia* is not so clear. By "the elements of the world" he may simply mean world order, the elementary truths of natural religion, expressed in basic ethical precepts, which structure the lives of ordinary people. The NIV translates "basic principles." Many commentators, however, believe that Paul had supernatural powers in mind (RSV "elemental spirits"). He certainly appears to personify the *stoicheia* (Gal. 4:3) and to link them with angel worship (Col. 2:18). Whether Paul meant to spiritualize the "elements" or not, the theological thrust of his argument is clear. The *stoicheia* stand for all religious and ethical practices, whether Jewish law-keeping or pagan worship (Gal. 4:3–5, 8–9), which belong to life outside Christ. Compared to him, they are all "weak and miserable" (Gal. 4:9). He has triumphed over them, and intends his followers to be free from bondage (Col. 2:20).

D. H. FIELD

Elohim. See GOD, NAMES OF.

El Shaddai. See GOD, NAMES OF.

Elyah. See GOD, NAMES OF.

Emanation. (Gk. *aporroia*, "a flowing down from") A technical term Greek philosophers such as Empedocles employed to convey the connection between external realities and mind perceptions. In Philo the Logos doctrine becomes the first stage in bridging the gap between the transcendent God and the world of sense perception or between the realm of unity and world of plurality. In the Middle Ages the Neo-Platonic ideas of Plotinus and others were mixed with Christian perspectives and gave birth to the mysticism of thinkers like John Scotus Erigena. The universal is real and a causal process gives birth to the particular. Thus, the created order is really God unfolded into particularities.

G. L. BORCHERT

See also NEO-PLATONISM; GNOSTICISM; MYSTICISM.

Ember Days. In Roman Catholicism and Anglicanism Wednesday, Friday, and Saturday of the four Ember weeks. They occur in the weeks after the Feast of St. Lucy (Dec. 13), Ash Wednesday, Pentecost, and Holy Cross Day (Sept. 14). The 12 days were seen as times for prayer, fasting, and almsgiving. They have been retained with modifications.

P. TOON

Emmanual. See IMMANUEL.

Empiricism, Empirical Theology. The philosophical theory that all ideas are derived from experience, asserting that internal and external experience are the sole foundation of true knowledge and of science. David Hume is the clearest representative of empiricism. In his *An Enquiry Concerning Human Understanding*, Hume maintained that all knowledge of the world is the product of experience. While we can know the relation between ideas, their actual reality cannot be established beyond probability. Thus, the true nature and scope of ordinary and scientific knowledge can be revealed only on experience and observation. Hume's empiricism established a criterion for meaning and significance which has been adopted by many since his time.

While "all ideas are derived from experience" is the crux of empiricism, the word "empirical" has been misapplied so frequently that in the last two centuries such ideological incompatibles as Francis Bacon, Thomas Hobbes, Immanuel Kant, William James, Henri Bergson, Rudolf Carnap, and Edmund Husserl have been designated as empiricists. Most of this confusion results from differences in definition and interpretation of "ideas," "derived from," and "experience."

Empiricism has been applied to theology in various ways. Hume believed in studying religion scientifically because there was nothing unique about religious experience. Friedrich Schleiermacher believed that religious experience was unique, and that theology could only provide symbols for describing the great diversity of human religious experiences. Therefore, every man must have a private description of his feelings, an individual theology. Schleiermacher is at least one source of the "religious experience" theories current today. Liberal theologians of the late 19th and early 20th centuries applied the scientific method to reconstruct the Christian faith in accordance with the findings of science.

D. A. RAUSCH

See also HUME, DAVID.

End of the World. See ESCHATOLOGY.

Energumen. See DEMON, DEMON POSSESSION.

Enlightenment, The. The Age of Enlightenment (Ger. *Die Aufklärung*) covers roughly the 18th century. It is sometimes identified with the Age of Reason, but the latter covers the 17th and 18th centuries.

In 1784 Immanuel Kant, answering the question, "What is enlightenment?" replied that enlightenment was a coming of age. Humans were emerging from immature reliance on such external authorities as the Bible, the church, and the state. No generation should be bound by the creeds and customs of bygone ages. To be so bound is an offense against human nature, whose destiny lies in progress. Kant admitted that the 18th century was not yet an enlightened age, but the barriers to progress were coming down. The motto of enlightenment was *Sapere aude*—"Have courage to use your own understanding."

Kant wrote his article midway between the American and French Revolutions. Both the Declaration of Independence of the United States of America (1776) and the Statement of Human and Civil Rights ratified by the French National Assembly (1789) bear the stamp of enlightened thinking. Both appealed to truths deemed to be self-evident. Reference to God or a Supreme Being was retained, but such concepts as life, liberty, and the pursuit of happiness (American) and freedom, property, security, and the right to protect oneself from violence (French) were regarded as naturally valid. These documents represent a middle stage between the traditional Christian view of the state and modern secular democracy. In general enlightened thinkers acknowledged God's existence as Creator but left the conduct of life to man and reason. The enlightened view proposed essentially humanistic goals for society, insisting that both ends and means should be determined by reason in accordance with nature. The theme of nature figured large. Nature embodied the beautiful and the good and was eminently accessible. The high esteem in which nature was held was linked to its self-evident reality and to the prestige of modern science, exemplified in Isaac Newton's mechanistic view of a world governed by rational laws.

Jean-Jacques Rousseau and François-Marie Voltaire attacked institutional Christianity while professing belief in a Supreme Being. Rousseau's religion denounced all creeds beyond the assertion that natural religion was based on feeling and that all beliefs should be brought "to the bar of reason and conscience." God was not a fit subject for argument and debate. God is known in the depths of our being. Voltaire professed a theism based on the order and rationality of the world. Just as a watch proves a watchmaker, so a universe proves a God. On this basis Voltaire urged tolerance of all religions except that of the institutionalized church, against which he directed his celebrated slogan, "Blot out the infamous one."

The ideas of the deists influenced Hermann Samuel Reimarus, the Hamburg schoolteacher credited with having initiated the quest for the historical Jesus. Reimarus wrote a private *Defence of the Rational Worshippers of God*, which portrayed Jesus as a simple Galilean preacher whose moral teaching got mixed up with politics and eschatology and who died a disillusioned man, having vainly tried to establish the kingdom of God on earth. Christianity is based on the fraudulent claims of the resurrection and the second coming of Christ, which the disciples invented after Jesus' death.

The Age of Enlightenment was characterized by the desire for a superior, more rational view of everything. It was a desire which contained the seeds of its own destruction. Scottish philosopher David Hume turned enlightened criticism back on itself. Hume used skeptical, empirical philosophy to question the powers of the human mind. Not only was Hume critical of religion; he was skeptical of human knowledge and of the power of the human mind to know anything for certain. Kant's philosophy of the mind was in part an answer to Hume, but Kant gave back Hume's problem as if it were the answer. Kant's philosophy was the last great attempt by an enlightened thinker to work out a truly enlightened philosophy of reality. He reduced religion to ethics and ethics to humanistic, rational principles. His teaching left unanswered the question of why man should base his behavior on the principles he proposed. It failed to do justice to religious experience, and it superimposed a rationalistic interpretation on the Bible.

C. BROWN

See also DEISM.

Ephesus, Council of (431). Known as the 3d ecumenical council, it was summoned by the Emperor Theodosius II. He hoped it would settle questions about the Person of Christ associated with Nestorius of Constantinople. Led by Cyril of Alexandria, the council condemned Nestorianism and, in so doing, approved the expression "Theotokos" (God-bearer) for Mary, mother of Jesus. The council also dealt with the ecclesiastical rights of the Church of Cyprus.

P. TOON

See also NESTORIUS, NESTORIANISM; THEOTOKOS.

Epicureanism. Ethical philosophy associated with Epicurus (341–270 B.C.). Epicurus established a school in ancient Athens which became famous for its teachings that the present life is all a person will have, and the good life is the one bringing the most pleasure or happiness now. The supernatural was rejected. The kinds of acts Epicurus held to be most pleasurable are those characterized by justice, honesty, and simplicity. Epicurus was evidently confused as to whether honesty is a means to an end—pleasure—or an end in itself. This confusion lies behind the fact that "Epicureanism" has come to be used for profligacy and luxury. Paul preached to a group of Epicureans in Athens, emphasizing the incarnation and resurrection of Jesus (Acts 17:16–32). They were evidently not very impressed.

S. R. OBITTS

Epiphany. A disclosure or unveiling. It has been used to refer to various occasions on which the incarnate Lord Jesus

Christ was revealed to various people at his birth, the coming of the magi, his baptism, and the wedding at Cana (first miracle), as well as when he will be revealed at his second coming. Liturgically Epiphany is the festival at which this revelation of Christ is celebrated. By the 4th century the Eastern Church observed the feast on Jan. 6. The Western Church (certainly in Rome) appears to have observed Dec. 25 as the birthday of Jesus from at least 336, and Jan. 6 was kept as a day for commemorating his manifestation to the Gentiles at the visit of the magi.

D. H. WHEATON

See also CHRISTIAN YEAR.

Episcopacy. See CHURCH GOVERNMENT.

Episcopius, Simon (1583–1643). Remonstrant leader. A native of Amsterdam and student at the University of Leiden under Jacobus Arminius, Episcopius was banished by the Synod of Dort for his able defense of the Arminian position. He published *Confessio* (1622) while in exile. Returning to Holland in 1634, he published a systematic exposition of Arminianism in four volumes, *Institutiones theologicae* (1650–51).

P. A. MICKEY

See also ARMINIANISM; DORT, SYNOD OF; REMONSTRANTS.

Equiprobabilism. See CASUISTRY.

Erasmus, Desiderius (1466?–1536). Christian humanist of the Reformation era. Erasmus was a prolific writer, and each main category of his work reveals something of his personality. He produced many scholarly books, including historical material, lexicons, translations, and critical editions of earlier works. He believed that truth was attainable through clarity of expression. In such satirical works as *The Praise of Folly* Erasmus ridicules humanists and scholars who take themselves too seriously, but he saves his most biting satire for bigoted churchmen, pompous lawyers, and war-mongering rulers. The more overtly Christian writings demonstrate that scholarship and humor were pursued to reach the goal of the restoration of primitive Christianity. Erasmus felt called to cleanse and purify the church by applying humanistic scholarship to Christian tradition. Truth and piety were not the result of ritual and sacraments but of historical research. Erasmus reached the height of his fame at the beginning of the Protestant Reformation. At first he encouraged Luther, but after the Leipzig debate (1519) he began to criticize him. Finally, he publicly broke with Luther in his *Diatribe on Free Will* (1524). In a sense, history passed Erasmus by, leaving him to defend his position against Reformers and Counter-Reformers.

R. G. CLOUSE

See also HUMANISM, CHRISTIAN.

Erastianism. Erastianism takes its name from Thomas Erastus (1524–83), who was born in Baden, studied theology at Basel, and later medicine, becoming professor of medicine at Heidelberg. He was a friend of Beza and Bullinger and was a Zwinglian. At Heidelberg Erastus emphasized strongly the right of the state to intervene in ecclesiastical matters. He held that the church has no scriptural authority to excommunicate any of its members. As God has entrusted to the civil magistrate (i.e., the state) the sum total of the visible government, the church in a Christian country has no power of repression distinct from the state. In practice, the term "Erastianism" is somewhat elastic. John Figgis calls it "the theory that religion is the creature of the state." Generally it signifies that the state is supreme in ecclesiastical causes, but Erastus dealt only with church discipline.

A. M. RENWICK

See also CHURCH AND STATE.

Erigena, John Scotus (ca. 810–ca. 877). Irish philosopher. Erigena played a significant role in interpreting Greek thought to the West. He was involved in a major theological controversy with the monk Gottschalk (ca. 805–869) over predestination; he also wrote on the Eucharist against Paschasius Radbertus (ca. 785–860). Erigena's views on nature and creation were portrayed in his greatest work, *De divisione naturae.* In the 13th century this work was condemned. It divided nature into four categories, urging a sharp distinction between God and creation and describing the emanation of the created order from God. While denying that creatures are part of God, Erigena claimed that God is the only true reality, introducing elements of pantheism in his thought.

D. K. McKim

See also Aristotle, Aristotelianism; Neo-Platonism; Scholasticism.

Error in the Bible. See Bible, Inerrancy and Infallibility of.

Eschatology. (Gk. *eschatos*, "last") The doctrine of "last things," in relation to human death, resurrection, judgment, afterlife, or the end of the world. In this latter respect eschatology is sometimes restricted to the absolute end of the world, excluding much that commonly falls within the scope of the term. The biblical concept of time envisions a recurring pattern of events in which divine judgment and redemption interact until God's final, definitive manifestation. Eschatology may therefore denote the consummation of God's purpose, whether it coincides with the end of the world (or of history) or whether the consummation is totally final or marks a stage in the unfolding pattern of his purpose.

Individual Eschatology in the OT. A shadowy existence after death is contemplated in much of the OT. The praises of Yahweh remained unsung in Sheol, which was popularly thought to be outside Yahweh's jurisdiction (Ps. 88:10–12; Isa. 38:18). Occasionally a more hopeful note is struck. According to Pss. 73:24–26 and 139:7–8, one who walks with God in life cannot be deprived of his presence in death.

The hope of national resurrection finds earlier expression than that of individual resurrection. In Ezekiel's vision of the valley of dry bones, where the divine breath breathes new life into corpses, a resurrection of Israel is in view (Ezek. 37:11). The persecution of martyrs under Antiochus Epiphanes gave a powerful impetus to resurrection hope. Henceforth belief in the future resurrection of at least the righteous dead became part of orthodox Judaism, except among the Sadducees, who claimed to champion the old-time religion against Pharisaic innovations. With this new emphasis goes a sharper distinction between the posthumous fortunes of the righteous and the wicked, in Paradise and Gehenna, respectively.

World Eschatology in the OT. Psalmists and prophets recognized that, while Yahweh was king, the reality fell short of his ideal. Yahweh's sovereignty was inadequately acknowledged, but one day the tension between ideal and reality would be resolved; on the day of Yahweh his kingship would be universally acknowledged, and the earth would be filled with the knowledge of the Lord (Isa. 11:9; Hab. 2:14). His effective recognition as "king over all the earth" is portrayed as a theophany in Zech. 14:3–9.

As the fortunes of David's house sank, there emerged with increasing clarity the figure of a coming Davidic king in whom promises made to David would be fulfilled and the vanished glories of earlier times would be restored and surpassed (Isa. 9:6–7; 11:1–10; 32:1–5; Jer. 23:5–6; 33:14–22; Amos 9:11–12; Mic. 5:2–4). Another form of eschatological hope appears in Daniel. Eternal and universal dominion is given at the end time to "one like a son of man," who is associated, if not identified, with "the saints of the Most High" (Dan. 7:18, 22, 27).

NT Eschatology. OT eschatology looks forward in hope and promise. The NT adds to hope the dominant note of fulfillment in Jesus. By his passion and resurrection Christ has begotten his people anew to a living hope (1 Pet. 1:3), because he has brought eternal life (2 Tim. 1:10). Jesus' Galilean preaching, summarized in Mark 1:15, declares the fulfillment of Daniel's vision in Dan. 7:22. In one sense the kingdom was present in Jesus' ministry (Matt. 12:28; Luke 11:20). In another sense it was future. Jesus taught his disciples to pray, "your kingdom come" (Luke 11:2). In this sense it would come "with power" (Mark 9:1)—an event variously associated with the resurrection of the Son of man or his advent "with great power and glory" (Mark 13:26).

In apostolic teaching eternal life may be enjoyed now, although its full flowering awaits a future consummation. The death and resurrection of Christ have introduced a new phase of the kingdom, in which those who believe in him share his risen life already, even while they live on earth in mortal body. There is an indeterminate interval between Christ's resurrection and parousia; during this interval the age to come overlaps the present age. Christians live spiritually in "that age" while they live temporally in "this age"; through the indwelling Spirit of God they enjoy the resurrection life in anticipation. This outlook has been called "realized eschatology." But the realized eschatology of the NT does not exclude an eschatological consummation to come.

Conclusion. Jesus' use of OT language cannot be confined to the meaning of that language in its original context. He probably did point forward to his personal coming to earth—not only to manifest his glory but to share that glory with his people, raised from the dead by his quickening shout. When the consummation to which his people look forward is described as their "hope of glory" it is their participation in Jesus' resurrection glory that is in view. That hope is kept bright by his indwelling presence (Col. 1:27) and sealed by the Spirit (Eph. 1:13–14, 18–21).

There is a tension between the "already" and the "not yet," but each is essential to the other. In the language of the seer of Patmos, the Lamb that was slain has by his death won the decisive victory (Rev. 5:5), but its final outworking, in reward and judgment, lies in the future (Rev. 22:12). The fact that we now "see Jesus crowned with glory and honor" is guarantee enough that God "has put all things under his feet" (Heb. 2:8–9). His people already share his risen life, and those who reject him are "condemned already" (John 3:18). For John the judgment of the world coincided with the passion (John 12:31); yet a future resurrection to judgment is contemplated as well as a resurrection to life (John 5:29).

Some questions, such as the chronological relation of the parousia to the great distress of Mark 13:19, to the manifestation of the man of lawlessness of 2 Thess. 2:3–8, or to the millennial reign of Rev. 20, relate to a detailed exegesis of the passages concerned rather than the thrust of their teaching, which is summed up in the words: "Christ Jesus our hope" (1 Tim. 1:1).

F. F. BRUCE

See also AGE, AGES; APOCALYPTIC; DAY OF CHRIST, GOD, THE LORD; ISRAEL AND PROPHECY; JUDGMENT; JUDGMENT SEAT; JUDGMENT OF THE NATIONS, THE; KINGDOM OF CHRIST, GOD, HEAVEN; LAST DAY, DAYS; MILLENNIUM, VIEWS OF THE; RAPTURE OF THE CHURCH; SECOND COMING OF CHRIST; THIS AGE, THE AGE TO COME; TRIBULATION.

Eternal Generation. The intertrinitarian relationship between the Father and the Son as taught by the Bible. "Generation" means a divine sonship existed prior to the incarnation (John 1:18; 1 John 4:9), that there is a distinction of persons within the one Godhead (John 5:26), and that between these persons there is a superiority and subordination of order (John 5:19; 8:28). "Eternal" reinforces the fact that the generation is not merely for the purpose of human salvation (see Luke 1:35), but essential to who God is and, as such, cannot be compared with natural or human generation. Thus it does not imply a time when the Son "was not," as Arianism argued.

G. W. BROMILEY

Eternality of God. See GOD, ATTRIBUTES OF.

Eternal Life. (Gk. *aiōnion*, "eternal"; *zōē*, "life") Though inferred in the OT, the concept of eternal life is a most emphatic NT revelation. "Eternal life" and "everlasting life," are found throughout the NT, especially in the Gospel of John and 1 John. The Scriptures describe, but do not formally define, eternal life. The nearest approach to a definition is given in John 17:3: "Now this is eternal life: that they may know you, the only true God, and Jesus Christ, whom you have sent" (NIV). Eternal life is described in its experiential aspect of knowing and having fellowship with God through Jesus Christ. Three word pictures are offered to describe receiving eternal life. (1) It is a new birth, being (John 1:13; 3:3). The bestowal of eternal life therefore relates the believer to God in a father and son relationship. (2) It is a spiritual resurrection "with Christ" (Col. 3:1; Rom. 6:13). (3) It is compared to the act of creation. As Adam became a living soul by the breath of God, so the believer becomes a new creation (2 Cor. 5:17; Eph. 2:10).

J. F. WALVOORD

See also LIFE; MAN, OLD AND NEW; NEW CREATION, NEW CREATURE; SALVATION; REGENERATION.

Eternal Punishment. Sin will be punished (Dan. 12:2; Matt. 10:15; John 5:28–29; Rom. 5:12–21), and the duration of this punishment is sometimes expressed in the NT by *aiōn* (an "age") or its derivatives (Matt. 18:8; 25:41, 46; 2 Thess. 1:9). The adjective (*aiōnion*) used of eternal life is also used of punishment (Matt. 25:46 has both). The one is no more limited than the other. Jesus also referred to hell (Gk. *geenna*), "where their worm does not die, and the fire is not quenched" (Mark 9:47–48, NIV). He spoke of fearing God because he "has power to throw you into hell" (Luke 12:5). He described a sin that "will not be forgiven, either in this age or in the age to come" (Matt. 12:32). Jesus spoke of hell more often than did anyone else in the NT. In the light of the cross we can be sure that God does all that can be done for a human's salvation. Beyond that, and the teaching of the permanence of the doom of the wicked, we cannot go. It is impossible to envisage the reality that is described so variously by Jesus. But we should beware also of a sentimentality which waters down such expressions.

L. MORRIS

See also ANNIHILATIONISM; APOKATASTASIS; HELL; UNIVERSALISM.

Eternal Security of the Believer. See PERSEVERANCE.

Eternal Sin. In Mark 3:29, instead of *kriseos* ("judgment"), the oldest Gk. MSS. have *hamartematos* ("sin"). So the best translation is not "in danger of eternal damnation" (KJV) but "guilty of an eternal sin" (NASB, NIV)—which is actually far worse morally. It is the sin of blasphemy against the Holy Spirit, for which there is no forgiveness (Matt. 12:31; Mark 3:29; Luke 12:10).

R. EARLE

See also BLASPHEMY AGAINST THE HOLY SPIRIT.

Eternal State. See FINAL STATE.

Eternity. (Heb. *'ôlām*; Gk. *aiōn*, "an age"; *aiōnios*, adj., "eternal") Eternity suggests transcendence of the temporal and is employed in various senses: durability ("the eternal hills"); time without end ("passing to his eternal reward"); time without beginning (speculative conceptions of the universe as "an eternal process"); infinite time (the ascription of temporality to the nature of God). Beyond this the term traditionally has been used by theology and philosophy to designate God's infinity in relation to time—i.e., to designate the divine perfection whereby God transcends temporal limitations of duration and succession and possesses his existence in one indivisible present.

Some recent theologians lodge time in the very nature of God instead of viewing it as in created dependency. Oscar Cullmann drops the whole idea of timelessness with reference to the eternal. He maintains that eternity is simply infinitely extended time: the former, boundless time; the latter, bound by creation at the one end and by eschatological events at the other.

No objection can be taken to Cullmann's aim, which is to preserve the absolute significance of redemptive history and to prevent a dissolution of the Christ-event as the decisive center of history from which both time and eternity are to be understood. But repudiation of the unique nontemporality of God is not required to preserve the reality and significance of historical revelation and redemption; indeed, the temporalizing of the Eternal poses theological problems all its own.

The nontemporality of God can be firmly supported. The constant use of *aiōn* for the spatial world (Gk. *kosmos*) suggests the concomitance of time and space; hence the nontemporality and also nonspatiality of God—an assumption objectionable to biblical theists—would seem to be implied by a one-sided reliance on *aiōn*. Instead it seems that time and space belong to the created order as distinct from the divine essence and that eternity is an incommunicable divine attribute. Moreover, the biblical contrast between divine and temporal duration frequently is qualitative rather than quantitative or proportional. Temporal categories are viewed as inapplicable to Jehovah (cf. Ps. 90:2). This qualitative connotation is more fully carried by the use of the pl. *'ôlāmîm* for God's eternity (as in Ps. 61:4; Dan. 9:24). Hebrew vocabulary does not express a qualitative differentiation, but the plural cannot literally mean a series of indefinite ages; it must refer poetically to a qualitative difference.

The NT translation of *'ôlām* by *aiōn* and *aiōnios* is significant. It shows that the primary thrust of the terms "eternal life" and "eternal death" is qualitative, and not simply quantitative. Eternal life is life fit for eternity, in which the believer already participates through regeneration (John 5:24). Although it does not imply nontemporality, the latter, eternal death, is spiritual death which, in the case of the impenitent unbeliever, is transmuted at physical death into an irrevocable condition. The attribute of eternity cannot be disjoined from God's other attributes. The biblical emphasis on divine omniscience supports the view of his supertemporal eternity. If God's knowledge is an inference from a succession of ideas in the divine mind, he cannot be omniscient. Divine omniscience implies that God knows all things in a single whole.

C. F. H. HENRY

See also AGE, AGES; GOD, ATTRIBUTES OF; GOD, DOCTRINE OF; THIS AGE, THE AGE TO COME; TIME.

Ethics. Inquiry into the moral nature of humanity to discover the individual's responsibilities and how to fulfill them. Ethics is a quest for truth, but it is different from other studies in its concern for applying the truth uncovered to behavior. It is not simply descriptive but prescriptive.

Ethical inquiry can be divided into philosophical, theological, and Christian ethics. Philosophic ethics seeks precepts from natural reason and temporal existence. Theological ethics deals with what may be gained from the insights of any given religious community. Christian ethics is the Christian instance of theological ethics. It weighs human moral obligations in the light of the distinctive revelation in Jesus Christ (Heb. 1:1–2).

It is also common to distinguish between personal and social ethics, although this is somewhat misleading because people are social beings and any conduct has social significance. However, social ethics deals with moral considerations that relate to our corporate identity, as we associate and establish society. The distinction reminds us that ethics involves not simply how one relates to others, but how groups associate responsibly.

Ethical inquiry is a reflective activity and, as such, human and fallible. Whatever the belief of the individual or group concerning a revelation of God, it is never thought to be exhaustive or all-encompassing. The features of life change with the times, so that we must continually weigh the implications of truth against present situations. There are also cross-cultural barriers that must be overcome in understanding obligation within a particular setting.

It has been customary to speak of conscience as an ethical faculty, but this has increasingly fallen into disuse since the demise of faculty psychology. The individual makes decisions, not simply with reference to strictly pragmatic concerns, but to what he perceives as right and proper. He reasons and acts in reference to some ethical norm.

There is within theological ethics as a rule and Christian ethics in particular a concern for "the higher order." One's religious commitment takes precedence over the obligation to human authority, legitimate as the latter might otherwise be. One must obey God rather than man (Acts 4:18–19). In any case, we see our responsibility within the scope of an integrating ideal.

M. A. Inch

See also Christian; Ethics, Biblical; Situation Ethics; Social Ethics.

Ethics, Biblical. Judeo-Christian ethics may not be separated from its theological base. Moral implications comprise the biblical ethic.

In the OT. In recognizing the OT as Scripture the church perceived the theocratic foundation of ethics as the will of God, holy, faithful, and good and based upon what God had already done as Creator and Redeemer of his people. Thus the Decalogue opens with "I am the Lord your God who brought you out of the land of Egypt, out of the house of bondage"; the covenant bound Israel to its God, not in a natural blood bond but in a moral relationship. It was God's choice, promise, and deliverance and Israel's response was grateful obedience and trust. This attitude lent an unparalleled quality of humility and confidence to Jewish ethical thought. Properly understood, obedience did not aim at divine favor but was inspired by it.

The Decalogue itself is a remarkable ethical document, its received form embraces a dual code of religious (Exod. 20:3–12) and social (vv. 13–17) duties. Both areas (worship, prohibition of idols, the oath, the sacred day, and filial piety on the one hand, and the sanctity of life, marriage, property, truth, and desire on the other) fall under divine authority.

Inevitably this form of commandment gave its tone to Judaic morality, although the final commandment against coveting enters a realm where legalism is helpless. Later Jewish moral teaching came to include (in Proverbs, Ecclesiastes, Job, Sirach) valuable ethical "wisdom." Its aim was to simplify duty into practical reverence for God (Ps. 111:10). Wisdom's ideal is eloquently expressed in Job 31.

In the NT. A long ethical tradition was summarized when John the Baptist demanded purity, righteousness, honesty, and social concern (Luke 3:10–14). Significantly, Jesus took up Judaism's ethical monotheism, social conscience, and the relation of religion to morality, while rejecting the tendency to self-righteousness, hard, external legalism, nationalism, cultivation of merit, and the failure to differentiate ritual from morality. Jesus then pressed the demand that righteousness transcend law, pointing to the mind and motive behind behavior (Matt. 5:17–48). Jesus stressed that behind the written code were original purposes of God (Mark 2:27; Matt. 19:3–9), and the overriding command to love God and neighbor (Matt. 22:35–40). In this summary of all duty as *love* lies Jesus' most characteristic contribution to ethical thought, even as his example of love's meaning and his death in love for men comprise his most powerful contribution to ethical achievement.

Paul's ethical concern was to counter the Jewish legalism which had failed in his own life and which threatened to make of the church just one more Jewish sect. He insisted on the sufficiency of faith to save Jew and Gentile alike and on the freedom of the Christians to follow the leading of the Spirit (the theme of Galatians). While handing on the tradition of ethical teaching (Rom. 6:17; 2 Thess. 2:15; 3:6), Paul explained the ethical significance of faith and the nature of life in the Spirit. Paul also taught that what the law can never do, through the weakness of human nature, Christ had accomplished, so that the law was fulfilled (Rom. 8:1–4). This transformation by the inner dynamic of the Spirit is a central ethical motif of Christianity.

Through all NT ethical teaching the imitation of Christ is yet another theme. The Synoptic Gospels present this as simply following Jesus. John expounds the ideal of *Christus Exemplar* as loving (13:34; 15:12), obeying (9:4; 15:10), standing firm (15:20), and humbly serving (13:14–15) as Jesus did for us. John links it with the Christian hope (3:2). Peter connects imitation with the cross (1 Pet. 2:21–25; 3:17–18; 4:1, 13). Paul makes it the goal of worship (2 Cor. 3:18), of ministry (Eph. 4:11–13), of exhortation (1 Cor. 11:1), and of God's providence (Rom. 8:28–29), defining its inmost meaning as having "the mind of Christ" (1 Cor. 2:16; Phil. 2:5), "the Spirit of God" (1 Cor. 7:40).

Summary. In contrast with philosophical systems, the enduring marks of biblical ethics are its foundation in relationship with God; its objective, imposed obligation to obedience; its appeal to the deepest in man; its down-to-earth social relevance, and its capacity for continual adaptation and development.

R. E. O. WHITE

See also ETHICAL SYSTEMS, CHRISTIAN; IMITATION OF CHRIST; KINGDOM OF CHRIST, GOD, HEAVEN; TEN COMMANDMENTS, THE.

Ethics, Sexual. See SEXUAL ETHICS.

Ethics, Situation. See SITUATION ETHICS.

Ethics, Social. See SOCIAL ETHICS.

Eucharist. See LORD'S SUPPER.

Euthanasia. (from Gk. *eu-* and *thanatos*, "easy" or "good death") Any attempt to shorten the process of death from being prolonged and/or ease its pain when it is inevitable. Often medical expenditures are a factor. The issue of euthanasia is in part a by-product of medical success. Persons are now kept alive to the point of contracting diseases of older age or experiencing the general physical deterioration which so often accompanies advanced years. With a rapidly increasing population of older persons in our society, euthanasia will become a larger issue.

Euthanasia may be classified on the basis of several criteria. It may be passive or active. Passive euthanasia involves simply allowing the person to die through withholding or discontinuing treatment that would prolong life. Active euthanasia involves some positive step to terminate life, such as administration of a toxic substance or injection of an air bubble into the bloodstream. Euthanasia may also be classified as voluntary or involuntary. Voluntary euthanasia is the case where the subject has indicated a desire for life to end. In involuntary euthanasia the decision is made for the subject by some third party, usually the closest relative. Thus there are four classes of euthanasia: voluntary passive, involuntary passive, voluntary active, and involuntary active.

Both revealed and nonreligious principles suggest that active euthanasia is less than God's best: the value of life; the finality of death; the possibility of diagnostic errors; the possible danger of abuse, and the biblical perspective that suffering may have a purifying or strengthening effect. It is desirable, therefore, that laws prohibiting euthanasia be retained while further thorough study is done. Other options, including the possibility of passive euthanasia, the use and development of painkillers, the sustaining power of God, and the encouragement of believers, should be explored and utilized.

M. J. Erickson

Eutychianism. See Monophysitism.

Evangelicalism. (from Gk. *euangelion*, "glad tidings," "good news," or "gospel") What is now usually identified as evangelicalism is a 20th-century Christian movement, transcending confessional boundaries, that emphasizes conformity to the basic tenets of faith and a missionary outreach of compassion and urgency. An "evangelical" believes and proclaims the gospel of Jesus Christ as defined in 1 Cor. 15:1–4, the message that Christ died for our sins, was buried, and rose again on the third day in fulfillment of the prophetic Scriptures and thereby provided the way of redemption for sinful humanity. Three times the NT calls one who preaches the gospel an *euangelistēs* ("evangelist").

Theological Meaning. Evangelicalism stresses God's sovereignty as a transcendent, personal, infinite Being who created and rules over heaven and earth. He is a holy God who cannot countenance sin, yet he has love and compassion for the sinner.

Evangelicals regard Scripture as the divinely inspired record of God's revelation, the infallible, authoritative guide for faith and practice. Denying the Enlightenment doctrine of humankind's innate goodness, they believe in the total depravity of human beings. All human goodness that exists is tainted by sin, and no dimension of life is free from its effects. Humanity was originally created perfect; but through the fall sin entered the race.

God himself provided the way out of the human dilemma by allowing his only Son, Jesus Christ, to assume the penalty and experience death on humanity's behalf. Christ made atonement for sin on the cross, thereby redeeming by dying in the place of those who trust him as Savior. When Christ arose from the grave, he triumphed over death and hell, demonstrating divine supremacy over the curse of sin and laying the foundation for redemption of all creation from sin's corrupting influence. Evangelicals believe that salvation is an act of unmerited divine grace received through faith in Christ, not through any kind of human work.

The Word of God is central within evangelicalism. The vehicle of God's Spirit is the biblical proclamation of the gospel, which brings people to faith. The written Word is the basis for the preached word, and holy living is part of witness, since life and word are inseparable elements of the message. Holiness involves confronting evil and overcoming its effects.

Finally, evangelicals look for the visible, personal return of Jesus Christ to set up his kingdom of righteousness, a new, unending heaven and earth.

Evangelicals share certain beliefs with all orthodox Christians: the Trinity; Christ's incarnation, virgin birth, and bodily resurrection; the reality of miracles and the supernatural realm; the church as the body of Christ; the sacraments as effectual signs or means of grace; immortality of the soul; and the final resurrection.

Historical Meaning. The evangelical spirit has manifested itself throughout church history. However, the 19th century clearly began a new evangelical age —especially in North America, Britain, and Germany.

Precursers to the modern movement arose in American revivalism in both urban and rural or frontier movements among Baptists, Methodists, Disciples of Christ, and Presbyterians. The growth of holiness perfectionism also helped to transform the U.S. This conservative Christianity reached to the grass roots of white America, and the black community was sustained by deep, personal faith. This influence shaped the nation's values and civil religion. Political leaders publicly expressed Christian convictions and suppressed non-Protestant and "foreign" elements who did not share in the national religious consensus. Not only unbelief but also social evil would be purged, and revivalism provided the reforming vision for a righteous republic. The antislavery and temperance campaigns, innumerable urban social service agencies, and even the nascent women's movements lay within it.

Protestant nations of the North Atlantic region shared in the missionary advance that carried the gospel to every corner of the earth, and revivals began to occur in Africa, Asia, and Latin America. The Evangelical Alliance was formed in London in 1846 to unite Christians (but not churches or denominations as such) in promoting religious liberty, missions, and other common interests. National alliances were formed in Germany, the U. S., and other countries, an international effort that in 1951 was replaced by the World Evangelical Fellowship (WEF).

In the early 20th century evangelicalism went into a temporary eclipse. But after World War II foreign missionary endeavors, Bible institutes and colleges, works among university students, and radio and literature ministries blossomed, while the evangelistic campaigns of the youthful Billy Graham had a global impact. A party of "conservative evangelicals" emerged in Britain and *Evangelikaler* in Germany, and their strength was reflected in such developments as the National Evangelical Anglican Congress and the German-based Conference of Confessing Fellowships. In the U.S. the foundation of the National Association of Evangelicals (1942), Fuller Theological Seminary (1947), and *Christianity Today* (1956) were significant expressions of the "new evangelicalism," a term coined by Harold J. Ockenga in 1947.

The Graham organization has been a major catalyst, especially in calling the World Congress on Evangelism (Berlin, 1966) and the International Congress on

World Evangelization (Lausanne, 1974). The subsequent consultations sponsored by the Lausanne committee, together with the activities of the WEF and regional organizations formed by evangelicals in Africa, Asia, Latin America, and Europe have fostered closer relations and cooperative efforts in evangelism, relief, and theological development. With the indigenization of mission societies, the multinational character of relief and evangelistic organizations, and the sending of missionaries by people in Third World countries themselves, what is now called evangelicalism has come of age and is truly a global phenomenon.

R. V. PIERARD

Evangelism. (From Gk. *euangelion*; verb, *euangelizomai*, to announce good news) The proclamation of the good news of salvation in Jesus Christ to bring about reconciliation of the sinner to God the Father through the regenerating power of the Holy Spirit.

According to the Lausanne Covenant, formulated by the International Congress on World Evangelization (1974): "To evangelize is to spread the good news that Jesus Christ died for our sins and was raised from the dead according to the Scriptures, and that as the reigning Lord he now offers the forgiveness of sins and the liberating gift of the Spirit to all who repent and believe. Our Christian presence in the world is indispensable to evangelism, and so is that kind of dialogue whose purpose is to listen sensitively in order to understand. But evangelism itself is the proclamation of the historical, biblical Christ as Saviour and Lord, with a view to persuading people to come to him personally and so be reconciled to God. In issuing the gospel invitation we have no liberty to conceal the cost of discipleship. Jesus still calls all who would follow him to deny themselves, take up their cross, and identify themselves with his new community. The results of evangelism include obedience to Christ, incorporation into his church and responsible service in the world."

Evangelism may, therefore, be broken down into component parts. First, there is the *message* based on the Word of God; it seeks to tell the story that God has already acted out. Second, there is the *method.* In the NT believers shared their faith through formal preaching and teaching, in their personal contacts and chance encounters. Consequently Christians have felt free to devise different ways of doing evangelism; to present the message clearly, honestly, and compassionately. Finally, there are the *goals* of evangelism. Though evangelism concentrates on the need to respond to God in initial repentance and faith, its message must also contain something about the obligations of Christian discipleship. Further, announcing the good news of salvation without showing the love of Christ in personal and social concern is not NT evangelism. In this holistic approach to evangelism we do not fail to distinguish between regeneration and sanctification, but hold the two closely together.

T. P. WEBER

See also CONVERSION; GOSPEL; REGENERATION.

Evangelism, Gift of. See SPIRITUAL GIFTS.

Eve. (Heb. *ḥawwâ*; Gk. *Heua*) Adam gave his wife the name Eve because she would become the mother of all the living (Gen. 3:20). The Heb. is very similar to the word "living," *ḥay* (fem. *ḥayyâ),* and the LXX actually translated her name as Life (*Zōē*). It was "not good for the man to be alone," so God made "a helper suitable for him" (Gen. 2:18, 20). The word translated "suitable" is a compound preposition meaning "corresponding to" or "opposite" him. It expresses the complementary nature of a person equal and able to respond to and even challenge him. Unfortunately, the joyful mutuality that marked this perfect relationship came to an end when Eve succumbed to the serpent's clever urging and ate the forbidden fruit (Gen. 3:1–6). Rather than obeying the simple command of God, she looked at the attractiveness of the fruit and its reward of "wisdom" and then shared the fruit with her husband. Sin now marred their relationship and the lives of their children (2 Cor. 11:3; 1 Tim. 2:11–14).

H. M. WOLF

See also ADAM; WOMAN, BIBLICAL CONCEPT OF.

Evening Prayer, Evensong. In the Anglican Church evening prayer or evensong refer to the evening service which is said or sung daily throughout the year. In origin this service is a conflation of the medieval services of vespers and compline. It is composed chiefly of Scripture—OT and NT lessons, biblical canticles (for example the Magnificat), biblical versicles, and responses with the Lord's Prayer. To these are added the Kyrie Eleison, creed, and prayers. In Roman Catholicism evening prayer is sometimes used to describe the evening office of vespers in the new breviary (1971).

P. TOON

Everlasting Life. See ETERNAL LIFE.

Everlasting Punishment. See ETERNAL PUNISHMENT.

Evidences of Christianity. See APOLOGETICS.

Evil, Problem of. Generally theists and atheists alike have perceived the problem of evil to be a problem about the internal consistency of the propositions: "God is all-loving," "God is all-powerful," and "Evil exists in a world created by such a God." It is generally assumed that all theologians within the Judeo-Christian tradition have the same understanding of God and evil and that only one problem of evil confronts such theists. Atheists are convinced that there is no way for a classical theist to solve the problem of evil. The problem, as atheists perceive it, is the inconsistency of the theistic positions: (1) God is omnipotent; (2) God is wholly benevolent, totally disposed to will and do those things which promote the happiness of others; (3) evil consequences resulting from actions and events befall humankind; (4) the omnipotent and wholly benevolent being of 1 and 2 eliminates every evil insofar as it can; (5) there are no nonlogical limits to what an omnipotent being can do; (6) therefore, God eliminates every evil which is logically possible for him to remove. Propositions 1, 2, 4, 5, and 6 entail the negation of 3, and thus the set of six is self-contradictory.

Nature of the Problem. Without a proper understanding of the nature of the problem any hope of resolving it is lost. The first mistake by the atheistic formulation is the idea that there is only one problem of evil confronting all theistic positions. As a matter of fact, there are many problems of evil; there are various kinds of problems of evil: (1) *The religious problem* relates to concrete instances of evil that people are actually experiencing. In view of the affliction, the individual's personal relation with God is strained, asking such questions as "Why is God allowing this to happen to me?" and "Can I worship a God who does not remove the evil which is besetting me?" (2) *The philosophical/theological problem* can be divided into two more specific areas, the problem of moral evil (produced by activities of moral agents) and the problem of natural evil (which occurs in the process of the functioning of the natural order). The philosophical/theological problem is abstract. It is not about a specific evil, nor about someone's relationship to God. It is a general question about why there should be any evil in a world created by an all-loving, all-powerful God. Even if there were no God and no evil, such a question could be posed as follows: How would the existence of an all-powerful, all-loving God, if such a God should exist, square with the existence of evil in the world, if there should be such evil?

There are also problems about the degrees, the intensity, and the gratuitousness of evil. That is, one can ask why God needs so much evil in the world to do whatever he is doing with evil. Could he not accomplish his ends with a lesser degree of evil? Answers to one kind of problem are not necessarily relevant to—or appropriate as—answers to another problem. If someone experiencing cancer, a concrete, religious problem, asks why this should be happening, the response that evil comes from the abuse of free will does not suffice. Free will is relevant to a problem of moral evil but inappropriate as an answer to questions about religious evil.

The Problem of Internal Consistency. A problem of evil is also a problem about the *internal* consistency of a theological position. The crucial question is not whether a theological position contradicts another theistic system or even whether it contradicts the atheist's views, but whether it contradicts *itself*. This point has important implications for both theists and critics of theism. The theist must so structure a theology as to contain views of God, evil, and human freedom which, when put together, do not contradict each other. In particular, theists must avoid a system in which God is said to be both good and able to remove evil, despite the system's admission of the existence of evil. Such a system will most assuredly succumb to its problem of evil. The critic of theism must specify a problem which actually arises within the views held by some theists. It is always possible to create a problem for the theist if the atheist is allowed to attribute his own views to the theist as proof that there is a problem. Obviously there will be a problem, but not a problem of internal inconsistency.

Perception of God. A final point in clarifying the nature of the problem of evil is that, while it is always an attack on a theological perception of God, it is not necessarily an attack on God himself. But if the theological position does reflect the true and living God, then the problem of evil which arises for that system is an attack on God himself. Thus, one needs verification independent of the discussions on the problem of evil that a particular system's God is the true and living God. Consequently, any use of a problem of evil to argue ultimately to the nonexistence of God would be misguided, unless it could be shown that the perception of God being attacked is the correct perception.

There have been many attempts to present answers to questions of evil. Such answers, known as theodicies or defenses, attempt to establish that God is just in spite of the evil present in the world. Generally speaking, the key premise in the argument about evil is that a good God removes every evil insofar as he can. The basic strategy of theodicists has been to suggest that while the premise is true, there is some key reason that God, though all-powerful and all-loving, still cannot remove the evil present in the world. Such a reason would justify the evil present in the world and resolve the theological position's problem of evil.

J. S. FEINBERG

See also EVIL; PAIN; THEODICY.

Evil One. See SATAN.

Evil Spirits. See DEMON, DEMON POSSESSION.

Evolution. Since publication of *The Origin of Species* by Charles Darwin in 1859, a storm of controversy has raged among theologians and scientists. Some proponents of Darwin's theory have made of it a paradigm for reinterpreting the human experience. Others have identified the theory of evolution as the work of the devil without any scientific merit. Most stand somewhere in between these two opinions.

Evangelical Positions. Evangelical Christians accept the Bible as the inspired Word of God, the only unerring guide of faith and conduct. However, there are at least four widely held theories in the contemporary dialogue among evangelicals relating interpretation of Genesis to science.

1. *Pre-Adamites Theories.* These take two forms. The "gap theory" states that after the creation of the heavens and the earth and before the situation described in Gen. 1:2, a long period of time elapsed in which a great cataclysm desolated the earth. Jer. 4:23–26; Isa. 24:1, and 45:18 are cited as evidence of this judgment of God. This theory attributes early human fossils to pre-Adamites, who were destroyed before the rest of the creation events in Gen. 1. The "two Adams theory" states that the first Adam of Gen. 1 was the old stone age Adam, which has since been extinct, and the second Adam of Gen. 2 was the new stone age Adam, the ancestor of humankind today. This theory suggests the rest of the Bible is concerned with the fall and salvation of the new stone age Adam and his descendants.

2. *Fiat Creationism.* This includes all of the literal views which insist on a 24-hour creation day. It demands a young earth approximately 10,000 years old and a universal deluge that accounts for most or all of the sedimentary deposits and fossils now found. It rejects scientific data pertaining to the concept of an ancient earth. Fiat creationists also reject any form of evolutionary development of life by attributing the differences in related organisms today to variations of the original stocks. They believe any evolutionary compromise in the interpretation of Gen. 1 is detrimental to the Christian faith.

3. *Theistic Evolutionism.* Theistic evolutionists accept the trustworthiness of the Scriptures but allegorize the Genesis account as a poetic representation of the spiritual truths of human dependence on God and symbolic acts of disobedience against God's grace. They accept processes of organic evolution as the ways God used to create humans. They believe that the Bible only tells us that God created the world but not how. Science provided a mechanistic explanation in evolution. The two levels of explanation should complement instead of antagonize each other. Despite the necessity to dispense with the historicity of the human fall, theistic evolutionists feel the fundamental Christian doctrines of original sin and the human need for redemption are unshaken by the incorporation of organic evolution into the Christian interpretation of life and origins.

4. *Progressive Creationism.* Progressive creationists interpret the Scriptures with the understanding that the Hebrew word for day may mean an "age" as well as a 24-hour solar day. Their idea, then, is sometimes called the "day-age theory" of the creation, and allows for an earth of unknown antiquity. Progressive creationists tend toward caution in their evaluation of the theory of evolution. Most accept only the microevolutionary theory, which states that mutations do give rise to the diversification of varieties within a biological species. They are skeptical of macroevolution (human-from-lower-forms) and organic evolution (human-from-molecule) as both unbiblical and unsubstantiated. There are at least three versions of the day-age theory: (1) day-geological age, which assigns different geological eras to the creation days in Gen. 1; (2) modified intermittent day, in which each creative era is preceded by a 24-hour solar day; (3) over-

lapping day-age, with each creative era delimited by the phrase, "There was evening and there was morning," and overlapping with each other.

Critique. *Pre-Adamites Theories.* According to J. Oliver Buswell, Jr., the gap theory is untenable. It has no exegetical evidence in the Bible, and it was invented by Christian geologists to harmonize apparent conflicts of the creation of light and vegetation before the appearance of the sun and the antiquity of human fossils.

Fiat Creationism. The major hurdle facing fiat creationists is considerable evidence for the antiquity of the earth. Since the dominant atheistic view of evolution requires a vast amount of time, fiat creationists maintain that the acceptance of the ancient-earth concept is a compromise with atheistic evolution. They reject the principle of uniformitarianism ("the present is the key to the past") and dating methods based on it, inferring instead that appearances of antiquity arise from a universal cataclysm.

Theistic Evolutionism. If human beings are a product of the chance events of natural selection, theistic evolutionists have the problem of convincing the secular world of the biblical basis of humans as created in the image of God and of the first sin. The figurative interpretation of the Genesis account of creation seems to weaken these two fundamental doctrines of the Christian faith. Theistic evolutionists also give too much credence to theory of organic evolution. In their efforts to reconcile the naturalistic and theistic approaches to the origin of life they inadvertently put themselves into the inconsistent position of denying the miracles of creation while maintaining the supernatural nature of the Christian message.

Progressive Creationism. Progressive creationists maintain that aside from the scientific data supporting the antiquity of the earth, there is adequate exegetical data to demonstrate that the days of Gen. 1 can be considered long, indefinite periods, and that the genealogies of the Bible were not intended for the construction of a chronology. Traditional day-age interpretation assigns days to various geological periods, which is difficult to align to what is known of fossil records. In addition, the creation of land plants that bear seeds and trees that bear fruits with seeds before the creation of land animals poses a problem, since many land plants depend on insects for pollination and fertilization. Both the modified intermittent day and overlapping day-age models overcome this problem by assuming the overlapping or contemporaneousness of the periods. The current popular star formation model of the origin of the earth and the solar system can be nicely harmonized with the Genesis account. This theory (the "big bang" theory of the galaxies) depicts the universe as expanding from a superdense state that exploded 13 billion years ago and subsequently cooled down to form the interstellar products, including the earth and planets. The events in the first three creative eras seem consistent with the scientific model of a dark nebula containing water vapor which eventually cleared up as oxygen was given off by plant photosynthesis.

All three models allow for processes of change after the creation of each prototype creature. In the interpretation of God's rest on the seventh day, the overlapping day-age model assumes creation was ended at the conclusion of the sixth day (Gen. 1:31) and God is now at rest from his creating. This agrees with the traditional view. However, the modified intermittent day model suggests that we are still living in the creative period initiated by the sixth creative solar day, which intervenes between the sixth and seventh days. God is still creating through the changes and developments of the inorganic and organic world. The seventh day, on which God absolutely rests (Heb. 4:1–11), will commence at the inception of the new heavens and new earth (Rev. 21:1–8). This seems to strain the interpretation of Gen. 2:1, which states, "Thus the heavens and the earth were completed in all their vast array" (NIV). The hurdles faced by progressive creationists are less than those confronting other models because there is a conscientious attitude in relating science to Scripture. Two of the more perplexing problems are: (1) How does the antiquity of humans fit in with the seemingly advanced civilization of Gen. 4? Despite the lack of artifacts associated with the early human fossils, physical anthropology suggests that humans have been on earth for perhaps millions of years. The large gap that exists between the first human and the advent of human civilization, which is dated to 9000 B.C., is a major problem. (2) What is the extent of the deluge? Since there is a lack of visible evidence for a universal flood, most progressive creationists subscribe to some form of local flood theories which suggest that the flood was confined to the Mesopotamia.

P. P. T. PUN

See also CREATION, DOCTRINE OF; EARTH, AGE OF; MAN, ORIGIN OF.

Exaltation of Jesus Christ. See STATES OF JESUS CHRIST.

Ex Cathedra. (Lat., lit. "from the throne") A description of authority given statements or pronouncements made by the pope in his capacities as head of the church on earth and vicar of Christ on earth. Such utterances are accepted by Roman Catholics as infallible, apostolic doctrine. Not all papal statements are regarded as *ex cathedra*, and there are no definitive criteria for ascribing this distinction.

P. TOON

See also INFALLIBILITY.

Excommunication. The exclusion of a wilfully disobedient sinner from the communion of the faithful, usually understood primarily as a medicinal measure to recall to repentance and obedience and secondarily to safeguard the community's purity.

Excommunication is said to have originated with the teaching of Jesus on binding and loosing (Matt. 16:19; 18:18; John 20:23). The sinner is bound in his sinful alienation from God's people and loosed following repentance. Excommunication came to be seen, then, as a responsibility of the true church derived from its Lord. The procedure for disciplining sinners and the three steps to be taken prior to excommunication were also delivered to the church by Jesus (Matt. 18:15–17).

Two related disciplinary practices are revealed in the writings of Paul. Private sins are to be corrected privately; open sins are to be corrected publicly (Gal. 2:14; 1 Tim. 5:20). Paul excommunicated a particularly scandalous sinner as soon as he was informed of the offense.

The practice of the church to the 6th century emphasized the close connection between excommunication and repentance. A grave offender who wished to make his peace with God presented himself to the bishop, who, by a liturgical excommunication, assigned him to the category of "penitent" and prescribed a period of public penitential works. When these were completed, the bishop lifted the excommunication and received the penitent back into communion.

From the 7th century a new form of excommunication developed. The strict requirement that all excommunicated persons should be avoided was relaxed so that, by the 15th century, a clear distinction was made between excommunicates (the *vitandi*) who were to be shunned, and less serious offenders (the *tolerati*) who were to be excluded only from the sacraments.

The Protestant Reformers recalled the church to a more biblical position on ecclesiastical discipline. Calvin maintained that discipline according to the Word, is the "best help" to sound doctrine, order, and unity, and that banishing blatant sinners is to exercise a spiritual jurisdiction invested by the Lord in the assembly of believers.

The Council of Trent also addressed the problem of abuses in the practice of excommunication. Bishops were not to allow themselves to be made tools of the state, excommunicating according to the wish of rulers. They were enjoined to be moderate in the use of excommunication, for the widespread use of the penalty for slight offenses provoked contempt. The primary medicinal function of excommunication was reconfirmed.

Modern Catholic teaching on excommunication, incorporated in canon law (*Codex Iuris Canonici*, 1917, canons 2257–67), denies to the excommunicate the sacraments, Christian burial, ecclesiastical office, and revenue from ecclesiastical sources. Formal excommunication is now rarely exercised in most Protestant churches.

F. S. PIGGIN

See also CHURCH DISCIPLINE.

Exemplarism. See ATONEMENT, THEORIES OF THE.

Exhortation, Gift of. See SPIRITUAL GIFTS.

Existence of God, Arguments for. See GOD, ARGUMENTS FOR THE EXISTENCE OF.

Existentialism. A variety of philosophies and attitudes which flourished in Germany from about World War I and in France during and immediately after World War II. In the postwar period its influence was felt in Britain, North America, and Western culture generally. Existentialism has been described as the attempt to philosophize as an actor rather than as a detached spectator, but the resultant philosophy varies enormously, depending on whether the philosopher is an atheist or a theist.

Origins. The origins of existentialism are frequently traced to the 19th-century Danish philosopher Søren Kierkegaard, the German philosopher and poet Friedrich Nietzsche, and the Russian novelist Fëdor Dostoevski. Whether any of these could be called an existentialist in the modern sense of the term is doubtful, but each anticipated ideas that became pronounced in existentialism. All three questioned the accepted values and philosophies of their day, and all three were concerned with the need of the individual to discover truth personally valid in the struggles of existence.

Although existentialism is associated with major philosophers such as Karl Jaspers and Martin Heidegger, many of its leading advocates have been writers, including Albert Camus and Jean-Paul Sartre, whose interests embraced literature as well as philosophy. To them the novel or the play was a better vehicle for describing and analyzing existence than was the scholarly paper. For existentialism has been concerned above all with the problems of human life in the modern, secular world.

Modern Existentialists. In some respects existentialism is characterized by protest against theological and metaphysical systems into which human life is made to fit. Both Heidegger and Sartre erected their own metaphysical systems on the basis of their analysis of existence. Existentialists frequently distinguish between authentic and inauthentic existence, but there seems to be no consensus as to how to define these ideas. It is questionable whether such a distinction is legitimate for an atheistic existentialist, since the idea of authentic existence implies that one form of existence is not merely preferable but right. It is difficult to see how one act is intrinsically better than another in a world in which humans alone determine values. Even the claim that authentic existence is characterized by the decision to choose rather than to allow a choice to be made by others is questionable. Having others choose could well be authentic for the person concerned, though not necessarily for someone else.

Existentialism and Theology. Existentialism has affected contemporary theology, notably in the teaching of Rudolf Bultmann, Paul Tillich, and Karl Barth. None of these was a pure existentialist. Bultmann used Heidegger's terminology, especially his distinction between authentic and inauthentic existence, to describe the distinction between the life of faith and life in the flesh in the context of his demythologizing program. But the framework of Bultmann's thought was a Neo-Kantian view of God that affirmed God's transcendence but questioned any human capacity to know God directly. Tillich also used existential categories, but in the context of an ontology that revived the philosophy of being, advocated by the early 19th-century German idealists. Barth's view of revelation was indebted to Kierkegaard, but his teaching, like Kierkegaard's, restated a theistic view of God and the world which was not characteristic of later existentialism.

C. BROWN

See also HEIDEGGER, MARTIN; KIERKEGAARD, SØREN; NEO-ORTHODOXY.

Ex Nihilo, Creatio. See CREATION, DOCTRINE OF.

Ex Opere Operato. (Lat., "from the work done") The historic Roman Catholic view of the way sacraments are effective. This position became official at the Council of Trent (1545–63). Canon VIII of the 7th session opposed the view that "grace is not conferred through the act performed, but that faith alone in the divine promise suffices for the obtaining of grace." The condition for the recipient is only that one does not place an obstacle (*obex*, sinful act or disposition) in the way of the sacrament's administration. Grace is given by God when the sacrament is conferred rightly by the church.

D. K. MCKIM

See also GRACE; OPUS OPERATUM; SACRAMENT.

Exorcism. See DEMON, DEMON POSSESSION.

Exorcist. See MINOR ORDERS.

Experience, Theology of. Experience can be a source of knowledge deriving from direct perception or apprehension of reality. Experiential knowledge can be gained either externally from the senses or internally from the inner world of the spirit. Experiencing something differs from reflecting about it or hearing a report on it. The experience has greater force ("You should have been there!") and provides a sense of certitude ("But I saw it!") that reflection and reportage do not. The personal nature of experience, however, is an important qualifier, for experience can never be fully transmitted or represented. Moreover, apart from authentic reflection, experience, however vivid, remains arbitrary, unclear, and open to false claims. Experience and reflection must be understood as complementary and interactive; no easy formula spells out their interrelation.

At the beginning of the 19th century liberal theology arose, formulating experience as the basis for Christian reflection. Friedrich Schleiermacher offered the classic formulation. Rather than emphasize God's action with regard to humankind, he sought to clarify Christianity in terms of human experience of God. Remembering the pietism of his youth and reacting to contemporary rationalistic and ethical reductions of religion in David Hume and Immanuel Kant, Schleiermacher wrote *On Religion:*

Speeches to Its Cultured Despisers (1799) to argue for the centrality of feeling in religion. Religion is not action (morality), nor metaphysics (theoretical knowledge). Rather, as he later characterized it, religion is based in the "feeling of absolute dependence."

Schleiermacher and those following his lead gave a one-sided stress to religious feeling. There is throughout his discussion, despite occasional disclaimers, a false compartmentalization of human activity into feeling, doing, and thinking. The result downplays or rejects orthodox Christian thought, for ideas about God are secondary and ultimately unimportant.

A theology based in experience need not deny orthodox Christian reflection, however. Such a theology is chiefly distinguishable, not by a liberal orientation but by a trinitarian emphasis on the Holy Spirit (on one's experience of God in creation and redemption).

Experiential theology has arisen historically within Christianity in reaction to a sterile intellectualism and/or a rote traditionalism. Its emphasis on the role of the Spirit continues to help the church attain a balanced trinitarian perspective. But there are also dangers: (1) Christian experience must never be viewed individualistically but nurtured and evaluated within the Christian community, past and present. (2) Experience and reflection must not become isolated from each other. Word and Spirit must remain complementary expressions of the Trinity. (3) The Spirit experienced cannot be reduced to only the Spirit in creation, or Christianity risks degeneration into psychology. Neither can theology be concerned only with the Spirit of redemption, or it may drift to isolationism and mysticism.

A biblically based theology of experience will stress the Spirit's ongoing role in creation and redemption (Acts 14:15–18; Rom. 8; Gal. 4:6–7). It will also recognize that a focus upon the Spirit will open naturally and authentically into an emphasis on Christ the Word (1 John 4:2; 1 Cor. 12:3). Finally, an experiential theology will always be a corporate church theology (1 Cor. 12; Rom. 12).

R. K. Johnston

See also Holiness Movement, American; Pentecostalism; Pietism; Revivalism; Schleiermacher, Friedrich Daniel Ernst.

Expiation. See Propitiation.

External Calling. See Call, Calling.

Ff

Faith. (Gk. *pistis*, "trust, firm persuasion"; verb., *pisteuō)* The many-sided relationship into which the gospel calls men and women—that of trust in God through Christ. A key NT concept, the complexity of this idea is reflected in the variety of Gk. constructions used with the verb *pisteuō* to express truth believed, restful reliance on that to which credit is given, or trust that reaches out for the object of its confidence. The last sense is the most common. The nature of faith, according to the NT, is to live by the truth it receives; faith, resting on God's promise, gives thanks for God's grace by working for God's glory.

General Conception. Three points must be noted for the circumscribing of the biblical idea of faith:

Faith in God Involves Right Belief about God. The word *faith* in ordinary speech covers confidence in propositions ("beliefs") as true and in persons or things. In the latter case trust logically involves some belief about the object trusted, a positive expectation about something's or someone's behavior. Rational expectation is impossible if the thing's capacities for behavior are wholly unknown. Throughout the Bible trust in God rests on an expectation that he will continue to act in harmony with what he has revealed concerning his character and purposes.

Faith Rests on Divine Testimony. Beliefs are convictions held because of testimony, not because they are self-evident. Whether particular beliefs should be treated as known certainties or doubtful opinions depends on the reliability of the testimony on which they are based. The Bible views faith's convictions as certainties and equates them with knowledge (1 John 3:2; 5:18–20), not because they spring from supposedly self-authenticating mystical experience, but because they rest on the testimony of a God who "cannot lie" (Titus 1:2).

Faith Is a Supernatural Divine Gift. Sin and Satan have so blinded fallen men (Eph. 4:18; 2 Cor. 4:4) that they cannot "come" in self-renouncing trust (John 6:44, 65), until the Holy Spirit has enlightened them (2 Cor. 4:6).

Biblical Presentation. Throughout Scripture, God's people live by faith; but the idea of faith develops as God's revelation of grace and truth enlarges. The OT variously defines faith as resting, trusting, and hoping in the Lord, cleaving to him, waiting for him, making him our shield and tower, taking refuge in him, and similar expressions. Psalmists and prophets, speaking in individual and national terms respectively, present faith as unwavering trust in God to save his servants from their foes and fulfill his declared purpose of blessing them. Isaiah, particularly, denounces reliance on human aid as inconsistent with such trust (Isa. 30:1–18). The NT regards the self-despairing hope, world-renouncing obedience, and heroic tenacity by which OT believers manifested their faith as a pattern to reproduce (Rom. 4:11–25; Heb. 10:39–12:2). Continuity is avowed here, but God has also uttered new words and deeds in Christ (Heb. 1:1–2), has become a knowledge of present salvation. Faith, so regarded, says Paul, first "came" with Christ (Gal. 3:23–25).

The Gospels show Christ demanding trust in himself as bearing the messianic salvation. John is fullest on this, emphasizing (1) that faith ("believing on," "coming to," and "receiving" Christ) involves acknowledging Jesus, not merely as a God-sent teacher and miracle worker (John 2:23–24) but as God incarnate (John 20:28), whose atoning death is the sole means of salvation (John 3:14–15; 6:51–58); (2) that faith in Christ secures present enjoyment of "eternal life" in fellowship with God (John 5:24; 17:3). The epistles echo this, and add further relationships. Paul shows that faith in Christ is the only way to a right relation with God, which human works cannot gain (see Romans and Galatians); Hebrews and 1 Peter present faith as the dynamic of hope and endurance under persecution.

J. I. PACKER

Faith, Gift of. See SPIRITUAL GIFTS.

Faith Healing. See HEAL, HEALING.

Fall of Man. Adam and Eve's disobedience and commission of sin which brought tragic spiritual, physical, and social deprivation to the human race. The record of the fall is set forth in stark simplicity in Gen. 3. Paul juxtaposes Adam, Moses, and Christ as historical figures (Rom. 5:12, 15–19; 1 Cor. 15:20–22) and assumes the reality of the tempter and temptation (2 Cor. 11:3; 1 Tim. 2:14). In addition, Luke traces the genealogy of Jesus from Joseph through David to Adam.

The Biblical Account. Gen. 1 and 2 depict man as a sinless being, created in the image of God for fellowship with his Creator. Adam and Eve were endowed with intellect, emotion, and a will which, although inclined toward God, was free either to obey or to disobey. God placed the first man in the garden under a probationary arrangement whereby his obedience and loyalty to God would be tested. The reward of obedience would be confirmation in holiness as a spiritual son of God; the reward of disobedience was spiritual and physical death. In the state of probation Adam acted not only for himself but represented the entire race.

Adam's probation centered around the trees of life and of the knowledge of good and evil (Gen. 2:9). God's command to Adam was clear. He could freely eat of every tree except the tree of the knowledge of good and evil. Should he eat of the latter he would die (Gen. 2:16–17). Through their choices Adam and Eve could accept or rebel against the will of God.

The record indicates that, although they possessed everything needed to realize their destiny, Adam and Eve were enticed by the serpent (Gen. 3:1). Was the serpent merely a figurative description for Satan (Buswell), or did a literal serpent become the instrumentality of the devil's dark workings (Hodge, Berkhof)? The latter seems preferable, since in judgment God permanently cursed the reptile (Gen. 3:14). Nevertheless, the real tempter was Satan (1 John 3:8; Rev. 12:9). The devil in the guise of a serpent sought to beguile Eve by tempting her first to distrust God's goodness (Gen. 3:1–3) and then to disbelieve God's Word (Gen. 3:4–5). The devil, as John would put it, was a liar from the beginning (John 8:44). Enticed by the serpent Eve saw that the tree was "good for food," "a delight to the eyes," and "to be desired to make one wise" (Gen. 3:6). The attraction of the tree of knowledge involved the material ("lust of the flesh"), esthetic ("lust of the eyes"), and intellectual ("pride of life") aspects of the world's allure (1 John 2:16). Eve was struck with ambition, pride, and the quest for self-realization apart from God. She took the fruit and gave some to Adam.

The Results. Immediately following their transgression, Adam and Eve experienced personal guilt, evidenced by attempts to make garments to cover their nakedness. They hid from the presence of the Lord because they felt the breached relation with him that accompanies spiritual death. The pair tried evasion and casting the blame on one another and the serpent, illustrating the depravity which had overcome their hearts. Finally, the fall resulted in physical death—the dissolution of body-soul unity (vv. 19, 22–24). Adam and Eve were driven out of the garden and prevented from eating of the tree of life, by means of which they would have lived forever. The cherubim and flaming sword guarding the tree of life symbolize the barrier between sinful humanity and a holy God.

Humankind after the fall suffers extensive spiritual deprivation. Although the image of God in man survives (Gen. 9:6), reason has lost its soundness (2 Cor. 4:4), the will is no longer free to choose God and the good (John 8:34), and man is both spiritually blind (1 Cor. 2:14) and spiritually dead (Eph. 2:1, 5). Because the reptile served as instrument of Satan's deception, God cursed the serpent above other animals (Gen. 3:14–15). The repulsion people sense when confronted with a snake would seem to be a consequence of this curse. The prophecy is then given that Satan is doomed to be crushed. The fall would have far-reaching implications for the female (Gen. 3:16). With the onset of sin and death as the law of human existence, women must bear additional children with the increase of physical pain; and in a sinful world there would be a functional subordination of the wife to the husband (for example, 1 Cor. 11:3; Eph. 5:22–24; 1 Pet. 3:1, 5, 6). For the male, the ground would offer resistance, and only toil and sweat would make it produce (Gen. 3:17–19). But in a fallen world labor would serve as a brake to sin. Moreover, in fulfillment of Gen. 3:17 humanity was condemned to death. Raised from the dust to live, sinful humans would return to the same dust in death.

The fall's effects impinge even upon the inanimate creation as God curses the ground upon which humanity treads. Paul teaches that since the rebellion of man the entire material universe languishes in a state of disfunction (Rom. 8:20–22). The effects of Adam's sin thus are truly cosmic in scope.

Finally, the fall of Adam and humanity in him (Rom. 5:12, 15–19; 1 Cor. 15:21–22) has an impact on the God who created man and woman (Gen. 3:21). God's act of making clothing of skins for Adam and Eve typifies the fact that God then began the long process of covering sin, first by the sacrifice of animals and then through the sacrifice of his own Son (2 Cor. 5:4).

B. A. Demarest

See also Adam; Depravity, Total; Sin.

Farrer, Austin (1904–1968). Chaplain of Trinity College, Oxford (1925–60), and warden of Keble College, Oxford (1960–68). He delivered the Bampton Lectures in 1948 and the Gifford Lectures in 1957. His published works include sermons, devotional books, theology, philosophy of religion, and Bible commentaries. These books reveal a man bringing together faith and reason and a philosopher-theologian-scholar concerned for matters of the heart as well as the mind. His sermons in particular show his concern for both theology and spirituality.

S. N. Gundry

Fast, Fasting. Total or partial abstinence from food for a limited period of time, usually for moral or religious reasons. In Judaism the day of atonement is the only public fast day prescribed by the law (Lev. 16:29–31; 23:26–32; Num. 29:7–11).

However, the OT also refers to many special public and private fasts, usually coupled with prayer, to signify mourning (1 Sam. 31:13; 2 Sam. 1:12), to show repentance and remorse (2 Sam. 12:15–23; 1 Kings 21:27–29; Neh. 9:1–2; Joel 2:12–13), or to demonstrate serious concern before God (2 Chr. 20:1–4; Pss. 35:13; 69:10; 109:24; Dan. 9:3). However, fasting that was not accompanied by genuine repentance and righteous deeds was denounced as an empty legal observance by the prophets (Isa. 58; Jer. 14:11–12).

Jesus himself apparently fasted in the wilderness as part of the preparation for his formal ministry (Matt. 4:1–2; Luke 4:1–2). However, the Gospels report that he spoke only twice about fasting—once to warn his disciples that it was to be a private act of simple devotion to God and once to indicate that it would be appropriate for his followers to fast after he left them (Matt. 6:16–18; 9:14–15; Mark 2:18–20; Luke 5:33–35). It is clear that he did not stress fasting, nor did he lay down any rules concerning its observance as had John the Baptist and the Pharisees for their disciples.

The early Christian community did not emphasize fasting but observed it in connection with certain occasions of solemn commitment (Acts 13:2–3; 14:23). Jewish Christians apparently followed the Jewish custom of fasting and prayer on Mondays and Thursdays until around the end of the first century when Wednesdays and Fridays were observed, probably in reaction against the Judaizers. However, such fasts were usually concluded by midafternoon and were not universally enforced. Also, from the 2d century on, two intensive fast days were observed in preparation for Easter.

In the 4th century, when Christianity finally became the only recognized faith of the Roman Empire, the consequent institutionalization of the church led to a much greater stress on form, ritual, and liturgy. Fasting became increasingly linked with a legalistic theology and the concept of meritorious works. In modern times there has been an attempt by Christians of different kinds to rediscover the true dynamic of fasting, as a way of pleasing God.

R. D. Linder

Fate, Fatalism. Fate, personified by the Greeks under the name of Moira, signified in the ancient world the unseen power that rules over human destiny. In classical thought fate was believed to be superior to the gods, since even they were unable to defy its all-encompassing power. Fate is not chance, which may be defined as the absence of laws, but instead a cosmic determinism that has no ultimate meaning or purpose. In classical thought as well as in Oriental religion fate is a dark, sinister power related to the tragic vision of life. Fate is blind, inscrutable, and inescapable. Christianity substituted for the hellenistic concept of fate the doctrine of divine providence. Whereas fate is the portentous, impersonal power that thwarts and overrules human freedom, providence liberates humans to fulfill the destiny for which they were created.

D. G. Bloesch

See also Freedom, Free Will, and Determinism; Providence of God.

Father, God as. It is chiefly in connection with Israel, the Davidic king, and Messiah that references to the fatherhood of God occur in the OT. By the historical event of deliverance from Egypt, God created the nation of Israel and subsequently cared for them, establishing a special relationship with them. His care for them is frequently compared to that of a father (Hos. 11:1; Deut. 14:1; 2 Sam. 7:14; Pss. 2:7; 89:26; Deut. 1:31; 8:5; Isa. 1:2). In a certain sense God is the Father of the God-fearing among the nation, rather than of the nation as a whole (Ps. 103:13; Mal. 3:17).

This later mode of thought finds expression also in the literature of the intertestamental period (Jubilees 1:24; Psalms of Solomon 13:8; 17:30; Ecclesiasticus 23:1, 4) and is endorsed by the teaching of Jesus. He gave increased prominence to the doctrine of the fatherhood of God. Two points in connection with Jesus' use of this title are of special interest. (1) He never joins his disciples with himself in allusions to his relationship with the Father in such a way as to suggest that their relationship to God is of the same kind (Matt. 11:27; John 3:25; 5:22; 8:58; 10:30, 38; 14:9; 16:28). (2) When he speaks of God as the Father of others he almost always refers to his disciples. While accepting the teaching of the OT that all persons are children of God by creation and receive his providential kindness (Matt. 5:45), he also taught that sin has brought about a change in people, necessitating rebirth and reconciliation to God (John 3:3; 8:42; 14:6). In accordance with this, the apostles teach that one becomes a child of God by faith in Christ and thus receives the Spirit of adoption (John 1:12; Gal. 3:16; 4:5; Rom. 8:15).

W. J. CAMERON

See also ABBA; GOD, ATTRIBUTES OF; GOD, DOCTRINE OF; GOD, NAMES OF.

Fathers, Church. Ecclesiastically, those who have preceded modern Christians in the faith. In this sense, ministers and particularly bishops are often referred to as fathers. More particularly the term has come to be applied to the first Christian writers of acknowledged eminence. Already in the 4th century it was used in this way of the teachers of the preceding epoch, and later all the outstanding theologians of at least the first six centuries have come to be regarded as fathers; for example Athanasius and Augustine. This is the normal current usage, although sometimes Protestants speak of the Reformation fathers (Luther, Zwingli, and Calvin).

G. W. BROMILEY

See also AMBROSE; AUGUSTINE OF HIPPO; CAPPADOCIAN FATHERS; CHRYSOSTOM, JOHN; CLEMENT OF ALEXANDRIA; CYPRIAN; CYRIL OF ALEXANDRIA; GREGORY I, THE GREAT; HIPPOLYTUS; ORIGEN; TERTULLIAN.

Federal Theology. See COVENANT THEOLOGY.

Feeling, Theology of. See EXPERIENCE, THEOLOGY OF.

Felix Culpa. See FORTUNATE FALL, THE.

Fellowship. (Gk. *koinonia*, "participation, fellowship, communion") The sense of sharing and self-sacrifice inherent in the word is evident in references to financial support in the early church as *koinonia* (verb, Rom. 12:13; 15:26; Gal. 6:6; Phil. 4:15; noun, 2 Cor. 8:4; 9:13; Heb. 13:16). Paul viewed the contribution for the needy Jewish Christians in Jerusalem, taken up from the poverty-stricken Gentile Christians in the hellenistic world, as the ultimate expression of fellowship among Christians. Then the true believer has fellowship in (participates in the implications of) the sufferings of Christ (Phil. 3:10; 1 Pet. 4:13), the sufferings of the apostles (2 Cor. 1:7), and the sufferings of his fellow man (Heb. 10:33).

There is a sense in which the Lord's Supper constitutes a fellowship or participation in the blood and body of Christ (1 Cor. 10:16). This is perhaps one of the meanings of the fellowship of the Spirit (2 Cor. 13:14; Phil. 2:1) and one of the ways we become partakers (*koinonia*) of the divine nature (2 Pet. 1:4) and of the glory that is to be revealed (1 Pet. 5:1).

J. R. MCRAY

Fideism. A school of thought at the turn of the century among Protestant modernists in Paris (Menegoz, Sabatier), but since used pejoratively to attack various strands of Christian "irrationalism." Fideists, following Immanuel Kant (who argued that reason cannot prove religious truth), are said to base their understanding of the Christian faith upon religious experience alone, understanding reason to be incapable of establishing either faith's certitude or credibility.

R. K. JOHNSTON

See also EXPERIENCE, THEOLOGY OF.

Filioque. (Lat., lit. "and from the Son") A phrase in the Western version of the Nicene Creed which says that the Holy Spirit proceeds from the Father *and the Son*. This was inserted into the confessions agreed to at Nicea (325) and Constantinople (381), apparently first at the local Council of Toledo (589). In spite of opposition the phrase gradually established itself in the West and was officially endorsed in 1017. Photius of Constantinople denounced it in the 9th century, and it was the main doctrinal issue in the rupture between East and West in 1054.

G. W. BROMILEY

Final State. The two eternal destinies of heaven and hell. Jesus spoke of both these eternal states in Matt. 25:46 .

J. K. GRIDER

See also HEAVEN; HELL; JUDGMENT; JUDGMENT SEAT.

Finney, Charles Grandison (1792–1875). American perfectionist, abolition leader, and revivalist. Between 1824 and 1832 Finney established the modern forms and methods of revivalism; he then spent his last 40 years constructing a theology of revival and Christian life as a professor at what was soon called Oberlin (Ohio) College (1836; president, 1851–66). His *Lectures on Revival* (1835) sought to preach a "right view of both classes of truths"—God's sovereignty and free human agency. In *Letters on Revival* (1845) he confessed he had been too optimistic in expecting a national revival. He nonetheless wished to use Oberlin to prepare "a new race of revival ministers" and, as he explained in *Lectures to Professing Christians* (1837) and later writings, to awaken people to the attainable duty of practicing Christian perfection as commanded by Matt. 5:48.

C. T. MCINTIRE

See also OBERLIN THEOLOGY; REVIVALISM.

Fire, Lake of. See LAKE OF FIRE.

Firstborn. Primogeniture, the exclusive right of inheritance belonging to the firstborn, is traceable to patriarchal times. The idea of firstborn in the NT is indicated by *prototokos*, which occurs eight times, most either historically or figuratively referring to Christ. That the term is a messianic title is suggested by the Greek of Ps. 89:27. The NT alludes to Christ as the firstborn in three aspects. (1) In Col. 1:15 he is said to be the "firstborn of all creation." (2) Col. 1:18 and Rev. 1:5 use firstborn in a sense similar to the first fruits of 1 Cor. 15:20. Christ is the firstborn from the dead because he was the first to be raised. (3) Rom. 8:29 teaches that Christ is the "firstborn among many brethren," which affirms that believers have joined the family of which Christ is the eldest Son.

D. H. WALLACE

First Day of the Week. See LORD'S DAY.

First Resurrection. See RESURRECTION OF THE DEAD.

Fixed Feasts. Feasts celebrated on the same calendar date each year. It differs from a movable feast among the various types of feasts celebrated in the Christian year. Easter is a movable feast; it may appear on various dates. Christmas is a fixed feast because it must fall on Dec. 25.

T. J. GERMAN

See also MOVABLE FEASTS; CHRISTIAN YEAR.

Flacius, Matthias (1520–1575). German Lutheran theologian. Flacius became involved in many disputes that plagued late 16th-century Lutheranism, including the adiaphoristic, the majoristic, and the synergistic controversies. Flacius and his supporters founded the Gnesio-Lutheran ("true Lutheran") faction, which attacked Philip Melanchthon and his followers as too conciliatory toward Roman Catholicism and proceeded to develop a Lutheran teaching distinct from Catholicism and more moderate Lutherans (Philippists). Flacius's well-known writings include the *Clavis*, or key to the Scriptures, which set forth his hermeneutical principles, and an anti-Roman history of the church, the *Magdeburg Centuries*.

R. G. CLOUSE

See also MAJORISTIC CONTROVERSY; MELANCHTHON, PHILIP; MONERGISM; SYNERGISM.

Flesh. (Heb. *šĕʾēr*, *bāśār*; Gk. *sarx*) The vehicle and circumstances of humanity's physical life in this world. In Phil. 1:22–24 Paul contrasts living in the flesh with departing to be "with Christ." Regularly, "flesh" is used along with "bones," "blood," or "body" (for example, Prov. 5:11; 1 Cor. 15:50) to isolate the physical aspect of human nature. Two modes of being are signified by "flesh" and "spirit" (Isa. 31:3; Jer. 17:5; John 1:13). Humankind as a race shares a common flesh (Gen. 6:12; Matt. 24:22; 1 Pet. 1:24).

In the NT. The term is most frequently used in the NT, especially by Paul, to refer to the sinful, unregenerate nature or lifestyle (Rom. 8:3, 5; Gal. 5:17; Jude 23). In the unregenerate, the flesh, with its passions (Gal. 5:24), works death (Rom. 7:5). The acts of the fleshly nature (Rom. 8: 12; Gal. 5:19) are characterized by lust (Gal. 5:16; 1 Pet. 4:2; 2 Pet. 2:10; 1 John 2:16), which enslaves the body and dominates the mind (Eph. 2:3), so that there is a complete mental state of the flesh (Rom. 8:5, 7). Very different are those who have experienced God's regeneration. They remain "in" the flesh, but they are no longer "after" the flesh (2 Cor. 10:3; Gal. 2:20).

The sinlessness of Jesus, the Word made flesh, is preserved by the careful statement that God sent his Son "in the likeness of sinful flesh" (Rom. 8:3; see Heb. 4:15); the Son became one with people at the point of their need (Heb. 2:14) in order to deal with sin at the point of its strength (see Rom. 8:3, ERV). "Flesh" is constantly used to teach the genuine humanity of the Savior (Rom. 1:4; 9:5; 1 Tim. 3:16; Heb. 5:7). Yet it is his flesh as "given" (John 6:51–56) which gives life. As an offering for sin he condemned sin in his physical body. The flesh is the sphere and instrument of redemption (Col. 1:22; 1 Pet. 3:18; 4:1) and was the sublime purpose of the incarnation (Heb. 10:5–20).

J. A. MOTYER

See also MAN, DOCTRINE OF; SIN.

Flood, The. The Noahic deluge as a catastrophic event involved tidal waves and heavy rain (Gen. 7:11) and perhaps underground springs. From southern Mesopotamia the flood stretched northward to the mountains of Urartu (Ararat), the peaks of which were covered. All living things died, and the storm only began to diminish after 150 days, the earth finally drying out 371 days from the beginning of the storms. The extent of the flood has aroused much debate. The word translated "earth" can mean a country, and "heaven" can describe the amount of sky visible within one's own horizon (1 Kings 18:45). While some arguments may suggest a limited flood, the fact that the mountains were submerged implies a more extended one (Gen. 7:19–20). Genesis thus supports arguments for both a local and a universal deluge, with traditional biblical teaching favoring the latter and regarding the flood as a punishment for unrepentent wickedness (Gen. 6:5).

R. K. HARRISON

Followers of the Way. See CHRISTIANS, NAMES OF.

Foot Washing. A religious act in some parts of the Christian church based upon the example and command of Jesus at the Last Supper. The wearing of open sandals, the dry climate, and dusty roads made foot washing upon entering a home a familiar practice in Eastern hospitality. The practice was given special prominence by Jesus when he washed his disciples' feet (John 13:1–20). His statement that the disciples "ought to wash one another's feet" (John 13:14) gave added importance to the act. The practice of the pedilavium may be seen in the early church from 1 Tim. 5:10 and from patristic notices in Tertullian (*De corona* 8) and Athanasius (*Canon* 66). The Synod of Toledo (694) prescribed it. Pedilavium has been observed by Roman and Greek churches and in such Protestant groups as Brethren, Mennonites, Waldensians, Winebrennarians, and some Baptists.

H. A. KENT, JR.

Foreknowledge. God's prescience or foresight concerning future events, an aspect of God's omniscience. All things, past, present, and future, external and internal, material, intellectual, and spiritual, are open to God. The Lord knows all things (1 Sam. 2:3) or everything (1 John 3:20). All creatures are open to his eyes (Heb. 4:13). Omniscience naturally includes prescience. God does not just know what is happening or has happened. He knows what is still to happen.

Foreknowledge stands in relation to the divine eternity. God is the "high and lofty One who inhabits eternity" (Isa. 57:15). Isa. 40 and succeeding chapters show that past, present, and future are present; he sees the end from the beginning and the beginning at the end (46:10). Being part of creation, time does not limit or condition God. His foreknowledge stands related to his will and power. He does not know merely as information; he is no mere spectator. When he foreknows he ordains. He knows because, willing, he has the power to do his will. "I have spoken, and I will bring it to pass" (46:11); "I work and who can hinder it?" (43:13). By reason of the totality of will and power in God's prescience, the "pre" in the word has more than temporal meaning. With his prior knowledge of things God is the presupposition of their being.

A collision seems to arise between divine foreknowledge and human freedom. God plainly foreknows and foreordains. Nothing outside him restricts or conditions his own freedom. Nevertheless, Scripture no less plainly teaches human responsibility in moral decision (Acts 4:27–28; Rom. 8:29–30; Eph. 1:11 for divine sovereignty; Deut. 30:19; 1 Kings 18:21 for human responsibility). Divine foreknowledge must not be confused with determinism or fatalism, difficult though the reconciling of prescience and human choice might be. The task of putting the two biblical truths together has led to some valid and important distinctions. God's necessary knowledge of himself is distinguished from his free knowledge of creatures. His speculative or contemplative knowledge is distinguished from his practical or active knowledge. His knowledge of possibility is distinguished from his knowledge of actuality. His approving knowledge of good is distinguished from his disapproving knowledge of evil (for example, the "I never knew you" of Matt. 7:23). All things are not known to God in the same way.

It is perhaps best to say that whether in providence or predestination, divine prescience means that God is in fact the presupposition of all things, including our wills, choices, and decisions. Nothing we do can inform or surprise him or impose conditions on him. He knows us omnipotently, yet he does not destroy us with this knowledge, but with it originates and guarantees authentic freedom. Only as sinners opposing God's will do we experience his foreknowledge as burden and bondage. True freedom does not imply the possibility of defying God but of serving him. We are foreknown and foreordained in the real self-determination which sees no problem in its being self-determination in and under the divine prescience.

G. W. BROMILEY

See also ELECT, ELECTION; SCIENTIA MEDIA.

Foreordination. See PREDESTINATION.

Forgiveness. In Heb. "forgiveness" is conveyed by *kāpar*, "to cover" (noun, *kippūr*, "atonement or covering"); *nāśā'*, "to bear" (guilt); *sālaḥ*, "to pardon." *Nāśā'* is used of both divine and human forgiveness. *Kāpar* and *nāśā'* describe only divine forgiveness. In the Gk. NT the words are *apolyein, charizesthai, aphesis,* and *paresis. Apolyein* is found numerous times as "to put away," (Matt. 5:31), but only once to signify forgiveness (Luke 6:37). *Paresis* (Rom. 3:25 only) suggests "putting aside" or "disregarding." In order for the righteous God to do this, Christ Jesus had to be "displayed publicly as a propitiation" (Rom. 3:25 NASB). *Charizesthai* is used only by Luke (Luke 7:21; Acts 3:14) and Paul, and only by the latter in the sense of "to forgive sins" (2 Cor. 2:7; Eph. 4:32; Col. 2:13; 3:13). It expresses the graciousness of God's forgiveness. It is used in connection with Christ's bestowing sight (Luke 7:21) and in describing that God freely gives us "all things" (Rom. 8:32). The most common NT word for forgiveness is *aphesis*. This noun is found 15 times and is generally translated "forgiveness" (Matt. 26:28). The verb is found about 40 times.

No book of religion except the Bible teaches that God completely forgives sin, but there it is frequently taught. For Christ's sake God has graciously forgiven [*echarisato*]" (Eph. 4:32), and remembers forgiven sins no more (Heb. 10:17). The initiative of forgiveness is with God, especially in Paul's use of *charizesthai* (2 Cor. 12:13; Col. 2:13). It is a ready forgiveness, as is shown in the prodigal son or "gracious father" parable (Luke 15:11–32).

There is only one sin for which the Father does not promise forgiveness: blasphemy against the Holy Spirit (Mark 3:29; Matt. 12:32). The contexts seem to suggest that this sin is attributing to unclean spirits the work of the Holy Spirit, but many interpreters (including Augustine) have understood it to include a deliberate persistence in such evil. This sin is also considered by some to be the unforgiving spirit (see Matt. 18:34–35). It might be the same as the "sin unto death" of 1 John 5:16.

There are to be no limitations whatever to the forgiveness of others (Luke 17:4; Matt. 18:22, both of which probably signify limitlessness). It is to be an attitude of mind even before the offending party requests forgiveness, as is implied by Jesus' statement, "unless you forgive your brother from your heart" (Matt. 18:35 NIV). For us to receive forgiveness, repentance is necessary (Luke 17:3–4). For the holy God to extend forgiveness the shedding of blood (Heb. 9:22) until no life is left (Lev. 17:11) is prerequisite—ultimately, the once-for-all (Heb. 9:26) spilling of Christ's blood and his rising again (Rom. 4:25).

J. K. GRIDER

See also ATONEMENT; ATONEMENT, DAY OF; PROPITIATION; SIN.

Formula of Concord. See CONCORD, FORMULA OF.

Fornication. Voluntary sexual communion between an unmarried person and one of the opposite sex. Fornicators (*pornoi*) are distinguished from adulterers (*moichoi*), as in 1 Cor. 6:9. In a wider sense *porneia* signifies unlawful cohabitation of either sex with a married person. In this meaning it is used interchangeably with *moicheia*, as in Matt. 5:32. The same use of *porneia* in the sense of adultery (*moichatai*) is found in Matt. 19:9. In its widest sense *porneia* denotes immorality in general, or every kind of sexual transgression. In 1 Cor. 5:1 *porneia* is rightly translated in the RSV by "immorality."

J. T. MUELLER

See also ADULTERY.

Forsyth, Peter Taylor (1848–1921). Scottish theologian. He was for 20 years principal of Hackney College, a Congregational theological seminary in London. In 1907 he gave the Lyman Beecher lectures at Yale University.

Forsyth sought to relate the gospel to the modern mind without surrendering its unique claims. He accepted the findings of historical criticism but differed from liberal theology in believing that criticism must be subjected to the scrutiny of a higher norm—the gospel. In Forsyth's view the heart of evangelical faith lies in the message of the cross. Soteriology was more important for him than Christology, the atonement more crucial than the incarnation. He saw the cross of Christ as the creative moral crisis of history, the point where divinity and humanity, time and eternity, judgment and grace met for a new creation.

Forsyth pioneered in the area of spirituality. It is holy souls who furnish the most potent argument for the gospel, apart from the gospel itself. The emphasis should be justification by holiness (by the holy God) and for holiness (life in communion with God). Forsyth saw prayer as supplication and intercession before a holy God. Forsyth is widely regarded as a forerunner of the neoorthodoxy of Karl Barth and Emil Brunner.

D. G. BLOESCH

Fortunate Fall, The. The concept of "fortunate fall" or *felix culpa* (happy crime) is rooted in early Christian liturgy, medieval and Reformed theology, and ultimately in the biblical text. It expresses the believer's confidence in God's beneficial control of evil. Augustine stated: "God judged it better to bring good out of evil than to suffer no evil to exist" (*Enchiridion* 8.27). Major theologians continued this concept, and Reformers made it a renewed emphasis. According to Musculus, "Through Christ we are more happily restored after the fall than we had been when created" (H. Heppe, *Reformed Dogmatics*, p. 304).

D. F. KELLY

See also EVIL, PROBLEM OF; FALL OF MAN; PROVIDENCE OF GOD; THEODICY.

Fosdick, Harry Emerson (1878–1969). American Protestant minister; Fosdick was the nation's most influential spokesman for classic theological liberalism. Born in Buffalo, N.Y., he was ordained in 1903 by the Madison Avenue Baptist Church and took a Baptist pastorate in Montclair, N.J., in 1904. He was professor of practical theology at Union Seminary (1908–46). From 1918 to 1924 he served as regular "guest minister" of First Presbyterian Church in New York where he became a lightning rod in the fundamentalist-modernist controversy, especially after 1922 when he preached and published his sermon: "Shall the Fundamentalists Win?" In 1926 Fosdick became pastor of the future Riverside Church, which he served until his retirement in 1946. A dynamic preacher and polished writer, Fosdick used his 30 books, a weekly radio ministry, and his pulpit to attack traditional Protestantism, evangelism, uncritical use of the Bible, and any lack of interest in scientific educational theory. He attempted to incorporate biblical criticism, insights from the psychology of religion, the teachings of evolution, and the values expressed in modern political and social movements into Christianity, accenting ethical aspects of Christian faith. Fosdick also stressed the personal peace and power of religion—as in his enormously popular *On Being a Real Person* (1943).

R. D. LINDER

See also FUNDAMENTALISM; LIBERALISM, THEOLOGICAL.

Four Spiritual Laws, The. An approach to personal evangelism written by Bill Bright, president of Campus Crusade for Christ. Originally prepared for staff of his worldwide evangelistic organization, the booklet "Have You Heard of the Four Spiritual Laws" has circulated widely. More than 25 million copies were distributed by 1980. The laws attempt to distill the essence of the gospel and to present it simply to the non-Christian. The four laws are: (1) God loves you and offers a wonderful plan for your life (John 3:16; 10:10). (2) Man is sinful and separated from God. Therefore, he cannot know and experience God's love and plan for his life (Rom. 3:23; 6:23). (3) Jesus Christ is God's only provision for man's sin. Through him you can know and experience God's love and plan for your life (Rom. 5:8; 1 Cor. 15:3–6; John 14:6). (4) We must individually receive Jesus Christ as Savior and Lord; then we can know and experience God's love and plan for our lives (John 1:12; 3:1–8; Eph. 2:8–9; Rev. 3:20).

R. K. JOHNSTON

Fox, George (1624–1691). English founder of the Society of Friends (Quakers). Son of a Leicestershire weaver, he announced in 1646 his reliance on the "Inner Light of the Living Christ." He rejected sacraments, paid clergy, even church attendance, and taught that truth is to be found, not in Scripture or creed, but in God's voice speaking to the soul. So emerged the "Friends of Truth." Their anticlerical views, disrespect of authority, and refusal to take oaths often led to arrest and imprisonment. His travels extended to the Netherlands, West Indies, and America (notably Maryland and Rhode Island). Whenever he could, he established local congregations. Fox was also a true pacifist, and his use of group silence was a brake on impetuous conduct. Later he moved his base from northwest England to London, where he spent his final years crusading against social evils, fighting for religious toleration and the promotion of education. His *Journal* gives insights into the turbulent conditions in England during the latter half of the 17th century.

J. D. DOUGLAS

See also FRIENDS, SOCIETY OF.

Franciscan Order. One of four 13th-century orders of mendicant (begging) friars (Franciscan, Dominican, Carmelite, Augustinian) established to meet the urgent challenge of spiritual decline, urban growth, and the rapid spread of heresy (especially in southern France and northern Italy). It was founded by Francis of Assisi and formally approved by Innocent III in 1210. Unlike earlier monasticism, the friars lived active lives as preachers and ministers to the needy. In 1517, Pope Leo X divided the Order into two independent branches—the Friars Minor of the Regular Observants (strict) and the Friars Minor Conventuals (moderate). Given their reforming instincts, the Observants soon divided into factions—Discalced (shoeless), Recollects, Reformed, and Capuchins (pointed cowl). Capuchins played a significant role in the Counter-Reformation and by 1619 had gained complete autonomy. In 1897 Pope Leo XIII united all Observant branches except the Capuchins, who retained their independence. Alongside the Order of Friars Minor, with the three independent branches of Observants, Conventuals, and Capuchins, there emerged two other Franciscan Orders—the Second Order of nuns (Poor Clares), founded by Francis and his follower Clare in 1212, and the Third Order (Tertiaries) of mainly laypersons.

R. K. BISHOP

See also FRANCIS OF ASSISI; MONASTICISM; MYSTICISM; SCHOLASTICISM.

Francis of Assisi (1182–1226). Francesco Bernardone, the universally admired founder of the Order of Friars Minor (Franciscans). The key of Francis's life was his uncompromising attempt to imitate Christ of the Gospels through absolute poverty, humility, and simplicity. He loved nature as God's good handiwork and had a deep respect for women (such as his beloved mother and Clare, his follower). At the same time, his willing obedience to the papacy and the priesthood allowed the church to embrace this otherwise radical reformer. Intense meditation on the suffering of Christ led to the famous experience of the stigmata—signs in his own flesh of the wounds of his Master. Although he was more a preacher than a writer, in 1223 he completed a second rule (adapted as the official Rule of the Order) and about 1224 his most famous piece, "Canticle of the Sun," a paean of praise for God and his creation.

R. K. BISHOP

See also FRANCISCAN ORDER; MONASTICISM; MYSTICISM.

Francke, August Hermann (1663–1727). One of the foremost leaders of pietism. Through the influence of P. J. Spener he became professor at the recently founded University of Halle in 1692 and taught there until his death. Halle became a center of pietism, with its stress on religious experience for the assurance of salvation. Francke's students carried his influence to various parts of Germany and to Scandinavia and Eastern Europe. Francke also pastored a nearby congregation. In 1695 he founded an orphanage, the first of several educational and charitable institutions funded entirely by contributions. He was active in supporting foreign mission work in India. His writings include exegetical, practical, and polemical works, a copious correspondence, and a few hymns.

J. M. DRICKAMER

See also EXPERIENCE, THEOLOGY OF; PIETISM; SPENER, PHILIPP JAKOB.

Freedom, Free Will, and Determinism. There are three basic positions concerning human choice: determinism; indeterminism, and self-determinism.

Determinism. The belief that human actions are the result of antecedent causes. Naturalistic determinism sees human beings as part of the machinery of the universe. In such a world every event is caused by preceding events, which in turn were caused by still earlier events, *ad infinitum.* Since each person is part of this causal chain, individual actions are determined by such antecedent causes as the environment and heredity. These are so determinative of human actions that no one could rightly say that any action could have been performed otherwise than it in fact was. According to determinism, the decision to sit on a brown chair rather than a blue sofa is not a free choice but is fully determined by previous factors. B. F. Skinner, the author of *Beyond Freedom and Dignity* and *About Behaviorism*, was a theorist in determinism.

Theistic determinism asserts that all events, including behavior, are caused (determined) by God. One of the more famous advocates of this view was the Puritan theologian Jonathan Edwards. He maintained that the concept of free will or self-determinism contradicted the sovereignty of God. If God is truly in control of all things, then no one could act contrary to his will, which is what self-determinism must hold. Hence, for God to be sovereign he must cause every event, including human action. Edwards argued that self-determinism is self-contradictory. If the will were in equilibrium or indifferent to any given event or decision, the will could never act, any more than a balanced weight scale can tip itself unless an outside force upsets the balance. Thus to speak of human acts as self-caused would speak of nothing causing something. Since every event must have a cause, self-determinism, which denies this, must be self-contradictory.

Indeterminism. The view that human behavior is totally uncaused. There are no antecedent or simultaneous causes of actions. All human acts are uncaused, and any given human act could have been otherwise. Some indeterminists extend their view beyond human affairs to the entire universe. In support of the indeterminacy of all events Heisenberg's principle of uncertainty states that it is impossible to predict where a subatomic particle is and how fast it is moving at any given moment. Since subatomic events are inherently unpredictable, how much more so are complex human acts. Human and nonhuman events are, therefore, uncaused. Two noted exponents of indeterminism are William James and Charles Peirce. Indeterminism is unacceptable for a Christian. If indeterminism is true, then either there is no God or no causal connection between God and the universe. The Christian position is that God created the world and providentially sustains it and intervenes in its affairs (Matt. 6:25–32; Col. 1:15–16).

Self-determinism. The view that a person's acts are caused by himself. Self-determinists accept that such factors as heredity and environment influence behavior. However, they deny that such factors are determining causes of behavior. Inanimate objects do not change without an outside cause, but personal subjects are able to direct their own actions. Self-determinists reject the notions that events are uncaused or that they cause themselves. Rather, they believe that human actions can be caused by human beings. Two prominent advocates of this view are Thomas Aquinas and C. S. Lewis. Forms of self-determinism seek to uphold the biblical views of God's sovereignty and of human responsibility.

N. L. GEISLER

Freewill Offering. See OFFERINGS AND SACRIFICES IN BIBLE TIMES.

Friend. See CHRISTIANS, NAMES OF.

Friends, Society of. Known also as Quakers. The founder was George Fox, who experienced a profound change in his religious life in 1652 when he said that he had a vision at a place called Pendle Hill. He thereafter based his faith on the idea that God speaks directly to any person.

Some of the first converts were called "Friends" or "Friends in Truth." The term "Quaker" was described by Fox as follows. "The priest scoffed at us and called us Quakers. But the Lord's power was so over them, and the word of life was declared in such authority and dread to them, that the priest began trembling himself; and one of the people said, 'Look how the priest trembles and shakes, he is turned a Quaker also.'"

The Quaker principle is simplicity in the manner of living. Women are encouraged to be ministers and there is spiritual democracy in meetings, and a stress on seeking truth and universal peace and brotherhood. Quakers have refused to remove hats to those in authority and used the singular "thee" and "thou" in their speech. They influenced the thought and social ethics of the English-speaking world far out of proportion to their numbers. Fox was imprisoned eight times, but he pioneered care for the poor, aged, and insane; advocated prison reform; opposed capital punishment, war, and slavery, and sought fair treatment of American Indians.

Probably the best known historical figure in the Society of Friends was William Penn. Born in 1644, he became a Quaker in 1667 and was an embarrassment to his father, Admiral Penn. King Charles II gave young William a grant of land in America to repay a debt to his father, launching Pennsylvania as a "holy experiment." By 1700 there were Friends meeting in all of the colonies.

A division occurred in the Society of Friends about 1827, with one group supporting the views of Elias Hicks, who believed that one should follow the inner light. The other group was influenced by the evangelical movement and put great emphasis on belief in the divinity of Christ, the authority of the Scriptures, and the atonement. Friends were also active in the antislavery movement. John Woolman, Anthony Benezet, Lucretia Mott, and John Greenleaf Whittier were involved in such activities as the underground railroad and the Colonization Society. The tradition of caring for others spurred humanitarian service during the American Civil War, and the American Friends Service Committee was formed in 1917.

The Society of Friends has no written creed and is optimistic about the purposes of God and the destiny of mankind. Their final authority for religious life and faith resides within each individual. Many, but not all, seek for this truth through the guidance of the inner light. They believe that they are bound to refuse obedience to a government when its requirements are contrary to what they believe to be the law of God, but they are willing to accept the penalties for civil disobedience.

J. E. JOHNSON

See also FOX, GEORGE.

Fullness. (Gk. *plērōma*) ***Theological Occurrences in the NT.*** (1) The "fullness" of Christ (John 1:16) is the inexhaustible resources of his grace on which his people may freely draw. (2) The "fullness" of Christ (Eph. 4:13) is also a spiritual maturity to which believers attain as members of his body. (3) The "fullness" of God (Eph. 3:19) is the full realization in believers of that eternal purpose toward which God is working. (4) The "fullness" which by God's decree resides in Christ (Col. 1:19) is the "fullness" of deity (Col. 2:9). (5) In Eph. 1:23, the church, the body of Christ, is called "the *fullness* of him who fills all in all"—or (as others translate) "the *complement* of him who is being perpetually filled" (with the fullness of deity). Whether the verb is middle ("fills") or passive ("is being filled"), "fullness" is probably in apposition with "body."

Gnostic Usage. In Valentinianism *plērōma* denotes the totality of the divine attributes. These attributes are expressed mythologically as 30 "aeons" emanating from God, but distinct from him and from the material world. They correspond to the Platonic "ideas"; sometimes each aeon is called a *plērōma* by contrast with the defectiveness of its earthly copies.

F. F. BRUCE

Fullness of Time. In Gal. 4:4 the period before Christ's birth. Israel had waited centuries for a Messiah. Paul uses the expression (which literally indicates the time set for a child's majority) to indicate that only when history had "matured" to the proper point was God ready to act. In Eph. 1:10, however, Paul is looking in the other direction: redemption was accomplished at the cross, but it is marked out in history. The "mystery"

(Rom. 16:25–26; Eph. 1:9; 3:4–5; Col. 1:26), which is this plan to unite all things in Christ, is being worked out in the church as the gospel spreads, people are joined to Christ, and the gospel transforms the social situation of the world.

P. H. DAVIDS

Fundamentalism. A movement reaffirming orthodox Protestant Christianity in order to defend it militantly against the challenges of liberal theology, German higher criticism, Darwinism, and other views regarded as harmful to American Christianity. It arose in the early 1900s and reached its height during and after World War I. Since then, the focus of the movement, the meaning of the term, and the ranks of those who willingly use the term to identify themselves have changed several times. Fundamentalism has gone through four phases of expression while maintaining an essential continuity of spirit, belief, and method.

Through the 1920s. The earliest phase involved articulating what was fundamental to Christianity and initiating an urgent battle to expel enemies of orthodox Protestantism from mainline churches. A series of 12 volumes called *The Fundamentals* (1910–15) identified a wide listing of enemies—Romanism, socialism, modern philosophy, atheism, Eddyism, Mormonism, spiritualism, and the like. Above all, liberal theology, which rested on a naturalistic interpretation of faith, and German higher criticism and Darwinism, which appeared to undermine the Bible's authority, were identified as threats. The writers represented a broad, interdenominational Christianity in both North America and the United Kingdom. The doctrines they defined and defended covered historical Christian teachings. They presented criticisms fairly, with careful argument and in appreciation of much their opponents said. Almost immediately, however, the list of enemies became narrower and the fundamentals less comprehensive.

The term "fundamentalist" was perhaps first used in 1920 by Curtis Lee Laws in the Baptist *Watchman-Examiner,* but it seemed to pop up everywhere in the early 1920s as an identification for someone who believed and actively defended the fundamentals of the faith.

Late 1920s to the Early 1940s. By 1926 or so, militant fundamentalists had failed to expel the modernists from any denomination. Moreover, they lost the battle against evolution. Orthodox Protestants, who still numerically dominated the denominations, began to struggle among themselves. During the 1930s the term "fundamentalist" came to apply to one party among those who believed the traditional fundamentals of the faith. New "pure" denominations emerged. The distinctive theological point that the fundamentalists made was that they represented true Christianity, based on a literal interpretation of the Bible, and that this truth ought to be expressed organizationally in separation from liberals and modernists; separatism was aligned with the maintenance of fundamental Christianity. Fundamentalists identified with purity in personal morality and American culture. Thus, the term "fundamentalist" came to refer largely to orthodox Protestants who left mainline northern denominations and established new denominations, joined conservative Southern churches, or started independent churches.

Early 1940s to the 1970s. From the early 1940s fundamentalists, thus redefined, divided gradually into two camps: Many voluntarily continued to use the term to refer to themselves. They equated fundamentalism with true Bible-believing Christianity. Others regarded the term as undesirable, connoting divisiveness, intolerance, anti-intellectualism, unconcern with social problems, even foolishness. This second group wished to regain fellowship with orthodox Protestants who still constituted the vast majority of clergy and people in the large Northern denominations—Presbyterian, Baptist, Methodist, and Episcopalian. They began during the 1940s to call themselves "evangelicals" and to equate that term with true Christianity. Beginning in 1948 a few preferred to take the name "neoevangelical." Organizationally many separatist fundamentalists formed the American Council of Christian Churches (ACCC) in 1941. Those desiring a more inclusive fellowship formed the National Association of Evangelicals (NAE) in 1942, which sought to embrace orthodox Protestants as individuals in all denominations.

The term "fundamentalist" now expressed a contrast from evangelicals or neoevangelicals, rather than merely with liberalism, modernism, or neoorthodoxy. Fundamentalists and evangelicals in the 1950s and 1960s shared much but remained apart because of a different ethos.

Late 1970s and the 1980s. By the late 1970s, and in particular by the 1980 campaign of Ronald Reagan for the U.S. presidency, fundamentalists entered a new phase. They became nationally prominent as offering an answer for what many regarded as a supreme social, economic, moral, and religious crisis in America. They identified a new and more pervasive enemy, secular humanism, which they believed was responsible for eroding churches, schools, universities, the government, and—above all—families. They fought those they considered to be offspring of secular humanism—evolutionism, political and theological liberalism, loose personal morality, sexual perversion, socialism, communism, and any turn from the absolute, inerrant authority of the Bible. They called Americans to return to the fundamentals of the faith and the fundamental moral values.

C. T. McIntire

See also Evangelicalism; Fundamentals, The.

Fundamentals, The. A series of 12 volumes of articles published in Chicago between 1910 and 1915 as a witness to the central doctrines and experiences of Protestant Christianity and a defense against modern movements, cults, and criticisms of orthodoxy. *The Fundamentals*, subtitled "A Testimony to the Truth," is associated with the founding of fundamentalism as a restatement of orthodox Christianity against liberal theology and modernism; 3 million copies were distributed free to English-speaking ministers, missionaries, and workers around the world. *The Fundamentals* originated out of, and was editorially controlled by, persons in the Bible school, revival, and independent church movements associated with the Bible Institute of Los Angeles and Moody Bible Institute. The authors included Presbyterians, Anglicans, Baptists, Independents, and others, and were from England, Scotland, Canada, and the U.S.

C. T. McIntire

See also Fundamentalism.

Gg

Gaebelein, Arno Clemens (1861–1945). Central figure in the development of the fundamentalist movement in the late 19th and early 20th centuries. Gaebelein was born in Thuringia (now part of eastern Germany) and emigrated to the U.S. in 1879. Following successful pastorates in Baltimore, Harlem, and Hoboken, Gaebelein returned to New York and began the Hope of Israel Movement, a mission dedicated to the Jewish people and their needs. *Our Hope* magazine (1894–1957) originated as an arm of this missionary enterprise and expanded into an influential Bible study magazine. It attracted readers from a broad spectrum of denominations and vocations. Gaebelein's special interest was prophecy. He was a consulting editor of the *Scofield Reference Bible.*

D. A. RAUSCH

Gallican Articles, The Four (1682). Articles drawn up at a specially convened assembly of the French bishops in Paris in March 1682 that delineated the respective powers of popes, kings, and bishops. They declared: (1) that popes have no control over temporal matters; (2) that the papacy is subject to the authority of general councils of the church; (3) that papal authority must be exercised with due respect for local and national church usages and customs; (4) that although the pope has "the principal part in questions of faith," pending the consent of a general council, his judgments are not irreformable. The articles were a classic expression of Gallicanism, and were taught as expressions of French Catholicism through the 18th century.

N. V. HOPE

See also GALLICANISM.

Gallicanism. Theory that asserted the freedom of the Roman Catholic Church, especially in France, from the authority of the papacy. It gained many supporters in France from the 15th century. In 1663 the Sorbonne endorsed Gallicanism. Bossuet drew up the Gallican Articles, which were published by the Assembly of the Clergy in 1682. These articles attempted to clarify the theological justification of the Gallican Liberties by appealing to the conciliar theory and reasoning that Christ gave Peter and the popes spiritual—not temporal—authority. The Gallican Articles became an obligatory part of the curriculum in every French school of theology. The movement flourished during the 17th century. The French Revolution struck a fatal blow to Gallicanism by forcing the French clergy to turn to Rome for help when they, along with the government, came under attack. Eventually the movement died out.

P. A. MICKEY

See also BOSSUET, JACQUES BENIGNE; GALLICAN ARTICLES, THE FOUR.

Gallic Confession (1559). French Protestant statement of belief. In May 1559, representatives of congregations met in Paris under the moderatorship of Francois de Morel for their first national synod. The representatives approved a system of church discipline. This assembly received a draft confession of faith in 35 articles, which they expanded into 40. This revamped confession was adopted by the synod, and in 1560 a copy was presented to King Francis II with a plea for tolerance for its adherents. At the 7th national synod, held at La Rochelle in 1571, the Gallic Confession was revised and reaffirmed. It remained the official confessional statement of French Protestantism for over four centuries.

N. V. HOPE

See also CONFESSIONS OF FAITH.

Gap Theory. Theory that attempts to reconcile the long geologic ages in the earth's history with the Genesis creation account. It maintains that Gen. 1:1–2 describes a condition that lasted an indeterminate length of time and preceded the six days of creation in Gen. 1:3–28. There was creation (1:1), followed by a catastrophe (1:2), in turn followed by a re-creation (1:3–28). All the geologic ages in earth's pre-Adamic history may be found either between 1:1 and 1:2 or during 1:2.

A. F. JOHNSON

See also CREATION, DOCTRINE OF; EVOLUTION.

Gehenna. Greek transliteration of the Aramaic *gêhinnām*, which itself goes back to the Hebrew *gê hinnōm*, "Valley of Ben Hinnom" (2 Kings 23:10; 2 Chron. 28:3). Originally Gehenna referred to Topheth, an early site of Baal worship and the abominable practice of sacrifice of children to Molech (see 2 Kings 16:3; 21:6 for the involvement of Ahaz and Manasseh; and 2 Kings 23:10 for condemnation of the practice by Josiah, the reformer king). Jer. 7:32 and 19:6 contain the prophecy that this place of shame will become the place of God's punishment. Because of such associations, by the 1st century B.C. Gehenna came to be used metaphorically for the hell of fire, the place of everlasting punishment for the wicked. This is the meaning of the 11 Synoptic uses by Jesus.

V. CRUZ

See also ETERNAL PUNISHMENT; HELL; SHEOL.

General Confession, The. Prayer at the beginning of matins and evensong to be said by all present. It is found in the Anglican *Book of Common Prayer*. The prayer contains confession of sins, request for forgiveness, and petition for grace to live better.

P. TOON

General Revelation. See REVELATION, GENERAL.

Generation, Eternal. See ETERNAL GENERATION.

Genevan Catechism (1537). Catechism published by John Calvin as the *Instruction and Confession of Faith according to the Use of the Church of Geneva* (Fr. 1537; Lat. 1538). Along with a confession of faith and articles on church government that appeared in 1537, the catechism was part of Calvin's original program for the reformation and organization of the church during his first period in Geneva. The catechism was in 58 sections, and was the first systematic exposition of Calvinist thought in the French language.

A. H. FREUNDT, JR.

See also CALVINISM; CATECHISMS.

Gerhard, Johann (1582–1637). Lutheran theologian. Gerhard taught at Jena, and wrote in many theological fields, including exegesis, dogmatics, history, polemics, and sermonic and devotional material. His sermons were well received. His devotional writings show that Lutheran orthodoxy was not at all dead but was conducive to vibrant Christian faith. The best known and most influential of his works was his multivolume dogmatics, *Loci Theologici*.

J. M. DRICKAMER

See also LUTHERAN TRADITION, THE.

Ghost, Holy. See Holy Spirit.

Gifts, Spiritual. See Spiritual Gifts.

Gladden, Washington (1836–1918). Popularizer of liberal theology and advocate of the social gospel. An ordained Congregational minister, Gladden served lengthy pastorates in Springfield, Massachusetts, and Columbus, Ohio. He also lectured widely and wrote more than 35 books. Theologically Gladden was in the vanguard of liberalism and was a tireless champion of social reform. He was also the author of hymns, including the well-known "O Master, Let Me Walk with Thee."

M. A. Noll

See also Liberalism, Theological; Social Gospel, The.

Glorification. Act of God when, at the parousia, those who have died in Christ and living believers will receive a final and full "redemption of our bodies" (Rom. 8:23), preparatory for and suited to the final state of Christian believers. At that time "the perishable" will "clothe itself with the imperishable," and "the mortal," the body, will put on immortality (1 Cor. 15:53). Then death, the Christian's last enemy (1 Cor. 15:26), will be swallowed up in victory (1 Cor. 15:54).

J. K. Grider

See also Heaven.

Glory. (Heb. *kābôd*; Gk. *doxa*) Comprehensive biblical term referring primarily to the respendence of God in relation to his people.

In the OT. Since *kābôd* derives from *kābēd*, "to be heavy," it lends itself to the idea that the one possessing glory is laden with riches (Gen. 31:1), power (Isa. 8:7), or position (Gen. 45:13). To the translators of the LXX it seemed that *doxa* was the most suitable word for rendering *kābôd*, since it carried the notion of reputation or honor, which was present in the use of *kābôd*. But *kābôd* also denoted the manifestation of light by which God revealed himself, whether in the lightning flash or in the blinding splendor that often accompanied theophanies. Of the same nature was the disclosure of the divine presence in the cloud that led Israel through the wilderness and became localized in the tabernacle. So *doxa*, as a translation of *kābôd*, gained a nuance of meaning that it did not possess before. At times *kābôd* had a deeper meaning, denoting the person or self. When Moses made the request of God, "Now show me your glory" (Exod. 33:18), he was not speaking of the light-cloud, which he had already seen, but he was seeking a special manifestation of God that would leave nothing to be desired (cf. John 14:8). In the prophets the word "glory" is often used to set forth the excellence of the messianic kingdom in contrast to the limitations of the present order (Isa. 60:1–3).

In the NT. In general the NT use of *doxa* follows the pattern established in the LXX. With reference to God, it denotes his majesty (Rom. 1:23) and his perfection, especially in relation to righteousness (Rom. 3:23). He is called the Father of glory (Eph. 1:17). The manifestation of his presence in terms of light is an occasional phenomenon. Jesus' transfiguration is the sole instance during his earthly ministry, but later manifestations include the revelation to Saul at the time of his conversion (Acts 9:3–8) and to John on the Isle of Patmos (Rev. 1:12–16). The fact that Paul is able to speak of God's glory in terms of riches (Eph. 1:18; 3:16) and might (Col. 1:11) suggests the influence of the OT upon his thinking. Paul labels the display of God's power in raising his Son from the dead as glory (Rom. 6:4).

Christ is the effulgence of the divine glory (Heb. 1:3). By means of him the perfection of the nature of God is made known to us. When James speaks of him as the Lord of glory (2:1), his thought seems to move along the lines of the revelation of God in the tabernacle. The glory of Christ as the image of God, the Son of the Father, was veiled from sinful eyes during the days of his flesh but was apparent to those of faith who gathered around him (John 1:14). Glory belonged to his suffering and completing the work given to him by the Father (12:23).

Eschatological glory is the hope of Christians (Rom. 5:2). In this future state we will have a new body patterned after Christ's glorified body (Phil. 3:21), superior to that with which we are presently endowed (1 Cor. 15:43). Christ within the believer is the hope of glory (Col. 1:27).

E. F. HARRISON

Glossolalia. See TONGUES, SPEAKING IN.

Gnesio-Lutherans. See FLACIUS, MATTHIAS.

Gnosticism. Late pre-Christian/early Christian thought characterized by claims to esoteric religious insights, an emphasis on knowledge, and the conviction that matter is evil. This general religious phenomenon of the hellenistic world was the product of the fusion of Greek culture and Oriental religion. Early Christian apologists like Irenaeus, Tertullian, Hippolytus, and Epiphanius are important sources of information concerning the Gnostics. These heresiologists were scathing in their denunciations of the Gnostics, who were perceived as leading Christians astray by the manipulation of words and the twisting of scriptural meanings. Further, they regarded Gnosticism as the product of the combination of Greek philosophy and Christianity.

The history of religions school, of which Hans Jonas is a contemporary exponent, has challenged this definition. The "Greek conceptualization" of Eastern religious traditions—that is, Jewish monotheism, Babylonian astrology, and Iranian dualism—is viewed as the basis for Gnosticism. While R. M. Wilson and R. M. Grant reject such a broad definition and affirm instead a primary basis in hellenistic Judaism or Jewish apocalyptic, the advantage of Jonas's view is that it recognizes the broad spectrum within Gnosticism. The weakness is that the definition encompasses almost everything under the rubric of hellenistic religions.

Types of Gnosticism. Despite a fluidity within Gnosticism, Jonas identifies two basic patterns or structures of Gnostic thought. Both are mythological structures that seek to explain the problem of evil in terms of its relationship to the process of creation.

Iranian. This branch of Gnosticism developed in Mesopotamia and reflects a horizontal dualism associated with Zoroastrian worship. It is epitomized in its later Gnostic form of Manichaeism. In this pattern light and darkness, the two primal principles or deities, are locked in a decisive struggle.

Syrian. This type of Gnosticism arose in the area of Syria, Palestine, and Egypt and reflects a much more complex vertical dualism. In this system the ultimate principle is good, and the task of the Gnostic thinkers is to explain how evil emerged from the singular principle of good. The method employed is the identification of some deficiency or error in the good.

The Gnostics obviously used sources such as Platonic dualism and Eastern religious thought, including ideas derived from Christianity. Their use of sources, however, often resulted in an attack upon those sources.

The question that still remains to be answered is: When did Gnosticism arise? Clearly by the middle of the 2d century A.D. Gnosticism had reached its apogee. But contrary to Schmithals (*Gnosticism in Corinth*) the opponents of Paul in Corinth were hardly Gnostics. Were the opponents he describes in Colossians or Ephesians Gnostics? Were the opponents in the Johannine letters Gnostics? It is hard to read the NT and gain any secure feeling at the present that canonical writers were attacking the Gnostic devotees or mythologizers.

G. L. BORCHERT

See also HERMETIC LITERATURE.

God, Arguments for the Existence of. The question of God's existence is a critical one in philosophy. It affects the whole tenor of human life, whether we are regarded as supreme beings in the universe or whether there is a superior being that we must love and obey—or perhaps defy. There are three basic arguments for the existence of God.

The* A Priori *Approach. This approach is the heart of the famous ontological argument adduced by Anselm of Canterbury. God cannot be conceived in any way other than "a being than which nothing greater can be conceived." Even fools know what they mean by "God" when they assert, "There is no God" (Ps. 14:1). But if the most perfect being existed only in thought and not in reality, then it would not really be the most perfect being, for the one that existed in reality would be more perfect. Therefore, concludes Anselm, "no one who understands what God is, can conceive that God does not exist." In short, it would be self-contradictory to say, "I can think of a perfect being that does not exist," because existence would have to be a part of perfection. It would be like saying, "I can conceive of something greater than that which nothing greater can be conceived"—which is absurd.

The ontological argument has had a long and stormy history. It fails to persuade most people, who seem to harbor the same suspicion as Kant that "the unconditioned necessity of a judgment does not form the absolute necessity of a thing."

The* A Posteriori *Approach. *The Cosmological Argument.* The most interesting—and persuasive—form of the cosmological argument is Aquinas's "third way," or the argument from contingency. Its strength derives from the way it employs both permanence and change. Hence, for there to be anything at all contingent in the universe, there must be at least one thing that is not contingent—something that is necessary throughout all change and self-established. In this case "necessary" does not apply to a proposition but to a thing, and it means infinite, eternal, everlasting, self-caused, self-existent. It is not enough to say that infinite time will solve the problem of contingent being. No matter how much time you have, dependent being is still dependent on something. Everything contingent within the span of infinity will, at some particular moment, not exist. But if there was a moment when nothing existed, then nothing would exist now. The choice is simple: one chooses either a self-existent God or a self-existent universe.

The most serious objection is that it is based on an uncritical acceptance of the "principle of sufficient reason," the notion that every event/effect has a cause. If this principle is denied, the cosmological argument is defanged. Hume argues that causation is a psychological, not a metaphysical, principle, one whose origins lay in the human propensity to assume necessary connections between events when all we really see is contiguity and succession. Kant follows Hume by arguing that causation is a category built into our minds as one of the many ways in which we order our experience. Sartre believes that the universe was "gratuitous." Bertrand Russell claims that the question of origins is tangled in meaningless verbiage and that we must be content to declare that the universe is "just there and that's all."

The Teleological or Design Argument. This is one of the oldest and most popular and intelligible of the theistic proofs.

It suggests that there is a definite analogy between the order and regularity of the cosmos and a product of human ingenuity. Voltaire puts it in rather simplistic terms: "If a watch proves the existence of a watchmaker but the universe does not prove the existence of a great Architect, then I consent to be called a fool."

No one can deny the universe *seems* to be designed; instances of purposive ordering are all around us. Almost anywhere can be found features of being that show the universe to be basically friendly to life, mind, personality, and values. Even the great critics of natural theology, Hume and Kant, betray an admiration for the teleological argument. Hume grants it a certain limited validity. Kant goes even further: "This proof will always deserve to be treated with respect. It is the oldest, the clearest and most in conformity with human reason. . . . We have nothing to say against the reasonableness and utility of this line of argument, but wish, on the contrary, to commend and encourage it."

The Moral Argument. The moral argument is the most recent of the theistic proofs. The first major philosopher to use it was Kant. Kant holds that the existence of God and the immortality of the soul are matters of faith, not ordinary speculative reason, which, he claims, is limited to sensation.

Kant reasons that the moral law commands us to seek the *summum bonum* (highest good), with perfect happiness as a logical result. But a problem arises when we contemplate the unpleasant fact that "there is not the slightest ground in the moral law for a necessary connection between morality and proportionate happiness in a being that belongs to the world as a part of it." The only postulate, therefore, that will make sense of our moral experience is "the existence of a cause of all nature, distinct from nature itself," that is, a God who will properly reward moral endeavor in another world. In a godless universe humankind's deepest experience would be a cruel enigma.

Many people will go part way and accept moral objectivism, but they want to stop with a transcendent realm of impersonal moral absolutes. They deny that one must believe in a Person, Mind, or Lawgiver.

The Question of Validity. How valid are the theistic proofs? This question raises issues in a number of fields: logic, metaphysics, physics, and theory of knowledge. If God truly exists, then we are dealing with a factual proposition, and what we really want when we ask for proof of a factual proposition is not a demonstration of its logical impossibility but a degree of evidence that will exclude reasonable doubt. Something can be so probable that it excludes reasonable doubt without being deductive or analytical or demonstrative or logically inevitable. We feel that the theistic proofs—excluding the ontological argument—fall into this category.

Natural theology, however, can never establish the existence of the biblical God. These proofs may make one a deist, but only revelation will make one a Christian. Reason operating without revelation always turns up with a deity different from Yahweh, the Father of our Lord Jesus Christ.

A. J. HOOVER

See also REVELATION, GENERAL.

God, Attributes of. Essential characteristics of the divine being, without which God would not be God. God is an invisible, personal, and living Spirit, distinguished from all other spirits by several kinds of attributes: metaphysically God is self-existent, eternal, and unchanging; intellectually God is omniscient, faithful, and wise; ethically God is just, merciful, and loving; emotionally God detests evil, is long-suffering, and is compassionate;

existentially God is free, authentic, and omnipotent; relationally God is transcendent in being, immanent universally in providential activity, and immanent with his people in redemptive activity.

Jesus told the Samaritan woman that she should worship God in spirit and in truth because God is spirit (John 4:24). As spirit, God is *invisible.* No one has ever seen God or ever will (1 Tim. 6:16). A spirit does not have flesh and bones (Luke 24:39).

As spirit, God is *personal.* Although some thinkers use "spirit" to designate impersonal principles or an impersonal absolute, in the biblical context the divine Spirit has personal capacities of intelligence, emotion, and volition. Christ's unique emphasis upon God as Father becomes meaningless if God is not truly personal. Similarly, the great doctrines of mercy, grace, forgiveness, imputation, and justification can only be meaningful if God is genuinely personal. God must be able to hear the sinner's cry for salvation, be moved by it, decide and act to recover the lost. In fact, God is suprapersonal, tripersonal. God is Father, Son, and Holy Spirit.

God as spirit is *living and active*. The God of the Bible actively creates, sustains, covenants with his people, preserves Israel and the Messiah's line of descent, calls prophet after prophet, sends his Son into the world, provides the atoning sacrifice to satisfy his own righteousness, raises Christ from the dead, builds the church, and judges all justly. Far from a passive being, the God of the Bible is an active architect, builder, freedom fighter, advocate of the poor and oppressed, just judge, empathetic counselor, suffering servant, and triumphant deliverer.

We need to be clear that in the Scriptures the divine attributes are not above God, beside God, or beneath God; they are *predicated of* God. God is holy; God is love. These characteristics do not simply describe what God *does*, they define what God *is*. To claim that recipients of revelation can know the attributes of God but not the being of God leaves the attributes ununified and belonging to nothing. The Scriptures do not endorse worship of an unknown God but make God known. The attributes are inseparable from the being of God, and the divine Spirit does not relate or act apart from the essential divine characteristics. In knowing the attributes, then, we know God as he has revealed himself to be in himself.

The Metaphysical Attributes. God is *self-existent.* All other spirits are created and so have a beginning. They owe their existence to another. God does not depend upon the world or anyone in it for his existence. Rather, the world depends on God for its existence.

God is *eternal* and omnipresent (ubiquitous). God's life is from within himself; he did not have a beginning in the space-time world. God has no beginning, period of growth, old age, or end. The Lord is enthroned as King forever (Ps. 29:10). God is our God forever and forever (Ps. 48:14). Although God is not limited by space or time, or the succession of events in time, he created the world with space and time. God sustains the changing realm of succeeding events and is conscious of every movement in history. God fills space and time with his presence, sustains it, and gives it purpose and value.

God is *unchanging* in nature, desire, and purpose. To say that God is immutable is not to contradict the previous truth that God is living and active. It is to say that all the uses of divine power and vitality are consistent with his attributes such as wisdom, justice, and love. God's acts are never merely arbitrary, although some may be for reasons wholly within himself rather than conditioned upon human response.

The Intellectual Attributes. God is *omniscient.* God knows all things (1 John 3:20). God knows all our inward thoughts and outward acts (Ps. 139). Nothing in creation is hidden from God's sight. Everything is uncovered and laid bare before him (Heb. 4:13). As omniscient, God's judgments are formed in the awareness of all the relevant data. God knows everything that bears upon the truth concerning any person or event. Although God's mind is unlimited and knows everything, it is not totally different in every respect from our minds made in his image. Our judgments are true insofar as they conform to God's by being coherent or faithful to all the relevant evidence.

God is *faithful* and true. Because God is faithful and true (Rev. 19:11), his judgments (Rev. 19:2) and his words in human language are faithful and true (Rev. 21:5; 22:6). There is no lack of fidelity in God's person, thought, or promise. God is not hypocritical and inconsistent. We may hold unswervingly to our hope because he who promised is faithful (Heb. 10:23). He is faithful to forgive our sins (1 John 1:9), sanctify us until the return of Christ (1 Thess. 5:23–24), strengthen and protect us from the evil one (2 Thess. 3:3), and not let us be tempted beyond what we can bear (1 Cor. 10:13). Even if we are faithless, he remains faithful, for he cannot disown himself (2 Tim. 2:13).

God is not only omniscient and consistent in person and word, but also perfectly *wise.* In addition to knowing all the relevant data on any subject, God selects ends with discernment and acts in harmony with his purposes of holy love. We may not always be able to see that events in our lives work together for a wise purpose, but we know that God chooses from among all the possible alternatives the best ends and means for achieving them. God not only chooses the right ends but also for the right reasons, the good of his creatures and thus his glory.

The Ethical Attributes. God is distinct from and transcendent to all his creatures, not only metaphysically and epistemologically, but also morally. God is morally spotless in character and action, upright, pure, and untainted with evil desires, motives, thought, words, or acts. God is *holy,* and as such is the source and standard of what is right. God is free from all evil, and loves all truth and goodness. He values purity and detests impurity and inauthenticity. God cannot approve of any evil, has no pleasure in evil (Ps. 5:4), and cannot tolerate evil (Hab. 1:13). God abhors evil and cannot encourage sin in any way (James 1:13–14).

God is just or *righteous.* God's justice or righteousness is revealed in his moral law expressing his moral nature and in his judgment, granting to all exactly what they deserve. His judgment is not arbitrary or capricious, but principled and without respect of persons. In the gospel a righteousness from God is revealed, a righteousness that is by faith from first to last (Rom. 1:17; 3:21). Believers are justified freely by God's grace that came by Jesus Christ, who provided the sacrifice of atonement (Rom. 3:24). God in his justice graciously provides for the just status of believers in Christ.

In mercy God withholds or modifies deserved judgment, and in grace God freely gives undeserved benefits to whom he chooses. All of these moral characteristics flow from God's great *love.* It is not that God is lacking something in himself (Acts 17:25), but that God desires to give of himself for the well-being of those he loves, in spite of the fact that they are unlovely and undeserving. God not only loves but *is* love (1 John 4:8). God so loved the world that he gave his one and only Son, that whoever believes in him shall not perish but have eternal life (John 3:16). God's love involves a responsible and faithful commitment for the well-being of others.

The Emotional Attributes. God is personal and ethical, and both senses call for healthy emotions or passions. One who delights in justice, righteousness, and holiness for the well-being of his creatures can only be repulsed by the injustice, unrighteousness, and corruption that destroys their bodies, minds, and spirits. Hence the Bible frequently speaks of God's righteous indignation at evil. Righteous indignation is anger aroused, not by overwhelming selfish emotions but by injustice and all the works of fallen "flesh." God *detests evil.*

God is patient and *long-suffering.* Properly jealous for the well-being of the objects of his love, God is angry at injustice done to them but suffers without losing heart. Long-suffering with evildoers, God, without condoning their sin, graciously provides them with undeserved temporal and spiritual benefits. Because Jesus himself suffered, he can help those who suffer and are tempted (Heb. 2:18). The God revealed in Jesus Christ is no apathetic, uninvolved, impersonal First Cause. The Father whom Jesus disclosed is deeply moved by everything that hurts his children. He is compassionate.

The Existential Attributes. God is *free.* From all eternity God is not conditioned by anything other than himself contrary to his purposes. God is not free to approve sin, to be unloving, to be unwise, to ignore the hard facts of reality, to be unfaithful to what is or ought to be, to be uncompassionate or unmerciful. God cannot deny himself. God is free to be himself, his personal, eternal, living, intellectual, ethical, emotional volitional self.

God is *authentic*—authentically himself. God is self-conscious, and knows who he is and what his purposes are (1 Cor. 2:11). He has a keen sense of identity, meaning, and purpose. God knows that he is the ultimate being, that there are in reality none to compare with him.

God is *omnipotent*. He is able to do whatever he wills in the way in which he wills it. God does not choose to do anything contrary to his nature of wisdom and holy love. God has not only the strength to effect all his purposes in the way in which he purposes them, but also the authority in the entire realm of his kingdom to do what he will. God is not a subject of another's dominion, but is King and Lord of all. By virtue of all his other attributes—his wisdom, justice, and love, for example—God is fit for the ruling of all that he created and sustains.

The Relational Attributes. As *transcendent,* God is uniquely other than everything in creation. A biblical theist not only believes that the one, living God is separate from the world, as against pantheism and panentheism, but also that God is continuously active throughout the world providentially (contra deists). God is not so exalted that he cannot know, love, or relate to natural law in the world of everyday experience.

While transcendent, God is nonetheless *immanent* in the lives of his people who repent of their sin and live by faith to accomplish the goals of his redemptive grace.

In summary, God is a living, personal Spirit worthy of whole-soul adoration and trust (because of his many perfect attributes), separate from the world, and yet continuously active in the world. Unlimited by space, God nevertheless created and sustains the cosmos, scientific laws, geographical and political boundaries. Beyond time, God nevertheless actively relates to time, to each human life, home, city, nation, and history in general.

Transcendent to discursive knowledge and conceptual truth, God nevertheless intelligently relates to propositional thought and verbal communication, objective validity, logical consistency, factual reliability, coherence and clarity, subjective authenticity and existential integrity. Unlimited by a body, God is nevertheless providentially related to physical power in nature and society. God knows and judges human stewardship in the use of all the earth's resources.

God transcends every attempt to achieve justice in the world, but righteously relates to every good endeavor of his creatures. Although free from unworthy and uncontrolled emotions, God cares about the poor, the unfortunate, the lonely, the sorrowing, the sick, the victims of prejudice, injustice, anxiety, and despair. Beyond all the apparent meaninglessness and purposelessness of human existence, God personally gives significance to the most insignificant life.

G. R. LEWIS

See also GOD, DOCTRINE OF; IMPASSIBILITY OF GOD; REVELATION, GENERAL; REVELATION, SPECIAL; TRINITY.

God, Doctrine of. Fundamental biblical/theological teaching that God exists and is ultimately in control of the universe.

The Biblical Concept of God. *God's Existence.* Questions concerning the reality of God are not discussed in Scripture; his existence is simply everywhere assumed. Scripture does recognize, however, the existence of a professed atheism. But such atheism is considered primarily a moral rather than an intellectual problem (Ps. 14:1).

Knowledge of God. God is known only through his self-revelation. Apart from his initiative in disclosing himself God could not be known by humankind. As the subject of his revelation God at the same time makes himself the object of human knowledge so that we can know him truly. God has also revealed something of himself in his creation and preservation of the universe (Rom. 1:20). To the extent that human reason yields a concept of a god it is undoubtedly related to this general or natural revelation. But sin and its alienating effect blind us from truly seeing God through this means (Rom. 1:18; Eph. 4:18).

While God communicates himself to us through a variety of means, including actions and words, human knowledge is fundamentally a conceptual matter and therefore the Word is the primary means of God's revelation. Even his actions are not left as mute works but are accompanied by the interpretive Word to give their true meaning. The revelation of God climaxed in the Person of Jesus Christ, who was not simply the bearer of the revelatory Word of God as were all who spoke God's Word prior to his coming, but the personal divine Word. In him "all the fullness of the Deity" dwelt in bodily form (Col. 2:9). In his work as Creator and Redeemer and through his words, God makes himself known to us.

The revelation of God does not totally exhaust his being and activity. He remains the incomprehensible One that we cannot totally fathom, both in his essence and ways (Job 36:26; Isa. 40:13, 28; cf. Deut. 29:29). In giving us a knowledge of himself God gives his Word a finite form compatible with human creatureliness. Despite this necessary accommodation to the limitations of human understanding, the revealed knowledge of God is nevertheless an authentic knowledge of God.

Definition of God. Instead of a general definition of God, the Bible presents descriptions of God as he has revealed himself. These are conveyed through express statements as well as through the many names by which God identifies himself. Fundamental to the nature of God, according to the biblical description, are the truths that he is personal, spiritual, and holy.

God Is Personal. Over against any abstract neutral metaphysical concept, the God of Scripture is first and foremost a personal being. He reveals himself by names, especially the great personal name "Yahweh" (cf. Exod. 3:13–15; 6:3; Isa. 42:8). He knows and wills self-consciously in accord with our concept of personality (1 Cor. 2:10–11; Eph. 1:11). Nowhere is the personhood of God more evident than in his biblical description as Father. Jesus constantly spoke of God as "my Father," "your Father," and "the heavenly Father."

God Is Spiritual. The Scriptures preclude the reduction of the personhood of God to a human level by the description of God as spirit (John 4:24). As the word "spirit" has the basic idea of power and activity, the spiritual nature of God refers to the infinite superiority of his nature over all created life. The weakness of the forces of this world, including humankind and animals, are contrasted to God who is spirit (cf. Isa. 31:3; 40:6–7). As spirit, God is the living God. He is the possessor of an infinite life in himself (Ps. 36:9; John 5:26). Matter is activated by spirit, but God is pure spirit. He is fully life. As such he is the source of all other life (Job 33:4; Ps. 104:30).

God Is Holy. One of the most fundamental features of God's being is expressed by the word "holy." He is the incomparable God, "the Holy One" (Isa. 40:25; cf. Hab. 3:3). In his holiness God is the transcendent Deity, infinitely exalted above all creation. The concept of revelation presupposes a transcendent God who must unveil himself to be known. The transcendence of God is frequently expressed biblically in terms of time and space. He exists before all creation (Ps. 90:2), and neither the earth nor the highest heavens can contain him (1 Kings 8:27). In a manner that exceeds our finite understanding God exists in his own infinite realm as transcendent Lord over all creaturely time and space. God's transcendent holiness is balanced by his immanence. He is wholly present in his being and power in every part and moment of the created universe. He is "over all and through all and in all" (Eph. 4:6). Not only does everything exist in him (Acts 17:28), but there is no place where his presence is absent (Ps. 139:1–10).

The Trinity. Crucial to the biblical doctrine of God is his Trinitarian nature. Although the term "trinity" is not a biblical word as such, Christian theology has used it to designate the threefold manifestation of the one God as Father, Son, and Holy Spirit. The formulated doctrine of the Trinity asserts the truth that God is one in being or essence who exists eternally in three distinct, coequal "persons." While the term "person" in relation to the Trinity does not signify the limited individuality of human persons, it does affirm the I-thou of personal relationship, particularly of love, within the triune Godhead.

The doctrine of the Trinity flows from the self-revelation of God in biblical salvation history. As the one God successively reveals himself in his saving action in the Son and the Holy Spirit, each is recognized as God himself in personal manifestation. It is thus in the fullness of NT revelation that the doctrine of the Trinity is seen most clearly. God is one (Gal. 3:20; James 2:19), but the Son (John 1:1; 14:9; Col. 2:9) and the Spirit (Acts 5:3–4; 1 Cor. 3:16) are also fully God. Yet they are distinct from the Father and each other. The Father sends the Son and the Spirit, while the Son also sends the Spirit (John 15:26; Gal. 4:4). This unified equality and yet distinctness is seen in the triadic references to the three persons. Christian baptism is in the name of the Father, Son, and Holy Spirit (Matt. 28:19).

The Trinitarian doctrine is thus central to the salvation kerygma of Scripture, according to which the transcendent God acts personally in history to redeem and share himself with his creatures.

R. L. SAUCY

See also GOD, ARGUMENTS FOR THE EXISTENCE OF; GOD, ATTRIBUTES OF; GOD, NAMES OF; TRINITY; REVELATION, GENERAL; REVELATION, SPECIAL.

God, Names of. While God is conceived of as revealing his attributes and will in a number of ways in Scripture, one of the most theologically significant modes of the divine self-disclosure is the revelation inherent in the names of God.

The Theological Significance of the Divine Names. *Yahweh.* The parallel structure in Exod. 3:14–15 supports the association of the name "Yahweh" with the concept of being or existence: "I AM has sent me to you" (v. 14); "The LORD . . . has sent me to you" (v. 15). The name "I AM" is based on the clause "I AM WHO I AM" found in Exod. 3:14 that, on the basis of the etymology implied here, suggests that "Yahweh" is the third-person form of the verb *hāya* The clause *'ehyeh 'aser 'ehyeh* has been translated in several ways: "I am that I am" (AV), "I am who I am" (RSV, NIV), and "I will be what I will be" (RSV marg.). Recently the translation "I am (the) One who is" has been suggested. The latter translation has much in its favor grammatically and fits the context well.

The main concern of the context is to demonstrate that a continuity exists in the divine activity from the time of the patriarchs to the events recorded in Exod. 3. The Lord is referred to as the God of the fathers (vv. 13, 15, 16). The God who made the gracious promises regarding Abraham's offspring is the God who is and who continues to be. The affirmation of v. 17 is but a reaffirmation of the promise made to Abraham. The name "Yahweh" may thus affirm the continuing activity of God on behalf of his people in faithfulness to his promise. Jesus' application of the words "I am" to himself in John 8:58 not only denotes his preexistence but associates him with Yahweh. Jesus is the fulfillment of the promise given to Abraham, the fulfillment that Abraham anticipated (John 8:56).

In the Pentateuch, the name "Yahweh" denotes that aspect of God's character that is personal rather than transcendent. It occurs in contexts in which the covenantal and redemptive aspects of God predominate. Cassuto says that "the name YHWH is employed when God is presented to us in His personal character and in direct relationship to people or nature; and *'Elohim*, when the Deity is alluded to as a Transcendental Being who exists completely outside and above the physical universe" (*Documentary Hypothesis*, p. 31). This precise distinction does not always obtain outside the Pentateuch, but "Yahweh" never loses its distinct function as the designation of the God of Israel.

'Elohim. This is the more general name for God. In the Pentateuch, when used as a proper name, it most commonly denotes the more transcendental aspects of God's character. When God is presented in relation to his creation and to the peoples of the earth in the Pentateuch, the name "'Elohim" is the name most often used. It is for this reason that "'Elohim" occurs consistently in the creation account of Gen. 1:1–2:42 and in the genealogies of Genesis. Where the context takes on a moral tone, as in Gen. 2:4b–25, the name "Yahweh" is used.

Throughout Genesis and the early chapters of Exodus *'elohim* is used most often as a proper name. After Exod. 3 the name begins to occur with increasing frequency as an appellative ("the God of" or "your God"). This function is by far the most frequent mode of reference to God in the Book of Deuteronomy. When used in this fashion the name denotes God as the supreme deity of a person or people. Thus, in the frequent expression,

"Yahweh your God," "Yahweh" functions as a proper name, while "God" functions as the denominative of deity.

The appellative *'elohim* connotes all that God is. As God he is sovereign, and that sovereignty extends beyond Israel into the arena of the nations (Deut. 2:30, 33; 3:22; Isa. 52:10). As God to his people he is loving and merciful (Deut. 1:31; 2:7; 23:5; Isa. 41:10, 13, 17; 49:5; Jer. 3:23). He establishes standards of obedience (Deut. 4:2; Jer. 11:3) and sovereignly punishes disobedience (Deut. 23:21). As God, there is no one like him (Isa. 44:7; 45:5–21). The same connotations obtain in the use of the shorter form *'el.* He is the God who sees (*'el rō'î*; Gen. 16:13) and he is *'el* the God of Israel (Gen. 33:20).

As *'El 'Elyon*, God is described in his exaltation over all things. In Ps. 83:18 Yahweh is described as "Most High over all the earth." Isa. 14:14 states, "I will ascend above the tops of the clouds; I will make myself like the Most High." In the majority of cases the attributes of this name are indistinguishable from other usages of *'el* or *'elohim*. God fixes the boundaries of the nations (Deut. 32:8). He effects changes in the creation (Ps. 18:13). *'El Shaddai* occurs most frequently in the Book of Job, where it functions as a general name for the deity. God disciplines (Job 5:17); he is to be feared (Job. 6:14); he is just (Job 8:3); he hears prayer (Job 8:5); and he creates (Job 33:4). This name occurs six times in the patriarchal narratives. In most of these instances it is associated with the promise given by God to the patriarchs. Yet the name is often paired with "Yahweh" in the poetic material, and thus shares the personal warmth of that name. He is known for his steadfast love (Ps. 21:7) and his protection (Ps. 91:9–10).

The root of *'Adonai* means "lord" and, in its secular usage, always refers to a superior in the OT. The word retains the sense of "lord" when applied to God (Gen. 15:2; Exod. 4:10).

The name *Abba* connotes the fatherhood of God. This is affirmed by the accompanying translation *ho pater* ("father"), which occurs in each usage of the name in the NT (Mark 14:36; Rom. 8:15; Gal. 4:6). The use of this name as Jesus' mode of address to God in Mark 14:36 is a unique expression of Jesus' relationship to the Father. Jeremias says, "He spoke to God like a child to its father, simply, inwardly, confidently. Jesus' use of *abba* in addressing God reveals the heart of his relationship with God" (*Prayers of Jesus*, p. 62). The same relationship is sustained by us with God. It is only because of our relationship with God, established by the Holy Spirit, that we can address God with this name that depicts a relationship of warmth and filial love. In a sense the relationship designated by this name is the fulfillment of the ancient promise given to Abraham's offspring that the Lord will be their God, and they his people (Exod. 6:7; Lev. 26:12; Jer. 24:7; 30:22).

T. E. McComiskey

See also Abba; Alpha and Omega; God, Attributes of; God, Doctrine of.

Godliness. Manner of life that is centered on God, with special reference to devotion, piety, and reverence toward him. Godliness is characterized by an attitude of devotion to God and right conduct. The idea of godliness is in many ways typically hellenistic, with its emphasis on reverence and devotion to God. Its closest OT equivalent is the "fear of God," which has as its central meaning a life of active obedience to the law (e.g., Lev. 19:14; 25:17; 2 Kings 17:34; Job 1:1; Ps. 128:1; Jer. 32:40).

The Greek word corresponding to godliness or piety is *eusebeia.* In the Pastoral Epistles *eusebeia* denotes a particular manner of life and comes close to the OT idea of "the fear of God." It does not focus upon the law, however, but upon the individual believer's faith in Christ (1 Tim. 3:16). The secret of the godly life is the revelation of God in Jesus Christ; godliness is basically following him in this life (Titus 2:12). It is thus presented as a Christian goal, to be earnestly sought after (1 Tim. 2:2; 4:7–8), even if it leads to persecution (2 Tim. 3:12). Godliness and sound doctrine are closely related. Godliness is one of the Christian virtues (2 Pet. 1:6–7); it is related to the power of God (1:3). The use of the word in the plural in 2 Pet. 3:11 suggests a reference to specific acts of piety.

Godliness is thus the honoring of God as Creator and Redeemer that is born of faith in Jesus Christ and expresses itself in daily living. It is the manifestation of faith in life and includes respect for the orders of creation, such as the family. As such, it is a criterion for soundness of doctrine, and should characterize all Christians.

F. Q. GOUVEA

See also ETHICS, BIBLICAL.

Gogarten, Friedrich (1887–1967). German Lutheran theologian. Gogarten was professor at Göttingen (1935–53). He associated himself with a young Swiss pastor, Karl Barth, who was similarly disengaging himself from the earlier theological idealism and charting a course that would be variously described as "crisis theology," "dialectical theology," and "neo-orthodoxy." Gogarten's polemic advocated rethinking the Christian faith along historical rather than metaphysical lines. History implied for him the process of interaction in which being and meaning are re-created. The nature of Christian responsibility consisted for Gogarten in receptivity (being-from-the-other), activity (being-for-the-other), and openness to "the absolute mystery which presses upon man's consciousness of responsibility for the world."

M. A. INCH

See also DEMYTHOLOGIZATION; NEO-ORTHODOXY.

Golden Rule. Jesus states what has come to be described as the Golden Rule: "So in everything, do to others what you would have them do to you, for this sums up the Law and the Prophets" (Matt. 7:12; cf. Luke 6:31). The negative form was widely expressed in Judaism. The 1st-century rabbi Hillel was reported to have taught, "Whatsoever you would that men should not do to you, do not that to them."

M. A. INCH

Gomarus, Francis (1563–1641). Dutch Calvinist theologian. In 1594 he was appointed professor of theology at Leiden. Here he emerged as a staunch upholder of Calvinistic orthodoxy against James Arminius, who joined him on the Leiden faculty in 1603. In 1611 he became minister of the Reformed congregation at Middleburg; from 1614 to 1618 he taught at the French Protestant seminary at Saumur; and from 1618 until his death he occupied a professorial chair at Groningen.

In 1610 the Arminians published *The Remonstrance*, a manifesto expounding their theological viewpoint. The Gomarists replied with a *Counter-Remonstrance.* This controversy dragged on until 1618, when the Synod of Dort was called to settle the dispute. Gomarus, who played a prominent role at Dort, was unable to persuade the synod to endorse his supralapsarianism (the idea that God's decree of election preceded the fall of humankind and contemplated humankind's fallen estate as part of the divine plan of predestination).

N. V. HOPE

See also ARMINIUS, JACOBUS; DORT, SYNOD OF; SUPRALAPSARIANISM.

Good, the Good, Goodness. The word "good" is a comprehensive term used to praise the excellence of something. To speak about a good book or good food is to use "good" in a typically nonmoral way. "Good" conveys a moral sense, however, when someone says "he is a good man" or "she did a good deed/work." The man is being lauded for his excellent moral character and the woman for her effort in fulfilling a human need. The morally good refers to various aspects of personhood, including deeds, character traits, motives, intentions, desires, and needs. When an action is commended because of transpersonal factors, such as its conformity to principles, the term "right" is generally employed. The relationship between the right and the good has been a persistent problem in ethics. The solution lies in the hotly contested search for the criteria or standards of goodness and has centered around the most compelling of all human questions, "What is the good?"

God Is All Good. For the Christian the meaning and unity of the good rests completely and absolutely in God as revealed in Scripture. Declarations that God is good, acts with goodness, and is the source of all good occur throughout Scripture and are usually tied to human gratitude and praise (e.g., 2 Chron. 5:13; 7:3; Pss. 25:8; 100:5; 106:1; Jer. 33:11; Nah. 1:7; Mark 10:18). The identity of the good with God is profoundly expressed by Amos in his unconventional use of the oft-repeated priestly teaching or call to worship, "Seek the LORD and live." He quotes this phrase three times; the third time he substitutes the word "good" for "the LORD" and admonishes the people to "seek good, not evil that you may live" (Amos 5:4, 6, 14). To seek God is to seek the good.

God's absolute goodness was no more powerfully affirmed than when Jesus was confronted by the man who flippantly addressed him as good and assumed that Jesus would redefine its meaning. Rather, Jesus insisted that God is perfect goodness and that God alone decides and, in fact, has already determined (in Scripture and in Jesus himself) what the good is (Matt. 19:16–22; Mark 10:17–22).

Being and Doing Good. God relates to humans in a covenantal way.(Gen. 6:18; 1 Sam. 20:8). Thus the good person is the one who lives in fellowship with the Lord and acts in accord with God's dictates for assuring human community (Mic. 6:8). The one who does good is of God (3 John 11). The faithful are exhorted to choose good; cling to the good (Rom. 12:9); diligently seek good (Prov. 11:27); love good (Amos 5:15); learn to do good (Isa. 1:17); and imitate good (3 John 11). Attainment of the good, however, is only possible with God's help, since no one does good but only evil continually (Rom. 3:12). As Jesus insisted, persons must be made good before they are able to produce good fruit (Matt. 12:33–35). According to Paul, Christians have been created in Christ Jesus for good works (Eph. 2:10).

Throughout Scripture the good is embodied in procedures of justice, deeds of kindness, and acts of liberation, all of which serve the poor and lowly in society (Isa. 1:17; Mic. 6:8). In these contexts the good becomes the right and is essentially linked to the practical goods of life. For the Christian, then, the right and the good are not finally at odds. The good as the right points to the necessary criteria for distributing natural goods. Nevertheless, these goods make the right worth pursuing. Since all good comes from God, goodness is, as Karl Barth correctly states, "the sum of everything, right, friendly and wholesome" (*Church Dogmatics,* 2.2.708).

D. J. MILLER

Good Friday. Friday before Easter. Its origins as a special holy day go back to the development of Holy Week in Jerusalem in the late 4th century. In the

East it came to be called "Great" and in the West "Good" Friday.

P. TOON

See also CHRISTIAN YEAR; HOLY WEEK.

Good News. See GOSPEL.

Good Works. See WORKS.

Gore, Charles (1853–1932). Bishop of Oxford (1911–19). Gore could be characterized as a "liberal catholic." To him this was Anglicanism at its best. He identified three marks of catholicism: apostolic succession, high sacramentalism, and a common rule of faith. Gore's liberalism is most clearly seen in his emphasis on giving reason wide reign, whether in philosophy or science, historical criticism, or the spiritual experience of humankind. Gore won national notoriety with his editing and contribution to *Lux Mundi* (1889). The Oxford Anglican contributors to this volume wished to bring the catholic faith into line with modern scholarship and moral problems.

Gore's views were expanded in his Bampton Lectures, *The Incarnation of the Son of God* (1891) and *Dissertations on Subjects Connected with the Incarnation* (1895). Gore maintained that the *kenosis* or self-emptying of Christ was the key to the incarnation, the central doctrine of Christianity. Gore wrote prolifically after he resigned his bishopric in 1919. His *Reconstruction of Belief* (1926) was a single-volume publication of three earlier works. His strong social views were summarized in *Christ and Society* (1928).

D. K. MCKIM

See also LIBERALISM, THEOLOGICAL; OXFORD MOVEMENT.

Gospel. (Gk. *euangelion*) The joyous proclamation of God's redemptive activity in Christ on behalf of sinners.

***Euangelion* in the Gospels.** The word *euangelion* is used only by Matthew and Mark. The concept, however, is not foreign to Luke. He uses the verb form 26 times in Luke-Acts, and the noun twice in Acts. In the Fourth Gospel there is no trace of either verb or noun. In all but one instance Matthew describes *euangelion* as the gospel "of the kingdom"; "this gospel" (Matt. 26:13) indicates that Jesus is alluding to his coming death. The phrase "preaching the good news of the kingdom" is twice used in summary statements of the ministry of Jesus (Matt. 4:23; 9:35). This gospel is to be preached throughout the entire world prior to the end of the age (Matt. 24:14; cf. Mark 13:10). The way in which Mark uses *euangelion* is suggested by his opening words, "The beginning of the gospel about Jesus Christ, the Son of God." Here *euangelion* is a semitechnical term meaning "the glad news that tells about Jesus Christ." This gospel is of such tremendous import that for its sake we must be willing to enter upon a life of complete self-denial (Mark 8:35).

The Gospel According to Paul. Over against the six occasions (discounting parallels) on which *euangelion* is used by the Gospel writers, it is found a total of 60 times in the writings of Paul. *Euangelion* is a favorite Pauline term. It is evenly distributed throughout his epistles, missing only in his note to Titus.

Paul's ministry was distinctively that of the propagation of the gospel. He was set apart for the gospel (Rom. 1:1); he had become a servant of the gospel by the gift of God's grace (Eph. 3:7). Paul regarded the preaching of the gospel as a sacred trust (Gal. 2:7). He was compelled to preach the gospel: "Woe to me if I do not preach the gospel!" (1 Cor. 9:16). For the sake of the gospel Paul was willing to become all things to all men (1 Cor. 9:22–23). No sacrifice was too great. Eternal issues were at stake. Those who were blinded and unable to see the light of the gospel were perishing and would be punished with everlasting destruction (2 Cor. 4:3; 2 Thess. 1:9). On the other hand, to those who believed, the gospel had effectively become the power of God for salvation (Rom. 1:16).

For Paul, the *euangelion* is preeminently the "gospel of God" (Rom. 1:1; 15:16; 2 Cor. 11:7; 1 Thess. 2:2, 8–9). It proclaims the redemptive activity of God. This activity is bound up with the person and work of God's Son, Christ Jesus. Thus it is also the "gospel of Christ" (1 Cor. 9:12; 2 Cor. 2:12; 9:13; 10:14; Gal. 1:7; 1 Thess. 3:2).

The Apostolic Preaching. There are two sources for the determination of the apostolic proclamation of the gospel. Of primary importance are the fragments of pre-Pauline tradition that lie embedded in the writings of the apostle (Rom. 10:9; 1 Cor. 12:3; 15:3–5; Phil. 2:6–11; 1 Tim. 3:16). A second source is the early Petrine speeches in Acts. These speeches (on the basis of their Aramaic background, freedom from Paulinism, and the general trustworthiness of Luke as a historian) can be shown to give reliably the gist of what Peter actually said and not what a second generation Christian thought he might have said. These two sources combine to set forth one common apostolic gospel. In briefest outline, this message contained: (1) a historical proclamation of the death, resurrection, and exaltation of Jesus, set forth as the fulfillment of prophecy and involving our responsibility; (2) a theological evaluation of the person of Jesus as both Lord and Christ; (3) a call to repent and receive the forgiveness of sins. This gospel is power (Rom. 1:16). As an instrument of the Holy Spirit it convicts (1 Thess. 1:5) and converts (Col. 1:6).

R. H. Mounce

Gospel, Social Implications of. The gospel is the proclamation and demonstration of God's redemptive activity in Jesus Christ to a world enslaved by sin. Redemption is personal; people make individual responses to the claims of Jesus Christ as Lord and Savior. Redemption is also social, but the nature, priority, and extent of the social implications of the gospel are not readily apparent.

Modern Period. The social implications of the gospel have been evident in every era of the church's life. The modern evangelical discussion about the social implications of the gospel, however, has been shaped by a variety of factors. Revivalism has been a crucial force in determining the nature of the discussion because of the prominence of revival leaders in molding modern evangelicalism. In the 19th century Charles G. Finney maintained that religion came first, reform second, but he sent his converts from the "anxious bench" into a variety of reform movements, including abolitionism. Energized by a postmillennial theology, Finney often said that "the great business of the church is to reform the world." Dwight L. Moody, on the other hand, saw little hope for society. As a premillennialist he pictured the world as a wrecked ship; he believed that God had commissioned Christians to use their lifeboats to rescue every person they could.

This shift in the relationship between revivalism and reform, present in Moody and even more pronounced in Billy Sunday, has been characterized by evangelical scholars as "the great reversal." Beginning at the end of the 19th century and continuing beyond the mid-20th century, the social implications of the gospel were neglected, sometimes abandoned, and most often declared to be of secondary importance by those who called themselves conservatives or fundamentalists. Groups that had once supported social reform retreated into a posture where the primary concern after conversion was the purity of individuals rather than justice in society.

At the same time, however, a movement was on the rise that challenged this uncoupling of evangelism and reform—the social gospel. Born in post-Civil War America and growing to maturity in the era of progressivism, the impact of the social gospel continued long after its formal demise following World War I. The social gospel has been defined by one of its adherents as "the application of the teaching of Jesus and the total message of the Christian salvation to society, the economic life, and social institutions . . . as well as to individuals." Interacting with the changing realities of an increasingly industrialized and urbanized nation, the social gospel viewed itself as a crusade for justice and righteousness in all areas of the common life.

Recent Discussion. In the contemporary period there are numerous attempts to return to a balance of individual and social emphases in the Christian faith. The civil rights crisis and the Vietnam War pricked the consciences of younger evangelicals who wondered whether their spiritual parents had not accommodated their faith to an American "civil religion." The last few decades have seen a rebirth of social concern. Evangelicals have been rediscovering their roots in Finney and earlier evangelical leadership. The Chicago Declaration of 1973 acknowledged that "we have not proclaimed or demonstrated [God's] justice to an unjust American society."

A new perspective is the liberation theologies emanating from Latin America, Asia, and Africa. The demand is for theological reflection that begins, not in the classroom, but in the midst of the poverty and injustice that defines the human situation for many of the peoples of the world today. The call is for a theology of "praxis" (practice).

In summary, historical study helps focus present options. As for priority the question remains: Are the social implications equal, secondary, or prior to the individual implications of the gospel? Continuing discussion about the nature and extent of social ministry revolves around such options as individual and/or social action; or charity and/or justice. However one chooses, the challenge is to translate love and justice into meaningful strategies so that proclamation becomes demonstration.

R. C. White, Jr.

See also Civil Rights; Evangelicalism; Liberation Theology; Social Ethics; Social Gospel, The.

Government. ***The Biblical Witness.*** From a biblical point of view government is one of the forms of human stewardship God has established to rule his creation (1 Pet. 2:13–3:17; 5:1–7).

God's call to stewardship is a call to obedience in particular realms of responsibility according to his normative law. This general framework of human stewardship under God's dominion is evident, for example, in God's choosing of Moses and David for government responsibility (Exod. 3:11–12; 18:13–26; Deut. 17:14–20; 1 Sam. 16:12–13; 2 Sam. 7:1–29), in his challenges to Israel's leaders through the prophets (1 Sam. 13:11–14; Isa. 10:1–4; Jer. 22:1–30; Dan. 2:20–23; 4:34–37; Zech. 7:8–14), and in NT teachings about government authority (John 18:33–37; 19:7–11; Rom. 13:1–7; Col. 1:15–16; Rev. 11:15–19).

Government has broad public responsibilities of distribution and retribution for the sake of the entire community or society over which it governs. While governments are called to look after the general public health and welfare of the whole society, that does not give them the authority to disrupt or destroy the proper responsibilities that God has given to parents, pastors, teachers, employers, and other stewards. Rules and regulations for sanitation, transportation, contracts, and the punishment of crimes, for example, are all public laws that belong to the proper domain of government. This domain of public responsibility, then, must be fulfilled as a trust from God, a stewardship of justice for the sake of the whole society.

Government is one of the means of God's self-revelation. God has revealed himself not only as Father, Shepherd, Husband, Counselor, Gardener, Brother, and Friend, but also as King, Judge, Governor, and Lord. Government, then, is not simply a human good that we have at our disposal for keeping some measure of peace and order on earth. Government is more than a this-worldly affair that may be discounted as less than important in God's overall plan for creation. Government is as important in God's self-revelation as family life, farming, worship, and every other aspect of creational life that was made in and through and for Jesus Christ to reveal the glory of God (Pss. 93; 94:1–3; 95:3; Isa. 9:6–7; Col. 1:16; Heb. 1:8–14; Rev. 1:5, 8; 19:11–21).

Political states today are largely secular states. Christians have many different opinions about how they should be related to these political authorities. States today are not simply disconnected from churches; in most cases they are based on ideologies that claim no relation to or dependence upon a biblical view of reality. Modern liberal, socialist, and communist ideologies all claim to be rooted in nothing more than the sovereignty and independence of human will and reason. Many Christians, therefore, spend their time trying to weigh or even justify the relative merits of one of these ideologies from a biblical viewpoint. Others accept the incompatibility of biblical Christianity with modern political establishments and seek a purer Christian life and witness apart from political engagement. Still others try to recover one of the earlier Catholic or Protestant traditions of life and thought as a basis for reforming or engaging in political life. A large number of Christians simply ignore or remain apathetic about government and politics, treating that realm as inconsequential for their Christian witness. In the realm of politics and government today there appears to be very little agreement among Christians about the nature and task of government from a biblical viewpoint.

Key Issues and Questions for Our Day. Considering the diversity of "Christian" approaches to political life in the light of the biblical witness, a few issues seem to stand out as most important for our consideration.

First, Christians should not expect to find in biblical revelation some kind of ideal or unchanging model of government (or the state) by which to evaluate their responsibility. Nowhere in the Bible does God put forward a political system that can serve as unchanging ideal. Rather than debate about competing ideals, Christians should turn to a critical assessment of their political traditions and ideologies in the light of a deeper understanding of biblical revelation about justice.

Second, the character of the modern state is a phenomenon that requires a thorough understanding of political and economic history. This means that the kind of education that we give our children is crucial. Without a grasp of the state's character and the modern ideologies that shape it, we cannot begin to consider a biblical view of it.

Finally, we must consider the meaning of the contemporary "global village." The world is rapidly becoming a closely interconnected network. Biblical revelation about the lordship of Christ over the whole earth, about the earth being God's footstool, about the challenge to Christ's sovereignty by Antichrist with a global design—all these dimensions of biblical revelation have direct bearing on contemporary political life and governments. The demand for justice is increasingly the demand for global justice, and Christians should be leading the way to an understanding of what the proper human stewardship of government means in response to Christ the King.

J. W. SKILLEN

Government, Church. See CHURCH GOVERNMENT.

Government, Gift of. See SPIRITUAL GIFTS.

Governmental Theory of the Atonement. See ATONEMENT, THEORIES OF THE.

Grace. Undeserved blessing freely bestowed on humankind by God. This concept is at the heart not only of Christian theology but also of all genuinely Christian experience. In discussing the subject of grace an important distinction must be maintained between common (general, universal) grace and special (saving, regenerating) grace, if the relationship between divine grace and the human situation is to be rightly understood.

Common Grace. Common grace is so called because it is common to all humankind. Its benefits are experienced by the whole human race without distinction among persons. Common grace is evident in God's continuing care for his creation, as he provides for the needs of his creatures, restrains human society from becoming altogether intolerable and ungovernable, and makes it possible for humankind, although fallen, to live together in a generally orderly and cooperative manner, to show mutual forbearance, and to cultivate together the scientific, cultural, and economic pursuits of civilization.

Special Grace. Special grace is the grace by which God redeems, sanctifies, and glorifies his people. Unlike common grace, which is universally given, special grace is bestowed only on those whom God gives eternal life through faith in his Son.

Prevenient grace is grace that comes first. It precedes all human decision and endeavor. Grace always means that it is God who takes the initiative and implies the priority of God's action on behalf of needy sinners. That is the whole point of grace: it does not start with us, it starts with God; it is not earned or merited by us, it is freely and lovingly given to us—even while we were yet sinners (Rom. 5:8, 10; 2 Cor. 8:9; 1 John 4:10, 19).

Efficacious grace is grace that effects the purpose for which it is given. It is efficacious simply because it is *God's* grace. What God purposes and performs cannot fail or come to nothing; otherwise he is not God. God's grace saves sinners; all those God gives to Christ will come to him, and whoever comes Christ will never drive away and will raise up at the last day (John 6:37, 39; cf. 17:6, 9, 12, 24).

Irresistible grace is grace that cannot be rejected. Irresistible grace is closely bound up with the efficacious nature of that grace. As the work of God always achieves the effect toward which it is directed, so also it cannot be resisted or thrust aside.

Sufficient grace is grace that is adequate for the saving of the believer both here and now and forever. As with the other aspects of special grace, its sufficiency flows from the infinite power and goodness of God. Those who draw near to him through Christ he saves "fully and completely" (Heb. 7:25, Phillips).

It is important to remember that the operation of God's grace is a deep mystery that is far beyond our limited human comprehension. God does not treat us as though we were puppets with no mind or will of our own. Our human dignity as responsible persons under God is never violated or despised.

P. E. HUGHES

See also GRACE, MEANS OF.

Grace, Means of. There are various media through which grace may be received. The primary means of grace is Scripture, from which our whole knowledge of the Christian faith is derived

(John 20:31; 2 Tim. 3:15). Preaching—the proclamation of the dynamic truth of the gospel—is an important means of grace (Luke 24:47; Acts 1:8; Rom. 1:16; 10:11–15; 1 Cor. 1:17–18, 23). Similarly, personal witness and evangelism are means for bringing the grace of the gospel to others.

While the above are essentially means of saving grace, there are also means of continuing or strengthening grace. The exposition of Scripture for the instruction and edification of Christian believers is one such means, as is the private study of the Bible. Another is prayer, in which Christians commune with God, experience his presence, and open themselves to his purpose and his power. Another is fellowship with other Christians in worship and witness. Yet another is participation in the sacrament of communion, which Christ instituted and commanded his followers to observe. It is of particular importance that the means of grace should be received with faith and gratitude; otherwise, instead of being means of grace they become means of condemnation.

P. E. HUGHES

See also BAPTISM; GRACE; LORD'S SUPPER.

Great Awakenings, The. The theological significance of America's first two Great Awakenings lies in the effect that intense revivalism had upon the shape of Christian thinking. The First Great Awakening (ca. 1735–43) is associated with the labors of the Dutch Reformed clergyman Theodore Frelinghuysen, the Presbyterian Gilbert Tennent, the Congregationalist Jonathan Edwards, and especially the itinerant Anglican George Whitefield—all Calvinists whose theological commitments provided a definite shape for their work. The Second Great Awakening (ca. 1795–1830) was more diffuse, with origins in the West under the leadership of Methodist, Baptist, and Presbyterian itinerants, and in the East with the Congregational ministers of New England and the special efforts of Yale President Timothy Dwight. The culminating theological figures of the Second Great Awakening were Yale divinity professor Nathaniel William Taylor, the driving organizational genius Lyman Beecher, and the dominant evangelist Charles Grandison Finney—all men who were far less Calvinistic than leaders of the earlier awakening and more closely attuned to the democratic assumptions of the new U.S.

The First Great Awakening. The soteriology of the First Awakening was exemplified in the practice of George Whitefield and the thought of Jonathan Edwards, who held that salvation belonged completely to God, and that humans did not possess the natural capacity to turn to Christ apart from God's saving call. In fact, Edwards' rejuvenation of a basically Calvinistic soteriology was the longest-lived theological result of the First Awakening.

The First Great Awakening also influenced theologies of the church and society. Under Edwards' leadership many New England Congregationalists and middle colony Presbyterians moved toward an ideal of a "pure church," the conviction that only professed believers should participate in the Lord's Supper or take their places as full members of a local congregation. Further, it stimulated the efforts of Separate Congregationalists and Baptists to organize churches that were entirely distinct from New England governments.

Finally, it also brought to an end the Puritan conception of society as a beneficial union of ecclesiastical and public life. The leaders of the Awakening called for purity in the churches, even if it meant destroying Puritanism's historically close association between church and state.

The Second Great Awakening. The Second Great Awakening stimulated religious life on an unprecedented scale at the turn of the 19th century and beyond. It breathed new life into exhausted denominations and provided the impetus for the creation of many newer bodies. It also had important theological consequences for ideas of salvation, church, and society. Particularly in the work of Nathaniel Taylor the soteriology of the Second Awakening moved away from that of Whitefield and Edwards. While Edwards and Whitefield had stressed the inability of sinful people to save themselves in order to preserve God's sovereignty in salvation, Taylor and the leading revivalists on the frontier tended to stress more the ability that God had bestowed on all people to come to Christ. This more Arminian approach to salvation received reinforcement from the increasing influence of Methodists in American life.

The Second Awakening also had a great impact on ecclesiology. Under the libertarian influence of the Revolutionary age individual Christians insisted that the Bible and the Bible only, free from traditional interpretations, was the standard for organizing churches. So it was that following the Bible only, Disciples, Free Will Baptists, Calvinistic Methodists, Universalists, "Christians," and other new groups employed private interpretation of Scripture to break from historical denominations and start their own. The more democratic spirit of the early U.S. also lay behind the great success of voluntarism. Voluntary societies, separate from the denominations and organized for a specific goal, were a product of the Second Awakening's energetic efforts to Christianize and reform America.

Finally, the Second Awakening contributed to a theology of society that emphasized the potential of America and the promise of a millennial hope. This vision inspired Christians to great feats of Christian service, due in no small part to the conviction that such a special outpouring of God's Spirit was a herald for the end of the age.

M. A. NOLL

See also DWIGHT, TIMOTHY; EDWARDS, JONATHAN; FINNEY, CHARLES GRANDISON; HALFWAY COVENANT; NEW ENGLAND THEOLOGY; REVIVALISM; STODDARD, SOLOMON; TAYLOR, NATHANIEL WILLIAM; WHITEFIELD, GEORGE.

Great Commission, The. The command of Jesus to go and make disciples of all nations, baptizing and teaching them (Matt. 28:16–20). The message to be conveyed includes the historical events of Christ's life, particularly his crucifixion (1 Cor. 15:3; Col. 2:14–15), his resurrection, his ascension (Luke 24:50–51; Rom. 4:25; 1 Cor. 15:3–4; Eph. 1:20–23), and his second coming (Acts 3:19–21).

W. H. MARE

Great Tribulation, The. See TRIBULATION.

Grebel, Conrad (ca. 1498–1526). Organizer of the first Free Church congregation. He was born in Zurich, at that time a solidly Roman Catholic city. Grebel founded the first modern free church and inaugurated believer's baptism on Jan. 21, 1525, after he and his followers faced fines and imprisonment for disrupting the religious unity of Zurich's new evangelical religious movement under Zwingli. He carried out earnest evangelization efforts in northern Switzerland. Grebel died of the plague a year and a half after founding his biblicist (now Mennonite) church.

J. C. WENGER

See also MENNONITES; ZWINGLI, ULRICH.

Gregory I, the Great (540–604). Pope whose papacy is generally considered the beginning of the medieval period. Gregory is especially significant for his role in increasing the power and authority of the papacy. He firmly believed the Roman pope was Peter's sole successor and therefore supreme head of the universal church, a view not accepted in some areas. In numerous ecclesiastical disputes he asserted the papacy's supremacy over the whole church. His efforts were not always successful, but by the time of his death the authority of the papal office had been greatly enhanced.

A different side of Gregory's character is seen in his pastoral and evangelistic concerns. He vastly increased the benevolent work of the church, supported in large part by his careful administration of vast estates owned by the church. His practical book on pastoral care, *Pastoral Rule*, had enormous influence for centuries. He also exhibited a deep concern for the evangelization of unbelievers. Theologically Gregory owed much to his study of the church fathers, especially Augustine. He held a high view of Scripture as the Word of God, emphasizing its importance not only for doctrinal truth but for individual spiritual nourishment. At the same time his teachings included many elements that would become standard in later Roman Catholic theology, including the sacrificial nature of the Mass and the dogma of purgatory.

J. N. AKERS

See also PAPACY.

Gregory of Nazianzus (ca. 329–ca. 389). Cappadocian father known as "the theologian." Gregory was born of aristocratic Christian parents near Nazianzus. During the Council of Constantinople (381) Gregory was elected bishop of Constantinople, but he resigned the see when his election was disputed. He retired to Nazianzus and then to his estate at Arianzus, where he died. Gregory's *Orations* constitute his most significant writings. Of these, the five "Theological Orations" (*Orat.* 27–31), preached at Constantinople in 380, are the best known.

Theologically Gregory's significance lies in his clarification of the doctrines of the Trinity and Christ. While maintaining against the Arians the essential unity of the three divine Persons, and therefore their equality, Gregory provided the terminology necessary to express the real distinctions among Father, Son, and Spirit, thereby safeguarding the Trinity from Sabellian perversion. The distinctive property of each person refers to the origin of each: the Father is unbegotten (*agennēsia),* the Son is begotten (*gennēsia*), the Spirit proceeds (*ekporeusis*). Against the Apollinarian denial of Christ's human soul Gregory insisted upon the complete manhood of Christ, for salvation is incomplete if the Son's incarnation is incomplete. Salvation is essentially deification, the complete participation of human nature in the divine; therefore, in Christ there must be two complete natures inseparably united in one person.

W. C. WEINRICH

See also CAPPADOCIAN FATHERS.

Gregory of Nyssa (ca. 335–ca. 394). Bishop of Nyssa, and one of the Cappadocian fathers. Gregory was born into a famous Christian family (father, Basil the elder; sister, St. Macrina; brothers, Basil of Caesarea and Peter of Sebaste).

Theological controversy influenced much of Gregory's writing. His *Against Eunomius* represents a detailed refutation of Arianism's subordination of the Word. In *To Ablabius* Gregory defends the Trinitarian doctrine against tritheistic misinterpretations. Against Apollinaris he argues for a full incarnation in the treatise *Antirrheticus*. Gregory's *Catechetical Oration* presents a systematic treatment of Christian doctrine for the instruction of catechumens. Gregory's *On Virginity* and *Life of St. Macrina* are classics of Christian asceticism.

Gregory ensured the triumph of Nicene orthodoxy by his detailed working out of Basil's distinction between *ousia*, the Godhead in which Father, Son, and Spirit share, and *hypostasis*, the individuality of each. The distinction among divine persons is maintained by their immanent mutual relations, while the true unity is seen by the oneness of attributes and external operation. His anthropology was an important contribution to Christian mysticism. Created in God's image, our soul is like God's nature, enabling us intuitively to know God and through purification to become like God.

W. C. WEINRICH

See also CAPPADOCIAN FATHERS.

Groningen Theology. Theological movement that takes its name from the theological faculty of the University of Groningen led by Petrus Hofstede de Groot (1830–60).

Its central doctrine was that God has revealed himself in all of creation and supremely in Jesus Christ so that humankind may be conformed to his image. While God had been active among all peoples, his work is seen especially in Israel and in the life of Jesus. The Groningen theology emphasized God's revelation in Jesus as an example to be followed. It claimed that Jesus had one spiritual nature that is shared by both God and humankind. It denied the doctrines of the Trinity and the atonement but accepted the miracles of Jesus as signs of his special mission. In Jesus' person, words, and works the nature of God, the holy Father of humankind, is seen. In Christ, God shows us ourselves, our depravity, and our destiny as his saved people. Faith in Christ saves from guilt and the dominion of sin, God's forgiving love is experienced, and the faithful are filled with his Spirit. Christ founded, preserves and perfects the church; it will triumph in the end.

M. E. OSTERHAVEN

Groote, Gerard (1340–1384). Dutch mystic who was the moving spirit behind the Brethren of the Common Life and the *Devotio Moderna*. After his conversion in 1374 he returned to his native Deventer. Finding self-discipline a problem, he entered a Carthusian monastery. He became a missionary preacher in the Utrecht diocese and beyond. He was widely accepted by the common people. He denounced abuses in the church, while upholding its traditional teaching and seeking reform from within. The establishment predictably reacted adversely to his criticism, and withdrew his license to preach. He retired to Deventer, founded the Brethren of the Common Life, but died of the plague before many of his ideas had been implemented. Much of Groote's thinking is reflected in the work of his most famous follower, Thomas à Kempis, author of *The Imitation of Christ*, a book earlier attributed to Groote himself.

J. D. DOUGLAS

See also BRETHREN OF THE COMMON LIFE; DEVOTIO MODERNA; THOMAS À KEMPIS.

Grotius, Hugo (1583–1645). Dutch jurist, statesman, theologian, and historian. Grotius is remembered as the "father of international law" on the basis of his *De jure belli et pacis (Concerning the Law of War and Peace)*, which appeared in 1625.

He was an ardent student of religion and wrote on theology, scriptural interpretation, and church government. One of his most popular books, *On the Truth of the Christian Religion* (1627), was intended as a missionary manual for those who had contact with pagans and Muslims. Another work, *De satisfactione Christi* (1617), espoused the governmental theory of the atonement. Grotius also published commentaries on the NT, treating it on a level with other literature and applying rules of textual criticism to it. In works such as *Via ad pacem ecclesiasticum* (1642) he expressed a desire for the unity of the church and was willing to make such extensive concessions to restore union with Rome that he was accused of converting to Roman Catholicism.

R. G. CLOUSE

Guardian Angel. See ANGEL.

Guilt. Legal and moral state of a person after the intentional or unintentional violation of a law, principle, or value. The law may have been established by a society's legal system, by God, or by an individual's personal code of ethics.

In the Bible. In a theological sense, guilt is a person's moral and legal state after the intentional or unintentional violation of God's law or principles (Lev. 4:2, 13, 22, 27; 5:2, 3, 15). The Bible shows a progressive development in the concept of guilt, from a corporate to a personal dimension. Jesus was concerned not only with the act and the inner attitude (Matt. 5:21–22), but he saw degrees of guilt dependent on knowledge and motive (Luke 11:29–32; 12:47–48). He made it clear that the law had been promulgated for our benefit. Guilt-producing sin not only brings suffering to the offender and those offended, but it also brings pain to the heart of God.

Management of Guilt. The word *guilt* carries with it the concept of deserved punishment or payment due—even payment by punishment. God made this clear in his indictment of the guilty Cain (Gen. 4:11–15). The principle of restitution was incorporated into Israel's written law (the sin offering; Lev. 4). The concept of payment for wrongdoing by punishment can be found in both Testaments. The concept of payment was significant in the atoning death of Christ upon the cross for the individual and collective sins of humankind.

Clouding the modern understanding of guilt is the common but erroneous use of the words *guilt* and *guilt feeling* as though they were interchangeable. Guilt is an after-the-fact reality or state that may or may not be accompanied by guilt feeling. Guilt feeling is a painful conglomerate of emotions that usually includes anxiety in anticipation of punishment; shame, with its sense of humiliation, dirtiness, and the need to hide; and grief, or depression, for the diminished sense of worth, dignity, and self-esteem. Although a source of intense emotional pain, the feelings of guilt can serve as an internal alarm system that alerts us to the fact that we have violated God's value system.

The most constructive, healthy response to the pain of guilt is repentance and acceptance of the grace of forgiveness offered by God through the person of Jesus Christ.

W. G. JUSTICE

Guilt Offering. See OFFERINGS AND SACRIFICES IN BIBLE TIMES.

Guyon, Madame (1648–1717). French mystic and quietist. Born Jeanne Marie Bouvier de la Mothe, in Montargis, France, she was compelled by her mother to marry Jacques Guyon in 1664. After being widowed in 1676, Madame Guyon entered more deeply into a life of religious devotion. She became an exponent of mystic quietism. She maintained that a true Christian must pray and strive for spiritual perfection, a state of inner blessedness that consists of a wholly disinterested love of God, submits implicitly to his will, and is indifferent to all outward things, even to the church and its sacraments. Her major writings were *A Short and Easy Method of Prayer, Autobiography,* and *The Song of Songs.*

N. V. HOPE

See also QUIETISM.

Hh

Hades. See DEAD, ABODE OF THE. *See also* HELL; SHEOL.

Halfway Covenant (1662). Attempt by Puritans in America to preserve a Christian commonwealth in the New World. Puritan leaders recognized that they had to preserve the church for professed believers, but they also wanted to keep as many people as possible under the influence of the church. Their solution was the "halfway" covenant. In this arrangement, second-generation New England Puritans could bring their children for baptism and halfway membership in the church. But no one in the second or third generation could participate in the Lord's Supper or exercise other privileges of church membership unless they testified that God had done a gracious work in their heart.

M. A. NOLL

Hallelujah. Liturgical expression urging worshipers to indulge in one of the highest forms of devotion that can be offered to God. The term is restricted to songs of praise in Scripture, occurring 24 times in the Psalter and four times in the Book of Revelation. In the synagogue period the "Egyptian Hallel" (Pss. 113–18) was recited as part of the passover ceremony in the home, the first two psalms preceding the meal and the rest sung at the conclusion. Pss. 135–36 were sung on the sabbath, while the "Great Hallel" (Pss. 120–36, or 135–36, or 145–50) was sung at the morning services in the synagogue. The NT closes with a heavenly choir's "Hallelujah."

R. K. HARRISON

Hallow, Hallowed. To make holy or honor as holy; to set apart for religious use, or to consecrate. The Bible speaks of setting apart many things or persons for sacred purposes, such as the priests (Exod. 29:1); the tabernacle and its equipment (Exod. 40:9); the children of Israel (Lev. 22:32); the sabbath (Jer. 17:22); the jubilee year (Lev. 25:10); the firstborn (Num. 3:13); and the temple (1 Kings 8:64).

H. F. VOS

Halloween (All Hallows Eve). Name given to Oct. 31, the eve of the Christian festival of All Saints Day (Nov. 1).

H. F. VOS

See also ALL SAINTS DAY.

Hands, Laying on of. See LAYING ON OF HANDS.

Hardening, Hardness of Heart. Action or state of persistent and sometimes hostile rejection of the Word of God. This involves not simply a refusal to hear the Word but a failure to respond in submission and obedience. The person with a hardened heart may also reject those who convey the Word, whether prophets, apostles, or the Logos himself, Jesus Christ. Individuals (Pharaoh [Exod. 4:21; 7:13, 22; 8:15, 19; 10:1]) or whole communities of peoples or nations (Israel [Isa. 6:10–11; 29:9–14; Rom. 11:7–25; 2 Cor. 3:14]; Gentiles [Josh. 11:20; Eph. 4:18]) may harden their hearts.

In Scripture both God and people are listed as agents of hardening. Pharaoh is said to harden his own heart (Exod. 8:15). But God is also said to harden Pharaoh's heart (Exod. 4:21; 10:1). Paul's comment on the incident is that God hardens whom he will and has mercy on whom he will (Rom. 9:18). Hardening is a complex phenomenon involving both divine and human agency. But instead of being the manifestation of predetermined reprobation, hardening is primarily presented in Scripture as a means of God's accomplishment of his purposes for history. Hardening is lifted only by God (2 Cor. 3:15–16; 4:3–6). Scripture expects the present hardening of Israel to be followed by new covenant ministries of the Spirit in which the hard heart of the nation is replaced by a new heart of faith and obedience (Jer. 31:33–37; Ezek. 36:26–37; Rom. 11:25–32).

C. BLAISING

Harnack, Adolf (1851–1930). German theologian and church historian. Harnack's principal contributions were in NT studies and patristics. Harnack's major works available in English include *History of Dogma* (7 vols., 1894–99), *The Mission and Expansion of Christianity in the First Three Centuries* (2 vols., 1904–5), *The Constitution and Law of the Church in the First Two Centuries* (1910), *Luke the Physician* (1907), *The Sayings of Jesus* (1908), *The Acts of the Apostles* (1909), and *The Date of the Acts and of the Synoptic Gospels* (1911). His historical scholarship broke new ground and in some respects actually undermined the views of contemporary liberal biblical critics.

In the theological best-seller *What Is Christianity?* (1901) Harnack argues that the kernel of Jesus' message is the kingdom of God, where the victory over evil provides the inner link with God and gives ultimate meaning to life. Here is demonstrated the fatherhood of God and the infinite worth of the human soul. Christians follow Jesus' example of the "higher righteousness" governed by the law of love, which exists independent of religious worship and technical observance.

R. V. PIERARD

See also LIBERALISM, THEOLOGICAL.

Hartshorne, Charles. See PROCESS THEOLOGY.

Head, Headship. In 1 Cor. 11:3 Paul designates God as "the head of Christ." This means that the incarnate Son of God is subject to the Father in his mediatorial office. Paul ascribes to Christ a double headship. First, he is the head of all things (Eph. 1:10, 22), over every power and authority (Col. 2:10). Christ's headship over creation is by virtue of his being its creator, sustainer, ruler, restorer, as well as nature's end and purpose (Eph. 1:10, 23; Col. 1:15–19). Second, Christ's headship over all things is exercised with a view toward the church, over which he is the head in a special sense (Eph. 1:22–23). The special character of Christ's headship over the church is indicated by the designation of the church as the body of Christ. Christ is the source of the church's life. Its life is in actuality a participation in his own (Eph. 1:23; 5:23; Col. 2:19); the union between Christ and the church is deep and profoundly spiritual (Eph. 5:28–32); Christ loves his church and is concerned for its welfare (Eph. 5:29–30); Christ is the provider of all things necessary for its growth and vitality (Eph. 4:7–16).

In Protestant theology in general and Reformed theology in particular the doctrine of Christ's headship over the church occupied an important place in the polemics of church polity. This headship is appealed to as the chief bulwark of the spiritual freedom of the church from either the authority of the pope or that of the magistrate. The idea of headship is also employed by Paul to describe the relationship between man and woman, husband and wife (1 Cor. 11:3).

R. S. RAYBURN

Heal, Healing. Restoration of health (Ps. 41:3), the making whole or well of an individual, whether physically, mentally, or spiritually. The Bible presents two basic views concerning healing and sickness. (1) In the OT Yahweh alone was considered the source of healing, just as he was the source of sickness. Deut. 32:39 portrays God as the direct dispenser of sickness and disease as punishment for sin (cf. Num. 12:9–15; 2 Chron. 21:18–19; 26:16–21), while healing is seen as a reward for obedience, a manifestation of God's forgiveness, mercy, and love (Gen. 20:17; Ps. 41:5). God heals not only individuals but also entire nations (Exod. 23:22–25; Lev. 26:14–21; Num. 16:47; Deut. 7:15).

(2) The second view of healing and sickness is prominent in the NT. Sickness is regarded as the consequence of the universal corrupt nature of humankind caused by original sin (Gen. 2:17; 3:19; Rom. 5:12–21). Thus as a result of the fall, humankind became naturally susceptible to disease. In the NT sickness and Satan are closely related (Matt. 12:22–28; Luke 13:16); however, Jesus' teachings, like the Book of Job, demonstrate that sickness is not always divine punishment for individual sins (although this remains possible; see John 5:14), nor is it normative for God to use sickness as punishment. Yet God does work through sickness to discipline and chasten his children (Prov. 3:7–8, 11–12; Heb. 12:6) and even to assist in developing faith, humility, and character (Job 40:4; 42:6; 2 Cor. 4:17). Nevertheless, sickness is basically an evil that contradicts and hinders God's will and desire for humankind.

In the healing ministry of Christ faith was a dominant factor (Matt. 8:13; 9:2, 22, 29; 13:58; 15:28; Mark 6:5–6). The most controversial theological aspect of divine healing is its relationship to the atonement. One view maintains that the privilege of physical healing is governed by the will and sovereignty of God—that is, God heals whomever he wills. The other claims that physical healing, like salvation, is an inheritance of every believer through the atoning death of Christ. Using Matt. 8:16–17 to interpret Isa. 53:4, this view concludes that Christ bore both our bodily and spiritual suffering on the cross. The healing ministry of Jesus was continued through his commissioning and sending out of the Twelve (Matt. 10:1–5; Mark 6:7–13; Luke 9:1–6) and the 70 (Luke 10:9). The Book of Acts and the Epistles provide clear evidence of the continuance of divine healing in the apostolic church. James 5:14–16 presents the healing of the sick through the prayer of faith as a permanent provision and promise. Throughout church history there has been a constant testimony and commitment to this teaching/practice.

P. G. CHAPPELL

See also SPIRITUAL GIFTS.

Healing, Gift of. See SPIRITUAL GIFTS.

Heart. ***Biblical Psychology.*** The biblical view of human nature was developed in a religious setting; there is no systematized or scientific psychology in the Bible. Nevertheless, certain fundamental conceptions are worthy of note. In the OT there is no marked emphasis on individuality but, rather, on corporate personality. Yet A. R. Johnson has shown that a fundamental characteristic of OT anthropology is the awareness of totality. The human person is not a body plus a soul, but a living unit of vital power, a psychophysical organism. The Hebrews thought of the human person as influenced from without—by evil spirits, the devil, or the Spirit of God—whereas in modern psychology the emphasis has tended to be on dynamic factors operating from within.

In the OT. In the English versions several Hebrew expressions are translated "heart," the main words being *lēb* and *lēbāb*. Like other anthropological terms in the OT, heart is also used very frequently in a psychological sense, as the center or focus of an individual's inner personal life. The heart is the source, or spring, of motives; the seat of the passions; the center of the thought processes; the spring of conscience. Heart, in fact, is associated with what is now meant by the cognitive, affective, and volitional elements of a person.

The Book of Proverbs describes the heart as the seat of wisdom (2:10); trust (or confidence) (3:5); diligence (4:23); deceit (6:14); wicked schemes (6:18); lust (6:25); folly (12:23); anxiety (12:25); bitterness (14:10); sorrow (14:13); happiness (15:13); discernment (15:14; 18:15); joy (15:30); pride (16:5); rage (19:3); and envy (23:17).

In the NT. The NT word for heart is *kardia*. This term has diverse psychological and spiritual connotations. Jesus emphasized the importance of right states of heart. The pure in heart see God (Matt. 5:8); sin is first committed in the heart (Matt. 5:28); evil thoughts and acts come out of the heart (Matt. 15:19); forgiveness must come from the heart (Matt. 18:35); we must love God with all our heart (Matt. 22:37); the Word of God is sown, and must come to fruition, in the heart (Luke 8:11–15). Paul's use of *kardia* is similar. While Paul uses other expressions, such as mind, soul, and spirit, to augment the conception of human nature, on the whole, it may be said that the NT word *kardia* reproduces and expands the ideas included in the OT words *lēb* and *lēbāb*.

Since the heart is regarded as the center or focus of a person's life, the spring of all desires, motives, and moral choices—indeed, of all behavioral trends—it is not surprising to note that in both Testaments the divine appeal is addressed to the "heart."

O. R. BRANDON

See also MAN, DOCTRINE OF.

Heaven. God's dwelling-place. Although some people envision heaven as a disembodied state where naked minds contemplate eternal, unchanging ideas, the Bible presents a different picture. According to Paul, the whole person survives. Even the body is raised again (1 Cor. 15:35–58). There is nothing in the Bible about disembodied spirits in the next world existing *in vacuo*. In heaven the redeemed will be in the immediate presence of God, beholding the Father's face. In the present life we "see but a poor reflection as in a mirror; then we shall see face to face" (1 Cor. 13:12). We will see Christ "as he is" (1 John 3:2). The childlike in faith will "always see the face" of the Father in heaven (Matt. 18:10). Heaven is God's house (John 14:2), where the redeemed will dwell, where "they will be his people" and where "God himself will be with them" (Rev. 21:3).

J. K. GRIDER

See also FINAL STATE.

Heavenlies, The. (Gk. *en tois epouraniois*) Term that occurs five times in the Book of Ephesians (1:3, 20; 2:6; 3:10; 6:12) and nowhere else in the NT. It is translated "in the heavenly places" (AV, RSV, NASB) or "in the heavenly realms" (NIV). God raised Christ to sit at his right hand in the heavenlies (Eph. 1:20; cf. Ps. 110:1; Heb. 8:1; 9:24; 1 Pet. 3:22). God also has raised believers with Christ so that, while they are living on earth, at the same time they are also seated with Christ in the heavenlies (Eph. 2:6), enjoying spiritual blessings (Eph. 1:3; the blessings are enumerated in 1:4–14). The heavenlies are also the arena of spiritual conflict. But we have won the victory because Christ is in control of all (Eph. 1:21–22; cf. Acts 4:12; 1 Cor. 15:24; Eph. 1:10; Phil. 2:10; Col. 1:16–20; 1 Pet. 3:22).

W. D. MOUNCE

See also PRINCIPALITIES AND POWERS.

Heavens, New. See NEW HEAVENS AND NEW EARTH.

Heave Offering. See OFFERINGS AND SACRIFICES IN BIBLE TIMES.

Hegel, Georg Wilhelm Friedrich (1770–1831). German philosopher. Hegel was the most influential of the German idealists. In his view only mind is real; everything else is the expression of mind. Philosophy became a kind of theology for Hegel, because he saw all reality as an expression of the Absolute, who is God. All that exists is the expression of divine mind, so that the real is rational and the rational is real.

Hegel divided religion into four different stages or ways of gaining knowledge of the Absolute. The first stage is natural religion, or animism, in which people worship trees, streams, and animals. The second stage represents God in human form. People build temples and worship statues. This stage also involves the development of self-consciousness in humans. Historic Christianity represents the third stage. Through the incarnation God is present in the world—God and humankind together. Jesus demonstrated that morals are a spontaneous expression of life—a participation in divine life. The fourth stage is the highest; it is Hegel's reformulation of Christian beliefs into concepts of speculative philosophy.

Interpretations of Hegel vary widely. Many consider his philosophical Christianity heretical, thinly veiled pantheism. For others, Hegel's system is a sincere attempt to articulate Christian truth in philosophical language.

P. H. DEVRIES

Heidegger, Martin (1889–1976). German philosopher. Heidegger was a central figure in modern existentialist thought, a prime mover for new directions in hermeneutics, and author of the influential *Being and Time* (1927). In 1933 he became the first National Socialist rector of the University of Freiburg. In this position he gave public and enthusiastic support for the Third Reich.

While Heidegger was not a theologian, deep religious concerns are evident in his writings. First, Heidegger focuses on our finitude and death. Heidegger believes that an awareness of death leads to authentic existence (although his idea of authentic existence is exclusive of any godly relationship). Second, Heidegger maintains that we are too concerned with factual details and not concerned enough with true being. Because our age focuses on research and planning, we see our tasks in terms of limited, neat, manageable functions. Third, Heidegger attacks Christianity for contributing to our self-betrayal. Christianity does not redeem but destroys genuine culture. Along with other movements Christianity has made truth a matter of propositions rather than of existence. Fourth, Heidegger gives central importance to language: "Language is the house of Being." The best of language is not found in logical or theological propositions but in the disclosures of poets. Heidegger attempts to reorient theological and philosophical talk away from the modern scientific ideal.

P. H. DEVRIES

See also EXISTENTIALISM; NEO-ORTHODOXY; BULTMANN, RUDOLF; TILLICH, PAUL.

Heidelberg Catechism (1563). Catechism written in Heidelberg at the request of Elector Frederick III, ruler of the influential German province of the Palatinate, to be used as a manual of instruction, a guide for preaching, and a confession of faith. The two commonly acknowledged architects of the catechism were Caspar Olevianus and Zacharias Ursinus. The German text, with a preface by Frederick III, was adopted by a synod in Heidelberg on Jan. 19, 1563. It was translated into Latin at the time of its publication.

The catechism is important for at least three reasons. (1) It was eventually translated into numerous languages and was adopted by many groups, making it the most popular of Reformed statements. (2) Although born in the midst of theological controversy, it is irenic in spirit, moderate in tone, and devotional and practical in attitude. It espouses Reformed theology as dictated by Frederick III, while not slighting Lutheran ideas. (3) The organization of the catechism is most unusual. The 129 questions and answers are divided into three parts patterned after the Book of Romans (sin-salvation-service).

R. V. SCHNUCKER

See also CATECHISMS; URSINUS, ZACHARIAS.

Heilsgeschichte. German term meaning the "history of salvation." The history of salvation perspective regards the Bible as essentially such a history. While the Bible says much about other matters, these are merely incidental to its single purpose of unfolding the story of redemption. *Heilsgeschichte* traces in history and doctrine the development of the divine purpose in the salvation of humankind. Considered as a somewhat different approach from the "proof-text" method, which uses the Bible as the raw material for the shaping of a systematic theology, *Heilsgeschichte* stresses a more organic approach. Oscar Cullmann is one of its most prominent exponents.

J. H. GERSTNER

Heim, Karl (1874–1958). German Lutheran theologian. Heim was a sensitive and perceptive observer of the modern world as well as a committed churchman. He was convinced that science and its attendant worldview are not equipped to answer our deepest existential questions. The reality of a personal God belongs to a dimension that is different from anything accessible to scientific investigation. We have essentially two choices open to us: skepticism or a decision of faith. The world's conceptual scheme can lead only to an empty skepticism, faith in Jesus Christ to intellectual and spiritual wholeness. During the traumatic years of the 1930s and early 1940s, Heim's sympathies were with the confessional church. Several of his works have been translated into English, including *God Transcendent* (1935) and *Christian Faith and Natural Science* (1953).

J. D. SPICELAND

Hell. Term generally used in Scripture to refer to a place of future punishment for the wicked dead. The word is used in some translations to refer to the grave or to the place of the dead. Also, "hell" is used to speak of the place of disembodied spirits, without any implication of either their bliss or torment. Gehenna, from the Greek *géenna*, is the eternal abode of the wicked. Whereas Hades is the intermediate state, Gehenna is eternal hell. Wherever it is used in the NT, it always means the place of eternal damnation. In the NT hell is portrayed as "unquenchable fire" (Matt. 3:12; cf. "fire of hell," 5:22; 18:9), a place of condemnation (Matt. 23:33), a "fiery furnace" (Matt. 13:42, 50), "blackest darkness" (Jude 13), a "fiery lake of burning sulfur" (Rev. 21:8), a place "prepared for the devil and his angels" (Matt. 25:41).

R. P. LIGHTNER

See also ABODE OF DEAD; ETERNAL PUNISHMENT; GEHENNA; SHEOL.

Helps, Gift of. See SPIRITUAL GIFTS.

Helvetic Confessions. The First Helvetic Confession (*Confessio Helvetica prior*) was written by Bullinger, Grynaeus, Myconius, and others delegated and assembled for that purpose in the city of Basel in 1536. It was the first confession that represented the faith of all the Swiss

Reformed cantons. It has sometimes (less suitably) been called the Second Confession of Basel (*Confessio Basileensis posterior*).

The Second Helvetic Confession began as Bullinger's personal confession, which he wrote in Latin in 1562. Peter Martyr Vermigli read it shortly before his death and agreed with it—a harbinger of its ultimate acceptance in the Reformed faith. By 1565, the Swiss again felt the need for a new common confession, and a conference was convened in Zurich. Bullinger's confession was considered and a few changes were made in it, to which Bullinger consented. It was published in German and Latin on March 12, 1566, and had the approval of Berne, Biel, Geneva, The Grisons, Mühlhausen, Schaffhausen, and St. Gall. The Second Helvetic Confession (*Confessio Helvetica posterior*) was soon translated into a number of languages ranging from French to Arabic. It was adopted by the Scots in 1566, the Hungarians in 1567, the French in 1571, and the Poles in 1578. The Second Helvetic Confession follows the order of the 27 articles of the First Helvetic Confession. It is an elaborate theological treatise with 30 chapters and over 20,000 words. Along with the Heidelberg Catechism, it is the most widely adopted and authoritative of the Reformed statements of faith.

R. V. SCHNUCKER

See also BULLINGER, JOHANN HEINRICH; CONFESSIONS OF FAITH.

Heresy. (Gk. *hairesis*) Deliberate denial of revealed truth coupled with the acceptance of error. The concept of heresy in 2 Pet. 2:1—divergent and destructive teachings promulgated by false teachers—came to predominate in Christian usage. The creeds were considered to contain the standard of truth and correct belief, and themselves formally contradicted various false teachings such as Arianism, Apollinarianism, Nestorianism, and Eutychianism.

M. R. W. FARRER

See also CHURCH DISCIPLINE; EXCOMMUNICATION; SCHISM.

Hermeneutic, The New. See NEW HERMENEUTIC, THE.

Hermetic Literature. Body of writings associated with Hermes Trismegistos. It is conjectured that most of these writings were written in the 2d and 3d centuries A.D. They are mystical, deeply influenced by Platonic and Stoic thought, and occasionally inconsistent. The Logos is a prominent feature, and there are striking parallels of language with John's Gospel. Direct borrowing either way is improbable, although Christianity perhaps influenced some Hermetica. This literature represents one aspect of the movement of Gnostic personal religion as the Christian mission began. It is therefore essentially syncretistic.

A. F. WALLS

See also GNOSTICISM; LOGOS.

Hesychasm. Contemplative movement in Eastern Orthodoxy known as "the way of stillness and repose." In the koine Greek, *hesychazō* meant "to be quiet, be at rest, remain silent." Originally the term was associated with certain Christian monastics who, although in communities, lived quietly in private cells. As it developed in the 11th century, hesychastic mysticism found its focus in spiritual exercises designed to produce a vision of God that could actually be seen with the physical eye. This vision consisted of an infusion of the "eternal, uncreated, divine light"—supposedly the same theophanic light that enveloped Jesus on the Mount of Transfiguration. The hesychasts believed this light to be communicable, gradually transforming seekers, until eventually they partook of the divine nature themselves.

Hesychasm was championed by the Mt. Athos leader, Gregory Palamas (1296–1359), who defended the distinction between the transcendent God—in essence unknowable and ineffable—and the immanent activity of divine energies or operations communicated to the seeking mystic by means of grace. The "divine and uncreated light," Palamas maintained, was an operation of the divine energy and not a direct communication of God's essence. In defense of a real communication between God and a person, he declared that a person "will experience the divine once the passions of the soul in accord with the body have been changed and sanctified though not deadened." After considerable conflict, the views of Palamas were finally accepted by the Councils of Constantinople in 1341, 1347, and 1351.

R. C. KROEGER

See also BEATIFIC VISION; MYSTICISM; UNIO MYSTICA.

Hierarchy. System of episcopal church government that (1) is distinct from the laity and has the exclusive right to administer the sacraments and govern the church; (2) claims an unbroken line of descent from Christ and the apostles and stands as their representatives in the church; (3) has a worldwide ordering of ranks or levels of authority (such as pope, bishops, priests).

The hierarchical system of church government is most fully developed within the Roman Catholic Church, where the hierarchy is divided into two parts: The hierarchy of *order* has authority to perform spiritual functions such as administering the sacraments and absolving sins; it consists of bishops (including the pope in his role as a bishop), priests, deacons, and several lesser offices (such as subdeacons and acolytes) instituted by the church. The hierarchy of *jurisdiction* (or pastoral government), on the other hand, has authority over church discipline and establishes rules of conduct and belief. This aspect of the hierarchy consists of the pope, bishops, cardinals, legates, and other lesser officers. Bishops thus belong to both aspects of the hierarchy.

W. A. GRUDEM

See also CHURCH GOVERNMENT; CHURCH OFFICERS; BISHOP; PAPACY.

High Church Movement. School of thought in Protestantism, particularly the Church of England (Anglicanism). The term "high" normally refers to a high view of the continuity of the church through history, and thus of its visibility. In accordance with this emphasis on visibility and continuity the sacraments of baptism and the Lord's Supper are viewed as indispensable means of grace. Other "signs" of being "high" include an emphasis on duly ordained and educated clergy, a respect for Catholic tradition (especially the ecumenical creeds), and a search for sound liturgy. Within Lutheranism (from the 17th century) and Methodism (from the 19th century) such an ethos or movement has often been found, although it has not necessarily been called "high church."

In Anglicanism, where the term has been used most frequently, it is important to distinguish between the High Church movement and the Tractarian (or Anglo-Catholic) movement. The former is much older than the latter. In the 17th century High Churchmen emphasized that the Church of England was a full member of the historical, continuing, and visible church of God, that its bishops could trace their "descent" back to the earliest times, that its liturgy contained original Catholic principles, that its sacraments were efficacious, and that its doctrine accorded with basic Catholic doctrine, being in harmony with that of the early centuries of the church. High Churchmen of distinction included Lancelot Andrewes (1555–1626), bishop of Winchester; George Herbert (1593–1633), a poet; Jeremy Taylor (1613–67), writer on spirituality; William Laud (1573–1645), archbishop of Canterbury; and Henry Hammond (1605–60), a biblical commentator.

The Tractarian movement was born in 1833 and proved much more positive about Roman Catholicism than the High Church party. By the end of the 19th century, however, the High Church movement had been absorbed by the Tractarian or Anglo-Catholic movement, and thus Tractarianism, High Church, and Anglo-Catholic functioned as rough equivalents, as they do to this day in Anglicanism.

P. TOON

See also ANGLO-CATHOLICISM; LAUD, WILLIAM; LOW CHURCH; OXFORD MOVEMENT.

Higher Criticism. Study of Scripture from the standpoint of literature, as opposed to lower criticism, which deals with the text of Scripture and its transmission. Higher criticism has three main concerns: (1) detecting the presence of underlying literary sources in a work; (2) identifying the literary types (*Gattungen*) that make up the composition; and (3) conjecturing on matters of authorship and date. Several other approaches have developed to assist the scholar in the use of higher criticism. Form criticism encourages the recognition of literary units according to their form. Tradition criticism examines the way in which specific traditions were interpreted by the various biblical writers. As with other disciplines, higher criticism needs to be used carefully. The improper use of higher criticism can result in purely speculative results lacking the support of external data.

R. K. HARRISON

See also ENLIGHTENMENT, THE; TÜBINGEN SCHOOL.

High Priest. See PRIESTS AND LEVITES.

Hinnom, Valley of. See GEHENNA.

Hippolytus (ca. 170–ca. 236). Greek-speaking presbyter in the church at Rome. Hippolytus wrote several important documents. The *Refutation of All Heresies* (*Philosophumena*) deals principally with Gnostic sects and traces their errors to philosophy. The *Apostolic Tradition* is the fullest source on the organizational and liturgical customs of the ante-Nicene church—covering baptism, the Eucharist, ordination, and the love feast. The *Commentary on Daniel* is the earliest commentary from the Orthodox Church; it sets forth a chiliastic eschatology. The *Against Noetus* opposes an early form of modalism.

E. FERGUSON

History of Religion School. See COMPARATIVE RELIGION.

Hocking, William Ernest (1873–1966). American philosopher. Hockings existentialist philosophy was known as objective idealism. It was his conviction that philosophy, if it is to be a worthwhile pursuit, must not be limited to academic circles. It must help to clarify and resolve issues in the wider world, including the world of religion, his area of special interest. He was a prolific writer, producing 18 books, including *The Meaning of God in Human Experience* (1912), *Human Nature and Its Remaking* (1918), *Re-thinking Missions* (1932), and *Living Religions and a World Faith* (1940).

J. D. SPICELAND

Hodge, Archibald Alexander (1823–1886). American Presbyterian scholar and theologian. He was the eldest son and successor of Charles Hodge from 1878. He continued the Calvinist tradition begun at Princeton Theological Seminary by Archibald Alexander, after whom he was affectionately named. In 1881 Hodge and Benjamin B. Warfield upheld Princeton's opposition to post-Enlightenment biblical criticism in their article "Inspiration." Affirming plenary verbal inspiration of the original autographs, Hodge and Warfield defined the doctrine of inerrancy, which dominated Presbyterianism in the 1890s. In *Popular Lectures on Theological Themes*, published posthumously in 1887, Hodge attempted to integrate his defense of Calvinism with cultural analysis.

W. A. Hoffecker

See also Hodge, Charles; Princeton Theology, Old; Warfield, Benjamin Breckinridge.

Hodge, Charles (1797–1878). American Presbyterian scholar and theologian. He taught biblical literature at Princeton Seminary from 1822 to 1840, when he became Archibald Alexander's successor as professor of exegetical and didactic theology, a position which he held until his death. Hodge used his position as editor of the *Biblical Repertory and Princeton Review* (founded 1825) to expound his own version of orthodox Calvinism and to attack theologies that deviated from it. But he is most remembered for his *Systematic Theology*, a three-volume, 2000-page work published in 1872–73. He was hard-working, earnest, prolific, and the most incisive of the conservative theologians who shaped education at Princeton Seminary from 1812 to 1929. Hodge's theology grew out of his commitment to an authoritative Bible, his respect for Reformed confessions and 17th-century European Reformed theologians, and his belief in the necessity of living piety.

M. A. Noll

See also Hodge, Archibald Alexander; Princeton Theology, Old; Warfield, Benjamin Breckinridge.

Hofmann, Johann Christian Konrad von (1810–1877). German Lutheran theologian. He was leader of the Erlangen School and professor at Erlangen from 1845 until his death. He espoused what has come to be known as the *heilsgeschichtlich* (salvation history) approach to biblical theology, stressing the history of the people of God, the inspiration of Scripture, and Jesus Christ as the goal of and key to the meaning of history. In his view, the purpose of biblical theology is to expound the history of salvation as contained in the books of the OT and NT. Only his *Biblische Hermeneutik* (1880) has been translated into English (*Interpreting the Bible* [1959]).

W. W. Gasque

Holiness. (Heb. *qōdeš*; Gk. *hagiasmos*) ***In the OT.*** Holiness in the OT is spoken of primarily in relation to God. Holiness refers to his essential nature; it is not so much an attribute of God as it is the very foundation of his being. "Holy, holy, holy is the Lord Almighty" (Isa. 6:3). God is thrice holy, intensely holy. Holiness, accordingly, is the background for all else declared about God. The first use of the word "holy" in the OT (Exod. 3:5) points to the fact that Moses was standing before the sacred presence of God. Holiness also reflects the majesty and awesomeness of God. He is majestic in holiness (Exod. 15:11). The very being of God provokes awe and fear. Thus holiness denotes the separateness, or otherness, of God from all his creation, and it signifies God's total apartness from all that is common and profane, from everything unclean or evil. Hence, holiness in relation to God refers climactically to his moral perfection. The holy God will show himself holy by his righteousness (Isa. 5:16). His eyes are too pure to look on evil (Hab. 1:13). This moral, or ethical, dimension of God's holiness becomes increasingly significant in the witness of the OT. Everything associated with God is also holy—an assembly of the people (Exod. 12:16); the sabbath (Exod. 16:23); heaven (Ps. 20:6); Zion (Ps. 2:6). God's name is especially holy, and never to be taken in vain (Exod. 20:7; Deut. 5:11). God's covenant people, chosen by him, are a holy people (Lev. 11:44; Deut. 7:6). Whatever is connected with the religious cultus is also holy. There are holy days, holy priests, holy anointing oil, holy firstfruits, holy utensils. The OT also stresses the need for inner holiness. In reply to the question, "Who may stand in his [God's] holy place?" the answer is given: "He who has clean hands and a pure heart" (Ps. 24:3–4).

In the NT. In the NT, for all that is said about God's grace and love, there is no less emphasis on his holiness. The NT highlights the ethical dimension of holiness. Holiness moves beyond any idea of a nation outwardly holy by virtue of divine election, and demonstrating such holiness through ritual and ceremony, to a people who are made inwardly holy. Basic to this is the witness of Jesus himself, the Holy One of God, who as the Son of man lived out a life of complete holiness, righteousness, and purity. Holiness (*hagiōsynē*) in the NT, accordingly, belongs to all believers. A common term for all believers is holy ones (*hagioi*), usually translated as "saints." "Saints" are not persons preeminent in holiness, but believers generally. All true believers are holy through Christ. In addition, holiness in the sense of transformation of the total person is now envisioned. So Paul writes: "May God himself, the God of peace, sanctify you [i.e., make you holy] through and through" (1 Thess. 5:23). Believers, as the saints of God, are "a chosen people, a royal priesthood, a holy nation" (1 Pet. 2:9). The holy nation is no longer Israel but the church. Holiness is no longer that to which a people are set apart and consecrated, but that which has now become an inward reality and in which they are being gradually transformed.

In Church History. In the history of the church, holiness has been viewed from many perspectives. In the Roman Catholic and Eastern Orthodox traditions several may be noted: (1) Ascetic. Holiness is pursued by fleeing the world (forsaking secular occupation, marriage, worldly goods). Hence it is limited to the few. (2) Mystical. Holiness is to be attained not so much by fleeing the world as by rising above it. Believers ascend a ladder of holiness with various stages (purgation, illumination, contemplation) until there is spiritual absorption in God. (3) Sacramental. Holiness is imparted through the supernatural grace of the sacraments; hence sacramental (unlike ascetic and mystical) holiness is available to all.

Classical Protestantism (16th century) was largely a movement away from ascetic, mystical, and sacramental views of holiness to a more biblical perspective. Soon, however, a number of diverging emphases were to emerge: (1) Disciplinary. The cultivation of a serious, often austere, life was viewed as the mark of a God-fearing and truly holy person (e.g., Scottish Presbyterians, English Puritans). (2) Experimental. In reaction against rigid orthodoxy, formalism, and the externals of faith, believers were encouraged to nurture the spiritual aspects of the faith (variously, Anabaptists, Quakers, Lutheran pietists). (3) Perfectionist. Total holiness, "entire sanctification," was regarded as possible not through works but by faith.

J. R. Williams

See also Spirituality.

Holiness Movement, American. Movement originating in the U.S. in the 1840s and 1850s as an endeavor to preserve and propagate John Wesley's teaching on entire sanctification and Christian perfection. Wesley held that the road from sin to salvation is one from willful rebellion against divine and human law to perfect love for God and humankind. Following Wesley, Holiness preachers emphasized that the process of salvation involves two crises. In the first, conversion or justification, the individual is freed from sins that have been committed. In the second, entire sanctification or full salvation, a person is liberated from the flaw in moral nature that causes people to sin. We are capable of this perfection even though we dwell in a corruptible body marked by numerous defects arising from ignorance, infirmities, and other creaturely limitations. It is a process of loving God with all one's heart, soul, and mind, and it results in the ability to live without conscious or deliberate sin.

In the mid-19th century several factors converged to contribute to the renewal of the Holiness emphasis, among them the camp meeting revivals that were a common feature in rural America, the Christian perfectionism of Charles Finney and Asa Mahan (the Oberlin theology), the "Tuesday Meeting" of Phoebe Palmer in New York, the urban revival of 1857–58, and protests within the Methodist Church about the decline of discipline. After the Civil War a full-fledged Holiness revival broke out within the ranks of Methodism, and in 1867 the National Camp Meeting Association for the Promotion of Holiness was formed. From 1893 it was known as the National Holiness Association (NHA) and in 1971 was renamed the Christian Holiness Association. Until the 1890s Methodists dominated the movement and channeled its enthusiasm into their churches.

By the 1880s the first independent Holiness denominations had begun to appear, and tensions between Methodism and the Holiness associations escalated. The gap between the two widened as Methodist practice drifted steadily toward a sedate, middle-class American Protestantism, while the Holiness groups insisted they were practicing primitive Wesleyanism and were the true successors of Wesley in America. The small schismatic bodies gradually coalesced into formal denominations, the largest of which were the Church of God, Anderson, Indiana (1880), Church of the Nazarene (1908), and Pilgrim Holiness Church (1897—merged with the Wesleyan Methodists in 1968 to form the Wesleyan Church).

The Holiness movement quickly spread beyond the bounds of Methodism. For example, a Mennonite group, the United Missionary Church (formerly Mennonite Brethren in Christ and since a merger in 1969, the Missionary Church), adopted the doctrine of entire sanctification and Holiness standards of personal conduct.

Numerical growth and material prosperity led inexorably to compromise with contemporary culture, and the relaxation of personal discipline was reflected in the wearing of fashionable dress and jewelry and secular entertainments such as participation in athletics and television viewing. As a result, several conservative splinter groups seceded from the Holiness denominations and joined together in an interchurch organization in 1947 known as the Interdenominational Holiness Convention. This organization presently regards itself as the defender of pristine Wesleyanism.

Pentecostalism is an offshoot of the Holiness movement. The Pentecostal revival made its greatest inroads in areas where Holiness movements were already prospering, and it attracted far more non-Methodists than had the earlier forms of perfectionism. Some Holiness denominations, most notably the Church of the Nazarene, flatly reject the use of tongues, while others, the largest being the Church of God, Cleveland, Tennessee, and the Pentecostal Holiness Church, teach both glossolalia and entire sanctification.

Despite its theological and practical weaknesses, the Holiness movement contributed to a deepening of the spiritual life in a materialistic age, and was a welcome contrast to the sterile intellectualism and dead orthodoxy that characterized so many churches at the time.

R. V. PIERARD

See also KESWICK CONVENTION; METHODISM; OBERLIN THEOLOGY; PENTECOSTALISM; PERFECTION, PERFECTIONISM; WESLEYAN TRADITION, THE.

Holiness of God. See GOD, ATTRIBUTES OF; GOD, DOCTRINE OF.

Holiness of the Christian. See GODLINESS.

Holl, Karl (1866–1926). German historian and theologian. He rose to the prestigious rank of professor of history at Berlin University in 1906. Holl's special interest was Luther studies. Holl stressed that the foundation of Luther's faith was a "religion of conscience." By this Holl meant that Luther responded to something that arose from deep inner feelings with which he felt impelled to deal. Those experiences, said Holl, are central to Luther's theology, for Luther felt that he was standing alone in his sins before God. From this confrontation with God, said Holl, came Luther's theology.

J. E. MENNELL

Holocaust, The. (LXX Gk. *holokautoma*, "complete burning") Nazi persecution, imprisonment, and eradication of 6 million Jews from 1933 to 1945. During the 1940s the annihilation of Jews and other prisoners became the primary goal of six Eastern European killing centers, inaugurating the industrialization of mass murder: Auschwitz, Belzec, Chelmno, Maidanek, Sobibor, and Treblinka. These centers were supplemented by a vast network of concentration camps, specializing in slave labor under the most deplorable physical and psychological conditions. Of an estimated 11 million civilians who died or were killed in these camps, 6 million were Jews. Thus, by 1945 the Nazis had eliminated two-thirds of the European Jews (a figure representing almost one-third of world Jewry).

After Hitler was appointed German chancellor on Jan. 30, 1933, the Nazi regime's policies toward Jews evolved and intensified through four stages:

1933–35. Sporadic economic and professional harassment included an economic boycott of Jewish businesses (Apr. 1, 1933), and the elimination of Jews from civil service posts (Apr. 7, 1933) and leading professions.

1935–38. Legal disabilities culminated in the Nuremberg laws (Sept. 1935), depriving Jews of German citizenship and prohibiting intermarriage. "Aryanization" of Jewish property and wealth also began.

1938–41. Deportations and pogroms started with "Crystal Night" (Nov. 9, 1938). Jewish businesses were expropriated and Jews were sent to concentration camps.

1941–45. The planned program of physical destruction of Jews began with the June 1941 German invasion of Russia, when Jews were systematically killed by means of mobile killing units and gas vans. After the Jan. 20, 1942, Wannsee conference in Berlin, extermination camps (with gas chambers and crematoria) became centers of the killing operations.

Many individual Christians helped Jews escape, but institutionalized Christianity failed through silence and lack of open, fearless, and concerted action to aid the oppressed. The German Protestant Confession Church focused its public efforts on the plight of baptized Jews, not on the persecution of Jews as Jews.

R. ZERNER

See also ANTI-SEMITISM.

Holy Communion. See LORD'S SUPPER.

Holy Ghost. See HOLY SPIRIT.

Holy of Holies. See TABERNACLE, TEMPLE.

Holy Saturday. The Saturday between Good Friday and Easter Sunday: liturgically a day of reflection and anticipation.

T. J. GERMAN

See also CHRISTIAN YEAR; EASTER; HOLY WEEK.

Holy Spirit. In the NT, the third person of the Trinity; in the OT, God's power.

The OT. The primary function of the Spirit of God in the OT is as the Spirit of prophecy. God's Spirit is the motivating force in the inspiration of the prophets—a power that sometimes moved prophets to ecstasy but always to the revelation of God's message, expressed by the prophets with "thus saith the Lord." The general implication in the OT is that the prophets were inspired by the Spirit of God. They anticipate a time when God, who is holy (or "other than/separate from" humankind; cf. Hos. 11:9) will pour out his Spirit on people (Isa. 11:1–2; Ezek. 36:24–27; Joel 2:28–29), who will themselves become holy. The Messiah/Servant of God will be the one upon whom the Spirit rests (Isa. 11:1–2; 42:1), and will inaugurate the time of salvation (Jer. 31:31–34).

Intertestamental Judaism. In the intertestamental period the messianic expectation of Judaism, which included the eschatological outpouring of God's Spirit (e.g., 1 Enoch 49:3, citing Isa. 11:2; cf. *Sybilline Oracle* 3.582, based on Joel 2:28–29), was bound up with the conviction that the inspiration of the Spirit had ceased in Israel with the last of the prophets; the Holy Spirit was understood as God's Spirit of prophecy, which would be given again in the new age to a purified Israel in conjunction with the advent of a messiah. The concept of the Holy Spirit was broadened through the Wisdom Literature, especially in the personification of wisdom as that idea came into contact with the idea of Spirit (Wisdom of Solomon; Wisdom of Ben-Sirach).

The NT. The NT teaching of the Holy Spirit is rooted in the ideas of the Spirit of God as the manifestation of God's power and the spirit of prophecy. The NT brings these ideas together in predicating them of the Holy Spirit, God's eschatological gift to humankind. Jesus returned from the Jordan full of the Holy Spirit (Luke 4:1), and after the temptation began his ministry "in the power of the Spirit" (Luke 4:14). Taking up the message of John the Baptist, Jesus proclaimed the coming of the kingdom of God (Matt. 4:17; cf. 3:1)—a coming marked by the presence of the Holy Spirit (Matt. 12:28 and pars.) as the sign of the messianic age of salvation (Luke 4:18–19; Acts 10:38).

Jesus understood the Holy Spirit as a personality. This comes out especially in John's Gospel, where the Spirit is called the "Paraclete," the Comforter (Counselor, Advocate). Jesus himself was the first Counselor (Paraclete, John 14:16), and he will send the disciples another Counselor after he is gone, the Spirit of truth, the Holy Spirit (14:26; 15:26; 16:5). The Holy Spirit will dwell in believers (John 7:38; cf. 14:17), and will guide the disciples into all truth (16:13), teaching them "all things" and reminding them of everything that Jesus had said to them (14:26). The Holy Spirit will testify about Jesus, as the disciples must also testify (John 15:26–27).

In Acts 2:14–18 Peter interprets the Pentecost phenomena as the fulfillment of Joel's prophecy of the outpouring of the Spirit upon all flesh in the messianic age (Joel 2:28–29). The outpouring of the Spirit upon all flesh was accomplished for the benefit of Jew and Gentile alike (Acts 10:45; 11:15–16), and individual converts have access to this gift of the age of salvation through repentance and baptism into the name of Jesus Christ (Acts 2:38).

Paul teaches that the Holy Spirit, poured out in the new age, is the creator of new life in the believer and the unifying force by which God in Christ is "building together" Christians into the body of Christ (Rom. 5:5; 2 Cor. 5:17; Eph. 2:22; cf. 1 Cor. 6:19). Paul identifies the spirit of God and the spirit of Christ with the Holy Spirit. These terms are generally interchangeable. Believers are being built together into a dwelling-place of God in the Spirit (Eph. 4:12). To each one grace has been given according to the measure of the gift of Christ (Eph. 4:7; cf. Rom. 12:3). The Spirit gives different kinds of spiritual gifts for different kinds of service (1 Cor. 12:4–5; 7), all for the common good. God has initiated a new covenant (Jer. 31:31–34; Ezek. 36:24–27) in the hearts of people by means of his eschatological Spirit (2 Cor. 3:6–8).

Patristic and Medieval Theology. The early church fathers did not move too far beyond the biblical ideas of the Holy Spirit. The Nicene Creed confesses faith in the Holy Spirit, but without any detailed exposition of the Spirit's divinity or essential relationship to the Father and the Son. This question became a major issue for the church in the late 4th century and following, and the Council of Constantinople added to the words of the Nicene Creed, describing the Holy Spirit as "the Lord and Giver of Life, proceeding from the Father, to be worshiped and glorified together with the Father and the Son." A controversy developed around the source of the Spirit, specifically whether he proceeded from the Son. Following Augustine's teaching, the phrase *filioque* ("and the Son") was eventually added to the Nicene Creed by the Western Church. The Eastern Church rejected the *filioque* doctrine. Although other aspects of the Spirit were occasionally discussed, the procession of the Spirit continued to occupy medieval theologians in the West.

The Reformation. It was not until the Reformation that the work of the Spirit in the church was truly rediscovered. While Luther rejected "enthusiasm" (the subjective claim of direct guidance by the Spirit independent of Scripture or church structure), he stressed Spirit over structure, and understood the Spirit to be at work through the Word (the gospel), primarily in preaching, and in the sacraments, and therefore in salvation. The Spirit works in salvation by influencing the soul to reliance, by faith, on Christ. The Word—primarily the incarnate Logos—is God's channel for the Spirit. A human messenger brings the Word of the Scripture to the ear, but God infuses his Spirit into the heart; the word of Scripture thus becomes the Word of God. No one can rightly understand the Word of Scripture without the working of the Spirit; where the Word is, the Spirit inevitably follows. Luther resisted the enthusiasts' sharp distinction between inward and outward Word. On the other hand, he rejected the Roman Catholic idea that the Spirit is identified with church office and that the sacraments are effective in and of themselves (*ex opere operato*). Thus the Spirit makes Christ present in the sacraments and in Scripture; only when the Spirit makes Christ present in the word is it God's own living Word. Otherwise the Scripture is letter, a law—it merely describes, it is only history. But as preaching, the Word is gospel (as opposed to law); the Spirit makes it so.

Calvin taught that the Spirit works in regeneration to illumine the mind to receive the benefits of Christ and seals them in the heart. By the Spirit the heart of a person is opened to the penetrating power of the Word and sacraments. Calvin went beyond Luther in asserting that not only is the preached Word the agent of the Spirit, but the Bible is *in its essence* the Word of God (Genevan Catechism). The Spirit works in the reading of Scripture as well as in the preaching of the Word, and the Word—preached or read—is efficacious through the work of the Holy Spirit. The divine origin of Scripture is certified by the witness of the Spirit; the Scripture is the Word of God given by the Spirit's guidance through limited human speech. Thus the exegete must inquire after God's intention in giving Scripture to us (e.g., in the modern application of the OT; *Inst.* 2.8.8). The highest proof of Scripture derives from the fact that God in person speaks in it, that is, in the secret testimony of the Spirit (*Inst.* 1.7.4). We feel the testimony of the Spirit engraved like a seal on our hearts with the result that it seals the cleansing and sacrifice of Christ. The Holy Spirit is the bond by which Christ unites us to himself (*Inst.* 3.1.1).

The Modern Period. While 17th-century radical Puritanism produced the Quakers with their emphasis on the subjective experience of the Holy Spirit (the Inner Light of George Fox)—such that Scripture is only a secondary source of knowledge for faith and practice (Robert Barclay, *Apology*)—18th-century Methodism expressed a more balanced approach to the work of the Spirit. The focus of later Methodism on the work of the Spirit after conversion as an experience of divine grace has found expression in the modern Holiness movement, represented by churches in the Christian Holiness Association. Another development that can be traced to Methodism's stress on sanctification is the 20th-century reawakening of Pentecostalism. Stemming from earlier emphases upon "second experience," Pentecostalism has placed great importance upon the "baptism of the Holy Spirit," which is seen as the completion of a two-stage process of salvation.

One of the most significant 20th-century developments in understanding the Holy Spirit is the teaching of Karl Barth. God's grace is manifested both in the objective revelation of God in Christ and our subjective appropriation of this revelation through the Spirit. According to Scripture, God's revelation occurs in our enlightenment by the Holy Spirit to a knowledge of God's Word. The outpouring of the Spirit is God's revelation. In this reality we are free to be God's children and to know, love, and praise him in his revelation. The Spirit as subjective reality of God's revelation makes possible and real the existence of Christianity in the world. For, Barth observes, "where the Spirit of the Lord is, there is freedom" (2 Cor. 3:17).

T. S. CAULLEY

See also BAPTISM OF THE SPIRIT; CHARISMATIC MOVEMENT; GOD, DOCTRINE OF; SPIRITUAL GIFTS; TONGUES, SPEAKING IN.

Holy Week. Week preceding Easter, set aside to observe in a special manner the passion and death of Jesus Christ. It may also be called the Greater Week, in remembrance of the great work performed by God during that week, or Paschal Week, in reference to the coming resurrection. Holy Thursday, or Maundy Thursday, as part of Holy Week is properly called Thursday of the Lord's Supper. Good Friday is the anniversary of the crucifixion of Christ; it is a somber day. Its full liturgical title is "Friday of the passion and death of the Lord." Holy Saturday is a quiet day of reflection and anticipation in preparation for the celebration of the resurrection of our Lord Jesus Christ on Easter Sunday.

T. J. GERMAN

See also EASTER; GOOD FRIDAY; HOLY SATURDAY; MAUNDY THURSDAY;.

Homoousion. Theological term employed by the Council of Nicaea in A.D. 325 to describe the relationship between the Son of God and the Father. Later it was used to describe the relationship of the Holy Spirit to the Father and the Son and thus was instrumental in the developing doctrine of the Trinity. *Homoousios* literally means same (*homo*) in substance (*ousia*) or, as it is sometimes translated, consubstantial.

In the teaching of Nicene and post-Nicene orthodoxy the essential relationship between the Father and the Son (and this was applied by extension to the Holy Spirit also in the post-Nicene period) was seen as one in which the Son derives his *ousia* from the Father, so that they are not numerically the same; the Father is thus properly the source of the Son's being. Nevertheless, it was asserted that in this (eternal) derivation, the Son is and remains *homoousios* with the Father, so that what the Father is and has is exactly what the Son is and has.

C. A. BLAISING

See also HYPOSTATIC UNION; NICEA, COUNCIL OF.

Homosexuality. Sexual desire directed toward members of one's own sex. Female homosexuality is frequently called lesbianism; the term is derived from Lesbos, where the Greek poetess Sappho (reputedly homosexual) lived ca. 600 B.C. Homosexuality was the sin for which Sodom was destroyed by divine judgment, hence the popular term "sodomy." Homosexuality is condemned both in Leviticus (18:22; 20:13), where it is abhorrent to God, defiling, and punishable by death, and in Deuteronomy (23:18), where it is forbidden to bring the earnings of a prostitute or homosexual into the house of God in payment of religious vows. It is usually assumed that the male cult prostitutes common in heathen shrines but forbidden in Israel (Deut. 23:17) were homosexuals.

An early Christian assessment of homosexuality is expressed by Paul: homosexuals "will not inherit the kingdom of God" (1 Cor. 6:9–10); because of idolatry God gave godless people up "to shameful lusts. Even their women exchanged natural relations for unnatural ones. In the same way the men also abandoned natural relations with women and were inflamed with lust for one another. Men committed indecent acts with other men, and received in themselves the due penalty for their perversion" (Rom. 1:26–27). Here the association with idolatry, the unnaturalness of the practice, and the divine judgment that abandons individuals to it (an echo of Sodom?) are all significant.

Causes of Homosexuality. (1) Since our earliest sexual curiosity and experience is usually with our own bodies, a pubescent phase of homosexual interest is normal. Some adult homosexual interest may simply be arrested development.

(2) An unhappy love affair, an illness, or a pathological fear of the opposite sex may cause an individual to return to the furtive but safer relief of early puberty.

(3) Environmental causes include an all-male milieu (a one-sex school, army, or prison) or a sexual relationship with the same-sex parent.

(4) Genetic or hormonal factors may condition an individual from birth to respond sexually to members of the same sex.

(5) Sensuality, exhibitionism, or the desire to shock may induce homosexual behavior.

A homosexual tendency arising from psychological, accidental, or environmental influences is sometimes amenable, as other deep-seated disorders, to psychological treatment. An involuntary predisposition to homosexual behavior, traceable to psychological problems, childhood experiences, accidental situations, or congenital factors, whether or not complicated by later experiences, is obviously not a fitting target for moral condemnation or contempt, but for sympathy.

A Christian View. The distinction between condition and conduct is critical to a responsible Christian view of homosexuality. The homosexual condition, *until indulged*, is not sinful. Like all congenital deviations from the norm, the condition of homosexuality should be accepted by the Christian community. The existence and acuteness of the problem represent a challenge to Christian compassion and ministry, and call for responsible sex education. The church should not ostracize but minister to those whose constitution and circumstances make the Christian walk difficult.

R. E. O. White

Hooker, Richard (1554–1600)**.** Anglican theologian. Hooker answered the Puritan critics of Anglicanism in his epoch-making *Laws of Ecclesiastical Polity* in eight books (only five were published in his lifetime). In order to defend the Anglican establishment Hooker circumvented both the Puritan appeal to Scripture and the Catholic appeal to tradition by going behind both to the primary source of authority: natural law, which is implanted in people's minds by God and comes to full expression in the state. Hooker's position tended to uphold Erastianism (state control over the church).

D. F. Kelly

See also Anglican Communion; Natural Law.

Hope. Trusting anticipation of the fulfillment of God's promises. In the OT God is "the Hope of Israel" (Jer. 14:8). Believers are to trust in him (Jer. 17:7), wait passively upon him (Ps. 42:5), and actively anticipate his blessing (Ps. 62:5). In the NT Christ is described as the Christian hope (1 Tim. 1:1). By his resurrection believers are filled with hope through the Spirit (Rom. 15:13). This hope relates to salvation, is an essential grace, like faith and love (1 Cor. 13:13), and includes the future (Rom. 8:24–25). Its object is the ultimate blessedness of God's kingdom (Titus 1:2). It produces joyful confidence in God (Rom. 8:28), patience in tribulation (Rom. 5:3), and perseverance in prayer.

D. H. Tongue

See also Hope, Theology of.

Hope, Theology of. Resurrection-centered theology that emerged in Germany in the late 1960s and regards Christ's resurrection as the beginning and promise of that which is yet to come. The Christian is a "hoper," who is impatient with evil and death in this present age. The church is a disquieting entity, confronting society with all its human securities, empires, and contrived absolutes. The church awaits a coming city and, therefore, exposes all cities made with human hands. This form of theology exists in dialogue with other visions of the future, especially Marxism, and it stands against the individualism of liberal pietist and existential theologies. In some ways it is orthodox, and yet politically it can be quite radical. Third World churches have been deeply influenced by the theology of hope. Undoubtedly a central figure of this new theology is Jürgen Moltmann, with his most influential book, *Theology of Hope* (1967). Other prominent representatives are Wolfhart Pannenberg, a Lutheran, and Johannes B. Metz, a Catholic.

Theologians of hope have made eschaton their conceptual center. Their first move is to use this center to affirm the meaning and significance of Jesus Christ. The eschaton is not an embarrassment; rather, it gives Christianity both personal and universal significance in a world that thinks, plans, and dreams in terms of future fears, hopes, and schemes. Further, this form of doing theology provides a way of seeing the mission of the church in terms of the larger issues of humankind in community and the question of revolution. The promise of this effort remains to be fully seen. Surely from their own perspective no theological model can be absolute. On the critical side, questions certainly arise. How do the creation and fall fit in? Is this theology no more than a sign of the times? Because our materialism and narcissism have blinded us to God as a living presence, have we now conjured up a theology to somehow account for this by putting him into the future?

S. M. SMITH

Host, Hosts of Heaven. Angels of God's council, also called "holy ones" or "sons of God" (1 Kings 22:19; cf. Job 1:6; 2:1; 38:7; Ps. 89:6–7). The word "host" (Heb. *ṣĕbāʾ*; Gk. *stratia*) is associated in the OT with God's heavenly throne, the created order, and divine and human warfare. While the heavenly host is as a whole subservient to God's will and offers him praise (Ps. 103:21), there are also elements of discord within its midst (1 Kings 22:21; Job 1:6–12; 15:15), leading to God's final judgment (Ps. 82; Isa. 24:21).

S. F. NOLL

See also ANGEL; PRINCIPALITIES AND POWERS.

Hosts, Lord of. See GOD, NAMES OF.

Household Salvation. The Bible demonstrates a family solidarity that is alien to Western individualistic thought. The Abrahamic, Mosaic, and Davidic covenants involved the household in the covenant blessings. The OT formula "he and his house" refers to parents and their children of all ages. Household baptisms in the NT show that the whole family was involved in salvation (Acts 16:15, 33; 18:8; 1 Cor. 1:16).

D. F. KELLY

Hubmaier, Balthasar (ca. 1480–1528). German Radical Reformer. Hubmaier wrote prolifically. In 1524 he issued his 18 theses, as well as his famous booklet against the burning of heretics. In 1525 he accepted baptism from Wilhelm Reublin, a colleague of the Zurich founder of Anabaptism, Conrad Grebel. By this time he had broken with Catholicism, as revealed in his marriage with Elisabeth Hügeline. He wrote several powerful defenses of the baptism of believers. His catechism for the instruction of catechumens appeared in 1526. The next year he issued treatises on church discipline, baptism, the Lord's Supper, and free will.

J. C. WENGER

Hügel, Friedrich von. See VON HÜGEL, FRIEDRICH.

Humanism. See SECULARISM, SECULAR HUMANISM.

Humanism, Christian. View that individuals and culture have value in the Christian life. Those who believe that the Christian revelation has a humanistic emphasis point to the fact that humankind was made in the image of God, that Jesus Christ became man through the incarnation, and that the worth of the individual is a consistent theme in the teaching of Jesus.

Christian humanists acknowledge the contributions of other forms of humanism, such as the classical variety that discovered the value of human liberty, and Marxism, which holds that people have been estranged from the good life because they are dispossessed of property and subordinated to material and economic forces. They caution, however, that these other forms can degenerate into excessive individualism or savage collectivism because they operate without God. The Christian humanist values culture but confesses that people are fully developed only as they come into a right relationship with Christ. When this happens, they can begin to experience growth in all areas of life as the new creation of revelation (2 Cor. 5:17; Gal. 6:15).

R. G. CLOUSE

See also ERASMUS, DESIDERIUS; MARITAIN, JACQUES.

Humanity of Christ. See CHRISTOLOGY.

Humiliation of Jesus Christ. See STATES OF JESUS CHRIST.

Humility. Quality or state of being humble. Totally dependent, and sinful, we have nothing to be proud of except God's being mindful of us and caring for us (Ps. 8:4–5). God lives with the humble (Isa. 57:15) and requires that we walk humbly with him (Mic. 6:8). Jesus requires that we humble ourselves as little children in order to receive the kingdom. Pure receptivity demands the unself-conscious, unassuming readiness to accept God's favor. Jesus provided an example for us when he washed the disciples' feet; he was a humble servant who "emptied himself" (Phil. 2:7–8). Whoever wants to become great must be slave of all (Mark 10:43). From humility toward God follows humility toward others ("in humility consider others better than yourselves" [Phil. 2:3]) and also toward oneself ("do not think of yourself more highly than you ought" [Rom. 12:3]). Christians must recognize that they possess nothing they have not received, are nothing but for the grace of God, and, apart from Christ, can do nothing.

R. E. O. WHITE

Hus, Jan (ca. 1372–1415). Czech reformer. Hus was appointed rector and preacher in Prague's Bethlehem chapel, the center of the Czech reform movement, in 1402. By 1407 his evangelical wing threatened not only the theological balance in Bohemia but also the ethnic status quo by challenging the power that Germans held in the Roman Catholic Church in Bohemia. Under pressure he left the city in 1412 to live in southern Bohemia. In 1414, with a promise of safe conduct, Hus traveled to the Council of Constance, where he was imprisoned and placed on trial for heresy. He was judged guilty and burned at the stake on July 6, 1415. For Czechs, Hus was not only a spiritual leader but also a focal point of national inspiration in the centuries following his death.

P. KUBRICHT

Hutchinson, Anne (1591–1643). Colonial American religious leader. Hutchinson came to Massachusetts in 1634 to remain under the preaching of her English pastor, John Cotton, who had migrated to Boston the year before. Her views began to display hints of antinomianism, the theological error that Christians do not need the law. She suggested that a believer possesses the Holy Spirit and thus is not bound by the law. Further, mere obedience to external laws (for example, of Massachusetts) does not mean that one is truly a Christian. The Massachusetts leaders soon demanded an explanation. After she and her followers were banished from the colony in 1638, she moved first to Rhode Island, then to Long Island, and finally to inland New York. Here she and most of her family were killed by Indians.

M. A. NOLL

Hyperdulia. Form of Roman Catholic veneration offered to the Blessed Virgin Mary as the Mother of God.

T. J. GERMAN

See also DULIA; LATRIA.

Hypocrisy. (Heb. *ḥānēp*, "polluted," "impious"; Gk. *hypokrisis)* Act or practice of pretending to be what one is not. In

Christ's stern denunciations of the scribes and Pharisees in the Synoptics (the only NT occurrences of *hypokritēs*), the OT meaning "godless" is strongly evident (Matt. 22:18; 23:13–29). As A. G. Hebert has noted, Jesus' point is not that the scribes were deliberately acting a part, but that, while outwardly religious, inwardly they were profane and godless (RTWB, 109). Elsewhere, the Greek idea of acting appears to be predominant. The term "hypocrite" in Matt. 6:2, 5, 16 seems to mean play-actor as does the sole occurrence of the verb *hypokrinesthai* in Luke 20:20. The adjective *anypokritos,* "genuine," "sincere," "without hypocrisy" (Rom. 12:9; 1 Tim. 1:5; James 3:17), also seems to reflect the influence of the Greek drama.

D. A. HUBBARD

Hypostasis. (Gk. *hypostasis,* "substance," "nature," "essence") Real personal subsistence or person. In philosophy it signifies the underlying or essential part of anything, as distinguished from attributes that may vary. As a theological term it describes any one of the three real and distinct subsistences in the one undivided substance or essence of God, and especially the one unified personality of Christ the Son in his two natures, human and divine. The classic definition of God is "one *ousia* in three *hypostaseis*."

W. E. WARD

See also CHALCEDON, COUNCIL OF; GOD, DOCTRINE OF; TRINITY.

Hypostatic Union. Doctrine first set forth officially in the definition of faith produced by the Council of Chalcedon (451) that concerns the union of the two natures (*physeis*) of deity and humanity in the one *hypostasis* or person of Jesus Christ. It can be stated as follows: In the incarnation of the Son of God, a human nature was inseparably united forever with the divine nature in the one person of Jesus Christ, yet with the two natures remaining distinct, whole, and unchanged, without mixture or confusion so that the one person, Jesus Christ, is truly God and truly man.

C. A. BLAISING

See also CHALCEDON, COUNCIL OF; COMMUNICATION OF ATTRIBUTES; MONOPHYSITISM.

Ii

"I AM" Sayings. The disclosure of Exod. 3:14, often rendered "I AM WHO I AM," may well be an instance of paronomasia; but more important, like the repeated "I am he" or "I myself am he" utterances (Deut. 32:39; Isa. 41:4; 43:10, 13, 25; 45:18; 46:4; 48:12; 51:12; 52:6), the formula is self-revelatory. Yahweh is not addressed in this way, but uses these expressions of himself, thereby demonstrating that he graciously chooses to reveal himself to humankind.

In the NT, many "I am" sayings are supplied with a subjective completion (e.g., "I am the light of the world" [John 8:12]) and therefore do not qualify as "I am" utterances in the absolute sense. Two, however, in the Fourth Gospel are undeniably absolute in both form and content (8:58; 13:19) and constitute Jesus' explicit self-identification with Yahweh who had already revealed himself to humankind in similar terms (see esp. Isa. 43:10–11). Jesus' opponents recognize this claim to unity with Yahweh and respond in anger (John 8:58–59); in 13:19–20, Jesus makes this identification explicit. These two occurrences of the absolute "I am" suggest that in several other passages in John, where "I am" is formally absolute but a predicate might well be supplied from the context (e.g., 4:26; 6:20; 8:24, 28; 18:5, 6, 8), an intentional double meaning may be involved.

D. A. CARSON

Ibn Rushd. See AVERROES.

Identification with Christ. Theological doctrine that derives from various passages in Scripture that regard Christians as being "in Christ." In a general way Christ is identified with humankind as the second Adam, and identified with Israel as the anticipated Son of David. In these cases the identity is a physical fact. In contrast to these relationships the theological concept of identification with Christ relates a Christian to the person and work of Christ by divine reckoning, by the human experience of faith, and by the spiritual union of the believer with Christ effected by the baptism of the Holy Spirit.

Identification with Christ is accomplished by the baptism of the Holy Spirit, an act of divine grace and power sometimes expressed as being baptized into (*eis*) the body of Christ, the church (1 Cor. 12:13), sometimes described as being baptized into Christ (Gal. 3:27). This new relationship of being "in Christ" was first announced by Jesus to his disciples in the upper room: "you are in me [*en emoi*], and I am in you" (John 14:20). The new relationship of the believer in Christ is defined as a new position, "in Christ," resulting from a work of God. That it is more than a mere position created by divine reckoning is revealed by the companion revelation, "I in you." The resultant doctrine is embraced in the word "union," which is commonly taken as a synonym for identification. Various figures are employed in Scripture to illustrate this union and identification (John 15:1–6; Eph. 1:22– 23; 4:12–16; 5:23–32).

J. F. WALVOORD

See also ABIDE; MURRAY, ANDREW; MYSTICISM; UNIO MYSTICA; UNITIVE WAY, THE.

Idolatry. Worship of an idol or deity represented by an idol, usually as an image. Idolatry, as a form of religious practice, was common in both OT and NT times. One of the most distinctive features of Hebrew religion during the OT period was the absence of idolatry. Its practice was prohibited among the Hebrews, and the archeological evidence indicates that this prohibition was observed for the most part.

There were two prevalent forms of idolatry in OT times, both banned by the Decalogue. (1) The first commandment prohibited the Israelites from worshiping any god other than the Lord (Exod. 20:3), thereby eliminating the false forms of idolatrous religion practiced by neighboring nations. (2) The second commandment forbade the worship of the God of Israel in the form of an image or idol (Exod. 20:4–6). Hence, the denunciation of idolatry in its various forms is a recurrent theme in both the law and the prophets (Deut. 7:25–26; 29:16–17; Isa. 40:18–23). In NT times idolatry was practiced in various forms throughout the Roman Empire and was steadfastly resisted by the early Christian church.

P. C. CRAIGIE

Ignatius of Loyola (1491–1556). Founder of the Society of Jesus (Jesuits). After his conversion he spent 11 months in prayer and fasting at Manresa in Catalonia. His religious experiences there became the basis and core of his classic *Spiritual Exercises*, published in 1548 after much revision. At the University of Paris, where he studied from 1528 to 1535, he attracted such compatriots as Francis Xavier and Diego Lainez, who were to be the founding fathers of the Society of Jesus. In 1534 Loyola and six colleagues vowed perpetual poverty and chastity and promised to undertake an evangelistic mission in Palestine. Loyola was ordained a priest in 1537. Gradually the men realized that only the structure of a religious order would preserve and perpetuate their union and apostolic work. Paul III authorized the Society of Jesus in 1540 and Loyola was elected the first superior general. He lived in Rome from 1537 until his death in 1556, writing the Jesuit *Constitutions* and supervising the rapid expansion of the new order.

J. P. DONNELLY

See also SOCIETY OF JESUS, THE.

Ignorance. Lack of knowledge, either in general or with respect to a particular fact or subject.

Ethical Implications. Ethicists have long sought an equitable mode for determining the extent of culpability for acts performed in ignorance. A useful formula is expressed by distinguishing between avoidable and unavoidable ignorance (some use the terms "vincible" and "invincible"). In events involving unavoidable ignorance we exonerate the agent from responsibility, as in the case of a man's failure to appear for an appointment because he was ignorant of the fact that he would be involved in an accident on the way. On the other hand, a judge does not excuse a defendant who claims he did not know that a gun was loaded for the agent could have taken the time to inform himself on this point, and since the gun is a lethal weapon, he should have informed himself before pressing the trigger. The Christian rejoices in the fact that final judgment resides with a mind more penetrating, a will more discerning, and a heart more loving than that of humankind.

Theological Synthesis. Sinners are constitutionally ignorant (Rom. 3:23). Having lost the pristine knowledge of God in the fall, they are aware of the existence of deity but totally incapable of knowing how to effect peace with him (Rom. 1:19–20; Eph. 2:12; 4:18). Human ignorance is most clearly expressed in this inability to recognize the Son of God when he appeared; this failure issued in Christ's rejection and death (Acts 3:17; 1 Cor. 2:7–8). Only divine intervention has prevented humankind from perishing in ignorance (Hos. 13:9). As the gospel is proclaimed (1 Cor. 15:1–3) faith is created (Rom. 10:17) and a knowledge provided that eventuates in salvation (John 17:3; 2 Tim. 3:15). In eternity, the ignorance of the redeemed will be superseded by consummate knowledge (the beatific vision, 1 Cor. 13:12).

F. R. HARM

See also ETHICS, BIBLICAL; RESPONSIBILITY.

Illumination. Spiritual enlightenment. Revelation is the unveiling of truth in the Scriptures; inspiration is the method by which the Holy Spirit superintended the writing of Scripture; and illumination is the ministry of the Spirit by which the meaning of Scripture is made clear to the believer. Jesus promised his followers that when the Spirit came on the day of Pentecost he would lead them into the truth (John 16:13–16), and this includes understanding the deep things of God (1 Cor. 2:9–10).

C. C. RYRIE

Illuminative Way, The. (Lat. *via illuminativa*) Second of the three stages of the mystic way, being intermediary between the purgative way, in which the person learns to reject sin, and the unitive way, in which the person enters the pure love of God, the mystic union.

P. H. DAVIDS

See also BEATIFIC VISION; JOHN OF THE CROSS; MYSTICISM; PURGATIVE WAY, THE; UNITIVE WAY, THE.

Illyricus. See FLACIUS, MATTHIAS.

Image of God. (Lat. *imago Dei*) That humankind by virtue of creation uniquely bears the image of God is a fundamental biblical doctrine—as is also that this image is marred by sin and that it is restored only by divine salvation.

Biblical Data. Hebrew-Christian theology frames the doctrine of the *imago Dei* in the setting of divine creation and redemption. While created in the image of God, people are nonethless creatures, distinct from their Creator. The Bible does not, therefore, simply affirm in a religious manner what speculative philosophies express more generally in their emphasis on the inherent dignity and worth of humankind, or on the infinite value and sacredness of human personality. For Scripture conditions human dignity and value upon the doctrine of creation, and not upon some sort of intrinsic divinity.

The biblical discussion turns on the Hebrew words *ṣelem* and *demût*, and the corresponding Greek terms *eikon* and *homoiosis*. Scripture employs these terms to affirm that humankind was fashioned in the image of God, and that Jesus Christ, the divine Son, is the essential image of the invisible God. The passages expressly affirming the *imago Dei* are Gen. 1:26–27; 5:1, 3; 9:6; 1 Cor. 11:7; Col. 3:10; James 3:9. Although we image God by virtue of our creation—a fact that the divine prohibition of graven images (which obscure the spirituality of God) serves pointedly to reinforce—the fall precludes all attempts to read off God's nature from ours. To project God in our image is but a heinous form of idolatry that confuses the Creator with the creature. This confusion reaches its nadir in the worship of the beast and his image or statue (Rev. 14:9–11).

Recent Theological Studies. Granted that the terms "image" and "likeness" denote an exact resemblance, in what respect does humankind reflect God? What of the vitiating effects of the fall into sin? Is the NT conception of the *imago* in conflict with the OT conception? Is it in conflict with itself? These questions are among those most energetically debated by contemporary theologians. The importance of a proper understanding of the *imago Dei* can hardly be overstated. The answer given to the *imago* inquiry soon becomes determinative for the entire gamut of doctrinal affirmation. The ramifications are not only theological, but affect every phase of the problem of revelation and reason, including natural and international law, and the cultural enterprise as a whole.

Evangelical biblical expositors find the created image of God to exist formally in human personality (moral responsibility and intelligence) and materially in the knowledge of God and his will for humankind. Hence the *imago Dei* is not reducible simply to the relation in which we stand in respect to God, but rather is the precondition of such a relationship. The fall did not destroy the formal image (human personality) although it involves the distortion (although not demolition) of the material content of the image. The biblical view is that we are made to know God as well as to obey him. Even in our revolt we stand condemned by the knowledge we have, and we are proffered God's redemptive revelation in the Bible. The objections that the admission of such a rational content to the *imago* implies pantheism, or a capacity for self-salvation by reflection through its supposed assertion of an undamaged spot in human nature, loses force when the support for such objections is seen to rest on exaggerations of divine transcendence from which the dialectical view itself arises, rather than on biblical considerations.

Although the two Testaments seem to conflict—since the former reiterates the survival of the *imago Dei* after the fall, while the latter stresses the redemptive restoration of the image—there is no real clash. The OT conception is presupposed in the NT, which is a legitimate development. While the NT speaks of the divine image in humankind (1 Cor. 11:7; James 3:9), its central message is redeemed humankind's renewal in the image of Christ.

C. F. H. HENRY

See also MAN, DOCTRINE OF.

Imago Dei. See IMAGE OF GOD.

Imitation of Christ. Christ-likeness is achieved not by legalistically trying to mold ourselves after the pattern Christ has set for us, but by the inward processes of salvation that change heart attitudes, producing good works and Christlike virtues (Rom. 12:1; Eph. 2:8–10; Phil. 2:12–13). We are transformed into Christ's likeness by the Spirit (2 Cor. 3:18). This process will not be finally completed until we see him on the day of resurrection (Rom. 8:29–30; 1 John 3:2). Paul constantly reminds us to imitate Christ's humility, sufferings, and death (e.g., Rom. 8:17–18, 36; Phil. 1:29–30; 2:5; 3:10–21) and Peter says explicitly (1 Pet. 2:21–23) that we are to follow in Christ's steps in suffering and death.

T. B. CRUM

See also BRETHREN OF THE COMMON LIFE; FRANCIS OF ASSISI; IDENTIFICATION WITH CHRIST; MYSTICISM; PIETISM; THOMAS À KEMPIS; UNIO MYSTICA.

Immaculate Conception. Roman Catholic doctrine that Mary, mother of Jesus, did not have original sin at her conception nor did she acquire elements of original sin during the course of her life. All other human beings, in contrast, have original sin from their conception due to the fall of Adam. The immaculate conception is an article of faith for Roman Catholics. Pius IX made it a dogma in 1854.

T. J. GERMAN

See also MARIOLOGY; MOTHER OF GOD.

Immanence of God. See God, Attributes of.

Immanuel. Symbolic name that literally means "with us [is] God." Occurring three times in the Bible (Isa. 7:14; 8:8; Matt. 1:23), the Hebrew word *'immānû 'ēl* (Gk. *Emmanouēl*) is employed as a proper name in all three verses, and as such is the name of the promised offspring of the *'almâ* ("unmarried woman") of Isa. 7:14 and the *parthenos* ("virgin") of Matt. 1:23; this offspring owns (Isa. 8:8) and protects (Isa. 8:10) the land and people of Israel. As a proper name "Immanuel" is also descriptive of both this child's divine nature and his messianic work of grace.

R. L. Reymond

Immersion. See Baptism, Modes of.

Imminence. Doctrine that Christ can return at any moment and that no predicted event must intervene before that return. This view is held primarily by those who believe the church will be raptured before the seven-year tribulation (also known as the 70th week of Daniel). It is the view typically held by dispensational premillennialists.

S. N. Gundry

See also Eschatology; Rapture of the Church; Second Coming of Christ; Tribulation.

Immortality. State of immunity from death typical only of God and resurrected believers. The concept of immortality is expressed directly in the Bible only in the NT. The words used are *athanasia, aphtharsia,* and its cognate adjective, *aphthartos. Athanasia* is the exact equivalent of the English word "immortality," It is used in 1 Cor. 15:53–54, where it describes the resurrection body as one that is not subject to death, and in 1 Tim. 6:16, where God is said to be the one who alone has immortality. He alone in his essence is deathless. *Aphtharsia* has the basic meaning of indestructibility and, by derivation, incorruption. It may be said, therefore, that immortality in the biblical sense is a condition in which the individual is not subject to death or to any influence that might lead to death. God is uniquely immortal in that he is without beginning or end of life and is not in any way affected by change or diminution. People, on the other hand, are immortal only by derivation and when their mortal body has been replaced by one that is immortal.

D. W. Kerr

See also Annihilationism; Conditional Immortality; Heaven; Intermediate State; Resurrection of the Dead; Sheol.

Immortality, Conditional. See Conditional Immortality.

Immutability of God. See God, Attributes of.

Impanation. (Lat. *impanare*, "to embody in bread") Explanation of Christ's presence in the Lord's Supper that maintains that he is embodied in the bread. Christ is locally and physically present in the host. Guitmund of Aversa (d. before 1195) taught this doctrine, comparing Christ's incarnation with his impanation in the Eucharist. John of Paris (d. 1306) said "the Body of Christ is 'impanated,'" that is, "has become bread." The Roman Catholic Church rejected this view, affirming instead transubstantiation.

C. G. Fry

See also Lord's Supper, Views of.

Impassibility of God. Doctrine that God is not capable of being acted upon or affected emotionally by anything in creation. Passibility, Thomists argued, involves potentiality and potentiality involves change. Unrealized potential and change in the Deity seems to contradict God's immutability, transcendence, self-existence, self-determination, and perfection. Suffering, furthermore, seems incompatible with perfect divine blessedness. Thus the Thirty-Nine Articles of the Church of England affirm that God is without body, parts, or passions.

The God of Abraham, Isaac, and Jacob, however, is not without feeling, not without the capability of loving and feeling the hurt of love spurned. The relationship of love to suffering stands out particularly in God's suffering servant (Isa. 53). With some things God is pleased, with others God is displeased. God pours out his righteous indignation upon the ungodly who persecuted his people (Isa. 63:1–6), but God suffered as his people suffered. The heavenly Father was so moved by human sin that he sent his Son into the world to suffer as humans suffer, to sacrifice himself for those who suffered.

God's immutability does not reduce the living, active, personal Lord of all to an impersonal, static principle. It affirms that God in all his thoughts, words, and acts dynamically moves in ways consistent with his own essence and purposes. Passibility may involve change. Change that does not deny any of God's essential attributes is in harmony with a biblical view of God. God is not only transcendent, but also immanent, relating to both the just and the unjust. Although God alone has life in himself, God has granted life to many others in order to participate in personal relationships with them.

G. R. Lewis

See also God, Attributes of.

Impeccability of Christ. See Sinlessness of Christ.

Imprecatory Psalms. Psalms that contain maledictions against an enemy (e.g., 5:10; 10:15; 55:15; 109:9–15). The question naturally arises whether these psalms can have any place in Christian Scripture. In a positive appraisal of the imprecatory psalms it must be noted (1) that all the imprecations are prayers. They are not a declaration of intent on the part of the psalmist, but a commitment of the problem to the Lord and a leaving of vengeance to him. (2) The imprecations express a holy, moral indignation. The psalmist longs for the vindication of God's name (9:19–20; 83:16–17), and cannot help hating those who hate God, abhorring those who rise up against him (139:21–22). (3) The imprecations are expressed in realistic acceptance of what God has revealed of his certain judgment (cf. 109:13 with Exod. 20:5) and awareness of the outworking of just retribution in the experiences of this life.

J. A. Motyer

Imputation. (Lat. *imputare*; Gk. *logizomai*) Charging or reckoning to an account. This broad theological concept finds its center in the atonement. The forensic notion of imputation has roots in the commercial and legal language of the Greco-Roman world. Imputation also has distinctively Hebraic roots (*ḥāšab*, "to count for, to reckon"), being used, for example, in reference to the sacrificial system (Lev. 7:18: "it will not be credited to the one who offered it"; Lev. 17:4).

In the NT, Christians are said to receive the righteousness of God as a "gift that came by the grace of that one man, Jesus Christ" (Rom. 5:15). God credited Abraham's belief to him as righteousness (Gen. 15:6; Rom. 4:3). Others are similarly blessed; the Lord never counts their sin against them (Ps. 32:1–2; Rom. 4:7–8). This divine judicial act is based, not on human merit, but on God's love (Rom. 5:6–8). In arguing for a forensic, communal grace rooted solely in Christ, through whom we receive reconciliation with God, Paul contrasts the work of Christ with the sin of Adam, by which sin, guilt, and death came into the world (Rom. 5:12–14). Just as it is in Christ that we are redeemed, so it is in Adam that we are judged sinners (Rom. 5:15–21; cf. 1 Cor. 15:21–22).

Although the exact nature of divine imputation remains a mystery, a biblically based understanding of the concept maintains the following: (1) The stress on the corporate and original nature of human sin, on the human solidarity of guilt, is but one pole of a full biblical understanding. Sin's social dimension needs the continual, yet paradoxical, balancing of sin's individual and personal dimensions (1 John 1:9–10). (2) The analogy between Adam and Christ is not simple or total. While the imputation of righteousness is *arbitrary*, a free and undeserved act of grace whose reality remains forensic, the imputation of guilt is *appropriate*, its consequences affirming the judgment. Paul himself emphasizes the danger of taking the analogy too far, distinguishing the free gift from the trespass (Rom. 5:15).

R. K. JOHNSTON

See also ADAM; FALL OF MAN; SIN.

Incarnation (Lat. *incarnatio*, "to enter into or become flesh") Doctrine that maintains that the eternal, preexistent Son of God became human in the person of Jesus.

The Nature of the Incarnation. The divine Logos did not simply take into union with himself a human person; otherwise, he would have been two persons, two egos, two centers of self-consciousness. When he refers to himself, Jesus never says "we" or "us" or "our"; he always uses "I" or "me" or "my." What the divine Logos, who was already and eternally a person, did do, through the operation of the Holy Spirit, was to take into union with himself a human nature with the result that Jesus Christ was one person with a divine nature (a complex of divine attributes) and a human nature (a complex of human attributes). This is not to say that the human nature of Christ is impersonal; rather, Jesus assumed that nature into personal subsistence with himself.

The Effecting Means of the Incarnation. The incarnation occurred through the virginal conception (a more accurate description than "virgin birth") of the Son of God by the Holy Spirit in the womb of Mary (Isa. 7:14; Matt. 1:16, 18, 20, 23, 25; Luke 1:27, 34–35; 2:5; Gal. 4:4). Due to the interpenetration of the persons within the Godhead (John 14:20; 17:21–23; Heb. 9:14), the Holy Spirit ensured the divine personality of the God-man without creating at the same time a new human personality.

Scriptural Representations of the Incarnate Person. Because Jesus Christ is the God-man (one person who took human nature into union with his divine nature in the one divine person), the Scriptures can predicate of his person whatever can be predicated of either nature. In fact, the person of Christ may be *designated* in terms of one nature while what is *predicated* of him so designated is true by virtue of his union with the other nature (Westminster Confession, 8.7).

R. L. REYMOND

See also CHRISTOLOGY.

Indian Theology. Attempt to reformulate biblical theology in Indian categories of thought, in a manner relevant to the Indian context. Until recently Western theology has dominated the Indian theological scene, and Christianity has come under criticism from Hindu thinkers in this regard. For Indian Christian leaders, Indian theology is an attempt to meet the criticism that Christianity is a foreign and dangerous denationalizing force. It represents a search for and an expression of self-identity in India and in the field of Christian theology. It is an attempt to conceptualize the urge for being Christian and Indian simultaneously. It faces the challenges of renascent Hinduism in its relegation of Christianity to a subordinate status. Moreover it stands for the concern of Indian theologians to communicate the gospel in thought patterns familiar to the Indian mind. It is to present "the water of life in an Indian cup."

Trends in Indian Theology. No uniform pattern or common trends can be traced in Indian theology. Corresponding to the diversified historical context and socioreligious needs, there are varied theological expressions of response to the gospel.

(1) There are attempts to harmonize Christianity, rather than Christ, with Hinduism.

(2) There is concern for dialogue. Christian theology in India finds itself in the midst of spirited and influential non-Christian religious systems, especially Hinduism, which claims the allegiance of more than 80 percent of Indians.

(3) There is frequently a polemic emphasis. God's special revelation is essential for knowing the truth, and Jesus is this divine special revelation.

(4) There is an apologetic emphasis. Renascent Hinduism stripped Christ and Christianity of everything that they claim and possess.

(5) There is concern for evangelism. Jesus Christ is not a monopoly of the West. He is equally for India too.

(6) There is emphasis on relevancy. Indian theologians want to erase the ghetto mentality of the minority Christians.

It is too early to make any meaningful judgment on the emerging variety of Indian theology.

C. V. MATHEW

Indulgences. Remission of punishment for sin due by virtue of divine justice. Basic to the theology of indulgences is the distinction between eternal and temporal punishment of sin. Roman Catholics believe that in absolution, given by the priest following repentance, the repentant sinner receives the remission of sins and removal of eternal punishment by God, for the sake of Jesus Christ. The matter of temporal punishment of sins remains, however, and this can only be removed by penitential acts. It is here that indulgences are believed to function, in that the church (via the pope or a bishop) grants indulgences to cover all or part of the temporal punishment of sins. In the case of an indulgence granted to a soul in purgatory, the effect is to guarantee for that soul the intercession of the saints.

P. TOON

Inerrancy and Infallibility of the Bible. See BIBLE, INERRANCY AND INFALLIBILITY OF.

Infallibility. State of being incapable of error. Christians of all traditions believe that Scripture is infallible. This common belief is further described and defined by the councils held in the early centuries, four of which command universal approval. The Orthodox Church continues to rely on councils; the Latin Church defines the seat of infallibility as the papacy; Protestants regard Scripture as the ultimate source of authority.

The doctrine of the infallibility of the pope was defined by the Roman Catholic Church in the year 1870. It declares that the pope is enabled by God to express infallibly what the church should believe concerning questions of faith and morals when he speaks in his official capacity as "Christ's vicar on earth," or *ex cathedra.*

Protestants ascribe infallibility to the OT and NT Scriptures as the prophetic and apostolic record. Infallibility has a fourfold sense: (1) the Word of God infallibly achieves its end; (2) it gives us reliable testimony to the saving revelation and redemption of God in Christ; (3) it provides us with an authoritative norm of faith and conduct; and (4) the infallible Spirit of God, by whom it is given, speaks through it.

In recent years concentration upon historical and scientific questions, and suspicion of the dogmatic infallibility claimed by the papacy, has led to severe criticism of the whole concept—even as applied to the Bible. It must be conceded that the term itself is not a biblical one and does not play any great part in actual Reformation theology. Yet in the senses indicated it is well adapted to bring out the authority and authenticity of Scripture. The church accepts and preserves the infallible Word as the true standard of its apostolicity; for the Word itself, the Scripture, owes its infallibility, not to any intrinsic or independent quality, but to the divine Subject and Author to whom the term "infallibility" may properly be applied.

W. C. G. PROCTOR AND J. VAN ENGEN

See also EX CATHEDRA; PAPACY; PETER, PRIMACY OF; ROMAN CATHOLICISM.

Infant Baptism. See BAPTISM, INFANT.

Infant Salvation. The doctrine of *limbo infantum* was developed in the medieval church to address the issue of the salvific status of infants dying unbaptized. The Council of Trent, which defined the position of the Roman Catholic Church against the Protestant position, held that infants dying unbaptized were damned, although it did not express a definite view about the kind and degree of their punishment. Moreover, the belief was expressed that the desire and intention of godly parents to have their children baptized might be accepted in lieu of actual baptism in the case of stillborn babies.

Zwingli took the position that all children of believers dying in infancy are saved, for they were born within the covenant, the promise being to believers and to their children (Acts 2:39). He even inclined to the view that all children dying in infancy are elect and saved. The Reformed confessions agree in teaching the possibility of infants being saved "by Christ through the Spirit, who worketh when, and where, and how he pleaseth" (Westminster Confession). They do not give confessional authority to the Zwinglian supposition that death in infancy may be taken as a sign of election, and thus of salvation, but cautiously suggest only that for which they can claim the clear authority of Scripture, namely, that all elect children will be saved by God's mysterious working in their hearts although they are incapable of the response of faith.

G. N. M. COLLINS

See also BAPTISM, INFANT; LIMBO.

Infralapsarianism. (Lat. for "after the fall," sometimes designated "sublapsarianism") Doctrine that God first decreed or permitted the fall and then decreed to save some and condemn others.

Infralapsarians argue for the following order of the divine decrees: (1) God decreed the creation of humankind—a good, blessed, creation, not marred or flawed. (2) God decreed humankind would be allowed to fall through its own self-determination. (3) God decreed to save some of the fallen. (4) God decreed to leave the rest to their just fate of condemnation. The key to the order of the decrees is that God decreed election to salvation *after* the fall, not before; hence the name of the view "infralapsarianism."

R. V. SCHNUCKER

See also ARMINIUS, JAMES; CALVINISM; DORT, SYNOD OF; PREDESTINATION; SUPRALAPSARIANISM.

Inheritance of Adam's Sin. See SIN; IMPUTATION.

Iniquity. See SIN.

Inner Man. (Gk. *ho esō anthrōpos*) Term used by Paul in Rom. 7:22; 2 Cor. 4:16; and Eph. 3:16 to express graphically the human focus of God's work of regeneration. Paul does not use this term to refer specifically to certain distinct areas near the center of the human personality. The term is deliberately vague and is used to express two paradoxical ideas: (1) the work of God is at present secret, to be revealed at the eschaton; and (2) the work of God must embrace the whole of human nature, penetrating every aspect of the person.

S. MOTYER

See also MAN, DOCTRINE OF; OUTWARD MAN.

Inspiration, Plenary. See PLENARY INSPIRATION.

Inspiration, Verbal. See VERBAL INSPIRATION.

Inspiration of the Bible. See BIBLE, INSPIRATION OF.

Intercession. See PRAYER.

Intercession of Christ. See OFFICES OF CHRIST.

Intermediate State. Period between an individual's death and the final judgment and consummation.

In the NT. The NT offers no sustained reflection on the intermediate state. This is probably because the parousia was perceived as so real and imminent that it would have seemed irrelevant to reflect upon the state of the dead (1 Thess. 4:13–18). Some have been so keenly aware of the importance of the parousia, the emphasis on human wholeness in Scripture, and the paucity of reflection on the intermediate state that they have taken other positions. Luther seemed sympathetic with the notion that the intermediate state was a kind of soul sleep. The parousia was a real awakening. Others have so emphasized our body/soul unity that death is seen to be total; the parousia would then be the re-creation of our body/soul.

Purgatory. The Roman Catholic doctrine of purgatory developed during the Middle Ages and hardened into dogma in reaction to the Protestant rejection of it. The Council of Trent (1545–63) declared that those who reject the doctrine of purgatory are anathema. Roman Catholics hold that the intermediate state is not only the place of fixed blessing and torment, but primarily the place of passage by purification toward blessing as postbaptismal sins are atoned for. Since some sins are more grievous than others, the time of punishment varies. The church here "below" can also aid those being punished through prayers and masses. Clear scriptural warrant is absent. The only possible supportive text is in the Apocrypha (2 Macc. 12:43–45).

S. M. SMITH

See also HADES; PURGATORY; SHEOL; SOUL SLEEP; SPIRITS IN PRISON.

Internal Calling. See CALL, CALLING.

Internal Testimony of the Holy Spirit. Holy Spirit's activity in bringing about the believing acknowledgment of Scripture's inherent authority. The internal testimony of the Spirit is one of the many facets of the illuminating work of the Spirit by which the eyes of a sinner's heart are enlightened (Eph. 1:17–18) to receive and respond to God's Word. In the succinct words of the Westminster Confession, "Our full persuasion and assurance of the infallible truth and divine authority [of Scripture], is from the inward work of the Holy Spirit bearing witness by and with the Word in our hearts" (1.5).

This doctrine of the internal testimony of the Spirit should not be confused with the Barthian view that regards Scripture as a fallible witness to revelation and acknowledges authoritative revelation only in an ever-recurring, present act of God. It should also be distinguished from existentialist views of revelation as well as from mystical and pietistic claims to new revelation. On the other hand, the classic doctrine may not be used to exclude the role of proper exegesis of the biblical text and sound hermeneutical principles for biblical interpretation.

The internal testimony of the Holy Spirit is related to, but distinguished from, both the text of Scripture and the subjective conviction of the believer. The internal testimony relates to the external testimony of Scripture itself; it does not bring new revelation to supplement Scripture. Scripture clearly testifies to its own inspiration and authority. It is self-authenticating (*autopistos*), inherently authoritative. The Spirit's internal testimony does not make Scripture authoritative; rather, it contributes to the believer's conviction that Scripture is truly what it claims to be. Thus the same Spirit who inspired the authoritative Word awakens that conviction and acknowledgment in a sinner's heart through this internal testimony "by and with the Word."

F. H. KLOOSTER

Interpretation of Tongues, Gift of. See SPIRITUAL GIFTS.

Invisible Church. See CHURCH, THE.

Invocation of the Saints. Requests to persons in heaven for their intercession before God in support of the petitioner's prayers. The practice derives from the doctrine of the communion of saints, the fellowship of all members of the body of Christ, including the terrestrial church militant and the heavenly church triumphant. If Christian fellowship impels believers on earth to bear one another's burdens in prayer, it seems reasonable to conclude that the compassion of those who have died disposes them even more to pray for those who still struggle with evil and suffering, especially as the former no longer face their own cares. Having begun in the 3d century, the practice of invocation intensified during the Middle Ages. The Council of Trent moderated the practice by declaring it "good and useful" to invoke the saints while not mandating invocation nor anathematizing those who denied its efficacy. Reformation theology denied the validity of the practice.

P. D. STEEVES

See also COMMUNION OF SAINTS, THE; VENERATION OF THE SAINTS.

Irenaeus (ca. 130–ca. 200). Bishop of Lyons in Gaul. Two of his treatises survive: the *Demonstration* (or Proof) *of the Apostolic Preaching* and *Against Heresies* ("Refutation and Overthrow of the Gnosis Falsely So Called"). Irenaeus's most original contribution to theology was his doctrine of recapitulation (*recapitulatio*). The divine Christ became fully man in order to sum up all humanity in himself. What was lost through the disobedience of the first Adam was restored through the obedience of the second Adam. Christ went through all the stages of human life, resisted all temptation, died, and arose a victor over death and the devil. Irenaeus extended the analogy with Adam to include Mary as a new Eve. The benefits of Christ's victory are available to believers through participation in him.

E. FERGUSON

Irish Articles (1615). Articles of belief adopted at the first convocation of the Irish Episcopal Church. The 104 articles are arranged under 19 heads. James Ussher, later archbishop of Armagh, wrote most of these articles. The articles affirm the absolute sovereignty of God, predestination, election and reprobation, and justification by faith, along with the importance of repentance and good works.

D. F. KELLY

See also THIRTY-NINE ARTICLES, THE; USSHER, JAMES; WESTMINSTER CONFESSION OF FAITH.

Ironside, Henry Allen (1876–1951). Bible teacher, evangelist, pastor, and author. Although essentially self-taught, he was always in high demand as an expositor at Bible conferences and institutes. From 1925 to 1943, he served as a visiting professor at Dallas Theological Seminary. From 1930 to 1948 he was pastor of Moody Memorial Church in Chicago. Ironside is best known for his prolific literary output; he was a major figure in the popularizing of dispensationalism among American evangelicals.

T. P. WEBER

See also DISPENSATION, DISPENSATIONALISM.

Irresistible Grace. See GRACE.

Irving, Edward (1792–1834). Church of Scotland minister. Irving sought to get back behind the anticharismatic stance of the Protestant Reformation and reintroduce the charismatic dimension to Protestantism. He moved to London in 1822. Here his pulpit gifts were soon recognized, and by 1827 the great Regent Square Church was erected to hold the crowds who came to hear him. With his exuberance and expectation he became the first major popularizer of 19th-century premillennialism, guiding such recognized exponents of the movement as J. N. Darby and other early Plymouth Brethren into this new understanding. He began to advocate a charismatic eschatology. The next stage in Irving's development was his conviction that the "extraordinary" gifts of the Holy Spirit would be given once again, just prior to the second coming of Christ. In the spring of 1830 word came that speaking in tongues had occurred in the west of Scotland, and within a year manifestations were present in Regent Square Church. Debarred from his pulpit by the presbytery and subsequently deposed by the Church of Scotland General Assembly (1833), Irving and his supporters, almost all former Evangelical Anglicans, found their way into what became known as the Catholic Apostolic Church.

I. S. RENNIE

Israel, The New. Description of the church arising from the conviction that the position of Israel as the elect people of God has been transferred to the church, so that the former can no longer claim it. The NT presents a picture of both continuity and discontinuity between itself and the OT.

Discontinuity. There are some horrifying expressions of judgment on the people of Israel for their failure to accept Christ (e.g., Matt. 23:37–38; Mark 13:2; Luke 19:41–44; John 8:24; Rom. 9:27–29; 11:8–10; 1 Thess. 2:16), as well as some strong expressions of the inadequacy and provisional nature of the OT law (Rom. 3:20, 8:3; Gal. 3:23–25; Phil. 3:6–7; Heb. 8:13) and a polemic against Israelite institutions (e.g., the teaching office—Matt. 23:2–4; the sacrificial system—Heb. 10:3–4, 11; the temple—John 2:13–22; Acts 7:48–53; synagogue worship—2 Cor. 3:14–15).

Continuity. The NT also affirms the divine origin of the OT and its compatibility with the gospel (Matt. 5:17–18; 22:41–46; John 5:37–39; 10:35; Rom. 3:2, 31; 7:12, 14; 13:8–10; 15:4). OT images, institutions, and prophecies are applied to Christ and the church. Paul asserts the certainty of Israel's ultimate salvation (Rom. 11:25–26), and the early church (following Jesus' example) initially felt completely at home in, or took over for itself, the institutions of Israel (the temple—Luke 2:49; Acts 3:1; teaching office and prophecy—Mark 1:21; Acts 13:15–16; the synagogue—Luke 4:16; Acts 13:5).

Reconciliation. How are these two attitudes to be reconciled?

(1) *Christ, not any particular group of people, is the center of God's purposes.* "For no matter how many promises God has made, they are 'Yes' in Christ" (2 Cor. 1:20). Paul pictures Christ as the "seed of Abraham" (Gal. 3:19); Abraham and his descendants ("seed") were given

the promise (Gen. 17:7–8), on which Israel's election was based (Gal. 3:16).

(2) *It follows that the people of God and the OT must be understood Christocentrically.* Christ provides the key to the right understanding of the OT. Its institutions and prophecies are applied to Jesus, and the law itself finds its meaning only in pointing to him (Rom. 3:21; 10:4; Gal. 3:24).

(3) *Judgment on Israel does not cancel God's election.* Paul insists that God has not rejected his people (Rom. 11:1) and that Israel will be saved (Rom. 11:25–26), for "God's gift and his call are irrevocable" (Rom. 11:29).

(4) *OT ways of understanding God's people may be applied to the church.* The saving events of the OT, especially the exodus, are used to illuminate salvation in Christ (e.g., 1 Cor. 10:1–11), and images for Israel are applied to believers (e.g., John 15:1; 1 Pet. 2:9).

S. Motyer

See also Church, The.

Israel and Prophecy. As the OT prophets were Israelites, and as their message concerned the chosen people, it follows that almost all prophecy, including prophetic eschatology, has as its primary focus Israel (including the united kingdom, and, after 922 B.C., the separate states of Judah and Israel). In contemporary discussions of the Bible's prophetic eschatology, frequent reference is made to Israel. But it is not always easy to determine in the sources whether the reference is to Israel in the OT sense (the nation of the chosen people), to Israel in some future nationalistic sense (a restored Israel), or to the church, the New Israel.

The Basic Prophetic Message Concerning Israel. Prior to the beginning of the exile (587–87 B.C.), the prophets' message was that Israel's failure in the covenant relationship had been so fundamental that if there were no repentance, judgment would come; the covenant would be brought to an end. The eventual failure of the nation to rediscover the essence of its covenant relationship with God culminated in the end of the independent state of Israel. During and after the exile, the prophets continued to address God's word to the remnant of Israel—not as a nation, but as a people. In part, their message was addressed to those in exile and to those returning to the promised land. The prophets continued to speak of coming judgment, but they also spoke of a future restoration of Israel after the judgment. In the interpretation of particular prophetic passages, it is difficult to know whether the restoration of which they speak is fulfilled in the return of Israel to the promised land after the exile or in a new and restored Israel in a transformed world.

From Prophecy to Apocalyptic. At the end of the OT period and continuing into intertestamental times, a transformation took place from prophecy to apocalyptic; that is, the proclamation of the divine Word in prophecy (especially that part having eschatological significance) gave way to apocalyptic writings in which the "secrets" of the future were affirmed in the account of visions, or in narratives written in the form of visionary accounts.

Problems of Interpretation. The place of Israel in prophetic eschatology and apocalyptic literature is difficult to interpret. During the course of Christian history, each age has had interpreters who have identified the prophetic and apocalyptic "predictions" with the persons and events of their own age. Time has shown them to be fundamentally wrong over and over again; thus, while retaining readiness and an openness to God's intervention in human history, a healthy skepticism may be adopted to some of the popular "prophets" of our own age, whose interpretations of the biblical texts are no less suspect than those of their predecessors.

In summary, the biblical perspective emerging from the writings of the prophets is that human history has a direction and movement within the providence of God in which Israel has a continuing place. From the NT perspective, faith in the second coming of Christ, coupled with the prophetic eschatology concerning Israel, is something to be grasped by faith. To retain the vital faith in the culmination of human history as we know it, and yet to refrain from tying the prophetic message concerning Israel to our own intricate schemes and timetables, are the challenges perpetually facing us in attempting to understand Israel's place in prophecy.

P. C. CRAIGIE

See also ESCHATOLOGY; MILLENNIUM, VIEWS OF THE; SECOND COMING OF CHRIST.

Jj

Jah. See GOD, NAMES OF.

Jahweh. See GOD, NAMES OF.

Jansen, Cornelius Otto (1585–1638). Dutch Roman Catholic theologian. In the early 1620s, believing that Augustine's theology of efficacious predestinating grace was being threatened by the humanitarian tendencies of the Jesuit theologians of the Counter-Reformation, Jansen embarked on an intensive study of Augustine's works, particularly his anti-Pelagian writings. The massive treatise that resulted from Jansen's undertaking, entitled *Augustinus*, was published posthumously in 1640. Its publication touched off a heated controversy in European Roman Catholic circles, particularly in France. Jansen's theology came to be called Jansenism, and the convent of Port Royal became an important center of Jansenist influence.

N. V. HOPE

See also PASCAL, BLAISE.

Jansenism. See JANSEN, CORNELIUS OTTO.

Jaspers, Karl (1883–1969). German existentialist philosopher. In such works as *Man in the Modern Age* (1932) and *Reason and Existence* (1935), Jaspers developed the central ideas of his existentialism. Jaspers maintained that the nature of the self is discovered through the "illumination of existence," which discloses the person as an entity seeking understanding and being. Existence is the authentic self and infinitely open to new possibilities. It is the eternal in a person and total freedom; but since life is a flux in which a person seeks to find mooring, existence is necessarily limited by "boundary situations" such as death, suffering, guilt, and struggle. People have freedom of choice, and when they choose, they act. In these and his major theological works—*Nietzsche and Christianity* (1946), *The Perennial Scope of Theology* (1948), and *Myth and Christianity* (1954)—Jaspers sees religious answers emerging from metaphysical descriptions of being. In effect he calls for a "philosophical faith" in human freedom and the transcendence that provides us with help and on which the world is grounded, and rejects the alleged "absolutism" of traditional Christianity for the openness and tolerance of this faith.

R. V. PIERARD

See also EXISTENTIALISM.

Jehovah. See GOD, NAMES OF.

Jehovah's Witnesses. Movement founded by Charles Taze Russell (1852–1916) in the 1870s (the name was adopted in 1931). At the age of 18 Russell started a Bible class in Pittsburgh; in 1908 he moved the headquarters of his organization to Brooklyn, New York, where it has been based ever since. Following Russell's death Judge Joseph Franklin Rutherford became the leader. An able organizer, he developed the group into its present organization. The group's magazine, the *Watchtower*, has a worldwide circulation of over 64 million.

As a religious organization the Jehovah's Witnesses are typical of many 19th-century groups. Although their theology bears some resemblance to that of the

Arians in early church history, they are essentially a modern group strongly influenced by rationalism. Their rationalistic attitude toward the Bible comes out in their literal interpretation of prophecy and failure to appreciate the symbolic character of biblical language. Their rejection of blood transfusions reflects the rejection of modern science as well as the extreme literalism of their exegesis. In attempting to justify their interpretation of Christianity and rejection of orthodoxy the Witnesses produced their own translation of the Bible—*The New World Translation of the Christian Greek Scriptures* and *The New World Translation of the Hebrew Scriptures*—in 1950. Probably the best introduction to the theology of the Jehovah's Witnesses is their book *Let God Be True.*

Today there are over 3 million Witnesses worldwide. They have an extensive missionary network throughout the world and operate in most countries. In some places, particularly in Africa, the Witnesses have suffered severe persecution. In others, especially North America, they are rapidly coming to resemble a reasonably sized religious denomination.

I. HEXHAM

See also CULTS.

Jerome (ca. 347–419)**.** Latin Church father. Jerome was a biblical scholar and translator who aimed to incorporate the best of Greek learning into Western Christianity. In 373 Jerome decided to travel to the East. He settled for a time in the Syrian desert southeast of Antioch. There he mastered Hebrew and perfected his Greek. After ordination at Antioch he went to Constantinople and studied with Gregory of Nazianzus. In 382 he returned to Rome. In 384, he went back to the East. After traveling first to Antioch then to Alexandria, he settled in Bethlehem, where he remained for the rest of his life. Jerome's greatest accomplishment was the Vulgate. The chaotic state of the older Latin translation of the Bible was notorious. Working from the Hebrew OT and the Greek NT, Jerome, after 23 years of labor, provided a new Latin translation of the Bible. Jerome is also known for his exposition of Scripture and for his vitriolic participation in theological controversies.

B. L. SHELLEY

Jerusalem. Principal city of ancient Israel. The origins of the city are lost in antiquity; but evidence of civilization on the site goes back to 3000 B.C., and the city is referred to by name in Egyptian texts as early as the beginning of the 2d millennium B.C. According to Ezek. 16:3, the site was once populated by Amorites and Hittites; and, if it is to be identified with Salem (Gen. 14:18; Ps. 76:2), it was ruled in Abraham's day by the petty king Melchizedek, who was also "priest of God Most High."

Jerusalem in History. At the time of the conquest Jerusalem (otherwise known as Zion, the name originally given to the southeast hill where the earliest fortress was located) was populated by the Jebusites. David decisively conquered the Jebusites (2 Sam. 5:6–10) and established Jerusalem (or Zion) as his strategic center and political capital. Calling it the City of David (2 Sam. 5:9), he fortified and beautified it until his death. His successor, Solomon, pursued the same course even more lavishly. After the division of the united kingdom, Jerusalem became the capital of the southern kingdom. Eventually the city was captured (597 B.C.) and destroyed (586 B.C.) by the Babylonians, and most of the inhabitants killed or transported. Persian rule brought the return of a few thousand Jews to the land and city, but the walls were not rebuilt until the middle of the 5th century B.C. Jerusalem's vassal status continued under the Greeks and it became the center of a brutal conflict between the Seleucid dynasty in the north and the Ptolemies of Egypt in the south. Infighting and corruption contributed to the decisive defeat of the city by the Romans in 63 B.C. and its pacification in 54 B.C.

Herod the Great came to power in 37 B.C. as a vassal king responsible to Rome, and embarked on the enlargement and beautification of the temple and other buildings. The Jewish revolt that began in A.D. 66 inevitably led to the destruction of the city by the Romans in A.D. 70. A further revolt under Bar Kochba in A.D. 132 led to the city's destruction once again (135). This time the Romans rebuilt the city on a smaller scale as a pagan center, banning all Jews from living there—a ban that was not lifted until the reign of Constantine. From the early 4th century A.D. on, Jerusalem became a "Christian" city and the site of many churches and monasteries. Successive occupiers—Persians, Arabs, Turks, Crusaders, British, Israelis—have left their religious and cultural stamp on the city, which since 1967 has been unified under Israeli military might.

The Centrality of Jerusalem. From the time that Jerusalem became both the political and the cultic capital of the children of Israel, it progressively served as a bifocal symbol: on the one hand it reflected the people and all their sinfulness and waywardness; on the other it represented the place where God made himself known and the anticipation of all the eschatological blessing that God had in store for his people.

Jerusalem's Sin. The prophets (especially Isaiah, Jeremiah, Ezekiel, and Micah) speak of Jerusalem as a prostitute, fallen away from God, guilty of idolatry and flagrant disregard of God's commandments. The city must stand under the judgment of God (Isa. 1:21; 29:1–4; 32:9–14; Jer. 6:22–23). Jerusalem's social and religious transgressions are so gross and persistent that Ezekiel labels it a "city of bloodshed" (Ezek. 22:2–3; 24:6). In its sin Jerusalem is counted as part of the pagan world (Ezek. 16:1–3) and it will certainly be destroyed (Ezek. 15:6). The citizens of Jerusalem are worse than those in Samaria and Sodom (Lam. 4:6; Ezek. 16:44–58; cf. Amos 2:4–5; Mal. 2:11). The city taken by David in victory will now be taken in judgment (Isa. 29:1–7).

Jerusalem's Glory. Yet all is not gloom. Promises for the restoration of Jerusalem following the exile become linked with promises of eschatological blessing (Isa. 40:1–5; 54:11–17; 60; cf. Hag. 2:19; Zech. 1:12–17). Yahweh can no more forget Jerusalem than a woman can forget her child (Isa. 49:13–18). Ezekiel anticipates the return of Yahweh to Zion (43:1–9). In Zion, Yahweh will inaugurate his eschatological rule (Pss. 146:10; 149:2; Isa. 24:23; 52:7; Obad. 21; Mic. 4:7; Zeph. 3:15; Zech. 14:9), whether personally or through the Messiah (Zech. 9:9–10), his servant (Isa. 40–66).

Jerusalem in NT Teachings. In the NT Jerusalem is still "the holy city" (Matt. 4:5; 27:53), the home of the temple and its priestly service, as well as the center of rabbinic authority. Jesus must die in the Jerusalem area (Matt. 16:21; Mark 10:33–34; Luke 9:31), in direct conflict with these central Jewish institutions. The temple had become a den of robbers (Mark 11:17), and Jerusalem lived up to its reputation as killer of the prophets (Matt. 23:37–39; cf. Luke 13:33). Jerusalem would be destroyed by foreign invaders (Matt. 23:38; Luke 19:43–44; 21:20, 24). In the Book of Acts, Jerusalem is the hub from which the gospel radiates outward (Acts 1:8), the site of Pentecost and of the apostolic council; but if it is the moral and salvation-historical center of Christianity, it is also the ideological home of Judaizers who wish to make the entire Mosaic code a precondition for Gentile conversion to Jesus Messiah—a position Paul condemns (Gal. 1:8–9). Paul himself, however, is quick to recognize how beholden all other believers are to the Christian remnant of Jerusalem (Gal. 2:10; 2 Cor. 8–9) which in a salvation-historical sense is truly the mother church.

A still deeper connection links OT treatment of Jerusalem to the "heavenly Jerusalem" (Heb. 12:22), to which Christian believers have already come, and to "Jerusalem above" (Gal. 4:26), which in an extended typology embraces new covenant believers and relegates geographical Jerusalem and its children to slavery: Jesus *fulfills* and to that extent *replaces* the OT types and shadows that anticipated him. Jesus enters Jerusalem as messianic king (Mark 11:1–11 and pars.) and is concerned to see Jerusalem's temple pure (Mark 11:15–17 and pars.), precisely because the city and temple anticipate his own impending death and resurrection—events that shift the focal meeting place between God and humankind to Jesus himself (Mark 14:57–58; John 2:19–22). This constitutes part of a broader pattern, worked out in some detail in the Epistle to the Hebrews, in which the gospel and its entailments simultaneously fulfill OT institutions and expectations and render them obsolete (Heb. 8:13). The ultimate goal is the new Jerusalem.

D. A. CARSON

See also JERUSALEM, THE NEW.

Jerusalem, The New. Term in the Book of Revelation (3:12; 21:2) used to describe the perfect and eternal dwelling-place of God. The New Jerusalem receives extended treatment in Rev. 21–22. The ultimate state of the church, and her reward, is presented under diverse metaphors: the church is simultaneously "prepared as a bride beautifully dressed for her husband"—indeed, she is "the bride, the wife of the Lamb" (21:2, 9), and "the Holy City, the new Jerusalem, coming down out of heaven from God" (21:2). The holy city is perfectly symmetrical (21:16) and is constructed with materials of fabulous wealth (21:18–21; cf. Isa. 54:11). It shines with the glory of God (21:11) and has foundations named after the 12 apostles and gates named after the 12 tribes of Israel (21:12, 14). The rich symbolism refers not only to the beatific vision but to a renewed and abundant existence. Perhaps the most moving element in the description is what is missing. There is no temple in the new Jerusalem, "because the Lord God Almighty and the Lamb are its temple" (21:22). Vastly outstripping the expectations of Judaism, this stated omission signals the ultimate reconciliation.

D. A. CARSON

See also JERUSALEM; CHURCH, THE.

Jesuits. See SOCIETY OF JESUS, THE.

Jesus Christ. Expression that is a combination of the name "Jesus" (of Nazareth) and the title "Messiah" (Heb.) or "Christ" (Gk.), which means "anointed." In Acts 5:42, this name/title combination is still apparent. As time progressed, however, the title eventually became so closely associated with the name that the combination was transformed from the confession "Jesus (who is) the Christ," to a confessional name, "Jesus Christ." The appropriateness of this title for Jesus was such that even Jewish Christian writers referred to "Jesus Christ" rather than "Jesus the Christ" (Matt. 1:1; Rom. 1:7; Heb. 13:8; James 1:1; 1 Pet. 1:1).

Sources of Information. *Non-Christian Sources.* There are essentially only three pagan sources of importance: Pliny (*Epistles* 10.96); Tacitus (*Annals* 15.44); and Suetonius (*Lives* 24.4). All three date from the second decade of the 2d century. The main Jewish sources are Josephus (*Antiquities* 18.3.3; 20.9.1) and the Talmud. The non-Christian sources provide meager information about Jesus, but they do establish the fact that he actually lived, that he gathered disciples and performed healings, and that he was condemned to death by Pontius Pilate.

Christian Sources. The nonbiblical Christian sources consist for the most part of the apocryphal gospels (A.D. 150–350) and the "agrapha" ("unwritten sayings" of Jesus, i.e., supposedly authentic sayings of Jesus not found in the canonical Gospels). Their value is quite dubious. The information that is not utterly fantastic (the Infancy Gospel of Thomas) or heretical (the Gospel of Truth) is at best only possible and not provable (see Gospel of Thomas 31, 47).

The biblical materials can be divided into the Gospels and Acts–Revelation. In the NT we learn much about the person and character of Jesus. Certain sayings of Jesus are known (Acts 20:35; 1 Cor. 7:10; 9:14), and possible allusions to his sayings are also found (Rom. 12:14, 17; 13:7, 8–10; 14:10).

The major sources for our knowledge of Jesus are the canonical Gospels. These Gospels are generally divided into two groups: the Synoptic Gospels (Matthew, Mark, and Luke) and John. Matthew, Mark, and Luke have largely the same order and wording (the term "synoptic" means "presenting a common view"). The literary relationship among the three is generally explained as follows: Mark wrote first. Matthew and Luke used Mark and another source (no longer extant), which mostly contained teachings of Jesus (called "Q"). Matthew and Luke used other materials as well ("M" = the materials found only in Matthew; "L" = the materials found only in Luke).

The Christ of Faith. The unique self-understanding of Jesus can be ascertained by two means: the implicit Christology revealed by his actions and words, and the explicit Christology revealed by the titles with which he described himself.

Implicit Christology. Jesus clearly acted as one who possessed a unique authority. He assumed for himself the prerogative of cleansing the temple (Mark 11:12–17), of bringing the lost into the kingdom of God (Luke 15), and of having divine authority to forgive sins (Mark 2:5–7; Luke 7:48–49). Jesus also spoke as one who possessed authority greater than the OT (Matt. 5:31–32, 38–39), Abraham (John 8:53), Jacob (John 4:12), and the temple (Matt. 12:6). He claimed to be Lord of the sabbath (Mark 2:28). He even asserted that the destiny of all people depended on how they responded to him (Matt. 10:32–33; 11:6; Mark 8:34–38).

Explicit Christology. Jesus referred to himself as the Messiah or Christ (Mark 8:27–30; 14:61–62), and his formal sentence of death on political grounds only makes sense on the basis of Jesus' having acknowledged that he was the Messiah. He also referred to himself as the Son of God (Matt. 11:25–27; Mark 12:1–9). Jesus' favorite self-designation, due to its concealing as well as revealing nature, was "Son of man" (Dan. 7:13; Matt. 10:23; 19:28; 25:31; Mark 8:38; 13:26; 14:62). Therefore, rather than being a title that stresses humility, this title reveals the divine authority Jesus possesses as the Son of man to judge the world and his sense of having come from the Father (cf. here also Matt. 5:17; 10:34; Mark 2:17; 10:45).

The Christology of the NT. In the NT numerous claims are made concerning Jesus Christ. Through his resurrection Jesus has been exalted and given lordship over all creation (1 Cor. 15:27; Phil. 2:9–11; Col. 1:16–17). The use of the title "Lord" for Jesus quickly resulted in the association of the person and work of Jesus with the Lord (Yahweh) of the OT. He is said to be preexistent (Phil. 2:6; Col. 1:15–16); he is referred to as creator (Col. 1:16); he is said to possess the "very nature" of God (Phil. 2:6) and be the "image" of God (Col. 1:15; cf. also 2 Cor. 4:4). He is even referred to explicitly in a number of places as "God" (John 1:1; 20:28; Rom. 9:5; 2 Thess. 1:12; Titus 2:13; Heb. 1:5–8; 1 John 5:20). Although the exegesis of some of these passages is debated, it is clear that some of them clearly refer to Jesus as "God."

The Quest for the Historical Jesus. The beginning of the quest for the historical Jesus can be dated to 1774–78, when Lessing published posthumously the lecture notes of Hermann Samuel Reimarus. The major problem that faces any attempt to discover the "historical Jesus" involves the definition of the term "historical." In critical circles the term is generally understood as "the product of the historical-critical method." This method for many assumes a closed continuum of time and space in which divine intervention, that is, the miraculous, cannot intrude. Such a definition will, of course, always have a problem seeking to find continuity between the supernatural Christ and the Jesus of history, who by such a definition cannot be supernatural. If "historical" means nonsupernatural, there can never be a real continuity between the Jesus of historical research and the Christ of faith. It is becoming clear, therefore, that this definition of "historical" must be challenged, and even in Germany scholars are arising who speak of the need for the historical-critical method to assume an openness to transcendence, that is, to the possibility of the miraculous. Only in this way can there ever be hope of establishing a continuity between the Jesus of historical research and the Christ of faith.

R. H. Stein

See also Christology; Logos; Messiah; Pre-existence of Christ; Resurrection of Christ; Second Coming of Christ; Sermon on the Mount; Sinlessness of Christ; Virgin Birth of Jesus.

John, Theology of. John was the disciple whom Jesus loved (John 13:23) and to whom the dying Jesus commended his mother (John 19:26–27). In the Gospels he is often associated with Peter and James; these three men were especially close to Jesus (Matt. 17:1; Mark 14:33; Luke 8:51). He and his brother James were called "sons of thunder" (Boanerges—Mark 3:17). The impression we get is that John knew Jesus more intimately than any of the other disciples. John is purported to be the author of the Gospel and three Epistles that bear his name and the Book of Revelation (of John).

God as Father. John uses the word "Father" 122 times to refer to God. John also tells us that God is love (1 John 4:8, 16); love is an important theme in both his Gospel and his epistles. The Father is constantly active (John 5:17); he upholds his creation and brings blessing on those he has created. He is a great God whose will is done, particularly in salvation. Throughout the Book of Revelation God is portrayed as a mighty God. He does what he wills and, although evil is strong, in the end he will triumph over it entirely.

Christology. The Gospel of John begins with a section on Christ as the Word. God has taken action in Christ for revelation and for salvation. Suffering and lowly service are not simply the path to glory; they *are* glory in its deepest sense. God is not concerned with what people regard as glorious. Even though Jesus lived his entire earthly life in a lowly manner, John can say, "We have seen his glory, the glory of the One and Only, who came from the Father, full of grace and truth" (John 1:14).

Miracles. John's treatment of the miracles is distinctive. He never calls them "mighty works" as do the synoptists, but "signs" or "works." They point us to significant truth, for God is at work in them.

The Holy Spirit. John tells us more about the Holy Spirit than do the other Evangelists. He was active from the beginning of Jesus' ministry (John 1:32–33), but the full work of the Spirit awaited the consummation of Jesus' own ministry (John 7:39). The Spirit is active in the Christian life (John 3:5, 8) and there are important truths about the Spirit in Jesus' farewell discourse. He is "the Spirit of truth" (John 14:16–17); he will never leave believers (John 14:16); he has a work among unbelievers, namely, that of convicting them of sin, righteousness, and judgment (John 16:8).

John's is a profound and deep theology, although expressed in the simplest of terms. It sets forth truths that no Christian can neglect.

L. MORRIS

John of the Cross (1542–1591). Spanish mystic and poet. John of the Cross was one of the leading teachers of Christian contemplation or the mystical way, as well as a founder of the Discalced Carmelite order. A friend of Teresa of Avila, he is best known for his *Dark Night of the Soul*, which is actually a second volume of *Ascent of Mount Carmel.* The latter work deals with the purgative way, while the former instructs the reader in the illuminative and unitive ways. John of the Cross's poetic gentleness is evident in *Spiritual Canticle*, and his wisdom as a spiritual guide and counselor shines through his work, which is invaluable to those interested in nonimaged mystical spiritual experience.

P. H. DAVIDS

See also ILLUMINATIVE WAY, THE; MYSTICISM; PURGATIVE WAY, THE; UNITIVE WAY, THE.

John the Baptist. First-century A.D. Jewish prophet. John was the son of Zechariah, a priest, and Elizabeth (also of priestly descent and a relative of Mary, the mother of Jesus). Born in the hill country of Judah, he spent his early years in the wilderness of Judea (Luke 1:80). His public ministry began in the 15th year of the emperor Tiberius (ca. A.D. 27), when he suddenly emerged from the wilderness. The Gospels present John as the fulfillment of the *Elijah redivivus* expectation (Mark 9:11–13; Luke 1:17). John's clothes made of camel's hair and his leather belt were similar to the dress of Elijah (Matt. 3:4; cf. 2 Kings 1:8).

John's message had a twofold emphasis: (1) the imminent appearance of the messianic kingdom, and (2) the urgent need for repentance to prepare for this event (Matt. 3:2). His message of repentance was directed particularly to the Jews, for God was going to purge Israel as well as the world (Matt. 3:7–12). When Jesus appeared on the scene John's role as a forerunner was completed. His recognition of this fact is expressed in his personal testimony to Jesus' messiahship (John 1:29). The baptism that John preached and practiced complemented his preparatory task. In its basic sense it was a symbolic act for the cleansing of sin; it was to be accompanied by repentance. The baptism of Jesus by John (Matt. 3:13–15) is to be explained not as a sign that Jesus needed repentance, but rather that by this act he was identifying himself with humankind in the necessary approach to God's kingdom. John's denunciation of Herod Antipas for his marriage led to his execution by beheading (Matt. 14:1–12). Josephus tells us that this took place at the fortress of Macherus near the Dead Sea.

R. B. LAURIN

Joy. Emotion resulting from the possession or expectation of good. In Scripture joy is presented as a consistent mark of both the individual believer and the believing community. It is a quality of life and not simply a fleeting emotion. It is grounded in God himself and flows from him (Ps. 16:11; Rom. 15:13). Joy is not an isolated or occasional consequence of faith but rather an integral part of one's whole relation to God (John 15:9–14; 1 Pet. 1:6). Fullness of joy comes when there is a deep sense of the presence of God in one's life. From that awareness flows the strong desire to share what one is experiencing with others.

C. DAVIS

Judaism. Religion and culture of the Jewish people. In the NT the word appears twice (Gal. 1:13–14) in reference to Paul's prior consuming devotion to Jewish faith and life.

Development. Hebrew religion began to give rise to Judaism after the destruction of the temple and the exile of Judah in 586 B.C. The biblical term "Jew" is almost exclusively postexilic. The Jewish religion of the biblical period evolved through such historical stages as the intertestamental, rabbinic, and medieval to the modern period of the 19th century with its Orthodox, Conservative, and Reform Judaism. Along the way Jewish religion took on new teachings and practices. Despite the shifting phases of its history, however, the essence of the religious teaching of Judaism has remained remarkably constant, firmly rooted in the Hebrew Scriptures (OT). Judaism is a religion of ethical monotheism. For centuries many Jews have sought to distill its essential features from the call to Israel "to act justly, and to love mercy and to walk humbly with your God" (Mic. 6:8).

Basic Doctrines and Beliefs. According to the teaching of Judaism there is no set of beliefs upon the acceptance of which the Jew may find salvation. In the Mishnah (Abot 1:2) one sees the broad philosophy that governed the minds of the early rabbis: "By three things is the world sustained: by the law, by the [temple] service, and by deeds of lovingkindness." This basic teaching is further underscored by the threefold function of the synagogue as a "house of study" (for learning of Torah), "house of prayer" (for worship of God), and "house of assembly" (for the care of community needs).

Contemporary Judaism often speaks of four foundational pillars of the Jewish faith, each interacting as a major force as part of the covenant: (1) the Torah, always a living law as the written Torah is understood in light of the oral Torah; (2) God—a unity (one), spiritual (not a body), and eternal; (3) the people (Israelites/Jews), called into being by God as members of one family, a corporate personality, a community of faith; and (4) the land (known today as Eretz Yisrael), a bond going back to Abraham, the father of the Hebrew people (Gen. 17:7–8).

M. R. WILSON

See also PHARISEES; SADDUCEES.

Judaizers. Gentiles who followed certain religious practices and customs of Judaism. The Greek verb *Ioudaizō*, "to judaize" (RSV "live like Jews"; NIV "follow Jewish customs") occurs in the NT only in Gal. 2:14. As "apostle to the Gentiles" (Rom. 11:13), Paul was against imposing a strict Jewish dietary code on non-Jews. Such legislation might imply that the belief of Gentile Christians was defective in comparison to that of Jewish Christians; it might suggest that conformity to Jewish custom must be added to faith in Christ (cf. Acts 15:1, 5). Paul thus was opposed to judaizing. It had the potential to distort salvation by grace alone, divide the body, and be an argument for developing two separate assemblies, one for Jews and one for Gentiles.

M. R. WILSON

Judgment. Because we are born in sin and cannot live up to God's righteous standards, we stand condemned (Rom. 1:18; Eph. 5:5–6; Col. 3:5–6; 2 Pet. 2:3).

God himself is the one who condemns (Job 10:2; Jer. 42:18; John 12:48). His condemnation is based on his justice, and such condemnation is deserved (1 Kings 8:32; Rom. 3:8; Gal. 1:8–9). Condemnation comes to the wicked and unrepentant (Matt. 12:41–42; Luke 11:31–32; John 5:29; Rom. 5:16, 18; 2 Thess. 2:12; Rev. 19:2) and results in eternal punishment (Matt. 23:33), but no OT believer who trusted in God (Ps. 34:22) or NT believer who trusts in Christ (John 3:18; 5:24) will be condemned. Jesus came to save rather than to condemn (John 3:17), and he frees us from final condemnation (Rom. 8:1–2).

Divine judgment is God's method of displaying his mercy as well as his wrath toward both individuals and nations (Exod. 6:6; 7:4; Eccles. 3:17; 12:14; Dan. 7:22; Joel 3:2; 2 Cor. 5:10). God is the true and only Judge (Gen. 18:25; Ps. 82:1; Eccles. 11:9), an office and function shared by the Father (Gen. 31:53; John 8:50; Rom. 3:6) and the Son (Acts 10:42; 17:31; Rom. 2:16). Retributive or negative judgment is a direct result of sin (1 Sam. 3:13; Ezek. 7:3, 8, 27; Rom. 2:12; Jude 14–15) and is therefore both just (Ezek. 33:20; 2 Tim. 4:8; 1 Pet. 2:23) and deserved (Pss. 94:2; 143:2; Ezek. 18:30). Rewarding or positive judgment relates to our stewardship of talents and gifts and is therefore characterized by divine compassion (Matt. 25:14–23; 1 Cor. 3:12–15; 1 Pet. 1:17). Although we experience judgment initially in this life, all of us are judged ultimately after death (Isa. 66:16; Jer. 25:31; Joel 3:12; John 12:48; Acts 17:31; Rom. 2:16; Rev. 20:12–13) at the judgment seat of God (Rom. 14:10) or Christ (2 Cor. 5:10).

R. YOUNGBLOOD

See also JUDGMENT SEAT.

Judgment, The Last. See LAST JUDGMENT, THE.

Judgment of the Nations, The. Amillennial teaching that there will be one general resurrection of all the dead at the end of the present age when Christ returns. This teaching implies that there is also only one final judgment, since the judgment is said to follow the resurrection (Rev. 20:11–15). The so-called judgment of the nations (Joel 3:1–3), then, is subsumed under this one final judgment. Consequently, all people who ever lived, both saved and unsaved, will appear before Christ in this final judgment. Premillennialists generally distinguish four judgments: the judgment of believers, the judgment of Israel, the judgment of the nations, and the "great white throne" judgment. These judgments are distinct from one another in subjects, time, and place. Premillenialists understand the judgment of the nations to be a judgment of the living Gentile nations by Jesus Christ following his return in glory to the earth (Isa. 2:4; Joel 3:1–3; Matt. 25:31–46).

S. N. GUNDRY

See also JUDGMENT SEAT; LAST JUDGMENT, THE; MILLENNIUM, VIEWS OF THE; SECOND COMING OF CHRIST.

Judgment Seat. (Gk. *bēma*, "step") Platform upon which the civil magistrate sat during judicial proceedings. Figuratively the term found use as a picture of the final confrontation between humankind and Jesus Christ where an accounting would be held for each person's earthly deeds. While the predominant nature of these judgments indicates they are held to announce condemnation to the wicked (Matt. 25:31, 46; John 3:18; 2 Thess. 1:7–10; Rev. 20:14–15), the judgment of Christians appears to be designed to evaluate the stewardship of their earthly life (Rom. 14:10; 1 Cor. 3:12–15).

S. E. MCCLELLAND

See also JUDGMENT; JUDGMENT OF THE NATIONS, THE; LAST JUDGMENT, THE.

Justice. (Heb. *ṣedāqâ, ṣedeq*; Gk. *dikaiosynē*) Communicable attribute of

God that manifests his holiness. Used of humankind, justice refers to right rule, to right conduct, or to people getting their due, whether good or bad. God's *relative* justice is his rectitude in and of himself; God's *absolute* justice is the rectitude by which he upholds himself against violations of his holiness. By *rectoral* justice he institutes righteous laws and establishes just rewards and penalties, as over against *distributive* justice, whereby he metes out just rewards (*remunerative* justice, expressive of his love) and punishments (*retributive* justice, expressive of his wrath).

B. L. GODDARD

See also GOD, ATTRIBUTES OF; RIGHTEOUSNESS.

Justification. Action of God by which he declares persons as righteous (i.e., in true and right relationship to himself). The basic fact of biblical religion is that God pardons and accepts believing sinners (Pss. 32:1–5; 130; Luke 7:47–48; 18:9–14; Acts 10:43; 1 John 1:7–2:2). As stated by Paul (most fully in Romans and Galatians, although see also 2 Cor. 5:14–15; Eph. 2:1–7; Phil. 3:4–11), the doctrine of justification determines the whole character of Christianity as a religion of grace and faith. It defines the saving significance of Christ's life and death by relating both to God's law (Rom. 3:24–26; 5:16–21). It displays God's justice in condemning and punishing sin, his mercy in pardoning and accepting sinners, and his wisdom in exercising both attributes harmoniously together through Christ (Rom. 3:23–24). It makes clear what faith is—belief in Christ's atoning death and justifying resurrection (Rom. 4:23–25; 10:8–10), and trust in him alone for righteousness (Phil. 3:8–9). It makes clear what Christian morality is—keeping the law out of gratitude to the Savior whose gift of righteousness made keeping the law needless for acceptance (Rom. 7:1–6; 12:1–2). It explains all hints, prophecies, and instances of salvation in the OT (Rom. 1:17; 3:21; 4:1–3). It overthrows Jewish exclusivism (Gal. 2:15–16) and provides the basis on which Christianity becomes a religion for the world (Rom. 1:16; 3:29–30). It is the heart of the gospel.

The Meaning of Justification. The biblical meaning of "justify" (Heb. *ṣādēq*; Gk. *dikaioō*) is to pronounce, accept, and treat as just, that is, as, on the one hand, not penally liable, and, on the other, entitled to all the privileges due to those who have kept the law. It is thus a forensic term, denoting a judicial act of administering the law—in this case, by declaring a verdict of acquittal, and so excluding all possibility of condemnation. Justification thus determines the legal status of the person justified. (See Deut. 25:1; Prov. 17:15; Rom. 8:33–34. In Isa. 43:9, 26, "be justified" means "get the verdict.") The justifying action of the Creator, who is the royal Judge of this world, has both a sentential and an executive, or declarative, aspect: God justifies, first, by reaching his verdict and then by sovereign action makes his verdict known and secures to those he justifies the rights that are now their due. What is envisaged in Isa. 45:25 and 50:8, for instance, is specifically a series of events that will publicly vindicate those whom God holds to be in the right.

Paul's Doctrine of Justification. The background of Paul's doctrine was the Jewish conviction that a day of judgment was coming, in which God would condemn and punish all who had broken his laws. That day would terminate the present world order and usher in a golden age for those whom God judged worthy. This conviction, derived from prophetic expectations of "the day of the Lord" (Isa. 2:10–22; 13:6–11; Jer. 46:10; Amos 5:19–20 Obad. 15; Zeph. 1:14–2:3) and developed during the intertestamental period under the influence of apocalyptic, had been emphatically confirmed by

Christ (Matt. 11:22–24; 12:36–37). Paul affirmed that Christ himself was the appointed representative through whom God would "judge the world with justice" on "the day when God will judge men's secrets through Jesus Christ" (Acts 17:31; Rom. 2:16).

Paul sets out his doctrine of the judgment day in Rom. 2:5–16. Against this dark background (cf. Rom. 1:18–3:20), Paul proclaims the present justification of sinners by grace through faith in Jesus Christ, apart from all works and despite all demerit (Rom. 3:21–26). This justification, although individually located at the point of time at which a person believes (Rom. 4:2; 5:1), is an eschatological once-for-all divine act, the final judgment brought into the present. The justifying sentence, once passed, is irrevocable. God's wrath will not touch the justified (Rom. 5:9). Those accepted now are secure forever. Inquisition before Christ's judgment seat (Rom. 14:10–12; 2 Cor. 5:10) may deprive them of certain rewards (1 Cor. 3:15), but never of their justified status.

Justification has two sides. On the one hand, it means the pardon, remission, and nonimputation of all sins, reconciliation to God, and the end of his enmity and wrath (Acts 13:39; Rom. 4:6–7; 5:9–11; 2 Cor. 5:19). On the other hand, it means the bestowal of a righteous person's status and a title to all the blessings promised to the just, a thought that Paul amplifies by linking justification with the adoption of believers as God's sons and heirs (Rom. 8:14–17; Gal. 4:4–7). Part of their inheritance they receive immediately through the gift of the Holy Spirit, whereby God "seals" them as his when they believe (Eph. 1:13), they taste that quality of fellowship with God that belongs to the age to come and is called "eternal life." Justification thus means permanent reinstatement to favor and privilege, as well as complete forgiveness of all sins.

The Ground of Justification. Paul's deliberately paradoxical reference to God as justifying the wicked (Rom. 4:5) reflects his awareness that this is a startling doctrine. Indeed, it seems flatly at variance with the OT presentation of God's essential righteousness, as revealed in his actions as Legislator and Judge—a presentation that Paul himself assumes in Rom. 1:18–3:20. The OT insists that God is "righteous in all his ways" (Ps. 145:17), a God who "does no wrong" (Deut. 32:4; cf. Zeph. 3:5). The law of right and wrong, in conformity to which righteousness consists, has its being and fulfillment in him. His revealed law, "holy, righteous and good" as it is (Rom. 7:12; cf. Deut. 4:8; Ps. 19:7–9), mirrors his character, for he "loves" the righteousness prescribed (Ps. 11:7; 33:5) and "hates" the unrighteousness forbidden (Ps. 5:4–6; Isa. 61:8; Zech. 8:17). As Judge, he declares his righteousness by "visiting" retributive judgment on idolatry, irreligion, immorality, and inhuman conduct throughout the world (Ps. 9:5–6, 15–16; Jer. 9:24; Amos 1:3–3:2). It seems unthinkable that a God who thus reveals just and inflexible wrath against all human ungodliness (Rom. 1:18) should justify the ungodly. Paul, however, takes the bull by the horns and affirms, not merely that God does it, but that he does it in a manner designed "to shew his righteousness, because of the passing over of the sins done aforetime, in the forbearance of God; for the shewing, *I say*, of his righteousness at this present season: that he might himself be just, and the justifier of him that hath faith in Jesus" (Rom. 3:25–16, ERV). The statement is emphatic, for the point is crucial. Paul is saying that the gospel that proclaims God's apparent violation of his justice is really a revelation of his justice. So far from raising a problem of theodicy, it actually solves one; for it makes explicit, as the OT never did, the just ground on which God pardoned and accepted believers before the time of Christ, as well as since.

Paul's thesis is that God justifies sinners on a just ground, namely, that the claims of God's law upon them have been fully satisfied. The law has not been altered, suspended, or flouted for their justification, but fulfilled—by Jesus Christ, acting in their name. By perfectly serving God, Christ perfectly kept the law (Matt. 3:15). His obedience culminated in death (Phil. 2:8); he bore the penalty of the law in our place (Gal. 3:13), to make propitiation for our sins (Rom. 3:25). On the ground of Christ's obedience, God does not impute sin, but imputes righteousness, to sinners who believe (Rom. 4:2–8; 5:19). "The righteousness of God" (i.e., righteousness *from* God: see Phil. 3:9) is bestowed on us as a free gift (Rom. 1:17; 3:21–22; 5:17, cf. 9:30; 10:3–10): that is to say, we receive the right to be treated and the promise that we shall be treated, no longer as sinners, but as righteous, by the divine Judge. Thus we become "the righteousness of God" in and through him who "knew no sin" personally, but was representatively "made sin" (treated as a sinner and punished) in our stead (2 Cor. 5:21). God justifies us by passing on us, for Christ's sake, the verdict that Christ's obedience merited. God declares us to be righteous, because he reckons us to be righteous; and he reckons righteousness to us, not because he accounts us to have kept his law personally (which would be a false judgment), but because he accounts us to be united to the one who kept it representatively . For Paul union with Christ is fact—the basic fact, indeed, in Christianity; and the doctrine of imputed righteousness is simply Paul's exposition of the forensic aspect of it (see Rom. 5:12–21). Covenantal solidarity between Christ and his people is thus the objective basis on which sinners are reckoned righteous and justly justified through the righteousness of their Savior. Such is Paul's theodicy regarding the ground of justification.

Faith and Justification. Paul regards faith, not as itself our justifying righteousness, but rather as the outstretched empty hand that receives righteousness by receiving Christ (Rom. 3:25–28).

Theologians on the rationalistic and moralistic wing of Protestantism—Socinians, Arminians, and some modern liberals—have taken Paul to teach that God regards human faith as righteousness (either because it fulfills a supposed new law or because, as the seed of all Christian virtue, it contains the germ and potency of an eventual fulfillment of God's original law, or else because it is simply God's sovereign pleasure to treat faith as righteousness, although it is not righteousness; and that God pardons and accepts sinners on the ground of their faith). In consequence, these theologians deny the imputation of Christ's righteousness to believers in the sense explained, and reject the whole covenantal conception of Christ's mediatorial work. The most they can say is that Christ's righteousness was the indirect cause of the acceptance of human faith as righteousness, in that it created a situation in which this acceptance became possible. Theologically, the fundamental defect of all such views is that they do not make the satisfaction of the law the basis of acceptance. They regard justification, not as a judicial act of executing the law, but as the sovereign act of a God who stands above the law and is free to dispense with it, or change it, at his discretion. The suggestion is that God is not bound by his own law: its preceptive and penal enactments do not express immutable and necessary demands of his own nature, but he may out of benevolence relax and amend them without ceasing to be what he is. This, however, seems a wholly unscriptural conception.

J. I. Packer

See also Faith; Sanctification.

Kk

Kabbalah. (Heb. *qābal*, "to receive, tradition") Jewish esoteric mystic philosophy that deals with the mysteries of God, the universe, and creation. The etymology of the name implies that this philosophy was received as special revelation by a select few chosen by virtue of their saintly character. They, in turn, transmitted this esoteric knowledge to those able to understand it properly. The first systematic development of Kabbalah took place during the Gaonic period of Babylonia (A.D. 600–1000). As the Babylonian center waned, other areas became prominent in its development, especially Italy, Spain, southern France, and Germany. Development continued in the 1100s and 1200s. The most prominent book of Kabbalah is the *Zohar* (Book of Splendor), allegedly written by Moses de León in Spain in the 13th century. In the 16th century in Safed, Israel, Isaac Luria's Kabbalah, with its practical emphasis, initiated a distinct redemptive and messianic perspective.

Kabbalah pictures God as being above all existence. The world was created through a series of 10 emanations of God's spiritual essence. The doctrine of reincarnation figures prominently in the teachings of Kabbalah. The pure soul, once the body dies, will be present among the emanations who control the world. An impure soul, however, must be reborn in another body. This process of rebirth continues until the impure soul has been made pure. What is most distinctive about this philosophy is the hermeneutical principle of finding hidden meanings in the texts of Scripture. Kabbalah influenced Jewish messianic movements, principally Hasidism.

L. GOLDBERG

Kähler, Martin (1835–1912). German theologian. His principal theological work, a volume on dogmatics entitled *Die Wissenschaft der christlichen Lehre* (1883), has the doctrine of justification as its primary theme. He is best known for a collection of essays entitled *Der sogenannte historische Jesus und der geschichtliche, biblische Christus* (1892), in which he resists the current scholarly trend of separating the historical Jesus from the apostolic proclamation. Kähler claims that the Christ of the kerygma attested to in the NT is the Jesus of history. In Kähler's thought there is no separation of the kerygmatic Christ from the historical figure of Jesus, nor is Jesus the mere starting point of the early Christian kerygma. Rather, Jesus is the basis and content of the kerygma, and hence the object of faith.

D. S. FERGUSON

See also BULTMANN, RUDOLF; DEMYTHOLOGIZATION; NEO-ORTHODOXY.

Kant, Immanuel (1724–1804). German philosopher. In 1784 Kant wrote an essay asking the question, "What is enlightenment?" For Kant, enlightenment is humankind's emergence from immaturity. Enlightened people learn to think for themselves without relying on the authority of the church, the Bible, or the state to tell them what to do. Kant's philosophy represents an attempt to reappraise human knowledge, ethics, aesthetics, and religion in the light of this ideal. As a necessary first step he undertakes an examination of the scope and limitations of the human mind in relation to these subjects. This is the common theme of his three great critiques: *Critique of Pure Reason* (1781), *Critique of Practical Reason* (1788), and *Critique of Judgment* (1790), dealing respectively with human knowledge, ethics, and aesthetics. He also deals with ethics in his *Groundwork of the Metaphysic of Morals* (1785). He sets out his enlightened view of religion in *Religion Within the Limits of Reason Alone* (1793). Kant regards Christianity as a way of teaching ethics for the philosophically unsophisticated. Jesus is an enlightened moral teacher whose life exemplified his teaching.

C. BROWN

See also ENLIGHTENMENT, THE.

Keble, John (1792–1866)**.** English clergyman and poet. Keble was the founder of the Tractarian (Oxford) movement. From 1823 until his death he was a parish priest. From 1831 to 1841 he combined that duty with the professorship of poetry at Oxford. His first major publication was a cycle of poems he called *The Christian Year* (1827). With Newman he wrote many of the 90 *Tracts for the Times* (1833–41). In 1838, he became one of the editors of the *Library of the Fathers*. To this he contributed a translation of the works of Irenaeus. His high view of the Eucharist is seen in his *Eucharistical Adoration* (1857).

P. TOON

See also ANGLO-CATHOLICISM; OXFORD MOVEMENT; PUSEY, EDWARD BOUVERIE.

Kenosis, Kenotic Theology. (Gk. *kenoō)* Theological term referring to the incarnation of Christ. It is taken from Phil. 2:7, where Christ is spoken of as having "emptied himself" (RSV) and taken human form. The main thrust of kenotic theology is that in the incarnation there was some form of self-limitation involved when the preexistent Son became man.

History. Kenotic theology began as a serious form of reflection on Christology in the works of Gottfried Thomasius (1802–75), a German Lutheran theologian. In general kenotic theology was formulated in the light of three crucial concerns: (1) to find a way of understanding the person of Christ that allowed his full humanity to be adequately expressed; (2) to affirm that God truly was in Christ; and (3) to face the problem of the consciousness of Jesus, the God-man.

Types. These concerns by no means force a uniformity of formulations; in fact, there is a variety of possibilities for a Christology in terms of the idea of a preincarnate self-limitation by God the Son. There are two broad categories for understanding kenotic theories. One concerns the relation of the kenotic theory to traditional orthodox formulas. A kenotic theory can function as a supportive modification of a traditional formula or it can be presented as an alternative. A second distinction within kenotic theories concerns the place of the concept within the larger understanding of God's being and relation to the world. For example, A. E. Garvie's *Studies in the Inner Life of Jesus* (1907) shows the influence of a conservative form of Hegelian speculation on the nature of the Trinity. Here there is seen to be a movement or dialectic within God between fullness (Father) and self-limitation/expression (Son) that finds its historic expression in the incarnation kenotically understood.

Criticism. Kenotic theology as formulated in Germany (1860–80) and England (1890–1910) was clearly not without challenge. Indeed, many believe that the criticisms evoked have proven fatal. First, kenotic theology is not faithful to the total biblical witness. Second, the credibility of the concept of a divine preincarnate act of self-limitation must be questioned. Third, the supposed strength of kenotic theology, the consciousness of Jesus, is dubious at best. Is there genuine continuity of consciousness in the pre- and postincarnate states of the eternal Son, if there is self-limitation?

S. M. SMITH

See also CHRISTOLOGY.

Kerygma. (Gk. *kērygma*) Term used to describe the content of the early Christian message. It contains within its scope the life and work of Jesus, with particular emphasis on his conflicts, suffering, death, and resurrection from the dead. In addition, the kerygma connects the events of Jesus' life and death with the history of Israel, seeing them as the climax of God's redemptive activity.

Kerygma is often distinguished from *didachē*, the former being the message of God's act in Christ in calling people to the decision of faith and membership in the community of faith, the latter being the instruction in belief and morals that the new converts receive within the church. The NT as a whole may be said to be kerygmatic in character, but certain passages appear to contain quite specific kerygmatic formulations (Acts 2:22–24; Rom. 1:1–4; 1 Cor. 15:1–11; 1 Tim. 3:16). These passages should be viewed as but examples of the way the kerygmatic proclamation came to be stated in specific form.

D. S. FERGUSON

See also BULTMANN, RUDOLF; GOSPEL; PREACH, PREACHING.

Keswick Convention. Annual summer gathering of evangelical Christians, held since 1875 at Keswick in the Lake District of northwest England. It had its origin in the Moody–Sankey evangelistic campaign in Britain in 1873–74 and in the writings of the American religious leaders Asa Mahan, W. E. Boardman, and especially Mr. and Mrs. Robert P. Smith. This convention is the prototype of similar conventions not only in England but in many other countries throughout the world. From the beginning the convention has had as its aim the deepening of the spiritual life. It differs from the average Bible conference in that it aims not merely to impart Bible knowledge and spiritual uplift, but to be a spiritual clinic where defeated and ineffective Christians may be restored to spiritual health. It stands for no particular brand of denominational theology. Its motto is "All One in Christ Jesus." The majority of Keswick speakers have been from England, but many have come from other parts of the world. Among the better known are Donald G. Barnhouse, F. B. Meyer, H. C. G. Moule, Andrew Murray, John R. W. Stott, Hudson Taylor, and R. A. Torrey. The addresses given at the convention are published annually in a volume entitled *The Keswick Convention* or *The Keswick Week*.

S. BARABAS

Keys of the Kingdom. Spiritual authority to preach the gospel and exercise church discipline on earth. The concept of a key implies the opening of a door and permitting entrance to a place or realm. The NT carries this concept of authority as well (Luke 11:52; Rev. 1:18; 3:7; 9:1; 20:1). The keys of the kingdom of heaven therefore represent at least the authority to preach the gospel of Christ and thus to open the door of the kingdom of heaven and allow people to enter.

Two factors suggest, however, that the authority of the keys in Matt. 16:19 is broader than just preaching the gospel. First, the plural "keys" suggests authority over more than one door. Thus, more than just entrance to the kingdom is implied; some authority within the kingdom is also suggested. Second, Jesus completes the promise about the keys with a statement about "binding" and "loosing," which means placing under church discipline and releasing from church discipline (cf. Matt. 18:15–17).

Jesus' conversation with Peter in Matt. 16:16–19 does not indicate whether the disciplining authority of the keys would later be given to others. But in Matt. 18:18 this authority is broadened to the church generally whenever it meets and corporately exercises church discipline (as in Matt. 18:17). Jesus is teaching that church discipline will have divine sanction. But it is not as if the church must wait for God to endorse its actions; rather, whenever it enacts or releases from discipline it can be confident that God has already begun the process spiritually.

W. A. GRUDEM

See also CHURCH DISCIPLINE; KINGDOM OF CHRIST, GOD, HEAVEN; PETER, PRIMACY OF.

Kierkegaard, Søren (1813–1855). Danish philosopher. Kierkegaard was the unintentional founder of existentialism. Although his life was filled with personal tragedy and loneliness, he was familiar with the major literary, artistic, and intellectual movements of his day. Further, his writings were significantly shaped by personal relationships. Perhaps the most important of these was his broken engagement to Regine Olsen. His early works include *Fear and Trembling* (1843), *Philosophical Fragments* (1844), *The Concept of Dread* (1844), and *Concluding Unscientific Postscript to the Philosophical Fragments* (1846). Later came *Christian Discourses* (1850) and *Training in Christianity* (1850).

Kierkegaard's philosophic target is Hegel's idealism. Whereas Hegel emphasizes universals, Kierkegaard argues for decision and commitment. Hegal seeks an objective theory of knowledge; Kierkegaard believes in the subjectivity of truth. This emphasis on the subjective explains Kierkegaard's paradoxical understanding of faith. Genuine faith calls for a "leap of faith," a passionate commitment to God in the face of uncertainty and objective reasoning. For Kierkegaard, the free choice of faith alone brings authentic human existence. During his lifetime Kierkegaard was little known or read outside of Denmark. In the 20th century, as his works have been translated, Kierkegaard has come to be widely appreciated for his affirmation of faith and critique of the human condition.

D. B. ELLER

See also EXISTENTIALISM.

King, Christ as. See OFFICES OF CHRIST.

King, Martin Luther, Jr. (1929–1968). American clergyman and civil rights reformer. King's personal prestige was at its height in the early to mid-1960s. His keynote sermon, "I Have a Dream," at the great march on Washington in August 1963, is one of the most memorable in American history. He also directed the well-publicized Selma to Montgomery march in the spring of 1965. The first of these events mobilized support for the Civil Rights Act of 1964, the second for the federal Voter Registration Act of 1965. King was awarded the Nobel Peace Prize in 1964.

During the 1950s and 1960s King's prominence gave many Americans their first glimpse of the richness of black preaching. His speeches and writings draw heavily on the vocabulary of black Christian history. Yet his thought reflects a number of influences. It draws upon an evangelical realism concerning the nature of evil and a scriptural defense of nonviolence ("love your enemies"). King makes little distinction between spiritual and social problems involved in the civil rights struggle, however. Other elements also enter his thinking—the pacifism of Gandhi, the civil disobedience of Thoreau, the existentialist theology of Paul Tillich, the personalistic idealism that King had studied at Boston University, and the American public faith in democratic equality.

M. A. NOLL

See also BLACK THEOLOGY; CIVIL RIGHTS.

Kingdom of Christ, God, Heaven. (Gk. *hē basileia tou theou*) Principal theme of Jesus' teaching.

Terminology. "The kingdom of God" and "the kingdom of the heavens" are linguistic variations of the same idea. Jewish idiom often substituted a suitable term for deity (see, e.g., 1 Macc. 3:50; Pirke Aboth 1:3). Matthew preserves the Semitic idiom while the other Gospel writers render it into idiomatic Greek. The kingdom of God is also the kingdom of Christ. Jesus speaks of the kingdom of the Son of man (Matt. 13:41; 16:28) and "my kingdom" (Luke 22:30; John 18:36).

The Kingdom Is God's Reign. The "kingdom of God" means primarily the rule of God, his divine kingly authority. It is the divine authority and rule given by the Father to the Son (Luke 22:29). Christ will exercise this rule until he has subdued all that is hostile to God. When he has put all enemies under his feet, he will return the kingdom—his messianic authority—to the Father (1 Cor. 15:24–28). The kingdom (not kingdoms) now exercised by people in opposition to God is to become the kingdom of our Lord and of his Christ (Rev. 11:15) and "he will reign for ever and ever." In Rev. 12:10 the kingdom of God is parallel to the salvation and power of God and the authority of his Christ.

The Kingdom Is Soteriological. The object of the divine rule is the redemption of humankind and their deliverance from the powers of evil (1 Cor. 15:23–28). Christ's reign means the destruction of all hostile powers, the last of which is death. The kingdom of God is the reign of God in Christ, destroying all that is hostile to the divine rule. It is the redemptive rule of God in Christ defeating Satan and the powers of evil and delivering humankind from the power of evil. It brings "righteousness, peace and joy in the Holy Spirit" (Rom. 14:17). Entrance into the kingdom of Christ means deliverance from the power of darkness (Col. 1:13). The believer enters the kingdom only through a second birth (John 3:3, 5).

The Kingdom Is Dynamic. The kingdom is not an abstract principle; the kingdom *comes.* It is God's rule actively invading the kingdom of Satan.

The Kingdom Comes at the End of the Age. Jesus teaches us to pray, "Your kingdom come" (Matt. 6:10). When the Son of man comes in his glory, he will sit on the throne of judgment. The wicked will go away to eternal punishment, while the righteous will "inherit the kingdom" (Matt. 25:31–46). The same separation at the end of the age is pictured in Matt. 13:36–43. This eschatological coming of the kingdom will mean the *palingenēsia* (Matt. 19:28), the rebirth or transformation of the material order.

The Kingdom Has Come into History. The kingdom, which will come in glory at the end of the age, has already come into history in Jesus' person and mission. The redemptive rule of God has already invaded the realm of Satan to deliver humankind from the power of evil. In the exorcism of demons Jesus asserted the presence and power of the kingdom (Matt. 12:28). While the destruction of Satan awaits the coming of the Son of man in glory (Matt. 25:41; Rev. 20:10), Jesus has already defeated Satan. The kingdom of God is already present in our midst (Luke 17:21).

The Kingdom Is Supernatural. As the dynamic activity of God's rule the kingdom is supernatural. It is God's deed. Only the supernatural act of God can destroy Satan, defeat death (1 Cor. 15:26), raise the dead in imperishable bodies to inherit the blessings of the kingdom (1 Cor. 15:50–53), and transform the world order (Matt. 19:28).

The Mystery of the Kingdom. The presence of the kingdom in history is a mystery (Mark 4:11). Before this eschatological consummation, before the destruction of Satan, before the age to come, the kingdom of God has entered this age and invaded the kingdom of Satan in spiritual power to bring to us in advance the blessings of forgiveness (Mark 2:5), life (John 3:3), and righteousness (Matt. 5:20; Rom. 14:16), which belong to the age to come. The righteousness of the kingdom is an inner, absolute righteousness that can be realized only as God gives it to us. The parables of Matt. 13 embody this new revelation.

The Kingdom as the Realms of Redemptive Blessing. A reign must have a realm in which its authority is exercised. Thus the redemptive rule of God creates realms in which the blessings of the divine reign are enjoyed. There is both a future and a present realm of the kingdom.

The Future Realm. In the Gospels the eschatological salvation is described as entrance into the kingdom of God (Mark 9:47; 10:24), into the age to come (Mark 10:30), and into eternal life (Matt. 25:46; Mark 9:45; 10:17, 30;). These three idioms are interchangeable. The consummation of the kingdom requires the coming of the Son of man in glory. Satan will be destroyed (Matt. 25:41), the dead in Christ raised in imperishable bodies (1 Cor. 15:42–50) that are no longer susceptible to death (Luke 20:35–36) to inherit the kingdom of God (Matt. 25:34; 1 Cor. 15:50). Before his death Jesus promised his disciples that they would share renewed fellowship and his authority to rule in the new order (Matt. 26:29; Luke 22:29–30).

A Present Realm. Because the dynamic power of God's reign has invaded this evil age it has created a present spiritual realm in which the blessings of God's reign are experienced. The redeemed have already been delivered from the power of darkness and brought into the kingdom of Christ (Col. 1:13). The present and future aspects of the kingdom are inseparably tied together in Mark 10:15. The kingdom has come among us and its blessings have been extended in the person of Jesus. Those who now receive this offer of the kingdom with complete childlike trust will enter into the future eschatological kingdom of life.

The Kingdom and the Church. The kingdom is not the church. The apostles went about preaching the kingdom of God (Acts 8:12; 19:8; 28:23); it is impossible to substitute "church" for "kingdom" in such passages. There is, however, an inseparable relationship. The church is the fellowship of those who have accepted the offer of the kingdom, submitted to its rule, and entered into its blessings. The kingdom of God, then, creates the church. The redemptive rule of God brings into being a new people who receive the blessings of the divine reign. The kingdom also works through the church. The disciples preached the kingdom of God and performed signs of the kingdom (Matt. 10:7–8; Luke 10:9, 17). The powers of the kingdom were operative in and through them. Jesus said that he would give to the church the keys of the kingdom of heaven with power to bind and loose (Matt. 16:18–19). When the church has proclaimed the gospel of the kingdom in all the world as witness to all nations, Christ will return (Matt. 24:14) and bring the kingdom in glory.

G. E. LADD

See also CHURCH, THE.

Knowledge. The problems of knowledge raised by the biblical revelation are chiefly two: first, the nature of God's knowledge, and, second, our knowledge of God.

God is omniscient: "His understanding has no limit" (Ps. 147:5). God's omnipotence, perfection, and blessedness require him to know all things always. His knowledge is eternal. Such an immediate and uninterrupted knowledge has frequently been designated as intuitive. God sees all things at a glance. He does not learn. He was never ignorant, and he can never come to know more.

Because of God's intuitive omniscience, as well as by reason of his omnipotence and omnipresence, God is incomprehensible. This idea, however, turns our attention from God's knowledge of himself to our knowledge of God. Of course God comprehends himself. In this respect God is not merely comprehensible but is actually known, understood, and comprehended. But God is incomprehensible to us. Unfortunately, the term "incomprehensible" carries undesirable connotations. The word sometimes means irrational, unintelligible, or unknowable. Now, obviously if we could know or understand nothing about God, Christianity would be impossible. It is absolutely essential to maintain that the human mind is capable of grasping truth. God's incomprehensibility therefore must be taken to mean that we cannot know everything about God. It is necessary to assert that we can know some truths about God without knowing everything that God knows.

"We *know* also that the Son of God has come and has given us *understanding*, so that we might *know* him who is *true*" (1 John 5:20, emphasis added; cf. 1 Kings 17:24; Pss. 25:5; 43:3; 86:11; 119:43, 142, 147; Eph. 1:13). We can grasp God's meaning, the truth can be known, and God can be known. Christianity is the religion of a Book; it is a message of good news; it is a revelation or communication of truth from God to us. Only if the propositions of the Bible are rationally comprehensible, only if human intellect can understand what God says, only if God's mind and the human mind have some content in common, only so can Christianity be true and only so can Christ mean something to us.

G. H. Clark

See also Epistemology; Truth; Revelation, General; Revelation, Special.

Knowledge, Gift of. See Spiritual Gifts.

Knox, John (ca. 1514–1572). Scottish religious reformer. Knox pursued a vigorous and prolonged career of preaching and writing on behalf of Protestantism. In Geneva from 1555 to 1559, he came under the effective influence of Swiss Reformed leaders, particularly Calvin. Knox returned to Scotland in 1559, preaching at St. Giles Church in Edinburgh and working tirelessly for the establishment of a Reformed Church. The principle that dictated Knox's theology is that of *sola Scriptura*, that the Bible is the only authoritative basis upon which doctrine can be founded. At Calvin's request in 1559, Knox wrote his only academic theological work, the *Treatise on Predestination*. In 1560 Knox coauthored the Scots Confession, a document that served as the confessional basis of the Scottish church until the drafting of the Westminster Confession of Faith (1647). In the same year Knox helped draft the First Book of Discipline, in which the authors formulated a plan for the ecclesiastical and social life of the nation.

Knox's most distinctive contribution to Reformation theology was his concept of the relation of church and state. Knox found a precedent in ancient Israel for the right of God's people to disobey civil authority when it contradicted the higher law of Scripture (*An Admonition or Warning*, 1554). He eventually taught that Christians are obliged to overthrow an idolatrous (i.e., Roman Catholic) monarch, just as the Israelites overthrew idolatrous kings. He propounded this idea in *The First Blast of the Trumpet Against the Monstrous Regiment of Women* (1558).

H. Griffith

See also Scots Confession.

Koinonia. See FELLOWSHIP.

Küng, Hans (1928–). Roman Catholic theologian. Küng helped to promote many of the reforms advocated by the Second Vatican Council. He was, however, prepared to go much further, as his *Council, Reform and Reunion* (1961) testifies. In *Justification* (1964) he advances the startling thesis that the Calvinist and Catholic views of justification are substantially the same, the Council of Trent's teaching being an extreme that is defensible only as a necessary answer to the opposite extreme of Luther. Reservations about the papacy as a true pastorate, along with the publication of *Humanae vitae* (on birth control), launched him into a fuller investigation of authority in *Infallible?* (1972), in which he claims that historical relativity rules out infallibility and that the papal claim is more a political tool than a true doctrinal reality. The threat thus posed to a basic Roman Catholic principle could not pass unnoticed. An inquiry began that eventually led to Küng's admonishment in 1975 and finally, when he refused to recant, to his deposition, not from the Tübingen faculty, but from his official status as a Roman Catholic teacher. Since then his views have become more liberal, as his apologetic works *On Being a Christian* (1971) and *Does God Exist?* (1980) reveal.

G. W. BROMILEY

Kuyper, Abraham (1837–1920). Dutch theologian and statesman. Following the death of Groen van Prinsterer in 1876, Kuyper became the leader of the small but growing Calvinist movement in both church and state. He wrote many books and hundreds of articles on theology, philosophy, politics, art, and social issues, in which he sought to express a Christian world and life view. Kuyper founded two newspapers, the daily political paper *De Standaard* and the weekly religious paper *De Heraut*. In 1874 he entered parliament as a representative of the newly formed Anti-Revolutionary party. In 1880 he founded the Free University of Amsterdam. Active in church politics, Kuyper led a secession movement from the state church in 1886 to form the independent Gereformeerde Kerk (Reformed Church). In 1900 Kuyper's Anti-Revolutionary party was elected to office and he became prime minister for five years. Kuyper is best remembered for his development of the theological doctrine of common grace and his emphasis on the importance of the kingdom of God in Christian thinking.

I. HEXHAM

See also MAURICE, JOHN FREDERICK DENISON; VAN PRINSTERER, GUILLAUME GROEN.

Ll

Labor. See WORK.

Lactantius (ca. 240–ca. 320). Christian apologist. He was also tutor to Emperor Constantine's son, Crispus. Lactantius used history, philosophy, and especially his own literary training to defend Christianity. His principal work is *The Divine Institutes*, of which he also prepared an epitome. Its first three books are a refutation of paganism, giving a systematic presentation of the themes of early Christian apologetics. Books 4 through 7 set forth a philosophy of religion, emphasizing the true worship of the one God, justice, moral conduct, and the immortality of the soul. Lactantius has been called the "Christian Cicero," both for the excellence of his style and his debt to Cicero.

E. FERGUSON

Laity. (Gk. *laos*, "people") The whole people of God. Historically, the term has come to be used of those who are not specifically ordained to the ministry (clergy).

G. W. BROMILEY

See also CLERGY.

Lake of Fire. Place of eternal punishment for the wicked. The phrase occurs six times in the Book of Revelation and nowhere else in the NT or in Jewish literature. The beast and false prophet are thrown alive into the lake of fire before the millennial reign (19:20). After the final battle they are joined by Satan (20:10), and after the final judgment Death and Hades are also cast in (20:14; cf. Isa. 25:8; 1 Cor. 15:26) as well as those whose names are not in the book of life (20:15) and evil men (21:8).

W. D. MOUNCE

See also DEATH, THE SECOND; ETERNAL PUNISHMENT; GEHENNA; HELL; JUDGMENT.

Lamb of God. Title for Jesus used twice by John the Baptist (John 1:29, 35). The Greek word *amnos* ("lamb") is found also in Acts 8:32; 1 Pet. 1:19; and Isa. 53:7 (LXX). The use of the genitive of possession—the lamb *of God*—specifically relates Christ to God in the act of sin bearing. He is at once the sacrificial victim presented to God and the victim provided by God. In this relationship he bears the world's sin; he removes it by taking it on himself. As in Isa. 53 he bears on himself alone the iniquity of us all, by being "led like a lamb to the slaughter, and as a sheep before her shearers is silent." In the Book of Revelation the unqualified designation "lamb" (*arnion*) occurs eight times in symbolic reference to Christ and unites the two ideas of redemption and kingship. On one side are such descriptions of the slain Lamb (5:6, 12; 7:14; 21:27). The stress here falls upon the redeeming work of Christ as the Lamb of God. On the other side, connected with the title is the idea of sovereignty (5:6–7; 6:16; 7:17; 17:14; 22:1, 3).

H. D. MCDONALD

Landmarkism. Convictions maintained by some Baptists, mostly in the southern U.S., concerning the nature of the church. The adherents of Landmarkism hold that the NT model for the church is the local and visible congregation and that it violates NT principles to speak of a universal, spiritual church. They also believe that a historic "Baptist succession" may be traced from John the Baptist to modern Baptist churches in which believer's baptism and Landmarkian principles have prevailed. The Landmarkian emphasis takes its name from a pamphlet by James M. Pendleton, *An Old Landmark Re-Set* (1856), based on Prov. 22:28 (KJV): "Remove not the ancient landmark." It is the position of the American Baptist Association, the United Baptists, and some independent Baptist churches.

M. A. NOLL

See also BAPTIST TRADITION, THE.

Last Adam, The. See ADAM, THE LAST.

Last Day. Biblical expression used to refer to the day of resurrection and judgment. The OT prophets often predicted that "in that day" the Lord would act in a mighty way to judge evil and redeem his people. The NT continues the OT theme of judgment/redemption and announces the inauguration of the final eschatological day or time. Jesus proclaims that the time is fulfilled and parallels that announcement with the news that the kingdom of God is at hand. There can be little doubt that Jesus saw the prophesied age of judgment/salvation as having been initiated by his invasion of the demonic realm (Matt. 12:28). Yet it is *inaugurated*, not fully *realized*, eschatology, for Jesus says that something greater than Jonah and Solomon is here (namely, himself), but that there is a coming judgment when the people of Nineveh and the queen of the South will arise and condemn the present generation. It is clear that the NT understands the last day to have begun in the person and work of Jesus Christ, as Peter attests on the day of Pentecost when he quotes Joel 2:28–32 and associates the fulfillment of the prophecy with the ministry of Jesus, calling upon his hearers to repent and be baptized (Acts 2:14–39). Yet because of the continuation of suffering and demonic opposition to the gospel the NT writers understand that the eschatological day had been initiated but not consummated by Jesus; hence a second coming of Christ will complete the day. Viewed in this manner, the last day, now inaugurated, is a time of testing for Christians, and is moving inexorably toward its conclusion when each will receive either judgment or fulfillment.

R. G. GRUENLER

See also AGE, AGES; DAY OF CHRIST, GOD, THE LORD; ESCHATOLOGY; KINGDOM OF CHRIST, GOD, HEAVEN; LAST JUDGMENT, THE; SECOND COMING OF CHRIST; TRIBULATION.

Last Judgment, The. Eschatological event at the end of history when Christ will judge the living and the dead and assign them their eternal destiny (heaven or hell). This last judgment will be the climax of a process by which God holds nations and individuals accountable to him as Creator and Lord. The OT centers ultimate judgment in the day of Yahweh (or "the day"), when the Lord rids the world of every evil (Isa. 2:12–20; Zeph. 1:8–12). The intertestamental period focuses on the punishment—usually by disaster—of God's enemies, both human and supernatural (Enoch 10:6; 105:3–4). The NT builds on both OT and intertestamental teaching, expanding it in the light of Christ's incarnation. In the Synoptics, Jesus proclaims himself as the eschatological judge and calls attention to the day of judgment (Matt. 10:15; 11:22, 24; 12:36, 41–42; 23:33), describing it as a final separation of the evildoers from the righteous (Matt. 13:41–43, 47–50). In John's Gospel final judgment, committed by the Father to the Son (5:26–27), will follow the resurrection of both the evil and the good (5:28–29), sealing the decree that human faith or disobedience has already determined.

Paul amplifies these themes: judgment is connected with Christ's coming and the resurrection of the dead (1 Cor. 15:22–25) and Christ is judge (2 Tim. 4:1). The rest of the NT affirms the same message.

The theological implications of the biblical teaching are that final judgment is (1) the ultimate triumph of God's will and the consummate display of his glory in history; (2) the cosmic declaration that God is just; (3) the climax of Christ's ministry; (4) the reminder that human and cosmic history move toward a goal, measured by the purposes of God; (5) the absolute seal of human accountability—all believers are held responsible for their works, all unbelievers for their rebellion; (6) the most serious motive for Christian mission—in the face of such judgment the world's only hope is Christ's salvation (Acts 4:12).

D. A. HUBBARD

See also DAY OF CHRIST, GOD, THE LORD; ESCHATOLOGY; JUDGMENT; LAST DAY; SECOND COMING OF CHRIST; TRIBULATION.

Last Supper. See LORD'S SUPPER.

Last Times. See LAST DAY, DAYS.

Latimer, Hugh (ca. 1485–1555). English religious reformer Latimer was a preacher rather than scholar. He was charged with criticism of traditional beliefs such as pilgrimages, the existence of purgatory, and the veneration of saints. He protested that his preaching agreed with that of the fathers, and said that he did not object to certain traditions but simply did not regard them as essential. He was excommunicated and jailed for three months until he made complete submission. He was appointed in 1534 to preach before Henry VIII every Wednesday in Lent and, through the influence of his friend Thomas Cromwell, was consecrated bishop of Worcester in 1535. Under Edward VI he declined to exercise his bishopric because he felt it might inhibit his preaching, which attracted large crowds. On the accession of the Catholic Mary (1553) he was arrested. In 1555 he was burned in Oxford with Nicholas Ridley, whom he encouraged with words that became famous: "We shall this day light such a candle, by God's grace, in England as I trust shall never be put out."

J. D. DOUGLAS

Latitudinarianism. Attitudes of a group of late 17th-century Anglican divines characterized by a high regard for the authority of reason and a tolerant, antidogmatic temper. They included John Tillotson, archbishop of Canterbury; Edward Stillingfleet, bishop of Worcester; Simon Patrick, bishop of Chichester and Ely; Gilbert Burnett, Reformation historian and bishop of Salisbury; and Thomas Tenison, archbishop of Canterbury. They reacted against Puritan Calvinism and were broadly Arminian in outlook. They aligned themselves with progressive and liberal movements in the contemporary intellectual world. Hostile to scholasticism and Aristotelianism, they drew their inspiration largely from Descartes's "mechanical" philosophy. Respect for "the theater of nature" led them to support scientific developments such as the Royal Society. Their comprehensiveness allowed only a narrow core of fundamentals in religion. They were also the precursors of the Broad Churchmen of the 19th century, and of the modernists and radicals of more recent Anglican divinity.

D. F. WRIGHT

See also LOW CHURCH; CAMBRIDGE PLATONISTS.

Latria. Adoration given to God alone. It differs in quality from any veneration given to either the Virgin Mary or the saints, a point settled by the Second Council of Nicea.

T. J. GERMAN

See also DULIA; HYPERDULIA.

Latter Days. See LAST DAY, DAYS.

Laud, William (1573–1645). English prelate. Archbishop of Canterbury and adviser to Charles I, Laud served at the same time as a member of the King's Privy Council, on the Court of High Commission, and as chief of the Star Chamber Court. He possessed a clear, if limited, vision of an efficiently ordered church, a uniformity of worship, and an obedient populace. His policies alienated both Puritans and Parliament in England and the general populace in Scotland. He was, however, a loyal member of the Church of England, diligently upholding the catholic nature of the Protestant reform in England against Roman Catholic claims. His name has been given to that High Church movement at the Restoration that was in reaction to the Puritan rule. Early Tractarians in the 19th century perceived themselves as building upon Laud's view of Anglicanism.

C. F. ALLISON

See also ANGLO-CATHOLICISM; CAROLINE DIVINES; HIGH CHURCH MOVEMENT.

Lauds. See OFFICE, DAILY (DIVINE).

Law, Biblical Concept of. The law of the Lord lies at the very heart of the OT. God's law is a delight (Ps. 119:92), an object of love (v. 97), venerated as truth (v. 142), a means of peace (v. 165) and liberty (v. 45), and a treasure above all earthly wealth (v. 72).

God's Law in God's World. From the beginning God's law has been at the center of his dealings with humankind. The major stress in Gen. 2—the Creator's benevolence and bounty toward Adam—does not obscure the fact that Adam was under law and that it was through obedience that he would enter into life. The rest of the OT perpetuates this view of humankind. Only by obedience to God's law can people live successfully and prosper in God's world.

The Two Images of God. *Humankind in the Image of God.* Humankind is the crown of God's creation. The threefold use of the verb "to create" in Gen. 1:27 marks humankind as both the creature par excellence and the perfect creative act. This human uniqueness is summed up in the description "in our image, after our likeness."

Law in the Image of God. God has provided another image of himself on earth. Every aspect of human experience is regulated by God's law, including filial duty (Lev. 19:3), religious commitment (v. 4), ritual exactness (v. 5), care of the needy (v. 9), and honesty in deed and word (vv. 11–12). Yet all this variety suspends from one central truth: "I am the Lord.," "I AM WHO I AM" (Exod. 3:14). The significance of the recurring claim is "You must do this or that because I AM WHO I AM"; every precept of the law is a reflection of "WHO I AM." Humankind is the living, personal image of God; the law is the written, preceptual image of God. The Lord longs for his people to live in his image, and to that end he has given them his law.

A Truly Human Life. When a person in the image of God and law in the image of God come together in the fully obedient life, then that person is living a truly human life. The law is given both to activate and to direct human nature into a truly human life; any other life is subhuman. Of course, it is true that in a world of sinners the law, regrettably, has to give itself to the task of curbing and rebuking antisocial and degrading practices, but OT law has, to a far greater extent, the function of liberating people to live according to their true nature.

The Pillars of True Religion. The full flowering of the law of God in the OT came through the ministry of Moses and in the context of that foundational series of events that began with the exodus and climaxed at Mount Sinai.

Grace and Law. Grace precedes law. The people of Israel who had been liberated from Egypt and redeemed by grace came to Mount Sinai to receive the law. The law of God is not a system of merit whereby the unsaved seek to earn divine favor but a pattern of life given by the Redeemer to the redeemed so that they might know how to live for his good pleasure.

The Way of Holiness by Obedience. The law that God gave through Moses had several aspects—civil, dealing with the legal system of the people of God considered as a state, with courts and penalties; moral, the law of holy living; and religious, the law of the ceremonies and sacrifices. It is the latter two aspects that concern us here. The first desire of God is that his redeemed people should be obedient. To keep the law is not a new bondage but a proof that the old bondage is past (Exod. 20:2). Law giving leads up to a pledge of obedience (Exod. 24:7) that matches the longing of the Lord (Deut. 5:29). In the OT as in the NT (Acts 5:32) obedience is a means of grace. A life based on the law of the Lord is constantly nourished by secret springs and is consistently fruitful (Ps. 1:2–3); it is under the blessing of God (Ps. 1:1), for by his law the Lord has made his people secure from bondage (Exod. 20:2). The way of obedience is the way of true liberty (Ps. 119:45).

The Way of Fellowship. Three main sacrifices were enjoined in OT law: the burnt offering, the peace offering, and the sin offering. The burnt offering expresses the double idea of acceptance before and dedication to God. Its aroma is pleasing to the Lord (Lev. 1:9), indicating his delight to accept it and the one who offers it (Gen. 8:20–21). The truth of acceptance is underlined when the burnt offering reappears in token form in the peace offering; the fat of the offering (Lev. 3:3–5) is regarded as a burnt offering in miniature and is regarded as "food" (Lev. 3:11; cf. 21:8). This means that the Lord, accepting both offering and offerer, is delighted to sit at table with the believer, condescending to participate in the feast of reconciliation. But the burnt offering also expresses dedication.

The peace offering looks both Godward and humankindward. Godward, it expresses thanksgiving and personal love (Lev. 7:12, 16), but it is commanded that this joyous response to God's goodness should be marked also by fellowship with others; the priest has his share (Lev. 7:31–34), and the command of Lev. 7:16 is fulfilled in the family celebration of Deut. 12:7. The object of the sin offering is forgiveness. Awareness of a particular fault brings individual sinners with their offering (Lev. 4:23), and the result is divine forgiveness (Lev. 4:20, 26, 31, 35). Two acts are common to all three main categories of sacrifice: the laying on of hands (Lev. 1:4; 3:2; 4:4) and the ritual of the blood (Lev. 1:5; 3:2; 4:5–6). In connection with burnt offerings and sin offerings these acts are explicitly linked with making atonement (Lev. 1:4; 4:20, 26). The sacrifices thus find their focus in the price-paying concepts of a substitution-based theology.

That the OT concept of law is, in fact, the biblical concept of law is nowhere seen more clearly than in the continuance throughout the Bible of the same pillars of true religion: grace and law. For the purpose of God remains the same, the obedience of his people, and it remains true that those who thus walk in the light find that the blood of Jesus Christ cleanses them from all their sin.

J. A. Motyer

See also Civil Law and Justice in Bible Times; Criminal Law and Punishment in Bible Times; Offerings and Sacrifices in Bible Times.

Law, William (1686–1761). English theologian and devotional writer. In 1714, for refusing to take the oath of allegiance to George I, he was deprived of his Cambridge fellowship and became a nonjuror (although remaining in communion with the Church of England). From 1723 until 1737 he acted as a tutor to Edward Gibbon, father of the historian. In 1740 he retired to King's Cliffe, where he remained until his death, living a disciplined life of prayer and good works, particularly the establishment of much-needed schools and almshouses. Law's most enduring contribution to English religion was in the realm of Christian devotion. His most important work was *A Serious Call to a Devout and Holy Life* (1729). Law argues that if Christians really desire to follow Christ, it must be in every area of activity, in business and leisure as well as in strictly devotional practices. The Christian life, he maintains, must be a continual practice of humility, self-denial, and renunciation of the world.

N. V. HOPE

See also MYSTICISM.

Law and Grace. See LAW, BIBLICAL CONCEPT OF.

Law and Justice in Ancient Times. See CIVIL LAW AND JUSTICE IN BIBLE TIMES.

Lawless One. See ANTICHRIST.

Laying on of Hands. Act of laying one's hands upon the head of another, generally as part of a religious rite. The laying on of hands is performed in different ways and with various meanings in the OT, NT, Judaism, and the Christian church. The simple placing of hands on a person was practiced when pronouncing a blessing (Gen. 48:14–22; Matt. 19:15; Mark 10:13, 16; Luke 18:15). Jesus and the disciples touched people in order to heal them (Matt. 8:15; Mark 1:41; 5:23; 6:5; 8:23, 25; Luke 4:40; Acts 28:8). The bestowal of the Spirit was also accompanied by the laying on of hands (Acts 8:14–17; 19:1–7). Ultimately the laying on of hands came to be associated mainly with ordination (Acts 6:6; 13:3; 1 Tim. 4:14; 2 Tim. 1:6).

Paul and Barnabas "appointed" (Gk. *cheirotoneō*, lit. "stretch out the hand") elders in every city (Acts 14:23), and a brother was "chosen" (same verb) by the churches to accompany Paul in carrying the collection (2 Cor. 8:18–19). This verb, *cheirotoneō*, which could mean "elect" or "point out," became, along with its cognate *cheirotonia*, the principal term for the laying on of hands at ordination. The laying on of hands, along with prayer, has continued in Christian ordination until today, whereas the laying on of hands ceased to be used for ordination in Judaism sometime after the 2d century. Various Christian churches have also used the laying on of hands in such ceremonies as confirmation, healing, and absolution.

W. L. LIEFELD

Lector. See MINOR ORDERS.

Leibniz, Gottfried Wilhelm (1646–1716). German philosopher and mathematician. From 1673 until the end of his life Leibniz worked for the Duke of Brunswick assembling and cataloging the vast archives of the House of Brunswick as he wrote a large history of the family. A man with many interests and intellectual contacts, he founded the Prussian Academy in 1700 and tried to promote peace between Protestant and Roman Catholic theologians. Leibniz viewed God as a free and rational being, a being who could have created any type of world that he desired. He believed that God must have created the best of all possible worlds, one in which people are rewarded and punished according to their conduct. God is not responsible for evil. Evil is the result of human freedom. In *Monadology* (1720) Leibniz agrees that matter consists of atoms, but contends that beyond and beneath the divisible physical atoms are the indivisible metaphysical atoms. These spiritual force centers he called *monads*. Leibniz has been viewed as Germany's greatest 17th-century philosopher and one of the most universal minds of all times. He is indicative of the great diversity within early modern rationalism.

D. A. RAUSCH

See also ENLIGHTENMENT, THE; RATIONALISM; SPINOZA, BENEDICT DE; THEODICY.

Leipzig Disputation (1519). Debate held at the University of Leipzig June 27–July 16, 1519, which involved Johann Eck, Martin Luther, and Andreas von Carlstadt. Topics included grace and free will, papal authority, and church councils. The debate was a tactical success for Eck because he succeeded in identifying Luther with Jan Hus (1372–1415), a condemned heretic. For Luther the Leipzig disputation was a turning point in his career, as it revealed the extent of his estrangement from the official position of the church and helped to clarify his thought on the central issues.

R. W. HEINZE

See also ECK, JOHANN; LUTHER, MARTIN.

Lent. Forty-day period of penitence and prayer that begins on Ash Wednesday and is preparatory for the feast of Easter. It is a form of retreat for Christians preparing to celebrate the paschal mystery. It became a 40-day retreat during the 7th century to reflect the 40 days spent by Christ in the desert; before this Lent usually lasted only a week.

T. J. GERMAN

See also ASH WEDNESDAY; CHRISTIAN YEAR; EASTER.

Leo I, the Great. Pope (440–461). Leo I was important in the development of the medieval papacy. He led the Western Church at the very end of imperial dominion in the West. It was a period ripe for the advance of papal power in both theory and reality. Leo put previous claims of papal supremacy based on the Petrine doctrine into a highly structured legal framework. His letters and decretals made clear his vision of a hierarchical church with everything converging on Rome. He provided the indispensable idea of *plenitudo potestatis* (plentitude of power) for the See of Peter where the pope, as heir of Peter, ruled over the whole church. His claims were rejected in the East, where in 451 the Council of Chalcedon gave the patriarch of Constantinople equal status. When he died in 461, Leo left in the papal archives powerful documentation upon which later popes from Gregory the Great to Innocent III could draw in order to achieve ultimate power in Western Christendom.

C. T. MARSHALL

See also PAPACY.

Lewis, Clive Staples (1898–1963). Anglican scholar, novelist, and Christian apologist. Lewis is perhaps best known for his literary fantasies that explore theological concepts. He was professor of Medieval and Renaissance English at Cambridge University. Converted in the late 1920s, first to theism and then to Christianity, he saw himself as an "empirical theist" who arrived at the existence of God through induction. In his two autobiographical works, *The Pilgrim's Regress* (1933) and *Surprised by Joy* (1955), he presents the concept of *Sehnsucht*, or sense of longing for the infinite, as the motivating factor in his conversion. This becomes a basic element in all his apologetics. Lewis's theological writings are renowned for their lucidity of style and force of logic. His theology is predominantly romantic. *Miracles: A Preliminary Study* (1947) and *The Problem of Pain* (1940) are his most well known volumes of direct theological exposition. *The Screwtape Letters* (1943) —which quickly sold over one million copies—and *The Great Divorce* (1946) are fictional explorations of the nature of temptation and of redemption. Impressive as these are, Lewis is at his best in his mythopoeic writings. He uses the term "myth" to designate that which is ultimately true but ineffable, that is, nondescribable in rational terms, able to be glimpsed only by the imagination. His chief mythopoeia are *Till We Have Faces: A Myth Retold* (1956); his trilogy of space travel, *Out of the Silent Planet* (1938), *Perelandra* (1943), and *That Hideous Strength* (1945); and his seven-volume *Chronicles of Narnia* (1950–56). Experts in children's literature rank the latter as among the finest stories of our time.

R. N. HEIN

See also MACDONALD, GEORGE.

Liberal Evangelicalism. Understanding of the Christian faith based on the evangelical tradition of the church, but also committed to a scientific worldview and its historical and psychological methodology. Used particularly in the early decades of the century by some within the Church of England (e.g., T. Guy Rogers, V. F. Storr, E. W. Barnes) to clarify their continuing evangelical orientation, the term has sometimes been adopted to describe other theological moderates who have sought a synthesis of the gospel and modern knowledge.

R. K. JOHNSTON

See also BAILLIE, JOHN; DENNEY, JAMES; EVANGELICALISM; FORSYTH, PETER TAYLOR; LEWIS, CLIVE STAPLES; LIBERALISM, THEOLOGICAL; MACKINTOSH, HUGH ROSS.

Liberalism, Theological. Major shift in theological thinking that occurred in the late 19th century characterized primarily by the desire to adapt religious ideas to modern culture and modes of thinking. It is also known as modernism. It is an extremely elusive concept. A variety of shades of liberal thinking exist, it has changed in character during the passage of time, and the distinctions between liberalism in Europe and North America are considerable.

Main Features. Liberals insist that the world has changed since the time Christianity was founded so that biblical terminology and creeds are incomprehensible to people today. Although most would start from the inherited orthodoxy of Jesus Christ as the revelation of a savior God, they try to rethink and communicate the faith in terms that can be understood by people today. Liberals maintain that Christianity has always adapted its forms and language to particular cultural situations and the "modernists" in any given age have merely been those who were most candid and creative in doing this. A second element of liberalism is its rejection of religious belief based on authority alone. All beliefs must pass the tests of reason and experience, and our minds must be open to new facts and truth, regardless of where these may originate. No questions are closed or settled and religion must not protect itself from critical examination. As the Bible is the work of writers who were limited by their times, it is neither supernatural nor an infallible record of divine revelation, and thus does not possess absolute authority.

A central idea of liberal theology is divine immanence. God is seen as present and dwelling within the world, not apart from or elevated above the world as a transcendent being. He is its soul and life as well as the creator. Thus God is found in the whole of life and not just in the Bible or a few revelatory events. Because he is present and works in all that happens, there can be no distinction between the natural and supernatural. The divine presence is disclosed in such things as rational truth, artistic beauty, and moral goodness. Immanence contributed to such common liberal beliefs as the existence of a universal religious sentiment that lay behind the institutions and creeds of particular religions and the superiority of good works (both in individual and collective terms) over professions and confessions. God is seen as the one who enables people to integrate their personality and thereby achieve perfection. This, of course, requires the restatement of many traditional Christian doctrines. The incarnation was the entrance into the world through the person of Jesus Christ of a molding and redeeming force in humanity, and it signified and ratified the actual presence of God in humanity. Jesus' prophetic personality is the clearest and most challenging demonstration of the divine power in the world, and he is both the revelation of God and the goal of humankind's longing. Just as Jesus' resurrection was the continuation of his spirit and personality, so it is with all mortals after the death of the physical body. Sin or evil is seen as imperfection, ignorance, maladjustment, and immaturity, not the fundamental flaw in the universe. These hindrances to the unfolding of the inner nature may be overcome by persuasion and education, and salvation or regeneration is their removal. Religion represents the dimension of life in which personal values receive their highest expression, and its power possesses spiritually therapeutic qualities. Prayer, for example, heightens spiritual sensitivity and confers the moral benefits of stability, self-control, and peace of mind.

Liberalism also manifests a humanistic optimism. Society is moving toward the realization of the kingdom of God, which will be an ethical state of human perfection. The church is the movement of those who are dedicated to following the principles and ideals set forth by Jesus, the one who provided the ultimate example of an unselfish life of love, and the members of this fellowship work together to build the kingdom. Liberal eschatology views God's work among us as that of redemption and salvation, not punishment for sin, and this end will be reached in the course of a continuous, ascending progress. Theological liberalism originated in Germany, where a number of theological and philosophical currents converged in the 19th century. German thought had a profound impact on British and American theology, but indigenous movements in both places, the Broad Church tradition in Britain and Unitarianism in America, significantly shaped liberalism's development there.

Decline and Persistence. By the time of World War I liberalism had made considerable inroads in the Protestant churches in Europe and North America, but it rested on shaky foundations. World War I shattered the heady optimism that was its stock in trade, while conservatives counterattacked. By the 1960s most liberals had abandoned humanistic optimism, progressive cultural immanentism, and the dream of an earthly kingdom, but they gave no ground on the nonliteral interpretation of the Bible. Many had a renewed interest in natural theology and stressed the importance of social change. The "radical" and "secular" theologians talked about the traditional concept of God as being "dead" in this secular age, and gloried in the God who comes to us in the events of social change. They were optimistic about the creative possibilities open to secular humankind, held up love as the sufficient norm of ethical behavior, and reaffirmed the lordship of Christ and his call to discipleship.

R. V. PIERARD

See also CATHOLICISM, LIBERAL; CHICAGO SCHOOL OF THEOLOGY; HIGHER CRITICISM; SOCIAL GOSPEL, THE; TÜBINGEN SCHOOL; UNITARIANISM.

Liberation Theology. Movement that attempts to unite theology and sociopolitical concerns. It is not actually a new school of theological theory but a movement. Furthermore, it is more accurate to speak of liberation theology in the plural, for these theologies of liberation find contemporary expression among blacks, feminists, Asians, Hispanic Americans, and Native Americans. The most significant and articulate expression of liberation theology to date has taken place in Latin America. Theological themes have been developed in the Latin American context that have served as models for other theologies of liberation.

There are at least four major factors that have played a significant role in the formulation of liberation theology. First, it is a post-Enlightenment theological movement. The leading proponents—such as Gustavo Gutiérrez, Juan Segundo, and José Miranda—are responsive to the epistemological and social perspectives of Kant, Hegel, and Marx. Second, liberation theology has been greatly influenced by European political theology and North American radical theology. Third, it is for the most part a Roman Catholic theological movement. After Vatican II (1965) and the conference of the Latin American episcopate (CELAM II) in Medellín, Colombia (1968), a significant number of Latin American leaders within the Roman Catholic Church turned to liberation theology as the theological voice for the Latin American church. Fourth, it is a theological movement specifically and uniquely situated in the Latin American context. Liberation theologians contend that their continent has been victimized by colonialism, imperialism, and multinational corporations.

Theological Method. Gutiérrez defines theology as "critical reflection on historical praxis." Doing theology requires theologians to be immersed in their own intellectual and sociopolitical history. Theology is not a system of timeless truths, engaging the theologian in the repetitious process of systematization and apologetic argumentation. Theology is a dynamic, ongoing exercise involving contemporary insights into knowledge (epistemology), humankind (anthropology), and history (social analysis). "Praxis" means more than the application of theological truth to a given situation. It means the discovery and the formation of theological truth out of a given historical situation through personal participation in the Latin American class struggle for a new socialist society.

Theological Interpretation. Liberation theologians claim that orthodoxy is dependent upon ancient Greek notions that perceived God as a static being who is distant and remote from human history. But, God cannot be summarized in objectifying language or known through a list of doctrines. God is found in the course of human history. God is not a perfect, immutable entity, "squatting outside the world." He stands before us on the frontier of the historical future (Assmann). God is the driving force of history causing the Christian to experience transcendence as a "permanent cultural revolution" (Gutiérrez). Suffering and pain become the motivating forces for knowing God. The God of the future is the crucified God who submerges himself in a world of misery. God is found on the crosses of the oppressed rather than in beauty, power, or wisdom.

The biblical notion of salvation is equated with the process of liberation from oppression and injustice. Sin is defined in terms of inhumane acts toward the oppressed. Biblical history is important insofar as it models and illustrates the quest for justice and human dignity. Israel's liberation from Egypt in the exodus and Jesus' life and death stand out as the prototypes for the contemporary human struggle for liberation. These biblical events signify the spiritual significance of the secular struggle for liberation. The church and the world can no longer be segregated. The church must allow itself to be inhabited and evangelized by the world. Joining in solidarity with the oppressed against the oppressors is an act of "conversion," and "evangelization" is announcing God's participation in the human struggle for justice. The importance of Jesus for liberation theology lies in his exemplary struggle for the poor and the outcast. The meaning of Jesus' incarnation is found in his total immersion in a historical situation of conflict and oppression. His life absolutizes the values of the kingdom—unconditional love, universal forgiveness, and continual reference to the mystery of the Father. Jesus' death is unique because he historicizes in exemplary fashion the suffering experienced by God on all the crosses of the oppressed.

Theological Critique. The strength of liberation theology is in its compassion for the poor and its conviction that the Christian should not remain passive and indifferent to their plight. Liberation theology is a plea for costly discipleship and a reminder that following Jesus has practical social and political consequences. Liberation theology's weakness stems from an application of misleading hermeneutical principles and a departure from historic Christian faith. Liberation theology rightly condemns a tradition that attempts to use God for its own ends but wrongly denies God's definitive self-disclosure in biblical revelation.

D. D. WEBSTER

See also HOPE, THEOLOGY OF.

Liberty, Christian. To live is to choose; to choose is to live. The exercise of choice, however, does not in itself make us free. Freedom, or liberty (the terms are here synonymous), is not *that* we can choose but *what* we choose. Indeed, the freedom of the Christian is a divine gift. Christian liberty thus bears two faces: (1) freedom *from* human disability and enslavement to the devil; and (2) freedom *for* striving to know and do the will of God.

Freedom From. "For he has rescued us from the dominion of darkness and brought us into the kingdom of the Son he loves" (Col. 1:13; cf. John 8:32, 36; Eph. 2:2). God liberates in Christ. In Christ we are liberated *from* servitude to the gods of this age, but we only enter into a full realization of this gracious liberty as we strive daily to live positively for God.

Freedom For. The pivot that hinges "freedom from" to "freedom for" is the divine law, written by God upon tablets of stone and the flesh of the human heart. First, the law causes us to acknowledge our sin (Rom. 3:20), and thus drives us through repentance to Christ (Gal. 3:24). Then, once liberated in Christ, we find in the law the goal, values, and purposes summed up in the term "love" (John 14:21, 23; Gal. 5:14). And love weaves, by the power of the Spirit, our choices into freedom. "Freedom from" by grace and through Christ becomes in the life of the believer a blessed "freedom for" by the Spirit and in Christ.

L. DE KOSTER

Liberty, Religious. See TOLERANCE.

Life. ***God as the Source.*** As the one being who has no cause outside himself, God is frequently disclosed in both the OT and NT as "the living God" (Deut. 5:26; Josh. 3:10; Ps. 84:2; Matt. 26:63; Rom. 9:26). It is specifically a positive description of him as present and active in the world, and in particular among his chosen people as Creator and Sustainer of their national existence, as well as being himself the never-failing energy of its physical and spiritual life.

In the OT. The two most important Hebrew words translated "life" by the English versions are *hayyîm*; and *nepeš*. The LXX distinguishes between them by translating the former as *zoē* and the latter as *psychē*. The term *rûaḥ*, often a synonym for *nepeš* (Isa. 26:9), means generally "life energy." As the "breath principle" of both people and animals (Eccles. 3:19; cf. Gen. 6:17; 7:15, 22) it has its source in God.

Human Life. Humankind has *ḥayyîm* (Gen. 7:21; Lev. 11:10 AV; Ezek. 47:9 AV; Acts 17:28). Ecclesiastes declares that this life is God-given (5:18; cf. 8:15), and the psalmist speaks of "the God of my life" (42:8). As living, humankind has *nepeš* or existence as a living being apart from God (Gen. 2:7). *Rûaḥ*, on the other hand, expresses humankind as drawing life from God. Yet humankind exists as a fully integrated being, a living psychosomatic unity. Life is thus God's supreme gift.

In the NT. Three words are translated "life": *bios, zoē,* and *psychē.*

Bios, the few times it is used, connotes life as the present state of existence (Luke 8:14; 1 Tim. 2:2; 2 Tim. 2:4; 1 Pet. 4:2; 1 John 2:16). *Zoē*, a frequently used word, corresponds generally with the OT *ḥayyîm* to denote the state of one possessed of vitality, one who is animate (Luke 12:15; Acts 8:33; 17:25; 1 Pet. 3:10). *Psychē* generally equates with the OT *nepeš* as the animating principle of life (Acts 20:10) and thus stands for one's "self" (Rom. 13:1).

Present Life. Jesus regarded life as a sacred trust from God, and in that realization he himself lived. He did not come to destroy life but to save it (Luke 9:56 AV) and to give it overflowing zest (John 10:10).

Eternal Life. The concept of eternal life is present in the teaching of Jesus (Matt. 19:29; 25:46; cf. 18:8–9; 19:17, and pars.), but it figures most prominently in the Johannine writings and means more than mere everlastingness. It is a life of a new quality—the God-type life. It is best understood in contrast to death, to that which is perishing (John 3:16; 5:24; 10:28). When expressing the significance of salvation in Christ in terms of life, Paul has the same general account as does John. He uses the phrase nine times. Of this life Christ is at once its source and mediator (Rom. 6:23)—indeed the two, Christ and life, are virtually identified (Gal. 2:20; Phil. 1:21; Col. 3:3–4).

Resurrection Life. Eternal life is not only a present possession, it carries the hope of future realization. Paul gives prominence to the future aspect and coordinates it with immortality (Rom. 2:7; cf. 2 Cor. 5:4; 2 Tim. 1:10), while contrasting it with death (Rom. 6:23) and corruption (Gal. 6:8). As himself the "resurrection and the life" (John 11:25), Christ has "destroyed death and has brought life and immortality to light through the gospel" (2 Tim. 1:10).

H. D. McDonald

See also Eternal Life; Resurrection of the Dead.

Life, Book of. See Book of Life.

Life, Everlasting. See Eternal Life.

Light. Ultimate blessedness that God gives to us. In the OT God is pictured as creating light (Gen. 1:3) and being clothed with light (Ps. 104:2). In the NT *phōs* is employed as an expression for the eternally real in contrast to the *skotos* of sin and unreality. In 1 John 1:5 it is stated absolutely that *ho theos phōs estin.* James calls God, as Creator of heavenly bodies, *patros tōn phōtōn* (1:17). By becoming incarnate the Logos becomes *phōs tou kosmou* (John 8:12). Paul's conversion is essentially an encounter with the *phōs ek tou ouranou* (Acts 9:3). The scales of sinful darkness fall from his eyes, and he is commissioned as a light for the Gentiles (Acts 13:47).

D. H. Tongue

Likeness of God. See Image of God.

Limbo. Roman Catholic concept adduced by medieval theologians as the place or state of those souls after death who did not fit into either heaven or hell. In fact there were two limbos. The limbo of the fathers (*limbus patrum*) was for the souls of OT saints; Christ's descent into hell in the creed was interpreted as his liberating these souls and taking them to heaven. More important was the limbo of unbaptized infants (*limbus infantum*), a perpetual state free from the pain of sense but without supernatural salvation and the enjoyment of God.

J. P. DONNELLY

See also INTERMEDIATE STATE.

Limited Atonement. See ATONEMENT, EXTENT OF THE.

Literalism. Commitment to strict exactness of words or meanings in translation or interpretation. Most often literalism is used in connection with biblical interpretation. Since the Reformation at least two main trajectories of thought have come to be associated with literalism. One approaches the text in such a strict, unimaginative way that word and letter are permitted to suppress the spirit of the text. Interpretation becomes a mechanical, grammatical, logical process.

The other employs different attitudes and methodologies, seeking to apply interpretative principles and rules with a sense of appropriateness and sensitivity. In addition to grammatical and philosophical investigations, it uses information about the author's historical and cultural situation that may aid in interpretation. Differing literary forms and genres are handled with methods suitable to their type. Here "literalism" means to seek the plain meaning without exaggeration, distortion, or inaccuracy.

J. J. SCOTT, JR.

Liturgical Year. See CHRISTIAN YEAR; WORSHIP IN THE CHURCH.

Liturgies. See WORSHIP IN THE CHURCH.

Logical Positivism. See POSITIVISM.

Logos. Most usual Greek term for "word" in the NT. It occasionally has other meanings (e.g., account, reason, motive); in the prologue to the Fourth Gospel (John 1:1, 14) and in other Johannine writings (1 John 1:1; Rev. 19:13) it is used of the second person of the Trinity.

Johannine Usage. According to John 1:1–18 the entire work of creation was carried out through (*dia*, "by," v. 3) the Logos. The source of life (1:4, probable punctuation) and light of the world (cf. 9:5) and of every person (1:9, probable punctuation), and still continuing (present tense in 1:5) this work, the Logos became incarnate, revealing the sign of God's presence and his nature (1:14). The prologue to the Gospel of John thus sets out three main facets of the Logos and his activity: his divinity and intimate relationship with the Father; his work as the agent of creation; and his incarnation.

Background of the Term. *OT.* In the OT God creates by the word (Gen. 1:3; Ps. 33:9). His word is sometimes spoken of semipersonally (Pss. 107:20; 147:15, 18); it is active, dynamic, achieving its intended results (Isa. 50:10–11). The wisdom of God is personified (Prov. 8—note especially vv. 22–31 on wisdom's work in creation).

Palestinian Judaism. The rabbis used the word *mēmrâ*, "word," as a periphrasis for "God." This usage occurs in the Targums.

Greek Philosophy. Among the philosophers the Logos is a shock absorber between God and the universe, and the manifestation of the divine principle in the world.

Hellenistic Judaism. In Alexandrian Judaism there was full personification of the Word in creation (Wisd. Sol. 9:1; 16:12). In the writings of Philo, the Logos is "the image"; the first form (*protogonos*), the representation of God; and even "Second God" (*deuteros theos*), the means whereby God creates the world from the great waste; and, moreover, the way whereby God is known (i.e., with the mind).

Sources of John's Doctrine. John's use of *logos* in the first chapter of his Gospel differs radically from philosophic usage. For the Greeks, Logos was essentially reason; for John, it is essentially word. Language common to Philo and the NT has led many to see John as in Philo's debt. But one refers naturally to Philo's Logos as "It," to John's as "He." The source of John's Logos doctrine is in the Person and work of the historical Christ. Its expression takes its suitability primarily from the OT connotation of "word" and its personification of wisdom. Christ is God's active Word, his saving revelation to fallen humankind.

Logos in Early Christian Use. The apologists found the Logos a convenient term in expounding Christianity to pagans. They used its sense of "reason," and some were thus enabled to see philosophy as a preparation for the gospel. The Hebraic overtones of "word" were underemphasized, although never quite lost. Some theologians distinguished between the *Logos endiathetos,* or Word latent in the Godhead from all eternity, and the *logos prophorikos,* uttered and becoming effective at the creation.

A. F. WALLS

See also JESUS CHRIST; JOHN, THEOLOGY OF; WORD, WORD OF GOD, WORD OF THE LORD.

Loisy, Alfred Firmin (1857–1940). French linguist, philosopher of religion, and biblical scholar. In 1902 Loisy published *L'evangile et l'eglise* (*The Gospel and the Church*). In 1903, along with four of his other books, it was put on the Index of prohibited books by the Roman Catholic Church. In 1904 he resigned his position at the Ecole Pratique, and in 1906 he ceased to exercise his priestly functions. In 1907 Pope Pius X, in his decree *Lamentabili* and his encyclical *Pascendi gregis* ("Against the Errors of the Modernists"), condemned Loisy's positions as "the synthesis of all heresies." Refusing to accept this papal condemnation, Loisy was excommunicated in 1908. From 1909 to 1930 Loisy was professor of the history of religions in the College de France, but drew no nearer to Catholic orthodoxy and died unreconciled to the Church.

N. V. HOPE

See also CATHOLICISM, LIBERAL.

Lombard, Peter. See PETER LOMBARD.

Lord. See GOD, NAMES OF.

Lord, Jesus as. Probably the earliest of the Christian confessions that eventually worked its way into the various acts of Christian worship (Rom. 10:9; 2 Cor. 12:3; Phil. 2:11). It is important to note that it is Jesus as the risen and exalted one who is Lord. The lordship of Jesus is confessed by the believing community in virtue of his exaltation to the right hand of God (Acts 2:36). According to Paul, Jesus as Lord is declared Son of God with power through his resurrection from the dead (Rom. 1:4). This must not be taken to mean that lordship is not to be ascribed to the earthly ministry of Jesus, but to reinforce the point that the significance of the title in the life of the church is linked to his exaltation. To underscore this, Ps. 110:1 is drawn on heavily in the NT affirmation of Christ's lordship (Matt. 22:44; 26:64 and pars.; Acts 2:34–35; Heb. 1:3). Having ascended on high he has given the church its charismatic leadership for the equipping of the saints and the perfecting of his body (Eph. 4:11–13). The diversity of gifts and the variety of services are the singular activity of the Lord (1 Cor. 12:4–5). In the church the risen Lord thereby continues his own ministry begun in the incarnation.

Prayer, praise, thanksgiving, and intercession are carried on in the church by virtue of the presence of the Lord at the right hand of the Father (Rom. 8:34). The church rejoices in the Lord (Rom. 5:11; Phil. 3:1; 4:4). The whole of the created order also comes under the lordship of Jesus. He is the sovereign firstborn over all creation, for it was created through him and is sustained by him (Col. 1:15–16; Heb. 1:3). The lordship of Jesus over history is carried out through the church and its proclamation. By virtue of his lordship the church is free to live in the world as servant. Being free from the necessity of power and achievement, for the victory is sealed, the church functions in terms of faithfulness and obedience, knowing that the conquest of death as the last enemy is a certainty in the light of the victory of Christ (1 Cor. 15:25–26). The consequence of the church's reflection on the lordship of Jesus was to establish—in spite of the threat it might have posed to monotheistic commitments—the oneness of Jesus with God. So a title whose basic thrust is to assert Jesus' present power and authority in the church and in the world leads the church to recognize that the authority is the direct, not mediated, authority of God himself.

R. W. Lyon

See also Christology; God, Doctrine of; Jesus Christ; Trinity.

Lord of Hosts. See God, Names of.

Lord's Day. (Gk. *kyriakē hēmera*) Probable designation of the first day of the week (Sunday). The term occurs only once in the NT (Rev. 1:10). In an early manual of church instruction, the Didache (ca. A.D. 120), Christians were directed to assemble on the Lord's day to worship (14:1). The attraction of the phrase was at least twofold. It expressed the Christian conviction that Sunday was a day when Christ Jesus conquered death and became Lord of all (Eph. 1:20–22; 1 Pet. 3:21–22) and a day that anticipated the return of that same Lord to consummate his victory (1 Cor. 15:23–28, 54–57). In the NT Sunday was usually designated as "the first day of the week" (Gk. *mia sabbaton*; Matt. 28:1; Mark 16:2; Luke 24:1; John 20:1).

Early Practice. That the early church customarily met on Sunday during the NT era cannot be unequivocally demonstrated. Two NT references, however, suggest that this was the case (Acts 20:7; 1 Cor. 16:2). Whether these meetings commenced according to the Jewish scheme of reckoning days (sunset to sunset) on a Saturday evening or according to the Roman pattern (midnight to midnight) on a Sunday is debated, but the latter was more likely. According to Pliny, a Roman governor in Asia Minor (ca. 95–110), Christians met at dawn on a regularly scheduled day (Lat. *stato die*) to worship Christ and then reassembled later the same day to eat a meal (*Letter to Trajan* 10.96.7), a practice that recognized the Roman day. According to Justin (*First Apology* 67.3–6) Sunday services included a reading of Scripture, exhortation, corporate and individual prayers, the Lord's Supper, and an offertory.

Theology of the Lord's Day. When the early church began Sunday worship is not known. Nor do the NT writers offer a rationale for the shift from Saturday's sabbath observance to Sunday's meetings, but two factors may be suggested. (1) The seventh day, Saturday, was no longer regarded as a day to be especially observed by worship and rest from labor (Rom. 14:5–6; Gal. 4:8–11; Col. 2:16–17;

cf. Acts 15:28–29). (2) The event of the resurrection, at the heart of the Christian gospel (Acts 2:31; 4:2, 10, 33; 10:40; 13:33–37; 17:18; Rom. 10:9; 1 Cor. 15:4, 12–19; 1 Thess. 1:10), occurred on a Sunday. Underlying each of these reasons, however, may have been the desire on the part of the early church to distinguish itself from Judaism and its distinctive sabbath observances.

Significance. Within Christianity there are differences of opinion on how the Lord's day should be observed. Three general distinctions may be noted. First, some Christians believe that the church as a whole was mistaken in leaving a Saturday observance for Sunday worship without a specific command to do so. They continue faithfully to "Remember the sabbath day by keeping it holy" (Exod. 20:8). The Seventh-day Adventists are the most visible members of this group. A second and larger group transfer the principles of sabbath observance to Sunday. The name "sabbatarian" is commonly given to this position. A classic expression of this is in the Westminster Shorter Catechism, in which Sunday is called "the Christian Sabbath" (Q. 59). Most Christians may be included in a third group, who believe that the sabbath commandment was a part of the ceremonial law of Israel and therefore not applicable to the church. This seems to have been the position of the early church. No hint of cessation from work on Sundays is found until Tertullian. While various factors, including Scripture (Ps. 92:2), may have led to an early morning and late evening meeting schedule, one likely explanation was the need to assemble at times that would not conflict with the workday. Most Christians, therefore, do not consider recreational activity or work on Sunday illegitimate, but they do stress the importance of gathering with other believers for worship, edification, and fellowship in the name of the risen Lord.

D. K. LOWERY

See also SABBATARIANISM; WORSHIP IN THE CHURCH.

Lord's Prayer. Jesus' pattern for prayer in Matt. 6:9–13. The meaning of the Lord's Prayer needs to be sought in the wider context of Matt. 6:1–18. Jesus is contrasting surface language with depth language in worship of God. The prayer is not a set form that he himself prayed or asked his disciples to pray, but illustrates the type of prayer appropriate to the person who worships deeply without hypocrisy. The entire Sermon on the Mount (Matt. 5–7) takes its cue from Jesus' declaration in 5:20: "For I tell you, unless your righteousness surpasses that of the Pharisees and the teachers of the law, you will certainly not enter the kingdom of heaven." The eschatological age has broken in with the coming of Jesus, and now the law is no longer inscribed in stone but in the heart (Jer. 31:33). True prayer is to be a deep and spontaneous response to God, not a superficial game played out in public simply to curry favor with the world. The flow of thought in the larger unit of 6:1–18, with the summary of 6:19–21, makes clear the serious contrast of opposites in which the Lord's Prayer is to be understood.

Luke's placement of the prayer (Luke 11:1–4) indicates his understanding of the underlying meaning of Jesus' ordering of values in the new age. Viewed in context of Jesus' eschatological contrasts, the Lord's Prayer provides a summary model for properly ordering the priorities of the kingdom. Both Matt. 6:9–13 and Luke 11:2–4 preserve Jesus' order: first God, then human needs. While Jesus makes use of Jewish sources in forming the prayer, he does not design it to be used as a set liturgical piece but as a model for the responsive heart in view of the demands of the new age.

R. G. GRUENLER

See also PRAYER; SERMON ON THE MOUNT.

Lord's Supper. There are four accounts of the Lord's Supper in the NT (Matt. 26:26–30; Mark 14:22–26; Luke 22:14–20; 1 Cor. 11:23–26). Jesus' words and actions are best understood in light of the Jewish passover. In the celebration of the passover the people of God not only remembered but relived the events of their deliverance from Egypt under the sign of the sacrificed paschal lamb as if they themselves participated in them (Exod. 12). Giving the bread and wine as his body and blood, Jesus points to himself as the true paschal Lamb and to his death as the saving event that will deliver the new Israel, represented in his disciples, from all bondage. His blood is to be the sign under which God will remember his people in himself. In his words at the table Jesus speaks of himself not only as the paschal Lamb but also as a sacrifice. In the sacrificial ritual of the OT the portion of peace offering not consumed by fire and thus not offered to God as his food (Lev. 3:1–11; Num. 28:2) was eaten by priest and people (Lev. 19:5–6; 1 Sam. 9:13) in an act of fellowship (Exod. 24:1–11; Deut. 27:7). In giving the bread and wine to his disciples, Jesus gives a sign of their own fellowship and participation in the event of his sacrificial death.

Jesus includes in the Last Supper the ritual of a covenant meal. In the OT the making of a covenant was followed by a meal in which the participants had fellowship and were pledged to loyalty one to another (Gen. 26:30; 31:54; 2 Sam. 3:20). The new covenant (Jer. 31:1–34) between the Lord and his people is thus ratified by Jesus in a meal. After the resurrection, in their celebration of the Supper (Acts 2:42–46; 20:7), believers would see the climax of the table fellowship that Jesus had had with publicans and sinners (Matt. 11:18–19; Luke 15:2) and of their own day-to-day meals with him. They would interpret it not only as a bare prophecy but as a real foretaste of the future messianic banquet, and as a sign of the presence of the mystery of the kingdom of God in their midst in the person of Jesus (Matt. 8:11). They would see its meaning in relation to his living presence in the church, brought out fully in the Easter meals they had shared with him (Luke 24:13–35; John 21:1–14; Acts 10:41). It was a supper in the presence of the risen Lord as their host. But they would not forget the sacrificial and paschal aspect of the Supper. The table fellowship they looked back on represented the fellowship of the Messiah with sinners that reached its climax in his self-identification with the sin of the world on Calvary. They had fellowship with the resurrected Jesus through remembrance of his death. As the Lord's Supper related them to the coming kingdom and glory of Christ, so did it also relate them to his once-for-all death.

R. S. WALLACE

See also LORD'S SUPPER, VIEWS OF.

Lord's Supper, Views of. ***Transubstantiation.*** In the 9th century Radbertus taught that a miracle takes place at the words of institution in the Supper. The elements are changed into the actual body and blood of Christ. The substance in the elements of bread and wine is changed into the substance of the body and blood of Christ while the accidents—that is, the appearance, taste, touch, and smell—remain the same. Transubstantiation was declared to be the position of the church in 1059, although the term itself was not used officially until the Fourth Lateran Council (1215). The medieval church further refined the doctrine of transubstantiation. The Council of Trent (1545–63) confirmed these teachings in its 13th and 22nd sessions, adding that the veneration given the consecrated elements is adoration (*latria*), the same worship that is given God.

Luther and Consubstantiation. The Reformers agreed in their condemnation of the doctrine of transubstantiation. They held it to be a serious error that is contrary to the testimony of our senses of sight, smell, taste, and touch; destructive of the true meaning of a sacrament; and conducive to gross superstition and idolatry. Luther's first salvo against what he considered to be a perversion of the Lord's Supper was *The Babylonian Captivity of the Church.* While he rejected transubstantiation and the sacrifice of the Mass, Luther believed that Christ is bodily present in the Lord's Supper and that his body is received by all who partake of the elements. While he acknowledged the mystery, Luther was certain of the fact of Christ's real corporeal presence inasmuch as he had said when he instituted the Supper, "This is my body." Luther's view became known as *consubstantiation.*

Zwingli. Luther's main opponent among the evangelicals was Ulrich Zwingli, whose reforming activity in Switzerland was as old as Luther's in Germany. Zwingli interpreted the words of Jesus, "This is my body," in harmony with John 6, where Jesus speaks of eating and drinking his body and blood, especially v. 63 ("The Spirit gives life; the flesh counts for nothing"). Zwingli not only opposed transubstantiation but also Luther's notion of consubstantiation, that somehow Christ is corporeally in, under, and with the elements. Zwingli found the idea of physical eating absurd and repugnant to common sense. Moreover, God does not ask us to believe that which is contrary to sense experience. The word "is" in the words of institution means "signifies," or "represents," and must be interpreted figuratively, as is done in other "I am" passages in the Bible. Christ's ascension means that he took his body from earth to heaven. Zwingli's shortcoming was his lack of appreciation for the real presence of Christ in the Supper in his Holy Spirit and a real feeding of the faithful on him. Zwingli's position lacks the reality of communion with Christ and a reception of him in the Supper.

Calvin. Calvin's view of the Lord's Supper appears to be a mediate position between the views of Luther and Zwingli, but it is in fact an independent one. Rejecting both Zwingli's "memorialism" and Luther's "monstrous notion of ubiquity" (*Inst.* 4.17.30), Calvin held that there is a real reception of the body and blood of Christ in the Supper, only in a spiritual manner. The sacrament is a real means of grace, a channel by which Christ communicates himself to us. With Zwingli, Calvin held that after the ascension Christ retained a real body, which is located in heaven. With Luther, Calvin believed that the elements in the Supper are signs that exhibit the fact that Christ is truly present. He repudiated Zwingli's belief that the elements are signs that represent that which is absent.

Inasmuch as the doctrine of the real presence of Christ in the Supper was the key issue in the eucharistic debate, it is obvious that Luther and Calvin agreed more than did Calvin and Zwingli. The latter's concept of Christ's presence was "by the contemplation of faith" but not "in essence and reality." For Luther and Calvin communion with a present Christ who actually feeds believers with his body and blood is what makes the sacrament. The question between them was the manner in which Christ's body exists and is given to believers.

M. E. Osterhaven

See also Lord's Supper.

Love. Asked which is the greatest commandment, Jesus replied, "'Love the Lord your God with all your heart and with all your soul and with all your mind.' This is the first and greatest commandment. And the second is like it: 'Love your neighbor as yourself.' All the Law and the Prophets hang on these two commandments" (Matt. 22:37–40; cf.

Mark 12:29–31; Luke 10:26–27). There is no other command greater than these two (Mark 12:31b). Love is therefore of preeminent importance in the Bible.

Biblical Terms. There are many Hebrew words that express the concept of love. By far the most prominent one (used over 200 times in the OT) is the verb *'āhab*, denoting both divine and human love as well as love toward inanimate objects.

Although not prominent in prebiblical Greek, the verb *agapaō* and the noun *agapē* are the most common NT words for love. This verb/noun combination is the most frequently used in the LXX in translating *'āhab*. Basically it is a self-giving love that is not merited. The second most frequently used word for love in the NT is the verb *phileō*. It is the most common word for love in prebiblical Greek.

God's Love. *The Attribute of Love.* God in his very essence is love (1 John 4:8, 16). God does not need to attain nor attempt to maintain love; it is his very substance and nature.

The Activity of Love. The activity of love comes from God's nature of love. Many verses speak of the Father's love for the Son; only John 14:31, however, explicitly states that Jesus loved the Father. The Holy Spirit's love for the other two persons of the Trinity is implied in John 16:13–15. The NT is replete with references of God's love for us. A central passage demonstrating this is 1 John 4:10: "This is love: not that we loved God, but that he loved us and sent his Son as an atoning sacrifice for our sins."

Our Love. On the basis of God's love for us, we are to love both God and other people. We are to love God with our whole being (Deut. 6:5; 10:12; 11:1, 13, 22; 13:3; 30:6, 16; Josh. 22:5; 23:11; Ps. 31:23). Jesus quotes the OT command to love God (Matt. 22:37; Mark 12:30; Luke 10:27).

Our love toward others has four dimensions: (1) We are to love our neighbor. The command to do so is stated often—first in Lev. 19:18, which is then quoted several times in the NT (Matt. 5:43; 19:19; 22:39; Mark 12:31, 33; Rom. 13:9; Gal. 5:14; James 2:8). (2) We are to love other believers. In Gal. 6:10 Paul exhorts us to do good to all people, but especially to those who belong to the family of faith. Jesus gives a new commandment: that we are to love one another as he has loved us (John 13:34–35; 15:12, 17; cf. 1 John 3:23; 5:2; 2 John 5). (3) We are to love our families. Husbands are commanded to love their wives (Col. 3:19) as Christ loves the church (Eph. 5:25–33). Wives are commanded to love their husbands (Titus 2:4) and parents to love their children (Titus 2:4). Children are admonished to honor and obey their parents (Exod. 20:12; Deut. 5:16; Prov. 1:8; Matt. 19:19; Mark 10:19; Luke 18:20; Eph. 6:1; Col. 3:20). (4) We are to love our enemies (Matt. 5:43–48; Luke 6:27–35). Rather than seeking revenge, believers are to love those who hate and persecute them (Rom. 12:14, 17–21; 1 Thess. 5:15; 1 Pet. 3:9).

H. W. HOEHNER

See also GOD, ATTRIBUTES OF.

Love Feast. Common meal of the Christian fellowship.

In the NT. In Acts 2:42–47 there is a description of the fellowship of the believers, which includes the breaking of bread in their homes and eating their meat (Gk. *trophē*) together with glad and sincere hearts. The first phrase may refer to the Lord's Supper, but the second term obviously indicates a typical meal. Similar communal behavior is mentioned in Acts 4:32. The growth of the Jerusalem church led to the appointment of the seven to serve tables (Acts 6:1–6), which presumably refers to the responsibility for organizing the common meals. Certainly by ca. A.D. 55 it is evident that that church observed the practice of meeting together for a common meal before partaking of the Lord's Supper (see 1 Cor. 11:17–34).

In Church History. Ignatius (*Smyr.* 8:2) refers to the *agapē*, as does the Didache (10.1; 11.9), the latter suggesting that it still preceded the Eucharist. By the time of Tertullian (*Apology* 39; *De Jejuniis* 17; *De corona militis* 3) the Eucharist was celebrated early and the *agapē* later at a separate service. This may be the practice referred to by Pliny in his letter to Trajan (*Epistles* 10.96), although his information is not altogether clear. Clement of Alexandria (*Paedagogos* 2.1; *Stromata* 32) also gives evidence of the separation of the two observances. During the 4th century the *agapē* became increasingly the object of disfavor, apparently because of disorders at the celebration and also because problems were raised by the expanding membership of the church. As a result, increasing emphasis was placed on the Eucharist.

In Modern Times. In the Eastern Church the rite has persisted, and is still observed in sections of the Orthodox Church, where it precedes the Eucharist, and in the Church of St. Thomas in India. From the Eastern Church it was continued through the Church of Bohemia to John Hus and the Unitas Fratrum, whence it was adopted by the Moravians. From them John Wesley introduced the practice within Methodism and it is occasionally observed today in Methodist churches.

D. H. WHEATON

See also LORD'S SUPPER.

Low Church. Those who do not place great emphasis on the corporate or historically continuous or doctrinally orthodox nature of the church (or a part or denomination within it), but who usually emphasize the rights and faith of the individual Christian. The technical usage relates to the 18th-century Church of England, where Low Church was contrasted with High Church as two schools of thought at each end of the Anglican spectrum of theological emphasis. To be Low Church was to be a latitudinarian or a broad churchman.

P. TOON

See also LATITUDINARIANISM.

Lucifer. See SATAN.

Luke, Theology of. ***Theological Themes.*** *Christology.* Luke presents Jesus as the Messiah (Luke 9:20) and Son of God (Luke 1:35; 2:49). Luke is unique in his presentation of Jesus as a prophet. Luke compares and contrasts Jesus with John the Baptist as a prophetic figure (Luke 4:24–27; 13:33).

Soteriology. Without question, Luke emphasizes the need and provision of salvation. The Gospel focuses on the cross through the passion predictions, especially through the sayings at the Last Supper (22:19–22). In the Book of Acts, Luke portrays the cross as God's will, although the crucifixion was carried out by sinful people (Acts 2:23). The Gospel of Luke presents the need of salvation and the progress of Jesus to the cross vividly; the Book of Acts declares the opportunity of forgiveness through Christ (2:38; 4:12; 10:43; 13:39).

Glory. Luke has a very strong theology of glory. He emphasizes the victory of the resurrection, with a declaration of the vindication of Jesus (Acts 2:24; 3:15; 4:10; 10:39–42; 13:26–37; 17:31). The ascension is stressed predictively in the middle of the Gospel (9:51) and in the middle of Luke's two-volume work, Luke 24 and Acts 1.

Doxology. This theology of glory finds practical expression in repeated ascriptions of glory to God. These occur especially at the birth of Christ (2:14) and on the occasions of healing (e.g., Luke 5:25–26; Acts 3:8–10).

The Holy Spirit. The Spirit is prominent from the beginning (Luke 1:15, 41; 2:25–35; 4:1, 18) and throughout the Book of Acts.

Prayer. This is especially significant at times of crisis in the life of Jesus (Luke 3:1; 6:12; 9:18) and in the early perilous days of the church (e.g., Acts 4:23–31; 6:4, 6; 8:15; 9:11; 10:2; 13:3).

The Power of God. Along with the other Gospels, Luke records the miracles of Jesus and uses the word *dynamis.* This emphasis continues throughout Acts.

Sense of Destiny; Prophecy and Fulfillment. This is a unique emphasis of Luke. The verb *dei,* "it is necessary," occurs frequently with reference to the things Jesus "must" accomplish (Luke 2:49; 4:43; 9:22; 13:33; 24:7, 26, 44–47). This is seen both in terms of accomplishment (Luke 1:1) and in terms of fulfillment of OT prophecy.

The Word of God. This is a more significant theme in Luke's writings than is generally recognized. *Logos* occurs in the Gospel prologue (1:2), in 4:22, 32, 36, and notably in the parable of the sower, which stresses obedience to the word of God (8:4–15). In the Book of Acts the growth of the "word" parallels the growth of the church (4:31; 6:7; 12:24).

Discipleship. Luke presents teachings not recorded in the other Gospels. In addition to 9:23–26, paralleled in Matthew and Mark, Luke has major sections on discipleship in 9:57–62 and 14:25–33.

Poverty and Wealth. The Gospel, addressed to a wealthy person, records Jesus' mission to the poor (4:18). Luke refers to a future reversal of social roles (1:46–55; 6:20–26). He emphasizes the church's generosity in sharing with those in need (Acts 2:44–45; 4:32–37; 11:27–30).

W. L. LIEFIELD

See also JOHN, THEOLOGY OF; MARK, THEOLOGY OF; MATTHEW, THEOLOGY OF; NEW TESTAMENT THEOLOGY.

Lust. Craving that which is forbidden, especially sexual passion. The word has been used in English versions, especially the AV, to translate several Hebrew and several Greek words that are basically neutral in ethical overtones and indicate only strong desire. In particular contexts these words may take on the negative aspect found in present usage of "lust." Some Hebrew words with the overtones of lust are *nepeš,* desire (Exod. 15:9; Ps. 78:18); *ḥāmad,* desire for the beauty of the evil woman (Prov. 6:25); and *'āwa,* to desire (Ps. 106:14). The Greek terms and their general meanings are *epithymia,* desire, longing; *epithymeō,* to desire, long for (Rom. 7:7; 13:9; Gal. 5:16; Eph. 2:3; 2 Pet. 2:18); *hēdonē,* pleasure, enjoyment (James 4:1, 3); *oregō,* to desire; *orexis,* longing, desire (Matt. 5:28; Rom. 1:24, 27); and *pathos,* passion (1 Thess. 4:5).

G. W. KNIGHT, III

See also DESIRE.

Luther, Martin (1483–1546). German religious reformer. While teaching at the University of Wittenberg (1507–12), Luther experienced intense spiritual struggles as he sought to work out his own salvation by careful observance of the monastic rule, constant confession, and self-mortification. Primarily through his study of the Scriptures as he prepared his university lectures, Luther gradually changed his view of justification. His fully developed doctrine, which viewed justification as a forensic act in which God declares the sinner righteous because of the vicarious atonement of Jesus Christ without any human merit rather than a lifelong process, was not clearly expressed in Luther's writings until his sermon *Of the Threefold Righteousness,* published toward the end of 1518.

The Reformation began in 1517, when Luther protested a major abuse in the sale of indulgences in his Ninety-Five Theses. These were translated into German, printed, and circulated throughout Germany, arousing a storm of protest against the sale of indulgences. In 1520 he wrote three pamphlets of great significance. The first, the *Address to the Christian Nobility of the German Nation*, called upon the Germans to reform the church and society, since the papacy and church councils had failed to do so. The second, *The Babylonian Captivity of the Church*, clearly put Luther in the ranks of the heterodox, because it attacked the entire sacramental system of the medieval church. Luther maintained there were only two sacraments, baptism and the Lord's Supper—or at most three, with penance possibly qualifying as a third—rather than seven sacraments. He also denied the doctrines of transubstantiation and the sacrificial Mass. The third pamphlet, *The Freedom of the Christian Man*, was written for the pope. It was nonpolemical and clearly taught the doctrine of justification by faith alone.

In April 1521, at the Diet of Worms Luther was asked to recant his teachings, but he stood firm, thereby defying also the authority of the emperor, who placed him under the imperial ban and ordered that all his books be burned. On the way home from Worms, Luther was abducted by friends who took him to the Wartburg castle, where he remained in hiding for nearly a year, and began his German translation of the Bible. In 1522 Luther returned to Wittenberg to deal with disorders that had broken out in his absence, and he remained there for the rest of his life. In 1525 he married Catherine von Bora, a former nun, who bore him six children. Throughout his life Luther maintained an overwhelming work load, writing, teaching, organizing the new church, and providing overall leadership for the German Reformation. Among his more important theological writings were the Smalcald Articles published in 1538, which clearly defined the differences between his theology and that of the Roman Catholic Church. Luther never viewed himself as the founder of a new church body, however. He devoted his life to reforming the church and restoring the Pauline doctrine of justification to the central position in Christian theology.

R. W. HEINZE

See also LEIPZIG DISPUTATION; LUTHERAN TRADITION, THE; LUTHER'S SMALL CATECHISM; MARBURG COLLOQUY; NINETY-FIVE THESES, THE; SMALCALD ARTICLES, THE.

Lutheran Tradition, The. Doctrine and practices authoritative in the Lutheran Church and those churches throughout the world in general. The term "Lutheran" was initially applied by the enemies of Luther in the early 1520s. The teaching of Luther—forged from his discovery that the righteousness of God is not a righteousness that judges and demands but a righteousness given by God in grace—found its systematic expression in the formularies incorporated in the *Book of Concord*. All these documents, with the exception of the Formula of Concord, were written between 1529 and 1537 by Luther and Philip Melanchthon. They reflect the emphasis on justification by grace and the correction of abuses in the life of the church while at the same time "conserving" the church's catholic heritage (through explicit commitment to the ancient creeds, traditional forms of worship, church government, etc.).

Doctrines. The distinctive doctrines of Lutheran theology have commonly been related to the classical leitmotifs of the Reformation: *sola Scriptura, sola gratia, sola fide.* The theology of Lutheranism is first a theology of the Word. Its principle of *sola Scriptura* affirms the Bible as the only norm of Christian doctrine. The Scripture is the *causa media* by which we learn to know God and his will; the Word is the one and the only source of theology. Furthermore, the Lutheran view of the Bible is to be distinguished from a legalistic orientation. Christ is at the center of the Bible. Essential to understanding the Word of God is accepting the promises of the gospel by faith. If this faith is lacking, the Scriptures cannot be correctly understood.

The second doctrinal distinctive of Lutheranism is the doctrine of justification. According to Luther there are two kinds of righteousness, an external righteousness and an inner righteousness. External (civil) righteousnes may be acquired through just conduct or good deeds. Inner righteousness consists of the purity and perfection of the heart. Consequently, it cannot be attained through external deeds. This righteousness is of God and comes as a gift of his fatherly grace. This is the source of justification. The ground for justification is Christ, who by his death made satisfaction for the sins of humankind.

Related to this teaching is the third significant hallmark of Lutheranism: *sola fide.* The means whereby justification accrues to the individual is faith. Justifying faith is not merely a historical knowledge of the content of the gospel; it is the acceptance of the merits of Christ. Faith, therefore, is trust in the mercy of God for the sake of his Son. Lutheranism has persistently refused to see faith itself as a "work." Faith is receptivity, receiving Christ and all that he has done. But faith cannot be apart from works. Where there is faith in Christ, love and good works follow.

In one way or another the three fundamental doctrines of Lutheranism—*sola Scriptura, sola gratia, sola fide*—determine the shape of other distinctive teachings.

History. In the 17th century these teachings were elaborated in a scholastic mold. Lutheran orthodoxy, whose classical period began about 1600, was an extension of the tradition represented by the Lutheran confessional writings. It was, however, profoundly influenced by the Neo-Aristotelianism that had secured a foothold in the German universities. The period of Lutheran orthodoxy gave way to the pietist movement in the late 17th century. Pietism was a reaction to what was perceived as an arid intellectualism in the orthodox theologians. Philipp Jakob Spener's *Pia desideria* called for a reform movement within Lutheranism. In the 18th century theological rationalism appeared in Germany and gained ground, threatening to undermine the historic faith.

Apart from Germany, where two-thirds of the population had accepted Lutheranism by the end of the 16th century, the expansion of Lutheranism into Sweden, Denmark, and Norway left national churches that have endured in strength. From these nations Lutherans migrated to the U.S. and Canada. The earliest Lutherans in America can be traced back to the 17th century. Swedish Lutherans settled in Delaware as early as 1638. In Georgia, almost 100 years later, a group of refugee Lutherans from Salzburg established residence. Colonies of Lutherans also settled in upper New York and in Pennsylvania by the time of the Revolution. Henry Melchior Muhlenberg organized the first American synod of Lutherans.

Contemporary Lutheranism seems to have entered an age of unification. The various waves of immigrants to America led to a proliferation of Lutheran bodies. There have been a number of mergers between these groups, which are now mainly represented by the Lutheran Church in America (1962), the American Lutheran Church (1960), and the Lutheran Church–Missouri Synod (1847). The Lutheran World Federation, founded in 1947, cultivates world unity and mutual assistance among its member churches. Lutheranism throughout the world constitutes the largest of the churches that have come out of the Reformation.

J. F. Johnson

See also CONCORD, BOOK OF; CONCORD, FORMULA OF; LUTHER, MARTIN; MELANCHTHON, PHILIP; MONERGISM; MUHLENBERG, HENRY MELCHIOR; PIETISM; REFORMATION, PROTESTANT; SYNERGISM; WALTHER, CARL FERDINAND WILHELM.

Luther's Small Catechism. Simple manual of instruction in the Christian faith written by Luther in 1529. In 1527 and 1528 Luther and his associates were asked by their prince to inspect the churches of Saxony. The results were profoundly disappointing. Ignorance reigned among clergy and laity alike, and the schools were in ruins. To meet the need for popular instruction Luther immediately drew up wall charts containing explanations in simple language of the Ten Commandments, the Lord's Prayer, and the Apostles' Creed. When his colleagues delayed in their own efforts at providing educational materials, Luther pulled together his wall charts and published them as a short, simple exposition of the faith. Much of the influence of Lutheranism around the world can be traced to the success of this catechism in expressing the profound truths of the faith in a language that all can understand.

M. A. NOLL

See also CATECHISMS; LUTHER, MARTIN.

Mm

M'Cheyne, Robert Murray (1813–1843). Scottish clergyman. M'Cheyne is widely considered one of the most Christlike men ever to have lived in Scotland. In 1836 he was called to St. Peter's Church of Dundee, which had some 4000 members. His ministry there was marked by deep personal holiness, prayer, concern for the salvation of the lost, powerful evangelical preaching, and tireless counseling. In 1839 he spent six months in Palestine, exploring possible missionary work among the Jews. Revival broke out in his congregation during his absence. Upon his return he threw himself into this work, which soon spread over the country, resulting in the conversion of thousands. He died at age 29. His biography retains its perennial popularity.

D. F. KELLY

MacDonald, George (1824–1905). Scottish novelist and poet. MacDonald is best known for his fairy tales for young people and his fantasies for adults. He wrote some 26 novels in which he scrutinized human behavior and commented on it from a Christian point of view. He also wrote a considerable amount of devotional poetry in the romantic tradition. In general, his convictions spring from a Scottish Calvinist base, strongly modified by German romantic thought as expressed mainly through the poetry and fantasies of the German writers Novalis and E. T. A. Hoffmann. MacDonald's best-known children's works are *The Princess and the Goblin* (1872), *The Princess and Curdie* (1883), and *At the Back of the North Wind* (1871). His most popular fantasies for adults are *Phantastes* (1858) and *Lilith* (1895). The fairy tale "The Golden Key" is considered to be his masterpiece.

R. N. HEIN

McGiffert, Arthur Cushman (1861–1933). American church historian. McGiffert was professor of church history at Union Seminary in New York in 1893. From 1917 to 1926 he served as president of that institution. McGiffert's assumptions about history had much to do with the shape of his theology. From study in Germany he returned to the U.S. with the idea that "scientific" history, which excluded the supernatural, was somehow more "objective" than that which allowed for the possibility of divine involvement in the events of the world. In accounting for this position he expressed the hope that one day people would not be "obliged to ask what Bible or church or creed require, but what the facts teach." Results of historical investigation were thus not to be subject to orthodox traditions. McGiffert's books—including *A History of Christianity in the Apostolic Age* (1897), *Protestant Thought before Kant* (1911), and *A History of Christian Thought* (1932)—remain forceful examples of church history from a liberal perspective.

M. A. NOLL

See also LIBERALISM, THEOLOGICAL; SOCIAL GOSPEL, THE.

Machen, John Gresham (1881–1937). American theologian. In 1915 Machen became professor of NT at Princeton Seminary, and in the intense struggles between fundamentalists and modernists during the 1920s and 1930s he emerged as an international champion of biblical authority and evangelical theology. The faculty of Princeton Seminary split over some of these issues, and ultimately the liberal forces in the Presbyterian Church "reorganized" Princeton Seminary in 1929 in such a way that their viewpoint prevailed administratively. This led to the resignation of Machen, Cornelius Van Til, Oswald T. Allis, Robert Dick Wilson, and others, who under the guidance of Machen founded Westminster Seminary in Philadelphia in 1929. Machen also founded the Independent Board for Presbyterian Missions in 1933 and in 1936 led in the organization of the Presbyterian Church of America (which soon changed its name to the Orthodox Presbyterian Church). Machen died while on a preaching tour in North Dakota. Among his most influential books are *The Origin of Paul's Religion* (Sprunt Lectures for Union Seminary in Virginia in 1921), *NT Greek for Beginners* (1923), *Christianity and Liberalism* (1923), *What Is Faith?* (1925), *The Virgin Birth of Christ* (Smyth Lectures for Columbia Seminary in 1927), and *The Christian Faith in the Modern World* (1936). Two of his booklets were very important: *The Attack upon Princeton Seminary—A Plea for Fair Play* (1927) and *Modernism and the Board of Foreign Missions* (1933).

D. F. KELLY

See also EVANGELICALISM; FUNDAMENTALISM; PRINCETON THEOLOGY, OLD.

Mackintosh, Hugh Ross (1870–1936). Scottish theologian and author. Mackinstosh was appointed professor of systematic theology at New College, Edinburgh, in 1904, a post that he held until his death. He was elected moderator of the Church of Scotland's General Assembly in 1932. Mackintosh had immense knowledge of and considerable sympathy for the liberal theological movement of 19th-century German Protestantism. His admiration was always mingled, however, with criticism for what he considered its errors. Much of his work was an endeavor to familiarize the British public with the results of German scholarship. His posthumous work, *Types of Modern Theology* (1937), is still a classic survey of German Protestant theology from Schleiermacher to Barth.

D. F. KELLY

McPherson, Aimee Semple (1890–1944). Pentecostalist revivalist and radio pioneer. McPherson's teaching was probably not as important as her personality in explaining her great success, but it did include standard fundamentalistic and Pentecostal emphases: sanctification, baptism of the Holy Spirit and the gift of tongues, Christ as Savior and healer, faith healing, and the imminent return of Christ. In 1922 she settled in Los Angeles, where she preached to thousands each week at her $1.5-million Angelus Temple. The International Church of the Foursquare Gospel arose as a result of her ministry in 1927. It continued under the direction of her son after she died, and now numbers well over 100,000 members worldwide.

M. A. NOLL

Majoristic Controversy. One of various controversies within Lutheranism between Luther's death in 1546 and the definitive formulation of the Lutheran platform in the *Book of Concord* (1580). Georg Major, a pupil of Melanchthon, claimed that good works are necessary to salvation. The counterattack of the Gnesio-Lutheran ("true Lutheran") party, led by Matthias Flacius and Amsdorf, was that good works are harmful to salvation. The bitter controversy was settled in article 4 of the Formula of Concord, which pointed out the excesses on both sides.

H. D. HUMMEL

See also AMSDORF, NICHOLAS VON; CONCORD, BOOK OF; CONCORD, FORMULA OF; FLACIUS, MATTHIAS.

Major Orders. Senior or higher ranks, classes, or grades of the ordained ministry in the church in contradistinction from minor orders (porters, lectors, exorcists, and acolytes). In the Roman Catholic Church there are three major orders—episcopacy, priesthood, and the diaconate.

P. TOON

See also CHURCH OFFICERS; MINOR ORDERS; ORDERS, HOLY.

Mammon. English transliteration of an Aramaic word for riches or wealth. In pre-Christian times the expression "the mammon of unrighteousness" had already become synonymous with the evils of money. The NT usage of this word is confined to Jesus' teachings (Matt. 6:24; Luke 16:9, 11, 13).

W. BROOMALL

Man, Doctrine of. ***In the OT.*** In the Genesis creation account humankind's presence in the world is attributed directly to God. God is the source of human life, and dust the material of human being.

People share physiological similarities with the rest of the created order and also depend on God's goodness for continuance. But however deeply related people are to the natural order, they are nonetheless different and distinctive from the rest of the created order; they enjoy a unique and special status in relation to God.

The three most significant words in the OT describing humankind in relation to God and nature are "soul" (*nepeš*, 754 times), "spirit" (*rûaḥ*, 378 times), and "flesh" (*bāśār*, 266 times). The term "flesh" has sometimes a physical and sometimes a figuratively ethical sense. In its latter sense it is used in contrast with God to emphasize human nature as contingent and dependent (Job 10:4; Ps. 78:39; Isa. 40:6). Both *nepeš* and *rûaḥ* denote in general the life principle of the human person, the former stressing more particularly individuality, or life, and the latter focusing on the idea of a supernatural power above or within the individual. By God's inbreathing, Adam, formed from the dust, became a living soul, a unified being in the interrelation of the terrestrial and the transcendental. Throughout the OT the two concepts of the human being as a unique and responsible individual and as a social and representative being are present. Adam was both a man and humankind. In him individual personhood and social solidarity found expression. From this perspective of racial solidarity in the first man it follows that Adam's sin involved every person, both individually and collectively.

In the NT. Jesus teaches that humankind is not just a part of nature, but more precious in God's sight than many sparrows (Matt. 10:31) and sheep (Matt. 12:12). Human distinctiveness lies in the possession of a soul, or spiritual nature, which to forfeit is an ultimate tragedy and final folly (Matt. 16:26). True human life is consequently life under God and for his glory.

The Pauline Anthropology. Paul's declarations regarding human nature are generally stated in relation to salvation so that his anthropology throughout serves the interests of his soteriology. Foremost, therefore, in his teaching is his insistence on our need of divine grace. Paul is emphatic about the universality of sin. Because of Adam's fall sin somehow got a footing in the world to make human life the sphere of its activity. Sin "entered the world through one man" (Rom. 5:12; cf. 1 Cor. 15:1–2). Because of Adam's sin, "all have sinned and fall short of the glory of God" (Rom. 3:23).

The most significant terms in Paul's anthropological vocabulary are "flesh" (*sarx*, 91 times), which he uses in a physical and an ethical sense; "spirit" (*pneuma*, 146 times), used to denote generally the higher, Godward aspect of human nature; "body" (*sōma*, 89 times), most often used to designate the human organism as such, but sometimes the carnal aspect of human nature; "soul" (*psychē*, 11 times), broadly employed to carry the idea of the vital principle of individual life. Paul has several words (translated as "mind" in the English versions) to specify our native rational ability that is seriously affected by sin (Rom. 8:6–7; Eph. 4:17; Col. 2:18; Titus 1:15). The mind transformed brings God acceptable worship (Rom. 12:2; Eph. 4:23) and so becomes in the believer the mind of Christ (1 Cor. 2:16; cf. Phil. 2:5). The term "heart" (*kardia*, 52 times) specifies for Paul the innermost sanctuary of psychical being either as a whole or with one or another of its significant emotional, rational, or volitional activities.

Historical Development. From these biblical statements about human nature, the history of Christian thought has focused on three main issues.

Content of the Image. The most enduring of these concerns is the content of the image of God. Irenaeus first introduced the distinction between "image" (Heb. *ṣelem;* Lat. *imago*) and "likeness" (Heb. *demût;* Lat. *similitudo*). The image of God he identified as the rationality and free will that inhere in humankind qua humankind. The likeness he conceived to be a superadded gift of God's righteousness that humankind, by virtue of reason and freedom of choice, had the possibility to retain and advance by obedience to the divine commands. But this probationary endowment Adam forfeited by an act of willful disobedience for both himself and his descendants. The Reformers denied this distinction between image and likeness upon which the works-salvation of medievalism was reared in their insistence upon the radical nature of sin and its effect upon the total being. The Reformed position is that the image of God consists in human rationality and moral competency, but that it is precisely these realities of being that were lost or marred through sin. Others consider personality as the ingredient of the image, while still others prefer to see it as sonship, contending that humankind was created for that relationship. Because of sin that relationship can be restored only in Christ.

The Origin of the Soul. The creationist doctrine holds that God is the immediate Creator of the human soul. First elaborated by Lactantius (ca. 240–ca. 320), it had the support of Jerome and Calvin. The alternative view, traducianism (Lat. *tradux*, "branch or shoot"), expounded by Tertullian, is that the substances of both soul and body are formed and propagated together. Favored by Luther, it was consequently generally adopted by later Lutheran theologians. In support of the view is the observation that Gen. 1:27 represents God as creating the species in Adam to be propagated "after its kind" (cf. Gen. 1:12, 21, 25).

The Extent of Freedom. Consonant with his idea of the *imago Dei* as grounded in human nature as rational and free, Justin Martyr set in motion the view that people are responsible for their own wrongdoing, which was to become a characteristic note of the Eastern Church. Thus Adam is seen as the primary type of each person's sinning, and Adam's fall is the story of every person. Western theology, by contrast, regards Adam's transgression as the fountainhead of all human evil. Tertullian traced sin to humanity's connection with Adam, through whom it has become a natural element of every person's nature. Yet he allowed some residue of free will to remain.

In Pelagius and Augustine these two views came into sharp conflict. Pelagius taught that humankind was unaffected by Adam's transgression, while Augustine maintained that Adam's sin has so crippled us that we can act only to express our sinful nature inherited from our first parents. The inevitable compromise appeared in the semi-Pelagian (or semi-Augustinian) synergistic thesis that while all people inherit a bias to sin, a freedom of decision remains that permits at least some to take the first step toward righteousness. In the Calvinist-Arminian controversy of the 17th century, the conflict was reenacted.

H. D. McDONALD

See also MAN, NATURAL; MAN, OLD AND NEW; MAN, ORIGIN OF.

Man, Natural. Term used by Paul in 1 Cor. 2:14, where "natural" is a translation of *psychikos* and stands in contrast to "spiritual" (*pneumatikos*, 1 Cor. 2:13, 15; 3:1) and thus in parallel with "fleshly" (*sarkinos*, 1 Cor. 3:1). The meaning of "natural man" indicates humankind in the "lower" aspects of being that mark people off as creatures, as temporally and spatially confined, as limited to this-worldly, "fleshly" modes of perception that cannot penetrate the world of the Spirit.

S. MOTYER

See also NATURAL THEOLOGY; MAN, DOCTRINE OF; MAN, OLD AND NEW.

Man, Old and New. Terms used by Paul to express the contrast between life without Christ and life in union with Christ (Rom. 6:6; Eph. 4:22–24; Col. 3:9–10). For Paul, Christ is the "new (Son of) man" of a new creation/kingdom/humanity established in contrast to that of Adam, who is the "old man." In union with Christ (through baptism into his death and resurrection, Rom. 6:3–5) we are transferred from the old creation to the new. Our "old man"—our membership in Adam—was crucified with Christ, and now we must seek to reflect in practice ("put on") the "image" of this new man, and to scour out ("put off") the remaining image of the old man (1 Cor. 15:45–49).

S. MOTYER

See also MAN, DOCTRINE OF; MAN, NATURAL; NEW CREATION, NEW CREATURE; SON OF MAN.

Man, Origin of. Evolutionists believe that humankind developed from lower organisms through a series of changes brought about by purely natural processes, and that this line of development can be traced from simple, presumably one-cell, living things, through more complex organisms, and finally through organisms that today would be classified as anthropoid apes, to humankind. Our closest relatives are believed to be the anthropoid apes because of the great number of similarities between apes and humans. While it is true that there are many similarities and that the similarities between people and the anthropoids are greater than those between people and other animals, it is also true that there are more than 100 differences between people and the anthropoids, some quite significant. Probably the most significant difference is the fact that people are able to communicate in abstract terms. We have developed language and a history. We are able to transmit culture from one generation to another and to profit from what has been learned by previous generations. These differences suggest a wide gap between us and the anthropoids.

The Book of Genesis indicates a "special" creation of humankind. It tells us that God fashioned Adam from the dust of the earth and breathed into his nostrils the breath of life so that he became a living soul (2:7); Adam was created in the image of God (1:27). The early chapters of Genesis clearly teach that from the beginning Adam was separate from animal species, that he was morally responsible, and that by his own choice he became alienated from God and a sinner. The Bible describes God's mercy in sending his Son to redeem us from sin. Scripture teaches that sin is the result of our choice; evolution suggests that it is the heritage of our animal ancestry.

J. W. KLOTZ

See also EVOLUTION.

Man, Son of. See SON OF MAN.

Manichaeism. Third-century dualistic religion, founded by Mani, who fused Persian, Christian, and Buddhist elements into a major new faith. Mani's religion was a complex Gnostic system offering salvation by knowledge. The main features of Manichaeism were enunciated in an elaborate cosmogonical myth of two absolute and eternal principles that manifest themselves in three eras or "moments."

The first moment describes a radical dualism in a previous age. Light and Darkness (Good and Evil), personified in the Father of Lights and the Prince of Darkness, were both coeternal and independent. In the middle moment Darkness attacked and became mixed with Light in a precosmic fall of primal humankind. This resulted in a second creation of the material world and humankind by the evil powers in which Light is trapped in nature and human bodies. Redemption of Light occurs by a cosmic mechanism in the heavens by which particles of Light (souls) are drawn up and fill the moon for 15 days. In the last phases of the moon Light is transferred to the sun and finally to Paradise. Ever since the fall prophets have been sent by the Father of Lights, such as Zoroaster in Persia, Buddha in India, and Jesus in the West. But Mani was the greatest prophet who, as the paraclete, proclaimed a salvation by knowledge (*gnosis*), consisting of strict ascetic practices. In the last days of the second moment a great war is to be concluded with judgment and a global conflagration lasting 1468 years. Light will be saved and everything material destroyed. In the third moment Light and Darkness will be separated forever as in the primordial division.

Manichaeism spread both east and west from Persia. In the West it was vigorously fought by both the Christian church and Roman emperors. Manichaeism survived into the Middle Ages through such sects as the Paulicians and Cathari, which probably developed from the original tradition.

W. A. HOFFECKER

Man of Lawlessness. See ANTICHRIST.

Man of Sin. See ANTICHRIST.

Marburg Colloquy (1529). Meeting that attempted to resolve the differences between Lutherans and Zwinglians over the Lord's Supper. The major participants were Luther, Melanchthon, Zwingli, and Oecolampadius. These differences had been expressed in a bitter pamphlet controversy between 1525 and 1528. While both Luther and Zwingli rejected the Catholic doctrines of transubstantiation and the sacrificial Mass, Luther believed that the words "This is my body, this is my blood" must be interpreted literally as teaching that Christ's body and blood were present in the sacrament "in, with, and under" the elements of bread and wine. Zwingli believed that Christ was present in and through the faith of the participants; this presence was not tied to the elements and depended upon the faith of the communicants.

R. W. HEINZE

Marcion (d. ca. 160). Christian Gnostic. Marcion rejected the OT and issued his own NT, which consisted of an abbreviated Gospel of Luke and 10 Pauline epistles (excluding the Pastorals) edited on a dogmatic basis. His *Antitheses* set forth contradictions between the Testaments. His positions are known principally from the five-book refutation by Tertullian, *Against Marcion.*

E. FERGUSON

See also GNOSTICISM.

Mariology. Theology of the Virgin Mary as the mother of the Son of God. The commonly held teachings of the doctrine of Mary are derived from her function as the mother of God (*Theotokos*), a term formally approved by the Council of Ephesus in 431. Mary, who enabled God the Savior to be born, holds a position more exalted than any other creature. She is the Queen of Heaven. Moreover, since her motherhood was indispensable to God's redemptive activity, Mary is essential to the final, spiritual perfection of every creature. Accordingly, although she was not involved in their original physical creation, Mary is, in this ultimate sense, the mother of God's creatures. Mary's involvement in salvation makes her coredemptrix along with Christ. Beginning in the 12th century, references appear to her redemptive work not only in Christ's birth but also at the cross. While Jesus offered his sinless person to appease God's wrath, Mary, whose will was perfectly harmonious with his, offered her prayers. Both atoned for our sins—although Christ's satisfaction was primary and wholly sufficient. Mary's mediatory role includes her present intercession for sinners. Further her immaculate conception, perpetual virginity, and bodily assumption into heaven are basic beliefs.

T. N. FINGER

See also MARY, ASSUMPTION OF; MOTHER OF GOD; MARY, THE BLESSED VIRGIN; IMMACULATE CONCEPTION.

Maritain, Jacques (1882–1973). French philosopher. Maritain's conversion to Christianity in 1906 was followed by his initiation into Thomism. He published his first philosophical article in 1910 and began his career of teaching philosophy a year later at the Collège Stanislas. In 1914 he moved to the Institut Catholique of Paris, and also published his first book, a critique of Bergson. Maritain wrote many books, each one devoted to shedding light on contemporary issues by means of Thomistic concepts. After World War II Maritain became the French ambassador to the Vatican. In 1948 he went to Princeton University. He stepped into an active retirement in 1956.

W. CORDUAN

See also NEO-THOMISM; THOMISM.

Mark, Theology of. ***Christology.*** The Gospel of Mark itself declares that it is "the gospel about Jesus Christ, the Son of God." In this Gospel, Jesus demands that his messiahship be kept secret. Here we find the primary critical problem of the Gospel. Every group with which Jesus is involved is forced to silence: the demons (1:23–25, 34; 3:11–12), those healed (1:40–44; 5:43; 7:36; 8:26), the disciples (8:30; 9:9). In addition, the leaders are kept from the truth (3:22; 4:10–12; 8:11–12), and Jesus withdraws from the crowds (4:10; 7:17; 9:28) and hides from them (7:24; 9:30). The crowds are not allowed to hear Jesus' teaching because they consider Jesus to be only a "wonder worker"; the disciples cannot proclaim it due to their own misunderstanding regarding the meaning of his office; the demons are silenced as part of the "binding of Satan" (3:27); and the leaders are kept from understanding as a sign of God's rejection of them. On the whole, Mark stresses that Jesus' messiahship is essentially incognito, hidden from all except those with spiritual insight.

The term "Son of God" occurs at the beginning of the Gospel (1:1) and at the climax in the centurion's cry (15:39). The stress on Jesus' sonship occurs at the baptism (1:11) and transfiguration (9:7) and is a key element in Jesus' control over the demonic realm (3:11). Further, Jesus is seen as omniscient (2:8; 5:32, 39; 6:48; 8:17; 9:4, 33; 11:2, 14; 12:9; 13:12) and omnipotent over demons, illness, death, and the natural elements. Yet at the same time Mark stresses his humanity: his compassion (1:41; 6:34; 8:2), indignation (3:5; 9:19; 10:14), and distress and sorrow (14:33–36). Jesus "sighs" (7:34; 8:12) and shows anger (1:43; 3:5); he becomes weary (4:38) and admits limitations regarding miracles (6:5–6) and knowledge (13:32). Mark's favorite designation for Jesus is "Son of man," a term that undoubtedly was Jesus' own self-designation but which also went beyond to picture the heavenly figure of Dan. 7:13. In Mark it speaks of his humanity (2:10, 27–28); his betrayal, suffering, and death (9:12; 14:21, 41); and his exaltation and future reign (13:26). Mark also portrays Jesus as teacher (4:38; 5:35; 9:17, 38; 10:51; 11:21). It is in his teaching that his true authority is manifest (1:22).

Eschatology. According to 1:15, the kingdom has already come, and the time of fulfillment is already here. Jesus' deeds and words demonstrate the presence of the kingdom within history, and Jesus will continue to mediate this end-time power until the final consummation of the divine plan (8:38; 13:24–27; 14:62). Mark's eschatology is "inaugurated"—it recognizes the "beginning" of the "end" and the fact that the believer lives in a state of tension between the two.

The Miracles and Soteriology. The miracle stories constitute one-fifth of the Gospel and 47 percent of the first 10 chapters of the Gospel. Mark is careful to stress that the miracles do not form apologetic proof that Jesus is the Christ. They can be known only *by* faith; they cannot *produce* faith. The disciples misunderstand them (4:40; 6:52; 8:17–18). Therefore, they need Jesus' teaching and person to understand properly. When faith is present, the miracles point to the salvific power of God in Christ.

Discipleship. Mark emphasizes the radical nature of the call to discipleship and the difficulties of achieving that goal. The disciples are amazingly obtuse with respect to Jesus' teaching and are both uncomprehending (6:52; 7:18; 8:17–18) and "hardened" (6:52; 8:17). This failure is not the final point, however, although Mark certainly stresses it at the very end, especially if the Gospel ends at 16:8. Yet in the last section of the Gospel before the passion narrative (8:31–10:52), the solution is seen in the presence of Jesus the teacher, who patiently and lovingly instructs the disciples. Discipleship is a call to the cross, and it cannot be understood until the cross. At the resurrection Jesus' followers still fail to understand (16:8) but this failure is obviated by the promise of Jesus' presence (16:7). As the reader identifies first with the problem of discipleship and then with Jesus (the solution), victory becomes an act of faith.

G. R. OSBORNE

See also JOHN, THEOLOGY OF; LUKE, THEOLOGY OF; MATTHEW, THEOLOGY OF.

Mark of the Beast. Term used in the Book of Revelation (13:16–18; 14:11; 15:2; 16:2; 19:20; 20:4) for the seal borne by the followers of Antichrist, acceptance of which is apostasy. This mark can be taken to be a brand, stamp, or tag having both economic (Rev. 13:17) and religious (Rev. 14:11) significance. Rev. 13:18 suggests that the mark of the beast is to be identified with the number of the beast, 666. John could be using an ancient system of numerology called gematria, in which the number concepts (e.g., 600, 60, 6, etc.) are identified with their alphabetic letter equivalents, to be translated then into proper names. In this connection, 666 has been identified with the emperor Titus or Nero.

W. H. MARE

See also ANTICHRIST.

Marpeck, Pilgram. See MENNONITES.

Marriage, Theology of. Biblical teaching on marriage is epitomized in the statement, "For this reason a man will leave his father and mother and be united to his wife, and they will become one flesh" (Gen. 2:24). This OT passage is quoted by Jesus (Matt. 19:5) and Paul (Eph. 5:31) to substantiate their teachings on marriage. The key phrase is the expression "one flesh" (Heb. *bāśār 'ehād*). "Flesh" here implies bodily and spiritual unity of man and woman.

Marriage is an exclusive relationship. The total unity of persons—physical, emotional, intellectual, and spiritual—comprehended by the concept of "one flesh" eliminates polygamy as an option. One cannot relate wholeheartedly in this way to more than one person at a time. It is also plain from the words of Jesus, "Therefore what God has joined together, let man not separate" (Matt. 19:6), that marriage is to endure for the lifetime of the two partners. Only under certain special conditions may the principle of indissolubility be set aside.

When is a couple married? Some, arguing from 1 Cor. 6:16, maintain that marriage is effected through sexual intercourse. A person is considered in the eyes of God to be married to that member of the opposite sex with whom he or she first had sex relations. The sex act is viewed as the agent through which God effects marriage in a manner apparently analogous to the way in which adherents of the doctrine of baptismal regeneration regard the sacrament of baptism as the agent in effecting regeneration. Others consider marriage to be brought about as the result of a declaration of desire to be married accompanied by the expression of mutual intentions of sole and enduring fidelity and responsibility toward the other, preferably undergirded by self-giving love, in the presence of accredited witnesses. It underscores the fact that marriage never has been regarded as solely the concern of the individual couple. To sunder parental relationships and join in intimate, lifelong union with another person demands a considerable degree of maturity—as expressed in a capacity for self-giving love, emotional stability, and the capacity to understand what is involved in committing one's life to another in marriage.

The chief contributions of the NT to the biblical view of marriage are to underscore the original principles of the indissolubility of marriage and the equal dignity of women (1 Cor. 7:4; 11:11–12; Gal. 3:28). By raising women to a position of equal personal dignity with men, marriage is made truly "one flesh," for the unity implied in this expression necessarily presupposes that both partners be given opportunity to develop their full potentialities. This equality need not raise difficulties with the biblical doctrine of subordination of married women (Eph. 5:22–23). This doctrine refers to a hierarchy of function, not of dignity or value. There is no inferiority of person implicit in the doctrine.

L. I. GRANBERG

See also ADULTERY; DIVORCE; SEPARATION, MARITAL.

Marriage Feast of the Lamb. Metaphor used in Rev. 19:7–9 to express the love of Christ for his people and the intimacy and richness of their fellowship in the coming age The imagery of the wedding banquet combines two distinct biblical figures. The consummation of the kingdom of God and the Messiah was depicted as a great feast in the OT and in Jewish literature (Isa. 25:6; 2 Apoc. Bar. 29:1–8; 1 Enoch 62:13–15). The metaphor is employed by Jesus as a description of the consummation of his own messianic reign (Matt. 8:11; 22:1–14; 25:10; Luke 14:15–23; 22:29–30). The other figure is that of the marriage between God and his people. Although already an important OT image, it is enriched in its NT form with Christ the bridegroom and the church his bride (John 3:28–29; 2 Cor. 11:2; Eph. 5:23–32). John joins the images of the messianic banquet and the marriage between Christ and his church so that in Rev. 19:7–9 the church is at once the bride and the guests at the wedding feast.

R. S. RAYBURN

Martyr, Peter. See PETER MARTYR VERMIGLI.

Mary, Assumption of. Roman Catholic doctrine that Mary, like both Enoch and Elijah in the OT, did not die but was assumed into heaven. The apostolic constitution *Munificentissimus Deus*, promulgated by Pius XII on Nov. 1, 1950, made it a doctrine necessary for salvation, stating, "The Immaculate Mother of God, the ever-Virgin Mary, having completed the course of her earthly life, was assumed body and soul into heavenly glory." Like Jesus, she is sinless, preserved from corruption, resurrected, received into heaven, and a recipient of corporeal glory. Thus Mary is crowned Queen of Heaven and assumes the roles of intercessor and mediator. There is no explicit biblical basis for this teaching.

W. N. KERR

See also IMMACULATE CONCEPTION; MARIOLOGY; MARY, THE BLESSED VIRGIN; MOTHER OF GOD.

Mary, The Blessed Virgin. Traditionally, Catholics have venerated Mary as entirely sinless and as the most glorious of God's creatures while Protestants have tended to neglect her role. Certain OT prophecies have been thought to refer to her (Gen. 3:15; Isa. 7:14; Jer. 31:22; Mic. 5:2–3). The symbolic drama of Rev. 12 has often been similarly interpreted. Paul mentions Mary specifically once (Gal. 4:4). While Matthew tells the nativity story, his references to Mary are brief. He does stress her virginity (Matt. 1:18–25). Luke records her encounter with the angel, her visit to Elizabeth, her song to God, the birth of Jesus, and her trips to Jerusalem with Jesus (Luke 1:26–2:51). Mary appears humbly obedient in the face of her responsibility (Luke 1:38), yet deeply thoughtful and somewhat perplexed as to its significance (Luke 1:29; 2:50–51). John records a misunderstanding between Jesus and Mary at the wedding feast in Cana (John 2:1–12). Yet John pictures Mary remaining faithfully beside the cross, while Jesus commends her to his "beloved disciple's" care (John 19:25–27). Luke lists Mary among the earliest post-Easter Christians (Acts 1:14).

T. N. FINGER

See also IMMACULATE CONCEPTION; MARIOLOGY; MARY, ASSUMPTION OF; MOTHER OF GOD.

Mass. The Eucharist or Lord's Supper. The term "mass" comes from the Latin *missio*. The expression *Ite, missa est* is the regular ending of the Roman rite. The term has been used in the West as a name for the whole of the service since at least the 4th century, and is presently used by Roman Catholics and some Anglicans and Lutherans.

P. H. DAVIDS

See also LORD'S SUPPER, VIEWS OF.

Mathews, Shailer (1863–1941). American Baptist theologian. Mathews taught at the divinity school of the University of Chicago. He was a champion of theological liberalism during the fundamentalist-modernist controversy. His *Faith of Modernism* (1924) was a widely read apology for reconstructing Christianity along liberal lines. Mathews was also an avid churchman. He advocated the social gospel (*The Social Teachings of Jesus*, 1897), served as president of the Federal Council of Churches (1912–16), and promoted the formation of the Northern

Baptist Convention, becoming its president in 1915.

T. P. WEBER

See also CHICAGO SCHOOL OF THEOLOGY; LIBERALISM, THEOLOGICAL.

Matins. See OFFICE, DAILY (DIVINE); MORNING PRAYER.

Matthew, Theology of. In order to understand the theology of Matthew's Gospel it is helpful to begin at the end of the book. Its climactic conclusion, the Great Commission (28:16–20), has been called the key to the Gospel's theology. Several important themes are brought together in these verses. First is the focus on the resurrected Christ. Prominent in Matthew's Gospel is the picture of Jesus as the Christ, the messianic Son of God who is also the suffering servant (3:15; 20:28; 26:39; 27:54). Second is the affirmation of Christ's spiritual presence with the disciples. Jesus assures the disciples, "surely I am with you always" (28:20). Jesus' promise to the disciples, "For where two or three come together in my name, there am I with them" (18:20), is confirmation of his presence.

Matthew is the only Gospel writer to use the word "church" (Gk. *ekklēsia*, 16:18; 18:17). Not without reason the Gospel of Matthew has been called "a pastoral Gospel." Matthew realizes that much of what Jesus taught the disciples is applicable to the church. Of great importance in this regard is the commission to make disciples of all nations (28:19). Further, Matthew records Jesus' commission to make disciples by "teaching them to obey everything I have commanded you" (28:20). This mission is to continue until the "end of the age" (28:20). When the gospel has been preached to all nations, then the end will come (24:14) and Christ will reign as king (25:31–34). Reference to a kingdom recurs throughout the Gospel.

A disciple is to be righteous, to be obedient to God. The model for the disciple is Jesus, the perfect Son who fulfilled all righteousness by rendering complete obedience to the Father's will (4:4, 10). That same righteousness is to characterize the disciple (5:20). Obedience to God is to be a priority in the disciple's life (6:33). Complete devotion to the Father is the goal (5:48). Matthew is under no illusion that knowledge alone will lead to righteousness. Teaching is essential, but it has to be met with faith. Those who believe in Jesus have their lives transformed (8:10; 9:2, 22, 29). Not so much the greatness but the presence of faith is important (17:20). Frequently Jesus addresses the disciples as ones of "little faith" (6:30; 8:26; 16:8). This is exemplified in Peter's experience. He boldly responds to Jesus' call to come to him on the water but then wavers in his faith because of the fearful circumstances (14:30).

The term "kingdom" in the Gospel of Matthew seems to have both a spiritual and a physical aspect. The spiritual aspect is present in the ministry of Jesus (12:28) but the physical consummation is anticipated at his return (19:28). Opposed to the kingdom of heaven is the kingdom of Satan (4:8–9; 12:26), from whom those with faith in Christ are delivered (12:27–28). While Satan is powerless before the Spirit of God (12:28), nonetheless he will actively hinder and counterfeit the work of God until the consummation (13:38–39). The ministry of the kingdom carried on by Christ is continued by the church (16:18). The Spirit who enabled Christ to carry out his work (12:28) will enable the disciples to continue it (10:20). The ministry of the church is thus a phase of the kingdom program of God. Ultimately God's program with Israel will also be completed with a positive response to the gospel of the kingdom (19:28; 23:39). Then the "end of the age" (28:20) will come. The king will separate the righteous from the unrighteous (7:21–23), the sheep from the goats (25:31–46), the wheat from the tares (13:37–43).

D. K. LOWERY

See also JOHN, THEOLOGY OF; LUKE, THEOLOGY OF; MARK, THEOLOGY OF.

Maundy Thursday. Thursday of Holy Week, said to be named from the command (Lat. *mandatum*) Christ gave his followers at the Last Supper that they love one another (John 13:34). Possibly the name derives from the Latin *mundo*, "to wash," referring to Jesus' washing the feet of the apostles, an event still commemorated by Christians, including the Church of the Brethren and Roman Catholics.

C. G. FRY

See also CHRISTIAN YEAR; HOLY WEEK.

Maurice, John Frederick Denison (1805–1872). Anglican theologian. In 1840 he became professor of English literature at King's College, London, with which he later combined a post in divinity, but was removed when his *Theological Essays* (1853) disclosed a denial of everlasting punishment. In 1866 he was elected professor of moral philosophy at Cambridge, and there produced his highly acclaimed *Social Morality* (1869). Amid all the controversies of his time (Tractarianism, the development of Broad Church theology, Darwin and evolutionary theory, Colenso and the issue of biblical criticism), Maurice made a profound contribution to theological thought and retained a surprisingly simple faith.

J. D. DOUGLAS

See also SOCIALISM, CHRISTIAN.

Means of Grace. See GRACE, MEANS OF.

Meat Offering. See OFFERINGS AND SACRIFICES IN BIBLE TIMES.

Mediating Theology. (*Vermittlungstheologie*) Theological stance adoped by widely differing thinkers, mostly in Germany, in the middle third of the 19th century, and characterized by an attempt to find truth on a middle ground between opposite extremes. These thinkers tried to mediate between the influences of Hegel and Schleiermacher, between rationalism and supernaturalism, and between innovation and tradition. For them, both feeling and thought were to be taken into account in theology. Christianity was seen as partly natural and partly supernatural in origin. The mediators tended to support the union of Lutherans and Reformed in the state churches of Germany. The most important members of the mediating school (*vermittelnde Schule*) were I. A. Dorner, Julius Koestlin, Julius Müller, C. I. Nitzsch, Richard Rothe, and Karl Ullmann. It can be dated from 1828 with the founding of the periodical *Theologische Studien und Kritiken*. The most important topic for mediating theology was Christology. This theological program was ambitious but vague and faded away once Ritschl and his disciples became influential in the late 19th century.

J. M. DRICKAMER

See also DORNER, ISAAC AUGUST; KENOSIS, KENOTIC THEOLOGY.

Mediation, Mediator. Act of intervention between two conflicting parties in order to promote reconciliation. In Scripture, mediation is the act of bringing sinful people to reconciliation with a holy God. Mediation in the OT is seen in the function of the offices of prophet and priest. The prophet spoke for God to people by way of revelation, instruction, and warning (Exod. 4:10–16; Jer. 1:7, 17; Amos 3:8). The priest spoke for people to God by way of intercession and sacrifice (Deut. 33:10; Heb. 5:1).

In the NT the word "mediator" is used six times. It is used twice in describing Moses as the mediator of the law (Gal. 3:19–20). The word is used three times in the Book of Hebrews, where Jesus is shown to be the mediator of a new or better covenant (8:6; 9:15; 12:24). After discussing the superiority of the new covenant over the old covenant, the author of Hebrews states that with the inauguration of the new covenant there needed to be a new mediator, who is identified as Christ (8:6). Christ as the mediator sacrificed his life in order to inaugurate the new covenant and thereby reconcile us to God. A central verse in the mediatorial work of Christ is 1 Tim. 2:5: "For there is one God and one mediator between God and men, the man Christ Jesus." Beyond the passages that explicitly use the terminology, the NT is replete with examples of Christ being mediator. He represented God to humankind as a prophet. He came from God and spoke the words of God (John 1:18; 6:60–69; 14:9–10). He was and is the greatest priest representing us to God. He was both the priest and sacrifice (Heb. 2:17; 7:26–27; 9:11–15). He offered prayers on behalf of himself (Matt. 26:39, 42, 44; Mark 14:36, 39; Luke 22:41, 44; John 17:1–5; Heb. 5:7) and on behalf of his disciples (Luke 22:32; John 17:6–26). He intercedes in our behalf (Rom. 8:34; Heb. 7:25; 9:24). Thus, he can be a true spokesman for God because he is God (John 1:1–5; 2 Cor. 5:19; Col. 2:9; Heb. 1:2; 5:5) and yet a true spokesman for us because he is man and can sympathize with us and our problems (Heb. 2:17; 4:15; 5:1–9).

H. W. Hoehner

See also Reconciliation.

Meister Eckhart (ca. 1260–1328). German Dominican mystical theologian. At Strasbourg and later at Cologne he developed a reputation as a preacher and spiritual director. Eckhart's significance lies in his elaboration of a mystical theology that stimulated widespread interest and directly influenced such men as J. Tauler and H. Suso. He was cited for heresy in 1326, but died before the proceedings were over. In 1329 John XXII condemned 28 of Eckhart's propositions as heretical. The essential doctrine that governs Eckhart's whole system is that of divine knowledge. God cannot truly be apprehended by any of the normal means of human knowing, for the unconditioned Godhead transcends all modes of individualized knowledge. Divine knowledge therefore must be an unrestricted knowledge suitable to its transcendent subject. This demands a detached intellection that views all of reality as it were from within the Godhead, from the standpoint of the divine subjectivity.

D. G. Dunbar

See also Mysticism.

Melanchthon, Philip (1497–1560). German scholar and religous Reformer. Melanchthon became a professor at the University of Wittenberg in 1518, and developed a close relationship with Luther. By 1521 he wrote *Loci Communes*, the first systematic statement of Luther's ideas. It gained widespread circulation due to its clear style and irenic tone—two characteristics of Melanchthon that were typical of his writing and were most helpful in his contacts with other Lutherans, Protestants, and Roman Catholics. In 1528 his "Visitation Articles" for schools was enacted into law in Saxony. He wrote numerous textbooks for use in schools and later was called "Preceptor of Germany." He wrote the Augsburg Confession in 1530 and its Apology in 1531. These two documents plus the Wittenberg Concord of 1536 soon became the key statements of Lutheran belief.

With the defeat of the Protestant forces at Mühlberg in 1547, Melanchthon proposed the Leipzig Interim, an attempt to salvage some Lutheran ideas in a basically non-Lutheran creedal statement. Melanchthon argued that certain

Roman Catholic rites and beliefs were adiaphora, nonessential to the faith, and thus could be accepted. For this effort he was attacked by Matthias Flacius as a traitor to the Lutheran cause. Melanchthon's final years were spent in controversy, and many Lutherans looked upon him with suspicion. His brilliant mind, love for Christian humanism, clarity in expression, gentle demeanor, and openness to new ideas made him an ideal coworker for Luther but also precipitated much of the controversy that filled his last years.

R. V. SCHNUCKER

See also AUGSBURG CONFESSION; MARBURG COLLOQUY; SYNERGISM.

Melchiorites. Term used for the followers of Melchior Hoffman (modernized in German as Hofmann), the radical Protestant Reformer who carried the gospel to Baltic areas such as Estonia and Livonia, to Emden in Friesland, and to Amsterdam. Hoffman was imprisoned for 10 years before dying in 1543. His Reformation in the Low Countries slowly matured into two wings. (1) The Peace Wing was led by Jan Volkerts Trypmaker (martyred in 1531) and Jacob van Campen (martyred in 1535). Later leaders in this Peace Wing in Friesland were Obbe Philips, his brother Dirk Philips, and from 1536 Menno Simons. (2) The apocalyptic and revolutionary Melchiorites were led by the unstable Jan Matthys, who set up a theocracy in Münster, Germany, and died violently in 1534, and the unscrupulous "King" Jan van Leyden, who was executed after the 1534–35 Münster "kingdom." Violent Münsterite "ultra-Melchiorism" was kept alive briefly by Jan van Batenburg (executed 1538) and by David Joris, who fled to Basel in 1544 under a false name and successfully posed for the rest of his days as a Zwinglian.

J. C. WENGER

See also RADICAL REFORMATION; ZWICKAU PROPHETS.

Melitian Schisms. Two schisms are known by this name, each revolving around a different individual named Melitius. The first involves Melitius, bishop of Lycopolis, who in 311 organized a schismatic church that by the time of the Council of Nicea is reported to have had 28 bishoprics. The Melitian church continued until the 8th century. The second schism concerns Melitius (also Meletius) of Antioch. It arose because of the presence of two rival orthodox parties at Antioch who refused to cooperate. Those who opposed Meletius secured the consecration of Paulinus in 362. This schism lasted until 415.

C. A. BLAISING

See also HOMOOUSION; NICEA, COUNCIL OF.

Mennonites. Large body of Anabaptist descendants of the 16th-century Dutch and Swiss Anabaptists (Swiss Brethren). The basic doctrines of the original Swiss Anabaptists, as well as the Peace Wing of the Dutch Anabaptists, are reflected in the *Programmatic Letters* (1524) of Conrad Grebel; in the Seven Articles of Schleitheim (1527); in the voluminous writings of Pilgram Marpeck (d. 1556); in the writings of Menno Simons and Dirk Philips (*Enchiridion or Handbook of the Christian Doctrine*); in the Swiss Brethren hymn book, the *Ausbund* (1564); and in the *Martyrs Mirror* (1660). The Swiss Brethren were the Free Church wing of the Zwinglian Reformation. Initially the pioneer leaders such as Conrad Grebel and Felix Mantz had nothing but praise for Zwingli. By the fall of 1523, however, they became increasingly uneasy about the tempo of the Reformation in Zurich, and became radical reformers who rejected the state church, infant baptism, and the use of the sword. In 1693 Jakob Ammann, a Swiss elder in Alsace, founded the most conservative wing of the Mennonites, the Amish.

Violent suppression of the Mennonites led to their near extermination in Germany. In Switzerland they survived chiefly in two areas, the Emme Valley of Berne and the mountainous areas of the Jura. William I of the House of Orange brought toleration of a sort to the Peace Wing of the Dutch Anabaptists about 1575. The severe persecution of the Swiss *Taufgesinnten*, the Dutch *Doopsgezinden*, and the Frisian *Mennists* effectively silenced their evangelistic and mission concerns for several centuries, but these were gradually revived in the 19th century, first in Europe and then in North America. Mennonite missions have been most successful in Africa, Indonesia, and India, and have started in Latin America.

J. C. WENGER

See also GREBEL, CONRAD; MENNO SIMONS; RADICAL REFORMATION.

Menno Simons (ca. 1496–1561). Founder of a loosely related group of Reformation believers known today as Mennonites. Menno was born in the Frisian village of Witmarsum and trained for the Roman priesthood. In the first year of his priesthood Menno came to doubt the doctrine of transubstantiation. As a result of reading the NT Menno renounced his Roman Catholicism on January 31, 1536, and went into hiding. He accepted baptism, probably from the leader of the Peace Wing of the Frisian Anabaptists, Obbe Philips, who also ordained Menno as an elder (bishop) in the province of Groningen in 1537. Menno served in the Netherlands (1536–43), in northwest Germany, mainly in the Rhineland (1543–46), and in Danish Holstein (1546–61). The first major collection of his writings appeared in 1646.

J. C. WENGER

See also MENNONITES.

Mercersburg Theology. Nineteenth-century Romantic Reformed theology that stood opposed to the main developments of American religious thought. Mercersburg theology was expounded principally by John Williamson Nevin (1803–86), a theologian, and Philip Schaff (1819–93), a church historian who taught at the seminary of the German Reformed Church in Mercersburg, Pennsylvania, in the 1840s and 1850s. For Nevin the Heidelberg Catechism, the doctrinal standard of the German Reformed, exhibited the Reformation at its best before its decline into a rationalistic and mechanical "Puritanism." He proposed a return to classic Reformed convictions about Christ and his work. *The Mystical Presence* (1846) argued that the views of the Reformers, especially Calvin, provided a means to overcome superficial and subjectivistic Protestantism. When Schaff came to Mercersburg in 1844 from the University of Berlin, he brought along an appreciation for Germany's new idealistic philosophy and its pietistic church renewal. His early work at Mercersburg urged Protestants toward a fuller appreciation of the Christian past. In *The Principle of Protestantism* (1844) he suggested, for example, that the Reformation carried forward the best of medieval Catholicism. He anticipated the day when Reformed, Lutheran, and even Catholic believers could join in Christian union. Such views led to charges of heresy, from which Schaff cleared himself only with difficulty. The influence of Nevin and Schaff was slight in the 1840s and 1850s. American Protestants were ill at ease with immigrants and with anyone who spoke positively about any aspect of Roman Catholicism.

M. A. NOLL

See also SCHAFF, PHILIP.

Merciful Acts, Gift of. See SPIRITUAL GIFTS.

Mercy. From a theological perspective the characteristic of mercy is rooted in God and experienced in relation to God, from whom it may be acquired as a Christian virtue and exercised in relation to fellow human beings. In the Bible a variety of Hebrew and Greek works are used that fall within the general semantic range of the English word "mercy." They include such terms as "lovingkindness" (Heb. *ḥesed*), "to be merciful" (Heb. *ḥānan*), "seat of compassion" (Heb. *rāḥam*), and "grace" (Gk. *charis*). In the OT mercy (in the sense of lovingkindness) is a central theme; the very existence of the covenant between God and Israel is an example of mercy, being granted to Israel freely and without prior obligation on the part of God. With the new covenant the mercy of God is seen in the death of Jesus Christ; Jesus' sacrificial death is in itself a merciful act, demonstrating the divine compassion and making possible the forgiveness of sins. From this fundamental gospel there follows the requirement for all Christians, who are by definition the recipients of mercy, to exercise mercy and compassion toward fellow human beings (Matt. 5:17; James 2:13). Throughout Christian history the awareness of the continuing human need for divine mercy has remained as a central part of Christian worship. The *kyrie eleison* ("Lord have mercy") of the ancient church has continued to be used in many liturgical forms of worship.

P. C. CRAIGIE

See also GOD, ATTRIBUTES OF.

Mercy Seat. (Heb. *kappōret*) Slab of gold, rectangular in shape, measuring approximately 3.5 feet by 2 feet. It was placed over the ark of the covenant, functioning as a cover or lid, in the innermost room of the tabernacle (and of the temple at a later date). On top of the mercy seat were two cherubim, facing each other, their wings extending over the mercy seat and meeting above it. A full account of the mercy seat is provided in Exod. 25:17–22; its construction is described in Exod. 37:6–9.

P. C. CRAIGIE

Merit. In theology a meritorious human act is one for which a reward from God is appropriate. Medieval theologians distinguished merit that strictly deserved a reward (*meritum de condigno*) from that for which a reward was merely appropriate (*meritum de congruo*). The latter could be gained by the nonjustified who heeded God's voice as known through reason and conscience or through the church. Although their actions were tainted with sin and, strictly speaking, could not deserve God's favor, God was pleased to reward them with sanctifying grace. But once aided by sanctifying grace individuals, through the exercise of their free wills, could produce merit *de condigno*, which strictly deserved divine rewards. Medieval theology also elaborated the doctrine of "supererogation." Saintly individuals accumulated merit exceeding that required for their own blessedness. These surplus merits were commonly thought to be stored in a heavenly "treasury" and to be available to others through prayers to saints, indulgences, and other pious acts. Contemporary Catholic theology still speaks of merit, but usually with a significant emphasis on divine grace. No one can merit original creation, final salvation, or God's acceptance of personal efforts *de congruo*. Ultimately Christ merited all the grace that God bestows (merit *de condigno*).

T. N. FINGER

See also GRACE; JUSTIFICATION; SALVATION; SANCTIFICATION; SUPEREROGATION, WORKS OF.

Messiah. (Heb. *māšîaḥ*; Gk. *messias*; Lat. *messias*) Anointed one.

In the OT. "Messiah" is the hellenized transliteration of the Aramaic *məšîḥāʾ*. The underlying Hebrew word *māšîaḥ* is derived from the verbal root *mšḥ*, "to anoint, smear with oil." The title was used most frequently of the king of Israel. The primary sense of the title is "king," as the anointed of God, but it also suggests election, that is, the king was chosen, elect, honored. After the death of David, Israel began to hope for another king like him who would maintain the power and prestige of the country. But Israel came into hard times with the division of the kingdom, and there arose a disillusionment concerning the hope for a king like David. After the exile, Zerubbabel, a descendant of David, took the leadership of Judah, but it was soon apparent that he was not another David. Gradually the hope was projected into the future, and eventually into the very remote future, so that the Messiah was expected at the end of the age. This is the mood of the messianic expectations in the latter part of the OT.

In Intertestamental Writings. The Apocrypha and Pseudepigrapha are the literary remains of the evolution of messianic hopes within Judah between the Testaments. Out of the welter of messianic hopes in this period there emerges a pattern: two kinds of Messiah came to be expected. On one hand, there arose an expectation of a purely national Messiah, one who would appear as a man and assume the kingship over Judah to deliver it from its oppressors. On the other hand, there was a hope for a transcendent Messiah from heaven, part human, part divine, who would establish the kingdom of God on earth. To the popular Jewish mind of the first two centuries before and after Christ these two concepts were not mutually exclusive, but tended rather to modify each other.

In the NT. It remained for Jesus to fuse the three great eschatological representations of the OT—Messiah, suffering servant, and Son of man—into one messianic person. There is no other explanation for the confusion of the disciples when he told them he must suffer and die (Matt. 16:21). That Jesus knew himself to be the Messiah is seen in his use of the title "Son of man"; in Mark 14:61–62 he equates the Christ and the Son of man. "Christ" is simply the Greek equivalent of the Hebrew "messiah." The first generation of the church did not hesitate to refer to Jesus as the Christ, and thereby designate him as the greater Son of David, the King. The word was used first as a title of Jesus (Matt. 16:16) and later as part of his personal name (Eph. 1:1). Peter's sermon at Pentecost acknowledges Jesus not only as the Christ, but also as Lord, and so the fulfillment of the messianic office is integrally linked to the essential deity of Jesus. Acts 2:36 affirms that Jesus was "made" Christ, the sense of the verb being that by the resurrection Jesus was confirmed as the Christ, the Messiah of God.

D. H. WALLACE

See also BRANCH; CHRISTOLOGY; SON OF MAN.

Messianic Banquet. See MARRIAGE FEAST OF THE LAMB.

Metaphysics. Branch of philosophy that inquires into the ultimate nature of reality. The term derives from Aristotle's *Metaphysics*, since it came after (*meta*) the book on physics. Since then, it has seemed especially appropriate to use the term to refer to such topics, since they are more fundamental and more abstract than questions about nature. Metaphysics is widely held to be the central issue in philosophy; central to metaphysics in turn is ontology. Ontology is concerned with being as its subject matter. Ontological questions include the following: What is real and what is mere appearance? Is there reality beyond the things that can be seen, tasted, touched, and heard? Are thoughts real? Is the mind real? Is time real? Is there a God? To accept a Christian perspective on reality necessarily involves making metaphysical commitments. A Christian worldview that is faithful to Scripture and Christian doctrine will involve, for example, the belief that reality includes far more than is amenable to direct empirical investigation. The Christian will be interested in God and his relation to the world, in the soul and its relation to the body, and in free will in relation to determinism. Insofar as Christians seek not only to give assent but also to exercise judgment and develop understanding they will pursue metaphysical inquiry.

D. B. FLETCHER

See also PHILOSOPHY, CHRISTIAN VIEW OF.

Metempsychosis. See REINCARNATION.

Methodism. Doctrines, polity, and worship practices unique to the Protestant denomination guided by the principles promulgated by John Wesley (1703–91). Around 1725, John and Charles Wesley and their colleagues/friends at Oxford formed the Holy Club, which stressed "inward religion, the religion of the heart." It earned its members the jeering title of "Methodists" by 1729. In 1738, after a visit to Georgia, the Wesleys had powerful experiences of the grace of God and felt the call to evangelize. By 1739 the distinct and aggressively evangelistic and highly disciplined Methodist movement spread like wildfire through field preaching, lay preaching, bands, and societies. The "Rules of Bands" demanded a highly disciplined life, an exacting schedule of meetings in which society members were expected to share intimate details of their daily lives, to confess their sins to one another, to pray for each other, and to exhort members of the class toward inner holiness and good works. The enthusiasm of the revivals came under the control of the bands or societies. The weekly prayer meetings; the use of an itinerary system of traveling preachers; the annual conferences; the establishment of chapels; the prolific outpouring of tracts, letters, sermons, and hymns; and the general superintendency of John Wesley became the hallmark of what emerged as a worldwide Methodist movement.

As the revivalistic awakening came to include Methodism, work extended from England to Ireland, Scotland, and Wales, where a Calvinistically oriented minority formally established themselves in 1764. Soon lay preachers were active in America, establishing circuits along the mid-Atlantic states under the supervision of Francis Asbury, who was sent by Wesley in 1771. In 1744 a conference was held in London and standards for doctrine, liturgy, and discipline were adopted. By 1784 Wesley concluded that no one individual would be a suitable successor. He therefore moved to record a "Deed of Declaration" in which he declared a group of 100 of his most able leaders (the "Legal Hundred") his legal successor. Methodist societies were now duly constituted as legal entities, conceived of as *ecclesicla in ecclesia* but formally separate entities from the Church of England. This also established the Annual Conference as the primary authority in the Methodist system.

In September 1784 Wesley yielded to American pressure to have his preachers administer the sacraments by ordaining two lay helpers as elders and Thomas Coke as general superintendent without consulting with his conference. At the Christmas Conference in Baltimore in 1784 Coke ordained Asbury, and the Methodist Episcopal Church was organized. Coke and Asbury were elected general superintendents. A Sunday Service based on the *Book of Common Prayer* and Twenty-Five Articles of Religion abridged by Wesley from the Thirty-

Nine Articles were adopted by the new denomination. Continuing his work among the various societies, Wesley ordained a number of presbyters in Scotland and England, and for the mission field. Unlike Methodism in America, no formal separation was consummated in England until after Wesley's death in 1791.

In the U.S. numerous Methodist-oriented bodies exist. Some came into being in disputes over doctrinal issues. Others arose out of social concerns. The largest is the United Methodist Church, formed in 1939 by the reunion of the Methodist Episcopal Church, South, the Methodist Protestant Church, and the Methodist Episcopal Church to form the Methodist Church and in 1968 by the addition of the Evangelical United Brethren (EUB) Church. Methodism today contains a wide variety of emphases, all united in practical faith and avoiding strict confessionalism.

P. A. MICKEY

See also WATSON, RICHARD; WESLEY, JOHN; WESLEYAN TRADITION, THE.

Methodism, Calvinistic. See CALVINISTIC METHODISM.

Metropolitan. See CHURCH OFFICERS.

Midtribulation Rapture. See RAPTURE OF THE CHURCH.

Millennium, Views of the. (Lat. *mille*, "thousand," plus *annus*, "year") Doctrine taken from Rev. 20:1–10, which describes the devil as being bound and thrown into a bottomless pit for 1000 years.

Major Varieties of Millennialism. For purposes of analysis and explanation Christian attitudes toward the millennium can be classified as premillennial, postmillennial, and amillennial. These categories involve much more than the arrangement of events surrounding the return of Christ. Premillennialists believe that the return of Christ will be preceded by certain signs, including wars, famines, earthquakes, the preaching of the gospel to all nations, a great apostasy, the appearance of Antichrist, and the great tribulation. These events culminate in the second coming, which will result in a period of peace and righteousness when Christ and his saints control the world. This rule is established suddenly through supernatural methods rather than gradually over a long period of time by means of the conversion of individuals. The Jews will figure prominently in the future age because they will be converted in large numbers and will again have a prominent place in God's work. Nature will have the curse removed from it, and even the desert will produce abundant crops. Christ will restrain evil during the age by the use of authoritarian power. Despite the idyllic conditions of this golden age there is a final rebellion of wicked people against Christ and his saints. This exposure of evil is crushed by God, the non-Christian dead are resurrected, the last judgment conducted, and the eternal states of heaven and hell established. Many premillennialists have taught that during the 1000 years dead or martyred believers will be resurrected with glorified bodies to intermingle with the other inhabitants of the earth.

In contrast to premillennialists, postmillennialists emphasize the present aspects of God's kingdom, which will reach fruition in the future. They believe that the millennium will come through Christian preaching and teaching. Such activity will result in a more godly, peaceful, and prosperous world. The new age will not be essentially different from the present, and it will come about as more people are converted to Christ. Evil will not be totally eliminated during the millennium, but it will be reduced to a minimum as the moral and spiritual influence of Christians is increased. During the new age the church will assume greater importance, and many economic, social, and educational problems will be solved. This period is not necessarily limited to 1000 years because the number can be used symbolically. The millennium closes with the second coming of Christ, the resurrection of the dead, and the last judgment.

The third position, amillennialism, states that the Bible does not predict a period of the rule of Christ on earth before the last judgment. According to this outlook there will be a continuous development of good and evil in the world until the second coming of Christ, when the dead will be raised and the judgment conducted. Amillennialists believe that the kingdom of God is now present in the world as the victorious Christ rules his church through the Word and the Spirit. They feel that the future, glorious, and perfect kingdom refers to the new earth and life in heaven. Thus Rev. 20 is a description of the souls of dead believers reigning with Christ in heaven.

The Rise of Millennialism. Early millennial teaching was characterized by an apocalyptic emphasis. In this view the future kingdom of God would be established through a series of dramatic, unusual events. Such teaching has been kept alive throughout the Christian era by certain types of premillennialism. Apocalyptic interpretation is based upon the prophecies of Daniel and the amplification of some of the same themes in the Book of Revelation. These works point to the imminent and supernatural intervention of God in human affairs and the defeat of the seemingly irresistible progress of evil. Such an outlook brought great comfort to believers who suffered from persecution by the forces of imperial Rome. Expressed in a form that has been called historic premillennialism, this hope seems to have been the prevailing eschatology during the first three centuries of the Christian era, and is found in the works of Papias, Irenaeus, Justin Martyr, Tertullian, Hippolytus, Methodius, Commodianus, and Lactantius.

Medieval and Reformation Millennialism. In the new age brought in by the acceptance of Christianity as the main religion of the Roman Empire it was Augustine, bishop of Hippo, who articulated the amillennial view that dominated Western Christian thought during the Middle Ages. The millennium, according to his interpretation, referred to the church in which Christ reigned with his saints. The statements in the Book of Revelation were interpreted allegorically by Augustine. No victory was imminent in the struggle with evil in the world. On the really important level, the spiritual, the battle had already been won and God had triumphed through the cross. Satan was reduced to lordship over the City of the World, which coexisted with the City of God. Eventually even the small domain left to the devil would be taken from him by a triumphant God. Augustine's allegorical interpretation became the official doctrine of the church during the medieval period. In defiance of the main teaching of the church, however, the earlier apocalyptic premillennialism continued to be held by certain counterculture groups. These millenarians under charismatic leaders were often associated with radicalism and revolts. Each of the three main Protestant traditions of the 16th century—Lutheran, Calvinist, and Anglican—had the support of the state and so continued the same Constantinian approach to theology. Both Luther and Calvin were very suspicious of millennial speculation. Calvin declared that those who engaged in calculations based on the apocalyptic portions of Scripture were "ignorant" and "malicious."

Modern Millennialism. It was during the 17th century that premillennialism of a more scholarly nature was presented. Two Reformed theologians, Johann

Heinrich Alsted and Joseph Mede, were responsible for the renewal of this outlook. They did not interpret the Book of Revelation in an allegorical manner but rather understood it to contain the promise of a literal kingdom of God to be established on earth before the last judgment. During the Puritan Revolution the writings of these men encouraged others to look for the establishment of the millennial kingdom in England. The collapse of the Cromwellian regime and the restoration of the Stuart monarchy discredited premillennialism. Yet the teaching continued into the 18th century through the work of Isaac Newton, Johann Albrecht Bengel, and Joseph Priestley.

As the popularity of premillennialism waned, postmillennialism rose to prominence. First expressed in the works of certain Puritan scholars, it received its most influential formulation in the writings of the Anglican commentator Daniel Whitby. It seemed to him that the kingdom of God was coming ever closer and that it would arrive through the same kind of effort that had always triumphed in the past. Among the many theologians and preachers who were convinced by the arguments of Whitby was Jonathan Edwards. Edwardsean postmillennialism also emphasized the place of America in the establishment of millennial conditions upon the earth.

During the 19th century premillennialism became popular once again. The violent uprooting of European social and political institutions during the era of the French Revolution encouraged a more apocalyptic climate of opinion. There was also a revival of interest in the fortunes of the Jews. A new element was added to premillennialism during this period with the rise of dispensationalism. Edward Irving, a Church of Scotland minister who pastored a congregation in London, was one of the outstanding leaders in the development of the new interpretation. Irving's apocalyptic exposition found support among the Plymouth Brethren and led many in the group to become enthusiastic teachers of dispensational premillennialism. Perhaps the leading early dispensational expositor among the Brethren was John Nelson Darby. He believed that the second coming of Christ consisted of two stages, the first a secret rapture or "catching away" of the saints that would remove the church before a seven-year period of tribulation devastates the earth, and the second when Christ appears visibly with his saints after the tribulation to rule on earth for 1000 years.

Darby's interpretation was accepted in America because of the work of individuals such as Henry Moorhouse, a Brethren evangelist, who convinced many interdenominational speakers to accept dispensationalism. Typical of those who came to believe in Darby's eschatology were William E. Blackstone, "Harry" A. Ironside, Arno C. Gaebelein, Lewis Sperry Chafer, and C. I. Scofield. It is through Scofield and his works that dispensationalism became the norm for much of American evangelicalism. His *Scofield Reference Bible*, which made the new eschatological interpretation an integral part of an elaborate system of notes printed on the same pages as the text, proved so popular that it sold over 3 million copies in 50 years. Bible schools and seminaries such as Biola, Moody Bible Institute, Dallas Theological Seminary, and Grace Theological Seminary, along with the popular preachers and teachers who have utilized the electronic media, have made this interpretation popular among millions of conservative Protestants. The new view replaced the older premillennial outlook to such an extent that when George Ladd restated the historic interpretation in the mid-20th century it seemed like a novelty to many evangelicals.

While the various forms of premillennialism competed for adherents in 19th-century America, a form of postmillennialism that equated America with the kingdom of God became very popular. Perhaps the most complete statement of this civil millennialism was presented by Hollis Read (*The Hand of God in History*). He believed that geography, politics, learning, the arts, and morality all pointed to the coming of the millennium to America in the 19th century. From this base the new age could spread to the entire earth. Whenever America has faced a time of crisis, there have been those who have revived civil postmillennialism as a means to encourage and comfort their fellow citizens. The biblical content of this belief has become increasingly vague as society has become more pluralistic.

R. G. CLOUSE

Miller, William (1782–1849). See ADVENTISM.

Mind. Totality of a person's mental and moral state of being.

What Is Mind? Plato was the first to make the distinction between mind and body. Plato held that the mind is capable of existence before and after its relationship to the body, and is able to rule over the body during its residence. Aristotle proposed a different schema, one that grew out of his understanding of form and matter. Aristotle's view was influential during the Middle Ages and was held by Aquinas and many scholastics. Descartes, however, was the first to systematically work out the nature and interrelationship of mind and body.

Mental Substance Theory. Descartes regarded both body and mind as substances. They are, however, utterly different in nature. Body is extended and unthinking. Mind, on the other hand, is unextended and thinking. Body is the more original and lasting. Mind is mental substance or pure ego. It is an enduring, immaterial, nonextended stuff that changes in the performance of certain acts. Mental acts are all acts of thinking, broadly defined. These acts include doubting, understanding, conceiving, affirming, denying, willing, refusing, imagining, and feeling. Mental substance, since its essence is to think, is always engaged in one of these acts.

Bundle Theory. Hume views the mind as nothing more than a bundle or collection of perceptions, which follow one another with incredible rapidity and are in constant flux and movement. If all these perceptions were removed, there would be nothing. Hume suggests that these perceptions are related to one another by resemblance, contiguity, and causation, but finally has to admit that he fails to explain the simplicity and identity of the mind.

Stream-of-Consciousness Theory. William James, developing a position somewhere between the mental substance and bundle theories, maintains that mind is a "stream of consciousness."

The Mind-Body Problem. *Monistic Theories.* Materialism is the oldest mind-body theory. It is the view that matter is fundamental, and that everything that exists is dependent upon it. When applied to mental events it means that all statements about mind are synonymous or translatable into statements about physical phenomena. A more sophisticated form of materialism, called identity theory, is widely held today.

Dualistic Theories. What unites dualistic theories is their emphasis on the fact that mentalistic and physicalistic statements differ not only in meaning but in reference. Interactionism was given its classical formulation by Descartes. He held that there are two kinds of substances in the world, mental and corporeal. Mental events can sometimes cause physical events and vice versa. Human beings are so constituted that events in one (e.g., fear) can cause events in the other (e.g., release of adrenalin). A second dualistic theory of the mind-body relationship is occasionalism. Occasionalists go beyond Descartes in claiming that because of their similarity, there can be no natural causal connection. Therefore, they propose God as the intermediary link between mind and body. An old but attractive dualistic theory is epiphenomenalism. Simply put, epiphenomenalism is the view that causality goes in only one direction, from body to mind. Mental events then are effects, never causes, of physical events. How is it that it sometimes appears that a mental event causes a physical change? That, it is argued, is an illusion. The mind-body problem has implications for a biblical anthropology. Traditionally Christian theologians have been dualistic at a minimum. Dichotomy, the view that people have a material and immaterial part, has been widely accepted. The chief alternative to dichotomy until recently has been trichotomy, which sees human beings as triparate, with body, soul, and spirit. More recently it has been popular to talk of a unitary view of human beings. Such discussions are characteristically ambiguous.

P. D. Feinberg

See also Dichotomy; Man, Doctrine of; Trichotomy.

Minister. One who serves. It is the consistent NT teaching that the work of the minister is "to prepare God's people for works of service, so that the body of Christ may be built up" (Eph. 4:12). The minister is called of God to a position of responsibility rather than privilege, as the Greek words for "minister" show (*diakonos*, "table waiter"; *hypēretēs*, "under-rower" in a large ship; *leitourgos*, "servant," usually of the state or a temple). There are two passages in the NT that are of special importance in understanding the ministries of the church: 1 Cor. 12:28 and Eph. 4:11–12. Included in the ministries exercised in the early church were those of apostleship, prophecy, teaching, working of miracles, healing, service, administration, speaking in tongues (possibly also interpretations [v. 30]), evangelism, and pastoral ministry. In every case these ministries appear to be the direct gift of God to the church. The NT also records other ministries in the church. Paul and Barnabas appointed elders in each church (Acts 14:23). Overseers and deacons worked in the early church (Phil. 1:1; 1 Tim. 3:1–10).

L. Morris

See also Church Officers; Ministry; Ordain, Ordination.

Ministry. Service rendered to God or to people (Eph. 4:7–16). Those entrusted with ministry in Scripture include priests and Levites, apostles, prophets, evangelists, pastor-teachers, elders, and all believers. The term "ministry" therefore refers to the work both of those commissioned to leadership and of the whole body of believers. The ideals of ministry are portrayed in the servant-leadership of Jesus. Acts 6:3 provides guidelines as to the spiritual qualities that must be sought in leaders, while 1 Tim. 3:1–13 (cf. Titus 1:6–9) specifies these necessary qualities in greater detail. There is a considerable difference of opinion regarding the historical development of ministry in the early church. Many have seen a development from a simple charismatic ministry, exercised by every Christian in an individual way, to an organized or "official" ministry restricted to a few, ultimately issuing in the monarchial episcopate in the postapostolic period. It is far from certain, however, that the NT church experienced a linear development from charismatic to institutional ministry, and even less plausible that there was an antithesis in the early church between these two forms of ministry.

There are a number of additional issues surrounding the theology of ministry. These include (1) whether the NT ever described a prerequisite "call" to ministry other than the general commands of Christ and the recognition of the local church; (2) whether women were admitted to ministry in the NT (and consequently should be today); (3) whether lifestyle (e.g., homosexuality) or prior experiences such as divorce should preclude ministry; and (4) what honor and authority should accrue to "full-time" ministers of Christ above those that belong to any faithful follower of the Lord. Some of these questions revolve around the institutional aspect of ministry. A further question is whether there is a sacramental aspect to ministry that is restricted to those ordained as priests by the church. A dual view of ministry—that all believers are to exercise a ministry in accordance with their spiritual gifts, but that authoritative teaching, leadership, and discipline are limited to a recognized body of elders—paves the way for an answer to the above questions.

W. L. LIEFELD

See also CHURCH OFFICERS; MINISTER; ORDAIN, ORDINATION.

Minor Orders. Those orders of ministry below the major orders in the Roman and Orthodox churches. In the former, subdeacons were usually reckoned as a minor order until they were officially classed as a major order in 1207. The minor orders since then are acolytes, exorcists, readers or lectors, and doorkeepers or porters. In the Eastern Church acolytes, exorcists, and doorkeepers have been merged with the subdiaconate, but readers and cantors remain. Today practically nothing of the functions of any of the minor orders survives. They were little more than a steppingstone to the higher orders and are all conferred at the same time.

L. MORRIS

See also CHURCH OFFICERS; MAJOR ORDERS.

Miracles. Events that run counter to the observed processes of nature. The word "observed" is particularly important here. Augustine, in his *City of God*, noted that Christians must not teach that miracles are events that run counter to nature, but rather that they are events that run counter to *what is known* of nature. Our knowledge of nature is a limited knowledge. Clearly there may be higher laws that remain unknown to us. In any case, miracles are not correctly conceived of as irrational disruptions of the pattern of nature in general, but as disruptions of the *known* part of that pattern.

Biblical miracles have a clear objective: they are intended to bring the glory and love of God into bold relief. They are designed, among other things, to draw our attention away from the mundane events of everyday life and direct it toward the mighty acts of God. In the context of the OT, miracles are viewed as the direct intervention of God in human affairs, and they are unquestionably linked to his redemptive activity on behalf of humankind. The most significant miracle of the OT is God's action on behalf of the Israelites in opening up the Red Sea as they escaped from the Egyptians. This miracle is the centerpiece of Hebrew history and of OT religion. It is a demonstration of God's power and love in action. This emphasis on miracles as the redemptive activity of God is continued in the NT, where they are a part of the proclamation of the good news that God has acted ultimately on our behalf in the coming of Jesus Christ into history. Miracles are a manifestation of the power that God will use to restore all of creation to its proper order, to restore the image of God in us to its full expression, and to destroy death. The central miracle of the Bible is the resurrection of Christ.

J. D. SPICELAND

Miracles, Gift of. See SPIRITUAL GIFTS.

Missiology. Study of the mission (in particular, the missionary activity) of the church. Missiology is an applied science. The underlying dynamic of the missiological process starts with an actual field situation confronting a church or mission, in which its problems, successes, and failures are clearly known; it ends with the application of missiological perspectives to this same field situation.

The three major disciplines essential to the missiological process are theology (mainly biblical), anthropology (mainly social, applied, and theoretical but including primitive religion, linguistics, cultural dynamics, and cultural change), and history. Other contributing disciplines include psychology, communication theory, and sociology. All these disciplines interact within the specific structures and problems of the given field situation and with the motivation of the gospel as the driving force of that interaction. Therefore, basic components that later become "missiology" are neither theology nor history, neither anthropology nor psychology, nor the sum total of these fields of study, but ethnotheology, ethnohistory, and ethnopsychology. The discipline of missiology then comes into its own, enriched and influenced by such ingredients as ecumenics, non-Christian religion, and even economics.

Missiology came into its own as an academic discipline in the 19th century. Karl Graul, director of the Leipzig Mission, was, according to Otto Lehmann, the first German to qualify himself for higher academic teaching in this field. Gustav Warneck, another German Lutheran, is regarded as the founder of Protestant missionary science. His *Evangelische Missionslehre* (1892) abundantly confirms this designation. Warneck significantly influenced the great Catholic missiologist Josef Schmidlin (1876–1944) and thereby initiated the sort of stimulating interaction between the two major segments of the church that has continued to the present. Warneck's death virtually coincided with the World Missionary Conference at Edinburgh in 1910. Since then, the International Missionary Council (until Ghana, 1958) and the Commission on World Mission and Evangelism of the World Council of Churches (after New Delhi, 1961) have continued to reflect on the science of mission.

Outstanding American evangelical missiologists include Rufus Anderson, the 19th-century popularizer of the indigenous church; Kenneth Scott Latourette and R. Pierce Beaver, two outstanding authorities on the history of missions and younger churches; Donald A. McGavran, the founder of the Church Growth movement; Eugene A. Nida, an expert on Bible translation and the cross-cultural communication of the Christian faith; J. Herbert Kane, the prolific writer of primary texts on all aspects of the Christian mission; and George W. Peters, the creative biblical theologian in the Mennonite tradition.

A. G. GLASSER

See also WARNECK, GUSTAV ADOLF.

Modalism. See MONARCHIANISM.

Moderator. See CHURCH OFFICERS.

Modernism. See LIBERALISM, THEOLOGICAL.

Modernism, Catholic. See CATHOLICISM, LIBERAL.

Moltmann, Jürgen. See HOPE, THEOLOGY OF.

Monarchianism. Third-century heresy that emphasized God's unity at the expense of Christ's divinity. (It is also called patripassianism or Sabellianism.) Monarchianism attempted to defend monotheism against suspected tritheism. It did so, however, by denying the personal distinctiveness of a divine Son and Holy Spirit in contrast to God the Father. Dynamic or adoptionistic monarchianism proposed a monotheism of God the Father. Jesus was regarded as a mere man who was endowed with the Holy Spirit. This view was first put forward in Rome about 190 by Theodotus of Byzantium and continued by his successor, Artemon (also called Theodotus). It is likely that Paul of Samosata held to a more advanced form of this dynamic monarchianism. A more sophisticated form of modalism was taught by Sabellius in Rome in the early 3d century. Sabellius taught the existence of a divine monad (which he named *Huiopator*), which by a process of expansion projected itself successively in revelation as Father, Son, and Holy Spirit. As Father it revealed itself as Creator and Lawgiver. As Son it revealed itself as Redeemer. As Spirit it revealed itself as the giver of grace. These were three different modes revealing the same divine person.

C. A. Blaising

See also Antiochene Theology; Homoousion; Paul of Samosata.

Monasticism. Lifestyle practiced by monks, characterized by the vows of chastity, poverty, and obedience. The term *monasticism* (also called monachism) literally means "living alone." The first monks were the so-called desert fathers, hermits living in the deserts of Egypt, Syria, and Palestine. Struggling with sin and fearful of damnation, these early monks left the towns for a solitary struggle against temptation. Some, like Simeon Stylites, lived very exotic lives and became tourist attractions. More typical, however, was Anthony of Egypt (ca. 250–356), whose commitment to salvation led him back to the community to evangelize unbelievers. His extreme asceticism deeply touched the sensibilities of the age. The desert fathers chose a life of lonely, individual struggle against the devil as opposed to the obvious support that came from living in some sort of community. Pachomius (ca. 290–346), an Egyptian monk, preferred a cenobitical monastic life to the eremitical lifestyle of the desert fathers. He wrote a rule of life for monks in which he emphasized organization and the rule of elder monks over the newly professed. Basil the Great (ca. 330–79) encouraged monks to care for orphans, feed the poor, maintain hospitals, educate children, and provide work for the unemployed.

From the 4th to the 6th centuries monasticism spread throughout the Christian world. From Asia Minor to Britain its ideal flourished. The Celtic monks tended to espouse the eremitical tradition, whereas Latin monasticism, under the Great Rule of Benedict of Nursia (ca. 480–ca. 547), codified itself into a permanent, organized communal form. To the traditional vows of poverty, chastity, and obedience to Christ the Benedictines added stability. Monks could no longer drift about from monastery to monastery but were bound to one for life. The great work of the monasteries of the Middle Ages was the *opus Dei*, the work of God, prayer and praise to the Almighty throughout the day and night. This "work" was organized into the offices of the monastic day. In addition, monks and nuns performed physical labor, provided charitable services, and kept learning alive.

In modern history monasticism has suffered three great blows; the Reformation, the Enlightenment, and 20th-century secularism. Generally, the leaders of the Reformation believed that the monastics did not in fact conform to a simple gospel rule of life, that their repetitive prayers, fasts, and ceremonies were meaningless and that they had no real value to society. In different terms the 18th-century Enlightenment would also argue that the monasteries were useless.

Modern liberals saw them as corrupt and unnatural, preserving the superstition of an obsolete age. The 20th century has seen the rapid decline of religious orders.

C. T. MARSHALL

See also BASIL THE GREAT; FRANCISCAN ORDER.

Monergism. Theological doctrine that the grace of God is the only efficient cause in beginning and effecting conversion. The opposite of synergism, this position is consistently upheld by the Augustinian tradition within Christianity. The implication of this doctrine is that if a person is saved, it is entirely the work of God; if an individual is lost, it is entirely the fault of that person, who, while not free to accept the gospel, is by nature able to reject it.

C. G. FRY

See also SYNERGISM.

Money. See WEALTH, CHRISTIAN VIEW OF.

Monism. Metaphysical view that there is only one substance or ultimate reality. Although the term was first used by the German philosopher Christian Wolff (1679–1754), monism actually dates back to the pre-Socratic philosophers, who appealed to a single unifying principle to explain all the diversity of observed experience. Substantival monism ("one thing") is the view that there is only one substance and that all diversity is ultimately unreal. This view was maintained by Spinoza and is also a tenet of both Hinduism and Buddhism.

Attributive monism ("one category") holds that there is one kind of thing but many different individual things in this category. Materialism and idealism are different forms of attributive monism. Many leading philosophers have been attributive monists, including Bertrand Russell and Thomas Hobbes on the materialistic side, and G. W. Leibniz and George Berkeley in the idealist camp. The Christian intellectual tradition has generally held that substantival monism fails to do justice to the distinction between God and creature, and that of attributive monisms only idealism is theologically acceptable.

D. B. FLETCHER

Monophysitism. (Gk. *monos*, "single," plus *physis*, "nature") Theological doctrine that the incarnate Christ had only a single, divine nature, clad in human flesh. It is sometimes called Eutychianism, after Eutyches (d. 454), one of its leading defenders. Since the Council of Chalcedon (451), which confirmed as orthodox the doctrine of two natures, divine and human, monophysitism has been considered heretical.

D. A. HUBBARD

Monotheism. Belief that there is only one God.

Monotheism and the OT. The Book of Genesis begins by assuming that there is only one true God, and that assumption is maintained throughout the OT. Against materialism, which teaches that matter is everything and eternal, Gen. 1 teaches that matter had a beginning and that God created it and is therefore above it. Against pantheism, which teaches that God is (or gods are) in everything, Gen. 1 teaches that God is above everything and separate from it. Against dualism, which posits a continuing struggle between two gods or principles (one evil and the other good), Gen. 1 posits one benevolent God who declares each of his creative works to be "good" and describes everything that he has created as "very good" (Gen. 1:31). Moses defines the nature of God in a clearly monotheistic fashion (Deut. 4:35, 39; 32:39). The writing prophets of the 8th century B.C. and afterward strengthened monotheistic doctrine by constantly reminding Israel of the vast gulf that separated Yahweh from pagan idols and the so-called gods that they represented.

Monotheism and the NT. Although the NT affirms Trinitarianism (see, e.g., Matt. 28:19; 2 Cor. 13:14), it is outspokenly monotheistic as well (see, e.g., Acts 17:22–31). For the NT writers no conflict exists between the teachings that God is one and that at the same time he is three in one. Paul can state with confidence that "there is no God but one" (1 Cor. 8:4), and in the very next breath, using a partial Trinitarian formula, can declare with equal confidence that "there is but one God, the Father, from whom all things came and for whom we live; and there is but one Lord, Jesus Christ, through whom all things came and through whom we live" (8:6).

R. YOUNGBLOOD

See also GOD, DOCTRINE OF; TRINITY; THEISM.

Montanism. Prophetic movement that broke out in Phrygia in Roman Asia Minor (Turkey) around A.D. 172. It attracted a wide following, chiefly in the East, but won its most distinguished adherent in Tertullian. After a period of uncertainty, especially at Rome, it was condemned by synods of bishops in Asia and elsewhere. A residual sect persisted in Phrygia for several centuries. The main associates of Montanus, who was a recent convert and held no church office, were the prophetesses Prisca (Priscilla) and Maximilla. What they called "the New Prophecy" was basically a summons to prepare for the return of Christ by heeding the voice of the Paraclete speaking, often in the first person, through his prophetic mouthpieces. They claimed to stand in the line of Christian prophecy well attested in Asia—for example, by John of Revelation—but their ecstatic manner of utterance was (falsely) alleged to run counter to the tradition of Israelite and Christian prophecy. They also incurred the hostility of church leaders by the unusual prominence of women, a boldness that seemed to court martyrdom, their confident predictions of the imminent consummation (shown in time to be false by virtue of their nonfulfillment), the hallowing of obscure Phrygian villages like Pepuza as harbingers of the new Jerusalem, and their stern asceticism that disrupted marriages, advocated protracted fasting, and allowed only a dry diet (xerophagy).

D. F. WRIGHT

Moon, Sun Myung. See UNIFICATION CHURCH.

Moral Argument for God. See GOD, ARGUMENTS FOR THE EXISTENCE OF.

Moral Inability. See DEPRAVITY, TOTAL.

Moral Influence Theory of Atonement. See ATONEMENT, THEORIES OF THE.

Moral Re-Armament. Modern name for the Oxford Group movement, founded by Frank Buchman (1878–1961). Before his conversion Buchman was a humanitarian dedicated to the welfare of his fellow human beings. He believed in God, but did not realize that people must be changed inwardly before there can be lasting changes in society. The conviction dawned on him that the disease that was eroding the moral fabric of society was sin in the human heart and that the only cure was Christ. Buchman became known for his "house parties" on university campuses (including Oxford, from which the movement derived its name).

Buchman was not wrong in his belief that the key to social reformation lies in personal transformation, but his tendency to downplay the continuing effects of sin in the believer tended to make his social policy simplistic and even utopian. When the Oxford Group movement became Moral Re-Armament in the late 1930s, the experience of personal conversion was even more disassociated from the objective work of Christ's atoning sacrifice on the cross, and a humanistic emphasis began to supplant the evangelical basis that remained central in Buchman's own life. To the end, Buchman insisted that "only God can change human nature"; yet the focus of attention in Moral Re-Armament was much more on the realization of the moral ideal than on divine grace. The first World Assembly of Moral Re-Armament was held at Caux, Switzerland, in 1946. Caux remains the center of MRA, but since Buchman's death the movement has lost much of its momentum.

D. G. BLOESCH

Mormonism. Doctrines and practices of the Church of Jesus Christ of Latter-day Saints. The Mormons, as they are usually known, represent one of the most successful of 19th-century religious movements. Today they are divided into two main groups: the Church of Jesus Christ of Latter-day Saints, organized from Salt Lake City, Utah, and the Reorganized Church of Jesus Christ of Latter-day Saints, based in Independence, Missouri. In addition to these major groups a number of smaller "fundamentalist" groups exist. Today the Utah church claims over 3 million members, while the Reorganized Church claims about 600,000 adherents.

The Church of Jesus Christ of Latter-day Saints was first organized on Apr. 6, 1830, at Fayette, New York, by Joseph Smith. Under the leadership of Brigham Young the Mormons left Nauvoo in 1847 and traveled westward to Utah. Here for more than 30 years Brigham Young ruled the Mormon Church and laid the foundation of its present strength. Mormonism has a dual foundation. The first is the claim of Joseph Smith to have received golden plates upon which ancient scriptures are alleged to have been written. Smith claimed to have translated these plates and subsequently published them in 1830 as *The Book of Mormon.* The second foundation is Smith's claim to have had an encounter with the living Jesus and subsequently to receive continuing revelations from God. The substance of these continuing revelations is to be found in the Mormon publication *The Doctrine and Covenants,* while an account of Joseph Smith's encounter with Jesus and the discovery of *The Book of Mormon* is to be found in *The Pearl of Great Price. The Book of Mormon, Doctrine and Covenants,* and *The Pearl of Great Price* form the basis of the Mormon continuing revelation. Since the death of Smith these revelations have been supplemented by what the church claims to be further revelations given to its leaders.

Mormonism teaches that God the Father has a body and that humankind's destiny is to evolve to Godhood. It claims that it is the only true church because its leaders continue to receive revelation from God. In addition it claims to possess the powers of the priesthood of Aaron and Melchizedek into which its male members are expected to be initiated. As a social organization the Mormon Church exhibits many admirable qualities. It promotes extensive welfare programs for its members, operates a large missionary and educational organization, and promotes family life. Mormons are expected to participate in what is known as "temple work." This involves proxy baptism for deceased ancestors and "celestial marriage." Mormons believe that in addition to temporal marriages church members may be sealed to their families "for time and eternity" through a process known as celestial marriage. As a new religious movement Mormonism represents a dynamic synthesis that combines frontier revivalism, intense religious experience, and popular evolutionary philosophies with a respect for Jesus and Christian ethics. This combination of beliefs holds strong attraction for many people uninterested or unschooled in Christian history and theology.

I. HEXHAM

Morning Prayer. "The Order for Daily Morning Prayer" from the *Book of Common Prayer* of the Church of England, long the principal service in Anglican and Episcopal churches. Morning prayer or English matins owes its origin to Thomas Cranmer.

C. G. FRY

See also BOOK OF COMMON PRAYER; WORSHIP IN THE CHURCH.

Mortality. Humankind's vulnerability to death and dissolution. The NT is clear: "The wages of sin is death" (Rom. 6:23); "Sin entered the world through one man and death through sin" (Rom. 5:12). Mortality is not a biological problem but a theological one. It is only through the substitutionary death and resurrection of Jesus Christ that the power of sin has been broken. The Christian is delivered from sin and death (Rom. 4:25; 5:6–8; 1 Cor. 15:3–4; 2 Cor. 5:14–15; 1 Thess. 5:10; Heb. 2:9; 1 Pet. 3:18; Rev. 1:17–18). Those who refuse God's offer of life through Christ choose instead "second death," an eternal and irrevocable existence separated from the God whom they have spurned (John 8:21, 24; 2 Thess. 1:8–9; Heb. 10:26–27, 31; Jude 12–13; Rev. 20:12–15).

F. R. HARM

See also ANNIHILATIONISM; CONDITIONAL IMMORTALITY.

Mortal Sin. See SIN, MORTAL.

Mother of God. (Gk. *Theotokos*) Title accorded to Mary, the mother of Jesus, at the Council of Ephesus (431). The council decreed that the title could rightly be given to Mary because Jesus was conceived of her by the Holy Spirit, and was the Son of God. Therefore Jesus was "God" from the moment of his conception.

W. C. G. PROCTOR

See also MARIOLOGY; MARY, THE BLESSED VIRGIN.

Movable Feasts. Those days of the church calendar that depend upon a phase of the moon and thus fall on different dates annually, such as Easter. They are in contrast to fixed feasts, which always occur on the same date, such as Christmas.

C. G. FRY

See also FIXED FEASTS.

Muhlenberg, Henry Melchior (1711–1787). American Lutheran clergyman. On his 30th birthday Muhlenberg had dinner with Johann Gotthilf Francke, son of the famed pietist. Francke shared with Muhlenberg a letter from "dispersed Lutherans in Pennsylvania" who needed a pastor. Muhlenberg's missionary fervor was stirred, and he decided to go to America. In 1748 he organized the first permanent Lutheran synod in America, later known as the Pennsylvania Ministerium. Muhlenberg is also known as "the father of Lutheran parochial education." In 1749 he purchased ground for a Lutheran seminary in Philadelphia. He established an orphans' home in Philadelphia. Muhlenberg commended the "Savoy Liturgy" of the Lutherans of London to American Lutherans in 1748, and in 1782 an American hymnal was prepared under his guidance. A model Lutheran church constitution was adopted by St. Michael's parish, Philadelphia, at his suggestion. Catechists, evangelists, and pastors were trained at his behest. Soon Muhlenberg had a "ministry of reconciliation" among Lutherans from New York to Georgia, speaking Dutch, German, Swedish, and English. By 1771 he was overseeing some 81 congregations.

C. G. FRY

Müntzer, Thomas. See ZWICKAU PROPHETS.

Murray, Andrew (1828–1917)**.** South African churchman, educator, and founder of the Dutch Reformed Church (DRC). In 1879 Murray began what was to become the first of seven great evangelistic tours. Adopting the methods of Moody and Sankey, he toured South Africa organizing revival meetings, which were an astounding success. These activities, plus his growing stature as a theological writer, led to his being invited to preach at the Northfield, U.S., and Keswick, U.K., conventions in 1895. In South Africa he took great interest in missionary work and education. Murray was a systematic thinker who wrote over 250 books and many articles. His best-known works are *Abide in Christ* (1882), *Absolute Surrender* (1895), and *With Christ in the School of Prayer* (1885). Throughout his life Murray took an active role in South African society. In 1852 he helped organize, and acted as the official interpreter for, the important Sand River Convention, which led to the British recognition of the South African Republic in the Transvaal. He took a keen interest in the welfare and education of Africans and held enlightened views on the race question.

I. HEXHAM

See also KESWICK CONVENTION; NORTHFIELD CONFERENCES.

Mystery. Secret plan that God shares only with believers. The concept of mystery has played an important role in Christian theology. The best theology has always maintained that the known must be balanced by the unknown, that God is a *mysterium tremendum et fascinans*, compelling the worshiper with awe toward him but remaining ultimately beyond the grasp of human reason and imagination. For Paul "mystery" is an important term. Of the 28 NT occurrences 21 are found in the Pauline writings. Paul frequently associates it with words for revelation (e.g., Rom. 16:25; Eph. 3:3–9); paradoxically, "mystery" is for Paul something no longer mysterious, but clearly revealed (Eph. 1:9; Col. 1:26–27) and accounts for the fact that "mystery" is often virtually identical with "gospel" (1 Cor. 2:1; Eph. 6:19; 1 Tim. 3:9). On the other hand, Paul does seem to use the term to convey the ideas of ultimate ungraspability (1 Cor. 2:7; 13:2; Eph. 5:32; Col. 2:2), or of present incomprehensibility (Rom. 11:25; 1 Cor. 14:2), or of something eschatological that transcends our present experience (1 Cor. 15:51; 2 Thess. 2:7). These two sides of Paul's usage—revealed and hidden—are not of course contradictory. They correspond to the two facets of all our knowledge of God, whose judgments are unsearchable and ways inscrutable (Rom. 11:33), even though "he had made known to us in all wisdom and insight the mystery of his will" (Eph. 1:9, RSV).

S. MOTYER

Mystery of Iniquity. (Gk. *to mysterion tēs anomias*) Phrase employed by Paul in 2 Thess. 2:7 to indicate the presence in the world now, in a veiled but active form, of that which will be the clear characteristic of the "man of lawlessness" when he appears.

S. MOTYER

See also ANTICHRIST.

Mystery Religions. During the NT and subsequent eras the most popular religious forms in the Greco-Roman world were those of the mystery religions. Some of these had been imported from Egypt and the Orient, while others were indigenous to Greece. Women in particular responded to the promise of a brighter future, as well as to the increased recognition and participation which were theirs in the mystery cults. The essence of the mysteries lay in their secrecy. Thousands of allusions to the mysteries remain in the form of literary references, vase paintings, reliefs, frescoes, inscriptions, and funerary statues.

Seasonal celebrations marked the birth and death of vegetation gods and of yearly changes in the forces of nature. The mystic rites reenacted a myth concerning a divine figure who suffered some sort of violence, was mourned, and then restored to grateful followers amid general jubilation. Beside the reenactment—which was usually accompanied with music, dancing, and sometimes stunning stage effects—there were acts performed, words spoken, objects revealed, a sacrifice offered, and a sacramental meal shared. Sexual symbols and activities were significantly present. Death, marriage, and adoption by the deity were often simulated, and in some cases the initiate was actually supposed thereby to attain divinity. While noise and wild tumult often accompanied the earlier stages of initiation, silence was attendant upon the ultimate unveiling of the truth.

Each of the mysteries had its distinctives, although there were great similarities and much syncretism in late antiquity. The most famous was that of Eleusis, whose cult was officially adopted by Athens. It centered upon Demeter, the Earth Mother, and her daughter Persephone, who was abducted to the underworld by its god, Hades. There she became his bride and queen of the dead. Each year she returned for nine months to her mother, who then caused the corn to grow and returned fertility to the earth. Demeter, bringing her gift of agriculture and civilization, had commanded Eleusis to establish her rites, to which anyone who spoke Greek—even women and slaves—might be admitted.

Scholars have been quick to note the similarities between Christianity and the mystery religions. It should be noted, however, that Christianity is based upon a historical person, while the mysteries were based upon myths of gods whose experiences were repeated yearly. Nevertheless, Christianity owed a debt to mystery religion especially in terms of vocabulary (Rom. 16:25–26; 1 Cor. 15:42–49; Phil. 3:12, 15; Col. 1:26–2:8; 2 Pet. 1:16). While there might be such borrowings of concept and language in the NT, actual vestiges of pagan religion were vigorously denounced.

R. C. Kroeger and C. C. Kroeger

See also Gnosticism.

Mystical Union. See Unio Mystica.

Mysticism. Mystical theology that seeks to describe an experienced, direct, nonabstract, unmediated, loving knowing of God, a knowing or seeing so direct as to be called union with God.

History. A distinct mystical or mystery theology emerged in the Alexandrian school of exegesis and spirituality with Clement of Alexandria and Origen and their search for the hidden meaning of Scripture and their exposition of the mystery of redemption. The Cappadocian fathers, especially Gregory of Nyssa; leading monastics, especially Evagrius of Pontus (346–99) and John Cassian (ca. 360–435); Augustine of Hippo; and the obscure personage known as Dionysius the Pseudo-Areopagite created the formative legacy for medieval mysticism. The term generally used until the 14th and 15th centuries to describe the mystical experience was "contemplation." In its original philosophical meaning this word (Gk. *theoria*) described absorption in the loving viewing of an object or truth. Only in the 12th and 13th centuries, with the writings of Richard of Saint Victor and Thomas Aquinas, do systematic descriptive analyses of the contemplative life appear. Late medieval concern with practical and methodical prayer contributed to a turning point in the 16th-century Ignatian and Carmelite schools (Ignatius Loyola, Teresa of 'Avila, John of the Cross). Spiritual writers from these traditions were concerned primarily with empirical, psychological, and systematic descriptions of the soul's behavior in order to assist spiritual directors.

Protestants generally rejected mystical theology.

The Nature of Mysticism. Beyond a general descriptive definition as offered above, explanations of the nature and characteristics of the mystical experience vary widely. Throughout Christian history and especially since the 16th century many Roman Catholic authors have distinguished ordinary or "acquired" prayer, even if occurring at a supraconceptual level of love, adoration, and desire for God, from the extraordinary or "infused" contemplation that is entirely the work of God's special grace. Only the latter is mystical in a strict sense, according to this view. Other writers, both Catholic and Protestant, would apply the term "mystical" to all communion with God. Many attempts have been made to describe the fundamental characteristics of mystical experience. Traditionally it has been asserted that the experiential union of creature and Creator is inexpressible and ineffable, although those who have experienced it seek imagery and metaphors to describe it, however imperfectly. As experienced union or vision, not abstract knowledge, it is beyond the level of concepts, for reasoning, ideas, and sensory images have been transcended (but not rejected) in an intuitive union. Thus it is suprarational and supraintellectual, not antirational or anti-intellectual. In one sense the soul is passive, because it experiences God's grace poured into itself. Yet the union is not quietistic, because the soul consents to and embraces the spiritual marriage.

The various stages of the mystical way have also been described in immensely varying ways. Virtually all writers agree, however, that purification (purgation or cleansing) and discipline are prerequisites. Each of the three classic stages—the path of purification, the phase of illumination, and the mystical union itself (not necessarily occurring in a fixed sequence but rather in interaction with each other)—may be described as consisting of various degrees or gradations. Scriptural sources for Christian mysticism are found largely in the Logos-incarnation doctrine of John's Gospel, in imagery such as that of the vine and branches (John 15) or Christ's prayer for union (John 17), as well as in aspects of the Pauline corpus. The latter include the description of Paul's rapture into the "third heaven" (2 Cor. 12:1–4) or statements such as that referring to a life "hidden with Christ in God" (Col. 3:3). In all of these the essential theological presuppositions involve belief in a personal God and in the centrality of the incarnation. For medieval mystics Moses' "vision" of God (Exod. 33:12–34:9) and his reflection of God's glory upon leaving Mount Sinai (Exod. 34:29–35; cf. 2 Cor. 3:7) served as prooftexts, and the allegorized spiritual marriage of the Song of Solomon, together with the other OT wisdom literature, provided unlimited scriptural resources until the shift from spiritual to literal-grammatical humanist and Reformation hermeneutics took place.

Anthropologically, Christian mystical theology presupposes a human capacity or fittedness for God, drawing especially upon the doctrine of human beings created in the image of God and on the doctrine of God becoming human in Christ. Christian mystics have traditionally understood mystical union as a restoration of the image and likeness of God that was distorted or lost at the fall from innocence. The image of God, distorted but not destroyed, remains as the foundation for the journey from the land of unlikeness to restored likeness and union.

D. D. Martin

See also Boehme, Jakob; Dionysius the Pseudo-Areopagite; Hesychasm; Illuminative Way, The; John of the Cross; Meister Eckhart; Purgative Way, The; Tauler, Johannes; Teresa of 'Avila; Underhill, Evelyn; Unio Mystica; Unitive Way, The.

Myth. (Gk. *mythos*) Term signifying the fiction of a fable as distinct from the genuineness of the truth (2 Tim. 4:4: "They will turn their ears away from the truth, and turn aside unto myths"). The term occurs five times in the NT (1 Tim. 1:4; 4:7; 2 Tim. 4:4; Titus 1:14; 2 Pet. 1:16). The NT meaning of the term is in complete harmony with its classical connotation, which from the time of Pindar onward always bears the sense of what is fictitious, as opposed to the term *logos*, which indicates that which is true and historical.

In contemporary theological discussion the term "myth" has achieved a special prominence. This is to a considerable degree the result of Rudolf Bultmann's demand for the "demythologization" of the NT—that is, for the excision or expurgation from the biblical presentation of the Christian message of every element of "myth." In Bultmann's judgment this requires the rejection of the biblical view of the world as belonging to "the cosmology of a prescientific age" and is therefore quite unacceptable to modern people. In effect, it amounts to the elimination of the miraculous or supernatural constituents of the scriptural record, since these are incompatible with Bultmann's own view of the world as a firmly closed system, governed by fixed natural laws, in which there can be no place for intervention "from outside."

It is Bultmann's contention that the central message or *kerygma* of Christianity is incredible to modern people so long as it is presented in the mythical setting of the biblical worldview. He accordingly finds it necessary to discard such obviously mythical elements as Christ's preexistence and virgin birth, his deity and sinlessness, the substitutionary nature of his death as meeting the demands of a righteous God, his resurrection and ascension, and his future return in glory; also the final judgment of the world, the existence of spirit beings, the personality and power of the Holy Spirit, the doctrines of the Trinity, of original sin, and of death as a consequence of sin, and every explanation of events as miraculous. It is self-evident that this process of demythologization, when carried through with the thoroughness Bultmann displays, mutilates the Christianity of the NT in so radical a manner as to leave it unrecognizable.

Bultmann's relativism goes hand in hand with subjectivism. The relevance of the Christ event assumes a merely subjective significance. The incarnation and resurrection of Christ, for example, are not to be understood as datable events of the past, but as "eschatological" events that are to be subjectively experienced through faith in the word of preaching. It is, in fact, only *my* experience, here and now, that can have any authenticity for me—not anything that has happened in the past or that will happen in the future. In short, the Christian message is compressed within an existentialist mold. History and eschatology are to be understood in terms of pure subjectivism. Pronouncements about the deity of Jesus are not to be interpreted as dogmatic pronouncements concerning his nature but as existential value judgments, not as statements about Christ but as pronouncements about *me*. Thus, for example, the objective affirmation that Christ helps me because he is God's Son must give place to the subjective value judgment that he is God's Son because he helps me. Truth, in a word, is identified with subjectivity.

Karl Barth, whose approach to the question of the authority of Scripture is governed by premises akin to those accepted by Bultmann, wishes to establish a distinction between myth on the one hand and saga or legend on the other. By "legend," however, he means what the other two understand by "myth." Legend, according to Barth, does not necessarily attack the substance of the biblical witness, even though there is uncertainty about what he calls its "general" historicity (i.e., its historical truth as generally conceived). Barth views myth as belonging to a different category that necessarily attacks the substance of the biblical witness inasmuch as it pretends to be history when it is not, and thereby throws doubt on, indeed denies, what he calls the "special" historicity of the biblical narratives (i.e., their special significance as history between God and humankind), thus relegating them to the realm of a "timeless truth, in other words, a human creation" (*Church Dogmatics* 1.1.375ff.). This however, is principally a matter of definition: where Bultmann uses the term "myth," Barth prefers to use "legend."

There is one further definition of myth to which attention must be drawn, one that in effect equates it with symbolism and relates it to the inherent inability of human language to express adequately the things of God. Thus Brunner maintains that "the Christian *kerygma* cannot be separated from Myth" since "the Christian statement is necessarily and consciously 'anthropomorphic' in the sense that it does, and must do, what Bultmann conceives to be characteristic of the mythical—'it speaks of God in a human way'" (*Dogmatics*, 2.268). And in the same connection Bultmann explains that mythology is the use of imagery to express the otherworldly in terms of this world and the divine in terms of human life, the other side in terms of this side (*Kerygma and Myth*). To eliminate myth in this sense would mean that it would become impossible for us to say anything about God or for God to say anything intelligible to us, for we have no other medium of expression than the terms of this world. But it certainly does not follow that the terms of this side must always be given a symbolical (mythological) meaning, or that they are always inadequate for the purpose intended. While there is indeed much symbolism in the NT, it is evident also that many things there are intended in a literal sense and that events like Christ's ascension are described phenomenally (i.e., from the quite legitimate point of view of the observer). Finally, it must be stressed that the concept of myth is incompatible with the classical doctrine of Scripture. The Christ of the Bible is the *Logos*, not a *mythos*; he needs no demythologization at the hands of human scholars.

P. E. HUGHES

See also BRUNNER, HEINRICH EMIL; BULTMANN, RUDOLF; DEMYTHOLOGIZATION.

Nn

Nations, Judgment of. See JUDGMENT OF THE NATIONS, THE.

Natural Law. Moral order divinely implanted in humankind and accessible to all persons through human reason. It should not be confused with the laws of nature, which became prominent in natural science during the 18th and 19th centuries—although there was, historically, some overlap and connection between the two. Natural law is chiefly a matter of ethics and is primarily associated with Roman Catholic theology. It has enabled the church to address socioeconomic, legal, moral, and political issues on what is held to be a philosophical foundation common to all humankind.

During the past century natural law theory experienced a renaissance in Roman Catholic circles. It underlies much of Pope Leo XIII's social legislation and influenced Pope Paul VI's famous ruling on matters of sexual conduct (*Humanae vitae*). American Catholic universities still have many institutes and journals that seek to apply natural law theory to contemporary social, moral, and legal issues. Several modern Protestant thinkers (e.g., certain Scottish commonsense realists, Emil Brunner, and, in their own distinctive way, Abraham Kuyper and his disciples) have seen the advantages of natural law theory in addressing social and ethical matters with non-Christians. But most Protestants, especially Karl Barth, continue to hold that ethical matters cannot be known in truth apart from the revelation of God's will in Jesus Christ and Scripture.

J. VAN ENGEN

Natural Man. See MAN, NATURAL.

Natural Revelation. See REVELATION, GENERAL.

Natural Theology. Truths about God that can be learned from created things (nature, humankind, the world) by reason alone. The importance of natural theology to Christian thought has varied widely from age to age, depending largely upon the general intellectual climate. It first became a significant part of Christian teaching in the High Middle Ages, and was made a fixed part of Roman Catholic dogma in 1870 at Vatican Council I. The council's Dogmatic Constitution on the Catholic Faith made it a matter of faith to believe that God has revealed himself in two ways, naturally and supernaturally, and that "God can certainly be known [*certo cognosci*] from created things by the natural light of human reason." The council sought to reaffirm, over against 19th-century secularized skeptics and especially philosophical movements since Kant, that God is indeed knowable by reason and that such philosophical truths are a legitimate and true form of theology.

The first great proponent of a natural theology distinguishable from revealed theology was Aquinas, the synthesizer of Greek philosophy and the gospel, who also laid the groundwork for the concept of natural law, the ethical equivalent of natural theology. Nearly all Catholic scholars of natural theology have built upon, refined, or qualified the position first articulated by Aquinas. In doing natural theology, first of all, they do not mean to have reason replace faith or philosophical discourse supplant the grace of God revealed in Christ. Faith and grace remain primary for all believers, but natural theology offers the opportunity to establish certain truths by means common to all persons. Second, these truths are not taken to be "grounds" or "foundations" for additional, revealed truths. Yet if these truths are established, it can be seen as "reasonable" to accept revealed truths as well. Consequently, Catholics are inclined to see a continuum between natural theology (that which is known of God by the light of natural reason) and revealed theology (that which is known by the light of faith).

The Protestant Reformers objected to the impact of philosophy upon theology and insisted upon a return to Scripture. They assumed that all people have some implicit knowledge of God's existence (Calvin's "sense of divinity"), but they declared it useless apart from the revelation of God's will and grace in Jesus Christ. Several early confessional documents (e.g., the Westminster and the Belgic confessions) do speak of God revealing himself in nature (citing Rom. 1:20–21), but this revelation is not fully comprehensible apart from Scripture.

In recent times natural theology has received comparatively little attention apart from a few Catholic philosophers. One interesting and related development has occurred in the field of the history of religions. Certain such historians (especially G. van der Leeuw and M. Eliade) have discovered patterns of religious belief and practice (a High God, a fall from a past Golden Age, various salvation motifs, etc.) that do not make up a natural theology in the traditional sense, but which they believe could yield an instructive prolegomenon to the study of Christian theology.

J. Van Engen

See also Thomas Aquinas; Neo-Thomism; Revelation, General.

Nazarene. See Christians, Names of.

Neander, Johann August Wilhelm (1789–1850). German church historian and theologian. Author of the *General History of the Christian Religion and Church* (6 vols., 1825–52) and several monographs on persons and movements in the early and medieval church, Neander is commonly regarded as the founder of modern church historiography. His works were based on extensive use of original sources, but tended to concentrate more on personalities than institutions. He saw the main theme of church history as the continuing conflict between the spirit of Christ and the spirit of the world. Neander's romantic conception of the role of church history was summed up in his famous phrase: "The heart (*pectus*) is the motivating force of theology."

R. V. Pierard

See also Mediating Theology.

Necessary Being. See Being.

Neoevangelicalism. See Evangelicalism.

Neo-orthodoxy. Twentieth-century Protestant theological movement characterized by a strong reaction against liberal Protestantism, an emphasis on key orthodox Reformation themes, and a stress on classic Protestant formulations as interpreted through biblical language and symbols.

History. The neo-orthodox movement began in the crisis associated with the disillusionment following World War I with a rejection of Protestant scholasticism and denial of the Protestant liberal movement, which had stressed accommodation of Christianity to Western science and culture, the immanence of God, and the progressive improvement of humankind. The first important expression of the movement was Karl Barth's *Römerbrief* (1919). Soon a number of Swiss and German pastors were involved. In the space of two years (1921–22) Friedrich Gogarten had published his *Religious Decision*, Emil Brunner his *Experience, Knowledge and Faith*, Eduard Thurneysen his *Dostoievsky*, and Barth the second edition of his *Commentary on Romans*. In the fall of 1922 they established *Zwischen den Zeiten*, a journal whose title characterized the crisis element in their thinking. They believed that they lived between the time when the Word was made flesh and the imminent reappearance of the Word. Although at this point most of the early members of the movement held to some common points of view, such as the absolute transcendence of God over all human knowledge and work, the sovereignty of the revelation in Jesus Christ, the authority of Scripture, and the sinfulness of humankind, it was not long before their dialectical approach led to disagreements and a parting of the ways. These disagreements, however, seemed to make the movement all the more vigorous and intriguing. Soon it spread to England, where C. H. Dodd and Edwyn Hoskyns became involved; in Sweden Gustaf Aulén and Anders Nygren became followers; in America the Niebuhr brothers were identified as neo-orthodox.

Methodology. The methodological approach of the movement involved dialectical theology, theology of paradox, and crisis theology. Barth and the early leaders were probably attracted to the dialectic as the result of their study of Søren Kierkegaard's writings. Kierkegaard believed theological assertions of the faith to be paradoxical. This requires the believer to hold opposite "truths" in tension. Their reconciliation comes in an existential act generated after anxiety, tension, and crisis, and which the mind takes to be a leap of faith. Some of the paradoxes identified by the neo-orthodox movement are the absolute transcendence of God in contrast with the self-disclosure of God; Christ as the God-man; faith as a gift and yet an act; humans as sinful yet free; eternity entering time. How is it possible to have a wholly other God who reveals himself? How is it possible for the man Jesus of history to be the Son of God, the second person of the Trinity? It is only in crisis/struggling that we can rise above the paradox and be grasped by the truth in such a way as to defy rational explanation. Crisis is that point where yes and no meet. It is that theological point where the human recognizes God's condemnation of all human endeavors in morals, religion, thought processes, and scientific discoveries, and the only release is from God's word. The neo-orthodox, in summarizing their methodology, used dialectics in relation to the paradoxes of the faith, which precipitated crises, which in turn became the situation for the revelation of truth.

Some Key Beliefs. Perhaps the fundamental theological concept of the movement is that of the totally free, sovereign God, the wholly other in relation to his creation. Next is God's self-revelation, a dynamic act of grace to which our response is to listen. This revelation is the Word of God in a threefold sense: Jesus as the Word made flesh; Scripture, which points to the Word made flesh; and the sermon, which is the vehicle for the proclamation of the Word made flesh. The movement also stressed the sinfulness of humankind. The sovereign, free God who reveals himself does so to a sinful fallen humanity and creation. There is a vast chasm between the sovereign God and humankind, and there is no way that we can bridge that chasm. All of our efforts to do so in religious, moral, and ethical thoughts and actions are as nothing. The only possible way for the chasm to be crossed is by God, and this he has done in Christ. And now the paradox and the crisis: when the paradox of the word's No against our sin is given along with the Yes of the Word of grace and mercy, the crisis we face is to decide either yes or no. The turning point has been reached as the eternal God reveals himself in our time and existence.

Significance. The neo-orthodox movement has made a number of important contributions to 20th-century theology. With its stress on Scripture as the container of the Word it emphasized the unity of Scripture and helped to precipitate a renewed interest in hermeneutics. With its rejection of 19th-century Protestant liberalism and its return to the principles of the Reformation it helped to rejuvenate interest in the theology of the 16th-century Reformers and in the early church fathers. With its threefold view of the Word the doctrine of Christology has been more carefully examined; and the concept of the Word as proclamation has reemphasized the importance of preaching and the church as the fellowship of believers. The use of dialectic, paradox, and crisis introduced an effort to preserve the absolutes of the faith from every dogmatic formulation and, by so doing, aided the cause of ecumenism. Finally, the urgency found in the writings and in the title of its first journal has encouraged a renewed interest in eschatology.

R. V. SCHNUCKER

See also AULÉN, GUSTAF EMANUEL HILDEBRAND; BARTH, KARL; BRUNNER, HEINRICH EMIL; BULTMANN, RUDOLF; GOGARTEN, FRIEDRICH; KIERKEGAARD, SØREN; NIEBUHR, REINHOLD.

Neo-Pentecostalism. See CHARISMATIC MOVEMENT.

Neo-Platonism. Principal form of Greek philosophy from the 3d to the 6th centuries A.D. Plotinus is usually identified as its founder (205–70), but perhaps a more accurate statement would be that Plotinus was the most creative thinker within later Platonism. Plotinus's system begins with the One, the supreme transcendent principle, which can be described only by negation. It is immaterial and impersonal. As the number one is different from all other numbers yet makes them possible, so the One is the ground of all being and source of all values. The One transcends all duality, both of thought and reality and of being and nonbeing. Out of the One, but without any change in the One, there proceeded by emanation Mind (*nous*), the intellectual principle. Mind is the principle of divine intelligence, the "eternal consciousness," the highest really knowable entity. This element already partakes of duality, for consciousness contains both the knower and the known. The next emanation was the World Soul (*psyche*). This is the moving power behind the whole universe. The World Soul is intermediary between Mind and bodily reality; it is the principle at work in the moving stars, animals, plants, and humankind, but transcends individual souls.

The lowest creative principle is Nature (*physis*). As the descent from the One is characterized by increasing individuation and multiplicity, so Nature finds itself in direct contact with matter. Bare matter is the limiting principle of reality. Humankind is a microcosm of reality, containing matter, nature, soul, and mind. Manifoldness longs to be reunited to the One, and by contemplation we have the possibility of return to the One. Contemplation is the most perfect human activity, and by it may be achieved a state of ecstasy, an experience of unification. The importance of mental concentration is the reason for describing Plotinus's view as intellectual mysticism.

After Plotinus and Porphyry, important later Neo-Platonists include Iamblichus (ca. 250–ca. 325), Sallustius, and Proclus (410–485). Neo-Platonism provided the philosophical basis for pagan opposition to Christianity in the 4th and 5th centuries. Porphyry, in addition to numerous philosophical treatises, wrote a massive work in 15 volumes, now lost, entitled *Against the Christians*. Julian, emperor from 361 to 363, besides official measures against the Christians wrote *Against the Galilaeans*, which can be reconstructed from Cyril of Alexandria's refutation of it. On the other hand, Neo-Platonism provided the intellectual framework for the thought of several Christian theologians: Gregory of Nyssa, Victorinus, Ambrose, Augustine, and especially Dionysius the Pseudo-Areopagite.

E. Ferguson

See also Augustine of Hippo; Dionysius the Pseudo-Areopagite; Erigena, John Scotus.

Neo-Thomism. Twentieth-century revival of the thought of Thomas Aquinas. Thomism was the dominant philosophy undergirding Roman Catholic theology from the 15th century. Under the pace-setting interpretations of such thinkers as Cajetan in the early 16th century, a complex system that spoke to the needs of both theology and contemporary philosophical questions developed. Thomism appeared to have triumphed in 1880 when Pope Leo XIII declared it to be the official (although not exclusive) philosophy of Catholic schools. At the same time, however, it became clear that Thomism's posture was threatened by the increasing popularity of Kantian philosophical principles. In the 20th century the movement bifurcated. Transcendental Thomism, represented by Joseph Maréchal, Bernard Lonergan, and Karl Rahner, self-consciously adapted itself to Kantian thought. But another wing, under the leadership of Étienne Gilson and Jacques Maritain, sought to recover a pure version of the teachings of Aquinas himself. The metaphysical distinctive of Neo-Thomism of the latter type may be found in its insistence on the maxim that "existence precedes essence." This means that one has to know that something exists before one knows what it is, and before one knows that something exists, one has to accept that anything exists. This latter conviction is not the result of a rational deduction; it is an immediate awareness.

This apprehension of being leads the Thomist to posit the existence of God via the cosmological argument. The understanding of God as unconditioned necessary existence goes far in providing the basis for Thomistic natural theology. For if God is uncaused, he is unlimited. Then he contains all perfections infinitely; for example, he is all-good, omnipresent, omniscient, all-loving, all-perfect. There can be only one such God, since a God who possesses all perfections cannot differ from any other God who would also possess all the identical possessions. The insistence on being over essence also makes itself felt in Thomism's understanding of the human person. With the understanding of the soul as the form of the body, the human is seen as a unit, composed of soul and body in mutual dependence. Thus, for instance, cognition combines both the physical/empirical (sensation) and the spiritual (abstraction). Thomistic writings have consistently defended the dignity and integrity of human personhood, particularly against totalitarian ideologies.

In theology Thomism has usually been linked to conservative expressions of orthodox doctrines, partially due to the close dependence on Aquinas's own formulations. Since the Second Vatican Council it has lost much ground in Catholic circles to philosophies of more recent origin, such as phenomenology or process thought, due to a certain impatience with Thomism's supposedly outmoded Aristotelianism. At the same time there has been some movement in evangelical Protestantism (e.g., Norman L. Geisler) to adopt Thomistic philosophical principles for purposes of apologetics and theological enhancement.

W. CORDUAN

See also MARITAIN, JACQUES; RAHNER, KARL; THOMAS AQUINAS.

Nestorius, Nestorianism. A native of Germanicia in Syria, Nestorius became patriarch of Constantinople in 428 and preached a series of sermons in which he attacked the devotionally popular attribution of the title *Theotokos* ("God-bearing") to the Virgin Mary. In place of *Theotokos,* Nestorius offered the term *Christotokos* ("Christ-bearing"). Nestorius's denunciation of *Theotokos* brought him under the suspicion of many orthodox theologians who had long used the term. His most articulate and vehement opponent was Cyril of Alexandria. When Cyril read of Nestorius's rejection of the term "hypostatic union" as an interpenetration and thus a reduction of both the divine and the human natures of Christ, he understood Nestorius to be affirming that Christ was two persons, one human, one divine. Cyril concluded that Nestorius rejected the union.

In August 430 Pope Celestine condemned Nestorius, and Cyril pronounced 12 anathemas against him in November of the same year. In 431 the Council of Ephesus deposed Nestorius, sending him back to the monastery in Antioch. Five years later he was banished to Upper Egypt, where he died, probably in 451. The dispute between Nestorius and Cyril centered in the relationship between the two natures in Christ and represents the divergence between the two major schools of ancient Christology, the Antiochene and the Alexandrian. The former emphasized the reality of Christ's humanity and was wary of any true communication of the attributes from one nature to the other; the latter emphasized Christ's essential deity and tended to affirm a real *communicatio*.

Ironically, modern research has discovered a book written by Nestorius, known as the *Book of Heracleides*, in which he explicitly denies the heresy for which he was condemned. Rather, he affirms of Christ that "the same one is twofold," an expression not unlike the orthodox formulation of the Council of Chalcedon (451). This points to the high degree of misunderstanding that characterized the entire controversy. After 433 a group of Nestorius's followers constituted themselves a separate Nestorian Church in Persia.

H. GRIFFITH

See also ALEXANDRIAN THEOLOGY; ANTIOCHENE THEOLOGY; COMMUNICATION OF ATTRIBUTES; CYRIL OF ALEXANDRIA.

New Birth. See REGENERATION.

New Commandment. See COMMANDMENT, THE NEW.

New Covenant. See COVENANT, THE NEW.

New Creation, New Creature. Translations of *kainē ktisis*, a term used in 2 Cor. 5:17 and Gal. 6:15. ("Creation" [RV, RSV; cf. NEB "new world"] is undoubtedly a better translation than "creature" [AV, Moffatt, NEB mg.]). Three factors contribute to the meaning of this expression: (1) *The OT background.* In the OT "new" is a word especially associated with the age to come, when God will do a "new thing" (Isa. 43:19), when he will make a "new covenant" (Jer. 31:31). Paul proclaims the fulfillment of these eschatological expectations. (2) *The balance between future and present in Pauline eschatology.* Because Christ is Christ, the promised new creation is *now* a reality: from the eternal perspective the person in Christ is "created" (past tense, Eph. 2:10), "justified" (Rom. 5:1), "sanctified" (1 Cor. 6:11), and "glorified" (Rom. 8:30), even though these things are not fully realized in experience. (3) *The balance between individual and corporate in Pauline anthropology.* Paul's terse "If any one is in Christ, he is a new creation" (2 Cor. 5:17a) invites us to see the individual participating in a much greater eschatological reality. In Christ, God has created "one new man" (Eph. 2:15).

S. MOTYER

See also CREATION, DOCTRINE OF; MAN, OLD AND NEW.

New England Theology. Theological tradition arising from the work of Jonathan Edwards (1703–58) and continuing well into the 19th century. The tradition was not unified by a common set of beliefs, for in fact Edwards' 19th-century heirs reversed his convictions on many important particulars. It was rather united in its fascination for common issues, including the freedom of human will, the morality of divine justice, and the problem of causation behind the appearance of sin.

Jonathan Edwards. Edwards' theological labors grew out of his efforts to explain and defend the colonial Great Awakening as a real work of God. In the process he provided an interpretation of Calvinism that influenced American religious life for over a century. Edwards was overwhelmed by the majesty and splendor of the divine. The major themes of his theology were the greatness and glory of God, the utter dependence of sinful humanity upon God for salvation, and the supernal beauty of the life of holiness. Edwards was not only a fervent Christian; he was also a theological genius unmatched in American history. Thus, it is little wonder that those who followed him were not successful in maintaining the fullness of his theology. What they did maintain was his revivalistic fervor, his concern for awakening, and his high moral seriousness.

The New Divinity. The next phase of the New England theology was known as the "new divinity." Its leading proponents were Joseph Bellamy (1719–90) and Samuel Hopkins (1721–1803), New England ministers who had studied with Edwards and had been his closest friends. Bellamy and Hopkins also introduced the first modifications of Edwards' ideas. For example, Bellamy propounded a "governmental" view of the atonement, the idea that God's sense of right and wrong demanded the sacrifice of Christ. Edwards, by contrast, had maintained the traditional view that the death of Christ was necessary to take away God's anger at sin.

The 19th Century. Modifications made in the New England theology by Hopkins and Bellamy were subtle ones. Their successors moved more obviously beyond the teaching of Edwards. Timothy Dwight (1752–1817), Edwards' grandson and president of Yale College, took a broader view of human abilities in salvation and emphasized the reasonable nature of the Christian faith. Jonathan Edwards, Jr. (1745–1801), who had studied with Bellamy, extended Bellamy's idea of a governmental atonement and also placed a stronger emphasis on the law of God for the Christian life. Both he and Dwight continued the general trend to view sin as an accumulation of actions rather than primarily a state of being issuing in evil deeds. By the time Dwight's best student, Nathaniel W. Taylor (1786–1858), assumed his position as professor of theology at Yale Divinity School in 1822, the movement from Edwards' specific convictions was very pronounced. Taylor's New Haven theology reversed the elder Edwards on freedom of the will by contending for a natural power of free choice.

The influence of the New England theology continued to be great throughout the 19th century. It set the tone for theological debate in New England and much of the rest of the country. Its questions dominated theological reflection at Yale until mid-century and at Andover Seminary even longer. The New England theology was at its best in careful, rigorous theological exposition. This strength sometimes turned into a weakness when it led to a dry, almost scholastic style of preaching. But with Edwards, Dwight, and Taylor, who did differ markedly among themselves on important questions, there remained a common ability to communicate a need for revival and ardent Christian living. The changes in the content of the New England theology, and indeed its passing, had much to do with the character of 19th-century America. A country convinced of the nearly limitless capabilities of individuals in the New World had increasingly less interest in a theology that had its origin in the all-encompassing power of God.

M. A. NOLL

See also DWIGHT, TIMOTHY; EDWARDS, JONATHAN; NEW HAVEN THEOLOGY; TAYLOR, NATHANIEL WILLIAM.

New Evangelicalism. See EVANGELICALISM.

New Hampshire Confession (1833). Baptist statement of faith. Published by a committee of the Baptist Convention in the state of New Hampshire, the New Hampshire Confession is one of the most widely used Baptist statements of faith in America. The confession was reissued with minor changes in 1853 by J. Newton Brown of the American Baptist Publication Society, and in this form attracted greater attention among Baptists in America. This confession has influenced many Baptist confessions since, including the influential Statement of Baptist Faith and Message of the Southern Baptist Convention (1925). The general tendency of the confession is moderately Calvinistic.

M. A. NOLL

See also BAPTIST TRADITION, THE; CONFESSIONS OF FAITH.

New Haven Theology. Late stage of the New England theology that originated in the efforts of Jonathan Edwards to defend the spiritual reality of the first Great Awakening (ca. 1740). It was also intended to address the needs of the Second Great Awakening (ca. 1795–1830). It thus served as a bridge between the Calvinism that dominated American Christianity in the 1700s and the more Arminian theology that came to prevail in the 19th century. Timothy Dwight, grandson of Jonathan Edwards and president of Yale College from 1795 to 1817, laid the groundwork for the New Haven theology. Dwight's best pupil, Nathaniel William Taylor, carried it to its maturity. The New Haven theology was a powerful force for revival and reform in the first half of the 19th century, particularly through the work of Taylor's fellow Yale graduate, Lyman Beecher. Beecher and like-minded colleagues employed the principles of the New Haven theology to promote moral reform, to establish missions and educational institutions, and to win the frontier for Christianity.

M. A. NOLL

See also DWIGHT, TIMOTHY; GREAT AWAKENINGS, THE; NEW ENGLAND THEOLOGY; TAYLOR, NATHANIEL WILLIAM.

New Heavens and New Earth. The biblical doctrine of the created universe includes the certainty of its final redemption from the dominion of sin. The finally redeemed universe is called "the new heavens and new earth." In the OT the kingdom of God is usually described in terms of a redeemed earth; this is especially clear in the Book of Isaiah, where the final state of the universe is already called a new heaven and a new earth (Isa. 65:17; 66:22). This vision is clarified in the NT. Jesus speaks of the renewal of all things (Matt. 19:28), Peter of the restoration of all things (Acts 3:21). Paul states that the universe will be redeemed by God from its bondage to decay (Rom. 8:18–21). This is confirmed by Peter, who describes the new heavens and the new earth as the home of righteousness (2 Pet. 3:13). Finally, the Book of Revelation includes a glorious vision of the end of the present universe and of the creation of a new universe, full of righteousness and the presence of God. The vision is confirmed by God in the awesome declaration, "I am making everything new!" (Rev. 21:1–8). The new heavens and the new earth will be the renewed creation that will fulfill the purpose for which God created the universe. It will be characterized by the complete rule of God and by the full realization of the final goal of redemption: "Now the dwelling of God is with men, and he will live with them" (Rev. 21:3).

F. Q. Gouvea

See also Eschatology; Kingdom of Christ, God, Heaven; New Creation, New Creature.

New Hermeneutic, The. Post-World War II theological development based on Bultmann's radical-critical methodology in interpreting Scripture. The new hermeneutic of Bultmann's disciples accepts the basic truth of his method and affirms the correctness of his interpretation of Luther's "justification by faith alone." Grace lies in the sphere of faith, not in the sphere of historical facts; hence radical biblical criticism can go on relatively unabated without danger to faith, since faith resides largely in a higher realm of history (*Geschichte* or *Urgeschichte*; primal history), while the relative events of the Bible reside in the changing realm of profane history (*Historie*). While Bultmann had extended the older view of hermeneutics far beyond its concern for detailed principles of exegesis and interpretation to a broad inquiry into the meaning of language as existential address, following Heidegger, his disciples felt he had not gone far enough. Ernst Fuchs and Gerhard Ebeling both sought to develop Heidegger's hermeneutical theory of language more comprehensively than had Bultmann and to see that speech itself is profoundly hermeneutical and existential. *Hermeneutik* becomes a deep inquiry into the function of speech and word. It listens and is submissibe to the call of being, as "being" graciously opens itself to *Dasein*, the person who "is there" in the world. For Heidegger, being is not God; but it is an easy step for the followers of Bultmann to adapt this language of "grace" and apply it to Christian proclamation.

The clearest exposition of this new development in post-Bultmannian hermeneutics is to be found in *The New Hermeneutic* (ed. James M. Robinson and John B. Cobb, Jr., 1964), which was written virtually on the scene and contains valuable focal articles by Ebeling and Fuchs, American reactions by Robinson, John Dillenberger, Robert Funk, Amos Wilder, and John Cobb, and a response by Fuchs. In brief, the new hermeneutic took a more positive turn toward the language of Jesus as mediating kerygma, not mere historiography as Bultmann had insisted. Fuchs and Ebeling saw the language of Jesus as "word-happening" or "speech-event" and were ready to argue, in the larger context of Heidegger's hermeneutic, that not just the Easter kerygma but Jesus' word as well mediates an eschatological self-understanding to the listener. Jesus' claim of authority is not limited simply to a point in Palestinian history, as Bultmann required, but speaks today with equal authority in the church's proclamation. Hence the word "kerygma," insofar as it had distinguished the proclamation of the church as over against the historical and no longer relevant proclamation of Jesus, is replaced by the word-event or language-event in the new hermeneutic.

Existentialist interpretation is therefore broadened to bridge the gap that had been created by Bultmann between *Historie* (Jesus) and *Geschichte* (the church's kerygma), to bring together historical and systematic theology in terms of the recurring language-event, which moves from Jesus to the contemporary preacher. Ebeling especially, as the historical and systematic theologian deeply immersed in Luther's hermeneutic as well as Heidegger and Bultmann, goes beyond the latter by insisting that all the words of Scripture have to do with the incarnate Son of God, Jesus Christ. Fuchs, his close friend and collaborator on the NT side, speaks of Jesus as standing in the place of God as he speaks of new possibilities for existential self-understanding.

All of the foregoing sounds like a return to orthodox concern for the Jesus of history and his identity with the Christ of faith. But the new hermeneutic is more subtle than to allow for a simple return to classical evangelicalism and too indebted to the basic methodology of Bultmannian radical criticism, which Bultmann himself inherited from his predecessors, notably Dilthey. The critical assumptions of the new hermeneutic remain basically unchanged, only broadened, from those of Bultmann. Fuchs continues to speak of Jesus primarily in terms of his language, but fails to appreciate that language does not have independent status apart from the person who speaks, and therefore cannot be apotheosized or separated from the intentionality of the speaker.

This serious fault in the later Heideggerian hermeneutic—to view language as something that speaks without reference to God or persons—feeds into the abortive attempt of the new quest for the historical Jesus. As long as the school of the new hermeneutic centered upon the event of Jesus' language and did not see that language as revelatory of Jesus' own self-understanding and messianic self-consciousness, it was bound to reflect the same fundamental skepticism regarding the person of Jesus as did Bultmann. James M. Robinson's attempt to undertake a new quest for the historical Jesus was soon abandoned, mainly because the quest focused upon the understanding of existence that emerges from Jesus' linguistic activity, not on Jesus' self-understanding that is disclosed in that activity. Similarly, Fuchs speaks of Jesus' language and his concept of time, but appears disinterested in what this says of Jesus as person. Amos Wilder has ably criticized Fuchs on this point. One of the foremost new questers, Ernst Käsemann, likewise shows a methodological fault in his desire to allow Jesus a more prominent position than did his mentor Bultmann. Conceding that Jesus makes many unusual claims that might suggest a messianic consciousness, Käsemann nonetheless holds back and declares that it is his personal opinion that Jesus did not think of himself in these terms.

This has led critics of the school who have been appreciative of the early promise of the new hermeneutic to bemoan the fact that the methodology is too closely allied to Heidegger's notion of language that mysteriously speaks on its own without reference to the intentionality of the speaker. A more adequate approach to Jesus' words and activity will need to employ a descriptive phenomenology that views the speaker, and perforce the self-understanding of the person who speaks, as standing within and revealed through what he says and does. Several helpful models may be employed in this more useful enterprise, among them the later Wittgenstein, Marcel, Polanyi, and the British school of person analysts, including G. E. M. Anscombe and P. F. Strawson. This approach is extremely valuable in bringing the new hermeneutic to a satisfactory conclusion in its search for the unity of the Jesus of history and the Christ of faith, and finding that solution in what all along has been the orthodox view of Jesus as the self-conscious Messiah who, in his speaking and acting, is the originator of the church's christological tradition.

That there have been gains in NT exegesis as a result of the renewed interest in the vitality of Jesus' language, especially the parables, should be gratefully acknowledged by all, in spite of the fact that Jesus' christological claims implicit in that language have not been widely appreciated. On the theological side of the new hermeneutic, recent developments have reached something of a stalemate over the question of "horizons." The most prominent exponent of the new hermeneutic in the Bultmannian tradition, Hans-Georg Gadamer, and a more recent evangelical interpreter, Anthony Thistleton, argue for a fusion of the church's horizon and ours. This, after all, lay at the center of the new hermeneutic as originally conceived, and it is popularly accepted in theological thought today that the text and the interpreter share in the meaning of the encounter. Evangelicals will want to be wary of speaking too hastily of a fusion of horizons of meaning, however, and will likely be more impressed with E. D. Hirsch's approach to hermeneutics, which allows the original meaning of the speaker or text to remain intact. There can be an appropriation of *significance* for the interpreter, which may vary depending on one's setting, but the authoritative *meaning* of the speaker or text is their prerogative to establish. The issue is a serious and fundamental one, for at stake is the very intentionality and authority of Jesus and the early church. There are signs that, at least from the NT side of the new hermeneutic, the intentionality of Jesus is beginning to receive renewed interest, a fact attested by two recent studies, David Hill's *New Testament Prophecy* and Ben Meyer's *Aims of Jesus*.

R. G. GRUENLER

See also BULTMANN, RUDOLF; KERYGMA.

New Jerusalem, The. See JERUSALEM, THE NEW.

New Light Schism. Division in the Presbyterian and Congregational denominations in the mid-18th century, primarily over practical matters of Christian experience. Presbyterian schism occurred in 1741 when the Old Lights, who were predominantly of Scotch-Irish heritage, ejected the New Light faction and formed the Old Side Synod of Philadelphia. The New Light party, with their English Puritan background, grew out of the Great Awakening and revived a more experiential interpretation of the Christian life. They organized the New Side presbyteries of New Brunswick and Londonderry. Both parties professed traditional Calvinist and Puritan doctrine, but they differed substantially on its practical implications. The Old Light majored on correct doctrine, the New Light on authentic piety.

Congregationalists also experienced schism over the Great Awakening. After George Whitefield's and Gilbert Tennent's evangelistic tours in 1740–41 brought a general revival to New England, James Davenport's incendiary preaching and incitement of emotional excesses brought sharp Old Light reprisals. Charles Chauncey argued that revivals were not the work of God because emotional outbursts were not produced by God's Spirit. Jonathan Edwards defended revivalism. But he argued that believers could distinguish between genuine and counterfeit awakenings by examining whether they brought love for Christ, Scripture, and truth and opposition to evil. Edwards defined the essence of true religion as "holy affections." This schism helped Edwards and his followers revive a balanced, vital Calvinism. Chauncey and other Old Lights, on the other hand, broke from Calvinism and began to advocate Arminianism and eventually Unitarianism.

W. A. Hoffecker

See also Edwards, Jonathan; Great Awakenings, The; Whitefield, George.

New Man. See Man, Old and New.

Newman, John Henry (1801–1890). English prelate and theologian. Newman was the most famous English convert to Roman Catholicism in the 19th century. In 1833 Newman, a Fellow of Oriel College, Oxford, together with such associates as John Keble and Edward Pusey, launched the movement of Catholic Anglicanism known as Tractarianism. When Newman realized that the Church of England as a whole would not follow the Tractarian program, he joined the Roman Catholic Church in 1845, taking some followers with him but leaving others to create major changes in large sections of Anglicanism. Eventually his intellectual brilliance was recognized and he was made a cardinal in his later years. Since his death, and particularly in more recent years, his influence has been of great importance for developments in Roman Catholic theology.

I. S. Rennie

See also Anglo-Catholicism; High Church Movement; Keble, John; Oxford Movement; Pusey, Edward Bouverie; Via Media.

New Morality. See Situation Ethics.

New School Theology. Modified Calvinist theology characterized by an enthusiasm for revivalism, moral reform, and interdenominational cooperation. New School Presbyterianism embodied mainstream evangelical Christianity in the mid-19th century. New School theology had its roots in the Calvinism of Jonathan Edwards, but its immediate predecessor was the New Haven moral government theology of Nathaniel Taylor. He synthesized moralistic elements from Scottish commonsense philosophy with reinterpretations of traditional Calvinism to construct a semi-Pelagian foundation for revivalism.

While Old School leaders roundly attacked Taylor's theology, revivalists and ministers such as Charles G. Finney, Lyman Beecher, and Albert Barnes popularized it. Finney used Taylor's theology to redefine revivals as works that we can perform using means that God has provided. This modified Calvinism was used to champion activism in American social life. Voluntary societies consisting of members from various denominations carried out missionary activity and battled social ills. These constructive crusades, in which New School Presbyterians played a leading role, were inspired by postmillennial expectations of progress. In the decades after 1840 New School theology became more conservative. Its proponents widely criticized Finney's perfectionism. They attacked Darwinism, early biblical criticism, and German philosophy and theology. Henry B. Smith of Union Theological Seminary emerged as the leading spokesman. His defense of systematic theology and biblical infallibility and his perceptions that New Schoolers had become more orthodox were influential in the reunion of the Northern branches of the Presbyterian Church in 1869.

W. A. Hoffecker

See also Auburn Declaration; Barnes, Albert; Finney, Charles Grandison;

NEW HAVEN THEOLOGY; OLD SCHOOL THEOLOGY.

New Testament. See BIBLE.

New Testament Canon. See BIBLE, CANON OF.

New Testament Theology. Theological discipline that traces themes through the authors of the NT and then amalgamates those individual motifs into a single comprehensive whole. NT theology studies the progressive revelation of God in terms of the life situation at the time of writing and then delineates the underlying thread that ties it together. This discipline centers upon meaning rather than application, that is, the message of the text for its own day rather than for modern needs. The true beginning of "biblical theology" came after the Enlightenment within German pietism. The mind replaced faith as the controlling factor, and the historical-critical method developed. J. F. Gabler in 1787 defined the approach in purely descriptive terms. After Gabler, critics treated the Bible like any other book.

Relationship to Other Disciplines. *To Systematic Theology.* Biblical theology forces systematics to remain true to the historical revelation, while dogmatics provides the categories to integrate the data into a larger whole. The organization itself, however, stems from the text; Scripture must determine the integrating pattern or structure. Biblical theology is descriptive, tracing the individual emphases of the writers and then collating them to ascertain the underlying unity. Systematics takes this material and reshapes it into a confessional statement for the church; it bridges the gap between "what it meant" and "what it means."

To Exegesis. There is a constant tension within biblical theology between diversity and unity, and a holistic consideration of the biblical material is a necessary corrective to a fragmented approach to the Bible. Thus biblical theology regulates exegesis. Yet exegesis also precedes biblical theology, for it provides the data with which the latter works. The theologian correlates the results of the exegesis of individual texts in order to discover their unity.

To Historical Theology. "Tradition" controls not only Roman Catholic dogma but Protestant thinking as well. All interpreters find their database in the community of faith. Historical theology makes the theologian aware of the ongoing dialogue and thus functions both as a check against reading later ideas into a passage and as a store of knowledge from which to draw possible interpretations.

Specific Problem Areas. *Unity and Diversity.* Certainly there is tremendous diversity in the Bible, since most of the books were written to defend God's will for his people against various aberrations. Further, there is a great variety of expressions, such as Paul's "adoption" motif and John's "newborn" imagery. This does not mean, however, that it is impossible to compile divergent traditions into a larger conceptual whole (see Eph. 4:5–6). Through all the diverse expressions a unified perspective and faith shine through. The key is linguistic/semantic; the differences can often be understood as metaphors that point to a larger truth. At this level we can detect unity.

Tradition-History. Many believe that doctrines and traditions developed in stages, and that inspiration should be applied to the originating event, the stages in the subsequent history of the community, and the final stage in which it was "frozen" into the canon. Traditio-critical speculation becomes, however, an end in itself, with very little in the way of fruitful results. Still, when placed within the context of the whole process, the method can highlight individual emphases, such as in the four Gospels.

Analogia Fidei and Progressive Revelation. If we place too much stress on unity, the tendency to apply any parallel (even if a wrong one) to a text can result. A better phrase would be *analogia Scriptura*, "Scripture interpreting Scripture." Here too we must exercise care and stress a proper use of parallels, studying the use of the terms in both passages in order to determine whether the meanings truly overlap. Progressive revelation ties together the seemingly disparate notions of tradition-history and *analogia Scriptura.* We must trace the historical process of revelation and determine the continuities among individual parts.

History and Theology. There is no reason that theology must be divorced from the possibility of revelation in history. Indeed, history and its interpretation are united, and recent approaches to historiography demonstrate not only the possibility of seeing God's revelation in history but the necessity of doing so. In Kings–Chronicles or the Gospels, for instance, history and theology are inseparable. We know Jesus as he has been interpreted for us through the Evangelists.

Language, Text, and Meaning. Recent theorists have drawn such a sharp contrast between modern conditions and the ancient world that the interpreter seems forever separated from the intended meaning of the text. Meaning in the text is open to the interpreter, who must place preunderstanding "in front of" the text (Ricoeur) and enter its own language game. Within this activity of interpretation, the original meaning is a possible goal. When we recognize the NT as stating propositional truth, the intended meaning becomes a necessary enterprise.

OT and NT. Any true biblical theology must recognize the centrality of the relationship between the Testaments. Again the issue is diversity versus unity. The various strata of both must be allowed to speak, but the unity of these strata must be recognized. Several aspects demand this unity: the historical continuity between the Testaments; the centrality of the OT for the NT; the promise–fulfillment theme of the NT; the messianic hope of the OT and its place as a "pedagogue" (Gal. 3).

Theology and Canon. Brevard Childs has made the final form of the canon the primary hermeneutical tool in determining a biblical theology. He believes that the parts of Scripture must maintain a dialectical relationship with the whole of the canon. There is no true biblical theology when only the individual voices of the various strata are heard. Many critics demur, however, saying that biblical authority and inspiration are dynamic rather than static, centering not only upon the final form of the text but also upon the individual stages within the tradition process, both before the "final" form and after it, even up to the present day.

Authority. Since biblical theology is descriptive, dealing with "what it meant," critical scholars deny its authority. True biblical authority, it is said, rests upon its "apostolic effectiveness" in fulfilling its task (Barrett), upon the community behind it (Knight), or upon its content (Achtemeier). In actuality the authority of Scripture transcends all these; as the revelation *of God*, it has propositional authority; as the revelation of God *to humankind*, it has existential authority. The text is primary, and the authority of the interpreter is secondary, that is, it derives its authority from the text.

A Proper Methodology. The *synthetic method* traces basic theological themes through the strata of Scripture in order to note their development through the biblical period. The *analytical method* studies the distinctive theology of individual sections and notes the unique message of each. The *historical method* studies the development of religious ideas in the life of God's people. The *christological method* makes Christ the hermeneutical key to both Testaments. The *confessional method* looks at the Bible as a series of faith statements that are beyond history. The *cross-section method* traces a single unifying theme (e.g., covenant or promise) and studies it historically by means of "cross-sections" or samplings of the canonical record.

The *multiplex method* (Hasel) combines the best of these methods and proceeds hermeneutically from text to theory. It begins with grammatical and historical analysis of the text, attempting to unlock the meaning of the various texts within their life settings. As the data are collected from this exegetical task, they are organized into the basic patterns of the individual books and then of the individual authors. At this stage the interpreter has delineated the emphases or interlocking forces in the strata. Once these various traditions (e.g., Markan, Johannine, Pauline) have been charted, the student looks for basic principles of cohesion between them, for metaphorical language that discloses larger patterns of unity among the authors. These larger unities are charted on two levels, first with respect to overall unity and then with respect to the progress of revelation. Finally, these motifs are compiled into major sections and subsections, following a descriptive (biblical) method rather than an artificial reconstruction. In other words, the data rather than the dogmatic presuppositions of the interpreter control the operation. From this emerges a central unifying theme around which the other subthemes gather themselves. Within this larger unity the individual themes maintain complementary yet distinct roles. The larger cohesive unity must result from rather than become the presupposition of the theological enterprise, that is, the texts determine the patterns.

Unifying Themes. Five criteria are necessary to the search for a central motif that binds together the individual emphases and diverse doctrines of the NT: (1) the basic theme must express the nature and character of God; (2) it must account for the people of God as they relate to him; (3) it must express the world of humankind as the object of God's redemptive activity; (4) it must explain the dialectical relationship between the Testaments; (5) it must account for the other possible unifying themes and must truly unite the theological emphases of the NT. Many proposed themes will fit one or another of the strata of OT and NT—the narrative or the poetic or the prophetic or the wisdom or the epistolary portions—but will fail to summarize all. This theme must balance the others without merely lifting one above its fellow motifs.

The *covenant* theme (Eichrodt, Ridderbos) has often been utilized to express the binding relationship between God and his people. The *God and Christ* (Hasel) theme has been stressed a great deal lately, noting the theocentric character of the OT and the Christocentric character of the NT. The *salvation history* theme (von Rad, Cullmann, Ladd) may be the best of the positions, for it recognizes God's/Christ's redemptive activity on behalf of humankind, in terms of both present and future communion.

G. R. Osborne

See also John, Theology of; Luke, Theology of; Mark, Theology of; Matthew, Theology of; Old Testament Theology; Paul, Theology of.

Niagara Conferences. Series of summer meetings for Bible study that marked the beginning of the Bible and Prophetic Conference movement in the U.S. The idea for holding summer Bible conferences originated in 1868 among a group of American evangelicals associated with the millenarian journal *Waymarks in the Wilderness*. For the next few years conferences were held in different cities, but in 1883 sponsors secured a permanent location at Niagara-on-the-Lake, Ontario. Because of the nonsectarian spirit of the sessions, the conferences were able to draw a cross-section of North American evangelicals. But the leadership of the meetings remained under the control of millenarian teachers and pastors. Men such as Nathaniel West, H. M. Parsons, A. J. Gordon, W. J. Erdman, A. T. Pierson, George Needham, Robert Cameron, and, most important, James H. Brookes made sure that the still suspect premillennialism was taught alongside more traditional evangelical theological fare. After the death of Brookes in 1897 the conference moved from Niagara-on-the-Lake. It eventually disbanded in 1901, when its leadership could no longer agree on the timing of the "rapture" in relation to the tribulation of the last days. Nevertheless, the Niagara Conference spawned other Bible and Prophetic Conferences and spread premillennial views, especially the dispensationalism of J. N. Darby. In addition, the conferences forged alliances among conservative evangelicals that played a significant role in the beginnings of the fundamentalist movement after World War I.

T. P. Weber

See also Dispensation, Dispensationalism; Fundamentalism; Millennium, Views of the.

Nicea, Council of (325). First ecumenical council in the history of the church convened by the emperor Constantine at Nicea in Bithynia (now Isnik, Turkey). The main purpose of the council was to attempt to heal the schism in the church provoked by Arianism. This it proceeded to do theologically and politically by the almost unanimous production of a theological confession (the Nicene Creed) by over 300 bishops representing almost all the eastern provinces of the empire (where the heresy was chiefly centered) and by a token representation from the West. The creed thus produced was the first that could legally claim universal authority as it was sent throughout the empire to receive the agreement of the churches (with the alternative consequences of excommunication and imperial banishment).

It should be noted that this creed is not that which is recited in churches today as the Nicene Creed. Although similar in many respects, the latter is significantly longer than the former and is missing some key Nicene phrases.

The theology expressed in the Nicene Creed is decisively anti-Arian. At the beginning the unity of God is affirmed. But the Son is said to be "true God from true God." Although confessing that the Son is begotten, the creed adds the words, "from the Father" and "not made." It is positively asserted that he is "from the being (*ousia*) of the Father" and "of one substance (*homoousia*) with the Father." A list of Arian phrases, including "there was when he was not" and assertions that the Son is a creature or out of nothing, are expressly anathematized. Thus an ontological rather than merely functional deity of the Son was upheld at Nicea. The only thing confessed about the Spirit, however, is faith in him.

Among other things achieved at Nicea were the agreement on a date to celebrate Easter and a ruling on the Melitian Schism in Egypt. Arius and his most resolute followers were banished, but only for a short time. In the majority at Nicea was Althanasius, then a young deacon, soon to succeed Alexander as bishop and carry on what would become a minority challenge to a resurgent Arianism in the East. The orthodoxy of Nicea would eventually and decisively be reaffirmed at the Council of Constantinople in 381.

C. A. BLAISING

See also ARIANISM; ATHANASIUS; CONSTANTINOPLE, COUNCIL OF; MELITIAN SCHISMS; MONARCHIANISM.

Nicea, Second Council of (787). Seventh ecumenical council providing the climax (although not yet the end) of the iconoclastic controversy by decisively authorizing the veneration of images of various sorts but especially those of Christ, Mary, angels, and saints. The controversy had begun when the emperors Leo III (beginning in 725) and his son after him, Constantine V, tried abruptly to end the practice of venerating images, which had been growing in the church for over three centuries. This seems to have been partly in response to the threat of Islam, which attributed its success to an unidolatrous monotheism. Irene, acting as regent for her son, Leo IV, convened the council, which met at Nicea in 787 and was attended by over 300 bishops. The iconoclasts were anathematized and the worship of images upheld.

C. A. BLAISING

See also DULIA; HYPERDULIA; LATRIA.

Niebuhr, Helmut Richard (1894–1962). American clergyman and theologian. The Niebuhr brothers were the leaders of a new "Christian realism" that represented an American counterpart to European neo-orthodoxy. H. Richard Niebuhr was ordained in the Evangelical and Reformed Church. In 1931 he accepted a position at Yale Divinity School, where he remained until his death. Niebuhr's interests ranged widely. Some of his works treated matters of the church in society. *The Social Sources of Denominationalism* (1929) demonstrated how thoroughly Christian institutions were intertwined with the cultural customs of the West. *The Kingdom of God in America* (1937) provided a brilliant portrait of the way in which the idea of God's kingdom had shifted in American history—from God's sovereignty in the time of Jonathan Edwards, to the kingdom of Christ during the 1800s, and finally to the coming kingdom for 20th-century liberals. *Christ and Culture* (1951) offered a classic schematization of the different ways in which believers over the centuries have interacted with their world.

M. A. NOLL

See also NEO-ORTHODOXY.

Niebuhr, Reinhold (1892–1971). American clergyman and theologian. Reinhold Niebuhr was the brother of H. Richard and the best-known spokesman for American "Christian realism" from the early 1930s until his death. Niebuhr was the son of a pastor in the Evangelical and Reformed Church. He moved from a pastorate in Detroit to New York's Union Theological Seminary in 1928, where he immediately entered a wider circle of activity. World War II led him to abandon his socialism and pacifism, but he remained a dedicated social activist—serving on scores of committees in the 1930s and 1940s, helping to form Americans for Democratic Action and New York's Liberal party, editing the journal *Christianity and Crisis*, and writing prolifically for newspapers and magazines.

His theological ethics were developed in a long list of major books, the most important being *Moral Man and Immoral Society* (1932) and *The Nature and Destiny of Man* (1941, 1943). The first repudiates liberal optimism concerning humanity. It points out that social groups are selfish almost by their very definition, and it rebukes the notion that human beings are perfectable as individuals or inherently good in groups. The second provides a more systematic discussion of what Niebuhr calls humankind's "most vexing problem: How shall he think of himself?" Here and elsewhere Niebuhr proposes a series of "dialectical" relationships to answer his own question: humanity is both "free and bound, both limited and limitless," sinner and saint, subject to history and social forces but also the shaper of history and society, creature of the Creator but potential lord of the creation, egotistical but capable of living for others. Niebuhr draws on the Bible to expound these paradoxes, especially what he calls the biblical "myth" of creation.

M. A. NOLL

See also NEO-ORTHODOXY.

Ninety-Five Theses, The (1517). Series of propositions dealing with indulgences that Luther drew up as the basis for a proposed academic disputation. They were written in reaction to abuses in the sale of a plenary indulgency by Johann Tetzel. Oct. 31, 1517, the day they were supposedly posted on the Wittenberg Castle Church door, has traditionally been considered the starting point of the Reformation. Recent scholarship has questioned both the dating of the theses and whether they were actually posted. Although the debate has not been resolved, most scholars still accept the traditional interpretation.

R. W. HEINZE

See also LUTHER, MARTIN.

Nonconformity. Refusal to conform to the established or majority religion. Episcopalians are a nonconformist body in Scotland, and Wycliffe and the Lollards are sometimes depicted as England's first nonconformists. The term "Nonconformists " is most specifically used of those Protestants who could not conscientiously conform to the established religion of the reformed Church of England, especially after 1662, when the Dissenters comprised Independents (Congregationalists), Presbyterians, Baptists, and Quakers. The first three became the main nonconforming denominations, being joined in the 18th century by the Methodists and later by other smaller bodies. Since the late 19th century they have been known as the English Free Churches.

After 1662, Nonconformists campaigned ardently for freedom of conscience and religion. Their fortunes varied with royal and parliamentary policies. But civil disabilities persisted. Until 1868 Nonconformists had to support the established religion by church rates, and not until 1871 could Nonconformists graduate from Oxford and Cambridge. After 1836 they no longer had to be married in an Anglican church, although until 1898 a chapel wedding needed a civil registrar. Behind these advances lay the lobbying of the Protestant Dissenting Deputies, drawn from the three main denominations and first organized in 1732. They aligned naturally with Whigs and later Liberals against Tories. Nonconformist church life was a proving ground for democratic aspirations. By the mid-19th century Nonconformity was a political force, having strongly supported Catholic Emancipation (1829) and the Reform Bill (1832). The Nonconformist conscience found expression in social reform and philanthropy, just as earlier Nonconformists were pioneers of the modern missionary movement, exporting worldwide England's church divisions. After decline in the late 18th century the Free Churches experienced considerable growth in the 19th century. Nonconformity's social and political contributions to English life are undoubted. Its significance has been greater for church ("a free church in a free state"), hymnody (Watts and Wesley), and religious experience (what B. L. Manning calls "intensity"—a Puritan legacy) than for theology.

D. F. WRIGHT

See also PURITANISM.

Northfield Conferences. Series of summer Bible conferences inaugurated by D. L. Moody in Northfield, Massachusetts, in 1880. Moody planned the conferences for laypeople to augment their understanding of the Bible and the Christian faith, to discuss methods of Christian work, and to promote spiritual renewal. He hoped men and women would return to their churches and exert a similar influence there. Although Moody was the dominant personality at these summer conferences, he was not the main speaker. He brought some of the best-known Bible teachers to the Northfield platform, including A. T. Pierson, A. J. Gordon, D. W. Whittle, George Needham, W. G. Moorehead, Nathaniel West, William E. Blackstone, James H. Brookes, C. I. Scofield, and R. A. Torrey. One outgrowth of the Northfield Conferences had an incalculable impact not just on American but world Christianity. In 1886 the Northfield Conference was expanded to include a month-long conference for college students. From this student conference, the first of many at Northfield, 100 men dedicated themselves to foreign missionary service when they completed college. By the following June this number had grown to 2000. Out of this grew the Student Volunteer Movement (SVM), which sought "the evangelization of the world in this generation." It spread across America to the British Isles and Europe with globe-circling effects. Collegians who visited the Northfield Student Conference and came under Moody's influence included Robert Speer, Robert Wilder, Sherwood Eddy, and John R. Mott. The Northfield student conferences were the birthplace of the SVM and, through that organization, of the early 20th-century ecumenical movement.

S. N. GUNDRY

See also KESWICK CONVENTION; MILLENNIUM, VIEWS OF THE.

Novatian Schism. Division in the Western Church that arose because of the effects of the Decian persecution (249–50). Pope Fabian was martyred in Jan. 250, but the church was in such dire straits that his successor was not elected until the spring of 251. The majority vote was cast for Cornelius, who favored full acceptance of those who had lapsed during the terrible peril. The choice was repudiated by those clergy who had been most staunch during the persecution, and in opposition they consecrated Novatian, a Roman presbyter who was apparently already acclaimed for his important and orthodox theological work, *On the Trinity*. Christendom was thus faced with two rival popes, each seeking support of the wider church.

When they were excommunicated by a synod of bishops at Rome, the Novationists, wishing to avoid compromise and complacency with sin, established a separate church with its own discipline and clergy, including bishops. The Novatian Church continued for several centuries and was received by the Council of Nicea as an orthodox although schismatic group. In particular its affirmation of Christ as being of one substance with the Father was applauded. Later the sect fell under imperial disfavor, was forbidden the right of public worship, and had its books destroyed. The majority of its members were reabsorbed into the mainstream of the Catholic Church, although the Novatian Church was an identifiable entity until the 7th century.

R. C. KROEGER AND C. C. KROEGER

See also CYPRIAN.

Numinous, The. Rudolf Otto's term for the most basic of human experiences. In his book *The Idea of the Holy* (1917), Otto investigates, among other things, this basic experience, which he regards as the "innermost care" of all religions. This is the experience of "the holy," and it contains a very specific element or "moment" that distinguishes it from our rational experience and that is in fact inexpressible. In his attempt to find a word that will capture this incomprehensible innermost core, and isolate it from the moral and rational aspects, Otto coins a word adopted from the Latin *numen*, "numinous." There is, then, a numinous state of mind that is perfectly *sui generis* and is irreducible to any other. It is absolutely primary and therefore cannot be strictly defined; it can only be discussed. This experience of the numinous is what lies behind all the world's great religions. It is the experience that generates all the moral and ethical responses of religion, as well as the dogmas and doctrines. It is the experience of the other, the holy, the incomprehensible, God.

J. D. SPICELAND

See also OTTO, RUDOLF.

Oo

Obedience. The whole of biblical theology centers on the notion of divine revelation and our receptive response: God speaks his word, we hear and are required to obey. The connection between hearing and obeying is essential. In the OT *šāma'* conveys the meaning of both to hear and to obey. Israel must hear Yahweh's voice and act in obedient response. In the Torah the theme of responsive obedience is underscored (Exod. 19:5, 8; 24:7; Deut. 28:1; 30:11–14). Abraham was blessed because he heard and obeyed the Lord's voice (Gen. 22:18). This theme lies behind the prophetic injunction, "Thus says the LORD." The prophetic word reveals both who God is and what he is calling Israel to do. In the LXX *šāma'* is regularly translated by words in the *akouein* word group, and this again expresses the inner relation between hearing and response. Emphatic forms *hypakouein* and *hypakoē* (lit. "to hear beneath") convey the meaning "obey/obedience" (in the NT the verb appears 21 times; the noun 15 times, especially in the writings of Paul).

Jesus stands in the OT prophetic tradition when he calls Israel to a discipleship that essentially involves "doing." When a person in the crowd praises Jesus' mother, Jesus replies, "Blessed rather are those who hear the word of God and obey it" (Luke 11:28; cf. John 10:16, 27; 15:5, 10). Paul regards obedience as being one of the constituent parts of faith. Initially Christ stands as the model of obedience (Phil. 2:5–8), and through his obedience, which is contrasted with Adam's disobedience, "many will be made righteous" (Rom. 5:19; cf. Heb. 5:8–9 for the parallel thought). Paul in fact views his task as bringing about the "obedience that comes from faith" among the nations (Rom. 1:5; 16:26).

G. M. BURGE

Obedience of Christ. The NT speaks explicitly of the obedience of Christ only three times: "through the obedience of the one man the many will be made righteous" (Rom. 5:19); "he humbled himself and became obedient to death" (Phil. 2:8); and "he learned obedience from what he suffered" (Heb. 5:8). But the concept that these verses contain is clearly alluded to in many other passages: (1) where Christ is portrayed as a "servant" (Matt. 20:28; Mark 10:45); (2) where he declares his purpose in coming to earth is to do his Father's will (John 5:30; 8:28–29; 10:18; 12:49; 14:31); (3) where his sinless and righteous life is asserted (Matt. 27:4, 19–23; Mark 12:14; Luke 23:4, 14–15; John 8:46; 18:38; 19:4–6; 2 Cor. 5:21; Heb. 4:15; 7:26); and (4) where his submission to authority is affirmed (Matt. 3:15; Luke 2:51–52; 4:16).

Christ's obedience can be characterized by the terms "preceptive" and "penal." Christ's preceptive obedience is his full obedience to all the positive prescriptions of the law; Christ's penal obedience is his willing, obedient bearing of all the sanctions imposed by the law that had accrued against his people because of their transgressions. By his preceptive obedience he made available a righteousness before the law that is imputed or reckoned to those who trust in him. By his penal obedience he took upon himself by legal imputation the penalty due his people for their sin. His preceptive and penal obedience, then, is the ground of God's justification of sinners, by which divine act they are pardoned (because their sins have been charged to Christ, who obediently bears the law's sanctions against sin) and accepted as righteous in God's sight (because Christ's preceptive obedience is imputed to them).

R. L. Reymond

Oberlin Theology. Nineteenth-century American revivalistic, perfectionistic, and reforming theology. It was closely associated with the work of Charles Finney, America's most famous antebellum revivalist, and with the faculty at Oberlin College, Ohio (founded 1833), of which Finney was a member. The theology contained emphases that were shared widely by New School Presbyterians, Methodists, many Baptists, members of Disciples and Christian churches, and even some Unitarians. Oberlin theology emphasized a belief in a second, more mature stage of Christian life. This second stage carried different names, such as "entire sanctification," "holiness," "Christian perfection," and "the baptism of the Holy Ghost." Oberlin theology represented an immensely important strand of 19th-century evangelical belief, not only because of its influential convictions but also because of its practical effects in revivalism (including the "anxious bench" and the protracted meeting) and its concern for reforming social ills, including slavery, intemperance, and economic injustice.

M. A. Noll

See also Finney, Charles Grandison; Holiness Movement, American; Pentecostalism; Perfection, Perfectionism.

Oblation. See Offerings and Sacrifices in Bible Times.

Obscenity. Anything that is filthy, repulsive, impure, lewd, offensive, and indecent. The U.S. Supreme Court, in the 1966 *Fanny Hill* case, gave three tests for obscenity: (1) obscene material appeals to prurient interest (i.e., it is intended to arouse lascivious thought and desire); (2) it is patently offensive to prevailing community standards; (3) it is utterly without redeeming social importance. Obscenity is wrong because it dehumanizes both the participant and the observer.

Since the perception of obscenity varies from one generation to the next, it is essential that moral discernment take place in prayerful Christian community. Out of genuine love for one's neighbor, however, it seems clear that Christians ought to struggle for restrictions, including censorship, on obscene material that portrays persons in cruel and dehumanizing fashion and contributes to the rapacious atmosphere of this era. It is also out of genuine neighbor love that Christians should struggle to protect children from the frontal assaults of obscene material on newsstands and television and through the mail.

While sexual sins receive full censure in Scripture, Christians must be careful not to allow their battle against sexual obscenity to overshadow their zeal to combat violence, dishonesty, greed, and other sins that are also condemned in the Bible. Finally, Christians must remember that their primary calling is not to act negatively as the restrainers of evil but to act positively as the promoters of the gospel and the good.

D. W. Gill

See also Pornography.

Occult, The. "Hidden" or "secret" wisdom that is beyond the range of ordinary human knowledge. The term is frequently used in reference to certain practices (occult "arts") that include divination, fortune telling, spiritism (necromancy), and magic. Those phenomena may be said to have the following distinct characteristics: (1) the disclosure and communication of information unavailable to humans through normal means (beyond the five senses); (2) the placing of persons in contact with supernatural powers, paranormal energies, or demonic forces; and (3) the acquisition and mastery of power in order to manipulate or influence other people into certain actions. The classical systems of occult philosophy and their more recent new age variants are fundamentally identical with the "cosmic humanism" that characterizes much of the contemporary world. Likewise, these ideas can be linked with such Eastern religious practices as yoga and meditation.

The occult/mystical worldview and its associated religious expression—especially in the Eastern cults presently active in the West—can be analyzed in terms of the following components: (1) *The promise of godhood—humankind is a divine being.* All forms of occult philosophy proclaim that the true or "real" human self is synonymous with God. (2) *The notion that "all is one"—God is everything* (pantheism). There is only one reality in existence (monism), and therefore everyone and everything in the material world is part of the Divine. (3) *Life's purpose is to achieve awareness of the Divine within—self-realization.* The path to salvation ("illumination," "enlightenment," "union") is an experiential one. (4) *Humankind is basically good—evil is an illusion or imperfection.* Ignorance, not sin, is at the root of the human dilemma. There is no need of redemption or forgiveness, only self-realization. (5) *Self-realization via spiritual technique leads to power—the God-man is in charge.* By employing spiritual technology such as meditation, chanting, and yoga, and through the application of universal laws, the realized being becomes master of personal reality. With this broad occult/mystical framework in mind, it can be said that the ultimate objective of psychic/occult power is to validate the lie of Satan—that humankind is God and that death is an illusion. In the deceptive quest for godhood and power, men and women are brought under the power of Satan himself. Both the OT and the NT proscribe such spiritually impure occultic activities as sorcery, mediumship, divination, and magic.

R. M. ENROTH

Ockham, William of. See WILLIAM OF OCKHAM.

Offerings and Sacrifices in Bible Times. A distinction must be made between offering and sacrifice. The word "offering" denotes several categories of gifts to the Lord: (1) a required offering to be burnt wholly or partially on the altar; (2) a voluntary offering to be burnt partially on the altar and to be consumed by the priests and the Israelites as a communal meal; (3) the tithe of the produce of the land and the offspring of the flocks. The word "sacrifice" denotes the particular way of presenting certain offerings. The word *zābah* ("sacrifice") is related to the word *mizbēaḥ* ("altar"), and both nouns are connected with the Hebrew verb meaning "to slaughter." Only three categories of offerings are to be considered sacrifices: the sin offering, the guilt offering, and the burnt offering. Thus, it can be said that all sacrifices are offerings, but not all offerings are sacrifices. The tithe was one of the tributary offerings imposed on Israel and there were strict regulations pertaining to it (Lev. 27:30–33; Num. 18:21–32; Deut. 14:22–29; 26:2–15).

Categories of Offerings. Offerings can be classified as (1) propitiatory (expiatory atonement): sin offering, guilt offering; (2) dedicatory (consecratory): burnt offering, cereal offering, drink offering; or (3) communal (fellowship): peace offering, wave offering, thanksgiving offering, vow, freewill offering. Several passages in the Pentateuch describe the offerings in great detail (Exod. 20:24–26; 34:25–26; Lev. 1–7, 17; 19:5–8; Num. 15; 28–29; Deut. 12). Lev. 1–7 sets forth the order of the various types of offerings.

Propitiatory Offerings. An expiatory offering was required when an Israelite had become ritually unclean or had unwittingly sinned against God or neighbor. The two types of expiatory offering are the sin offering and the guilt offering.

The Sin Offering (ḥaṭṭā't, Exod. 29:14, 36; Lev. 4). Every Israelite, whether commoner or high priest, was required to make a sin offering. What was offered depended upon the individual's status within the community. A poor person could satisfy the requirements by sacrificing two pigeons or turtledoves (Lev. 5:7), or one-tenth of an ephah of fine flour (Lev. 5:11; cf. Heb. 9:22). The Israelite of modest income could bring a female goat (Lev. 4:28) or a lamb (4:32) to the altar. The leaders in the community were expected to offer a male goat (4:23) and the high priest as well as the people as a congregation had to sacrifice a young bull (4:3, 14). A sin offering was presented under three circumstances. First, it was required for ritual cleansing (Lev. 12:6–8; 14:13–17, 22, 31; 15:15, 30; Num. 6:11, 14, 16). A second occasion for which a sin offering was required was when an Israelite unintentionally sinned against the law of God (Num. 15:25–29). Finally, sin offerings were made at each of the Hebrew festivals such as passover (Num. 28:22–24) and the feast of weeks (Num. 28:30).

The Guilt Offering ('āšām, Lev. 5:14–6:7; 7:1–7; AV, "trespass offering"). The second kind of expiatory offering was the guilt offering, which consisted of a payment of damages or a fine. The guilt offering was a means of making restitution when social, religious, or ritual expectations had not been observed. It was required of any Israelite who had defrauded God or a fellow Israelite. Whether the offense was against God or another person, the guilty party had to pay full restitution. Furthermore, the offender was required to pay a penalty of one-fifth of the value of the goods defrauded. This additional offering was usually a ram (Lev. 5:15).

Dedicatory Offerings. Three offerings are characterized as being "pleasant" to the Lord. These are the burnt offering (Lev. 1), the cereal offering (Lev. 2), and the peace offering (Lev. 3). The phrase "an aroma pleasing to the Lord" (NIV) or a "sweet savor" (AV) is a standardized idiom denoting God's acceptance of and pleasure with Israelite offerings.

The Burnt Offering ('ōlā, Lev. 1:3–17; 6:8–13). Any Israelite could present a burnt offering. A bull (1:3–5), a sheep or goat (1:10), and a bird (1:14) were all considered to be appropriate sacrifices. The offering was made by having the offender place a hand upon the animal before it was killed (1:4). After the animal was killed its blood was drained on the altar (1:5) or on the side of the altar (1:15). The priest then carefully washed and cut the offering into pieces and arranged the pieces on the altar (1:6–9, 12–13). The Scriptures indicate a close association between the burnt offering and the sin offering. These two types of offerings were required together during the new moon festival (Num. 28:11–14), passover (Num. 28:19–24), the feast of weeks (Num. 28:26–29), the festival of trumpets (Num. 29:2–4), day of atonement (Num. 29:8), and the feast of booths (Num. 29:12–38). The association suggests that before worshipers can fully devote themselves to the Lord (symbolized by the burnt offering), they must know that their sins have been atoned for (symbolized by the sin offering).

Cereal Offering (minḥâ, Lev. 2:1–16; AV, "meat offering," NIV, "grain offering").

The cereal offering was presented by all Israelites, including priests. It consisted mainly of fine flour (Lev. 2:1–3), wafers, unleavened bread, and cakes (2:4–10), or ears of grain (2:14–16). A portion of the cereal offering was burned together with incense (2:1–2). The offering was generally made together with the burnt offering (cf. Num. 28–29) and peace offering (Lev. 7:12–14; Num. 15:4–10).

Drink Offering (nesek, Num. 28:14; 29:6). As with the cereal offering, anyone could present a drink offering. It accompanied both burnt and peace offerings (Num. 15:1–10).

Communal Offerings. In addition to the required offerings the worshiper could present voluntary offerings.

Peace Offering (šelāmîm, Lev. 3; 7:11–36; NIV, "fellowship offerings"). Any Israelite could make a peace offering in addition to the sacrifices made for atonement and consecration. The animal was killed at the entrance of the outer court (Lev. 3:1–2, 7–8, 12–13) and its blood was thrown against the altar (3:2, 8, 13). The entrails were completely burned. The priest was permitted to take the breast and eat it with his family in a clean place. Before taking it as his own, the priest was required to recognize it as a heave offering (*terûmâ*). He was expected to lift up his portion to signify that it was the Lord's (Lev. 7:34; Exod. 29:27–28). Then he would wave it as a wave offering (*tenûpâ*) to symbolize that it was the Lord's and that it became his for food by divine appointment. The last stage of the peace offering was the communal meal, where the offerer and his family would enjoy those parts of the offering that had not been burned or taken by the priest (Lev. 7:15–17). It was to be eaten by ritually clean people in a place near the sanctuary (a ritually clean place); strict rules dictate the time period during which the food could be enjoyed. The peace offering was regularly made during the feast of weeks (Lev. 23:19–20) as a token of gratitude to God.

Voluntary Offerings. The votive offerings included those gifts presented in fulfillment of a vow (Lev. 7:16–17; 22:21; 27; Num. 6:21; 15; 3–16; 30:11). The vow was made either as part of a request of God and then fulfilled when the request was granted, or it could be a voluntary response to the goodness of God. The fulfillment of the latter vow falls together with the thanksgiving offering (*tôdâ*, Lev. 7:12–13, 15; 22:29; 2 Chron. 33:16; Pss. 50:14, 23; 116:17). Another type of voluntary offering was the freewill offering (*nedābâ*, Exod. 35:27–29; 36:3; Lev. 7:16; Num. 15:3; Deut. 12:17; 16:10; 23:23; Ezek. 46:12). Because of the voluntary nature of the freewill offering, an imperfect ox or sheep was acceptable (Lev. 22:23). The emphasis on sacrifices and offerings in the OT is God's revelation for Israel. It signifies the gravity of sin and the grace of God. By the shedding of blood sins can be expiated so that the Israelites could know they were reconciled with God. The complex system of sacrifices and offerings made the point that people must know what God requires of them and that they must be sure to please God by the renewal of their heart and motivations as they give of their possessions to God. The expiatory sacrifices did not atone for all sins. Only unintentional sins, inadvertent acts of default, and particular cases of dishonesty could be atoned for, but any trespass of the Decalogue required the death penalty.

Sacrifices and Offerings in the NT. Jesus upheld the sacrificial system. He went to the temple at passover and participated in the passover meal. He commanded the lepers to go to the priests to undergo ritual cleansing and to bring the required offerings (Matt. 8:4; cf. Luke 17:14). In the Sermon on the Mount Jesus did not reject offerings, but stressed that one must first be reconciled to one's brother before one can be reconciled with God (Matt. 5:23–24). Following the crucifixion and ascension of Jesus, the apostles applied the OT language of sacrifice and expiation to Jesus' sacrifice of himself (Rom. 3:25; 8:3). The Epistle to the Hebrews shows how the OT sacrificial system is fulfilled by Jesus as the high priest of the new covenant, by whose blood all sins can be atoned for and by whom the Christian can be strengthened to do works pleasing to God (Heb. 13:20–21). Paul likewise exhorted the Christians in Rome to offer themselves as a living sacrifice to God as a dedicatory offering (Rom. 12:1–2).

W. A. VAN GEMEREN

Officers, Church. See CHURCH OFFICERS.

Offices of Christ. As the only Redeemer of his church, Jesus Christ performed his saving work in the threefold role of prophet (Deut. 18:15; Luke 4:18–21; 13:33; Acts 3:22), priest (Ps. 110:4; Heb. 3:1; 4:14–15; 5:5–6; 6:20; 7:26; 8:1), and king (Pss. 2:6; 45:6; 110:1–2; Isa. 9:6–7; Luke 1:33; John 18:36–37; Heb. 1:8; 2 Pet. 1:11; Rev. 19:16). Theologians refer to these as the three offices of Christ, with all the other christological designations such as apostle, shepherd, intercessor, and head of the church being subsumed under one of these three general offices. In filling these offices Christ fulfills all the needs of humankind. "As prophet he meets the problem of man's ignorance, supplying him with knowledge. As priest he meets the problem of man's guilt, supplying him with righteousness. As king he meets the problem of man's weakness and dependence, supplying him with power and protection" (J. B. Green, *A Harmony of the Westminster Presbyterian Standards*, pp. 65–66).

R. L. REYMOND

Oil, Anointing with. See ANOINT, ANOINTING.

Old Lights, The. See NEW LIGHT SCHISM.

Old Man. See MAN, OLD AND NEW.

Old Roman Creed. See APOSTLES' CREED.

Old School Theology. Orthodox Calvinist (Presbyterian) theology in the ascendance from the 1830s to the 1860s. Princeton theologians Archibald Alexander and Charles Hodge believed that their theology faithfully reflected Reformed beliefs and should be central in American Presbyterianism. They contended that their Calvinism was historically aligned with the Westminster Confession of Faith, Calvin, Augustine, and the Bible itself. The very term "Old School theology" indicates that its adherents wanted to retain traditional Reformed doctrines. They wanted a "consistent Calvinism" and developed distinct views on confessionalism, revivalism, and church polity. Because of their stand on these issues, the Old School faction expelled the New School from the church in 1837 for having diverged from them. In 1869 New and Old Schools in the North reunited, primarily because during the schism New School theology had become more orthodox.

W. A. HOFFECKER

See also ALEXANDER, ARCHIBALD; HODGE, CHARLES; NEW HAVEN THEOLOGY; NEW SCHOOL THEOLOGY.

Old Testament. See BIBLE.

Old Testament Canon. See BIBLE, CANON OF.

Old Testament Theology. Despite its wealth of affirmations about God, the OT does not contain any systematized theological statements about such matters as sin, redemption, and divine grace. On the basis of a knowledge of Hebrew, an objective historical method, and a recognition that the OT is God's word written, it may be possible to outline some of the more important concepts that could be included in an OT theology.

Doctrine of God. God is the ground of all existence, and reveals himself creatively by deeds such as the making of the world and humankind as well as by the verbal communication of his nature and will. While his nature is that of infinite spirit, he permits himself to be described periodically in anthropomorphic terms. He thus has a face—a presence, from which people can be alienated because of their sin (Gen. 4:14). He has hands, with which he creates his marvelous works (Ps. 143:5). His voice may be heard directly (Exod. 3:4) or through the prophets (Isa. 8:1; Jer. 1:4; Ezek. 31:1) as his word is proclaimed.

The personality of God is also expressed by a variety of names, which in ancient Near Eastern tradition signified a range of character and function. He is the God Most High (Gen. 14:18), God Almighty (Exod. 6:3), "a God who sees" (Gen. 16:13), the God of Israel (Gen. 33:20), and YHWH ("I AM WHO I AM" or "I WILL BE WHAT I WILL BE"). This name, often transliterated "Jehovah" or "Yahweh," establishes God's existence beyond question and identifies him as the only true and living God, who binds the Israelites to himself in a covenant relationship.

Throughout the OT God is conceived of as an omnipotent being who possesses a complete personality and who can be known fully as God at every stage of the historical process. He is omniscient and has total knowledge of all future events until the end of time. Characteristic of his purposes and deeds is love or mercy (*ḥesed*), which surrounds creation and creature alike (Ps. 145:9) and finds its supreme expression in altruistic activities of blessing and redemption. The idea of God as the Father of his people is connected with the establishing of the covenant nation, who become his adopted children, and is also expressed in relationship to the work of the Messiah, who will ultimately enlarge the family of believers by his work of redemption. As Father, God requires a response of filial love and obedience from his children (Mal. 1:6), and will punish them if they become apostate.

The OT also describes the activities of God in terms of a vitalizing Spirit (*rûaḥ*) who sustains creation (Job 34:14; Ps. 104:30) and gives distinctive existence to humankind (Gen. 2:7).

Doctrine of Man and Sin. The OT teaches that humankind has been created in the image of God (*imago Dei*). Two Hebrew terms, *ṣelem* and *demût*, are used (Gen. 1:26–27; 5:1, 3; 9:6) as synonyms to indicate that humankind reflects God in a unique manner. Human beings are thus different from other forms of created organic life, over which they have been given dominion (Gen. 1:28). It is obvious that the concept of the *imago Dei* must be grasped firmly before the significance of other OT observations about sin, grace, human salvation, and the like can be appreciated properly. The *imago Dei* is defaced but not destroyed by human rebellion against God in Eden, an episode that defined sin for humanity as a process culminating in rejection of, or disobedience to, the known, revealed will of God. From this point humankind was recognized as "mortal" (Gen. 6:3), a term implying frailty, self-centeredness, and transience.

Because of sin the penalty of death was imposed upon the human race (Gen. 3:19), but the breach between Creator and creature was repaired to some extent by sacrificial procedures, which found their fullest definition in the Mosaic period. Levitical law prescribed the restoration of fellowship between sinners and God in great detail (Lev. 1–7), and one of the most prominent sacrificial observances in Hebrew covenantal religion was the day of atonement (Lev. 16), by which the sins of accident, error, or omission of the nation were forgiven. These offenses were inadvertent transgressions and were distinguished from presumptuous sins, which constituted open rebellion against known covenant spirituality and for which there could be no forgiveness.

Doctrine of Redemption. The OT shows clearly that animal sacrifice as such has no intrinsic efficacy, but that when the sacrificial offering was presented to God in the manner prescribed, its blood made atonement for the sinner (Lev. 17:11), and fellowship with God was restored. The guilt offering was regarded as "most holy" (Lev. 7:1) because it served to fulfill the holiest of duties. While some prophets appeared to criticize sacrifice (Isa. 1:11; Hos. 6:6; Amos 5:21), they were more concerned with the motivation that prompted the rite than with the institution itself. The restoration of the sinner is an act of God's grace; the characteristic OT term is *ḥesed.* It is often translated as "mercy" or "lovingkindness," and represents the motivating force behind the covenant of love God established with his chosen people (Deut. 7:12).

Covenantal theology is of the greatest importance in OT thought because it provides a dimension of formal discipline and spirituality for a people that was expected to exemplify in national life the character of their God. Against this background the ideal of the long-promised Messiah comes gradually to fruition. From the beginning this personage was a fact of history, a being conceived of in regal terms, first as an ideal ruler such as David but subsequently as an anointed figure ("messiah") who would appear at the end of the age to usher in the divine kingdom. The splendor of such a person was indicated by Isaiah (9:6–7; 11:1–5), while the historical continuity was especially stressed by Jeremiah (33:14–15). The nature of the messianic kingdom was foretold by Zechariah (9:9–10; 12:7–9), and the precise birthplace of this royal individual was predicted centuries before the event by Micah (5:2).

In the OT teachings concerning redemption and restoration there appear some rather enigmatic references to a "servant of the Lord." These are particularly prominent in the Book of Isaiah, but in the prophecy they are distributed between an individual and the idea of the nation as the servant, which makes the matter of identification problematic. The nation of Israel as servant (41:8; 42:19; 44:1) is replaced elsewhere (42:1; 49:1; 52:13; 53:11) by an individual who will restore the nation (49:5–6) and glorify God throughout the earth. The servant was to be a prophet of God, empowered by the Spirit (42:1; 61:1) for the work of establishing divine justice in the earth (42:4). In his mission he would suffer for others' sins and die dishonorably (53:3, 9). His atonement would be that of the guilt offering (Isa. 53:10), which when accepted by God would lead many to be accounted righteous, whatever their race. The servant's work would thus change the old corporate concept of salvation that existed under the Sinai covenant and broaden the scope of God's redemptive activity. It would include the whole human race and place response to God's invitation to forgiveness and fellowship on an individual rather than a corporate basis (cf. Jer. 31:29–30).

The suffering servant obviously has much in common with the Messiah, Israel's ideal ruler. Both emerge from the Davidic line (2 Sam. 7:15–16; Isa. 11:1) and have a special anointing for their task (Isa. 11:2; 42:1). The ruler, through the Davidic covenant, witnesses about God's nature and saving purposes to those outside the covenant (Isa. 55:3), a function that is also assigned to the servant (Isa. 49:6). Finally, the Messiah, spoken of as the "Branch," is equated with the servant in postexilic prophecy (Zech. 3:8).

Eschatology. At death the individual Hebrew was deemed to have gone to Sheol, an underworld region of vague dimensions where the dead existed as shadows of their former selves. Some passages suggest a diminished consciousness of God's presence and activities there (Ps. 88:10–11; Isa. 38:18), but others proclaim God's nearness even in Sheol (Ps. 139:8). Teaching about individual resurrection is stated most clearly in Dan. 12:2.

Because Israel's national life was based upon the covenant at Sinai, a corporate concept of survival formed an attractive prospect, especially when associated with the leadership of the Messiah. The possibility of national revival through God's power was seen clearly in Ezekiel's vision (Ezek. 37:1–14), in which a new act of human creation comparable to the first (cf. Gen. 2:7) took place. Despite this encouraging prospect, earlier prophets had pointed sternly to Israel's rebellion against the covenant provisions and had spoken of an apocalyptic day of the Lord, in which impenitent Israel would be punished, not blessed (Amos 5:18–20). Other prophets promised that on that day the whole earth would acknowledge God's righteous overlordship (Isa. 11:9). The scene is thus set for God to inaugurate a new age of grace by a sudden revelation of himself in power as he smites the nation's enemies from the Mount of Olives (Zech. 14:3–4). Then he will rule as King over all the earth, and will make his name one among humankind (Zech. 14:9) as he judges in righteousness (Pss. 96:13; 98:9).

R. K. Harrison

See also God, Attributes of; God, Doctrine of; God, Names of; Image of God; Man, Doctrine of; Messiah; Offerings and Sacrifices in Bible Times; Sin; Son of Man.

Oman, John Wood (1860–1939). British theologian. Oman spent most of his career in the service of the English Presbyterian Church, first in a lengthy pastorate at Alnwick, Northumberland (1889–1907), and then as professor of systematic theology and apologetics at Westminster, the Presbyterian theological college at Cambridge (1907–35). He was strongly influenced by liberal German thought, especially that of Schleiermacher, whose *Speeches on Religion* he translated (1893) and whose emphasis upon the importance of subjective, personal religious experience he reflected in his major writings, including *Grace and Personality* (1918) and *The Natural and the Supernatural* (1931).

W. C. Ringenberg

Omission, Sins of. Sin committed when one fails to do right. Sins of omission are to be contrasted to sins of commission, which are when individuals do that which is wrong. Negligence can also be sin. Ignorance of an offense does not absolve one from guilt (Lev. 4:13, 22, 27; 5:2–4, 17, 19; 6:4; cf. James 4:17). In Scripture terrible punishments are given because of ignorance and/or negligence. Failure to "help the Lord" resulted in a curse (Judg. 5:23), and an anathema is pronounced upon those who do not love the Lord (1 Cor. 16:22). Failure to minister to others results in everlasting destruction and damnation (Matt. 25:45–46).

R. P. Lightner

Omnipotence. See God, Attributes of.

Omnipresence. See God, Attributes of.

Omniscience. See God, Attributes of.

Ontological Argument for God. See God, Arguments for the Existence of.

Ontological Ethics. See Duty.

Ontology. See Metaphysics.

Oppression. The sin of man's inhumanity to man. It is the violation of human rights and dignity, the exploitation of human labor, the repression of moral values, and the robbery of self-identity. Oppressors may arise from an elite who have the power to subjugate others because of their wealth and privileged position, or they may arise from the masses who have the power to oppress a minority because of the strength of their number. Oppression may occur in the family or at the factory or in society at large. Oppressors may be conscious of their efforts to hold down others or they may be oblivious to the consequences of their sinful activities. Their primary motive may be fear, pride, or greed. Oppression is a complex evil bearing psychological, spiritual, economic, and political consequences, and frequently renders the oppressed unaware of their true situation and defenselessness.

Economic and political oppression is a major concern in contemporary theological thought. Theologies of liberation share the conviction that the essence of the gospel is the liberation of the oppressed from sociopolitical exploitation. Black theologian James Cone speaks for many theologians of liberation when he writes, "To know Jesus is to know Him as revealed in the struggle of the oppressed for freedom" (*God of the Oppressed*, p. 34). For Cone, oppression is social oppression, and freedom is brought about by political struggle—a struggle in which "the poor recognize that their fight against poverty and injustice is not only consistent with the gospel but is the gospel of Jesus Christ."

The emphasis on social oppression has challenged evangelicals to examine biblical perspectives on oppression and become more aware of the influence of social conditioning in shaping theological perspectives. In the past many evangelicals have tended to spiritualize clear biblical references to social and economic oppression. There are a number of reasons for this position, including the biblical stress on patience in suffering, the association of economic struggle with greed and covetousness, the long-standing Christian tradition of obedience to the ruling powers, and the reduction of social concern to works of compassion.

While the Bible acknowledges that poverty may result from laziness and divine punishment, both the OT and NT make clear that its major cause is injustice, exploitation, and class conflict. God is continually portrayed as the defender and refuge of the oppressed. God upholds their human rights and promises judgment on the oppressor. The biblical meaning of oppression exposes the complexity of evil and traces injustice back to a fundamental rejection of God (Rom. 1:18–21). Oppression may be political, racial, sexual, economic, generational, religious, spiritual, or demonic. It is not simply economic, nor is it confined to one social class.

Evangelical theology should not obscure the practical social dimensions of oppression. Poverty results from sin and evil. It is to be neither accepted nor idealized. Concern for humankind's spiritual condition of lostness and separation from God does not justify indifference toward the justice and well-being of those who are economically poor or racially outcast. The evident complexity of evil in human history does not rationally or spiritually allow for a one-dimensional view of oppression that divorces social realities from personal sin and rebellion against God, and from the dominating and destructive influence of the principalities and powers. Christians are called to work for social justice in the certain hope that the living Lord Jesus will one day rule and reign. Until that day Christians are required to work for the liberation of the oppressed through the power and wisdom of the Spirit.

D. D. WEBSTER

See also LIBERATION THEOLOGY; SOCIAL GOSPEL, THE.

Opus Operatum. Term used in Roman Catholic sacramental theology to express the doctrine that the sacraments confer the grace of God "by the working of the work" (*ex opere operato).* The view thus rejects all suggestion of dependence not only on the minister (*ex opere operantis*) but also on the receiver. So much is grace and rite conjoined that the due administration of the latter must necessarily involve the former.

G. J. C. MARCHANT

See also EX OPERE OPERATO; SACRAMENT.

Ordain, Ordination. These words come from the Latin meaning "to set in order," "to arrange." In later Latin they came to mean "to appoint to office." The AV uses the verb "to ordain" to render about 30 different Hebrew and Greek words, which shows that the English word has many different shades of meaning. Converted Israel will sing of the peace that Yahweh will "ordain" (appoint) for it (Isa. 26:12). God has "ordained" the moon and stars (Ps. 8:3); these heavenly bodies were prepared by God for their work. Yahweh "ordained" Jeremiah to be a prophet to the Gentile nations (Jer. 1:5); he gave Jeremiah to the nations along with his ministry. Certain truths were set aside by the apostles and elders as essential to the faith; these "decrees" were "ordained" of God (Acts 16:4). God "ordained" a specific place for his people to dwell (1 Chron. 17:9); he reserved it exclusively for them. Jesus "ordained" 12 men to serve in special ways (Mark 3:14). He set them apart for a specific office and duties; he appointed them.

There is a nontechnical sense in which local churches and sometimes denominations "ordain" those who minister among them. This is usually accompanied by the laying on of hands. Support is often found for this from the following: (1) Traditionally, group approval has thus been given. (2) The OT speaks of priests, Levites, prophets, and kings being set aside for their work in this way. (3) Christ called, appointed, and commissioned the twelve, although without formal ordination. (4) The apostles gave special recognition to the choice of Matthias to take the place of Judas Iscariot.

The Roman Catholic and Orthodox churches regard ordination as a sacrament instituted by Christ and conferring grace upon the recipient. Anglicans give great prominence to ordination, some believing in apostolic succession. Church bodies associated with what might be called the Free Church movement usually view ordination in a less rigid way and practice it simply as group approval upon the individual after doctrinal examination.

R. P. LIGHTNER

See also ORDERS, HOLY; PREDESTINATION.

Order of Salvation. (Lat. *ordo salutis*) Order in which God brings salvation to the sinner. The term was apparently brought into theological usage in 1737 by Jakob Karpov, a Lutheran. There are differences not only between Catholics and Protestants but also between Lutheran and Reformed in how they regard the order of salvation. For example, the Reformed order may be taken as (1) effectual calling, issuing in (2) regeneration, (3) faith, leading to (4) justification, and (5) sanctification, ultimately resulting in (6) glorification. Some of these experiences are synchronous, however, and the stages in such cases must be regarded as of logical rather than of chronological sequence.

G. N. M. COLLINS

Orders, Holy. Major orders of the ministry in an episcopal church. In the Anglican and the Orthodox churches, these are the bishops, priests, and deacons. In the Roman Catholic Church, where the episcopate and the presbyterate are counted as one order, the three are bishop-priests, deacons, and subdeacons. Admission to holy orders is by ordination, the important ceremony being the laying on of hands.

L. MORRIS

See also MAJOR ORDERS; ORDAIN, ORDINATION.

Orders, Major. See MAJOR ORDERS.

Orders, Minor. See MINOR ORDERS.

Ordo Salutis. See ORDER OF SALVATION.

Origen (ca. 185–ca. 254). Christian author and teacher. Origen fused Greek thought with biblical exposition. The Catechetical School at Alexandria reached its zenith under his tutelage. At the request of a church challenged by a plethora of deviant doctrines, he traveled widely and defended the orthodox faith against pagans, Jews, and heretics. His *Against Celsus*, a response to a pagan treatise attacking Christianity, stands as a monument of Christian apologetic. Although three centuries later (553), he was declared a heretic, Origen must chiefly be remembered for the power and understanding with which he developed, propounded, and defended the major doctrines of the Bible.

C. C. KROEGER

See also SUBORDINATIONISM.

Original Righteousness. See RIGHTEOUSNESS, ORIGINAL.

Original Sin. See SIN.

Origin of Man. See MAN, ORIGIN OF.

Origin of the Soul. See SOUL.

Origin of the Universe. Heb. 11:3 tells us that the universe was created by God and implies that our full comprehension of this awesome event or process comes by faith. The first law of thermodynamics states that neither energy nor matter can be created or destroyed, but that both are eternally existent in some form. The second law of thermodynamics holds that in a closed system, disorder is always increasing. There are, of course, those who doubt the existence of a God who supernaturally created the universe. If there is no God, the first law of thermodynamics demands that the universe has always existed. But, by the second law, if the universe has always existed, it would have become disordered, or run down, completely by now. Obviously, this is not the case. Therefore naturalism leads to a dilemma. Either the laws of thermodynamics are not correct, or the universe is not a closed system. A common method of bypassing this dilemma is to propose that the universe began with a giant explosion. The "big bang" theory, however, does not solve the dilemma. For the Christian there is no dilemma. The universe is not a closed system, but has been acted on by an external God. Belief in a timeless God, who created the universe from nothing, is certainly intellectually defensible as well as taught by Scripture. God is separate from, preexistent to, but intimately involved in, the universe he created.

M. LA BAR

See also CREATION, DOCTRINE OF.

Orr, James (1844–1913). Scottish theologian. Orr was professor of apologetics and dogmatics in the newly formed Trinity College of Glasgow in 1900, and retained this position until his death. An influential writer as well as lecturer, Orr won a prize for *The Sabbath: Scripturally and Practically Considered* (1886). More famous was his *The Christian View of God and the World* (1893). In 1897 he gave two series of lectures in the U.S., which were later published as *The*

Progress of Dogma (his masterpiece) and *Neglected Factors in the Study of the Early Progress of Christianity.* Orr had profound firsthand knowledge of modern German and British philosophy and theology. Like his colleagues George Adam Smith and James Denney he held a basic evangelical position, but wished to restate the faith in interaction with modern trends in philosophy and theology.

D. F. KELLY

Orthodox Tradition, The. Theological tradition generally associated with the national churches of the eastern Mediterranean and eastern Europe and principally with the Ecumenical Patriarchate of Constantinople. The distinguishing characteristic of this tradition is its preservation of the integrity of the doctrines taught by the fathers of the seven ecumenical councils of the 4th through 8th centuries. Through medieval times the churches of the Orthodox tradition were mainly Greek-speaking; in modern times they have been predominantly Slavic.

Nature of Orthodox Theology. The first two councils, Nicea I (325) and Constantinople I (381), laid the foundation of Orthodox theology by adoption of the statement known commonly as the Nicene Creed. This formula established the primary principle of Trinitarianism, declaring the substantial equality of God the Son with God the Father, specifically in refutation of Arianism. The third council, Ephesus (431), rejected Nestorianism by affirming that in Christ divinity and humanity united in a single person, the Word made flesh. In its primary thrust this affirmation set the premise of Orthodox Christology; it also set the premise for the development of doctrine concerning Mary. In that the Christ was God incarnate, the Virgin was "Mother of God" (*Theotokos*, "god-bearer"); she was not simply mother of an ordinary human. In consequence of this declaration, Orthodoxy expressed high regard for Mary, positing her perpetual virginity and sinless life while remaining skeptical of the later Catholic dogmas of the immaculate conception and assumption.

The next three councils, Chalcedon (451), Constantinople II (553), and Constantinople III (680), confronted the heresy of monophysitism in its evolving forms, further defining for Orthodoxy its Christology, which states that in the one person of Christ there are two entire natures, the human and divine, including two wills. The seventh council, Nicea II (787), in the midst of the struggle over iconoclasm, defined the doctrine of images representing Christ and the saints, requiring that the faithful venerate, but not worship, them. In a special way painted icons became symbols of Orthodoxy, inasmuch as they united correct doctrine and correct worship—the twin meanings of the word—and this perception led to the designation of the final restoration of icons in Byzantine churches on the first Sunday of Lent in 843 as the "triumph of Orthodoxy." For Orthodoxy, the artistic image reiterated the truth that the invisible God had become visible in the incarnate Son of God who was the perfect image of God; the image channeled the presence of the person depicted to the one contemplating it, as the incarnate Word had brought God to humankind. Since Nicea II no genuinely ecumenical council has been possible, owing to the defection (in Orthodoxy's view) of the Roman See, and thus no new absolutely definitive declaration of Orthodox dogma has been possible. From this fact derives Orthodoxy's self-conscious identity as the church of the seven councils and its sense of mission in preserving the faith of the ancient fathers of the church.

The most celebrated point of controversy between Orthodoxy and Western theology arose over the insertion by the latter of the *filioque* clause into the

Nicene Creed sometime after the 8th century. Its doctrine of the church distinguishes Orthodoxy most clearly from all other theologies. According to this doctrine the visible church is the body of Christ, a communion of believers, headed by a bishop and united by the Eucharist, in which God dwells. As such, although individual members are fallible sinners, the church is held to be infallible. This true church by definition is the Orthodox Church, which is "one, holy, catholic, and apostolic," from which other churches are separated. That is, the church consists of those believers who remain in fellowship with, and submission to, the concert of historic patriarchates, Jerusalem, Antioch, Alexandria, Constantinople, and Rome. (When Rome separated from the concert, Moscow assumed membership in the pentarchy, although Rome's place remains reserved for it to resume if it will renounce its obstinacy.) The infallibility of the church validates the authority of tradition on a par with that of Scripture. Moreover, tradition established both canon and interpretation of that Scripture and thus takes logical precedence over it.

History of Orthodox Theology. The history of Orthodoxy may be divided into two periods: Byzantine and modern. During the millennium of the Empire of Byzantium, to 1453, Orthodox theology matured in close association with it. Emperors convoked councils, after the example of Constantine I and the Nicene Council, and pronounced on theological matters, providing some weak basis for speaking of "caesaropapism" in the Byzantine age. In this period three distinctive emphases of Orthodoxy emerged: theology as apophacticism, knowledge as illumination, and salvation as deification. Relying principally on the 6th-century writer Dionysius the Pseudo-Areopagite, Orthodox writers insisted that God in his nature is beyond any understanding. Humans can know nothing about the being of God, and therefore all theological statements must be of a negative, or apophactic, form: God is unchanging, immovable, infinite, and the like. Even a seemingly positive affirmation has only negative significance; for example, to say, "God is Spirit," is actually to affirm his noncorporeality. Theology, then, is not a science of God, which is impossible, but of his revelation. That which is known is not necessarily true of God but is what God chooses to disclose, although in that sense it is indeed true knowledge.

Such a theology of negation led to the elevation of spiritual experience to at least an equal role with rationality as an epistemological principle in theology. Maximus Confessor, Orthodoxy's chief 12th-century teacher, affirmed: "A perfect mind is one which, by true faith, in supreme ignorance knows the supremely unknowable one." Knowledge of God comes from illumination, the inner vision of true light, for "God is light." From this perception derived Orthodoxy's characteristic fascination with the transfiguration of Jesus, when the light of his deity was supremely revealed to the apostles. It also fostered heyschasm, in which the mystic's vision of divinity became a theologically significant enterprise. It is for this reason that what is called Orthodox theology is also designated with equal validity "Orthodox spirituality." The chief synthesizer of this aspect of Orthodoxy was Gregory Palamas in the 14th century. The Orthodox concept of salvation as deification undergirded the contemplative methodology implied in the illumination view. Only the "pure in heart" see God, and purity comes only by divine grace in the economy of redemption. Those who are redeemed through the incarnation, whom the NT designates "sons of God" and "partakers of the divine nature," are deified; that is, they become created, in contrast to uncreated, gods.

In the period after 1453 the two events which most influenced the evolution of Orthodoxy were the fall of the Byzantine Empire and the division of Western Christianity. Termination of imperial patronage increased the autonomy of the episcopacy and promoted the Russian contribution to the Orthodox heritage; the presence of Reformation theology made it possible for Orthodoxy to select from several alternative expressions of Christian doctrine. After the middle of the 19th century the most creative developments within Orthodoxy came from Russian writers, such as Vladimir Solovyev, Nikolai Berdyaev, Sergei Bulgakov, Georges Florvosky, and from professors of the Russian seminaries in Paris and New York, notably Alexander Schmemann and John Meyendorff. Their work is too recent for it to be incorporated into the essence of Orthodoxy, but it testifies to the continuing vitality of the tradition.

P. D. STEEVES

Orthodoxy. (Gk. *orthodoxia*) Right belief, as opposed to heresy or heterodoxy. The term expresses the idea that certain statements accurately embody the revealed truth content of Christianity and are therefore in their own nature normative for the universal church. This idea is rooted in the NT insistence that the gospel has a specific factual and theological content (1 Cor. 15:1–11; Gal. 1:6–9; 1 Tim. 6:3; 2 Tim. 4:3–4), and that no fellowship exists between those who accept the apostolic standard of christological teaching and those who deny it (1 John 4:1–3; 2 John 7–11). The idea of orthodoxy became important in the church in and after the 2d century, through conflict first with Gnosticism and then with other Trinitarian and christological errors. The preservation of Christianity was seen to require the maintenance of orthodoxy in these matters.

J. I. PACKER

See also HERESY.

Osiander, Andreas (1498–1552). German theologian and Reformer. Osiander was a follower of Martin Luther. A biblical scholar, Osiander prepared a revised version of the Vulgate and a harmony of the four Gospels. Osiander's refusal to consent to the Augsburg Interim caused his removal as preacher and reformer in Nürnberg. He became a professor of theology at the newly founded University of Königsberg in Prussia and afterward was appointed vice-president of the bishopric of Samländ. His *De justificatione* (1550) involved Osiander in disputes within Lutheranism over the nature of justification. He taught that to be justified is both to be declared righteous by God and to receive the impartation of righteousness in the soul.

C. G. FRY

See also ANTINOMIANISM; IMPUTATION; MAJORISTIC CONTROVERSY; SYNERGISM.

Otherworldliness. See WORLDLINESS AND OTHERWORLDLINESS.

Otto, Rudolf (1869–1937). German theologian. Otto taught theology at Göttingen, Breslau, and Marburg. His interest in universal religious experience and worship led to the research that culminated in *Das Heilige* (1917; ET *The Idea of the Holy*), which was his major work and was hailed as one of the classics of religious psychology. The book went through 14 German editions and was translated into several languages. This work attempts to understand and explain those uncommon but very real moments when the soul is captured by an "ineffable Something." This dramatic religious experience is both nonrational and universal—we all encounter it at some time. Otto's claim is that this experience is the innermost core of all religions. Otto's other works include *The Philosophy of Religion* and *Science and Religion.*

J. D. SPICELAND

See also MYSTICISM; NUMINOUS, THE.

Outward Man. AV translation of *ho exo anthropos*, an expression used by Paul in 2 Cor. 4:16. The contrast between inner and outer is illuminated by that between "the new man" and "the old man" in Eph. 4:22–24 and Col. 3:9–10. These terms characterize the old and the new lifestyle; similarly, the outward parts of our human makeup are for Paul not merely physical but embody (literally) the power of sin and "the flesh," with which we have to reckon in every part of our nature.

S. MOTYER

See also INNER MAN; MAN, DOCTRINE OF; MAN, OLD AND NEW.

Owen, John (1616–1683). Puritan theologian. Owen was committed to the congregational way of church government. In 1651 he was appointed dean of Christ Church, Oxford. He added to this duty that of the vice-chancellorship of the university from 1652 to 1657. Owen was very influential not only at Oxford but also in matters of state in London. His commitment to congregational church government is seen in the part he played in the writing of the Savoy Declaration of Faith and Order (1658). With the change of political and religious direction in England in 1660, Owen was ejected from Christ Church and became a Nonconformist. He is remembered today not primarily because of his important career as an educator and statesman but because of his theological writings.

P. TOON

Oxford Group Movement. See MORAL RE-ARMAMENT.

Oxford Movement. Nineteenth-century development within the Church of England in response to the critical rationalism, skepticism, lethargy, liberalism, and immorality of the day. Emphasizing a return to the traditions of the church, the leaders of the movement longed for a higher standard of worship, piety, and devotion among clergy and church members. Guided by and receiving its impetus from Oxford University, the movement also protested state interference in the affairs of the church. On July 14, 1833, in response to the English government's bill reducing bishoprics in Ireland, John Keble preached the sermon "National Apostacy" from the university pulpit. He accused the government of infringing on "Christ's Church" and of disavowing the principle of apostolic succession of the bishops. Insisting that salvation was possible only through the sacraments, Keble defended the Church of England as a divine institution. During the same year John Henry Newman began to publish *Tracts for the Times*, a series of pamphlets by members of the University of Oxford that supported and propagated the beliefs of the movement. They were widely circulated, and the term "Tractarianism" has often been used for the early stages of the Oxford Movement or, indeed, as a synonym for the movement itself.

After Newman became a Roman Catholic in 1845 the movement was no longer dominated by Oxford and became more fragmented in its emphases. Edward B. Pusey, professor of Hebrew at Oxford and a contributor to *Tracts*, emerged as the leader of the Anglo-Catholic party. It greatly influenced Anglicanism. Eucharistic worship was transformed, spiritual discipline and monastic orders were revived, social concern was fostered, and an ecumenical spirit has developed in the Church of England. Those who opposed it believed it was imitative of Roman Catholicism.

D. A. RAUSCH

See also ANGLO-CATHOLICISM; KEBLE, JOHN; NEWMAN, JOHN HENRY; PUSEY, EDWARD BOUVERIE.

Pp

Pacifism. (Lat. *pax*, "peace") Spectrum of positions covering nearly all attitudes toward war, but specifically that part of the spectrum that includes a refusal to participate in war. Those individuals who refuse to do so are called conscientious objectors.

History. Pacifism is one of three historic attitudes of the church toward war. In some form it has existed throughout the entire history of the Christian church. Since the 4th century it has often been overshadowed by the just war theory and the concept of crusade, or aggressive war for a holy cause. The early church was pacifist. Prior to A.D. 170–80 there are no records of soldiers in the Roman army. During the Middle Ages the sectarians kept alive the pacifist tradition. Groups of Waldensians and Franciscan Tertiaries refused military service. The Cathari were pacifist. The Hussite movement developed two branches, a crusading one under Jan Zizka and a pacifist one under Peter Chelciky.

Alongside the wars of religion of the 16th and 17th centuries arose the pacifist traditions that for the most part have preserved their opposition to war. Pacifism emerged as the dominant position of the Anabaptists, who not only rejected the sword of war but also refused to engage in political life. Although their identification of two kingdoms paralleled Luther's analysis closely, the Anabaptists denied that Christians could in any way exercise the sword of the magistrate in the worldly kingdom. When Alexander Mack organized the Church of the Brethren in 1708, Anabaptism was the major impulse in dialectic with pietism. While Quakers, who emerged in the mid-17th century, distinguished the kingdom of God from that of the world, they did not utterly despair of the world and involved themselves in its political processes up to the point of war. Appeals to individual conscience played an important role in Quaker nonviolent political activity on behalf of justice and peace. Anabaptists, the immediate predecessors of the Mennonites, were the most withdrawn from participation in government, with the Quakers the least separated. The Brethren occupied a median position.

The 19th century saw the formation of a number of national and international pacifist societies. The Fellowship of Reconciliation was founded as an interdenominational and international religious pacifist organization on the eve of World War I and established in the U.S. in 1915. It continues today as an interfaith activist force for peace. Further, in addition to the historic peace churches, denominations that have traditionally accepted the just war theory or the crusade idea have recently issued declarations accepting pacifist positions within their traditions. Two significant examples are Vatican II's *Pastoral Constitution on the Church in the Modern World*, which for the first time endorsed pacifism as compatible with Catholic teaching, and the declaration of the United Presbyterian Church (USA), *Peacemaking: The Believer's Calling.*

Intellectual Basis for Pacifism. Pacifism encompasses many kinds of opposition to war, deriving support from a variety of overlapping philosophical, theological, and biblical sources, not all of which are explicitly Christian. Christian pacifists appeal to the authority of the Bible, using specific texts such as the Decalogue and the Sermon on the Mount. The incarnation and the priestly office of Jesus make his specific teachings authoritative and therefore binding on his followers. Pacifism also finds support in broader biblical injunctions, such as the call to express God's love to all persons or to witness to the presence of the kingdom of God on earth. Theological motifs central to Christianity also support pacifism. For example, since life is sacred and a gift from God, no individual has the right to take it. This divine source of life leads directly to the idea of the family of God. With every human being either actually or potentially a child of God, no Christian may take the life of a fellow member of the family of God. The presence of the kingdom of God on earth similarly links all persons under God's rule and therefore proscribes violence toward anyone.

J. D. WEAVER

See also WAR.

Paedobaptism. See BAPTISM, INFANT.

Pain. The biblical data concerning pain can be organized around three major topics: (1) the biblical words for pain, anguish, and affliction; (2) the biblical usage of such terms; and (3) the biblical teaching concerning the purposes of pain and affliction. We shall be concerned with the latter.

In regard to the unbeliever and the disobedient, Scripture teaches that often God sends pain and affliction as a means of judgment for sin (Job 4:7–9). Sometimes such pain and affliction may turn the individual back to the Lord (e.g., Jonah) or bring a person or nation to salvation (e.g., Israel in the tribulation, Zech. 12).

Sometimes the believer is afflicted as a means of chastisement (Ps. 94:12–13; cf. Heb. 12:6). God uses affliction to keep his servants humble (2 Cor. 12:7). On some occasions the purpose of affliction is to demonstrate to Satan that there are those who serve God because they love him, not because it pays to do so (Job 1–2). According to Peter, suffering promotes sanctification (1 Pet. 4:1–2). It does so in various ways such as refining our faith (1 Pet. 1:6–7), educating us in such Christian virtues as endurance and perseverance (Rom. 5:3–4; James 1:3–4), teaching us more about the sovereignty of God so that we understand the Lord better (Job 42:2–4), and giving us an opportunity to imitate Christ (1 Pet. 3:17–18).

Affliction and pain offer an opportunity for the believer to minister to others who are undergoing affliction (2 Cor. 1:3–4). On some occasions God's purpose in afflicting the righteous is to prepare them for judgment of their works for the purpose of rewards. We will someday have to give account of our works before the Lord, and affliction helps prepare us so that on that day our faith may be proved genuine and may result in praise, glory, and honor when Jesus returns (1 Pet. 1:7). Finally, God uses affliction as a prelude to our exaltation. The theme of suffering and glory is prevalent throughout Scripture, especially in 1 Peter. The example of Christ is the pattern (Phil. 2:5–11; 1 Pet. 3:17–22), and God wants to do the same for us, even if that humbling involves affliction (1 Pet. 5:6).

J. S. FEINBERG

See also EVIL, PROBLEM OF; THEODICY.

Pain of God Theology. Indigenous Japanese theology introduced by Kazoh Kitamori, a Japanese theologian teaching at the Tokyo Theological Seminary, in his *Theology of the Pain of God* (1946). Kitamori maintains that there are four constituents in the pain of God. First, God's love and forgiveness for sinners who deserve his wrath and judgment engender pain in God. The second constituent is simply human suffering and pain—hunger, thirst, exhaustion, fear, rejection, and the excruciating pain of the historical Jesus at his crucifixion. This pain can be healed, redeemed, and made meaningful only when it unites with the pain of God. The suffering of the historical Jesus as the Son of God is expressed in the pain of God. Third, God the Father suffers when he lets his only beloved Son suffer and die on the cross. This suffering of the Father is expressed in the pain of God. Fourth, God becomes immanent in the historical reality of human suffering.

The significance of the pain of God theology is twofold. First, Kitamori took the tragedies of World War II and sufferings of the Japanese people very seriously. His attempt to contextualize the gospel in the life situation of Japanese at a crucial time was one of the first in Asia. Furthermore, the concept of suffering and pain is at home in Japan, where the traditional Buddhist teaching of suffering (*dukka*) has been prevalent. Second, Kitamori developed the first significant Asian contextual theology to be widely publicized in the West. His theology pioneered a string of other Asian theologies existing today.

B. R. RO

See also ASIAN THEOLOGY.

Paley, William (1743–1805). Anglican theologian and archdeacon of Carlisle from 1782. His most notable work was *A View of the Evidences of Christianity* (1794), which for more than a century was required reading for entrance to Cambridge University. In *Natural Theology* (1802) he argued teleologically for God's existence.

J. D. DOUGLAS

Palm Sunday. The Sunday before Easter Sunday. Palm branches symbolize the entry of Jesus into Jerusalem before his crucifixion, during which the people strewed branches in his path as a sign of reverence.

T. J. GERMAN

See also CHRISTIAN YEAR; HOLY WEEK.

Panentheism. Doctrine that God includes the world as part of his being, that is, the world is God, although God is more than the world. Panentheism represents the attempt to combine the strengths of classical theism with those of classical pantheism. The term is particularly associated with the work of Charles Hartshorne. According to Hartshorne, God, while including an element that may be described as simple, is a complex reality. God knows the world—a world in which change, process, and freedom are real elements. For this freedom and change to be real, and for God's knowledge of this freedom and change to be perfect, Hartshorne reasons that God's knowledge must itself grow and change. That is, as new facts come into being, God comes to know these new facts (some of which are the result of genuinely free will), and thus God's knowledge grows. A perfect knower includes within himself the object which is known. Through perfectly knowing the world, God therefore includes the world (as it comes to be) within himself. As the world grows, God grows. God becomes. Through perfectly knowing and including the world, God is the supreme effect. That is, everything that happens affects God and changes God—God's knowledge changes. Therefore, the concrete God, the complex God who is actual, is the God who knows, includes, and is changed by the world. This, according to Hartshorne, is the God who loves the world and who shares the joys and sorrows of each creature in the world. This type of theology has only attracted a minority of Christian thinkers since it is so different than classical theism.

S. T. FRANKLIN

See also PROCESS THEOLOGY.

Pantheism. (Gk. *pan* plus *theos*, "everything is God") Doctrine that the universe is God. The term was coined by John Toland in 1705 to refer to philosophical systems that tend to identify God with the world.

Pantheism is not a monolithic position. There are several important forms of pantheism. *Hylozoistic pantheism:* The divine is immanent in, and characteristically regarded as the basic element of, the world, giving movement and change to the whole. The universe, however, remains a plurality of separate elements. This view was popular among some of the early Greek philosophers. *Immanentistic pantheism:* God is a part of the world and immanent in it, although his power is exercised throughout its entirety. *Absolutistic monistic pantheism.* God is both absolute and identical with the world. Thus, the world is also changeless although real. *Relativistic monistic pantheism:* The world is real and changing. It is, however, within God as, for example, his body. God is nevertheless changeless and unaffected by the world. *Acosmic pantheism:* God is absolute and makes up the totality of reality. The world is an appearance and ultimately unreal. *Identity of opposites pantheism:* Discourse about God must of necessity resort to opposites. That is, God and his relationship to the world must be described in formally contradictory terms. Reality is not capable of rational description. One must go beyond reason to an intuitive grasp of the ultimate.

From a biblical standpoint pantheism is deficient to a greater or lesser degree on two points. First, pantheism generally denies the transcendence of God, advocating his radical immanence. Second, because of the tendency to identify God with the material world, there is again a lesser or greater denial of the personal character of God.

P. D. FEINBERG

See also NEOPLATONISM; THEISM.

Papacy. (Lat./Gk. *papa*) Office of the pope. As head of the Roman Catholic Church the pope is considered the successor of Peter and the vicar of Christ. He is also, and first of all, the bishop of Rome and, for Eastern Christians, the patriarch of the West. The term *papa*, from which the word "pope" is derived, originated in ancient colloquial Greek as an endearing term for "father," and was then applied, beginning in the 3d century, to Eastern patriarchs, bishops, abbots, and eventually parish priests (of whom it is still used today). In the West the term was never very common outside Rome (originally a Greek-speaking church), and from the 6th century became reserved increasingly for the bishop of Rome, until in the later 11th century Pope Gregory VII made that practice official. The term "papacy" (*papatus*), meant to distinguish the Roman bishop's office from all other bishoprics (*episcopatus*), also originated in the late 11th century. For Catholics the papacy represents an office divinely instituted by Christ in his charge to Peter (Matt. 16:18–19; Luke 22:31–32; John 21:15–17), and therefore something to be revered and obeyed as a part of Christian faith and duty. The papal role has in fact varied from age to age, and a historical survey is required to put papal claims in perspective.

History. Over against emperors and patriarchs in Constantinople, who claimed that their church in "new Rome" virtually equaled that of "old Rome," the popes asserted vehemently that their primacy derived from Peter and not from their political setting, making theirs the only truly "apostolic see." Siricius (384–98) and Innocent (401–17) issued the first extant decretals, letters modeled on imperial rescripts in which popes ruled definitively on matters put to them by local churches. Leo the Great (440–61) was the first to appropriate the old pagan title of *pontifex maximus*. Gelasius (492–96), finally, over against emperors inclined to intervene at will in ecclesiastical affairs, asserted an independent and higher pontifical authority in religious matters. Throughout the early Middle Ages (600–1050) papal claims remained lofty, but papal power diminished considerably.

The papacy emerged during the High Middle Ages (1050–1500) as the real leader of Western Christendom, beginning with the so-called Gregorian reform movement, culminating initially in the reign of Pope Innocent III (his reforms are permanently inscribed in the Fourth Lateran Council), and waning again during the Great Schism and the conciliar movement. In 1059 a new election law (with modifications made in 1179, the same as that in force today) raised the pope above all other bishops, who were in principle still elected by their clergy and people. Henceforth the pope would be elected solely by cardinals, themselves papal appointees given liturgical and administrative responsibilities, and he could be chosen from among all eligible clergy (preferably cardinals) rather than, as the older law held, only from among Romans. Papal decretals replaced conciliar canons as the routine and normative form of regulation, and this "new law" (little changed prior to the new codes issued in 1917 and 1982) reached down uniformly into every diocese in the West. The papal curia or court, reorganized and massively expanded, became the center of ecclesiastical finance and administration. Legates carried papal authority into all parts of Europe. Above all, this revitalized papacy constantly asserted the priority of the spiritual over the material world, and adopted for itself a new title as head of the church, that of "vicar [or placeholder] of Christ."

The early modern papacy (1517–1789) began with a staggering defeat. Protestant Reformers, persuaded that the papacy had corrupted the gospel beyond all hope of reform, revolted. The so-called Renaissance papacy had largely lost sight of its spiritual mission, and was forced reluctantly into the reforms articulated by the Council of Trent (1545–63). The papacy then took charge of deep and lasting reforms, such as training clergy, upholding new standards for the episcopal and priestly offices, and providing a new catechism. The number of cardinals was set at 70 (until the last generation), and "congregations" were established to oversee various aspects of the church's mission.

The critical attack of Enlightenment thinkers (Josephinism in Austria) together with growing national (Gallicanism in France) and episcopal (Febronianism in Germany) resistance to papal authority culminated in the French Revolution and its aftermath, during which time two popes (Pius VI and Pius VII) endured humiliating imprisonments. But the forces of restoration, combined with the official indifference or open hostility of secularized governments, led to a strong resurgence of centralized papal authority known as ultramontanism. Pope Pius IX (1846–78) made this the program of his pontificate, codified it as a part of the Catholic faith in the decrees on papal primacy and infallibility in Vatican Council I (1869–70), and enforced it with an unprecedented degree of Roman centralization that characterized the Catholic Church into the 1960s. Throughout the last century mass media, mass transportation, and mass audiences have made the popes far better known and more highly reverenced as persons (as distinguished from their office) than ever before. Vatican Council II (1962–65) brought deep reforms, in particular a much greater emphasis on bishops acting collegially with one another and the pope.

Papal primacy rests upon the power of the keys, which it is claimed Christ conferred upon Peter and his successors, although it has obviously varied in principle and especially in practice throughout the centuries. Leo the Great and the high medieval popes claimed for themselves a "fullness of power" that Vatican Council I defined as "ordinary" and "immediate" jurisdiction over the church and all the faithful in matters of discipline and ecclesiastical authority as well as faith and morals, thus potentially transforming the pope into a supreme bishop and all other bishops into mere vicars, an imbalance that Vatican Council II sought to redress with far greater emphasis upon the episcopal office.

J. Van Engen

See also Infallibility; Keys of the Kingdom; Vatican Council I; Vatican Council II.

Paraclete. See Holy Spirit.

Paradise. Term probably of Persian origin, appearing as *pardēs* in the OT three times ("orchard," Song of Sol. 4:13, asv; "forest," Neh. 2:8, asv; "parks," Eccles. 2:5). The NT employs *paradeisos* three times, to denote the place of blessedness promised to the thief (Luke 23:43), the third heaven (2 Cor. 12:4), and the location of the promised tree of life (Rev. 2:7).

H. A. Kent, Jr.

See also Abraham's Bosom; Heaven.

Paradox. Assertion that is self-contradictory, or two or more assertions that are mutually contradictory, or an assertion that contradicts some very commonly held position on the matter in question.

Paradoxes may be either rhetorical or logical. A rhetorical paradox is a figure used to shed light on a topic by challenging the reason of another. The NT contains many examples of this use of the paradox (e.g., Matt. 5:39; 10:39; John 11:24; 2 Cor. 6:9–10). Logical paradoxes arise from the attempt to unify or coordinate the multiple facets of experience. Because of the diversity and complexity of reality and also because of the limitations of finite and sinful human reason, our best efforts to know reality bring us only to the production of equally reasonable (or apparently so) yet irreconcilable (or apparently so) truths. In such cases we may be nearer the truth when we espouse both sides of a paradoxical issue than when we give up one side in favor of the other.

In modern theology the concept of paradox has assumed a prominent role in the writing of Kierkegaard and his 20th-century followers, Karl Barth, Reinhold Niebuhr, and others. The infinite, timeless, and hidden God can reach into finite time of human history through events that can be discerned only by faith, and even then necessarily appear as logical paradoxes. For theists of any period, of course, a paradoxical "setting aside" of the laws of logic is understood as provisional; a true synthesis is always to be found in the mind of God.

K. S. Kantzer

Paradox, Theology of. See Neo-orthodoxy.

Pardon. See Forgiveness.

Parousia. See Second Coming of Christ.

Pascal, Blaise (1623–1662). Mathematician, scientist, and religious thinker. Pascal relied upon the experimental method, and among his contributions were the first mechanical calculator, basic research on vacuums and hydraulics, the formulation of probability theory, and the establishment of foundations for differential and integral calculus. In 1654 he experienced a "second conversion" to the Jansenist doctrine at

Port-Royal, and he fervently embraced the Christian faith, as seen in his later works, the *Provincial Letters* (1657) and the posthumously published *Pensées (Thoughts on Religion and Some Other Subjects).* In his religious writings Pascal was an apologist rather than a systematic thinker. In effect he argues psychologically, believing that the heart is the key. God can be perceived intuitively by the heart, not through reason. This involves combining knowledge, feeling, and will and establishing the personal, mystical relationship with Christ that gives life. As Pascal brings out in his wager argument, probability compels us to take the risk of faith in God.

R. V. PIERARD

See also JANSEN, CORNELIUS OTTO; PASCAL'S WAGER.

Pascal's Wager. Famous apologetic advanced by Blaise Pascal in his *Pensées.* Moving from rational knowledge to reasonable surmise, Pascal affirms that "either God exists, or he does not," and proposes that we wager on the matter. To bet that he is, means a modest surrender of reason; but, to opt for divine nonexistence, is to risk the loss of eternal life and happiness. The stake (one's reason) is slight compared to the prize that may be won. If we gamble for God we will win everything, but we lose nothing should this turn out to be wrong.

R. V. PIERARD

See also PASCAL, BLAISE.

Passion of Christ. See CROSS, CRUCIFIXION.

Passover. First of three annual Hebrew festivals at which all men were required to appear at the sanctuary (Exod. 23:14–17). The historical passover is related to the 10th plague—the death of the firstborn in Egypt. Israel was instructed to prepare a lamb for each household. Blood was to be applied to the lintel and doorpost (Exod. 12:7). The sign of the blood would secure the safety of each house so designated. On the evening of the 14th of Nisan (Abib) the passover lambs were slain. After being roasted, they were eaten with unleavened bread and bitter herbs (Exod. 12:8), emphasizing the need for a hasty departure and reminiscent of the bitter bondage in Egypt (Deut. 16:3). The passover was a family observance. In the case of small families, neighbors might be invited to share the paschal meal.

The initial instructions concerned the preparation for the historical exodus (Exod. 12:21–23). Subsequent directions were given for the observance of the seven-day festival of unleavened bread (Exod. 13:3–10). The passover experience was to be repeated each year as a means of instruction to future generations (Exod. 12:24–27). In subsequent years a passover ritual developed incorporating additional features. Four successive cups of wine mixed with water were used. Psalms 113–18 were sung at appropriate places. Fruit, mixed with vinegar to the consistency of mortar, served as a reminder of the mortar used during the bondage. The death of Christ at the passover season was deemed significant by the early church. Paul calls Christ "our passover" (1 Cor. 5:7). The command not to break a bone of the paschal lamb (Exod. 12:46) is applied by John to the death of Christ (John 19:36). The Christian must put away the "old yeast" of malice and wickedness, and replace it with "bread without yeast, the bread of sincerity and truth" (1 Cor. 5:8).

C. F. PFEIFFER

See also LAMB OF GOD; OLD TESTAMENT.

Pastor. See SPIRITUAL GIFTS.

Patriarch. Ecclesiastical title used in both Roman Catholic and Eastern Orthodox churches to describe a bishop who has been exalted over other bishops (patriarchs reside in Rome, Alexandria,

Antioch, Constantinople, and Jerusalem). This term recalls the OT patriarchs who were heads of their families or tribes.

W. L. LIEFELD

See also BISHOP; CHURCH OFFICERS.

Patripassianism. See MONARCHIANISM.

Pattern. See TYPE, TYPOLOGY.

Paul, Theology of. Paul gives two different accounts of the source of his theology. In Gal. 1:11–12 he insists that he did not receive it from people but "by revelation from Jesus Christ," referring to his experience on the Damascus Road. But in 1 Cor. 15:3–8 he pictures himself as simply passing on the tradition he had received about Christ's atoning death, burial, and resurrection. Paul felt himself empowered, as an apostle of Christ, to speak in Christ's name (2 Cor. 13:3) under the inspiration of the Holy Spirit (1 Cor. 2:12–13, 16) in ways in which the earthly Christ had never spoken. In fact, Paul's thought is a fantastically creative combination of elements drawn together, under the orchestration of the Spirit, from many different sources: from Jesus' earthly teaching (1 Cor. 7:10–11; 9:14), from his own background in Pharisaism (Rom. 10:6–9; Gal. 4:22–26), from earlier Christian traditions (Rom. 3:24–25; 1 Cor. 15:3–7; Phil. 2:6–11), from secular Greek thought (Rom. 2:15; Col. 3:18–4:1), from his own insight (Eph. 3:4), and above all from the OT (Rom. 15:4; 2 Tim. 3:15–16).

The Nature of God. Two key words highlight the center of Paul's thinking about God.

Creation. His belief in the one God, Creator of all that is, shapes Paul's theology fundamentally. His belief in the equality of Jews and Gentiles before God (Rom. 1:16; 10:12; Gal. 3:28) is based on the oneness of God (Deut. 6:4), who, unlike pagan deities, cannot be bound to a particular geographical area or nation but extends his saving love to all people equally (1 Tim. 2:3–5). Paul's whole ministry as apostle to the Gentiles (rejected by many Jewish Christians) grew out of this presupposition. The foundation for this new Jew-Gentile unity is to be found in the person of Christ, who is a second Adam (1 Cor. 15:47), the head of a newly created humanity balancing and repairing the old. God is the one who "calls things that are not as though they were" (Rom. 4:17). The light of the gospel, shining in believers' hearts, is comparable to the original light of creation (2 Cor. 4:6). Against this background Paul's thought moves on a cosmic scale. God has something more glorious in mind than just a new humanity: the transformation of creation is his ultimate goal (Rom. 8:18–25; Eph. 1:9–10; Col. 1:15–20).

History. For Paul history is purposeful, developing toward a goal and along a route predetermined by its one Lord. He accepts the OT as the Word of God and argues strenuously that the "new" in Christ must be integrated into the "old" previously given. Behind all his epistles lies a concern to establish this subtle balance between old and new.

The Son of God. The OT helps Paul to understand how Christ is the last Adam in God's purposes, and leads him to see Christ's death as the vital turning point between the two ages. For example, Isa. 53 demonstrates that Christ's death was substitutionary, for our sins, so that God's people could be made righteous through his righteousness (Rom. 4:25; 5:18; Phil. 2:7–8). His reflection on Jesus' use of Daniel's "Son of man" vision (Dan. 7) leads Paul to see that, paradoxically, the death that looked like a final defeat was actually a tremendous victory over the powers of this world (Rom. 8:31–39; 1 Cor. 2:6–8; Gal. 6:14; Col. 2:15). The resurrection Paul comes to see as God's response to Christ's death (Rom. 1:4; 6:4; 1 Cor. 15:15; Phil. 2:9–11), and thus as God's response to the whole new humanity, which will likewise be raised to glory

(Rom. 6:5; 8:11; 1 Cor. 6:14; 15:20–22; Eph. 2:4–7; Phil. 3:8–11; Col. 2:13–14; 1 Thess. 4:14) and must begin to express that new life now (Rom. 6:4, 11; Col. 2:20–3:5).

The People of God. Paul's conversion took him from one "people of God" to another. The tension inevitably produced by these rival claims meant that he had to establish his theology of the church from first principles upward. The most important issue in this struggle was justification, because of the common conviction that God will one day judge the world (Rom. 3:6). Who will then be acquitted, "justified"? Paul rejected his Jewish contemporaries' view (which he had previously accepted) that God's covenant with his people assured Israel of forgiveness and acquittal. If this alone were necessary, why did Christ die (Gal. 2:21)? The bald fact of the death of God's Son showed Paul that justification could not come through "works of the law" (Gal. 2:16; 3:10; Rom. 3:20)—that is, through mere dependence, however heartfelt and zealous, on the status conferred by God's gift of the law. Christ alone could give assurance of justification, because Christ alone had overcome the sin that has made the law incapable of giving the promised blessing (Rom. 7:7–8; 8:3). But this dethroning of the law as the central salvific principle demolished the barriers of Israel and opened justification to all who would simply embrace Christ and, through reception of his Holy Spirit, begin to evidence the faith and love for God for which the OT longed in vain (Deut. 6:4; 9:13–14; 29:4; Ezek. 18:31; 36:26; Rom. 5:5; 6:17; Gal. 3:14, 23–26). Paul was thus able to claim that he, with his "law-free gospel" offered to all alike, was more faithful to the law (Rom. 3:31) than were those who urged that salvation could be enjoyed only within the borders of Israel. Through Christ, who is its "end" (Rom. 10:4), the law is delivered from its bondage to sin (Rom. 7:10–11) and its nationalist limitations (Gal. 5:3) and restored to its proper role as the guide of the people of God. Hence Paul's confident handling of the OT, and the "therefore" of Rom. 12:1 (introducing the practical section of the epistle) is truly logical, and continues the exposition of justification in Rom. 1–11.

The new Christian lifestyle is thus integral to Paul's theology. Its keynotes are the outworking of the love principle (Rom. 12:9–21; 1 Cor. 13; Eph. 5:2; Col. 3:14) through the formation of a Christian mind (Rom. 8:5; 12:2, 17; 1 Cor. 2:15–16; Eph. 4:17–24; Phil. 4:8) under the empowering presence of the Holy Spirit (Rom. 8:13; 12:11; Gal. 5:22–25; Eph. 3:14–18; 5:18–20; 1 Thess. 1:6) in the context of an interdependent community life (Rom. 12; 1 Cor. 12; Eph. 4:1–16; Col. 3:12–4:1) inspired by a constant awareness of the imminent eschatological goal (Rom. 8:23–25; 13:11–14; 1 Cor. 7:29–31; 2 Cor. 5:9–10; Gal. 6:8; Phil. 3:12–14; 1 Thess. 5:4–11).

S. Motyer

Peace. (Heb. *šālôm*; Gk. *eirēnē*) Completeness, soundness, wholeness. "Peace" is a favorite biblical greeting, and is found at the beginning or end of all of the NT epistles except James and 1 John. To this day it is one of the commonest words among the Semites.

Peace is a condition of freedom from strife, whether internal or external. Security from outward enemies (Isa. 26:12) and calmness of heart (Job 22:21; Isa. 26:3) are implied by the term. Peace is so pleasing to the Lord that the godly are told to seek it diligently (Ps. 34:14; Zech. 8:16, 19). It is to be a characteristic of the Christian (Mark 9:50; 2 Cor. 13:11). Peace is a comprehensive and valued gift from God, and the promised and climactic blessing in messianic times (Isa. 2:4; 9:6–7; 11:6; Mic. 4:1–4; 5:5). The innumerable blessings of the Christian revolve around the concept of peace. The gospel is the gospel of peace (Eph. 6:15). Christ is our peace (Eph. 2:14–15); God the Father is the God of peace (1 Thess. 5:23). The inalienable privilege of every Christian is the peace of God (Phil. 4:9) because of the legacy of peace left by Christ (John 14:27; 16:33). These blessings are not benefits laid up in eternal glory only, but are a present possession (Rom. 8:6; Col. 3:15).

C. L. FEINBERG

Peace Offering. See OFFERINGS AND SACRIFICES IN BIBLE TIMES.

Pelagius, Pelagianism. Pelagianism was a 4th-century teaching that stressed human ability to take the initial steps toward salvation by virtue of personal effort, apart from special grace. Pelagianism was sharply opposed to Augustinianism, which emphasized the absolute necessity of God's grace for salvation. Pelagius was an eminently moral person who became a teacher at Rome late in the 4th century. British by birth, he was a zealous ascetic. He came to oppose passionately Augustine's quietism, reflected in his prayer in the *Confessions*: "Give what thou commandest—and command what thou wilt" (10.31. 45). The keystone of Pelagianism is the idea of unconditional free will and moral responsibility. In creating humankind, God did not subject people, like other creatures, to the law of nature but gave them the unique privilege of accomplishing the divine will by their own choice. This possibility of freely choosing the good entails the possibility of choosing evil.

According to Pelagius there are three features in human action: power (*posse*), will (*velle*), and realization (*esse*). The first comes exclusively from God; the other two belong to humankind. Thus, as people act, they merit praise or blame. Whatever his followers may have said, Pelagius himself held the conception of a divine law proclaiming to people what they ought to do and setting before them the prospect of supernatural rewards and punishments. If we enjoy freedom of choice, it is by the express bounty of our Creator; we ought to use it for those ends that God prescribes. The rest of Pelagianism flows from this central thought of freedom. First, it rejects the idea that human will has any intrinsic bias in favor of wrongdoing as a result of the fall. Second, it considers grace purely an external aid provided by God. This grace is offered equally to all. God is no respecter of persons. By merit alone we advance in holiness. God's predestination operates according to the quality of the lives God foresees we will lead. Although Pelagianism reflects an awareness of our high calling and the claims of the moral law, its one-sidedness renders it an inadequate interpretation of Christianity.

B. L. SHELLEY

See also AUGUSTINE OF HIPPO.

Penal Theory of the Atonement. See ATONEMENT, THEORIES OF THE.

Penance. (Lat. *poena*, "penalty") Disciplinary measures adopted by the church against offenders. Initially the term applied to those guilty of such glaring offenses as apostasy, murder, and adultery. These individuals were allowed only one chance of restoration after undergoing fastings; they were expected to make a public confession of their sin in renewal of the baptismal profession, and had to accept certain lasting prohibitions, such as continence in the case of the unmarried.

Two notable developments took place in the Middle Ages. First, penance at least once a year was made compulsory from 1215. Second, the whole understanding was developed in a new way that ultimately found codification at the Council of Trent, when penance was officially accepted as a sacrament. It was still agreed that the eternal guilt of mortal sins after baptism could be met only by the atoning work of Christ, true contrition, and the word of absolution. From this angle penance properly speaking remained disciplinary. But it was now argued that the temporal guilt of either mortal or venial sin may be met in part by the actual penances, thus mitigating the final expiation demanded in purgatory.

The Reformers cut through the whole falsification of theory and practice by insisting that what the NT demands is not penance but penitence or repentance, although they saw real value in the restoring of true discipline and the counseling of those troubled in conscience.

G. W. BROMILEY

See also PENITENCE; REPENTANCE.

Penitence. Repentance, sorrow for sin, and the turning away from it to lead a new life. Jesus' message, as well as that of his disciples, was characterized by the call for people to repent (Mark 1:15; 6:12; Luke 10:13).

B. L. SHELLEY

See also REPENTANCE.

Pentecost. (Gk. *pentekostos*, "fiftieth") Fiftieth day after the passover. Pentecost was the culmination of the feast of weeks (Exod. 34:22; Deut. 16:10), and included the offering of two loaves of unleavened bread, representing the first products of the harvest (Lev. 23:17–20; Deut. 16:9–10). After the exile it became one of the great pilgrimage feasts of Judaism. In the Christian church Pentecost is the anniversary of the coming of the Holy Spirit (Acts 2). The term "Pentecost" is now used of the period of the church year from Pentecost Sunday to Advent.

M. C. TENNEY

See also CHRISTIAN YEAR.

Pentecostalism. Evangelical charismatic reformation movement that usually traces its roots to an outbreak of tongues-speaking in Topeka, Kansas, in 1901 under the leadership of Charles Fox Parham, a former Methodist preacher. Parham formulated the basic Pentecostal doctrine of "initial evidence" after a student in his Bethel Bible School, Agnes Ozman, experienced glossolalia in Jan. 1901. Of special importance also is the Azusa Street revival, which occurred in an abandoned African Methodist Episcopal church in downtown Los Angeles from 1906 to 1909 and which launched Pentecostalism as a worldwide movement. The Azusa Street services were led by William J. Seymour, a black Holiness preacher from Houston, Texas, and a student of Parham. The Topeka and Los Angeles events took place in a turn-of-the-century religious environment that encouraged the appearance of such a Pentecostal movement. The major milieu out of which Pentecostalism sprang was the worldwide Holiness movement, which had developed out of 19th-century American Methodism. Leaders in this movement were Phoebe Palmer and John Inskip, who emphasized a "second blessing" crisis of sanctification through the "baptism in the Holy Spirit."

After 1906 Pentecostalism spread rapidly in the U.S. and around the world. Despite its origins in the Holiness movement, the majority of Holiness leaders and older Holiness denominations rejected Pentecostal teachings outright. These included the Church of the Nazarene, the Wesleyan Methodist Church, the Church of God (Anderson, Indiana), and the Salvation Army. Other Holiness groups, however, were Pentecostalized rapidly as leaders went to Azusa Street to investigate the phenomena in evidence there. Among the Azusa Street "pilgrims" were G. B. Cashwell (North Carolina), C. H. Mason (Tennessee), Glen Cook (California), A. G. Argue (Canada), and W. H.

Durham (Chicago). The first Pentecostal denominations emerged from these struggles from 1906 to 1908, and included the Pentecostal Holiness Church, the Church of God in Christ, the Church of God (Cleveland, Tennessee), the Apostolic Faith (Portland, Oregon), the United Holy Church, and the Pentecostal Free-Will Baptist Church. Most of these churches were located in the Southern states and experienced rapid growth after their Pentecostal renewal began. The Church of God in Christ and the United Holy Church were predominantly black.

Pentecostalism also spread rapidly to Europe and South America. Further, successful Pentecostal missions were also begun by 1910 in China, Africa, and many other nations of the world. The missionary enterprise accelerated rapidly after the formation of major missions-oriented Pentecostal denominations in the U.S. after 1910. The Assemblies of God, formed in 1914, soon became the largest Pentecostal denomination in the world. Most of the Pentecostal groups that began after 1914 were based on the model of the Assemblies of God. They include the Pentecostal Church of God, the International Church of the Foursquare Gospel (founded in 1927 by Aimee Semple McPherson), and the Open Bible Standard Church. As there was rapid growth, there was also much controversy and division.

The greatest growth for Pentecostal churches came after World War II. With more mobility and greater prosperity, Pentecostals began to move into the middle class and to lose their image of being disinherited members of the lower classes. The emergence of healing evangelists such as Oral Roberts and Jack Coe in the 1950s brought greater interest and acceptance to the movement. The television ministry of Roberts also brought Pentecostalism into the homes of average Americans. The founding of the Full Gospel Business Men in 1948 brought the Pentecostal message to a whole new class of middle-class professionals, helping to change the image of the movement even further. In the post-World War II period the Pentecostals also began to emerge from their isolation, not only from each other but from other Christian groups as well. In 1943 the Assemblies of God, the Church of God (Cleveland, Tennessee), the International Church of the Foursquare Gospel, and the Pentecostal Holiness Church became charter members of the National Association of Evangelicals (NAE), thus clearly disassociating themselves from the organized fundamentalist groups that had disfellowshiped the Pentecostals in 1928. They thus became part of the moderate evangelical camp that grew to prominence by the 1970s.

Intrapentecostal ecumenism began to flourish also during the late 1940s both in the U.S. and elsewhere. In 1947 the first World Pentecostal Conference (WPC) met in Zurich, Switzerland, and has since met triennially. The next year the Pentecostal Fellowship of North America (PFNA) was formed in Des Moines, Iowa, and has met annually since then. Pentecostalism entered a new phase in 1960 with the appearance of "Neo-Pentecostalism" in the traditional churches in the U.S. The first well-known person to openly experience glossolalia and remain within his church was Dennis Bennett, an Episcopal priest in Van Nuys, California. This new wave of Pentecostalism soon spread to other denominations in the U.S. and also to many other nations. Other well-known Neo-Pentecostal leaders were Brick Bradford and James Brown (Presbyterian); John Osteen and Howard Irvin (Baptist); Gerald Derstine and Bishop Nelson Litwiler (Mennonite); Larry Christenson (Lutheran); and Ross Whetstone (United Methodist). In 1966 Pentecostalism entered the Roman Catholic

Church as the result of a weekend retreat at Duquesne University led by theology professors Ralph Keiffer and Bill Story. As glossolalia and other charismatic gifts were experienced, other Catholic prayer groups were formed at Notre Dame University and the University of Michigan. By 1973 the movement had spread so rapidly that 30,000 Catholic Pentecostals gathered at Notre Dame for a national conference. The movement had spread to Catholic churches in over 100 nations by 1980.

In order to distinguish these newer Pentecostals from the older Pentecostal denominations, the word "charismatic" began to be used widely around 1973 to designate the movement in the mainline churches. The older Pentecostals were called "classical Pentecostals." By 1980 the term "Neo-Pentecostal" had been universally abandoned in favor of "charismatic renewal." By 1980 the classical Pentecostals had grown to be the largest family of Protestants in the world, according to the *World Christian Encyclopedia.* The 51-million figure attributed to the traditional Pentecostals did not include the 11 million charismatic Pentecostals in the traditional mainline churches. Thus, 75 years after the opening of the Azusa Street meeting there were 62 million Pentecostals in over 100 nations of the world.

V. SYNAN

See also AZUSA STREET REVIVAL; BAPTISM OF THE SPIRIT; CHARISMATIC MOVEMENT; KESWICK CONVENTION; SPIRITUAL GIFTS; TONGUES, SPEAKING IN.

Perfection, Perfectionism. ***The Biblical Emphasis.*** The OT roots for religious perfection signify wholeness and perfect peace. The most frequently used Hebrew term for "perfect" is *tāmîm*, which occurs 85 times and is usually translated *teleios* in the LXX. Of these occurrences 50 refer to sacrificial animals and are usually translated "without blemish" or "without spot." When applied to persons the term describes an individual who is without moral blemish or defect (Job 1:1, 8; 2:3; 8:20; Ps. 101:2, 6). Another Hebrew term for perfect is *šālēm*, an adjectival form of the root *slm*, which means "peace." This term has a covenant background and indicates the loyalty and purity of motive that are characteristic of a moral and intellectual life of integrity before God (1 Kings 8:61; 11:4; 15:3). The root idea connotes fellowship between God and his people and a right relationship with the One who is the model of perfection.

The NT vocabulary reflects the OT interpersonal concepts rather than the Greek ideal of static and dispassionate knowledge. The emphases are on obedience, wholeness, and maturity. The Greek words derived from *telos* connote the idea of design, end, goal, or purpose. Paul uses *teleios* to describe moral and religious perfection (Col. 1:28; 4:12). He contrasts it to *nepios*, "childish," which connotes moral immaturity and deficiency. The "perfect man," *teleion*, is the stable person who reflects "the whole measure of the fullness of Christ," in contrast to children who are tossed about by every new wind of doctrine (Eph. 4:13–14). James uses *teleios* to describe the end result of spiritual discipline. The trying of faith develops patience and character so that the disciple may be "mature and complete, not lacking anything" (James 1:3–4).

Responsible, spiritual, intellectual, and moral development that conforms to the desired pattern is perfection. In the Sermon on the Mount, Jesus uses *teleios* to exhort believers to be perfect as the heavenly Father is perfect (Matt. 5:48). This use of the future tense indicates a moral obligation, however, and not an absolute perfection identical to that of God. The concept of corporate perfection seen in a community united in love is expressed by the Greek verb *katartizein*. Interrelatedness in love is a necessary part of the "perfecting of the saints" (1 Cor. 1:10; Eph. 4:12; Heb. 13:21). The biblical emphasis on perfection, then, does not imply absolute perfection but an unblemished character that has moral and spiritual integrity in relationship to God. The goal of spiritual maturity is set forth, and the believer is charged with making sincere and proper use of the spiritual resources available through Christ in order to attain this maturity in fellowship with Christ and the Christian community.

Theological Issues and Historical Heritage. The command of Jesus in the Sermon on the Mount, "Be perfect, therefore, as your heavenly Father is perfect" (Matt. 5:48), is central to the issue of human perfection. This text has been variously interpreted and even rejected as inauthentic in the attempts to arrive at theological understanding.

One of the most extensive attempts at attaining Christian perfection is found in monasticism. Antony of Egypt and Pachomius went into solitude to practice their disciplines with the aim of achieving spiritual perfection. They were overwhelmed by the sense of their own unworthiness and by the increasing worldliness of the church. The attaining of their goal involved renouncing all encumbrances of the world, taking up their cross, and praying without ceasing. The ideal of perfection became socialized as expressed in the rules of Basil and Benedict. Monastic communities developed that not only sought perfection by resignation from the world and asceticism, but also attempted to transform the world through extensive missionary efforts and the preservation of spiritual, esthetic, and intellectual life.

Aquinas was convinced that although Adam lost the gift of divine grace that enabled humankind to enjoy God fully, the free grace of God can restore humanity to God's favor and enable the Christian to follow God's precepts in perfect love. Final perfection and the beatific vision of God are reserved for the life to come, but through contemplation a perfect vision of God and perfect knowledge of truth can be enjoyed in this life. His concept of perfection, however, involved a disparagement of the world and an understanding of the desires of flesh as evil. Thus the elimination of bodily desires is a prerequisite to perfection, and in this aspect Aquinas equates perfection with renunciation. Furthermore, he saw perfection as carrying with it human merit and thus contributed to the idea of the treasury of merits from which the imperfect can draw at the discretion of the church. Finally, he formed a hierarchy of the state of perfection that corresponded to the levels of the religious orders. Although he did not deny the possibility of perfection for all persons, religious vows were certainly the shortcut to meritorious perfection. He thus perpetuated the spiritual dichotomy beteen clergy and laity.

Both the Lutheran and Calvinist Reformers reflected the Augustinian position that sin remains in humanity until death, and therefore spiritual perfection is impossible in this life. Calvin explicitly stated that, while the goal toward which the pious should strive is to appear before God without spot or blemish, believers will never reach that goal until the sinful physical body is laid aside. Since the body is the residence of the depravity of concupiscence, perfection and physical life are mutually exclusive. Luther also retained the connection between sin and the flesh. He did, however, emphasize a new center of piety—the humanity and work of Jesus Christ. While the previous seekers after perfection focused on the knowledge and love of God that was grasped through contemplation, Luther focused on the knowledge of God through God's revelation in Christ. Faith in Jesus Christ therefore brings an imputed perfection that truly worships God in faith. This true perfection does not consist in celibacy or mendicancy. Luther rejected the distinction between clerical and lay perfection and stressed that proper ethical behavior was not found in renunciation of life, but in faith and love of one's neighbor.

With the pietists arose a Protestant rejection of the pessimism with which the Lutherans and Calvinists viewed the quest for perfection. Marked by the quest for personal holiness and an emphasis on devotion rather than doctrine, 17th-century leaders such as Jakob Spener and A. H. Francke stressed personal holiness marked by love and obedience. Perfection was reflected in works done solely for the glory of God and in the ability to distinguish good from evil. While tending toward narrowness and provincialism and often deteriorating into a negative scrupulosity, the pietists developed strong community contexts for nurture and motivated extensive missionary endeavors.

John Wesley was inspired by the perfectionist themes of the early saints and by the devotional literature of Thomas à Kempis, Jeremy Taylor, and William Law. Seeing self-love, or pride, as the root of evil, Wesley taught that "perfect love" or "Christian perfection" can replace pride through a moral crisis of faith. By grace, the Christian can experience love filling the heart and excluding sin. Wesley did not see perfection as sinlessness, nor did he understand it to be attained by merit. He thus combined some aspects of the Catholic emphasis on perfection with the Protestant emphasis on grace. In contrast to Augustine's Platonic view of sin as being inseparably related to concupiscence and the body, Wesley saw it as a perverted relationship to God. In response to God's offer of transforming grace, the believer in faith is brought into an unbroken fellowship with Christ. This was not only an imputed perfection but an actual or imparted relationship of an evangelical perfection of love and intention. In this life the Christian does not attain absolute Christlikeness but suffers numerous infirmities, faults, prejudices, and involuntary transgressions. These, however, were not considered sin, for Wesley saw sin as attitudinal and relational. In *A Plain Account of Christian Perfection* he stressed that Christian perfection is not absolute, nor sinless, nor incapable of being lost; is not the perfection of Adam or the angels; and does not preclude growth in grace.

In removing from the idea of perfection any idea of meritorious effort, Wesley resisted any tendency to exclusiveness and elitism. His relational understanding of sin resisted the hellenistic equation of sin with humanity. A reform of personal and social morality resulted to a large degree from the spiritual renewal that accompanied his work. Thus perfection for Wesley was not based on renunciation, merit, asceticism, or individualism. It was instead a celebration of the sovereignty of grace in transforming the sinful person into the image of Christ's love. Wesleyan perfectionist thought was, however, not without liabilities. Although Wesley defined sin as involving relationships and intentions, he did not adequately guard against allowing it to become understood as a substance or entity that was separate from the person and must be extricated. Some of his followers did develop this substantialist understanding of sin and a resulting static concept of sanctification. Wesley also tended to narrow sin to include only conscious will and intent. Consequently, some of his interpreters have been led to rationalize serious attitudinal aberrations as expressions of unconscious or unintentional human faults. Finally, Wesley expressed an inward asceticism that tended to denigrate the esthetic, and his emphasis on simplicity was too easily distorted by his followers into a legalistic externalism. Wesley's emphasis on perfection has been preserved in some circles of Methodism, and continues to be promoted in the denominations associated with the Christian Holiness Association.

R. L. SHELTON

See also GODLINESS; SANCTIFICATION.

Perichoresis. (Lat. *circumencessio, circuminsessio*) Mutual interpenetration. Trinitarian perichoresis begins with the unity of natures or a strict consubstantiality and affirms a reciprocal interrelation. Each person has "being in each other without any coalescence" (John of Damascus). Perichoresis is a necessary implication of orthodox Trinitarian thought.

For christology the complementary use of perichoresis was based on the affirmation of the unity of person (hypostasis) and sought to describe the relation of Christ's two natures as a mutual interpenetration. The interpenetration of the incarnate Son, however, is not strictly mutual, since the movement is from the divine to the human. During the Reformation the interpenetration of the two natures became a burning issue and focused on the nature of Christ's presence in the Lord's Supper. Luther affirmed that the exalted humanity of Christ participated in the omnipresence of his deity in such a way as to communicate his presence at the Lord's Supper.

Jürgen Moltmann has recently given considerable thought to this issue in relation to the cross. He contends that because of the perichoresis of the divine in the human it can and must be affirmed that God suffered in the death of Christ.

S. M. SMITH.

See also COMMUNICATION OF ATTRIBUTES.

Perseverance. Continuing steadfastness in the faith. Perseverance is an an essential virtue in the face of persecution. Yet believers are never left to suppose their future depends wholly upon their own endurance. If Jude (v. 21) urges "keep yourselves in God's love," Peter (1 Pet. 1:5) declares that we "through faith are shielded by God's power until the coming of the salvation that is ready to be revealed in the last time." Final perseverance in a state of grace by no means depends entirely on the virtue of persevering. Believers need assurance, not only encouragement—"once a Christian, always a Christian."

History of the Doctrine. In the dual stance of the NT there obviously lay opportunity for divergent views as to whether Christians can be sure they will continue in a state of grace to the end. In the postapostolic centuries the baptized were urged, "Let none of you be found a deserter," and the prevailing rigorism denied all comfort to those who fell from the purity conferred in baptism. Hermas and Tertullian (initially) allowed postbaptismal repentance once, Cyprian and others not at all. By the 4th century some delayed baptism until late in life because postbaptismal sin incurred such dire responsibilities. The classification of apostasy with murder and fornication as unpardonable (later, pardonable only after public penance) shows the same deep awareness of the possibility of total defection.

With Augustine a new theme entered the discussion. Convinced of our utter helplessness by virtue of original sin, Augustine traced every thought and motion Godward to the operation of divine grace within those elected to salvation. Nothing was ascribed to human initiative, or even to human response. Electing, effectual grace includes not only the call to salvation, the impulse of faith to respond, the inspiring of a good will, but also the *donum perseverantiae*, the gift of enduring to the end. Calvin reaffirmed that Christ died only for the elect and their salvation was guaranteed. God would never allow any to fall away; they are kept in the faith by the almighty power of God. All the regenerate are eternally secure; they have been predestined to eternal glory and are assured of heaven. They do fall into temptation and commit sin, but they do not lose salvation or suffer separation from Christ. Such dogmatic assurance provoked the Arminian arguments (1) that election itself was conditional, depending upon God's foresight of who would respond in faith of their own free will; and (2) that believers, truly saved, can lose salvation by failing to maintain their faith—the regenerate can, by grieving the Spirit, fall away and perish.

Value of the Doctrine. Difficult as it is to frame a defensible statement, the Christian values here at stake are precious. If we fall, we know that is our fault; if we are upheld, we know it is because of God's grace. The warnings, exhortations, and tragic examples of the NT do still speak directly to our hearts; had it depended upon us, our waywardness would long ago have snatched us out of God's hands, separated us from God's love. But it has not depended upon anything in us, except our desire to be saved. In this sense God himself, in his freedom, has made perseverance, like salvation, dependent upon human response—so most modern Christians would probably say. But the condition is simply wanting to endure; thereafter, "the perseverance of the saints is nothing else but the patience of God."

R. E. O. White

See also Assurance; Backsliding.

Person, God as. See God, Attributes of.

Person of Christ. See Christology.

Peter, Primacy of. Peter's primacy or leadership among the 12 apostles and in the primitive church generally is accepted by Protestant and Catholic scholars alike. Differences on this matter arise rather between conservative biblical scholars, who accept the texts essentially as they stand, and more liberal ones who argue that a role Peter developed later was projected, somewhat inaccurately, back into the Gospel accounts. Protestants and Catholics do continue to differ, however, on what the implications of Peter's leadership are for later ages and structures of the church.

Simon, son of Jona or John, was among the first of the apostles called by Jesus (Matt. 4:18–20; Mark 1:16–18); appears first in all biblical lists of apostles (see esp. Matt. 10:2); became part of an inner group especially close to Jesus; and was probably the first apostle to see the resurrected Jesus (Luke 24:34; 1 Cor. 15:5). He served as the impetuous spokesman for all the apostles, and he also represented their collective desertion. Peter first confessed that Jesus was the Messiah (Matt. 16:16; Mark 8:29; Luke 9:20) or Holy One of God (John 6:69); Jesus surnamed him the "rock" upon which he would build his church (Matt. 16:18; Mark 3:16; John 1:42); and the risen Lord charged Peter with the pastoral office (John 21:15–17). In the primitive church, as described in the Acts of the Apostles, Peter clearly emerges as leader, the preacher at Pentecost, the one who receives the vision that opens the way to Cornelius and other Gentiles, and the decisive speaker at the Council of Jerusalem (Acts 15:7–11).

Roman Catholics believe that Peter's was a permanent office instituted by Christ and conferred upon the apostle's successors in the see of Rome, and that his primacy in the primitive church has fallen now to the bishops (popes) of Rome. Most pointedly, and defined at Vatican Council I in 1870, its *First Dogmatic Constitution on the Church of*

Christ, also known as *Pastor aeternus*, made it a matter of Catholic faith to believe that Christ conferred primacy of jurisdiction over the whole church directly and without mediation (this against conciliarists) upon Peter, that the Petrine office and its primacy persist through the ages in the bishops of Rome, and that they therefore possess universal, ordinary jurisdiction over all of Christ's church. Vatican Council II, in its constitution on the church (*Lumen gentium*), reaffirmed the foregoing, but then went on in fact to place great stress upon all bishops acting together collegially. This Catholic claim to Petrine and Roman primacy rests upon two bases, one historical and the other theological.

The historical claim is that Peter died a martyr as the first bishop of Rome and passed to succeeding bishops there his office and primacy. Singular emphasis upon Peter as the founder and first bishop of Rome first emerged in the 3d century and became prominent in the late 4th century, especially as articulated by the popes who reigned between Damasus (366–84) and Leo (440–61). Theologically the Roman Catholic Church bases its position on Matt. 16:18, claiming that Peter is the "rock" upon which the church is founded, thus giving it the full power of binding and loosing. The first certain application of this text to the Roman Church was by Pope Stephen I (254–57) in argument with Bishop Cyprian of Carthage over the baptism of heretics. This interpretation prevailed in Rome and has been the mainstay of papal documents and claims to this day.

Modern exegesis has produced some surprising twists. Some Protestants say the rock clearly refers to Peter and only by extension to his faith, while liberal Protestants and Catholics claim that this is not an authentic saying of Jesus but rather reflects the advent of "early Catholicism" in the primitive church. Progressive Catholic theologians concede that this saying, whatever its exact meaning and referent, cannot serve as a direct proof text for the Roman papacy and its primatial claims. Conservative Protestants continue to focus upon Peter's confessional recognition of Jesus as the Messiah as the foundational rock of the church and its disciplinary powers.

J. Van Engen

See also Papacy; Peter the Apostle.

Peter Lombard (ca. 1100–1160). Medieval theologian. Lombard taught at the Cathedral School in Paris and later became bishop of Paris (1159). His fame rests on his *Book of Sentences* (1158). The book is divided into four sections: God, the creation, the Trinity, and the sacraments. Lombard was one of the first to insist on the view that there are seven sacraments, and he distinguished between sacraments and sacramental signs.

R. G. Clouse

See also Scholasticism.

Peter the Apostle. Simeon (or Simon) bar-Jonah (Matt. 16:17; John 21:15) was known in the apostolic church principally by the name that Jesus conferred on him, "the rock," in either its Aramaic form *Kepa'* (1 Cor. 1:2; 15:5; Gal. 2:9) or Graecized as *Petros* (Gal. 2:7; 1 Pet. 1:1; 2 Pet. 1:1). Matthew associates this with the confession of Caesarea Philippi (Matt. 16:18).

Peter was a fisherman from Bethsaida (John 1:43), but had a home in Capernaum (Mark 1:29). One of the original 12 disciples, he is depicted by the Synoptic tradition as their leader and natural spokesman (Matt. 15:15; Mark 1:36; 9:5; 10:28; 11:20; Luke 5:5), particularly in crises. Christ chooses him, with James and John, as an inner circle (Mark 5:37; 9:2; 14:32). Peter undoubtedly leads the first Jerusalem church. He is the first witness of the resurrection (1 Cor. 15:5; cf. Mark 16:7). He leads in the gathered community before Pentecost (Acts

1:15–22), and is the first preacher (Acts 2:14–41) and the representative preacher of the early chapters of Acts (3:11–26; 4:8–12). He presides in judgment (Acts 5:1–9; 8:20–24). Paul regards him as a "pillar" of the early church (Gal. 2:9).

There is no evidence that he was bishop of Rome or stayed long in the city. First Peter was written there (so probably 1 Pet. 5:13), doubtless after Paul's death, for Silvanus and Mark were with him. Probably (see Eusebius, *Ecclesiastical History* 3.39) Mark's Gospel reflects Peter's preaching. Peter died in Rome in the Neronian persecution (1 Clement 5–6), probably by crucifixion (cf. John 21:18). Recent excavations reveal an early cultus of Peter, but the original grave is unlikely ever to be found.

A. F. Walls

See also Peter, Primacy of.

Pharisees. Jewish religious party that flourished in Palestine from the late 2d century B.C. to the late 1st century A.D.

Sources. Virtually all our knowledge about the Pharisees is derived from three sets of sources: the works of the Jewish historian Flavius Josephus—*The Jewish War* (ca. A.D. 75), *The Antiquities of the Jews* (ca. A.D. 94), and *Life* (ca. A.D. 101); the various compilations of the rabbis (ca. A.D. 200 and later); and the NT. It should be noted, however, that the sources provide neither a complete nor a straightforward picture of the Pharisees.

Name. Various etymologies have been proposed for the name "Pharisee." The only one to receive general approval is that which derives the name from the Aramaic passive participle *periš*, *perišayya'*, meaning "separated." The consensus is that the Pharisees regarded themselves, or were regarded, as the "separated ones."

Nature and Influence. The fundamental issue in Pharisaic studies is the twofold question of the nature of the group and its influence within broader Judaism. Two basic positions have been taken on this question. The traditional view holds that the Pharisees were the creators and shapers of late second temple Judaism. They were not so much a sect as a dominant party within Judaism. The second point of view is a relatively recent development. Proponents of this position argue that when the inherent limitations and tendencies of our sources are taken into account, the Pharisees come across not as the creators and shapers of Judaism but merely as one of its many expressions. In essence, according to this view, the Pharisees were a rather tightly knit sect organized around the observance of purity and tithing laws; on most other issues the Pharisees reflected the range of views present within Judaism. Of course, not all scholars subscribe to one of these two views; many hold mediating positions. Nevertheless, these two views constitute the foundations upon which the modern study of Pharisaism is based.

History. The origin of the Pharisaic movement is shrouded in mystery. It is likely that the Pharisees were one of several groups to grow out of the revival and resistance movement of the Maccabean period (ca. 166–60 B.C.). Whatever its origins, the Pharisaic movement seems to have undergone a two-stage development. During the reign of Salome Alexandra the Pharisees as a group were heavily involved in politics and national policy making. Sometime after this, possibly when Herod the Great rose to power (37 B.C.), the Pharisees withdrew from politics. Individual Pharisees remained politically involved, but there was no longer any official Pharisaic political agenda. This seems to have been the situation during the time of Christ. After the Jewish revolt of A.D. 70 many scholars with Pharisaic leanings gathered at the city of Jamnia to form a school for the preservation and redefinition of Judaism. Thus they played an important role at the beginning of the century-long process that transformed second temple Judaism into rabbinic Judaism.

Beliefs. The Pharisees were strongly committed to the daily application and observance of the law. They accepted the traditional elaborations of the law that made daily application possible. They believed, moreover, in the existence of spirits and angels, the resurrection, and the coming of a Messiah. They also maintained that the human will enjoyed a limited freedom within the sovereign plan of God. Yet there is little evidence to suggest that these were distinctively Pharisaic beliefs.

The Pharisees and Jesus. The NT does not present a simple picture of the relationship between the Pharisees and Jesus. Pharisees warn Jesus of a plot against his life (Luke 13:31); in spite of their dietary scruples they invite him for meals (Luke 7:36–50; 14:1); some of them even believe in Jesus (John 3:1; 7:45–53; 9:13–38); later, Pharisees are instrumental in ensuring the survival of Jesus' followers (Acts 5:34; 23:6–9). Nevertheless, Pharisaic opposition to Jesus is a persistent theme in all four Gospels. The disputes between Jesus and the Pharisees center primarily on the validity and application of purity, tithing, and sabbath laws (e.g., Matt. 12:2, 12–14; 15:1–12; Mark 2:16; Luke 11:39–42). In the end, the Pharisees could not reconcile Jesus' actions and claims with their own understanding of piety and godliness.

S. TAYLOR

See also SADDUCEES.

Philippists. See CRYPTO-CALVINISM.

Philosophy, Christian View of. Focusing on the most fundamental and general issues facing humankind, philosophers traditionally have attempted to synthesize all knowledge into a coherent, consistent system. No scientist or group of scientists can accomplish this task, however, for they are all limited in the scope of their investigations to just parts or certain aspects of the experienced world. The dominance of the scientific method in the modern era has brought with it skepticism about the possibility of going beyond the methods of science in describing reality. Consequently the synthetic and synoptic function of philosophy is considered less than attainable by some philosophers today. More in vogue presently is the other characteristic associated with the philosophers from the time of the ancient Greeks onward, namely, their attempt to be analytical. In this role the philosopher gives leadership in the careful evaluation of the assertions, concepts, assumptions, methods, and conclusions of anyone who claims to be describing reality or prescribing human behavior.

The Four Types of Philosophical Problems. *Logic.* The philosophical field of logic seeks to ascertain the principles of the thought patterns one ought to follow if reality is to be reflected adequately. Thus logic is the normative discipline of correct reasoning as such.

Theory of Knowledge. The issues here include the definition, criteria, and sources of knowledge. Equally significant is the question of whether there is a foundational structure of directly known principles of evidence upon which reasoning can be built.

Metaphysics and Ontology. Although the etymology and traditional use of the term "ontology" makes it a synonym of "metaphysics," its meaning has become narrowed in contemporary philosophy. In the analytically oriented philosophy of today's English-speaking world metaphysics amounts to a rigorous examination of the concepts used when referring to the basic categories of being. The term "ontology" is usually preferred, leaving "metaphysics" for the largely discredited speculative account of reality as a whole. By way of contrast, Continental philosophy considers ontology to be the disclosure of the world of appearance that is reality.

Value Theory. The fourth major department of philosophy includes ethics and aesthetics. The primary focus of the study of aesthetics is upon the question of whether beauty is relative to the observer. Ethics is mainly concerned with the grounds warranting human actions to be judged right or wrong, and persons and events good or evil.

The Christian Attitude Toward Philosophy. Paul's warning to the Colossian believers is clear: "See to it that no one takes you captive through hollow and deceptive philosophy" (Col. 2:8). Such a warning was to be expected in light of what passed for philosophy in Paul's time. But he makes a philosophical assertion himself by continuing in the same passage to point out that in Christ "all the fullness of the Deity lives in bodily form" and that Christ is "the head over every power and authority" (Col. 8:9–10).

Secular philosophers began losing the initiative to Christian thinkers within a few centuries after Paul's death. Indeed, during the 1000 years prior to the modern era virtually all European philosophers were Christians. They took seriously the need of providing an interpretation of divine revelation in nature, Christ, and Scripture for a culture built on the framework of the ancient Greek philosophers. The basic questions every human must ask had been so clearly articulated by the Greeks that the Christian philosophers sought to formulate equally cogent answers from the standpoint of God's general and special revelation. Secular philosophy, often anti-Christian, however, has regained the leadership in the modern period.

As much has been learned from and about both God's and humankind's creative work since the origin of the human race, the Christian thinker must contemplate more than the problems of concern to the biblical writers. Moreover, in order to encompass as much of God's truth as possible from natural revelation within a comprehensive view of the universe created and sustained by the merciful, loving God of Scripture, the Christian must engage in philosophical speculation. All that a Christian must do to pursue philosophy properly is critically to scrutinize the discoveries, insights, and theories that have increased our knowledge of God's universe, and coherently to weave this knowledge into an adequate whole consistent with Scripture. This will involve a consideration, assessment, and evaluation from the scriptural viewpoint of every area of the human quest for knowledge, for control of the environment, for human governance, and for artistic expression.

The Christian philosopher should be able to assist the theologian in two important ways. One is to provide leadership in developing techniques of rigorous, critical analysis of cultural and theological assumptions, concepts, and doctrines and their implications. The other line of assistance is in the formulation of a synthetic and synoptic scheme of thought in order that the systematic theologian, particularly, can show Scripture to be relevant to contemporary life and thought. The simple fact that any systematic theologian must adopt a philosophical system makes it crucial that Christian philosophers make available guidance in the selection and use of one consistent with the teachings of Scripture.

S. R. Obitts

See also Aesthetics, Christian View of; Metaphysics; Philosophy of Religion.

Philosophy of Religion. The philosophical investigation of the nature and grounds of religious beliefs is one of the oldest and most persistent areas of philosophical endeavor. Religious belief and practice give rise to a variety of philosophical issues, posing epistemological questions about the justification of religious belief, metaphysical questions about the nature of God and the soul, and ethical questions about the relation of God to moral values. So many are the intersecting major philosophical concerns in the religious arena, and so immediate is the interest, that philosophy of religion is one of the most significant fields of philosophical endeavor to both Christian philosophers and those of other persuasions. The classic problems in the philosophy of religion center on the grounds for belief in God, the immortality of the soul, the nature of miracles, and the problem of evil.

Grounds for Belief in God. The classical arguments for God's existence are the five ways of Aquinas and the ontological argument of Anselm of Canterbury. Aquinas's arguments are variations of two major forms, the cosmological and teleological arguments. The cosmological argument is based upon the contention that the existence and activity of the universe demand an explanation in an entity beyond itself. The teleological or "design" argument advanced by Aquinas and William Paley, among others, urges us to infer from the well-orderedness of nature the existence of a supreme designer. Both cosmological and teleological arguments have come under sustained criticism, notably by the noted empiricist and skeptic, David Hume.

Anselm's ontological argument is the only theistic proof to proceed a priori, that is, by reflection on the concept of God alone, with no reference to such external evidence as the existence or nature of the world. Anselm observed that if God is defined as "the Being greater than whom nothing can be conceived," then to deny the existence of such a being lands one in a contradiction. One is thus implying that "something greater than God" can be conceived, that is, an *existing* God. This conceivable being would have, in addition to God's properties, a quality lacked by God—existence—and so would be greater than the being greater than whom nothing could be conceived. In addition to the use of arguments for God's existence, philosophers of religion traditionally have been interested in another avenue of possible knowledge about God—religious experience.

Status of the Soul. The nature of the soul, its relation to the body and its fate at death have been constantly studied from Plato to the present.

The Miraculous. The concept of miracle has received significant attention in philosophy. Christianity stresses the importance of biblical miracles to Christian faith and doctrine, especially the resurrection of Christ from the dead. Hume's monumental work, *An Essay Concerning Human Understanding*, depicts miracles as contradictions of our "firm and unalterable" experience in the regularity of natural laws, rendering them improbable in the extreme. This has led to intense debate.

The Problem of Evil. The most potent criticism of theism, both philosophically and personally, arises from the so-called problem of evil. A significant intellectual problem is posed for theism by virtue of the fact that it asserts the existence of a God with unlimited power, wisdom, and goodness in the face of the existence of a world acknowledged to be rife with both moral evil and suffering.

Contemporary Emphases. Much contemporary philosophy of religion focuses on questions surrounding the use of language in referring to God. Following Hume, contemporary philosophers such as A. J. Ayer and A. G. N. Flew have raised critical questions about religious language. In particular, they have argued that talk about God is as cognitively meaningless as mere gibberish, since it is incapable of empirical verifiability or falsifiability. Also of interest on the contemporary front is the logical coherence of the doctrine of God as he is traditionally understood in Judeo-Christian thought.

D. B. FLETCHER

See also EVIL, PROBLEM OF; GOD, ARGUMENTS FOR THE EXISTENCE OF; MIRACLES.

Photian Schism. Ninth-century dispute between Eastern and Western Christianity. It began when Photius was appointed patriarch of Constantinople by the emperor Michael III in 858, after the previous incumbent had been deposed. The latter's followers questioned the legality of this deposition and found support from Pope Nicholas I, who took the opportunity to claim dominion also over the Eastern Church. The breach was widened by doctrinal differences.

J. D. DOUGLAS

See also FILIOQUE.

Pietism. Recurring tendency within Christian history to emphasize more the practicalities of Christian life and less the formal structures of theology or church order. Its historians discern four general traits in this tendency: (1) its experiential character—pietists are people of the heart for whom Christian living is the fundamental concern; (2) its biblical focus—pietists are, to paraphrase John Wesley, "people of one book" who take standards and goals from Scripture; (3) its perfectionistic bent—pietists are serious about holy living and expend every effort to follow God's law, spread the gospel, and provide aid for the needy; (4) its reforming interest—pietists usually oppose what they regard as coldness and sterility in established church forms and practices.

Spener and Francke. Modern pietism is usually traced to the work of Philipp Jakob Spener, known often as the father of pietism, who was called in 1666 to be the senior minister in Frankfurt am Main. He appealed for moral reform in the city. He initiated a far-flung correspondence, which eventually won him the title "spiritual counselor of all Germany." Most important, he also promoted a major reform in the practical life of the churches. In 1670 Spener instituted a *collegia pietatis* ("pious assembly") of laity to meet on Wednesdays and Sundays to pray, discuss the previous week's sermon, and apply passages from Scripture and devotional writings to individual lives. Spener took a major step toward reviving the church in 1675 when he was asked to prepare a new preface for sermons by Johann Arndt. The result was the famous *Pia Desideria* (*Pious Wishes*). This brief work examined the sources of spiritual decline in Protestant Germany and offered proposals for reform. The tract was an immediate sensation.

Spener left Frankfurt for Dresden in 1686, and from there he was called to Berlin in 1691. His time in Dresden was marked by controversy, but it was not a loss, for in Dresden he met his successor, August Hermann Francke. In Berlin, Spener helped to found the University of Halle, to which Francke was called in 1692. Under Francke's guidance the University of Halle showed what pietism could mean when put into practice. In rapid succession Francke opened his own home as a school for poor children, he founded a world-famous orphanage, he established an institute for the training of teachers, and later he helped found a publishing house, a medical clinic, and other institutions.

Francke experienced a dramatic conversion in 1687, the source of his lifelong concern for evangelism and missions.

Under his leadership Halle became the center of ambitious missionary endeavors. The university established a center for Oriental languages and also encouraged efforts at translating the Bible into new languages. Francke's missionary influence was felt directly through missionaries who went from Halle to foreign fields and indirectly through groups like the Moravians and an active Danish mission that drew inspiration from the leaders of pietism.

The Spread of Pietism. Spener and Francke inspired other varieties of German pietism. Count Nikolas von Zinzendorf, head of the renewed Moravian Church, was Spener's godson and Francke's pupil. Zinzendorf organized refugees from Moravia into a kind of *collegia pietatis* within German Lutheranism, and later shepherded this group in reviving the Bohemian Unity of the Brethren. These Moravians, as they came to be known, carried the pietistic concern for personal spirituality almost literally around the world. This was of momentous significance for the history of English-speaking Christianity when John Wesley was thrown into a company of Moravians during his voyage to Georgia in 1735. What he saw of their behavior then and what he heard of their faith after returning to England led to his own evangelical awakening. Another group under the general influence of Spener and Francke developed pietistic concern for the Bible within German Lutheranism at Württemberg. Its leading figure, Johann Albrecht Bengel (1687–1752), represented a unique combination of scholarly expertise and devotional commitment to Scripture.

Influences radiating from Halle, Württemberg, and the Moravians moved rapidly into Scandinavia. Pietism exerted its influence through Wesley in England. The father of American Lutheranism, Henry Melchior Muhlenberg, was sent across the Atlantic by Francke's son in response to requests for spiritual leadership from German immigrants. In addition, pietism also influenced the Mennonites, Moravians, Brethren, and Dutch Reformed in early America.

An overall evaluation of pietism must take into consideration the circumstances of its origin in 17th-century Europe. Whether in its narrow German usage or its more generic sense, pietism represented a complex phenomenon. It partook of the mysticism of the late Middle Ages. It shared the commitment to Scripture and the emphasis on lay Christianity of the early Reformation. It opposed the formalism and cold orthodoxy of the theological establishment. And it was a child of its own times with its concern for authentic personal experience. It was, in one sense, the Christian answer to what has been called "the discovery of the individual" by providing a Christian form to the individualism and practical-mindedness of a Europe in transition to modern times.

In more specifically Christian terms pietism represents a significant effort to reform the Protestant heritage. Some of the fears of its earliest opponents have been partially justified. At its worst the pietistic tendency can lead to inordinate subjectivism and emotionalism; it can discourage careful scholarship; it can fragment the church through enthusiastic separation; it can establish new codes of almost legalistic morality; and it can underrate the value of Christian traditions. On the other hand, pietism was—and continues to be—a source of powerful renewal in the church. At its best it points to the indispensability of Scripture for the Christian life; it encourages religious freedom and cooperation among believers; and it urges individuals not to rest until finding intimate fellowship with God himself.

M. A. Noll

See also Francke, August Hermann; Spener, Philipp Jakob.

Plato, Platonism. Plato (ca. 427–347 B.C.) came from an aristocratic background. He was given an excellent education, which was followed by several years spent as a member of the Socratic Circle, abruptly ended by the death of Socrates in 399. After Socrates' death, an event that certainly had a profound effect on Plato, he traveled extensively and was also widely exposed to Pythagoreanism and Heraclitianism. Upon returning to Athens (the date is not exactly known), he set up his famous school of philosophy, the Academy, and taught there until his death. During his career Plato wrote more than 24 philosophical works that are still extant; almost all of these are written in dialogue form, often with Socrates as the major personality.

For Plato, sense experience is not a valid means of ascertaining reality, since it is often in error and at best can only perceive facts in this changing world. Rather, he stresses the proper use of reasoning and mathematics, which he holds to be much more reliable than the pursuit of natural science. Methodologically, the innate knowledge that we are physically born with is rationally reflected upon and extracted from others by means of the so-called Socratic method. This was illustrated by Socrates' well-known dialogue with the slave boy in *Meno* (82–87). Since the boy had no way of learning the principles of geometry, his perception of these truths must have been due to the skillful questioning of Socrates, who drew out the innate knowledge already in the mind of the boy. Through such rational means we may discover the other world of forms. Three of the most important contributions that Plato made to the philosophy of religion are his theory of forms, his cosmology, and his teaching concerning the immortality of the soul.

Forms. For Plato, forms are not physical objects nor are they simply logical or mathematical symbols. Rather, they have objective existence and provide the reality for the physical objects in the sense world, which can only imperfectly imitate these forms. The forms are ordered according to a hierarchy, of which the highest form is good.

Cosmology. Much of Plato's cosmology is found in *Timaeus*. The Demiurge ("craftsman"), who appears to be God, fashions preexisting matter by patterning it after the forms. By the inclusion of mind or soul, the creation shares a small part of divine essence.

Immortality of the Soul. Plato's beliefs on this topic are chiefly set forth in *Phaedo*. Death is marked by the separation of the body and the soul. Until this time the body is a hindrance, as it opposes and even imprisons the soul. After death the just will be rewarded with a better destiny than the unjust.

Influence of Platonic Thought. Plato's academy was closed by Justinian in A.D. 529. Both before and after this time Platonism in various forms has been one of the most influential philosophies. Its influence on Judaism may be seen in Philo in the 1st century B.C. It inspired the Neo-Platonism of Plotinus in the 3d century A.D., which emphasized the mystical implications of Plato's thought. Christian thought also came under the influence of Platonism, as scholars of the 3d century such as Clement of Alexandria and Origen mixed this Greek philosophy with their theology. In particular, Augustine's interpretation of Plato dominated Christian thought for the next 1000 years after his death in the 5th century. The Renaissance was partially characterized by a revival of Platonic thought, led by scholars such as Marsilio Ficino and Giovanni Pico of Florence. Later, the 17th-century Cambridge Platonists promoted these ideas. In modern philosophy Platonism has inspired the works of thinkers such as A. E. Taylor and A. N. Whitehead.

G. R. Habermas

See also AUGUSTINE OF HIPPO; CAMBRIDGE PLATONISTS; NEO-PLATONISM.

Pleasure, God's Good. See WILL OF GOD.

Plenary Inspiration. The doctrine of plenary inspiration emerged first among the Jesuits, and was to remain a viable view in certain Roman Catholic circles into the 19th century. Among Protestants plenary inspiration was particularly prominent among English-speaking evangelicals. The main principles of plenary inspiration are as follows. (1) God is the author of the Bible, in varied ways. (2) The focus of inspiration is the writers of the Bible. There is author rather than text orientation. (3) The writers have been inspired in all that they have written, although in varied ways. The inspiration of *suggestion* deals with matters of content that can be known only by divine revelation and in which the writers were inspired in a fashion similar to that of verbal inspiration. The inspiration of *elevation* relates to humanly accessible knowledge, from which inferences and conclusions have to be drawn. In this mode of inspiration the mental processes are elevated and sharpened. The inspiration of *superintendence* operates when copying from extant documents, affording accuracy of transmission. As evangelicalism began to lose some of its dynamic in the second quarter of the 19th century, and as new pressures began to be felt, many plenarists shifted to either partial or verbal inspiration, although among some conservative Wesleyans the theory appears never to have entirely disappeared.

I. S. RENNIE

See also BIBLE, INERRANCY AND INFALLIBILITY OF; BIBLE, INSPIRATION OF; BIBLE, VERBAL INSPIRATION.

Pleroma. See FULLNESS.

Plotinus. See NEO-PLATONISM.

Polygamy. Practice of having more than one wife at one time. Islam permits a man to have four wives, but in recent times in some Mohammedan countries, notably in Turkey, this practice has been abolished by state law. According to the divine institution, lawful marriage consists of one man and one woman (Gen. 2:18, 24). Christ supported monogamy as the only proper form of marriage (Matt. 19:4–6). While the Bible does not directly condemn the plural marriages that occurred in the OT, it candidly reports the evil effects of polygamy (or polygyny), as in the families of Jacob (Gen. 35:22; 37:18–28), David (2 Sam. 13; 15), and especially Solomon (1 Kings 11:1–12).

J. T. MUELLER

See also MARRIAGE, MARRIAGE CUSTOMS IN BIBLE TIMES.

Polytheism. Belief in a multitude of distinct and separate deities. It is formally contrasted with pantheism, the belief in an impersonal God identical with the universe, although the two doctrines can sometimes be found in the same religious tradition. Polytheism is distinguished from theism, also called monotheism, on the basis of polytheism's claim that divinity, while personal and distinguished from the universe, is many rather than one. Except for the great monotheisms of Judaism, Christianity, and Islam, the world's religions are overwhelmingly polytheistic. Polytheism characterizes Hinduism, Mahayana Buddhism, Confucianism, Taoism, and Shintoism in the East, and also contemporary African tribal religions. In the ancient world Egyptians, Babylonians, and Assyrians worshiped a plurality of deities, as did the ancient Greeks, Romans, and Norse. Belief in several distinct deities serves to provide a focus for popular religious devotion when the official deity or deities of the religion are remote from the common person.

D. B. FLETCHER

See also THEISM; MONOTHEISM.

Pope. See PAPACY.

Pornography. Literally, the writing of harlots; the depiction of erotic behavior intended to cause sexual excitement. Since sex is of almost universal interest, allusions to it are legitimate and necessary if dramatic or literary descriptions of human life are to be truthful or educative; but an enormous market exists for those who exploit sex for gain. Psychologically, the overstimulation of imagination by sexual images renders the whole personality oversexed by disproportionately concentrating thought and desire, often to the point of pornographic addiction; it coarsens feelings and attitudes toward the other sex as tools for sexual indulgence, unrefined by affection, tenderness, or respect; it inverts the sex drive into sterile, self-absorbed, physical pleasure alone—"mental masturbation"; and because overstimulation brings diminishing effects, it leads readily to mental indulgence in increasingly coarser, sadistic perversions—"hard-core" pornography.

Socially, the problems are protection of the immature and unstable; the danger that the emotions stimulated may erupt in antisocial sexual aggressiveness; the tendency to devalue women (mainly) and marriage; and the effect of sensualist displays and opportunities on the whole tone of society. Legally, suppression of "obscenely offensive" materials has been difficult to enforce because of variable public taste and the unanswerable statement, "The offensiveness is all in the viewer's mind."

Christians acknowledge the obligation to preserve purity of mind and heart. Jesus condemned the lustful look as equivalent to adultery, and declared the only defilement was that which comes from within (Matt. 5:28; Mark 7:20). The NT abounds in warnings concerning lust of the flesh, lust of the eyes, concupiscence, uncleanness, following the inclination to sensuality, and "the cravings of our sinful nature" (Eph. 2:3) on the principle that as we think, so we are. The Christian response to pornography is: "Clothe yourselves with the Lord Jesus Christ, and do not think about how to gratify the desires of the sinful nature. . . . Whatever is pure, whatever is lovely, whatever is admirable—if anything is excellent or praiseworthy—think about such things"

R. E. O. WHITE

See also OBSCENITY.

Porter. See MINOR ORDERS.

Possession, Demon. See DEMON, DEMON POSSESSION.

Postlapsarianism. See SUPRALAPSARIANISM.

Postmillennialism. See MILLENNIUM, VIEWS OF THE.

Posttribulation Rapture. See RAPTURE OF THE CHURCH.

Power, Powers. See PRINCIPALITIES AND POWERS.

Praise. Homage rendered to God by his creatures in worship of his person and in thanksgiving for his favors and blessings. Praise is rendered to God by Israel, especially in the "Hallel" psalms (Pss. 113–18). Not only Israel, but all who serve God, both heaven and earth, the seas and all that moves in them—in fact, everything that has breath—must rightfully render praise to the Lord (Pss. 69:34; 135:1–2; 150:6). God may be praised with musical instruments and song (Pss. 104:33; 150:3–5). Sacrifice (Lev. 7:13), testimony (Ps. 66:16), and prayer (Col. 1:3) are also praise-filled activities. Praise may be public as well as private (Ps. 96:3); it may be an inward emotion (Ps. 4:7) or an outward utterance (Ps. 51:15). It is rendered to God for his salvation (Ps. 40:10) as well as for the greatness of all his marvelous works

(Rev. 15:3–4). He should be praised for his inherent qualities, his majesty (Ps. 104:1) and holiness (Isa. 6:3). Paul sought the glory of God rather than the praise of other people (1 Thess. 2:6), but recognized legitimate praise for true Christian service (2 Cor. 8:18). Such praise may become an incentive to holy living (Phil. 4:8).

G. B. STANTON

Prayer. Address of God in word or thought involving praise, thanksgiving, confession, petition, and intercession.

Heiler's Typology. Probably the most significant work on the phenomenology of prayer is Friedrich Heiler's *Das Gebet* [*Prayer*], written toward the end of the First World War. Heiler makes a convincing case that prayer takes quite divergent forms, depending on the kind of religion or spirituality in which it is found. He sees six types of prayer: primitive, ritual, Greek cultural, philosophical, mystical, and prophetic.

The two highest types of prayer are the mystical and the prophetic. Mysticism in its Christian context represents a synthesis of Neo-Platonic and biblical motifs, but it is also a universal religious phenomenon. Here the aim is union with God, who is generally portrayed in suprapersonal terms. Mysticism sees prayer as the elevation of the mind to God. Revelation is an interior illumination rather than the intervention of God in history (as in biblical faith). Mystics often speak of a ladder of prayer or stages of prayer, and petition is always considered the lowest stage. The highest form of prayer is contemplation, which often culminates in ecstasy. Prophetic prayer involves importunity—begging and even complaining. In this category of prophetic religion Heiler places not only the biblical prophets and apostles but also the Reformers, especially Luther, and the Puritans. Judaism and Islam at their best also mirror prophetic religion, although mysticism is present in these movements as well.

The spirituality that Heiler did not consider and that is really a contemporary phenomenon can be called secular spirituality. It signifies a this-worldly mysticism where the emphasis is not on detachment from the world but immersion in the world. J. A. T. Robinson describes secular prayer as the penetration through the world to God. The liberation theologian Juan Luis Segundo defines prayer as reflection on and openness to what God is doing in history. Dorothy Sölle speaks of "political prayer," which is oriented toward praxis rather than either adoration or petition.

Hallmarks of Christian Prayer. In biblical religion prayer is understood as both a gift and a task. God takes the initiative and we must respond. This kind of prayer is personalistic and dialogic. It entails revealing our innermost selves to God but also God's revelation of his desires to us (Prov. 1:23). In the Bible petition and intercession are primary, although adoration, thanksgiving, and confession also have a role. Yet the petitionary element is present in all these forms of prayer. Biblical prayer is crying to God out of the depths; it is the pouring out of the soul before God (1 Sam. 1:15; Pss. 88:1–2; 130:1–2; 142:1–2; Lam. 2:19; Matt. 7:7–8; Phil. 4:6; Heb. 5:7). It often takes the form of importunity, passionate pleading to God, even wrestling with God. Meditation and contemplation have a role in biblical religion, although not, however, as higher stages of prayer (as in mysticism) but as supplements to prayer. Further, biblical spirituality makes a place for silence, yet silence is to be used not to get beyond the Word but to prepare ourselves to hear the Word.

The Paradox of Prayer. Prayer in biblical or evangelical spirituality is rooted in both the experience of Godforsakenness and in the sense of the presence of

God. It is inspired by both the felt need of God and gratitude for his work of reconciliation and redemption in Jesus Christ. Christian prayer is both corporate and individual. We find God in solitariness, but we never remain in this state. Instead, we seek to unite our sacrifices of praise and our petitions and intercessions with those of the company of fellow believers. The person of prayer may find God in both solitude and fellowship. Even in solitude we believe that the petitioner is not alone but is surrounded by a cloud of witnesses (Heb. 12:1), the saints and angels in the church triumphant. We are called to present personal and individual needs to God, but at the same time we are urged to intercede for the whole company of the saints (John 17:20–21; Eph. 6:18) and also for the world at large (1 Tim. 2:1–2). The goal of prayer is not absorption into the being of God but the transformation of the world for the glory of God. We pray not simply for personal happiness or for protection (as in primitive prayer) but for the advancement and extension of the kingdom of God.

D. G. BLOESCH

Prayer, The Lord's. See LORD'S PRAYER.

Prayers for the Dead. No passage in OT or NT enjoins or even implies this practice. Of the single passage in the Apocrypha that appears to allude to it, it may be said that text, translation, and interpretation of 2 Macc. 12:44 are all uncertain. In the Roman Catholic Church the practice is particularly connected with teaching on purgatory, indulgences, and the Mass. The liturgies and confessions of Protestant churches do not countenance prayers for the dead.

O. R. JOHNSTON

See also PURGATORY.

Preach, Preaching. In the NT a preacher is a person who has the inner call from the Holy Spirit and the external call from the church and has been duly set apart to proclaim the gospel. The preacher's task is to speak as a personal witness to God's revelation, interpreting it, explaining it, and applying it to the needs of the people. The most common definition of preaching is one composed from two quotes from Phillips Brooks: "Preaching is the communication of truth through personality." Bishop Manning gives a more theological definition when he calls preaching "the manifestation of the Incarnate Word from the written word through the spoken word."

Preaching in the Bible. In the OT the words used are *qōhelet*, preacher; *bāśar*, to tell good news; *qārā*, to call or proclaim; *qerî'â*, preaching. The NT uses *euangelizō*, to announce good news; *kēryx*, herald; *kēryssō*, to proclaim as a herald; *diangellō*, to proclaim or publish abroad; *katangellō*, to proclaim solemnly. In both Testaments the words used to denote preaching have the essential element of proclamation or announcing. The preacher is one who tells forth the message that has been received from God. John the Baptist was the connecting link between the OT and the NT. He was the last and greatest of the prophets and the first preacher of the new era. He announced the immediate coming of the promised reign of God and his Messiah.

In distinction from John, Jesus calls to faith in the Lord who has now come. He offers himself and his work to the acceptance of his hearers. He is the revelation and embodiment of God's gracious ways with persons, and as such he is to be received and trusted. Jesus preached in various locations and to various sized audiences. Sometimes he spoke to small groups and at other times to vast crowds. Sometimes he interpreted the Scriptures in a synagogue service, while on other occasions he preached in the field or by the sea. The preaching of Jesus was marked by authority and by quiet confidence in God, in himself, and in his mission and message. Sometimes he thundered judgment, and at other times he issued a tender invitation. In his preaching he blended parable, aphorism, argument, and scriptural exposition. Two occasions are recorded in the Gospels when Jesus sent out groups of disciples on preaching missions. He gave them their message, together with practical instructions as to how they should carry out their ministry. The Book of Acts depicts the disciples waiting at Jerusalem for the promise of the Spirit. Acts and the Epistles give traces of the apostolic preaching following Pentecost. In the preaching of the apostles is found the two permanent elements of Christian preaching, evangelism and instruction. There is a free presentation to all people of the claims and demands of the gospel. There is also orderly public instruction of believers in worship based upon the Scriptures.

Preaching in Church History. After the death of the apostles and their fellow workers in the early church there was a decline in preaching, until gradually it rose in power to a high level in the 4th and early 5th centuries. Then preaching fell into a long night of obscurity and weakness; with the preaching of the Crusades and the rise of scholasticism it began to revive. It reached its height in the 13th century. Then again there was a general falling off in purity and power. The Reformation represented another high wave gathering forces slowly to its crest in the early part of the 16th century. After the Reformation, with the fracturing of the visible church: preaching was marked by diversity as it spread from country to country and denomination to denomination. Each country, and each denomination, has had its peaks of power in preaching.

Contemporary trends in preaching include liturgical preaching, holistic preaching, preaching based on communications theory, liberation preaching (some homileticians include black and feminist preaching in this category), preaching built around language theory, life-situation preaching, inductive preaching, and narrative preaching. There is renewed interest in theological preaching. The Christian church will grow, flourish, and accomplish God's purposes for it only as there are those who respond to God's call to preach that word which brings faith and life. P. T. Forsyth was correct when he said, "With preaching Christianity stands or falls, because it is the declaration of a gospel."

J. S. BAIRD

Prebendary. See CHURCH OFFICERS.

Predestination. The doctrine of predestination has both a wider and a narrower aspect. In its wider reference it refers to the fact that the Triune God foreordains whatsoever comes to pass (Eph. 1:11, 22; cf. Ps. 2). From all eternity God has sovereignly determined whatever happens in history. The narrower aspect or use of the term is that God from all eternity has chosen a body of people for himself, that they should be brought into eternal fellowship with him, while at the same time he has ordained that the rest of humanity should be allowed to go their own way, which is the way of sin, to ultimate eternal punishment. These are known as the doctrines of election and reprobation. While some may accept the idea of God choosing some to eternal life, they reject completely any idea of a decree of reprobation (Rom. 9:16–19).

The foundation of the doctrine of predestination is the biblical doctrine of God. He is the Eternal One, above and beyond time and space, for there never was a time when he did not exist, so he is not subject to changes of time and place (Deut. 33:27; Isa. 57:15; Mal. 3:6; Rom. 1:20–21). Furthermore, God is sovereign over all things as the Creator, Sustainer, and Ruler of the universe. He is Lord over all (Isa. 45; Dan. 4:34–35; Rom. 9:17–18; Eph. 1:11). God is also sovereignly righteous, so that all that he does is according to the perfection of his nature (Jer. 23:6; 33:16; Rom. 1:17; 10:3; 2 Pet. 1:1). In eternity he sovereignly established his own plan and purpose, which is far above anything that we can think of, conceive, or understand. We may know God's plan only as he reveals it (Deut. 29:29; Ps. 33:11; Isa. 46:10; 55:7–9; Jer. 23:18; Heb. 6:17).

Throughout the OT the doctrine of election is set forth with increasing clarity. On the one hand it is stated that Israel was chosen, not because of anything it had to offer, but solely because of the grace of God and by his sovereign choice (Deut. 7:7–8; Isa. 41:8–9; Ezek. 20:5). From both Israel and other nations God freely chose individuals who would do his will in history for the blessing of Israel (1 Sam. 16:1–13; 1 Chron. 28:1–7; Isa. 45:1–6). On the other hand, not all Israel was elect, but only a faithful remnant whom God had chosen (Isa. 1:9; 10:21–22; 11:11; Jer. 23:3; 31:7). These Paul calls "a remnant chosen by grace" (Rom. 11:5). Those not of the elect remnant were rejected because of their sin to suffer ultimate punishment.

In the NT the OT doctrines of election and predestination are expanded and clarified. There is no attempt to reject or alter them, but they are given a more clearly universal scope. Christ claimed that he was the mediator spoken of in the OT, and that to him the Father had given his elect people (Mark 1:15; Luke 4:21; John 5:39; 10:14–15). Furthermore, he stated very clearly that he had come to lay down his life as redeemer for his people. This is the theme of both his sermon in John 10 and his prayer for his own in John 17. He promised that his people would all come to him and would persevere in their faith unto eternal life (John 6:39, 65; 10:28–29).

Paul gives the clearest exposition of the doctrine. While he refers to the doctrine of predestination in passing in a number of places, he expounds it in detail in Rom. 8:29–11:36 and throws further light on it in Eph. 1. In these passages he stresses our hopelessly sinful condition and the fact that because of our disobedience and rebellion God not only turns from us but hardens us in our sinfulness (Rom. 9:14–16). At the same time, however, he reaches out and draws to himself those whom he has chosen from all eternity, redeeming and justifying them in Jesus Christ (Rom. 10:11–13; Eph. 1:4–14). Yet in all of this is the mystery of God's sovereign action and human responsibility (Rom. 9:19; 11:33). And in all things the glory of God's righteousness is made manifest (Rom. 9:16–18).

The doctrine of predestination has continued to raise questions ever since the days of the apostles, but especially since the Protestant Reformation of the 16th century, when they were formulated most precisely.

W. S. Reid

See also Elect, Election; Preterition; Reprobation.

Preexistence of Christ. Concept that Christ had existence before his incarnation in a human body.

John, assuming that Christ came from God and went to God (John 13:3), emphasizes Christ's being sent by the Father on a divine mission, expressing divine love (John 3:16; 1 John 4:9–10), a revelation of the unseen Father by one belonging "at the Father's side" (John 1:18)—a divine Word, present when God spoke at creation and now again conveying meaning and power to the world (John 1).

Paul appeals for generosity because Christ, although rich, became poor. (2 Cor. 8:9). He pleads that converts live as children of God because God sent his

Son (Gal. 4:4); argues for self-effacement from the fact that Christ, being in the form of God, "emptied himself" (Phil. 2:5–6); contends, against the Gnostics' *plerōma* filling the gulf between God and creation, that all things were created in, through, and for Christ, who is before all things (Col. 1:15–16).

The implications of preexistence are a concern of subsequent Christian thought. Christ's preexistence does not impair the manhood of Jesus, as two real natures coexist in one person. Nor does Christ's preexistence imply continuity of memory between the eternal Son and Jesus. Modern scholars assert that Jesus had a *growing* consciousness of his unique status.

R. E. O. White

See also Christology; Jesus Christ.

Preexistence of the Soul. See Soul.

Premillennialism. See Millennium, Views of the.

Presbyter. See Church Officers; Elder.

Presbyterianism. See Church Government.

Presence, Divine. In the Bible the word "face" or "countenance" (Heb. *pānîm*; Gk. *prosōpon* or *enōpion*, "in the face of") is normally used to indicate presence. As applied to God there seem to be three main senses. First, there is the general and inescapable presence of God (Ps. 139:7–12). Second, there is the special presence of God among his people or among the nations to save or to judge (Exod. 33:14; Nah. 1:5). This is further expressed by the divine dwelling in the tabernacle and temple, and especially by the coming of Jesus Christ as Immanuel (Matt. 1:23; John 1:14), his continued presence in and with his disciples by the Holy Spirit (Matt. 28:20; John 14:16–17), and his final coming in glory (1 Thess. 2:19). Third, there is the presence of God in heaven, before which the angels stand (Luke 1:19) and believers will be presented faultless in virtue of the work of Christ (Jude 24), thus enjoying, as the psalmist dared to hope, the fullness of joy (Ps. 16:11; cf. 73:23–24).

G. W. Bromiley

See also God, Doctrine of; God, Attributes of.

Preservation. See Conservation.

Preterition. (Lat. *praeter*, "beyond or past," plus *praeteritus*, "that which is passed over") God's passing over of the nonelect, whom he allows to go their own way and perish for their sins.

W. S. Reid

See also Reprobation; Elect, Election; Predestination.

Pretribulation Rapture. See Rapture of the Church.

Prevenient Grace. See Grace.

Priest, Christ as. See Offices of Christ.

Priesthood. Religious official whose main function is the offering up of sacrifices. The term is identical in origin with the word "presbyter," which literally means "elder"; in the English language its connotations are largely sacrificial. The English Reformers of the 16th century hoped that the retention of the term "priest" in the *Book of Common Prayer* would effect the restoration of its proper meaning of elder. The Christian doctrine of priesthood and the relationship between the priesthood of the OT and that of the NT is most fully expounded in the Epistle to the Hebrews, which has been called "the Epistle of Priesthood."

The Necessity of Priesthood. It is the universal sinfulness of humankind that makes a sacrificing priesthood a necessity. The sacrifices offered up effect, or symbolize the means of effecting, reconciliation between sinful people and their holy Creator. The function of priesthood, accordingly, is a mediatorial one.

OT Priesthood. The priesthood of the old covenant could not effect the reality of reconciliation portended by its sacrificial function. Its character was preparatory; it portrayed the principle of propitiatory sacrifice but not the fulfillment of that principle. Its imperfection, which aroused the longing for and the expectation of the provision of the perfect priesthood, was apparent for the following reasons. (1) In the midst of its activity a new priesthood of a different order, that of Melchizedek, was prophetically spoken of (Ps. 110:4; Heb. 7:11–17). (2) During the period when the old or Mosaic covenant was in operation the promise of a new covenant was given, the inauguration of which would mean the placing of God's law in the hearts of his people and the removal of their sins forever (Jer. 31:31–34; Heb. 8:7). (3) Not only were the priests of the old order mortal, they were also sinful, and thus themselves in need of redemption and reconciliation. Consequently, before offering sacrifices for the people they were obliged to offer sacrifices for their own sins—an action that plainly attested the imperfection of their priesthood (Heb. 5:3; 7:27).

Christ as Priest. The purpose of the old order of priesthood was to teach the people that atonement for sins requires the provision of an innocent victim in the sinner's place and the shedding of blood as that victim dies the death due to the sinner. The Levitical order could not accomplish this atonement, but it kept alive the expectation of the coming of the perfect priest and the offering of the perfect sacrifice in fulfillment of the gospel promises contained in the Scriptures of the OT. The new order of priesthood is that of Melchizedek, and it is comprehended in the single person of our Redeemer Jesus Christ (Heb. 7). The perfection of his priesthood is confirmed by the fact that it is forever (Ps. 110:4), that the sacrifice he offered is once for all (Heb. 7:27), and that, his work of atonement completed, he is now enthroned in celestial glory (Heb. 1:3; 10:12; 12:2). The perfection of his priesthood is established by the sinlessness of his earthly life as the incarnate Son, our fellow human being. The new order of priesthood fulfilled in the single person of Christ has completely superseded the old order. With Christ as our one great high priest who lives forever there is now no place or need for any succession of sacrificing priests.

The Priesthood of Believers. There remains, however, a priesthood that belongs to those who through faith have been united to Christ. This has commonly been designated "the priesthood of all believers." Thus Peter describes Christians as "a holy priesthood" whose function is to offer "spiritual sacrifices acceptable to God through Jesus Christ" (1 Pet. 2:5; cf. v. 9). These spiritual sacrifices are not in any sense redemptive sacrifices but sacrifices of gratitude to God for the one all-sufficient redemptive sacrifice of Christ's self-offering at Calvary for sinners. Thus we are exhorted to "present our bodies," ourselves, "as living sacrifices, holy and pleasing to God" (Rom. 12:1); and as we willingly offer ourselves we express our spiritual priesthood in acts of praise and thanksgiving and in the selfless service of other people as we minister to their needs. The exercise of this priesthood is summed up in the words of Heb. 13:15–16: "Through Jesus, therefore, let us continually offer to God a sacrifice of praise—the fruit of lips that confess his name. And do not forget to do good and to share with others, for with such sacrifices God is pleased."

P. E. HUGHES

See also OFFERINGS AND SACRIFICES IN BIBLE TIMES; OFFICES OF CHRIST.

Princeton Theology, Old. Dominant theology of American Presbyterianism, and one of the most influential theologies in the U.S. from the founding of Princeton Seminary (1812) until the reorganization of that institution in 1929. The first professor at Princeton Seminary, Archibald Alexander, epitomized a great deal of the Princeton tradition in his own life. He was a person of piety and Christian warmth, but his main emphases in theology were the reliability of Scripture and the ability of human reason to understand Christian truth. His intellectual sources were Calvin, the Westminster Confession and catechisms, the Swiss theologian Francois Turretin, and the Scottish philosophy of common sense.

Alexander's pupil, Charles Hodge, extended the Princeton point of view during his 56 years at Princeton Seminary. Although he shared many of Alexander's concerns, Hodge had a fuller place in his theology for the work of the Holy Spirit. He was also a more effective polemicist in expounding a traditional Calvinism against innovations in American theology. Hodge's successors, on the other hand, were called upon to deal with the issues posed by liberalism. Hodge's own son, Archibald Alexander Hodge, and Benjamin B. Warfield addressed these critical issues forthrightly, especially where they concerned the Bible.

The last of the major Princeton theologians was J. Gresham Machen, a theologian of wide interests who became best known as a defender of traditional orthodoxy. His *Christianity and Liberalism* (1923) was one of the strongest 20th-century statements against modernistic trends in American churches. Yet Machen was not successful in preserving his point of view at Princeton. After the Princeton board was reorganized to the disadvantage of the conservatives in 1929, Machen left to help found Westminster Theological Seminary in Philadelphia. With him went a theological tradition stretching back to Archibald Alexander.

M. A. NOLL

See also ALEXANDER, ARCHIBALD; HODGE, ARCHIBALD ALEXANDER; HODGE, CHARLES; MACHEN, JOHN GRESHAM; WARFIELD, BENJAMIN BRECKINRIDGE.

Principalities and Powers. Pauline expression taken from late Jewish apocalyptic thought, where it was applied to intermediate beings lower than God and higher than humankind. Apart from passages where the reference is unmistakably to human authorities (Rom. 13:1–3; Titus 3:1), principalities (*archai*) and authorities (*exousiai*) or powers (*dynameis*) refer to cosmic intelligences, occasionally angelic, but usually demonic (Rom. 8:38; 1 Cor. 15:24; Eph. 1:21; 3:10; 6:12; Col. 1:16; 2:10; 2:15). Other similar spirit powers are dominions (*kyriotētes*, Eph. 1:21; Col. 1:16), thrones (*thronoi*, Col. 1:16), and the rulers (*archontes*) of this age (1 Cor. 2:6). It is not possible on the basis of NT evidence to rank these spirit powers or to attribute distinctive meanings to each.

Six acts in the drama of the principalities and powers may be delineated: 1. *Creation.* In the creation plan these powers were designed as good spirits (Col. 1:16). 2. *Fall.* Some spirit powers separated from Christ (Jude 6) in a rupture of cosmic proportions (2 Pet. 2:4), necessitating atonement (Col. 1:20). 3. *Defeat by Christ.* In his death Jesus disarmed the forces of evil (Col. 2:14–15). In his resurrection and exaltation he subjected them to his lordship (Eph. 1:20–22; 4:8; 1 Pet. 3:22). 4. *Learning.* The spirit powers, who are not omniscient, learn the manifold wisdom of God by witnessing the historic experience of the church (Eph. 3:10). 5. *Continuing warfare.* Although defeated and under instruction, the spirit powers have not yet surrendered. The vestiges of their power continue to corrupt the disobedient (Eph. 2:2). The

Christian's most powerful and deceitful enemies are still demonic (Eph. 6:12). 6. *Total defeat.* The days of this warfare are numbered and the outcome certain. With the consummation of the kingdom of God the evil powers will be robbed of all malignant efficacy (1 Cor. 15:24).

It is possible, however, that Paul intended his reference to thrones, dominions, principalities, and authorities in Col. 1:16 to embrace earthly as well as heavenly powers. The matter invites further research. But for the present, while allowing that all human systems are wide open to corruption from demonic forces, it is safest to avoid identifying principalities and powers with sociopolitical structures, as some theologians have done recently.

F. S. PIGGIN

See also DEMON, DEMON POSSESSION.

Probabiliorism. See CASUISTRY.

Problem of Evil. See EVIL, PROBLEM OF.

Procession of the Spirit. See FILIOQUE.

Process Theology. Contemporary theology that teaches that God is dipolar, or has two natures, and that he is integrally involved in the endless process of the world. God has a "primordial" or transcendent nature, his timeless perfection of character, and he has a "consequent" or immanent nature by which he is part of the cosmic process itself. This process is "epochal," that is, not according to the motion of atoms or changeless substances but by events or units of creative experience that influence one another in temporal sequence.

The method of process theology is more philosophically than biblically or confessionally based, although many of its proponents use process thought as a contemporary way of expressing traditional Christian teachings or seek to relate biblical themes to process concepts. Also the method emphasizes the importance of the sciences in theological formulation. Thus process theology generally stands in the tradition of natural theology, and in particular is associated with the empirical theology tradition in America (Shailer Mathews, D. C. Macintosh, Henry Nelson Wieman) that championed the inductive, scientific approach in liberal theology. Also process theology has some philosophical kinship with the evolutionary thinking of H. Bergson, S. Alexander, C. Lloyd Morgan, and P. Teilhard de Chardin. But its true fountainhead is Whiteheadian philosophy.

Alfred North Whitehead (1861–1947), the famed mathematician-philosopher, sought a set of metaphysical concepts that would explain all individual beings, from God to the most insignificant thing. He held that God is radically immanent in the world process itself, leading it on toward greater value and aesthetic intensity, not by coercion but by sympathetic persuasion. Although God in his primordial nature transcends the world, he as actual entity includes the world consequently within himself, and suffers and grows along with it through the creativity that he and the world possess.

The Contributions of Hartshorne. Although Whitehead's philosophy had already reached maturity with the publication of *Process and Reality* in 1929, only a few used Whitehead as a source for theological thought before the 1950s. It was Charles Hartshorne (1897–) who developed the theological implications of Whitehead's thought and acted as the chief catalyst for the process theology movement of the 1960s and 1970s. Hartshorne took up Whitehead's metaphysical system and, with some modifications, defended it as the most coherent and viable alternative. He agreed with Whitehead on the primacy of becoming (which is inclusive of being, in contrast to classical philosophy), and he emphasized even more than Whitehead the category of feeling as a quality of every entity (panpsychism).

In accordance with the "law of polarity" Hartshorne developed his dipolar view of God, although somewhat differently from Whitehead. Rejecting Whitehead's notion of eternal objects, Hartshorne called the mental pole of God the "abstract nature" of God, which is simply the abstract self-identity of God or his enduring character through all the stretches of time. The consequent nature Hartshorne called God's "concrete nature," which is God in his actual existence in any given concrete state, with all the wealth of accumulated values of the world up to that present state. The attributes of God's abstract nature are those divine qualities that are eternally, necessarily true of God regardless of the circumstances; whereas the qualities of God's concrete nature are those particulars of God's being that he has gained by his interaction with the world in accordance with the circumstances. God in his concrete actuality is a "living person" *in process*; his life consists of an everlasting succession of divine events or occasions.

According to Hartshorne, God's perfection should not be seen exclusively in terms of absoluteness, necessity, independence, infinity, and immutability wholly in contrast to the relativity, contingency, dependence, finitude, and changeability of the creatures. For Hartshorne this is the great mistake of classical theism (of such theologians as Aquinas), resulting in all sorts of problems like the contradiction of God's necessary knowledge of a contingent world, or God's timeless act of creating and governing a world that is temporal, or God's love for humankind that supposedly involves God in history yet in no way makes him relative to or dependent on humankind. Hartshorne contends that if temporal process and creativity are ultimately real, then God himself must be in process in some sense and must be dependent upon the free decisions of the creatures.

In opposition to classical theism, then, Hartshorne develops his "neoclassical" theism in which perfection is understood to mean that God is unsurpassable in social relatedness. God is the "self-surpassing surpasser of all." God is more than just the world in its totality (contra pantheism) because he has his own transcendent self-identity; yet God includes the world within himself (contra classical theism) by his knowledge and love, which are simply his perfect prehension or taking in of the creative events of the world. Such a view of God is thus termed "panentheism" (all-in-God-ism).

Christian Process Thought. After 1960, as the influence of neo-orthodoxy was waning, an increasing number of theologians turned to Whitehead and Hartshorne as new philosophical sources for a contemporary expression of Christian faith. Beginning with the doctrine of God, such theologians as John Cobb, Schubert Ogden, Daniel D. Williams, and Norman Pittenger sought to show that the process view of God is more in accord with the biblical view of God (as dynamically related to human history) than is the more traditional Christian view of classical theism.

Process theologians then began to concentrate on Christology, especially in the 1970s, although Pittenger led the way by writing several works on the subject from a process view, the first in 1959. For Pittenger the uniqueness of Christ is seen in the way he actualized the divine aim for his life. David Griffin has spoken similarly, suggesting that Jesus actualized God's aims in such a way that he became God's decisive revelation. Cobb emphasizes a Logos Christology. The Logos as the primordial nature of God is present (incarnate) in all things in the form of initial aims for creatures. But Jesus is the fullest incarnation of the

Logos because in him there was no tension between the divine initial aim and his own self-purposes of the past. Lewis Ford places emphasis on the resurrection as the basis for Christology. The resurrection is of a spiritual kind; it is a new emergent reality, the "body of Christ," in which humankind is transformed into a new organic unity by the living spirit of Christ. Although process theology has not yet become a major force in the church pew, it is very influential in the intellectual world of the seminaries and graduate schools, and no doubt is the most viable form of neoliberal theology now in the U.S.

Evaluation. By philosophical or rational standards process theology has several commendable points: (1) it emphasizes metaphysical coherence; (2) it integrates science and theology; (3) it provides a tenable answer to the charge that theological language is meaningless; (4) it eloquently champions natural theology; (5) it gives clear and plausible form to a dynamic, personal view of God.

By rational standards process theology also has its weaknesses or questionable features. First, one may question whether the process model does justice to the self-identity of an individual person in process. Second, process theology has some problems concerning the finitude and temporality of God—the problem of relating God's infinite, nontemporal, primordial nature to God's finite, temporal, growing, and consequent nature, or the problem of seeing unity of experience in each moment of God's omnipresent existence in view of the teaching of relativity physics that there is no simultaneous *present* throughout the universe. Third, there is the question of the religious adequacy of panentheism. Is the most worthy object of worship a God who needs the world in order to be a complete personal being or a God who is a complete personal being *prior* to the world?

D. W. Diehl

See also Panentheism.

Promise. The most common NT word for promise is *epangelia*. Its NT uses may be classified into three groups. There are, first, the frequent references to God's promises to Abraham concerning an heir (Rom. 4:13–16, 20; 9:8–9; 15:8; Gal. 3:16–22; 4:23; Heb. 6:13–17; 7:6; 11:9, 11, 17). The second major group of references are to David's seed, the Savior God had promised (Acts 13:23, 32). It is to this group that we must assign Paul's allusion to that which was promised, given through faith in Jesus Christ (Gal. 3:22). The third group of promises concerns the gift of the Holy Spirit after Christ's ascension (not actually referred to as a promise until after the resurrection; [Luke 24:49; cf. Acts 1:4; 2:33; Eph. 1:13]). Other subjects related to the promises of God are mentioned only incidentally in the NT: the promise of rest (Heb. 4:1); the fulfillment of the promises of a new heaven and a new earth (2 Pet. 3:13; cf. Isa. 52:11; Hos. 1:4); the promise of the resurrection (Acts 26:6); "the first commandment with a promise," regarding obedience of children to their parents (Eph. 6:2; cf. Exod. 20:12).

W. M. Smith

See also Hope; Prophecy, Prophet.

Prophecy, Gift of. See Spiritual Gifts.

Prophecy, Prophet. A prophet is one who speaks "before" in the sense of proclaim, or the one who speaks "for," that is, in the name of (God). In the OT there are three terms for the prophet: *rō'eh*, *nābî'*, and *ḥōzeh*. The first and last are distinguished by nuances bearing on the habitual or temporary character of the vision. *Nābî'* ("one who witnesses or testifies") is best adapted to characterize the prophetic mission.

Prophetic Inspiration. The originality of biblical prophecy derives from the phenomenon of inspiration. It is God who invites, summons, and impels the prophet (Jer. 20:7). By inspiration God speaks to the *nābî'*, who has to transmit exactly what God conveys. The mode of inspiration is verbal (Deut. 18:18; Jer. 1:9; cf. Gal. 1:11–12; 1 Cor. 15:1–4; 1 Thess. 2:13; 4:8). Yet inspiration does not suppress individuality.

The Prophets. The writing prophets of the OT are well known. There are four Major Prophets (Isaiah, Jeremiah, Ezekiel, Daniel) and 12 Minor Prophets (Hosea, Joel, Amos, Obadiah, Jonah, Micah, Nahum, Habakkuk, Zephaniah, Haggai, Zechariah, Malachi), classified according to the length of their writings. In addition there were many other prophets. Moses, who wrote the law of God, was regarded as a *nābî'* without equal (Deut. 34:10–12). Prophetic voices were also raised in the days of the judges (Judg. 2:1–5; 3:9–11; 4:4; 6:8; 1 Sam. 3:1). Samuel came as a second Moses (Ps. 99:6; Jer. 15:1), and his work was continued by Gad and Nathan (2 Sam. 12, 24; 1 Kings 1). After the division of the kingdom Ahijah (1 Kings 2), Elijah, and Elisha call for particular mention. After four centuries of prophetic silence John the Baptist is the last of the prophets of the old covenant and the precursor of Jesus (Matt. 19:1; cf. Matt. 3:7–12; Luke 3:16–18; John 1:23, 29). In addition to the Baptist, the NT also refers to a prophetic ministry exercised by both men and women. After Pentecost, mention is made of Agabus (Acts 2:28; 21:10), Jude and Silas (Acts 15:32), and the four daughters of Philip (Acts 21:8–10).

The Prophetic Message. The prophecies of the writing prophets of the OT may be divided into three main groups: (1) Prophecies concerning the internal destiny of Israel declare the judgment of God on the unbelief and iniquities of the people, but promise restoration after the testing period of the exile. (2) Messianic prophecies point to the coming Redeemer of Israel and the world. They attain an astonishing clarity and precision in the case of Micah (5:1) and especially Isaiah. The latter gives us a striking summary of the saving life and work of Christ (52:13–53). (3) Eschatological prophecies refer to the last days when the kingdom of God will be set up on earth.

Prophets and Prophecy of the NT Period. Early Christian prophets (Acts 11:27–28; 15:30–32; 21:10) were powerful persons within the church who spoke the word of the risen Lord with authority. (1) Their presence and activity were widespread (cf. Acts 20:23 with 21:10–11). (2) They worked within the framework of the church, perhaps becoming active only when Christians were at worship (Acts 13:1–2). (3) They ranked in importance second only to the apostles (1 Cor. 12:28–31; Eph. 2:20; 4:11). (4) They belonged to and worked out from bands or brotherhoods that could be considered exclusive groups of charismatics (Acts 11:27; 13:1; 1 Cor. 12:29; Rev. 19:10; 22:9; cf. Barnabas 16:9). (5) They were people whose minds were saturated with the OT Scriptures (Acts 7; cf. Rom. 11:27 with Isa. 27:9; 1 Cor. 15:51, 54–55, with Isa. 25:8; Hos. 13:14). (6) Their ministry was distinguished from that of apostle, miracle worker, and the like (1 Cor. 12:28–29), but closely associated with that of teacher (Acts 13:1; Rev. 2:20). (7) They were people whose words and actions were especially prompted by the Spirit (Acts 11:27–28; 21:11).

A. Lamorte and G. F. Hawthorne

Prophet, Christ as. See Offices of Christ.

Propitiation. The turning away of wrath by an offering. In the NT this idea is conveyed by the use of the Greek terms *hilaskomai* (Heb. 2:17), *hilastērion* (Rom.

3:25), and *hilasmos* (1 John 2:2; 4:10). In the OT the principal Hebrew verb is *kipper*, usually rendered in the LXX by *exilaskomai*. Outside the Bible the word group to which the Greek words belong unquestionably has the significance of averting wrath.

While God's wrath is not mentioned as frequently in the NT as the OT, it is there. Human sin receives its due reward, not because of some impersonal retribution, but because God's wrath is directed against it (Rom. 1:18, 24, 26, 28). The whole of the argument of the opening part of Romans is that all people, Gentiles and Jews alike, are sinners, and that they come under the wrath and the condemnation of God. When Paul turns to salvation, he thinks of Christ's death as *hilastērion* (Rom. 3:25), a means of removing the divine wrath. The paradox of the OT is repeated in the NT that God himself provides the means of removing his own wrath. The love of the Father is shown in that he "sent his Son as an atoning sacrifice [a propitiation] for our sins" (1 John 4:10). The purpose of Christ's becoming "a merciful and faithful high priest" was to "make atonement [propitiation] for the sins of the people" (Heb. 2:17). His propitiation is adequate for all (1 John 2:2).

L. MORRIS

See also ATONEMENT; WRATH OF GOD.

Protestantism. Movement within Christianity that originated in the 16th-century Reformation and later focused in the main traditions of Reformed church life—Lutheran, Reformed (Calvinist/Presbyterian), and Anglican-Episcopalian. The term derives from the "protestation" submitted by a minority of Lutheran and Reformed authorities at the German Imperial Diet at Speyer in 1529 in dissenting from a clamp-down on religious renewal. The "protestation" was at once objection, appeal, and affirmation. Lutherans and other advocates of reform became known as Protestants. The English word originally had the force of "resolute confession, solemn declaration," standing for gospel truth against Roman corruption.

Fundamental Principles. The fundamental principles of 16th-century Protestantism included the following: *Soli Deo Gloria*: the justification of God's wisdom and power against papal usurpation and manmade religion, honoring God's sovereign transcendence and providential predestination. *Sola Gratia*: redemption as God's free gift accomplished by Christ's saving death and resurrection. *Sola Scriptura*: the freedom of Scripture to rule as God's Word in the church, disentangled from papal and ecclesiastical *magisterium* and tradition. *The Church as the Believing People of God*: the church constituted not by hierarchy, succession, or institution, but by God's election and calling in Christ through the gospel. *The Priesthood of All Believers*: the privileged freedom of all the baptized to stand before God in Christ "without patented human intermediaries." *The Sanctity of All Callings or Vocations*: the rejection of medieval distinctions between secular and sacred or "religious" (i.e., monastic) with the depreciation of the former, and the recognition of all ways of life as divine vocations.

Protestant Developments. Protestantism has developed a distinctive ethos in each of the several traditions derived from the Reformation and also within their historical, cultural, and geographical variations. On some issues, such as the manner (not the reality) of Christ's presence in the Supper, Protestants have disagreed from a very early stage, while agreeing in rejecting transubstantiation and the sacrifice of the Mass and insisting that living faith alone feeds upon Christ's flesh and blood. On others, such as church order, diversity of practice has not always involved disagreement in principle.

Another pattern of Reformation in the 16th century, generally called Anabaptist or Radical despite its diversity, sought to restore the precise shape of apostolic Christianity. Pentecostalism has a similar aim, along with other movements, including some Baptists and (Plymouth) Brethren. Some African Independent churches have pursued a restorationist approach even to the OT. Although Anabaptism gave birth to no major Protestant tradition (but note the Mennonites), its rejection of the Constantinian state-church and all its works (endorsed unreservedly by all three primary Protestant traditions) became in time the common property of most of Protestantism, especially outside Europe.

Despite its divisions the community of Protestantism is still discernible in cross-denominational movements—missionary expansion, Bible translation, biblical criticism and modern theological study, welfare and relief agencies, and the ecumenical movement itself. Protestants are also held together by common convictions, chief among them the acceptance of the Reformation as an indispensable part of their history. Protestantism's scriptural principle finds expression in the axiom *Ecclesia reformata sed semper reformand* ("a church reformed but always open to further reformation"). Subjection to the Word of God means that no traditions or institutions, secular or religious, not even Reformation or Protestant ones, can be absolutized. Finally, Protestantism seeks to draw its life from the gospel of God's grace in Christ. True to its heritage it can tolerate no do-it-yourself Christianity, no ground for human self-confidence before God's face. It will ultimately always value the Christ of faith more than the church of history.

D. F. WRIGHT

See also REFORMATION, PROTESTANT.

Providence of God. The doctrine of providence may be viewed from three different aspects. (1) The creation is the stage on which are enacted God's dealings with humankind. Providence is God's gracious outworking of his purpose in Christ that issues in his dealings with humankind. We are not at this point slipping over into the doctrine of predestination, but are saying that from the beginning God has ordered the course of events toward Jesus Christ and his incarnation. From the biblical point of view world history and personal life stories possess significance only in the light of the incarnation. (2) According to Acts 14:17; 17:22–30 and Rom. 1:18–23, God's providence bears witness to God among the heathen. (3) The God who gives life also preserves it. God is not a God of the soul alone, but of the body also. In Matt. 6:25–34 the disciples are reminded (by their Creator himself) of their creaturely relationship to God, and are freed from all anxiety about their earthly future. In sum, the doctrine of providence tells us that the world and our lives are not ruled by chance or by fate but by God, who explicates his purposes of providence in the incarnation of his Son.

T. H. L. PARKER

Psychology and Christianity. Throughout history people have reflected on human thoughts and behavior and have attempted to make sense out of these. Psychology has been a distinct discipline, however, only since the last half of the 19th century. Since then it has quickly grown to a position of considerable importance and visibility.

The Pre-1900 Era. Long before psychology developed as a separate discipline from philosophy, Christianity was actively involved in the study, development, and understanding of psychology. Such work is to be found in the theological study of the soul, an important topic in theology since earliest times. Tertullian's 3d-century *De anima* is a good early example. The works of John Flavel in the 17th century and of Jonathan Edwards in the 18th century made particularly strong contributions, worthy of the careful study of any modern Christian interested in psychology. Franz Delitzsch's *System of Biblical Psychology* might represent the capstone of this tradition.

1900 to the Present. The end of the first era was clearly tied to the emergence of psychology as a separate discipline and, in particular, its scientific emphasis. Empiricism, determinism, relativism, and reductionism became the major characteristics of modern psychology, and Christians felt immediately alienated from the discipline. Freud's reductionistic views of religion were particularly offensive and threatening. Added to this was the rise of radical behaviorism as led by John B. Watson and B. F. Skinner. Psychology seemed less and less relevant to theology, and the fruitful interaction of Christians with psychological topics that characterized previous centuries came to a rather abrupt halt.

It has been hard for Christians not to respond to such challenges defensively. To many, psychology has seemed the enemy of the faith. Similarly, believers have come to regard many psychologists as enemies of personal well-being. Rather than viewing psychology as the enemy, with irreconcilable differences between the two realms, others maintain that there is much common ground between the two. Christians whose writings reflect this position include Seward Hiltner and John Sanford. Proponents of such a view have been influential in breaking down much of the mistrust of Christians toward psychology. Because they have tended to come from theologically liberal religious traditions, however, many conservative Christians have remained unconvinced.

Closely associated with these developments has been a movement within conservative Protestant Christianity identified by the catch phrase "the integration of psychology and theology." The integrationists have begun with an assumption of the unity of truth. They expect that all knowledge can be interrelated into a single body of truth that will represent a harmonizing of biblical revelation and psychology. Paul Tournier and Gary Collins are two well-known writers in this tradition. The *Journal of Psychology and Theology* and the *Journal of Psychology and Christianity* contain the writings of many more.

Current Status. Recently there has been an enormous thawing in the climate of mistrust between Christianity and psychology. Christian pastors, often having received some training in pastoral counseling during seminary, are now much more open to use the services of psychologists (particularly Christian psychologists) and to see that psychological insights can be beneficial to their ministry. Young Christian psychologists now have the option of training in a Christian context that explicitly addresses the integration of psychology and theology and usually includes some formal study of theology. All of this has resulted in an upsurge of publications on the relationship between Christianity and psychology.

D. G. BENNER

See also PSYCHOLOGY OF RELIGION.

Psychology of Religion. Religion has provided an important focus for applied psychology in the past century. Currently there is keen interest in the understanding of religious phenomena from the viewpoint of contemporary psychology, that is, the scientific study of religion from a social science perspective. Such aspects as the origins, the motivations, the expressions, the dynamics, the development, and the effects of religion are popular topics. Broadly defined as the scientific study of faith and/or religion using psychological methods, the psychology of religion is a rich and diverse field that has much to offer individuals concerned with more fully understanding human nature and behavior. The psychology of religion is of particular interest to many Christians in the mental health disciplines.

Definitions. Psychology can be understood as a group of generic efforts to study human behavior scientifically. Religion can be understood in terms of either its functional or substantive definition. The functional definition of religion emphasizes the process wherein humans attempt to answer the enigmas and meaning of life through faith. The substantive definition of religion stresses the product of faith wherein those who gather themselves together around a transpersonal idea are labeled religious. Considerable tension within the field is due to the failure to clarify the manner in which psychology and/or religion is being perceived.

There have been a variety of ways in which psychology and religion have been related, distinguishable by the preposition used to tie the terms together. The psychology *of* religion is defined as either the effort to reduce religion to psychological dynamics or the attempt to more fully understand the significance of these processes for religion. Psychology *through* religion is the reverse of the foregoing, whereby religion or normative analysis of human nature informs the psychological understanding of persons. The psychology *with* religion approach is best understood as an effort to offer psychological and religious interpretation of the same phenomena without engaging in reductionism. Finally, the psychology *for/against* religion perspective is defined as the attempt to use psychology either to authenticate or to invalidate religion. All these approaches are distinguishable in the large literature in the field.

History and Trends. The field can best be understood in terms of three phases: (1) the "psychology of religion" movement, which flourished from 1880 to 1930. Conversion and religious experience were the most frequently studied topics. Perhaps the most significant work to come out of the movement was William James' *Varieties of Religious Experience.* (2) The "pastoral psychology" movement, which began in the 1920s and is still strong; and (3) the "psychology and religion" movement, which can be traced back to the publication of Gordon Allport's *Individual and His Religion* (1950). This approach is concerned with exploring areas of mutual concern to both theologians and psychologists (e.g., moral development, maturity, dimensions of religiosity, altruism, prejudice).

Methodology. Psychology has become an enormously sophisticated enterprise methodologically. Techniques of data collection have been varied, but foremost among these have been the use of questionnaires, interviews, analysis of biographical material, the use of introspection, direct observation, psychological testing, experimental manipulation, participant-observer study, and longitudinal or cross-sectional analysis of attitudes and/or behavior.

Orientations to Religion. People differ widely in the way they think about religion, the importance they place on it, and the reasons they state for being religious. Numerous scales have been developed to assess religious orientation. Researchers argue that it is not enough to state that someone is religious unless one attempts to clarify the precise manner in which an individual incorporates or introjects those beliefs.

Psychodynamics and Religion. Researchers ask: How does one's emotionality interact with one's religious faith commitment, and vice versa? What kinds of persons are religious? How do persons differ with respect to personalities, traits, and underlying attitudes in light of their religious commitments? Then conversion has been extensively studied since the beginnings of the psychology of religion movement. A recent work by two evangelical psychologists (Johnson and Malony, 1982) is an example of the sophisticated work being done today by theologically informed and psychologically sensitive researchers. The model they propose to understand the conversion process merits serious attention.

Religious Experience. Researchers ask: How does one decide if what he is experiencing is religious? Is there such a thing as a special religious sense? How does one understand being religious?

Religious Development. A final theme in the psychology of religion has been the function of faith throughout the life span. Elkind has written extensively on the origins of religion in the child, Oraker on the religiosity of adolescents, Feldman on changes and stability of religious orientations in college, and Clippinger on adult religious behavior. But perhaps the most significant recent proposal on faith development has been J. Fowler's *Stages of Faith* (1981), a six-stage model of the development of faith throughout the life span. An emerging theme in the developmental literature is the nature of mature religion, and those factors that facilitate its development or retard its realization.

Conclusion. Religion is more than mere psychological dynamics. Yet the behavioral sciences provide us with many insights into the multifaceted nature of faith.

The psychology of religion, then, attempts to bring into the scientific study of religion and/or faith a mutual respect for the insights of both theology and psychology in order to more fully understand human nature and behavior.

R. E. Butman

See also Psychology and Christianity.

Punishment, Everlasting. See Eternal Punishment.

Purgative Way, The. Teaching embodied in the classic Christian mystical tradition, especially John of the Cross and Teresa of 'Avila, that before one can receive the vision of God one must first purify oneself from all sin and spiritual hindrances.

P. H. Davids

See also Illuminative Way, The; Unitive Way, The.

Purgatory. Roman Catholic and Greek Orthodox concept of an intermediate realm where all those who die at peace with the church but who are not perfect must undergo penal and purifying suffering. Only those believers who have attained a state of Christian perfection are said to go immediately to heaven. The great mass of partially sanctified Christians dying in fellowship with the church but nevertheless encumbered with some degree of sin go to purgatory where, for a longer or shorter time, they suffer until all sin is purged away, after which they are translated to heaven.

L. Boettner

See also Intermediate State; Limbo.

Purification. Israel, chosen by a holy Jehovah to be his people, was required to be holy (Lev. 11:44–45; 19:2; 21:26). Under the Mosaic legislation the holiness of Israel was from the first recognized as moral separation from sin (Lev. 20:22–26), but it was expressed outwardly by separation from objects designated as unclean. Israelites who had contracted uncleanness had to separate themselves from the congregation, the length of time depending on the nature of the uncleanness (see Lev. 12; 15:11–13; Num. 5:2–3). They were to wash themselves in water, and for the more serious forms of uncleanness they were required to offer sacrifice (e.g., Lev. 12:6). As revelation progressed, the concept of holiness deepened. Ps. 51:7 and Ezek. 36:25 both use terms drawn from the purification ritual to describe the cleansing of the heart from sin. The NT writers confine purification to cleansing from sin through the blood of Christ (Heb. 1:3; 9:14; 1 John 1:7;) and interpret OT ritual as foreshadowing this cleansing (Heb. 9:13–14, 23).

D. B. KNOX

Puritanism. Loosely organized reform movement originating during the English Reformation of the 16th century. The name came from efforts to "purify" the Church of England by those who felt that the Reformation had not yet been completed. Eventually the Puritans went on to attempt purification of the self and of society as well.

History. From William Tyndale (d. 1536), the Puritans adopted an intense commitment to Scripture and a theology that emphasized the concept of covenant; from John Knox they absorbed a dedication to thorough reform in church and state; and from John Hooper (d. 1555) they received a determined conviction that Scripture should regulate ecclesiastical structure and personal behavior alike. Puritans achieved a measure of public acceptance in the early years of Queen Elizabeth's reign. They then suffered a series of reverses that lasted through the reigns of her successors James I and Charles I. In the days of James I some Puritans grew discouraged about their reforming efforts and separated entirely from the Church of England. These Separatists included the "Pilgrims," who, after a sojourn in Holland, established the Plymouth Colony in what is now southeastern Massachusetts in 1620.

When Charles I attempted to rule England without Parliament and its many Puritan members, and when he tried systematically to root Puritans out of the English church, a larger, less separatistic body emigrated to Massachusetts Bay (1630), where for the first time Puritans had the opportunity to construct churches and a society reflecting their grasp of the Word of God. In England other Puritans continued the struggle for reform. When war with Scotland forced Charles I to recall Parliament in 1640, civil war was the ultimate result. That conflict ended with the execution of the king (1649), the rise of Oliver Cromwell to the protectorate of England, the production of the Westminster Confession and catechisms, and the erection of a Puritan Commonwealth. Yet Cromwell, for all his abilities, found it impossible to establish a Puritan state. After his death (1658), the people of England asked the son of Charles I to return, a restoration marking the collapse of organized Puritanism in England. Across the Atlantic a vital Puritanism survived only a little longer. By the time of Cotton Mather (d. 1728) Indian warfare, the loss of the original Massachusetts charter, and a growing secularization had brought an end to Puritanism as a way of life in America.

Convictions. Puritanism generally extended the thought of the English Reformation, with distinctive emphases on four convictions: (1) that personal salvation was entirely from God, (2) that the Bible provided the indispensable guide to life, (3) that the church should reflect the express teaching of Scripture, and (4) that society was one unified whole.

The reason that Puritan beliefs concerning salvation, Scripture, and the church created such upheaval was their fourth basic conviction, that God had sanctioned the solidarity of society. Most Puritans believed that a single, coordinated set of authorities should govern life in society. The result was that Puritans sought nothing less than to make all England Puritan. Only late during the Puritan Commonwealth did ideas of toleration and of what is known today as pluralism arise, but these ideas were combated by most Puritans themselves and firmly set to rest for another generation by the restoration of Charles II.

From a modern vantage point the intolerance entailed by a unified view of society has harmed the Puritans' reputation. From a more disinterested perspective it is possible also to see great advantages. The Puritans succeeded in bursting the bonds of mere religiosity in their efforts to serve God. Puritanism was one of the moving forces in the rise of the English Parliament in the early 17th century. For good and for ill, it provided a foundation for the first great political revolution in modern times. It gave immigrants to Massachusetts a social vision whose comprehensively Christian character has never been matched in America. And, for such a putatively uncreative movement, it liberated vast energies in literature as well.

Notable Puritans. The Puritans enjoyed a great number of forceful preachers and teachers. William Ames explained "the doctrine of living to God" in *The Marrow of Theology*, a book used as a text during the first 50 years of Harvard College. The sermons and tracts of William Perkins outlined with sympathy the steps that a repentant sinner should take to find God. John Preston preached the severity of God's law and the wideness of his mercy fearlessly in the courts of James I and Charles I. John Owen, adviser to Cromwell and vice-chancellor of the University of Oxford, wrote theological treatices on the atonement and on the Holy Spirit that still influence Calvinistic thought in the English-speaking world. His contemporary, Richard Baxter, published nearly 200 works expounding the virtues of theological moderation and the truths of what C. S. Lewis would call "mere Christianity." In America, Boston's John Cotton labored to present God's glory in conversion, and Hartford's Thomas Hooker glorified God in the labors of the converted.

Important as the contributions of ministers were, the greatest contribution of Puritans to Christian history probably resided with its laypersons. The English-speaking world has never seen such a cluster of thoroughly Christian political leaders as the Lord Protector Oliver Cromwell, the governor of Massachusetts John Winthrop, or the governor of Plymouth William Bradford. These leaders erred, perhaps often, but they devoted their lives to public service, self-consciously and whole-heartedly, out of deepest gratitude to the God of their salvation.

Evaluation. The Puritans resemble other groups in Christian history who, in forsaking all for God, have won back not only God but much of the world as well. They stand with the early Franciscans, the Protestant Reformers, the Jesuits, the Anabaptists, the early Methodists, and the Reformed Dutch of the late 19th century who, in their own separate ways, were transfixed by the glories of redemption and who went far in redeeming the world around themselves. With these groups the Puritans also verified the truth of the gospel words: they sought first the kingdom of God and his righteousness, and much more was added to them besides.

M. A. Noll

Pusey, Edward Bouverie (1800–1882). Leader of the Tractarian movement in the Church of England. Pusey was also Regius Professor of Hebrew at Oxford. His initial opposition to liberalism was expressed by his active involvement in the Tractarian movement from its inception in 1833. When Newman and others, sensing the hostility to their program in much of the Church of England, entered the Roman Catholic Church in 1845, Pusey was the acknowledged leader of the remaining Tractarians, who were often called Puseyites. His conservatism was further evidenced by his espousal of verbal inspiration, clearly evidenced in his famous commentaries on Daniel and the Minor Prophets.

I. S. RENNIE

See also KEBLE, JOHN; NEWMAN, JOHN HENRY; OXFORD MOVEMENT.

Qq

Quakers. See Friends, Society of.

Quicunque Vult. See Athanasian Creed.

Quietism. Emphasis on human inactivity and passivity that accompanies the mystic experience. More specifically, the term refers to a manifestation of Roman Catholic mysticism in the 17th and 18th centuries. This movement was inspired by the teachings of Miguel de Molinos, for whom the goal of Christian experience was the perfect rest of the soul in God. Molinos was accused of despising Christian virtue and of moral aberration because he believed that in a state of contemplation the soul is unaffected by either good works or sin. The Jesuits led the attack on his doctrine, claiming that it was an exaggerated and unhealthy form of mysticism. Through their efforts he was arrested and imprisoned. Despite opposition quietism spread to France, where it found an outstanding proponent in Madame Guyon whose teaching, elaborated in *A Short and Easy Method of Prayer*, emphasized passive prayer as the major Christian activity.

R. G. Clouse

See also Guyon, Madame; Mysticism; Spirituality.

Quimby, Phineas Parkhurst. See Church of Christ, Scientist; Eddy, Mary Baker.

Qumran. See Dead Sea Scrolls.

Rr

Racovian Catechism (1605). Catechism prepared by the followers of Faustus Socinus and one of the earliest statements of anti-Trinitarian belief. The Racovian Catechism was published in Polish in Racov, Poland. The catechism was divided into eight sections and was intended more as a collection of beliefs than a confessional creed. Christ was represented in it as more than a great man, but not divine until after his resurrection.

P. KUBRICHT

See also SOCINUS, FAUSTUS.

Radical Reformation. All reforming elements not identified with the magisterial Reformation. The Radical Reformation is also known as the Left Wing of the Reformation and the Third Reformation. Common to all its participants were disappointment with moral aspects of territorial Protestantism and the rejection of some of its doctrines and institutions. While various interlocking historical connections and doctrinal variations limit the validity of typological and ideological classifications, three main groupings of radicals have been identified: Anabaptists, spiritualists, and evangelical rationalists.

Anabaptists. The Anabaptist movement had a varied cast of characters. From it has evolved the Free Church tradition. Anabaptist origins are to be sought in the circle of Conrad Grebel, which left Zwingli's reformation when Zwingli compromised its biblical basis. From Zurich the movement was spread by missionaries from Switzerland to Austria and Moravia, South Germany, and the Low Countries.

Swiss Anabaptism. Anabaptism in Switzerland developed from Zwingli's early supporters. These future radicals included the Grebel circle, which gathered in the home of Andreas Castelberger for Bible study, and priests from the outlying towns of Zurich. For different reasons the urban and rural radicals became disillusioned with Zwingli's reform. The rebaptisms that occurred first on Jan. 21, 1525, and from which come the name "Anabaptism," originally expressed an anticlerical opposition to civil and religious authority outside of the local parish rather than a Free Church theological concept. The Schleitheim Articles of 1527, edited by Michael Sattler, consolidated this Swiss Anabaptism.

South German Anabaptism. In spite of the mutual practice of adult baptism, Anabaptism in South Germany was a quite different movement from the Swiss Brethren. It stems from the reformulation of ideas from Thomas Münzer by Hans Hut and Hans Denck (ca. 1500–27).

Denck's concept of inner transformation was pacifist in expression, with focus more on the renewal of individuals than of society. This inner, transforming Christ served Denck as an alternative authority both to the Roman hierarchy and to the learned exegesis of the Reformers. Hut understood the inner transformation to be accomplished through the experience of both inner and outer struggle and suffering. Hut modified Münzer's revolutionary outlook, commanding the transformed believers to keep the revolutionary sword sheathed until God called for it. Unlike the Swiss Brethren, Hut's practice of rebaptism was not to form separated congregations, but rather to mark the elect for the end-time judgment. Hut's movement gradually died out following his death in a jail fire, but his legacy continued in various ways.

Low Countries Anabaptism. The third major Anabaptist movement was planted in the Low Countries by Melchior Hofmann (ca. 1495–1543). He believed in the near inbreaking of God's kingdom into the world, with divine vengeance upon the wicked. The righteous would participate in this judgment, not as agents of vengeance but as witnesses to the coming peace. Hofmann's baptism served to gather the elect into an end-time congregation to build this new Jerusalem. He died after 10 years of imprisonment in Strasbourg. Two lines carried on in transformed fashion the Hofmann legacy. The revolutionary Melchiorites founded the short-lived kingdom of Münster (1534–35), while the pacifist line runs through Menno Simons, whose name 20th-century Mennonites carry. After the fall of Münster, Menno rallied the peaceful Melchiorites as well as the surviving Münsterites disillusioned with violence and developed concepts of the transformation of the individual and of the assembly of a spotless church.

The heirs of the various Anabaptist groups came to recognize their common emphases on the Bible, adult baptism, pacifism, and sense of separation from the state church and worldly society. They had contacts and discussions and divisions. While they never united into one homogeneous body, some sense of unity developed, as represented by the Concept of Cologne signed in 1591 by 15 preachers, the first confession of faith accepted simultaneously by Dutch and High and Low German Mennonites.

Spiritualists. Radicals characterized as spiritualizers downplayed significantly or rejected altogether external forms of church and ceremonies, opting instead for inner communion through the Holy Spirit. Thus, for example, Silesian nobleman Kasper Schwenckfeld held that there had been no correct baptism for 1000 years, and in 1526 he recommended suspension of the observance of the Lord's Supper—the *Stillstand* observed by his followers until 1877—until the question of its proper form could be settled.

Evangelical Rationalists. Other radicals, given significant weight to reason alongside the Scriptures, came to reject aspects of traditional theology, principally in christological and Trinitarian matters. Michael Servetus, burned in Geneva for his views, is a noteworthy example of Anti-Trinitarianism, which attained institutional form in the pacifistic Polish Brethren, later known as Socinians, and in the Unitarian churches in Lithuania and Transylvania.

J. D. WEAVER

See also GREBEL, CONRAD; HUBMAIER, BALTHASAR; MELCHIORITES; MENNO SIMONS; MENNONITES; RACOVIAN CATECHISM; SOCINUS, FAUSTUS; ZWICKAU PROPHETS.

Radical Theology. See DEATH OF GOD THEOLOGY.

Rahner, Karl (1904–). Jesuit theologian. Rahner was one of the leading thinkers behind the Second Vatican Council. In 1949 he formally became a member of the theological faculty at Innsbruck. He moved to Munich in 1964 and taught there from 1967 to 1971.

Rahner's early work in philosophy gives a clear view of the principles underlying his theology. He is committed to a form of transcendental Thomism, which combines the thought of Aquinas with insights from Kant, Hegel, Heidegger, and Rahner's most immediate intellectual predecessor, Joseph Maréchal. The essence of this philosophy is that being is discovered, not in external objectivity, but in the subjectivity of a human knower.

Rahner puts a new face on Christology. He sees Jesus Christ as representing the unique fulfillment of the *potentia obedientialis* within human nature. Thus Rahner attempts to avoid the problem of reconciling the apparent paradox of two natures in Christ; the human nature is inherently open to reception of the divine. Further it enables Rahner to place Christ at the pinnacle of human evolution. It may be observed here that Rahner's humanism needs to be tempered in respect to the fallenness of humanity and the consequences of sin.

W. Corduan

Ramus, Peter (1515–1572). French Protestant philosopher. Ramus presented himself as an educational reformer dedicated to saving Christianity from the errors of Aristotelianism and scholasticism.

Ramus held that all knowledge must be related to God, and having been created by God, the entire spectrum of knowledge (encyclopedia) can be divided into the individual liberal arts. Each liberal art has a particular sphere of knowledge, delineated by a Ramist doctrine known as technometry (Lat. *technometria* or *technologia*). Dialectic is the art of discoursing well, grammar the art of speaking well, and so on. Ramus also applied his ideas to religion in a methodical book, *Commentaries on the Christian Religion* (Lat. ed., 1576). Religion is "the art of living well" and takes its place alongside the other liberal arts. Ramus had his greatest influence among 16th- and 17th-century English Puritans (William Ames, William Perkins) and in New England at Harvard University. Ramus died with other Protestants in the St. Bartholomew's Day Massacre in Paris. Puritans considered him the great Protestant martyr of France.

K. L. Sprunger

See also Scholasticism, Protestant.

Ransom. Metaphor employed by the early church to speak of the saving work of Christ. Jesus uses the metaphor of ransom in Mark 10:45/Matt. 20:28. Paul also states that Christ gave himself as a "ransom for all men" (1 Tim. 2:6). The metaphor of ransom is supported by such concepts as purchasing, price (1 Cor. 6:20), and redemption (1 Pet. 1:18–19). When the NT, therefore, speaks of ransom with reference to the work of Christ, the idea is not one of transaction, as though a deal is arranged and a price is paid. Rather the focus is on the power of the cross to save (1 Cor. 1:18). In the famous ransom saying of Mark 10:45 Jesus speaks of his coming death as the means of release for many. The contrast is between his own solitary death and the deliverance of many. In the NT the terms of ransom and purchase, which in other contexts suggest an economic or financial exchange, speak of the consequences or results (cf. 1 Cor. 7:23). The release is from judgment (Rom. 3:25–26), sin (Eph. 1:7), and death (Rom. 8:2).

R. W. Lyon

See also Atonement, Theories of the; Redeemer, Redemption.

Rapture of the Church. Phrase used by premillennialists to refer to the church being united with Christ at his second coming (from the Lat. *rapio*, "caught up"). The main biblical passage upon which the teaching is based is 1 Thess. 4:15–17.

The major divisions of interpretation of Paul's words center on the relationship of the time of the rapture to the tribulation period, which marks the end of the age. Pretribulationists teach that the church will be removed before this seven-year period and the revelation of the Antichrist. The midtribulationists contend that the church will be raptured during the tribulation after the Antichrist's rise to power but before the severe judgments that prepare the way for Christ's return to establish his rule on earth. The post-tribulationists hold that the church will continue to exist in the world throughout the entire tribulation and will be removed at the end of the period when Christ returns in power.

Pretribulationism and the Origin of the Rapture Debate. Until the early 19th century those believers who discussed the rapture believed it would occur in conjunction with the return of Christ at the end of the tribulation period. It was the contribution of John Nelson Darby to eschatology that led many Christians to teach that the return of Christ would occur in two stages: one for his saints at the rapture and the other with his saints to control the world at the close of the great tribulation. According to this interpretation, between these two events the 70th week predicted by Daniel (9:24–27) would be fulfilled and the Antichrist would come to power. With the church removed from the scene, God would resume his dealings with Israel.

Darby's ideas had a wide influence in Britain and the U.S. Many evangelicals became pretribulationists through the preaching of the interdenominational evangelists of the 19th and 20th centuries. The *Scofield Reference Bible* and the leading Bible institutes and graduate schools of theology such as Dallas Theological Seminary also contributed to the popularity of this view. During the troubled 1960s there was a revival of the pretribulational view on a popular level through the books of Hal Lindsey and the ministries of preachers and Bible teachers who use the electronic media.

The Midtribulation View. This modified view, advocated by Harold John Ockenga and others, involves the limitation of the wrath of God upon the world (Rev. 16–18) to the first three and a half years prior to the battle of Armageddon. Influenced by the repeated mention of three and a half years (42 months) in Dan. 7, 9, and 12 and in Rev. 11 and 12, they argue for a shortened tribulation period. Midtribulationists claim that the rapture is to take place after the fulfillment of certain predicted signs and the preliminary phase of the tribulation as described in Matt. 24:10–27. The event will not be secret but will be accompanied by an impressive display including a loud command and a trumpet call (1 Thess. 4:16; Rev. 11:15; 14:2). This dramatic sign will attract the attention of unsaved people, and when they realize that the Christians have disappeared they will come to Christ in such large numbers that a major revival will take place (Rev. 7:9, 14).

The Post-tribulation View. Many other interpreters are uncomfortable with the sharp distinction that the pretribulationists draw between the church and Israel. Christ, they believe, will return to rapture his saints and establish his millennial rule at the same time. They cite numerous passages that indicate that Christ's second coming must be visible, public, and following the tribulation. This is based upon the fact that much of the advice given to the church in Scripture relative to the last days is meaningless if it does not go through the tribulation. Advocates of the post-tribulation position differ among themselves on the application of the prophetic Scriptures and the details about the return of Christ. John Walvoord has detected four schools of interpretation among their number.

The Partial Rapture Interpretation. A small group of pretribulationists teaches that only those who are faithful in the church will be caught up at the beginning of the tribulation. The rest will be raptured sometime during or at the end of the seven-year period.

R. G. CLOUSE

See also DARBY, JOHN NELSON; DISPENSATION, DISPENSATIONALISM; ESCHATOLOGY; MILLENNIUM, VIEWS OF THE; SECOND COMING OF CHRIST.

Rationalism. Philosophical position that holds that reality is actually rational in nature and that making the proper deductions is essential to achieving knowledge. Such deductive logic and the use of mathematical processes provide the chief methodological tools. Thus, rationalism has often been held in contrast to empiricism. It is usually associated with Enlightenment philosophers such as Descartes, Spinoza, and Leibniz. It is this form of Continental rationalism that is the chief concern of this article.

Innate Ideas. Descartes enumerates different types of ideas, such as those derived from experience, those drawn from reason itself, and those that are innate and thus created in the mind by God. This latter group is a mainstay of rationalistic thought. Innate ideas are those that are the very attributes of the human mind, inborn by God. As such these "pure" ideas are known a priori by all humans, and are thus believed by all. Descartes maintains that, without innate ideas, no other data could be known.

Epistemology. Rationalists had much to say about knowledge and how one might gain certainty. They usually asserted that God was the ultimate guarantee of knowledge. Perhaps the best example of this conclusion is found in the philosophy of Descartes. Beginning with the reality of doubt he determines to accept nothing of which he cannot be certain. At least one reality, however, can be deduced from this doubt: *he* is doubting and must therefore exist. In the words of his famous dictum, "I think, therefore I am."

From the realization that he doubts, Descartes concludes that he is a dependent, finite being. He then proceeds to the existence of God via forms of the ontological and cosmological arguments. In meditations 3–4 of his *Meditations on First Philosophy* Descartes argues that his idea of God as infinite and independent is a clear and distinct argument for God's existence. In fact, Descartes concludes that the human mind is not capable of knowing anything more certainly than God's existence. A finite being is not capable of explaining the presence of the idea of an infinite God apart from his necessary existence.

Next Descartes concludes that since God is perfect, he cannot deceive finite beings. Furthermore, Descartes's own facilities for judging the world around him were given him by God and hence will not be misleading. The result is that whatever we can deduce by clear and distinct thinking (such as that found in mathematics) concerning the world and others must therefore be true. Thus the necessary existence of God both makes knowledge possible and guarantees truth concerning those facts that can be clearly delineated. Beginning with the reality of doubt Descartes proceeds to his own existence, to God, to the physical world.

This rationalistic methodology, and the stress on mathematics in particular, was an important influence on the rise of modern science during this period. Galileo held some essentially related ideas, especially in his concept of nature as being mathematically organized and perceived as such through reason.

Biblical Criticism. Of the many areas in which the influence of rationalistic thought was felt, higher criticism of the Scriptures is certainly one that is relevant to the study of contemporary theological trends. Spinoza not only rejected the inerrancy and propositional nature of special revelation in the Scriptures, but he was also a forerunner of both

David Hume and some of the English deists who rejected miracles. Spinoza held that miracles, if defined as events that break the laws of nature, do not occur.

Evaluation. Although rationalism was quite influential in many ways, it was also strongly criticized by scholars who noticed a number of weak points. First, Locke, Hume, and the empiricists never tired of attacking the concept of innate ideas. Second, empiricists also asserted that reason could not be the only (or even the primary) means of achieving knowledge when so much is gathered by the senses. Third, reason alone leads to too many contradictions, metaphysical and otherwise. For example, Descartes's dualism, Spinoza's monism, and Leibniz's monadology have all been declared as being absolutely knowable, in the name of rationalism. Fourth, rebuttals to rationalistic and deistic higher criticism appeared quickly from such able scholars as John Locke, Thomas Sherlock, Joseph Butler, and William Paley. Special revelation and miracles were especially defended against attack.

G. R. HABERMAS

See also DEISM; DESCARTES, RENÉ; ENLIGHTENMENT, THE; LEIBNIZ, GOTTFRIED WILHELM; SPINOZA, BENEDICT DE.

Rauschenbusch, Walter (1861–1918). American clergyman and "father of the social gospel." In 1886 he became pastor of New York City's largely immigrant Second German Baptist Church, which was located on the lower East Side in an area aptly called Hell's Kitchen. What Rauschenbusch saw there of the immigrants' sordid living conditions, of labor exploitation by industrial giants, and of government indifference to the suffering of the poor led him to rethink his religious categories.

When Rauschenbusch returned to Rochester in 1897 as a professor at the seminary, he did not forget his New York experience. His first book, *Christianity and the Social Crisis* (1907), was his response to America's social crisis. It was an immediate sensation. In subsequent books Rauschenbusch fleshed out the contours of a social gospel. *Christianizing the Social Order* (1912) contained his most sustained criticism of American capitalism which, according to Rauschenbusch, blinded its practitioners to human needs in a drive for profit, tyrannized over the weak and defenseless, and fostered values through mass marketing that debased the spirit. In the place of capitalism, he called for a social order characterized by justice, collective ownership of most property, democracy in the organization of industry, and a much more equal distribution of goods. Rauschenbusch frequently called himself a Christian socialist, but he also took pains to disavow Marxist formulas for reconstructing American economic life. His last major work, *A Theology for the Social Gospel* (1917), appeared shortly before his death. It set out systematically a Christian theology to address the needs of modern society. He was undoubtedly the most influential American Christian thinker in the first third of the 20th century.

M. A. NOLL

See also LIBERALISM, THEOLOGICAL; SOCIAL GOSPEL, THE.

Reader. See MINOR ORDERS.

Realism. Theory of knowledge that maintains that "universals" (general concepts representing the common elements belonging to individuals of the same genus or species) have a separate existence apart from individual objects. It stands in contrast to nominalism, which holds that universals have no reality apart from their existence in the thought of an individual. Plato's insistence that there is a realm of universals above the material universe as real as individual objects themselves had a great influence on medieval thought. Realism had a great effect on the "natural theology" of medieval scholasticism. It affected both the method of demonstration and the shape of resulting theological dogmas. One notes its influence to a lesser extent after the Reformation in both Roman Catholic Neo-Thomist circles and among Protestants who emphasize the "unity" of the human race in the passing on of original sin.

D. A. Rausch

See also Anselm of Canterbury; Duns Scotus, John; Nominalism; Thomas Aquinas.

Realism, Scottish. See Scottish Realism.

Realized Eschatology. Eschatological position that maintains that the heart of Jesus' message was not the future kingdom, but that the kingdom of God was already realized in his ministry. This concept should be contrasted with futurist or thoroughgoing eschatology, in which the teaching of Jesus about the kingdom of God is viewed as significantly influenced by Jewish apocalyptic. While Continental scholarship has focused on the latter, the Anglo-American tradition has often urged that the futurist aspects of the kingdom be reduced to a bare minimum.

C. H. Dodd is often identified with realized eschatology because of his epoch-making challenge to the apocalyptic interpreters of Jesus. Dodd's chief contribution was *The Parables of the Kingdom* (1935), in which he examined various texts that spoke of the kingdom as already present. This does not mean that Jesus merely pointed to the sovereignty of God in human history and labeled this the kingdom, but rather that Jesus viewed the kingdom as arriving in an unparalleled, decisive way. The eschatological power of God had come into effective operation within his present life and was released through his death.

Realized eschatology has been subject to many criticisms. Most interpreters have argued for a synthesis of realized and futurist components in eschatology. Dodd convincingly demonstrated that Jesus' appearance brought to bear on history an eschatological crisis in the present; history, however, still awaits its consummation in the future, when the kingdom will come in apocalyptic power.

G. M. Burge

See also Eschatology.

Real Presence. Theologically, the word "real" indicates a particular form or understanding of the presence of Christ in the sacrament of communion in terms of realist philosophy. On this view, the so-called substance of Christ's body is a reality apart from its "accidents" or specific physical manifestations.

G. W. Bromiley

See also Concomitance; Lord's Supper, Views of; Transubstantiation.

Reason. Capacity of the human intellect to carry out organized mental activity such as the association of ideas, induction and deduction of inferences, or value judgments. Biblically, the existence of an efficacious human reason is assumed. There has been a wide diversity of opinions within systematic theology, however, on the capabilities of reason, particularly in comparison with the faculty of faith.

Throughout the history of the church few theologians have espoused pure rationalism, namely, the idea that pure reason can without benefit of faith deduce all Christian truth. In the few instances where this approach may have been used (e.g., Socinianism, deism, Hegelianism), technical heresies were almost invariably the direct consequence. Guarding against potential abuse of reason has led a significant array of Christian thinkers to disparage reason strongly, often specifically by attacking the systematic expression of reason in a philosophical system. Tertullian asked the celebrated question, "What has Athens to do with Jerusalem?" Many noted writers utilizing a Platonic expression of Christian theology have held to the clear precedence of faith over reason. "I believe that I may understand," was the slogan attributed to Augustine of Hippo and adopted by Anselm of Canterbury. Aquinas and his disciples have attempted to maintain a delicately balanced view on reason and faith. Reason is seen here as a viable avenue of Christian knowledge, but it is far from omnicompetent.

Despite all of this diversity, however, it is possible to formulate some principles that should be generally valid within all of conservative Christian theology.

(1) Human reason is capable of fulfilling certain tasks.

(2) Human reason is finite. There are some tasks that human reason cannot fulfill because of its limitations. Our reason stands in contrast to the divine intellect with its omniscience.

(3) Human reason is affected by sin (Rom. 1:20–23).

(4) The recognition that we are lost and need to place our faith in Jesus Christ as the sole source of salvation is a reasonable one. But salvation does not occur until we actually exercise our will and believe in Christ. Thus, contrary to a Gnostic scheme, redemption can never be due simply to a mental activity.

(5) One of the goals of the Christian life is the renewing of the mind (Rom. 12:2). Hence as we grow in Christ, our reasoning becomes increasingly captive to the Spirit of God.

W. Corduan

Rebaptism. During the 2d century, the church in Asia Minor, faced with considerable heresy, refused to recognize the validity of heretical baptism. Converts to the orthodox faith from heretical groups were accordingly rebaptized. The church at Rome, however, took the position that the rite of baptism was valid when properly performed, that is, with the correct formula and with the right intention, despite the erroneous views of its administrator. The Roman position was endorsed by the Council of Arles (314) and was championed by Augustine in his controversy with the Donatists. The Council of Trent (1545–63), in its fourth canon on baptism, reaffirmed the Catholic position. In Reformation times the Anabaptists insisted on baptism for those who had been baptized in infancy, and this has continued to be the position of the Baptist churches.

E. F. Harrison

Recapitulation. (Lat. *recapitulatio;* Gk. *anakephalaiosis*; a "summing up") Doctrine derived from Eph. 1:10 that holds (1) that Christ retraced the steps of Adam and humanity; and (2) that Christ comprehended in himself the whole of humanity. The doctrine of recapitulation is especially associated with Irenaeus, although later authors picked up its themes. The doctrine was especially important in the context of the Gnostic controversy because it emphasized the reality of the incarnation, the unity of humankind, and the certainty of redemption.

E. Ferguson

See also Irenaeus.

Reconciliation. Change of attitude or relationship. Paul speaks of a wife's reconciliation to her husband (1 Cor. 7:11), Jews and Gentiles becoming reconciled to each other in being reconciled to God (Eph. 2:14–22), and the alienated, divisive elements of a fragmented universe brought together again under one head (Christ) (Eph. 1:10; Col. 1:20). His illustrations include those far off made nigh, strangers made fellow citizens of the household, and dividing walls removed. His testimony to reconciliation's results dwells especially upon peace with God (Rom. 5:1; Eph. 2:14; Col. 1:20); access to God's presence (Rom. 5:2; Eph. 2:18; 3:12; see Col. 1:22) in place of estrangement; joy in God replacing the dread of "wrath" (Rom. 5:9, 11); and assurance that God is for us, not against us (Rom. 8:31). Since a right relationship with God is the heart of all religion, reconciliation, which makes access welcome and fellowship possible, may be regarded as the central concept in Christianity.

Our sense of estrangement from God witnesses to a barrier on God's side, precluding fellowship—not, certainly, any reluctance in God's mind, that Jesus must change, but a moral, even judicial, barrier that requires the death of Jesus, not merely his message or example, to remove. In the NT the basis of reconciliation is the death of Christ on the cross (Rom. 5:10; Eph. 2:16; Col. 1:20, 22), who became sin for us (2 Cor. 5:18, 21). "God was reconciling the world to himself in Christ" (2 Cor. 5:19), an accomplished fact that we are urged to accept. "We have now received reconciliation" (Rom. 5:11). As Christ is our peace; as we are reconciled by his death; as God presented Christ as an atoning sacrifice (Rom. 3:25); and as the sin that separates is ours, not God's—only God *could* reconcile.

R. E. O. White

See also Atonement; Man, Old and New; Paul, Theology of; Propitiation.

Rector. See Church Officers.

Redeemer, Redemption. Although closely related to the concept of salvation, redemption is more specific, for it denotes the means by which salvation is achieved, namely, by the payment of a ransom. As in the case of salvation it may denote temporal, physical deliverance.

In the OT. In Israel both property and life could be redeemed by making the appropriate payment. God's deliverance of his people from Egypt is spoken of as a redemption (Exod. 6:6; 15:13); he is Israel's Redeemer (Ps. 78:35). The language of redemption is used in connection with Israel's release from captivity in Babylon (Jer. 31:11; 50:33–34). The occurrence of numerous passages in the OT where redemption is stated in terms that do not explicitly include the element of ransom has led some scholars to conclude that redemption came to mean deliverance without any insistence upon a ransom as a condition or basis. The manifestation of the power of God in the deliverance of his people seems at times to be the sole emphasis (Deut. 9:26). On the other hand there is no hint in the direction of the exclusion of a ransom. The ransom idea may well be an assumed factor that is kept in the background by the very prominence given to the element of power needed for the deliverance.

In the NT. This observation affords the necessary bridge to the NT use of the term "redemption." Certain passages in the Gospels reflect this somewhat vague use of the word as implying divine intervention in behalf of God's people without specific reference to any ransom to be paid (Luke 2:38; 24:21). Mark 10:45, although it does not contain the word "redeem," is a crucial passage for the subject, because it records Jesus' conception of his mission. His life of ministry would terminate in an act of self-sacrifice, which would serve as a ransom for the many who needed it. The most complete development of the doctrine in the NT comes in the writings of Paul. Christ has redeemed us from the curse of the law (Gal. 3:13; 4:5; Gk. *exagorazein* in both cases). In Paul's most concentrated section on the work of Christ he couples redemption with justification and propitiation (Rom. 3:24; cf. 1 Cor. 1:30). One prominent feature of Paul's usage is the double reference to the word—with a present application to the forgiveness of sins based on the ransom price of the shed blood of Christ (Eph. 1:7; cf. 1 Pet. 1:18–19), and a future application to the deliverance of the body from its present debility and liability to corruption (Rom. 8:23).

E. F. HARRISON

See also MESSIAH; SALVATION.

Redemption, General. See ATONEMENT, EXTENT OF THE.

Redemption, Particular. See ATONEMENT, EXTENT OF THE.

Reformation, Protestant. Wide-ranging movement of religious renewal in Europe occurring primarily in the 16th century but anticipated by earlier reform initiatives—the Waldensians in the Alpine regions, Wycliffe and Lollardy in England, and the Hussites in Bohemia. Although inseparable from its historical context—political (the emergent nation-states and the tactical interplay of forces and interests in Imperial Germany and in the loose Swiss Confederation), socioeconomic (particularly urban growth, with expanding trade, the transition to a money economy, and new technologies, notably printing, promoting a new assertive middle class, alongside persistent peasant discontents), and intellectual (chiefly the Renaissance, especially in the Christian humanism of northern Europe)—it was fundamentally religious in motivation and objective.

Luther was no doubt the most important of the early Reformers. Yet he borrowed much from Erasmus. In fact, most Reformers were trained humanists, skilled in the ancient languages, grounded in biblical and patristic sources, and enlightened by Erasmus's pioneer Greek NT (1516). Although Luther's thought proved to have a catalytic effect throughout Europe, reform was astir in numerous centers. Probably independent in origin was Zwingli's radical reform in Zurich, provoking the thoroughgoing Anabaptist radicalism of the Swiss Brethren. Strasbourg under Bucer's leadership illustrated a mediating pattern of reform, while Geneva, reformed under Berne's tutelage, had by mid-century become an influential missionary center, exporting Calvinism to France, the Netherlands, Scotland, and elsewhere. Much of Germany and Scandinavia followed Luther's (or perhaps Melanchthon's) Lutheranism, while England welcomed a welter of Continental currents, at first more Lutheran, later more Reformed, to energize indigenous Lollard undercurrents.

Protestant Objections. The Reformers' target may be generally described as degenerate late medieval Catholicism, over against which they set the faith of the apostles and the early fathers. There was proliferating abuse, both theological and practical, connected with penance, satisfactions, and the treasury of merit. These practices were the basis of indulgences, to which were directed Luther's Ninety-Five Theses with their pivotal affirmation that "the true treasure of the Church is the most holy gospel of the glory and grace of God." The Reformers attacked the false basis for papal authority. They also challenged the Church's refusal to allow laypersons access to the Scriptures. The Reformers maintained a tireless polemic against monasticism, one of the most prominent features of Latin Christianity. They rejected the distinction between the inferior life of the secular Christian and the higher "religious" world of monk and nun. The mediation of Mary (although not necessarily her perpetual virginity) and the intercession of the saints were denied by the Reformers. Christ alone was exalted as our advocate before God and God's appointed priest to bear our sins and minister to our frailty. By rejecting all but two—baptism and the Lord's Supper—of the seven medieval sacraments, the Reformation liberated the faithful from the power of the priesthood. In response to allegations of innovation and disruption of the church's long-lived unity, the Reformers claimed to be renovators, restorers of the primitive face of the church. Reformation theology was strongly theocentric, and clearly reasserted the distinction between Creator and creation. Confusion between the two blighted medieval doctrine in various spheres—Eucharist, church, papacy—and made its influence felt in other areas, such as mysticism and anthropology.

The Legacy of the Reformation. Quite apart from the varying hues and shades of their theologies, which owe much to different intellectual and religious formations as well as to temperament, sociopolitical setting, and conviction, the Reformers were not agreed on all issues. Most notoriously they parted company on the Lord's Supper.

Separate attention must be paid to the orthodox Anabaptist Radicals whose Reformation was more sweeping than the "new papalism," as they called it, of the magisterial Reformers. Believers' baptism identified and safeguarded the bounds of the church, the gathered community of the covenanted band. As Christendom died out in the West, the attraction of the Radical Reformation option appears in a clearer light.

At times it seemed as though reform-minded Catholics might prevail. Rome thought otherwise, and in theology the Catholic reforms of Trent were in large measure a counter-Protestant reaction. If renewal was more evident elsewhere, in the new Jesuit order, the Spanish mystics, and bishops like Francis of Sales, not until the 20th century and Vatican Council II did the Roman Church take to heart the theological significance of the Reformation.

D. F. WRIGHT

See also COUNTER-REFORMATION; LUTHER, MARTIN; PROTESTANTISM.

Reformed Tradition, The. The term "Reformed" is used to distinguish the Calvinistic from the Lutheran and Anabaptist traditions. The Reformed tradition finds its roots in the theology of Ulrich Zwingli, the first reformer in Zurich, and John Calvin of Geneva, who in his biblical commentaries and pamphlets, but especially in the *Institutes of the Christian Religion,* developed a Protestant theology. Calvin's teachings have been followed by many different individuals and groups who came out of the Reformation down to the present day, but they have not always followed exactly the same line of thinking or development.

The Reformation and the Reformed Tradition. The first line of development in the Reformed tradition was that which has been common to northwest Europe, Switzerland, France, Holland, and Germany, and has also had an influence to the east in Hungary and to the south in the Waldensian church in Italy. The Reformed churches in the first-named areas were very active in producing the early confessions of faith and catechisms still held as doctrinal standards in many of the churches. The Heidelberg Confession of 1563 is still a standard confessional document in most European Reformed churches. The Helvetic Confession (1536, 1566), the Gallic Confession (1559), and the Belgic Confession (1561) also set forth a Calvinistic doctrinal position.

Across the channel in the British Isles, Calvinism was a dominant influence in the Reformation, reaching its heights in the 1640s. Much influenced by the Canons of the Synod of Dort (1618) the Westminster Assembly produced the Westminster Confession of Faith, catechisms, Form of Church Government, and Directory of Worship, which have become the standards of all English-speaking Presbyterian churches. The Presbyterian church in Scotland, the

Church of Scotland, which had originally used the Scots Confession (1560) and the Genevan Catechism, adopted the Westminster standards in 1647, after the English Parliament, dominated by the Independents, had refused to agree to their becoming the standards of the Church of England.

In the European and British colonies throughout the world Reformed and Presbyterian churches from the late 17th century on were founded by the colonists who emigrated to Massachusetts, New York, South Africa, Australia, New Zealand, and other places.

While the Reformed tradition has had its conflicts, it also has had a very positive influence in the world. In the 18th century it was one of the principal centers of the evangelical revival. In Scotland the movement had begun by 1700 through the influence of Thomas Boston and the Marrow Men, so called because they had been greatly influenced by the Puritan work *The Marrow of Modern Divinity*. The revival associated with the work of this group eventually merged with the Evangelical revival in England through the influence of George Whitefield. At the same time in the American colonies Jonathan Edwards was involved in the Great Awakening, which was again linked to the English movement through Whitefield. In all these cases Calvinistic theology was the underlying influence.

The Reformed Tradition in Recent Times. The revival of evangelical preaching and power did not stop there, for through Scottish influence it was carried to Europe in 1818, when Robert Haldane visited Switzerland on an evangelistic tour. He greatly influenced such men as César Malan and Merle d'Aubigné, and through them the Evangelical revival spread to other parts of Europe. In Holland it had a particularly strong impact, resulting in the labors of Groen van Prinsterer, Herman Bavinck, and Abraham Kuyper.

This Reformed practice of social and political involvement in Britain and Holland was carried to America, where those in the Reformed tradition have taken a considerable part in such matters. Many in the Presbyterian and Reformed churches were participants in the movement to abolish slavery, and more recently have been prominent in civil rights and similar movements. Unfortunately in South Africa the Reformed tradition has been involved in support of racial apartheid policies and their application.

The Reformed tradition has always been strongly in favor of the education of church members. Calvin's insistence upon catechetical training of the young and his establishment of what is now the University of Geneva, was imitated in Scotland by John Knox in the educational provisions in the *First Book of Discipline*, in the Netherlands by the establishment of such institutions as the University of Leiden, and in France by the founding of various seminaries. Similarly in America this educational tradition was responsible for the founding of universities such as Harvard and Yale. In more recent years Calvin College in Grand Rapids, Michigan, Redeemer College in Hamilton, Ontario, and similar institutions indicate that the Reformed tradition in education is still functioning and is fulfilling an important part in developing an educated, Christian citizenry.

From 1850 another noticeable development has been the endeavors of the various Reformed and Presbyterian churches to cooperate in many ways. In 1875 the World Alliance of Reformed Churches holding the Presbyterian system was organized, and still continues. As some of the churches in the alliance, however, have drifted away from a truly Reformed theological position, a new body, the Reformed Ecumenical Synod, was established to ensure that a fully Reformed witness would be maintained.

W. S. Reid

See also Calvin, John; Calvinism; Dort, Synod of; Edwards, Jonathan; Kuyper, Abraham; Whitefield, George; Zwingli, Ulrich.

Regeneration. Inner re-creating of fallen human nature by the gracious sovereign action of the Holy Spirit (John 3:5–8). Regeneration in Christ changes the disposition from lawless, godless self-seeking (Rom. 3:9–18; 8:7), which dominates humankind in Adam, into one of trust and love, of repentance for past rebelliousness and unbelief, and loving compliance with God's law. It enlightens the blinded mind to discern spiritual realities (1 Cor. 2:14–15; 2 Cor. 4:6; Col. 3:10), and liberates and energizes the enslaved will for obedience to God (Rom. 6:14, 17–22; Phil. 2:13).

The use of the figure of new birth to describe this change emphasizes two facts about it. The first is its decisiveness. The regenerate person is a new creature in Christ, buried with him out of reach of condemnation and raised with him into a new life of righteousness (see Rom. 6:3–11; 2 Cor. 5:17; Col. 3:9–11). The second fact emphasized is the monergism of regeneration. Spiritual vivification is a free, and to us mysterious, exercise of divine power (John 3:8), not explicable in terms of the combination or cultivation of existing human resources (John 3:6), not caused or induced by any human efforts (John 1:12–13) or merits (Titus 3:3–7).

Biblical Presentation. The noun "regeneration" (Gk. *palingenesia*) occurs only twice. In Matt. 19:28 it denotes the eschatological restoration of all things (Acts 3:21) under the Messiah for which Israel was waiting. In Titus 3:5 the word refers to the renewing of the individual. Elsewhere, the thought of regeneration is differently expressed.

In OT prophecies regeneration is depicted as the work of God renovating, circumcising, and softening hearts, writing his laws upon them, and thereby causing their owners to know, love, and obey him as never before (Deut. 30:6; Jer. 31:31–34; 32:39–40; Ezek. 11:19–20; 36:25–27). In the NT the thought of regeneration is more fully individualized, and in John's Gospel and First Epistle the figure of new birth—"from above" (*anothen*: John 3:3, 7, Moffatt), "of water and the Spirit" (i.e., through a purificatory operation of God's Spirit: see Ezek. 36:25–27; John 3:5; cf. 3:8), or simply "of God" (John 1:13, nine times in 1 John)—is integral to the presentation of personal salvation.

Paul specifies the christological dimensions of regeneration by presenting it as (1) a lifegiving coresurrection with Christ (Eph. 2:5; Col. 2:13; cf. 1 Pet. 1:3); (2) a work of new creation in Christ (2 Cor. 5:17; Eph. 2:10; Gal. 6:15). Peter and James make the further point that God "begets anew" (*anagennaō*: 1 Pet. 1:23) and "brings to birth" (*apokyeō*: James 1:18) by means of the gospel. It is under the impact of the word that God renews the heart, so evoking faith (Acts 16:14–15).

J. I. Packer

See also Call, Calling; Elect, Election; Salvation; Salvation; Order of.

Regeneration, Baptismal. See Baptismal Regeneration.

Regula Fidei. See Rule of Faith.

Reid, Thomas. See Scottish Realism.

Reincarnation. Belief that an individual human soul passes through a succession of lives. The idea of reincarnation had its origin in northern India (1000–800 B.C.) in the early Hindu scriptures (Upanishads). The concept of reincarnation has always been an integral part of classical

Buddhism. Reincarnational thinking was expressed by some Greek philosophers, including Pythagoras and Plato. Because of the influence of the 1st-century Greek mystery religions, the Gnostics, and the Roman Stoics, the theory of transmigration, or reincarnation, became firmly established as a Western as well as Eastern doctrine.

The modern Western expression of reincarnation emerged during the Enlightenment of the 18th century and was revived by such 19th-century occultic movements as Theosophy, founded by Madame H. P. Blavatsky. This Westernized version of reincarnation was later popularized by such psychics as Edgar Cayce, Helen Wambach, and Jeanne Dixon. The Christian's disavowal of reincarnation is anchored in the biblical assertion that "man is destined to die once, and after that to face judgment" (Heb. 9:27).

R. M. ENROTH

Relics. Objects preserved as memorials of the earthly lives of saints, Mary, or Jesus, including their bodies and items that they had contact with. Belief in relics spread widely among Christians by the 4th century, receiving approval from Ambrose, Augustine, and Chrysostom. Initially this belief focused on graves of martyrs, which became choice sites for building churches. The seventh ecumenical council decreed that no new church be consecrated without relics in its altar. The cult of relics expanded enormously in the Middle Ages, leading to a multitude of pilgrimages and inevitable superstitions and commercial abuses. The forerunners of Protestantism, Hus and Wycliffe, inveighed against the cult of relics as idolatry, and the Reformers echoed them. The Council of Trent confirmed the veneration of relics as established by tradition. Catholic canon law now regulates relics through the Congregation of Rites, requiring that relics be authenticated by episcopal certification and forbidding their sale.

P. D. STEEVES

Religion, Religious. "Religious" is in general the adjective of the noun "religion"; but it is also used as a noun in a specialized sense to indicate connection with a monastic order. Thus, a monk may be called a "religious."

The large number, and often contradictory character, of the definitions to be found in modern discussions of religion suggest that scholars find it impossible to formulate a generally acceptable definition. Perhaps a satisfactory definition can be attained only by confining attention to one or a few of the "higher" religions, the others being treated as defective and so not normative. Such a method would yield, as definitive characteristics of religion, the acknowledgment of a higher, unseen power; an attitude of reverent dependence on that power in the conduct of life; and special actions, such as rites, prayers, and acts of mercy, as peculiar expressions and means of cultivation of the religious attitude.

A. K. RULE

Religionless Christianity. See BONHOEFFER, DIETRICH.

Religious Liberty. See TOLERANCE.

Remarriage. The question of remarriage is a difficult one, touching, as it does, upon matters of biblical exegesis, moral judgment, and pastoral psychology. Does Scripture allow remarriage? In any particular case would remarriage be morally right? In such a case would remarriage be pastorally wise?

The Exegetical Question. The exegetical question is closely related to the issue of divorce. Remarriage is presupposed in the Deuteronomic legislation (Deut. 24:1–4), although return to a first husband is forbidden in the one case of a woman also divorced by a second husband. In the Synoptic Gospels (Matt. 5:31–32; 19:3–4; Mark 10:2–3; Luke 16:18) is Jesus forbidding all remarriage because it is adultery? Does the "exceptive clause" ("except for the case of *porneia*") in Matt. 5:32 and 19:9 mean that in this one case a husband is free to separate from his wife, but without the right of remarriage? Or is Jesus in these passages both affirming God's ideal for marriage as a permanent covenant and also recognizing that sometimes divorce is a tragic reality because of sin? If one takes the latter view, it is arguable that the right of remarriage is also presupposed.

The Moral Question. The primary moral question is whether remarriage cuts into any outstanding covenant obligations of the first marriage that are still capable of fulfillment. If there is any possibility of reconciliation with the first partner, that consideration is decisive. Parental obligations to any children are also of the highest priority, and constitute yet another moral issue affecting the decision concerning remarriage. Furthermore, the social dimensions of marriage require that we also consider the overall stability of marital and family patterns in society.

The Pastoral Question. There remains the pastoral question, which may still mean that even if remarriage were judged permissible, it may not be judged wise. Many marriages are broken because of some sort of personal inadequacy in commitment. A good Christian marriage can provide one of the most fruitful contexts for healing personal immaturities and childhood hurts, but a bad marriage may serve only to deepen wounds and expose hurts undealt with to the consciousness. To add the pain, guilt, and tragedy of divorce to a stock of personal insecurity and need is to make some people very vulnerable indeed, and it is by no means a straightforward question that a second marriage will necessarily be any more successful than the first, unless personal help has been received. A failed marriage should raise the question of personal need and the possibilities of therapy or pastoral ministry on the one hand, and the serious consideration of future celibacy on the other.

However proper remarriage in any particular case may be judged to be, that does not remove from the church one of its primary responsibilities in this area: that of finding ways in which to foster and encourage those personal qualities that make for covenant faithfulness and commitment, even faced with the pressures of contemporary society, and of finding ways of minimizing in social terms those factors that militate against the permanence of marriage.

D. J. ATKINSON

See also DIVORCE; MARRIAGE, THEOLOGY OF; SEPARATION, MARITAL.

Remission of Sins. See FORGIVENESS.

Remnant. Translation of several Hebrew words in the OT, only two of which are of consequence: *yeter* and *še'ērît*. The NT Greek equivalents, *loipos* and *leimma*, are infrequent. In the majority of cases these words are used in a literal and self-explanatory way. They refer merely to things or people left over after famine, conquest, division, or passage of time. In the OT prophetic books, however, the hope promised for those of the nation left over after the fall of Jerusalem crystallizes into a promise not only of preservation for the few people remaining, but also a promise for the kernel of the nation that will be preserved and at length returned to their land and privileged status in messianic times. For this concept the Hebrew word *še'ērît* is principally used.

R. L. HARRIS

Remonstrants. Dutch Protestant followers of the theological views of Arminius. The Remonstrants presented to the States General in 1610 a "Remonstrance" that reflected their divergence from Calvinism. When the matter came before the Synod of Dort it had become a political as well as a theological issue. The Remonstrants, who upheld the principle of free investigation, were ousted from their pulpits. Many of them were expelled from the Netherlands, and their theological position was declared contrary to Scripture. They were not officially tolerated until 1795. The movement has retained its appeal and has had a significant influence on orthodox Dutch Calvinism and on other Christian denominations.

J. D. DOUGLAS

See also ARMINIANISM; DORT, SYNOD OF.

Renan, Joseph Ernest (1823–1892). French Semitic philologist and historian of religion. Renan was a major representative of French theological liberalism. In 1860–61 he went on an archeological expedition to Lebanon and Palestine, where he wrote his celebrated *Life of Jesus* (1863), the opening volume of the seven-volume *History of the Origins of Christianity*. In this book Renan replaces D. F. Strauss's myth theory of the origins of Christianity with a legend theory. Appointed professor of Hebrew at the Collège de France in 1862, Renan was removed two years later because of the controversy swirling about him but was reinstated in 1870 and became its administrator in 1884.

R. V. PIERARD

Renewal. All those processes of restoration of spiritual strength subsequent to and proceeding from the new birth. The concept of renewal has its roots in the OT (Pss. 5:10; 103:5; Isa. 40:31; 41:1). The main NT Greek words are *anakainizō* and *ananeoō*. In Rom. 12:2 this renewal (*anakainōsis*) is applied to the mental faculties, and indicates the reinvigorating effect of Christian commitment on conduct. This is further illustrated by Paul's teaching regarding the new man (Col. 3:10), which is represented as in constant need of renewal (2 Cor. 4:16). A more specific description is found in Eph. 4:23, where the phrase "made new in the attitude of your minds" shows the spiritual character of this renewal. In the subapostolic age the idea of renewal tended to become linked with that of baptism (Barnabas 6:11; Acts of Thomas, 132). Another word, *palingenesia*, is used of the event of rebirth that leads to renewal (Titus 3:5).

D. GUTHRIE

See also BAPTISM; REGENERATION.

Renewal, Church. Phenomenon that has been described by such words as revival, awakening, and reform and that represents one of the dominant concerns of the 20th-century American church. "Renewal" has such diverse components as mass evangelism; efforts to promote personal witnessing; revivals (in the sense of outpourings of the Holy Spirit); the Faith at Work, charismatic (or Neo-Pentecostal), and Church Growth movements; the awakening among young people; renewal efforts that have emanated from individual congregations; and the larger evangelical renaissance.

Present-Day Renewal. The centrality of the Bible in present-day renewal is reflected in almost all facets of the movement, including increased scholarly activity. Rather than being largely an object of study, Scripture is seen as the light for life's pathway, as the Word of God to be understood in order to be obeyed. Prayer and the life of devotion, including such elements as praise and intercession, have formed another prominent theme. Prayer is grounded in the larger resurgence of a supernaturalism that not only accepts the possibility but emphasizes the necessity of divine intervention in human life. The hope of authentic renewal itself rests in the possibility of the appropriation of God's resources through prayer and Bible study.

The experiential dimension of Christian faith, centered in a meaningful personal relationship with God continues to be a major current in the stream of vital Christianity. That primary relationship in its turn transforms all other relationships, creating personal wholeness as well as community among believers. The Holy Spirit stands at the heart both of the possibility of divine resources and of the experiential dimension of renewal. Both the fruit and the gifts of the Spirit have received strong emphasis as part of the larger empowering or outpouring without which there can be no authentic and powerful renewal of the church.

Renewal and Social Concern. Social concern and action, practical responsiveness to the entire range of human need, a prominent feature of late 20th-century church renewal, represents a return to the biblical pattern of historic evangelicalism and a reversal of this century's "great reversal" of that tradition. Partly to counter the centrifugal pressures inherent in the attention devoted separately to devotion, social action, and other emphases, a holistic Christian message has emerged as an additional theme. The Christian person in the modern world must be one whose life reflects a balance of prayer/devotion, evangelism, social concern/action, and rigorous intellectual endeavor.

N. A. Magnuson

See also Church Growth Movement.

Repentance. In the OT the Hebrew verb *nāḥam* ("repent") is usually used to signify a contemplated change in God's dealings with people for good or ill according to his just judgment (1 Sam. 15:11, 35; Jon. 3:9–10) or, negatively, to certify that God will not swerve from his announced purpose (1 Sam. 15:29; Ps. 110:4; Jer. 4:28). In five places *nāḥam* refers to human repentance or relenting.

The background of the NT idea of repentance lies not primarily in *nāḥam* (except in Job 42:6; Jer. 8:6; 31:19), but rather in the Hebrew verb *šûb*, meaning to turn back, away from, or toward in the religious sense. Repentance follows a turning about that is a gift of God (Ps. 80:3, 7, 19; Jer. 31:18–20). Isa. 55:6–7 gives the typical OT call to repentance and conversion.

In the NT the Greek noun *metanoia* occurs 23 times and the verb *metanoeō* 34 times. Repentance is the theme of the preaching of John the Baptist (Matt. 3:1, 8; Mark 1:4). Jesus continues John's theme but adds, significantly that "The time has come" (Mark 1:15). His coming is the coming of the kingdom in person and is decisive (Matt. 11:20–24; Luke 13:1–5). All life relationships must be radically altered (Matt. 5:17–7:27; Luke 14:25–35; 18:18–30). Sinners, not the righteous, are called to *metanoia* (Matt. 9:13; Mark 2:17; Luke 5:32), and heaven rejoices over their repentance (Luke 15). The preaching of repentance and remission of sins must be joined to the proclamation of the cross and the resurrection (Luke 24:44–49). The apostles are true to this commission (Acts 2:38; 3:19; 17:30; 20:21). Unfaithful churches must repent (Rev. 3:5, 16). Apostates crucify the Son of God all over again; it is impossible for them to be brought back to repentance (Heb. 6:5–6).

C. G. Kromminga

See also Conversion; Salvation; Order of Salvation; Penitence.

Reprobation. Doctrine that God has eternally condemned the nonelect to eternal punishment for their sins. Calvin set forth this doctrine very clearly and precisely in his *Institutes* (3.23.1ff.), and while he regarded it as a dreadful (*horribile*) doctrine, he denied that it was to be avoided or rejected, for it is clearly taught in Scripture (Gen. 25:21–23; Exod. 4:21; 10:21, 27; Mal. 1:2–3; Rom. 9:10–13).

W. S. Reid

See also Elect, Election; Predestination; Preterition.

Responsibility. Relation a free moral agent has to a decision or act for which that agent is answerable, accountable, or responsible. The counterpart to responsibility is imputability, in which the decision or act is chargeable, attributable, or imputable to the agent. Assumed here in both cases are a law imposing an obligation and a sanction enforcing the obligation. A sanction is a promise of reward and the threat of punishment. The lawbreaker deserves the punishment, and the law keeper is entitled to the reward because of merit or the right of payment. Responsibility and imputability, or culpability, are particularly concerned with the extent to which a decision or act owes its origin to an agent's will guided by reason. Responsibility for a bad act is called guilt. There is no corresponding designation of responsibility for a good act.

Responsibility and Freedom. No one holds a person responsible for a decision or act when that person's will is not free. For those who hold the will to be free, a practical criterion is that for any act an agent may be considered to have the freedom required for responsibility if that person can choose to do otherwise. To be able to choose to do otherwise may be taken to mean that more than one alternative is open to the agent, and the alternative actualized is the one chosen by the agent. The focus here is upon being able to put into effect a decision once it is made. Another condition necessary for moral responsibility is knowledge of what is expected. A person who is ignorant of a rule or law is either not held responsible or is thought to have a reduced degree of responsibility, as long as that person did not willfully bring about that ignorance.

Responsibility and Scripture. Specific biblical teachings relative to responsibility include the following: (1) Every human being is held responsible by God for the sin of the first human being (Rom. 5:12). (2) God's giving of the law through Moses created a much greater sense of responsibility in Israel (Rom. 7:7). (3) The rest of the human race is no less responsible, however, for when they do by nature the things required by the law, they demonstrate that the requirements of the law are written on their hearts (Rom. 2:14–15). (4) Unless sinners acknowledge responsibility for sin and repent, they cannot be forgiven by God (Acts 3:19).

S. R. Obitts

See also Ethics, Biblical; Freedom, Free Will, and Determinism.

Restoration of Israel. See Israel and Prophecy.

Resurrection of Christ. That Jesus Christ died and afterward rose from the dead is both the central doctrine of Christian theology and the major fact in a defense of its teachings.

The Centrality of the Resurrection. It is the witness of the NT that the resurrection of Jesus is the pivotal point of Christian theology and apologetics. Paul records an early creed in 1 Cor. 15:3–5, which highlights the resurrection as an integral part of the gospel. Paul also reports several eyewitness appearances. Then Paul relates the importance of this event, for if Jesus did not literally rise from the dead, then the entire Christian faith is fallacious (v. 14) and ineffective (v. 17). Furthermore, preaching is valueless (v. 14), Christian testimony is false (v. 15), no sins have been forgiven (v. 17), and believers have perished without any Christian hope (v. 18). The conclusion is that, apart from this event, Christians are the most miserable of all people (v. 19).

Similarly, Luke's writings relate several instances where the resurrection provided the basis for the Christian proclamation. Jesus taught that his death and resurrection constituted the central message of the OT (Luke 24:25–27). Peter held that the miracles that Jesus performed, and his resurrection in particular, were the chief indications that God approved of his teachings (Acts 2:22–32). Paul's teaching frequently utilized the resurrection as the basis of the gospel message (Acts 13:29–39; 17:30–31). Other NT writings share the same hope. Jesus pointed to his resurrection as the sign vindicating the authority of his teachings (Matt. 12:38–40). This event both ensures the believer's salvation (1 Pet. 1:3) and provides the means by which Jesus serves as the believer's high priest (Heb. 7:23–25).

The Resurrection and Contemporary Theology. There is virtual agreement, even among most critical theologians, that the resurrection of Jesus is the central claim of Christianity. Yet a major issue is the question of whether all that is required is the message of the resurrection, or the literal event itself. This is not only a dispute between evangelicals and higher critical theologians, but also among these critical scholars as well. The pivotal fact, recognized as historical by virtually all scholars, is the original experiences of the disciples. It is nearly always admitted that the disciples had real experiences and that "something happened."

First, more radical critics hold that the nature of the original eyewitnesses' experiences cannot be ascertained. A second group of scholars is distinguished from the first not only by exhibiting some interest in the nature of the disciples' experiences, but often by the acceptance of the literal resurrection itself. Yet while the naturalistic theories are usually rejected, this group still insists that the event can be known only by faith completely apart from any verification.

The third position is characterized by a significant interest in more historical aspects of the resurrection. Not only are naturalistic theories usually rejected, but the empty tomb is often held to be a historical fact. These scholars proceed a step further by setting forth a more or less abstract reconstruction of the historical nature of the appearances. The fourth approach to the resurrection is that the available historical evidence demonstrates the probability that Jesus was literally raised from the dead.

It is important to note that of these four critical positions only the first is generally characterized by a rejection of or agnostic attitude toward the literal resurrection of Jesus. Just as significant is the observation that the first position not only appears to be losing ground, but varying positions that support the facticity of the resurrection are presently quite popular.

The Resurrection as History. Historical arguments for the resurrection have traditionally been based on two lines of support. First, naturalistic theories have failed to explain away this event, chiefly because each is disproven by the known historical facts. Second, historical evidences for the resurrection are often cited, such as the eyewitness testimony for Jesus' appearances, the transformed lives of the disciples, the empty tomb, the inability of the Jewish leaders to disprove these claims, and the conversion of skeptics such as Paul and James, the brother of Jesus. When combined with the absence of naturalistic alternative theories these evidences are quite impressive. Contemporary apologetics has moved even beyond these important issues, however, to other arguments in favor of the resurrection. One crucial center of attention has been 1 Cor. 15:3–4, where Paul records material that he had "received" from others and then "passed on" to his listeners. It is agreed by virtually all contemporary theologians that this material contains an ancient creed that is actually much earlier than the book in which it is recorded.

Another extremely strong argument for the resurrection is derived from the known facts that are admitted as historical by virtually all critical scholars who deal with this subject. Events such as Jesus' death by crucifixion, the subsequent despair of the disciples, their experiences that they believed to be appearances of the risen Jesus, their corresponding transformations, and the conversion of Paul due to a similar experience are five facts that are critically established and accepted as historical by most scholars. Of these facts the nature of the disciples' experiences is the most crucial. Historical investigation demonstrates that the earliest eyewitnesses were convinced that they had seen the risen Jesus.

G. R. HABERMAS

Resurrection of the Dead. ***In the OT.*** The OT evidences certain universal, animistic ideas about postmortem survival that underlay the practice of necromancy (1 Sam. 28:8–9), funeral provisions, directions for the dead, and the concept of the shadowy underworld of Sheol/Hades (see Ezek. 32:17–32). By the 1st century most Jews believed there would be a general resurrection; the rabbis argued that Abraham reasoned that God could raise the dead (see Heb. 11:19). The Pharisees, Essenes, and Qumran covenanters expected the resurrection of the just (Acts 23:8). The Sadducees denied resurrection because it was not "Mosaic" and represented a foreign idea (Mark 12:18; Josephus says they believed the soul died with the body). A few, holding matter evil, denied the concept of resurrection altogether.

In the NT. Jesus raised others to resume life and predicted his own rising. His own resurrection is, in fact, the key event in Christian history and the basis of Peter's (Acts 2:32) and Paul's (Acts 17:18; 23:6; 26:6–8) message. Apostolic testimony (Acts 3:26; 4:2, 33; Rom. 10:9; 1 Cor. 15:3–11) makes it clear that resurrection is essential to the Christian gospel.

Pauline reflection begins from contemporary Pharisaic views: the departed share the coming glory (1 Thess. 4:15); there will be a general resurrection and judgment (Acts 24:15; 17:31; Rom. 2:5–11; 2 Cor. 5:10). Paul goes on, however, to develop three themes: (1) Redemption will be complete; it will include our bodies. (2) "We will all be changed." Paul first establishes the bodily resurrection of Jesus (1 Cor. 15:1–11). He then points out the variety of bodily forms in nature (birds, fishes, grain), each adapted to its environment, and asserts that God will provide the risen soul with a new body, glorious, incorruptible, immortal (1 Cor. 15:35–49; cf. 1 Thess. 4:16–17). The key words "we will be changed" imply both continuity and difference. Paul did not expect such transformation at death, but at the second advent of Christ (1 Cor. 15:23, 51–57; 1 Thess. 4:14–17), following an intermediate state that is far better but not final glory (Phil. 1:23; cf. Acts 7:60 "sleep," Luke 23:43 "today"). (3) We are already, but not yet, raised with Christ. The victory of his resurrection is ours.

Johannine reflection moves even nearer than Paul's toward incorporeal immortality. Eternal life is experienced now (John 3:36); the faithful never see death (8:51); believers have already "crossed over" from death to life (5:24).

R. E. O. WHITE

See also RESURRECTION OF CHRIST.

Retaliation. See VENGEANCE.

Revelation, General. Divine disclosure to all persons at all times and places by which they come to know that God is, and what he is like. General, or natural, revelation may be divided into two categories: internal (the innate sense of deity and conscience) and external (nature and providential history).

Summary of Positions. Some scholars flatly deny any reality to general revelation. Karl Barth, for example, refused to acknowledge any revelation outside the Word of God. Others, such as Abraham Kuyper, G. C. Berkouwer, and Cornelius Van Til, concede the givenness of general revelation, but deny that it registers as actual knowledge in the sin-darkened mind of the unregenerate. On the other extreme many liberal scholars insist that the light afforded by general revelation is sufficient for salvation. A second liberal tradition claims that the human mind, utilizing the scientific method, is capable of ferreting out all the truth we need to order our lives. The Thomistic tradition claims that the rational mind, aided by the analogy of being between God and humankind and the law of cause and effect, is capable of proving God's existence and the infinity of his perfectness. Augustine, Luther, Calvin, Charles Hodge, B. B. Warfield, and Carl F. H. Henry argue for the objective reality of general revelation and its limited utility in mediating an elemental knowledge of God's existence and character.

Biblical Data. According to Ps. 19 God reveals himself through the two-volume book of nature (vv. 1–6) and book of the law (vv. 7–13). In the first volume we read, "The heavens declare the glory of God; the skies proclaim the work of his hands" (v. 1). That which the created order shows forth is the divine "glory" (*kābôd*), namely, the external manifestation of God's inner being and attributes. The revelation of God's glory through the heavens is declared to be perpetual or uninterrupted (v. 2), wordless or inaudible (v. 3), and worldwide in scope (v. 4).

In the prologue to his Gospel, John makes two assertions about the eternal Word. First, "in him was life, and that life was the light of men" (1:4). Second, "the true light that gives light to every man was coming into the world" (1:9). It seems likely that John has in mind the universal work of the Logos whereby the human mind is divinely illumined so as to perceive God as a first principle, much the same as Calvin's "sense of divinity" or "seed of religion."

The clearest teaching that all people possess a rudimentary knowledge of God as Creator occurs in Rom. 1:18–21. Paul argues that through the universal revelation in nature God is "clearly seen" (v. 20), "understood" (v. 20), and "known" (v. 19; cf. v. 21). That which we gain knowledge of is defined as God's invisible qualities—his eternal power and divine nature (*theiotes*).

B. A. DEMAREST

See also REVELATION, SPECIAL.

Revelation, Special. God's communication to humankind of divine truth, that is, his manifestation of himself or of his will. The essentials of the biblical view are that the Logos is the divine agent in all revelation, this revelation being further discriminated as general or universal (i.e., revelation in nature, history, and conscience) and special or particular (i.e., redemptive revelation conveyed by wondrous acts and words). Special revelation is crowned by the incarnation of the living Word and the inscripturation of the spoken word. The gospel of redemption is therefore not merely a series of abstract theses unrelated to specific historical events; it is the dramatic news that God has acted in saving history, climaxed by the incarnate person and work of Christ (Heb. 1:2), for the salvation of lost humankind. Yet the redemptive events of biblical history do not stand uninterpreted. Their authentic meaning is given in the sacred writings—sometimes after, sometimes before the events. The series of sacred acts therefore includes the divine provision of an authoritative canon of writings—the sacred Scriptures—providing a trustworthy source of knowledge of God and of his plan.

Special revelation is redemptive revelation. It publishes the good tidings that the holy and merciful God promises salvation as a divine gift to sinful people who cannot save themselves (OT) and that he has now fulfilled that promise in the gift of his Son in whom all people are called to believe (NT). The gospel is good news that the incarnate Logos has borne the sins of doomed sinners, has died in their stead, and has risen for their justification. This is the fixed center of special redemptive revelation.

False Views of Revelation. Christian theology has had to protect the biblical view of special revelation against many perversions. Since Schleiermacher's day Protestant theology has been influenced repeatedly by anti-intellectualistic strands in modern philosophy, especially by such thinkers as Kant, James, and Dewey. Schleiermacher's formulas, that we know God only in relation to us and not as he is in himself, and that God communicates life and not doctrines, have been influential in encouraging an artificial disjunction in many Protestant expositions of special revelation. Although often striving to advance beyond these restrictions, more recent existential and dialectical expositions nonetheless do not consistently rise above the quicksands of a merely relational theology.

Revelation as Rational. Because of its implications for rational revelation the traditional identification of the Bible as the word of God written has been especially repugnant to contemporary neo-orthodox theology. It is contended that Jesus Christ alone should be identified as the Word of God, and that to speak of Scripture in this way demeans Christ. The evangelical Protestant, however, distinguishes carefully between the *logos theou* and the *rhema theou*, that is, between the ontological Word incarnate and the epistemological word inscripturate. The OT prophets consistently speak of their words as the words of God, using the formula "Thus saith the Lord" with untiring regularity. The NT apostles, moreover, speak of divine revelation in the form of definite ideas and words. The neo-orthodox tendency to look upon Scripture as simply witness to revelation, in fact, contravenes the historic Christian view that the Bible itself is a form of revelation specially provided for sinful humankind as an authentic disclosure of the nature and will of God.

From all this it is clear how significant is the Christian assertion that the laws of logic and morality belong to the *imago Dei*. Christian theology has always been under biblical compulsion to affirm the identity of the Logos with the Godhead, and to find a connection between God as rational and moral and the form and content of the divine image in humankind. That Jesus Christ is himself the truth; that we bear the divine image on the basis of creation and that this image while distorted by sin is not destroyed; that the Bible is a rational revelation of the nature of God and his will for fallen people; that the Holy Spirit uses truth as a means of conviction and conversion—all these facts indicate in some measure the undeniable premium assigned to rationality by the Christian religion. Yet human reason is not viewed as a source of truth; rather, we are to think God's thoughts after him. Revelation is the source of truth, and reason, as illuminated by the Spirit, the instrument for comprehending it.

C. F. H. Henry

See also BIBLE, AUTHORITY OF; BIBLE, INSPIRATION OF; REVELATION, GENERAL.

Revenge. See VENGEANCE.

Revivalism. Movement that maintains that vital Christianity begins with a response of the whole being to the gospel's call for repentance and spiritual rebirth by faith in Jesus Christ. This experience results in a personal relationship with God.

The 18th-Century Birth. The appeal for a personal, public response to the gospel that came to characterize revivalism sprang up almost simultaneously in both England and America in the 18th century. The initial signs of the First Great Awakening in the American colonies occurred in the congregation of the Dutch Reformed pastor Theodore J. Frelinghuysen in northern New Jersey in 1725. In 1726 William Tennent, the Presbyterian leader of the Great Awakening, started his "log college" to prepare ministers to preach a personalized message that called men and women to repentance.

By the time George Whitefield began recurrent revivalistic tours of the American colonies in 1738, Jonathan Edwards, the theologian of the colonial awakening, had already experienced revival in Northampton, Massachusetts. Edwards accepted the validity of much of the religious emotion that accompanied the conversions among his parishioners and wrote in defense of the proper role of emotion in true religion. The revival continued to move south until it touched all the colonies. In England the recognized leader of the "Evangelical Revival" was John Wesley, founder of Methodism and close friend of Whitefield. Whitefield had encouraged Wesley to take up the field preaching that brought the gospel directly to the masses of working people.

The Definitive Stage. The pre-Revolutionary revivals demonstrated the general patterns that characterized all subsequent awakenings; however, it was the Second Great Awakening at the beginning of the 19th century that defined the theology and method of the tradition. The revival began at Hampden-Sidney and Washington colleges in Virginia in 1787. It continued at Yale under Timothy Dwight and at Andover and Princeton at the end of the 18th century. It was popularized in the great camp meetings on the frontier. The Cane Ridge, Kentucky, camp meeting in Aug. 1801, became the most famous of all. The strange emotional phenomena evident in the earlier colonial revival reappeared in intensified form. "Falling," "jerking," "rolling," and "dancing" exercises engaged many of the 20,000 worshipers present. These demonstrations moderated as the revival continued, but physical phenomena have always existed in some measure in popular revival movements.

The outstanding figure in early 19th-century revivalism was Charles Grandison Finney. Finney took the revival ethos of the frontier camp meeting to the urban centers of the Northeast. His success there and his widespread influence as a professor and later president of Oberlin College gave him a platform for propagating a theology and defense of the revival methods he espoused.

A significant new development in revivalism between 1835 and 1875 was the rise of perfectionist revivalism. Finney introduced a perfectionist note into his evangelism after his move to Oberlin College in 1835. He and his colleague Asa Mahan, president of Oberlin, joined perfectionist leaders in Methodism, such as lay leaders Walter and Phoebe Palmer, in a new Holiness revivalism in the churches. The movement used revivalistic methods to call Christians to a second crisis of faith and total commitment subsequent to conversion.

Institutionalization and Decline. Dwight L. Moody dominated the revival movement from 1875 until his death in 1899, even though most of the revivalism of the time was carried on in the local churches and camp meetings of the rapidly growing Baptist and Methodist denominations. Ira Sankey, his musical director, became the best known of the many gospel musicians who formed an essential part of the revivalistic teams that sprang up during this period.

Large audiences continued to attend the revival campaigns of William "Billy" Sunday, R. A. Torrey, Gypsy Smith, and others after the turn of the century. The change of national mood resulting from the economic upheavals that followed World War I, the persistent attacks of such social critics as H. L. Mencken, and the turn toward a gospel of social concern among the larger denominations, however, led to a decline in the influence of revivalism in the churches and in American life. Nevertheless, the Pentecostal revival that spread swiftly from its center in Los Angeles after 1906 and the effective use of radio by Charles Fuller and other radio evangelists indicated the continuing strength of the revivalist tradition in the churches.

The Modern Period. The rise of Billy Graham in the 1950s and his subsequent recognition as one of the most influential religious leaders of the post-World War II period signaled the latent residual strength of revivalism in the Christian churches. Graham's success in working with a broad spectrum of Protestant churches as well as significant segments of Catholicism reiterated the fact that revivalism is not a sporadic phenomenon in the Christian tradition but rather a steady force that breaks into public prominence whenever churches and society ignore its concerns for experiential religion.

The Theology of Revivalism. The intimate historical relationship between the growth of evangelicalism and revivalism indicates many common theological presuppositions. Evangelicalism's commitment to the reliability and authority of Scripture is the basis for revivalism's direct preaching and appeal; the former's belief in the universal need for spiritual rebirth is the basis for the latter's direct call for repentance and faith in Christ. The evangelical's acceptance of Christ's final commission to his disciples as a mandate for personal witness and world mission reinforces the urgency that characterizes revival movements.

M. E. Dieter

See also Edwards, Jonathan; Finney, Charles Grandison; Great Awakenings, The; Pietism; Wesley, John; Whitefield, George.

Reward. The two chief passages of Scripture that discuss rewards at length are 1 Cor. 3:8–15 and 1 Cor. 9:16–27. Additional information can be found in those passages where rewards for service are depicted as crowns (1 Cor. 9:25; Phil. 4:1; 1 Thess. 2:19; 2 Tim. 4:8; James 1:12; 1 Pet. 5:4; Rev. 2:10; 3:11). Various types of service merit rewards, such as enduring temptation (James 1:12), diligently seeking God (Heb. 11:6), dying for Christ (Rev. 2:10), dedicated pastoral work (1 Pet. 5:4), faithfully doing God's will and longing for his appearing (2 Tim. 4:8), soul winning (1 Thess. 2:19–20), faithful stewardship (1 Cor. 4:1–5), acts of kindness (Gal. 6:10), and hospitality (Matt. 10:40–42). Rewards can be lost (Rev. 2:10; 2 John 8). It is possible to be busy in the Lord's service and receive no rewards at all (1 Cor. 3:15; 9:27) or to receive little when one should receive much (2 John 8).

H. Z. Cleveland

See also Crown.

Riches. See Wealth, Christian View of.

Righteousness. (Heb. *ṣādaq*; Gk. *dikē*)
OT Usage. The God of Israel is revealed as a God of righteousness, who "does right" in all his works and judgments

(Gen. 18:25; Deut. 32:4; Ps. 11:7; Dan. 9:14). The OT concept of righteousness is closely linked with God's judgeship (Pss. 9:8; 50:6; 143:2). God judges equitably; he does not clear the guilty or forsake the righteous, and the judges of Israel are commanded to act according to his example (Exod. 23:7; Deut. 1:16–17; 10:17–18; Ps. 98:9). The righteousness of God is revealed in his punishment of the wicked and disobedient (Neh. 9:33; Ps. 7:9–17; Lam. 1:18; Dan. 9:14). But more emphatically God's righteousness is made known in his deliverance of his people from their enemies and oppressors (1 Sam. 12:6–11; Pss. 9:7–9; 51:14; Isa. 46:11–13). God as Judge comes to the rescue of the poor and the oppressed, delivering them from injustice and restoring their rights (Pss. 34:16–22; 72:1–4; 82; Isa. 11:4). He even treats them as righteous, in the relative sense that they are in the right as over against their wicked oppressors (Pss. 7:6–11; 143:1–3, 11–12). Consequently God's righteous judgment is often expressed in terms of his saving acts. Righteousness many times is closely related to God's salvation, mercy, and lovingkindness, especially in the psalms and the Book of Isaiah (Pss. 40:10; 85:9–10; 98:2–3; Isa. 45:8; 46:13; 51:5; cf. Jer. 9:24). The climax of this positive aspect is found in the theme of Messiah, the one who will be a truly righteous king and will fulfill God's covenant purpose for Israel, bringing it and all nations to God's final righteousness (Ps. 72; Isa. 9:7; 11:3–5; 42:6; Jer. 23:5–6; 33:15–16; Zech. 9:9).

NT Usage. Much of the NT is taken up with the purpose of showing that Jesus of Nazareth is indeed the promised Messiah, and thus God's purposes of righteousness and salvation are spoken of as centered in him. Jesus spoke of a false righteousness found in those who trust in themselves as righteous or justified because of their moral accomplishments (Matt. 23:28; Luke 16:15; 18:9), but he taught that the truly justified are those who acknowledge their sin and trust in God for forgiveness and his righteousness (Matt. 5:36; Mark 2:17; Luke 18:14).

Following the teaching of Christ, Paul explains that no one seeking to be righteous by the works of the law can be justified in God's sight, since everyone is a sinner and has fallen short of God's righteous standard (Rom. 3:9–10, 20, 23; Gal. 2:16). Therefore the righteousness of God comes as a gracious declaration in which God pronounces righteous those who put their faith in Jesus Christ (Acts 13:39; Rom. 3:22; 5:1, 18). God forgives the sins of the justified on the basis of Christ's atoning death, so that God himself is vindicated as just in his justification of sinners (Rom. 3:25–26; 5:8–9; cf. 1 John 1:9; 2:2).

The NT also makes it clear that the one who by faith is declared righteous also by faith seeks to do the deeds of righteousness and to grow in righteousness by God's grace (Rom. 6:12–18; Eph. 4:24; 5:9; Phil. 1:11; Heb. 11; James 2:17–26; 1 Pet. 2:24; 1 John 2:29). God's righteousness, which expresses itself in wrath and judgment against unrepentant sinners (2 Thess. 1:5–9; Rom. 2:5–9; Rev. 19:2), triumphs through love in the form of salvation from sin for those who repent and claim God's covenant promise fulfilled in Christ.

Theological Concepts. In systematic theology righteousness or justice is seen, first of all, as an attribute of God's being (one of the moral and communicable attributes), and then derivatively as an attribute of humankind created in God's image.

God's Righteousness (Justice). Righteousness is that attribute by which God's nature is seen to be the eternally perfect standard of what is right. It is closely related to God's holiness (or moral perfection), on the one hand, and to God's moral law or will as an expression of his holiness, on the other hand.

Our Righteousness. Doctrinally, human righteousness can be analyzed in four ways: (1) Original righteousness. God made humankind upright or morally good (Gen. 1:31). (2) Christ's righteousness. Since Adam's fall Christ is the only human being who has perfectly fulfilled God's moral law and has maintained a righteous nature (Matt. 5:17; John 8:29, 46; Heb. 4:15; 1 Pet. 2:22). (3) Imputed righteousness (justification). God declares the believer righteous. (4) Renewed righteousness (sanctification). Having been declared righteous, the believer grows in the likeness of Christ (being renewed in the image of God) and becomes righteous in actual moral character, that is, becomes sanctified.

D. W. DIEHL

See also GOD, ATTRIBUTES OF; JUSTIFICATION; RIGHTEOUSNESS, ORIGINAL; SANCTIFICATION.

Righteousness, Original. Original moral state or condition of humankind prior to the fall into sin (Gen. 1:31; Eccles. 7:29; Eph. 4:24; Col. 3:10). Roman Catholicism sees original righteousness as a *donum superadditum*, a gift added to the "natural" image of God. In the fall original righteousness (by which humankind had supernatural communion with God) was lost, but the natural image (consisting of human reason, freedom, and spirituality) remained relatively intact. The Protestant Reformers rejected this twofold distinction and taught that original righteousness was the very essence of humankind's original nature or image, not a supernatural addition to it. The fall meant the thorough corruption of the image but not its total loss.

D. W. DIEHL

See also FALL OF MAN; IMAGE OF GOD; RIGHTEOUSNESS.

Righteousness of God. See GOD, ATTRIBUTES OF.

Ritschl, Albrecht (1822–1889). German Protestant theologian. Ritschl was professor of systematic theology at Göttingen. Here he wrote his most important works, *The Christian Doctrine of Justification and Reconciliation* (1870–74), *Instruction in the Christian Religion* (1875), *Theology and Metaphysics* (1881), and *History of Pietism* (3 vols., 1880–86), and founded the important journal, *Zeitschrift für die Kirchengeschichte.* Central to Ritschl's system is his notion of justification. He defines Christianity as an ellipse with two foci—Jesus, who reveals the love of God for us and reconciles us, and the church, which is the spiritual and ethical community he founded and whose goal is the transformation of human society into the kingdom of God. Justification is the forgiveness of sins, the divine act of lifting the consciousness of guilt (both sin and punishment), but it is achieved in and through the church, the community for which Jesus died.

R. V. PIERARD

See also LIBERALISM, THEOLOGICAL.

Roman Catholicism. Term in general use since the Reformation to identify the faith and practice of Christians in communion with the pope. Although it has a reputation for conservatism and reaction, Roman Catholicism is a genuinely evolving religious system, valuing the deepening and development of its understanding of the Christian faith. This development sometimes goes beyond biblical data, but Catholic scholars contend that certain pivotal church doctrines—the sacraments, the blessed Virgin Mary, and the papacy—are suggested by a "trajectory of images" in the NT; postbiblical developments are said to be consistent with the "thrust" of the NT. At other times this evolution has involved the rediscovery of truths that the church once possessed but lost in the course of its long history. The church has even at times recognized as error what it had earlier decreed authoritatively.

Although Roman Catholicism cannot be fixed within a single monolithic theological system, it is nevertheless helpful to distinguish between two traditions within Catholicism. The mainstream tradition has stressed the transcendence of God and the church as a divinely commissioned institution (the "vertical church"). This authoritarian, centralizing tradition has been variously labeled, mainly by its critics, as "medievalism," "Romanism," "Vaticanism," "papalism," "ultramontanism," "Jesuitism," "integralism," and "neoscholasticism." A minority reformist tradition has stressed the immanence of God and the church as community (the "horizontal church"). Reform Catholicism has nourished such movements as Gallicanism, Jansenism, liberal Catholicism, and modernism.

The two traditions coalesced at Vatican II, facilitated by John XXIII's dictum, "The substance of the ancient doctrine is one thing . . . and the way in which it is presented is another." An understanding, then, of modern-day Roman Catholicism requires a description of the characteristics of conservative Catholicism that dominated the church especially from the Council of Trent (1545–63) until Vatican II, plus an outline of the changes in emphasis inaugurated at Vatican II.

The Church. The most distinctive characteristic of Roman Catholicism is its ecclesiology. Supernatural life is mediated to Christians through the sacraments administered by the hierarchy to whom obedience is due. Pre-Vatican II theology taught that the Roman Catholic Church is the only true church of Christ, since it alone has a permanent, apostolic hierarchy and Petrine primacy to ensure the permanence of the church as Christ instituted it. The most important document of Vatican II, the *Dogmatic Constitution on the Church*, transformed rather than revolutionized the church's ecclesiology. The traditional emphasis on the church as means of salvation was supplanted by an understanding of the church as a mystery or sacrament, "a reality imbued with the hidden presence of God" (Paul VI). The conception of the church as a hierarchical institution was replaced by a view of the church as the whole people of God.

In the *Decree on Ecumenism* the council recognized that both sides were at fault in the rupture of the church at the Reformation, and it sought the restoration of Christian unity rather than a return of non-Catholics to "the true Church."

The Pope. The dogmas of papal primacy and infallibility were promulgated as recently as Vatican I (1869–70), but they have a long history that Roman Catholics trace ultimately to the will of Christ (Matt. 16:18–19; Luke 22:32; John 21:15–17) and the roles exercised by the apostle Peter (fisherman, shepherd, elder, rock, etc.) in the NT church. Vatican II stressed the role of the pope as "perpetual and visible source and foundation of the unity of the bishops and of the multitude of the faithful." It also revived the collegiality of bishops, thus modifying the monarchical governance of the church: "Together with its head, the Roman Pontiff, and never without its head, the episcopal order is the subject of supreme and full power over the universal church."

The Sacraments. The sacramental system worked out especially in the Middle Ages by the schoolmen and subsequently at the Council of Trent envisaged sacraments primarily as causes of grace that could be received independent of the merit of the recipient. Recent Catholic sacramental theology emphasizes their function as signs of faith. Sacraments are said to cause grace insofar as they are intelligible signs of it, and that the fruitfulness, as distinct from the validity, of the sacrament is dependent on the faith and devotion of the recipient. Sacramental rites are now administered in the vernacular, rather than in Latin, to increase the intelligibility of the signs.

Conservative Catholicism connected sacramental theology to christology, stressing Christ's institution of the sacraments and the power of the sacraments to infuse the grace of Christ, earned on Calvary, to the recipient. The newer emphasis connects the sacraments to ecclesiology. We do not encounter Christ directly, but in the church, which is his body. The church mediates the presence and action of Christ. The number of sacraments was finally fixed at seven during the medieval period (at the councils of Lyons 1274, Florence 1439, and Trent 1547). In addition, Roman Catholicism has innumerable sacramentals—baptismal water, holy oil, blessed ashes, candles, palms, crucifixes, and statues. Sacramentals are said to cause grace not *ex opere operato* like the sacraments, but *ex opere operantis*, through the faith and devotion of those using them.

Revelation. The Council of Trent declared tradition to be equally authoritative with Scripture and the definitive interpretation of both to be the preserve of the church. In its *Dogmatic Constitution on Divine Revelation* Vatican II sought to remove the sharp distinction perceived by Protestants between Scripture and tradition by defining tradition as the successive interpretations of the Scriptures given by the church throughout the ages. That the church somehow stood above both sources of revelation was specifically denied: "This teaching office is not above the word of God, but serves it. . . . It is clear, therefore, that sacred tradition, sacred Scripture, and the teaching authority of the Church . . . are so linked and joined together that one cannot stand without the others."

The failure of post-Vatican II Catholicism to give a clear preeminence to the Bible leaves some Protestants dissatisfied, but there is no doubt that the scholarly and popular study of the Bible by Roman Catholics has increased markedly since 1965. Roman Catholicism is no longer simply reacting and polemical, devoted to defending truth through the condemnation of error. It is now an innovative and irenical movement, more devoted to illustrating the Christian faith than defining it.

F. S. PIGGIN

See also CATHOLICISM, LIBERAL; COUNTER-REFORMATION; EXCOMMUNICATION; GALLICANISM; INFALLIBILITY; PAPACY; TRENT, COUNCIL OF; ULTRAMONTANISM; VATICAN COUNCIL I; VATICAN COUNCIL II.

Roman Creed, Old. See APOSTLES' CREED.

Romanticism. (Old Fr. *romanz*) Movement in art, literature, philosophy, and religion in the late 18th and early 19th centuries. The Romantic movement arose in the 1790s as a reaction against the classicism and rationalism of the Enlightenment. Among the major Romantic authors are Coleridge, Wordsworth, Byron, Shelley, Keats, Scott, and Blake in Britain; Madame de Staël, Musset, George Sand, and Victor Hugo in France; and Goethe, August, Friedrich von Schlegel, Novalis, Eichendorff, Kleist, Tieck, the Grimm brothers, and E. T. A. Hoffmann in Germany. There were also Romantic composers (Chopin, Schubert, Schumann), painters (Delacroix, Turner), and philosophers (Fichte, Schelling, Hegel, Schopenhauer). The main Romantic theologian was Schleiermacher. The movement had run its course by the end of the 1830s, but some features continued even past midcentury.

Romanticism generally stresses emotionalism, sensualism, fantasy, and imagination over rational order and control. Reality is found not by rational thought but through feeling, immediate experience, spiritual illumination, brooding, and listening to inner voices. There is a subjectivism that emphasizes self-consciousness, the activity of the ego, introversion, and originality. A sense of mystery arises out of an inner longing for that which is unexperienced and unknown. Each personality should be allowed to unfold freely, according to its own genius, individual impulses, and idiosyncrasies. Romantics seek beauty, color, and adventure in out-of-the-way places and events and among common people. The exotic is preferred over the familiar, rural life over that of the city. Prescribed unities and forms are rejected for that which is different, unconventional, novel, and spontaneous. Romantics had a deep interest in the past, especially the Middle Ages, as well as nonclassical (Nordic) mythology, folklore, and primitivism, and they contributed greatly to recovering and publishing long-forgotten medieval historical records and literature. Finally Romantic art seems on the one hand to be sensuous, concrete, and down to earth, yet simultaneously it is much more visionary and even mystical. As Novalis put it, in the Romantic view of life "world becomes dream, dream becomes world."

The impact of Romanticism on religious and theological developments is significant. To be sure, its emphasis on human self-consciousness, personal creative powers, the natural goodness of humankind, and the pantheistic interfusion of real and ideal, finite and infinite, spirit and matter leads to a glorification of human powers of self-expression and to pride. Many Romantics refused to believe in any power superior to their own genius, and the objects of their devotion—nature, liberty, beauty, love, brotherhood—essentially circle back to the worshiper and function as ways of asserting human self-sufficiency.

Nevertheless, some did embrace Christianity, such as Schlegel and Novalis. In turn both Schlegel and Novalis deeply influenced the young preacher Friedrich Schleiermacher, who moved freely in Berlin's salons. At Schlegel's urging he wrote *On Religion: Addresses to Its Cultured Despisers*, a general analysis and defense of religion commending it to the intellectuals of the day who tended to dismiss it as mere superstition. In this and his main theological work *The Christian Faith* Schleiermacher charts a middle course between traditional orthodoxy and cold rationalism. It reflects his Romantic preference for the vital, inward, and spontaneous over the static, outward, and formal. Romanticism also influenced Hegel, but he went in a different direction and subsumed theology under philosophy, giving the highest place to reason.

From a historical perspective Romanticism affected trends in the church. In Britain the Romantics tended to view the church with indifference. In Germany a number of figures turned to Christianity. Some became Roman Catholics, including Friedrich Schlegel, Adam Müller, and Karl Haller, while Clemens Brentano and Joseph Görries returned to Catholicism. The dogmatic church offered a secure resting point for those weary of the restless and vain wanderings into the uncertain, and they viewed it in Novalis's sense as the mystical affirmation of Christianity. The French writer Chateaubriand glorified the Catholic faith in *The Spirit of Christianity* (1802) as a great cultural and moral force. Romanticism thus contributed to the Catholic revival of the early 19th century. Interestingly, these converts identified with a conservative view of the state.

R. V. Pierard

See also Schleiermacher, Friedrich Daniel Ernst.

Rule of Faith (Lat. *regula fidei*). Term referring to the sure doctrine of the Christian faith. The expression was first used in the theology of the church in the last quarter of the 2d century. Synonymous expressions were "canon of truth," "rule of truth," "the canon of the church," and "the ecclesiastical canon." This "canon of truth" is the official church teaching that is in agreement with Scripture and is a summary of it.

M. E. OSTERHAVEN

Rural Dean. See CHURCH OFFICERS.

Ss

Sabaoth. See God, Names of.

Sabbatarianism. View that insists that one day of each week be reserved for religious observance as prescribed by the OT sabbath law. Strict or literal sabbatarianism contends that God's directive concerning the OT sabbath law is natural, universal, and moral; consequently the sabbath requires people to abstain from all labor except those tasks necessary for the welfare of society. In this view the seventh day, the literal sabbath, is the only day on which the requirements of this law can be met. The Seventh-day Adventist Church teaches a strict sabbatarianism. Their arguments for the universally binding character of the sabbath law are as follows: (1) it is part of the moral law; (2) it was given at the creation; and (3) it was not abrogated in the NT.

Semisabbatarianism holds a view essentially the same as strict sabbatarianism but transfers its demands from Saturday, the seventh day, to Sunday, the first day of the week. Organizations such as the Lord's Day Observance Society (est. 1831), and the Imperial Alliance for the Defense of Sunday (England) have sought to preserve the principles of semisabbatarianism, but with decreasing success since World War II.

F. R. Harm

See also Adventism; Lord's Day.

Sabbath. Seventh day of the week in which God ceased from his work of creation and declared the day blessed and holy (Gen. 2:1–3). By outlining certain prohibitions about the gathering of the manna (Exod. 16), God underscored the sacred nature of the day to the Israelites. The Decalogue forbids work on the sabbath, for both the Israelites and for their servants and guests (Exod. 20:8–11). Deut. 5:12–15 implies that there is a humanitarian motive in the sabbath concept. In God's sight, no person or animal should be required to work seven days a week and to be enslaved as the Israelites were in Egypt. The sabbath is therefore a direct indication of God's consecration of Israel, as well as of his creation. The OT also made provision for a sabbath year so that the land might rest, the needy might feed on the aftergrowth, and the animals might eat the surplus (Exod. 23:10–11; Lev. 25:1–7, 18–22; Deut. 15:1–11).

Jesus observed the sabbath, not only worshiping but also by teaching in the synagogue during that time of the week (Mark 6:2). His disciples' plucking ears of grain and his healing on the sabbath were not violations of the sabbath law, but indications that Jesus recognized the import of the commandment. Not only his disciples, but also Paul and the early Jewish Christians observed the sabbath. Jewish tradition has maintained the aspects of Torah observance, community worship, and joyful family participation to the present day.

D. A. Rausch

See also Lord's Day; Sabbatarianism.

Sabellianism. See Monarchianism.

Sacrament. Religious rite or ceremony. Baptism and the Lord's Supper were given a prominent place in the fellowship of the early church (Acts 2:41–42; 10:47; 20:7, 11), along with proclamation (*kerygma*) and teaching (*didachē*). Both rites were regarded as means appointed by Jesus Christ to bring the members of the church into communion with his death and resurrection, and thus with himself through the Holy Spirit (Matt. 28:19–20; Acts 2:38; Rom. 6:3–5; 1 Cor. 11:23–27; Col. 2:11–12). The sacraments were linked together in Jesus' teaching (Mark 10:38–39) and in the mind of the church as having such significance. They were the visible enactment of the word proclaimed in the kerygma, and their significance must be understood as such.

A sacrament came to be defined (following Augustine) as a "visible word" or an "outward and visible sign of an inward and spiritual grace." The similarity between the form of the sacrament and the hidden gift tended to be stressed. Five lesser sacraments—confirmation, penance, extreme unction, order, and matrimony—became traditional in the church. But the church has always reserved a special place for baptism and the Lord's Supper as the chief mysteries. At the Reformation these were regarded as the only two sacraments that had the authority of Jesus himself, and therefore as the only true sacraments.

R. S. WALLACE

See also BAPTISM; BAPTISM, BELIEVERS'; BAPTISM, INFANT; BAPTISM, MODES OF; BAPTISMAL REGENERATION; *EX OPERE OPERATO*; LORD'S SUPPER.

Sacrifice. See ATONEMENT; OFFERINGS AND SACRIFICES IN BIBLE TIMES.

Sadducees. Jewish group that flourished in Palestine from the late 2d century B.C. to the late 1st century A.D.

Name and Nature. Ever since Abraham Geiger argued that the Sadducees were the priestly aristocracy, the majority of scholars have held that their name was derived from "Zadok," the name of the high priest during Solomon's reign (1 Kings 2:35; cf. Ezek. 44:15; 48:11). Thus the Sadducees are thought to have been the party of the Zadokite priestly elite. More recently, many scholars have argued that the Sadducees were essentially a loose confederation of wealthy and powerful men (this would include members of the priestly aristocracy) who took a secular-pragmatic, rather than a religious-ideological, stance with regard to the nation and its laws.

History. The meager evidence suggests the following outline. The Sadducees solidified as a group soon after the Maccabean revolt (167–160 B.C.). They were heirs to a persistent tendency within the Jewish aristocracy to see Judaism as a temple-centered religion rather than a law-centered way of life. Because they supported the Hasmonean policy of military and economic expansion, they gradually came to exercise tremendous influence in John Hyrcanus's court (134–104 B.C.). Their influence predominated until the end of Alexander Jannaeus's reign (76 B.C.). Under Queen Alexandra (76–67 B.C.) the Sadducees lost their power, and their numbers were greatly reduced. They fared little better under Herod the Great (37–4 B.C.), who deeply mistrusted the native Jewish aristocracy. With the imposition of direct Roman rule (A.D. 6), Sadducean fortunes revived. Between A.D. 6 and 66 the Sadducees not only became a major power within the Sanhedrin, but, for many years, they were able to control the high priesthood as well. The revolt of 66–70 spelled the end for the Sadducees.

Beliefs. The Sadducees are said to have rejected all Jewish observances not explicitly taught in the pentateuchal law. In their legal debates, the Sadducees consistently pushed for a strict and narrow application of the law. They repudiated the notions of resurrection and rewards and punishments after death, and denied the existence of angels and preterhuman spirits.

Sadducees and the NT. Unlike the Pharisees, the Sadducees are consistently painted in a bad light by the NT writers. Their opposition to Jesus and the early church is presented as monolithic and constant. Reasons for the hostility are not hard to imagine. To the Sadducees, Jesus and his early followers would have appeared as destabilizing forces in the delicate balance between limited Jewish freedom and totalitarian Roman rule. But just as significantly, the Sadducees could not have had anything but contempt for a movement that proclaimed the present reality of the resurrection and the unconditional necessity of repentance.

S. TAYLOR

See also PHARISEES.

Saint, Saintliness. Saints acquire their status by divine call (Ps. 85:8; Rom. 1:7). Latent in the use of this term is the idea that relationship to God involves conformity to his will and character (Eph. 5:3). In the Book of Revelation, where separation unto God leads to Satan-inspired persecution from the world (Rev. 13:7; 14:12) and even to martyrdom (16:6; 17:6), are the seeds for the Roman Catholic concept of the saint as a peculiarly holy or self-sacrificing person who is worthy of veneration. In the NT, however, the term "saint" is applied to all believers. It is a synonym for a Christian "brother" (Col. 1:2). The saints are the church (1 Cor. 1:2). In the Book of Ephesians, where there is a strong emphasis on the unity of the church, "all the saints" practically becomes a refrain (1:15; 3:8, 18; 6:18).

E. F. HARRISON

See also CANONIZATION; GODLINESS.

Sainthood. See CANONIZATION.

Saints, Invocation of. See INVOCATION OF THE SAINTS.

Saints, Veneration of. See VENERATION OF THE SAINTS.

Salvation. Redemption from the power and effects of sin.

The Biblical Idea. The common Hebrew words for salvation, deriving from the root *yāša'*, (width, spaciousness, freedom from constraint, hence—deliverance) obviously lend themselves to broad development in application. Literally, they cover salvation from any danger, distress, and enemies.

The Greek term *sōtēria* gathered a rich connotation from LXX to carry into NT. There, too, it means deliverance, preservation, from any danger (Acts 7:25; 27:31; Heb. 11:7).

The Comprehensiveness of Salvation. The comprehensiveness of salvation may be shown:

(1) By what we are saved from. We are saved from sin and death; guilt and estrangement; ignorance of truth; bondage to vices; fear of demons, of death, of life, of God, of hell; despair of self; alienation from others; pressures of the world; a meaningless life. Paul's own testimony is almost wholly positive: salvation brings peace with God, access to God's favor and presence, hope of regaining the glory, endurance in suffering, steadfast character, an optimistic mind, inner motivations of divine love and power of the Spirit, ongoing experience of the risen Christ, and joy in God (Rom. 5:1–11). Salvation extends also to society, aiming at realizing the kingdom of God; to nature, ending its bondage to futility (Rom. 8:19–20); and to the universe, attaining final reconciliation of a fragmented cosmos (Eph. 1:10; Col. 1:20).

(2) By noting that salvation is past (Rom. 8:24; Eph. 2:5, 8; Titus 3:5–8), present (1 Cor. 1:18; 15:2; 2 Cor. 2:15; 6:2; 1 Pet. 1:9; 3:21), and future (Rom. 5:9–10; 13:11; 1 Cor. 5:5; Phil. 1:5–6; 2:12; 1 Thess. 5:8; Heb. 1:14; 9:28; 1 Pet. 2:2). Salvation includes that which is given, freely and finally, by God's grace (forgiveness—called in one epistle justifica-

tion, friendship; or reconciliation, atonement, sonship, and new birth); that which is continually imparted (sanctification [growing emancipation from all evil, growing enrichment in all good], the enjoyment of eternal life, experience of the Spirit's power, liberty, joy, advancing maturity in conformity to Christ); and that still to be attained (redemption of the body, perfect Christlikeness, final glory).

(3) By distinguishing salvation's various aspects: religious (acceptance with God, forgiveness, reconciliation, sonship, reception of the Spirit, immortality); emotional (assurance, peace, courage, hopefulness, joy); practical (prayer, guidance, discipline, dedication, service); ethical (new moral dynamic for new moral aims, freedom, victory); personal (new thoughts, convictions, horizons, motives, satisfactions, self-fulfillment); social (new sense of community with Christians, of compassion toward all, overriding impulse to love as Jesus has loved).

R. E. O. WHITE

See also SAVIOR.

Salvation Army. See BOOTH, CATHERINE; BOOTH, WILLIAM.

Sanctification. Process of making holy. The Hebrew (*qdš*) and Greek (*hagias-*) roots—represented in the AV by the translations "sanctify, holy, hallow," and in the RSV by "consecrate, dedicate"—are applied to any person, place, occasion, or object "set apart" from common, secular use as devoted to some divine power.

The Nature of Sanctification. Jesus prays that God's name be "hallowed"; God "sanctifies" the Son, the Son "sanctifies" himself (John 10:36; 17:19). Christians are set apart for God's use (1 Cor. 1:2; 1 Pet. 1:1–2).

The most common understanding of sanctification is the growth in holiness that should follow conversion (Eph. 1:4; Phil. 3:12). Paul prays that the Thessalonians be sanctified wholly—spirit, soul, and body being kept sound and blameless—as something still to be accomplished. *Everything* is to be sanctified (1 Tim. 4:4–5). We are to be holy, righteous, and blameless before God and the world (Phil. 2:14–15; Col. 1:22; 1 Thess. 2:10).

Theology and Sanctification. Justification and sanctification are not separate in time (1 Cor. 6:11), for God's justifying act sets the sinner apart for service. Justification by faith is the moral dynamic of salvation (Rom. 1:16); forgiveness itself has moral force, creating the will to goodness in the forgiven. The two experiences must not be identified. In justification, God, at the beginning of Christian life, declares us acquitted. In sanctification, God accomplishes his will in us as Christian life proceeds. Sanctification never replaces justification.

Sanctification is of the Spirit (Rom. 15:16; 1 Cor. 6:11; Eph. 4:30; 1 Thess. 4:7–8; 2 Thess. 2:13; 1 Pet. 1:2). Sanctification is the outflow of an overflowing life within the soul, the "fruit" of the Spirit (Gal. 5:22–23), summed up as "sanctification" (Rom. 6:22 lit.).

How far does sanctification go? The Greek root *telei-* does not mean "sinless," "incapable of sinning," but "fulfilling its appointed end, complete, mature" (even "all-inclusively complete," Matt. 5:48). Such maturity is clearly part of the Christian's goal. Paul's denial that he is already "perfect," and his exhortations to ongoing sanctification, show that he does not think a final, complete sanctification can be claimed in this life.

Historical Considerations. In the apostolic church, the essence of sanctification was Christlike purity; in the patristic church, withdrawal from the contaminations of society. This hardened, in the medieval church, into asceticism: "sanctity" and "saintliness" came to be applied only to the "religious" person (priest, monk), whereas a lower attainment, compromising with the world, was tolerated in the "ordinary, secular, or lay" Christian. Luther sought to annul this double standard, making sanctification a matter of inward attitude toward all the affairs of the outside world; he made much, in his expositions, of the transformation in the life of the believer by the work of the Spirit.

Calvin's insistence upon divine sovereignty and self-discipline made sanctification a question of ever more complete obedience to the Decalogue as the core of biblical ethics. John Wesley, and Methodism after him, laid great emphasis upon complete sanctification, and often on the necessity that Christians seek perfection.

R. E. O. WHITE

Satan. (Heb. *śāṭān*, "adversary") Angelic creature who, before the creation of the human race, rebelled against the Creator and became the chief antagonist of God and humankind. Isa. 14:12–14 and Ezek. 28:12–15 paint Satan's past career in all its prefall splendor. They also portray his apostasy in drawing with him a great multitude of lesser celestial creatures (cf. Rev. 12:4), making him "the Evil One" or "the Tempter." These fallen angels (demons) fit into two classes: those that are free and those that are bound. The former roam the heavenlies with their prince-leader Satan (Matt. 12:24) and as his emissaries are so numerous as to make Satan's power practically ubiquitous. The angels (demons) that are bound are evidently guilty of more heinous wickedness and are incarcerated in Tartarus (2 Pet. 2:4; Jude 6).

Satan caused the fall of the human race (Gen. 3). His judgment was predicted in Eden (v. 15), and this was accomplished at the cross (John 12:31–33). Although Satan, even after his judgment in the cross (Col. 2:15), continues to reign as a usurper (2 Cor. 4:4), and tempts and accuses humankind (Rev. 12:10), he is to be ousted from the heavenlies (vv. 7–12) as well as the earth (5:1–19:16), and is to be confined to the abyss for 1000 years (20:1–3). When released from the abyss at the end of the 1000 years, he will make one last attempt to lead his armies against God (Rev. 20:8–9). This will result in his final doom when he is cast into the lake of fire (v. 10), which has been prepared for him and his wicked angelic accomplices (Matt. 25:41).

Satan's present work is widespread and destructive. God permits his evil activity for the time being. Demons must do Satan's bidding. The unsaved are largely under Satan's authority, and he rules them through the evil world system over which he is head and of which the unregenerate are a part (Isa. 14:12–17; 2 Cor. 4:3–4; Eph. 2:2; Col. 1:13). As far as the saved are concerned, Satan is in continued conflict with them (Eph. 6:11–18), tempts them, and seeks to corrupt and destroy their testimony and their physical life (1 Cor. 5:5; 1 John 5:16).

M. F. UNGER

See also ABADDON; BAAL-ZEBUB; DEMON, DEMON POSSESSION; OCCULT, THE; SATANISM AND WITCHCRAFT.

Satanism and Witchcraft. Worship of Satan and the use of sorcery with evil intent. The neopagan movement consists of a large number of small, diverse groups that share the common belief that they are inheritors of ancient religious traditions. Some of these groups are violently anti-Christian, but others claim to be the true inheritors of Gnostic Christianity. The traditions to which they appeal in their attempts to legitimate themselves vary greatly. Some claim to be a revival of Druidism, others of Greek religions, or of ancient Egyptian mysteries. Many simply claim to belong to what they call WICCA, which they assert is the ancient witchcraft religion of Europe. A few groups claim to be satanists who worship the devil of the Christian tradition.

For the new pagans, religion is a practical activity carried out through ritual and ceremonial acts to align the participants with the cosmic order and thus release the mystical power within them. The exact rituals, techniques, and beliefs of the new pagan groups vary greatly. But all are concerned with a quest for power and the desire that humans control their own destiny. One of the most important figures in the growth of modern paganism is Alphonse Louis Constant (1810–75), who called himself Eliphas Levi. An ex-Roman Catholic seminarian, he claimed to be an occult initiate and wrote many books that purported to reveal ancient mysteries and occult law. He drew upon theories of magic and the kabbalah, which is an ancient system of Jewish mysticism.

I. HEXHAM

See also DEMON, DEMON POSSESSION; SATAN.

Satisfaction. Compensation or reparation. The English translation "satisfaction" occurs only twice in the AV (Num. 35:31–32) as the rendering for the Hebrew *kōper*, literally meaning "a price paid as compensation." Theologically the term has played a significant part in the theory of the atonement, especially since the time of Anselm (1033–1109). Prior to his *Cur Deus Homo*, the most prevalent view of Christ's death was that it was a ransom paid to the devil in order to deliver the souls of people over whom Satan had a legal claim. Anselm by contrast stressed the fact that the death of Christ was a satisfaction rendered to God's justice and honor. Since his time this view has become one of the essential ingredients in the orthodox theory of the atonement for both Roman Catholics and Protestants. In the subsequent Protestant discussion, a distinction has been made between Christ's active and passive obedience. In the former he satisfied the demands of the law by rendering perfect obedience, and in the latter he satisfied the curse of the law by submitting himself to the ignominious death of the cross.

P. K. JEWETT

See also ATONEMENT, THEORIES OF THE; BLOOD, SACRIFICIAL ASPECTS OF; OFFERINGS AND SACRIFICES IN BIBLE TIMES; PROPITIATION.

Satisfaction Theory, The. See ATONEMENT, THEORIES OF THE.

Sattler, Michael. See MENNONITES.

Saumer Academy. See AMYRALDIANISM.

Savior. One who saves or delivers.

In the OT "savior" represents a participle of the Hebrew *yāša'* ("delivers, sets free"), used frequently of God (Isa. 43:11; 45:21). In the NT and LXX "Savior" represents the translation of the Greek term *sōtēr* ("deliverer, preserver"). Emphasis upon God as Savior can be found in Luke 1:47; Jude 25; and the Pastoral Epistles (six times). The title is applied to Christ as constituting, not merely exhibiting, salvation (Luke 2:11; John 4:42; Acts 5:31; 13:23; Eph. 5:23; Phil. 3:20–21; 1 John 4:14).

R. E. O. WHITE

See also JESUS CHRIST; MESSIAH; SALVATION.

Savonarola, Girolamo (1452–1498). Italian religious reformer. Savonarola came to Florence in 1490 to serve as public speaker at San Marco. He rose to prominence by predicting the coming of divine judgment. The French invasion of 1494 seemed to be a fulfillment of his prophecy, and when the Medici abandoned the city he gained great influence through his preaching. His uncompromising nature, however, made many enemies and brought him into conflict with Pope Alexander VI. Unresponsive to papal warnings, he was excommunicated. He was charged with treason, convicted, and burned at the stake. Many early Protestants such as Luther and Beza regarded him as a martyr for the gospel.

R. G. CLOUSE

Savoy Conference (1661). Series of meetings held at the Savoy in the Strand, London, with the aim of reviewing the contents of the *Book of Common Prayer* and hearing criticism of it by leading Presbyterian divines. The meetings lasted from Apr. 15 to July 24, 1661, and included 12 bishops, 12 Presbyterian clergy, and assessors from each party. This attempt to keep the Presbyterians in the national church failed, and a large number of them became Nonconformists in 1661–62. Certain of their requests for change were granted and embodied in the 1662 edition of the *Book of Common Prayer*. This allowed a minority of Presbyterians to stay within the church.

P. TOON

See also BOOK OF COMMON PRAYER.

Saxon Confession (1551). Exposition of the Augsburg Confession written by Philip Melanchthon in 1551 for presentation to the Council of Trent. Originally entitled *Repetition of the Augsburg Confession,* it appeared in print in 1552 under the title *The Confession of Doctrine of the Saxon Churches*. It was considerably less conciliatory than the Augsburg Confession. In addition to stating evangelical doctrine, it specifically detailed the errors of the Roman Catholic Church in 23 sections.

R. W. HEINZE

See also AUGSBURG CONFESSION; CONFESSIONS OF FAITH; MELANCHTHON, PHILIP.

Saybrook Platform (1708). Articles committing Connecticut Congregationalists to the doctrine of the Savoy Declaration (1658). The leaders of the colony had been troubled by forces that seemed to be fragmenting Connecticut society and undermining traditions in the churches. In Sept. 1708, four laymen and 12 ministers met at Saybrook in response to the General Court's appeal. They prepared 15 *Articles for the Administration of Church Discipline*. This "platform" also incorporated some presbyterian features.

M. A. NOLL

See also CREED, CREEDS; CONFESSIONS OF FAITH.

Sayers, Dorothy Leigh (1893–1957). English author. As writer of detective fiction, author of religious plays, translator of Dante, arbiter of English usage, and lay theologian, Sayers was an influential exponent of orthodox Christian faith during the middle third of the 20th century. A lifelong member of the Church of England, she published her learned, yet eminently readable, theological essays to promote a basic understanding of historic orthodoxy. In *The Mind of the Maker* Sayers provided extended exposition of a theme that she had treated in several occasional papers. The creative process, she argued, can be regarded profitably as an analogy to the way in which the Trinitarian God governs the world.

M. A. NOLL

Scapegoat. See ATONEMENT, DAY OF.

Schaff, Philip (1819–1893). American church historian. Schaff was called in 1844 to a professorship at the obscure theological seminary of the German Reformed Church in Mercersburg, Pennsylvania. With his colleague John W. Nevin, Schaff quickly became known as the exponent of the intellectually profound and controversial Mercersburg theology. In his inaugural address, *The Principle of Protestantism* (1844), he set forth the developmental principle, arguing that the Reformation was a flowering of the best in medieval Catholicism and that Protestantism and Catholicism would eventually merge into a renewed, evangelical faith. In *What Is Church History?* (1846) he identified with the new "historical school" that united past and present in the development of the church. Schaff insisted that the most dangerous enemy was not the Roman pope but the "numberless popes" who would enslave Protestantism to human authority. Noteworthy are his eight-volume *History of the Christian Church*, the *Creeds of Christendom* (3 vols., 1877), a multivolume edition of the church fathers, and the *Schaff-Herzog Encyclopedia of Religious Knowledge* (1884).

R. V. PIERARD

See also MERCERSBURG THEOLOGY.

Schism, The Great (1054). First permanent severing of the Christian community.

Two fundamental differences between the Latin Catholic and Greek Orthodox traditions developed during the early Middle Ages. The first was the Petrine doctrine—absolute in the West but resisted in the East. The second was a Western addition to the Nicene Creed—*ex Patre Filioque*—which provoked the *filioque* controversy. Other divisive issues, such as the celibacy of the priesthood, the use of unleavened bread in the Eucharist, episcopal control over the sacrament of confirmation, and priestly beards and monkish tonsures, were the source of conflict but not schism.

It was the fusion of the *filioque* controversy with the rise of papal power that created the great crisis of 1054. The "reform" papacy of the 11th century established itself on the right of the pope, as apostolic heir of Peter, to absolute power over all Christian people and institutions. Such claims had been rejected by the early church councils. To Eastern patriarchs Christ's charge to Peter in Matt. 16:18–19 was shared by all the apostles and their spiritual heirs, the bishops. In 1054 Pope Leo IX (1048–54) sent a delegation headed by Cardinal Humbert of Silva Candida to discuss the problems between the papacy and Constantinople. Disaster followed. The patriarch of Constantinople, Michael Cerularius, rejected both papal claims and the *filioque*. The Western legates accused Constantinople of having altered the Nicene Creed. In the end, Cardinal Humbert deposited a Bull of Excommunication against Michael Cerularius on the altar of the Hagia Sophia, and the Great Schism was official. In 1965, Pope Paul VI lifted the ban of excommunication against Michael Cerularius. The problem of papal rule has been rendered more difficult, however, by 19th-century Roman declarations of papal infallibility. The wording of the Nicene Creed has not been settled.

C. T. MARSHALL

See also FILIOQUE.

Schlatter, Adolf von (1852–1938). German NT scholar and theologian. Schlatter was professor at Tübingen (1898), where he spent his most productive years. Schlatter was one of the most respected voices of conservative scholarship in early 20th-century Germany. He felt that a precise knowledge of the religion of late Judaism and history of the intertestamental period was necessary for a proper understanding of the NT, and his research opened new paths for NT exegesis. Besides several large commentaries and numerous *Erläuterungen* designed to assist ordinary Bible readers, he wrote major historical studies of Israel (1901) and the early church (*The Church in the NT Period* [1926]). He distinguished himself in systematics with substantial works in dogmatics (1911), ethics (1914), and NT theology (1921–22).

R. V. PIERARD

Schleiermacher, Friedrich Daniel Ernst (1768–1834). German theologian and philosopher. Schleiermacher's intellectual development was profoundly influenced after 1796 by his association in Berlin with the flowering Romantic movement, which revolted against classical norms in literature and art and the arid rationalism of the Enlightenment. Prodded by Friedrich Schlegel, a leader of the new movement, Schleiermacher wrote *On Religion: Speeches to Its Cultured Despisers* in 1799 to address his fellow Romantics. He claimed that they had renounced religion because rationalists had wrongly reduced its essence either to knowledge acquired through reason and expressed in doctrines, or morality perceived through conscience and demonstrated in moral behavior. In doing so they had ignored feeling, not only a primary component of Romanticism, but the very essence of religion. Schleiermacher therefore redefined religion as a unique element of human experience, not located in the cognitive or moral faculties, which produce only an indirect knowledge of God by inference, but in feeling, which yields immediate experience of God.

Schleiermacher recast Christian theology in *The Christian Faith* (1821) in keeping with his Romantic redefinition of religion. In his mature thought he defined religion as "the feeling of absolute dependence" or "God-consciousness." Theological statements do not describe God in any objective manner but rather are ways in which the Christian feeling of absolute dependence is related to God. Theology is a historical discipline whose task is to record the religious experience of each new generation.

Schleiermacher's revision of Christian theology had its most radical impact on the issue of authority. No external authority, whether it be Scripture, church, or historic creedal statement, takes precedence over the immediate experience of believers. This contributed to a more critical approach to the Bible by questioning its inspiration and authority, and to a rejection of doctrines Schleiermacher believed were unrelated to people's religious experience of redemption such as the virgin birth, the Trinity, and the return of Christ—tenets that implied a cognitive and thus indirect knowledge rather than immediate God-consciousness.

These ideas gained wide acceptance in the 19th century. Schleiermacher's influence was evident not only in the demise of Enlightenment deism in Europe, but also in the rise of theological liberalism in America. His ideas were sharply challenged after World War I by the neo-orthodox theologian Karl Barth, who charged that not only were essential doctrines reinterpreted, but Christianity's uniqueness was compromised by making it merely one among many forms of religion.

W. A. HOFFECKER

See also LIBERALISM, THEOLOGICAL; ROMANTICISM.

Schleitheim, Seven Articles of. See MENNONITES.

Schmucker, Samuel Simon (1799–1873). Proponent of "American" or "New School" Lutheranism. As opposed to "European" or "Old" Lutheranism, Schmucker sought an accommodation between American Protestantism and traditional Lutheran distinctives. He was a founder, professor of theology, and president of Gettysburg Lutheran Seminary and a vital force in the General Synod of Lutheran churches that had been formed in 1820. At the same time, he moved beyond traditional Lutheranism by supporting revivalism and aiding the development of interdenominational agencies like the American Sunday School Union.

M. A. NOLL

Scholasticism. Medieval European Christian philosophical and theological system. Scholasticism attempted to synthesize ideas expressed in classical Roman and Greek writings, the Scripture, the writings of the patristic fathers, and other Christian writings preceding the medieval period. Aristotle's views helped give scholasticism a systematic structure, but Platonism also played a large part in the enterprise.

The method of scholasticism sought to understand the fundamental aspects of theology, philosophy, and law. Apparently contradictory viewpoints were offered in order to show how they possibly could be synthesized through reasonable interpretation. A problem would first be "exposed," and then it would be "disputed" in order to cause a new "discovery" in the mind of the person who was seeking new personal knowledge. Each text investigated had a commentary. The master helped the student to read the text in such a way that the student could really understand what it was saying. This experience was to be much more than just memorative. There were yes-and-no positions to various texts, which sought to keep the student from merely memorizing the text. Abelard developed the yes-and-no method with great precision. The two most exciting types of disputations were the *quaestio disputata*, which was a disputed question, and the *quodlibet*, which was a very subtle form of disputed question that could be publicly disputed only by a truly great master, whereas the disputed questions could be talked about by lesser minds still growing in knowledge.

Aquinas represents the apogee of scholastic thought. His great effort was to combine what could be called non-Christian philosophy with both Christian philosophy and theology. Scholasticism went into decline in the 15th century, but was revived in the 16th century. The 20th century has experienced a renewed attempt to make the Thomistic form of scholasticism credible as a system of thought. This movement within Roman Catholic circles has been partially successful.

T. J. German

See also Abelard, Peter; Albertus Magnus; Anselm of Canterbury; Bonaventure; Duns Scotus, John; Peter Lombard; Thomas Aquinas; William of Ockham.

Scholasticism, Protestant. Method of thinking developed in early Protestantism that became especially prominent in the 17th century and became a widely accepted way to create systematic Protestant theologies. Several factors account for the growth of Protestant scholasticism: formal education, confidence in reason, and religious controversy.

Protestant scholasticism used reason as a means to develop coherent theology out of biblical texts. The use of scholastic techniques and attitudes served to keep Protestants in the mainstream of early modern philosophy, which, although it moved away from deductive logic, maintained confidence in reason. Protestant theologians, especially Calvinists, could use scholastic methods to inquire beyond biblical texts into the intricacies and implications of Protestant theology, especially when divine election and the will of God were considered.

The influence of Protestant scholasticism was both immediate and long-range. Among Lutherans, the essential doctrine of justification by faith was transformed into a rather complicated theory of conversion by the most famous Lutheran scholastic, Johann Gerhard (1582–1637). Gerhard used Aristotelian and biblical proofs in his *Loci theologicae* (9 vols.). The dominant Reformed scholastics, however, were Beza, Vermigli, Adrianus Heerebout, and Francis Turretin (1623–87). Turretin's *Institutio* became the standard work for modern Protestant scholastics, as it was used as a textbook to shape the modern Princeton theology. Reformed scholasticism in this tradition led to what is generally labeled Calvinist orthodoxy.

The impact of Protestant scholasticism's methods and outlook was threefold: it created a systematic, well-defined, and aggressive Protestant theology; it led to a reaction from those who emphasized the emotional character of Christian piety; and it encouraged accommodation to early modern philosophy.

R. J. VANDERMOLEN

See also BEZA, THEODORE; GERHARD, JOHANN; PETER MARTYR VERMIGLI; RAMUS, PETER; TURRETIN, FRANCIS.

Schoolmen. See SCHOLASTICISM.

Schwabach, Articles of (1529). Lutheran confessional document prepared by Melanchthon and other Wittenberg theologians. In their final form the 17 constituent articles provided the basis for the first part of the Augsburg Confession (1530). They were directed against Roman Catholics, Zwinglians, and Anabaptists, and set forth the Lutheran understanding of the Eucharist.

J. D. DOUGLAS

See also AUGSBURG CONFESSION; CONFESSIONS OF FAITH; MARBURG COLLOQUY.

Schweitzer, Albert (1875–1965). German theologian, medical missionary, and musicologist. Schweitzer's early theological work was devoted to the messiahship and suffering of Jesus (*The Mystery of the Kingdom of God* [1901]), and his most noteworthy book, *The Quest of the Historical Jesus* (1906), established his theological reputation. He also distinguished himself as a student of the Baroque organ with *J. S. Bach* (1908), an eight-volume critical edition of Bach's organ works, and a book on German and French organ construction (1906).

After eight years of study and completion of a dissertation refuting the theory that Jesus was paranoid (*The Psychiatric Study of Jesus*), he received an M.D. at Strasbourg in 1913 and left immediately for the mission at Lambaréné in Gabon. With his wife, a nurse, he founded a jungle hospital which eventually became world-famous. He received the Nobel Peace Prize in 1952 and in later life was a strong opponent of atomic weapons. Schweitzer's work in Africa was a monument to his understanding of what following the spirit of Jesus means. Although he was uncertain about traditional Christian dogma, he strongly emphasized the ethical side of life and the necessity for discipleship.

R. V. PIERARD

Schwenckfeld, Kasper von Ossig (1489–1561). Mystic, lay theologian, and Silesian nobleman. Schwenckfeld was a university-educated courtier and early supporter of Lutheran reforms in Silesia (ca. 1520–26). He broke with Luther and other Reformers initially over the nature and meaning of the Lord's Supper and advocated a suspension of reforms until the major parties could agree. His own spiritualized concept of the Supper focused on an inward partaking of Christ's heavenly flesh, and was denounced by Luther. Schwenckfeld hoped to develop a "royal" or middle course between Lutheranism and Catholicism, both of which he felt were overly concerned with outward practices; but he was condemned by both. Although Schwenckfeld's evangelical spiritualism anticipated later developments in pietism and the Society of Friends, he refused to organize his followers. A Schwenckfelder Church was developed after 1540 by spiritualists who treasured his numerous writings. Small groups of "Confessors of the Glory of Christ" developed in Silesia, Swabia, Prussia, and elsewhere.

D. B. ELLER

Scientia Media. (Lat. "middle knowledge") Sixteenth-century theological concept that Jesus introduced a third form of divine knowledge of what *would* happen under such-and-such conditions based upon neither God's nature nor his decree but upon the free decisions of created beings. Thus God knew what would happen if David had remained in Keilah, and what would happen if he had not (1 Sam. 23:1–13); God knows such things not because he controls the course of history, but because he knows what free decisions people will make independently of his controlling decree. The concept of *scientia media* was held by Lutherans and Arminians seeking to restate Roman Catholic theology in opposition to the challenges of Protestantism and Jansenism. The Reformed agree that God knows what might happen under all conditions, but they reject the notion that this knowledge is ever ultimately based on our autonomous decisions. Human decisions, they argue, are themselves the effects of God's eternal decrees (see Acts 2:23; Rom. 9:10–18; Eph. 1:11; Phil. 2:12–13).

J. M. Frame

See also Foreknowledge.

Scofield, Cyrus Ingerson (1843–1921). Congregational minister and writer. His pastoral ministry, both in Dallas (1882–95) and, at D. L. Moody's urging, in East Northfield, Maine (1895–1902), was marked by strong public response.

As impressive as his pulpit ministry was, Scofield's greatest impact came through his writings. In 1885 he issued *Rightly Dividing the Word of Truth.* This work set the direction for his teaching and, through numerous editions, the agenda for a major segment of American fundamentalism. Two publications reinforced this basic work. *The Comprehensive Bible Correspondence Course*, first issued in 1896, supplied a curricular base for churches and Bible schools. *The Scofield Reference Bible* was his most important work. Nine years were devoted to this project prior to publication by Oxford University Press in 1909, and over 2 million copies have been sold. Scofield's system is dispensational, premillennial, and pretribulational. The dispensations, seven in number, are periods of time, each governed by a particular principle. These are innocence, conscience, human government, promise, law, grace, and kingdom. For Scofield the dispensations are seen in the light of God's program of redemption.

Scofield enthusiastically promoted world missions and founded the Central American Mission. In an age when denominational missions suffered from liberal malaise, Bible school people in large numbers went into all the world taking Scofield's works with them. Today his teachings form the theological core in Bible schools around the world.

W. N. Kerr

See also Dispensation, Dispensationalism; Fundamentalism.

Scopes Trial (1925). Legal confrontation over the teaching of evolution in a Tennessee high school and one of the turning points in American religious history. The state of Tennessee in Mar. 1925 passed a law forbidding the teaching of evolution in its schools. The next month, John T. Scopes, a biology teacher at Rhea County High School in Dayton, assigned a text that linked humankind with the evolution of vertebrate mammals. Scopes was indicted, tried in July, convicted by a jury that deliberated a total of nine minutes, and given a $100 fine by Judge John Raulston. The conviction was later overturned by the Tennessee Supreme Court on the technical grounds that the jury, rather than the judge, should have set the amount of the fine. Tennessee's antievolution law continued on the books, although not enforced, until 1967.

The real confrontation at Dayton, however, involved the counsel imported into Tennessee for the event—for the prosecution, three-time presidential candidate William Jennings Bryan, who had emerged as the champion of antievolutionary forces after World War I; for the defense, the famous Clarence Darrow, who had only recently defended the Chicago murderers Leopold and Loeb. Bryan seemed to stand for traditional American values—a simple trust in the Bible, a commitment to "simple facts," and a distrust of new "hypotheses"; Darrow seemed to represent enlightened science, modern thought, and urbane culture. The Scopes Trial had a major impact on American religious life. It gave fundamentalists a reputation for cultural backwardness that lingers to the present. It solidified the issue of evolution as a focus for concern among theological conservatives. And, although the reality may have been different, it fixed in the popular mind a sharp distinction between rural, evangelical, traditional America and an urban, educated, and secular counterpart.

M. A. NOLL

See also EVOLUTION; FUNDAMENTALISM.

Scots Confession (1560). First confession of faith of the Reformed Church of Scotland. It was drawn up in four days by six Scottish Reformers—Knox, Spottiswood, Willock, Row, Douglas, and Winram, each of whom bore the Christian name of John. Knox undoubtedly played the predominant role in this preparation. The Scottish Parliament adopted the confession in 1560 with little opposition. Queen Mary, who still resided in France, refused to ratify the decision, with the result that it did not become the official confession until 1567, when Parliament reenacted it after her deposition. The Scots Confession remained the official confession of the Church until it adopted the Westminster Confession of Faith in 1647. The theology of the Scots Confession is Calvinistic and in general agreement with other creeds of the Reformed churches.

R. KYLE

See also CONFESSIONS OF FAITH; KNOX, JOHN; WESTMINSTER CONFESSION OF FAITH.

Scottish Realism. British 18th-/19th-century movement that attempted to overcome the epistemological, metaphysical, and moral skepticism of the Enlightenment philosophy of David Hume (1711–76) with a philosophy of common sense and natural realism. The founder of Scottish Realism was a moderate (as opposed to evangelical) Presbyterian clergyman, Thomas Reid (1710–96), who became professor at King's College, Aberdeen, in 1751 and at Glasgow in 1764. He wrote *Essays on the Intellectual Powers of Man* (1785) and *Essays on the Active Powers of Man* (1788).

Reid argued that the mind perceives external objects directly through intuitive knowledge. We know reality, not by a "conjunction" of separated sense experiences, but by immediate "judgments of nature," which we make because our mind is constituted by God to know reality directly. These "original and natural judgments" (by which we know real objects) "make up what is called *the common sense of mankind*; and what is manifestly contrary to any of those first principles is what we call *absurd*" (*Inquiry*, 7.4). These first principles, of course, cannot and need not be proved; they are "self-evident" to common human experience. Among these principles are the existence of external objects, cause and effect, and the obligations of morality. Any philosophy that denies these commonly accepted principles on which all people must base their lives is of necessity defective. The Scottish philosophy exercised supreme influence over American theological thought, providing the epistemological structure utilized by both "liberals" and "conservatives" in 19th-century America.

D. F. KELLY

See also HUME, DAVID; PRINCETON THEOLOGY, OLD.

Scripture. (Gk. *graphē)* Term occurring in the NT in reference to the canonical OT literature. Its plural form denotes the entire collection of such compositions (Matt. 21:42; 1 Cor. 15:3–4), but when used in the singular, *graphe* can mean either a specified passage (Mark 12:10) or the constituent body of writings (Gal. 3:22). The Scriptures are referred to by the term *hiera grammata* on one occasion (2 Tim. 3:15), while in the Pauline literature the word *gramma* ("writing") refers consistently to the Hebrew Torah or law. The content of a particular verse, or group of verses, is sometimes described as *to gegrammenon* (Luke 20:17; 2 Cor. 4:13).

R. K. HARRISON

See also BIBLE.

Scripture, Authority of. See BIBLE, AUTHORITY OF.

Second Advent of Christ. See SECOND COMING OF CHRIST.

Secondary Separation. See SEPARATION.

Second Chance. Another chance after death to profess Christ. Some theologians have argued that some (or all) who die unsaved will have a second chance. The Jehovah's Witnesses also maintain this view. Chief arguments for it include (1) general considerations about divine love and justice; (2) the position (defended by texts like John 3:18, 36) that conscious, deliberate unbelief in Jesus is the only legitimate ground for condemnation; therefore, those at least who have never heard of Christ or who have not seriously considered him ought to have another chance; (3) texts like Matt. 12:32; 1 Pet. 3:19; 4:6 taken to teach a probation after death.

This view is rejected by all orthodox Protestant churches. The mainstream of Protestant theology urges that death is the *end* of probation and that the spiritual condition after death is fixed, not fluid (Luke 16:19–31; John 8:24; Heb. 9:27). God's judgment is based upon deeds done in the body (Matt. 7:22–23; 10:32–33; 25:34–46; 2 Cor. 5:9–11; Gal. 6:7–8; 2 Thess. 1:8). The idea of a second chance is inconsistent with the urgent call in Scripture to repentance and obedience *now* (2 Cor. 6:2; Heb. 3:7–19; 12:25–29).

J. M. FRAME

Second Coming of Christ. Doctrine that Jesus Christ, who left earth and ascended to the Father, will one day again return to earth.

The Fact of the Second Coming. Jesus, in his great discourse on the last things (Matt. 24–25), speaks of his return in parables and more direct teaching. He promises the disciples that he is going to prepare a place for his followers and will one day come again to receive them to himself, that they might be together forever (John 14:3). The angels at the time of the ascension tell the disciples that the Lord will come again in the same manner in which he had gone away (Acts 1:11). The return of Christ is part of the kerygma (Acts 3:21). It is mentioned in Paul's writings (1 Cor. 15:23; Phil. 3:20; Col. 3:4; 1 Thess. 2:19; 3:13; 4:15–17; 2 Thess. 1:7; 2 Tim. 4:8; Titus 2:13; Heb. 9:28).

The Nature of the Second Coming. The second coming will be personal and bodily. Jesus suggests that his coming will be spectacularly visible and unmistakable: "For as the lightning that comes from the east is visible even in the west, so will be the coming of the Son of Man" (Matt. 24:27). The Son of man will be seen "coming on the clouds of the sky, with power and great glory" (v. 30). Paul's description of the second coming includes similarly unmistakable circumstances: "For the Lord himself will come down from heaven, with a loud command, with the voice of the archangel and with the trumpet call of God, and the dead in Christ will rise first" (1 Thess. 4:16).

Terms for the Second Coming. Several NT terms represent the event. The most frequently used term is *parousia*, meaning literally "being by." It means "presence, coming, or arrival" (1 Thess. 3:13; 4:15; 2 Thess. 2:8). *Apocalypse* means, literally, "revelation." Paul speaks of waiting for the revealing of Christ (1 Cor. 1:7). *Epiphany* means "manifestation." This will be a coming of Christ at the end of the tribulation (1 Tim. 6:14; 2 Tim. 4:8; Titus 2:13–14).

The Purpose of the Second Coming. The purpose of Christ's second coming is the establishment, in the fullest sense, of the kingdom of God. The time is coming when "every knee should bow, in heaven and on earth and under the earth, and every tongue confess that Jesus Christ is Lord, to the glory of God the Father" (Phil. 2:10–11). Jesus' coming will involve joyous celebration by Christians, but also reluctant submission by unbelievers. Even the devil, the beast, and the false prophet will be thrown into the lake of fire (Rev. 20:10).

Preparation for the Second Coming. Watchfulness is urged. Because no one knows the time of Jesus' coming, it is essential that we be alert to the possibility at any time (Matt. 24:42). Waiting is the precaution against the error of believing that it must necessarily be soon (see Matt. 25:1–13; cf. 2 Pet. 3:3–4). Finally, the follower of the Lord is to be working in view of the certain fact of his return. The parable of the talents (Matt. 25:14–30) makes this especially clear. Watchful waiting is not to be idleness. Paul's words to the Thessalonians (2 Thess. 3:6–13) underscore this.

Millennial Views. Various positions are taken on the question of the relationship of Christ's return to the 1000-year period of which John writes in Rev. 20:4–6.

Amillennialism. This view does not expect any earthly reign of Christ between his return and the final judgment. It maintains that the 1000 years are symbolic, either of the completeness of Christ's reign when he returns, or of the condition of believers during the intermediate state between death and resurrection. *Postmillennialism.* Through the successful preaching of the gospel, the reign of God will gradually become complete upon earth, evil will cease, and peace will come. At the end of this period, which is not necessarily exactly 1000 years, Christ will return. *Premillennialism.* Christ will return at the beginning of the millennium and will resurrect dead believers; they, together with believers still alive at Christ's coming, will reign with him on earth. At the end of this period of time there will be a brief flareup of evil, followed by the resurrection of unbelievers and the final judgment.

Tribulational Views. A number of positions are adopted relative to the relationship between the second coming and the great tribulation of Matt. 24. *Pretribulationism.* Christ will come for the saints to remove them from the world (the rapture) before the seven years of tribulation, returning with the saints at the end of the tribulation. *Post-tribulationism.* The church will not be removed from the world, but will go through the tribulation, although preserved within it. *Midtribulationism.* The church will go through the first three and a half years (the tribulation) but will be removed before the great tribulation (or wrath of God).

Conclusion. The doctrine of the second coming has often become a source of controversy among Christians. It should instead, as Paul indicates, serve as an encouragement to hope and comfort (1 Thess. 4:18).

M. J. ERICKSON

See also JUDGMENT; JUDGMENT OF THE NATIONS, THE; JUDGMENT SEAT; MARRIAGE FEAST OF THE LAMB; MILLENNIUM, VIEWS OF THE; RAPTURE OF THE CHURCH; RESURRECTION OF THE DEAD; TRIBULATION.

Second Death, The. See DEATH, THE SECOND.

Second Great Awakening. See GREAT AWAKENINGS, THE.

Sect, Sectarianism. The term "sect" has regularly been applied to groups that break away from existing religious bodies, such as the early Christians who separated from Judaism or the Protestants who separated from Roman Catholicism. The term has also been applied to groups that maintain their identity without separating from the larger religious body, for example, the Pharisees among the Jews or the Puritans in the Church of England.

"Sectarianism" in a narrow sense denotes zeal for, or attachment to, a sect. Likewise, it connotes an excessively zealous and doctrinaire narrow-mindedness that would quickly judge and condemn those who disagree. In a broader sense, however, "sectarianism" denotes the historical process by which all the divisions in major world religions have come about. In the history of Christianity, for example, sectarianism is a prevalent theme from the Judaizers and Nicolaitans of the NT to the many new denominations emerging in recent times.

Sociologists of religion have appropriated the term "sect" as a label for a specific type of religious movement. In the typology of religious movements that has developed from the pioneering work of Ernst Troeltsch, the sect is a formally organized religious body that arises in protest against and competition with the pervasive religion of a society.

H. K. GALLATIN

See also CULTS; DENOMINATIONALISM.

Secular Clergy. Roman Catholic clergy not bound by the rules of any particular religious community such as the Society of Jesus or the Benedictines. They are directly supervised by a local bishop, or "ordinary." Secular clergy are viewed as working quite directly *in* the world, while yet not being *of* the world.

T. J. GERMAN

Secularism, Secular Humanism. Way of life and thought pursued without reference to God or religion. In general terms, secularism involves an affirmation of immanent, this-worldly realities, along with a denial or exclusion of transcendent, other-worldly realities. It is a worldview and lifestyle oriented to the profane rather than the sacred, the natural rather than the supernatural. Secularism is a nonreligious approach to individual and social life.

Secularism as a comprehensive philosophy of life expresses an unqualified enthusiasm for the process of secularization in all spheres of life. Secularism is fatally flawed by its reductionist view of reality, denying and excluding God and the supernatural in a myopic fixation on the immanent and the natural. In contemporary discussion, secularism and humanism are often seen in tandem as secular humanism—an approach to life and thought, individual and society, which glorifies the creature and rejects the Creator. As such, secularism constitutes a rival to Christianity.

From the perspective of biblical Christian theology, secularism is guilty for having "exchanged the truth of God for a lie, and worshiped and served created things rather than the Creator" (Rom. 1:25). Having excluded the transcendent

God as the Absolute and the Object of worship, the secularist inexorably makes the world of humankind and nature absolute and the object of worship. In biblical terms, the supernatural God has created the world and sustains its existence. This world (Lat. *saeculum*) has value because God has created it, continues to preserve it, and has acted to redeem it. While God is Lord of history and the universe, he is not identifiable with either (pantheism). Men and women exist in freedom and responsibility before God and for the world. Stewardship and partnership define our relationship to God and the world.

The relationship of the church to the society around it is one of loving service and witness, proclamation and healing. In this sense, then, secularization of society is a Christian calling. That is, society must not be divinized or absolutized, but viewed as something historical and relative. Only God is finally sacred and absolute. Reestablishing the sacredness of God will, however, imply the proper, relative valuation of this world.

D. W. Gill

See also Death of God Theology; Enlightenment, The; Humanism, Christian; Liberalism, Theological; Situation Ethics.

Security of the Believer. See Perseverance.

Self-Esteem, Self-Love. Estimate that one makes of oneself. To make a sensible appraisal of self-worth is to evaluate oneself in terms of both strengths and weaknesses, potential for growth and vulnerabilities. Self-love involves an acceptance of oneself, yet is not complacency. It involves a comfortableness with one's being, but is not devoid of impetus for growth.

For the Christian the old nature, that which is fallen and judicially condemned by God, has been put away by the blood of Christ (Rom. 6). Thus without compromise the Scriptures can command us to love our neighbor as we love ourselves, implying a degree of legitimate self-love. For in such self-love we are praising the work of God in us, a work that has established a new nature that is of God. This is the principle of self-love as declared by the Bible, which is full of examples of people of God who dared to experience and express self-love. For example, in Genesis the story of Joseph and his brothers illustrates one who knew he was right and acted accordingly, in spite of the accusations of his brothers. God's appraisal of such behavior is indicated by Joseph's vindication. We must evaluate ourselves honestly before other people and God. God's aim is that we be in his image and have a high sense of self-esteem that is not contrived or phony but real.

E. R. Skoglund

See also Humility; Love.

Self-Examination. Scrutiny of one's inner self to determine spiritual status, motives, and attitudes. In the OT the searching of innermost thoughts and intents was primarily the responsibility of God (Exod. 20:20; Deut. 8:2, 16; 13:3; Ps. 26:2). Believers are to examine (Gk. *dokimazō*) themselves to make sure they are in proper relationship to God and others so that they may partake of the Lord's Supper (1 Cor. 11:28). Christians must judge (*diakrinō*) themselves lest they be judged (1 Cor. 11:31–32). Self-judgment leads to confession and forgiveness.

V. R. Edman

Self-Existence of God. See God, Attributes of.

Self-Righteousness. Concept of a personally developed ethic as one's standard for salvation. In Judaism, self-righteousness could be understood as a necessary evaluation of "balance" with regard to merit accumulated through good works as opposed to inherited sinfulness. Conformity to the Torah, plus active development of good impulse and restraint of evil impulse, were standards by which to evaluate self-righteousness. This is precisely the type of righteousness, coveted by the Pharisees, which Jesus rejects in contrast to the righteousness of the kingdom (Matt. 5:20; 6:33; cf. Luke 18:9–14). The shocking news of the gospel is that God has declared us righteous only in Christ. Thus any attitude of self-righteousness is excluded (Eph. 2:9) and categorically condemned (Matt. 6:1).

S. E. McClelland

Semi-Arianism. Fourth-century doctrine of Christ's sonship. Semi-Arianism was espoused by theologians reluctant to accept either the strict Nicene definition or the extreme Arian position. After the Council of Nicea (A.D. 325) a single term came to identify each position. Orthodox theologians, led by Athanasius, used the term *homoousios*; the Arian party used *anomoios*. Semi-Arians avoided either extreme and adopted the term *homoiousios*, which defined Christ as "of like substance" with the Father, but left vague the extent to which Christ differed from other created beings. Semi-Arians called Christ "divine," but in effect denied that he is truly God, that he is "equal to the Father as touching his Godhead."

B. L. Shelley

See also Arianism; Athanasius; Nicea, Council of.

Semi-Pelagianism. Doctrinal position, upheld from 427 to 529, that rejected the extreme views of both Pelagius and Augustine in regards to the priority of divine grace and human will in the initial work of salvation. The label "Semi-Pelagian," however, is a relatively modern expression, which apparently appeared first in the Lutheran Formula of Concord (1577), and became associated with the theology of the Jesuit Luis Molina (1535–1600). It would be more correct to call the proponents of the theological position Semi-Augustinians. While rejecting the doctrines of Pelagius and respecting Augustine, they were not willing to follow the ultimate consequences of his theology.

The Semi-Pelagians agreed with Augustine as to the seriousness of sin, yet regarded his doctrine of predestination as in conflict with tradition and dangerous because it makes all human efforts superfluous. In opposition to Augustinianism, Cassian, for example, taught that although a sickness is inherited through Adam's sin, human free will has not been obliterated. Divine grace is indispensable for salvation, but it does not necessarily need to precede a free human choice, because, despite the weakness of human volition, the will takes the initiative toward God. In other words, divine grace and human free will must work together in salvation. In opposition to the stark predestinarianism of Augustine, Cassian held to the doctrine of God's universal will to save, and that predestination is simply divine foreknowledge.

The debate about Semi-Pelagianism continued well into the 6th century, when Caesarius of Arles convened the Synod of Orange (529). Caesarius succeeded in dogmatizing a number of principles against the Semi-Pelagians. In doing so, however, the synod did not accept Augustine's full doctrine of grace, especially not his concept of divine grace that works irresistibly in the predestinated. In 531, Boniface II approved the acts of this council, thus giving it ecumenical authority. Semi-Pelagianism, as a historical movement, subsequently declined, but the pivotal issue of Semi-Pelagianism—the priority of the human will over the grace of God in the initial work of salvation—did not die out.

R. Kyle

Senses of Scripture. See INTERPRETATION OF THE BIBLE.

Sensus Deitatis, Sensus Divinitatis. Term used by Calvin to describe innate knowledge of God. The sense of deity is not merely a capacity for the knowledge of God, nor is it the product of reflection upon natural revelation. It is an immediate intuition of the existence and majesty of the one true God, which, though obscured by human sinfulness, can never be completely eradicated.

D. G. DUNBAR

See also REVELATION, GENERAL.

Sentences. (Lat. *sententiae*) Exposition of thought that attempts to make the beliefs of the faith partially reasonable within the framework of *fides quaerens intellectum* ("faith seeking to understand"). The notion of sentences originated from the writings of the early Christian fathers, who wished to explain in a disciplined and authoritative manner the various truths that emanate from the Scripture as the Word of God. The sentences of the medieval period sought to organize more clearly the thoughts of the fathers of the church. Those of Peter Lombard were the most interesting and unusual of the period.

T. J. GERMAN

See also PETER LOMBARD.

Separation. Negative aspect of sanctification. Having been redeemed and regenerated, the Christian's life is to be different from that of the non-Christian.

Primary Separation. In the OT, the people of Israel were to practice separation of life in several ways. They were, for instance, not to engage in the religious practices of the neighboring heathen nations: offering their children as sacrifices, practicing various means of fortune telling, and consulting mediums, witches, and the like (Deut. 18:9–14). In the NT, the emphasis is even stronger on the fact that God has called his people to be unique; believers have been selected by him as his temple, to be indwelt by him. The emphasis upon this choosing is expressed in terms of abstaining from sinful desires (1 Pet. 2:11), putting off the old nature and the practices of the Gentiles (Eph. 4:17–32), and putting to death whatever belongs to the earthly nature (Col. 3:5).

There are whole lists of activities that are not the fruit of the Spirit, but rather are the works of the flesh (Gal. 5:19–21), which the believer is to shun. Further, many of the sins of the flesh that Paul speaks against are not primarily physical or bodily but attitudinal or spiritual (e.g., strife, jealousy, anger, selfishness, dissension, party spirit, envy). His appeal to believers not to be conformed to the world speaks of the renewing of minds (Rom. 12:1–2).

Secondary Separation. Paul talks about not being mismated with unbelievers (2 Cor. 6:14). Paul encourages us to take note of those who create dissensions and difficulties—who, in other words, are engaged in certain works of the flesh—and to have nothing to do with them (Rom. 16:17). He instructs the Corinthian church to drive out the immoral wicked person, who is living in sin, from the church (1 Cor. 5:13), delivering him to Satan for the destruction of his sinful nature (v. 5).

Ecclesiastical Separation. The Bible clearly states that heresy is not to be tolerated (Gal. 1:8–9; 2 Tim. 3:5; Titus 3:10–11; 1 John 4:1–6; 2 John 7–11; Rev. 2:14). Members of the church share in the responsibility for it. Remaining in the church, people have the opportunity to influence, and perhaps reform, those who are straying and perhaps even win them back. Separation often leads to additional splitting, fragmenting the body of Christ even further. While Christians may differ at some points regarding the nature and proper areas of separation, they agree that the motivation stems from their belonging to the Lord. In the OT, places, buildings, articles, and days were holy, set apart for the exclusive use of the holy God. In the NT, this God dwells, not in temples made with human hands, but in Christians (1 Cor. 3:16; 6:19). Christians, as a consequence, should desire their lives to be pure and clean, appropriate to his habitation and use.

M. J. ERICKSON

Separation, Marital. Legal dissolution in whole or in part of a marriage. Some Christian churches have forbidden divorce with right of remarriage (divorce *a vinculo*), although they have recognized legal separation "from bed and board" (*a thoro et mensa*) as permitted in some circumstances of marital breakdown. This was apparently the view of most of the early fathers. The Church of Rome does not recognize divorce, but does allow legal separation without right of remarriage.

It is extremely unlikely that legal separation from bed and board without right of remarriage was known to the writers of the OT or the NT. In Deut. 24, the reference is to divorce with (restricted) right of remarriage.

D. J. ATKINSON

See also DIVORCE; MARRIAGE, THEOLOGY OF; REMARRIAGE.

Separation of Church and State. See CHURCH AND STATE.

Septuagesima. (Lat. for "seventieth") Third Sunday before Lent. Septuagesima, sexagesima, and quinquagesima are the names traditionally assigned in the calendar of the Western Christian Church to the three Sundays leading up to Lent.

D. H. WHEATON

See also CHRISTIAN YEAR; LENT.

Seraph, Seraphim. See ANGEL.

Sermon on the Mount. Discourse in Matt. 5–7 containing the epitome of Jesus' ethical teaching. The shorter but parallel sermon in Luke 6:20–49 is usually known as the Sermon on the Plain because of a different description of the setting. No other block of Jesus' teaching has enjoyed such wide influence and undergone such intense examination. Various attempts to place the sermon precisely in Jesus' ministry have proven problematic, but it certainly is early. That it bears some relationship to Luke's Sermon on the Plain is evident, especially from the overall agreement in the ordering of parallel material. The greatest difference is the absence in Luke of the Palestinian Jewish or OT background to the sayings and of the whole block of material where Jesus' teaching is set over against some of contemporary Judaism (5:17–6:18). Of the various explanations of the relationship between the two sermons, the most satisfactory one is that they represent two separate teaching occasions reflecting different versions of a discourse Jesus gave on several occasions, but adapted to each situation. This allows for the redactional activity in Matthew, but ascribes the basic sermon as it stands to Jesus himself.

Theological Assessment. Three parts of the sermon have wielded considerable influence in their own right. The Beatitudes have the kingdom as their primary theme, but they also introduce other emphases. In contrast to their consoling nature in Luke, in Matthew they assume the character of ethical demands, and the focus of the blessings themselves is eschatological. The Matthean version of the Lord's Prayer is poetic and has had a significant influence on Christian liturgy. The Golden Rule (7:12) brings to their apex the sermon's earlier teachings on interpersonal relations.

Several of Jesus' precepts are presented in such an absolute form that many interpreters have questioned the sermon's value for the average Christian. For example, the person who literally destroys an eye or a hand (5:29–30) has not solved the problem, because the left member is still there. Hyperbole here serves to underscore the urgency of radical action to remove the source of a temptation. Jesus' forbidding of judging (7:1) has led some to conclude that a Christian cannot be a judge or serve on a jury; however, he is not giving the word a legal meaning, but is talking about being judgmental in interpersonal relations.

Influence and Interpretation. Since the 2d century no block of Scripture of comparable size has exerted as great an influence as the sermon. In the pre-Nicene period, passages from this discourse were quoted or alluded to more than from any other part of the Bible. To the present day these words still profoundly challenge Christians and non-Christians alike.

The arresting nature of the sermon has produced numerous diverging efforts to explain, or even explain away, Jesus' words. Many have resisted efforts to limit the sermon's applicability. One approach sees Jesus teaching an obedience-righteousness that cannot be reconciled with Paul. Anabaptists did not go so far, but insisted that Jesus' words are so absolute that their obedience precludes Christian participation in certain social and political institutions. Luther attempted to avoid what he regarded as the extremes of both the Roman and Anabaptist interpretations and stressed the obligation to keep the sermon's commandments. Liberal Protestantism has seen the sermon as the heart of the gospel and as Jesus' program for reforming society.

Two approaches limit the full applicability of the sermon to the breaking in of the kingdom, but with different results: Albert Schweitzer saw Jesus primarily as an eschatological figure, so he coined the term "interim ethics" to emphasize that the stringent requirements of the sermon could apply only to the stress-packed times immediately before God introduced his kingdom, an event that never occurred, so the sermon does not apply to the modern situation. Dispensationalists also limit the sermon's focus to the kingdom, so for them Jesus' teachings will fully apply only at its future coming.

Jesus concludes the sermon by setting up certain requirements that relate directly to salvation. He divides humankind into three classes: those who (1) follow him (7:13–14, 17, 21, 24–25), (2) do not follow him (vv. 13–44, 26–27), and (3) pretend to follow him (vv. 15–20, 21–23). To be saved people must actually follow the teachings of the sermon, but Jesus does not say those actions must be performed perfectly. The saved are those who accept and actually attempt to direct their lives by the sermon; the lost are those who pretend to follow or who reject these teachings.

G. T. Burke

See also Golden Rule; Jesus Christ; Logia; Lord's Prayer; Parables of Jesus.

Serpent. See Satan.

Servant of the Lord. (Heb. *'ebed yhwh*, "servant of Jehovah") Divinely appointed figure who appears in the so-called servant oracles in the Book of Isaiah. Twenty times in Isa. 40–53 the *'ebed yhwh* is prophesied, even as vividly present, spoken to, or speaking. The identity of the servant varies. Sometimes the term refers to the whole nation, "Israel, my servant" (41:8), although sinfully deaf and blind (42:19). In Isaiah's "servant songs" (42:1–7; 49:1–9; 50:4–9; 52:13–53; and probably 61:1–3), however, this national meaning disappears; the servant is a righteous individual who restores Jacob (49:5).

The mission of the servant is (1) that of a humanly born prophet (49:1–2; cf. Jer. 1:5), empowered by God's Holy Spirit (Isa. 42:1; 61:1; Luke 4:21), with a non-self-assertive ministry (Isa. 42:2–3; Matt. 12:18–21). (2) He suffers vicariously, bearing the cares of others (Isa. 53:4; cf. Christ's healings, Matt. 8:17). (3) Meeting disbelief (Isa. 53:1), he becomes subject to reproach (49:7; 50:6; Matt. 26:67; 27:26). (4) Condemned as a criminal, he gives up his life, punished for the sins of others (Isa. 53:5–8; 1 Pet. 2:22–25), God making his soul a priestly guilt offering (Isa. 53:10). He atoningly "sprinkles" many nations (52:15; Heb. 12:24; 1 Pet. 1:2). (5) The servant accomplishes God's pleasure, is buried honorably with the rich (Isa. 53:9–10; Matt. 27:57), and is resurrected in glory (Isa. 53:10, 12). (6) His divine sacrifice justifies many (v. 11), and avails for Gentiles as well (42:6; Luke 2:32). (7) He establishes ultimate justice in the earth itself (Isa. 42:4; Rom. 15:21). (8) The servant thus becomes the incarnation of God's redemptive covenant or testament (Isa. 42:6; 49:8), effectuating it by his death and constituting in his own resurrected life its inheritance for the saints (Col. 1:27). Christ conclusively revealed his identity, both as Messiah (4:25–26) and as suffering servant (Luke 22:37).

J. B. PAYNE

See also BRANCH; CHRISTOLOGY; MESSIAH.

Service, Gift of. See SPIRITUAL GIFTS.

Session. (Lat. *sessio*) A sitting. The OT portrays God as seated on the throne of the universe, thereby signifying sovereignty (1 Kings 22:19; Pss. 2:4; 99:1). In Ps. 110:1 the Messiah is invited to occupy the position of honor at God's right hand (Mark 12:36; Acts 2:34; Heb. 1:13). To this position God exalted Christ at his ascension (Eph. 1:20–23; Phil. 2:9–11). Heb. 1:3; 10:12; 12:2 describe the session as the sequel to his one complete sacrifice on earth. He sits as high priest after the order of Melchizedek (Heb. 8:1; 10:12), exercising his priesthood of sympathetic assistance to and intercession for humankind (Heb. 2:17–18; 4:14–16; 7:17–27) until all is finally subjected to him (Heb. 10:13). His session also points toward his future judgment (Matt. 19:28; 2 Cor. 5:10).

D. H. WHEATON

See also ASCENSION OF CHRIST; STATES OF JESUS CHRIST.

Seven Articles of Schleitheim. See MENNONITES.

Seventh-day Adventism. See ADVENTISM.

Sexual Ethics. Field of moral obligation and duty in sexual relationships. We presently live in the wake of two movements that have done much to unsettle the traditional Judeo-Christian understanding of sexual roles: the sexual revolution and the women's liberation movement.

General Issues. There are numerous issues and subissues that fall under the larger category of "sexual ethics" and that need to be examined in a context faithful to the broad Judeo-Christian tradition. The personal perspective necessarily has its center of gravity in the clear biblical teaching that Christians are called to personal morality. Sexual relations are in the exclusive province of the marriage relationship, which itself serves as a model, or symbol, of the relationship of Christ to his church. The sexual revolution and the women's liberation movement have challenged traditional Christian teaching. It remains an important task for Christians to apply the counsel of Scripture and the wisdom of Judeo-Christian tradition to the current sociocultural situation. The Judeo-Christian ethic is particularly under siege at the public policy level. Whose values should be reflected in the law and public policy of our pluralistic society?

Specific Issues. Perhaps the most significant question raised by the apparent excesses of the sex education movement concerns the right of parents to guide the moral and character development of their children. When public programs directly offend and undermine that right, what is the appropriate remedy? When controversial views on such topics as homosexuality, abortion, and extramarital sex are taught in public schools, what are the parents who hold more traditional beliefs to do? Certainly, it cannot be considered an imposition to require public programs to be accountable to the public they serve. Yet, the myth that the struggle is between conservatives who seek "to impose morality" and an otherwise neutral public policy is a persistent one. This perception is reinforced by media coverage of conservative Christian attempts to influence the values reflected in public institutions such as public schools.

Although the vast majority of Americans reject homosexuality as normative, morally acceptable, or worthy of protection by custom or legislation, the homosexual rights movement has become increasingly entrenched in recent years. Once again, the question is, Whose values should be reflected in our law and public policy?

Conclusion. Whether sexual ethics are examined in the context of personal morality, in terms of the proper role of men and women in the church and society, or in regard to current public policy questions, the conclusion is much the same. The traditional answers from Judeo-Christian history, philosophy, and theology are often dismissed without a hearing, and our heritage—including the moral roots of our legal and political systems—is being exchanged for the views that the enlightened secularists offer in its place. While the biblical values affirmed by evangelicals and other orthodox Christians and Jews may not, ipso facto, be appropriate for legislation, there are numerous instances in which these traditions do offer the best alternative for public affirmation.

C. HORN, III

See also ADULTERY; COHABITATION; DIVORCE; HOMOSEXUALITY; MARRIAGE, THEOLOGY OF; SEPARATION, MARITAL.

Shaddai. See GOD, NAMES OF.

Shedd, William Greenough Thayer (1820–1894). American systematic theologian. In 1863 Shedd became a professor of Bible and theology at New York's Union Seminary, where he remained for over 30 years. The best-known of Shedd's many works was the *Dogmatic Theology* (3 vols., 1888–94). Shedd defends the "high Calvinism" of the Westminster Confession against Arminianism, Roman Catholicism, and modern rationalism. Shedd's interests extended well beyond theology to take in literature, church history, homiletics, and biblical commentary. He testified to his interest in the idea of organic historical development by publishing *Lectures on the Philosophy of History* (1856), and by editing the complete works of Samuel Taylor Coleridge, published in seven volumes in 1853.

M. A. NOLL

See also CALVINISM.

Shekinah. Visible manifestation of God's glory. The shekinah first appeared when God led Israel from Egypt and protected them by a pillar of cloud and fire (Exod. 13:21; 14:19). Specifically, God appeared in the cloud over the atonement cover of the ark (Exod. 25:22; Lev. 16:2; cf. Heb. 9:5). The shekinah guided Israel through the wilderness (Exod. 40:36–38); and, although the ark's loss meant "Ichabod [no glory]" (1 Sam. 4:21), the cloud again filled Solomon's temple (1 Kings 8:11; cf. 2 Chron. 7:1). Ezekiel visualized its departure because of sin (10:18) before this temple's destruction, and Judaism confessed its absence from the second temple. The shekinah reappeared with Christ (Matt. 17:5; Luke 2:9), true God localized (John 1:14: *skēnē*, "tabernacle"; cf. Rev. 21:3, = *šekînâ*?), the glory of the latter temple (Hag. 2:9; Zech. 2:5). Christ ascended in the glory cloud (Acts 1:9) and will some day so return (Mark 14:62; Rev. 14:14; cf. Isa. 24:3; 60:1).

J. B. PAYNE

See also GLORY.

Sheol. Intermediate state in which souls are dealt with according to their lives on earth. In the OT there are six ways "Sheol" is used. (1) A place from which individuals can save themselves (Ps. 89:48). Once there, a person has no hope of returning to the realm of the living (Job 7:9; 17:13–16). (2) The place where all people go upon death. The phrase "in mourning will I go down to the grave" occurs four times in Gen. (37:35; 42:38; 44:29, 31). (3) A place where the wicked go upon death (Job 21:13; 24:19; Pss. 9:17; 31:17; 49:14). (4) A place from which the righteous are saved (Ps. 49:15; 86:13; Prov. 15:24). (5) A place over which God has absolute sovereignty. Sheol "lies open ["naked"] before" God (Prov. 15:11; Job 26:6) so much so that he is there (Ps. 139:8). (6) A metaphor or image for greed (Hab. 2:5; Prov. 27:20; 30:16), murder (Prov. 1:12), jealousy (Song of Sol. 8:6), troubles of life (Ps. 88:3), near-death situations (2 Sam. 22:6; Pss. 18:5; 30:3; 116:3; Jon. 2:2), and great sin (Isa. 28:15, 18; 57:9).

Jewish apocaplyptic writings during the intertestamental period begin to make a moral distinction with respect to Sheol (2 Bar. 54:15). Many apocalyptic books teach that our final destiny is determined in this earthly life (1 Enoch; 2 Enoch 62:2; 53:1). In other words, Sheol is a place where individuals experience rewards or punishments that will come to them in a final judgment (2 Esd. 7:75ff.). Some books even state that Sheol is the final state of punishment for the wicked (Jub. 7:29; 22:22; 24:31).

W. A. VAN GEMEREN

See also DEAD, ABODE OF THE; HADES; INTERMEDIATE STATE.

Shepherding Movement. See DISCIPLESHIP MOVEMENT.

Shroud of Turin. See TURIN, SHROUD OF.

Shrove Tuesday. Name traditionally given to the day before Ash Wednesday. On this day in the Middle Ages the faithful were expected to attend confession in order to be absolved (shriven) in order to begin Lent in the right spiritual state.

D. H. WHEATON

See also CHRISTIAN YEAR; LENT.

Signs. See MIRACLES.

Simons, Menno. See MENNO SIMONS.

Simplicity of God. See GOD, ATTRIBUTES OF.

Sin. ***The Biblical Understanding of Sin.*** From the biblical perspective, sin is not only an act of wrongdoing but a state of alienation from God. Sin means refusing to repent and believe in the promises of God (Ps. 95:8; Heb. 3:8, 15; 4:7). Sin is inherent in the human condition. We are not simply born into a sinful world, but we are born with a propensity toward sin; this inherent sinful tendency is universal (Ps. 58:3; cf. 51:5; Rom. 3:23). This spiritual infection is in some mysterious way transmitted from generation to generation. Sin does not originate from human nature, but it corrupts this nature. Sinful acts have their origin in a corrupt heart (Gen. 6:5; Isa. 29:13; Jer. 17:9). The chief manifestations of sin are pride, sensuality, and fear. Other significant aspects of sin are self-pity, selfishness, jealousy, and greed. We become most aware of our sinfulness in the presence of the holy God (Ps. 51:1–9; Isa. 6:5; Luke 5:8). The effects of sin are moral and spiritual bondage, guilt, death, and hell (Rom. 6:23; James 1:14–15).

Historical Controversy over Sin. In the 5th century, Augustine challenged the views of Pelagius, who saw sin basically as an outward act transgressing the law and regarded humankind as free to sin or desist from sin. Appealing to the witness of Scripture, Augustine maintained that sin incapacitates us from doing the good, and because we are born as sinners we lack the power to do the good. Yet because we willfully choose the bad over the good, we must be held accountable for our sin.

Pelagius held that we can raise ourselves by our own efforts toward God, and therefore grace is the reward for human virtue. Augustine countered that we are helpless to do the good until grace falls upon us, and when grace is thus given we are irresistibly moved toward God and the good.

At the time of the Reformation, Luther powerfully reaffirmed the Pauline and Augustinian doctrine of the bondage of the will against Erasmus, who maintained that we still have the capacity to do the right, although we need the aid of grace if we are to come to salvation. Luther saw us as totally bound to the powers of darkness—sin, death, and the devil. What we most need is to be delivered from spiritual slavery rather than inspired to heroic action.

The 20th-century debate between Karl Barth and Emil Brunner on human freedom is another example of the division in the church through the ages on this question. Although firmly convinced that we are sinners who can be saved only by the unmerited grace of God as revealed and conveyed in Jesus Christ, Brunner nonetheless refers to an "addressability" in us, a "capacity for revelation," that enables us to apprehend the gospel and to respond to its offer. For Barth, not even a capacity for God remains within our fallen nature; therefore, we must be given not only faith but also the condition to receive faith.

Modern Reappraisals of Sin. In the 19th century, theologians under the spell of the new world consciousness associated with the Enlightenment and Romanticism began to reinterpret sin. For Schleiermacher, sin is not so much the revolt of humankind against God as the dominance of the lower nature within us. It is the resistance of our lower nature to the universal God-consciousness that needs to be realized and cultivated in every human soul. Sin is basically a minus sign, the inertia of nature that arrests the growth of God-consciousness.

Albrecht Ritschl understood sin as the product of selfishness and ignorance. He did not see the human race in bondage to the power of sin, but instead believed that people could be effectively challenged to live ethical, heroic lives. His focus was on actual or concrete sins, not on our being *in* sin.

In 20th-Century America. Reinhold Niebuhr taught that sin is inevitable because of the tension between human freedom and human finitude, but it is not a necessary implication of human nature. Our anxiety over our finitude provides the occasion for sin; our ability to transcend ourselves is the source of the possibility of sin. We are tempted either to deny the contingent character of our existence (in pride) or to escape from the responsibilities of our freedom (in sensuality). Niebuhr sought to preserve the paradox of the inevitability of sin and human culpability for sin. Paul Tillich saw the sin of humankind as consisting in estrangement from his true self and the ground of his selfhood. In liberation theology, sin is redefined in terms of social oppression, exploitation, and acquiescence to injustice. Closely related is feminist theology, which sees the essence of sin in passivity to evil, in timidity and cowardice in the face of intimidation. Sin consists not so much in self-affirmation as in self-contempt.

The understanding of sin has also undergone a profound transformation in popular culture. Under the influence of "new thought" and other neotranscendentalist movements, media religion reinterprets sin as negative thinking or defeatism. In some other strands of culture religion, also showing the impact of "new thought," sin is equated with sickness or instability. The cure lies in self- or group therapy rather than in a sacrifice for sin. The way to overcome guilt is through catharsis rather than repentance. Atonement is reinterpreted to mean at-one-ment with the self or the world.

Overcoming Sin. Christian faith teaches that sin cannot be overcome through human ingenuity or effort. The solution to the problem lies in what God has done for us in Jesus Christ. The penalty for sin is death, judgment, and hell, but the gospel is that God has chosen to pay this penalty himself in the sacrificial life and death of his Son, Jesus Christ (John 3:16–17; Acts 20:28; Rom. 3:21–26; 5:6–10; 2 Cor. 5:18, 19; Col. 2:13–15).

Through his atoning sacrifice on Calvary, Christ set humankind free by taking the retribution of sin upon himself. He suffered the agony and shame that we deserve to suffer because of our sin. He thereby satisfied the just requirements of the law of God and at the same time turned away the wrath of God from fallen humankind. His sacrifice was both an *expiation* of our guilt and a *propitiation* of the wrath of God.

Reformation theology insists that Christ saves us, not only from the power of sin, but also from its dire consequences—physical and eternal death. We are given both immortality and the remission of sins.

Sin in Evangelical and Legalistic Religion. Sin, in evangelical perspective, is not so much the infringement of a moral code as the breaking of a covenantal relationship. Sin is not an offense so much against law as against love. In legalistic religion, sin is the violation of a moral taboo. In evangelical religion, sin is wounding the very heart of God. The opposite of sin is not virtue, but faith.

Biblical faith acknowledges the legal dimension of sin, recognizing that the just requirements of the law have to be satisfied. Yet it also perceives that sin is basically the sundering of a personal relation between God and humankind and that the greatest need is not the payment of debt but reconciliation.

D. G. BLOESCH

See also AUGUSTINE OF HIPPO; GUILT; IDOLATRY; JUSTIFICATION; OMISSION, SINS OF; PELAGIUS, PELAGIANISM; SANCTIFICATION.

Sin, Conviction of. "Exposing" and "correcting," "proving wrong," or "showing the guilt of."

Conviction originates with the persons of the Godhead: the Father (Heb. 12:5), the Son (Jude 15; Rev. 3:19), and the Holy Spirit (John 16:7–11). It is mediated through Christian witnesses, especially preachers, as they spread and implement the word of God (Matt. 18:15; John 16:7, 8; Eph. 5:11, 13; 1 Tim. 5:20; 2 Tim. 4:2; Titus 1:9, 13; 2:15), as an outworking of brotherly love (Lev. 19:17–18, LXX). Their witness intensifies the convicting work already present through the Mosaic law (James 2:9) and self-revelation to the conscience resulting from illumination by Christ's first advent (John 3:20).

Conviction of sin implies an educative discipline. The inflexible standard of divine righteousness is brought to bear on sin, and a turning in obedience to God is shown to be the desirable alternative to remaining in a sinful state.

R. L. THOMAS

See also SIN.

Sin, Man of. See ANTICHRIST.

Sin, Mortal. Sin causing spiritual death. All sin is mortal inasmuch as its intrusion into human experience is the cause of every person's death (Rom. 5:12; 6:23). Roman Catholic moral theology sees sin as twofold: mortal sin extinguishes the life of God in the soul; venial sin weakens, but does not destroy that life. Mortal sin involves people totally. They determine not only to act in a specific manner, but to express therein the type of individual they wish to be in and through that action. The result is spiritual death.

F. R. HARM

See also SIN, UNPARDONABLE; SIN UNTO DEATH.

Sin, Unpardonable. Christian teaching about the unpardonable sin stems from a saying of Jesus recorded in all three Synoptic Gospels (Matt. 12:31–32; Mark 3:28–29; Luke 12:10). The meaning of this sin in Christian thought is best viewed as a total and persistent denial of the presence of God in Christ. It reflects a complete recalcitrance of the heart. Rather than a particular act, it is a disposition of the will. The unpardonable sin is not a particular act for which one may later feel regret, but instead a blatant hostility toward God and a serious rejection of Jesus after one has been exposed to the knowledge of the truth.

G. M. BURGE

See also SIN UNTO DEATH.

Sin, Venial. (Lat. *venia*, "pardon, favor, kindness, forgiveness") Sin that can be forgiven. The term does not occur in Scripture, but the basic idea does. Essentially a Roman Catholic concept, venial sin is invariably used in contrast with mortal sin. Mortal sins are those sins that exclude people from the kingdom; venial sins are those sins that do not exclude people from it (cf. Gal. 5:19–21; Eph. 5:5; with James 3:2; 1 John 1:8). Venial sin differs from mortal sin in the punishment it entails. Venial sin merits temporal punishment expiated by confession or by the fires of purgatory, while mortal sin merits eternal death.

F. R. HARM

See also SIN, MORTAL.

Sinlessness of Christ. Teaching that Jesus Christ was sinless (impeccable). This has been a universal conviction of the Christian church. Even heretics in the early centuries and during the later period of rationalism (1650–1920), who attacked the orthodox Christology of Nicea and Chalcedon, left this teaching alone. Based on the apostolic witness (2 Cor. 5:21; Heb. 4:15; 7:26; James 5:6; 1 Pet. 2:22; 3:18; 1 John 3:5), it has both a negative and a positive meaning. Negatively, it means that Christ was kept free from all transgression of the law of God. He whose "food" it was "to do the will of him who sent [him] and to finish his work" (John 4:34) could challenge his enemies to convict him of sin (John 8:46). Positively, this implies the holiness of Christ (Luke 1:35; 4:34; John 6:69; 10:36; Acts 3:14; 4:27, 30; Heb. 7:26), that is, his wholehearted commitment to his Father (John 5:30; Heb. 10:7) and to that mission for which he had been sent into the world (John 17:19).

M. E. OSTERHAVEN

See also CHRISTOLOGY; JESUS CHRIST.

Sin Offering. See OFFERINGS AND SACRIFICES IN BIBLE TIMES.

Sin unto Death. Unpardonable sin. The precise nature of *hamartia pros thanaton* in 1 John 5:16 may be surmised in its exegetical context to mean some form of final impenitence, since every sin repented of is forgiven. Two major sins of impenitence are mentioned in the NT: (1) the unforgivable blasphemy against the Holy Spirit (Matt. 12:22–32); and (2) the "crucifixion" of Christ by those who were once enlightened by the Holy Spirit but who through unbelief hold him up to contempt (Heb. 6:4–6; 10:26–29).

R. G. GRUENLER

See also BLASPHEMY AGAINST THE HOLY SPIRIT.

Sins, Seven Deadly. At an early stage in the life of the church, the influence of Greek thought (with its tendency to view sin as a necessary flaw in human nature) made it necessary for the church to determine the relative seriousness of various moral faults. This ultimately gave rise to what is commonly referred to as the seven deadly sins—pride, covetousness, lust, envy, gluttony, anger, and sloth. They are to be understood as "capital" or "root" sins rather than "deadly" or "mortal" (sins that cut people off from their true last end). The list represents an attempt to enumerate the primary instincts that are most likely to give rise to sin.

R. H. MOUNCE

Sins of Omission. See OMISSION, SINS OF.

Situation Ethics. Position that every significant moral decision has to be taken "in the light of the circumstances."

Consequences, cost, risk, contrary considerations—all have to be weighed to make moral decisions. There never are exact precedents; every situation is unique. Every system of moral rules, laws, and principles therefore gives rise to casuistry, formal and authoritative, like the Jesuit *Summae de poenitentia*, or informal and advisory, like Baxter's *Christian Directory*. These adjust general principles to particular circumstances, allow exceptions, and discuss "cases of conscience." There can be no absolute, invariable moral rules that govern all situations; even so brief a law as "Thou shalt not kill" did not apply equally to murderers, adulterers, war, sacrifices, or food. "Circumstances alter cases," it is said, and from this it is an easy step to pronounce all moral codes out of date in a world "come of age."

This lack of adequate, predetermined directions is the essential truth that situation ethics erects into the *only* principle in ethical theory. It builds thereon a so-called new morality, which repudiates all rules, guidelines, laws, principles, or enshrining of past experience or superior authority, and reduces morality to instant, individual, intuitive, and isolated decisions, varying with every situation.

To distinguish "moral" behavior from merely capricious, anarchic, amoral reactions to circumstances, it is necessary to presuppose some standard or "norm" of morality, by reference to which the quality of a given decision may be described. Various single norms have been proposed—self-consistency, compassion, utility, truth, pleasure—or even a scale of norms; but situation ethics has generally selected *love* as the sole and all-sufficient norm of moral action.

In its popularized form, situation ethics does not, however, depend upon Christian insights. Its chief exponent, Joseph Fletcher, quotes scriptural phrases and precedents whenever convenient, and cites eight "proof texts" for his "love norm," including words of Jesus about the great commandment and Paul on love's fulfilling the law, but he sees nothing particularly different or unique in a Christian's choices. "Lovingness" is the motive at work with full force behind the decisions of many non-Christians.

On the surface there is much that is attractive to Christians. "The only law is Christ's law of love"; but the master criterion remains essentially vague, because what love aims at is left undefined. It is wholly individualist, impulsive, born-of-the-situation; all obligations are dissolved in loving impulse.

If the norm is claimed to be the love taught by Jesus, then it is inconsistent to desert his concept of love as the fulfilling, not the abrogating, of divine law; to argue that Jesus was right only about love, but wrong on chastity, divorce, self-discipline, the commandments of God; and quite false to claim his authority for whatever "love" excuses—abortion, extramarital sex, lies, and the rest. Where Christ's authority is claimed, Christ's meaning must be retained.

Christians confront every situation with mind and heart already shaped by Christian experience, inheriting (to some degree) the long Christian tradition of what is right, and committed to Christian belief and obedience. With the example of Jesus before them, they enter every new situation having "the mind of Christ." Their norm of behavior, therefore, although it must certainly be applied to varied and unprecedented situations, is in fact rooted in the past, expressed in the incarnation of the ideal in Christ.

R. E. O. WHITE

See also ETHICAL SYSTEMS, CHRISTIAN; ETHICS, BIBLICAL; LOVE.

Six Articles, The (1539). One of a series of regulations designed to maintain unity in the Church of England under Henry VIII, during that period when the church was independent of the pope but still not officially Protestant.

The articles reaffirmed transubstantiation, ordered laypeople to refrain from the cup in communion, and upheld the celibacy of the clergy. They also proclaimed the immutability of monastic vows, defended the saying of private masses, and stressed the importance of auricular confession. Protestants, understandably, called this "the bloody whip with six strings." The Six Articles were eloquent testimony to Henry's desire to slow the pace of reform in England and to preserve order in his country.

M. A. NOLL

See also TEN ARTICLES, THE.

Slavery. State of involuntary servitude. Slavery was an accepted fact in the ancient world and a significant factor in economic and societal life. Slaves were frequently the product of defeats in wars. Often entire populations, as well as soldiers, were enslaved. The sale of slaves became a cornerstone of business in the Greco-Roman world, reaching its peak in the pre-Christian 2d century.

The state of the slave varied. Some were impressed into gangs that worked the fields and mines. Others were highly skilled workers and trusted administrators. Frequently slaves were far better off than free laborers. Roman laws were passed to protect slaves and to allow rights, even of private possessions, which were sometimes used to ransom the slave and his family (Acts 22:27–28). By the 1st century the slave population had become so large in the Roman world it created problems. Uprisings were frequent and owners were fearful and suspicious.

In the OT slavery was a legally prescribed institution and generally more humanitarian than in the Near East. Slaves generally performed household duties or labored with the family in the fields. Slaves were acquired by purchase, in payment of debt, by inheritance, by birth, and as prisoners of war. OT instances show a father selling a daughter (Exod. 21:7; Neh. 5:5), a widow selling children (2 Kings 4:1), people selling themselves (Lev. 25:39; Deut. 15:12–17). A person might be freed by purchase (Lev. 25:48–55), sabbatical year law (Exod. 21:1–11; Deut. 15:12–18), the jubilee year (Lev. 25:8–55), or the death of the master (Gen. 15:2). Slaves were considered part of the owner's family and, if Israelites, had the right to the sabbath rest and to participate in the religious feasts.

The early church did not attack slavery as an institution. It did, however, reorder the relationship of slave and masters (Phil.), indicate that in God's sight there was neither "slave nor free"

(Gal. 3:28), and state that both were accountable to God (Eph. 6:5–9).

In the 15th century the modern slave trade emerged, principally under the Portuguese. The discovery of America called for black labor, causing the trade to flourish. Some 15 million slaves were transported to the Americas mostly to the West Indies and South America. Under the efforts of evangelical leaders such as Granville Sharp, William Wilberforce, and Thomas Clarkson slavery was outlawed in Britain in 1807 and 1827 in the empire. The U.S. Congress brought the slave trade to an end in Jan. 1808, but interstate slave trade and the breeding of slaves flourished. In the U.S. the Roman Catholic and Protestant Episcopal churches did not take a stand on slavery, but most other bodies split North and South on the issue.

W. N. KERR

Smalcald Articles, The (1537). Articles of belief named for the town in Hesse-Nassau, Germany, where they were presented to Protestant leaders. They are now part of the *Book of Concord*, the normative collection of Lutheran confessions. Luther wrote them in Dec. 1536. Together with his Small and Large catechisms, they comprise his contribution to the *Book of Concord*. The Smalcald Articles are grouped in three parts: (1) those concerning "the chief articles" of "the Divine Majesty"; (2) those concerning "the articles which refer to the office and work of Jesus Christ or our redemption"; (3) those concerning miscellaneous matters. The articles were valued as a bold, clear-cut testimony of the Lutheran position and as a testimony of Luther's personal faith, for he wrote them at a time when he felt his death was near.

C. G. FRY

See also AUGSBURG CONFESSION; CONCORD, BOOK OF.

Small Catechism, Luther's. See LUTHER'S SMALL CATECHISM.

Smith, Hannah Whitall (1832–1911). Writer, teacher, and social reformer. Her best-known book is *The Christian's Secret of a Happy Life* (1875). It has gone through numerous editions and been translated into most of the major languages of the world. Smith explains the secret of a happy, Christian life as "a life of inward rest and outward victory." It exists when a Christian is saved not only from sin's "guilt" but "from the power and dominion of sin." She speaks of "the infiniteness of God's power for destroying that which is contrary to Him (which is 'sin')" and extols "God's power," which "comes to help us and to redeem us out of sin." Consistent with failures, and with temptation, it is something the believer receives through faith, with consecration to God as a prerequisite to faith.

Hannah married Robert Pearsall Smith, also a Quaker. They joined successively the Methodists, the Plymouth Brethren, and the Baptists; and then they set out to preach the Higher Life. The Smiths both preached extensively in Europe and played an important part in founding the Keswick Convention.

J. K. GRIDER

See also HOLINESS MOVEMENT, AMERICAN; KESWICK CONVENTION.

Social Ethics. Study of questions of good and evil, right and wrong, obligation and prohibition as these arise in a social context.

As in the case of other subfields of ethics, social ethics may be approached descriptively (What is the character of this morality? This ethical language?) or prescriptively (I propose this set of values, these norms and principles, this way of resolving an ethical dilemma). A further distinction must be made between ethical discernment and ethical implementation. Social ethics includes reflection both on the problem of analysis and discernment of the social good and on the problem of strategy and implementation of the social good.

It is impossible to maintain a clear and precise distinction between social ethics and personal (individual) ethics. No individual behavior is without social implications. No social situation or problem is without individual repercussions. Nevertheless, for analytical purposes it is helpful to treat social ethics as a field in its own right and to direct primary attention to the ethical aspects of social groups, institutions, and corporate problems (racial, economic, political, etc.). By contrast, then, personal ethics focuses on the individual moral agent.

The first task of Christian social ethics is the analysis of structures and situations and the discernment of good and evil in relation to these.

Christian social ethical analysis proceeds in a dialectic between revelation, the word of God "from above," and observation and experience "from below." A sociological realism must probe beneath surface problems to a correct discernment of the fundamental forces and problems of our society. At the same time, analysis and discernment are informed by biblical revelation. God not only illuminates, corrects, and deepens our observations of social reality, he also raises new issues and problems often undetected by even the most realistic sociological analysis.

Much of traditional theological social ethics has been shaped by appeals to orders of creation (or "spheres" or "mandates"). The orders of the family and marriage, politics and the state, work and economics have been understood not only by reference to biblical revelation but also by common sense, reason, and natural law.

Whether or not social ethics is founded primarily on orders of creation, certain elements of the biblical revelation on creation have ongoing importance for Christian social ethics. The ethical "good" is defined by the will, word, and work of God. Humanity is intended to be cohumanity: a social, joyful partnership of human beings before God.

The fall (Gen. 3) indicates that evil originates in rebellion against God and disobedience to his command. Evil is manifested in accusation, division, and the domination of one human being over another. Its essential characteristics are pride, disobedience to God, accusation, division, domination, exploitation, violence, and the will to power.

Social structures and forces can have a demonic, corporate aspect. Evil is not merely an individual phenomenon but a corporate, structural matter. In this light, the state (or work, or money) is ethically ambiguous: it can be the promoter of cohumanity, the restrainer of social evil, or the habitat of the rebellious powers.

Justice (righteousness, judgment) is one of the most important ethical norms for Christian social ethics. "I am the Lord who exercises kindness, justice and righteousness on earth, for in these I delight" (Jer. 9:24). God "works . . . justice for all who are oppressed" (Ps. 103:6). Biblical justice is more than fairness and equality. It is a redress of grievances on the part of the oppressed. It is not so much in tension with love as inclusive of love and mercy.

It is in Jesus Christ that the word of God is most clearly and fully revealed—for social ethics as for everything else. The social teaching of Jesus is given in his "platform" statement (Luke 4:18–21), in the temptation (Matt. 4), in his parables and discourses, in the Sermon on the Mount (Matt. 5–7), in his farewell discourse (John 13–17), and in the events of the crucifixion and resurrection. The great commands to love God and love one's neighbor, the call to unqualified servanthood and sacrifice, the Golden Rule, the call to simplicity and away from worship of mammon give the essential dimensions of Jesus' social ethics. Christian social ethics must reflect not only on the traditional, mainline interpretations of the meaning of Jesus Christ, the kingdom of God, and the love command, but also on the interpretation and application of this social teaching by Franciscans, Anabaptists, Quakers, and others who have developed a social ethic based on Jesus Christ.

Christian social ethics leans toward the future and complete arrival of the judgment and grace of God. More than the original creation, it is the new creation that is invoked for ethical guidance in the NT. History moves toward the new Jerusalem, not back to a golden age in Eden. For these reasons, the Apocalypse has particular social ethical significance in revealing God's final ethical judgment on human society in terms of Babylon (Rev. 18) and the new Jerusalem (Rev. 21).

It is the task of the church to reflect on the relation between Christ and culture—that is, between the ethical command of God and the social situation.

Contemporary reflection on how Christian (or religious) conviction relates to society has been influenced a great deal by social historians and social scientists. While Marx, Durkheim, and others have also had considerable influence, this reflection is most often indebted to pioneering studies done by Max Weber, Ernst Troeltsch, and H. Richard Niebuhr. Reflection of contemporary strategy and implementation is greatly impoverished without taking into account these traditional perspectives.

Basic to the Judeo-Christian world view is the conviction that God participates and intervenes in human history, partly, at least, in response to the prayer of the people. Entreaties, prayers, petitions, and thanksgivings are to be made in behalf of all people, including those with political authority (1 Tim. 2:1–2). Prayer is thus a political and social activity of great importance. Evangelism also brings about social change by means of the transformation of social actors, individual moral agents.

Far from being an uncaring, irresponsible withdrawal from social responsibility, the formation of alternative Christian community plays an important role in implementing social ethical change. The primary alternative community is the church (in both its local and broader senses). Intentionally Christian businesses, schools, political groups, and other associations are other means by which this strategy may be employed.

Direct participation in the political (and other) structures and institutions of society is another strategy available for the implementation of social ethical concern. Especially in circumstances where Christians are invited to exercise political and social responsibility, it is appropriate to regard institutional participation as a valid means of implementing ethical conviction.

Under no circumstances are evil means justified or permissible (Rom. 6). The Christian is called to "overcome evil with good" (Rom. 12:21). Since the means chosen affect the character of the end, a good end can be achieved only by the use of good means. Justice will be achieved only with just means; peace with peaceful means; freedom or equality with means that are characterized by freedom and equality. Christian reflection on strategy and implementation of the good that is discerned will always stress this indissoluble relationship between means and ends.

D. W. Gill

See also Abortion; Ethics, Biblical; Situation Ethics.

Social Gospel, The. Protestant effort to apply biblical principles to the growing problems of the emerging urban-industrial America during the decades between the Civil War and World War I.

Considered to be probably a uniquely American movement in theology, the social gospel also stands as part of a rich Judeo-Christian heritage of response to human need, with roots in the OT and the NT and antecedents in every era of church history. Its more immediate debt included the writings and programs with which English and Continental churchmen and theologians like Charles Kingsley and John Frederick Denison Maurice had begun responding to similar social distress. In the U.S., social gospel roots included such 19th-century clergymen as Stephen Colwell, whose *New Themes for the Protestant Clergy* was published in 1851, and the revivalists whose story Timothy L. Smith has related in *Revivalism and Social Reform in Mid-Nineteenth Century America.*

The uniqueness of the social gospel resided, then, not in its discontinuity from the past, but in its resourcefulness in applying Christian principles to complex and massive problems during a critical transition in American social history.

The distinctive ideas of the social gospel clustered around the prevailing social and economic crises, and the responses contained within the Bible and Christian history. Opposing the dominant laissez-faire individualism in economic life, with its sanctioning of unrestrained competition, social gospelers pressed for brotherhood that included cooperation between management and labor. They saw in the OT prophets' denunciation of injustice, in the life and teachings of Jesus, and in the immanence of a God of love in human society the sanctions for a contrasting human order. That order would be realized in the kingdom of God, a kingdom in which God's will would be done as human lives expressed his love across the range of their relationships and of society's institutions. And because humankind was essentially good and perfectible, marked by sin that was a quite curable selfishness, the kingdom would indeed come. To social gospel advocates the early years of the 20th century appeared to be ushering it in with increasing rapidity.

Walter Rauschenbusch burst into national prominence with his *Christianity and the Social Crisis* (1907), followed a few years later by *The Social Principles of Jesus* (1916), and *A Theology for the Social Gospel* (1917). The major supporting denominations—Baptists, Congregationalists, Episcopalians, Methodists, and Presbyterians—established commissions, while the churches in concert in 1908 formed the Federal Council of Churches, an agency that gave high priority to the social gospel as expressed in its "social creed." A new and Christian century appeared to be well underway.

The deaths of Washington Gladden and Rauschenbusch in 1918 symbolized the dramatic change that came with World War I and its aftermath of political and economic chaos abroad and isolationism and reaction in the U.S. While the social gospel continued into the 1930s, it was increasingly undermined by a changing national temper that included the gradual decline of liberal theology in the mainline churches.

The demise of the social gospel movement did not mean the death of its central emphasis upon applying Christian principles to social problems and to human need. In the civil rights and antiwar movements of recent decades, and in the radical social stance of the National and World councils of churches, some see continuity with the classical social gospel. Evangelicals have returned, meanwhile, to the social concern and action that had marked them until near the eve of World War I. In both cases the ongoing social Christianity appears to be less marked by utopianism and narrowly industrial concerns, and more by social action than was the social gospel itself.

N. A. Magnuson

See also GLADDEN, WASHINGTON; LIBERALISM, THEOLOGICAL; RAUSCHENBUSCH, WALTER.

Social Implications of the Gospel. See GOSPEL, SOCIAL IMPLICATIONS OF.

Socialism, Christian. Application of the social principles of Christianity. The concept had unconventional origins in the French social reformer Henri de Saint-Simon (1760–1825), who in his *Nouveau Christianisme* held that religion "should guide the community toward the great aim of improving as quickly as possible the conditions of the poorest class." Having seen what France had suffered first under the Revolution in all its ferocity, and then under Napoleon, he urged European rulers to unite for the suppression of war, and to return to true Christianity, which concerns itself with the plight of the poor. Saint-Simon's views were to influence an improbable combination of thinkers that included Thomas Carlyle, John Stuart Mill, Heinrich Heine, Auguste Comte, Friedrich Engels, and Walter Rauschenbusch, and were to find echoes in the work of the more recent American theologians Paul Tillich and Reinhold Niebuhr.

As well as having an impact on France, Christian socialism was a force in many other European countries, prompting the founding of groups that held that the working class had a right to social and economic justice, and that these were areas in which Christians should be active. The term "Christian socialism" was popularized in mid-19th century England when, after the failure of the Chartist movement, a group of Anglicans sought the application of Christian principles in the organization of industry. Its leaders were J. M. F. Ludlow (who had been educated in France), J. F. D. Maurice, and Charles Kingsley.

J. D. DOUGLAS

Society of Jesus, The (Jesuits). Roman Catholic religious order founded by Ignatius of Loyola and officially approved by the Church in 1540. The Jesuits are classified as mendicant clerks regular. In 1534 Loyola and six companions, all students of theology at the University of Paris, took vows of poverty and chastity and promised to devote their lives to missionary work in Palestine if that were possible. They gathered new recruits, and since they wished to give permanent structure to their way of life, they sought approval from Pope Paul III as a religious order. Loyola was elected the first superior general in 1540 and spent his remaining years directing the new order and writing its Constitutions. The new order had several distinctive features. The superior general is elected for life and appoints all subordinate superiors; hence the Jesuits are highly centralized. Obedience is especially stressed. There is no distinctive religious habit or uniform, such as earlier orders had, no special fasts or bodily austerities, no common singing of the divine office.

Loyola stressed quality rather than quantity, but the Society of Jesus grew rapidly. There were about 1000 Jesuits by the founder's death in 1556, mainly in Spain, Italy, and Portugal, but also in France, Germany, and Belgium, as well as missionaries in India, Africa, and Latin America. By 1626 there were 15,544 Jesuits. Growth was steady but somewhat slower until 1773 when Clement XIV, under pressure from the Bourbon monarchs of France, Spain, and Naples, suppressed the society. A few Jesuit houses survived in Prussia and Russia where the monarchs refused to promulgate the suppression. In 1814 Pius VII restored the Jesuits worldwide. Despite being exiled from most European Catholic countries at one time or another, the Jesuits grew steadily in numbers during the next century and peaked at 36,038 in 1964. Membership declined after the Second Vatican Council, reaching 27,027 in 1981 with roughly one-third in Europe, one-third in the U.S. and Canada, and one-third in Asia, Africa, and Latin America.

Education quickly became the largest single Jesuit apostolate and remains a major commitment today. The society adopted Aquinas as their official theologian but freely modified his system, as in the theology of Francisco Suárez (1548–1617). Prominent among recent Jesuit theologians are Pierre Teilhard de Chardin, Karl Rahner, and Bernard Lonergan. Traditionally the Jesuits have reserved their highest regard for missionary work. Francis Xavier (1506–52), the first and greatest Jesuit missionary, laid the basis for Jesuit activity in India, Indonesia, and Japan.

Although the Jesuits were not founded to combat Protestantism, they were quickly drawn into the struggle. Many Jesuits published controversial works, for instance, Peter Canisius and Robert Bellarmine, both of whom also wrote catechisms that enjoyed wide use for three centuries. Other Jesuits influenced policy as court preachers or as confessors to the emperor; the kings of France, Spain, and Poland; and the dukes of Bavaria. Well over 1000 Jesuits died as martyrs both in Europe and in the missions. The Roman Catholic Church has canonized 38 Jesuits, including 22 martyrs.

J. P. DONNELLY

See also IGNATIUS OF LOYOLA.

Socinus, Faustus (1539–1604). Anti-Trinitarian theologian. After spending time in several European countries, in 1578 Socinus settled in Poland, where a strong Anti-Trinitarian community existed. Eventually he was recognized as their principal leader. His stay in Poland was not altogether peaceful; from time to time he faced persecution for his beliefs from both Catholics and Protestants. Socinus's ideas laid the foundation for later unitarian movements, although he did not go as far as future Anti-Trinitarians in denying the miraculous or divine role of Jesus. He was also among the first who subjected Scripture to rational criticism.

P. KUBRICHT

See also RACOVIAN CATECHISM.

Solafidianism. (Lat. *sola fide*, "faith alone") Doctrine that salvation is by faith only. The term emerged as a consequence of Luther's translation of Rom. 3:28 in which he added the word "alone" to the phrase "man is justified by faith [alone] apart from works of the Law" (NASB). He was severely castigated for this, but Erasmus defended him. Implicit in solafidianism is the doctrine of divine monergism, which declares that salvation is totally dependent upon God's activity and is in no way conditioned by our actions.

F. R. HARM

Solidarity of the Race. Theological teaching that all humans are of the same species and shape, with Adam as a common ancestor. This teaching is not so much positively affirmed as it is assumed in all of Scripture. Most of the scriptural evidence for the solidarity of the race is found in passages dealing with the imputation of Adam's sin to all his posterity (Gen. 3:15–19 Rom. 5:12–21). Even prior to NT teaching on the significance of Adam's sin, however, the OT established the unity of the human race. The very use of the Hebrew term *'ādām* presents strong evidence that the word refers to the class of people (Gen. 6:1). Therefore, *'ādām* can be translated by "Adam" and by "humankind" or the plural "men." If the human race has a common ancestor in Adam, then all humans have the image of God. For this reason, then, the one gospel of salvation in Christ is truly relevant to all people not only because it proclaims that God's wrath is propitiated by the sacrifice of his Son, and hence that there is hope for our "human" condition. There is also a proclamation of hope in that it calls us to be a part of the new humanity in Jesus Christ.

W. A. VAN GEMEREN

See also MAN, DOCTRINE OF.

Son of God. (Gk. *huios tou theou*) The Christian uses of the expression "Son of God" as referring to Jesus can be explained only in light of a Jewish background and peculiarly Christian additions.

In the OT. Israel's unique relationship with God enabled it to be referred to in the singular as God's firstborn son (Exod. 4:22) or simply as his son (Exod. 4:23; Jer. 31:20; Hos. 11:1). In Ps. 2:7 God is quoted at the coronation of the king as saying, "You are my Son; today I have become your Father" (cf. Ps. 89:26–27; 2 Sam. 7:14).

In the NT. *Jesus' Own Claims.* Although Jesus preferred to refer to himself as the Son of man, there is sufficient evidence that his identity as Son of God goes back ultimately to his own assertions. This is especially true of John (John 10:30, 36, 38), but instances of it are also found in the Synoptics (Mark 14:61–62; Matt. 11:25–27 = Luke 10:21–22; cf. John 10:36).

Others' Recognition of Jesus' Divine Sonship. The NT presents a remarkably large and diverse group of individuals who referred to Jesus as the Son of God. These include God the Father (Mark 1:11; 9:35) and Satan (Matt. 4:3, 6). Understandably, the assertion and development of Jesus' divine sonship in the NT came principally from his disciples. During his ministry they did this as a group (Matt. 14:33) and as individuals: Peter (16:16), Nathanael (John 1:49), and Martha (11:27). Paul's initial preaching in Damascus emphasizes this point (Acts 9:20). "His Son" or "Son of God" appears in most of his epistles, especially in contexts dealing with eschatology, Jesus' messianic rule, and salvation. The Johannine epistles represent a special case, where Jesus' divine sonship is constantly asserted as a corrective to the Docetic heresy. The author of Hebrews applies OT messianic texts to Jesus as God's Son, but more important, Jesus' sonship is at the heart of his argument that Jesus is superior to angels, Moses, and the Levitical priests.

Associated Themes. The key to understanding what NT writers mean by the title "Son of God" is found in the contexts in which the title occurs. Heading the list are those passages that connect Jesus' divine sonship with his royal office as Messiah. Jesus did this himself in response to the high priest's question (Mark 14:61–62), as God had earlier done at his baptism and transfiguration, using the language of Ps. 2:7. Paul (Acts 13:33) and the writer of Hebrews (1:5; 5:5) also apply this verse to Jesus.

Sons of God. Just as Israelites in the OT were sons of God, so are disciples of Jesus in the NT, although Jesus is Son in a unique sense (John 3:16, 18; 1 John 4:9). Jesus himself uses this phrase of his followers (Matt. 5:9, 45), but it is in Paul that the doctrine is most fully developed (Rom. 8:14–17; Gal. 4:1–7).

G. T. BURKE

See also CHRISTOLOGY; JESUS CHRIST; MESSIAH.

Son of Man. (Heb. *ben-'ādām*; Gk., *huios tou anthropou*) Title for the Christ or Messiah. This christological title appears 69 times in the Synoptic Gospels and 13 times in the Gospel of John and meets the most demanding tests of authenticity because of its original use by Jesus. There is no evidence of a well-defined Son of man Christology in Judaism before the time of Jesus, although the occurrence of the term in Dan. 7:13 seems to be the natural background for

Jesus' creative use of the expression as an enigmatic title.

The first intentional use of the title by Jesus functions as a substitute for the personal pronoun "I," and as such conveys extraordinary claims of authority on his part, quite different from its ordinary and simple reference to "man" in the psalms and as a form of address in the Book of Ezekiel. As Jesus uses the title in Mark 2:10, he claims the authority to forgive sins, indicating that he is consciously and creatively investing the title with deep christological meaning, tantamount to sharing the prerogatives of God. Similarly his use of the title in Mark 2:28 indicates his authority over the sabbath, another claim of correlativity with God. The explicitly redemptive character of his ministry is evidenced by his personal claim that "the Son of man did not come to be served, but to serve, and to give his life as a ransom for many."

Occasionally the title is used in a prophetic sense. Of the 11 passages in this category, eight are in Mark (8:31; 9:12, 31; 10:33; 14:21, 41) and all disclose Jesus' messianic awareness that he is to suffer as a ransom for many. In considerable detail Jesus foretells his betrayal, condemnation, death, and resurrection.

Jesus also refers to the Son of man in the third person. There are 19 of these sayings, all of which portray the Son of man as a glorified divine being, whereas in the first two groupings, Jesus generally speaks of himself in terms of humility and suffering. Among the Markan sayings in this category (8:38; 9:9; 13:26; 14:62), 9:9 clearly refers to his own rising as the Son of man from the dead; and 14:62, the scene before the high priest, couples his "I am" confession that he is the Christ, the Son of the Blessed One with the surrogate for "I," the Son of man, "sitting at the right hand of the Mighty One and coming on the clouds of heaven."

Matt. 12:40 also clearly refers to Jesus as Son of man, and there is no good reason for not accepting the other Q sayings as authentic (Matt. 24:27, 37, 39, 44), as well as special M (13:41; 19:28; 24:30; 25:31) and L sayings (12:8; 17:22; 18:8; 21:36). Matt. 19:28 is especially instructive on the matter of who the glorified Son of man is, for Jesus promises his disciples with the authoritative "I tell you the truth, at the renewal of all things, when the Son of Man sits on his glorious throne, you who have followed me will also sit on twelve thrones, judging the twelve tribes of Israel."

At the completion of his earthly ministry when Jesus' redemptive work was fulfilled and the Holy Spirit was poured out in power at Pentecost, the disciples realized that Christ was now to be preached openly without reference to the enigmatic title "Son of man" or the veiled connotations of the kingdom of God. Obediently they proclaimed Christ, and true to form Son of man and kingdom of God virtually disappear from the apostolic vocabulary.

R. G. GRUENLER

See also CHRISTOLOGY; JESUS CHRIST.

Soteriology. See SALVATION.

Soul. Living being, life principle, person, or individual spiritual nature. In general terms it can be said that in Scripture the soul is conceived to be an immaterial principle created by God, which is usually united to a body and gives it life; the soul continues to exist after death, however, in human beings (Matt. 10:28; James 5:20; Rev. 6:9; 20:4), a condition that is ended at the close of this age (1 Cor. 15:35–55).

Speculation about the soul in the subapostolic church was profoundly influenced by Greek philosophy. Augustine taught that the soul is a rational-spiritual substance made "like God," and made by him, sustaining and directing the body (*Greatness of the Soul,* 13.22).

Most early fathers accepted the creationist view that God created each individual soul at the moment that he gave it a body, while some, like Tertullian, held the traducianist theory—that each soul is derived, along with the body, from one's parents. Arguments cited in favor of creationism were (1) that Scripture distinguishes the origin of soul and body (Eccl. 12:7; Isa. 42:5; Zech. 12:1; Heb. 12:9); (2) that creationism preserves the idea of the soul as a simple, indivisible substance better than traducianism, which requires the idea of the division of the soul and its derivation from the parents; and (3) that it makes more credible Christ's retention of a pure soul than does traducianism.

In behalf of traducianism it was said (1) that certain Scripture passages support it (Gen. 2:2; Heb. 7:10; cf. 1 Cor. 11:8); (2) that it offers the best theory for the whole race having sinned in Adam; (3) that it is supported by the analogy of lower life in which numerical increase is obtained by derivation; (4) that it teaches that parents beget the whole child, body and soul, and not just the body; and (5) that it was necessary for Christ to have received his soul from the soul of Mary in order to redeem the human soul.

M. E. Osterhaven

See also Body, Biblical View of the; Dichotomy; Man, Doctrine of; Spirit; Trichotomy.

Soul Sleep. Psychopannychy or the doctrine that the soul sleeps between death and resurrection. The doctrine of soul sleep has been held sporadically in the church. It is not a heresy in the narrower sense, due to the paucity of biblical teaching on the intermediate state, but it may be called a doctrinal aberration. The case for soul sleep rests principally on these considerations: (1) Human existence demands the unity of soul and body. If the body ceases to function, so must the soul. (2) The use of the term "sleep" in Scripture for death is alleged to point to the cessation of consciousness. (3) A state of consciousness between death and resurrection, characterized by bliss or woe, unwarrantably anticipates the judgment of the last day, when the basis for these experiences is provided.

On the contrary view, while the normal human state is admittedly a union of soul and body, the possibility of disembodied conscious existence is firmly held, both on the analogy of God's existence as pure spirit (humankind being made in his image) and on the basis of such passages as Heb. 12:23 and Rev. 6:9–11. As to the word "sleep," it is intended to apply to the body, even though the individual as such may be said to sleep in death. The exclusion of the possibility of bliss or woe from the intermediate state, on the ground that the divine judgment that justifies such reactions will not yet have been pronounced, would logically rule out the joyful assurance of salvation in this life as well as the foreboding of judgment to come.

E. F. Harrison

See also Adventism; Conditional Immortality; Intermediate State.

Sovereignty of God. Biblical teaching that God is King, supreme Ruler, and Lawgiver of the entire universe.

Biblical Statements. God "has established his throne in heaven, and his kingdom rules over all" (Ps. 103:19). As the "Most High," God is sovereign over the kingdoms of the world and gives them to anyone he wishes (Dan. 4:17, 25, 34; 5:21; 7:14). God is the "only Ruler, the King of kings and Lord of lords" (1 Tim. 6:15; cf. Rev. 19:16). The sovereignty of God thus expresses the very nature of God as all-powerful and omnipotent, able to accomplish his good pleasure, carry out his decreed will, and keep his promises.

Several divine names express God's sovereignty. He is called "God Most High" (*'elyôn*, Gen. 14:18–20), "God almighty" (*'ēl šadday*, 17:1; cf. Exod. 6:2), "sovereign Lord" (*'adōnāy yhwh*, Gen. 15:2; Deut. 3:24 NIV), and "Lord God Almighty" (*kyrios pantokrator*, Rev. 1:8). God's sovereignty is expressed in the comprehensive plan or decree for world history; he "works out everything in conformity with the purpose of his will" (Eph. 1:11). His sovereignty is exercised and displayed in history in the works of creation, providence, and redemption. After the resurrection Christ claims "all authority in heaven and earth" (Matt. 28:18), and the ascended Christ is exalted "far above all rule and authority, power, and dominion" (1 Cor. 15:24–28; Eph. 1:19–21; Phil. 2:9–11; Rev. 5:9–14). Hence the earliest Christian confession was simply: "Jesus is Lord" (Rom. 10:9).

Theological Considerations. Sovereignty is an inherent characteristic of God. A distinction is sometimes made between "sovereign will" and "sovereign power." God's sovereign will and power are not arbitrary, despotic, or deterministic; his sovereignty is characterized by his justice and holiness as well as by his other attributes. Divine sovereignty and human responsibility are paradoxical and beyond human comprehension, but not contradictory. Divine sovereignty and human *sovereignty* are certainly contradictory, but divine sovereignty and human *responsibility* are not. God uses human means in history to accomplish his purposes, yet such means do not involve coercion. The doctrine of the sovereignty of God is emphasized especially in the Augustinian-Calvinistic tradition.

F. H. KLOOSTER

See also CALVINISM; DECREES OF GOD; ELECT, ELECTION; GOD, ATTRIBUTES OF; GOD, DOCTRINE OF; GOD, NAMES OF; PREDESTINATION; REFORMED TRADITION, THE; REPROBATION; SUPRALAPSARIANISM.

Special Revelation. See REVELATION, SPECIAL.

Spener, Philipp Jakob (1635–1705). Founder of German pietism. Spiritual rebirth and ethical concerns became important factors in Spener's preaching as he assumed successive pastoral positions in Strasbourg (1663), Frankfurt-on-Main (1666), Dresden (1686), and Berlin (1697). Although Spener deemphasized the theological dogmatism and controversies of the Protestant scholastics, his view of conversion and its necessary implementation were controversial wherever he preached. His attacks on ignorance and moral laxness among the clergy were not welcomed by that group, and his proposed system of reform was a real threat to established Lutheran churches. These ideas were first published in 1675 in *Pia desideria (Heartfelt Desires for a God-Pleasing Reform of the True Evangelical Churches)*. The theology in this work stressed the unity of faith and works. Equally important was the means Spener proposed for implementing change—a church within the church. Spener founded small groups (*collegia pietatis*) to advance the participants' closeness to God through prayers, songs, spiritual reading, and discussion.

R. J. VANDERMOLEN

See also PIETISM.

Spinoza, Benedict de (1632–1677). Dutch philosopher. Spinoza's reputation as philosopher and ethicist was established by his *Principles of Descartes' Philosophy Geometrically Demonstrated* (1663), and his most famous work, *Tractatus Theologico-Politicus* (1670). As a philosopher Spinoza alienated many religious contemporaries by removing biblical ideas about God and many religious beliefs (such as acceptance of miracles) from the supernatural sphere; further, he alienated empiricists with his emphasis on geometrical order and his denial that physical facts are the basis of true generalizations about reality. Spinoza's method, contrary to that of the empiricist followers of Locke, was to arrive at truths from axioms by using deductive logic.

R. J. VANDERMOLEN

Spirit. The spirit of humankind fulfills its true destiny when it lives in conscious relationship to God its Creator. Himself the eternal Spirit who out of nothing made everything by the breath (spirit) of his mouth, God is called "spirit" and "Father of our spirits" (John 4:24; Heb. 12:9). Humankind has breath, or spirit, because it has been given by God's Spirit (Job 27:3; 33:4; 34:14); when a person dies the spirit is returned to God (Eccles. 12:7). Life and death, therefore, are represented in the Bible as a giving and a withdrawing of God's breath, or spirit, for all created life, including humanity, is utterly dependent on him (Ps. 104). The NT carries forward the teaching of the OT. For example, the human spirit is seen even more sharply as having been made by God and for him so that his children may live in fellowship with him through the Holy Spirit. Thus the Spirit of God witnesses to our spirits that we are children of God (Rom. 8:16–17).

M. E. OSTERHAVEN

See also GOD, DOCTRINE OF; HOLY SPIRIT; MAN, DOCTRINE OF.

Spirit, Holy. See HOLY SPIRIT.

Spirit, Unclean. See DEMON, DEMON POSSESSION.

Spirits, Discernment of. See SPIRITUAL GIFTS.

Spirits in Prison. Enigmatic phrase occurring in 1 Pet. 3:19. Some have held that the reference is to people of Noah's time who at the time Peter was writing were disembodied spirits imprisoned and awaiting final judgment. Others see in the passage a preaching by Christ to the dead between his death and resurrection, whether simply to announce his victory to OT saints or to give further opportunity for people who died unrepentant. There is much to commend the view that the spirits are the angels who sinned in the time of Noah (Gen. 6:1–5). To these Christ proclaimed his triumph. The context appears to support this (see 1 Pet. 3:22).

E. F. HARRISON

Spiritual Body. (Gk. *sōma pneumatikon*) The resurrected spiritual body in contrast to the physical body (*sōma psychikon*), which is subject to sin and death (1 Cor. 15:44). Jesus in his resurrection appearances embodies the new imperishable existence, and although not of flesh and blood of the old order, nor limited by physical parameters of that order (John 20:19–20), nevertheless has identifiable physical characteristics and can eat food (Luke 24:36–43). *Sōma pneumatikon* is Paul's way of saying that the believer's personal identity as a body-spirit unity will be raised to a new life like that of Christ himself.

R. G. GRUENLER

See also RESURRECTION OF THE DEAD.

Spiritual Gifts. Gifts of God enabling Christians to perform (sometimes specialized) service. There are several Greek words in the NT used for spiritual gifts. *Dōrea* and *doma* are so used but are rare (Eph. 4:8; Acts 11:17). *Pneumatikos* and *charisma* are frequently found, with *charisma* being the most common. The term *charisma* ("spiritual gift"), except for its occurrence in 1 Pet. 4:10, is used only by Paul. *Charisma* signifies redemption or salvation as the gift of God's grace (Rom. 5:15; 6:23) and a gift enabling Christians to perform their service in the church (1 Cor. 7:7), as well as defining a special gift enabling Christians to perform a particular ministry in the church. Paul offers instruction on spiritual gifts in Rom. 12:6–8; 1 Cor. 12:4–11, 28–30; Eph. 4:7–12. Spiritual gifts were unusual manifestations of God's grace (*charis*) under normal and abnormal forms.

There are five gifts of the Spirit.

Working of Miracles (1 Cor. 12:10, 28–29). "Miracles" is the rendering of *dynameis* (powers). In the Book of Acts *dynameis* refers to the casting out of evil spirits and the healing of bodily ailments (8:6–7, 13; 19:11–12). This may explain "working of powers," but this gift is not synonymous with "gifts of healing." Probably the former was much more spectacular than the latter, and may have signified raising the dead (Acts 9:36–42 20:9–12).

Gifts of Healing (1 Cor. 12:9, 28, 30). These resemble "working of miracles" (powers)—witness the ministry of Jesus (Matt. 4:23–24), of the Twelve (Matt. 10:1), and of the Seventy (Luke 10:8–9). Gifts of healing were also prominent in the church after Pentecost (Acts 5:15–16; cf. James 5:14–15). "Gifts" (plural) indicates the great variety of both the sicknesses healed and the means used in the healings.

The Gift of Helpers (1 Cor. 12:28). This gift is mentioned in Acts 20:35, where Paul exhorts the Ephesian elders to labor "to help the weak" and constantly to remember the Lord's own words, "It is more blessed to give than to receive." Paul supports this exhortation with his own example. The early church seems to have had a special concern for the needy, and those who helped the indigent were considered to have been endowed by the Spirit for this ministry.

The Gift of Governments or Administration (1 Cor. 12:28; cf. Rom. 12:8). The early church's organization was fluid. Official offices had not been established, nor were duly appointed officials yet ruling the churches. It was necessary, therefore, that certain members should receive and exercise the gift of ruling or governing the local assembly of believers. This gift would take the form of sound advice and wise judgment in directing church affairs.

The Gift of Faith (1 Cor. 12:9). The Spirit's gift of faith could effect mighty things (Matt. 17:19–20), and keep believers steadfast in persecution.

These five spiritual gifts, then, had special reference to the practical aspects of the church's life, the physical well-being of believers, and orderliness of their worship and conduct. The remainder of the gifts of the Spirit concern the ministry of the Word of God.

Apostleship. Paul gives pride of place to the grace of apostleship: "God has appointed first of all apostles" (1 Cor. 12:28). The designation "apostle" began to be applied to NT personalities other than the Twelve, especially to Paul. The apostles believed that they had received this spiritual gift to enable them to fulfill the ministry of the Word of God; nothing, therefore, should be allowed to prevent their fulfilling that all-important function (Acts 6:2). We also gather from Paul that the gift of apostleship was to be exercised principally among unbelievers (1 Cor. 1:17). Paul's apostleship was to be fulfilled among Gentiles; Peter's ministry of the word was to be exercised among Jews (Gal. 2:7–8).

Prophets. Prophets stand next in importance to apostles in Paul's enumeration of the spiritual gifts (1 Cor. 12:2–30). Prophets in the NT church (Acts 11:28) seem often to have been itinerant preachers. Moving from church to church, they built up believers in the faith by teaching the Word. Their ministry would probably be characterized by spontaneity and power, since it seems to have included speaking by revelation (1 Cor. 14:6, 26, 30–31).

The Gift of Discernment of Spirits. Believers had to be able to discriminate between the false and the true spirits, when an itinerant prophet claimed to be inspired to speak by revelation (1 Cor. 14:29).

The Gift of Teaching. Clearly related to, but carefully distinguished from, the gift of prophecy is the gift of teaching (Rom. 12:7; 1 Cor. 12:28–29). In Eph. 4:11 Paul adds the idea of pastor to that of teacher, because no one is able to communicate effectively (teach) without loving those who are being instructed (pastor). Likewise, to be an effective pastor, one must also be a teacher.

The Gift of Exhortation (Rom. 12:8). The possessor of the gift of exhortation would fulfill a ministry closely allied with that of the Christian prophet and teacher.

The Gift of Speaking the Word of Wisdom (1 Cor. 12:8). This gift would communicate ability to receive and explain "the deep things of God."

The Gift of Speaking the Word of Knowledge (1 Cor. 12:8). Speaking the word of knowledge suggests a word spoken only after long and careful consideration.

The Gift of Tongues. The Spirit gives "kinds of tongues" (1 Cor. 12:10, 28). The nature of this gift is explained in 1 Cor. 14.

The Gift of Interpretation of Tongues (1 Cor. 12:10, 30). A necessary corollary to speaking in tongues was the interpretation of tongues. The tongue speaker might also exercise the gift of interpreting, but usually others exercised it (vv. 26–28; 12:10).

The Evangelist. Timothy is called an evangelist in 2 Tim. 4:5, as is Philip, one of the seven, in Acts 21:8. The task of preaching the gospel, although theoretically everyone's responsibility, is entrusted specifically to certain individuals by the Holy Spirit.

Service (Gk. *diakonia*). Called a gift in Rom. 12:7, it is perhaps a generalized gift of power to anyone exercising a specific function in the church.

Contributing (Rom. 12:8). All are to give to the needs of the church, its ministry, and the poor, but a special gift enables some to make joyous sacrifice in this area.

Acts of Mercy (Rom. 12:8). Merciful acts are to be performed with cheerfulness under the guidance of the Spirit.

Giving Aid (Rom. 12:8). Giving aid is to be exercised with zeal.

In instructing Christians on the exercise of these gifts, Paul is concerned to stress their practical nature. The Spirit bestows *charismata* for the edification of the church, the formation of Christian character, and the service of the community. The reception of a spiritual gift, therefore, brings serious responsibility, since it is essentially an opportunity for self-giving in sacrificial service to others. The more spectacular gifts (tongues, healings, miracles) necessitate some degree of order that will prevent their indiscriminate use (1 Cor. 14:40). The spirits of the prophets must be subjected to the prophets (v. 32). Paul clearly insists that spectacular gifts are inferior to those that instruct believers in faith and morals and evangelized non-Christians.

J. G. S. S. Thomson and W. A. Elwell

See also Baptism of the Spirit; Charismatic Movement; Holy Spirit; Tongues, Speaking in.

Spiritual Healing. See Heal, Healing.

Spirituality. State of deep relationship to God. At one time terms such as "holiness," "holy living," "godliness," "walking with God," and "discipleship" captured the tenure of the Christian experience—commitment, a deepening relationship with Christ, and a life of personal obedience to the Word of God. "Spirituality" is a more abstract term, even misleading, when used of the asceticism of any religion, including specific traditions of Roman Catholic devotion. But the contemporary decline of the sacred, even among evangelical Christians, and the invasion of secularism into every aspect of life emphasize the need to reconsider devotion to Christ much more seriously.

Modern exemplars of spiritual life remind us that all humankind has the potential for being spiritual. The advanced standards of asceticism in Eastern religions today are often contrasted favorably with the self-interest, materialism, and hedonism of Western life. Asian religions are often marked by a contempt for materialism and a concept of spirituality as a sustained and consistent way of life that shames Western Christians. The endless vigil, the extreme asceticism, and the simplicity of a mullah, guru, or fakir seem to excel any standards of ascetic spirituality in the West.

Christian spirituality is Christocentric. Paul frequently describes the life of the believer "in Christ" to emphasize the union Christians enjoy with Jesus Christ. This is a dynamic union, which the Synoptic writers describe as following Jesus, the Johannine writings as union in love, and Hebrews and 1 Peter as a pilgrimage. These and other metaphors imply the growth and dynamism of the life of Christ in the believer. God's original purpose to create humankind in his image and likeness (Gen. 1:26–28) is reinterpreted by redemption as being "conformed to the likeness of his Son" (Rom. 8:29). Christian spirituality is life in the Trinity. Christians live in the acceptance of sonship knowing God as Father. They realize this in the Sonship of Jesus Christ, his saving work of forgiveness, and his gift of eternal life. He actualizes this by the gift of the Holy Spirit, who enables the believer to cry "Abba Father" (Rom. 8:15; Gal. 4:6). Christian spirituality is the outworking, then, of the grace of God in the human soul, beginning with conversion and concluding with death or Christ's second advent. It is marked by growth and maturity in a Christlike life. It implies community and fellowship (Eph. 4:15–16), a life of prayer (Matt. 6:5–15; 1 Thess. 5:17), a sense of the eternal dimension in all of existence (Gen. 50:19–20; Rom. 8:28), and an intense awareness of life lived in the present before God (Matt. 6:34). The Spirit-filled life is one that manifests practically the Spirit of Jesus, with the fruit of love that is joyful, peaceful, patient, kind, good, faithful, gentle, and self-controlled (Gal. 5:22–23). This is true spirituality. It is a continuous command, "Be filled with the Spirit," that should be neither quenched (1 Thess. 5:19) nor grieved (Eph. 4:30).

Christian spirituality engenders fellowship, and the communion of saints deepens its character. As social beings, the reality of our spirituality is tested by the quality of our public worship (Acts 2:42). Godliness and spiritual friendship reinforce each other, as a horizontal and a vertical way respectively, to inspire and to embody the love of God in human hearts. For Christian worship is not primarily a matter of special practices but of lifestyle (Rom. 12:1; 14:6; 1 Cor. 10:31).

Orthodox (Greek) Spirituality. The creation of a school for catechumens in Alexandria in the 3d century stimulated an intellectual and speculative type of spirituality. It owed much to Philo, who sought to combine Judaism and Platonism. This led to a dualistic view of matter and spirit, scriptural allegorism, the method of abstraction in apophatic attitudes and in a tendency to think dialectically.

To this was added a Christocentric mysticism by Athanasius (296–373) completing what Irenaeus had emphasized beforehand, of the recapitulation of humankind's purpose in Christ. There is also a strong asceticism, influenced by the desert fathers such as John Cassian (ca. 360–435), Evagrius (ca. 346–399), and John Climacus (ca. 570–649), who considered the monastic model of *apatheia* as the ideal. This is not the apathy of the Stoics, but the fiery love of God, that both burns up human passions and possessiveness and flames in living desire for God. Orthodox piety is also deeply liturgical in its dispensing of the sacraments and the celebration of the church calendar, which frames the whole year with its commemoration of all the stages of the Savior's earthly life and ministry. There is the strong contemplative element in the tradition of hesychasm (*hesychia*, "quiet"). "Prayer without ceasing" goes back to the contemplative life of the desert fathers, but it was richly developed by Symeon the New Theologian (949–1022).

Western Medieval Spirituality. Gregory the Great (540–604) is the father of medieval spirituality. He systematized Western monasticism, and developed the imagery of the vision of God. To experience this, he emphasized the need of purity of heart, with the associated virtue of humility. Practical service was another Western trait of Gregory's teachings. Isidore (ca. 560–636), bishop of Seville, and the Venerable Bede (673–735) developed Gregory's ideas further, with stress on reading (*lectio*), meditative memory (*meditatio*), prayer (*oratio*), and practice (*intento*), as guides for the spiritual life in the dark ages of the barbarians. Maximus the Confessor (ca. 580–662) was the first to give expression to the Catholic tradition of the three ways to God (purgation, illumination, and union).

The High Middle Ages (1000–1300) was primarily concerned with monastic reform, the clash between scholasticism and the contemplative life, and the role of the laity in the church. An intensely affective expression of spirituality was promoted by Bernard of Clairvaux (1090–1153) and his followers. The imitation of Christ was aroused by the examples of the friars, notably Francis of Assisi (1181–1226) and his followers, Bonaventure (1221–74) and Raymond Lull (1235–1315).

The Late Middle Ages (1300–1500) was marked by a dramatic change of mood to one of pessimism in Western life with famines, plagues, intellectual sterility, and skepticism, and the break-up of feudal society. Individual mysticism deepened, although regional associations of mystics were discernible.

In the Rhineland, the Dominicans Meister Eckhart (1260–1328), Johannes Tauler (ca. 1300–1361), and Henry Suso (ca. 1295–1366), with the Augustinian John Ruysbroeck (1293–1381), all exerted a profound influence. Gerard Groote (1340–84) and his disciple Thomas à Kempis (1379–1471) gave birth to the *Devotio Moderna*, whose classic, *The Imitation of Christ*, had an immense influence on subsequent generations. In northern Italy, Catherine of Genoa (1447–1510) and Lorenzo Scupoli (*The Spiritual Combat*) had profound influence.

Modern Catholic Spirituality. More than anywhere else, the founders of the tradition of modern Catholic spirituality are the Spanish mystics. Ignatius of Loyola (1491–1556) was the founder of the Jesuits and author of *The Spiritual Exercises*. Teresa of 'Avila (1515–82) and John of the Cross (1542–91) were Carmelite reformers.

In France there was sharp conflict between the more rationalistic views of men like Bossuet and the quietist views of Francis Fénelon (1651–1715). Before him the great influence on French spirituality was Francis of Sales (1567–1622), who followed the combined influences of Ignatius and Teresa. Sales focused on the spiritual needs of the laity. A more theological emphasis on spiritual renewal of the clergy was made by Pierre de Brulle (1575–1629), who founded the Oratory for that purpose in 1611.

Caroline (Anglican) Spirituality. In England, the spirituality of the Anglican Church is associated with the *Book of Common Prayer*. Although "Caroline" refers to the reign of Charles I and II, it is still characteristic of much Anglicanism today. Its balance between the contemplative life of prayer and the vocal liturgy of communal prayer is the genius of its spiritual continuity in the life of the church.

(Protestant) Puritan Spirituality. While the Reformation of Martin Luther (1483–1546) and John Calvin (1509–64) developed into classical Protestantism, the subsequent reforms of Puritanism, pietism, and Methodism were distinct, and sometimes divergent. To Luther the essence of spiritual life could be sustained on the actualization of the Ten Commandments, the Lord's Prayer, and the Apostles' Creed. Calvin is a much more sophisticated spiritual guide, and in the third book of his *Institutes* he has left rich teaching on the spiritual life. He gave his own distinctive alternative to the Catholic model of purgation-illumination-union with the biblical themes of justification-sanctification-glorification.

It was out of Calvinist teaching that Puritan spirituality developed in England and later in New England. It focused on the centrality of the Word of God and its preaching, the preparation of heart to receive the Word, the need for a godly walk and accountability to God, and the strength and watchfulness required in pilgrimage and conflict. The heavenly hope of believers enabled them to anticipate heaven while still on earth.

German Pietism. In reaction to the sterile theology of Lutheranism in the 17th and 18th centuries, pietism was somewhat anti-intellectual and reactionary. Philipp J. Spener (1635–1705) was its classical exponent, although Johann Arndt (1555–1621) was its founder. Arndt's *True Christianity* was widely read as an inspiration for "a new life." August H. Francke (1663–1727) was the organizing genius of the lay movement. Both Spener and Francke practiced their devotion in the establishment of poor schools, orphanages, farms, printing shops, and other enterprises.

Methodism and Modern Holiness Movements. John Wesley (1703–91), who lived and died an Anglican priest, founded the Methodist movement. While preaching was the main emphasis of his ministry, he developed hymnody with his brother Charles as an instrument of spirituality, and developed class organization as a means of instruction. The aim was to achieve Christian perfection/scriptural holiness.

The Keswick Convention was established in England in the late 1800s to promote the message of victorious Christian living.

Pentecostalism, beginning in the early part of this century out of holiness teaching, and the more interdenominational charismatic movement since World War II have been significant renewal movements. The release of self-consciousness, the exercise of touch, the emphasis on spiritual gifts, the strong awareness of the satanic and the need of exorcisms, the ministry of all believers—these have marked the character of its spirituality. There is a felt vibrancy in the reality of the living and present God, like children rediscovering the reality of the fatherhood of God.

In spite of the renewal movements, there is a dearth today of spiritual leadership and direction in the evangelical world. Catholics can look to Mother Teresa in Calcutta, and the Orthodox to the unnamed martyrs of modern Russia, but evangelical Protestants are largely secularized by their politics, their obsession with growth, and their interests in administration and parachurch activities. The loss of the practice of prayer, the ignorance of the rich traditions of spirituality, and the need to develop a cultural framework for the practice of devotion are challenges worthy of the most serious consideration at the end of the 20th century.

J. M. HOUSTON

See also BEATIFIC VISION; BOEHME, JAKOB; BRETHREN OF THE COMMON LIFE; DEVOTIO MODERNA; FRANCIS OF ASSISI; GODLINESS; HESYCHASM; HOLINESS MOVEMENT, AMERICAN; ILLUMINATIVE WAY, THE; KESWICK CONVENTION; MYSTICISM; PERFECTION, PERFECTIONISM; PIETISM; PURGATIVE WAY, THE; QUIETISM; SANCTIFICATION; UNITIVE WAY, THE.

Sprinkle, Sprinkling. See BAPTISM, MODES OF.

Spurgeon, Charles Haddon (1834–1892). English Baptist minister.

In Apr. 1854, Spurgeon accepted a call to the Baptist chapel at New Park Street in London and began a ministry that lasted 38 years. He received some unfavorable publicity at first because of his lack of formal education and rural origins. The congregation began to grow, however, and soon he was preaching at Exeter Hall while the church building was being enlarged. Then some members of the church rented the Surrey Gardens Music Hall, and at age 22 Spurgeon became perhaps the most popular preacher of his day.

In 1861 the Metropolitan Tabernacle at Elephant and Castle streets was built, a church that would seat 6000 people. The building was completely paid for when the congregation occupied the site, and Spurgeon ministered there continually until his death. The tabernacle became a center for the religious life of the area, housing a pastor's college and a colportage society that emphasized the distribution of religious literature. The congregation grew yearly, and it has been estimated that 14,000 members were added during Spurgeon's ministry.

A prolific writer, he published some 2241 of his weekly sermons during his lifetime; some 3800 in all were published. From 1865 on he edited a monthly magazine entitled *The Sword and the Trowel.* His primary emphasis was always evangelism. Often criticized for not having received formal college training, his sermons revealed that he did a great deal of reading, and his personal library contained more than 10,000 volumes.

J. E. JOHNSON

State. See GOVERNMENT.

States of Jesus Christ. Different relationships Jesus Christ had to God's law for humankind, to the possession of authority, and to receiving honor for himself. Generally two states (humiliation and exaltation) are distinguished. Thus, the doctrine of the twofold state of Christ is the teaching that Christ experienced first the state of humiliation, then the state of exaltation. Within each of these states four aspects may be distinguished.

The Humiliation of Christ. *Incarnation.* The incarnation, or Christ's taking to himself a human nature, was itself a step of humiliation. He gave up the honor and glory that belonged to him in heaven (John 17:5). He also gave up his right to exercise divine authority for his own benefit and the right to enjoy his lordship over all things in heaven and on earth (2 Cor. 8:9; Phil. 2:6–7; Heb. 2:9). Thus he gave up the status of ruler and took on the status of a servant. Furthermore, he subjected himself to the demands of living under the law (Gal. 4:4), thus making it necessary for him to obey perfectly the OT laws that God had commanded of his people (John 8:46; Matt. 3:15). He took on himself the obligation to obey God perfectly *as a man*, as our representative, in order to earn salvation for us through a record of perfect lifelong obedience (Rom. 5:18–19).

Suffering. Jesus' sufferings lasted throughout his whole life, although they culminated in his trial and death on the cross. He experienced the ordinary sufferings of living in a fallen world. He was weary (John 4:6), thirsty (19:28), hungry (Matt. 4:2), sorrowful (John 11:35), and lonely (Matt. 26:56). He felt great grief at human sin and its terrible effects (Matt. 23:37; Mark 3:5; 8:12; John 11:33–35, 38). He endured human opposition and intense hatred against himself (Luke 11:53–54; John 15:18, 24–25). He was "a man of sorrows and familiar with suffering" (Isa. 53:3).

Jesus' humiliation increased in intensity at the time of his trial and death. Physical sufferings connected with crucifixion were terrible, as were the mocking and shame connected with such a death. But even worse were the sufferings in spirit that Jesus experienced when God the Father put on him the guilt of our sins (2 Cor. 5:21; Gal. 3:13; 1 Pet. 2:22; cf. Isa. 53:6).

Death. Jesus' physical body died (Matt. 27:50), and his human spirit (or soul) was separated from his body and passed into the presence of the Father in heaven (Luke 23:43, 46). By virtue of union with Jesus' human nature, his divine nature experienced what it was like to go through death.

Burial. Jesus' body was laid in a tomb (Matt. 27:59–60), and he continued under the state of death for a time. Thus, Jesus' humiliation was complete in that he suffered all the punishment and shame due to fallen humankind as a result of sin.

The Exaltation of Christ. *Resurrection.* The resurrection was the transition point into Jesus' state of exaltation. It was the person of Christ that was exalted, not just his human nature, but the focus of this activity of exaltation was the change in his human nature to a new, much more glorious state.

The resurrection was not just a restoration to life, but the beginning of a new, better kind of life, a "resurrection life" (Rom. 6:9–10). After the resurrection, Jesus still had a physical body that could be touched and held (Matt. 28:9; John 20:17, 27), could break bread (Luke 24:30), prepare breakfast (John 21:12–13), and eat (Luke 24:42–43). It was a body of "flesh and bones," for Jesus said, "A ghost does not have flesh and bones, as you see I have" (v. 39).

Yet this physical body of Jesus was no longer subject to weakness, sickness, aging, or death. It was imperishable and glorious and powerful (1 Cor. 15:42–44; the term "spiritual" here means not "nonmaterial" but "conformed to the character of the Holy Spirit").

Ascension. Forty days after his resurrection (Acts 1:3), Jesus ascended to heaven and entered more fully into the privileges of his state of exaltation.

When Jesus ascended into heaven he received glory, honor, and authority which were not his before as God-man (Acts 2:33, 36; Phil. 2:9–11; 1 Tim. 3:16; Heb. 1:3–4; 2:9), especially the authority to pour out the Holy Spirit on the church in greater fullness and power than before (Acts 1:8; 2:33).

After Jesus ascended into heaven he also began his high priestly work of representing us before God the Father (Heb. 9:24) and of interceding for us before God (7:25; Rom. 8:34).

Sitting (Session) at the Father's Right Hand. A further stage in the exaltation of Christ was his sitting down at the right hand of the Father in heaven (Acts 2:33; Eph. 1:20–22; Heb. 1:3). This action shows both the completion of Christ's work of redemption and his reception of new authority as God-man to reign over the universe.

Return in Glory. When Jesus Christ returns to the earth in glory, his exaltation will be complete, and he will receive all the glory that is due to him as the

God-man who has purchased our redemption and is worthy of eternal and infinite honor. Then his kingdom will be established forever, and, exalted with the Father and the Holy Spirit, "he will reign for ever and ever" (Rev. 11:15; 22:3–5).

W. A. GRUDEM

See also JESUS CHRIST; OFFICES OF CHRIST.

Steiner, Rudolf (1861–1925). See ANTHROPOSOPHY.

Stewardship (Gk. *oikonomia*, "management of a household"). Administration of duties or goods in one's care.

The idea that we are stewards of God in relation to the world and our own life is inherent in the creation story (Gen. 1–3). Adam was appointed lord of all things except himself. In the NT, the word (when not used in its ordinary sense) refers to the administration of the gifts of God, especially preaching the gospel. By metonymy, stewardship may refer to God's provision for the Christian age (Eph. 1:10; 3:9), the context implying that this plan includes the entrustment of the gospel message to humankind. This idea is explicit in 1 Cor. 4:1–2; 9:17; Eph. 3:2; Col. 1:25; Titus 1:7. Stewardship is broadened to include all Christians and all the gracious gifts of God in 1 Pet. 4:10.

The modern emphasis on the stewardship of possessions, while true, may tend to obscure the fact that our primary stewardship is that of the gospel and includes the use of our whole life as well as our money.

F. L. FISHER

Stoddard, Solomon (1643–1729). American clergyman. Stoddard was one of the most influential leaders in American Protestantism from the settlement of Massachusetts (1630) to the colonial Great Awakening (ca. 1740). From his pulpit in Northampton, Massachusetts, where he served from 1672 to 1729, Stoddard's ideas exerted a powerful influence, not only in the Connecticut River valley, but in Boston and in New England as a whole.

He regarded the Lord's Supper distributed at an open communion as a converting ordinance. He claimed that participation in communion was an excellent way for people to "learn the necessity and sufficiency of the Death of Christ in order to [find] Pardon." Stoddard's concern for revival was shared by his grandson, Jonathan Edwards, who became his associate minister in 1724 and his successor in 1729.

M. A. NOLL

Stoics, Stoicism. Major school of hellenistic thought. The Stoics derived their name from the Painted Porch (Gk. *stoa*) in Athens where their founder taught. Although the school, begun by Zeno of Citium (335–263 B.C.), continued to maintain its headquarters in Athens, throughout the more than half a millennium of its existence, its major thinkers and practitioners lived elsewhere—Cleanthes of Assos (331–232), Chrysippus of Soli (ca. 280–207), Panaetius of Rhodes (ca. 185–110 B.C.), and Seneca (ca. 4 B.C.–A.D. 65), Epictetus (ca. 55–ca. 135) and Marcus Aurelius (A.D. 121–180) from Rome.

Stoic influence on Jewish writers is seen principally in Philo, who, as other Middle Platonists, borrowed both Stoic terminology and concepts. Of principal interest in the NT is Paul's sensitivity to his Stoic auditors' belief in divine immanence, as he in his Areopagus speech quoted from Zeno's friend Aratus to support the doctrine (Acts 17:28).

While some Stoic influence on later Christian theologians is detectable, it is Christian Middle Platonists of the 2d century like Justin and Clement of Alexandria and Western theologians like Minucius Felix and Tertullian who exhibit the greatest debt to the Stoa. It is in the area of ethics, however, that the strongest affinities are found. Galen, the 2d-century physician-philosopher, provided ample testimony to this when he classed Christians with philosophers on the basis of their ethics, in spite of the fact that they could not follow a demonstrative argument. Christians, however, differed with Stoics on suicide and found certain other Stoic teachings objectionable, including their materialism, fatalism, doctrine of endless world cycles, and belief in total divine immanence.

G. T. BURKE

Storch, Nicholas. See ZWICKAU PROPHETS.

Strong, Augustus Hopkins (1836–1921). American theologian, educator, and author.

From 1865 to 1872 Strong was pastor of the First Baptist Church of Cleveland, Ohio, which numbered John D. Rockefeller among its members. In 1872, Strong was elected president of the Rochester Theological Seminary and professor of theology. In these dual roles he served for 40 years, retiring in 1912 as president emeritus.

Strong's great influence was due to his personal contact with students and prominent laypersons and to his writings. Through the various editions of his books, *Systematic Theology* (1886, 1907–46), *Philosophy and Religion* (1888), *Christ in Creation and Ethical Monism* (1899), and *What Shall I Believe?* (1922), one can trace the development of Strong's theology. By 1894 Strong abandoned federal theology for what he termed ethical monism, or qualitative monism, metaphysical monism, and personalistic idealism. He considered his most original contribution to theology to be his explanation of the imputation of the sins of the race to Christ.

W. R. ESTEP, JR.

Stübner, Markus. See ZWICKAU PROPHETS.

Subdiaconate. Order of ministry found in the church from the 3d century. In the hierarchy of ordained clergy the subdeacon followed the bishop, priest, and deacon. The subdeacon's duty was primarily liturgical, especially at High Mass, when he chanted the Epistle reading, presented the bread (paten) and wine (chalice) to the presiding priest, and cleaned the holy vessels afterward.

The churches of the Reformation in the 16th century abolished this order, but it was retained by the Roman Church until 1972. It is still found, however, in the Orthodox and Eastern churches.

P. TOON

See also CHURCH OFFICERS; MAJOR ORDERS.

Sublapsarianism. See INFRALAPSARIANISM.

Subordinationism. Doctrine that assigns an inferiority of being, status, or role to the Son or Holy Spirit within the Trinity. Condemned by numerous church councils, this doctrine has continued in one form or another throughout the history of the church.

The Nicene fathers ascribed to the Son and Spirit an equality of being or essence, but a subordination of order, with both deriving their existence from the Father as primal source. Athanasius insisted upon the coequality of the status of the three Persons of the Trinity, and Augustine that these Persons are coequal and coeternal. Yet ancient and modern theologians have argued for a subordination in the role of Son and Spirit to the Father and cite in support such passages as Matt. 11:27; John 5:26–27; 6:38; 8:28; 14:28.

R. C. KROEGER AND C. C. KROEGER

See also ARIANISM; MONARCHIANISM; NICEA, COUNCIL OF.

Substance. (Lat. *substantia*; Gk. *hypostasis*, "standing under" + *ousia*) Essential nature, essence.

The matter of substance played an important role in Christian theology in both the patristic and medieval periods. In defining the nature of the Godhead, the East generally emphasized its threefold nature, while in the West the stress was on its unified substance. This and translation problems between Greek and Latin made it difficult to realize that an actual consensus was being reached. In Greek, *hypostasis* and *ousia* were synonyms, as can be seen in the Creed at Nicea (325). The Cappadocian fathers found them too ambiguous. Hence, they arrived at a Trinitarian formula that distinguished them: three *hypostaseis* (individuals), one *ousia* (substance). In the West, where in the 4th century the formula was expressed as one *substantia* (substance), three *personae* (persons), this caused difficulties. Augustine regarded *essentia* (essence) and *substantia* (substance), which usually translated *ousia* and *hypostasis* respectively, as synonyms, so when the Eastern fathers talked of three *hypostaseis*, it sounded as if they meant three substances. The difference, however, was merely semantic.

Since the patristic period, substance has been important in connection with the eucharistic doctrine of transubstantiation. Aquinas has given the doctrine its most extensive theoretical development, beginning from, but not limited to, Aristotle's distinction between substance and accident. According to the doctrine, which received formulation before Aquinas at the Fourth Lateran Council (1215) and after him at the Council of Trent, in the Eucharist the substance of the bread and wine are changed into the substance of the body and blood of Christ. At the level of accidents or species, however, no change takes place, because such accidents as color, shape, taste, and the like remain. Hence, it is only at the level of faith that one can know that this actual change in substance has taken place.

G. T. BURKE

See also TRINITY, HOMOOUSION, TRANSUBSTANTIATION.

Suffering. See EVIL, PROBLEM OF; PAIN.

Suffering Servant. See SERVANT OF THE LORD.

Sufficient Grace. See GRACE.

Suffragan Bishop. See CHURCH OFFICERS; BISHOP.

Sunday. See LORD'S DAY.

Supererogation, Works of. Voluntary works over and above what God commands. In Roman Catholic theology *supererogatio* means doing more than God requires. The term goes back to the Vulgate of Luke 10:35 (*quodcumque supererogaveris*), but was not used in its present technical sense until the Middle Ages. The conception is based upon a distinction between works that are necessary for salvation and those that are voluntary. In doing the latter (such as accepting vows of poverty, celibacy, and obedience), a person can do more than God requires.

R. J. COATES

Superintendent. See CHURCH OFFICERS.

Supper, Lord's. See LORD'S SUPPER.

Supplication. See PRAYER.

Supralapsarianism. Doctrine that God decreed both election and reprobation before the fall.

Theodore Beza, Calvin's successor at Geneva, was the first to develop supralapsarianism in the modern sense. By the time of the Synod of Dort in 1618–19, a heated intraconfessional controversy developed between infra- and supralapsarians; both positions were represented at the synod. Francis Gomarus, the chief opponent of James Arminius, was a supralapsarian.

The question of the logical, not the temporal, order of the eternal decrees reflected differences on God's ultimate goal in predestination and on the specific objects of predestination. Supralapsarians considered God's ultimate goal to be his own glory in election and reprobation, while infralapsarians considered predestination subordinate to other goals. The object of predestination, according to supralapsarians, was uncreated and unfallen humanity, while infralapsarians viewed the object as created and fallen humanity.

The term "supralapsarianism" comes from the Latin words *supra* and *lapsus*; the decree of predestination was considered to be "above" (*supra*) or logically "before" the decree concerning the fall (*lapsus*), while the infralapsarians viewed it as "below" (*infra*) or logically "after" the decree concerning the fall.

Although supralapsarianism never received confessional endorsement within the Reformed churches, it has been tolerated within the confessional boundaries. In 1905 the Reformed churches of the Netherlands and the Christian Reformed Church in 1908 adopted the Conclusions of Utrecht, which stated that "our Confessional Standards admittedly follow the infralapsarian presentation in respect to the doctrine of election, but that it is evident . . . that this in no wise was intended to exclude or condemn the supralapsarian presentation." Recent defenders of the supralapsarian position have been Gerhardus Vos, Herman Hoeksema, and G. H. Kersten.

F. H. KLOOSTER

See also CALVINISM; DECREES OF GOD; ELECT, ELECTION; INFRALAPSARIANISM; PREDESTINATION; REPROBATION; SOVEREIGNTY OF GOD.

Swedenborg, Emanuel (1688–1772). Swedish scientist and religious teacher. For much of his adult life he was an assessor of the Royal Board of Mines in his homeland and wrote works on science and philosophy. In his 1750s his interest shifted to religion and theology as he claimed to have special communication with angels and spirits. Holding that he had been granted by God a special knowledge in the interpretation of the Bible, he wrote several works unfolding a system of thought that rejects or alters many traditional Christian beliefs.

Swedenborg's theological views include the following: (1) Monopersonal Trinity. The Godhead consists, not of three persons, but of three essential principles. The Father is the inmost principle, the "ineffable Love" of God; the Son is the divine Wisdom; and the Holy Spirit is the divine Power. All three principles are the same divine person, Jesus Christ himself. (2) The continuance of true marital love in heaven. (3) The spiritual realization of the second advent and last judgment in 1757 (from which doctrine the Church of the New Jerusalem was formed).

D. W. DIEHL

Synagogue. Jewish house of assembly, study, and prayer. Its origins are shrouded in mystery. While some have suggested that it dates back to Moses and others have identified the "meeting places" in Ps. 74:8 as synagogues, it has been traditionally traced to the period of the Babylonian exile, when the Jewish people were deprived of the temple and assembled together for worship in a strange land. Jewish tradition has maintained that the reference to "little sanctuary" in Ezek. 11:16 is a direct reference to the synagogues of these exiles and that Ezekiel's repeated allusion to the assembly of the elders (8:1; 14:1; 20:1) also indicates synagogue worship.

By the first Christian century the synagogue was a well established institution, giving every indication of centuries of growth as a center of religious and social life of the Jewish community. Before the destruction of the temple by the Romans in A.D. 70, the synagogue maintained an important functioning relationship with the temple. After the destruction, the synagogue emerged as the central institution. The NT documents both Jesus' use of the synagogue and that of the disciples and early Christians. Missionaries, such as Paul, made great use of the 1st-century synagogues as well. The synagogue service, in turn, had a major impact on Christian worship and church government (cf. the office of "elder").

The reading of both the law and the prophets was a central element in the synagogue service. In addition, the basic structure included the recitation of the *Shema* ("Hear O Israel: The LORD our God, the LORD is one," Deut. 6:4–9) and the *Amidah,* a central silent prayer contemplating God and thanking him for the sabbath and human blessings.

D. A. RAUSCH

Syncretism. Process by which elements of one religion are assimilated into another religion, resulting in a change in the fundamental tenets or nature of those religions. It is the union of two or more opposite beliefs, so that the synthesized form is a new thing. It is not always a total fusion, but may be a combination of separate segments that remain identifiable compartments. Syncretism of the Christian gospel occurs when critical or basic elements of the gospel are replaced by religious elements from the host culture. The NT canon and the recognized creed became the church's two greatest weapons against the growth and transmission of syncretism. Church history is filled with the story of struggle against syncretism from political, social, religious, and economic sources.

In the striving by missionaries for an indigenous national church with a contextualized gospel, the danger of syncretism is ever present in attempts at accommodation, adjustment, and adaptation. Three steps in biblical adaptation have been suggested: (1) discriminating selection of words, symbols, and rites (e.g., "Logos"); (2) rejection of that which is clearly incompatible with biblical truth; (3) reinterpretation by a complete refilling of the selected rite or symbol with a truly Christian meaning. The supracultural teachings of Scripture must be judge of both culture and meaning as God works through people using various forms to bring all creation under his lordship.

In the history of theology the term "syncretism" is used specifically to define two movements aimed at unification. In the Lutheran tradition, George Calixtus (1586–1656) attempted to reconcile Lutheran thought with Roman Catholicism on the basis of the Apostles' Creed. This precipitated a syncretistic controversy that was to last for many years. In Roman Catholicism "syncretism" refers to the attempt to reconcile Molinist and Thomist theology.

S. R. IMBACH

Synergism. (Gk. *synergos,* "working together") Reference to the doctrine of divine and human cooperation in conversion. Synergism seeks to reconcile two paradoxical truths: the sovereignty of God and human moral responsibility. Nowhere do these two truths so intersect as in the theology of conversion. The Augustinian tradition emphasizes the sovereignty of God in conversion (monergism or divine monergism). The other emphasizes cooperation of God and humankind. During the Lutheran Reformation the synergistic controversy occurred arising from statements made by Philip Melanchthon. In the second edition of his *Loci* (published in 1535), Melanchthon wrote that in conversion "Three causes are conjoined: The Word, the Holy Spirit and the Will not wholly inactive, but resisting its own weakness. . . . God draws, but draws him who is willing . . . and the will is not a statue, and that spiritual emotion is not impressed upon it as though it were a statue." His followers were called Philippists. His opponents were called Gnesio- or Genuine Lutherans.

Matthias Flacius, professor at Jena, became the major adversary of the Philippists. He taught that the "natural man" is comparable to a block of wood or a piece of stone and is hostile toward the work of God. The Formula of Concord (1577) rejected synergism, endorsed Augustinianism, avoided the rhetoric of Flacianism and the tendencies of Philippianism, teaching "through . . . the preaching and the hearing of his Word, God is active, breaks our hearts, and draws man, so that through the preaching of the law man learns to know his sins . . . and experiences genuine terror, contrition and sorrow . . . and through the preaching of . . . the holy Gospel . . . there is kindled in him a spark of faith which accepts the forgiveness of sins for Christ's sake."

C. G. Fry

See also Concord, Formula of; Flacius, Matthias; Melanchthon, Philip; Monergism.

Synod. (Gk. *synodos*, "a group of people traveling together") Calling together of the clergy of a diocese. It is believed that the first official synod was held by Bishop Siricius in Rome in 387. Subsequently Pope Benedict XIV ruled that a synod was a convocation of the diocese, while the gathering of all the bishops of the Catholic world was to be called a council.

Different denominations use the word in different ways today. Episcopalians have varying systems of synodical government in their various provinces, while since Vatican II the Church of Rome has had biennial synods (starting in 1969) of representative bishops. Presbyterians use the synod, composed of ministers and elders from the presbyteries, as the next stage up in their chain of church government. Lutheran churches also organized themselves originally in regional synods.

D. H. Wheaton

Systematic Theology. Attempt to reduce religious truth to an organized system.

The word "theology" does not occur in Scripture, although the idea is very much present. Etymologically theology derives from the Greek words *theos* (God) and *logos* (reason or speech), and thus means rational discussion about God. B. B. Warfield advanced the classic short definition: "Theology is the science of God and his relationship to man and the world." In greater detail theology might be defined as the discipline that (1) presents a unified formulation of truth concerning God and his relationship to humanity and the universe as this is set forth in divine revelation and that (2) applies such truths to the entire range of human life and thought. Systematic theology thus begins with divine revelation in its entirety, applies the Spirit-illumined mind to comprehend the revelation, draws out the teachings of Scripture via sound grammatical-historical exegesis, provisionally respects the development of the doctrine in the church, orders the results in a coherent whole, and applies the results to the full scope of human endeavor.

The discipline sometimes is designated "dogmatic theology" (Shedd, Pieper, Bavinck, Barth), the leading idea being truth established by competent authority. The governing authority is variously viewed as inspired Scripture, creedal standards, or the church's *magisterium.* Other common designations are Christian theology (Clark, Headlam, Wiley) and Christian faith (Rahner, H. Berkhof, and many Dutch theologians). Some mistakenly view systematic theology as a deposit of divine truths that is timeless and unalterable. Although the Scriptures are inviolable, fresh theological understanding and reformulation are required in every generation. First, because as language and cultural forms change the body of Christian truth must be clad in contemporary dress to remain intelligible; and second, because new issues and problems continually arise to challenge the church.

The church undertakes the task of constructing a systematic theology for three principal reasons: (1) That the church might be edified. The people of God are spiritually enriched by those teachings that systematic theology upholds as to be believed (2 Tim. 3:16). (2) That the gospel in its fullness might be proclaimed. Without the foundation of a solid theology there can be no effective gospel preaching, evangelism, missionary outreach, or Bible translation. And (3) that the truth content of the faith might be preserved. It is the express task of systematic theology to expound the whole counsel of God as given by divine revelation.

One way of doing systematic theology is the so-called confessional method, by which the teachings of Scripture are expounded and proclaimed. Thus Lutheran confessional theologies, Reformed confessional theologies, and neo-orthodox confessional theologies have been produced from the perspectives of the host system. The difficulty of the confessional method is that few reasons are given *why* one confessional position should be accepted as the norm vis-à-vis all the others. Preferable is the method that respects all the confessional views as hypotheses to be tested by the criteria of logical consistency, coherence with the facts of revelation, and existential viability. The task of the theologian is to show that the body of truth as it is formulated from revelation fits the facts with fewest problems and satisfies human needs to a greater degree than the alternatives.

B. A. DEMAREST

See also DOGMA; DOGMATICS.

Tt

Tauler, Johannes (ca. 1300–1361). Medieval mystic. Tauler spent his life as a Dominican preacher and spiritual counselor, primarily in Strasbourg, but also in Basel and Cologne. Tauler's literary legacy consists of German sermons. His approach may with caution be described as that of a pastoral *Lebemeister* ("master of living") rather than that of a pastoral *Lese-* or *Lehrmeister* ("lector or scholastic-mystical master of teaching"). Tauler's mystical theology is based less explicitly on a metaphysical system than on the existence of the image of God in humans focusing on a transforming or "hyperforming" (*Überformung*) of the human being in the divine image. Tauler's mystical theology is personalistic and anthropological, stressing the affective resources of the soul (the *Gemüt* or "basic will") to a greater degree than the intellectual faculties of the soul. Tauler also pays greater attention to the preparation for union, to the purgative path of growth in love and in freedom from selfness and creatureliness; a person cannot run before walking. His sermons were widely transmitted and frequently printed. They were read and recommended by subsequent spiritual writers, including Luther and various pietists.

D. D. MARTIN

See also MEISTER ECKHART; MYSTICISM.

Taylor, Nathaniel William (1786–1858). Founder of the New Haven theology. Taylor contributed to the rise of evangelical theology by modifying Calvinism, rendering it compatible with revivalism in the opening decades of the 19th century. In 1822 Taylor was appointed Dwight Professor of Didactic Theology at Yale, where he taught until his death in 1858. Taylor was prompted to revise Calvinism by the increasing charges from Unitarians that Calvinistic determinism actually promoted immorality by denying human freedom. In response to these attacks he altered the Reformed doctrines of revelation, human depravity, God's sovereignty, Christ's atonement, and regeneration in order to harmonize Calvinist theology with actual revival practices. Taylorism was popularized by revivalists such as Charles G. Finney, who demonstrated wide appeal to New School Presbyterians and Congregationalists anxious for revivals in their parishes. Old School opponents such as Charles Hodge at Princeton Theological Seminary accused Taylor of Pelagianism and Arminianism and defended traditional Calvinism.

W. A. HOFFECKER

See also NEW HAVEN THEOLOGY.

Teaching, Gift of. See SPIRITUAL GIFTS.

Teilhard de Chardin, Pierre (1881–1955). Jesuit paleogeologist and theologian. After 20 years in Asia, where his work included participation in the discoveries of Sinanthropus (Peking Man) and Pithecanthropus, he lectured widely in Europe and America to acclaim from outside of the church. Most of Teilhard's published views from his lifetime are scientific; his major theological works saw print only posthumously. Teilhard's central work is *The Phenomenon of Man* (1938). It is divided into three parts corresponding to Teilhard's tripartite conception of evolution: prelife, life, and thought. For him, the evolutionary process is orthogenetic: evolution, rather than merely the result of chance adaptation. This evolution proceeds along a "correct" line that the universe is compelled to follow. Thus the material realm already tends toward consciousness. Physical matter, however, is enveloped by the "biosphere," the manifestation of all the various forms of life beginning with the simplest and concluding with the most complex, the human being.

In the area of human development the most remarkable features of evolution are accented. All along, evolution has defied the second law of thermodynamics by increasing complexity in the system and by raising similarity in forms. But now in the human person complexity is highly intensified, and all of human evolution converges into the development of culture and thought. Thereby is created the third layer beyond matter and the biosphere: the "noosphere." The noosphere is the ever-increasing collectivity of human knowledge as well as of humanistic attitudes, especially love. It too develops, and has a goal: the unification of all humankind under the commitment of love. Teilhard refers to this certain destiny as "omega point." It becomes identical with Jesus Christ. Teilhard has few true disciples, but his thought has been a great stimulant for dialogue. Many of his ideas are reflected in the Vatican II documents. Scientists have found inspiration in his transmaterial view of the world.

W. CORDUAN

See also EVOLUTION.

Teleological Argument for God. See GOD, ARGUMENTS FOR THE EXISTENCE OF.

Temple, William (1881–1944). English theologian. Temple was ordained priest in 1909. His appointments included: fellow of Queen's College, Oxford (1904–10); headmaster of Repton (1910–14); rector of St. James's, Piccadilly (1914–17), where his preaching through the Gospel of John laid the foundation for his most popular devotional work, *Readings in St. John's Gospel* (1939); canon of Westminster (1919–20); bishop of Manchester (1921–29); archbishop of York (1929–42); and archbishop of Canterbury (1942–44).

Of massive intellectual and spiritual power, Temple's most important writings are on philosophical theology (*Mens Creatrix* [1917]; *Christus Veritas* [1924]; *Nature, Man and God* [1934]) and social theology (*Christianity and Social Order* [1942]). Influenced by the Neo-Hegelian idealism of T. H. Green and Edward Caird, Temple sought a unifying spiritual principle by which apparently contradictory or independent intellectual and social movements might be reconciled or related. This principle, he believed, was the Christian doctrine of the Logos. Consistent with his position, Temple was committed to a large number of social, political, economic, and ecclesiastical movements. He was first president of both the World Council of Churches "in process of formation" (1938) and of the British Council of Churches (1943). In spite of his brilliance, Temple's was a serene and simple faith, grounded in a life of prayer.

F. S. PIGGIN

Temptation. Act of tempting or the state of being tempted. In the OT the specific verb indicating the act of tempting is the piel form of the Hebrew verb *nāsâ*. In Gen. 22:1 this verb characterizes God's command to Abraham to offer Isaac as a burnt offering in the land of Moriah. A similar use of the term is used in reference to God's testing of people (Exod. 16:4; 20:20; Deut. 8:2, 16; 13:3; 2 Chron. 32:31; Ps. 26:2). The term is rarely, if ever, applied in the OT to Satan's act of enticing people to sin. Nevertheless, the essence of temptation in this sense is clearly revealed in the account of the fall and in the record of Satan's role in the affliction of Job (Gen. 3:1–13; Job 1:1–2:10).

The NT reflects the translation of *nāsâ* with the Greek verb *ekpeirazō* in the LXX (Matt. 4:7; 1 Cor. 10:9; Heb. 3:8–9). In these passages the sinful tempting of God is referred to by way of the OT. The same sense is employed by Peter in connection with the sin of Ananias and Sapphira (Acts 5:9) and the prescriptions to be given to Gentile Christians (Acts 15:10). The additional use of *peirazō* and related forms is complex. The words may refer to exterior circumstances that try the believer's faith and are designed to strengthen that faith (James 1:2; 1 Pet. 1:6). Although these circumstances are held to be under the absolute control of God, the explicit causal ascription of them to God is not prominent. While Satan's role in temptation is usually assumed rather than stated, in 1 Cor. 7:5 Paul explicitly warns Christians to observe his charge with respect to marital relationships, "that Satan will not tempt you because of your lack of self-control" (cf. Matt. 4:1; Mark 1:13; Luke 4:2).

Jesus teaches the disciples to pray, "And lead us not into temptation, but deliver us from the evil one" (Matt. 6:13), and the Bible is replete with warnings to be watchful because of the ever-present danger of falling into temptation (Luke 22:40; Gal. 6:1; 1 Pet. 5:8–9). Very likely Jesus was subject to temptation throughout his ministry (cf. Luke 4:13; 22:28). The temptation of Christ is the crucial temptation in redemptive history (Matt. 4:1, and pars.). The necessity of the temptation in view of Adam's fall is evident. Jesus triumphed over Satan with his immediate and obedient use of the Word of God. He thereby proved that he was qualified to be the "last Adam." "The reason the Son of God appeared was to destroy the devil's work" (1 John 3:8b).

C. G. KROMMINGA

Tempter. See SATAN.

Ten Articles, The (1536). After declaring himself supreme head of the English Church in 1534, Henry VIII strove for a middle way between Roman Catholicism and Lutheranism: the English Church would still be Catholic, but without the pope. In deference to his Protestant supporters, Henry's Ten Articles reduced the number of sacraments from seven to three; denied the efficacy of prayers for souls in purgatory; and condemned religious images, prayers to the saints, and the use of holy water and ashes. Protestants increasingly demanded more reforms; so in 1539 Henry was forced to issue the Six Articles to restrain them. These essentially prohibited any Protestant reforms beyond the Ten Articles. As a result, Henry was able to maintain a precarious balance between the two theologies for the rest of his reign.

J. E. MENNELL

See also SIX ARTICLES, THE.

Ten Commandments, The. Basic law of the covenant formed between God and Israel at Mount Sinai. Although the date of the event is uncertain, the commandments may be dated provisionally to the early part of the 13th century B.C. In Hebrew, the commandments are called the "Ten Words," which (via Greek) is the origin of the alternative English title of the commandments, namely, the Decalogue. The commandments are recorded twice in the OT—first in the description of the formation of the Sinai Covenant (Exod. 20:2–17) and in the renewal of the covenant on the plains of Moab (Deut. 5:6–21).

The commandments are described as having been written on two tablets. Each tablet contained the full text. One tablet belonged to Israel and the other to God, so that both parties to the covenant had a copy of the legislation. The first five commandments pertain basically to the relationship between Israel and God; the last five are concerned primarily with the forms of relationships among human beings.

Because God was the one who enabled Israel to move toward statehood, as a consequence of his liberating the chosen people from slavery in Egypt, he was also to be Israel's true King. As such, he had the authority to establish Israel's law, as is made clear in the preface to the commandments. Thus, the commandments were initially part of a constitution and served as state law of the emerging nation of Israel. The fundamental principle upon which the constitution was established was love.

(1) ***The Prohibition of Gods Other Than the Lord*** (Exod. 20:3; Deut. 5:7). The first commandment is in negative form and expressly prohibits the worship of foreign deities. The essence of the covenant was a relationship, and the essence of that relationship was to be faithfulness. At the heart of human life today, there must be a relationship with God. Anything in life that disrupts the primary relationship breaks the commandment. Foreign "gods" are thus persons, or even things, that would disrupt the primacy of the relationship with God.

(2) ***The Prohibition of Images*** (Exod. 20:4–6; Deut. 5:8–10). The temptation for Israel to worship God in the form of an image must have been enormous, for images and idols occurred in all the religions of the ancient Near East. But the God of Israel was a transcendent and infinite being, and could not be reduced to the limitations of an image or form within creation. In the modern world, the shape of the temptation has changed. For example, one can construct an image of God with words. If we use words about God and say, "This is exactly what God is like no less" (and, we imply, no more), and if we work out the minute details of our understanding of God, then we are in danger of creating an image of God no less fixed or rigid than the image of wood or stone. The second commandment thus guards the ultimate greatness and mystery of God.

(3) ***The Prohibition Against the Improper Use of God's Name*** (Exod. 20:7; Deut. 5:11). God had granted to Israel an extraordinary privilege; he had revealed to them his personal name. The name is represented in Hebrew by four letters, *yhwh*, variously rendered in English Bibles as Lord, Yahweh, or Jehovah. Yet knowledge of God's personal name could be abused. In the ancient Near Eastern religions, magic was a common practice, involving the use of a god's name, which was believed to control the god's power, in certain kinds of activity designed to harness divine power for human purposes. Thus the kind of activity prohibited by the third commandment is attempting to control God's power through his name for a personal and worthless purpose. Within Christianity, it is in the name of God that the privilege of access to God in prayer is granted. The abuse of the privilege of prayer, involving calling upon the name of God for some selfish purpose, is tantamount to the magic of the ancient world. The third commandment is a positive reminder of the enormous privilege given to us in the knowledge of God's name; it is a privilege not to be taken lightly or abused.

(4) ***The Observation of the Sabbath*** (Exod. 20:8–11; Deut. 5:12–15). The holiness of the sabbath is related to the reason for its establishment; two reasons are given, and there is a common theme linking them. In the first version (Exod. 20:11), the sabbath is to be kept in commemoration of creation; God created the world in six days and rested on the seventh day. In the second version (Deut. 5:15), the sabbath is to be observed in commemoration of the exodus from Egypt. The theme linking the two versions is creation; God created not only the world, he also "created" his people, Israel, in redeeming them from Egyptian slavery. For Christianity, the concept of sabbath has been moved from the seventh to the first day of the week, Sunday. The move is related to a change in Christian thought, identified in the resurrection of Jesus Christ on Sunday. The change is appropriate, for Christians now reflect each Sunday, or sabbath, on a third act of divine creation, the "new creation" established in the resurrection of Jesus Christ from the dead.

(5) ***The Honor Due to Parents*** (Exod. 20:12; Deut. 5:16). The fifth commandment forms a bridge between the first four, concerned primarily with God, and the last five, concerned primarily with interhuman relationships. On first reading, it appears to be concerned with family relationships only; children were to honor their parents. It also is concerned with transmission of faith in God throughout subsequent generations. Today, when so much education is undertaken beyond the confines of the family unit, the commandment serves a solemn reminder, not only of the need for harmonious family life, but also of the responsibilities with respect to religious education that rest upon both parents and children.

(6) ***The Prohibition of Murder*** (Exod. 20:13; Deut. 5:17). This prohibits murder, the taking of another person's life for personal and selfish gain. Stated positively, this preserves for each member of the covenant community the right to live. In the modern world, a similar statute, prohibiting murder, exists in almost all legal codes; it has become a part of state law, rather than purely religious or moral law. Jesus, however, pointed to the deeper meaning implicit in the commandment (Matt. 5:21–22).

(7) ***The Prohibition of Adultery*** (Exod. 20:14; Deut. 5:18). The act of adultery is fundamentally an act of unfaithfulness. One or both persons in an adulterous act are being unfaithful to other persons. Thus the seventh commandment is the social parallel to the first. The relevance is apparent, but again, Jesus points to the implications of the commandment for the mental life (Matt. 5:27–28).

(8) ***The Prohibition of Theft*** (Exod. 20:15; Deut. 5:19). A person had a right to certain things, which could not be violated by a fellow citizen for personal advantage. But while the commandment is concerned with property, its most fundamental concern is human liberty. The worst form of theft is "manstealing" (somewhat equivalent to modern kidnapping); that is, taking a person (presumably by force) and selling that person into slavery. The crime and the related law are stated more fully in Deut. 24:7. It prohibits a person from manipulating or exploiting the lives of others for personal gain.

(9) ***The Prohibition of False Witnessing*** (Exod. 20:16; Deut. 5:20). The ninth commandment prohibits perjury, the giving of false testimony within the proceedings of the law court. Thus, it establishes a principle of truthfulness and carries implications with respect to false statements in any context.

(10) ***The Prohibition of Coveting*** (Exod. 20:17; Deut. 5:21). It is curious to find such a commandment in a code of criminal law. The first nine commandments prohibit *acts*, and a criminal act can be followed by prosecution and legal process (if the act is detected). But the 10th commandment, in contrast, prohibits *desires*, or covetous feelings. Under human law, it is not possible to prosecute upon the basis of desire (proof would be impossible!). And yet Hebrew law was more than a human system, for there was a chief Judge, God. The genius of the commandment lies in its therapeutic nature. The root of almost all evil and crime lies within the self; it lies in the desires of the individual. Thus evil desires are prohibited; if the 10th commandment is fully and profoundly understood, then the significance of the first nine is much better understood.

The Ten Commandments functioned first as a part of the constitutional law of a nation; in the teaching of Jesus, they became the ethic of the kingdom of God, adding substance and direction to the "first and great commandment," that we love God with the totality of our beings (Matt. 22:37–38). The commandments as such are not the basis of salvation; rather, to those who have found salvation in the gospel of Jesus Christ, they are a guide toward that fullness of life in which love for God is given rich expression.

P. C. Craigie

See also Civil Law and Justice in Bible Times; Law, Biblical Concept of.

Tennant, Frederick Robert (1866–1957). English theologian. Tennant spent his academic career as a Fellow of Trinity College Cambridge and university lecturer in the philosophy of religion from 1913 until his retirement in 1938. His greatest work was his two-volume *Philosophical Theology* (1928–30) in which he argued that there is a theistic worldview that can be shown to be more reasonable than other interpretations of reality and more congruent with the knowledge by which life and science is guided.

Tennant's philosophical and apologetic works were based solidly in the British empirical tradition. He rejected the efforts of rationalism, religious a priorism, and revelation to provide the groundwork for belief in God and religious faith. Instead, belief should be constructed in the same general way as the laws of science. For Tennant, theology is the final link in a chain of belief that begins with interpretations of empirical data. Theistic belief is a continuation of the curve of knowledge constructed by natural science and is built upon the hypotheses of these sciences. Metaphysics and science should not be separated, for "science and theism spring from a common root."

D. K. McKim

Teresa of ´Avila (1515–1582). Spanish mystic. After a prolonged spiritual struggle, accompanied by poor health, she entered the Carmelite Convent of the Incarnation at ´Avila on Nov. 2, 1535. Here she was treated with deference because of her personality and family status. In 1555 her spiritual pilgrimage took a more serious turn. This second conversion, as it is sometimes called, was marked by "mental prayer" and ecstatic visions. Later, on Aug. 24, 1562, the resolute nun founded the convent of Discalced ("barefoot") Carmelite Nuns of the Primitive Rule of St. Joseph. After a visit by the General of the Carmelites, she was encouraged in her work and given permission to form other houses of the Discalced Carmelites, not only for nuns, but for monks also.

Teresa was a remarkable person, combining mystic contemplation and a fervent activism with a literary career. She wrote two autobiographical works, the *Life* and the *Book of Foundations*. Two books were written for her nuns: *The Way of Perfection* and *The Interior Castle*. It was her conviction that contemplation should lead to action, not lethargy. In spite of a frail body, beset by continuing bouts of illness, she became the personification of this conviction. Teresa was canonized by Gregory XV in 1622.

W. R. Estep, Jr.

See also Mysticism.

Terminism. Doctrine that God has eternally determined a time limit (Lat. *terminus*) in the life of the individual after which he no longer wills the conversion and salvation of that person. After that time the individual may no longer repent and come to faith. As expressed by the pietist J. C. Boese (d. 1700), terminism led to a controversy between the pietists and the orthodox Lutherans in the late 17th and early 18th centuries. Terminism is best considered a peculiar point of historic pietism, although a similar idea has been held by some Quakers.

J. M. DRICKAMER

See also PIETISM.

Tertullian (ca. 155–220). First Latin father of the church. Converted to Christianity at Rome and returning to Carthage, he gave himself passionately to the propagation and defense of the gospel. Ultimately disenchanted with the laxity of the Roman Church, he broke away and espoused the rigorous asceticism and enthusiasm of Montanism. A man of vast erudition, he employed the classical rhetorical arts and freely cited Greek and Latin authors, although he disclaimed a reliance on Greek philosophy. Increasingly he wrote in the Latin vernacular and became the first great Latin church father. He set the concepts of Scripture in new language, and much of his terminology became normative in the theological discussions of the Western Church. He was peculiarly apt at pithy sayings, the most famous of which is, "The blood of Christians is the seed of the church." It was Tertullian who coined the term "Trinity." His postulation that the Godhead was "one substance consisting in three persons" helped spare the West much of the bitter christological controversy that raged in the Eastern Church.

R. C. KROEGER AND C. C. KROEGER

See also MONTANISM.

Testament. Division of Scripture. As used in biblical theology, the term may denote the era from the arrangement given through Moses (Exod. 19:5–8; Jer. 31:32; Heb. 8:9) to the death of Christ. This is the old testament, or covenant, in contrast to the new, which began legally with the death of Christ, as may be inferred from Luke 22:20 and 1 Cor. 11:25. The AV uses the term "testament" as well as "covenant" for the Hebrew and Greek originals *berît* and *diathēkē*, but the ASV uses the word "covenant" regularly, apart from the exceptional use of "testament" in Heb. 9:16–17.

M. J. WYNGAARDEN

See also COVENANT.

Testimonium Spiritus Sancti Internum. See INTERNAL TESTIMONY OF THE HOLY SPIRIT.

Testimony. See WITNESS, WITNESSING.

Tetragrammaton. Designation for the four (*tetra*) letters (*grammata*) in the Hebrew Bible for the name of the God of Israel, *yhwh.* The name was God's particular revelation to Moses and the Israelites (Exod. 6:2–3). It signifies that the God of Israel, unlike pagan deities, is present with his people to deliver them, to fulfill his promises to them, and to grant them his blessings. The pronunciation of the tetragrammaton *yhwh* was lost when the Jews avoided its usage for fear of desecrating the holy name (Exod. 20:7). The translators of the LXX consistently avoided the name and substituted the title *Kyrios* ("Lord"). In the Hebrew text the vowels of *'ădōnāy* (*ă-ō-ā*) were placed under the tetragrammaton to remind readers that they were not to pronounce *yhwh* but instead to read the word as *'ădōnāy*. Christians who were unaware of this substitution read the vowels as if they actually belonged to *yhwh*, which resulted in the English form "YeHoWaH" or "JeHoVaH" (the *ă* of *'ădōnāy* having been reduced to *ĕ* under the *y* of *yhwh*). The ASV of 1901 adopted the practice of using the name "Jehovah," whereas most English versions continued the established practice of translating the tetragrammaton by LORD (capital letters) to distinguish it from "Lord" (*Adonai*). Many scholars accept the widely held opinion that the tetragrammaton is a form of the root *hyh* ("be") and should be pronounced as "Yahweh" ("He who brings into being"; cf. Exod. 3:12, "I will be with you" and "I AM WHO I AM," v. 14).

W. A. VAN GEMEREN

See also GOD, NAMES OF.

Tetrapolitan Confession (1530). Confession composed during the Diet of Augsburg by Martin Bucer and Wolfgang Capito on behalf of four southern German cities—Strasbourg, Constance, Memmingen, and Lindau (i.e., four cities = tetrapolitan)—not represented at the Diet of Augsburg. The confession's structure parallels the 23 chapters of the Augsburg Confession, but it attempts to provide a compromise treatment of the Lord's Supper (chap. 18) that might hold the Lutheran and Reformed sacramental theories in working tension. As a theological formula it failed in its attempts to gain a Protestant and evangelical union.

P. A. MICKEY

See also BUCER, MARTIN; CONFESSIONS OF FAITH.

Thank Offering. See OFFERINGS AND SACRIFICES IN BIBLE TIMES.

Theism. Literally, belief in the existence of God.

God as Ultimate Reference Point. In its broadest sense theism denotes a belief in some ultimate reference point that gives meaning and unity to everything. The God postulated in this sense is, however, totally depersonalized and thoroughly transcendent, almost an abstract concept. Paul Tillich's concept of theism is that God is whatever becomes a matter of ultimate concern, something that determines our being or nonbeing. Consequently, God is identified as the ground of all being, or being-itself. This broad sense of theism is also found in Hegel, who actually has several concepts of God, but at least one that fits this category. Philosophy, he says, rises to divinity or a divine viewpoint. Here "God" seems to be equivalent to transcendent, all-encompassing thought, but is not a personal God.

God as Immanent. A narrower concept of theism sees God also as depersonalized and as the ultimate reference point, but gives God some kind of concrete manifestation. Nevertheless, the God of such theistic views is entirely immanent. One example is pantheism, the view that everything is God. The most famous philosophical form is that of Spinoza, who held there is only one substance in the universe—God. Consequently, everything is merely a mode of that one substance. Such a God is not abstract but immanent.

Another example of this concept is process theism, based on the process metaphysics of Alfred North Whitehead (*Process and Reality*), sometimes known as bipolar or dipolar theism. Some of the better-known process theologians are Charles Hartshorne, Schubert Ogden, John Cobb, and David Griffin. According to this school, there are in God two poles: a primordial, eternal, potential pole, and a temporal, consequent, actual pole. A final example of this form of theism is found in Georg Hegel's conception of God as Spirit. This notion of Spirit does not allow God to be a person in the Judeo-Christian sense, but sees him as a force, or general consciousness, uniting all finite consciousnesses. In other words, he is not just all finite consciousnesses taken together, but rather the force that underlies and unites all intersubjectivity.

God as Personal. Two examples will illustrate this sense of theism.

(1) Polytheism, of which the best known is perhaps the Greco-Roman pantheon of gods. Here there is a multiplicity of gods, each representing and personifying some aspect of life or of the created universe. In spite of the fact that each god may represent only one quality of life (love, war, etc.), each is perceived as a person.

(2) Deism. Here, God is an individual being (personal in that sense), but one who does not interact with the world. He initially created the world, but since then has withdrawn himself from it (impersonal in that sense). He does not act in the world or sustain it, but remains thoroughly transcendent from it.

God as Personal Creator and Sustainer. A final perception is of God as Creator and Sustainer of the universe. He is infinite in attributes, and he is the only God. This monotheistic concept of God is held within the Judeo-Christian tradition, and there are three ways in particular that have appeared.

(1) *Theonomy.* God is the law in the universe, and in particular, his will is law. Whatever rules of ethics, epistemology, and the like, there are result from what God wills and could be otherwise if he so chose.

(2) *Rationalism.* According to Leibniz, all the laws of logic, ethics, and the like are necessary laws in the universe and are so in virtue of the principle of sufficient reason in accord with which everything must happen. In such a system God must create a world, and he must create the best of all possible worlds (for Leibniz, the best world is intelligible).

(3) *Modified Rationalism.* This does not demand that God create a world, but asserts that creating a world is something fitting for God to do. Modified rationalism differs from theonomy in that it claims that certain things are intrinsically good and intrinsically evil, apart from what God says about them. In such a universe, things are as they are according to reason, and in many cases one can discern why something is the case and what the case is by means of reason, though some things can be known only by revelation, a view historically typical of Judeo-Christian theologies.

Conclusion. More needs to be said about theism as a philosophy, especially about certain questions traditionally attached to the philosophy of theism. For example, in speculating on theism, one of the questions that arises is about the relation of human language to God, that is, How is human language (with its reference to finite beings) predicable of an infinite being? Another question deals with whether it is possible to demonstrate rationally, or at least to justify rationally, belief in God's existence. Philosophers of religion also ask whether a particular mode of experience is specifically religious. Likewise, they ask about the relation of the providence and sovereignty of God to human freedom and responsibility. Finally, there is the question about the internal consistency of theological systems that hold to the existence of an all-powerful, all-loving God along with the presence of evil in the world.

J. S. FEINBERG

See also DEISM; GOD, ARGUMENTS FOR THE EXISTENCE OF; GOD, ATTRIBUTES OF; GOD, DOCTRINE OF; PANENTHEISM; PANTHEISM; POLYTHEISM.

Theistic Evolution. See EVOLUTION.

Theodicy. (Gk. *theos*, "God," and *dikē*, "justice") Term used to refer to attempts to justify the ways of God to humankind. A successful theodicy resolves the problem of evil for a theological system and demonstrates that God is all-powerful, all-loving, and just, despite evil's existence.

Six basic points are relevant to the nature of a theodicy. (1) A theodicy is a response to a problem of the logical consistency of a theological position. Most attacks on theistic systems charge that their key theological claims (for example, God is omnipotent, God is all-loving, and evil exists in a world created by God) taken together are self-contradictory. (2) A successful theodicy must be relevant to the problem of evil it addresses—moral evil, physical evil, the problem of an individual's relation to God in view of experiencing specific evil, as well as problems of the degree and intensity of evil. (3) A theodicy must be relevant to the specific theology it addresses. Each theological position incorporates a particular concept of divine benevolence, divine power, the nature of evil, and the nature of free human action. The theodicist must construct a defense of God's ways as they are portrayed in a given theological system.

(4) The problem of evil in its various forms is always a problem of logical consistency, and as such is intellectually interesting only for theologies that incorporate a notion of God's omnipotence according to which he may do any logically consistent thing. (5) Most theodicies (and systems of ethics in general) adopt a particular axiom with regard to moral agency and moral blameworthiness; namely, that people are not morally responsible for that which they cannot do or which they do under constraint or compulsion. (6) The pattern of most theodicies is indicated by the preceding principles. They attempt to resolve the apparent contradiction by arguing that God, in spite of his omnipotence, cannot remove evil. Since he cannot remove evil, he is not morally responsible for its presence in the world. Such an argument rests on the concept of God's omnipotence according to which God can do only the logically consistent.

Several interesting theodicies have been offered by well-known thinkers for the moral problem of evil. For example, Gottfried Leibniz's theodicy was structured for his extreme rationalistic theological system. Given the basic tenets of this system, Leibniz does not contradict himself with his theodicy. Consequently, he has solved his problem of evil, a problem of internal consistency. One may reject his theodicy and his theology, but not on grounds that it fails to remove the alleged contradiction.

Other well-known theodicies rest upon a modified rationalistic theology. Such a metaphysic lies behind the free will defense, the basic theodicy in the Augustinian tradition of theodicy; and also behind the soul-building theodicy, the basic theodicy in the Irenaean tradition. There are four basic points here. (1) In a modified rationalist's universe, God is not obligated to create any world, for his own existence is the supreme good. (2) Creating a world is a fitting thing for God to do, but not the only fitting thing for him to do. Whatever he chooses to do is done on the basis of reason, but such reasons are not necessary laws in this universe. (3) There is an infinite number of finite contingent possible worlds. Some by their very nature are inherently evil, so God could not create them. There is, however, more than one good possible world that God could have created. There is no such thing as a best possible world. (4) God was free with respect to whether or not he should create and with respect to which of the good possible worlds he would create, if he chose to create. For such a theological position, the problem of evil arises as follows: Is the contingent possible world that God created one of the good possible worlds (despite the evil in it)? The modified rationalist theologian must specify a reason that this world is one of those good possible worlds.

The theodicist using the free will defense begins by pointing out that God is not the cause of evil in the world; the abuse of human free will is. Then, the question is whether God is not guilty for giving humankind free will when he knew that we could abuse it to commit evil. The answer is no. Free will is a value of the highest order, which God should have given. God is not the one who uses such free will to commit evil; we do, so we are responsible for evil. Moreover, God is still good for giving us something which he could, and in fact did, abuse because a world in which there are significantly free beings (even though they produce evil) is a far better world than one that contains no evil but is populated by automatons. In other words, God cannot both create significantly free beings *and* make it the case that they always freely do good. On the free will defender's account of free human action, if God makes it the case that we do anything, we cannot do it *freely*. Genuine free will, then, involves evil, but God is justified in what he did, for free will is a good that far overbalances any evil produced by the use of such a will.

Soul-building theodicy also rests on a modified rationalist theology, but it incorporates a consequentialist ethic. The most noteworthy form of this view in recent years is that of John Hick, who begins by suggesting that God's intent in creating humankind was not to create a perfect creature, but rather to create a being in need of moral development. God intended for our time on earth to be spent in building moral and spiritual character in preparation for participation in the kingdom of God. Hick asks, What sort of environment would be most conducive to soul building? Would a world in which no evil ever confronts us be better for developing character, or would we be more likely to develop spiritually if we lived in a world where we would be confronted by problems and evil? Hick argues that the answer is obviously the latter. If God wants to use the world to build souls, he cannot place us in an Edenic paradise where nothing ever goes wrong. Consequently, there is evil in the world, but God is not to be blamed for it, since he intends to use it to build souls and ultimately develop us to a point where we are ready for the kingdom of God. Hick recognizes that if God's purpose with the world is to build souls, many will argue he has severely failed. Evil in the world often turns people away from God rather than encouraging them to grow spiritually. Therefore, it does not seem that the evil in the world accomplishes its purpose, and God must be guilty for creating such a world. Hick answers that though it seems that souls are not being built, God will nonetheless see to it that everyone ultimately makes it to the kingdom of God. No soul will finally go unbuilt; no evil will prove to be unjustified or unjustifiable.

The theodicies presented above render their theologies internally consistent and thereby solve their problem of evil. As a result, atheists are mistaken who claim that all theistic positions are hopelessly irrational because self-contradictory on this matter. Moreover, their claims that no theist can solve his problem of evil are contradicted by the fact that many theists can do so. The ways of God are defensible, and they are defensible in such a way that no theist should have to give in to the charge of irrationality due to a problem of evil.

J. S. Feinberg

See also Evil, Problem of; Pain.

Theologia Crucis ("Theology of the Cross"). Luther's most profound contribution to theological thought. Before the fall (*lapsus*) Adam was capable of knowing God directly or immediately. God was the *Deus revelatus* who communed with Adam in Eden's garden. The consequence of the fall included much more than personal death and moral deterioration; it also changed our ability to know and commune with the Creator. The revealed God became the hidden God (*Deus absconditus*). The only way the shattered fellowship could be restored was by means of redemption. Throughout the OT period, the only place God met with his people was at the mercy seat (Exod. 25:22), the place of sacrifice and redemption. God's consummate meeting place was unveiled at the cross of Christ. God is known and understood, not in strength, but in weakness, not in an awesome display of majesty and power, but in the exhibition of a love willing to suffer in order to win us back to himself.

F. R. HARM

See also LUTHER, MARTIN; *THEOLOGIA GLORIAE.*

Theologia Gloriae ("Theology of Glory"). Antithesis of the theology of the cross. So strongly did Luther feel about the distinction between these theologies that he stated unequivocally that only those who hold to and teach the theology of the cross deserve to be called theologians. The theology of glory feels that it knows God immediately through his expressions of divine power, wisdom, and glory; whereas the theology of the cross recognizes him in the very place at which he has hidden himself—the cross and its suffering, all of which is esteemed to be weakness and foolishness by the theology of glory.

F. R. HARM

See also LUTHER, MARTIN; *THEOLOGIA CRUCIS.*

Theophany. A visible or auditory manifestation of God. Visible manifestations include an angel appearing in human form (Judg. 13); a flame in the burning bush (Exod. 3:2–6); or fire, smoke, and thunder on Mount Sinai (Exod. 19:18–20). Auditory manifestations include the voice of God in the garden (Gen. 3:8), the still small voice to Elijah (1 Kings 19:12), or the voice from heaven at the baptism of Jesus (Matt. 3:17). Normally the physical aspects are not described in any detail because it is the message of God that is emphasized. The physical aspects are there to impress the recipients and authenticate the revelation. This is not to imply that everything is immediately obvious to the recipients. God takes the initiative in theophany, never revealing himself completely, and usually only in a temporary, rather than a permanent way. A permanent manifestation like the incarnation of Christ made theophanies less necessary and accounts for their diminished importance in the NT.

J. C. MOYER

See also ANGEL OF THE LORD.

Theotokos. See MOTHER OF GOD.

Thirteen Articles, The (1538). Doctrinal statement by a committee of German Lutheran and English theologians, written in Latin at London in the summer of 1538. The product of negotiations that had been carried on since 1535, they were based on the Augsburg Confession (1530) and on a set of articles drawn up in Wittenberg in 1536 at an earlier stage in the discussions. The Thirteen Articles were never accepted by the civil or ecclesiastical authorities in England, but Thomas Cranmer preserved them, and they became in part the basis for the Forty-Two Articles approved during the reign of Edward VI.

J. M. DRICKAMER

See also AUGSBURG CONFESSION.

Thirty-Nine Articles, The (1563). Historical doctrinal standard of the Church of England and most of the Anglican Communion of Churches. The articles arose as one of the manifestations of the 16th-century English Reformation. Shortly before Edward VI's death,

Thomas Cranmer presented a doctrinal statement consisting of 42 topics, or articles, as the last of his major contributions to the development of Anglicanism. These Forty-Two Articles were suppressed during the Catholic reign of Edward's successor, Mary Tudor, but became the source of the Thirty-Nine Articles that Elizabeth and her Parliament established as the doctrinal basis of the Church of England. The 1563 Latin and 1571 English editions of the articles are the definitive statements. Elizabeth promoted the articles as an instrument of national policy (to solidify her kingdom religiously) and as a theological *via media* (to encompass as wide a spectrum of English Christians as possible). Since her day much controversy has swirled over their theological significance.

The Thirty-Nine Articles remain a forthright statement of 16th-century reform. They are Protestant in affirming the final authority of Scripture. They are at one with common Reformation convictions on justification by grace through faith in Christ. They lean toward Lutheranism in permitting beliefs and practices that do not contradict Scripture. They contain statements that, like Zwingli in Zurich, give the state authority to regulate the church. They are "catholic" in their respect for tradition and in their belief that religious ceremonies should be everywhere the same within a realm.

M. A. NOLL

See also ANGLICAN COMMUNION; CONFESSIONS OF FAITH.

This Age, The Age to Come. Terms characterizing the biblical concept of time. Biblical thought views time as linear (or horizontal) and contrasts the present age with a future age to come. Among the evangelists Matthew clearly brings out his horizontal dualism (12:32). In the climax to the parable of the wheat and tares (13:36–43), "the end of the age" is viewed in terms of apocalyptic. There will be a climactic conclusion to the present historical order: the Son of man/Jesus Christ will return, initiate judgment, and establish his kingdom (cf. Matt. 24:3; Luke 20:34–35). Paul similarly emphasizes this two-age structure (Eph. 1:21) and affirms that the two ages are interlocked; Jesus Christ is the turning point in eschatology. And yet an aspect of the future age is already present. Especially in the Fourth Gospel, a vertical eschatology is evident that claims a present reality for elements of the age to come (e.g., eternal life, judgment; 3:19; 5:24). Christ's reign is here in the present world, but his rule is incomplete; his realm is still coming in the future.

G. M. BURGE

See also AGE, AGES.

Thomas à Kempis (ca. 1379–1471). German monk and spiritual writer. Thomas Hemerken (Hämmerlein or "little hammer") entered the monastery at Agnietenberg (Mount Saint Agnes near Zwolle), which was affiliated with the Windesheim Congregation of Augustinian regular (monastic) canons. He spent most of his life at Mount Saint Agnes, where he was ordained priest (1413–14) and served as subprior and director of novices. He was a prolific copyist. Thomas wrote or compiled more than 30 works, which may be arranged in the following categories: (1) several volumes of monastic sermons; (2) biographies of the founders of the *Devotio moderna* (Gerard Groote, Florent Radewijns, and others) intended for the edification of novices; (3) a chronicle of his monastery that includes much historical and biographical information on the *Devotio moderna*; and (4) numerous works on the spiritual life (e.g., *Prayers and Meditations on the Life and Passion of the Lord*). He is best known, however, for the compilation of the four books of the *Imitation of Christ.*

D. D. MARTIN

See also BRETHREN OF THE COMMON LIFE; *DEVOTIO MODERNA*; SPIRITUALITY.

Thomas Aquinas (1225–1274). Italian Dominican theologian. Aquinas taught in Paris and Italy. He was canonized in 1326, made a Doctor of the Church in 1567, commended for study by Pope Leo XIII (*Aeterni patris*) in 1879, and declared patron of Catholic schools in 1880.

Major Writings. Aquinas is credited with some 98 works, although nine are of doubtful authenticity. The greatest and most influential was *Summa theologiae*, a systematic presentation of Christian doctrine in philosophical terms.

Thought. The views of Aquinas cover most philosophical and theological categories.

Faith and Reason. Aquinas believed faith is based in God's revelation in Scripture. Support for faith is found in miracles and probable arguments. There are five ways to demonstrate God's existence by reason: (1) from motion to an Unmoved Mover, (2) from effects to a First Cause, (3) from contingent being to a Necessary Being, (4) from degrees of perfection to a Most Perfect Being, and (5) from design in nature to a Designer. There are, however, mysteries (e.g., Trinity, incarnation) that cannot be known by human reason but only by faith.

Epistemology. All knowledge begins in experience. We are, however, born with an a priori, innate capacity to know. Nothing is in the mind that was not first in the senses—*except the mind itself* with its capacity to know by means of first principles. These first principles are self-evident, once they are understood.

Metaphysics. The heart of Aquinas's metaphysics is the real distinction between essence and existence in all finite beings. Only God is pure being, pure actuality, with no potentiality whatsoever. God alone is pure act(uality) without form. Angels are completely actualized potentialities (pure forms), and humankind is a composition of form (soul) and matter (body) with progressive actualization.

God. God alone *is* being (I Am-ness). Everything else *has* being. God's essence is identical to his existence, it is of his essence to exist. God is a necessary being. He cannot *not* exist. Neither can God change, since he is without potentiality to be anything other than he is. Likewise, God is eternal, since time implies a change from a before to an after.

Analogy. God is known by analogy. We must take only the perfection signified (goodness, truth, etc.), without the finite mode of signification, when we apply it to God. So the attribute will have the same definition for creatures and Creator, but it will have a different application or extension, since creatures are finitely good, while God is infinitely good. So before we can appropriately apply the term "good" to God we must negate the finite *mode* (how) in which we find good among creatures and apply the *meaning* (what) to God in an unlimited way.

Creation. God created the world out of nothing (*ex nihilo*). Time did not exist before God created—only eternity. God did not create *in* time; rather, with the world there was the creation *of* time. So there was no time before time began.

Humankind. Humankind is a hylomorphic unity of soul and body. Adam was directly created by God at the beginning, and God directly creates each new soul in the womb of its mother. Despite this unity of soul and body, there is no identity between them. The soul survives death and awaits the reunion with the body at the resurrection.

Ethics. Just as there are first principles of thought, so there are first principles of action called laws. Aquinas distinguishes four kinds. *Eternal* law is the plan by which God governs creation. *Natural* law is the participation of rational creatures in this eternal law. *Human* law is a particular application of natural law to a local community. *Divine* law is the revelation of God's law through Scripture and the church.

Virtues are in two classes: natural and supernatural. The former include prudence, justice, courage, and temperance. These are part of the natural law. Supernatural virtues are faith, hope, and love.

N. L. GEISLER

See also NEO-THOMISM; THOMISM.

Thomism. School of philosophy and theology following the thought of Thomas Aquinas. It developed in various phases and has experienced periods of support and neglect. When Aquinas died he left no direct successor, but his system was adopted by various individuals, most notably by many of his confreres in the Dominican order and by his own original teacher, the eclectic Albertus Magnus.

Thomism became one of the several competing schools of medieval philosophy. In particular, it set itself off against classical Augustinianism with its reliance on Aristotle, most eminently by insisting on a unified anthropology whereby the soul is the form of the body. What Aquinas was to the Dominicans, Duns Scotus became to the Franciscans, and Scotism debated with Thomism on such issues as freedom of the will and the analogy of being. Finally, Thomism, along with the other two schools mentioned, maintained a moderate realism in contrast to nominalism.

A central figure of developing Thomism was Thomas de Vio Cardinal Cajetan (1469–1534). His high ecclesiastical standing contributed to the authoritativeness of his expositions of Aquinas. Thomism became the leading school of Catholic thought in the 16th century. Several factors contributed to its ascendancy. The Jesuit Order (approved in 1540), known for its aggressive teaching, aligned itself with Aquinas; the Council of Trent (first convened in 1545) self-consciously styled many of its pronouncements in Thomistic phraseology. Thomism entered the 17th century triumphantly, but exited void of power and originality. Due to lack of competition Thomism became too self-contained to cope with the rise of rationalism and empirical science on their own ground. Consequently, although Thomism was still alive, primarily in Dominican circles, in the 18th century, it was essentially a spent force.

The early 19th century saw another abrupt change in the fortunes of Thomism. Catholic thinkers increasingly began to see that in Aquinas's works there were viable responses to topical questions not answered elsewhere. Particularly the questions of human dignity in the face of rising industrialism revived Thomism. Dramatically the schools returned to the authority of Aquinas. By the time of Vatican I (1869/70), Thomistic principles were again in vogue. And Thomism triumphed in 1879 when Pope Leo XIII in *Aeterni patris* recalled the church to Aquinas. The result was the movement known as Neo-Thomism, which has persisted well past the middle of the 20th century.

W. CORDUAN

See also NEO-THOMISM; SCHOLASTICISM; THOMAS AQUINAS.

Tillich, Paul (1886–1965). Protestant theologian. Born and ordained in Germany, he spent his professional life teaching theology and philosophy. In the troubled late 1920s he became interested in the religious-socialist movement, and his open opposition to Hitler and the political-cultural views he represented led to Tillich's dismissal from the philosophy faculty at the University of Frankfurt in 1933. Not long after leaving Frankfurt he came to the U.S. His academic career in America spanned 33 years, during which he taught at Union Theological Seminary (New York), Columbia University, Harvard University, and the University of Chicago. He became an American citizen in 1940.

His interests and research were wide ranging, and the influences on his thought were correspondingly diverse. They include Platonism, medieval mysticism, German idealism, and existentialism. Perhaps the most important work of his career was the three-volume *Systematic Theology* (1963). Here it is argued that God should be viewed as the ground of being, known to humankind as ultimate concern. It is by participation in this ground of being that we receive our own being. Tillich was a prolific writer in both German and English. His published works include *Interpretation of History* (1936); *The Protestant Era* (1936); *The Courage to Be* (1952); *The New Being* (1955); *Theology of Culture* (1959); and *Morality and Beyond* (1963). *On the Boundary* (1966) is a revision of part 1 of *The Interpretation of History*. It is a brief and very readable autobiographical sketch.

J. D. Spiceland

Time. (Gk. *chronos*) Created sphere in which God's redemptive plan is actualized. The Bible presents a distinctive conception of time, reflected especially by its peculiar use of the Greek terms *kairos* and *aiōn*. In the usual secular sense, *kairos* refers to a definite point of time especially appropriate for a given undertaking (Acts 24:25), *aiōn* to an extent of time (stipulated or unstipulated). The NT builds on this usage with a special eye toward redemptive history (John 7:6), in which divine determination (Acts 1:7), not human deliberation, constitutes a given moment or age the appropriate time of God's working.

While the NT gives prominent scope to the future *kairoi* associated with the eschatological drama, its central *kairos* is the life, death, and resurrection of the incarnate Christ, which is decisively significant for the kingdom of God. The terms "day [of the Lord]" and "hour," "now," and "today" likewise gain dramatic significance in the NT context whenever the eternal order and redemptive history impinges upon the sweep of ordinary events. The interconnected redemptive *kairoi* supply the threadline of salvation history. Yet the divine *kairoi* at the same time secretly enfold the entire secular movement of time (Acts 17:26) for the fulfillment, often unwittingly, of God's ultimate purposes. As the *kairos* is a decisive momentary unveiling of the eternal, so the *aiōn* discloses the Lord of ages who divides the long sweep of time according to his own purposes. The *kairoi* are decisive turning points within the larger *aiōna*. The Bible brackets history with an eye on the age of promise, the age of fulfillment, and the age to come.

Modern philosophy characteristically affirms that it takes time more seriously than did ancient or medieval philosophy. Classic Greek thought dissolved the significance of the temporal world, depicting it as illusory shadow alongside the eternal ideas and forms. In fact, virtually the whole movement of ancient religion and philosophy depreciated the significance of the temporal order. Nowhere does the importance of time come into view as in biblical teaching. While time is not ultimate, it is the divinely created sphere of God's preserving and redemptive work, and the arena of human decision. History moves toward a divine goal involving the redemption of the elect by the Creator and Lord of the universe. Within this historical matrix, every thought, word, and deed have repercussions in the eternal moral order.

C. F. H. HENRY

See also AGE, AGES; ETERNITY; THIS AGE, THE AGE TO COME.

Tithe. See OFFERINGS AND SACRIFICES IN BIBLE TIMES.

Tithing. Practice of giving one-tenth of one's property or produce to support religious institutions. It is an ancient practice, widespread in antiquity and found in Judaism as well as in surrounding cultures of the ancient Near East. OT commandments to tithe emphasize the quantity (one-tenth) of the gift. God is entitled to share directly in the grain, wine, and oil that humans are permitted to produce. At different times in Israel's history, varying regulations governed the tithe (see Deut. 14:22–29; Neh. 10:37–38). There are few NT references to the tithe. Jesus attacked the Pharisees for paying the tithe (Gk. *apodekatoō*) while neglecting the more important parts of the law: justice, mercy, and faith (Matt. 23:23; cf. Luke 11:42). The Pharisee in Jesus' parable says, "I fast twice a week and give a tenth of all I get" (Luke 18:12).

The early church prescribed a tithe for its members. Yet this differed from OT regulations in that the tithe was seen as an absolute minimum, and it was to be given from one's total income. The Didache prescribed that firstfruits be given of "money, clothes, and of all your possessions" (13:7). In the later history of the church, the obligation to tithe was always held in tension with Christ's command to sell all and renounce possessions (Matt. 19:21) along with Paul's teaching that Christ brings freedom from legal prescriptions (Gal. 5:1). By the 5th and 6th centuries, the practice of tithing was well established in the West. Medieval tithes were divided into *predial*, due from the fruits of the earth; *personal*, due from labor; and *mixed*, due from the produce of livestock. These were further divided into *great*, derived from corn, hay, and wood to go to the rector or incumbent priest of the parish; and *small*, from all other predial tithes, plus mixed and personal tithes to go to the vicar. Although the legal tithe has now disappeared, many churches teach tithing of money today as a minimum duty to God.

D. K. MCKIM

Tolerance. Indulgence of belief or conduct other than one's own. The term is variously defined from being an attitude of forbearance in judging the beliefs and behavior of others to one of respect for the opinions and practices of others when they are in conflict with one's own. The problem of tolerance is deeply rooted in the history of religions, in which coercion, intolerance, and persecution have played a prominent role. Religious intolerance, generally born out of the denial of the right of dissent in faith or practice, is as old as religious diversity.

Throughout human history, religion and tolerance have not been natural allies. Intolerance, not tolerance; conformity, not nonconformity; and assent, not dissent have been hallmarks in the history of religions. More wars have been fought, more persecutions have been carried out, and more lives have been lost in the name of religion than for any other single cause. Religious intolerance has, in turn, been made the basis of racial prejudice and acts of political and social discrimination against nonadherents or nonconformists to established religious faith. Among the causes of religious intolerance are the following: (1) a religion that is viewed as false and/or dangerous to the prevailing religious community; (2) a religion perceived to be in conflict with the mores and moral values of a particular society; (3) a religion judged to be subversive because its teachings threaten the pattern of political authority or the political policy being advanced, and (4) a religion believed to be alien to the culture in which it is being promulgated or one identified with a foreign power.

Tolerance in History. The ultimate concerns of religious traditions have in a sense precluded the tolerance of opposing views of faith and practice. Because of the will to demand conformity to unify the empire or nation, religious differences or expressions of dissent were treated with intolerance which became the basis of persecution. Generally speaking, diversity was abhorred because it represented a threat to the unity and solidarity of the tribe, the state, the empire, or the nation. The denial of tolerance is usually characterized by the following: (1) the absolutizing of the formulations of a particular faith and the necessity of defending it; (2) fear of the consequences of tolerating moral and religious error; (3) abhorrence of unorthodox views and practices; and (4) intense hostility toward those who are nonconformists with respect to the legally and socially accepted norms of religious faith and practice. These characteristics, deeply embedded in interfaith and international relations throughout the history of religions, have been manifestly present in the waves of intense persecution carried on throughout the centuries in Christianity's relations with Jews and Judaism, in the confrontations between Islam and Christianity, and in the encounters between Catholicism and Protestantism.

Tolerance in Modern Times. The concept of tolerance, rooted in the concept of "liberty of conscience," a phrase of modern origin, emerged slowly. The major advances toward tolerance came not from church confessions of faith, councils, or synods, but from constitutions, legislatures, and courts of law. While the Protestant Reformation did not espouse tolerance as such, it did represent a revolt against authority in the final dismemberment of a united Christendom or *mundus Christianus*, and it fostered the emergence of new nation-states and a new national spirit throughout Europe. Ecclesiastical or religious authority was weakened to a degree beyond which it could never recover. Religious liberty came to be proclaimed as both a natural and a divine right. The spirit of tolerance was greatly accelerated in principle and in practice by international relations that resulted in the ratification of treaties between states, and by the emergence of pluralistic societies resulting from constitutional governments and the shifting of many large and ethnic communities. Since the adoption in 1948 of the Universal Declaration of Human Rights, religious tolerance has been recognized as a part of international law.

J. E. Wood, Jr.

Tongues, Gift of. See Spiritual Gifts.

Tongues, Speaking in ("Glossolalia"). One of the nine *charisma*, or "grace-gifts," of the Spirit in 1 Cor. 12:4–11. It has two functions: in the Acts of the Apostles, it is an initiation or authentication gift meant as a divine affirmation of a new group entering the church; and in 1 Cor. 12–14 and Rom. 12 it is a "spiritual gift" bestowed upon sovereignly chosen individuals within the church. It is vigorously debated whether the NT favors unknown or known languages, with a slight majority favoring the former. Many others opt for a both/and rather than an either/or.

The Biblical Data. *NT Evidence.* Pentecost (Acts 2) has been the focus of much debate. Some argue that the miracle was one of hearing rather than speaking and that this ecstatic utterance was meant as the obverse to the Babel incident regarding the confusion of tongues (Gen. 11:1–9). This is unlikely, for the tenor of the passage favors a miracle of speaking. While the Babel theme may be present, the major theological emphasis deals with the universal mission. The catalogue of nations in Acts 2:9–11 sweeps from east to west, stressing the future redemptive mission of the church (cf. 1:8). The rest of Acts builds upon this; there is the Samaritan Pentecost (8:14–19), the Gentile Pentecost (10:44–46), and the Ephesian Pentecost (19:6).

In 1 Cor. 12–14, the purpose of the gift has obviously changed drastically. It is no longer apologetic proof, but has now become part of the cultic worship of the church. The problem at Corinth was the tendency of enthusiasts to elevate glossolalia to the greatest of the gifts. Paul in these chapters corrects this error and puts the gift in its proper place. The gifts are given, not to everyone, but only to those sovereignly chosen by the Spirit (12:11). Moreover, in any hierarchical order, tongues is the least of the gifts; the use of "first, second, third" in v. 28 reflects just such a pattern. In vv. 29–30 it is clear that Paul denies the contention of the enthusiasts that everyone truly spiritual should speak in tongues: "All are not apostles, are they? All do not speak in tongues, do they?"

Chapter 13 explores the basic problem of this group, the lack of love, and chapter 14 stresses the problematic value of this gift for the church. Without "interpretation" it is incomprehensible and will not "edify" like the gift of prophecy. Moreover, as a "sign" it seems to the outsider to typify madness (vv. 21–23). Paul at the same time recognizes the validity of glossolalia as a spiritual gift (v. 12) and rejoices that he has been chosen to excel in it (v. 18). Nevertheless, tongues are often best relegated to private devotions (v. 28) and must be utilized in corporate worship with dignity and order (vv. 26–33). Finally, Paul commands that in spite of the problems enumerated above, the church dare not "forbid" glossolalia, so long as it is expressed in a "fitting and orderly" manner (vv. 39–40). In other NT epistles, there are perhaps references to tongues in Eph. 5:19, Col. 3:16, and Rom. 8:26.

Church History. The supernatural gifts like glossolalia gradually declined during the patristic period. Several fathers spoke favorably of it, and groups like the Montanists made it central to their worship experience. The Eastern Church, with a more mystical and enthusiastic religious experience, continued to be open to tongues, and many believe that it was practiced unabated in Greek Orthodox monasteries throughout the Middle Ages. The next widespread outbreak occurred among a group of persecuted Huguenots in southern France at the end of the 17th century. This lasted a little over a decade. The Irvingites from the 1830s to the end of the century made speaking in tongues the hallmark of their church life. The example of the Huguenots and the Irvingites led to similar occurrences among the Shakers and the Mormons in America, and in Russia a pentecostal-type movement began in the 1850s and apparently continued throughout the century.

Modern Pentecostalism developed out of the revivalist movement, within which several such experiences were recorded in the 19th century. In 1901, in a small Bible school in Topeka, Kansas, a group made up of several Baptist ministers and students in a Bible study came to the conclusion that tongues always accompanied Spirit baptism in the Book of Acts. After much prayer they apparently received the gift. For the first few years, in spite of much publicity, only sporadic outbreaks occurred. The "breakthrough" came in Los Angeles in 1906, and the resulting Azusa Street Mission became the center for Pentecostalism. Meanwhile, glossolalia arose in the 1904 Welsh revival and in Pentecostal meetings throughout both Europe and America in ensuing years. In the first half of this century Pentecostals were rejected by the other denominations. The normal result of such an occurrence was a church split. In the 1960s, however, the phenomenon simultaneously developed within both mainline Protestant and Roman Catholic groups, and what has become known as the charismatic movement began. Today there are movements within both Pentecostalism and the charismatic groups toward a mediating position on tongues.

The Current Issue. We may delineate three basic positions today with respect to the tongues controversy, and there are two issues within the positions. (1) Are tongues for every age? (2) Are tongues the necessary sign of baptism by the Holy Spirit?

The Positive School. Pentecostals and most charismatics answer yes to both questions. They make clear distinction between baptism (in Acts) and the gift of tongues (1 Cor.). The former is for everyone, while the latter is given only to those whom the Spirit chooses. Even in the latter instance, however, the common belief is that all the gifts are open to everyone, and it is only a matter of the faith to claim it. Since glossolalia is the *only* initial evidence of Spirit baptism, everyone must seek the gift in that sense. It is the key to greater spiritual power in one's life and so must be sought.

The Negative School. This group answers no to both questions above. There are two basic approaches. (1) The Reformed scholar Benjamin B. Warfield at the turn of the century argued that glossolalia was among the sign gifts intended to authenticate the message of the apostles. Therefore, when the NT message was complete, they no longer were necessary. (2) The dispensational scholar Merrill F. Unger asserted that the "perfect" in 1 Cor. 13:10 meant the canon, and therefore at the close of the canon tongues "ceased in and of themselves" (the middle voice).

The Middle Position. A growing number take a position similar to that of A. B. Simpson, founder of the Christian and Missionary Alliance: "This gift is one of many gifts and is given to some for the benefit of all. The attitude toward the gift of tongues held by pastor and people should be, 'Seek not, forbid not.'" Those of this persuasion would answer yes to the first question, no to the second.

G. R. Osborne

See also Charismatic Movement; Holy Spirit; Pentecostalism; Spiritual Gifts.

Torgau Articles, The. Three documents composed by Lutheran theologians in the 16th century. They are named for a town on the Elbe River in Germany. (1) The Torgau Articles of 1530 were prepared by Martin Luther, Philip Melanchthon, and Justus Jonas and presented to Elector John the Constant in anticipation of the Diet at Augsburg. They contained an introduction and 10 articles, dealing primarily with abuses in Roman Catholic practice and defending worship in the vernacular. (2) The Torgau Articles or Confession of 1574 were prepared by various Lutheran theologians and subscribed by the Wittenberg faculty. They dealt with the Lord's Supper. (3) The Torgau Articles or Book of Torgau of 1576 were occasioned by controversies within the Lutheran churches and composed by a convention held at Torgau between May 28 and June 7, 1576, which included Jacob Andreae, Andreas Musculus, Martin Chemnitz, David Chytraeus, and Nicholas Selnecker.

C. G. Fry

See also Concord, Formula of.

Total Depravity. See Depravity, Total.

Tractarianism. See Oxford Movement.

Tradition. Entire process by which normative religious truths are passed on from one generation to another. As such, tradition is found in all religious communities, whether its form be oral or written, its contents embodied in a closed canon or a living organism. Even evangelical Protestants, inclined though they may still be to overlook it, must recognize that oral tradition preceded and shaped the canon of written Scripture and that their own understanding of Scripture and consequently their own community life have been molded, consciously or unconsciously, by particular traditions.

Most scholars see recorded in the OT numerous traditions regarding persons, places, events, and cults crucial to the full story of God's dealings with his chosen people. The act of handing these on is specifically enjoined or mentioned only rarely (Deut. 6:20–25; 26:5–9; Josh. 24:2–13), but the very text entirely presupposes it. In the NT the Greek word for tradition (*paradosis*) is used, in the main, negatively by Christ and positively by the apostles. Christ repudiated "human traditions" (Matt. 15:3; Mark 7:9, 13). But the apostles, sometimes in the style of rabbis, passed on and explicated the gospel tradition they had received from the Lord. Often in formulaic utterances taken up into his text (Rom. 1:1–4; 6:7; Phil. 2:5–11; 1 Thess. 4:14–17; 1 Tim. 3:16), Paul repeats this tradition and enjoins his flock to receive and keep it (1 Cor. 11:2; Col. 2:6; 2 Thess. 2:15). Sometimes this tradition is the very heart of the gospel (esp. 1 Cor. 15:1–9), while elsewhere it concerns cultic matters such as the Lord's Supper (11:23) or ethical matters such as divorce (7:10). In writings that some critics consider later this tradition comes to be called the received "deposit of faith" (1 Tim. 1:10; 6:20; 2 Tim. 1:12, 14; Titus 1:9). The power of the apostolic witness is that what they were called to "pass on" was not of men but of God (Gal. 1:1).

The question of how the apostolic witness came to be written down and the canon of inspired texts formed is a very complicated and controversial one. Well into the 2d century, the OT remained the early Christians' only authorized text, but the needs of churches and the assaults of heretics led to a relatively rapid formation of the canon of the NT by the late 2d century and its fixation by the middle of the 4th century. The essential criterion was that these writings contain authentic *apostolic tradition.*

Once the NT canon was fixed and the whole Bible complete, the great church fathers of the 4th and 5th centuries distinguished tradition and Scripture more clearly, but not antithetically. Tradition was understood as the church's enriching and interpretative reflection on the original deposit of faith contained in Scripture.

The Eastern Orthodox came to define tradition as the whole of the church's witness, based on Scripture, but expressed chiefly in the seven ecumenical councils, the writings of the fathers, and liturgical worship. In principle, Scripture remained fundamental and the church alive with its witness; in practice, the weight of tradition became preponderant and the church tended to stagnate in its fixation on what had been promulgated between the 4th and 7th centuries. Outside Scripture, ecumenical councils represented the highest authority in defining tradition.

During most of the Middle Ages, the Western view differed only slightly, placing somewhat greater emphasis upon written Scripture as fundamental and an ever-increasing emphasis upon the papacy (rather than councils) as the normative spokesman for apostolic tradition. But in the 14th century the realization that certain doctrines (e.g., Mary's immaculate conception) could not be proved even remotely from Scripture, together with theologians' increased sophistication about their sources, inspired several of them to posit tradition as a separate, unwritten *source* handed down by apostolic succession, especially through an infallible papacy. The Protestant revolt against all tradition transformed this view, despite protest, into the church's official position at the Council of Trent: The truths and discipline of the gospel are contained in written Scripture *and* in unwritten traditions given to the church by Christ or the Spirit through the apostles, and both deserve *equal* respect. Vatican Council I completed this line of thought when it declared the church's teaching office to be centered in an infallible papacy.

Protestants have nearly always rejected tradition in principle, while necessarily allowing it to reappear in practice in some other form. Luther rejected ecclesiastical traditions as distortions of the true gospel found in Scripture alone, and he thus, and for nearly all Protestants ever since, radically sundered apostolic authority from ecclesiastical tradition, now rendered merely human.

In practice, most Protestant groups formed traditions nearly as binding as the Catholics and established similar sets of authorities: ecumenical councils, confessional creeds, synodical legislation, church orders, and theologians (esp. founders) of a particular church. Those free churches, particularly in America, that claim to stand on Scripture alone and to recognize no traditional authorities are in some sense the least free because they are not even conscious of what traditions have molded their understanding of Scripture. Yet there is a decided difference between Protestants and Catholics. All Protestants insist that these traditions must ever be tested against Scripture and can never possess an independent apostolic authority over or alongside of Scripture. In recent years, scholarly research into the formation of Scripture and the course of church history has inspired greater thoughtfulness and honesty among Protestants on the subject of tradition. The Word of God does not and cannot operate in a vacuum, as an isolated text; it comes alive through the Spirit in the context of gathered believers who make up Christ's church. Preaching is in fact the chief Protestant form of perpetuating tradition, that is, authoritative interpretations and applications of the word.

J. Van Engen

Traducianism. Theory that the soul, as well as the body, comes from the parents. Direct biblical evidence is nonexistent, and conclusions must be based on deductions. In favor of traducianism: (1) God's breathing into Adam the breath of life is not said to be repeated after Adam (Gen. 2:7); (2) Adam begat a son in his own likeness (Gen. 5:3); (3) God's resting (Gen. 2:2–3) suggests no fresh acts of creation *ex nihilo*; and (4) original sin affects the whole person, including the soul; this is simply accounted for by traducianism. Traducianism was held by Tertullian, Lutherans, and the Eastern Church.

J. S. Wright

See also Soul.

Transcendence of God. See God, Attributes of; God, Doctrine of.

Transcendentalism. Idealistic philosophy that in general emphasizes the spiritual over the material. By its very nature, the movement is difficult to describe and its body of beliefs hard to define. Its most important practitioner and spokesman in its New England manifestation, Ralph Waldo Emerson, called it "the Saturnalia or excess of Faith." That which is "popularly called Transcendentalism among us," he wrote, "is Idealism; Idealism as it appears in 1842."

This description mentions two of the very elements—an emphasis upon heightened spiritual awareness and an interest in various types of philosophical idealism—that make transcendentalism so difficult to describe.

The transcendentalists were a loosely knit group of authors, preachers, and lecturers bound together by a mutual loathing of Unitarian orthodoxy, a mutual desire to see American cultural and spiritual life freed from bondage to the past, and a mutual faith in the unbounded potential of American democratic life. Located in the Concord, Massachusetts area in the years between 1835 and 1860, the transcendentalists formed not a tight group but, rather, a loose federation, with Emerson (1803–82) clearly its central figure. The publication of his *Nature* in 1836 is generally considered to mark the beginning of an identifiable movement. The next two decades were to see numerous new works from Emerson and poems, essays, and books from other transcendentalist figures, such as Henry David Thoreau (1817–62), Orestes Brownson (1803–76), Amos Bronson Alcott (1799–1888), Margaret Fuller (1810–50), George Ripley (1802–80), and Theodore Parker (1810–60). These figures and others banded together for the formation of an informal discussion group called the Transcendental Club; the publication of the transcendentalist literary and philosophical journal, *The Dial*; and the establishment of an experiment in utopian communal living, Brook Farm.

Transcendentalism marked the first substantial attempt in American history to retain the spiritual experience and potential of the Christian faith without any of the substance of its belief. By claiming an essential innocence for humankind, by substituting a direct intuition of God or truth for any form of revelation, and by foreseeing a future of ill-defined but certain glory for humankind, transcendentalism paved the way for the many romantic notions about human nature and destiny that have become such a central part of the American experience in the last 100 years.

R. LUNDIN

See also EMERSON, RALPH WALDO.

Transcendental Meditation (TM). Eastern meditative practice popularized in the West by Maharishi Mahesh Yogi. Born in India in 1918, Maharishi (which means "great sage") was a disciple of Swami Brahmananda Saraswati (or "Guru Dev") before he began teaching in the West as a Hindu holy man. As part of a series of world tours, Maharishi first came to the U.S. in 1959. The TM movement has become the largest and fastest growing of the various Eastern spiritual disciplines that have taken root in the West. The simplified and Westernized set of yoga techniques that Maharishi has introduced and marketed in the West is presented to the public as a nonreligious practice designed to enable a person to make use of full mental potential while at the same time achieving deep rest and relaxation. TM claims to offer people absolute happiness, perfect bliss, and "restful alertness" through a technique that requires a minimum of meditation—20 minutes twice a day.

The claim that TM is not religious, that it is merely a scientific technique, has been questioned by Christian and secular observers alike. Maharishi and his carefully trained instructors assert that the benefits of TM can be enjoyed without compromising one's religion. Critics of the TM movement argue that transcendental meditation is essentially Hindu religious practice in disguise. Transcendental Meditation is in reality a form of pantheism. It does not teach the existence of one eternal, personal God, the Creator of the universe. It is part of the monist tradition in that it teaches belief in the essential oneness of all reality and therefore the possibility of our unity with the divine. The practice of TM itself leads the meditator toward the idolatry of self-worship because of the identification of the self with the higher "Self" of the creation. In short, TM promotes an experience involving the loss of one's distinctive identity under the false pretense of a scientific technique.

R. M. ENROTH

Transgression. See SIN.

Transmigration of Souls. See REINCARNATION.

Transubstantiation. Roman Catholic theory of the Lord's Supper defined as a dogma in 1215. The theory of transubstantiation attempts to explain the statements of Christ: "This is my body" and "This is my blood" (Mark 14:22, 24) as applied to the bread and wine of the Lord's Supper. It is insisted that the "is" must be taken with the strictest literalism. But to our senses the bread and wine seem to remain exactly as they were even when consecrated. There is no perceptible miracle of transformation. The explanation is found in terms of a distinction between the so-called substance (or true reality) and the accidents (the specific, perceptible characteristics). The latter remain, but the former, the substance of bread and wine, is changed into that of the body and blood of Christ. This theory carries with it many serious consequences. If Christ is substantially present, it is natural that the elements should be adored. It can also be claimed that he is received by all who communicate, whether rightly to salvation or wrongly to perdition. There also arises the idea of a propitiatory immolation of Christ for the temporal penalties of sin, with all the associated scandals of private masses. The weaknesses of the theory are obvious. It is not scriptural. On sharper analysis it does not even explain the dominical statements. It contradicts the true biblical account of Christ's presence. It has no secure patristic backing. It stands or falls with a particular philosophical understanding. It destroys the true nature of a sacrament. And it certainly perverts its proper use and gives rise to dangerous superstitions inimical to evangelical faith.

G. W. BROMILEY

See also CONCOMITANCE; LORD'S SUPPER, VIEWS OF; REAL PRESENCE.

Trent, Council of (1545–1563). Official Roman Catholic response to the Lutheran Reformation. The Council of Trent did not begin until 25 years after Luther's symbolic rejection of papal authority when he publicly burned *Exsurge Domine* (1520), the papal bull condemning his teachings. This fateful delay in the history of Christianity permitted the consolidation of Protestantism and ensured that, when the council did eventually meet to define doctrines, it would do so in conscious reaction to Protestant doctrines. Although some Protestants attended the council, the majority of those attending were motivated by a desire to counter, rather than conciliate, the Protestants. Hence, even Catholic historians who emphasize the continuity of Trent's doctrinal definitions with traditional Catholic theology concede that Trent did not restore the medieval equilibrium so much as evolve a new system synthesizing Catholic tradition and the altered historical situation. The new system was rigid and exclusive, but also rich and energetic, drawing on the spiritual and theological revival that characterized the Counter-Reformation.

The council's history has three periods: (1) Sessions 1–10 (Dec. 13, 1545–June 2, 1547), during the pontificate of Paul III; (2) Sessions 11–16 (May 1, 1551–Apr. 28, 1552), under Julius III; (3) Sessions 17–25 (Jan. 17, 1562–Dec. 4, 1563), under Pius IV.

It was decided at the outset to deal with both disciplinary reforms (which Holy Roman Emperor Charles V, saw as the first priority) and the definition of dogma (the primary concern of Paul III).

The article on justification was perceived as the most difficult of the doctrinal issues, partly because it had not been dealt with in previous councils. Thirty-three canons condemned Protestant errors concerning justification. The Tridentine doctrine on justification was expressed in 16 chapters. Justification results not only in the remission of sin but also in "sanctification and renewal of the whole man."

In the belief that Lutheran heresy was based on a misunderstanding of the sacraments, the council devoted more time to them than any other doctrinal issue. The council confirmed that there are seven sacraments instituted by Christ (baptism, confirmation, communion, penance, unction, orders, marriage) and condemned those who said that sacraments are not necessary for salvation or that through faith alone, and without any sacrament, man can be justified. Sacraments contain the grace they signify and confer it *ex opere operato*, irrespective of the qualities or merits of the persons administering or receiving them.

The Tridentine decrees enjoyed great prestige and determined Catholic belief and practice for four centuries.

F. S. PIGGIN

See also COUNTER-REFORMATION; PAPACY.

Trespass. See SIN.

Trespass Offering. See OFFERINGS AND SACRIFICES IN BIBLE TIMES.

Tribulation. General biblical term denoting the suffering of God's people.

In the NT tribulation is the experience of all believers and includes persecution (1 Thess. 1:6), imprisonment (Acts 20:23), derision (Heb. 10:33), poverty (2 Cor. 8:13), sickness (Rev. 2:22), and inner distress and sorrow (Phil. 1:17; 2 Cor. 2:4). Tribulation may be a means by which God disciplines his people for their unfaithfulness (Deut. 4:30). More often, especially in the NT, tribulation occurs in the form of persecution of believers because of their faithfulness (John 16:33; Acts 14:22; Rev. 1:9). The sufferings of Christ provide the model for the believer's experience (1 Pet. 2:21–25), and in some sense we participate in the sufferings of Christ (Col. 1:24). Tribulations are viewed by Scripture as entirely within the will of God, serving to promote moral purity and godly character (Rom. 5:3–4). Jesus promised tribulation as the inevitable consequence of his followers' presence in the evil *kosmos* (John 16:33), something they could expect as a way of life.

The Great Tribulation. *The Teaching of Jesus.* The precise expression, "great tribulation" (Matt. 24:21; Rev. 2:22; 7:14—Gk. *thlipsis megalē*), serves to identify the eschatological form of tribulation. These words are Jesus' description of a worldwide, unprecedented time of trouble that will usher in the parousia, Jesus' return to earth in great glory (see pars. Mark 13:19, "days of distress," and Luke 21:23, "great distress"; also Rev. 3:10, "hour of trial"). This period of time will be initiated by the "abomination of desolation" (Matt. 24:15) predicted in Dan. 9:27, a desecration of the "holy place" by one whom many scholars believe is the same as the "man of lawlessness" of 2 Thess. 2:3–4. Jesus gives specific instructions to inhabitants of Judea for their escape and warns that the intensity of its calamities would almost decimate all of life (Matt. 24:15–22).

Views of the Great Tribulation. Although some modern interpreters, along with many ancient commentators and early fathers, are inclined to regard Jesus' predictions as totally fulfilled during the destruction of Jerusalem in A.D. 70, the words of Matt. 24:29, "Immediately after the distress of those days," seem to connect them with the parousia.

Adherents of the major millennial views place the great tribulation at different points in relation to the millennium. Both postmillennialists and amillennialists regard it as a brief, indefinite period of time at the end of the millennium, usually identifying it with the revolt of Gog and Magog of Rev. 20:8–9. Postmillennialists view history as moving toward the Christianization of the world by the church and a future millenium of undetermined length on earth culminating in the great tribulation and final return of Christ. In contrast, amillennialists consider the millennium to be a purely spiritual reality from the first advent to the second, a period lasting already 2000 years and to culminate in the great tribulation—a somewhat less optimistic view of history and the progress of the gospel witness.

To premillennialists the millennium is a future, literal 1000 years on earth, and the great tribulation a chaotic period toward which history is even now moving, a decline, that is, to be terminated by the return of Christ before the millennium. One group, which describes itself as "historic" premillennialists, understands the great tribulation to be a brief but undetermined period of trouble. Another group, dispensational premillennialists, connects it with the 70th week of Dan. 9:27, a period of seven years whose latter half pertains strictly to the great tribulation.

W. H. Baker

See also Last Judgment, The; Millennium, Views of the; Rapture of the Church; Second Coming of Christ.

Trichotomy. Theological term referring to the tripartite division of human nature into body, soul, and spirit. This view developed from Plato's twofold division, body and soul, through Aristotle's further division of the soul into an (1) animal soul, the breathing, organic aspect of human being, and a (2) rational soul, the intellectual aspect. Early Christian writers, influenced by this Greek philosophy, found confirmation of their view in 1 Thess. 5:23, "May your whole spirit, soul, and body be kept blameless at the coming of our Lord Jesus Christ." Present theological and psychological emphasis is almost altogether upon the fundamental wholeness or unity of human being as against all philosophical attempts to divide it.

W. E. Ward

See also Body, Biblical View of the; Dichotomy; Man, Doctrine of; Soul; Spirit.

Trinity. Term designating one God in three Persons. Although not itself a biblical term, "the Trinity" has been found a convenient designation for the one God self-revealed in Scripture as Father, Son, and Holy Spirit. It signifies that within the one essence of the Godhead are three "persons" who are neither three gods on the one side, nor three parts or modes of God on the other, but coequally and coeternally God.

The main contribution of the OT to the doctrine is to emphasize the unity of God. God is not himself a plurality, nor is he one among many others. He is single and unique (Deut. 6:4), and demands the exclusion of all pretended rivals (Deut. 5:7–11). Hence there can be no question of tritheism.

In the NT there is no explicit statement of the doctrine (apart from the rejected 1 John 5:7), but the Trinitarian evidence is overwhelming. God is still preached as the one God (Gal. 3:20). Yet Jesus proclaims his own deity (John 8:58) and evokes and accepts the faith and worship of his disciples (Matt. 16:16; John 20:28). As the Son or Word, he can thus be equated with God (John 1:1) and associated with the Father. The Spirit or Comforter is also brought into the same interrelationship (John 14–16).

It is not surprising, therefore, that while we have no dogmatic statement, there are clear references to the three persons of the Godhead in the NT. All three are mentioned at the baptism of Jesus (Matt. 3:16–17). The disciples are to baptize in the name of Father, Son, and Holy Ghost (Matt. 28:19). The developed Pauline blessing includes the grace of the Son, the love of God, and the communion of the Holy Ghost (2 Cor. 13:14). Reference is made to the election of the Father, the sanctification of the Spirit, and the sprinkling of the blood of Jesus Christ (1 Pet. 1:2) in relation to the salvation of believers.

The fact that Christian faith involves acceptance of Jesus as Savior and Lord meant that the Trinity quickly found its way into the creeds of the church as the confession of faith in God the Father, Jesus Christ his only Son, and the Holy Ghost. The implications of this confession, especially in the context of monotheism, naturally became one of the first concerns of patristic theology, the main aim being to secure the doctrine against tritheism on the one side and monarchianism on the other.

In the fully developed doctrine the unity of God is safeguarded by insisting that there is only one essence or substance of God. Yet the deity of Jesus Christ is fully asserted against those who would think of him as merely adopted to divine sonship, or preexistent, but in the last resort created. The individuality of Father, Son, and Holy Spirit is also preserved against the notion that these are only modes of God for the various purposes of dealing with humankind in creation or salvation. God is one, yet in himself and from all eternity he is Father, Son, and Holy Ghost, the triune God.

G. W. Bromiley

See also God, Attributes of; God, Doctrine of.

Troeltsch, Ernst (1865–1923). German theologian, philosopher of history, and social theorist. In 1915 he became professor of philosophy at Berlin. A liberal, he was active in politics as a state legislator and held a post in the Prussian ministry of cultural affairs. Troeltsch grappled with problems raised by the scientific historical method, and saw the modern awareness of history as the key to understanding culture. He regarded all religion as a reflection and intimation of the ultimate reality of God, and from a rational standpoint Christianity is valid since its ethical values are shaped by living decisions made by its adherents in the historical setting of Western culture. His concern with social and political questions led to a sociological treatment of the history of Christianity in his best-known work, *The Social Teaching of the Christian Churches* (1912). It examined the areas of family, economics, politics, and learning and revealed Christianity as exhibiting two contradictory but complementary tendencies—compromise and rejection of compromise.

R. V. Pierard

Trust. See Faith.

Truth. Fundamental or spiritual reality. The first Christian theologian to attempt any systematic exposition of the concept of truth was Augustine. His immediate aim was to refute skepticism. If the human mind is incapable of grasping truth, particularly the truth about God, then morality and theology are impossible. Augustine distinguished four senses of the term "truth." First, truth is the affirmation of what is (e.g., three times three is nine, and David was king of Israel). Second, every reality (particularly the immutable, supersensible ideas) can be considered as an affirmation of itself; it is true when it merits the name it claims. In this sense beauty and wisdom are truth. Third, the Word of God, Jesus Christ, is the Truth because he expresses the Father. Finally, in the realm of sensible objects, such as plants and animals, there is a resemblance, but only a resemblance, to the primary realities of point 2. Strictly speaking, a visible tree is not a true tree. But as the resemblance is real, even sensible objects have a degree of truth.

The differences between the Hebrew Scriptures and the Greek philosophies are to be sought in the nature and the method of the salvation proclaimed, in the concepts of sin, of redemption, and the specific norms of morality; and not in the usage of the word "truth." The relation between God and truth in the Scriptures is indisputably quite different from anything found in Greek philosophy, mainly because the concept of God is so different. It is in such theological content, not in philological usage, that the important distinctions are to be found.

G. H. CLARK

Tübingen School. Conservative school of theology fostered by G. C. Storr (1746–1805) that stressed the supernatural character of revelation and biblical authority. Also, a Catholic "Tübingen school" attempted in the late 19th century to reconcile the church's teaching with modern philosophy and biblical studies. By far the best known, however, is the one headed by Ferdinand Christian Baur (1792–1860), which opened up new avenues in NT study and was the most controversial movement in biblical criticism in the mid-19th century. Its major contribution was calling attention to the distinct strands and theologies within the NT itself and establishing the principle of a purely historical understanding of the Bible.

Although Baur began teaching at Tübingen in 1826, the school's founding is properly dated from the appearance of his pupil D. F. Strauss's *Life of Jesus* in 1835. This marked the formal break between the old conservative school and the new radical antisupernaturalism. Soon a circle of young lecturers formed under the leadership of Eduard Zeller and in 1842 founded the principal mouthpiece of the school, the *Tübinger theologische Jahrbücher.* Although relatively short-lived, the school, with its emphasis on dialectical conflict within the early church, rejection of Pauline authorship of most of his epistles, and completely antisupernaturalistic outlook, contributed significantly to the development of a historical-critical approach to the Bible that completely ignored the divine element in it.

R. V. PIERARD

See also LIBERALISM, THEOLOGICAL.

Turretin, Francis (1623–1687). Calvinist theologian. Turretin was born and died in Geneva, but was educated in a variety of theological centers, including Geneva, Leiden, Utrecht, Paris, Saumer, Montauban, and Nimes. In 1647 he became pastor to the Italian congregation in Geneva, and in 1653 he was named a professor of theology as well. He was known for his mild and friendly personality as well as for his unbending interpretation of Calvinism. In 1675 he published the *Formula Consensus Helvetica*, and in 1688 his famous four-volume work, the *Institutio*, one of the fullest expressions of Calvinist scholasticism. His theology was revived in the 19th century by the American Presbyterians of the Princeton school of theology, most notably Charles Hodge. Turretin's *Institutio* was reprinted in 1847, and became a standard textbook for orthodox training in American Presbyterianism.

R. J. VANDERMOLEN

See also PRINCETON THEOLOGY, OLD; SCHOLASTICISM, PROTESTANT.

Twelve Articles of the Peasants (1525). Southern German demand for religious, social, and economic rights in the face of continuation of the manorial system under which the peasant was virtually a slave. The articles emerged as the Christian Union of peasants attempted to establish an evangelical state in which special privileges were to be abolished and all people were to be equal. The peasants took the NT quite literally, applying its teachings to society at large. Unfortunately, radical elements under Thomas Müntzer became violent, causing a crusade by the princes who crushed the peasant forces. In the end, towns and peasants suffered and the Reformation lost face. Only the princes profited. The witness of the peasants to the civil rights implicit in the gospel was at least 100 years ahead of its time. The *Twelve Articles* stand with Balthasar Hubmaier's *Heretics and Their Burners* as a call for religious liberty and social justice.

W. N. KERR

See also HUBMAIER, BALTHASAR; RADICAL REFORMATION; ZWICKAU PROPHETS.

Twofold State of Jesus. See STATES OF JESUS CHRIST.

Two Swords Theory. See CHURCH AND STATE.

Type, Typology. From the Greek word for form or pattern, which in biblical times denoted both the original model or prototype and the copy that resulted. In the NT the latter was labeled the antitype, and this was especially used in two directions: (1) the correspondence between two historical situations like the flood and baptism (1 Pet. 3:21) or two figures like Adam and Christ (Rom. 5:14); (2) the correspondence between the heavenly pattern and its earthly counterpart, e.g., the divine original behind the earthly tent/tabernacle (Acts 7:44; Heb. 8:5; 9:24). There are several categories—persons (Adam, Melchizedek), events (flood, brazen serpent), institutions (feast), places (Jerusalem, Zion), objects (altar of burnt offering, incense), offices (prophet, priest, king).

In addition we might note the parallel use of image along with type to denote a moral example to be followed. This latter is an important part of the NT stress on imitation of the divinely ordained pattern exemplified first in Christ (John 13:15; 1 Pet. 2:21), then in the apostolic band (Phil. 3:17; 2 Thess. 3:9), the leaders (1 Tim. 4:12; Titus 2:7; 1 Pet. 5:3), and the community itself (1 Thess. 1:7). As such all believers are to consider themselves models or patterns of the Christlike life.

Hermeneutical Significance. It has increasingly been recognized that typology expresses the basic hermeneutic, indeed the attitude or perspective, by which both OT and NT writers understood themselves and their predecessors. Each new community in the ongoing development of salvation history viewed itself analogously in terms of the past. This is true within the OT as well as in the NT use of the OT. The two major sources, of course, were creation and the exodus. Creation typology is especially seen in Rom. 5 and the Adam-Christ parallel, while exodus or covenant typology predominates in both Testaments. Positively, the exodus was behind the redemptive imagery in Isa. 51–52 as well as NT salvific concepts. Negatively, the wilderness wanderings became the model for future admonition (Ps. 95:7–8; Heb. 4:3–11).

The church fathers combined typology and allegory, linking the former with general religious truths expressed in terms of Greek philosophical concepts. The Reformers espoused a system which viewed the OT literally with a christological hermeneutic, that is, as pointing forward messianically to Christ. During the critical period after the 17th century, the whole concept of promise-fulfillment was played down and the OT was thought to reflect religious experience rather than history. In recent decades, however, typology properly conceived has become again a valid tool, based upon the biblical perspective regarding the recurring pattern in God's acts within history, thereby establishing continuity between the stages of redemptive history.

G. R. OSBORNE

Tyrrell, George (1861–1909). Roman Catholic modernist. Tyrrell was born in Dublin. He became a Jesuit and was ordained priest in 1891. Removed to Yorkshire (1900–1905), he attacked his church's view of authority and suggested that Roman Catholicism, like Judaism, might "have to die in order that it may live again in a greater and grander form." Rather than recant and submit, Tyrrell chose dismissal from the Jesuits, and complained that "mendacity seems to have eaten into the whole heart of the system." In 1907 he was deprived of the sacraments. He rejected papal infallibility and defended modernism in his *Medievalism* (1908). He developed his thought in *Christianity at the Cross-Roads* (1909), but refused to join Roman Catholic priests who were received into the Church of England.

J. D. DOUGLAS

See also VON HÜGEL, FRIEDRICH.

Uu

Ubiquity of God. See GOD, ATTRIBUTES OF.

Ultradispensationalism. Dispensationalists distinguish Israel from the church and so look for a point in history at which God's redemptive program changed from the one form of administration to the other. The most common dispensationalism finds the beginning of the church in Acts 2 with the Spirit's coming at Pentecost. From the standpoint of Acts 2 dispensationalism two other views seem extreme, or "ultra." According to Acts 13 dispensationalism the church began when Paul started his mission to Jews and Gentiles (Acts 13:2). According to Acts 28 dispensationalism the church began toward the end of Paul's ministry and was introduced when he referred to Israel's rejection of the kingdom of God and the sending of God's salvation to the Gentiles (Acts 28:26–28).

Acts 28 dispensationalism is sometimes called Bullingerism after its leading proponent, Ethelbert William Bullinger (1837–1913). Other writers holding this position include Charles H. Welch, A. E. Knoch, Vladimir M. Gelesnoff, and Otis R. Sellers. Proponents of the Acts 13 dispensationalism are J. C. O'Hair, C. R. Stam, and Charles F. Baker, author of a major textbook, *A Dispensational Theology*. Baker's name is associated with the Grand Rapids Grace Bible College, which prepares people for ministry in Grace Gospel Fellowship and the Worldwide Grace Testimony.

G. R. LEWIS

See also DISPENSATION, DISPENSATIONALISM.

Ultramontanism. Literally "beyond the mountains" (Alps), the term usually refers to a 19th-century movement within the Roman Catholic Church that opposed conciliar and nationalist decentralization and advocated centralization of power in the papacy in order to restore the spiritual vigor of the church. The concept itself actually dates from the Middle Ages, when the papacy sought increased power in order to free itself from secular control, as in the investiture controversy of the 11th century—a movement that some call "old ultramontanism." Coined as a term of derision in the 17th century, "ultramontanism" was resurrected in the post-Napoleonic era to refer to an attempt spearheaded by French Catholic romantics to terminate the influence of Enlightenment rationalism and secular governments in church affairs and to restore papal power—a movement that some call "new ultramontanism."

R. D. LINDER

See also PAPACY; VATICAN COUNCIL I; VATICAN COUNCIL II.

Unbelief. Turning away of individuals and groups from the traditional Christian faith and worldview. Unbelief can be understood from a broad cultural perspective as the secularization of Western society and a defection from belief in the theistic, personal God of the Judeo-Christian heritage. We may also speak of a relative unbelief within the church that is in evidence when certain cardinal doctrines of the faith are denied and attacked from within Christendom. In this sense theological liberalism in at least its extreme forms represents a sort of unbelief.

Unbelief in Western culture began to constitute a serious challenge during the Renaissance with the rise of science and in the Enlightenment. While 18th-century unbelief challenged the intellectual grounds for faith, 19th-century unbelief moved beyond this and assumed the falsehood of theism. The spread of unbelief in the 20th century has continued apace. Atheists, among others, turned to existentialism in Europe, as advocated by Jean-Paul Sartre, while Anglo-American thinkers entertained logical positivism, as represented by A. J. Ayer. Sartre argued that God's existence was to be denied because it was incompatible with human freedom, while Ayer and Anthony Flew urged that it was linguistically meaningless even to refer to God in language. Varieties of Marxism have risen to power in major areas of the world, invariably antagonistic to religious belief.

D. B. Fletcher

See also Agnosticism; Atheism; Death of God Theology.

Unchangeability of God. See God, Attributes of.

Underhill, Evelyn (1875–1941). British spiritual writer. The appearance of *Mysticism* (1911) marked the beginning of her life's work of explaining the mystical traditions. Initially she intentionally avoided an explicitly Christian viewpoint in order to reach a broader readership. *The Mystic Way* (1913) attempted what *Mysticism* had not: to establish the mystical character of NT Christianity. Her *Practical Mysticism* (1920) appeared at the same time as several translations and studies of medieval mystical writings. Underhill translated or edited a few of these; for most of them she provided encouragement for other translators and wrote introductions to their translations. She also published two volumes of mystical verse (*Immanence* [1912]; *Theophanies* [1916]). After World War I Underhill became active in the Church of England, while placing herself (1922–25) under the spiritual direction of the Roman Catholic Friedrich von Hügel. Called upon to give numerous retreats, she shifted her focus increasingly toward the liturgical life of the church; this culminated in her second main work, *Worship* (1936).

D. D. Martin

See also Mysticism; Spirituality.

Understanding. Cognitive activity that surpasses in depth and richness mere acquaintance with facts or events. Whereas "to know" generally signifies perception and observation in an impersonal, objective mode, "to understand" means to grasp the meaning of phenomena that are meaningful to persons either because they are expressions of persons or because they form an important part of persons' lives. To understand means to see the cause-and-effect relations and the purposes of the phenomenon in question, and to be able to place this phenomenon into the broader context of human choices and actions.

Biblical understanding is a very lively field of intellectual interest, as philosophers and theologians have come to realize that there is more to understanding the biblical texts than merely to exegete them. To understand is to engage in a hermeneutical task involving an attempt to enter into the "horizon" of interpretations and presuppositions of the biblical writer while retaining our own "horizon." Any naïve view of understanding Scripture is to be rejected, such as those that see the text as having a single, transparent meaning for all persons in all times, merely awaiting proper exegesis to be manifest. The questions in biblical understanding have now become, To what extent is there a definite and objective meaning in Scripture? To what extent do our own personal "horizons" of contemporary concepts shade our understanding? Can there be a biblical message to be understood, or does our act of understanding either create or radically shape the message?

D. B. FLETCHER

Unforgiveable Sin. See SIN, UNPARDONABLE.

Unification Church. Religious movement founded by the Rev. Sun Myung Moon (also known as the Holy Spirit Association for the Unification of World Christianity). Despite its relatively small size (less than 500,000 members worldwide), it has received considerable publicity and media attention because of its controversial beliefs and practices. Moon was born to Presbyterian parents in Korea in 1920. He claims that on Easter Sunday, 1936, while in prayer on a Korean hillside, Jesus appeared to him and revealed that he had been chosen to complete the work that Jesus had begun. This experience was the first in a series of revelatory encounters with God in which Moon states that he received new truth for a new age. The new revelations and teachings of Rev. Moon were subsequently set forth in the *Divine Principle*, first published in 1957. Moon officially established his new church in 1954 with the avowed purpose of bringing salvation to the world and initiating a truly international family.

The doctrine of the Unification Church is highly eclectic and spiritistic in nature. It reflects the peculiarities of Korea's religiously fertile soil and Moon's lifelong interest in spiritualistic phenomena. The presence of much biblical and Christian terminology in Unification theology has led casual observers to conclude that Moon's church is just another variant of Christianity. Moon himself, however, has admitted that his teachings are heretical from the standpoint of traditional, orthodox Christianity. He maintains that because of sectarian divisions and the inability of conventional churches to meet the needs of today's complex world, God desires to communicate a new revelation of truth which, assisted by the spirit world and the movement's loyal followers (popularly known as "Moonies"), will bring about a spiritual revolution. Such a movement will result in the true, lasting unification of the world.

R. M. ENROTH

Uniformity, Acts of. Four parliamentary enactments designed to ensure uniformity of theology and worship in the Church of England on the basis of required use of the *Book of Common Prayer*. The Act of 1549 (Edward VI) established the first *Book of Common Prayer*, prepared by Thomas Cranmer and others, for exclusive use in the Mass and all public services. The Act of 1552 (Edward VI) reflected a shift in Cranmer's position, as the Prayer Book was revised in a Zwinglian direction. It eliminated the requirement for ministers to wear ecclesiastical vestments in services of worship. The Act of 1559 (Elizabeth I) reestablished the Prayer Book of 1552 as of June 24, 1559, repealing the legislation of Mary's reign which had restored Roman practice in worship. The Act of 1662 (Charles II) reestablished Anglicanism as part of the Restoration settlement after the collapse of the Puritan revolution. It required universal adoption of a somewhat revised version of the Elizabethan Prayer Book of 1559, including a public declaration of support as well as episcopal ordination for those not already so ordained, before the ensuing St. Bartholomew's Day (Aug. 24). As a result of the Act of 1662 about 2000 nonconforming clergy were ejected from the English church. The Toleration Act of

William and Mary (1689) restricted the act to conforming Anglican ministers.

N. A. MAGNUSON

Unio Mystica. Direct union or communion with God that is quite different from the general union in Christ that is the privilege of all believers. Students of Christian mysticism have assembled various categories for the mystical unions described by mystics. One set of categories distinguishes between a habitual or frequently recurring union and an ecstatic, transient union. Some authors also speak of a unitive life, a more or less permanent state of living in bliss in God's presence that is granted in the present life on earth to a very few as a sort of extension of habitual union. Another distinction is that between abstractive union that removes the human spirit from consciousness of the ordinary world of sense phenomena and a nonabstractive union that is fully compatible with ordinary consciousness.

D. D. MARTIN

See also MYSTICISM.

Union, Hypostatic. See HYPOSTATIC UNION.

Union with Christ. See IDENTIFICATION WITH CHRIST.

Union with God. See UNIO MYSTICA.

Unitarianism. The origin of this ancient heresy, sometimes called antitrinitarianism, is to be found in the Arian controversy of the early 4th century A.D.,when Arius, presbyter in the church at Alexandria, set forth the system of thought that bears his name. It reappeared in a somewhat different guise in the writings of Michael Servetus in the 16th century, and received a new impetus and theological foundation in the Socinianism of Laelius and Faustus Socinus and in the Racovian Catechism of 1605. With the coming of the Enlightenment and the appearance of deism, Unitarianism in the hands of Joseph Priestly and others became more rationalistic and less supernaturalistic in its outlook. Nature and right reason replaced the NT as the primary sources of religious authority, and what authority the Scriptures retained was the result of their agreement with the findings of reason.

Unitarianism came to New England as early as 1710, and by 1750 most of the Congregational ministers in and around Boston had ceased to regard the doctrine of the Trinity as an essential Christian belief. The triumph of Unitarianism in New England Congregationalism seemed complete with the election of Henry Ware, an avowed opponent of the Trinitarian position, to the Hollis chair of divinity at Harvard. In the 19th century, under the impact of transcendentalism, Unitarianism became steadily more radical. Its later leaders such as Ralph Waldo Emerson and Theodore Parker rejected those remaining supernatural elements which William Ellery Channing had seen fit to retain. Modern Unitarianism has become increasingly humanistic.

C. G. SINGER

See also ARIANISM; CHANNING, WILLIAM ELLERY; RACOVIAN CATECHISM; SOCINUS, FAUSTUS; TRANSCENDENTALISM.

Unitive Way, The. Final and highest stage of the three ways of the spiritual life in classical mystical theology, following on the purgative and illuminative ways. While the basis of these categories is found in the NT (e.g., 1 Cor. 3:1–3; Heb. 5:12–14; 1 John 2:12–14), they developed in the later fathers, especially Evagrius Pontieus and Augustine. The classic expression of the unitive way is in John of the Cross's *Dark Night of the Soul.*

P. H. DAVIDS

See also ASCETICAL THEOLOGY; ILLUMINATIVE WAY, THE; MYSTICISM; PURGATIVE WAY, THE.

Universalism. Belief that affirms that in the fullness of time all souls will be released from the penalties of sin and restored to God. Historically known as *apokatastasis*, it denies the biblical doctrine of eternal punishment and is based on a faulty reading of Acts 3:21; Rom. 5:18–19; Eph. 1:9–10; 1 Cor. 15:22; and other passages. The first clearly universalist writings date from the Greek church fathers, most notably Clement of Alexandria, his student Origen, and Gregory of Nyssa. In Western Europe universalism almost completely disappeared during the Middle Ages, save for the Irish scholar John Scotus Erigena and some of the lesser-known mystics. Some spiritualist and Anabaptist writers of the Radical Reformation revived the doctrine. In the 16th century it was embraced by the German scholar Hans Denck and spread through his convent Hans Hut.

Universalism that was explicit and the center of doctrine emerged out of Calvinism in England. Several sects that embraced final salvation developed out of 17th-century Puritanism, among them the Philadelphians, founded by Jane Lead. It was not, however, until a century later, when James Relly broke with the Wesley–Whitefield revival, that an organized universalist movement appeared. His *Union* (1759) rejected Calvinism and argued that all souls are in union with Christ. One of Relly's converts was John Murray, who arrived in New England in 1770 and organized the first Universalist congregation at Gloucester, Massachusetts, in 1779. A General Convention was formed a few years later. Organized Universalism thus became primarily an American phenomenon.

The former Baptist Elhanan Winchester founded a Universalist congregation in Philadelphia in 1781 and developed a compelling restorationist position in his *Dialogues on the Universal Restoration* (1788). Winchester, an Arminian, argued that future punishment is measured for each sin and results ultimately in the eternal happiness of all souls. Hosea Ballou, another former Baptist, proved to be the dominant theological spokesman for the movement in the early 19th century. His *Treatise on the Atonement* (1805) posited a "moral" view of Christ's sacrifice rather than the "legal" or substitutionary position of Relly and Murray. Christ suffered on behalf of humankind but not in their place. Nineteenth century universalism took on the familiar characteristics of an American denomination. It grew steadily in several midwestern and New England states, and in frontier and rural areas it assumed a more evangelical posture than has commonly been recognized. Several periodicals were started and state or regional associations formed. Tufts College (1852) and a theological school (1869) at Medford, Massachusetts, became the leading educational institutions.

Twentieth-century universalism, now clearly a liberal faith, was largely shaped by the theologian Clarence Skinner. A wider conception of universalism was articulated, which rejected the deity of Jesus and sought to explore the "universal" bases of all religions. Accordingly, closer ties were sought with the major world non-Christian and native American religions. Universalists continue to stress such beliefs as the dignity and brotherhood of humankind, tolerance of diversity, and the reasonableness of moral actions.

D. B. Eller

See also Apokatastasis; Unitarianism.

Universalism, Hypothetical. See Atonement, Extent of the.

Universe, Origin of. See Origin of the Universe.

Unpardonable Sin. See Sin, Unpardonable.

Ursinus, Zacharias (1534–1583). Reformed theologian. Ursinus was born in Breslau and studied in Wittenberg under Melanchthon and then with Calvin in Geneva. He became head of Collegium Sapientiae, Heidelberg, holding the main theology chair there. He also preached, and was charged by Frederick III to develop a new Reformed church liturgy. Ursinus wrote a *Summa theologica* and a *Catechismus minor* in preparation for this task. He worked closely with one of the leading preachers of the city, Caspar Olevianus, and others, including Frederick, in writing what came to be called the Heidelberg Catechism.

R. V. SCHNUCKER

See also HEIDELBERG CATECHISM.

Ussher, James (1581–1656). Irish Protestant churchman and scholar. Born in Dublin, he was one of the earliest graduates of the newly founded Trinity College, and gained appointment there as professor of theological controversies in 1607. He drafted the articles approved by the first convocation of the Irish Episcopal Church in 1615. In 1621 he was appointed bishop of Meath and in 1626 archbishop of Armagh (primate of Ireland). His authority declined after 1633, however, when Thomas Wentworth became deputy and pursued Archbishop Laud's policy of enforcing conformity with England. He nonetheless remained on good terms with both men, even while opposing their efforts. He left Ireland in 1640.

Ussher was a vehement opponent of Roman Catholicism and denounced toleration as a "grievous sin," yet he was respected by all parties for his even temper. In patristic studies he distinguished the genuine parts of the epistles of Ignatius from the spurious. Undoubtedly he is best known for his scriptural chronology (with the creation of the world dated in 4004 B.C.) since it was eventually inserted in the marginal notes of the AV. Ussher was regarded as an outstanding preacher in the "plain" style. He also collected a magnificent library of books and manuscripts (including the famous Book of Kells) now housed at Trinity College, Dublin.

R. K. BISHOP

See also IRISH ARTICLES.

Utilitarianism. Ethical theory according to which the rightness of actions is determined by the net balance of benefits produced. The principle of utility is seen by utilitarians as the sole moral criterion by which to judge actions, this principle being that we should always produce the greatest possible balance of good over evil. Utilitarianism is a teleological or consequentialist moral theory, holding that rightness of actions is a function of the consequences, "the greatest good for the greatest number." Consequences are to be distributed as widely as possible; the moral agent is not to look only to personal welfare nor to that of those especially cared for, but to all persons. In some versions the class of beneficiaries is extended to include nonhuman sentient beings as well.

Utilitarianism is traced historically to Jeremy Bentham (1748–1832), although David Hume was a significant precursor of the theory. Bentham advanced utilitarianism as an ethic primarily for social reform. Christian utilitarians such as John Austin (1790–1859) attempted to see God's law as pointing the way to utility. In John Stuart Mill (1806–73) utilitarianism emerged as a specifically personal ethic. Utilitarianism's most careful and articulate spokesman was Henry Sidgwick (1873–1958), who saw utilitarianism as capable of reconciling the various "methods of ethics" (intuitionism or deontology, egoism, and utilitarianism itself) and thus of philosophically justifying "common sense morality."

Utilitarianism is very much in the midst of philosophical debate at the present time. Detractors argue that it fails to provide an adequate protection for the claims of justice, since it would seem that on utilitarian principles the rights of the few could be violated to realize a gain in utility for the greater number. Its defenders argue that utilitarianism fares far better than any deontological system in commanding one's allegiance and in providing a reason to do as morality requires. Contemporary Christian ethicists are generally disinclined to see utilitarianism as an adequate Christian moral theory.

D. B. FLETCHER

See also ETHICS, BIBLICAL; SOCIAL ETHICS.

Utrecht, Declaration of (1889). Policy statement made by the five Old Catholic bishops, which in 1897 was adopted as the doctrinal basis of the Old Catholic Churches. It affirmed loyalty to Catholicism rightly understood—that is, as found in the beliefs of the primitive church and the decrees of the ecumenical councils up to the Great Schism between Rome and Constantinople in 1054. Made at a time soon after Vatican Council I controversies had augmented the ranks of dissidents, the declaration condemned what it regarded as Roman deviations from orthodoxy. Prominent among these were the decrees on immaculate conception (1854) and papal infallibility (1870), and the Syllabus of Errors (1864), which had condemned liberal doctrines. The Declaration of Utrecht was in large part the work of those who had earlier unsuccessfully tried to persuade Roman Catholicism to subject its history and traditions to modern criticism.

J. D. DOUGLAS

Vv

Vatican Council I (1869–1870). Council convened by Pope Pius IX in Rome and reckoned by Roman Catholics to be the 20th ecumenical church council. It was the first to meet since the Council of Trent (1545–63). Its work was cut short by the Franco-Prussian War and the invasion and capture of Rome by the army of the Italian government in Sept. 1870. The council with its 737 members completed only two major doctrinal statements, leaving another 51 unfinished. Vatican I is remembered almost exclusively for its doctrinal definition of papal infallibility.

Constitution "De Fide Catholica." The first doctrinal definition, "On the Catholic faith" (approved Apr. 1870; also called *Dei Filius*), expressed a consensus of the Catholic revival concerning God, faith, and reason. In its four chapters it defined as a doctrine of divine revelation the existence of a free, personal, Creator God who was absolutely independent of the universe he created. The religious truth concerning the existence of this God, it affirmed, could be known by human reason alone, so that all people had no excuse for unbelieving. Nevertheless, other truths about God and this creation could only be known by faith through divine revelation via Scripture and the tradition of the church. Properly understood, faith and reason were not in conflict. The errors that were specifically mentioned in an appendix—notably atheism, pantheism, rationalism, fideism, biblicism, traditionalism—were either utterly wrong (atheism) or wrong in emphasizing merely one element of the whole truth (rationalism). This definition provided the basis for Catholic theology and philosophy for the next several generations.

Constitution "On Papal Primacy and Infallibility." The passage on papal infallibility, after crucial amendments, carefully circumscribed in what sense the *magisterium* (doctrinal authority) of the pope was infallible: "The Roman Pontiff when he speaks *ex cathedra*, that is, when, exercising the office of pastor and teacher of all Christians, according to his supreme Apostolic authority, through the divine assistance promised to him in St. Peter, he defines doctrine concerning faith and morals to be held by the universal Church, then under those circumstances he is empowered with that infallibility with which the divine Redeemer willed his Church to be equipped in defining doctrine concerning faith and morals." The statement concluded, against Gallicanism and conciliarism, that "such definitions by the Roman Pontiff were in themselves, and not by virtue of the consensus of the Church, not subject to being changed."

Eighty-eight bishops voted against the definition in the first round, and 55 bishops formally absented themselves at the final vote (July 18, 1870). Eventually, after the council, every bishop submitted to the definition, and the debate transmuted into differences over its interpretation. The definition encouraged Catholic revival, gave Protestants new evidence of papal superstition, and convinced secularists that the papacy was indeed utterly incompatible with modern civilization. To this day the doctrine of papal infallibility continues to trouble many Catholics and to complicate Roman Catholic consultations with Anglicans, Lutherans, and others.

C. T. McIntire

See also Infallibility; Papacy.

Vatican Council II (1962–1965). Twenty-first ecumenical church council and deliberate attempt to renew and bring up to date (*aggiornamento*) all facets of church faith and life. It was convened in Oct. 1962 by Pope John XXIII, and reconvened in Sept. 1963 by his successor, Pope Paul VI. Altogether the council held four annual fall sessions, finally adjourning after approving 16 major texts that were promulgated by the pope. At the opening session 2540 bishops and other clerical members of council attended, and an average of 2300 members were present for most major votes. The council took on a profound and electrifying life of its own. Before the eyes of the world it succeeded in initiating an extraordinary transformation of the Roman Catholic Church.

Chief among the council's characteristics was a pastoral spirit that dominated throughout. There was also a biblical spirit. From the very beginning the bishops indicated that they would not accept the rather abstract and theologically exact drafts prepared for them. Instead, they desired to express themselves in direct biblical language. Moreover, there was an evident awareness of history—the history of salvation, the pilgrim church, the ongoing tradition, the development of doctrine, the openness to the future. The council was ecumenical in its outreach to non-Catholic Christians (represented by observers from 28 denominations) and humble in relation to non-Christian religions. It was remarkably open to the whole world, especially through massive global press coverage and by directly addressing the world in an opening "Message to Humanity," and in a series of closing messages to political rulers, intellectuals and scientists, artists, women, the poor, workers, and youth. Yet the council kept the church thoroughly consistent with its Roman Catholic identity and tradition.

Undoubtedly the central theme of the promulgated documents was the church. The *Dogmatic Constitution on the Church* (Nov. 1964) was the pivotal doctrinal statement of the entire council. A second dogmatic constitution was *On Divine Revelation*. A third, called simply a constitution, was *On Liturgy*, and a fourth, called a pastoral constitution, was *On the Church in the Modern World*. In addition, nine practical decrees and three declarations of principle were promulgated. Of these, five concerned the vocations of the church as fulfilled by bishops, priests (two), members of religious orders, and the laity. Three treated education, missions, and the media. Four covered the church's relations with Eastern Catholics, ecumenism, non-Christian religions, and civil governments (religious liberty).

C. T. McIntire

Veneration of Relics. See Relics.

Veneration of the Saints. Celebration of the virtuous life or heroic death of persons whose souls reside in heaven with Christ. Such honor includes the respectful memory and imitation of the virtues of departed believers as well as verbal communion with them. It includes both private and public devotion. Veneration of saints began as recognition of early martyrs, at whose graves Christians conducted memorial services of worship of God. By the 4th century Christians inaugurated similar honor of other deceased, called "confessors," whose piety they esteemed as a sacrifice equivalent to that of martyrs. Subsequently use of images and relics as conveyers of personal presence multiplied the places where this form of the communion of saints was practiced by Orthodox and Catholic faithful. To differentiate between worship of God and veneration of saints Augustine proposed the distinction, elaborated by later writers, between *latria* and *dulia*. *Latria* ("worship") belongs to deity alone (Matt. 4:10); *dulia* ("honor") may be merited by human beings by virtue of their office or deeds (Rom. 13:7).

P. D. STEEVES

See also LATRIA; DULIA; BEATIFICATION; CANONIZATION; INVOCATION OF THE SAINTS.

Vengeance. In Jewish-Christian thought vengeance is seen as the deliberate act of God: "O LORD, the God who avenges, O God who avenges, shine forth"(Ps. 94:1). In Deut. 32:35, 43 God is praised precisely because vengeance is his. Jesus also recognized that God brings about justice for his chosen ones (lit. "make vengeance for them" [Luke 18:7–8]). Throughout Scripture a final "day of vengeance" is foreseen, associated with avenging God's people, with requital, recompense, anger, wrath (Mic. 5:15), not leaving the guilty unpunished (Nah. 1:3), repayment of wrong (Rom. 12:19), and punishment (2 Thess. 1:8–9).

Among people, instinctive personal revenge aims at relief of anger, self-defense, and deterrence. But Christian teaching outlaws revenge entirely; the Christian reaction to injury is forgiveness, love, turning the other cheek, and overcoming evil with good. Incentives to this total repudiation of private vengeance are four: (1) feelings of anger, hatred, and malice being forbidden (Sermon on the Mount), no action for emotional release is contemplated; (2) retaliation changes nothing in the situation, producing only a vicious circle, injury breeding further injury; (3) Christ's superb example (Luke 9:51–56; 19:41; 23:34); (4) our own dependence as sinners on God's forgiving love—only the merciful obtain mercy, only the forgiving are forgiven (Matt. 5:7; 6:14–15).

Nevertheless, protection and vindication of others oppressed, out of love toward them and indignation against wrong, remain a Christian duty. This is implemented wherever possible through the community's judicial system, as God's agency of vengeance (Rom. 13:1–4; 1 Pet. 2:13–14), helping to insure impartiality, equity, punishment without malice, examination of circumstances, motive, and background of the offender. Ultimate vindication of the moral order of the world is in God's hands (Rom. 12:19; 1 Thess. 4:6). By such careful distinctions Christianity effectively eschews all personal vengeance, without sentimentally destroying the moral basis of social order.

R. E. O. WHITE

Venial Sin. See SIN, VENIAL.

Verbal Inspiration. Belief that every word of the Bible was inspired by God himself.

The Nature of Verbal Inspiration. The exponents of verbal inspiration in the late 16th and 17th centuries usually shared in the Aristotelian philosophical orientation that was once again sweeping Europe, while in most cases they also shared Augustinian theological propensities. Both Continental Protestants and Roman Catholics were involved.

The doctrine of verbal inspirations espouses the following beliefs: (1) God is the author of the Bible in the sense of being the formal cause. (2) The focus of inspiration is the words of the Bible; it is text- rather than author-oriented. (Plenary inspiration, in contrast, focuses on the writers.) (3) All the words and all the verbal relationships are inspired by God. This includes all seemingly peripheral statements as well as those more obviously germane to the matter under consideration. (4) The data of the Bible are claimed as the source of the theory—not the data in the sense of the phenomena, but the teaching of the Bible about its own nature. (5) Dictation is not involved; there is no violation of the personality of the writer. God had sovereignly and concursively been preparing the writers for the instrumental task so that they willingly and naturally recorded God's revelation in the way he required. Thus the Bible may be described as all of God and all of human writers. (6) Conscious accommodation on God's part accounts for any apparent lapse, infelicity, or inexactitude. (7) The autographs of the biblical books are solely thus inspired. (8) Inerrancy is the quality of such a Bible; it speaks with exactitude on all matters, save where accommodation has obviously taken place. (9) Authority flows from such a Bible on all matters which it touches, thus guaranteeing that divine teaching is communicated on all matters concerning what Christians are to believe and how they are to live.

Verbal Inspiration in History. The forces that drove Christians to produce theories of inspiration continued in such strength that during the 18th century they virtually engulfed verbal inspiration except in certain restricted quarters. Partial inspiration became a common view during this century among those who made significant accommodation to the Enlightenment, whereas the Christians of the dynamic first and second evangelical awakenings, from 1735 to 1825, almost invariably held to plenary inspiration. During their two finest generations the evangelicals, although they adhered to the full inspiration of the Bible, did not propagate the verbal theory.

In the English-speaking world, Robert Haldane, the wealthy Scottish lay evangelist, determined that a new line of biblical defense was necessary. He introduced verbal inspiration in his frequently reprinted *Books of the Old and New Testaments Proved to be Canonical and Their Verbal Inspiration Maintained and Established.* In the U.S., Charles Hodge introduced the verbal theory—silently jettisoning the plenary view of his venerated predecessor at Princeton Seminary, Archibald Alexander—making it the accepted view among Old School Presbyterians in the middle Atlantic and southeastern states and a position of long continuance among Northern and Southern Presbyterians of Old School lineage.

Perhaps the most important individual in the popular spread of verbal inspiration was Haldane's Genevan convert, Louis Gaussen, whose *Theopneustia* is still reprinted. And while this was happening in the English-speaking world, Lutheran confessionalism was resuscitating verbal inspiration in the Germanic lands. On the other hand, the majority of mid-19th-century evangelicals clung to plenary inspiration. Among denominations such as Methodists and Congregationalists there was little concern with verbal inspiration.

The second wave of reaction to liberalism was fundamentalism, which emerged in the late 19th and carried on into the 20th century. Although it differed from confessionalism in certain important aspects, they were at one in championing verbal inspiration and worked together for the dissemination of this concept. One of the ablest upholders of verbal inspiration was B. B. Warfield of Princeton Seminary. Although he added nothing particularly new to the theory, his numerous articles and book reviews shed the light of his brilliant mind upon this specially chosen theme.

I. S. Rennie

See also Bible, Authority of; Bible, Inerrancy and Infallibility of; Bible, Inspiration of; Enlightenment, The; Fundamentalism; Liberalism, Theological; Plenary Inspiration.

Vermigli, Peter Martyr. See PETER MARTYR VERMIGLI.

Vermittlungstheologie. See MEDIATING THEOLOGY.

Vespers. See OFFICE, DAILY (DIVINE); EVENING PRAYER, EVENSONG.

Via Analogia. Approach to the human conceptualization about God that uses analogy. It seeks to escape the limitations imposed by the *via negativa*, which denies all positive attribution of God. The direct opposite of the *via negativa* is the *via eminentia*, according to which all positive qualities in the world have their origin in God, who thus possesses them preeminently, thereby allowing us to predicate properties directly of God, knowing that they are first of all his as Creator.

The *via eminentia* by itself, however, does not take into account the limitations of finitude in contrast to divine infinity. Hence it must be said that God possesses properties in compliance with his essence, infinitely in both quality and quantity, whereas creatures possess them finitely and only as derived from God. Thus analogy seeks to steer a middle course between univocity (where the properties are all alike) and equivocation (where the properties are entirely dissimilar).

Analogy has been widely criticized among Protestants for its apparent reliance on natural theology, particularly since analogy is devised by Aristotle and adapted by Thomas Aquinas. Karl Barth in particular claims that analogy denies God's free self-expression in his revelation.

W. CORDUAN

See also VIA NEGATIVA.

Via Eminentia. See VIA ANALOGIA.

Via Illuminativa. See ILLUMINATIVE WAY, THE.

Via Media. Doctrinal justification for the Anglican Church as representing a middle way between the Roman Catholic Church and dissenting Protestantism. Although the term first appeared in the 17th century, it was made most popular by John Henry Newman during his career as tractarian with the Oxford Movement (1833–41). As Newman himself tells it in *Apologia pro vita sua*, the *via media* was based on three ideas: dogma, sacrament, and anti-Romanism. The first is directed against liberalism, the second against evangelicalism, and the third against the papacy. The *via media*, which was after all only a theoretical notion, was to die at Newman's own hands. He became increasingly convinced that his own arguments were working against him.

W. CORDUAN

See also NEWMAN, JOHN HENRY; OXFORD MOVEMENT.

Via Negativa. Approach to the knowledge of God that denies the strict applicability of any human concepts to God. Originating in the Neo-Platonic tradition, it became an important consideration in the Christian theology of the Middle Ages. A leading advocate of the *via negativa* was Dionysius the Pseudo-Areopagite. He summarized his views in his short work *The Mystical Theology*. Dionysius recognized a way of affirmation in which it is realized that God possesses all attributes as First Cause; he explained this notion in *On Divine Names*. This way of affirmation begins with God and sees all creaturely attributes as derived from him. But if we attempt to reverse this process and try to reapply those attributes to God, we find that he is beyond such predication, and all we have left is the darkness of skepticism concerning his attributes.

Aquinas and other later medieval scholars retained the idea of the *via negativa*, but only insofar as it reveals to us the uniqueness of God. Rather than leading to skepticism, they saw the remoteness of God as necessitating analogical predication.

W. CORDUAN

See also DIONYSIUS THE PSEUDO-AREOPAGITE; NEO-PLATONISM; *VIA ANALOGIA*.

Via Purgativa. See PURGATIVE WAY, THE.

Via Unitiva. See UNITIVE WAY, THE.

Vicar. See CHURCH OFFICERS.

Vicarious Atonement. See ATONEMENT.

Violence. Ruthless exercise of power, by actions involving physical force or unlawful intimidation, resulting in loss, injury, or constraint to the unprotected. Its condemnation as evil and retrograde is assumed to follow, alike from its irrationality and its injustice. But violence may also be both rational and just—in duly authorized, impartial, and controlled law enforcement, in restraint of unlawful violence such as rioting, and in benevolent constraint of the insane.

Violence has always been present in society, in law enforcement and in war, and may always be so until all humankind share identical intellectual convictions. Christian moralists will therefore distinguish the springs, grounds, and aims of violence before condemning all violent actions for reasons of academic superiority, cultural taste, or fear. Christians will sympathize with (but not approve) the violence that expresses personal frustration of the physically or mentally handicapped, but will still insist that for a rational and moral creature, violence will always be subnormal. For society, violence will ever breed insecurity, never arriving at truth, justice, or equilibrium, but always reproducing endless counterviolence.

Christian wisdom will condemn the exploitation of violence for entertainment, rejecting the claim that theater and literature may "reflect society" without incurring responsibility for portraying the intolerable as "normal," and so lowering social standards. Most of all, the Christian must condemn the manipulation, by the social and intellectual activist, of the frustrated and envious passion of the mob for selfish or political ends.

R. E. O. WHITE

Virgin Birth of Jesus. Matt. 1:18, 22–25 and Luke 1:26–38 teach that the birth of Jesus resulted from a miraculous conception. He was conceived in the womb of the Virgin Mary by the power of the Holy Spirit without male seed.

The NT Accounts. The two accounts in Matthew and Luke are generally thought to be independent of each other and thus to be based on a tradition antedating both. Confirming the antiquity of this tradition is the remarkably "Hebraic" character of both birth accounts: the theology and language of these chapters seem more characteristic of the OT than the NT, as many scholars have noted. This fact renders very unlikely the hypothesis that the virgin birth is a *theologoumenon*—a story invented by the early church to buttress its christological dogma. The writers draw no inference from the virgin birth concerning Jesus' deity or ontological sonship to God; rather, they simply record the event as a historical fact and (for Matthew) as a fulfillment of Isa. 7:14.

The Rest of Scripture. Much has been said concerning the "silence" of Scripture about the virgin birth outside of the passages mentioned. This silence is real, but it need not be explained by any ignorance or denial of the virgin birth by other NT writers. It is significant that even the Gospels of Matthew and Luke are "silent" about the virgin birth through 50 of their combined 52 chapters. The silence of the rest of the NT can be explained in essentially the same ways as one would explain the partial silence of Matthew and Luke. The main function of the virgin birth in the NT, to show the fulfillment of prophecy and to describe the events surrounding Jesus' birth, is appropriate only to birth narratives, and only two birth narratives have been preserved in the canon. We must also assume that the early church maintained a certain reserve about public discussion of these matters out of respect for the privacy of Jesus' family, especially Mary.

Is Isa. 7:14 a prediction of the virgin birth? Matt. 1:22 asserts that the virgin birth "fulfills" that passage, but much controversy has surrounded that assertion, turning on the meaning of the Isaiah passage in context, its LXX translation, and Matthew's use of both. E. J. Young has mounted one of the few recent scholarly defenses of the traditional position. For Matthew the concept of "fulfillment" sometimes takes on esthetic dimensions that go beyond the normal relation between "prediction" and "predicted event" (cf. his use of Zech. 9:9 in 21:1–4). For Matthew, the "fulfillment" may draw the attention of people to the prophecy in startling, even bizarre ways that the prophet himself might never have anticipated. It "corresponds" to the prophecy in unpredictable but exciting ways, as a variation in music corresponds to a theme. It may be that some element of this takes place in Matt. 1:23, though Young's argument may prevail in the long run.

Doctrinal Importance. The consistency of this doctrine with other Christian truth is important to its usefulness and, indeed, to its credibility. For Matthew and Luke the chief importance of the event seems to be that it calls to mind (as a "sign," Isa. 7:14) the great OT promises of salvation through supernaturally born deliverers, while going far beyond them, showing that God's *final* deliverance has come. But one can also go beyond the specific concerns of Matthew and Luke and see that the virgin birth is fully consistent with the whole range of biblical doctrine. For example, the virgin birth is important because of: (1) The doctrine of Scripture. If Scripture errs here, then why should we trust its claims about other supernatural events, such as the resurrection? (2) The deity of Christ. While we cannot say dogmatically that God could enter the world only through a virgin birth, surely the incarnation is a supernatural event if it is anything. To eliminate the supernatural from this event is inevitably to compromise the divine dimension of it. (3) The humanity of Christ. This was the important thing to Ignatius and the 2d-century fathers. Jesus was *really* born; he *really* became one of us. (4) The nature of grace. The birth of Christ, in which the initiative and power are all of God, is an apt picture of God's saving grace in general of which it is a part. It teaches us that salvation is by God's act, not our human effort. The birth of Jesus is like our new birth, which is also by the Holy Spirit; it is a new creation (2 Cor. 5:17).

Is belief in the virgin birth "necessary"? To reject the virgin birth is to reject God's Word, and disobedience is always serious. Further, disbelief in the virgin birth may lead to compromise in those other areas of doctrine with which it is vitally connected.

J. M. FRAME

See also CHRISTOLOGY; JESUS CHRIST.

Virgin, Assumption of the. See MARY, ASSUMPTION OF.

Virtue, Virtues. The classical pagan concept of virtue (*aretē*) and its achievement differs radically from the biblical view. For Plato there were four inherent virtues: wisdom, courage, temperance, and justice. Aristotle extended the number and taught that these were learned. Stoicism, common in NT times, concurred with the Platonic view. All omitted "benevolence," which is foundational in Christian morality. As classical learning entered the church, leaders like Ambrose of Milan adapted the Platonic view of virtue to the Christian system. During the Middle Ages the four "natural" virtues were combined with the "theological" virtues (faith, hope, and love) and were called the seven cardinal virtues. Christian theology universally insists that virtue comes from above and is not the product of human effort.

The biblical use of *aretē* gives the scope of the concept. It is variously translated virtue (Phil. 4:8; 2 Pet. 1:5, KJV), excellence (Phil. 4:8, RSV, NIV), wonderful deeds (1 Pet. 2:9, RSV), goodness (2 Pet. 1:3, 5, NIV). The NT gives several lists of qualities that can be called virtues (1 Cor. 13; Gal. 5:22–23; Phil. 4:8; Col. 3:12–16). These are more personal than a "household table" (Eph. 5:21–6:9) or a "community table" (1 Tim. 2:1–15; 5:1–21; 6:1–12). Jonathan Edwards in *Charity and Its Fruits* writes that "all virtue that is saving, and that distinguishes true Christians from others, is summed up in Christian love." Such virtue is practical and marked by inward sanctity and outward charity (Eph. 2:8–10).

W. N. KERR

Visible Church. See CHURCH, THE.

Vision of God, *Visio Dei*. See BEATIFIC VISION.

Vocation. (Lat. *voco*) God's calling to his people, both individually and corporately. In the OT God is seen as calling individuals to special tasks of obedience and leadership; Abraham, Moses, Samuel, David, and Jeremiah are differing examples of this activity. He also called Israel as a nation to enter into covenant with him at Sinai.

Jesus called people to follow him as disciples. For some this meant leaving all they had in order to join his band, while others were left to continue witnessing for him in their natural locality. The teaching of the NT epistles is consistent in maintaining that the Christian's call to follow Christ has a moral dimension. The Christian is to be like Jesus, to grow into his likeness (2 Cor. 3:18; 1 Pet. 1:16; 1 John 3:2–3). So Paul stresses that the Christian is called to be a saint (Rom. 1:7; 1 Cor. 1:2) and also partakes of a holy calling (2 Tim. 1:9). Christians are also encouraged to see their daily occupations, however menial, as God's vocation for them in this world. Finally, in the most restricted and technical sense, the word has been used to refer to God's call to the work of Christian ministry in its various aspects, including the "religious" life of the monk or nun.

D. H. WHEATON

See also CALL, CALLING.

Voluntarism. (Lat. *voluntas*, "will") General name for a variety of philosophical positions united in their emphasis on will. In contrast to the dominant rationalistic, intellectualist stream of Western thought reaching back to Plato and beyond, voluntarism boldly asserts the superiority or importance of the exercise of will to the deliberations of reason. Voluntarism is expressed in the work of David Hume, who argued that the conflict since Plato between reason and will was strictly impossible; reason is capable of selecting only means toward ends, not the ends themselves. Will alone by affirming them can choose ends, and reason is to be the "slave" of the will in helping to achieve those willed ends.

In theology and religious philosophy voluntarism is significant in several contexts. Some hold that we need not have rational grounds for religious belief, but may justifiably assert our wills to make a religious commitment, a view titled fideism. Such a doctrine in various forms has a long history in Christian thought, and finds expression in Pascal,

Kierkegaard, William James, and many contemporary evangelicals of a pietistic leaning.

Theological voluntarism with respect to ethics is generally called the "divine will" or "divine command" theory. This view is held by William of Ockham, Carl F. H. Henry, Emil Brunner, and many others, and was criticized as early as Plato's *Euthyphro*. Theological voluntarists argue that God's mere assertion of a command to do or refrain from doing an action or type of action renders these either right or wrong.

D. B. FLETCHER

Von Hügel, Friedrich (1852–1925). Roman Catholic philosopher and writer. Multilinguist and biblical and patristics scholar, he lamented his church's modern retreat from intellectual culture and rich mental training and its reluctance to wrestle with contemporary problems. He greatly admired Augustine, wrote a definitive study of Catherine of Genoa (1908), and often referred to the saintliness of the Middle Ages. This gifted layman was a leader of the modernist movement within his church, and to it gave generously of his money, learning, and advice. He ministered through correspondence with the highly placed, as his *Selected Letters* (1928) shows, and he is chiefly remembered as a wise counselor of souls.

J. D. DOUGLAS

See also CATHOLICISM, LIBERAL; TYRRELL, GEORGE.

Vow. Voluntary obligation or promise made to God. It is generally taken on condition of receiving special favors from God. Often during sickness or other kinds of affliction the vow is made to God. It is then to be carried out when the calamity is over or the desire is granted (Gen. 28:20–22; Num. 21:2; 1 Sam. 1:11; 2 Sam. 15:8). The conditions of the vow are the following: (1) a consciousness of entire dependence upon the will of God and of obligation of gratitude; (2) that it is something which in itself is lawful; (3) that it is something which is acceptable to God; (4) that it is something that tends to the spiritual edification of the one who makes the vow. Who may take such a vow? (1) The person assuming the vow must be competent, that is, having sufficient intelligence. A child or a person with an unbalanced mind may not take it. (2) The vow may be assumed only after due deliberation. Being an act of worship, it may not be taken rashly. (3) It must be voluntary and be taken cheerfully.

W. MASSELINK

Ww

Waldenses. A fervent evangelistic movement with uncertain roots but which is named for the group that began in the city of Lyons, France, in the decade 1170–80. A wealthy merchant, Peter Waldo, underwent a deeply personal religious experience. Following this, he gave away his property and adopted a life of strict gospel simplicity and poverty. Many men and women became his followers. These "Poor Men of Lyons" did not intend to challenge the authority of the church, but the hostility of first the local clergy and finally the papacy drove them into opposition. Their condemnation by the archbishop of Lyons in 1181 was formalized in 1184 when Pope Lucius III declared the movement heretical and called for its destruction. Thereafter, although they were subject to violent persecutions, the Waldenses developed quickly in Languedoc and the Piedmont. From here they spread throughout central and eastern Europe.

As most popular religious movements of the period, the Waldensian ethic was personal and anticlerical. In search of an authentic gospel ethic, they translated the NT, the prophets, and selections from the fathers into the vernacular. Ultimately the Waldenses declared themselves a counterchurch, the "true church," in opposition to the Roman Church, whose clergy and sacraments were renounced as invalid. Waldensians believed in the divinity of Jesus Christ and in salvation by Christ. They accepted that all true believers were entitled to preach, evangelize, and give the sacraments. They condemned prayers for the dead and indulgences. In spite of persecution by the revived and militant medieval papacy, they survived to stimulate the atmosphere in which the Protestant Reformation began. Many Waldensian beliefs entered the mainstream of the Protestant tradition.

C. T. MARSHALL

Waldo, Peter. See WALDENSES.

Walloon Confession. See BELGIC CONFESSION.

Walther, Carl Ferdinand Wilhelm (1811–1887). Lutheran clergyman and theologian. Born in Langenschursdorf in Saxony, where his father served as pastor, in 1838 Walther joined a group of approximately 700 Lutherans emigrating to the U.S. under Martin Stephan. Most settled in Perry County, Missouri. Stephan's fanaticism led to his expulsion from the community and Walther succeeded him as spiritual leader. With others Walther founded a log college in Dec. 1839, which was moved to St. Louis in 1850 and named Concordia Theological Seminary.

In 1841 Walther moved to St. Louis, where he served as pastor of the Trinity congregation and as professor of theology at Concordia Seminary. Walther also established Concordia Publishing House. In 1844 he founded a biweekly publication, *Der Lutheraner*, as the voice of a strict confessional Lutheranism. The publication became the rallying point for Lutherans of similar convictions and soon led to the organization of the German Evangelical Lutheran Synod of Missouri, Ohio, and Other States, familiarly known as the Missouri Synod. Walther served as its president from 1847 to 1850 and from 1864 to 1878. A prolific author, powerful preacher and debater, and masterful organizer and leader, Walther emerged as the most influential Lutheran clergyman of the 19th century.

R. L. TROUTMAN

See also LUTHERAN TRADITION, THE.

War. A struggle between rival groups, carried on by arms, which can be recognized as a legal conflict. By this definition riots or individual violence are not wars, but armed rebellion within a nation and violent struggles between nations are included.

Scriptural Background. Many OT statements support armed conflict, including Deut. 7 and 20 and Joshua, Judges, and Samuel. These passages have been cited to justify war, but others have cautioned that many laws given to ancient Israel are not meant to be applied to later times. In the teaching of Jesus the kingdom is no longer confined to a single state but exists in an international body, the Christian church.

The NT says little about war, but one can draw some principles about conflict. In the Sermon on the Mount, Jesus encouraged his followers to live in a nonviolent manner (Matt. 5:39, 44). Yet Jesus seemed to accept war as part of the world system (Matt. 24:6), and followers who were soldiers were not condemned (Acts 10). The first disciples included Zealots, although Jesus tried to channel their energies into nonpolitical tasks. Individual soldiers were recognized as heroes of faith (Heb. 11:32), but Jesus explained that the cause of God was not to be advanced through physical force (John 18:36) and he criticized Peter for violently defending him at his arrest (Matt. 26:52–54).

The Just War. Roman society was Christianized during the 4th and 5th centuries, making the pacifist position difficult to maintain. Earlier believers had benefited from Rome but had largely ignored imperial claims upon them. As long as the church was a minority, its attitudes could be overlooked; but when believers became numerous, pressure increased for them to serve in the army. Augustine expressed a new attitude toward conflict by formulating the just war theory. He adapted rules of warfare developed by classical thinkers such as Plato and Cicero to the Christian position. War, he taught, should be fought to secure justice and reestablish peace. It must be conducted by the ruler and characterized by an attitude of love for the enemy. Promises to the opposition should be honored and the lives and property of noncombatants respected. Those engaged in God's service, including monks and priests, were not to take part. Augustine's argument for war was still influenced by the nonviolent approach of the early church. There is a mood of gloom and resignation in much of his teaching regarding the state and its coercive powers.

The Crusade and Medieval Christianity. In the 11th century the pacifism of the early church changed to the glorification of the fighting knight. A reason was evangelization of Germanic peoples, who retained their martial spirit. The Crusades were the most obvious example of the merger between violence and holiness in the medieval church. The liturgy was expanded to include the blessing of battle standards and weapons. Knights were consecrated in sacral fashion through ceremonies based on old pagan customs. New religious orders such as the Templars were founded to fight the enemies of God. Western peoples came to look upon all who professed another faith as enemies of God who should be destroyed or converted. It was wrong to show mercy, and the code of the just war could be suspended when fighting them. A favorite Crusader text was "Cursed is he who keeps back his sword from bloodshed" (Jer. 48:10).

Renaissance and Reformation Developments. The technological and political changes of 15th- and 16th-century Europe forced many Christians to reconsider their attitudes toward war. The major technological change was the development of cannons able to destroy medieval fortresses. When adapted for field use, artillery made the knight obsolete. Christian humanists such as Thomas More and Desiderus Erasmus condemned the new violence. Erasmus reminded his readers that once wars are accepted as just, they tend to become glorious. The humanists accused the church of missing the true meaning of Scripture becoming instead the obedient servant of the ambitious and the bloodthirsty. Early Reformers (Martin Luther, Ulrich Zwingli, and John Calvin) did not add their voices to this protest, however. When religious fanaticism was added to the new munitions, the religious wars following the Reformation were some of Europe's most violent. Only the Anabaptists practiced nonresistance. They advocated a literal return to the Sermon on the Mount and an imitation of the peacefulness of Christ.

Total War and the Modern World. Christians in the 19th century responded to new armaments by encouraging international cooperation and humanitarian endeavors. Despite a strong current of nationalism these attempts led to international gatherings, including the Hague Conferences of 1899 and 1907, which produced recommendations protecting the rights of prisoners of war, insisting on care for the sick and wounded, ensuring the rights of neutrals, and attempting to generally limit the cruelty of war. The attitude of Christians toward World War II was closer to the just war theory. The struggle differed from the World War I because it was a clash between antagonistic social and political systems. The bizarre biological racism of fascism led many former Christian pacifists, including Reinhold Niebuhr, to urge participation in the conflict. New technology produced weapons that made war more destructive than ever before. The atomic bomb seemed to represent the ultimate in destructive capability. When the war ended, the rivalry between the U.S. and the Soviet Union continued to threaten world peace. The United Nations has tried to keep peace, but the arms race has become a fact of life and the production of weapons woven into the texture of modern technological society. The situation is made even more difficult because of a decline in Christian influence.

Christian Responses to War. It is difficult to formulate one Christian position on war. The early church, certain Christian humanists, and most Anabaptists have taken a nonresistant or pacifist stance. Most, however, followed Augustine's limited justification for certain wars. One of the more interesting developments in recent times is the effect the threat of global conflagration is having on Christian attitudes. Leaders have come to realize that the use of nuclear bombs makes a mockery of the just war position because noncombatants are inevitably slaughtered. These "nuclear pacifists" say the nature of current weapons invalidates war as a rational policy.

R. G. CLOUSE

See also PACIFISM.

Warfield, Benjamin Breckinridge (1851–1921). American Calvinist theologian. Warfield was the last of the great conservative theologians in the chair of theology at Princeton Seminary. As professor of didactic and polemic theology, Warfield wrote a vast number of articles, reviews, and monographs for the popular press and learned journals. His scholarship was precise, wide-ranging, and well grounded in scientific literature. He was one of the great academic theologians at the turn of the century. Like his Princeton predecessors, Archibald Alexander and Charles and A. A. Hodge, Warfield was a strict Calvinist. He wrote numerous studies on Calvin, Augustinian theology, and the Westminster Confession, both to illuminate and to defend the theological history. Warfield is best remembered for his painstaking efforts to defend the inerrancy of the Bible. In 1881 with A. A. Hodge he wrote a famous essay, "Inspiration," which reasserted traditional Protestant belief in the full infallibility and truthfulness of Scripture. In countless essays and reviews thereafter Warfield labored to clarify the Bible's testimony to its inspiration and to oppose those who detracted from Scripture's authority. This work on the Bible has made Warfield an important guide for all modern conservative evangelicals.

M. A. NOLL

See also HODGE, ARCHIBALD ALEXANDER; HODGE, CHARLES; PRINCETON THEOLOGY, OLD.

Washing of Feet. See FOOT WASHING.

Watson, Richard (1781–1833). English Wesleyan theologian. In his commitment to Wesleyan orthodoxy and the Arminian position he continually defended the proposition: "Our Lord Jesus Christ did so die for all men, as to make salvation attainable by all men." A major argument in his *Theological Institutes* (1823) was that Christ died for all, that his death was for those who obtain salvation as well as for those who reject Christ and thereby fail to obtain salvation. Watson's *Institutes* was the first systematic treatment of the theological motifs of Wesley's thought and became the required core text in the Course of Study School in both the Methodist Episcopal Church and the Methodist Episcopal Church, South, from the 1870s until about 1900. Watson's theological orthodoxy and social activism in opposing slavery influenced both British and American Wesleyan thought.

P. A. MICKEY

See also WESLEYAN TRADITION, THE; METHODISM; ARMINIANISM.

Watson, Thomas (d. ca. 1686). Puritan minister and writer. Educated at Emmanuel College, Cambridge, he became rector of St. Stephen's, Walbrook, London, in 1646, where he combined learning with popular preaching. He was ejected from St. Stephen's as a nonconformist under the 1662 Act of Uniformity. For several years he ministered secretly until the easing of repressive legislation permitted Nonconformists to conduct public worship in their own meeting places, in one of which Watson was for a time copastor with Stephen Charnock. A prolific writer, he is remembered chiefly for his *Body of Practical Divinity*, published posthumously in 1692.

J. D. DOUGLAS

See also UNIFORMITY, ACTS OF.

Watts, Isaac (1674–1748). English hymn writer. Born in Southampton and educated at the famous nonconformist academy in Stoke Newington, he ministered in a London church (1699–1712), during which time he wrote *Horae Lyricae* (1706), a book of religious poetry that ensured his inclusion in *Johnson's Lives of the Poets*. His hymns first appeared in *Hymns and Spiritual Songs* (1707) and ran through numerous editions in his lifetime. He was a pioneer in writing for the young. His *Divine Songs Attempted in Easy Language for the Use of Children* (1715) aimed to be "a constant furniture for the minds of children, that . . . may sometimes give their thoughts a divine turn, and raise a young meditation." In *The Psalms of David Imitated in the New Testament* (1719) he aimed to make David a Christian. This work included "Our God, Our Help in Ages Past" (from Ps. 90), still used on great national occasions, and "Jesus Shall Reign" (Ps. 72). "When I Survey the Wondrous Cross" was called by Matthew Arnold the finest hymn in the English language. Though Edinburgh University gave him an honorary D.D. (1728), Watts was an uneasy Calvinist, unhappy with the doctrines of total depravity and reprobation.

J. D. Douglas

Wave Offering. See Offerings and Sacrifices in Bible Times.

Way, Follower of the. See Christians, Names of.

Wealth, Christian View of. Individual wealth signifies well-being resulting from outward rather than inward causes. Adam Smith used the word to signify material well-being produced and consumed in the community. Whether pertaining to an individual or a community, wealth involves an evaluation of things according to priorities.

Individual Wealth. For the Christian, wealth is not the greatest good, but it can be a good if used for godly service. God entrusts his wealth to individuals and institutions; as compassionate stewards of God's property we are fully responsible to him for the proper administration of his wealth. At the same time we are the legitimate owners during the period of stewardship. Complete economic self-sufficiency is difficult, if not impossible, because of the curse of the ground. This forces us to cooperate with others to increase our own wealth, demonstrating interdependence. How we manage our cooperation with others determines the value of our wealth. Wealth can be enjoyed for the prospect of family continuity it offers, the status it provides, and the opportunity for the exercise of power.

One's worldview affects individual attitudes toward wealth and its accumulation. When the highest purpose is seen as attaining spiritual union with God, wealth may be regarded with disdain. The accumulation of wealth beyond the minimum to keep an ascetic alive may subvert the individual's spiritual union with God. Because the desire for wealth and the things wealth allows can defile the spirit, the struggle of life is to mortify any desire for wealth and to escape its entanglements. This antagonism between spirit and wealth is unnecessary, however, and may ultimately be understood as anti-Christian.

When the Christian begins with the fact of God's creation, which is described as good, all the earth becomes a setting of beauty, goodness, and love of a holy God. The worlds of spirit and wealth flow together in oneness. Through Jesus Christ all wealth is clean, and both spirit and wealth are to be respected. The Christian way of unity is for people to be fulfilled and expressed through material wealth in an abundant life. In the biblical view the Spirit of God naturally flows through everything the Christian is and does, and the Christian is a blessing purely because he or she is. The Christian works as unto the Lord, realizing that nothing is secular.

The view that God is active in wealth and present in the whole of creation removes any sense of guilt associated with accumulating and using wealth. It is in the use of wealth that we learn to choose between the wrong passions of the flesh and the pure passions of the spirit through which we grow to be fully human. John Wesley advised Christians to "Make as much as you can; save as much as you can; give as much as you can." The Christian view frees the pursuit of wealth and permits us to bring a greater sense of well-being to the hungry as part of bringing the kingdom of God to reality on earth.

The benefits a wealthy person derives depend on what forms of wealth are most valued—individual priorities. Different benefits accrue, depending upon whether a person stresses wealth in the form of (1) money, (2) securities, (3) equities, (4) physical nonhuman goods, or (5) human capital.

Community Wealth. Under the free enterprise system the variety of products and services available to the public increases constantly as a result of scientific discovery, experimentation, and risk taking. The possibility of accumulating wealth stimulates individuals to develop products and produce more efficiently, while competition stimulates management to improve production. Workers are free to select their occupations and offer their services to whomever they wish; businesses are free to choose their products, workers, manufacturing techniques, and locations. Consumers who are free to buy determine what and how much will be produced. Businessmen must respond to this competition or fail. While no nation has ever had wholly unrestricted free enterprise, the most rapid economic progress has occurred in nations which have given it the most latitude.

Unfortunately, the wealth accumulated in England and the U.S. under this freedom was not used compassionately. The greater flow of goods was accompanied by increasing exploitation of women and children, the rise of slums, and a growing inequality. Our ability to produce enough to meet the basic needs of all did not lead to shared well-being. It was not that the majority of people were worse off but that the dignity of many suffered. New economic problems such as unemployment and depressions arose. Individual efforts of charity did not suffice. Churches were silent about the Bible's emphasis on a compassionate use of wealth.

If the church had been faithful through the Industrial Revolution, it might not have lost so many workers and intellectuals. If it had spoken clearly against the uninhibited use of wealth, the "survival of the fittest" concept might not have taken over. Pessimism in the face of abuses and mistrust of businessmen have led to the growth of government corporations and regulation. In the past 50 years government regulation has opened a new set of problems, limiting the freedom spawned by the Reformation and retarding economic growth.

Conclusion. Because God made the world and everything in it, wealth as a part of God's creation is not inherently evil and therefore to be refused. In the Bible it is often depicted as a blessing from God and a sign of his favor. However, because this is a fallen world, wealth also partakes of our fallenness. If it is used to exploit, dominate, or persecute, it becomes a great evil. Covetousness is equivalent to idolatry (Col. 3:5), and the love of money is the root of all evil (1 Tim. 6:10). Thus the Bible admonishes us not to become anxious over our possessions, exhausting ourselves to pile up treasures on earth where moth and rust corrupt. Our heavenly Father knows we have needs, and whether we abound or suffer want, we should be content with what his kind hand has provided (Phil. 4:11–13).

D. K. Adie

Wesley, John (1703–1791). An 18th-century evangelical revival leader and founder of Methodism. Wesley was one of 19 children born in Epworth, England, to Samuel and Susanna Wesley. He spent his early years under the direction of his remarkable mother, who sought to instill a sense of vital piety leading to a wholehearted devotion to God.

Life. Wesley was educated at Christ Church, Oxford. Although a serious student in both logic and religion, Wesley was not to experience his "religious" conversion until 1725. He was then confronted with what to do with the rest of his life. Through the influence of his mother, a religious friend, and the reading of Jeremy Taylor and Thomas à Kempis, he was inspired to make religion the "business of his life." He was ordained and became leader of a small band of students organized by his younger brother, Charles. This band, dubbed the "Holy Club," would later be called "Methodist" for their prescribed method of studying the Bible and for their rigid self-denial which included many works of charity. During this period (1729–35) both John and Charles fell under the influence of the nonjuror and mystic William Law.

In 1735 Wesley went to Georgia as a missionary to the Indians. After a disastrous experience, he returned to England (1738) and met the Moravian Peter Böhler, who exhorted him to trust Christ alone for salvation. What had earlier been merely a religious conversion now became an "evangelical" conversion. At a Moravian band meeting on Aldersgate Street (May 24, 1738), as he listened to a reading from Luther's preface to his commentary on Romans, Wesley felt his "heart strangely warmed." With George Whitefield, a former member of the Holy Club, he began preaching salvation by faith. This "new doctrine" was considered redundant by the sacramentalists in the established church, who thought people sufficiently saved by virtue of their infant baptism. The established churches soon closed their doors to their preaching. The Methodists (a name which carried over from their Oxford days) began preaching in the open air.

In 1739 Wesley followed Whitefield to Bristol, where a revival broke out among the miners of Kingswood. At that point Wesley's true genius surfaced through his ability to organize new converts into Methodist "societies" and "bands" which sustained both them and the revival. The revival continued under Wesley's leadership for over 50 years. He traveled 250,000 miles throughout England, Scotland, Wales, and Ireland, preaching 40,000 sermons. His influence also extended to America as he (after considerable reluctance) ordained several of his preachers for the work there, which was officially organized in 1784. Wesley literally established "the world as his parish" in order to spread "scripture holiness throughout the land." He remained fearlessly loyal to the established church all his life. Methodism in England did not become a separate denomination until after his death.

Theology. Although Wesley was not a systematic theologian, his theology can be described with reasonable clarity from the study of his published sermons, tracts, treatises, and correspondence. In essence, Wesley's theology affirms God's sovereign will to reverse our "sinful, devilish nature," by the work of his Holy Spirit, a process he called *prevenient, justifying,* and *sanctifying* grace (grace being nearly synonymous with the work of the Holy Spirit).

Sanctifying grace described the work of the Holy Spirit in the lives of believers between conversion and death. Faith in Christ saves us *from* hell and sin *for* heaven and good works. Imputed righteousness, according to Wesley, entitles one to heaven; imparted righteousness qualifies one for heaven. It is here that Wesley goes to great lengths to describe his views on Christian perfection.

The process of sanctification or perfection culminates in an experience of "pure love" as one progresses to the place where love becomes devoid of self-interest. This second work of grace is described as the one purpose of all religion. If one is not perfected in love, one is not "ripe for glory." It is important, however, to note that this perfection was not static but dynamic, always improvable. Neither was it angelic or Adamic. Adam's perfection was objective and absolute, while Wesley's perfection was subjective and relative, involving, for the most part, intention and motive.

Generally speaking, Wesley was a practical theologian. In a very practical way his theology was geared primarily to his own needs and to the needs of those given into his care.

R. G. TUTTLE, JR.

See also ARMINIANISM; METHODISM; WESLEYAN TRADITION, THE; WHITEFIELD, GEORGE; REVIVALISM.

Wesleyan Tradition, The. In the broad sense of the term, the Wesleyan tradition identifies the theological impetus for many movements and denominations with roots to John Wesley. This primarily means the various Methodist denominations (Wesleyan Methodist, Free Methodist, African Methodist Episcopal, African Methodist Episcopal Zion, Christian Methodist Episcopal, and United Methodist). The tradition has been a catalyst for other movements and denominations as well—for example, Charles Finney and the Holiness movement; Charles Parham and the Pentecostal movement; Phineas Bresee and the Church of the Nazarene.

Wesleyan Distinctives. The Wesleyan tradition seeks to establish justification by faith as the gateway to sanctification or "scriptural holiness." Humans were created in the image of God's own eternity. They were upright and perfect. They dwelt in God and God dwelt in them. God required full and perfect obedience, and they were (unfallen) equal to the task. When they disobeyed their righteousness was lost. We, as their seed, inherited a corruptible and mortal nature. We became dead in spirit, in sin, and to God, so that in our natural state we hasten on to death everlasting. God, however, was not to be undone. While we were yet sinners Christ died for the ungodly. The ungodly, therefore, are justified by faith in the full, perfect, and sufficient sacrifice. This is not the end, but the beginning. Ultimately for the true Wesleyan, salvation is completed by our return to original righteousness by the work of the Holy Spirit. Although we are justified by faith alone, we are sanctified by the Holy Spirit.

The Wesleyan tradition stresses that Jesus came to fulfill, not destroy, the law. God made us in his perfect image, and he wants to return us to a full and perfect obedience through sanctification. As we continually yield to the Spirit's impulse, he roots out what would separate us from God, from ourselves, and from those around us. Christians are not justified *by* good works but *for* good works. Good works are the inevitable fruit of justification. Wesley insisted that Methodists who did not fulfill all righteousness deserved the hottest place in the lake of fire. Being restored to original righteousness became the hallmark of the Wesleyan tradition.

Wesleyanism. The Wesleyan tradition's defense normally rests on four basic proofs: Scripture, reason, tradition, and experience. While only a construct of Wesley's theology, the following principles can be identified:

Scripture. Scripture is the first authority and the measure whereby all other truth is tested. It was delivered by men divinely inspired. It is a rule sufficient of itself. It neither needs, nor is capable of, addition.

Reason. Although Scripture is sufficient and is the foundation of true religion, without reason we cannot understand the essential truths of Scripture. Reason must be assisted by the Holy Spirit if we are to understand the mysteries of sanctification.

Tradition. Although other evidence is perhaps stronger, Wesley insists: "Do not undervalue traditional evidence. Let it have its place and its due honour. It is highly serviceable in its kind, and in its degree" (*Works*, 10.75). For Wesley tradition supplies a chain linking Christians today to the apostles.

Experience. Apart from Scripture, experience is the strongest proof of Christianity. Wesley states that Christianity is an experience of holiness and happiness, the image of God impressed on a created spirit. We cannot have reasonable assurance of something unless we have experienced it.

R. G. TUTTLE, JR.

See also ARMINIANISM; HOLINESS MOVEMENT, AMERICAN; METHODISM; SANCTIFICATION; WESLEY, JOHN.

Westcott, Brooke Foss (1825–1901). English NT scholar. Westcott did some of the 19th century's great NT work after 1870 as Regius Professor of Divinity at Cambridge. With F. J. A. Hort he worked in textual criticism, publishing the Westcott–Hort edition of the Greek testament, and he produced commentaries on the Gospel of John, the Epistles of John, and the Epistle to the Hebrews. His approach was conservative and spiritual. He was also deeply involved in social issues and was the first president of the Christian Social Union. Abhorring the raw brutalities of unfettered capitalism, he found his answer in an organic view of society based on an incarnational model similar to that of F. D. Maurice. After two decades at Cambridge, Westcott succeeded J. B. Lightfoot as bishop of Durham in 1890. His social consciousness, intelligence, scholarship, and spirituality made him a force in England's industrial northeast.

I. S. RENNIE

See also SOCIALISM, CHRISTIAN.

Westminster Catechisms. The Westminster Confession of Faith and Larger and Shorter catechisms are standards of doctrine subordinate to Scripture, within the Reformed tradition. After the Westminster Assembly completed its confession, a consensus developed that two catechisms would be needed, "one more exact and comprehensive, another more easie and short for new beginners." The Larger was intended for pulpit exposition, while the Shorter was intended for the instruction of children. The Shorter was completed in 1647 and the Larger in 1648. The Larger has, to a considerable extent, fallen into disuse, while the Shorter remains greatly used and loved among churches holding fast to Reformed doctrines. The theology of the catechisms is the same as that of the confession.

J. M. FRAME

See also WESTMINSTER CONFESSION OF FAITH; CATECHISMS.

Westminster Confession of Faith (1647). The Westminster Assembly (so called because of its meeting place) was summoned by the English Parliament in 1643 to advise Parliament in restructuring the Church of England along Puritan lines. Its historical context was the English civil war. To the assembly were invited 121 ministers (the "divines"), 10 members of the House of Lords, 20 of Commons, plus 8 nonvoting (but influential) representatives from the Church of Scotland, which was allied to the English Parliament by treaty, the "Solemn League and Covenant." Different views of church government were represented, presbyterianism being dominant. In theology, however, there was virtual unanimity in favor of a strong Calvinistic position, unequivocally rejecting what the assembly saw as the errors of Arminianism, Roman Catholicism, and sectarianism. The assembly's Confession of Faith, completed in Dec. 1646, is the last of the classic Reformed confessions and by far the most influential in the English-speaking world. Though it governed the Church of England only briefly, it has been widely adopted (sometimes with amendments) by

British and American Presbyterians, and by many Congregational and Baptist churches. It is known for its thoroughness, precision, conciseness, and balance.

J. M. FRAME

See also CONFESSIONS OF FAITH; WESTMINSTER CATECHISMS.

White, Ellen Gould (1827–1915). Seventh-day Adventist leader. Reared a Methodist, she became an Adventist follower of William Miller in 1843 and a "sabbathkeeper" in 1846, soon after her marriage to James White. The Seventh-day Adventist Church as an official denomination was established at Battle Creek, Michigan, in 1863, with Ellen as leader and her writings and counsels accepted as the "spirit of prophecy" (Rev. 19:10). Before her death she was said to have experienced "two thousand visions and prophetic dreams." Her early followers regarded these visions as partially fulfilling Joel 2:28–32. Among her publications are the nine-volume *Testimonies for the Church* (1855–1909) and *Steps to Christ*, which has sold more than 20 million copies in more than 100 languages. Having lectured throughout America, Mrs. White took Seventh-day Adventism to Europe (1885–87) and Australia (1891–1900).

J. D. DOUGLAS

See also ADVENTISM.

Whitefield, George (1714–1770). English 18th-century evangelist. Whitefield is regarded as one of the greatest itinerant preachers in the history of Protestantism. An ordained minister of the Church of England, he cooperated with John and Charles Wesley in establishing "Holy Club" at Oxford in the 1720s, a group of young men dedicated to seriousness in religion and a methodical approach to Christian duty. Whitefield showed the way to the Wesleys in preaching out of doors and in traveling wherever he could to air the message of salvation. He visited Georgia briefly in 1738 to aid in the founding of an orphanage. When he returned to the colonies in 1739, his reputation as a dramatic preacher went before him. His visit became a sensation, especially during a preaching tour of New England during the fall of 1740 when Whitefield addressed crowds of up to 8000 people nearly every day for over a month. This tour, one of the most remarkable episodes in the history of American Christianity, was the key event in New England's Great Awakening. Whitefield returned often to the American colonies, where in 1770 he died as he had wished, in the midst of yet another preaching tour. Whitefield was a decided, if unscholarly, Calvinist. In his one visit to Northampton, Massachusetts, in 1740 he moved Jonathan Edwards to tears by the emotional and evangelistic power of his Calvinistic message. The 15,000 times that he preached in a ministry of 33 years remain his most enduring monument.

M. A. NOLL

See also AWAKENINGS, THE GREAT; REVIVALISM.

Whitehead, Alfred North. See PROCESS THEOLOGY.

Whitsunday. See PENTECOST.

Wicked, Wickedness. Sinfulness, want of conformity to God's law as a God-dishonoring state. "Wicked" (wickedness) is the rendering of more than a dozen Heb. and of five Gk. words. In Hebrew, it most frequently renders *rāšāʿ* (252 times). Wicked apparently always involves a moral state, unlike *raʿ* (usually rendered by "evil"), which may describe misfortunes and distresses resulting from sin as well as sin itself. Wicked is contrasted with "righteous" (*ṣaddîq*), especially in Proverbs (for example, 12:5; 13:5; 29:2) and in Ps. 37. Wickedness is an active, destructive principle (Prov. 21:10; 29:16). This active opposition to God and his people causes suffering and distress (Ps. 10). But it is vain; the wicked shall perish in his wickedness (Ps. 9:16). "Wicked" is used less frequently in the NT, where it usually renders the strong word *ponēros* (for example, Matt. 13:19, 38, 49).

O. T. ALLIS

See also EVIL; SIN.

Will. (*'ābâ*, inclination; *rāsôn*, *hāpēs*, good pleasure; Gk. *thelō*, *boulomai*) The Scriptures manifest greater interest in the will of God than in the will of man. The latter is not treated in analytic fashion any more than are heart or other psychological terms. In the NT the chief verbs mean to wish or to will. The noun *thelēma* is used mainly of God. Decision or plan is the force of the rarely used *boulē* (Acts 5:38). To will in the sense of coming to a decision is sometimes expressed by *krinō* (1 Cor. 5:3). Among the more striking passages in which *thelēma* is used of man are Eph. 2:3, where the word has the force of desire, and 2 Pet. 1:21, where it denotes an act of the will. Of supreme import is Luke 22:42, the Gethsemane declaration of Jesus' submission to the will of the Father. Here is the pattern for the capitulation of the will of the believer to God.

E. F. HARRISON

See also FREE WILL, AND DETERMINISM; FREEDOM; MAN, DOCTRINE OF; WILL OF GOD.

William of Ockham (ca. 1280–1349). Medieval English theologian, born in Ockham, Surrey. Ockham's first major work was his commentary on the *Sentences* of Peter Abelard. It created a sensation at Oxford. The chancellor of the university, John Lutterell, remanded selections from the commentary to the papacy at Avignon. There Ockham's ideas were censured, and he was summoned to explain his views in person. While at Avignon, he continued to write. Of special importance were his *Summa logicae* and *De sacramento altaris*. Ockham insisted that faith and reason could never be reconciled, that reason could construct universals with regard to nature alone. Nothing about God, faith, or doctrine could be known in this way. Knowledge of God came by way of revelation and intimate personal experience. His ideas stimulated the growth of mysticism and fed the spiritual environment in which the Reformation occurred. Ockham was reconciled to the Roman Church before his death.

C. T. MARSHALL

See also NOMINALISM.

Will of God. (Heb. *'ābâ*, *rāsôn*, *hāpēs*; Gk. *thelō/thelēma*, *boulomai/boulē*, and *eudokia)* To will, desire, favor, enjoy, have pleasure, counsel. In Eph. 1:5, 9, 11 all three major Gk. words are used. Paul often attributes his calling as an apostle to the will of God (1 Cor.1:1; 2 Cor. 1:1; Eph. 1:1; Col. 1:1; 2 Tim. 1:1), and the expression is used elsewhere to teach that God's will as the final ground of all things. Most allusions to the divine will refer to God's redemptive purpose, but in some God's will is seen as the ultimate cause of the entire created world (for example, Rev. 4:11).

It is necessary to make distinctions within the will of God. God's will may be said to be both necessary and free. It is necessary with respect to himself; it is free in relation to creation. God's necessary will means that he cannot deny himself but must act consistently with his own nature. There are some things which he wills necessarily, some things he cannot do (2 Tim. 2:13; Heb. 6:18; James 1:13; 1 Sam. 15:29; Num. 23:19). Herman Bavinck observes: "God's will is identical with his being, his wisdom, his goodness, and with all his attributes. And it is for this reason that man's heart and mind can rest in that will, for it is the will not of blind fate, incalculable fortune, or dark energy of nature, but of an omnipotent God and merciful Father" (*The Doctrine of God*, 235).

God's will is free with respect to creation. He did not have to make the world; to deny this is to slip into pantheism. Creation, preservation, and salvation are free acts of God. The will of God is also distinguished as decretive and preceptive, or hidden and revealed. God's decretive, or hidden, will, sometimes called his secret will, is that by which he has determined what he will do; it is known to him alone. His preceptive, or revealed, will is that attribute by which he tells us what to do. The latter is revealed in Scripture; thus the law of God is correctly said to be an expression of God's holy will. Deut. 29:29 refers to this distinction within the will of God; Ps. 115:3; Dan. 4:17, 25, 32, 35; Rom. 9:18–19; 11:33–34; Eph. 1:5, 9, 11 refer to his secret will; and Matt. 7:21; 12:50; John 4:34; 7:17; Rom. 12:2; 10:8; Deut. 30:14 refer to his revealed will.

Much is obscure about God's will; Scripture affirms that no one can plumb the depths of the counsel of God (Job 9:10; 38; Rom. 11:33). The importance of doing God's will and the detailed exposition of his preceptive will, though, are crystal clear. God's children are called to obedience. Faith, by which one is accepted of God (Heb. 11:6; Rom. 3:24–28; Gal. 2:16), means trusting in God's promise of salvation in Christ and obedience. That which is to be obeyed is the will of God expressed in his law. The law is set forth in a variety of forms in the Ten Commandments; Beatitudes and other teachings of Jesus; summaries given by Christ (for example, Mark 12:30–31), Paul (for example, Rom. 13:8–10), and John (1 John 4:7–21).

M. E. OSTERHAVEN

Wisdom, Gift of. See SPIRITUAL GIFTS.

Witness, Witnessing. Properly, a "witness" (Gk. *martys*) is "one who testifies" (*martyreō*) by act or word his "testimony" (*martyrion*) to the truth. This act of testifying is called his "testimony" (*martyria*). In ancient days, as at the present, this was a legal term designating the testimony given for or against one on trial before a court of law. In Christian usage the term came to mean the testimony given by Christian witnesses to Christ and his saving power (Luke 24:48; Acts 1:8; 2:4; 10:39–43; 2 Tim. 2:2). Because such testimony often means arrest and scourging (see Matt. 10:18; Mark 13:9), exile (Rev. 1:9), or death (see Acts 22:20; Rev. 2:13; 17:6) the Greek was transliterated to form the English word "martyr," meaning one who suffers or dies rather than relinquish witness.

F. L. FISHER

Witness of the Holy Spirit. See INTERNAL TESTIMONY OF THE HOLY SPIRIT.

Wittenberg, Concord of (1536). An agreement on the doctrine of the Lord's Supper between Saxon Lutherans and southern German Protestants. Articles of the concord declared: (1) That the Eucharist has both an earthly and a heavenly reality; thus Christ's body and blood are "truly and substantially present and presented and received" with the bread and wine. (2) That, while no transubstantiation takes place, "by the sacramental union the bread is the body of Christ . . . present and truly presented." (3) That the sacrament is "efficacious in the Church" and independent of the worthiness of minister or recipient. This achieved a substantial measure of agreement; the only point unsettled was that of ubiquity. It was this which prevented the Swiss Protestants from accepting the concord.

J. D. DOUGLAS

See also BUCER, MARTIN.

Woman, Biblical Concept of. The place of women in the family, in society, and in the church has been the object of much attention. Scripture provides a wholesome contrast with the oppressive attitude and practice which prevailed in biblical times in the nations surrounding the Jews and which often yet prevail.

The Creation of Woman. The supreme dignity of human beings is expressed in the concept that they are created "in the image of God." This is immediately related to male and female (Gen. 1:27). The creation of Eve accompanies the institution of monogamous marriage. The unity between husband and wife as "one flesh" is asserted in Gen. 2:24 and referred to in the NT (Matt. 19:5; Mark 10:8; 1 Cor. 6:16; Eph. 5:31; see Luke 16:18). This unity is the fundamental bond of society.

The rift which opened up at the fall has poisoned even the beneficial institution of marriage. In the punishment meted out to Eve is the statement, "Your desire will be for your husband and he will rule over you" (Gen. 3:16). This was a divine description of what would occur, not a mandate. Subordination is not enjoined, any more than it is mandated that women should suffer a maximum of pain in childbearing, or men a maximum of toil in earning their living. God provided means to alleviate the effects of the curse, and those who wish to carry out his will can and should counteract evil. Also, the promise of the redeemer through a descendant of Eve precedes the statement of the curse incurred by women (Gen. 3:15).

The Mosaic Economy and Onward. The Mosaic economy recognized the dignity of women, the significance of motherhood and the importance of their welfare and security of women, a great advance over the surrounding civilizations. Mothers are frequently recognized along with fathers, for example in the fifth commandment (Exod. 20:12) and Proverbs (1:8; 6:20; 10:1). Women are protected in slavery (Deut. 21:10–14) and widowhood (Exod. 22:22; Deut. 14:29; 24:17, 19; 27:19). Sins against women are seriously dealt with (for example, Lev. 20:10; Deut. 22:20–24).

OT women occupied such positions as prophetess (Miriam in Exod. 15:20 and Num. 12:2, Deborah in Judg. 4:4, Huldah in 2 Chron. 34:22); judge (Deborah shared with Barak this office, Judg. 4–5); and queen (Athaliah in 2 Kings 11, Esther). OT society was patriarchal, and the word "father" is used in OT Scripture about five times as often as the word "mother." God is represented as a male; to do otherwise would have undoubtedly severely curtailed the understanding of his majesty. The licentious developments in religions where female deities are found would manifest the appropriateness of avoiding this representation. Outside the canon the Jewish attitude toward women was severely discriminatory. Quotations are often cited from Jewish writings that show contempt. While this may at times be exaggerated, there is a tendency to demean women.

Jesus and Women. The birth and infancy narratives feature a remarkable number of women. From the start the record stresses a place for women well beyond what was ordinary in Jewish life. Jesus spoke to women (as in the conversation with the Samaritan woman in John 4), taught women (as at the home of Martha and Mary in Luke 10:38–42), and accepted women as followers (Luke 8:2–3) in spite of objections that might arise. His teaching featured women as central figures in some parables (Matt. 13:33; 25:1–13; Luke 15:8–10; 18:1–5). He pointed to the place of women in the descriptions of the times of the end (Matt. 24:19, 41); he observed the significance of the widow's mite (Luke 21:1–4). Jesus safeguarded the rights of women in his instructions on marriage and divorce (Matt. 5:27–32; 19:3–9). After the resurrection our Lord first appeared to women and made them the bearers of the good news even to the apostles (Matt. 28:8–10; John 20:14–16).

Women in the Early Church. The attitude of Jesus is reflected at many levels in the early church. Mary the mother of Jesus is listed among those who worshiped in the upper room (Acts 1:14). Baptism—the sign and seal of the covenant of grace—is administered to women as well as to men (Acts 8:12; 16:15). Women were prophets (Acts 2:18; 21:9; 1 Cor. 11:5). Widows were recognized in the church, almost to the point of having a special office (1 Tim. 5:3–16). Paul was surrounded by women coworkers. In Rom. 16 it would appear that 10 of the 29 persons mentioned are women. This whole approach is climaxed by Paul's great declaration that "in Christ there is . . . no male or female" (Gal. 3:28).

Passages Articulating Distinction. In the light of these practices and specific texts certain passages that appear to enjoin some distinctions need to be considered—1 Cor. 7; 11:3–16, and 14:33–36; Eph. 5:22–33; 1 Tim. 2:9–15, and 1 Pet. 3:1–7.

The clearest restrictions are found in 1 Tim. 2, so that passage deserves special attention. The context is a series of directions applying to church life, although the mention of childbearing might also suggest that the reference is to life in the home and in society. Certainly the instructions concerning a woman's attire have relevance beyond the church. Paul's reasoning is, generally speaking, that Eve was created second and her yielding to Satan qualitatively differed from Adam's in some way; therefore, women are under restriction. If this is the correct understanding, what exactly is restricted?

There are some areas where the prohibition cannot be lodged: (1) Paul could not forbid mothers to teach their children since this is enjoined in Prov. 1:8; 6:20; 31:26 and implicitly in Deut. 6:7. This would also conflict with the commendation given to Lois and Eunice in 2 Tim. 1:5. (2) Paul seemingly does not refer here to teaching as such, since many teachers have been women and have often been blessed in this function. In Paul's day teachers were often slaves, so teaching did not involve great authority. We simply do not understand this passage well enough to safely apply it. It is not clear, for instance, why only men are enjoined to pray (2:8) when this activity surely should be open to women both at home and in the church (1 Cor. 11:5). It is not clear why the fact that Eve was deceived when Adam was not warrants a restriction on women. The person who sins with eyes open would appear to be even less reliable than one who is deceived. One interpretation might be that the order of the fall rather than a special type of failure is in view. Verse 15 furthermore has a strange shift in the number of the verb. The first verb, "she shall be saved," agrees with the previous statement, "the woman . . . was deceived." But afterward a plural verb is used. Paul certainly does not teach salvation by childbearing instead of by faith, but precisely what he does mean is difficult to say. Since he deals with the early chapters of Genesis, it appears plausible that his reference to childbearing points to the protevangel and the entrance of our Lord into humanity through a woman, the Virgin Mary. If this be correct, Paul would then complete his discussion with a reminder of the dignity of women and their place in the saving economy of grace to counterbalance a restriction previously imposed.

Some assumption about teaching appears to be in view, but it is not clear under what circumstances. When we read in 2 Tim. 3:16–17 that all Scripture is God-breathed and is useful for "teaching, rebuking, correcting and training in righteousness," the language Paul uses applies to women as well as to men.

Conclusion. It is clear that the Scripture provides for women a place of dignity and significance. It never demeans the activities of wife, homebuilder, mother, or educator of children. In this respect some of the emphases of feminism are doing a great disservice to a large number of women by failing to recognize the worth and dignity of their tasks.

Meanwhile, there is no scriptural reason to consider women as inferior. Created in the image of God to be man's helpmate, "not made out of his head to rule over him, nor out of his feet to be trampled upon by him, under his arm to be protected and near his heart to be beloved" (Matthew Henry), woman has a place in God's purpose. Although encompassed in the ruin of the fall, she is the object of God's compassion and grace. It is through a woman, the Virgin Mary, that the Lord Jesus Christ made his entrance into our race. Women were among the first to respond to his ministry and the first to witness his resurrection. Women, in even greater number than men, have responded to the invitation of the gospel and to the mandate of the Great Commission. In Revelation, the concluding book and climax of Scripture, the church as the body of all God's redeemed people is represented as a woman, the bride of Jesus Christ.

R. NICOLE

See also EVE; WOMEN, ORDINATION OF; WOMEN IN THE CHURCH.

Women, Ordination of. The ordination of women to Christian ministry has become a topic of importance in the second half of the 20th century. The issue is complicated by the fact that biblical guidelines are sparse, and ancient traditions have often been molded by fear and prejudice. Ordination itself is a rite by which a community appoints an individual to a leadership role. In the NT period this was often associated with the laying on of hands (Acts 6:6; 13:3), although such an act did not always imply public office (Acts 28:8). In this way the community demonstrated visibly its acceptance of the leader. The act also signified God's gracious bestowal of spiritual power (Acts 8:17; 19:6).

NT Evidence. Women feature in the NT as leaders of community worship, as specially appointed church officials, and as coworkers with the apostles. In 1 Cor. 11:2–16 Paul gives careful directives concerning how men and women leading congregational worship were to be dressed. He assumes that women will be leading mixed congregations in prayer and prophecy. Prophecy involves preaching and teaching (1 Cor. 14:3, 24–25). Paul refers to Phoebe as a deacon of the church in Cenchrea (Rom. 16:1). The word here translated "deacon" may mean "minister," and it is often so translated (Eph. 6:21; Col. 1:7; 1 Tim. 4:6). Probably Phoebe was entrusted with the letter to the church in Rome. The matters which she had in mind as the purpose of her visit merited the cooperation of the whole church. Paul speaks of women as his coworkers (Rom. 16:7; Phil. 4:3).

The Problem of Women's Leadership. One factor which adversely affected the ordination of women was the gradual trend toward regarding the leadership role as a priestly office. In OT times women were not members of the priesthood. Another factor was the low regard in which sexuality was held in the early centuries. Women came to be viewed as objects of temptation, and men who devoted to a life of "purity" were to avoid their company. Monasticism encouraged this trend. Although it was not originally intended that the monastic communities should be the training schools for priests, it worked out that way. Church leadership was perpetuated by appointments from the leaders themselves. As these leaders were all men, the result was that women had no voice.

Conclusion. The church of today is reassessing traditions and is seeking to come to grips with the Bible. There seems to be no biblical basis for the common practice placing both men and women in leadership positions but reserving ordination and pay only for men. Consequently many denominations are placing women in ordained ministries on a basis of equal salary and responsibility.

E. M. HOWE

See also WOMAN, BIBLICAL CONCEPT OF; WOMEN IN THE CHURCH.

Women in the Church. ***In the Bible.*** The first women in the church were female followers attached to Jesus (Matt. 27:55–56; Mark 15:40–41; Luke 8:1–3). Theirs was a significant ministry, and some are named and appear to form a cohesive unit (Luke 8:2; Acts 1:13–14). Luke notes that these women, along with others, followed Jesus to Jerusalem, the cross, and the tomb (23:27, 49, 55–56). They maintained watch over it and noted the exact location (Matt. 27:59–61; Mark 15:47). They were instructed by an angel to proclaim the resurrection, a task for which Christ had prepared them (Luke 24:6–8). Jesus showed himself first to Mary Magdalene, then to the other women, with the specific direction that they convey the news to the male disciples. Thus women are attested as the primary witnesses of the birth, crucifixion, burial, and resurrection of Jesus Christ. This witness, together with their confession of him as Messiah and Son of God (John 4:27–42; 11:27), was testimony essential to the formulation of the church's beliefs.

Women were present at the choice of Matthias (Acts 1:13–14). On the day of Pentecost the Holy Spirit fell equally upon men and women (Acts 2:17–18), and women had a pronounced role in the ministry of the early church (Acts 9:36–43; 21:8–9; Rom. 16). Churches are identified as meeting in the homes of women, who apparently had leadership (Acts 12:12; 16:40; Rom. 16:3–5; 1 Cor. 1:11; 16:19; Col. 4:15; 2 John). Euodia and Syntyche are mentioned as colleagues of Paul (Phil. 4:2–3), as is Priscilla with her husband, Aquila, whose name usually stands second (Acts 18:1–4, 18–28; Rom. 16:3–4; 1 Cor. 16:19; 2 Tim. 4:19). The early fathers understood Junia (Rom. 16:7) to be a female apostle. There was a strong tradition that Thecla was an associate of Paul, and there is evidence for her life and ministry.

In Church History. Tertullian wrote of four orders of female church officers, all mentioned in the Bible: deacons, virgins, widows, and eldresses. Some of these women were considered clerics, given ecclesial authority, and seated with the other clergy (*Testament of the Lord* 1.23). The NT speaks twice of women deacons (Rom. 16:1–2; 1 Tim. 3:11), and Pliny reports two deaconesses as leaders of a Christian community (*Epistles* 10.96.8). The ordination service of deaconesses is still preserved in the Apostolic Constitutions (8.19–20). Women elders are mentioned in 1 Tim. 5:2 or Titus 2:3, where they must be *hieroprepeis*, "worthy of holy office." The title "eldress" was applied by the early church to those in the order of widows, whose qualifications are given in 1 Tim. 5:5–10. Early catacomb paintings show women in the authoritative stance of a bishop, conferring blessing on Christians of both sexes. Two frescos appear to show women serving communion. Beginning about 350 prohibitions were issued against women's activities: Council of Laodicea (serving as priests or presiding over churches, establishing presbyteresses or presidents in the churches, approaching the altar), Fourth Synod of Carthage (teaching men or baptizing), 1st Council of Orange and the councils of Nîmes, Epaons, and Orleans (ordination of deaconesses). These prohibitions prove the previous existence of such offices for women.

Although deprived of official status, women continued to serve the church. The responsible behavior of Christian wives and mothers won from the pagan Libanius the exclamation, "What women these Christians have!" Jerome once referred a hermeneutical dispute to the Bible scholar Marcella. Empress Pulcheria, a prime mover in the Council of Chalcedon, was declared by Pope Leo I to be the major defender of orthodoxy against Nestorianism and Eutychianism. Women exerted tremendous influence in the Reformation, Counter-Reformation, and Great Awakenings. In the American church they were in the forefront of evangelism and of the Sunday school, missionary, holiness, and Pentecostal movements. The first woman to be ordained by a recognized denomination was Antoinette Brown (1853), a convert of Charles Finney. The ordination of women remains a controversial issue in evangelical churches.

In Evangelical Thought. Within Protestant evangelicalism there are significantly differing views on the activities, role, and status of women in the church. Three major stances may be discerned:

(1) Subordinate status. Proponents argue that the priority of man's creation gives him a superiority over woman (1 Cor. 11:8–9; 1 Tim. 2:13). As she led him into sin, God has ordained that he should rule rather than she (Gen. 3:16; 1 Tim. 2:14). Because of Eve's misdemeanor the earlier church fathers, notably Tertullian, concluded that women were weak, degraded, depraved, and an obstacle to the spiritual development of men. Although considerably modified, the doctrine of woman's inferiority has been eloquently expressed by some modern theologians who view women as less capable of good judgment. There is a strong emphasis on the prohibition against women teaching or exercising authority over men (1 Tim. 2:11–14), and there is the command for them to be silent in the congregation (1 Cor. 14:34–35; 1 Tim. 2:12).

(2) Equal status but headship by male leaders. The subordination of Christ to the Father and headship concepts of 1 Cor. 11:3–15 are models. The subjection of wife to husband in marriage (Eph. 5:22; Col. 3:18; 1 Pet. 3:1) is transposed to the church. In some groups women who have no husbands are encouraged to seek out a male figure, such as a father or pastor, to serve as intermediary in her access to God. Certain evangelicals hold that the submission of wife to husband must extend even to obedience if he commands her to perform a sinful act and that the moral choice and guilt are his rather than hers.

(3) The position sometimes called biblical feminism. Although the roots of this stance predate them, D. L. Moody, A. J. Gordon, C. G. Finney, and J. Blanchard promoted equality as a biblical concept and urged full utilization of women in the church. Phoebe Palmer, an associate evangelist with Moody and herself credited with the conversion of 25,000, declared the church to be a potter's field in which the talents of women are buried. One contemporary group lays great stress on Gen. 1:27; 1 Cor. 11:11–12, and Gal. 3:28 in affirming women as equals of men in Jesus Christ. These universal statements, it is maintained, supersede the narrower dictates of Paul. The apparent contradiction of Paul's statements is explored and a distinction made between those which are universally normative and those which are culturally relative. Just as certain statements regarding slavery are no longer applicable, so certain statements regarding women better served another age. God is affirmed as no respecter of persons (Acts 10:34) and as having maternal aspects (Deut. 32:18; Ps. 131:2;

Isa. 42:14; 49:15; 66:9–13; Matt. 23:37). For some, theological justification for ordination rests upon the leadership roles of women in both the OT and the NT. Egalitarian marriage is set forth as a biblical and humanitarian principle involving mutual submission (Eph. 5:21). Allied in some respects with liberation theology, this group has produced a radically new theology that is highly controversial in the evangelical world.

A more irenic school of thought, seeking to uphold both the authority of Scripture and sexual equality, holds that the "difficult" passages are no less inspired by God than 1 Cor. 11:11–12 and Gal. 3:28. Adherents demand that texts be studied in their linguistic, religious, historical, social, and geographical setting. The Greek word for "head," for instance, unlike its English and Hebrew counterparts, did not convey the meaning of "chief" or "boss." Thus the concept of "head" in 1 Cor. 11:3 and Eph. 5:23 must be studied in the light of its accepted Greek meanings (Eph. 4:15–16; Col. 2:19), topmost bodily member (Eph. 1:22–23), interdependent with the body (1 Cor. 12:21; Eph. 5:23–30), and the part which is usually born first (Col. 1:15–18). Gen. 3:16 is viewed as a divine prediction of sinful dominance (Matt. 20:25–28; Mark 10:42–45; Luke 22:24–27) rather than a divine decree and is countered with Jer. 31:22, 31–34 in the new covenant.

Research into the cult patterns of ancient women has a high priority in an understanding of Paul as missionary to the Gentiles. The ceremonial shouts of women, obligatory in certain pagan practices, contained no meaning but aroused considerable religious awe in the hearers. These sacred cries are attested in Corinth; thus it is understandable that the apostle, in seeking to curtail meaningless noise and confusion during worship (1 Cor. 14), would ask women to refrain from such utterances while allowing them to pray and prophesy meaningfully (1 Cor. 11:5). The possibility of alternative translations of 1 Tim. 2:12 is raised, especially since *authentein*, generally rendered "to bear rule," had several more common meanings in the NT era. Proponents suggest that it may be a directive against women involved in false teaching (1 Tim. 4:7; 5:15; 2 Tim. 3:3–7; Rev. 2:20). The entire passage (1 Tim. 2:5–15) must be studied in the wider context of the Pastoral Epistles with their concern over heretical opposition to the truth and need for suppression of false teachers (1 Tim. 1:3–4; Titus 1:10–11). In particular there is evidence that there may have been a distortion of the Adam and Eve story (1 Cor. 11:2–4, 13–15; 1 Tim. 1:4; 2 Tim. 4:4; Titus 1:14) similar to Gnostic theologies which portrayed Eve as a celestial power and as the one who brought life and light to Adam through the serpent's gift of knowledge. 1 Tim. 2:11–15 may then be a refutation of such doctrines rather than a rationale for the restriction of women.

In any event, the proper utilization of the talents of gifted Christian women remains a pressing contemporary issue and one that requires much thought, study, and reflection.

R. C. KROEGER AND C. C. KROEGER

See also WOMAN, BIBLICAL CONCEPT OF; WOMEN, ORDINATION OF.

Wonders. See MIRACLES.

Woolman, John (1720–1772). Quaker social reformer and mystic. Woolman was one of the most effective advocates for peace and the abolition of slavery in colonial America. Woolman's *Considerations on the Keeping of Negroes*, written in two sections in 1754 and 1762, contended that slavery affronted common humanity and the "inner light of Christ" that had been placed in all people. His mystical piety represented an important development in Quaker thought as well as in Quaker social action. His *Journal* reveals one who saw physical life as an intimate reflection of the spiritual world, and who devoutly reverenced the work of God in both nature and other humans.

M. A. NOLL

See also FRIENDS, SOCIETY OF.

Word, Word of God, Word of the Lord. ***Old Testament.*** Of Hebrew terms used to express God's communications, *peh* ("mouth"), generally translated "word" in these contexts, is most vivid. It specifies the source of the declaration as coming directly from God. Both Moses (Num. 3:16, 51; cf. 4:5; Josh. 22:9) and Joshua (Josh. 19:50) received instructions from the mouth of the Lord for their people.

Every instance of the term *'imrâ*, including the one occurrence of its plural form (Ps. 12:6), has God's Word in view, while the term itself focuses on the act of speech as such. As the speech of God his word is "tried" (Ps. 18:30, AV), or "proves true" (RSV, see Pss. 105:19; 119:140; 2 Sam. 22:31), having "stood the test" (Prov. 30:5, NEB).

There are 394 occurrences of the word *dābār* to characterize a communication as the *word* "of God" or "of the Lord." Here the emphasis falls upon the matter of the utterance, on the what is said. As *dābār*, God's word is the virtual concrete expression of his personality. This *dābār* of the Lord can be trusted (Ps. 119:42) as the source of life (Ps. 119:25), light (Ps. 119:105), and understanding (Ps. 119:169).

In the LXX the words *rhēma* and *logos* are used to translate *dābār*. The NT uses both *rhēma* and *logos* with apparent indifference to any significant nuance of meaning. In addition to the word "of God" and "of the Lord" there is that "of Jesus" (Matt. 26:75; John 2:22; 4:50) and "of Christ" (John 5:24; 17:17; Col. 3:16). One and the same, then, with "the word of God" and "the word of the Lord" is the "Word"—the *logos*—of Jesus Christ; so are his words (*rhemata*) spirit and life (John 6:63).

The first disciples spoke "the word of God" with boldness (Acts 4:31) and so "the word of God" increased (Acts 6:7; cf. 19:20). At Salamis, Paul and Barnabas "proclaimed the word of God in the synagogues" (Acts 13:5), which "word of God" Sergius Paulus desired to hear (vs. 7). This "good word of God" (Heb. 6:5, KJV) is "the word of truth" (Col. 1:5) and is consequently God's gospel (Acts 20:24; Rom. 1:1; 15:16; 1 Thess. 2:2, 8, 9; 1 Tim. 1:11; 1 Pet. 4:17) and Christ's (Mark 1:1; Rom. 1:16; 15:19; 1 Cor. 9:18; 2 Cor. 2:12;). The word of God proclaimed orally by its first witnesses is one with the Word finally embodied in written form in the NT.

In Rev. 19:13 the exalted Christ is "The Word of God." The title associates itself with the same author's *logos* doctrine, either by way of an approach to it or as an application of it. In John 1:1–2 the term *logos*—Word—is used in an absolute sense of Christ as the incarnate Son of God. In the person of Christ God's essential being became actual, comprehensive, and historical. As the Word, Christ was among men as the incarnate speech of God; and communicates eternal life to those who receive him. John declares that this Word had an existence beyond the limits of time. He stresses both his separate personality—"the Word was with [*pros*, lit. "toward"] God" in the intimacy of an eternal relationship—and his true deity—"the Word was God." Because the Word was personally distinct from God and yet truly God, he made God known.

In several NT passages "the word of God" is used to designate in principle the written Scriptures themselves. Our Lord authenticated this use by declaring that Scripture, as the Word of God, cannot be broken (John 10:35). It is "the sure word of prophecy" of which Peter speaks

(2 Pet. 1:19, AV) because it results from God's outbreathing (2 Tim. 3:16; 2 Pet. 1:21). By characterizing the Scriptures of the OT as the Word of God, Jesus incidentally affirmed that what is Scripture is the Word of God, and vice versa. Into this category the canonical writings of the NT eventually came. Its writers frequently allude to the divine revelation preserved in the OT as the Word of God, and they regarded the message of the gospel as the true meaning and fulfillment of that former testament. They learned from their Lord himself that Moses and all the prophets wrote of him (Luke 24:27). The fathers of the early church and the Reformers of the later church affirmed faith in the biblical writings as the Word of God.

H. D. McDonald

See also Logos.

Work. Some terms used to designate work in the Bible have no moral or physical implications, as when God works in creation, or in general reference to human labor: Heb. *mĕlā'kâ* (Gen. 2:2; Exod. 20:9; 1 Chr. 4:23; Hag. 1:14) and *ma'ăśeh* (Gen. 5:29; Exod. 5:13; Prov. 16:3; Eccles. 1:14), and Gk. *ergon*. On the other hand, Heb. *yĕgîa'* (Gen. 31:42; Deut. 28:33; Ps. 128:2; Ezek. 23:29) and *'āmāl* (Ps. 90:10; Eccles. 1:3; 2:10; Jer. 20:18) and Gk. *kopos* (Matt. 11:28; John 4:38; 1 Cor. 4:12; 15:58; 1 Thess. 1:3; 2 Thess. 3:8) imply weariness, trouble, and sorrow.

Work and labor of themselves are never held to be evil, but rather are thought of as a natural occupation in the world. Even in the state of innocency the representative of all creation before God (Gen. 2:15), was given work to perform. That sin corrupted and degraded work is continually repeated in the Bible, however. Gen. 3:17–18 states that work will, because of sin, change its character to become the cause of man's ultimate physical disintegration. Work in the Bible frequently embodies the idea of weariness, yet it does have eternal significance. Paul makes this plain in speaking to both servants and masters (Eph. 6:5–9; 1 Tim. 6:1–2), summing it all up in his instruction to Christians to be not "slothful in business, but fervent in spirit serving the Lord" (Rom. 12:11), and in his exhortation to do all things to the glory of God (1 Cor. 10:31). The Christian must thus regard work as a divinely appointed means of serving God.

W. S. Reid

See also Vocation.

Works. The works of both God and people are prominent in the Bible. God's works consist of creation, providence (including the preservation and government of the world), and redemption. Jesus' comment that his Father was still working (John 5:17) is reinforced by Paul (Phil. 1:6; Rom. 14:20), who considered his activity as an aspect of the work of God (1 Cor. 16:10; Phil. 2:30; cf. Acts 13:2).

Although human labor originated as a divine commission and privilege (Gen. 2:15), the intervention of sin gave it a negative connotation. Humans live by the sweat of their brow (Gen. 3:17–19; cf. 5:29), and work is marked by vanity and sin. This negative attitude toward mere human action was accentuated by an emphasis in late Judaism on the righteousness of works and their reward. NT teaching must be seen against this background. Human activities are characterized in general as of the devil (John 8:41), of darkness (Rom. 13:12), of the flesh (Gal. 5:19), as evil (Jude 15; Matt. 23:3), lawless (2 Pet. 2:8), and dead (Heb. 6:1; 9:14). The only works that will stand the scrutiny of God are those effected by his Spirit and grounded in faith (John 6:29; 1 Thess. 1:3; Rom. 2:6–7; Acts 26:20). Such are not only approved by Jesus (Matt. 5:16; 7:21; 21:28–43) and Paul (Rom. 2:6–7) but expected of God's people (Matt. 25:37–40). What is condemned is the expectation of payment from God for doing what he has commanded. After doing all that is commanded—if that were possible—believers must still say, "We have only done our duty" (Luke 17:10). The chief work God desires is the obedience of humble belief (John 6:29), which begets a life full of good deeds (Titus 3:14).

M. E. OSTERHAVEN

World. (Heb. *'ereṣ*, earth in contrast to heaven; *tēbēl*, planet; Gk., *oikoumenē*, world's people; *aiōn*, an age in time and space; *kosmos*, order or system) While *'ereṣ* is used in Gen. 1:1, the more usual term is *tēbēl*, which signifies the planet with its topographical features, people, and fruits (Pss. 19:4; 90:2). *Oikoumenē* denotes the populated world (Luke 4:5); *aiōn*, usually rendered age, occasionally combines the concepts of time and space (Heb. 1:2; 11:3).

The most striking fact about the NT use of *kosmos* is the readiness with which the term is employed in an evil sense. Especially in the Johannine writings, the world is presented as hostile to God and in disorder. How, then, can *kosmos* describe such a state of affairs? The powers of spiritual evil, with Satan as their head, appear to be organized on a vast scale and with great efficiency (Eph. 6:12) to dominate the lives of unredeemed humanity. Satan rules a kingdom which is opposed to the kingdom of God (Luke 11:18). This does not express a hopeless dualism between equally powerful gods. Even in a world marred by evil, God is sovereign. Satan's kingdom exists by permission, not because of divine helplessness. Reconciliation has been provided for the world (2 Cor. 5:19), whereby people may leave the *kosmos* system and enter the kingdom of God.

E. F. HARRISON

See also AGE, AGES; THIS AGE, THE AGE TO COME; WORLDLINESS AND OTHERWORLDLINESS.

Worldliness and Otherworldliness. Israel's world-affirming outlook—God is creator and ruler of *this* world—was reinforced by the incarnation of Jesus Christ. Nevertheless, Peter and Paul exhorted converts to separate from the world, while stressing involvement in human needs and the mission to save the world. John insisted that love of the world contradicts love for the Father; yet Christ, the Savior of the world God loves, died for the world (1 John 2:2).

Tension grew between ministry to the world and world-renouncing concentration upon the world above (mysticism) or the world to come (adventism). Christians resisted the theaters, games, and debauchery rampant in the Roman world yet cared for the world's unwanted. Separation became rejection and ultimately escape. Anchorites and monastics despised marriage, cleanliness, and all human comforts, in an otherworldly search for deeper truth and the vision. Simultaneously, the conversion of Rome fostered a new kind of worldliness, ambition for the rewards of power. Two types of Christians emerged—the religious, withdrawn from the world, and the lay, active in the world. In the proper tension the Christian lives redeemed from the world and independent of it, but yet sent into it to minister, living within it in the power of the world to come, knowing that the world is God's.

R. E. O. WHITE

Worldwide Church of God. See ARMSTRONGISM.

Worms, Diet of (1521)**.** In one of the most dramatic events of the Reformation Martin Luther confessed his faith before Charles V, scion of the house of Hapsburg, Holy Roman Emperor. April 17 at 4 P.M. Luther entered the diet to be questioned by the archbishop of Trier, who pointed to a table of writings and asked if the Reformer had written them and if he recanted. "The books are all mine, and I have written more," Luther responded. "Do you defend them all, or do you care to reject a part?" he was asked. "This touches God and his Word. This affects the salvation of souls. . . . To say too little or too much would be dangerous. I beg you, give me time to think it over," Luther answered. Allowed a day for reflection, Luther reappeared at 6 P.M. on April 18. The same questions were posed. Luther explained that his books were of several types—pastoral, polemical, theological. Denied the opportunity to further explain, Luther was asked for a simple reply. He stated: "Since then your Majesty and your lordships desire a simple reply, I will answer without horns and without teeth. Unless I am convicted by Scripture and plain reason—I do not accept the authority of popes and councils, for they have contradicted each other—my conscience is captive to the Word of God. I cannot and I will not recant anything, for to go against conscience is neither right nor safe. God help me. Amen." Worms marked Luther's complete break with the Roman Church—excommunicated by pope and banned by emperor—and the birth of Lutheran Protestantism.

C. G. FRY

See also LUTHER, MARTIN.

Worry. See ANXIETY.

Worship in the Church. To worship God is to ascribe to him the worth he is due. The church of Jesus Christ is by definition a worshiping community called into being by God as "a spiritual house to be a holy priesthood, offering spiritual sacrifices acceptable to God through Jesus Christ" (1 Pet. 2:5 NIV). The Christian church has from its beginning gathered regularly to worship. The most basic acts of worship in the early church—the reading and exposition of Scripture; the prayers; the singing of psalms, hymns, and spiritual songs; and the observance of the sacraments—are all derived from the example and command of Jesus. However, except for the celebration of the Lord's Supper, these practices were derived from synagogue worship.

The Early Church. What distinguished early Christians from other Jews was their conviction that Jesus was the promised Messiah and that salvation was found only in him. They continued to worship in a basically Jewish fashion, but added the Lord's Supper (Acts 2:42, 46) and prayers in the name of Jesus (Acts 4:24–30). Although the Christians gathered daily for prayer, fellowship, preaching, and teaching (Acts 2:46; 5:42), the chief day for services of worship in the church was changed from the Jewish sabbath to the first day of the week almost from the beginning, because it was the day of resurrection.

The *Didache* (ca. A.D. 95–150), describes in detail how the Lord's Supper was celebrated, including prayers and liturgical direction. Fixed forms of prayer were included, but provision was made for free prayer. Confession of sin was required before partaking of the Lord's Supper (*Didache* 14.1). In primitive church gatherings baptized believers celebrated the Lord's Supper along with a full-scale meal. At an early date, however, the meal was separated from the sacrament (Clement of Alexandria *Paedagogos* 2.1; *Stromata* 3.2; Tertullian *Apology* 39.3) and called the *agapē* or love feast. By the 4th century the observance of the feast had largely died out because of disorders in its conduct (Augustine *Letter to Aurelium* 22.4).

The Middle Ages and Reformation. When the Emperor Constantine made Christianity the official religion of the Roman Empire in 313, the new public image of the Christians encouraged the building of splendid churches and the creation of longer and more colorful services. The results were not uniformly beneficial. As many pagans professed to embrace Christianity, they began to influence, in particular, an emphasis upon the "mystery" of the Lord's Supper. Rather than simple worship, form and ceremony became important until eventually the Lord's Supper grew into the Roman Mass, with all its abuses in the medieval Roman Church.

The Reformers were more concerned with doctrine than with worship, and most of them gave comparatively little attention to the development of liturgy. A wide variety of worship services came into being. Calvin's aim was to return to the worship practices of the primitive church. He endorsed congregational singing, especially the metrical versions of the Psalms and gave the sermon utmost importance. His liturgy became the norm in the Calvinistic churches of Europe. In England the *Book of Common Prayer* (1549; 1552; 1662) was produced.

American Churches. Three principal types of worship came to American colonies. (1) Some retained a fixed liturgy, as in the Anglican Church. This allowed maximum opportunity for formal corporate participation. While deemphasizing preaching, it encouraged frequent communion. (2) A characteristic of churches that arose out of radical Puritanism was rejection of all forms in worship as quenching the Spirit. This guarded the freedom to personally praise God and communicate his message to others. (3) Calvinistic churches sought to worship according to the Word, following the dictum that nothing was to be allowed in worship except what Scripture commanded.

As the frontier was pushed westward, most American denominations arising from European churches were influenced by revivalism. Many of America's free churches have their roots in the revival tradition. The revival meeting began with a song service of three or more songs chosen to raise the emotional pitch of the congregation. Intensely personal prayers were offered and an offering received. After a highly subjective musical number, usually a solo, the congregation was prepared for the climax of the service, the evangelistic sermon, always followed by some form of "altar call." Strong revivalistic and judgmental preaching tended to completely overshadow the experience of corporate worship. The Lord's Supper was limited to semiannual or quarterly or sometimes monthly observance. There was little common prayer. The pastor's sermon was the all-important part of the service.

Another movement which had a strong effect upon worship was the Chautauqua, which rose in the 19th century to raise the cultural level of the country. Chautauqua spread over the country and churches began to be built like theaters with banked seats, so what was taking place in the pulpit and choir loft could be more readily observed. People became more and more mere spectators in worship.

The combination of the highly subjective emphasis of revivals and the entertainment aspect of the Chautauqua has been felt strongly in the evangelical America. The choir and soloists often seem to provide Christian entertainment, while individual participation in the service is limited to the singing of hymns. The central part of the service is the sermon, in line with an appropriate emphasis on the Word of God, but the potential richness of common worship for the individual worshiper is often unrealized.

R. G. RAYBURN

See also CHRISTIAN YEAR.

Wrath of God. Wrath, anger, and indignation are integral to the biblical proclamation of God's opposition to sin. While God's love is spontaneous to his own being, his wrath is called forth by the wickedness of his creatures. The wounding of his gracious love and rejection of his mercy, evokes his holy wrath. God's act of wrath is his "strange work" (Isa. 28:21). In the OT wrath expresses the personal, subjective free will of Yahweh, who actively punishes sin. In such NT passages as John 3:36; Rom. 1:18; Eph. 5:6; Col. 3:6; Rev. 6:16; 11:18; 14:10; 16:19; 19:15, wrath is specifically described as God's wrath or the wrath of the Lamb. The wrath of God is being continually revealed from heaven, actively giving the wicked up to uncleanness, to vile passions, to reprobate minds, and punishing them in the day of wrath and revelation of the just judgment of God (Rom. 1:18–2:6; Rom. 9:22). In 2 Thess. 1:7–9 Paul writes as personal a description of the Lord Jesus' action in directly punishing the disobedient as can be penned. Accordingly, man's puny efforts to escape divine wrath are insufficient, but God's own heart of love provides a way of salvation. He calls men to repent, to return unto himself, to receive his forgiveness and renewal.

W. C. Robinson

See also Eternal Punishment; Judgment.

Würtemberg Confession (1552). A Lutheran statement of faith used alongside the Augsburg Confession and Formula of Concord in Swabia. It was mainly the work of theologian John Brenz (1499–1570). Viewed by many Lutherans as a restatement of the Augsburg Confession, the Würtemberg Confession was described as an excellent statement of positive Lutheranism, mild, popular, and moderate in tone toward Roman Catholics. By 1559 the confession was incorporated into the Great Church Order, which was used by Lutherans in Würtemberg for centuries.

C. G. Fry

See also Confessions of Faith; Lutheran Tradition, The.

Wycliffe, John (ca. 1330–1384). English scholar and theologian; often called "the Morning Star of the Reformation." He spent most of his life teaching at Oxford University. A brilliant scholar who mastered the late medieval scholastic tradition, he performed diplomatic duties for the Crown and wrote in support of civil government. His work denied the validity of clerical ownership of land and property, as well as papal jurisdiction in temporal affairs. The doctrine of dominion, which he set forth in *On Divine Dominion* (1375) and *On Civil Dominion* (1376), declared that all people are the tenants of God and only the righteous as God's true stewards ought to have political authority because they alone have the moral right to rule and hold possession.

These views led to his condemnation in a series of papal bulls issued in 1377, which declared that Oxford should stop such teaching. Opposition drove Wycliffe to more extreme positions, and he moved from an attack on the wealth and temporal power of the church to criticism of central dogmas of medieval Catholicism. Wycliffe's writings, in addition to his work on the problems of church and state, include logical and metaphysical treatises and numerous theological books and sermons. He is best known, however, for instigating a translation of the Vulgate into English. He spent the last few months of his life on that task, leaving completion to his followers. Made up of scholars from Oxford, the lesser gentry, and poor people from rural and urban areas, these followers, called Lollards, faced brutal persecution but survived over a century after Wycliffe died. If Wycliffe's influence on English Protestantism is difficult to trace, it is clear in Continental thought. His ideas spread to Bohemia through Czech students who attended Oxford University. In Prague, John Hus adopted his teachings, and the Hussites kept them alive for many years.

R. G. Clouse

Yy

Yahweh. See GOD, NAMES OF.

Zz

Zinzendorf, Nikolaus Ludwig von (1700–1760). German reformer and founder of the Moravian Church. In 1722 he invited a group of Bohemian Brethren (*Unitas Fratrum*) refugees to settle on his estate in Saxony, organizing them into the community of Herrnhut (The Lord's Watch). He was formally ordained a bishop in 1737. In numerous trips to other lands, including two visits to America, he founded and nurtured churches and kindled a missionary vision among Protestants. He wrote hymns and prayers, created liturgical forms, and prepared daily "watch words" (*Losungen*) to foster spiritual growth. Zinzendorf held to essentials of Lutheran theology. His distinctive emphasis, however, was on "heart religion." Zinzendorf envisioned the revitalization of the existing Lutheran Church through the cultivation of an intense community religious life. This included frequent worship services, organizing the community into groups with spiritual supervisors, schools, the use of choral and instrumental music, and actively evangelizing the world.

R. V. Pierard

See also Pietism.

Zurich Agreement (1549). The statement on the Lord's Supper that prevented a split between Calvinists and Zwinglians in Switzerland; also called *Consensus Tigurinus*, after the Latin name of the city. Calvin was the main author, but Bullinger's influence was evident throughout. In 26 articles the agreement presented a unified doctrine that became the basis for unity among all the Reformed in Switzerland.

J. M. Drickamer

Zwickau Prophets. The "Zwickau prophets" were Nicholas Storch, Markus Stübner, and Thomas Drechsel, three refugees from the conventicle movement of Zwickau, who visited Wittenberg shortly after Christmas, 1521. Their extravagant claims perplexed and excited the Wittenbergers. They formed the image of Anabaptists for Martin Luther and Philip Melanchthon, who believed that the prophets, along with Thomas Müntzer and Andreas Carlstadt, were the fathers of Anabaptism.This view prevailed until the 20th century, until historian Harold S. Bender argued that Anabaptists' origins were not from these radicals.

J. D. Weaver

Zwingli, Ulrich (1484–1531). After Martin Luther and John Calvin, the most important early Protestant reformer. Zwingli was ordained a priest and served parishes in Glarus (1506–16) and Einsiedeln (1516–18) until called to be the people's (or preaching) priest at the Great Minster in Zurich.

Sometime around 1516, after diligent study in Erasmus's Greek NT and after long wrestling with the moral problem of sensuality, he experienced an evangelical breakthrough. This turned him even more wholeheartedly to the Scriptures, and he became particularly hostile to the medieval system of penance and relics, which he attacked in 1518. One of the great moments of the Reformation occurred early in 1519 when Zwingli arrived in Zurich and announced his intention to preach exegetical sermons, beginning with the Gospel of Matthew. In the final decade of his life he shepherded Zurich to its declaration for reform (1523). He wrote numerous tracts and aided in the composition of such confessions as the Ten Theses of Berne (1528). He established solid relationships with other Swiss reformers, including Oecolampadius in Basel; he inspired and then broke with the rising Anabaptist movement. An attempt at unity with Luther ended at the Colloquy of Marburg (1529), despite only one momentous disagreement—over the Lord's Supper. Zwingli lost his life while serving as a chaplain to Zurich troops engaged in warfare with other Swiss cantons.

M. A. NOLL

See also MARBURG COLLOQUY.